Mac OS® X Panther™

UNLEASHED

John Ray and William C. Ray

SAMS 800 East 96th Street, Indianapolis, Indiana 46240 USA

Mac OS X Panther Unleashed

International Standard Book Number: 0-672-32604-3

Library of Congress Catalog Card Number: 2003094093

Printed in the United States of America

First Printing: January 2004

06 05 04 4 3 2

Trademarks

All terms mentioned in this book that are known to be trademarks or service marks have been appropriately capitalized. Sams Publishing cannot attest to the accuracy of this information. Use of a term in this book should not be regarded as affecting the validity of any trademark or service mark.

Warning and Disclaimer

Every effort has been made to make this book as complete and as accurate as possible, but no warranty or fitness is implied. The information provided is on an "as is" basis.

Bulk Sales

Sams Publishing offers excellent discounts on this book when ordered in quantity for bulk purchases or special sales. For more information, please contact

U.S. Corporate and Government Sales

1-800-382-3419

corpsales@pearsontechgroup.com

For sales outside of the U.S., please contact

International Sales

1-317-428-3341

international@pearsontechgroup.com

Acquisitions Editor
Scott Meyers

Managing Editor
Charlotte Clapp

Project Editor
George E. Nedeff

Copy Editor
Geneil Breeze

Indexer
Larry Sweazy

Proofreaders
Carla Lewis
Linda Seifert

Technical Editor
Terrence Talbot

Publishing Coordinator
Vanessa Evans

Multimedia Developer
Dan Scherf

Designer
Gary Adair

Contents at a Glance

Table of Contents

Part V Advanced Command-Line Concepts

About the Authors

John Ray is an award-winning application developer and security consultant with more than 20 years of programming and administration experience. He has worked on projects for the National Regulatory Research Institute, The Ohio State University, Xerox, and the state of Florida, as well as serving as the IT director for a multimillion dollar design and technology firm. A Macintosh owner and programmer since 1984, John has written/contributed to numerous titles including *Maximum Mac OS X Security, Sams Teach Yourself Macromedia Studio MX 2004 All in One, Sams Teach Yourself Mac OS X*, and *Panther All In One*.

John currently serves as the Senior Systems Engineer for the College of Food, Agricultural, and Environmental Sciences at The Ohio State University. He maintains a cluster of Linux, Mac OS X, and Mac OS X Server machines and associated CommuniGate Pro and Apache servers.

William Ray is a mathematician turned computer scientist turned biophysicist who has gravitated to the field of bioinformatics for its interesting synergy of logic, hard science, and human-computer-interface issues. A longtime Macintosh and Unix enthusiast, Will has owned Macs since 1985 and has worked with Unix since 1987. Prior to switching his professional focus to the biological sciences, Will spent five years as a Unix programmer developing experimental interfaces to online database systems. Shortly after migrating to biophysics, Will developed a Macintosh and Unix-based computational biology/graphics laboratory and training center for The Ohio State University's College of Biological Sciences. At the facility, which he managed for five years, Will introduced hundreds of students and faculty to Unix, and provided training and assistance in the development of productive computing skills on the paired Macintosh and Unix platforms. Will is currently a Professor of Pediatrics at the Columbus Children's Research Institute Children's Hospital in Columbus, Ohio, and the Department of Pediatrics, The Ohio State University, where he is investigating tools that work at the interface between humans, computers, and information, and working to build a core computational research and training facility for his institute.

Joan Ray (Contributing Author) is a Unix system administrator and Webmaster for the College of Biological Sciences at The Ohio State University. Joan has a degree in French from OSU and is working toward additional degrees in Japanese and geology.

When not helping with this or other books, Joan is administering a cluster of SHI and Sun Unix workstations and servers; helping and providing training for users with Unix, Classic Mac OS, and Mac OS X questions; and serving as college Webmaster.

Dedication

This book is dedicated to the fine folks at Williams Street/Adult Swim. If you ever need a 1,500 page script for "Aqua Teen Hungerforce: Unleashed" or "Home Movies: Unleashed," let me know. — John

Acknowledgments

Many thanks to Terrence Talbot for identifying the changes in the ever-evolving Panther software, Carla Lewis for an excellent job identifying discrepancies and finding all the words we made up, and George Nedeff for pulling it all together.

We Want to Hear from You!

As the reader of this book, *you* are our most important critic and commentator. We value your opinion and want to know what we're doing right, what we could do better, what areas you'd like to see us publish in, and any other words of wisdom you're willing to pass our way.

You can email or write me directly to let me know what you did or didn't like about this book—as well as what we can do to make our books stronger.

Please note that I cannot help you with technical problems related to the topic of this book, and that due to the high volume of mail I receive, I might not be able to reply to every message.

When you write, please be sure to include this book's title and author as well as your name and phone or email address. I will carefully review your comments and share them with the author and editors who worked on the book.

Email: networking@samspublishing.com

Mail: Mark Taber
Associate Publisher
Sams Publishing
800 East 96th Street
Indianapolis, IN 46240 USA

Reader Services

For more information about this book or others from Sams Publishing, visit our Web site at `www.samspublishing.com`. Type the ISBN (excluding hyphens) or the title of the book in the Search box to find the book you're looking for.

Introduction

Here's To the Crazy Ones...

So...you've decided to start using a Mac, or are starting out for the first time in Mac OS X. Coming from Windows, Linux, or even the Classic (OS 7/8/9) Macintosh operating system to OS X can pose a bit of culture shock to any user. You'll be surprised at how *pretty* it is on the outside, and how powerful it is on the inside. This is *not* the Macintosh of ten or even five years ago.

For many people, the Macintosh has always been either a machine that worked the way it should or one that quickly spiraled into a nightmare of freezes, lockups, and completely unexplainable behavior. If you were lucky enough to experience a machine that performed the way you wanted, you loved your Mac. If not, you went the Windows (or possible Linux) path and watched the Mac users in bewilderment as they rallied around their computers.

Those of you who have been following the Macintosh over the years have seen Apple go through its share of up and downs. The company buried itself in controversy over hardware and operating system uncertainties only to rise again with the introduction of Mac OS X and (finally) the G5.

To fully comprehend the magnitude of the Apple comeback, you need to understand the corner that the company had painted itself into. The Macintosh OS was being rapidly overtaken by competing operating systems, and Apple's plans to modernize the existing Mac OS had failed.

- 1991—Apple introduces System 7.0. System 7.0 provides the first seamless multitasking environment for the Macintosh. At the time, System 7.0 provides better stability and a far better user experience than Windows.
- 1994/1995—Apple updates to System 7.5. System 7.5 provides new features above the earlier Mac OS release but is still based on the same system as 7.0 and carries many of the same problems. After five years, the base OS is still very much the same. To address the need for better stability and speed, Apple announces Copland—the next-generation operating system that would be numbered Mac OS 8.
- 1995—Microsoft introduces Windows 95. Windows 95 provides many of the features of Mac OS, as well as preemptive multitasking and an early form of memory protection. Windows 95 proves to be more responsive and stable than Mac OS.

- 1995/1996—Microsoft Windows NT takes hold. Featuring the Windows 95 interface, Microsoft's Windows NT operating system offers vastly increased speed and stability over Windows 95. Capable of running weeks without a crash, Windows NT is heralded as the next big thing.
- 1996—Apple scraps Copland. A few short weeks after the 1996 developer conference, Apple announces that it is abandoning the Copland project. Developers cry—a lot. BeOS and OpenStep become candidates for replacement. In late 1996, Apple acquires NeXT.
- 1997—Apple introduces System 8.0, and Microsoft introduces Windows 98. Using pieces of the Copland project, Apple builds Mac OS 8. Unfortunately, the basis of the operating system is rapidly approaching ancient in industry terms. To replace the dying Mac OS, Apple introduces Rhapsody at the 1997 Developer conference. Based on OpenStep, Rhapsody is proclaimed to be the future of Mac OS—modern, crash-proof, and years away. Developers begin to feel heart palpations.
- 1998—Apple appears to scrap the Rhapsody project by announcing Mac OS X at its May developer conference. Those attending the conference were, again, in shock. Luckily it turned out that Apple really wasn't switching gears again. Rhapsody was becoming the basis for Mac OS X—not replacing it.
- 1999—The first developer release of Mac OS X appears. It has little resemblance to the existing desktop Mac operating system. Several months later, it is followed up with the second developer release. This time, it is apparent that Apple was on to something. The Macintosh user experience returns. Developers breathe a sigh of relief.
- 2000—Steve Jobs demonstrates the Mac OS X "Aqua" interface for the first time. Ooohs and ahhhs are heard from those attending the speech and from the thousands of Internet viewers tuned in. Later in the year, Apple releases a public beta of Mac OS X.
- Saturday, March 24, 2001—After almost five years of delays, false starts, and public unrest, Apple rolls out Mac OS X. The new operating system keeps the promises that Apple made six years earlier: It provides a revolutionary user experience, modern foundation, easy development, and backward compatibility.

For more than six years, developers and users alike waited for a sign of a *real* shipping modern operating system—all the while watching Windows systems get friendlier, faster, and more stable than the Mac and watching users leave in droves. When Mac OS X finally shipped in 2001, no one knew whether anyone would actually use it.

Thankfully users like yourself have embraced the platform as did the software developers. Apple bridged together the friendliness of the original Macintosh along with the stability and power of Linux and the Windows NT/2000/XP operating systems. Each successive release of the operating system turns new heads and converts users who had sworn off the Macintosh forever.

The current release, Panther, provides features such as a revamped user interface (really, those striped windows were very annoying), faxing, Samba 3, and a brand-new Finder. Whether you're new to the Mac, new to OS X, or upgrading from a previous version, you'll find Panther is yet another home-run in Apple's system releases.

Mac OS X Panther Unleashed

By its very design, Mac OS X accomplishes two seemingly contradictory goals. It creates an easy-to-use system that is crash-resistant and resilient to user error. First-time users can sit down in front of the system, find the tools they need, and immediately start working. At the same time, advanced users have complete access to an underlying Unix subsystem, advanced networking capabilities, and a wealth of Open Source technologies including the Apache Web server, Perl, Postfix, and many other powerful applications.

Much of the difficulty in creating a Mac OS X book is deciding which portions of the system should be detailed and which should be left to other, more in-depth resources. For example, for the first time ever, Apple is shipping a full, world-class development environment with every copy of Mac OS X. Documenting this environment alone could take an entire volume. Additionally, literally thousands of command-line applications make up the BSD subsystem under the Aqua interface. We've worked to create a text that provides focused information on those topics most likely to provide the most benefit to the reader.

This book gives you the knowledge to use Mac OS X to its fullest—both from the perspective of a traditional Mac user and that of a seasoned Unix administrator. The book is arranged so that you can quickly find the topics that interest you without reading through tons of extraneous information. As your familiarity with the operating system grows, you'll find the tips and tricks you need to perform everything from interface customization to shell scripting and creating a fully capable Internet server system.

Reading through the book, you may be surprised to find that we've questioned how a number of OS features have been implemented, and sometimes are vocally critical of Apple's design decisions. Although there are many things we love about the OS, there are still plenty of headache-inducing "gotchas" that crop up from time to time, and we'll do what we can to steer you clear of them.

Mac OS X will grow and update rapidly as Apple continues its efforts to optimize the OS X system performance and user experience. As we work to create this resource, we will make every attempt to provide the latest and most accurate Mac OS X information available.

Be aware that to get this book on the shelves before Apple releases 10.4, we often have to work with software that is beta quality. In addition, Apple provides periodic updates to Mac OS X throughout the year. If you find an example that no longer works as you'd expect, drop us a note, and we'll try to find an answer for you.

Comments, suggestions, and questions, are always welcomed.

Sincerely,

John Ray (jray@macosxunleashed.com)

William Ray (wray@macosxunleashed.com)

PART I

Introduction to Mac OS X

IN THIS PART

CHAPTER 1

Panther System Elements

IN THIS CHAPTER

Mac OS X has had a long and rocky birth process. In late 1996, Apple purchased NeXT Computer, Inc., with the thought of using its OpenStep operating system as the basis for the next-generation Mac OS. Developed initially under the moniker Rhapsody, this new operating system was little more than a graphic makeover for OpenStep. Mac OS users were left without support for existing software, and developers were left without support for existing code. Steve Jobs touted the component model of the new operating system as being the future of the Macintosh, but people weren't buying it.

Thankfully, Apple listened to the feedback of its users and developers, and slowly but surely molded the architecture of the new system to create a powerful and compatible system. Today we have Panther, the latest release of Mac OS X with the features that users want and the technologies that developers need.

The Mac OS X Layers

Apple typically presents Mac OS X as a series of layers. Each layer represents an independent component of the Mac OS X operating system. The lower levels (such as Darwin and QuickTime) provide the foundation of technologies on higher levels.

The Mac OS X architecture consists of 11 components (as represented in Figure 1.1):

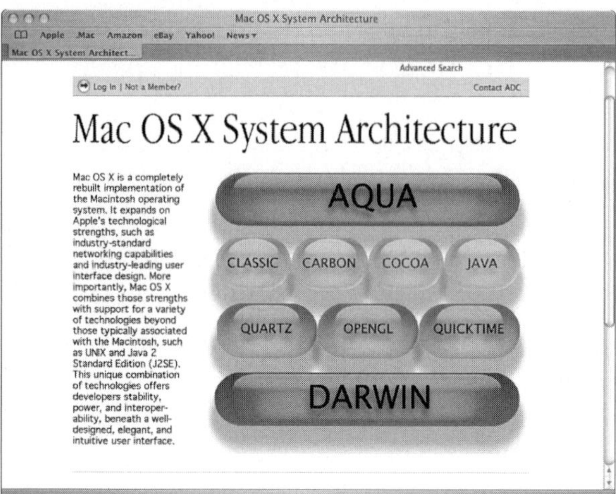

FIGURE 1.1 The Mac OS X architecture can be represented using a layered, component-based model.

- Darwin—The open source core operating system. Darwin includes a full BSD implementation (more on that later in the chapter).
- Quartz and Quartz Extreme—Apple's new 2D imaging framework and window server based on the PDF format. Quartz breaks new ground in handling the onscreen interface. Quartz Extreme builds on Quartz by coupling the image manipulation capabilities of Quartz with the powerful graphic transformation features of OpenGL. (OpenGL, although powerful for 3D rendering, can also manipulate 2D images with ease.) Today's video cards, such as the Radeon and GeForce, perform the work of OpenGL rendering using the card's dedicated processor (GPU) virtually eliminating the burden of Quartz from your Macintosh's CPU.
- OpenGL—OpenGL is the industry standard created by SGI (formerly known as Silicon Graphics, Inc.) for 3D graphics. Although OpenGL is heavily challenged by Direct3D on the Microsoft platform, even Microsoft grudgingly supports the standard.
- QuickTime—Apple's award-winning multimedia technologies are built in to the graphics foundation of Mac OS X. Jaguar's QuickTime 6.0 includes the new standard for Internet video—MPEG-4.
- CoreAudio—Apple's new professional Audio component provides wide-ranging MIDI support, native multichannel support, a plug-in audio effects system, 3D positional sound, and much more.
- Cocoa—Cocoa (originally called Yellow Box in Rhapsody and derived from NeXTSTEP and OpenStep) is the robust modern API that enables applications to be built from scratch in a fraction of the time it would take traditionally.

- Java 2—For the first time ever, the Mac OS is a player in the Java development and deployment arena. Java 2SE v1.4.1 is a first-class citizen and distributed with each copy of Mac OS X.
- Carbon—An application programming interface (API) to ease the transition to Mac OS X for traditional Mac programmers. This is based on the original Mac OS API and can be used to create programs that run on Mac OS 8/9 as well as Mac OS X.
- Classic—The Classic environment (originally called Blue Box in the Rhapsody implementation) enables existing Mac OS applications to run under Mac OS X.
- Aqua—Aqua uses the Quartz imaging engine to create the most astoundingly beautiful user interface available on any platform. Applications written in Cocoa, Carbon, or Java can access the capabilities of the Aqua GUI.
- AppleScript—Lying at the top of the Mac OS X technologies is AppleScript. AppleScript is a deceptively easy-to-use but powerful scripting language that enables users to script Mac OS X applications and automate workflows. Advanced programmers can take advantage of AppleScript Studio (part of the Apple Developer Tools) to build full GUI applications with AppleScript.

NOTE

If you're interested in the Mac OS X architecture from a developer's viewpoint, you can download an overview from `http://developer.apple.com/macosx/architecture/`.

What Is an API?

An *Application Programming Interface*, or API, is a collection of procedures and functions that a programmer can use when writing software. APIs are usually specific to a particular task; for example, the QuickTime API can be employed to add multimedia to applications. The system-level API for traditional Macintosh programming is called the Macintosh Toolbox. In Mac OS X, the Carbon API has replaced the Toolbox.

What's New in Panther

Panther is Apple's third release of Mac OS X (or fourth if you count the public beta). It continues the trend of yearly major updates, which, although not entirely friendly on the pocketbook, is a welcome change to the years of stagnation the operating system underwent in the mid to late '90s.

Over the past several years we've worked to keep this book up-to-date with the latest additions to the operating system, and Panther is no different. In this section, we'll briefly cover what we consider to be the major changes from Jaguar to Panther, and where you can read about them (if appropriate). This isn't an all-inclusive list—just the elements that we've found to be the most compelling.

Aqua refinement—The original release of Mac OS X sported a bright blue interface with stripes. It was unlike anything anyone had seen. Unfortunately, it proved just a bit garish for even the most die-hard fan. Since that time, Apple has slowly toned down the colors and shading, and greatly reduced the contrast of the stripes. In Panther, common interface elements have been replaced by more streamlined alternatives—elegant button bars replace bulky tabs, and menus are separated into sections by horizontal lines rather than empty space. The end result is that Panther is much easier on the eyes than any other release of Mac OS X. (Throughout)

Finder—The Panther Finder has been rewritten to use the metal appearance (the jury is still out on this). It includes easier network browsing, searching, labels, and a new sidebar to enable users to quickly navigate to important locations on their system. The biggest benefit of the new sidebar feature is that Open and Save dialog boxes also inherit the sidebar—providing a "Finder-like" experience for file navigation. (Chapter 2)

Fast user switching—Mac OS X is (and has been) a multiuser system, capable of running multiple processes for multiple users simultaneous. Unfortunately, prior to 10.3, the only way to really do this was through the command line. Panther provides *fast user switching*—a means of allowing users to turn over their computer to another person without having to exit their applications. (Chapter 2)

Exposé—Probably the most "visual" change of Panther is Exposé. This new System Preferences pane enables a user to quickly find a specific window and bring it to the front, no matter how many they have scattered across their screen. Besides being useful, Exposé uses the scaling features of Mac OS X to work its magic in an absolutely mesmerizing way. (Chapter 2)

Internet experience—The Panther "Internet experience" has improved greatly over previous versions of the operating system with the inclusion of Safari 1.0, iChat AV (with videoconferencing features), a greatly improved version of Mail (that doesn't feel like you're working in mud), and a revised version of Sherlock that makes finding third-party channels extremely easy.

Utilities—Almost all the Mac OS X utilities have had a face-lift or been consolidated with other, similar, utilities. Preview, Disk Utility, and Activity Monitor all have new features and a new look. A new tool, Font Book, has been added to provide basic Font management features to the new OS. (Chapters 3–10)

Component installation—Although not an "in-your-face" feature per se, Panther greatly simplifies installation of components such as screensavers and fonts. Instead of needing to know where to place these items, a user can simply double-click the item she wants to install, and Panther automatically does it for her. This brings back an OS ease-of-use not seen since System 9.x. (Throughout)

Faxing—Although free faxing utilities were available for previous versions of Mac OS X, Apple has included its own utility in Panther. Everything you need to send and receive faxes with a fax-modem equipped Macintosh are included in Panther (Chapter 10).

Unix subsystem—Panther updates the BSD subsystem from release 4.4 to 5.0. This change brings with it new features in the command-line utilities. Apple has also included Linux APIs for ease of software porting and made a switch to bash—a shell made popular largely by Linux distributions. (Chapters 12–32)

X11—Although available as a free download from Apple's site for Jaguar, the Apple X11 X Windows distribution is included on the CDs that come with the operating system. X11 is the windowing system common to the Unix platform and can be used to compile and run thousands of GUI Unix applications on your Macintosh. (Chapter 19)

Postfix—Sendmail is gone! If you're running a mail server, Postfix is now the default MTA for Mac OS X. Although some users may lament the change, it bodes well for those who want to create a secure mail server without stumbling through the nightmare of Sendmail configuration. (Chapter 29)

Networking—Network configuration has improved with Wizard-based setup, direct support for IPv6, increased functionality such as GUI support for renewing DHCP leases, and interoperability with VPNs. (Chapters 9 and 30)

Security—Apple has consolidated several user-level security features within the System Preferences and has added the File Vault utility, which can transparently encrypt your home directory, making it difficult to steal information, even if a thief has physical access to your hard drive. (Chapters 3, 11, and 31)

Windows integration—Integration with Windows operating systems is improved with significantly better file browsing, sharing (via Samba v3), and Active Directory support. Working well with Windows continues to be a big focus of Mac OS X development. (Chapter 30).

New Chess!—Yes, after years of including a barely updated (over its NeXT counterpart), visually buggy (try setting your piece colors), and somewhat lackluster Network configuration application, Apple has included a new fully 3D chess game in Panther. If you need one good reason to push you over the edge to purchase the Panther update, this is it (unless you hate chess, in which case you'll have to find another reason).

There are many tweaks and refinements throughout the operating system, and Apple is guaranteed to make more as the 10.3.x releases appear throughout the year. If Apple adds it to the OS, we'll do our best to include the information in *Mac OS X Unleashed*.

Mac OS X Basics

When using Mac OS X, shown in Figure 1.2, you'll interact with many different programs operating in different ways.

FIGURE 1.2 The Mac OS X workspace is similar to Windows, Linux, and traditional Mac OS desktops.

Constant throughout the operating system, however, are a number of components that you should become familiar with to best exploit the capabilities of the operating system. If you've been with Mac OS X since the beginning, you may want to skip ahead. Otherwise, read through these pages to get a feel for the OS elements and terminology you'll be encountering throughout the book:

- The filesystem—Where did everything go? Mac OS X imposes a strict structure on the filesystem. Learn where you can find your files and applications.
- The Apple menu—The Apple menu provides access to recent applications, documents, and common systemwide functions. Gone are desk accessories and access to individual control panels.
- Windows—The Mac OS X windows have controls that are similar to both traditional Mac OS and Windows, but not quite the same as either.
- The Application menu—In Mac OS X, each application has its own self-named menu that contains functions common to any program, such as setting preferences or showing version information.
- Menu extras—Many of the system preferences panes and applications (Sound, Date and Time, Network, iChat, and so on) offer the capability of adding a menu extra to the menu bar for quick access to settings.
- Additional components—Additional components that you're likely to encounter throughout Mac OS X applications include features such the Color Picker and Spell Checking.

NOTE

Obviously the Dock and Finder are important interface elements as well, but they go far beyond being simple components of Mac OS X, and, as such, get their very own chapter—Chapter 2, "Managing the Panther Workspace."

The Filesystem—Where Did Everything Go?

Mac OS X radically changes the way that Mac users interact with their files by imposing structure on a system that previously allowed a user to delete just about every file and folder on his hard drive before complaining. For those who have been using the Mac OS for 15 years, this change might come as an unwelcome surprise. Interestingly, Windows 2000/XP and Linux users are likely to be more accustomed to these restrictions already.

The goal of the OS X project is to provide system stability and ease of use to as wide a range of users as possible. To do this, Apple created sets of directories that must exist on each Mac OS X installation. This produces consistency across different copies of the operating system and makes it simple for application installers to choose the appropriate place for storing files. Users cannot modify the system-level directories or move them out of their default location. Anyone with experience using Mac OS 8 or 9 will, at one point in time, have installed a piece of software only to ask "Where in the world did that file just go?" Under Mac OS X, you'll know.

The "Computer Level" of the Filesystem Hierarchy

Like the My Computer icon in Windows, Mac OS X provides a topmost view of the storage devices accessible to the machine. You can still see your drives and network volumes mounted on the desktop, but you can also access them by looking at the Computer view of your system. Figure 1.3 shows a Finder window that is viewing the top level of the system.

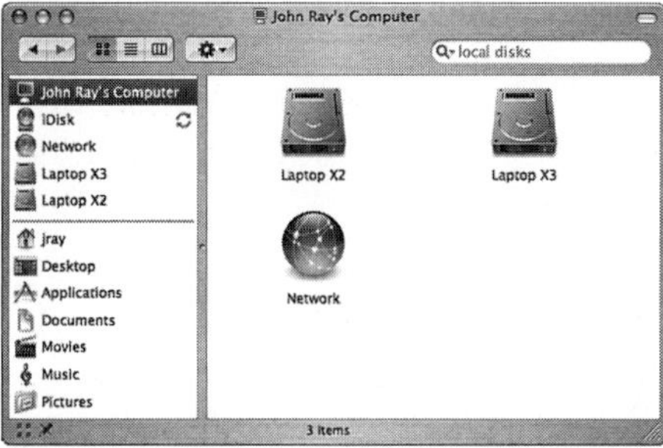

FIGURE 1.3 Mac OS X provides access to your drives and network within a Finder window, as well as on the desktop.

Within these locations are all the files accessible by my system. Any additional FireWire or USB drives plugged into the computer will appear in this location, as well as be mounted directly on the desktop.

The purpose of the hard drive icons should be obvious: to navigate the filesystem just as you would in Mac OS 8/9 or Windows. The Network icon works much like Network Places in Windows. Double-clicking Network allows you to browse and access file servers on your local network.

NOTE

Linux and Unix users might recognize the Computer level of the filesystem as being the same as the root level of a Unix filesystem. In reality, the root level starts with the Mac OS X boot disk—all other volumes use mount points below that volume (under the `/Volumes` directory). The Computer view of the filesystem is an artificial construct created by Apple to provide a top-level view of all resources available on the computer.

The Top-Level Mac OS X Filesystem

When you open your Mac OS X boot drive, you see a collection of four permanent folders (Applications, Library, System, and Users), similar to those shown in Figure 1.4. These directories contain all the preinstalled applications, utilities, and configuration files for your system. If you've installed Xcode (recommended if you intend to use the Unix features discussed in this book), you'll also see a Developer folder containing the development tools.

FIGURE 1.4 The Mac OS X top-level filesystem contains several permanent folders.

NOTE

If you have installed Mac OS 9 on your machine, you will also see several folders related to that operating system:

- Desktop (Mac OS 9)—An alias of the Mac OS 9 desktop
- Applications (Mac OS 9)—Mac OS 9's support applications

- System Folder—The Mac OS 9 System Folder
- Documents—Mac OS 9 Documents and Information files

These locations are not "part" of Mac OS X per se, but part of Classic, covered in Chapter 3, "Applications and Utilities."

As a normal Mac OS X user, you cannot modify these folders by moving, renaming, or deleting them. In addition, you cannot create new folders at this level of the drive. Don't worry too much about this. If you really want to create a new folder, there are ways to do it by using the superuser account or `sudo` (discussed later in the book), but it shouldn't be necessary.

Applications

The Applications folder contains all the preinstalled Mac OS X applications, such as iChat AV, Mail, QuickTime Player, and many others. Any application located within this folder will be accessible to any user on the system. If you're installing an application that should be accessed by only a single person, it might make more sense to store the application within the user's home directory (home directories will be covered shortly).

Perhaps more interesting than the applications in the Applications folder is the Utilities folder, which is also located within the Applications folder. The Utilities folder contains tools necessary to set up your printers, calibrate your display, and perform other important tasks.

Library

The Library folder demonstrates the modular construction of the OS X system. Although it does not have a strict definition, you can think of the Library as a storage location for systemwide application preferences, application libraries, and information that should be accessible to any user.

Some of the `/Library` folders are used by applications to store data such as preferences, whereas others hold printer drivers or other system additions made by the user. The default Library folders you'll find upon installation include the following:

- Application Support—Contains files that are used by, but are not necessarily part of, an application. For example, the StuffIt engine is used globally by several compression utilities. Instead of having multiple copies of the engine for each program, a single copy of the engine is located in the Application Support folder.
- Audio—Contains application or user-added sounds and plug-ins for the Mac OS X audio system.
- Caches—Stores cached system information.
- ColorSync—Stores ColorSync output device profiles as well as scripts to work with ColorSync information. Mac OS X includes a large number of AppleScripts that can be used immediately, including the ability to mimic the color settings of a typical PC monitor.

- Desktop Pictures—Although desktop pictures can be loaded from any picture file, the Desktop Pictures directory provides a central storage area for all users to access picture files.
- Documentation—If a third-party application installs documentation beyond traditional program help files, it should automatically be added to this folder.
- Fonts—User-installed fonts can be added to the Fonts folder.
- Frameworks—Shared libraries used by one or more applications.
- Image Capture—Mac OS X includes an extensible utility for retrieving images from digital cameras and other forms of digital media. This folder contains scripts that can automatically crop images or create Web page galleries.
- Internet Plug-Ins—Rather than multiple browsers needing multiple copies of the same plug-in, or multiple users each needing a copy, the Internet Plug-Ins directory stores a single copy, accessible by any program that needs them.
- Java—Java is an integral portion of Mac OS X. If there are Java class libraries that should be available to anyone using the system, they can be stored in the Java folder.
- Keyboard Layouts—Plug-ins for alternative keyboard layouts.
- Keychains—Files containing authentication information for system services.
- Logs—Log files generated by user-level services, such as file sharing, are stored here.
- Modem Scripts—The scripts necessary to initialize all the Mac OS X–supported modems are stored here. These scripts are simple text files that can easily be modified to work with unlisted modems.
- Perl—Perl module information is stored within the Perl directory. Users should never need to manually update the contents of this folder.
- Preferences—Systemwide preference files. Because Mac OS X supports multiple users, each user should have his own preferences file (located in his home directory). This folder contains preferences that are global; that is, across all users.
- Printers—Drivers and utility software to manage third-party printers. Printer page description files can also be found here.
- Python—Third-party Python packages can be added to this directory.
- QuickTime—QuickTime plug-ins, such as third-party codecs live here.
- Receipts—When an application uses the Apple installer to copy files to the system, it leaves behind a `.pkg` (package) file that contains a complete list of all the files installed on the system and where they are located. Chapter 32, "System Maintenance," contains information on how to read the "Bill of Materials" from a `.pkg` file.

- Screen Savers—Screensavers accessible by all users can be added either manually or automatically (by double-clicking) to this directory.
- Scripts—A number of useful AppleScripts are stored in the Scripts folder. Everything from Finder to email automation is included.
- StartupItems—If a StartupItems folder doesn't exist on your system, you can create one. Any properly configured services will be executed from this location automatically. Note: This is not to be used in the same manner as the Startup folder on Mac OS 9. Applications placed here will not start when the computer is booted.
- User Pictures—This folder contains custom user pictures that can be used to identify individual accounts at login.
- WebServer—CGIs (executable programs designed to work with a Web browser) and HTML documents are stored here. These can be used to build an industrial-strength Web server.

If you plan to run a system with multiple user accounts, these folders affect all users on the system. For example, if you purchase a screensaver module for yourself, putting it in the `/Library/Screen Savers` folder gives access to all users.

As you work your way through the OS, you'll discover two other Library folders, one in your home directory, and another in the System directory. Each of these folders is similar in function to `/Library` but affects different parts of the system.

The `/System/Library` folder should never be touched by you, or third-party installers—it is reserved for Apple's system-level settings. The `/Users/<your user name>/Library` folder (in your home directory, which we'll discuss shortly, is for your own personal settings and items (such as screensavers) that should be accessible only by *you*—not every user on the entire machine.

TIP

If your computer is being used as a personal workstation, it's best to leave the Mac OS X installation as "untainted" as possible. Almost all the items contained in the Library folder can also exist within your home directory. As you'll soon learn, your home directory is yours to configure however you see fit. Keeping systemwide configuration as simple as possible helps to make backing up and restoring a system very straightforward.

System

Next up on the list is the Mac OS X System folder. By default, the System folder contains one other folder, called Library. This is similar to the Library folder that contains the Fonts folder and other resources, but is reserved for use by Apple's software. Within the System's

Library folder are contained the components that make up the core of the Mac OS X experience. Even though it is possible to perform some interesting hacks to the operating system by changing these files, be aware that any modifications you make could result in your computer becoming unbootable.

Users

The Users directory, for newcomers, typically requires the most explanation.

Mac OS X is based on an underlying Unix operating system. Within Unix, each file and folder belongs to a specific user and group. The *owner* of a file is exactly what it sounds like—the person to whom that file belongs. If you create a file, you own it. As the owner, you have the right to decide whether you want other people to be able to view or edit it. A file or directory's *group* is similar to the owner, but an owner is a single person, whereas a group can consist of many different people.

For example, assume that you (Joe) are working with team members on an annual budget report. The members of the team who should be able to read the file are Betty, Bob, and Sue. Because there can be only one owner, Betty, Bob, and Sue can be given access to the file by assigning them to a group, such as `ReportReaders`, and then providing `ReportReaders` the ability to read the files.

Chapter 11, "Additional System Components," and Chapter 24, "User Management and Machine Clustering," discuss how new groups can be added to the system and users assigned to them. After they've been added, you can assign arbitrary groups and permissions to files/folders within the Finder (see Chapter 2) or via the command line.

There is another possibility for allowing multiple people to have access to a single file: granting access to "others." In the event that everyone should be able to read a file, you can also grant access to anyone. This is the typical mode of operation for the traditional Mac operating system—everyone has access to everything.

These three attributes for allowing access to a file (owner, group, and world) are controlled via three sets of permissions:

- Owner permissions—Also called *user permissions*, these control whether a file's owner can read, write, or execute a file or application.
- Group permissions—These control read, write, and execute access for members of the group assigned to the file. If only the owner should have access to the file, the group permissions can be set to "none."
- Other permissions—These permissions affect everyone else—that is, those not in the file's group and not the owner. If a file has world read/write/execute access turned on, anyone with access to the system will be able to edit or delete the file.

NOTE

The owner of a file can always change the permissions associated with that file—even if they've turned off read or write access for themselves. Why would a file's owner want to shut off the ability to read or write his or her own file? Possibly to prevent accidental changes from being made. You'll find that the BSD layer of Mac OS X has a number of "why would you want to do that?" features. Creating special cases, such as limiting a file owner's ability to disable his own read access, is against the Unix philosophy of keeping the operating system consistent and flexible. If a file's owner doesn't want to be able to read his file, that's his decision, and Mac OS X isn't going to stop him!

Of the three permissions that can be set for the owner, group, or world, the read and write attributes should be obvious. They control the capability to read from files and write to them. The execute attribute controls whether a file should be capable of being launched by someone on the system. Some applications should be accessible by only certain users, and this attribute provides a means of selectively enabling a program to execute in the same way you can enable reading or writing. Unfortunately, because the Mac OS X Finder only supports setting read and write attributes directly, you'll need access to the command line to test execute permissions.

NOTE

As mentioned earlier, Mac OS X does not allow normal user accounts the capability to modify the folders at the top level of the hard drive. This is because those folders are owned by an account called the *root* or *superuser account*. Although it's tempting to use the root account to gain complete control over the system, it's also highly dangerous. For this reason, Apple has disabled the root account in Mac OS X. Enabling the account will be covered, but isn't recommended unless you're comfortable making changes that could affect your system's capability to boot.

The Home Directory

So, the system allows users to own their own files and provides a means of controlling other users' access to these files—what does that have to do with the Users directory that we're discussing? The Users directory contains the home directories of all the users on the machine. A user's home directory can be considered that user's workspace. It is hers, and hers alone. Files and folders stored within a user's home directory are protected from other users.

If you've been a Mac user for a long time, you should start to think of your home directory as the place where you can make all your modifications to the folder arrangement and structure. Your home directory is the start of your personal area on Mac OS X. You can add documents, applications, fonts, screensavers—just about anything you can think of. Best of all, no one can mess with your configuration; conversely, you can't mess with anyone else's!

Within the Users directory are directories for each of the users on the system—these are the home directories themselves. Your directory will be named using the short name that you chose when you created your Mac OS X user account. Apple has created several default folders in your home directory, as shown in Figure 1.5.

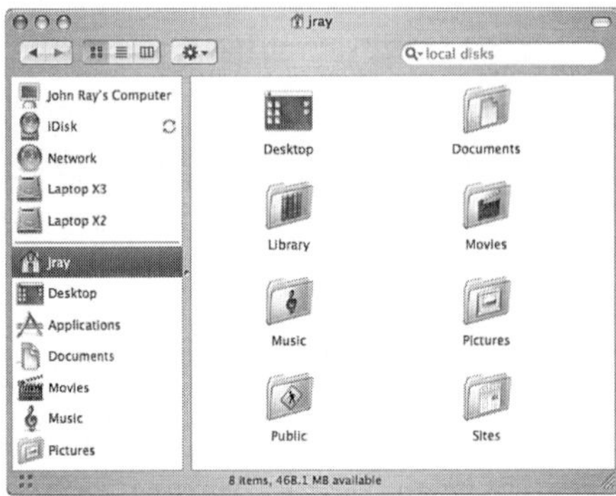

FIGURE 1.5 The home directory is filled with several default folders.

- Desktop—The Desktop folder is much like what it always has been: a folder that contains everything that shows up on your desktop. In older versions of the Mac OS, this folder is invisible unless you are connecting to a remote Macintosh AppleShare server, in which case you could see the remote machine's Desktop folder. In Mac OS X, the Desktop folder is always visible in your home directory.
- Documents—A generic store-all location for any documents that you create. This is just a recommended storage location to help organize your files.
- Library—The Library folder is the same as the top-level Library folder and the Library folder within the System folder. Within the directories in this directory, you can store fonts, screensavers, and many other extensions to the operating system.
- Movies—This is another generic storage location where you can keep your iMovies and other media.
- Music—A generic location for storing your MP3s and various audio files. This is the default music library location for iTunes 4.
- Pictures—A suggested location for storing pictures. Apple's iPhoto software stores its image files here, as do other applications you work with, but there's nothing stopping you from storing your files elsewhere.
- Public—If you plan to share your files over the network, you can do so by placing them in the Public folder and activating file sharing within the Sharing System

Preferences pane. This is discussed in Chapter 9, "Network Setup." Inside the Public folder is another folder called Drop Box. Other users can place items inside your drop box, but they cannot open the Drop Box folder itself. A small down arrow is located at the lower-right corner of the Drop Box icon to identify it visually.

- Sites—The Sites folder contains your personal Web site, starting with the document index.html.

TIP

The top-level Library folder, the System folder's Library folder, and the Library folder in the user's home directory are all similar. Each can hold components used by other parts of the operating system.

The operating system evaluates these in the order of `/System/Library`, `/Library`, and then the `Library` in each user's folder. To keep files as consolidated as possible, it's best to store components in your home Library folder. If some items should be accessible to all the operating system's users, place these within the top-level Library.

You should never need to change the contents of the System folder.

Even though Apple has been kind enough to include specific folders for different file types, feel free to do anything you want with your home directory. The only folders that should not be modified (renamed or deleted) are the Desktop and Library folders. These are critical to system operation and must be maintained.

NOTE

By default, a user can access only the Public and Sites folders within another user's home directory. Other folders appear with a red minus symbol in the lower-right corner. This indicates that no access is available to that location.

The Apple Menu

In 1984, Apple introduced the Apple menu, similar to what many MS Windows users now call the Start menu. The Apple menu provided an access point for small applications and system controls. Originally, the Mac OS allowed only special applications called Desk Accessories to exist in the Apple menu. Later, the menu became a simple folder that a user could place an application or folder in, and then access that item from within any application, at any time.

Under Mac OS X, the Apple menu is restricted to performing systemwide tasks or launching System Preferences. Figure 1.6 shows the Mac OS X Apple menu.

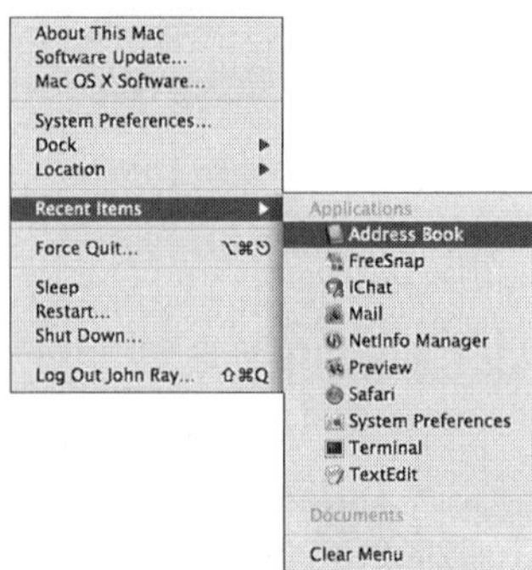

FIGURE 1.6 The Mac OS X Apple menu can be used to access common systemwide functions.

The choices now available from the Apple menu are as follows:

- About This Mac—Displays information about the computer. This shows the current version of the operating system, the amount of available memory, and the type of processor the system is using.
- Software Update—Launch the Mac OS X auto-update feature to check for new versions of installed Apple software.
- Mac OS X Software—Launches the user's preferred Web browser and loads the URL `http://www.apple.com/downloads/macosx/`. There, you can download third-party applications from Apple's list of available OS X software.
- System Preferences—The equivalent of the traditional control panels, the System Preferences selection launches the application used to control almost all aspects of the Mac OS X configuration.
- Dock—The Mac OS X Dock is one of the most visible additions to the new operating system—it is also one of the most controversial. This submenu provides quick access to common functions, such as the ability to hide the Dock. These functions, as you might expect, are also located in System Preferences.
- Location—The Location submenu allows you to quickly reconfigure the Mac OS X network settings. Locations are configured within System Preferences.
- Recent Items—Displays the most recently launched applications and documents. This submenu is visible in Figure 1.6.
- Force Quit—Opens a window where you can choose to quit an application, regardless of its current state. Forcing an application to quit in Mac OS X does not disrupt operating system stability but will lose any unsaved data. This is equivalent to the BSD command `kill` **`-kill`** ***`<process ID>`***. See Chapter 12, "Introducing the BSD Subsystem," for more information on the command line.

- Sleep—Places your computer in a sleep state that requires very little power and can be started in a matter of seconds without the need for a full reboot.
- Restart—Closes all applications, prompts the user to save open files, and gracefully reboots the computer.
- Shut Down—Closes all applications, prompts the user to save open files, and shuts down the computer.
- Log Out—Closes all applications, prompts the user to save open files, and then returns to the Mac OS X login screen.

TIP

Three of the eleven Apple menu items can be accessed by pressing Control-Eject on the new Apple keyboards. This keystroke displays a dialog box with Restart, Shutdown, and Sleep options.

Pressing the power button on an Apple monitor or computer has the same effect.

TIP

The menu options Logout, Restart, and Shutdown can be invoked without a confirmation dialog box if you hold down the Option key while selecting them.

Windows

There's no getting around it—the Aqua interface is unlike any other. One of the most obvious places that you'll deal with the interface is through onscreen windows, demonstrated in Figure 1.7. There are a number of differences between Mac OS X window controls and other operating systems. Let's take a look at a Finder window and see what's different.

FIGURE 1.7 Mac OS X windows are familiar, but the position of common elements has changed, and a few new ones have been added.

Close/Minimize/Zoom

In the upper-left corner of each window are located the Close (red X), Minimize (yellow –), and Zoom (green +) buttons. Differentiated only by color and position, the corresponding character symbol appears in each bubble button when the mouse cursor nears.

Clicking the Close button closes the open window. The OS X Minimize button shrinks the window into an icon view contained within the Dock. This icon is a full representation of the original contents of the window, and sometimes might even update its appearance as the parent application generates new output. To help differentiate between different minimized windows, the icon of the controlling application will be superimposed in the lower-right corner of the minimized icon. Clicking the icon in the Dock restores the window to its original position and size on the screen.

TIP

Double-clicking the title bar of a window has the same effect as clicking the Minimize button.

The Zoom (maximize) button does not perform in the way to which most Windows users are accustomed. Instead of filling the entire screen (which has always bothered me to no end), Maximize opens the window to the size necessary to display the available information. If three icons need to be shown, you don't need to waste your entire screen showing them.

TIP

Holding down Option while clicking the Minimize or Close button results in all the windows in the current application being minimized or closed.

Hide/Show Toolbar

In the upper-right corner of certain windows (such as the Finder and Mail windows) is an elongated button that can be used to quickly show or hide toolbars in applications. Apple has stressed ease of use within Mac OS X and is advocating customizable toolbars within applications.

Window Moving and Resizing

A noticeable new window feature, or lack thereof, is the borderless content area. As seen in Figure 1.8, the display in most "non-metallic" OS X application windows goes directly to the edge of the content window.

Although this creates a more attractive and more integrated feeling, all window dragging must take place from the title bar. Luckily, Apple has prevented users from completely dragging the title bar of a window off the screen. Title bars will not extend past the menu bar; several pixels of the edge of the window remain if you attempt to push a window off the edge of the screen.

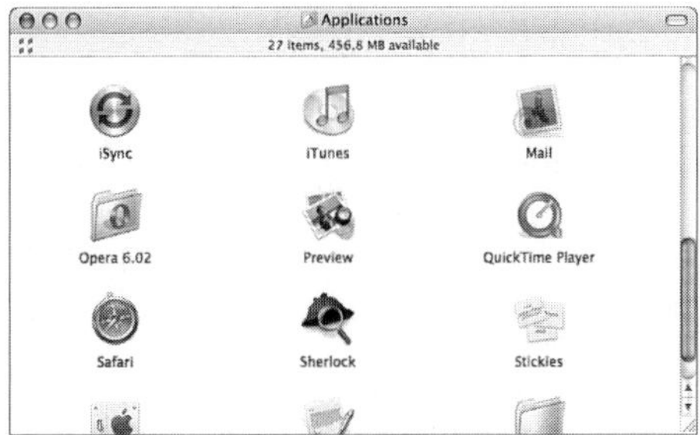

FIGURE 1.8 The content in a window goes right up to the edge.

Resizing windows works as you're accustomed: Click and drag on the resize icon in the lower-right corner of each window. Many applications in Mac OS X take advantage of *live resizing*; that is, as you resize the window, the contents of the window change. Unless you have a fast machine or blazing video card, live resizing is, sadly, painfully slow in content-heavy applications such as Web browsers.

TIP

In Mac OS X, if you hold down the Command key, you can drag nonactive windows that are located behind other windows. In fact, holding down Command enables you to click buttons and move scrollbars in many background applications.

Another fun trick is to hold down the Option key while clicking on an inactive application's window. This hides the frontmost application and brings the clicked application to the front.

Finally, rather than switching to another window to close, minimize, or maximize it, positioning your cursor over the appropriate window controls highlights them—allowing you to get rid of obtrusive windows without leaving your current workspace.

Although slightly improved in Panther, Apple's new window design has brought much criticism from those accustomed to the Mac's platinum appearance. With Mac OS X, the window controls have taken on much of the appearance of their Windows counterparts. Creating an environment that is comfortable for all users, regardless of what they've used before, is an important part of Apple's strategy to attract new users.

Window Widgets

A number of *widgets* make up the Mac OS X interface, such as buttons, sliders, and check boxes. Although most users will be familiar with these items, there are a few that may leave people scratching their heads. Figure 1.9 shows samples of many of the OS X Aqua interface elements.

Aqua interface elements include the following:

- Button bars—New in Panther, button bars replace the traditional windows "tabs." Clicking an area within a button bar displays new information within the same window. In the current Apple UI guidelines, these are called *beveled button mosaics*—we'll call them *button bars*.
- Pushbuttons—Pushbuttons are rendered as translucent white or aqua-colored ovals with the appropriate label text. These are typically used to activate a choice or to respond to a question posed by the operating system or application. The default choice, activated by pressing the Return key, pulses for easy visual confirmation.
- Check boxes/Radio buttons—These elements perform identically to their OS 8/9 counterparts aside from an update in coloring. Check boxes are used to choose multiple attributes (AND), whereas radio buttons are used to choose between attributes (OR).

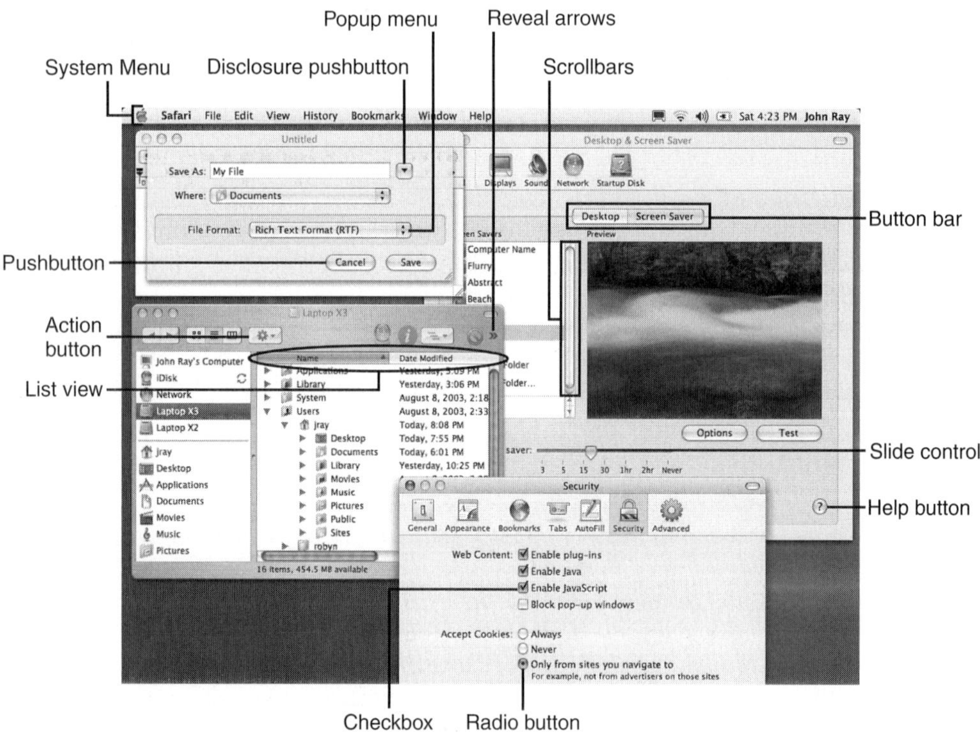

FIGURE 1.9 These are the Mac OS X window widgets.

- List views—List views are also similar to early Mac OS implementations. Clicking a column sorts by that selection. Clicking again reverses the direction of the sort (ascending to descending, or vice versa). Columns can be resized by clicking the edge of the heading and dragging in the direction you want to shrink or expand the column.
- Pop-up/down menus/System menus—Single-clicking a menu displays a menu until a selection is made. Menus can be navigated with the mouse, or the arrow keys—pressing Return when the correct selection is highlighted. Incidentally, there are "pop-up" and "pop-down" menus. The difference, according to Apple, is that pop-up menus extend up and down from the item you've clicked, whereas pop-down menus only extend down.
- Disclosure arrows—Disclosure arrows hide information that may be considered "extraneous""hide" adhide information within. Click the arrow to reveal additional information about an object.
- Disclosure pushbuttons—Like disclosure arrows, these pushbuttons are used to reveal all possible options (a full, complex view), or reduce a window to a simplified representation. This feature is used in the File Open/Save dialog boxes.
- Reveal arrows—Shown at the edge of a toolbar, reveal arrows, when clicked, display information that normally does not fit in the available onscreen space.
- Scrollbars—Scrollbars visually represent the amount of data within the current document by changing the size of the scrollbar handle in relation to the data to display. The larger the handle, the less data there is to scroll through. The smaller the handle, the more information to display.
- Sliders—Displayed in either horizontal or vertical orientation, slide controls are used to visually choose a value from a given range, such as choosing a size between two extremes.
- Help buttons—Clicking a Help ("?") button opens Mac OS X Help to information specific to the window where you clicked the button.

Sheet Dialogs and Drawers

Two other unique interface elements in Mac OS X are sheet dialogs and drawers. The sheet-style dialogs are used in place of traditional dialog boxes. Normally, when a computer wants to get your attention, it displays a dialog box with a question, such as "Do you want to save this document?". If you have ten open documents on your system, how do you know which one needs to be saved?

Sheets appear directly from the title bar of an open window. Instead of being "application-centric" or "system-centric," sheets are "document-centric." Figure 1.10 demonstrates a sheet-style dialog used to confirm saving the contents of a text document.

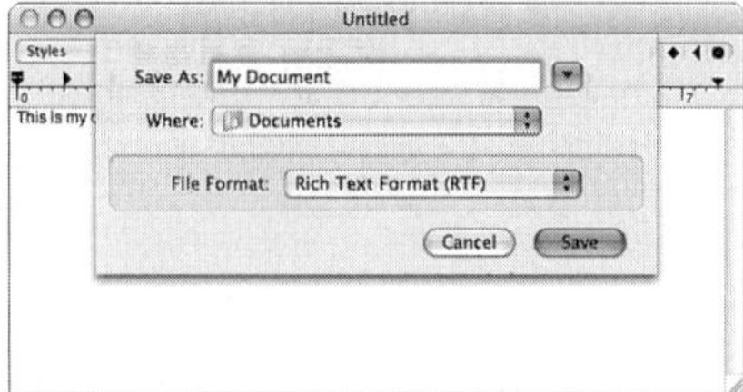

FIGURE 1.10 The sheet-style dialog appears to drop from an open window's title bar.

Sheet dialogs are used just like any other dialog box, except they are attached to a document. Unlike many dialog boxes, which keep you from interacting with the system until you interact with *them*, sheets only limit access to the window that the dialog box is related to.

Apple has included a few gee-whiz features in the implementation of these new styled dialog boxes. If a window is too close to the edge of the screen or too small to hold the entire sheet that appears, it will spring from the edge of the screen or scale the sheet appropriately so that it fits. This is just a visual effect but quite amusing in action.

Another new interface element introduced in Mac OS X is the window *drawer*. The drawer appears from the edge of an application window and is used to store commonly used settings and options that might need to be accessed while a program is running. Figure 1.11 shows the OS X Mail application's drawer, containing a list of active mailboxes.

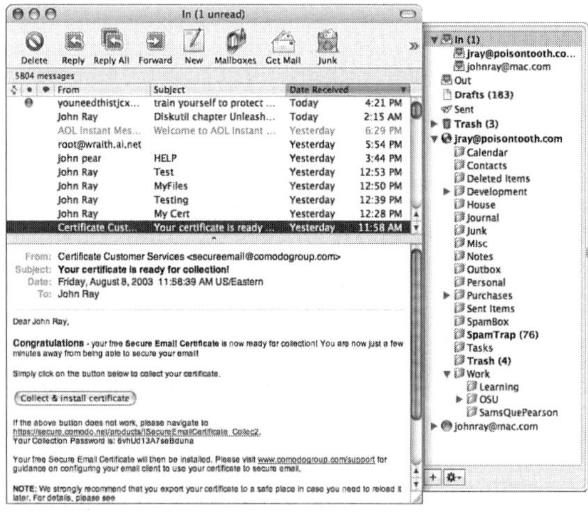

FIGURE 1.11 The drawer holds options often needed during a program's execution.

Applications supporting the use of a drawer typically activate it when you click a button in the toolbar. After a drawer is open, you can drag the edge to change its width.

TIP

There are two standards in how the drawer operates. By default, the tray slides out from the right of the main window after you click a button to activate it. If the window is too close to the side of the screen, the tray either is forced out of the other side of the window or pushes the main window over to make room.

If you're using an application in which the tray can appear from either side, you might be able to force the side that the tray uses in the future. For example, in the Mail application, if you position the window near the right side of the screen and then display the mailbox tray, it appears from the left side of the window. This position change will be remembered for future activations of the tray.

The Application Menu

When an application launches in Mac OS X, it creates a menu based on its own name and places it in the first position after the Apple on the menu bar. For example, if you start an application named TextEdit, the first menu item after the Apple will be TextEdit.

This menu contains items that act on the entire application rather than on its files. For example, traditionally, you would quit an application by choosing Quit from the File menu. Even though we're all familiar with this, it doesn't really make sense. Quitting an application has nothing to do with a file—it affects the running application. Because of this, the application menu was created to consolidate all the application-specific menus into one location. Figure 1.12 displays the application menu for DVD Player—an included application.

FIGURE 1.12 Application menus contain the functions that act on an entire application.

Seven default items make up the application menu:

- About—The About menu, which reveals information about the running program, used to be located under the Apple menu. The Apple menu is now reserved for systemwide options, so About has been placed within the application menu.

- Preferences—For many years, preferences haven't really had a home. Some applications placed the option under the File menu; others under the Edit menu.
  The application menu provides a convenient location for preferences because they apply to the entire application.
- Services—Services are one of the more interesting, but rarely mentioned, features of Mac OS X. A service is installed by an application and can act on a selected item on the system. For example, if you want to email some text from a Web page, you could select it and then choose Mail Text from the Mail service menu. This would launch the Mail application and start a new message containing your text.
- Hide—Hides the current application. This command hides all the windows in the active application. This was previously located within the application switcher menu—in the upper-right corner of Mac OS 8 or 9. Command-H is usually a shortcut for Hide.
- Hide Others—Hides all applications other than the active application. This effectively clears the screen except for the program you're currently using. In earlier versions of the operating system, this was also located in the application switcher menu.
- Show All—Shows all hidden applications.
- Quit—Quits the current application. Command-Q is the universal Quit shortcut.

NOTE

Although part of the application menu, Services deserve special attention because, even though they do work with information in the current application, they do so by sending it to other programs on the system.

For example, your Mac OS X system includes a Speech service with the option to speak selected text. If you happen to be reading an email message and would rather have it read aloud to you, you could select the message and then choose Start Speaking Text from Speech service. Mail passes the selected text to the Speech service, which subsequently reads it.

A few of the more useful services include

- Make New Sticky Note—Turns selected text into a Sticky Note.
- Mail—Starts a new email message that includes selected text or files.
- Speech—Reads selected text aloud.
- Summarize—Summarizes selected text by removing unnecessary content (this one is very cool).

Unfortunately Services don't always work in Carbon applications and never within applications running in Classic.

The application menu is a wise addition to the Apple menu but does take a while to get used to. I still find myself hunting through the menus looking for preferences, even when I know where I should be looking. Unfortunately, just because there is a place for a preferences menu, it doesn't mean that developers will fully use it. If applications are not modified to take advantage of this new menu, you might have to continue searching through your software's menu bar to find the real location of your preference menu item.

Menu Extras

Menu extras are GUI elements that appear in the right side of the Mac OS X menu bar. The time displayed in the upper-right corner of your screen, for example, is a menu extra. These handy additions provide quick access to common system settings or functions. Figure 1.13 shows a number of menu extras.

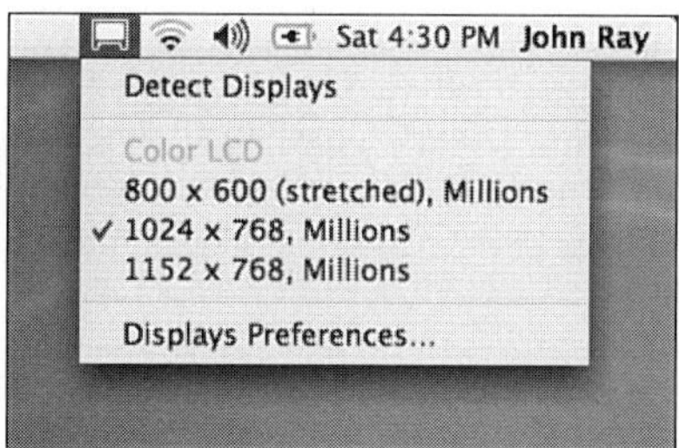

FIGURE 1.13 Menu Extras provide quick access to system settings.

Each extra is added to the menu bar through System Preferences panes that correspond to the item's function. A few of the extras provided in 10.3 include

- Displays—Adjusts the resolution and color depth from the menu bar.
- Volume—Changes the sound volume.
- AirPort—Monitors AirPort signal strength and quickly adjust network settings.
- IChat AV—Controls your connection to the AIM (AOL Instant Messenger) network. Provides quick access to online buddies and an easy way to change your AIM status.
- Date and Time— Displays date and time graphically as a miniature clock or using the standard text format.
- Battery—Keeps track of battery usage and recharge time.
- Modem Status—Displays modem connect time as well as options for initiating/terminating connections.

Clicking a Menu Extra opens a pop-down menu that displays additional information and settings. Items such as Battery and Date/Time can be modified to show textual information rather than a simple icon status representation.

Users can alter the position of Menu Extras by holding down the Command key and dragging the icons to the desired position. Menu extras can be removed entirely by dragging them off the menu bar.

Additional OS Components

A few other OS components don't quite fit into the categories we've looked at. To provide a simple point of reference, they'll be included here:

- Open/Save dialogs—Choosing a document to open and where to save a file, have changed drastically in Mac OS X.
- Color Picker—The Mac OS X Color Picker is intuitive, simple, and available globally.
- Font window—Applications can now take advantage of a global Mac OS X Font window. This eliminates the myriad of font-choosing devices (menus, windows, and so on) previously employed in the OS.
- Volume and brightness—Controls for your volume and screen brightness are available globally, even on desktop systems.
- Screen captures—Screen captures can be created easily within Mac OS X and offer unprecedented flexibility.
- Alternative input methods—Onscreen character sets and handwriting recognition give you new ways to enter information into your computer.
- Text tools—Built-in text tools for spell checking and search and replace provide advanced text features in the most unlikely places (such as Stickies!).

Apple's embracing of OS-wide component technologies bodes well for the operating system from the perspective of both a user and a developer.

Open/Save Dialog Boxes

Open and Save dialog boxes now feature the Mac OS X column and list displays—mirror two of the Finder's views. In addition, these dialogs also take advantage of the shortcut pane introduced in the Panther Finder (see Chapter 2 for details).

Open

When opening a document from within an application, you'll see a window similar to the one in Figure 1.14.

At the top of the window is a pop-up menu that displays your current position in the Mac OS X file hierarchy. Using this menu, you can choose any of the folders leading up to your current position.

Also in the toolbar are back/forward arrow buttons for moving back and forth to previously visited locations in the filesystem, and buttons for choosing List or Column view. These views and their interaction are discussed fully in Chapter 2.

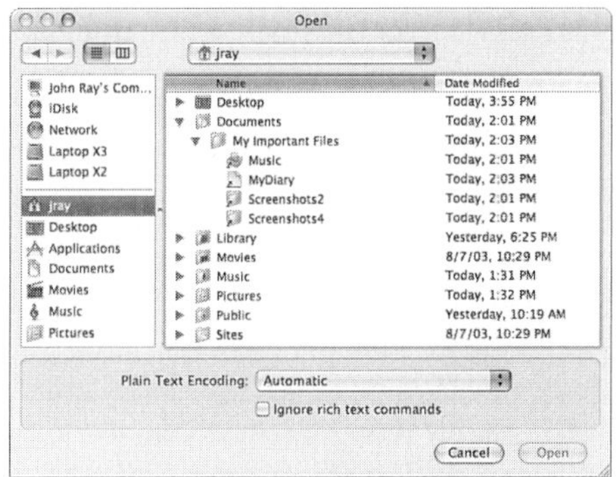

FIGURE 1.14 The default Open dialog box.

The center of the window contains the shortcut pane on the left and file navigation on the right. Any shortcuts defined within the Panther finder's sidebar automatically appear in the list in the dialog box. Clicking a shortcut refreshes the dialog box with the selected location. You can even drag to the dialog box's sidebar to add a new iem.

> **TIP**
>
> The Open and Save dialog boxes are resizable. When resized, additional columns are added to the column navigation view, making navigation even easier.

Save

The new style of file system navigation also carries over to the Save dialog box, shown in Figure 1.15.

In its default minimal state, the Save dialog contains only a Save As field for a filename and a Where pop-down menu that shows elements added to the Finder sidebar.

If the location to which you want to save your files isn't in the pop-up menu, you can click the disclosure pushbutton to the right of the Save As field. The dialog box expands to a full-sized Save box, shown in Figure 1.16.

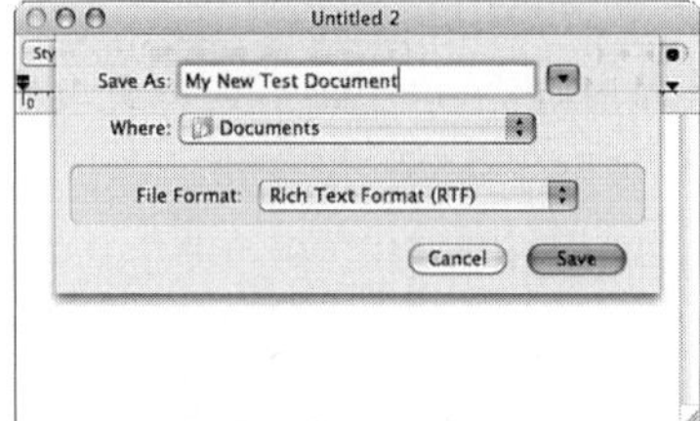

FIGURE 1.15 The default Save dialog contains only a filename and location pop-down menu.

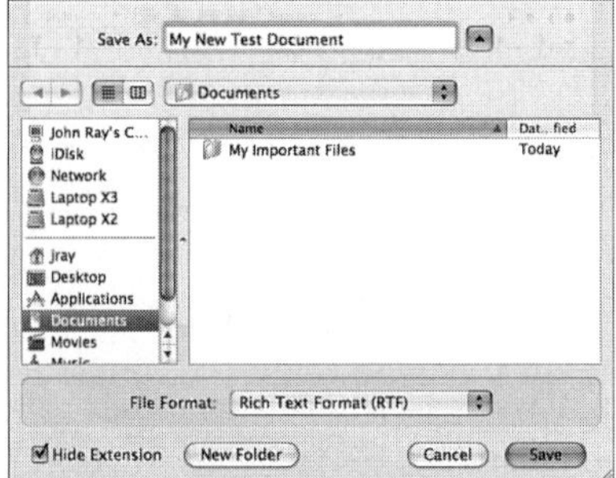

FIGURE 1.16 The Save dialog has an expanded view as well.

The file navigation within the Save dialog box works identically to the Open dialog. Clicking the New Folder button creates a new folder in the current folder.

One interesting new feature here is the Hide Extension check box. Clicking this displays the file without an added file extension. In the case of Figure 1.16, it removes the `.pdf` from the end of the filename. This is the way Macintosh users are used to seeing files, and might make some people more comfortable in the new operating system. If you prefer to see the entire filename, including the extension, leave this box unchecked.

When you've located the folder in which you want to store your file and entered a name in the Save As field, click the Save button to save the file.

Colors Window

Mac OS X has adopted a new color picker shared throughout Carbon and Cocoa applications.

Along the top of the window are five default color selection methods—color wheel, color sliders, color palettes, image palettes, and crayons—represented by a row of toolbar icons. Clicking one of the icons switches the selection method. Figure 1.17 displays a sample of the Colors window.

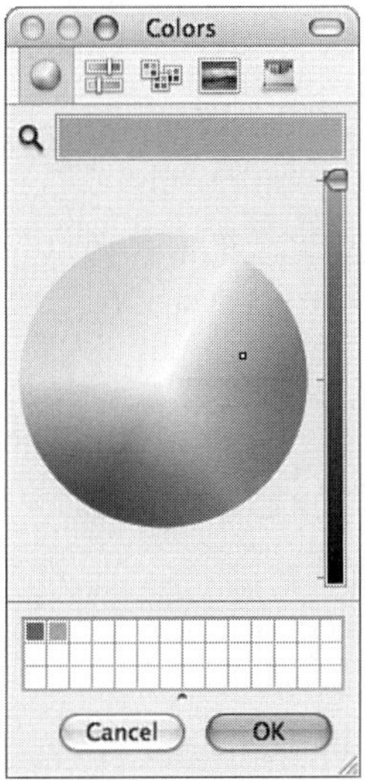

FIGURE 1.17 The Colors window provides several systemwide methods of picking your colors.

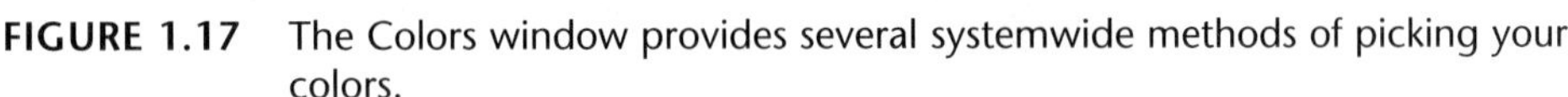

NOTE

Most of the color selection methods are self-explanatory. The image palette method, however, allows you to drag any Mac OS X–supported image format (including PDFs!) into the window to choose a color from that image. This might not be immediately obvious, but it is useful.

Three features are common to all the color selection methods:

- Magnifying glass—The magnifying glass can be used to choose a color from any window or location on the screen, even the menu bar.
- Color Well—To the right of the magnifying glass is the Color Well, which contains the currently selected color. Some applications support dragging colors directly from this rectangle to the object that should take on the color.
- Favorite Colors—At the bottom of the window is a Favorite Colors pane that you can use to store commonly used colors. Drag them from the Color Well into any of the squares to store them.

The Color Picker has two forms —it appears either as a standard window, with OK and Cancel buttons, or as a floating palette as determined by the software that invokes it. When in the window mode, you can simply click OK after you've picked a color. In palette mode, however, the Colors window does not automatically close after you pick a color—if you want to choose additional colors, this can be helpful.

Font Window

The Mac OS X Font window is a new method of choosing and organizing fonts on your system that eliminates the need for third-party utilities. Unfortunately, just because the window exists doesn't mean that applications use it.

The Font window is covered in detail in Chapter 10 "Printer, Fax, and Font Management." For now, let's take a look at a few of its modes of operation. By default, the Font window looks similar to that shown in Figure 1.18.

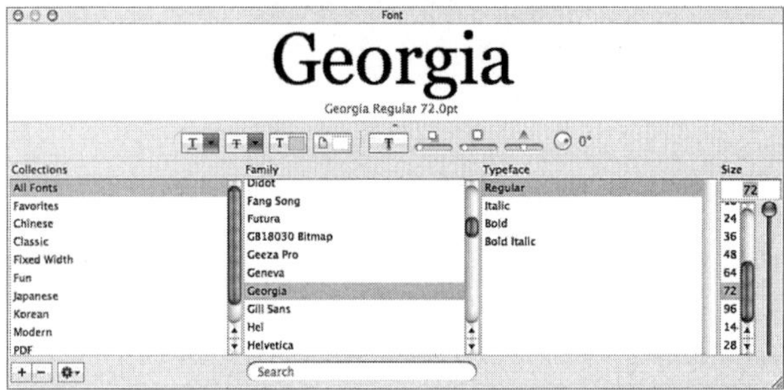

FIGURE 1.18 The Font window displays available font families, typefaces, and sizes in a single floating window.

You can easily see the available font families, the typefaces, and sizes. Much like the Finder's column navigation, you start at the left and work your way to the right. Each choice in a column limits the choices in the next column, and so on. If you want more control over the fonts, just drag the bottom-right corner of the window to expand it. A new column, Collections, appears. Collections are user-customizable font sets that help you keep track of the hundreds of available system fonts.

If, on the other hand, the Font window is too bulky for your tastes, resize the window into its smallest possible form. It takes on a new look, shown in Figure 1.19. Each of the columns is reduced to a single pop-up menu, conveying a maximum amount of information in a minimum amount of space.

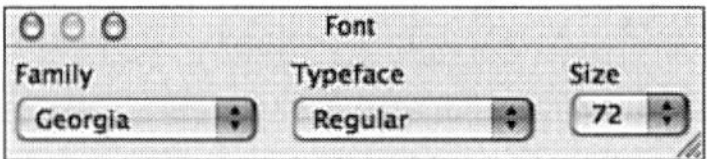

FIGURE 1.19 When resized, the Font window adjusts its appearance accordingly.

There are many other new features of the Font window, accessed through the buttons at the bottom and top of the window, including full drop shadow effects for any Font window aware application. These options are covered in Chapter 10.

Volume and Brightness

Finally those volume controls on your Apple keyboard are useful! Mac OS X includes support for adjusting screen brightness and system volume. Although this is not overly exciting in and of itself, Apple's implementation is elegant.

Pushing the sound keys on your keyboard displays a transparent overlay of the current sound level on your screen, as shown in Figure 1.20.

FIGURE 1.20 Users can adjust volume and brightness from their keyboards.

The keyboard brightness controls work in much the same way—providing instant access to your screen settings. Although these keys are not labeled on desktop keyboards, the dim/brighten controls are accessible by pressing F14 and F15, respectively.

Screen Captures

After three years of release, I still find users who don't know how to take screen captures in Mac OS X. This built-in function is an example of another slick feature barely mentioned by Apple.

To make a simple screenshot and save it to a PDF file (sequentially labeled `Picture 1`, `Picture 2`, ... , `Picture` *n*, as you take them), use Command-Shift-3. You hear a camera shutter sound, and the picture file appears on the desktop. To save directly to the Clipboard rather than a file, use Control-Command-Shift-3. These can be customized in the Keyboard and Mouse System Preferences pane, discussed in Chapter 11.

NOTE

If you have multiple monitors attached, each screen will be a page within the saved PDF file.

The fun doesn't stop there. Two additional screenshot modes allow you to choose a portion of the screen to image.

The first, Command-Shift-4 displays a crosshair that you can drag across the screen to select the area you want to save. After drawing the region, let go of the mouse button, and the screen area will be saved. Again, including Control in the equation (Control-Command-Shift-4) saves the picture to the Clipboard rather than a file.

Finally, the last mode of screen capture takes a picture of a given window or screen element (Dock icon, menu bar, and so on). To activate this mode, bring up the crosshairs by pressing Command-Shift-4 or Control-Command-Shift-4. Before doing anything else, press the *spacebar*—the crosshair changes to a camera. Using the mouse, point the camera at the element you want to capture—it will highlight—and then press the mouse button to take the picture.

Alternative Input Methods

In Mac OS X 10.2, Apple introduced two new methods of getting information into your computer. You've used your mouse and keyboard for years; perhaps it's time to try something different. If you have a supported graphics tablet (currently Wacom), and have installed the appropriate drivers, you can "write" into all your favorite applications using Apple's Inkwell technology. Alternatively, if you're looking for a specific character, you can invoke the new global character palette to find any character in any font on your system.

Inkwell

Built from the remains of the Newton recognition engine, the new *Apple Recognition Engine* (also known as Inkwell) provides global handwriting recognition within Mac OS X. Adaptive to a wide variety of printing styles, Inkwell can insert text and graphics or execute commands based on the penstrokes you enter on your graphics tablet.

For example, you can easily start the Mail application, write a message to your friend using your own handwriting, switch to Inkwell's graphics mode, create a digital graphical signature for the message, and send it—all without touching a mouse (or trackpad, for laptop users). Figure 1.21 shows Inkwell adding text to the TextEdit application.

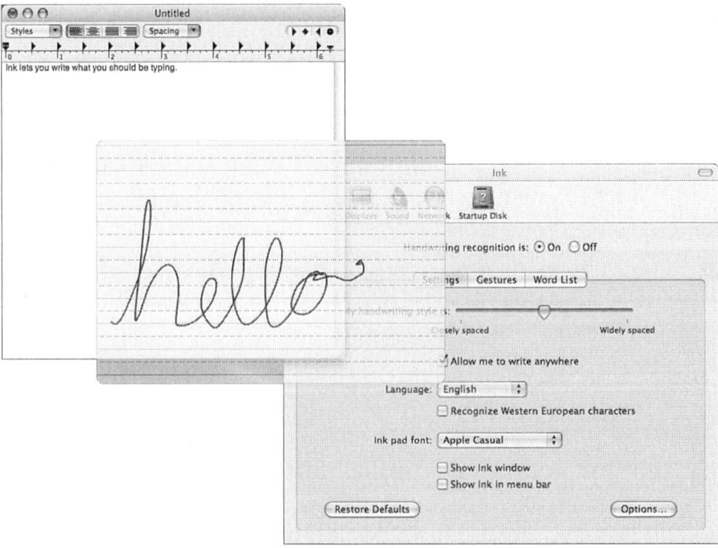

FIGURE 1.21 Inkwell turns tablet input into text.

NOTE

Inkwell does not work with laptop trackpads and currently is limited to third-party graphics tablets. You must download and install the latest Mac OS X tablet drivers from the manufacturer before using Inkwell.

Inkwell is activated and controlled through the Ink System Preferences pane, covered in Chapter 3.

Character Palette

For those who need access to any font, any glyph, anywhere, you can now add the systemwide Character Palette to your menu bar. Accessed through either the International System Preferences pane or the Action font window pop-down menu, the Character Palette option adds a global menu to the system that can be used to open a palette containing all system-accessible characters, as shown in Figure 1.22.

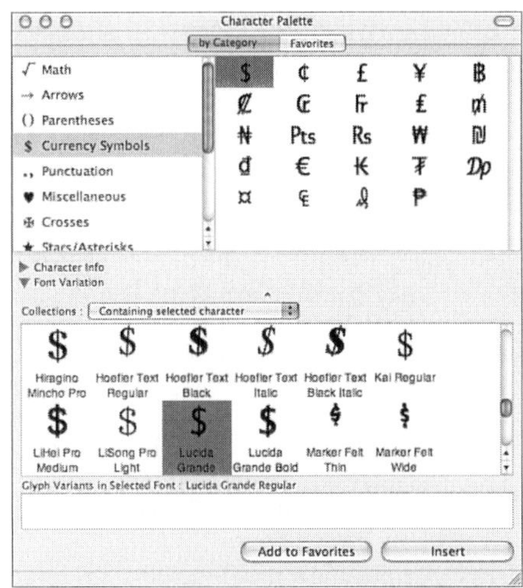

FIGURE 1.22 The Character Palette can provide direct character entry into any application.

After you locate the character you want, you can insert it into the active application without having to cut or paste. This advanced feature is discussed in Chapter 10.

Text Utilities

Because of the object-oriented component nature of Mac OS X, complex functions such as search and replace and spell checking are available from applications that you'd hardly expect to have any options. As you use the operating system, you'll find that many programs—even Safari—offer the capability to spell-check and find/replace inputs, saving you the trouble of typing into a word processor or other application to handle your text processing.

Find and Replace Dialog Boxes

Using the Edit, Find submenu you can perform a full-text search of all the open notes. You can search and replace any or all the notes, as well as choose to perform case-sensitive or whole-word searches, as shown in Figure 1.23.

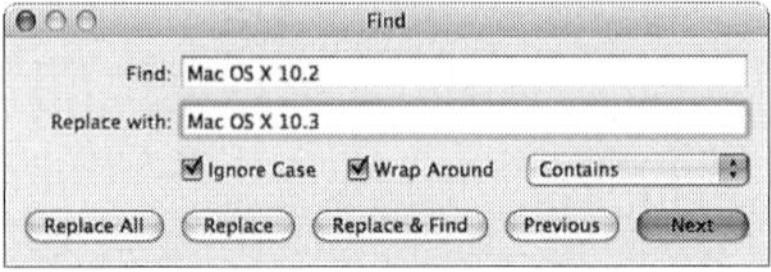

FIGURE 1.23 Search and Replace features are available throughout Mac OS X.

The Find pane has two fields: Find and Replace With. Enter the text you want to locate in the first, and what, if anything, you want to replace it with in the second.

To ignore the case of characters while searching, click the Ignore Case check box. Use the Wrap Around check box to force the entire document to be scanned, regardless of your cursor position. Finally, use the pop-up menu to determine what part of the word should be matched (full word, any word containing the string, and so on). When the search is defined, use one of the five buttons at the bottom of the pane to start an action:

- Replace All—Replaces all occurrences of the text with the supplied string. You will not be prompted for each replacement.
- Replace—Replaces the currently found item with the replacement string.
- Replace & Find—Replaces the currently selected item, and then finds and highlights the next occurrence.
- Previous—Jumps backward to a previously matched string.
- Next—Finds and highlights the next matched string in the document.

After starting a search (Command-F), you can use the shortcuts Find Next (Command-G) and Find Previous (Shift-Command-G) to continue searching without the Find pane open.

NOTE

Using the Find submenu, you can also quickly enter a new search term without opening the Search dialog box. Use Enter Selection (Command-E) to make the currently selected string the search term. Additionally, if you resize your window and lose the selected text, use Scroll to Selection (Command-J) to find your place.

Spell Checking

As with find and replace, spell checking is another common activity implemented in many Mac OS X applications.

In a supported application (such as TextEdit), choose Edit, Spelling, Spelling (Command-:). This opens a basic spell-checking window, as shown in Figure 1.24.

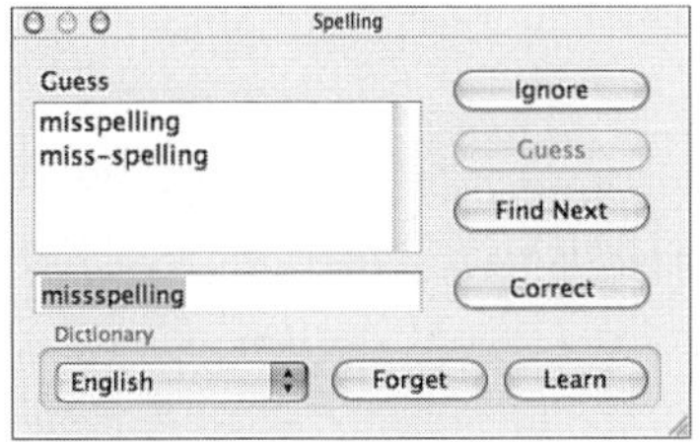

FIGURE 1.24 The Spelling window can locate and correct common missspellings in your work (yes, I meant that).

You can use the pane by itself by entering words that you want to correct into the field by the Correct button and then choosing Correct. Alternatively, navigate through the potential spelling errors using the buttons in the Spelling window:

- Ignore—Click Ignore to skip a word that you don't want to fix.
- Guess—Finds other words similar to the misspelled word.
- Find Next—Skips from word to (misspelled) word in your note.
- Correct—Fixes the error. If multiple possibilities are shown, choose the correct word from the list on the left and then choose Correct.
- Learn—Adds the currently selected word to the Mac OS X dictionary. Switches default dictionaries using the Dictionary pop-up menu.
- Forget—Removes the currently selected word from the dictionary.
- Dictionary—Chooses from multiple installed dictionary files. The Default Mac OS X installation includes a number of dictionaries.

Another way to visually check your spelling skills is to choose Edit, Spelling, Check Spelling (Command-;). This highlights misspelled words with a red underline. Control-clicking a highlighted word gives you the option of correcting it. To make the spell-checking process even more interactive, choose Edit, Spelling, Check Spelling As You Type to highlight misspelled words as they are entered.

Help Center

Finishing up the intro to Panther System Elements is the Mac OS X Help Viewer. The Help Viewer provides a simple browserlike interface to help files for many OS Apple and third-party applications. For example, Figure 1.25 shows the basic Finder Help.

FIGURE 1.25 The Help system works exactly like a Web browser.

You can click through the browser information just as you would a Web browser. Put your mouse over something of interest (it should underline or already be underlined if it is clickable) and then click.

The Mac OS X help is divided into guides automatically installed with your applications. To browse a guide for a particular program, choose it from the Library menu. You can return to the "top" of the guide you are browsing by clicking the "home" button. The arrows in the window's toolbar moves you forward and backward through the pages you've viewed.

To locate specific information, type a few keywords in the Search field, such as "open PDFs", and then press Return. A few seconds later, the Help Center application displays all matching documents that it found, along with a relevance rating and the guide that it was located in. Click the blue hyperlinks in the bottom pane of the Help Viewer to open the corresponding documents.

NOTE

Using View, Customize Toolbar from the menu, you can add a button to choose between which help guide you are browsing. You can also add buttons to increase or decrease the size of the help text.

TIP

The guide index is generated by aliases to individual applications' HTML help folders placed in `~/Library/Documentation/Help`. You can copy these aliases to the systemwide `/Library/Documentation/Help` directory to make them available to all users, or delete them if you don't want the help guide to appear in the list.

Unfortunately, the Mac OS X Help system is pretty sparse. Apple has linked the Mac OS X help to an online server (`http://helposx.apple.com/`) for automatic updates, but for the time being, help is not consistently implemented throughout the OS. That's why you need this book!

Summary

This chapter provided the basic information you need to find your way around the Mac OS X operating system. It is not meant to explain every possible feature but to provide an overview of what features have been added to Panther, and what you should know to successfully use the operating system.

Subsequent chapters will assume that you've familiarized yourself with the pointing and clicking aspects of using the system and will focus on all available features, starting with the Finder, Dock, and Exposé in Chapter 2.

CHAPTER 2

Managing the Panther Workspace

IN THIS CHAPTER

- Using the Finder
- Finder Windows
- Finder Views
- The Go Menu
- Browsing Network Volumes
- Finder File Operations
- Getting File Information
- The Desktop
- Burning CD/DVDs
- Using Fast User Switching
- Finder Preferences
- Using the Dock
- Customizing the Dock
- Process Manager: Force Quitting Applications
- Window Management with Exposé

You're now ready to take an inside look at Mac OS X and its operation. This chapter covers the Finder, Dock, and Exposé. Together, these three components of Panther help you manage your files, applications, and the plethora of windows you're bound to have covering your screen.

Using the Finder

Simply put, Finder is the application that Mac OS X uses to launch and manipulate files and applications. The Finder handles all common tasks such as creating, deleting, moving, and copying files and folders. It is, in effect, the "portal" of the Mac OS X operating system.

Unlike other tools and utilities, the Finder is always active and is automatically launched immediately after logging in to the system. Much of the Macintosh's legendary ease of use is attributed to the Finder and its intuitive interface to the filesystem.

The Panther Finder offers new features beyond what was available in previous versions of Mac OS X. This section provides an in-depth look at these new capabilities and how the Finder is used to navigate through the operating system.

Finder Windows

The Finder offers many ways to navigate through your data using windows, menus, and the keyboard. All navigation takes place inside a Finder window. To open a new Finder window, double-click a folder or disk icon that is on your desktop. Alternatively, you can use the New Finder Window selection from the Finder's File menu (Command-N).

Two non-file-browsing related elements of the Finder window help organize and navigate your workspace: The Sidebar and Toolbar.

Sidebar

Introduced in Panther, the Finder Sidebar pane puts all your commonly used folders in a single place—the Sidebar pane found at the left side of the Finder window, as shown in Figure 2.1. You can shrink and expand the width of the Sidebar using the vertical bar separating the Sidebar and content panes. Double-clicking the vertical line closes the pane entirely; double-clicking again restores it.

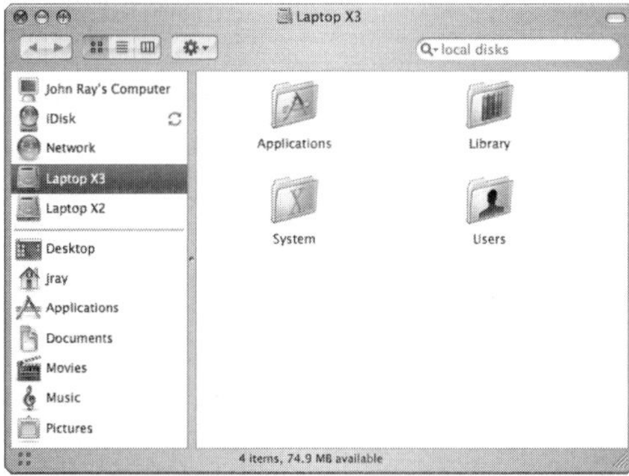

FIGURE 2.1 The Sidebar provides access to different areas of the filesystem.

Storage Volumes

As disks are inserted or network volumes mounted, the Sidebar refreshes to show the new entries. Removable media can be ejected by clicking the Eject icon that appears to the right of their entry in the list.

NOTE

You cannot use the Sidebar to unmount partitions that aren't recognized as removable media. To unmount any partition or drive that isn't your startup disk, drag it to the trash can in the Dock.

Clicking an entry in the list refreshes the right side of the Finder window with the contents of the chosen item. For disks, this is (obviously) the contents of the disk. However, three additional storage elements behave a bit differently from a normal disk: Computer, iDisk, and Network.

- Computer—A "top-level" view of your computer and attached storage devices. When viewing the computer, you will see all drives, mounted, servers, and so on that are accessible.

- iDisk—Your Internet-based personal storage that comes with your $100/year .Mac subscription. For more information on iDisk and .Mac, see Chapter 4, "Internet Applications."
- Network—A convenient means of browsing network NFS/AppleTalk/CIFS volumes within the familiar comfort of the Finder interface. We'll discuss network browsing and connections further in this chapter and throughout the book.

User-Defined Elements

The bottom portion of the Sidebar comes with a few predefined shortcuts to your home directory, along with the system Applications folder and your personal Documents, Movies, Music, and Pictures folders.

Again, clicking an entry in the list of user-defined elements also refreshes the right portion of the window to display the contents. You can drag additional folders, files, or applications to the list. As you drag, a horizontal bar is displayed in the list to show where the new item will be inserted. If you drag directly on top of an existing folder or application you've added to the Sidebar, the list entry highlights to "accept" the element you're dragging. You can use this to put items in folders, or drag documents onto applications to launch them.

NOTE

As you add entries to the Sidebar, the icons automatically shrink to make room. When the list finally extends beyond the bounds of the window, a scrollbar appears.

TIP

Elements added to the Finder Sidebar automatically show up in the sidebar of Open/Save dialog boxes.

Sidebar Defaults

To Change the default items that are displaced in your Finder Sidebar, choose Finder, Preferences; then click the Sidebar icon to open the Sidebar preferences pane, shown in Figure 2.2.

Use the check boxes to enable or disable the default storage devices and personal folders automatically added to the Sidebar. Close the preferences window to save and enabled your changes.

FIGURE 2.2 Choose the default items for your Sidebar.

Finder Toolbar

The Finder toolbar holds useful functions that you might want to access from wherever you are in the Finder. Like the Sidebar, the Finder toolbar can hold shortcuts to files, but it can also be used to carry out actions on files, folders, and the navigation process itself.

There are two ways to customize the Mac OS X toolbar: by using the supplied buttons (shortcuts) and by adding your own applications and folders.

Toolbar Components

By default, the Finder comes with four active toolbar components:

- Backward/Forward—Move back to the previously visited folder, or forward again. These buttons work just like the controls of a Web browser.
- View—Set a viewing style for the Finder's file listings. We'll cover the views shortly.
- Action—Perform an action on the selected file(s) or folder(s) such as opening, moving to the trash, and so on.
- Search—Search the Finder for a file or folder.

To customize your Finder windows with additional Apple-defined options, choose View, Customize from the Finder's menu. A display of all the available buttons appears, as shown in Figure 2.3.

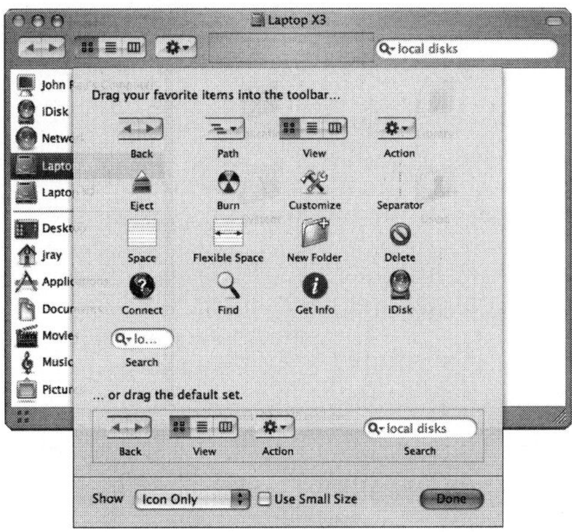

FIGURE 2.3 Finder buttons give single-click access to applications, folders, and special features.

To add one of these buttons to the toolbar, simply drag it from the window to wherever you want it to appear in the toolbar. If the number of shortcuts in the toolbar exceeds the size of the window, the shortcuts that can't be displayed appear in a pop-up menu (look for the ">>" icon) at the right side of the toolbar. These are the available toolbar buttons:

- Back/Forward—Navigate through previously visited folders. This is part of the default toolbar set.
- Path—Adds a pop-up menu to the toolbar that contains all the folders in the current path. Choose an item from the menu to jump to that folder. This is virtually identical to holding down the Command key while clicking on the title of a Finder window but doesn't require a modifier key.
- View—Quickly toggle between the three available Finder views. This is part of the default Finder toolbar.
- Action—Perform an action on the selected item. Actions are, for the most part, the same things you can find under the File menu, or by Control-clicking on an icon.
- Eject—Eject drive media (CDs, DVDs, and so on). If you have a modern Apple keyboard, you already have an Eject key, so this added button really won't be necessary. This is the same as pressing Command-E or dragging a disk icon to the Dock's trash can.
- Burn—Burn the currently active CD—if available. CD burning is covered later in this chapter.
- Customize—The Customize shortcut takes you to the shortcut menu.

- Separator—Serves to separate icons in the Finder's toolbar. Does not have an active function. A separator is included after the View element in the default toolbar.
- Space—A fixed-size blank space. This button does not perform an action.
- Flexible Space—A flexible-sized blank space that grows and shrinks with the width of the window; does not perform an action.
- New Folder—Creates a new folder within the current Finder window. This is the same as pressing Shift-Command-N.
- Delete—Moves the currently selected Window item (or items) to the trash. This command does not empty the trash.
- Connect—Opens the file server connection window. This is the same as choosing Go, Connect To Server (Command-K).
- Find—Opens a window to search for files/folders.
- Get Info—Gets information about the selected file or folder (Command-I).
- iDisk—If you've set up a .Mac account and given the system your username and password (either during installation or in the Internet System Preferences pane), this shortcut automatically mounts your Apple iDisk.
- Search—Adds a search field for quick file searches. This is part of the default Finder toolbar.
- Default Set—Replaces the existing toolbar icons with the Mac OS X defaults.

At the bottom of the toolbar customization pane, you can choose how you want the toolbar displayed using the Show pop-up menu. You can pick Icon Only, Text Only, or Icon & Text if you prefer both. The default selection is Icon & Text. You can also shrink the size of the toolbar icons by checking the Use Small Size box.

TIP

In applications other than the Finder, you can toggle through each of the different toolbar states by holding down Command or Shift-Command and clicking the toolbar button in the window's title bar. The Finder, for some reason, does not support this feature.

You can however, Control-click in *seemingly* any toolbar to access a contextual menu to change the toolbar options.

As you are editing your toolbar, you might want to reorder the existing icons or remove them entirely. Just drag the toolbar elements into the order you want—they will automatically move to adjust to the new ordering. To remove an element, drag it outside the current toolbar, and it disappears. Click Done when you're satisfied with the results.

NOTE

The toolbar buttons can be rearranged at any time by holding down the Command key and dragging them. User-defined shortcuts can be moved at any time.

User-Defined Buttons

In addition to the many predefined customizations, the toolbar also supports user-defined shortcuts, just like the Sidebar. Users can drag common applications, documents, or folders to any place in the toolbar.

When folders and applications are added to the toolbar, a single click on the icons opens or launches the respective element. Users can also drag documents onto toolbar application and folder icons to open the file using the application or to move the file into a folder.

Toolbar and Sidebar customization is done on a per-Finder, per-user account basis. When you modify your toolbar, it is modified for all Finder windows in your workspace, not just the currently open folder. Because these changes happen on a per-user basis, customizations you make to your Finder will *not* affect other users.

TIP

Clicking the toolbar button in the upper-right corner of the Finder window, or choosing View, Hide Toolbar (Option-Command-T) hides *both* the toolbar and the Sidebar *and* reverts to an aqua-style appearance.

In this mode, the Finder works as it did in pre-Mac OS X versions of the OS—double-clicking a folder *always* opens a new window with the contents.

Status Bar

Not quite the toolbar but useful nonetheless, the status bar has long supplied Mac users with important information about their systems. The Finder's status bar shows the number of items contained in a folder and the amount of space available on the drive. In Panther's Finder, the status bar is at the bottom of the window and can be seen in Figures 2.1 and 2.2.

In addition to the storage usage information, the status bar can also contain one of three icons in the left corner of the bar:

- Grid pattern—If a small grid pattern appears, the view is set to snap to grid, allowing minimal flexibility in the movement of icons.
- Arranged icons—If you've chosen to keep the icons automatically arranged, you'll see four tiny folders.

- Slash pencil—A pencil with a line through it means that you can read the items in the directory but not store files within it (in other words, the directory is read only).

CAUTION

Even if you add up the sizes of all the folders that you use, you're probably going to come up short. Many hidden Unix directories also count when calculating the amount of available space. Unfortunately, to an end user, it's going to appear as if he's lost several hundred megabytes on his hard drive.

When the Finder is operating in the aqua-style mode, the status bar appears at the top of the Window and can subsequently be hidden by choosing View, Hide Status Bar. It *cannot* be hidden when the Sidebar and toolbar are active.

Finder Views

Although the Finder shortcut pane and toolbar aid in navigation, they aren't the "meat" of the Finder. The content pane of the Finder contains a view of all the files and folders in your current location. Depending on the View mode of the content pane, you can browse your files in a traditional icon-style mode, columns, or a hierarchical list. To switch between these modes, use the three-button View control in the Finder toolbar (icons, list, columns, respectively), or choose your poison from the View menu.

Icon View

The first time you log in, the Finder will be using the Icon view. If you have already been using the Finder and are no longer in Icon view, you can quickly switch to Icon view by choosing View, Icons (Command-1), or by clicking the first icon in the View area of the toolbar. Figure 2.4 shows a Finder window in Icon view.

FIGURE 2.4 The default view mode is the Icon view.

Within the Icon view mode, you can navigate through the folders on your drive by double-clicking them. If you prefer to use the keyboard, you can move between the icons in the frontmost Finder window by pressing the arrow keys or by typing the first few letters that start the name of the folder or file you want to select. To open a selected item, choose File, Open, or press Command-O on the keyboard.

By default, if the toolbar and shortcut pane are displayed in the window, moving from folder to folder refreshes the current window. You can switch to a multiwindow view by clicking the toolbar button in the upper-right corner of the Finder window or by using the Finder Preferences.

TIP

To momentarily switch to a multiwindow mode, hold down Command when double-clicking a folder. This opens the folder in a new window.

TIP

To toggle between open Finder windows, press Command-`. Note that the desktop itself is considered a Finder window.

Another method of navigating your drive is to Command-click the icon or text in the center of the Finder window's title bar. You will then see a pop-up menu (as shown in Figure 2.5), which displays a bottom-to-top hierarchy of the folder path required to reach the current directory. You can choose any of the folders in the list to quickly jump to that location.

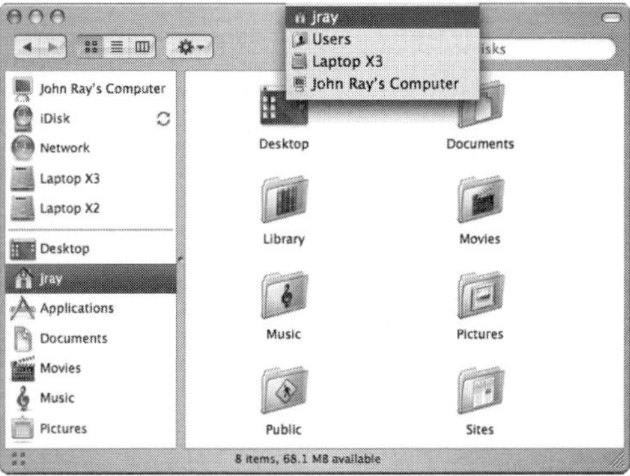

FIGURE 2.5 The pop-up folder list gives quick access to folders above the currently open directory.

NOTE

By default, opening a new Finder window takes you to your home directory. If you would prefer to be taken to a top-level view of all the volumes on your system, use the Finder application preferences to set new Finder Windows to Show Computer.

Why Are All My Filenames Cut Off?

At long last, the Mac OS supports long filenames. The Finder, however, displays only two lines of each name, abbreviating the middle with an ellipsis (...).

Thankfully, there is a way to view more of the name of the file. Select the icon and leave your mouse cursor over an abbreviated title, or hold down Option while moving your mouse over the title. Without the Option key, a ToolTip with the full name of the file will be displayed under the icon in 3 or 4 seconds. If you hold down the Option key, the expanded name will be shown instantly.

Icon View Options

You can customize the Icon view by dragging the icons around to suit your tastes. This is the most basic form of customization offered. To add more dramatic effects to a window in Icon view, choose View, Show View Options from the menu, or press Command-J. Figure 2.6 shows the View Options window for the Icon view.

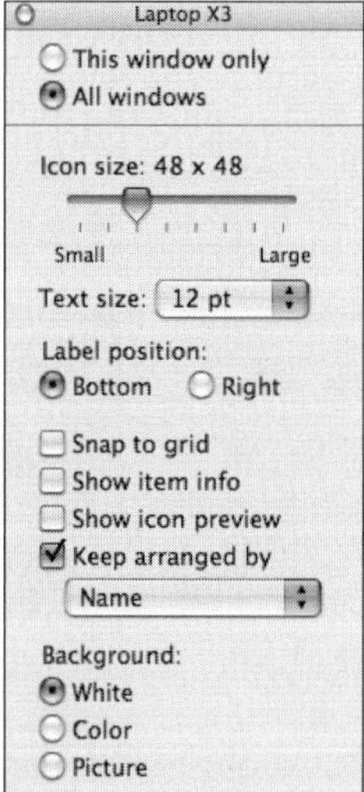

FIGURE 2.6 The Icon view options let you create a different look for the Finder window.

The first decision you must make when adjusting view options is whether to inherit global settings, or apply the changes to the current window. At the top of the View Options window are two choices: This Window Only and All Windows. Choosing the first setting tells Mac OS X that the changes you make to the view are specific to that window—no other windows will be changed. For example, using This Window Only, you can set your home directory and each of the directories within it to their own style independently of one another. On the other hand, picking All Windows applies a systemwide view option to the window and indicates that any changes made to the view options will affect any other windows set to inherit the global settings. This is a great way to create a common look and feel across multiple folders without having to maintain separate settings for each.

TIP

If you are setting the attributes for multiple Finder windows, you can speed up the process by opening all the windows to adjust and then opening the View Options window. As you click between the different Finder windows, the contents of the View Options window change to reflect the settings of the current window. There is no need to close View Options after setting up a window—just click the next Finder window to work with, adjust its settings, and so on.

A window that behaves in this manner is typically called an "*Inspector*" in Mac OS X because it allows you to inspect the attributes of multiple objects—in the case of the Finder, windows.

There are three primary settings for the view, the first being icon size. Mac OS X supports icon sizes from 16×16 pixels all the way up to 128×128 (the standard Mac size was previously 32×32). The large icons are impressive and are far more detailed than any icons you've ever seen before. You can scale the icons from their smallest size to the largest size by dragging the Icon Size slider from the left to the right. Figure 2.7 shows the Applications folder of the Mac OS X drive using the largest icon size.

FIGURE 2.7 The largest icon size allows for detailed, photo-realistic icons.

Next, you can control the size of the icon label font with the Text Size pop-up menu. Apple allows a selection between 10 and 16 points but does *not* provide a means of changing the label's font. The positioning of the icon's label can be changed from on the bottom to the right using the Label Position setting.

TIP

If you find the Mac OS X antialiased fonts difficult to read, use the Appearance System Preferences pane to set the smallest font size that Mac OS X will antialias and the style of antialiasing used.

If you're still displeased with the settings, you can manually set the antialiasing threshold to anything you want using the Terminal application and the command:

```
defaults write .GlobalPreferences AppleAntiAliasingThreshold <fontsize>
```

Find out more about the Terminal starting in Chapter 12, "Introducing the BSD Subsystem."

TIP

The smallest icon size is extremely tiny, especially on high resolution displays, and leaving the label underneath the icon results in huge gaps between icons. To maximize your window space, position the icon's label on the right when using small icons.

The next group of settings control icon arrangement, which determines how the icons are displayed and laid out on the screen.

To keep your icons straight and neat all the time, choose Snap to Grid. Mac OS X maintains an invisible grid within Finder windows that is used to keep icons evenly aligned with one another. Unfortunately, there are no provisions for changing the spacing on the grid. As a result, Mac OS X icons that are aligned to the grid might seem more loosely spaced than you want.

NOTE

If you take advantage of the Icon view with no preset arrangement, you might find that your icons get a bit messy after a while. To quickly align your icons to the Finder's grid, choose View, Clean Up from the menu.

You can also choose to display additional information in the icon and its label. The Show Icon Preview setting displays thumbnails of recognized image formats—even PDF files! Show Item Info, on the other hand, adds a count of the number of files contained within each folder directly under each folder's icon and displays information about media files (resolution, duration, and so on).

A final form of icon arrangement is to keep the icons arranged by attributes of the files that they represent. Click the Keep Arranged By check box and then choose from the list of available options:

- Name—Sorts the icons by the alphabetical order of their names.
- Date Modified—Sorts the icons by the day and time they were last modified. Newly modified files and folders appear at the bottom of the list.
- Date Created—Sorts the icons by the date and time they were created. The first time a file is saved, the created and modified times are identical.
- Size—Sorts by the size of the files or the size of the files contained within folders.
- Kind—Sorts the files by their type (that is, folders, applications, images, and so on).
- Label—Sort the files by a user-defined color label. We'll look at the label features in Panther shortly.

TIP

To quickly arrange icons in a Finder window, choose View, Arrange. This allows you to arrange your icons by any of the aforementioned attributes. It's a quick way to add some order to your life without opening View Options.

Note that if you have an arrangement set for a given window, the Arrange menu will be dimmed and cannot override your View Option settings.

Finally, the Background option offers you the capability to choose a background color or picture on a per-folder basis. This enables you to create a visually impressive system and can also provide quick cues for your current location within the operating system.

The default folder background is None. This uses a standard white background for all windows. To choose an alternative color, just click the Color radio button. A small square appears to the right of the button. Click this square to launch the Mac OS X Color Picker. You can learn more about the Color Picker in Chapter 1, "Panther System Elements." Figure 2.8 shows a Finder window with a tinted background.

An even more impressive effect is to use a background picture for the window rather than just a color. Background images can be based on any of the QuickTime-supported formats (GIF, JPEG, TIFF, and so on). Click the Picture radio button and then click the Select button that appears. You are prompted to open an image file from the system. Using the Open and Save dialog boxes is covered in Chapter 1.

After you choose a picture, a thumbnail of your choice is shown in the small square (image well) to the left of the Select button. Your Finder window refreshes with the chosen image in the background. Figure 2.9 shows a Finder window with an image in the background.

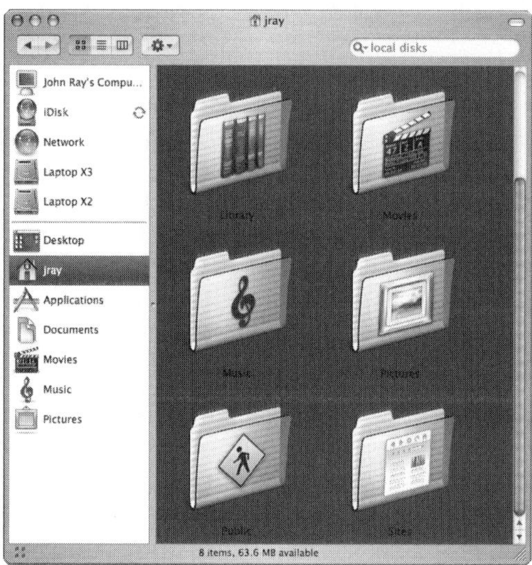

FIGURE 2.8 You can use the OS X Color Picker to choose your window background color.

In the current release of Mac OS X, pictures cannot be scaled to match the size of a window. Instead, Finder background pictures are tiled, much like a repeating background on a Web page.

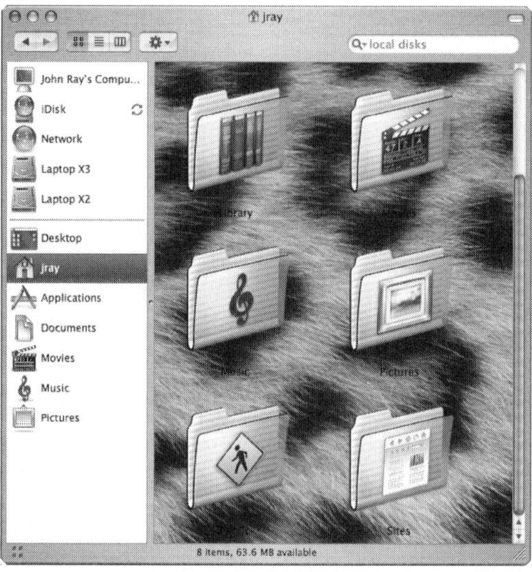

FIGURE 2.9 Any image can be used as a background in a Finder window.

NOTE

The Icon view is presently the only view that supports background colors or images.

List View

The next view to explore is the Finder's List view. You can switch to List view by clicking the middle icon in the Finder toolbar's View area, or, if the toolbar isn't present, by choosing View, As List from the Finder's menu. Demonstrated in Figure 2.10, the List view is a straightforward means of displaying all available information about a file or folder on a multicolumn screen.

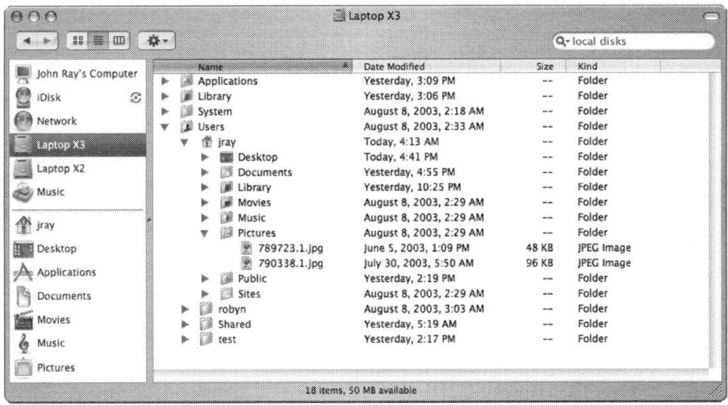

FIGURE 2.10 List view packs a lot of information into a small amount of space.

The columns in the List view represent the attributes of each file. You can contract or expand the columns by placing the mouse cursor at the edge of the column and click-dragging to the left or right. Clicking a column highlights it and sorts the file listing based on that column's values. By default, the column values are listed in descending order. Clicking a column again toggles the sorting order. An arrow pointing up or down at the right of each column represents the current sort order.

You can reposition the columns by clicking and dragging them into the order you want. However, the first column, Name, cannot be repositioned.

When a folder appears in the file listing, a small disclosure arrow precedes its name. Clicking this arrow reveals the file hierarchy within that folder. You can drill down even further if you want, revealing multiple levels of files. Figure 2.10 shows three levels of files displayed simultaneously. Windows users might find a level of comfort in this view because it is similar to the Windows Explorer.

As with the Icon view, double-clicking a folder anywhere within this view either opens a new window (toolbar/Sidebar-less mode) or refreshes the contents of the existing window with the new location.

If keyboard navigation is your thing, the same rules as the Icon view apply. You can navigate up and down through the listing using the up-arrow key and the down-arrow key. In addition, you can use the left-arrow key and right-arrow key to move in and out of folders in the hierarchy. Holding down Command-Option along with the right-arrow key or left-arrow key expands or collapses all folders inside the currently selected folder. Typing the first few characters of an object's name highlights that object in the listing. You can then use Command-O to open it.

Finally, Command-clicking on the title of the window reveals the same pop-up list of folders as the Icon view. Choose one of the items in the list to jump to it.

List View Options

As with the Icon view, there are a number of options that you can use to customize the appearance and functionality of the List view. To alter the options for a window, make sure that it is the frontmost Finder window and then choose View, Show View Options (Command-J). Figure 2.11 shows the List View Option window.

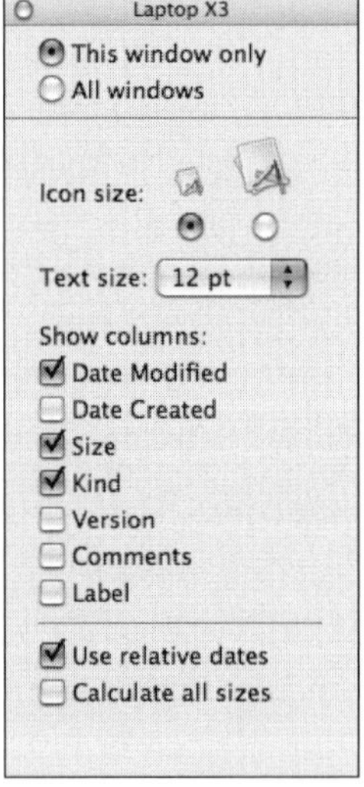

FIGURE 2.11 The list view also can be customized.

The Icon Size option offers a choice of two icon sizes: small or large. To change the size of the icon that precedes every line in the list, click the radio button below the size that you want. Unlike the Icon view, the List view icons cannot be scaled beyond the two presets. Text size for the list can also be chosen from 10 to 16 points.

The Show Columns option offers seven different attributes that can be displayed in each List view:

- Date Modified—Shows the date that a file or folder was last changed.
- Date Created—Shows the date that a file or folder was created.
- Size—Shows the size of a file on the system.
- Kind—Shows an abstract representation of a file (image, application, and so on).
- Version—Displays the version of an application. Not always available in Mac OS X.
- Comments—Shows any comments set for the file or folder. Comments are set from the Get Info (Command-I) window.
- Label—Shows the color label (if any) assigned to the file or folder.

By checking or unchecking the box in front of each option, you can add or remove the corresponding column in the List view.

TIP

To determine a file's type from the command line, try `file <filename>`:

```
% file jeans1024x768.jpg
jeans1024x768.jpg: JPEG image data, JFIF standard
```

For more information about the command line, see Chapter 12.

Two additional settings affect the column display:

- Use Relative Dates—Relative dates are a way of representing dates *relative* to the current day. For example, items modified during the current day are listed as Today, whereas files modified a day earlier are listed as Yesterday. Clicking the Use Relative Dates check box displays the Created and Modified columns using these conventions.
- Calculate All Sizes—By default, folder sizes are not calculated and displayed in the file listing. Checking this box enables folder sizes to be displayed in the file listing.

CAUTION

Calculating folder sizes might seem like a good idea, but it can bog down your system tremendously. If you have multiple file listing windows open, and each is calculating folder sizes, it can slow down Finder operations and application responsiveness.

A quick way to display the usage of each directory is the du command from the command line:

```
% du -s *
40    Addresses
0     Assistants
0     Audio
4096  Caches
0     ColorPickers
8     Documentation
16    Favorites
2520  Fire
```

Column View

The final type of window view is the Column view. This will be recognized by NeXT-heads as almost identical to the original File Browser used on the NeXT system. There are two primary advantages of this view: ease of navigation and file identification. You can switch to the Column view style by choosing View, As Columns from the menu, or by clicking the third icon in the View area of the toolbar. Figure 2.12 shows a Finder window in Column view.

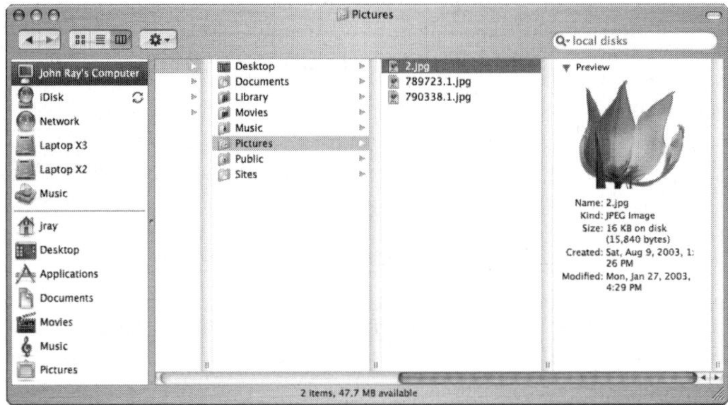

FIGURE 2.12 The Column view uses...columns.

The key feature of the Column view is its navigation. Unlike the other views, which can either overwhelm you with information or require multiple windows to move easily from point to point, the Column view is designed with one thing in mind: ease of navigation.

The concept is simple: Click an item in the first column, and its contents will be shown in the next column. This would be less than useful if the programmers stopped at this point, so they didn't. You can continue to drill down further into the filesystem by choosing a folder that was within your original folder. The display will then do one of two things: If your window is open wide enough, it will display the contents of the second folder in yet another column. If no other columns are available, the columns will slide to the left, and a scrollbar will appear at the bottom of the window. Using this scrollbar, you can quickly trace the steps you've taken to reach a file. If you want to adjust the width of the columns, grab the handle (represented by two vertical lines) and drag it—all the columns resize accordingly.

TIP

Holding down Option while dragging the handle resizes only the columns to the left or right of the divider line.

Option-Double-clicking the handle at the right side of a column auto-resizes that column so that the column fits the largest icon name string. Double-clicking without the Option key resizes *all* columns to the smallest size needed to fit the largest icon name string.

TIP

If you use the horizontal scrollbar to move back along a path, the folders you've chosen remain highlighted in the columns. You can, at any time, choose a different folder from any of the columns. This refreshes the column to the right of your choice. There is no need to start from the beginning every time you want to change your location.

If at first glance this seems too complicated or awkward, I urge you to try it. The Column mode is a fast and efficient means of finding what you're looking for.

TIP

When you use one of the shortcut pane items to jump to a location on your system, *that* becomes the top level of the filesystem. You will not be shown any directories preceding that point.

As with the other views, Command-clicking on the title of the window reveals the same pop-up list of folders as the Icon view. Choose one of the items in the list to jump to it.

There is one other big bonus of using the Column view: the ability to instantly see the contents of a file without opening it. You already know that as you choose folders, their contents appear in the column to the right, but what happens if you choose a file or application instead?

The answer is that a preview or description of the selected item will appear in the column to the right. For an example, take a look at Figure 2.13, where the front page of a PDF file is displayed.

This is a convenient way of viewing pictures and other forms of supported QuickTime media. When an application or a file that cannot be previewed is chosen, information about the file is displayed, such as the creation/modification dates, size, and version.

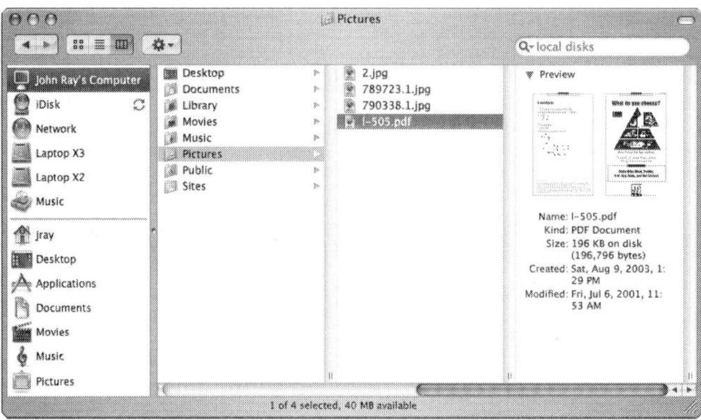

FIGURE 2.13 When a file is selected, a preview is shown in the rightmost column.

TIP

Do not underestimate the power of this feature. Not only can you view pictures, you can also view QuickTime movies and other media using this same technique.

In fact, if you have a large collection of MP3s (legally obtained, of course) and you're using the Column view mode, you can actually listen to your MP3s without launching an MP3 player application. Unfortunately, the MP3 does not continue to play if you switch off the selected file, but that's hardly worth mentioning considering the added functionality.

Column View Options

The Column view options, shown in Figure 2.14, are sparse. As usual, the text size is adjustable, and you can also choose to show the small icons in each column, and whether the far right column is used for a preview, or will just act as a file list. There are no global view options for the Column view mode.

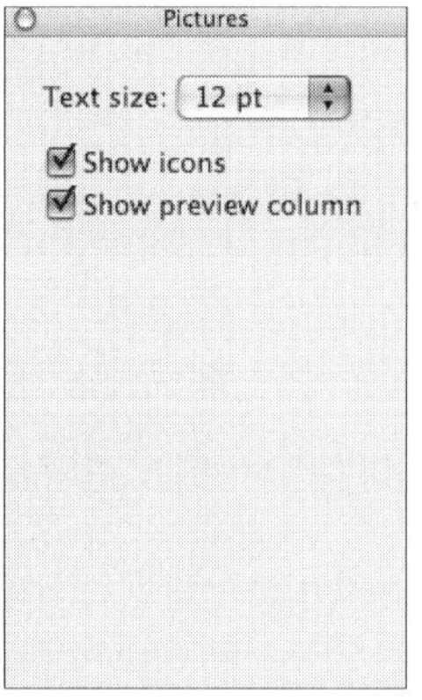

FIGURE 2.14 Choose whether to display icons in each column and whether a preview is displayed.

The Go Menu

If you want to navigate quickly from any view, you can use the folder shortcuts contained in the Go menu. This menu enables the user to jump the Finder to one of several predefined locations, or to manually enter the name of a directory to browse:

- Computer—Jump to the Computer level of the file hierarchy. At the Computer level, you can browse connected storage devices and network volumes (Shift-Command-C).
- Home—Go to your home directory (Shift-Command-H).
- Network—Open the network browser (Shift-Command-K).
- iDisk—Choose to open your, or another user's, iDisk or iDisk public folder (if you have .Mac). For more information, see Chapter 4.
- Applications—Jump to the System-level Applications folder (Shift-Command-A).
- Utilities—Open the Mac OS X Utilities folder, found in `/Applications/Utilities`. Many tools for managing and monitoring your system are found here.
- Recent Folders—The Recent Folders submenu contains a system-maintained list of the last 10 folders you visited.

The second-to-last quick-navigation option is the Go to the Folder dialog box (Shift-Command-G). For now, this is as close as we're going to come to the command line. Mac users beware, and Windows/Linux users rejoice. You're about to tell the Finder where you want to be, based on a pathname you enter! Figure 2.15 shows the Go to the Folder dialog box.

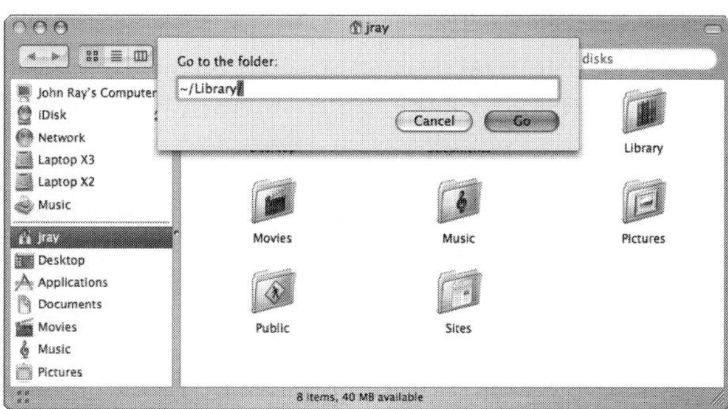

FIGURE 2.15 Go to the Folder lets you enter your destination by hand!

You can type any folder pathname into the Go to the Folder field. Folder names are separated by the / character. Think of it as being similar to a Web URL. Table 2.1 shows a few shortcuts you can use to navigate your drive.

TABLE 2.1 Shortcuts To Help You Navigate Your System

Path	Purpose
`/`	The root (top) level of your hard drive.
`~/`	Your home directory.
`~<username>`	Replace `<username>` with the name of another user to jump to that user's home directory.
`/<directory>`	Move to a directory relative to the root of the filesystem.
`<directory>`	Move to a directory relative to the directory you're currently in.

As you type in your pathname, Mac OS X watches what you're typing and attempts to autocomplete the name of the directory. Click Go or press Return when you've finished typing the directory you want to visit.

NOTE

This function is provided mostly for those users who are comfortable dealing with pathnames. It can be used to jump to the hidden Unix directories on your system, such as `/etc`, `/usr`, and so on.

If you want to make all the BSD subsystem viewable within the Finder, you can do so within the Finder application preferences. You can learn more about the Mac OS X Defaults system in Chapter 20, "Command-Line Configuration and Administration," and more about the command line in Chapter 12.

TIP

The Mac and Unix systems make strange bedfellows. The Mac has traditionally used a colon (:) to separate folder names in a path; therefore, it didn't allow colons within filenames. Unix, on the other hand, doesn't allow / within filenames, but it does allow colons.

In the Mac OS X Finder, the : character still isn't allowed (it is replaced with a hyphen [-] if you try to use it in a file or directory name), but / can be used in a name. Unfortunately, the Go to the Folder dialog box cannot deal with directories that include the / because it is thinking in terms of Unix directories. The moral of the story is, "Don't name your directories with a / and expect to be able to navigate to them using the Go to the Folder dialog box."

The final "Go" menu option, Connect to Server is discussed in the next section.

Browsing Network Volumes

A new feature of Panther is the capability to browse network volumes directly in a Finder window. The Network icon located at the My Computer level of your system or in the Finder shortcut pane provides a direct link to the available NFS/CIFS/AppleTalk servers on your network.

To look for available servers, click the Network icon. After several seconds, your screen refreshes with any results that it found, as shown in Figure 2.16.

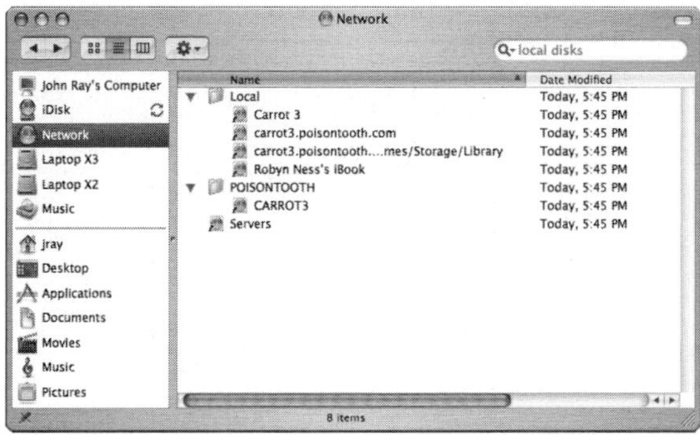

FIGURE 2.16 Browse network volumes directly in the Finder.

AppleTalk Zones and Windows Workgroups are represented by folders, whereas machines registered through Rendezvous can be found under the "Local" folder. Double-clicking the icon of a shared resource attempts to connect and mount that device.

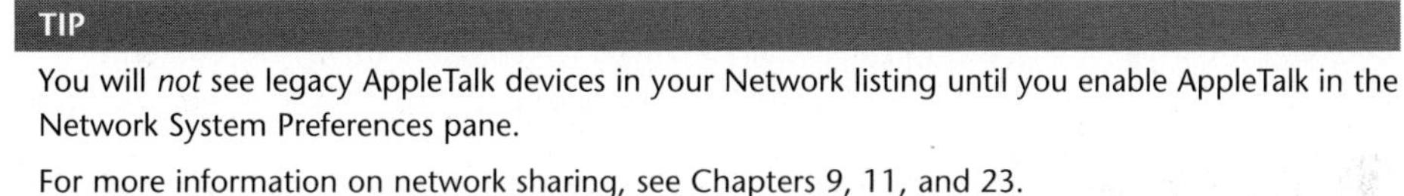

TIP

You will *not* see legacy AppleTalk devices in your Network listing until you enable AppleTalk in the Network System Preferences pane.

For more information on network sharing, see Chapters 9, 11, and 23.

In previous versions of Mac OS X, connecting to remote servers was performed through Go, Connect To Server. Although this option still remains, as shown in Figure 2.17, it serves a different purpose.

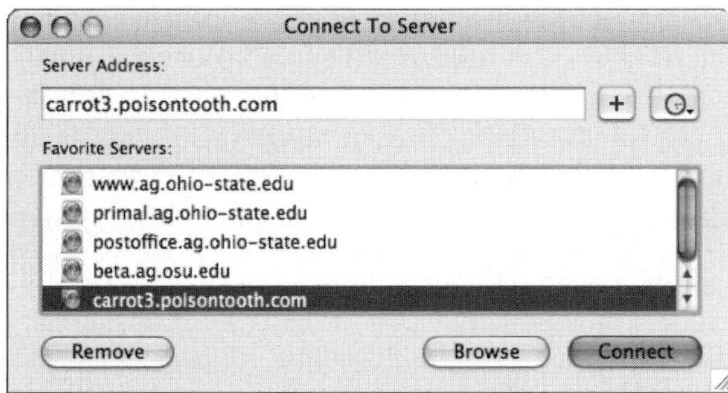

FIGURE 2.17 Connect to and store commonly used server URLs here.

Rather than browse servers, the Connect To Server feature allows you to type the URL of a network resource to connect to:

- **afp:<*machine IP/hostname*>[/<volume>]**—Standard AppleShare IP or Mac OS X Server shares.
- **http://<*WebDAV URL*>**—WebDAV shares. See Chapter 27, "Web Serving," for details.)
- **cifs://<*machine IP/hostname*>[/<volume>]**—Or smb://; see Chapter 30, "Windows Interoperability," for details.
- **ftp://<*machine IP/hostname*>[/<volume>]**—See Chapter 25, "FTP Serving," for details.
- **nfs://<*machine IP/hostname*>[/<volume>]**—See Chapter 23, "File and Resource Sharing with NFS and NetInfo," for details.

After entering a URL, click Connect to connect to the network resource.

You can also choose "+" to add a URL to the list of Favorite servers (where it can subsequently just be clicked to access). Use the Remove button to remove a URL from the Favorite Servers list. Frequently used URLs are held in the "clock" icon drop-down menu to the right of the "+".

We'll discuss network connections in-depth throughout the book, such as in Chapters 23, 25, and 27. Most users will rarely need the Connect To Server feature and can simply use the Network icon in the Finder shortcut pane to browse and connect to their resource.

TIP

New to Panther is the capability to connect directly to FTP servers with read *and* write capabilities. FTP volumes appear and act just like any other network volume.

Finder File Operations

Because you're reading an *Unleashed* title, you probably already know the basics of most graphical operating systems: Click and drag files to move them; double-click applications to launch them. Mac OS X doesn't break any new ground in the handling of files. Everyone who has used Windows, KDE/GNOME, or an earlier version of Mac OS will be able to carry their existing knowledge over to the new operating system. To be thorough, this portion of the chapter serves as a quick reference to standard file and application operations.

Adding/Removing Labels

Starting with Panther, Apple has reintroduced the popular "label" feature of Mac OS. Labels are a color code that you can assign to an arbitrary file or group of files in Mac OS

X. Your important work files, for example, might be labeled with the color red, whereas personal files are labeled green. Rather than having to separate the files into different folders, you can simply apply different labels. The Finder highlights the name of each icon with the color of the chosen labels so that you can easily pick them out. In addition, you can use the View Options in List mode to sort by assigned labels or even use the Finder's search feature to search by label. (Searching is discussed later in this chapter in the section "Performing File and Content Searches.")

To assign a label to an icon or group of icons, select the object(s) and then use File, Color Label; the Toolbar Action button; or the contextual (Control-click) menu to choose one of the seven different color options, shown in Figure 2.18. The meaning is entirely up to the user—labels have no effect on how the operating system manages the files.

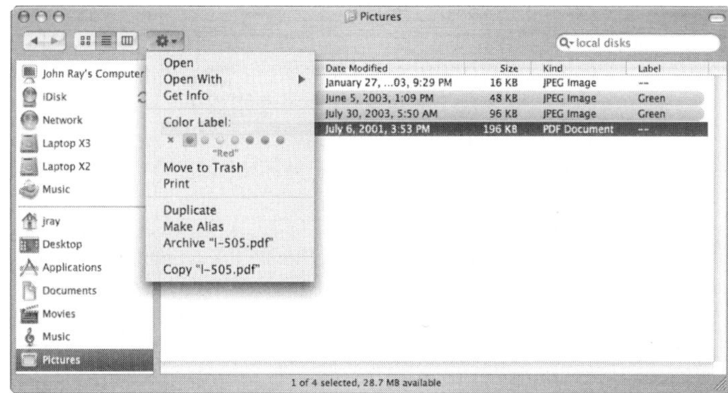

FIGURE 2.18 Choose one of seven different color labels to apply to the file(s).

When setting a label, you may notice that directly to the left of the color options is an "X" icon. Choosing the "X" removes the label (if any) from the selected item(s).

Each label also has an associated word (the label "name") displayed along with the highlight color in the Finder List view. To change the names (defaulted to the color names) associated with each label, choose Finder, Preferences; then click the Labels icon to open the Label name preferences pane, shown in Figure 2.19.

Type into the fields beside each color to change the label names. Close the preferences window to save and activate your changes.

Compressing/Uncompressing Files

Another new Panther Finder feature is the capability to zip and unzip files from the Action toolbar button or contextual menus. To zip, choose the files or folders to include in the archive and then use the Action button, or Control-click and choose Archive.

FIGURE 2.19 Assign names to each of the color labels.

To uncompress, select a zip file and choose Unarchive from the Action button or contextual menu. The files will be unarchived in your current location.

NOTE

Zipping/unzipping does not affect the original files or the archive. These files are left untouched.

Moving Files and Folders

Moving a file changes its location, but does not alter the contents of the file or its creation and modification dates. To move a file in Mac OS X, drag its icon to the folder or location where you want it to reside. If you are dragging within a Finder window, the window automatically scrolls as your cursor reaches the border, allowing you to move around within the view without having to drop the icon and manually scroll the window.

If you attempt to move a file from one device (such as a disk) to another, the cursor changes to include a "+" sign, and the file is *copied* rather than moved. The original file stays in its current location, and a new version is created on the other storage media. You must delete the original copy of the file if you do not want to keep multiple versions of the file.

TIP

Finder (and some application) windows include a proxy icon in the title bar. If you click and hold this miniature icon for a few seconds, it becomes draggable. The icon represents the currently open folder or document and can be used just like dragging the item's icon within the Finder window.

Copying Files and Folders

Copying a file creates an exact duplicate of an original file. The new file sports a new creation and modification date, although the contents are identical to the original. There are a number of ways to create a copy on Mac OS X:

- Drag a file to a different disk—Dragging a file to a disk other than the one it is currently stored on results in a copy of the file being created at the destination. The copy has the same name as the original.
- Drag a file while holding down Option—If you drag a file to a folder on the same disk it is currently located on while holding down the Option key, a duplicate of that file is created in the new location. If the Option key is not held down, this normally just moves the file. The copy has the same name as the original.
- Choose Duplicate from contextual/Finder menu—If you want to create an exact duplicate of a file within the same folder, highlight the file to copy and then choose File, Duplicate (Command-D). Or, alternatively, Control-click the icon and choose Duplicate from the pop-up contextual menu. A new file is created with the word "copy" appended to the name.
- Use the Finder contextual menus—Control-click on a Finder icon (or selection of multiple icons); then choose Copy. Next, locate where you want to copy the files to and then choose Edit, Paste from the menu. You can also use the toolbar's Action menu to perform a Copy and Paste action. Windows users will recognize this immediately.

TIP

Mac OS X recognizes many two-button mice and automatically maps the second button to the Control-click command. Additionally, many mice that include scroll-wheel functionality automatically work in Cocoa-based applications.

In addition, the scroll wheel on many mice can be used to control the scrolling of windows. If you have this feature, you can also scroll horizontally by holding down the Shift key while using your scroll wheel.

As the file copies, the Finder displays a window, like that in Figure 2.20, where you can see the progress of the copy operation. If multiple copies take place at the same time, the status of each operation is shown stacked on one another in the copy status window. In Figure 2.20, two copies are taking place. If you want to collapse the copy to show only summary information about the copy (time remaining), click the disclosure triangle at the left of the copy status.

If you attempt to copy over existing files, the Finder prompts you whether you want to replace them and provides an Apply to All check box to apply your decision to any other conflicting files it finds during the operation. Remember that under Mac OS X, you cannot alter certain system files and directories or another user's files. If you attempt to replace existing files to which you do not have access, the copy operation will fail.

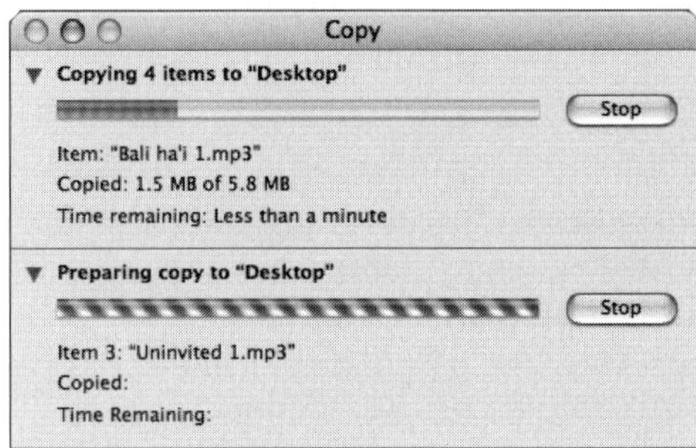

FIGURE 2.20 A single window contains all the status information for multiple copy operations.

Dragging with Spring-Loaded Folders and Windows

Using the spring-loaded folder feature of Mac OS X, you can drag items onto closed folders, and after a few seconds, those folders "spring" open, allowing you to continue the drag operation. To force the "spring" action to occur immediately, press the spacebar while hovering over the folder you want to open.

Mac OS X also includes *spring-loaded windows*. Spring-loaded windows "spring" onto the screen when an icon is dragged over them. To demonstrate this effect, drag a Finder window to the bottom of your screen until only the title bar is showing. Next, drag an icon over the title bar—the window springs up from the bottom of the screen and then disappears when you release the item or move your mouse off the window. You can force a window to "spring" immediately by pressing the spacebar.

TIP

The amount of time it takes a folder to spring open is controlled through the General Finder preferences, discussed later.

Deleting Files and Folders

Deleting files and folders permanently removes them from your system. Although the Mac OS X Finder has an Undo menu, it cannot undo the effects of erasing a file from your system. Like copying a file, there are a number of ways to delete:

- Drag to Dock trash—Dragging an icon from a Finder window into the Dock's trash can is one of the most obvious and easy ways to get rid of a file.
- Move to Trash contextual/Action/Finder menu—You can move a selected item to the trash by Control-clicking the icon and choosing Move to Trash from the contextual menu, or choosing the option of the same name from the Finder's File menu or Action toolbar button.
- Finder toolbar—A Delete shortcut can be added to the Finder's toolbar. Any items selected can be quickly moved to the trash by clicking the Delete shortcut. Delete is not one of the default toolbar icons.

Moving an item to the trash does not delete it permanently from your drive. Instead, it places the item inside an invisible folder in your home directory called `.Trash`—you cannot see or access this folder directly from the Mac OS X GUI. If you're interested in getting to the contents of the folder, check out the discussion of command-line navigation, starting in Chapter 12. The trash can icon in the Dock fills with crumpled paper when it contains items waiting to be deleted.

Although Mac OS X doesn't give you a true representation of the `.Trash` folder, it does let you view the contents of the trash by clicking the trash can icon in the Dock. The Trash window works identically to other Finder windows. If you want to rescue a file you've accidentally sent to the trash, you can drag the file's icon out of the trash.

To completely remove a file from your system, choose Empty Trash from the Finder's application menu, or press Shift-Command-Delete. Alternatively, you can Control-click or click and hold on the trash can, and choose Empty Trash from the resulting pop-up menu. Holding down Option when Emptying the Trash (including via the keyboard shortcut) bypasses the Finder's warning messages.

Emptying the trash might take a few moments if you are deleting many files. During this time, the Finder brings up a dialog box similar to the Copy dialog box. You can click Stop to cancel the trash operation, sparing the files that haven't yet been erased.

Secure Empty Trash

By default, when Mac OS X empties the trash, it simply removes pointers to the files from the filesystem. The data itself remains on the drive and can be recovered by a number of available data forensics tools. If you work for the NSA or any other organization that requires high level security, this poses a security threat in that even if you've deleted sensitive information from your computer, *someone* can recover it.

In Panther, Apple provides a Secure Empty Trash feature, also available under the Finder's Application menu. Using the Secure Empty Trash option overwrites your files several times to ensure that they cannot be recovered.

Why Isn't Once Enough?

Magnetic media at its most basic level is an analog storage medium. If you've ever erased a cassette tape with a tape eraser, you may notice that you can *very* faintly hear the original recording. The same holds true for magnetic computer media. To be absolutely certain that no data can be recovered, multiple passes must be made—eliminating any trace of the original data.

For an excellent discussion of the topic, read "Secure Deletion of Data from Magnetic and Solid-State Memory" by Peter Gutmann (`http://www.safedelete.com/a-gutmann.phtml`).

Creating Aliases

An *alias* is a representation of a file that, for all intents and purposes, appears to be the file. Windows users will recognize it as being similar to a shortcut.

Suppose that you have a document called `My Diary` buried deep in your drive, but you want to leave a copy of the icon on your desktop. Instead of duplicating the file and maintaining two copies, you can create an alias of the original file and then place the alias wherever you want. Accessing the alias is the same as accessing the real file. The Finder uses aliases for Recent Folders. Rather than having to move the real directories, it can just create aliases of them. You can tell an alias from the original by the arrow in the lower-left corner of the icon. Figure 2.21 shows several aliases to other files.

You can create aliases in two ways:

- Drag a file while holding down Option-Command—If you drag a file to a folder while holding down the Option-Command keys, an alias of that file is created in the new location.
- Choose Make Alias from contextual/Finder /Action menu—If you want to create an alias of a file within the same folder, highlight the file to alias and then choose File, Make Alias (Command-L), Control-click the icon and choose Make Alias from the pop-up contextual menu, or use the Make Alias option under the Action toolbar button. A new file is created with the word "alias" appended to the name.

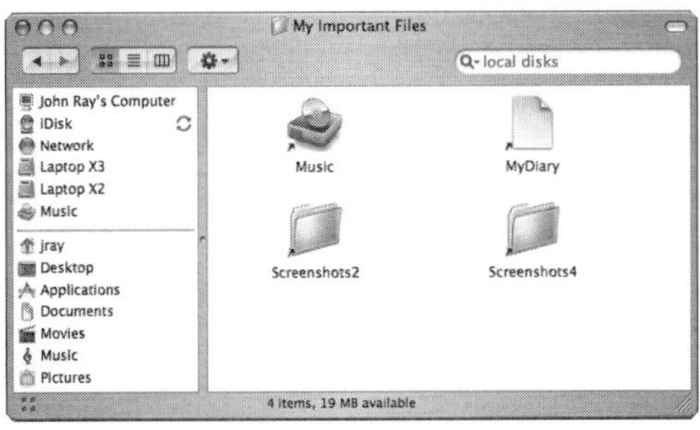

FIGURE 2.21 Aliases represent real files on your system.

Although aliases can be used to represent the original file, throwing them away does not delete the original file. Alternatively, deleting the original file doesn't delete the alias. If the original file is erased, the alias simply becomes broken. Double-clicking a broken alias displays a dialog box similar to the one in Figure 2.22.

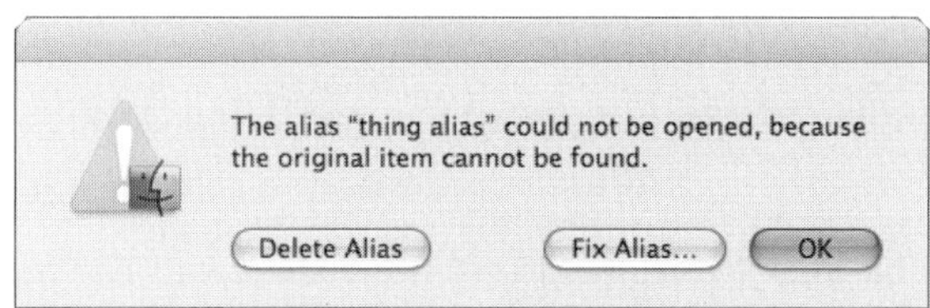

FIGURE 2.22 Broken aliases can be deleted or fixed.

If you just want to get rid of a broken alias, click the Delete Alias button. If you want to point the alias to a different file, choose Fix Alias and locate the file you want to use, and the alias will be reattached. To leave things the way they are, click OK.

NOTE

Aliases aren't quite the same as symbolic links in Linux/Unix. The Mac filesystem assigns a unique identifier to each file. Aliases reference that identifier and can be used to locate a file wherever it is on your drive. If the original is moved, the ID does not change, and the alias continues to work. Aliases do not translate to the BSD subsystem in any form and *cannot* be substituted for `ln -s`.

Show Original

To locate the file to which an alias points, select the alias and choose Show Original (Command-R) from the Finder's File menu, from the icon's contextual menu, or use the toolbar's Action button. The original file is highlighted in the Finder.

Launching Applications/Opening Documents

We saved the easiest for last. Launching an application or loading a document is a matter of double-clicking its icon, or dragging a document on top of the application's icon. In the latter case, the application starts and loads or processes the document that was dropped on it.

You can also launch an application by selecting it and then choosing File, Open; by choosing Open in the icon's contextual menu; or by using the toolbar Action button. If you're opening a document and want it to load into an application other than its default application, use File, Open With; or choose Open With in the item's contextual menu; or use the toolbar Action button. To set a file to always open with an alternative application, hold down Option when the Open With menu selection is visible onscreen, and it will change to Always Open With.

NOTE

If you use a contextual menu or the Action button to open applications and documents, you might notice a Show Package Contents selection in the menu as well. Only available in certain cases, this effectively opens the file as if it were a folder, showing the various resources (images, sounds, and so on) that the application uses.

While an application is launching, its icon will bounce in the Dock.

Unrecognized Files

If you attempt to double-click a document that the system does not recognize, Mac OS X warns you that there is no application available to open the document you've tried to access, as demonstrated in Figure 2.23. If you're sure that a program on your system is capable of viewing the file, select the Choose Application button. You are prompted to choose the application that will open the file. If the system does not allow you to pick the appropriate application, change the selection in the Show pop-up menu to read All Applications rather than Recommended Applications. By default, the system tries to guess the best application for the job—sometimes it fails miserably.

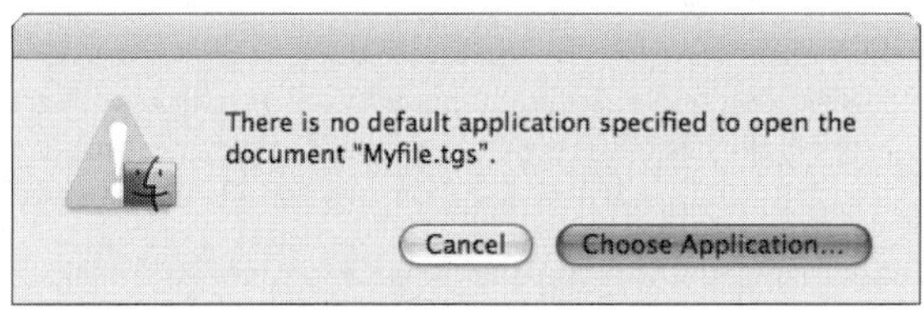

FIGURE 2.23 If a file can't be opened, you can choose an application to open it with.

You can also fix unrecognized files by setting the application to open them through the Get Info Finder command, discussed later in this chapter.

Renaming Files

To rename a file in the Finder, click on the file's icon label. The filename becomes editable in a few seconds. If you're the impatient sort, just press Return after selecting an icon; you'll immediately find yourself in Edit mode.

Alternatively, you can use File, Get Info in the Finder menu to edit the name in a larger field.

The Edit Menu

The Edit menu is used universally in almost every application that you'll run under Mac OS X. It has been duplicated on Linux, Windows, and just about every other GUI-based OS on the planet. The Edit menu allows a user to quickly select, copy, and cut information from one place in the system and paste it somewhere else. While the information is waiting to be added to another document, it is temporarily housed in the *Clipboard*.

Mac OS X has seven basic features available from the Finder's Edit menu:

- Undo/Redo—The Undo command allows you to reverse just about any action you've taken in the Finder, aside from emptying the trash. If you've moved a file or created a copy you don't need, just undo it. If you find that you've undone something you didn't mean to, the Undo menu changes to Redo—effectively enabling you to undo your undo. Although useful, this command has little in common with the other Edit menu options (Command-Z).
- Cut—Cuts a piece of information (text, graphic, sound, and so on) from a document. The information is removed from the current file and placed in the Clipboard for reuse (Command-X).
- Copy—Like Cut, but leaves the information in the original document and creates a copy of the data within the system Clipboard. If Copy (Command-C) is chosen when a Finder icon is selected, that file is prepared for duplication. The process is completed by choosing Paste.
- Paste—Pastes the contents of the Clipboard back into the frontmost document or field. If the receiving element cannot handle the type of data you are attempting to paste (pasting a sound into a text field, for example), the Paste operation will fail. If you've previously used Copy while a Finder file icon was selected, the file will be copied to the location represented by the currently active Finder window (Command-V).
- Select All—Highlights all selectable items within a window or document (Command-A).
- Show Clipboard—Choosing Show Clipboard displays a small Finder window with the data that has been cut or copied from an application. Restarting your computer or logging out will lose the contents of the Clipboard.
- Special Characters—Displays the character selection palette for selecting characters from any installed language and font.

NOTE

The Edit menu works to cut and copy information between native Mac OS X applications and applications running in the Classic environment (discussed in Chapter 3, "Applications and Utilities"). Unfortunately, the integration between these two effectively separate operating systems is such that you might need to wait a second or two between a cut/copy and a paste for the information to find its way to the appropriate destination.

Performing File and Content Searches

In addition to organizing your files, the Finder enables you to find applications by filename or documents by filename or their contents. But the best part is that the search results are interactive. You can launch located programs and applications by double-clicking their icons in the results pane. Also, dragging a file or folder to the desktop or a Finder window moves that object to a new location. This is a quick way to clean up when you've accidentally saved a file to the wrong folder.

The Finder window provides a quick means of performing a name-search. Type your search term in the Search field in the toolbar (upper-right corner, by default). As you type, the search results are displayed almost instantly within your window in two panes. The top pane displays all the located files, whereas the bottom pane shows the folder hierarchy that contains a selected file, as shown in Figure 2.24.

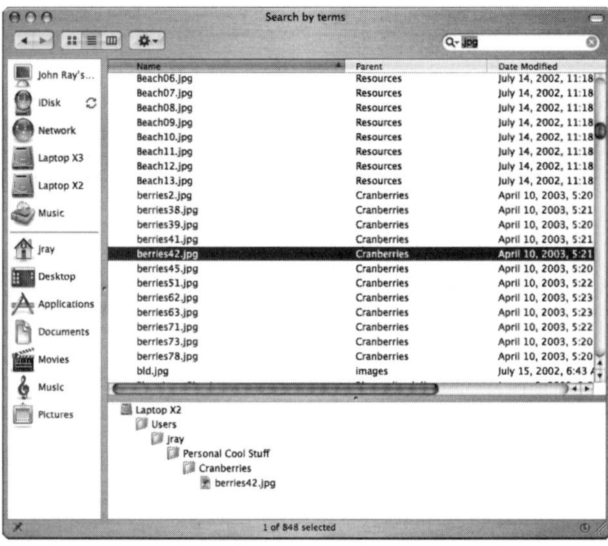

FIGURE 2.24 Search results are returned almost instantly.

To cancel a search in-progress, click the "X" icon at the end of the search field. To return to the file listing you were viewing before the search, use the toolbar's Back arrow.

Using the pop-up menu inside the search field (click the magnifying glass icon), you can choose where the search will take place.

Advanced Searches

If searching by name isn't enough, you can gain even greater control by using the *full* find feature: File, Find (Command-F). This opens a separate search window, shown in Figure 2.25.

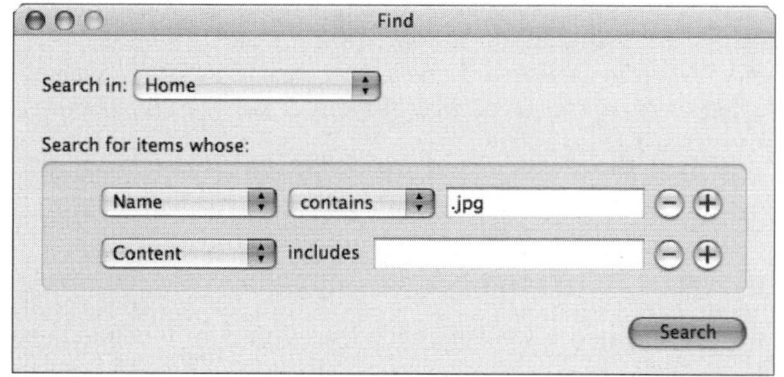

FIGURE 2.25 Gain more control over your searches with an advanced search.

Use the Search In pop-up menu to choose where the search takes place:

- Everywhere—Examines all accessible drives and user accounts.
- Local Disks—Examines only the current drive, but all user accounts.
- Home—Examines only the home directory of the person currently logged in.
- Selection—Displays a list of available drives for you to choose. You can also click the Add/Remove button to insert or remove specific folders.

Choose whether to search for filenames, contents, or both. Enter your search text into the appropriate field(s). If you want to add additional search terms in these categories, click the "+" buttons beside the fields to add additional conditions, or the "-" button to remove them. Use the comparison pop-up menu to choose what determines a file "match"—such as "contains," "starts with," or "ends with" the given text.

Finally, click the Search button to start the search. In a few moments, the search results are displayed in a new window.

NOTE

Although the advanced search result window *appears* to be a specialized window, it is actually just a Finder window with the toolbar and shortcut pane hidden. Clicking the toolbar button in the upper-right corner "unhides" everything.

As with a simple search, Find lists the filename, parent directory, the date the file was modified, file size, and the kind of file. After an item has been highlighted, its path is shown in the details pane at the bottom of the window. Double-clicking opens the file, folder, or application.

NOTE

Searching for file contents requires that the directory containing the file be indexed, or cataloged. You can index a folder, or check for the last date of last indexing, using the Get Info window.

Getting File Information

The Mac OS has always returned a wealth of information about a file via the Get Info option from the Finder's File menu. In Mac OS X, this is no different. Unlike Mac OS 8/9, the Mac OS X Info window can display a great deal more information about your files and folders, such as graphical previews and user permissions.

Let's take a look at each one of the views, the information it contains, and what it means to you.

General

The default Get Info window can be displayed by selecting the file you want to examine within the Finder and then choosing File, Get Info (Command-I). As shown in Figure 2.26, the initial information window provides basic facts about the selected resource. The Get Info window can display additional information about a selected resource by expanding hidden portions of the window via the disclosure arrows located along the bottom of the window.

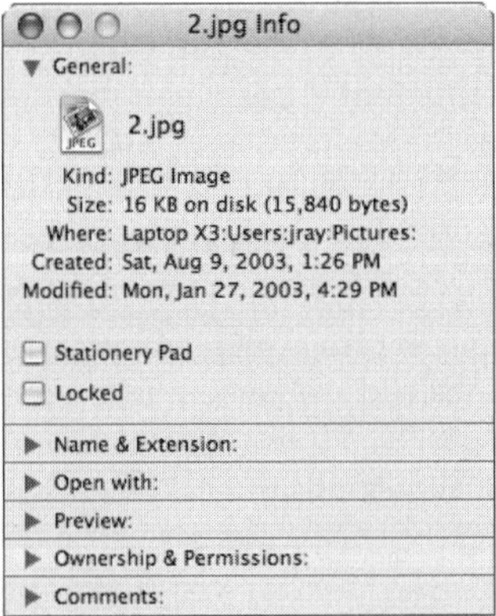

FIGURE 2.26 The General Information pane provides basic size, location, and type information about a file.

Selecting a file and choosing Get Info displays data about that file and has several options for revealing additional information:

- Kind—The type of file being examined (application, movie, and so on).
- Size—The size of the file or folder.
- Where—The full path to the selected resource.
- Created—The day and time the item was created.
- Modified—The day and time the item was last modified.
- Version—The version of the document. Usually available only on application files.
- Stationery Pad—Available for document files only. If the Stationery Pad check box is checked, the file can be used to create new files but cannot be modified itself. This is used to create template files for common documents.
- Locked—If this option is checked, the file cannot be modified or deleted until it is unlocked. For Linux/Unix users, this is equivalent to setting the immutable flag for the file.

If the file you are viewing is an alias file, the General Information pane also shows the location of the original file along with a Select New Original button that lets you pick a new file to attach the alias to.

Changing Icons

If you're unhappy with the icon of the resource you're examining, you can click the object's icon within the General Information pane, and then use the Copy and Paste options in the Edit menu to move icons or images from other files onto the selected item. The Cut option can be used to remove a custom icon from a file and restore the default.

> **TIP**
>
> An excellent source for high-quality Mac OS X icons is Iconfactory at `http://www.iconfactory.com` or Xicons, located at `http://www.xicons.com`.

Name & Extension

Mac OS X shares something with Windows: file extensions. Although it is still possible for files to have the traditional Macintosh file types and creators, it is no longer the norm. To shield users from the shock of seeing extensions to the names of their files, Apple added the option to hide file extensions in Mac OS X. Users can turn off this option on a file-by-file basis by accessing the Name & Extension portion of the Get Info pane, as shown in Figure 2.27.

To edit the filename itself (including the extension) make modifications within the Name & Extension field. Turn on (or off) file extensions by clicking the Hide Extension check box.

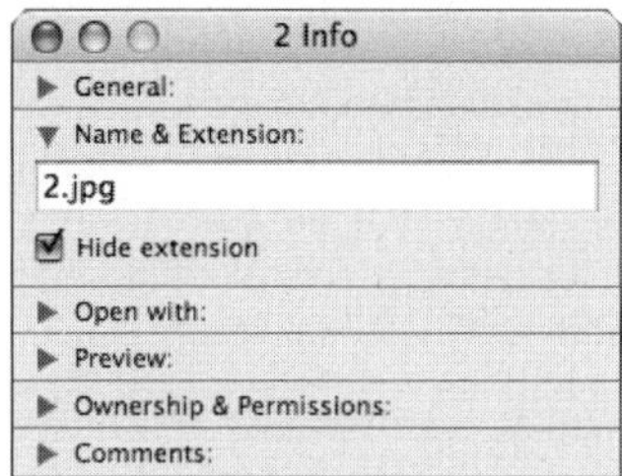

FIGURE 2.27 The Name & Extension pane can hide or reveal file extensions.

> **NOTE**
>
> Mac OS X functions identically whether or not file extensions are visible. This is simply a change in appearance, not functionality.

Content Index

When you're getting info on a folder, the Content Index option is available, as demonstrated in Figure 2.28.

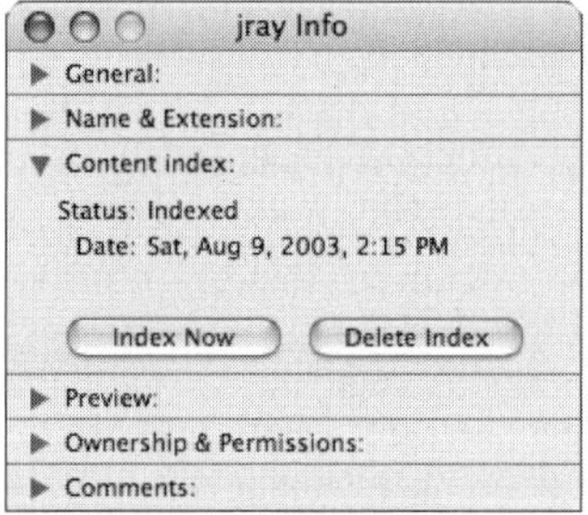

FIGURE 2.28 Index folder contents for quick searches.

Using the Index Now button, you can index a folder's contents so that the Finder's Find function can quickly search for text within the folder's files. You must index a folder before you can perform a content search.

Click the Delete Index button to remove an index that is outdated (because you've removed/changed files within the folder) or no longer needed.

Open With

If you have selected a document icon (not an application or a folder), you should be able to access the Open With pane within the Get Info window. This is used to configure the applications that open certain types of documents on the system. Unlike previous versions of Mac OS, which relied on a hidden creator and file type, Mac OS X can also use file extensions or creator/file-type resources. If you download a file from a non-Mac OS X system, your computer might not realize what it needs to do to open the file. The Open With pane, shown in Figure 2.29, lets you configure how the system reacts.

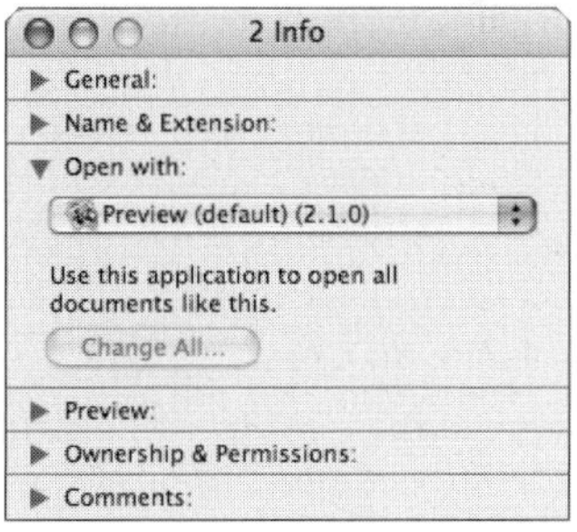

FIGURE 2.29 The Open With option allows you to choose what application will read a particular file or type of file.

The default application name is shown at the top of a pop-up menu containing alternative application choices. If the application you want to use isn't in the menu, choose Other, and then use the standard Mac OS X File dialog box to browse to the application you want to use.

If you have a group of files that you want to open with a given application, you can select the entire group and use the Open With settings to adjust them all simultaneously. Alternatively, click the Change All button to set the default application for all files of that type on your system. This beats selecting each file and making the setting individually.

Languages

If you have an application selected, you might be able to choose Languages within the Get Info window. Applications can have multiple internal resources that change the application to the appropriate system conditions—the Language pane allows you to adjust the language resources used by an application.

In early versions of the Mac OS, resources were contained within a file's resource fork. Unfortunately, resource forks are unique to the Mac filesystem. To store Mac files and applications on a non-Mac filesystem, various contortions had to be made. Typically, the data portion of an application would be stored like a normal file, and the resource fork would be converted to a second file stored elsewhere.

Although this has worked for many years, it requires computers that interact with Mac files to understand the unusual quality of Mac files. In Mac OS X, files can still have resources, but they have been bundled in an entirely new way. First introduced in

Mac OS 9, the Mac OS now supports a new concept called a *package*. A package is nothing more than a folder structure that appears to the user to be a single file. In reality, a package is a folder that contains individual files for all the resources it might need. Other operating systems need not understand the specifics of the Mac filesystem to store package files. The Languages pane, shown in Figure 2.30, displays the language resources available for each application, allowing a user to immediately localize software with the appropriately packaged resources. The Add and Remove buttons can be used to add additional language resources to the software.

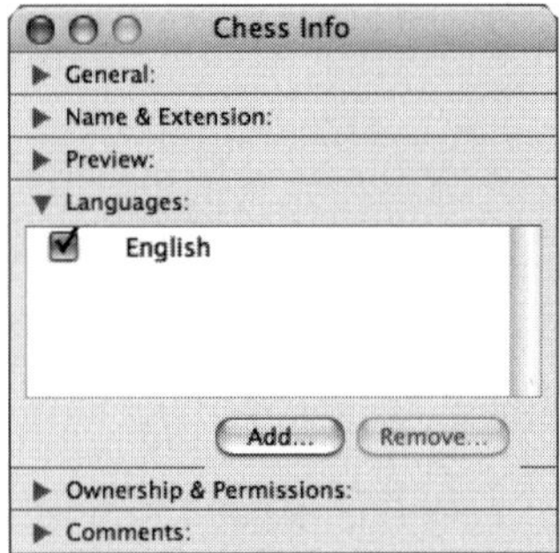

FIGURE 2.30 Language resources can be examined in this view.

NOTE

Although only language resources are shown in the current version of Mac OS X, you might find interesting things appearing in the future. When NeXT Computer was shipping OpenStep, the operating system could run on multiple CPU architectures, such as x86, Motorola 68000, and Sparc. Applications for OpenStep could contain resources for each of the different CPUs, allowing a single application file to run unchanged on multiple different computers.

Even though Intel support for Mac OS X is currently only a dream (or a behind-closed-doors reality if you believe the "Marklar" rumors), it is possible that Apple might reintroduce this feature in the future.

Preview

If a QuickTime-recognized document is selected, there will be another available Get Info option: Preview. Preview provides a quick look at the contents of a wide variety of media files including MP3s, CD audio tracks (AIFF), JPEGs, GIFs, TIFFs, PDFs, and many more.

If you are previewing a video or audio track, the QuickTime player controls will appear and enable you to play the contents of the file. This is a great way to play your CDs or listen to MP3s without starting up a copy of iTunes. Figure 2.31 shows a CD audio track being played in the Preview pane.

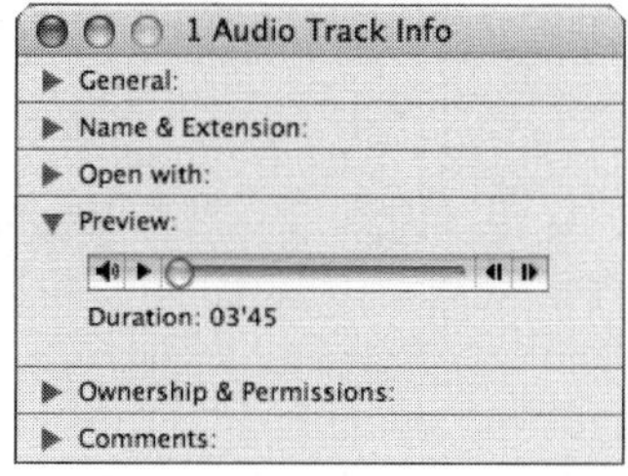

FIGURE 2.31 Play your CD tracks using the Finder's Get Info Preview pane.

Ownership & Permissions

Mac OS X enables you to take control over who can view your files. Without your password (or the system administrator `[root]` password), other users can be completely restricted from accessing your folders and files. Choose the Ownership & Permissions pane of the Get Info window after selecting the file or folder you want to adjust. Your screen should look similar to Figure 2.32.

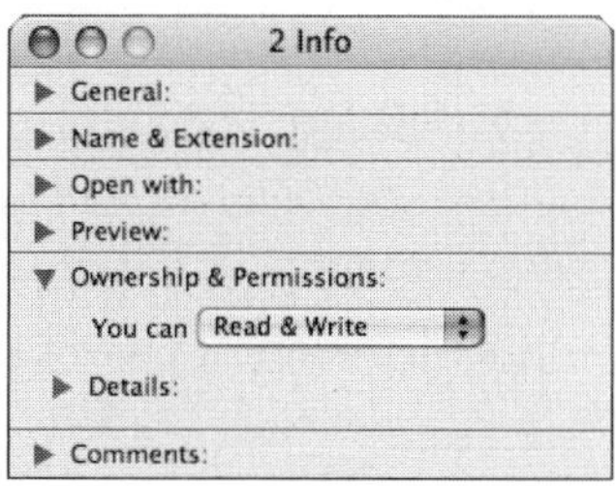

FIGURE 2.32 Choose what you can do to a file.

Mac OS X makes it easy to adjust permissions without getting into nitty-gritty details such as file ownership. By default, the pop-up menu labeled You Can allows you to choose what *you* want to be able to do with a file. Choose from the following:

- Read Only—The file or folder can be read but not modified in any way.
- Write Only (Drop Box)—Available only as an option for folders, write-only access allows users to add files to a folder but not to read what is inside the folder.
- Read & Write—The file or folder can be read, written to, or deleted.
- No Access—The file or folder may not be read, written to, deleted, or modified in any way.

If this doesn't suit your fancy, you can gain finer grained control by expanding the "Details" section of the Ownership & Permissions pane, as shown in Figure 2.33.

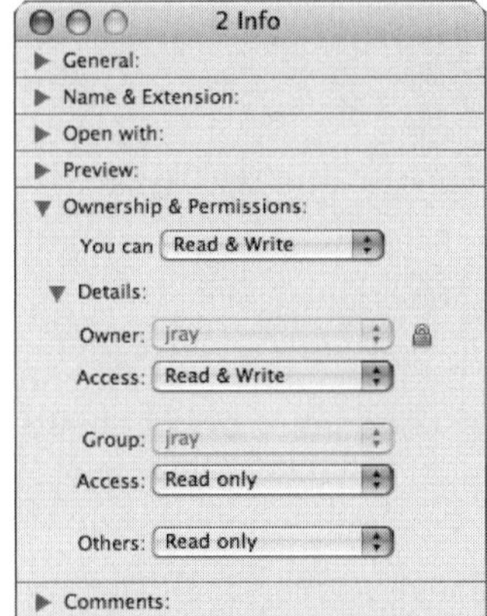

FIGURE 2.33 Get complete control over file ownership and permissions.

Here, there are three levels of access you can adjust:

- Owner—The person who owns a file. Most files on a default Mac OS X installation are owned by a system user. You own files that you create.
- Group—By default, you are a member of your own group (with the same name as your username). Chapter 24, "User Management and Machine Clustering," discusses the creation of additional groups.
- Others—Users who are not the owner and not part of the default group.

For each of these levels of access, there are multiple user rights. Adjusting these rights controls what the owner, group, and everyone else can do to a file or folder.

When viewing the file information for a folder, the window also shows an Apply to Enclosed Items button that copies all the access rights on the folder to the files underneath. If a folder does not have read permissions, the files inside the folder may still be accessed or modified unless they too have removed read permissions.

A final setting exists for non-boot storage volumes. If a disk is selected while viewing privilege information, an Ignore Ownership on This Volume check box appears. Clicking this box causes the volume to appear as wide open to the operating system. Users can modify anything on the drive—just as in previous versions of the Mac OS. Activating this setting is not recommended.

Comments

The final area within the Get Info window, Comments, provides a text field for you to enter comments about the selected file. Some applications generate file comments automatically to help you remember where the file was downloaded, and so forth.

TIP

By default, the Get Info window opens a separate window for each item you request information about. To display a single "inspector-style" window that switches as you move between items, use the Show Inspector option that appears in the File menu when you hold down Option.

The Desktop

The desktop is, for all intents and purposes, a global Finder window that sits behind all the other windows on the system. You can copy files to the desktop, create aliases on the desktop, and so on. The primary difference is that the desktop is available only in the Icon View mode.

TIP

The contents of the desktop are also accessible from the Desktop folder contained within your home directory (path: `~/Desktop`).

Like other Finder windows, the desktop layout is controlled by the View Options located in the View menu. Use the Icon Size slider and arrangement settings exactly as you would adjust any other window within Icon View mode.

Desktop & Screen Saver: System Preferences Pane

A more visually exciting change that you can perform on your Finder desktop is changing the background image. To do this, you can access the Desktop pane within the System Preferences application (path: `/Applications/System Preferences`).

To open the System Preferences, you have a number of options:

- Click the System Preferences icon in the Dock—it resembles a light switch with an Apple logo.
- Choose System Preferences from the Apple menu.
- Launch System Preferences manually. It is located in the system's Applications folder (path: `/Applications/System Preferences`).

After System Preferences is running, click the Desktop & Screen Saver icon, located within the Personal category of the Preferences window.

Desktop Backgrounds

After launching, make sure that the Desktop button is selected. Figure 2.34 shows the Desktop portion of the Desktop & Screen Saver Preferences pane.

TIP

To quickly enter the Desktop Preferences, Control-click on the Desktop background and choose Change Desktop Background from the contextual menu that appears.

FIGURE 2.34 Set your background image using the Desktop Preferences pane.

To change the current background, drag an image file from the Finder into the image well within the pane. Alternatively, you can browse Collections of images by choosing from the Collection list and then using the scrollbar to move through the available options. A collection is nothing more than a folder of images. There are six preset collections: Apple backgrounds, Nature, Abstract, Solid Colors, Pictures, and Desktop Pictures. The Pictures option selects your personal `~/Pictures` folder. To browse an arbitrary folder, choose the Choose Folder item, and then select the folder you want to use (If you've created albums in iPhoto, these will also be displayed in the collection list. See chapter 6 for more information on iPhoto).

To have your desktop picture change automatically, click the Change Picture check box and then pick the change interval from the pop-up menu.

TIP

To run the screensaver (discussed in the next section) as your desktop background, use the command `/System/Library/Frameworks/ScreenSaver.framework/Resources/ScreenSaverEngine.app/Contents/MacOS/ScreenSaverEngine -background` or use a utility such as Xback (`http://www.gideonsoftworks.com/xback.html`).

NOTE

The Apple image collections are located within `/Library/Desktop Pictures` and can be added to or modified by any administrative user on the system.

Screensavers

Screensavers are like desktop backgrounds for when you're lazy. Screensavers were traditionally invoked to save monitors from suffering burn-in. Today, screensavers are largely for "show" only and in reality are only serving to shorten the life span of your LCD's backlight. Even so, they're fun to look at and, in Mac OS X, a screensaver engine is built-in.

To access the screensaver functions of the Desktop & Screen Saver pane, click the Screen Saver button within the preferences pane. Your display should resemble Figure 2.35.

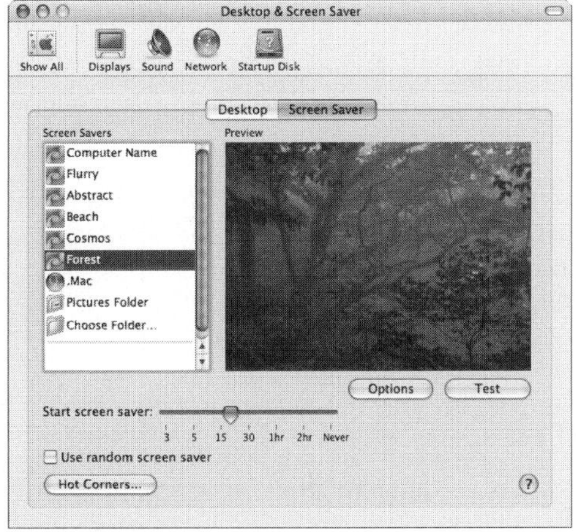

FIGURE 2.35 Set your computer to display pretty pictures when you're not working.

From the list on the left, choose the screensaver that sounds "interesting." The Pictures Folder saver uses images in your Pictures directory to create an onscreen slideshow, or the Choose Folder saver allows you to choose an arbitrary folder to use for a slideshow. The .Mac option is discussed in Chapter 4. After choosing a screensaver, a preview appears in the pane on the right. If you want a random screensaver to display each time it starts, click the Use Random Screen Saver check box (If you've created albums in iPhoto, these will also be displayed in the screensaver list. See chapter 6 for more information on iPhoto).

Many screensavers offer configuration for fine-tuning their graphics and performance. Click the Options button to display a dialog containing advanced configuration for the selected saver. The Test button can be used to test the screensaver fullscreen.

To set up *when* the screensaver is displayed, use the Start Screen Saver slider to choose when (if ever) the screensaver starts. Because a screensaver doesn't actually turn off your display, this is largely meaningless; it is simply how long you have to wait until you see pretty pictures.

NOTE

Use the Energy Saver preferences pane to completely turn off your monitor after a set period of time. This is discussed in Chapter 11, "Additional System Components."

Finally, to enable and choose corners where you can place your cursor to immediately (or never) start a screensaver, click the Hot Corners button. A dialog appears allowing you to choose a screen corner to disable or start the screensaver as well as what corners activate the Exposé effect discussed shortly. Positioning your mouse in the chosen corner will have the selected effect.

TIP

Screensavers are plentiful for Mac OS X (visit `http://www.versiontracker.com` or `http://www.macupdate.com` and search for screen saver).

To install a new screensaver, manually copy the `.saver` file to `/Library/Screen Savers` or `~/Library/Screen Savers` for use by all users on the system or for personal use, respectively. Or, take advantage of Panther's capability to install it for you by double-clicking the file and then following the onscreen instructions.

Burning CD/DVDs

Burning CD-Rs, CD-RWs, or DVDs within the Mac OS X Finder is easy and similar to working with any other storage device. To make the process as transparent as possible, Mac OS X creates a hidden CD/DVD-sized temporary storage area on your hard drive. Applications, files, and folders that are added to a CD/DVD are actually copied to this location until the user tells the system to burn the CD/DVD. Only after the burn starts are files actually transferred to the CD/DVD media.

To write your own CD/DVD, first insert media into the writer. The Mac OS X Finder prompts you to choose how you want to use the disc, as shown in Figure 2.36. Again, this doesn't actually write anything to the media just yet, but it tells the computer what your intentions are for the disc.

Enter a name for the disc you are writing—it will appear with this name on the desktop. Next, choose an action. Four are provided:

- Open Finder—An HFS+/ISO 9660 disk image for storing Macintosh data and files is mounted in the Finder.
- Open iTunes—Opens iTunes so that the CD can be used for burning MP3s. A CD image is not mounted.
- Open Other Application—Open another application to work with the CD (such as Roxio's Toast).
- Run Script—Run an AppleScript.

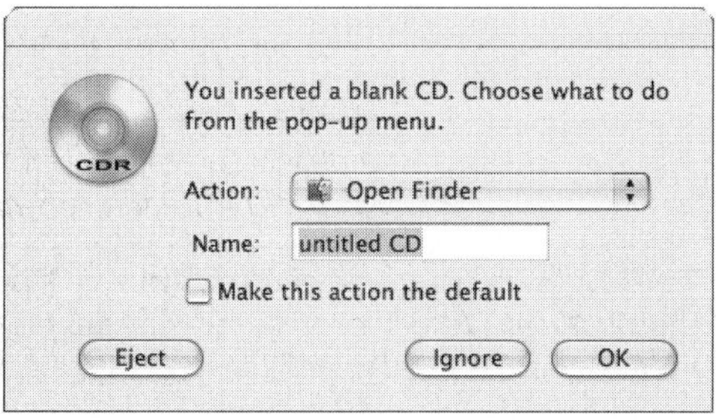

FIGURE 2.36 Before you can start using a CD, you must tell Mac OS X what type of CD it will be.

If you want to leave the CD in the drive but not prepare it, click Ignore. You can also choose to make the current settings the default with the Make This Action the Default check box.

Because this chapter focuses on the Finder, choose Open Finder and then click OK. You'll learn about iTunes in Chapter 7, "Audio."

After a few seconds, an icon representing the CD appears on your desktop. You can interact with this virtual volume as you would any other under Mac OS X—copy files to it, delete files, and so on.

When you've created the CD layout that you like, you can start the burn process by choosing File, Burn Disc. In addition, dragging the CD to the trash also prompts for burning to begin. Mac OS X displays the dialog box shown in Figure 2.37.

NOTE

To choose File, Burn Disc from the menu, the frontmost Finder window must be the CD's window. If the CD is not the active window, the menu item will be disabled.

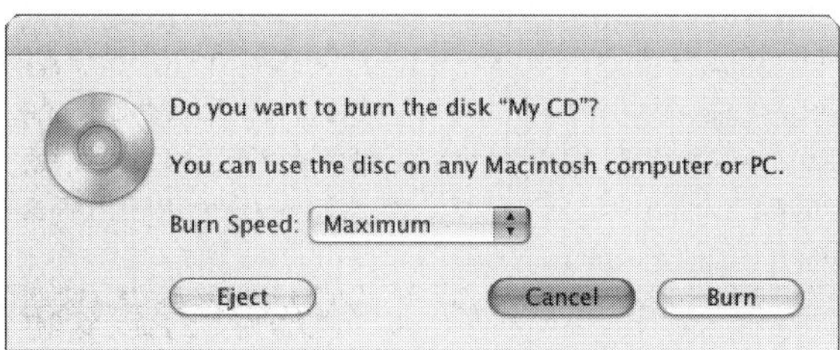

FIGURE 2.37 Choose Burn to write the CD.

Choose your Burn speed and click the Burn button to start the process of writing the CD. This will take a few minutes and will be tracked by the Finder much like a normal copy operation. If you've decided against writing the CD, click Eject to remove the media and erase the CD layout you've created.

Using Fast User Switching

Introduced in Panther is *fast user switching*, a feature borrowed from Windows XP and useful for families of shared computers. By default, if you've added multiple user accounts to your computer (see Chapters 11 and 24 for information), you have to close your applications and then choose Log Out from the Apple menu to allow another user to access the system. In Panther, fast user switching can preserve your current desktop, let another user log in and use their account, and then return you to where you left off.

To enable fast user switching, open the Accounts system preferences pane, authenticate by clicking the lock icon in the lower-left corner, and then click the Login Options button. Your screen should resemble Figure 2.38.

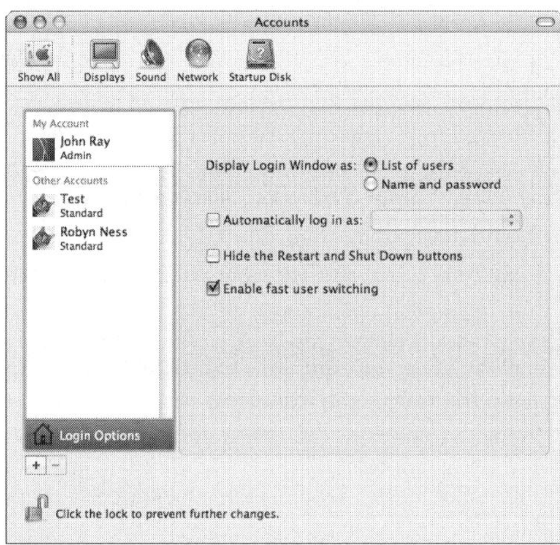

FIGURE 2.38 Enable fast user switching.

Click the Enable Fast User Switching check box and then quit the System Preferences application. A menu item appears with your name in the upper-right corner of the menu bar—the switching menu. Displaying the menu reveals a list of local user accounts with login enabled along with a Login Window option. Choosing a user's name prompts for that user's login information and then switches to the user's desktop. Choosing the Login Window selection leaves your applications running but displays the login window, allowing other users to log in without disrupting your workspace.

TIP

If you want to be able to switch to another user account without entering that user's password, the user *must* have a blank password. See Chapters 11 and 24 for more information on setting up user accounts.

User accounts that are "active" (have running applications) are denoted with an orange check mark in front of their name in the switching menu and the login screen, as shown in Figure 2.39. Switching to an active account is almost instantaneous.

FIGURE 2.39 Active sessions are denoted by an orange check mark in the switching menu and login screen.

CAUTION

Users should log out (Shift-Command-Q) completely when finished using the computer. Shutting down or restarting your computer while there are active sessions could result in lost data for users who are still logged in.

Finder Preferences

The remaining Finder Preferences can be used to adjust a few more settings that control how you will interact with your desktop and icons. Open the General preferences by choosing Finder, Preferences. Figure 2.40 shows the General pane.

Use the General Finder Preferences to configure these elements:

- Show These Items on the Desktop—Choose whether different storage devices will be mounted automatically on the desktop. Use the Hard Disks, Removable Media, and Connected Servers check boxes to display the associated devices on the desktop. If an item is not mounted on the desktop, it will be accessible by moving to the Computer level of the filesystem hierarchy.
- New Finder Window Shows—Determine what location a new Finder window opens in. Choose Computer to open a window displaying all mounted storage devices or Home to start in your home directory.

- Always Open Folders in a New Window—Clicking this option forces a new window to open each time a folder is double-clicked. This is the only way to make the toolbar-mode Finder windows behave like the traditional Finder.
- Open New Windows in Column View—Force all Finder windows being opened into the Column view.
- Spring-Loaded Folders and Windows—Choose the length of time a folder or window waits before "springing open" while your mouse hovers over it. See "Moving Files and Folders" earlier in this chapter.

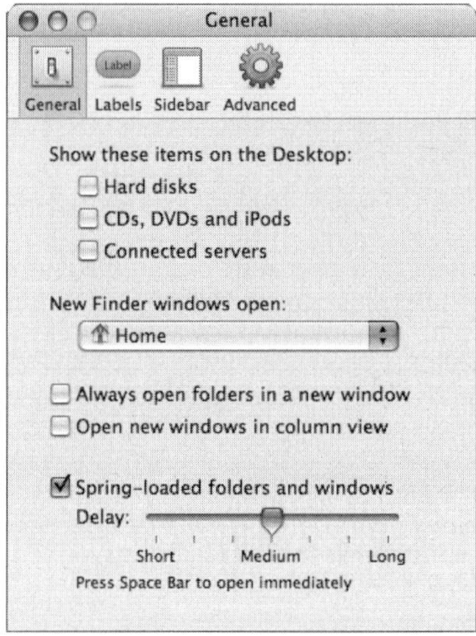

FIGURE 2.40 Finder Preferences control file extensions, trash warnings, and more.

The Advanced pane provides a few more choices that ordinarily you won't need to change:

- Show All File Extensions—Turn on this setting to force all file extensions to be shown in the Finder and other windows. Most Mac users won't want to do this.
- Show Hidden Files—Display *all* files, including Unix directories normally hidden.
- Show Warning Before Emptying the Trash—When emptying the trash can, Mac OS X displays a warning message. To bypass this dialog, deselect this check box. Alternatively, hold down Option when choosing Empty Trash to temporarily bypass the warning.
- Languages for Searching File Contents—Choose the languages that will be indexed when indexing the contents of a folder. By default, Mac OS X has several languages selected. You may want to deselect all but your primary language to speed up the indexing process.

Close the Finder Preferences window when you're satisfied with your settings.

A Simpler Finder?

I'd like to introduce my child (husband, wife, mother, father) to Mac OS X, but she's not ready for the Finder; what can I do? A Simple Finder mode can be activated on a per-user basis within the Accounts System Preferences pane. The Simple Finder removes much of the complexity (and feature set) of the standard Finder but makes operating the computer much easier for those who just want to launch applications. See Chapter 11 for information on the Mac OS X System Preferences panes.

Using the Dock

The Dock is "constant" within the Mac OS X interface. No matter what application you're in, the Dock is present on your screen, or a mouse motion away. The Dock supplements the Finder operations by enabling you to launch applications, open documents, and delete items without having to dig through (or under) dozens of windows. Figure 2.41 shows the Dock.

FIGURE 2.41 The Dock acts as application launcher, switcher, and more.

Application Switcher and Launcher

To use the Dock as an application launcher, commonly used applications can be added to the Dock, much like a Finder toolbar, by dragging them to the position you want on the left side (or top in vertical mode) of the Dock divider bar. This half of the bar contains all docked and currently running applications. A running application is denoted by a small triangle under its icon.

To switch between the active programs, just click the icon of the application that you want to bring to the front. Holding down Option as you click on an application brings the application to the front and hides the previously active process. Simultaneously holding down both Option-Command while clicking brings the clicked application to the front and hides all other applications.

To switch between open programs from the keyboard, use Command-Tab—this should seem familiar to Windows users. This displays a list of active icons, shown in Figure 2.42, that you can cycle through with the Tab key or via the arrow keys (as long as the Command key is held down).

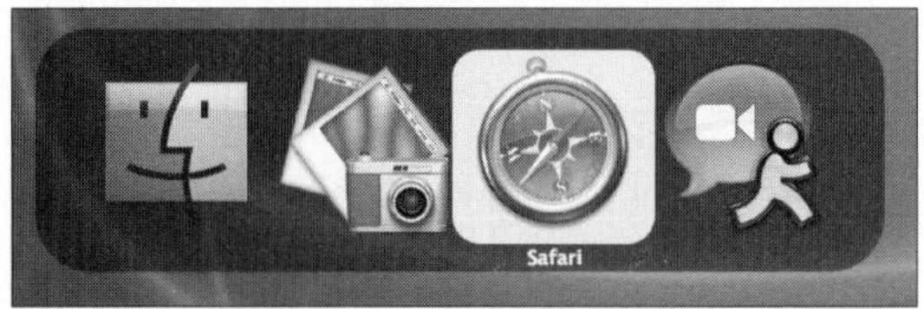

FIGURE 2.42 Switch between active applications with Command-Tab.

Finally, if you have placed an application on the Dock, you can launch it by single-clicking the icon. The application icon begins bouncing (unless configured not to in the Dock System Preferences pane) and continues to do so until the software is ready for user interaction.

> **TIP**
>
> To add an application currently running to a permanent spot in the Dock, just click and hold (or Control-click) the icon, and then choose Keep in Dock from the pop-up menu.

Interacting with Running Applications

Common functions, such as quitting an application, hiding it, or jumping to one of its open windows, can be accessed by clicking and holding a running application's Dock icon or by Control-clicking on the icon. Some applications, such as iTunes, allow basic controls (playback controls, in the case of iTunes) to be accessed through the Dock pop-up menu. After the menu has appeared, you can press the Option key to reveal hidden menu options; this particular key/mouse combination changes a Dock icon's Quit selection to Force Quit when used.

Application icons also serve as proxy drop points for documents. You can drag documents on top of an application's Dock icon to open them in that application.

> **TIP**
>
> Dragging a document to a running application or to the trash is a bit of a pain in Mac OS X. In an effort to accommodate the icon you're dragging with the assumption that you're adding it to the Dock, the other icons move out of its way. For a user, this means that the icon she's headed for might not hold still long enough for a traditional drag-and-drop. To keep the Dock icons from sliding, hold down the Command key during the drag.

TIP

To force a docked application to accept a dropped document that it doesn't recognize, hold down Command-Option when holding the document over the application icon. The icon immediately highlights, allowing you to perform your drag-and-drop action.

File and Folder Shortcuts

Shortcuts to files and folders that are used frequently can be stored to the right (or bottom in vertical mode) of the Dock separator bar. When a folder is added to the Dock, it can be single-clicked to open a Finder window containing the contents of that folder. Clicking and holding (or Control-clicking) a folder in the Dock creates a pop-up hierarchical menu displaying the contents of the folder. Any elements added to the folder will be immediately visible in the pop-up menu.

NOTE

Moving an icon to the Dock does not change the location of the original file or folder. The icon within the Dock is just an alias to the real file.

TIP

To locate an application, file, or folder that you've dragged to the Dock, hold down Command and click the Dock icon, or choose Show in Finder while Control-clicking or click-holding the icon. The Finder opens a window and highlights the original file or folder.

Dock Extras

Dock extras (Docklings) are small, always-on applications that provide instant-access features from within the Dock. Unlike other applications, a Dock extra lives its whole life within the Dock and does not have a user interface that extends beyond the Dock icon and a pop-up menu. Unlike other Dock elements, Dock extras can be positioned anywhere on the Dock, except after the trash can. To activate a Dock extra configuration menu, either click-and-hold or Control-click the icon. Although the original Mac OS X releases came with a few Docklings, they've since been replaced by menu extras. The Dockling appears to be largely a thing of the past, but if you're interested in trying one, they can still be found on VersionTracker (`http://www.versiontracker.com`) or MacUpdate (`http://www.macupdate.com`).

The Trash Can

The Mac OS trash can lives on the right side of the Dock. You can drag files and folders directly from the Finder into the Dock's trash can. If you want to remove an item from the trash, click the trash can icon, and a window appears containing all the items waiting to be deleted. You can drag files from this window just as you can in any other Finder window.

To empty the trash, use the Finder's application menu and choose Empty Trash (Shift-Command-Delete); or click-and-hold or Control-click the Trash can icon, and choose Empty Trash from the pop-up menu. Holding down Option while emptying the trash bypasses any system warning messages. The Finder preferences can permanently disable the Empty Trash warning.

TIP

If you're not completely in love with Apple's new Trash icons, you can replace them (along with several other built-in Dock icons) by opening `/System/Library/CoreServices/Dock.app/Contents/Resources` and editing the assorted `.png` image files located there. The `trashempty.png` and `trashfull.png` icons define the two states of the trash can.

Even easier is to use CandyBar, by Panic Software (`http://www.panic.com`) to swap icon sets in and out for your computer.

NOTE

Although not available from the Dock trash can's Empty Trash pop-up menu—keep in mind that the Secure Empty Trash option is available from the Finder's application menu.

Ejecting Media

There are a number of ways to eject disks under Mac OS X. Control-clicking on a mounted volume opens a contextual menu with an Eject option. Alternatively, you can highlight the resource to remove and choose File, Eject (Command-E) from the Finder's menu; press the Eject key on most Apple keyboards; or use the Eject icon beside each removable resource in the Finder's shortcut pane.

The final method of ejecting a disk might seem a bit unusual to some users, but it has been a standard on the Macintosh for many years. Disks can be safely unmounted and ejected by dragging them to the trash can. To get around the obvious "Hey, isn't that going to erase my disk?" reaction that many have, Mac OS X conveniently changes the trash can icon into an eject symbol during a drag operation that includes a storage volume.

Windows

Minimized windows are placed in a thumbnail view beside the trash can. Depending on the application, these iconified windows might continue to update as their respective applications attempt to display new information. The QuickTime player, for example, can continue to play miniaturized movies in the Dock.

TIP

There are three built-in minimizing effects for Mac OS X, two of which (Genie and Scale) are accessible in the Dock Preferences pane. You can switch between the three effects manually by using the following commands within the Terminal window:

- The standard Genie effect:

```
defaults write com.apple.Dock mineffect genie
```

- An aptly named suck effect:

```
defaults write com.apple.Dock mineffect suck
```

- A simple window scaling:

```
defaults write com.apple.Dock mineffect scale
```

Customizing the Dock

After the initial "gee whiz, that's pretty" reaction to the Dock wears off, you'll probably want to customize the Dock to better suit your Finder settings. Depending on your screen size, you might be looking at a Dock that, by default, eats up about one-third of the available desktop space on your machine. Don't worry, there are ways to rectify the situation.

Instant Resizing

The easiest and fastest way to resize the Dock is to click and hold on the divider line that separates the right and left sides of the Dock. With your mouse held down, drag up and down. The Dock dynamically resizes as you move your mouse. Let go of the mouse button when the Dock reaches the size you want.

TIP

As the Dock grows or shrinks, the icons change size with it, and the divider line shifts to the left or right as needed. After the resize has started, you do not need to keep your mouse cursor centered over the divider line—the resize continues until the mouse button is released, regardless of your pointer position.

After playing with different Dock sizes, you might notice that some sizes look better than others. This is because Mac OS X must interpolate between several different native icon graphics to scale the images. To choose only native icon sizes, hold down the Option key while using the separator bar to resize.

Dock: System Preferences Pane

For more fine-tuning of the Dock, you must turn to the System Preferences application. The Dock has a settings pane within System Preferences that you can use to adjust its size, adjust its icon magnification, and make it disappear when not in use. Users of Apple's Titanium PowerBooks or Cinema-aspect displays, such as the 17-inch iMac, will be pleased to find that the Dock can even move into a vertical mode, occupying space along the sides of the screen.

Open System Preferences; then click the Dock icon within System Preferences. Your screen should now resemble Figure 2.43.

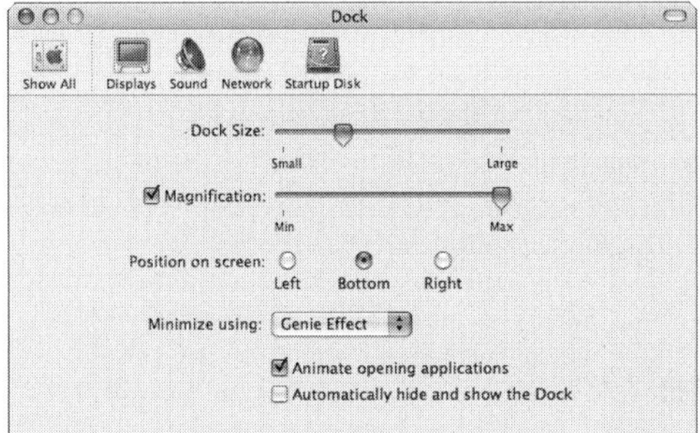

FIGURE 2.43 Customize the Dock's appearance from the System Preferences application.

Within this pane, you can choose how you want the Dock to look and act on your computer. There are six settings:

- Dock Size—This sets the size of the Dock icons. Moving this slider from left to right increases the size of the default Dock icon and is identical to dragging the separator bar discussed earlier in the section "Instant Resizing." Keep in mind that the Dock does not expand beyond the edges of the screen and shrinks automatically to make room for additional icons.
- Magnification—If you activate Dock magnification by clicking the check box, the Dock icons automatically scale as you move your cursor over them. You can use the magnification slider to adjust the maximum size that a magnified icon will take. Although this is useful if you have an extremely small Dock, its main purpose seems to be eye candy. If you haven't seen this effect demonstrated, turn it on—you're in for a treat.
- Position on Screen—Use these radio buttons (Left, Bottom, Right) to control where the Dock appears on your desktop. The default position is at the bottom of the screen, but many users may find that a vertical orientation (left or right) is more useful and appealing.
- Minimize Using—Audiences were wowed when they first saw the Dock's Genie effect for minimizing windows. Although nifty, it isn't exactly the fastest thing on the planet. Starting in Mac OS X 10.1, Apple includes a second minimization effect: Scale. This effect is much less dramatic but also much faster. Use the Minimize Using pop-up menu to choose your minimization style.

- Animate Opening Applications—By default, when an application is starting, the Dock bounces the application's icon up and down. This provides visual feedback that the system hasn't stalled. Shutting off this feature might result in a small speed increase but is likely to be a bit frustrating when you can no longer tell whether the system is starting the application you selected.
- Automatically Hide and Show the Dock—If this check box is set, the Dock automatically disappears when you move your mouse out of it. To make the Dock reappear, just move your cursor to the bottom of the screen—it will grow back into the original position. You can toggle this at any time from the Finder by pressing Option-Command-D.

Easy access to several of the Dock's configuration options is also available through the Dock submenu in the Apple menu or by Control-clicking the dock right/left separator line to show a Dock contextual menu.

How Can I Configure Dock Sounds?

What you're hearing when the Dock makes a "poof" are the Mac OS X interface sounds, which can be turned on from the Sound Preferences pane. The individual sound files are located at `/System/Library/Components/CoreAudio.component/Contents/Resources/SystemSounds` and can be replaced (at your own risk) with customized sound files. See Chapter 7 for information on recording audio on Mac OS X.

Process Manager: Force Quitting Applications

For a long time, the Macintosh didn't have an effective and reliable method of quitting a "hung" application. Windows users are accustomed to pressing Control-Alt-Del to force an application to exit, but Mac users were stuck pressing Option-Command-Escape and hoping for the best. If a force quit working without completely crashing Mac OS, it usually made the system unstable and forced a reboot within minutes.

With Mac OS X, the Option-Command-Escape keystroke still works, but now it brings up a process manager with a list of running applications, as shown in Figure 2.44. Applications that your Mac has identified as crashed are highlighted in red.

To force an application to exit, just choose it from the list and click Force Quit. This terminates the application without reducing your system stability. If the Finder seems to be misbehaving, you can choose it from the application list, and the Force Quit button becomes Relaunch, allowing you to quit and restart the Finder without logging out.

You can also access the Force Quit feature from the Apple menu, or by opening the pop-up Dock menu for a running application and then pressing the Option key to toggle the standard Quit selection to Force Quit.

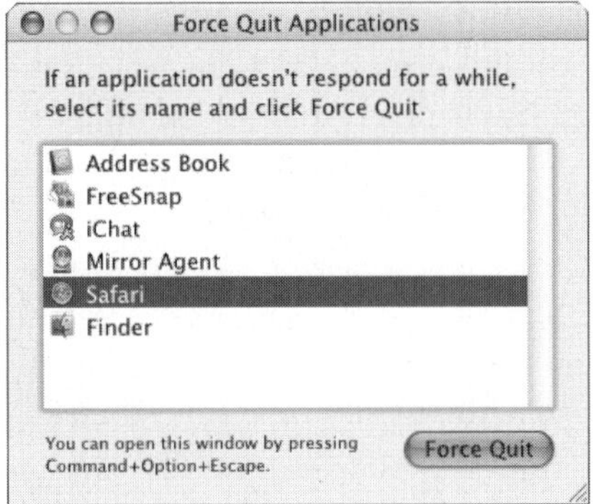

FIGURE 2.44 Choose an application to kill and then click Force Quit.

CAUTION

Forcing an application to quit does not save any open documents. Be sure that the application is truly stalled, not just busy, before you use this feature.

TIP

Forcing an application to quit is the same as using the command-line functions `kill` or `killall`. Learn more about the command line starting in Chapter 12.

Mac OS X offers another utility that can also force applications, including system processes, to quit. This program, Activity Monitor, is discussed in Chapter 3.

Window Management with Exposé

As you use your Mac OS X-based computer, you'll find that way too often, you've buried yourself in open windows. Although you can minimize and maximize windows to find what you want, this is not an efficient way to deal with the clutter.

Apple recognized this and introduced a feature in Panther called Exposé. Rather than rearrange your workspace to find a specific window, Exposé temporarily rearranges *all* your windows so that you can see them simultaneously and find what you want. After you've located the window you want, you can select it by positioning your mouse over the top of it and clicking, shown in Figure 2.45. All the onscreen windows return to their original positions with the chosen window on top.

What makes Exposé unique is that it does not change your working environment (your windows stay exactly where they are), and it allows you to choose a window based on its content as well as its title (minimized windows are often too small to recognize the content).

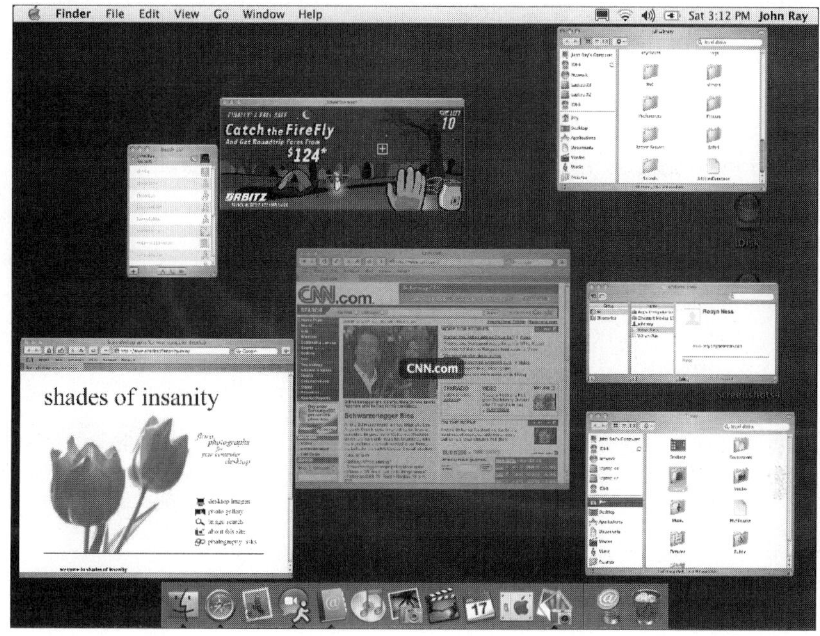

FIGURE 2.45 Itty-bitty windows, everywhere…

Besides quickly locating windows, Exposé can be used to hide all active windows so that you can see your desktop; then make them instantly reappear. This is useful for dragging and dropping icons that would normally be obscured from the desktop into your active applications.

To configure Exposé, open the Exposé System Preferences pane, shown in Figure 2.46.

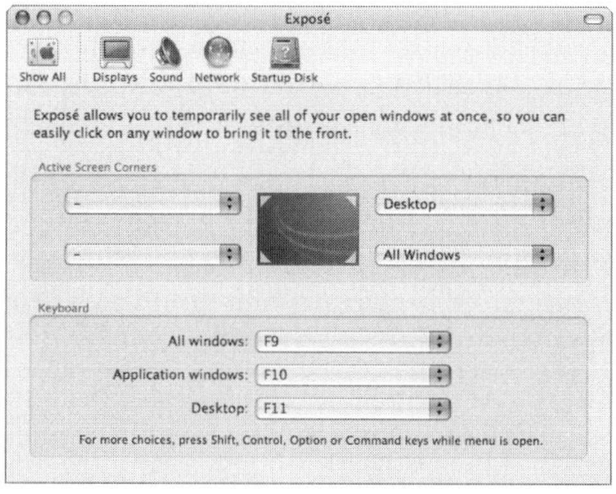

FIGURE 2.46 Use Exposé to manage your window clutter.

At the top of the Exposé pane, choose whether the Exposé effect will be activated by moving the mouse into any of the four screen corners. Moving the mouse into a corner starts Exposé; moving back into the corner returns the windows to normal. There are three separate Exposé effects to choose from:

- All Windows—Shrinks all onscreen windows to locate a specific one.
- Application Windows—Shrinks all the current application's windows to find a window within your chosen program.
- Desktop—Moves all windows temporarily offscreen to access the desktop.

Setting a screen corner to "-" removes any action previously attached to that corner.

NOTE

Because both Exposé and the Screen Savers can be activated by placing your mouse in a screen corner, you'll notice that you can configure the screensaver corners in Exposé and the Exposé corners in the Screen Saver pane.

At the bottom of the Exposé pane, you can choose keyboard shortcuts for each of the three Exposé modes, eliminating the need to mouse across the screen. Holding down Shift, Control, Option, or Command when choosing a keyboard shortcut sets a modifier key that must also be held down to activate the Exposé mode.

TIP

When using Exposé in All Windows or Application Windows modes, pressing the Tab key cycles through each active application's windows. This is an *extremely* useful feature if you have dozens of open windows and working through them all in the All Windows mode proves to be a bit overwhelming.

Summary

The Mac OS X Finder continues to evolve with new features and capabilities. The Finder shortcuts open up new possibilities in filesystem navigation, whereas Exposé provides a means of managing the ever-growing problem of window clutter. With each release of Mac OS X, Apple continues to improve the Macintosh user experience and add features never before seen on *any* operating system.

CHAPTER 3

Applications and Utilities

IN THIS CHAPTER

- Address Book
- iCal
- ISync
- Preview
- DVD Player
- Keychain Access
- Apple Custom Profiler
- Activity Monitor
- Console
- Disk Utility
- The Classic Environment
- Ink
- The Bluetooth Suite
- Other Tools and Utilities
- Summary

Mac OS X comes with dozens of utilities and applications—many of which can be easily cataloged, such as the Internet and media tools discussed in the upcoming chapters. Many applications, however, can't easily be assigned a category. This chapter covers the *useful* Mac OS X applications and utilities that you're likely to use regularly. If you're a big fan of Stickies, sorry; it gets an honorable mention, but we have to draw the line somewhere!

Address Book

The Mac OS X Address Book is more than a simple contact manager or a mailing label printer. It is a systemwide database that stores all your contact information and is accessible from other applications that require you to "contact people." So, you, ask, what are these other applications; email is the only place where it could be useful, right? Wrong. Address Book data is available in Safari, Mail, Sherlock, iCal, Fax, iChat, and more! A properly maintained Address Book can organize your data and streamline how you use your computer.

Standards-Based

With the LDAP protocol (Lightweight Directory Access Protocol) and vCard 3.0 Personal Data Interchange format, the Address Book is based entirely on open standards and can be used in a cross-platform environment.

vCards

The most common way to send contact information with an email is by adding a signature. Unfortunately, there is no standard for signatures, so picking up contact information from one is an exercise in futility. The vCard (`.vcf`) format attempts to change this by defining a simple cross-platform MIME standard for an electronic business card. vCards can be used on PDAs such as the Palm Pilot, and then copied to your system and used directly within the Address Book application.

Mac OS X uses version 3.0 of the vCard standard, developed by the Internet Mail Consortium and documented in RFC2426 (`http://www.ietf.org/rfc/rfc2426.txt`). A sample vCard, generated by Michael Heydasch's vCard CGI (`http://www.vicintl.com/vcf/`) is shown here.

```
BEGIN:VCARD
  FN:Mr. John P. Smith, Jr.
  TITLE:General Manager
  ORG:XYZ Corp.;North American Division;Manufacturing
  ADR;POSTAL;WORK:;;P.O. Box 10010;AnyCity;AnyState;00000;U.S.A.
  LABEL;POSTAL;WORK;ENCODING=QUOTED-PRINTABLE:P.O. Box 10010=0D=0A=
  Anywhere, TN 37849=0D=0A=
  U.S.A.
  ADR;PARCEL;WORK:;133 Anywhere St.;Suite 360;AnyCity;AnyState;00000;U.S.A.
  LABEL;POSTAL;WORK;ENCODING=QUOTED-PRINTABLE:133 Anywhere St.=0D=0A=
  Anywhere, TN 37849=0D=0A=
  U.S.A.
  TEL;Work;VOICE;MESG;PREF:+1-234-456-7891 x56473
  TEL;Home:+1-234-456-7891
  TEL;Pager:+1-234-456-7891
  TEL;Cell:+1-234-456-7891
  TEL;Modem;FAX:+1-234-456-7891,,*3
  EMAIL;Internet:webmaster@anywhere.com
  URL:http://www.anywhere.com/mrh.vcf
  UID:http://www.anywhere.com/mrh.vcf
  TZ:-0500
  BDAY:1997-11-29
  REV:20010510T104344
  VERSION:2.1
END:VCARD
```

The vCard defines a person object based on X.520 and X.521 directory services standards—implemented on a large scale in enterprise directory systems. Even encoded images can be included in vCards!

After a vCard is generated, it can be attached to email messages for easy importing into remote address books. In the case of Mac OS X, you can simply drag the vCard from an Email message window into the Address Book, and it will be added to your contact list. To attach your own vCard, you can drag from the Address Book into a message Compose window.

LDAP

The Lightweight Directory Access Protocol defines a means of querying remote directory systems that contain personnel data. Linux, Windows, and Mac OS X computers all have the capability to poll LDAP servers for account information, such as login and password.

The Address Book uses LDAP server connectivity to retrieve contact information from network servers. You can add your own LDAP server to the mix as long as you know the name or IP address of the server, and the search base.

The *search base* defines a starting point in the LDAP hierarchy to begin looking for information. Companies might have their LDAP directories built based on a per-department schema or other arrangement. Unless you are the LDAP administrator, it is impossible to guess the appropriate search base. Your best bet is not to use a search base, or to contact your network administrator for the correct value. Bases are specified in the following format:

```
<key name>=<base string>
```

NOTE

Exchange users will be happy to know that Address Book now supports Exchange synchronization. This is covered in detail in Chapter 30, "Windows Interoperability."

Using Address Book

The main Address Book window, shown in Figure 3.1, has two viewing styles—Card and Column view and Card Only view. To toggle between them, use the View buttons at the upper left. You will do most of your work with Address Book in Card and Column view. The Card view displays only a single contact at a time, making the usefulness debatable.

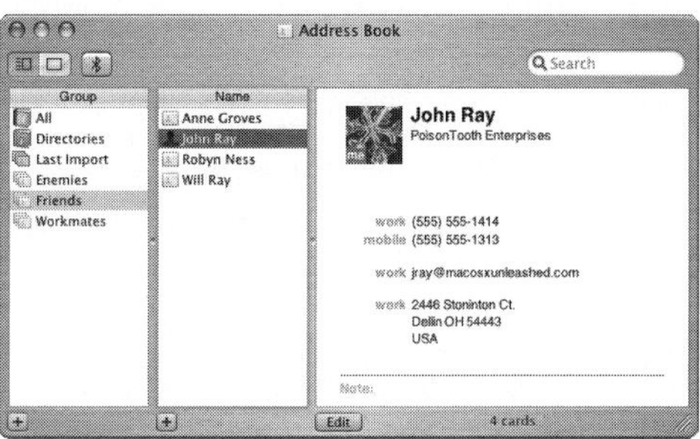

FIGURE 3.1 The Address Book, shown here in Card and Column view, keeps track of your contact information with a simple uncluttered interface.

The Card and Column view displays a three-column view of the Address Book with these columns:

- Group—A list of all the groups of contacts on your system. The three predefined groups are All, which shows the contents of all your group, Directories (LDAP Servers), and Last Import, which contains the last card/cards you imported via LDAP or from an external source.
- Name/Directory—The contacts (or available directory servers) within the selected group.
- Contact Card—A "business" card view of the currently selected contact.

At the bottom of the Group and Name columns are "+" buttons that add new Groups and Contacts to the system. Under the Contact Card pane is an Edit button that switches the current contact to Edit mode.

You can browse through your contacts much like using the Finder's column view. Choose a group and then a contact within the group, and view their information in the contact pane. The Search field at the top of the Address Book window searches the currently selected group for a string of your choice.

Working with Cards

Because Address Book maintains contact information, the base "unit" of information is a single person stored in an Address Book card. Address cards can store multiple addresses, phone numbers, and contact information for an individual, making it unnecessary to maintain multiple cards for a single person.

Adding/Editing Cards

To add a card, select the group that should contain the contact and then click the + button below the Name column. This opens a blank card in the right column where you can type the information you want to save.

There are fields for name, work and mobile phone, email address, home page, names of friends/relatives, AIM handle, and addresses as well as a space at the bottom for notes. You can Tab between fields or click into the ones you want to insert. You can add as much or as little information as you want, but an email address is required if you plan to use the card with Mail, and an AIM handle is required for iChat.

NOTE

vCards are a standard across multiple platforms and are often included in email messages. You can drag vCard attachments from within the Mail application into Address Book to add them.

If the label to the left of the field doesn't match the information you want to add, you can adjust it by clicking the up/down arrows icon. This opens a pop-up menu with several common labels as well as an option to customize. In some cases, such as adding a phone number, you may want (or need) to add multiple values. When you're editing a field that supports multiple entries, plus and minus buttons appear to the left of the field. Clicking plus adds a new field of the same type; minus removes the field. To add completely new fields, choose Card, Add Field; then choose from any of the available fields.

TIP

The default template for creating new cards can be changed in the Address Book application preferences, or by choosing Card, Add Field, Edit Template.

In the upper-left corner of the Card column is the card picture well. If you want to add a custom picture, you can paste it into the well, or double-click the picture well (choose Card, Choose Custom Image) to open a window where you can drag an image file and zoom/crop the image, or even take a video snapshot. This process is *identical* to setting your Buddy icon in iChat, which is covered in detail in Chapter 4, "Internet Applications." To clear a custom image, choose Card, Clear Custom Image.

When you're finished adding information, click the Edit button again, and the unfilled fields disappear.

To edit a card you've already created, select the name of the individual from the Name column and click the Edit button below the Card column, or choose Edit, Edit Card (Command-L) from the menu.

To delete a card, select it and press the Delete key on your keyboard or choose Edit, Delete Person. You are asked to confirm the action before it is carried out.

Special Card Settings and Functions

When editing a card, a few special properties and functions can be applied. The first, Card, Make this My Card, sets the current card so that it represents *you*, the owner of the active system account. Your address book card is represented with a "head" icon in Address Book listings, unlike other cards.

A second property, set by choosing Card, This is a Company, or by clicking the Company check box when editing a card, swaps the Company and Contact information in the card display and alters the card icon in the listing to resemble a small building.

If you are displeased with the first/last name ordering in a card, choose Card, Swap First/Last Name, and they are reversed in the Card view. To reset to the default ordering, choose Card, Reset First/Last Name to Default.

A final option, Card, Merge Cards (Command-I) is useful if you've accidentally created multiple cards for the same person. You can merge information in two or more cards by selecting them in the Name column and then choosing the Merge Cards option.

Viewing Cards

When a card is not in Edit mode, many of the labels in the Card view provide links to useful functions. Clicking a "friend/relation" name displays the option to jump to that person's contact card, if it exists.

A unique feature Apple provides is the capability to display a Web-based map of any street address in your address book. Click the label to the right of any address field and choose Map Of from the pop-up menu. Your Web browser opens to a map of the location. You can also choose to copy the URL of the map, or copy an address-label form of the address to the Clipboard.

If you have the Apple BlueTooth adapter, you can click the button in the Address Book to locate paired BlueTooth phones within range. You can then click a phone number within an address card and choose Dial from the pop-up menu to dial your phone.

In addition, BlueTooth-paired phones automatically trigger Address Book to display the Address card (if available) for incoming calls, and provide the capability to answer the call or send the call to voicemail.

Adding/Editing Groups

You can arrange your cards into your own custom groups, which, besides creating organization, can be used to send email to a common collection of people.

> **TIP**
>
> If you have many cards to work with but no need for mailing to custom groups, you can enter keywords in the Notes section of the cards and then use the Search function, located at the upper right of the Card and Column view, to see only those cards that contain your chosen keyword.

To create a group, click the "+" button under the Group column and type a name for it. You can then start adding contacts to the group, either by adding them using the method discussed previously, or by selecting another contact group (such as All) and dragging contacts from the Name column to populate the new group. You can hold down the Command key to select more than one addressee at a time.

> **NOTE**
>
> The controls for adding and managing groups in Address Book are shared with many applications throughout the operating system. You should familiarize yourself with their use.

Distribution Groups

An Address Book group can be used with Mail to send messages to a group of people simultaneously by dragging the group into the Address field in Mail. When used in this manner, the group is considered a *Distribution Group*. All Address Book groups can be used as Distribution Groups, but before using them, you may want to choose which email address each contact in the group uses when the message is sent. To do this, highlight your group in Address Book; then choose Edit, Edit Distribution List. A window similar to that shown in Figure 3.2 appears.

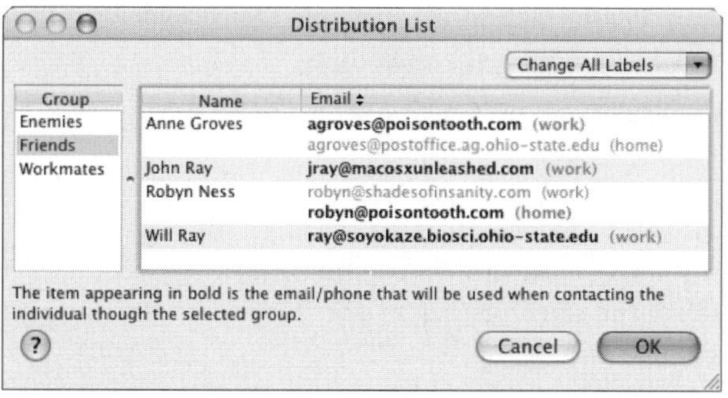

FIGURE 3.2 Choose the address to use if a group is used to send email.

Use the pop-up menu in the upper right-corner of the Distribution List window to switch all contacts in the group to their work, home, or other addresses. To switch on a person-by-person basis, simply click the correct contact address in the list to highlight it.

When all the correct addresses are selected, click OK. You can now use your Address Book group as a mailing distribution list.

LDAP Servers

To set up Address Book for LDAP queries, open the LDAP pane in the application preferences. The LDAP pane allows you to configure multiple LDAP servers to query. The "+" button opens a sheet for configuring your server, as shown in Figure 3.3.

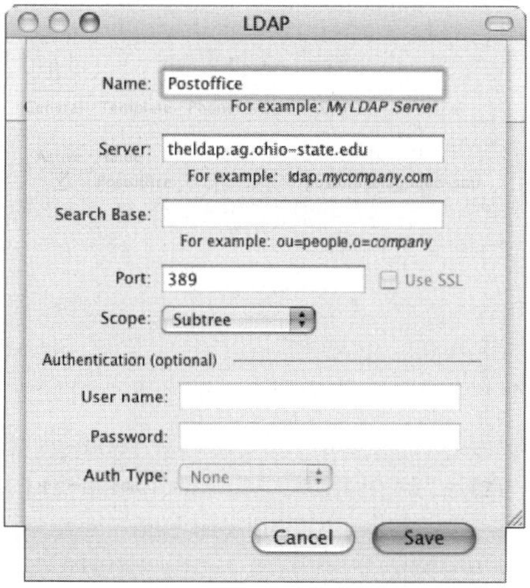

FIGURE 3.3 Set up your LDAP server in the LDAP preferences pane.

Add a name for the server that will be displayed in the Address Book, along with the necessary information for querying the directory.

Click Save to save the LDAP server. You can use the "+", "-", and Edit buttons in the LDAP tab to manage your LDAP servers.

Search an LDAP Server

After adding an LDAP server, you can choose the Directories group in the Address Book window and then select the directory server you added. Finally, type a query string in the Search field and press Return.

The results are displayed in a list, as shown in Figure 3.4.

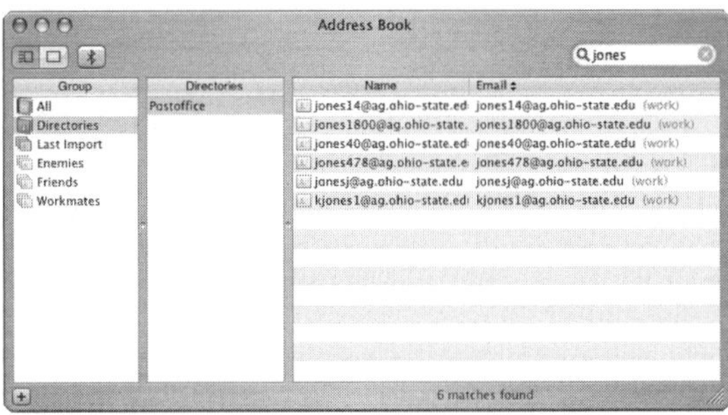

FIGURE 3.4 Search an LDAP directory for contact information.

You can drag any entry in the result list to the All group, or one of your personally defined groups. It will be added and can be edited like any other address card.

Printing Mailing Labels

Built into Panther's Address Book is the capability to easily print labels. To print labels, first select the group you want to print and then Choose File, Print. Address Book displays the dialog box shown in Figure 3.5.

Use the Style pop-up menu to choose between a mailing label layout and a simple list of names. When printing lists, you are given the option of choosing which attributes are printed in the list and what font to use.

Mailing labels (the style chosen in Figure 3.5) provide settings for controlling your paper layout under the Layout button bar option and include several label standards, such as Avery. The Label button displays settings for choosing between which Address Book addresses are printed (Home or Work), sorting, font options, and an image that can be printed beside each address.

Make your setting choices and view the results in the preview on the left side of the window; then click Print to start printing.

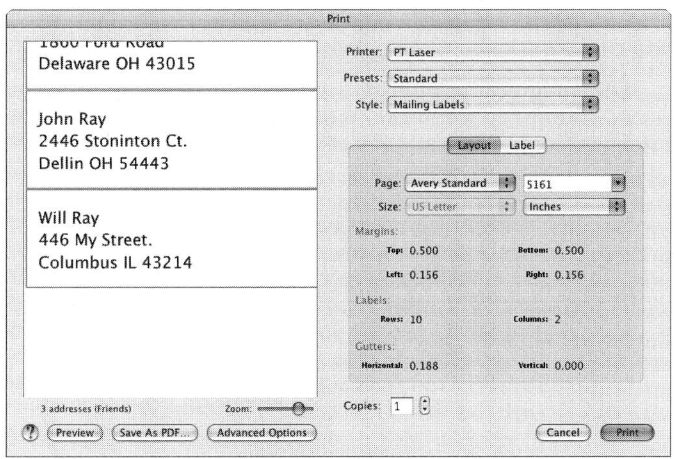

FIGURE 3.5 Print lists and mailing labels with ease.

Preferences

The Address Book preferences, accessible from the application menu, are used to choose sorting display and vCard preferences and to configure LDAP servers for use with the Address Book directory services.

General

The General pane, shown in Figure 3.6, allows you to choose the Display order for names (first or last name first), how the contacts should be sorted, the Address format, and display font.

FIGURE 3.6 The Address Book General preferences.

To automatically send updates made to your personal card to a group of people in your Address Book, click the Notify People When My Card Changes check box. When you change any piece of information in your card, you are prompted whether you want to email the update to your contacts. You can choose the groups to send email to, and type a brief message to them, as shown in Figure 3.7.

FIGURE 3.7 Have Address Book automatically notify other people when updates take place.

Finally, Address Book now supports simple synchronization with Exchange—covered in detail in Chapter 30.

Template

The Template preferences pane provides control over the "default" Address Card format. Using the same controls available when creating a card entry, you can create your own custom template, as shown in Figure 3.8.

Use the Add Field pop-up menu to add additional fields to the template.

Phone

The Phone preferences pane, shown in Figure 3.9, enables you to create and choose custom phone layouts and activate/deactivate automatic formatting of phone numbers in Address Book. Note that autoformatting must be enabled for you to use the custom defined layouts.

Use the Formats menu to choose from one of the predefined formats, or click the disclosure button to display the format editor (visible in Figure 3.9). To use the format editor, click "+" to add a new format and type the number format as you want it to appear, substituting the pound (#) sign for the actual phone number digits.

Use the "-" button to remove phone number formats or the edit button to edit existing formats. The formats can also be dragged in the listing to change their order.

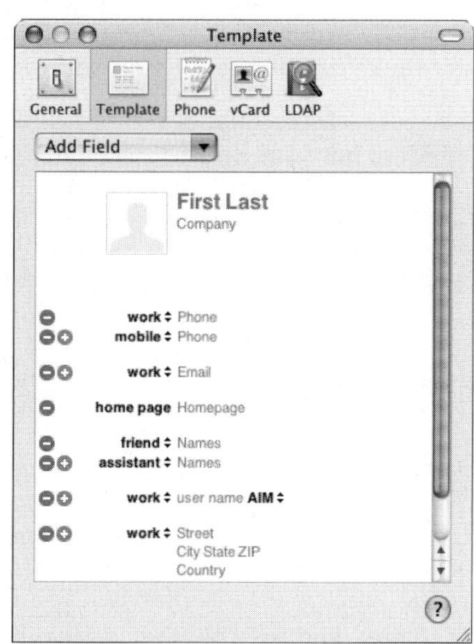

FIGURE 3.8 Define a custom Card template.

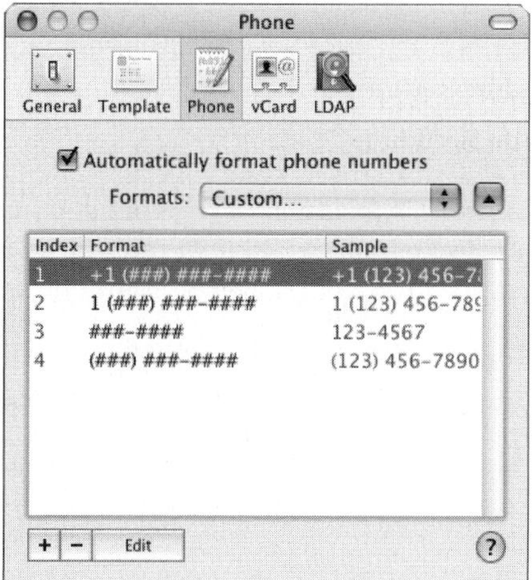

FIGURE 3.9 Add or choose custom telephone formats.

vCard

Use the vCard pane to choose the default format of your address cards (2.1 or 3.0).

You can also ensure the privacy of your personal card by enabling the Enable Private 'Me' Card option. This keeps everything but your *work* contact data from being exported with your card.

Use the Export Notes in vCards option to include the notes field when exporting cards. Because notes are typically personal information, they are not exported by default.

LDAP

Because we already covered LDAP configured in the course of the Address Book discussion, it won't be included here.

Menus

The Address Book menus have a few features that we haven't covered yet.

File

Use the File menu to export, import, and back up your Address Book database.

- New Card (Command-N)—Create a new Contact card.
- New Group (Shift-Command-N)—Create a new Contact group.
- New Group from Selection—Create a new group based on the contacts currently selected within the Address Book.
- Import—Import contact information from vCards or LDIF data.
- Export vCard/Group vCard—Depending on whether you have a single contact or group selected, this function exports a single or multiple contact `.vcf` file. Alternatively, you can just drag the group or contact from the Address Book to the Finder.
- Backup Database—Back up the Address Book database.
- Revert to Database Backup—Load the Address Book backup information.
- Send Updates—Send a notice to your contacts that your personal card has been updated.

Edit

The Edit menu, among other things, sports a working Undo feature that actually works to undo changes, including deletes, in the Address Book.

- Undo/Redo—Undo/redo the last change made to the Address Book.
- Delete Person/People—Delete the selected contact(s).
- Remove from Group—Remove the selected contact(s) from the group they're in. The contact itself is not deleted.
- Rename Group—Rename the selected group.

- Edit Card (Command-L)—Edit the currently selected card.
- Edit Distribution List—Resolve multiple email address conflicts when using a group as a mailing list.

View

The View menu toggles between the Card and Columns view (Command-1), Card view (Command-2), and the Directories view (Command-3).

Card

Finally, the Card menu is used to move between cards and customize their appearance.

- Next Card (Command-])—Move to the next card within a group.
- Previous Card (Command-[)—Move to the previous card within a group.
- Merge Cards—Merge the information within the selected cards.
- Add Field—Add a special field (IM, Phonetic spelling, or Birthday) to the current contact.
- This is a Company/Person—Choose to display the card in a person-centric or company-centric card.
- Swap First/Last Names—Swap the contact's first and last name fields.
- Make This My Card—Set the currently highlighted contact to be you.
- Go To My Card—Show the contact card that is marked as identifying "you."
- Clear Custom Image—Clear any image that has been set for the current contact.
- Choose Custom Image—Set a custom image for the current card, including taking a photo through an active FireWire camera.
- Open in Separate Window (Command-I)—Open the current card in a single separate window.

NOTE

Many applications, including Address Book, have a Scripts menu that provides access to many prebuilt AppleScripts. Address Book includes scripts for importing addresses from other applications.

iCal

The iCal calendaring solution is Apple's first in-house calendar for the Macintosh and one of the only available standards-based scheduling applications for the Macintosh. iCal supports network calendar publishing and subscribing, event notifications and invitations, and, of course, a lovely Aqua interface.

Open Standards

iCal gets its name from both Apple's i marketing department and the calendar standard it supports—iCalendar. The iCalendar standard is defined in RFC 2445: `http://www.ietf.org/rfc/rfc2445.txt`. For a change, we can blame someone else for adding the "i" in front of an otherwise perfectly usable title. The iCalendar format is an object-oriented description language that can define a series of event objects within a calendar object, and a series of alarms within each event.

For example, a single one-calendar, one-event, one-alarm iCal file looks like this:

```
BEGIN:VCALENDAR
CALSCALE:GREGORIAN
X-WR-TIMEZONE;VALUE=TEXT:US/Pacific
VERSION:2.0
BEGIN:VEVENT
SEQUENCE:1
UID:1380303474
DTSTAMP:20020910
SUMMARY:MS PACMAN Auction
DESCRIPTION: A Classic Ms. Pacman Arcade Game. Mint Condition
DTSTART;TZID=US/Pacific:20020917T121631
DURATION:PT1H00M
BEGIN:VALARM
TRIGGER;VALUE=DURATION:-PT15M
ACTION:DISPLAY
DESCRIPTION:Event reminder
END:VALARM
END:VEVENT
END:VCALENDAR
```

The `BEGIN` and `END` statements mark the start and end of an iCal object definition. In this example, a calendar object in the Pacific time zone is created; then an event is defined for a Ms. Pacman arcade game auction that starts on 09/17/2002 at 12:16:31AM and lasts for 1 hour and 00 minutes. Within that event, an alarm is defined that displays a warning when the current time is equal to the auction time minus 15 minutes.

By basing iCal on a standard, Apple has opened up the door to integration with enterprise calendaring solutions (including MS Exchange) and the exchange of information to and from a wide variety of platforms such as the Windows Outlook client.

Using iCal Calendars and Views

On starting iCal, you see a three-paned window, shown in Figure 3.10. This serves as your workspace while using the application.

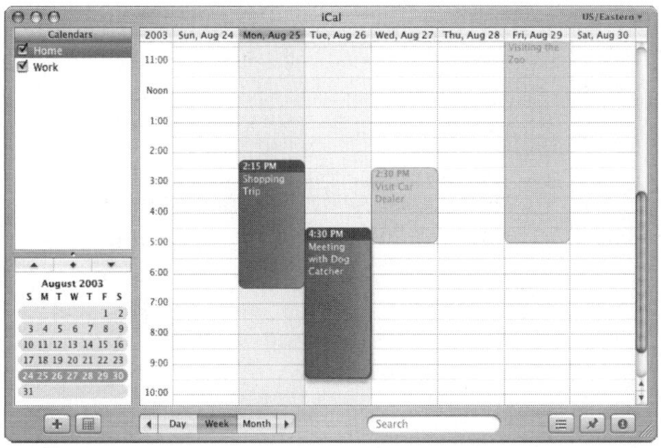

FIGURE 3.10 The iCal workspace gives you complete control over your schedule.

The upper-left corner contains the Calendars list. Each calendar that you've added or subscribed to is displayed here. By default, iCal comes with two Calendars—Home and Work. You can feel free to delete these or use them. New calendars are added by clicking the "+" button at the bottom of the left-hand pane, or by choosing File, New Calendar (Option-Command-N). Calendars can be deleted by highlighting them in the list and pressing the Delete key, or by choosing Edit, Delete from the menu.

Calendars with a checked check box in front of them are "active" and are displayed in the main calendar view to the right of the Calendars list.

Directly beneath the Calendars list is a mini-month view. Move through the months using the three icons (up arrow, diamond, and down arrow) to move back, to the current day in the calendar view, or to the next month, respectively. Clicking a date within one of the mini-months jumps the main calendar view to that day. You can collapse this view dragging the divider line between the Calendars list and the by-month view, or click the calendar icon at the bottom of the iCal window.

Along the bottom of the iCal window are several additional controls. The Day, Week, and Month buttons determine the view-style of the main calendar—whether you're looking at a single Day, Week, or Month. The arrows to either side of these buttons move forward and back to the next appropriate calendar "unit" (Day, Week, or Month).

In the bottom center of the window is a single Search field. Typing in this field displays (as you type) a list of events that match the string you've entered. Figure 3.11 shows a calendar search in action. The search works only across the calendars currently checked in your calendar list.

Click an event in the search results that you want to jump to, and it will be highlighted in the main calendar view pane.

Finally, to the right of the Search field are three additional buttons. The first button hides or shows the search results. The second shows or hides a new pane to the right of the main calendar view containing To Do items. The third opens a window drawer containing detailed information about the currently selected event, calendar, or To Do item.

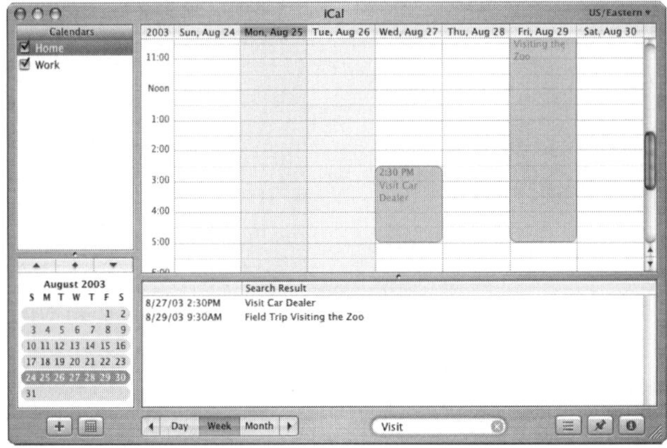

FIGURE 3.11 Search for an event in your calendars.

Adding and Editing Events

Adding an event is easiest within the Day or Week calendar views. Highlight the calendar that should hold the event, navigate in the main calendar view to the day where you want to create an event, and then click and drag from the start time to the end time. As you drag, the event end time will be displayed near your cursor.

A New Event box is drawn that covers the selected time, and, when you release the mouse button, the subject (title) is highlighted. Start typing immediately to enter a new subject (title), or double-click the event subject to edit it after it has been deselected. Figure 3.12 shows a day view with a new event (Meeting with Anne G.) added.

After an event is added, it can be dragged between different time slots, or days. The event duration can be changed by putting the cursor at the bottom edge or top edge of the event block and dragging it to resize the box. You can also add new events using File, New Event (Command-N). This creates a new one-hour event starting one hour after the *current* time but on the selected day. Use the editing techniques discussed previously to position and change its duration.

NOTE

Although events on the same calendar cannot be "drawn" over the same time slot, you can make two events at the same time with the same duration by creating them in separate time slots and then dragging them to the same slot.

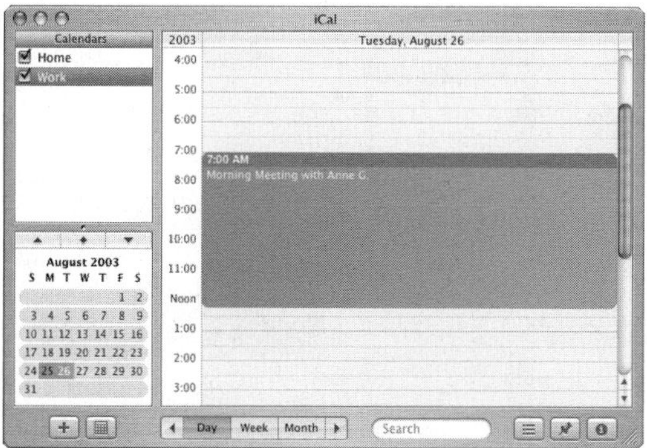

FIGURE 3.12 Add new events by clicking and dragging to cover the desired time span.

If you prefer working within the Month view, you can add new events in this view by double-clicking on the calendar cell of a given day. This creates a new event and extends the Information drawer, which provides convenient access to the time/duration values for the event.

> **TIP**
>
> If you'd prefer to edit the event duration by dragging, you can quickly jump to the Day view by double-clicking the date (number) in the Month view.
>
> To set these attributes, quickly jump to the Day view by double-clicking the day's number within the Month view.

To remove any event, highlight it in any of the three calendar views; then press your Delete key, or choose Edit, Delete.

Event Invitations

Events don't usually happen in a vacuum. If you're planning a party and no one else is invited, you may have a problem. iCal supports the notion of event invitations and acceptance. After creating an event, you can invite other people listed in your address book to the event, and they, in turn, can accept or decline. All without having to type a thing or interpret someone's cryptic response.

To send an invitation, switch to the Day or Week calendar view so that the event you want to send invitations for is visible. Next, open the Information drawer. You should see a field called Attendees. Here, you can simply start typing email addresses or names. If they are recognized as an Address Book entry, they will be automatically completed. Press Return between multiple addresses. After an address is added and "recognized," it becomes an object in iCal. You can use the small pull-down menu attached to each attendee to choose between multiple email addresses stored for them, or to remove them or manually edit their email addresses, as shown in Figure 3.13.

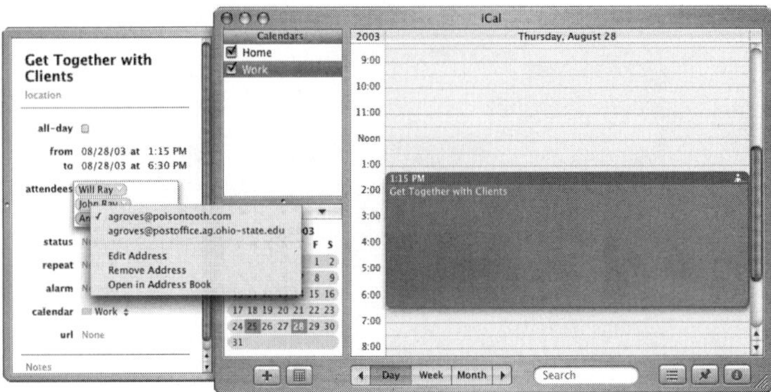

FIGURE 3.13 Enter the attendees of your event.

Alternatively, you can invite people in your Address Book to the event by opening the People window (Window, Show People, Option-Command-A) and dragging their individual vCard or a group vCard onto the event within the Calendar View pane. An icon of a person appears in the upper-right corner of the event in Day or Week view mode.

At this point, you've officially told iCal that you want to invite the listed people, but you haven't yet sent invitations. To do this, you must click the Attendees label in the Information window—a drop-down menu appears with the option to send invitations. Choose Send Invitations.

When you click the Send Invitations button, iCal works with Mail to send an invitation file to the people on the list. You'll also notice the attendees are displayed with a "?" icon in front of their names. This indicates that they are not yet confirmed as attending the event. Confirmed attendees are displayed with a check mark, whereas declined attendees show an "X."

The recipient of an invitation, assuming that he has iCal installed, can double-click the invitation icon in his email. The iCal application on his system displays the dialog box shown in Figure 3.14.

Here the invitee can choose to accept or decline the invite, what calendar to add it to, and whether he should respond to the mailed invitation. If he chooses to respond, another automatically generated message is sent back to the event creator. Clicking the included icon, this time, changes the person's invitation status to "confirmed" for the event. Nifty.

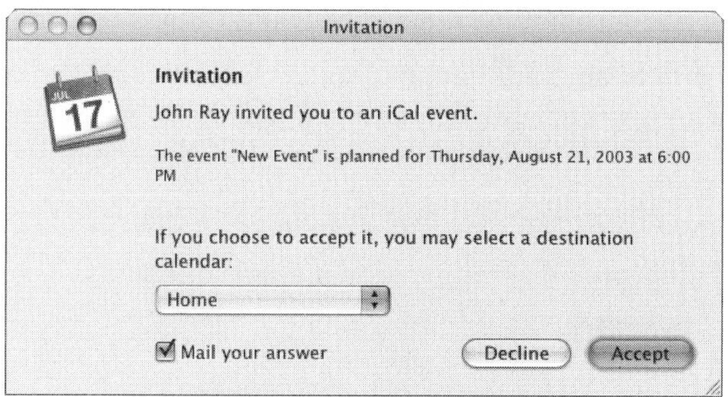

FIGURE 3.14 An invitation is in progress.

Event Info

As you've seen, invitation management is one of the uses of the Information drawer as it applies to events. You can also use the Info drawer to change event descriptions, durations, and schedules. Eleven fields are available when an event is selected:

- Event Title—The name of the event being edited.
- Event location—An arbitrary value, presumably where the event is taking place.
- All-day—Whether it is an all-day event (not scheduled for a specific time).
- From/to—The date/time/duration of the event.
- Attendees—Covered previously.
- Status—The status of the event (Tentative, Confirmed, or Cancelled).
- Repeat—If an event occurs over several days, weeks, months, or years, use the Repeat field to set how often it appears on your calendar. You can also choose when the recurrences will end, if ever.
- Alarm—Choose to display a message, send an email, or play a sound. After choosing an action, a second field appears allowing you to set the number of minutes, hours, or days before an event starts that the action will take place.
- Calendar—The calendar the event is stored on.
- URL—A URL pertinent to the given event.
- Notes—General notes and other information you might want to store about an event.

TIP

If you want to store time zone information with events, you can add a Time Zone field to the Event Information display using the iCal application preferences.

To Do Lists

A To Do item differs from an event in that it doesn't take place at a certain time, but often must be completed by a given date. iCal can track your To Do items using the To Do List. Click the pushpin icon in the lower-right corner of the iCal window to display the To Do List, demonstrated in Figure 3.15.

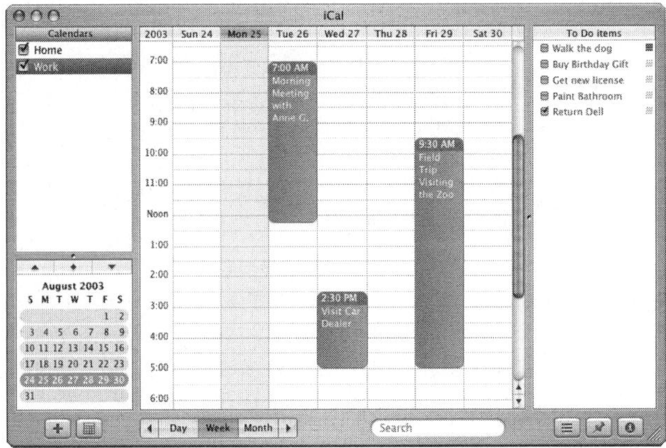

FIGURE 3.15 The To Do List contains a list of things to do.

To add a new item to the list, highlight the calendar that should contain the To Do item, and then double-click within the To Do List pane, or choose File, New To Do (Command-K). A new item is added to the list. By default, new To Do items have no deadline and can be flagged as "finished" by simply clicking the check boxes in front of them. To the right of each To Do item is a small three-line graph. You can drag your mouse over these lines to set a priority for the item (or use the item's contextual menu).

To Do Info

To add additional notes about a To Do entry and set a deadline, highlight the item in the To Do List and then open the Information Window drawer.

The To Do Info window allows you to enter extended text information about the item, choose whether it has been completed, pick a due date, assign it a priority, pick the calendar it should be a part of, and assign an appropriate URL for extended information.

Calendar Publishing and Subscribing

One of the most useful features of iCal is the capability to publish calendars to a .Mac account or WebDAV share (see Chapter 27, "Web Serving," for information on setting up WebDAV on your computer) and for others to subscribe to your calendar.

To publish an existing calendar to the Internet, highlight the calendar within your calendar list and then choose Calendar, Publish from the menu. The dialog box shown in Figure 3.16 appears.

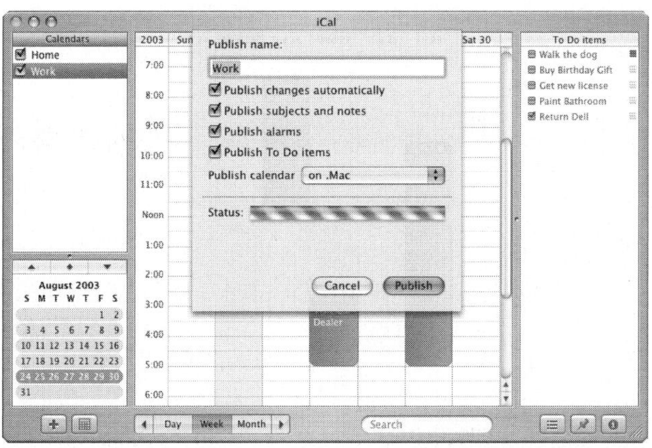

FIGURE 3.16 Publish your calendar to a .Mac account or WebDAV share.

First, choose whether you're using a .Mac account or a Web server (WebDAV). If you're using .Mac, iCal automatically uses the account information contained in the Internet System Preferences pane. Otherwise, it prompts for the WebDAV URL, login, and password.

Next, choose the information you want to be published:

- Publish Name—The name that the subscribers see when viewing your calendar.
- Publish Changes Automatically—Automatically update your published calendar when you make local changes in iCal.
- Publish Subjects and Notes—Publish the subject and note fields for events.
- Publish Alarms—Publish alarm information (alarm type, time, and so on) along with your events.
- Publish To Do Items—Include any To Do items in the Calendar as part of the publication.

TIP

You can change any of these attributes later by selecting the calendar and opening the Information drawer.

Click the Publish button to send your calendar to the remote server. Published calendars are denoted by a "transmission" icon appearing after their name in the Calendar list.

After publishing, you are prompted with the option to Send Mail with your calendar information to those who might be interested in subscribing. You can also choose Visit Page to see a Web view of your Calendar. The Visit Page option is available only to .Mac subscribers for the purpose of publishing and provides a fully interactive Web view of your calendar;

users who are not Mac.com members can still visit the Web page just to see the calendar but cannot update it.

TIP

If you have your own Web Server and want to publish calendars online, visit `http://sourceforge.net/projects/iwebcal/` for a free, Open Source solution.

You can update a published calendar with the latest changes by choosing Calendar, Refresh (Command-R) or Calendar, Refresh All (Shift-Command-R) to refresh *all* published calendars. To completely remove a Published calendar, use Calendar, Unpublish.

TIP

If you start publishing your calendars to a .Mac server and then want to move to a WebDAV server or vice versa, you can easily "move" your published calendars using the Calendar, Change location menu option.

Subscribing to a Calendar

To manually enter a subscription, choose Calendar, Subscribe (Option-Command-S) from the menu. The subscription window shown in Figure 3.17 appears.

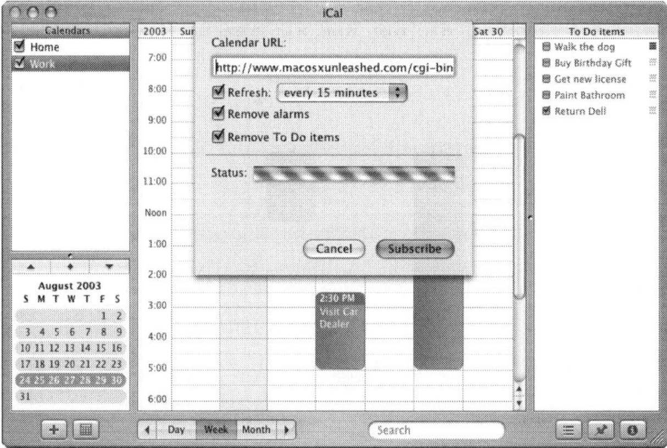

FIGURE 3.17 Enter a URL to subscribe to a calendar.

Enter the URL of an appropriately prepared iCal source, choose how often the calendar should automatically refresh, and choose whether to remove the creator's alarms and To Do items from the calendar.

Click Subscribe after you've configured the subscription to suit your needs. After a few seconds, the subscribed calendar appears in your calendar list (differentiated from local calendars by the "shortcut" arrow following its name). You can refresh a subscribed calendar using the Calendar, Refresh (Command-R) or Calendar, Refresh All (Shift-Command-R) options.

NOTE

I've created a few dynamic iCal calendar scripts that automatically monitor eBay auctions you're bidding on. If you're interested in getting a copy, email me at `jray@macosxunleashed.com`.

Preferences

A few final preferences can be set from the iCal application preferences, shown in Figure 3.18.

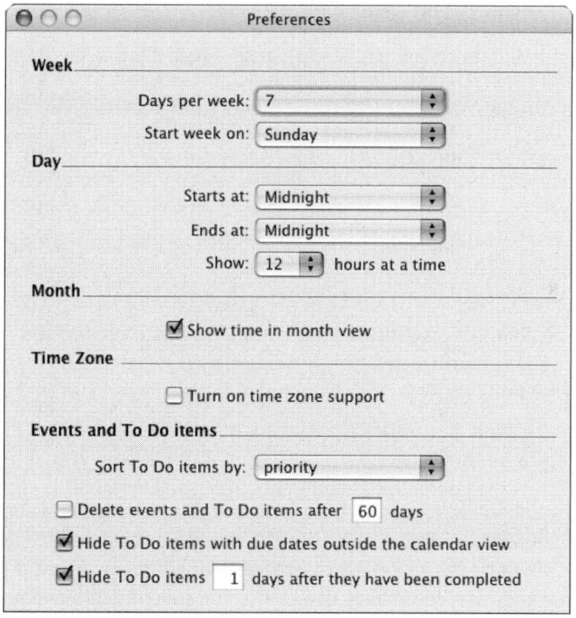

FIGURE 3.18 Set a few additional iCal preferences.

Within the Week category, choose whether iCal recognizes a work (5 day) or normal (7 day) week, and what day of the week the calendar should use as the start day.

Use the Day settings to define how many hours are shown in a day, and of those hours, how many are visible onscreen simultaneously without scrolling.

To add a display of the event time within the Month view, click the Show Time in Month View check box.

Add time zone support to the Information window using the Turn on Time Zone Support check box. Turning on time zone support adds a pop-down menu to the upper-right corner of the iCal window where you can choose your zone, *and* adds a time zone attribute that can be set for events.

Finally, the Events and To Do Items options provide control over how To Do Items are sorted, and when To Do items and events should be deleted or hidden from the Calendar view.

Menus

A few minor additional features are available from the iCal File menu that were not covered in the course of this discussion.

As usual, the File menu is used to create new calendars, events, and To Do items. It can also, however, export, import, and print calendar files.

- Import—Import calendar data from Entourage and iCalendar or vCal format files.
- Export—Export the active calendar to an iCalendar format file.
- Print—Print a copy of the active calendar view.

iSync

Most people's lives extend beyond their home to their workplace (or vice versa). Information should be available wherever you go, on whatever device you use. To this end, Apple has created the iSync software. Since its initial introduction, iSync has grown to support dozens of mobile phones, Palm devices, your iPod, iCal, Safari, Address Book, and more. If you have a .Mac account, no matter what Macintosh you're using, your critical information is only a "sync" away.

NOTE

Although an iCal Calendar subscription may seem like the perfect way to share information between your home and work computers, you can't edit a subscribed calendar. iSync allows you to have local calendar files that are synchronized automatically between your different workstations.

The iSync Interface

The iSync window, shown in Figure 3.19, provides the control over what you're syncing and when you're syncing it. On the left side of the window are the devices (data sources) that have been "registered" with iSync, and on the right is the Sync Now button to start the synchronization process. Clicking a device icon in the iSync window opens a pane with all available synchronization settings for that device.

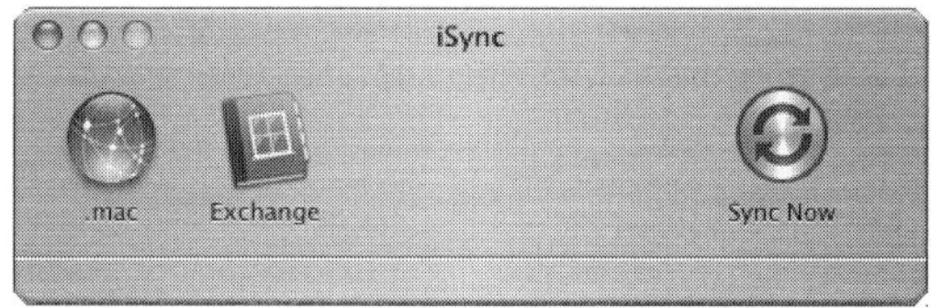

FIGURE 3.19 Devices to sync and a big shiny button.

Setting Up .Mac Synchronization

By default, only one item is available for synchronizing—your .Mac account. This is a "special" device in that it provides a holding area for multiple computers to send and then retrieve information. If you have a .Mac account, it can be used with each of your Macintosh workstations to synchronize Bookmarks and other data.

For each computer that will be synchronized through the .Mac account, you must "register" that computer with the iSync service. To do this, first make sure that you've successfully added your .Mac account information to the .Mac control panel (discussed in Chapter 4). If you do not have a .Mac account, you will *not* be able to synchronize machines and devices over the network.

Assuming that your .Mac settings are in order, highlight the .Mac icon, and click the Register button, choose a unique name for the computer, and click the Continue button (see Figure 3.20).

Configuring Device Sync Options

Each time you register a device, you must also choose what happens on the first "sync"—whether information should be copied from the computer to the device, or whether information should be merged with what is currently stored on .Mac.

For the .Mac sync options, you also can choose what items are being synchronized (Safari Bookmarks, Address Book Contacts, and iCal information).

At the bottom of the .Mac sync pane is a list of all computers that have been registered through iSync with your iMac account. You can select a computer in the list and click the Unregister Selected Computer button to remove it.

> **NOTE**
>
> Removing a selected computer does not delete any information from it. It does effectively disable its capability to sync until it is re-registered, but you won't lose any information.

To automatically synchronize your chosen items with .Mac every hour, click the Automatically Synchronize Every Hour check box. Click the .Mac icon to close the configuration pane.

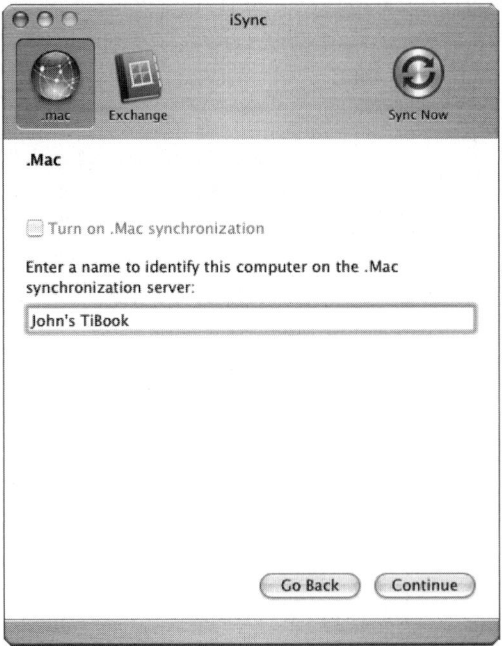

FIGURE 3.20 Register each computer to be synchronized with .Mac.

Adding Other Devices to iSync

To add other devices to iSync, choose Devices, Add Device from the menu. Click Scan if nothing is initially detected. iSync scans for iPods, PDAs, and Bluetooth-paired devices within the range of your computer, as shown in Figure 3.21.

FIGURE 3.21 Scan for other iSync-capable devices.

Double-click the found devices to add them to the iSync window and "register" them with the iSync process. Choosing a registered device in the iSync window displays the synchronization options specific to that device. For example, Figure 3.22 shows the synchronization options for my iPod.

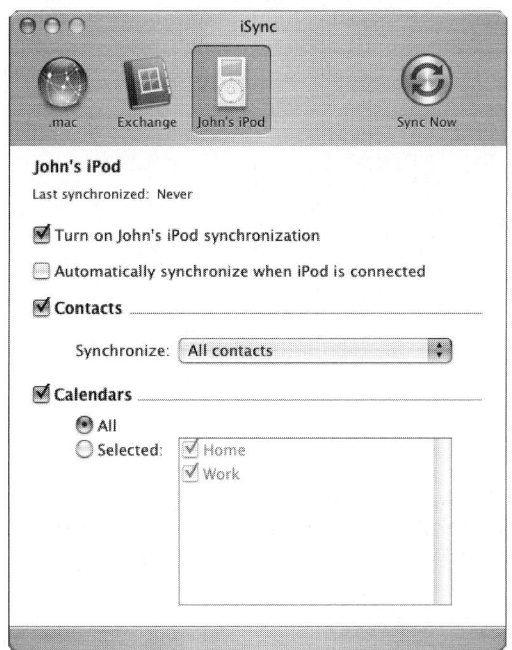

FIGURE 3.22 Synchronization options are unique for each device.

For the iPod, you can choose to automatically synchronize each time your iPod is connected as well as what contacts and calendars should be synchronized. The options for your devices are likely to vary from what you see here. It simply depends on the type of device and the features it supports.

NOTE

If you're a Palm user, you *must* have the iSync-Palm conduit and the Sync Manager from the Palm Desktop installed for iSync to work. The conduit is available from `http://www.apple.com/isync/download/`.

Pocket PC users can use the excellent The Missing Sync in conjunction with iSync to synchronize their handheld devices with Mac OS X. (`http://www.markspace.com/pocketpc.html`).

Synchronizing

After choosing the sync options for each of the devices you want to use, click the Sync Now button, or choose Devices, Sync Now (Command-T) from the menu, to synchronize all of them. iSync often displays a confirmation message with the changes it is about to make, allowing you to stop or apply the modifications (this warning is configurable in the iSync Preferences). Figure 3.23 shows the synchronization process.

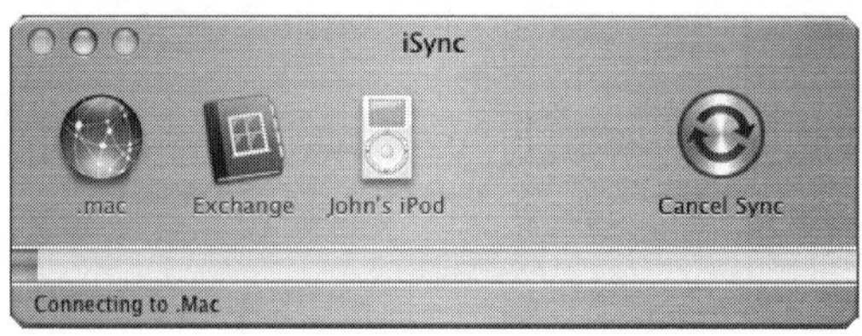

FIGURE 3.23 iSync gathers information from your devices and software and then synchronizes it.

After a few seconds, all your devices will have a copy of the latest calendars and contacts.

Safety Features

To safeguard your data (in case of accidental or malicious synchronizing), Apple had built in a few features that can help you recover from an "oops" situation. Using Devices, Revert to Last Sync, you can revert to the information stored on your computer *before* the last time it was synchronized.

Perhaps even more useful is the ability to take a "snapshot" of your computer's synchronization data using Devices, Backup My Data. You can do this at any time—presumably when you have your computer set up in a critical state that you wouldn't want to lose. To revert *back* to the backed up state if something goes awry, you simply choose Devices, Revert To Backup.

Resetting All Devices

The Devices, Reset All Devices option can come in handy in two situations:

If you've been working on your computer and have configured it to be the way you want it and *don't* want to synchronize for fear of messing up your settings, Reset All Devices allows you to override the information stored on your other devices with what is contained on your local computer.

Alternatively, if your local machine isn't the way you want it, and you don't want its configuration to mess up anything else, you can use Reset All Devices to reset its data with what is currently stored in your .Mac account, overriding anything that would have been synchronized with other devices.

The iSync Log

To view a log of what iSync has done, when it was done, and the result, choose Window, Show Logs. Figure 3.24 shows the log window.

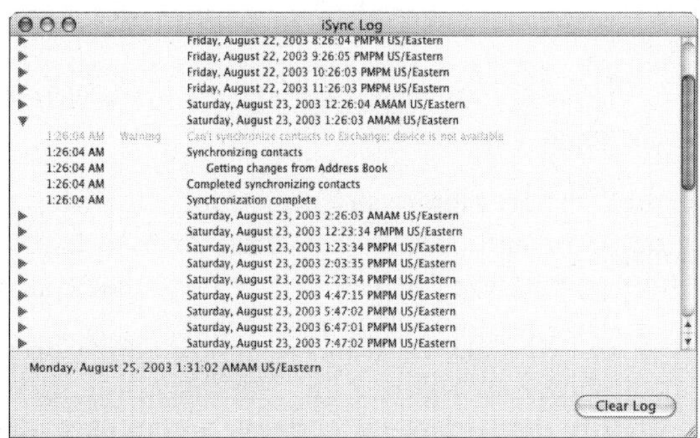

FIGURE 3.24 iSync logs each synchronization.

Use the disclosure arrows in front of each log line to expand or collapse details about each entry.

Removing Devices

To remove registered devices from iSync, simply highlight them in the iSync window and then use Devices, Remove Device from the menu. .Mac registered computers can remove their registrations by using the Remove options under the Devices menu. A removed device will not be "seen" by iSync and will have to be manually added to be used again. Alternatively, you can disable synchronization for a registered device by using the device configuration pane to temporarily disable synchronizing.

Preferences

The iSync application preferences, shown in Figure 3.25, allow you to add an iSync menu extra to your menu bar. From the menu extra, you can synchronize your devices, open iSync, or view any warnings that occurred during the last synchronization process.

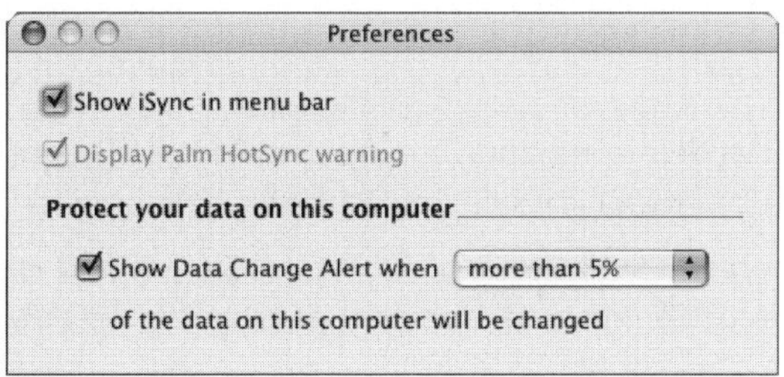

FIGURE 3.25 Use the iSync preferences to add a menu extra to your menu bar.

Within the preferences, you can also choose the amount of data that has to change for iSync to display a warning message.

Preview

For viewing PDF files and images of all sorts, Mac OS X comes with the Preview application (path: `/Applications/Preview`).

Preview can be launched by either double-clicking a supported file, or by selecting a group of files and then dragging them onto the Preview icon. Preview is also integrated into the Mac OS X printing system, so clicking Preview in any Print dialog box starts it.

When you open an image or PDF document in Preview, it shows up in a window with a toolbar across the top, as shown in Figure 3.26. The following options are located in the toolbar. (These change slightly depending on whether you're viewing an image or PDF; this is an all-inclusive list):

- Drawer (Command-T)—Opens and closes a drawer that displays thumbnail images of the pages or files open in the current Preview window. Clicking a thumbnail image shows it the main viewing area.
- Back and Forward—If you've viewed several pages in a multipage file out of sequence, you can page back through in the order you visited using the Back/Forward arrows.
- Page—When you're viewing a multipage TIFF or PDF file, Page Number enables you to enter a page number to jump directly to that page.
- Page Up (Command-left arrow) and Page Down (Command-right arrow)—If you're viewing a multipage file, you can move through the pages sequentially using the Page Up and Page Down arrows. Unlike Back and Forward, Page Up and Down move between multiple documents that you may be viewing.
- Zoom In (Command-+) and Zoom Out (Command--)—These two options enable you to view a larger or smaller version of the selected image or PDF. If the image is larger than the Preview window, scrollbars appear.
- Scroll tool (Tool Mode, Command-1)—The Scroll tool can be used to grab the image and move it around the page. This is a convenient way to handle horizontal as well as vertical scrolling.
- Text Mode (Tool Mode, Command-2)—The Text Mode tool is used with PDFs to select the text within a PDF for copying and pasting.
- Selection Tool (Tool Mode, Command-3)—The Selection tool can be used with images to select a portion of an image for copying, pasting, or cropping (Command-K).

To get information about the active PDF document or image, choose Window, Document Info, as shown in Figure 3.27.

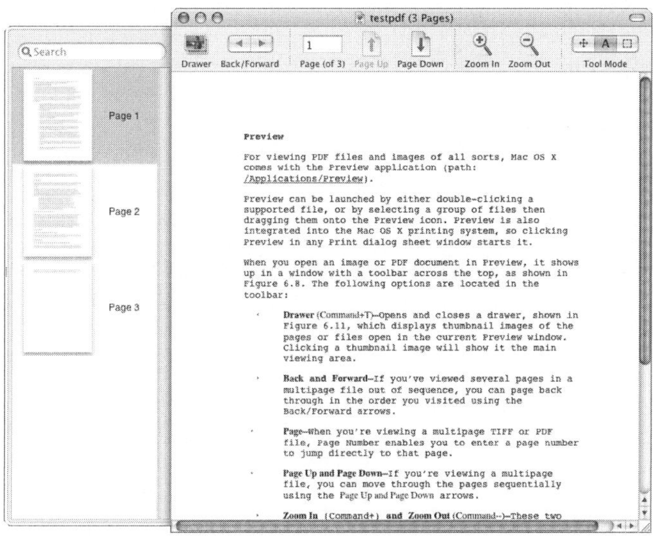

FIGURE 3.26 The Preview window includes a toolbar where you can easily alter the viewing style of your files or move between pages.

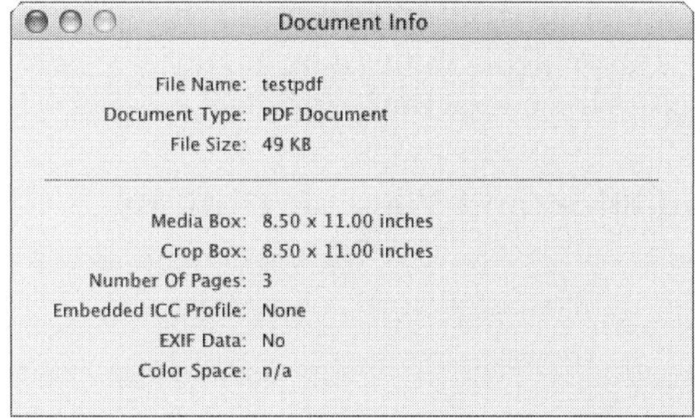

FIGURE 3.27 The Document Info feature displays extended information about the image or PDF you have loaded.

PDF Text Selection and Searching

The Panther version of Preview has a number of new features for manipulating PDFs. First, the Text tool can be used to highlight text within a PDF and subsequently copy and paste it into another application.

Preview can also search through the PDF text much like you can search through a word processor document. To search, open the Preview drawer. A Search field is displayed at the top of the thumbnail list, as shown in Figure 3.28.

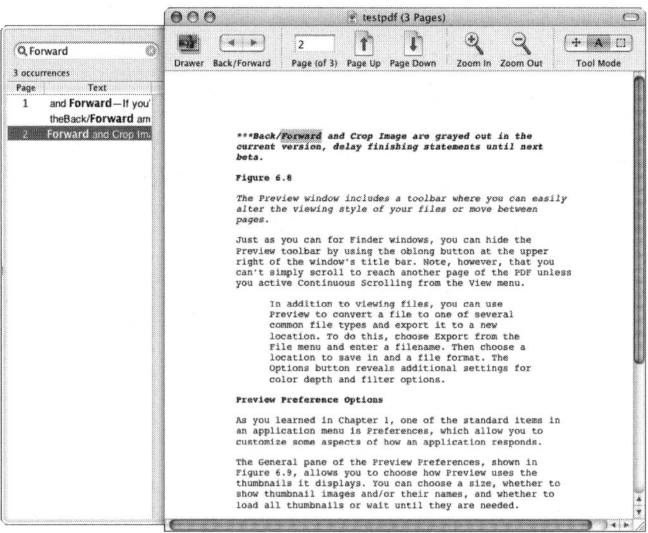

FIGURE 3.28 Search the text content of your PDF files.

To search, type a text string into the Search field and then press Return. The results are returned in the drawer. Each page is listed, along with each instance found on the page. Click on a search result line to highlight that line in your document. To clear the search results, click the "X" icon at the end of the Search field.

Image/PDF Manipulation and Viewing Options

Images and PDFs can be manipulated using the View menu. If you're viewing backward or upside-down images, Preview has simple controls to help out.

- Actual Size (Command-0)—View the image at its actual size, not zoomed in or out.
- Zoom In (Command-+)—Zoom in (enlarge) the image/PDF in the viewing area.
- Zoom Out (Command--)—Zoom out of the image/PDF in the viewing area.
- Zoom to Fit—Zoom the image or PDF to fit the size of the Preview window.
- Zoom to Selection (Command-*)—Zoom the area of the page marked with the Selection tool to fill the Preview window.
- Rotate Left (Command-L)—Rotate the PDF page or image to the left.
- Rotate Right (Command-R)—Rotate the PDF page or image to the right.
- Flip Horizontal—Flip the image/PDF about a vertical axis, reversing it horizontally.
- Flip Vertical—Flip the image/PDF about a horizontal axis, reversing it vertically.

- Continuous Scrolling—When active, the scrollbar scrolls through all the pages of the PDF sequentially. If disabled, you must jump from page to page using the Forward/Backward controls and then use the scrollbar to scroll through the contents of a single page.
- Full Screen—Display the image or PDF in a full-screen mode against a black background. Press Esc to exit full-screen mode.

NOTE

Many of these controls can be added to the toolbar by using the View, Customize Toolbar feature.

TIP

Images can be exported to a variety of formats using the File, Export option.

Preview Preferences

The General pane of the Preview Preferences, shown in Figure 3.29, allows you to choose how Preview uses the thumbnails it displays. You can choose a size, whether to show thumbnail images and/or their names, and whether to load all thumbnails or wait until they are needed.

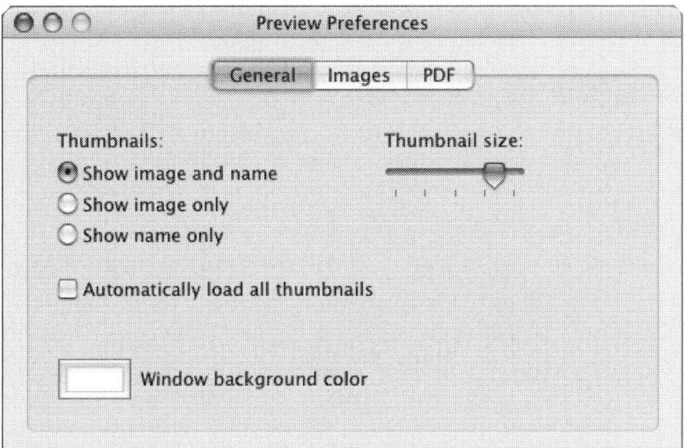

FIGURE 3.29 The Preview Preferences pane.

In the Images and PDF preference panes, you can choose the default size at which images and PDF documents are opened—fit to screen or some other size. You can also choose rendering options, including disabling antialiasing for PDFs.

DVD Player

Included with Mac OS X is DVD Player, an application for displaying DVD content on computers equipped with internal DVD drives. To start DVD Player, simply insert a video DVD into your system, or double-click the application icon in the Applications folder.

By default, Mac OS X launches DVD Player automatically when it detects a DVD in the drive. At startup, the DVD begins to play, and a playback controller appears onscreen, as shown in Figure 3.30.

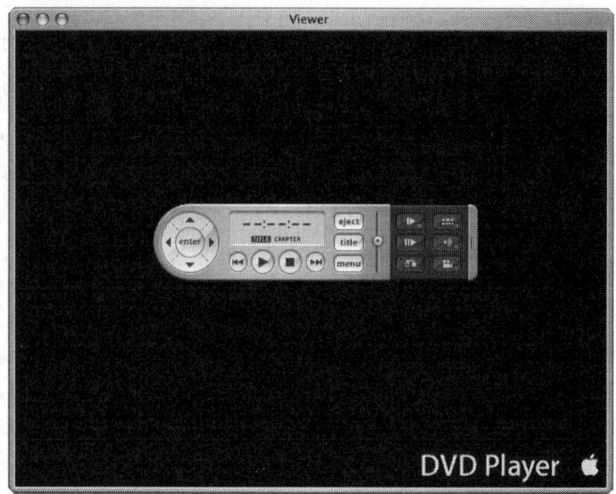

FIGURE 3.30 DVD Player's controller window keeps all the needed controls in one convenient place.

> **NOTE**
>
> Unlike for QuickTime movies, if you minimize a DVD Player window, the picture won't play in the Dock. However, the sound continues to be audible.

Use the controller window as you would a standard DVD remote. Basic playback buttons (play, stop, rewind, and fast-forward) are provided, along with a selection control and a volume slider. Also available are buttons to access the menu, display the title of the current scene, and eject the DVD.

> **TIP**
>
> Typically, viewers navigate through DVD menus with arrow keys on their DVD controllers. Because your DVD Player is run on your computer, you have additional options. To navigate onscreen selections without the use of the controller, you can simply point-and-click at a DVD menu item to select it. To navigate with the keyboard, use the arrow keys and press Return.

Six additional advanced controls are accessible by clicking the far right edge of the controller window. In Figure 3.30, the controller window is shown with the window tray extended. This opens a window drawer containing two columns of buttons that control playback or special features of DVDs. Those controls, from top to bottom, left to right, are Slow, Step, Return, Subtitle, Audio, and Angle buttons.

TIP

If you use iChat frequently, you can use the Player pane of the DVD Player application preferences to force playback to pause or mute when a conference takes place.

If you prefer a vertically oriented player control, choose Controls, Use Vertical Control (Option-Command-C) from the menu. You can switch back to the horizontal layout at any time by choosing Controls, Use Horizontal Control (Option-Command-C) from the same menu.

Although the onscreen controller can be used for most everything, DVD Player also provides keyboard commands for controlling playback. The following options are available under the Controls menu:

- Use Vertical/Horizontal Controller—Toggles between horizontal and vertical orientations with Option-Command-C.
- Open/Close the Control Drawer (Command-])—Toggles the extra features drawer open and closed on the controller.
- Add Bookmark—Prompts for a bookmark name and then saves a bookmark with the exact location of the current DVD playback. If you choose to make a bookmark the *default* bookmark, you can automatically have DVD Player initiate playback from that point when the DVD is inserted (see the "DVD Player Preferences" section later in the chapter for more information). Press Shift-Command-8 to skip to the default bookmark at any time.
- Edit Bookmark—Provides a point-and-click interface for editing, renaming, removing, and setting as default the bookmarks that you've stored for the currently active DVD.
- Play/Pause(Spacebar)—Play or pause the video.
- Stop (Command-.)—Stop the current video from playing.
- Scan Forward (Shift-Command-right arrow)—Speed through the video playback.
- Scan Backward (Shift-Command-left arrow)—Move backward through the video playback.
- Previous Chapter (right arrow)—Skip to the previous chapter on the DVD.
- Next Chapter (left arrow)—Skip to the next chapter on the DVD.

- DVD Menu (Command-`)—Stop playback and load the menu for the active DVD.
- Volume Up (Command-up arrow)—Increase the volume.
- Volume Down (Command-down arrow)—Decrease the volume.
- Mute (Option-Command-down arrow)—Mute the sound.
- Closed Captioning On/Off (Option-Command-T)—Toggle closed captioning on and off.
- Play Closed Caption in Window (Option-Command-W)—Plays the closed captioning in a separate window from the video.
- Play Closed Caption over Video (Option-command-V)—Plays the closed captioning directly over the video.
- Eject (Command-E)—Eject the current DVD.

TIP

When fast-forwarding or rewinding, the view is displayed at an accelerated rate. Use the Controls, Scan Rate option to set the speed to two, four, or eight times faster than normal.

DVD Player Preferences

The preferences for DVD Player are split into four sections. The Player pane, shown in Figure 3.31, enables you to set how DVD Player reacts on system startup and insertion of a DVD. You can also choose the viewer size. If you have created bookmarks, you may want to check the option to start playback from the default bookmark.

The Disc Setup pane contains settings for default language and the option to enable DVD@ccess, which allows DVD Player to recognize and react to embedded hot spots that link to Internet Web sites. You can also change audio output settings.

The Full Screen pane allows you to set a viewer size (maximum, normal, half, or current) and to decide whether the viewer can be resized. Options are also available for dimming other windows while DVD Player is active, remaining in full screen when DVD Player is inactive, disabling the menu bar (kiosk mode) so that viewers can't exit the program, and hiding the controller after a set period of time.

NOTE

If you disable the menu bar, you can exit the DVD Player by ejecting the DVD.

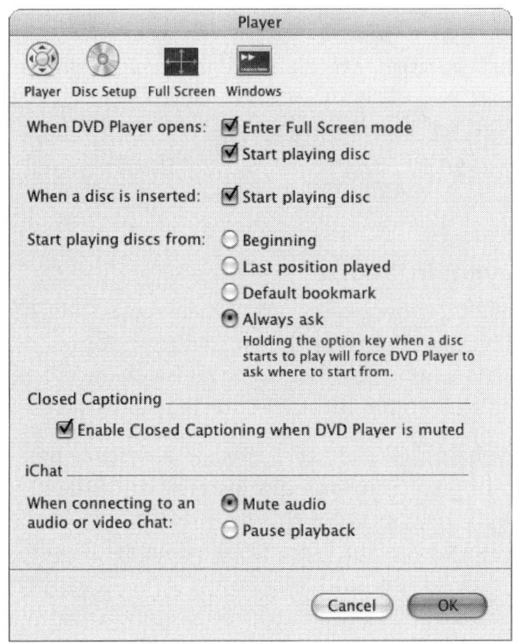

FIGURE 3.31 Change how DVD Player is activated and the size of the viewing window.

The Windows pane controls whether the controller fades away or just disappears when it is hidden and turns on and off status information, which appears while a movie is playing. You can also choose the color and transparency of these messages, as well as the color and transparency of closed captioning.

> **NOTE**
>
> Gradual fade of the controller upon hiding and transparent text are features enabled through the use of Quartz Extreme, which allows some graphics cards to take some of the graphics-processing load off Mac OS X.

Keychain Access

Using the Internet is a never-ending struggle to keep track of passwords for email servers, file servers, Web sites, and other private information. The Keychain Access software (path: `/Applications/Utilities/Keychain Access`) automatically stores passwords from Keychain-aware applications such as Mail and Safari. Users can also manually add their own passwords to the keychain. Later, the keychain can be unlocked to reveal the original cleartext password.

CAUTION

The default keychain is unlocked by your account password. Sensitive information is best placed in a secondary keychain with a different password; otherwise, a single compromise of your account unlocks access to all your information.

Read how to add new keychains in the "Managing Keychains" section later in the chapter.

Keychains and Keychain Scope

By default, all users have their own keychain named `login`. This is called the *User* keychain. Additional User keychains can be created to store specific information, such as credit card numbers, PINs, and so on. Think of the keychain as a database of your most sensitive information, all accessible through your Mac OS X account password.

In addition to User keychains, Global keychains are accessible by all users on the system. A Global keychain can be created by an administrator and shared to the other users on the system. An example of the usefulness of this feature is creating a keychain with corporate login data for intranet file servers that should be available to everyone.

User keychains are stored in `~/Library/Keychains`, whereas Global keychains are located in `/Library/Keychains`.

Automated Access

Launching Keychain Access displays the contents of your default keychain—named `login`. For an account that has been using the keychain to store file server passwords, HTTP authentication information, and so on, the Keychain Access window should look similar to that shown in Figure 3.32.

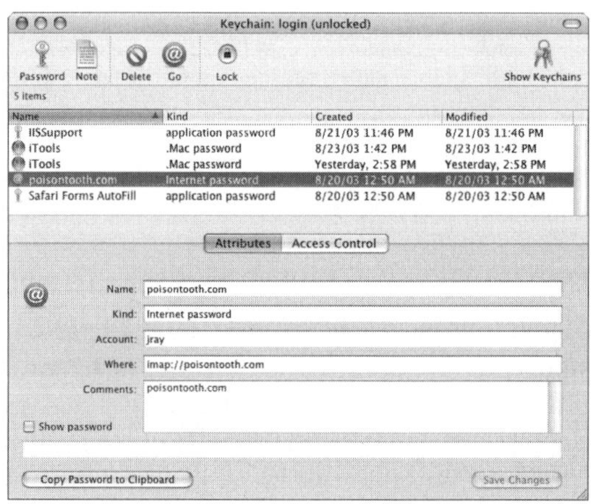

FIGURE 3.32 The Keychain Access window displays a list of stored passwords and other information.

The obvious question is, "How did these items get here?" They were added by Mac OS X applications. Typically, when an application wants to store something in the keychain, you'll be given the option of storing it. For example, when accessing a site that requires HTTP authentication, some Web browsers present a dialog box requesting a username and password, and offering to "remember" it or "add to keychain." Choosing these options automatically adds the entered password to the default keychain. Over time, your keychain could become populated with hundreds of items, and you might not ever know it!

When an application wants to access information from your keychain, it must first make sure that the keychain is unlocked. Your default Mac OS X keychain is automatically unlocked when you log in to your account, making its passwords accessible to the applications that stored them. To manually lock or unlock a keychain, click the Lock button at the top of the Keychain Access window. The Keychain Access window, along with its Dock icon, changes to reflect its security status. If an application attempts to access information on a locked keychain, it displays a dialog box, as shown in Figure 3.33. Entering the correct password (your account password for the default keychain) unlocks the keychain that your application is attempting to access. Clicking the Details disclosure pushbutton displays what keychain is being unlocked and the application making the keychain request.

FIGURE 3.33 If an application attempts to access data in a locked keychain, you are prompted for the keychain's password.

Even after a keychain is unlocked, an application might still need a bit more help before it can retrieve the information it needs from the keychain. Each stored piece of information can be controlled in a way that makes it accessible to only specific applications. Mail passwords, for example, are accessible only by the Mail application. If a program you just downloaded off the Internet attempts to unlock your Web or email passwords, you'll know something nefarious is afoot. Sometimes, usually after a system upgrade, you will have to re-educate your Mac OS X computer about what applications can access what passwords. This is a simple process.

When the keychain notices an unauthorized application attempting to access a piece of information, it prompts the user with a window to deny the access, allow it only once (Allow Once), or allow the application to access the information whenever it wants (Always Allow), demonstrated in Figure 3.34.

Before making a choice, always click the Details disclosure pushbutton to view which keychain is being accessed and which application wants the data. If you don't recognize the application, click Deny to disallow access.

FIGURE 3.34 Each application must be authorized to access a specific piece of information.

Working with Keychain Items

Users who want to access stored data, or manually add new information to a keychain, can do so through the Keychain Access program. Each item listed in the Keychain window can be viewed by selecting it. Web entries can be launched in a Web browser by selecting the resource and clicking the Go toolbar button. You can sort the Keychain item list by using View, Sort or by clicking the headings in the List view.

The lower portion of the window displays information about a keychain entry using a button bar with two entries: Attributes and Access Control.

Attributes

The Attributes button as its name suggests, provides basic information about the stored information. For example, Figure 3.35 shows the attributes for an IMAP password in my default keychain. The Kind field identifies the type of information, Where shows the resource that stored the information, and Account displays the creating user account. Users can add any additional comments about the item by typing in the Comments field. Click the Show Password button to display the password in cleartext.

NOTE

When you click Show Password, you often are prompted to allow Keychain Access to retrieve the data. Although this might seem strange, it is because Keychain Access itself must obey the same rules as the rest of the system. Because Keychain Access isn't listed as having unlimited access to stored items, it asks each time it needs to retrieve the information.

You can edit any of the item attributes within the Attributes pane. Click the Save Changes button in the lower-right corner to save any modifications you've made.

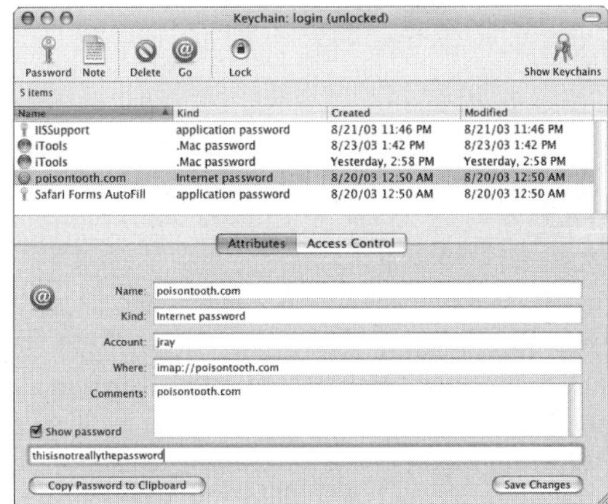

FIGURE 3.35 The Attributes pane displays what type of data is stored, and when it was added to the keychain.

Access Control

The Access Control pane enables the user to pick and choose which applications can access a given piece of information in the keychain. Shown in Figure 3.36, the controls of this pane are straightforward. Click Allow All Applications to Access This Item to transparently provide access to the resource with no user interaction.

You can specify individual applications by clicking the Confirm Before Allowing Access radio button; then use the Add and Remove buttons to add and remove applications from the list. Leave the application list blank to always force a confirmation. Finally, check the Ask for Keychain Password check box to force the user to enter a password each time access is confirmed.

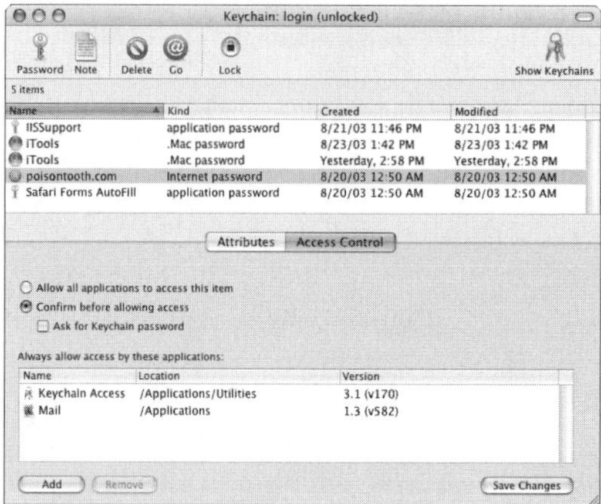

FIGURE 3.36 The Access Control pane provides control over what applications can access a piece of data.

Adding New Entries

New pieces of information can be added to the keychain by clicking the Add button in the main Keychain window or choosing File, New, then Password Item or Secure Note from the menu or clicking the Password or Note buttons in the toolbar. This action opens a new window, such as that shown in Figure 3.37, for entering the data to be stored. Enter the name or URL of the stored item in the Name field, the account name associated with the data in the Account field, and, finally, the sensitive data in the Password field. By default, the password is hidden as you type. To display the password as it is typed, click the Show Typing check box. Click Add when finished. When creating a Secure Note, only a name and note field are displayed.

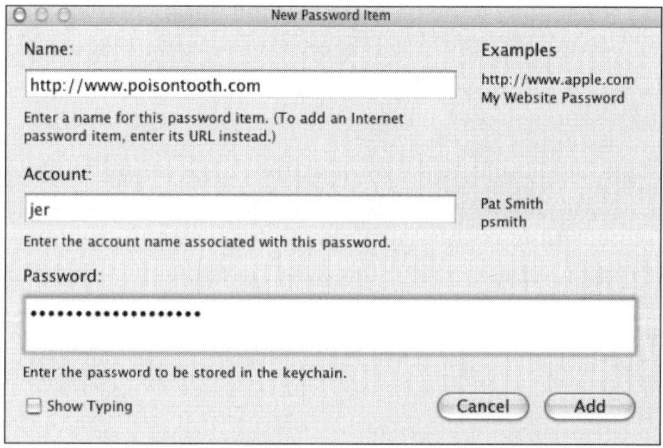

FIGURE 3.37 New items can easily be added manually to an existing keychain.

To remove any item from the keychain (either automatically or manually entered), select its name in the list and then click the Delete toolbar button, or choose Edit, Delete.

Adding Certificates

Digital certificates are used to provide authoritative identification information for people and services online. Secure Web sites use certificates to prove that they are legitimate (as you'll see in Chapter 27). Another use, fully supported in Panther, is that of providing secure mail services to and from clients that support the S/MIME standard (see `http://www.rsasecurity.com/standards/smime/faq.html` for details).

To support encryption in mail, you must add an X.509 digital certificate containing a private and public key. The public key is used to *sign* outgoing messages so that other users can encrypt mail to you, which, subsequently is decrypted with your private key. Other users who sign their outgoing messages with their public key (using the S/MIME standard) can send you mail, and the Mac OS X Mail application *automatically* saves a certificate with their public key to your keychain. This, in turn, allows you to send encrypted messages to that person.

To obtain a certificate for signing mail, contact a Certificate Authority (CA), such as `http://www.verisign.com/products/class1/index.html` or `http://www.thawte.com/html/COMMUNITY/personal/`. Or do a Google search for "free email certificate" to turn up several dozen free options.

Unfortunately, not many certificate services (if any) can easily provide the certificates in a format that is Mac OS X "Mail" ready. As a result, it is difficult to predict how you will "get" your certificate. Some users in similar situations report success importing the certificates into browsers such as Netscape (`http://www.netscape.com`) or Opera (`http://www.opera.com`) and then using the export options in these browsers to save the certificate in a `.cer`, `.crt`, or `.p7c` (among others) file. I've personally had success importing the certificate into Outlook (most certificate services are already set up to import into Outlook) and then exporting from Outlook. Whatever your technique, you should eventually end up with a certificate that can be imported into Keychain Access.

To import a certificate, double-click it (if it is a recognized type), or choose File, Import and choose the file. Keychain Access displays an import dialog box, as shown in Figure 3.38.

FIGURE 3.38 Import a digital certificate into Keychain Access.

Choose the keychain to add the certificate to and then click OK. If you want to view the certificate before saving it, click the View Certificates button. After an S/MIME certificate has been added, the encryption features "appear" in Mail, as described in Chapter 4.

Certificates can be selected in the Keychain element list to view their contents and change their Trust settings. Trust Settings can be altered such that permission is required each time a certificate is accessed, or a certificate is always trusted.

Managing Keychains

Each user account can have as many keychains as needed, including systemwide Global keychains. Click the Keychains toolbar button to manage the keychains stored in your user account; the window drawer shown in Figure 3.39 appears.

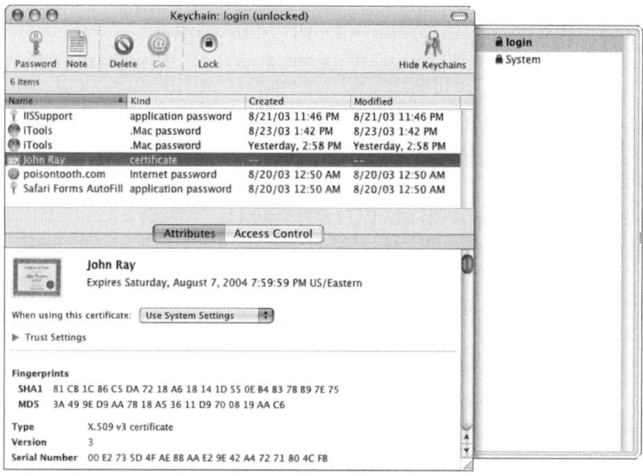

FIGURE 3.39 Use the Keychain List to manage your available keychains.

As mentioned earlier, a default keychain is generated for each user account named `login`. Also included is a default Global keychain named `System` shared throughout all user accounts.

New keychains can be created by choosing File, New Keychain. You are prompted for a name and a save location for the keychain. The default for a User keychain is `~/Library/Keychains`; Global keychains should be stored in `/Library/Keychains`.

Next, you need to enter a passphrase that unlocks the new keychain. It's best to choose something different from your account password to prevent people who might gain access to your account from seeing your most sensitive information. If you want to add an existing keychain file (perhaps from your account on another Mac OS X machine), use File, Add Keychain from the menu, and then choose the keychain file on your drive.

When the new keychain is added or created within an account, you can switch to it by choosing its name from the Keychain window drawer. You can make a keychain your default keychain (displacing `login`), by choosing File, Make Keychain Default.

NOTE

To move entries from one keychain to another, select the items you want to move and then drag them to the appropriate keychain in the keychain drawer.

To remove a keychain from the system, highlight its name in the list and then press the Delete key.

Unlock or lock keychains in the drawer using the Lock/Unlock toolbar icons.

TIP

You can add a Keychain menu extra to your menu bar by choosing View, Show Status in the menu bar. This extra provides the capability to lock and unlock any one of your keychains at any time.

Creating Global Keychains

Global keychains are identical to User keychains but have a flag toggled to make them available to all users—the Global flag (surprise). You can convert any keychain to or from Global keychain status using the Keychain List (Window, Keychain List; Command-Option-L). The Keychain List is shown in Figure 3.40.

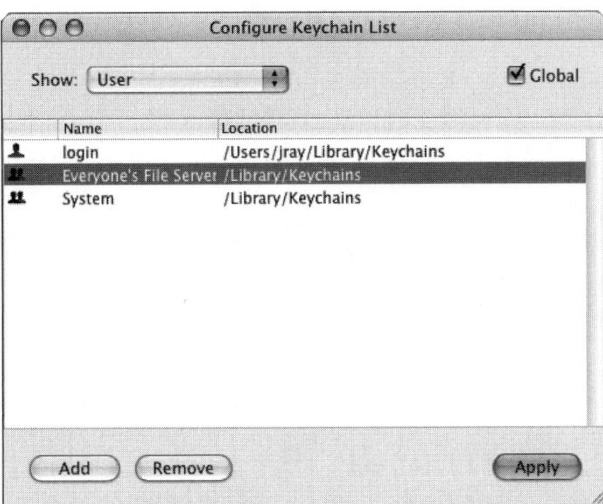

FIGURE 3.40 Manage User and Global keychains.

The pop-up menu at the top of the list enables you to choose between User (your keychains) and System keychains. System keychains are keychains stored at the System (`/Library/Keychains`) level but *not* necessarily Global keychains. If installing a keychain for everyone on the system, it should be stored as a System keychain and should *also* be set as a Global keychain.

To convert a keychain to or from global status, highlight it in the Keychain List; then use the Global check box to change its status. System Global keychains automatically show up in other users' Keychain Lists.

Keychain Settings and Passwords

The Keychain Access application has no preferences, but it does allow some control over each keychain file, such as modifying the password that unlocks the keychain. To open the settings, highlight the appropriate keychain from the Keychains drawer and then choose Edit, Change Settings for Keychain. You should see a new window, much like the one shown in Figure 3.41.

FIGURE 3.41 Set your keychains to lock after a certain length of time.

Within the Settings window, you can use the Lock After XX Minutes of Inactivity setting to force Mac OS X to lock a keychain if it isn't used for a certain length of time. Clicking Lock When Sleeping causes the keychain to be locked if the computer goes to sleep.

Use Edit, Change Keychain Password to edit the password that unlocks the keychain.

NOTE

If you change the password on your default keychain to something other than your Mac OS X account password, it will not be automatically unlocked when you first log in.

Keychain First Aid

As you work with keychains, a variety of problems can occur, such as passwords getting out of sync and improper keychains being set as the default. The Keychain First Aid tool can repair some of these common problems for any user account on the system.

To access Keychain First Aid, choose Window, Keychain First Aid (Option-Command-A). The First Aid window, shown in Figure 3.42, appears.

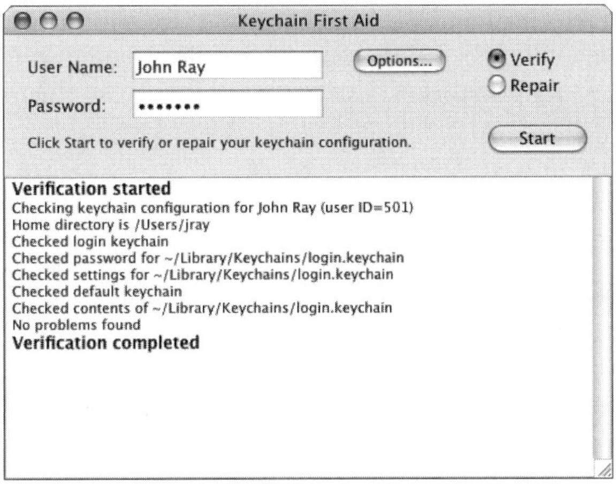

FIGURE 3.42 Keychain First Aid can repair common Keychain problems.

To verify a user's keychain, click the Verify radio button, enter the username and password, and click the Start button. If problems are found, switch to Repair mode and then click Start again.

The options button can be used to configure what "repairs" will take place and also offers an option to reset to a "factory fresh" default keychain.

The First Aid features are best for fixing problems for users who have accidentally messed up their default `login` keychain. It does not fix a keychain that has suffered data corruption or recover information that has otherwise been lost. It is a tool to help you, as an administrator, handle keychain problems for your users without logging in to their accounts.

Menus

Keychain Access menus provide little additional control over what is offered in the toolbar buttons. Use the File menu to quickly lock all keychains and reset the default keychain for your account. All other functions are readily accessible from the Keychain Access window.

Apple System Profiler

The Apple System Profiler (path: `/Applications/Utilities/System Profiler`) is a tool for browsing the hierarchy of components in your computer, connected to your computer, and installed on your computer. A typical use of this utility is to provide detailed configuration information for error reports to hardware and software manufacturers. Other uses include surveying the applications that are installed, along with their version information, and checking the status of USB or FireWire devices plugged in to your machine.

The profiler collects information about your computer when initially launched. Information is divided into four major categories (labeled Contents): Hardware, Software, Network, and Logs, which are listed in a pane on the left side of the window.

In the initial display, Hardware is highlighted, providing an overview of your system hardware, as shown in Figure 3.43.

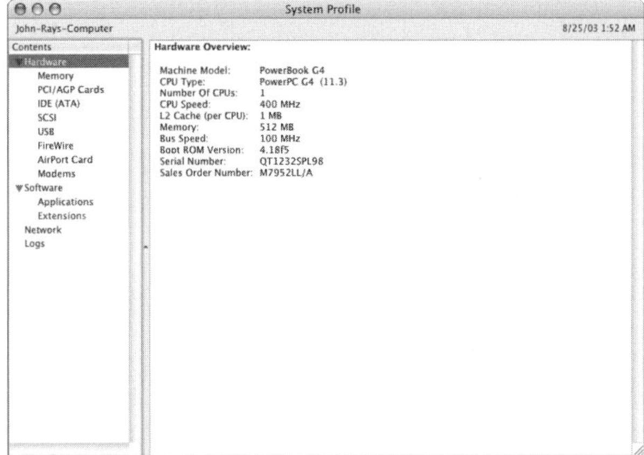

FIGURE 3.43 The System Profiler collects and displays your system's hardware configuration.

Each of the categories can be expanded or collapsed by clicking the disclosure arrow in front of the topic. Disclosure arrows are used extensively throughout the application, so be sure to click around—you'll be surprised at the total amount of available information.

NOTE

The View menu offers the capability to switch between three levels of reported information (Short, Standard, and Extended). The information in this section assumes that Extended (Command-3) is selected.

Hardware Profile

The Hardware category, displayed in Figure 3.43, contains a summary of the base computer. By expanding Hardware to show each of the subtopics, you can find everything from the serial and sales order number assigned when your machine was first built to the Vendor IDs of devices plugged in to your USB bus.

TIP

To access the System Profile information quickly, you can run `/usr/sbin/system_profiler` from the command line or open About this Mac in the Apple menu and click the More Info button.

For example, to see the internal disks and ATA storage devices, click the ATA (IDE) hardware category. The content area of the screen refreshes with a list of devices at the top and a detail view of the selected device at the bottom. Figure 3.44 shows an example of this screen.

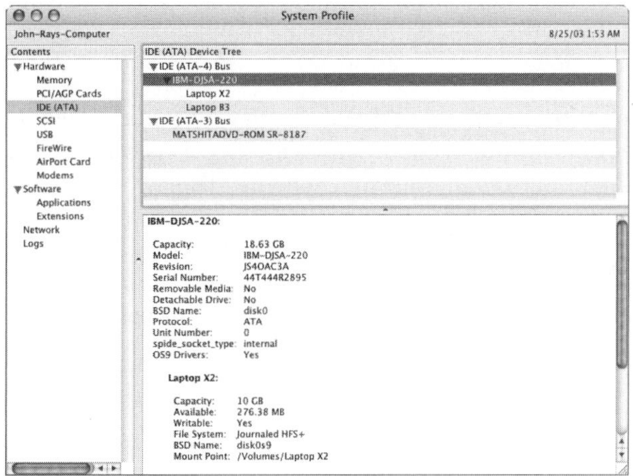

FIGURE 3.44 View details of a given piece of hardware.

If you're unfamiliar with the standard Macintosh bus types, this list may provide some insight:

- USB—Universal Serial Bus. In its initial implementation (version 1), USB is a slow (12Mbps) bus used for connecting external peripherals such as low-speed storage, scanners, printers, cameras, mice, and keyboards. USB 2.0, now included on new Macs, supports much faster speeds and can be much like FireWire.
- FireWire—An Apple-developed bus technology that supports speeds of 400Mbps and 800Mbps, hot-swappable devices such as high-speed storage, and digital-video cameras. The FireWire bus is also known by its IEEE name 1394 and Sony's iLink.
- PCI—Peripheral Component Interconnect. The PCI bus was developed by Intel (yes, that Intel) and is the standard for connecting internal video cards, sound cards, and so on.
- ATA—Integrated Drive Electronics. The IDE standard was developed by Western Digital and is used for internal CD-ROM and disk storage.
- SCSI—Small Computer System Interface. A fast bus for high-speed storage devices, typically used on server-class computers.

Software Profile

Selecting the Software profile category displays information about your Mac OS X system configuration, including version, kernel, boot volume, and active user. You can use the three categories within Software to display extended information about installed components of the OS.

Applications

The Applications selection scans your drive to display all the installed applications (the BSD subsystem is not taken into account). You can view version, creator, and modification dates in the upper pane. Selecting an entry in the list displays details, including location in the bottom pane.

Frameworks

Selecting Frameworks displays a list of libraries installed on your computer, in a view identical to Applications.

There are dozens of frameworks in the base installation of Mac OS X—ranging from AppleShare to Speech Recognition.

> **What Is a Framework?**
>
> A *framework* is a collection of shared object libraries. Instead of each application reimplementing code, the operating system can provide commonly used functions in the form of a shared library.

Extensions

Extensions, like frameworks, provide functionality to the operating system. Unlike frameworks, they work directly with the hardware to enable the operating system to access devices such as network cards, sound cards, and other components. Mac users are familiar with extensions. In Mac OS 8 and 9, extensions had similar capabilities but often made the operating system unstable. In Mac OS X, the traditional extension is replaced by a `.kext` (kernel extension). These plug-ins for the Mach kernel cannot be installed by unprivileged users and are no longer appropriate for creating cool (but crash-causing) additions to the system.

The layout of the Extensions view is identical to that of the Frameworks.

Network

The Network category provides an overview of your installed network configurations, their interface IDs, and IP addresses (if any), as shown in Figure 3.45.

Selecting a configuration displays additional information including MAC address and subnet mask in the lower details pane.

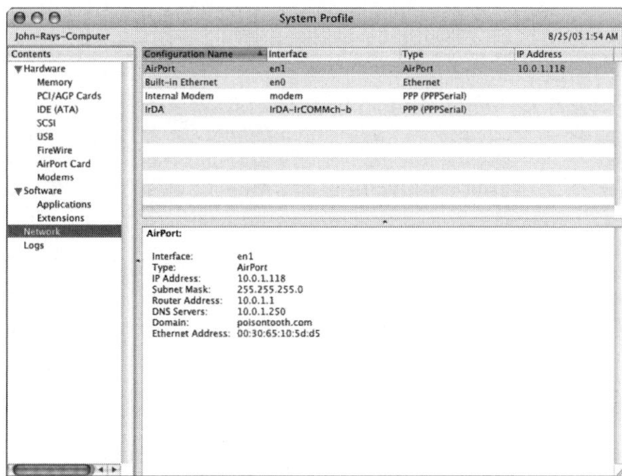

FIGURE 3.45 The Network category gives you a quick overview of your network status.

Logs

Finally, the Logs category allows you to view the Mac OS X Console and System log. This functionality is replicated in a number of locations, such as the Console utility, so its inclusion here is a bit curious.

Menus

The menus provide little additional functionality beyond what can be accessed directly in the System Profiler window.

The File menu operates on reports generated from the Profiler's data. You can use the regular Open command to open existing report files; use Save to save reports in System Profiler, RTF, or plain text; and use the Print function to print the report window.

The View menu offers the option of switching between Short (Command-1), Standard (Command-2), and Extended (Command-3) report types. If you aren't seeing a piece of information that should be displayed, switch to the Extended report.

Activity Monitor

In Chapter 2, "Managing the Panther Workspace," you learned how pressing Option-Command-Escape opens a process list and enables you to force-quit open applications on the system. The Activity Monitor application is similar but contains information on all the system's processes, not just the GUI software that is running. Figure 3.46 shows the default Activity Monitor display.

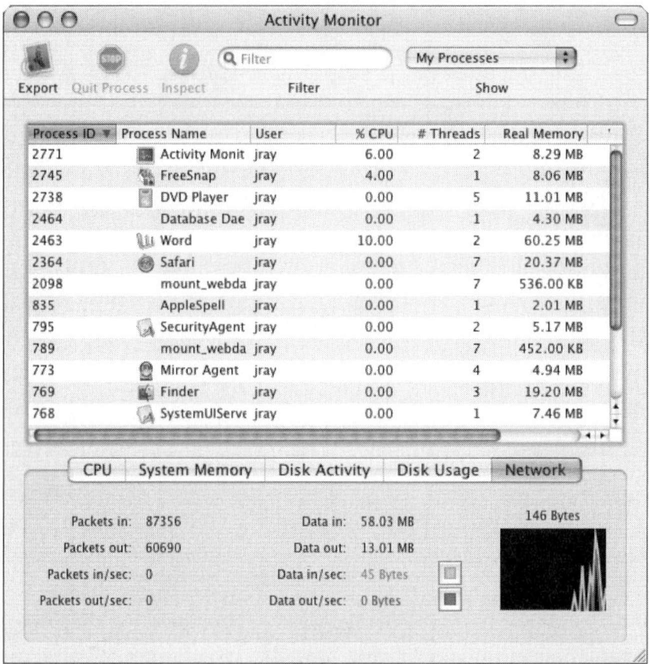

FIGURE 3.46 The Process Listing can show you everything that is running on your computer.

Controlling the Process Listing

Using the controls in the Process Listing screen, you can configure the type of output and amount of the information displayed.

The Filter and Show features help limit the amount of data shown within the process listing. Typing into the Find field filters processes that match the given string. For example, typing **Internet** would limit the displayed processes to those that have the word "Internet" in their name, such as Internet Explorer. The Show pop-up menu filters processes based on the owner. You can change the setting to show the following categories:

- All Processes—All the processes running on the system.
- All Processes Hierarchically—All the processes running on the system, sorted into a parent/child hierarchy.
- My Processes—The processes running under your user account.
- Administrator Processes—The processes running with administrative rights.
- Other User Processes—Processes running from other user accounts (not including `root`).
- Active Processes—Processes that are currently running and active.

- Inactive Processes—Processes that are running, but sleeping (not consuming CPU time).
- Windowed Processes—Processes running under the Mac OS X windowing system. (Your GUI applications.)

The process listing is not, as you might first think, a real-time view of the programs running on the system. The process information is always changing. To avoid overwhelming the user with a list that jumps all over the place, the process list is only updated every few seconds. Using the Monitor, Update Frequency menu selection, you can change the rate at which the list is refreshed. The larger the number, the longer you must wait for updates.

Processes are listed based on seven columns: Process ID, Name, User, % CPU, Threads, Real Memory, and Virtual Memory. Each column can be sorted by clicking on the column heading. Click the small triangle in the upper-right corner of the process list to reverse the sorting order.

Using the toolbar icons, you can export a process listing as an XML file, quit a process, or view details about a process using Inspect (Command-I).

CAUTION

If you use the Quit button to force a process to quit, make absolutely sure that it isn't a critical process. Because you now have access to the processes that control Mac OS X, be aware that your actions could result in making your system inoperable.

Process Details

If you want even more information about a process, you can double-click it within the listing or highlight it and click the Inspect ("I") icon in the toolbar, or choose Process, Inspect (Command-I). A detail window, shown in Figure 3.47, appears.

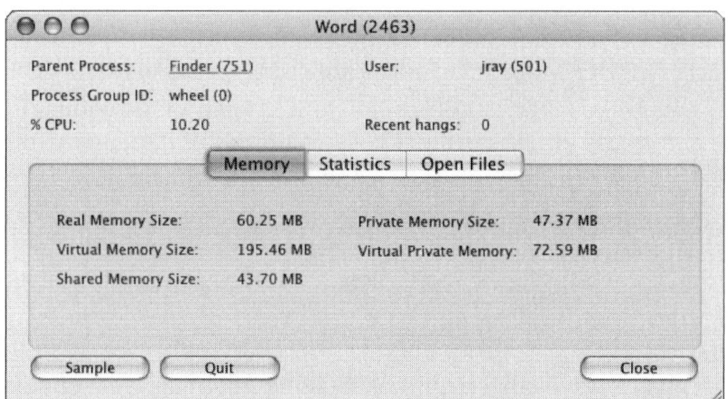

FIGURE 3.47 View details about a selected process

At the top of the detail window you can view the following information:

- Parent Process ID—The process that started the selected process. For example, if a user starts a program from the command line (the "shell"), the ID of the shell is listed as the program's parent process ID. Processes started at boot time list the parent process ID of 1 (`init`). Note that the Parent process name is a hyperlink—clicking it opens the details window for the parent process.
- Group ID—The ID of the group used to start the process.
- %CPU—The amount of CPU time that the process is taking.
- User—The user who owns the process.

The middle portion of the process details window displays information about one of three categories, depending on which button in the button bar is highlighted: Memory, Statistics, or Open Files:

- Memory—The amount of memory (real and virtual) being used by the process. For information on memory "types" visit (`http://developer.apple.com/documentation/Performance/Conceptual/Performance/VirtualMemory/Virtual_Mem_on_Mac_OS_X.html`).
- Statistics—Information about how the process is behaving on your system, including threads, CPU time used, and the number of Unix system calls processed.
- Open Files—A list of files that are open and in-use by the process.

At the bottom of the details window are three buttons: Sample, Quit, and Close. The Sample button takes a sample trace of the process execution over several seconds (this is mostly only useful for developers). The Quit button will force-quit the process, and Close will close the details window.

Displaying System Statistics

At the bottom of the Activity Monitor window are controls for viewing CPU usage, System Memory, Disk Activity, Disk Usage, and Network activity. These provide an overview of activity and usage across the entire system; they are not at all dependent processes selected in the process listing. Let's run through each pane and the information it contains.

CPU Usage

The CPU usage pane, shown in Figure 3.48. displays the current activity level of the CPU(s) on your system.

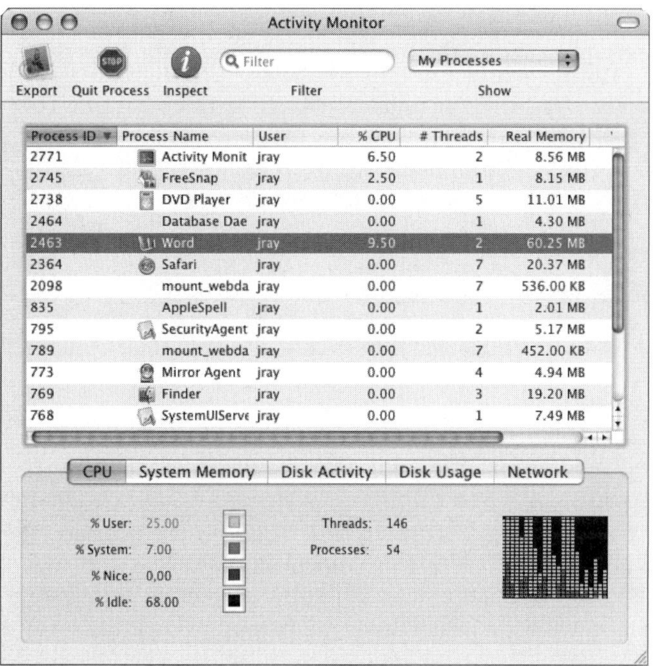

FIGURE 3.48 View your system activity level in the CPU pane.

Three types of "activity" are monitored:

- User—CPU time that is used by user-started processes and applications.
- System—Processor usage by the system processes, such as the WindowServer and other components of the operating system. The System CPU time often correlates directly to the user activity. Dragging objects within an application, for example, places a load on the application and on the Mac OS X graphics and event-processing subsystem.
- Nice—CPU time used by processes running with an altered scheduling priority. All user processes start with the same priority of execution. This priority can be adjusted with the `nice` and `renice` commands to provide them with more or less access to CPU time.

The fourth value (idle) is actually just a "lack" of activity (100% minus the other three values). The total number of threads and processes is also displayed.

To the right of the readouts is a scrolling graph that displays the three types of CPU activity.

> **TIP**
>
> In the CPU pane and any other pane, you can alter the colors used in the graph by clicking the color wells to the right of each readout.

System Memory

The System Memory pane shows the overall memory usage for the system, as displayed in Figure 3.49.

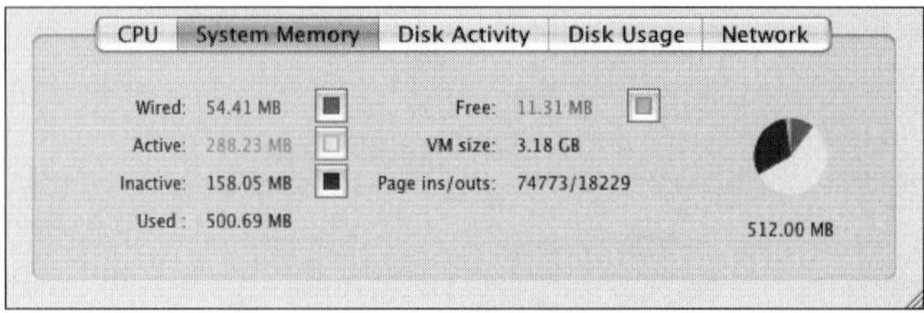

FIGURE 3.49 Monitor your system's memory usage.

Although most of the data labels should be obvious (active memory, inactive memory, total used, and so on), the Wired reading may be confusing if you've never encountered it before. Wired memory cannot be written to virtual memory and *must* remain in real memory by the system. A properly operating idle system should not display an increase in real memory over an extended period of time. If it *does*, a memory leak in a system component (such as a device driver) may be slowly eating away at your resources.

Disk Activity

The third pane, Disk Activity, tracks your disk usage—reads/writes on your drives. This pane is demonstrated in Figure 3.50.

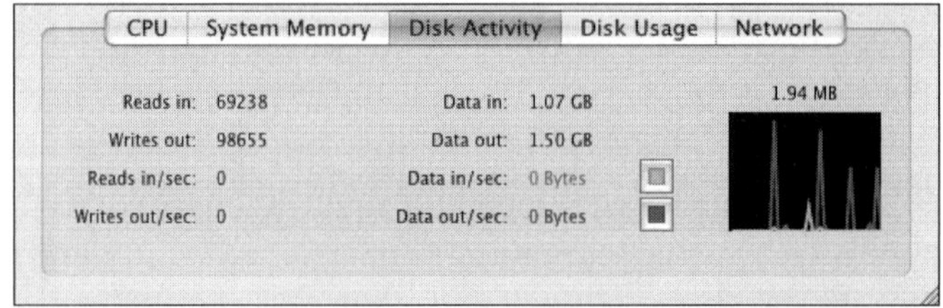

FIGURE 3.50 View the read/write activity on your local drives.

Disk Usage

The Disk Usage pane, shown in Figure 3.51, displays the amount of available free space on any of your currently mounted volumes.

Use the pop-up menu in the Disk Usage pane to choose the drive you want to monitor.

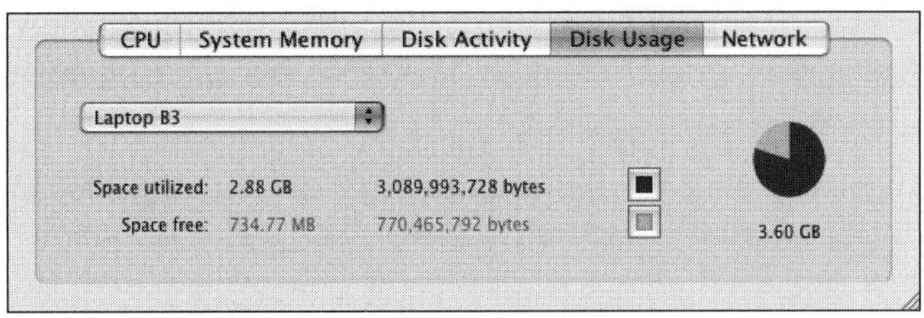

FIGURE 3.51 Monitor how much remaining space is available on your local and network volumes.

Network

The final pane, Network, displays the amount of data and packets going in and out of your active network interfaces. Figure 3.52 shows the Network pane.

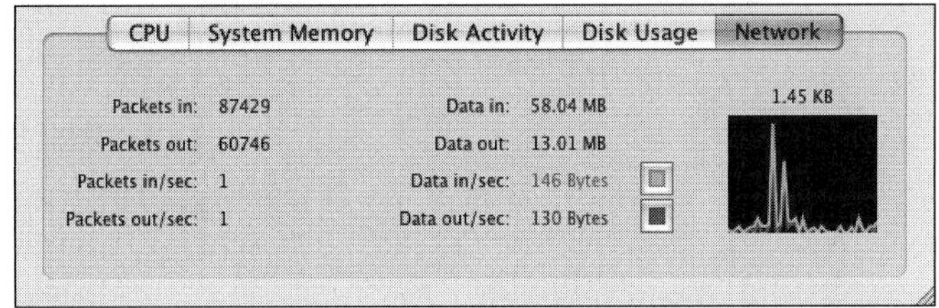

FIGURE 3.52 The Network pane can be used to monitor incoming and outgoing data.

Displaying Monitor Graphs

You've already seen that the Activity Monitor is capable of producing graphs to display your CPU usage, among other things. Keeping the Activity Monitor window open to view the graphs, however, isn't realistic if you plan to use your computer for actual work.

Thankfully, Apple provides a number of ways of displaying *some* of the information in floating windows or within the Dock icon. The Monitor menu provides access to all these functions:

- Show CPU Usage (Command-2)—Displays a floating window with an instantaneous view of the CPU usage.
- Floating CPU Window—Changes the appearance of the CPU window. Display it horizontally (Command-4) or vertically (Command-5).
- Show CPU History (Command-3)—Displays a growing graph of CPU usage over time, just like the CPU pane discussed earlier. This display can be seen in Figure 3.53.
- Clear CPU History (Command-K)—Clears the current CPU history graph.
- Show CPU Monitors on Top of Other Windows—If selected, the floating windows will always be on top of any other application windows.

- Dock Icon—If you'd rather display CPU Usage, CPU History, Memory Usage, or Network usage in the Activity Monitor Dock icon, this submenu allows you to choose what the icon will display.
- Update Frequency—As mentioned earlier, the Update frequency changes how frequently the process list is updated as well as the individual graphs.

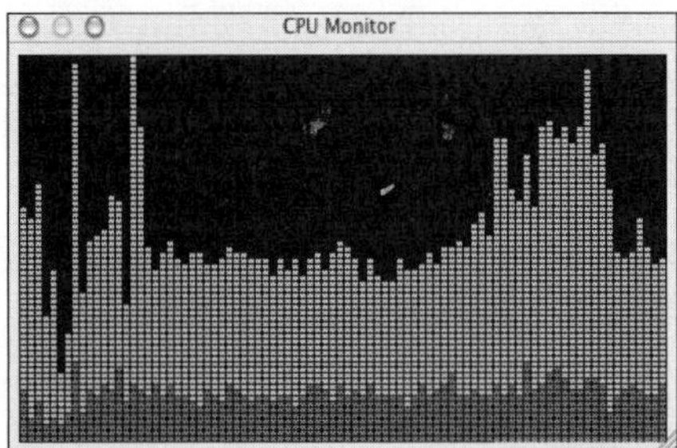

FIGURE 3.53 Display your CPU usage in a floating window or in the Dock icon.

Menus

The Process Viewer's menus provide a bit more control over the application, such as exporting the current process list to an XML file and sorting the output list.

Use the File menu options to print or export the list of processes. These options can be useful for creating a record of normal system activity to refer to if you think your system is misbehaving:

- Save (Command-S)—Exports the current list of processes as an XML file that can be viewed with Apple's XML editor (included with the Developer tools). You can also export the process list with the Export button in the toolbar. Learn more about XML's role in Mac OS X in Chapter 20, "Command-Line Configuration and Administration."
- Print (Command-P)—Prints the process list. Only the processes in the visible portion of the window are printed!

Console

The Console application (path: `/Applications/Utilities/Console`) is literally a window into the other side of Mac OS X. While the system is running, the GUI hides a tremendous amount of information from the user. Important information is sent to the Unix Console device (`/dev/console`). On many Unix systems, the console actually is a separate device, such as a VT100 terminal display that displays any data sent to it. This exists as a virtual device on Mac OS X and is responsible for reporting information as it arrives.

Viewing Console Logs

The Console application enables you to watch error and status messages as they appear. If your computer appears to be stalled or is acting in an unusual manner, the Console might be producing information that can help debug the problem. Figure 3.54 shows the Console application.

Even on a properly working Mac OS X system, the Console displays error and warning messages. You'll often see a large amount of information related to system processes such as `lookupd`. `lookupd` is a system process that handles network DNS service, user information lookups, and anything else that accesses the Mac OS X NetInfo database. Each request for information from `lookupd` is given a time-to-live. If that time is exceeded, the request fails and is logged to the console. In a networked environment, such failures are common, and the system simply repeats the action until it succeeds.

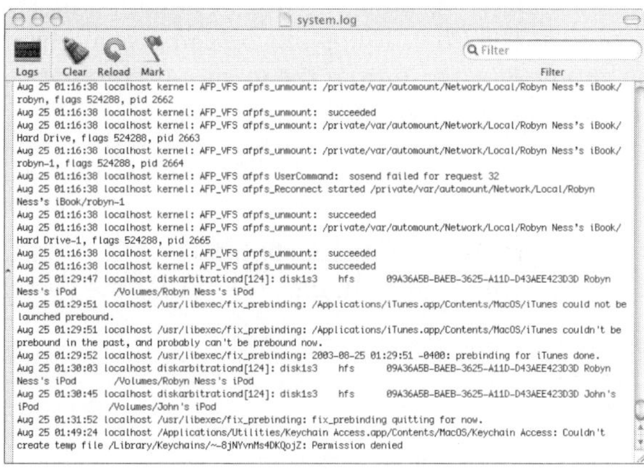

FIGURE 3.54 The Console shows internal system error and status messages as they appear.

What Is NetInfo?

NetInfo is a database system that stores most of the functional information about the Mac OS X's base configuration. This database can be set up to distribute information across a Mac OS X network—enabling a single user to access his resources from anywhere on the network. Windows users will find a similarity between NetInfo and the Windows registry. NetInfo, however, is easier to work with and existed many years before the registry (in the form of NeXT Computer's NeXTSTEP). More information on NetInfo is provided later in this book.

Managing the Log View

To filter the Log view, use the filter field in the upper-right corner to enter a string that each line must match to be displayed. For example, to display information from the Safari Web browser, you would type **Safari**.

To clear the filter, either remove the string, or click the "X" icon at the end of the field.

You can also use the toolbar icons to Mark the log, which enters a time stamp into the log display, or to clear the display entirely. This does *not* modify the actual log files, just the information display. To reload the full log at any time, click the Reload button, or use File, Reload (Command-R).

> **TIP**
>
> Additional functions (such as a full Find pane) can be added to the toolbar using View, Customize Toolbar.

Viewing Other Log Files

The Mac OS X System maintains a great deal of log information in addition to what is sent directly to the console. The Console application can display the contents of any log that you want if you choose File, Open from the menu. As you read through the book, you'll find that many BSD services create their own log files.

Logs are stored in three key locations: Your home directory (`~/Library/Logs`), the System log directory (`/Library/Logs`), and the BSD log directory (`/var/log`). Console is already "aware" of these locations and allows you to browse logs stored here by clicking the Logs icon in the toolbar. This opens a pane on the left side of the window, as shown in Figure 3.55.

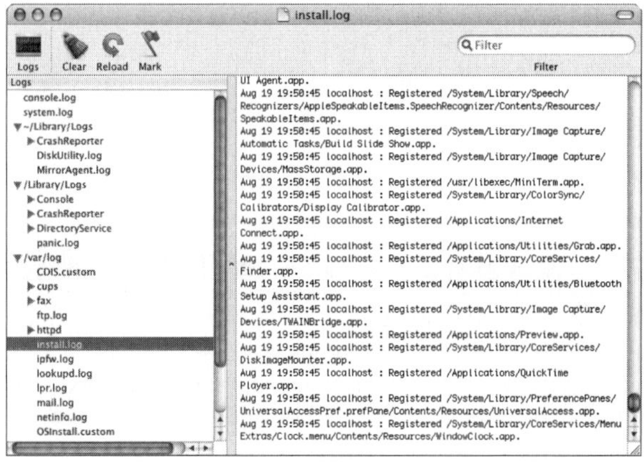

FIGURE 3.55 Browse other logs on your system.

Use the disclosure arrows to browse to other logs located on your drive. Alternatively, you can use File, Open Quickly to also browse the log hierarchy to a log of your choosing.

To save a copy of the log you are viewing, or a portion of it, choose File, Save a Copy As or File, Save Selection As (Option-Command-S).

Preferences

Use the Console application preferences to pick a delay that will be used for displaying log information as it comes in. If the console application is running but hidden when incoming information is received, clicking the Bring Updated Log Window to Front check box causes the application to appear and display the new information. The Send Back slider is used to set the length of the delay before the Console application hides itself.

Click Bounce Icon When Log Is Updated to cause the dock icon to bounce when there are incoming messages.

Disk Utility

In Panther, Apple has combined its two disk-related utilities—Disk Copy and Disk Utility—into a single application (still named Disk Utility). Disk Utility (path: `/Applications/Utilities/Disk Utility`) can still be used to create disk images and repair volumes, and has gained a few additional features as well. To discuss Disk Utility, we'll approach it from two sides: the disk imaging aspect and disk repair features.

Disk Operations

Disk Utility combines disk repair with disk formatting and partitioning. As with Mac OS 9, you cannot use either of these functions on your startup partition. If you only intend to work with a secondary disk or partition, launch Disk Utility from the Finder. To use Disk Utility to work on your primary disk, follow these steps:

1. Insert your Mac OS X Install CD into your computer.
2. Start (or restart) your Macintosh while holding down the C key.
3. Wait for the Installer to boot.
4. Choose Open Disk Utility from the Installer application menu.

After launching Disk Utility, the application opens to display a list of your disk resources in a pane on the left side of the window, as shown in Figure 3.56. To the right of the disk list is the content pane, which displays controls for operating on the selected disk item.

Disks are listed with each of their partitions displayed. Grayed out partitions are system partitions that do not contain files that you can verify or repair.

When a disk is selected, up to five button bar selections appear in the content area: First Aid, Erase, Partition, RAID, and Restore. Each button opens a pane that performs a different function within the application, as you might guess from their names.

At the bottom of the Disk Utility window is a display of the details of the selected disk object. Although most of this information is self-explanatory, of interest is the S.M.A.R.T. (Self-Monitoring Analysis and Reporting Technology) status. A disk that supports S.M.A.R.T. can report potential problems before they occur, warning you of imminent drive failure.

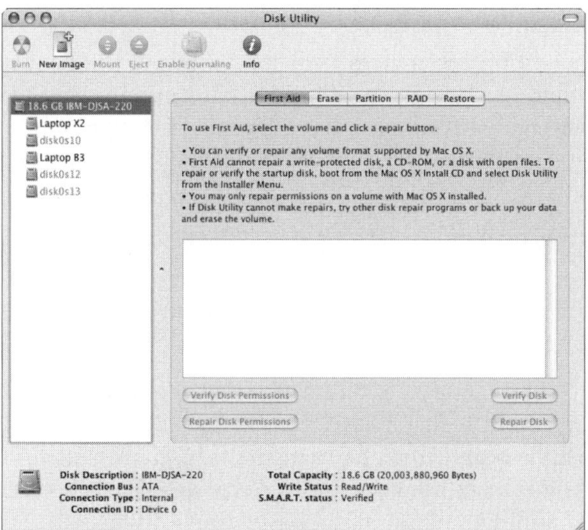

FIGURE 3.56 The left pane contains your disk resources; the right pane displays the operation you are performing on your disk.

TIP

To get more information about a disk or partition, select it in the list and then click the Info icon in the Disk Utility toolbar.

Choose the disk or partition that you want to work with and then click the tab to move to the appropriate pane. We'll start with the First Aid.

NOTE

The button bar changes depending on the object you've selected. If you choose a disk, for example, you see *all* the control areas. If you choose a partition, you do *not* see the partition controls because you can't very well partition a partition—nor can you apply RAID settings to a partition and so on.

First Aid

The First Aid pane, shown in Figure 3.57, can perform basic repair operations on a drive. It functions on UFS, HFS+, and HFS volumes—meaning that you can repair both types of Mac OS X partitions and both types of Mac OS 8/9 partitions. Unfortunately, Disk First Aid is not capable of repairing extensive disk damage, so third-party utilities such as Micromat's Drive 10 and TechTool Pro (`http://www.micromat.com/`) are still important parts of every software library. In addition to basic disk repair, the First Aid tools can also fix any file permissions that may accidentally have been changed while using your computer.

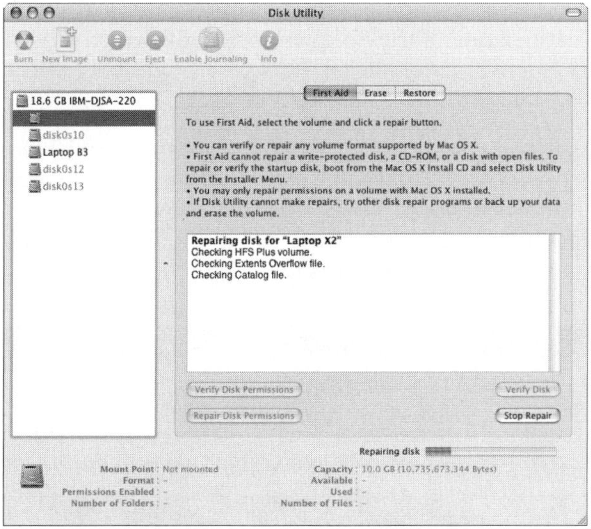

FIGURE 3.57 Use Disk First Aid to repair damaged volumes.

To check or verify a disk, select the disk and partition from the volume list at the left of the window. Next, click the appropriate action button:

- Verify Disk—Displays any errors found in your disk but does not attempt to repair them.
- Repair Disk—Performs the same tests as Verify but automatically fixes any errors it might find. You can only repair volumes other than your boot disk.
- Verify Disk Permissions—Check to make sure that your Mac OS X volume has the proper permissions set. If you're having trouble installing applications or deleting files, you may have a permissions problem.
- Repair Disk Permissions—Repair any incorrectly assigned permissions. Permissions can only be repaired on your current boot disk.
- Stop—Halts the current action (Verify or Repair).

If errors are found, they will be reported. Several things are checked during this process:

- Extents overflow file—The Extents file keeps track of file information that could not be placed contiguously on a disk. As files become fragmented, the locations of the fragments are stored here.

- Multilinked files—Files incorrectly linked to the same allocation blocks on the disk.
- Catalog—Contains the information that forms the structure (files, folders) of the disk.
- Bitmap—A binary picture of the disk, which records which blocks are allocated to files and which are free space.

If errors cannot be repaired, Disk Utility warns you that it is incapable of fixing your system. If this happens, try rerunning the repair—Disk First Aid often requires two passes to work correctly. If the repair does not work, Apple's suggested course of action is to back up the drive, erase it, and then restore your files. I'd recommend trying another disk repair tool before resorting to such desperate measures.

TIP

You can batch-repair multiple volumes by selecting several disks from the volume list. Just press Command and click the disks/partitions to add to the selection list.

NOTE

Volumes are repaired from the command line by using the `fsck` tool in single-user mode, as discussed in Chapter 32, "System Maintenance."

Apple also offers a command-line utility for mounting, unmounting, ejecting, and renaming disks: `disktool`. Learn more about the command line starting in Chapter 12, "Introducing the BSD Subsystem."

Erase

The next pane, Erase, does exactly what you would think it should: It erases drives and partitions. This is essentially a quick-and-dirty partitioning and initialization tool; it creates a single empty partition on the selected device and erases anything that was previously there. Figure 3.58 shows the Erase pane.

Use the Volume Format pop-up menu to choose between Journaled and non-Journaled Mac OS Extended partition types. Enabling Journaling does add a minor speed hit to the drive but helps protect your machine from data corruption if the system crashes or is otherwise interrupted.

TIP

You can enable journaling for a partition at any time by selecting it in the Disk/partition list and clicking the Enable Journaling button in the toolbar, or by using File, Enable Journaling (Command-J).

Journaling can be *disabled* by choosing Window, Customize Toolbar to add a Disable Journaling button to the toolbar and then applying it to a disk/partition, or by choosing File, Disable Journaling (Command-J).

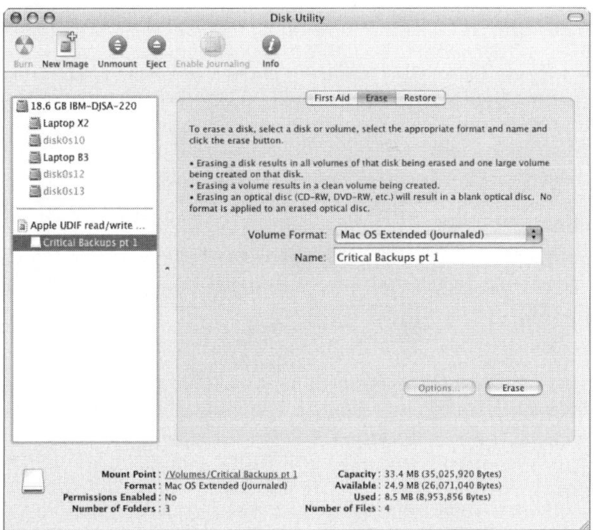

FIGURE 3.58 The Erase pane is used to quickly erase volumes and create a single empty partition.

Next, enter a name for the new volume. This appears as your disk label on the desktop.

TIP

If you want to securely erase the volume, click the Options button to force Disk Utility to zero all data on the drive and write random data over the drive eight times.

See Chapter 2 for more information on why multiple writes are required for a secure erasure.

Finally, click Erase to remove all existing information from the device and install the selected filesystem.

Partition

To create a more complex drive layout, use the Partition pane. Shown in Figure 3.59, this is the control center for working with your drive. Be warned—changes here will erase any information on the target drive!

The Volume Scheme section of the Partition pane contains a visual representation of the partitions on the system. Each box is a partition. The highlighted box is the active partition.

You can change a partition's size by dragging the dividers between the partitions up and down to shrink or grow the available space. As you drag the bar, the size field on the right portion of the pane changes to show the current settings.

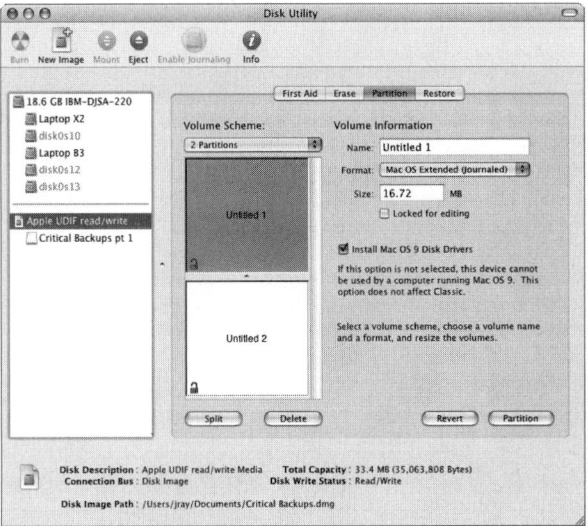

FIGURE 3.59 Partitioning your drive erases any existing information.

In addition to working with the visual view of the partition, you can use the various pop-up menus, fields, and buttons to set other parameters:

- Scheme—Quickly divides your drive into 1–8 equally sized partitions.
- Name—Sets the name of the highlighted partition.
- Format—Sets the highlighted partition to be either HFS, HFS+, HFS+ Journaled, UFS, or free space.
- Size—Manually enter a new size for the selected partition.
- Locked for Editing—When checked, the Locked for Editing setting freezes the current partition's settings. You can continue to work with other partitions but not one that is locked. Clicking the lock icon in the visual view of the partitions also toggles the lock.
- Install Mac OS 9 Disk Drivers—If this option is unchecked, the device is not usable on Mac OS 9.
- Split—Splits the current partition into two equally sized partitions.
- Delete—Removes the active partition.
- Revert—Returns the partition map to its original state.
- Partition—Commits the partition table design to the drive. This destroys all current data on the device.

Clicking the Partition button is the final step to designing your volume's layout. After you click the Partition button, you are prompted with a final confirmation, and then the changes are written to the disk.

RAID

RAID, or Redundant Array of Independent Disks, is a collection of multiple drives that function together as a single drive. By using drives performing in parallel, the computer can write and read information from the RAID set at a much higher rate than a single drive. Four common types of RAID are available:

- Level 0 – Disk striping—This increases I/O speed by reading and writing to multiple drives simultaneously. It offers no fault tolerance.
- Level 1 – Disk mirroring—Creates a fault-tolerant system by creating an exact mirror of one drive on another drive.
- Level 3 – Disk striping with error correction—This RAID type uses three drives: two operating identically to level 0, and a third containing error correction information for fault tolerance.
- Level 5 – Striped data and error correction—RAID level 5 offers the best balance between performance and fault tolerance.

Unfortunately, Panther only supports Level 0 and Level 1 in software.

RAID capabilities are easy to configure if you have multiple drives within a machine.

To set up a RAID set, drag the icons of the drives to add to a set from the volume list to the RAID pane's disk listing. Using the RAID scheme, choose what type of RAID support is enabled for the disks and provide a name for the resulting virtual drive that represents the combination of devices.

Finally, choose a volume format for the RAID set—this is identical to choosing a format for any volume—and click the Create button to generate the RAID set.

The new volume will be mounted on the desktop.

NOTE

If a drive in a RAID set ever becomes corrupted, this is reported in Disk Utility, and you are given the option of rebuilding the drive set.

Restore

The Restore pane, shown in Figure 3.60, is a new feature in the Panther release of Disk Utility. Restore enables you to completely replace the contents of a disk with a disk image that you've created previously. The disk image can even be stored on a Web server for retrieving over the network. To use restore, you must first create a disk image (we're getting there, don't worry).

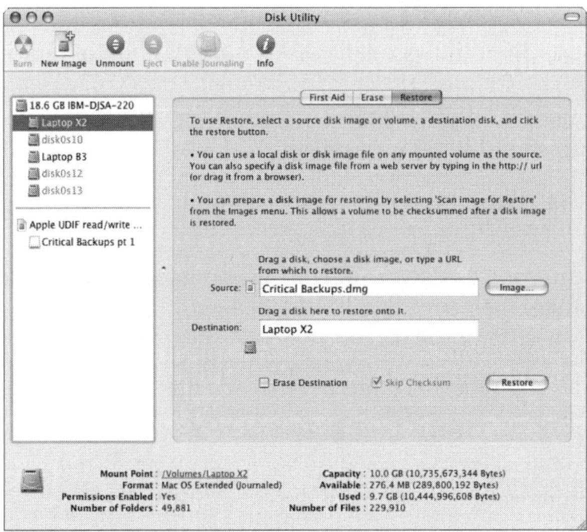

FIGURE 3.60 Restore volumes from disk images.

After an image is created, click the Image button to select it, drag it to the Source field, or type in a URL that can be used to retrieve the image.

Next, drag a disk or partition to the Destination field. If you want to erase the destination before copying the image to the drive, click the Erase Destination check box.

Finally, click Restore to start the restoration process.

> **TIP**
>
> The Restore feature of Disk Utility uses a command-line tool called `asr`. Apple has provided *excellent* step-by-step instructions for using `asr` and disk images to clone computers for classroom/workplace environments.
>
> Rather than repeat those here, use `man asr` from the command line and read the section entitled "HOW TO USE ASR." Read more about the command line starting in Chapter 12.

Additional Disk Operations

The toolbar contains options for unmounting/mounting volumes. After selecting a disk or partition from the list, you can choose to Mount (Option-Command-M), Unmount (Option-Command-U), or Eject (Command-E) the volume.

Disk Imaging

Disk images have become a common and convenient way to distribute software for Mac OS X. Rather than create an archived folder, developers write their applications to a virtual disk that is loaded into memory when used. This disk appears to the computer as a real disk and can be manipulated like any other disk. For the end user it is a simple way to work with new applications. A single disk image file can contain applications, support files, and any other data a program might need—and it never needs to be decompressed. In fact, many applications can actually run directly from disk images, without needing to be copied to your hard drive at all. Disk Utility even has built-in CD burning capabilities to make turning a disk image into a real CD a matter of a few clicks.

Adding Disk Images to the Interface

To work with an existing disk image, drag the image file into the disk list pane of Disk Utility or use Image, Open (Option-Command-O). It is added to an area below your standard hard disks and remains there until you drag it back out (even between executions of Disk Utility).

To mount an image you've added to Disk Utility, either double-click its name in the disk list pane, or select it and choose Open from the toolbar.

From this point, you can work with the disk image much like you would with any other disk in Disk Utility. You can verify it, repair it, repartition it, and so on.

Creating Disk Images

Disk Utility can create images as well as mount them. This is useful for creating an exact duplicate of software you don't want to lose, or for making a master image for distributing software over a network with `asr`.

There are three ways to generate an image: Copy an existing volume/partition; copy an existing folder; or create an empty image file, mount it, and then copy files to it.

To create an empty image file, choose Images, New, Blank Image. Figure 3.61 shows the disk image creation dialog box.

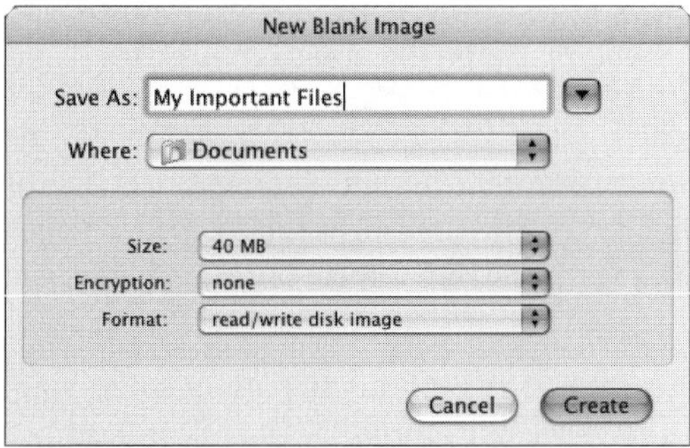

FIGURE 3.61 Generate a new blank image; then copy files to it.

Fill in the Save As field as you normally would—this is the name of the image file, not the volume that is going to be created. Choose a size for the image from the Size pop-up menu. There are a variety of preset sizes for common media, such as Zip disks, CDs, and DVDs, and a Custom setting for arbitrary sizes.

Next, choose a volume format with the Format pop-up menu. You can choose between a read/write disk image, which occupies the exact amount of space you've set for the image, or a *sparse* image that grows to accommodate the files you add.

Finally, if you want to encrypt the disk image, choose AES-128 from the Encryption pop-up menu and then click Create. The new disk image is created and added to the Disk Utility disk pane immediately.

Creating an image from an existing drive is even easier. Highlight the partition you want to use; then choose Images, New, Image From *Device* where *Device* is the name of your selected partition.

You are prompted for the location to save the image. Using the Image Format pop-up menu, choose the type of image to create: read-only, read-write, compressed, or CD/DVD master. Apply encryption to the image file by choosing AES-128 from the Encryption pop-up menu. Click Save to copy an image of the device onto your hard drive.

TIP

Read-only images are a good way to distribute software because they do not allow any changes to be made to the image. This results in an image that cannot be modified or tainted and can always be assumed to be a working master copy.

The third way to create an image is to copy the contents of a folder or volume. This is the easiest means of building a disk image if you have all the files in a subfolder of your volume, or want to create an image of a mounted network share. It also results in a disk image that is unfragmented because it isn't based off a direct device copy.

Choose Images, New, Image from Folder; then use the Mac OS X file browser to pick the folder or volume that you want to use. As with the other two imaging methods, choose the image file and format when prompted, and click Save to create the disk image file.

Burning CDs

To burn a CD from within Disk Utility, you must have your CD writer connected and powered on. Select the Image you want to burn; then choose Images, Burn or click the Burn toolbar icon. If the image is suitable for CD burning, Disk Utility displays the dialog shown in Figure 3.62.

Click the disclosure pushbutton to choose the maximum speed you want to use during the burn process, along with whether you want to burn additional copies of the image, verify the burn, and eject or mount the disk after it has finished.

When you're satisfied with your settings, click the Burn button, and Disk Utility begins writing the CD.

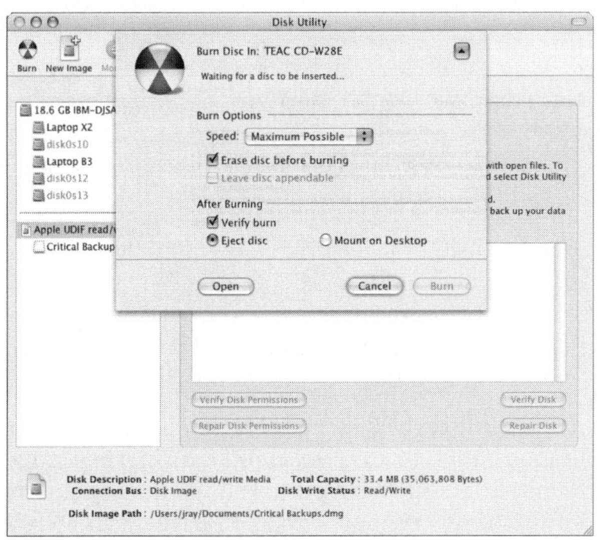

FIGURE 3.62 Insert a CD and click Burn.

Other Disk Image Operations

Using the Images menu, you can Verify disk images, Convert them to other formats (such as read/write to read-only), calculate checksums, and scan the image for restore. Scan the Image for Restore is a step required before using the image with the Restore feature of Disk Utility.

Disk Utility Menus

Although most options for Disk Utility are found in the toolbar or via controls in the various panes, two additional features are located in the File menu.

The first, File, Log, displays a log of the Disk Utility operation, including repairs, partitioning, and so on. The second—File, Fix OS 9 Permissions—can be used to solve permission problems that may cause OS 9 not to boot or function correctly. Choosing Fix OS 9 Permissions automatically fixes the permissions on the appropriate volume; you do not need to select a volume or partition first.

The Classic Environment

The Classic environment is a complete implementation of Mac OS 9.x on top of Mac OS X. To Mac OS X, Classic is nothing but another application; to a user, however, Classic is a gateway to his older software programs.

TIP

You must have at least 128MB of memory to use Classic, an installed copy of Mac OS 9.x, and a 400MHz G3 (or faster) is recommended. Because Mac OS 9.x no longer comes with Mac OS X, you must order it from Apple.

Classic is a process under Mac OS X. Mac OS X must be running for Classic to work. In essence, you're booting two operating systems simultaneously.

When using the Classic environment, the 9.x operating system must access all hardware through the Mac OS X kernel. This means that software that accesses hardware directly will likely fail. Users of 3Dfx video cards, hardware DVD playback, video capture cards, and even some CD writers will find that their hardware no longer functions correctly.

On the other hand, Classic brings the benefit of Mac OS X's virtual memory underpinnings to legacy applications. Each Mac OS 9.x application can be configured for a much larger memory partition than was possible previously. To the Classic environment, the virtual memory appears to be real memory. Programs have much more breathing room in which to function.

Working with the Classic environment is a somewhat unusual experience. Depending on the application running, there can be graphic anomalies and confusing filesystem navigation. This chapter shows what you'll see and what to do when things don't seem to work right.

Launching Classic

The Classic environment is typically launched once during a Mac OS X login session—either manually or automatically. After it is running, Classic remains active until you log out or manually force it to shut down.

NOTE

Classic does not gain all the stability features of Mac OS X, such as protected memory. If an application crashes in Classic, it can bring down all applications running in Classic. The Mac OS X system will be unaffected, but you might need to manually restart the Classic environment.

There are two ways to launch the Classic environment: by double-clicking a Classic application and through the Classic pane within System Preferences.

Classic applications appear to the Mac OS X Finder just like any other application. To verify that a piece of software is indeed a Classic application, you can select the icon and choose File, Get Info or choose Get Info from the contextual or action menus. Figure 3.63 shows the General Information pane for the Graphing Calculator, a Classic application.

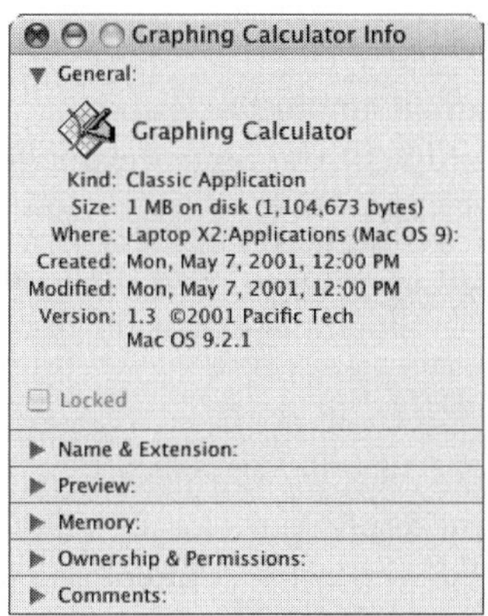

FIGURE 3.63 The General Information pane identifies Classic applications.

Memory Settings

Classic applications, because they still use the Mac OS 9.x Memory Manager, require a preferred and minimum memory size to be set. Because you have no direct access to the 9.2 Finder under OS X, Classic applications have an additional Get Info pane called Memory, as shown in Figure 3.64.

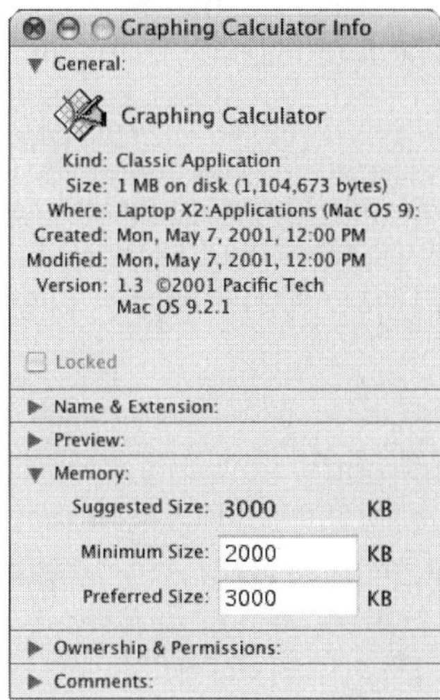

FIGURE 3.64 Classic applications allow memory limits to be set.

Two limits can be set:

- Minimum Size—The minimum amount of memory that an application must have to run. The Mac OS 9.x environment prohibits the application from launching unless the minimum memory size can be met.
- Preferred Size—The amount of memory that you want the application to have. This is the upper limit of the memory partition that will be requested from Mac OS 9.x.

To take advantage of the new Mac OS X memory architecture, set these values higher than you would in older versions of the Mac OS. If you do, be aware that your settings here will carry over if you boot directly into Mac OS 9.x, where you might not have as much real or virtual memory available.

Forcing Carbon Applications into Classic

Carbon applications are a special case of Mac OS X application. They are capable of running natively on Mac OS X, and on Mac OS 9.x through the use of CarbonLib. If you want to use the Classic environment to launch a Carbon application, a setting within the General pane of the Get Info pane can force a Carbon-compliant package to launch through Classic.

To launch a Carbon application in Classic, check the Open in the Classic Environment check box and then close the info pane. Double-clicking the application launches it in Classic rather than in Mac OS X until the box is manually unchecked.

Configuring Classic

If you have multiple Mac OS 9.x installations, or want to manually start or stop the Classic environment, you can do so from the Classic System Preferences pane. First, open System Preferences (path: `/Applications/System Preferences`) and then click the Classic icon.

Start/Stop

The Classic Preferences pane can control how and when Classic boots. As shown in Figure 3.65, the following options are found in the Start/Stop pane of the Classic pane:

- Select a Startup Volume for Classic—Mac OS X can start the Classic environment by booting any available Mac OS 9.x system. It is recommended that you use a separate drive or partition for Mac OS 9.x, as you will be able to boot to the Mac OS 9 partition, bypassing Mac OS X in case of an emergency.

- Start Classic When You Log In—If you want Classic to start up immediately after you log in to your computer (or immediately at startup, if you're using Mac OS X as a single-user system), click this button. Be warned; the Classic environment takes a few minutes to start, and your system performance will be degraded during this time.
- Hide Classic While Starting—The Classic startup window will be hidden while the Classic environment boots.
- Warn Before Starting Classic—Use this option to force Mac OS X to prompt you each time it launches the Classic environment. If you find yourself accidentally starting Classic by double-clicking legacy files, and so on, this can be helpful.
- Show Classic Status in Menu Bar—Adds a menu extra, shown in Figure 3.66, that can start and stop Classic and provides access to the Classic Apple menu items.
- Start/Stop—Click the Start button to launch Classic manually or Stop to shut it down.
- Restart—Is equivalent to choosing Restart from the Mac OS 9.x Finder. Open applications prompt you to save open documents and then exit. The Classic environment will reboot.
- Force Quit—If Classic becomes unresponsive (that is, it crashes), the only option is to force it to quit. Open documents are lost, exactly as if Mac OS 9.x crashed (as it tends to do from time to time). You can also use the Control-Option-Escape keystroke to force it to quit.

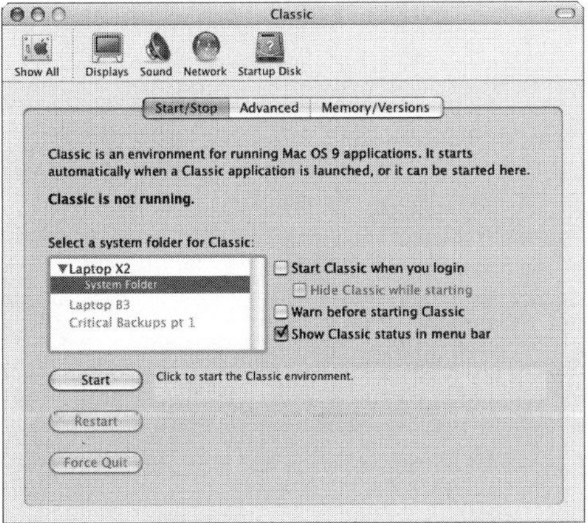

FIGURE 3.65 The Classic System Preferences pane configures the startup volume and allows manual startup and shutdown.

FIGURE 3.66 The Classic menu extra provides feedback on the status of Classic as well as provides controls for stopping/starting and restarting the environment.

Advanced Settings

Use the advanced startup options to provide control over the boot sequence and basic Classic operation. Figure 3.67 shows this pane.

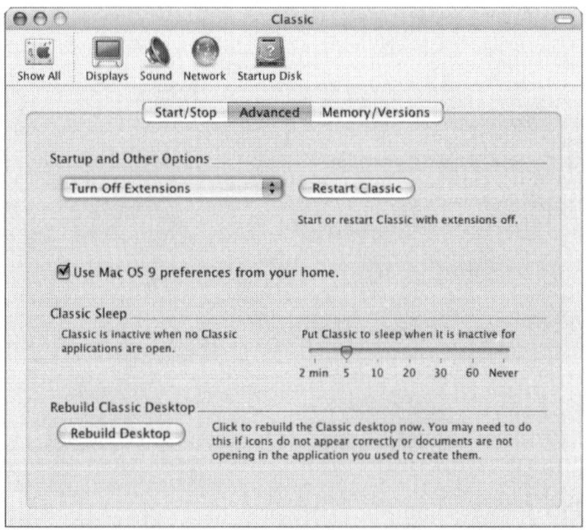

FIGURE 3.67 Advanced settings control the boot and runtime features of Classic.

You can make four modifications to the startup process:

- Turn Off Extensions—Turning off the extensions is the equivalent of pressing Shift while booting into Mac OS 8 or 9. This prohibits additional control panels and extensions—beyond those needed by the 9.2 operating system—from loading.
- Open Extensions Manager—This opens the Mac OS 9.x Extensions Manager control panel during the boot process, allowing you to disable extensions that appear to be causing system instability.
- Use Key Combination—This unusual option enables the user to choose up to five keys that will be kept in pressed state while Classic boots. Some extensions can be individually disabled by certain keystrokes; this feature lets you target those processes.
- Use Mac OS 9 Preferences from Your Home—If selected, Classic maintains a separate set of preferences for your account. If unchecked, a systemwide preferences location is used.

After choosing your startup options, click the Start or Restart button to implement the selection.

NOTE

The first time you boot Classic, the advanced options will not be available. Subsequent executions will enable all the advanced features.

Apple has also kindly included two features in the Advanced pane that help fix a common problem and speed up overall system functions—the ability to rebuild the desktop and put Classic to sleep if it is inactive:

- Put Classic to Sleep When It Is Inactive For—When Classic is running, it is using your system resources. The Classic environment continues to use CPU time even if you aren't running a Classic application. This is because Mac OS 9.x must keep up the basic system maintenance and monitoring processes that happen behind the scenes. If you choose to put Classic to sleep, it stops using these resources after the length of time you choose.
- Rebuild Desktop—Rebuilding the Mac OS 9.x desktop can help solve "generic icon" problems (files that should have custom icons show up as generic white icons in the Finder), as well as issues with documents that can't find the appropriate Classic application to open them. If your Classic environment starts to act in unusual ways, rebuilding the desktop is a good place to start.

TIP

Classic functions best when it is used as a means of accessing legacy applications and data. You should maintain as minimal a system software installation as possible. Extensions and control panels that are not needed should be removed. If possible, use the Open Extensions Manager startup option to choose one of the base extension sets from within the Extensions Manager and stick with it.

Memory/Versions

With Classic running, the Memory/Versions pane displays the processes that are active and how much memory they are consuming, as shown in Figure 3.68.

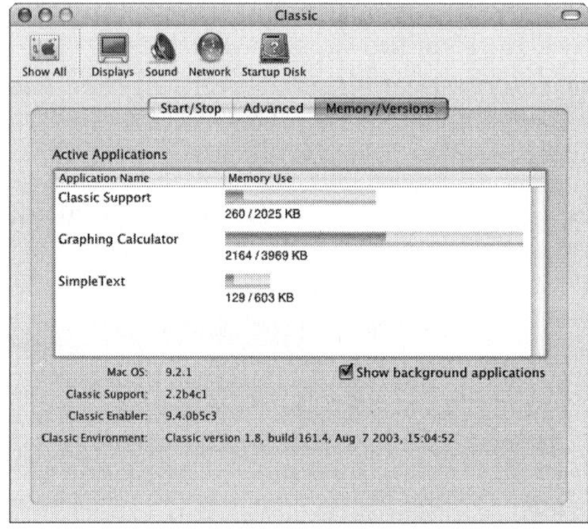

FIGURE 3.68 The Memory/Versions pane gives feedback on active Classic processes.

To display information about background Classic processes, click the Show Background Processes check box. Information about the version of Classic and its supporting software is displayed at the bottom of the pane.

Direct Booting Mac OS 9.x

To boot directly into Mac OS 9.x, use the Startup Disk System Preferences pane, shown in Figure 3.69.

After searching the mounted disks (this can take a while) for viable systems, each of the accessible system folders is listed in the Startup Disk pane. Each icon lists the OS version and volume name. To select one, click the icon; a status message appears at the bottom of the screen describing your choice.

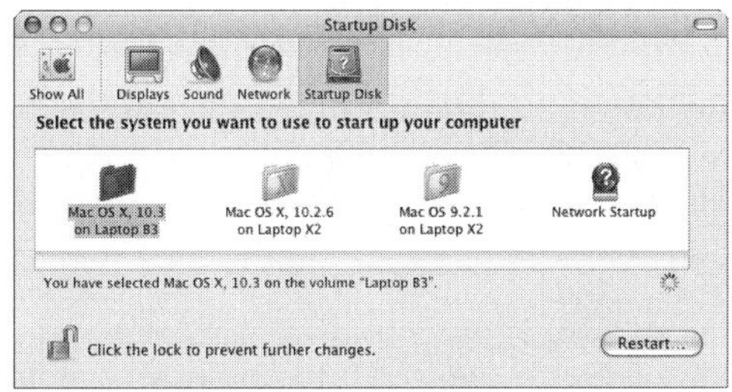

FIGURE 3.69 Boot directly into Mac OS 9.x using the Startup Disk pane.

Quit the System Preferences application when you're finished or click Restart. The next time your computer boots, it boots into the operating system you selected.

Booting into OS X

To switch back to OS X after running 9.2, you follow a similar process as switching from Mac OS X to Mac OS 9. From the Apple menu, choose Control Panels; then select and open the Startup Disk control panel.

Each mounted disk is displayed on a line in the control panel. Disks that include a bootable system folder have a disclosure arrow directly in front of them. Clicking the disclosure arrow displays the operating systems located on that disk, along with their path and version.

To boot into OS X, highlight the OS X installation within the list and then click the Restart button in the lower-right corner. If you don't want to restart immediately, close the control panel. The next time the system restarts, it boots into the selected system.

TIP

Advanced users may want to use the `bless` command, which chooses what folders can (and should) boot your computer. In short, on a two-partition system, `bless` can be invoked like this to set your Mac's OpenFirmware to boot from OS 9:

```
sudo /usr/sbin/bless/
Â-folder9 '/Volumes/<path to Mac OS 9 System Folder>' -setOF
Or, from Mac OS X:

sudo /usr/sbin/bless/ -folder '/System/Library/CoreServices' -setOF
```

Familiarize yourself with the command line (see Chapter 12) and read the `bless` man page before attempting to use the command.

TIP

One final alternative means of choosing your startup devices is to hold down Option when restarting your computer. The boot manager built into your Macintosh firmware will load, displaying all recognized boot devices.

Ink

Panther includes a handwriting recognition feature called Ink, which allows you to provide text input to any application by writing rather than typing. Built on Apple's Recognition Engine (originally the Newton Recognition Engine), Ink requires no special "graffiti" alphabet—though people with messy handwriting may require practice to understand how Ink interprets characters.

When a recognized graphics tablet is plugged into one of your computer's USB ports, an icon called Ink shows up under the Hardware section of the System Preferences. The Ink preferences pane, shown in Figure 3.70, gives you the option to turn handwriting recognition on or off and to change several settings.

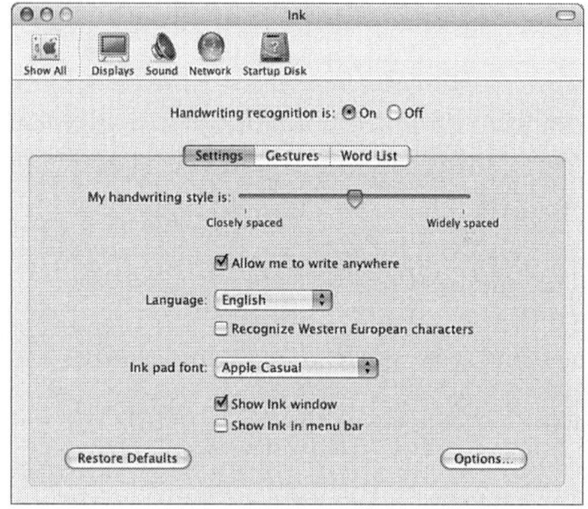

FIGURE 3.70 Ink allows you to set your keyboard and mouse aside.

Turning on handwriting recognition launches the InkBar, a toolbar that floats on top of all other application windows. From the InkBar, you can toggle between handwriting recognition mode and pointer mode, select common menu commands and keyboard shortcut characters (Command, Shift, Option, Control), or open the InkPad, as shown in Figure 3.71. With the Inkpad open, you can switch between the writing and drawing modes using the buttons at the lower left.

The text or drawings you create in the InkPad can be inserted into other documents. Simply create the content of your choice in the workspace and click the Send button to add it to the active document at the current insertion point. For example, when finished typing a message in Mail, you could sign your name in the drawing view of the InkPad and insert your signature at the bottom of your message. Obviously, the application must support graphics input to accept graphic images.

FIGURE 3.71 The InkPad appears below the InkBar to provide a space for you to write or draw.

Although InkPad lets you compose your additions before you add them to a document, you can also write directly into a program. To add text directly to an application, touch the stylus to the tablet to open a writing space with guiding lines and begin writing words. If a writing space doesn't appear, try touching the stylus to the graphics tablet in a different place. Your stylus can also act as a mouse, so some areas of the screen, such as window controls or menus, activate commands instead of opening a writing space.

Ink doesn't require you to learn special letter forms, but you must write linearly as if you were using paper rather than write overlapping letters as you would on a PDA. When you pause, your markings will be converted to text at the top of the writing space. To correct a mistake, draw a long horizontal line from right to left, and the last character disappears. If you have larger sections to delete, switch to the pointer mode in the InkBar, select the part you want to redo, and switch back to writing mode to try again.

NOTE

Some applications that don't use standard OS X text controls behave unpredictably with Ink's text recognition. If you are using an application in which spaces don't appear between words as needed, try writing your content in the Inkpad and use Send to insert it in the other application.

Ink Preferences

Ink's preferences can be changed to suit individual users' writing styles and increase reliability. The following adjustments can be made under the Settings pane:

- Allow Me to Write—Choose whether you can write within all programs or only the InkPad.
- My Handwriting Style Is—Move the slider to describe your handwriting as closely spaced, widely spaced, or somewhere in between.
- InkPad Font—Set a font for InkPad. For greatest accuracy, Apple recommends keeping the font set to Apple Casual, which contains letter shapes that are the most similar to those recognized by Ink, so that you can model your writing after it.
- Play Sound While Writing—Check this box to activate the sound of pen scratching against paper while you write.

Clicking the Options button opens a sheet with additional handwriting recognition options, including the amount of delay before writing is converted to type, how much the stylus must move before a stroke is recorded, how long the pen must be held still to act as a mouse, whether the pointer should be hidden while writing, and whether to recognize Western European characters. If you change your mind about configurations you've made in either the Settings tab or the Options sheet, choose Restore Defaults to revert to the originals.

The Gestures pane displays shapes that have special meaning in Ink, such as vertical or horizontal spaces, Tab, and Delete. Click on an item to see both a demonstration of drawing the shape and a written description of it. You can also activate or deactivate Gesture actions using the check box in front of each item. Note that Apple recommends you provide extra space in front of Gesture shapes and exaggerate the ending stroke so that the system does not confuse them with letters.

The Word List pane allows you to add uncommon words that you use frequently. Ink uses a list of common words to help decipher people's input. If you come across a word that Ink doesn't know, click the Add button and type it in the text box.

The Bluetooth Suite

Bluetooth is an emerging wireless technology that allows you to form a wireless *PAN—Personal Area Network*. Using this wireless network, you can synchronize PDAs, connect to the Internet through your cell phone, print to printers, use Apple's wireless keyboard and mouse, and so on. Although Bluetooth *is* an accepted standard, few devices currently use it, and not all Macintosh systems come with Bluetooth enabled. If you're interested in Bluetooth, you can purchase a Bluetooth USB dongle for about $40 that will Bluetooth-enable your Mac.

NOTE

Most third-party USB Bluetooth transceivers work just fine on Panther. Even Microsoft's Bluetooth adapter is recognized without a hitch.

Panther comes with a suite of Bluetooth tools, including a System Preferences pane, menu extra, File Exchange utility, Bluetooth serial utility, and Bluetooth Setup Assistant. Although this may seem like a lot of support software just to use a wireless mouse, it isn't as convoluted as it might seem. You should be familiar with two basic terms to use Bluetooth devices:

- Discoverable—A device is considered *discoverable* if it can be "seen" on a Bluetooth network. Nondiscoverable devices are hidden from other Bluetooth devices.
- Pairing—To speak to a Bluetooth device, your computer must be *paired* with it. This prevents any random person from walking into a room with a Bluetooth device and using it to access your computer. Pairing often, but not always, requires a password to be entered on the computer and the device connecting to it.

With that knowledge, and a compatible Bluetooth adapter, you're ready to get started.

Bluetooth System Preferences

After plugging a Bluetooth transceiver into your computer, Panther displays a new Bluetooth System Preferences pane, as shown in Figure 3.72.

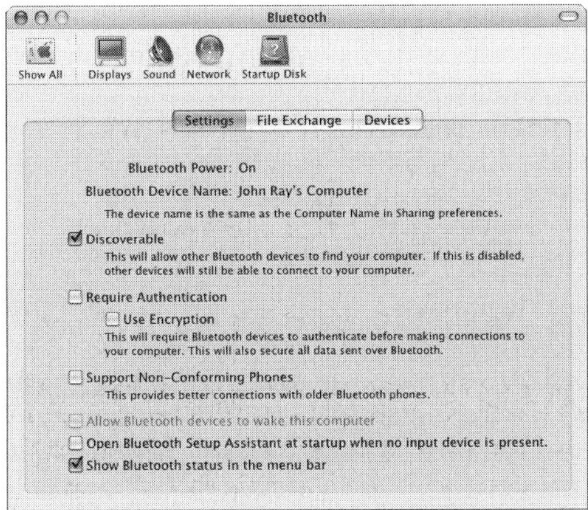

FIGURE 3.72 The Bluetooth System Preferences provide control over your wireless devices.

Settings

Three panes are used to control Bluetooth operation. The first pane, Settings, is shown in Figure 3.72. Here you can see the status of your Bluetooth adapter and make changes to your first Bluetooth device—your Macintosh. After your Macintosh has an adapter plugged in, it becomes simply another Bluetooth device on your network. It can speak to other devices, and they, in turn, can speak to it. That being the case, you may want to adjust the discoverability and authentication requirements to keep unauthorized users from seeing or pairing with your computer.

- Discoverable—Enables other Bluetooth devices to see your computer on the Bluetooth network. They can, quite literally, browse to your computer. If unchecked, your machine will be invisible to other devices.
- Require Authentication—Enable this setting to require other devices to authenticate with your computer before pairing. Click the Use Encryption check box to force authentication transmissions to be encrypted.

Although these are the primary settings for how your computer presents itself on the Bluetooth network, a few additional settings aid in device compatibility and setup:

- Support Non-conforming Phones—When checked, Panther supports earlier Bluetooth-enabled phones that do not conform to the current spec. If you have trouble pairing your phone, try using this setting.
- Allow Bluetooth Devices to Wake This Computer—If enabled and supported by your system, external devices will be able to wake your computer from sleep.
- Open Setup Assistant at Startup When No Input Device Is Present—If Bluetooth is enabled but no input device is paired with your computer, this setting causes the setup assistant to run automatically.
- Show Bluetooth Status in the Menu Bar—Adds a menu extra that can be used to quickly access many of the Panther Bluetooth settings.

File Exchange

The next pane, Bluetooth File Exchange (shown in Figure 3.73), is used to configure how your computer exchanges files with other Bluetooth devices. Although not quite the equivalent of File Sharing between Macs, Bluetooth File Exchange allows simple point and click file transfers between active paired devices.

The first set of preferences control what happens when a Bluetooth device transfers files *to* you. You can force it to prompt for each item, or refuse them altogether. PIM (Personal Information Manager (that is, PDA) items and other recognized data formats can be set to simply save the information, ask (the default) what to do, or automatically open it with a helper application. Use the Choose Folder button to select a folder that contains the items transferred to your computer.

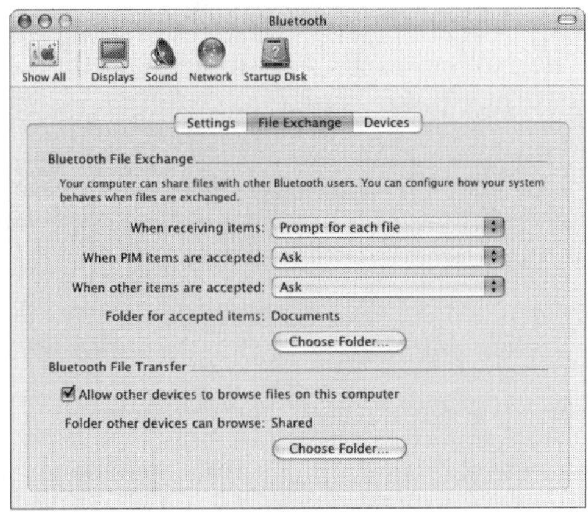

FIGURE 3.73 Set up how your Macintosh handles Bluetooth file sharing.

To allow other devices to transfer files *from* your machine, enable the Allow Other Devices to Browse Files on This Computer check box. You can use the Choose Folder button to limit their browsing to a single folder (by default, the Shared folder).

Devices

The Devices pane, shown in Figure 3.74, is the control center for pairing Bluetooth devices with your machine.

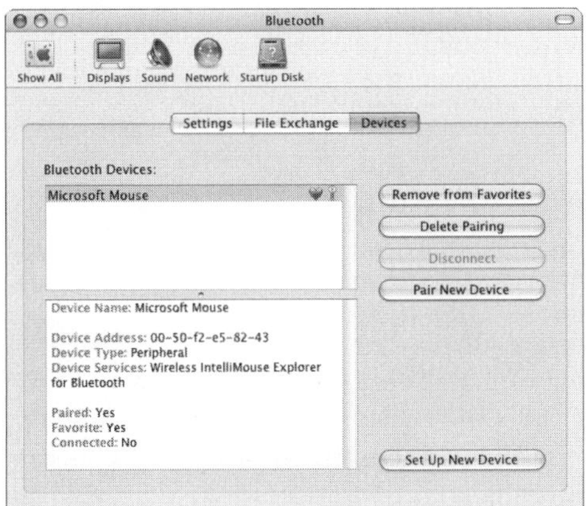

FIGURE 3.74 Use the Devices pane to connect Bluetooth devices to your computer.

In the upper-left corner of the pane is a list of Bluetooth devices paired with your computer. Below the list is a detailed display showing information about the selected device. To the right of the selected device are five buttons used to control the device pairings:

- Add to Favorites/Remove from Favorites— Toggles the device as a "favorite."
- Delete Pairing—Removes a device from your list of known Bluetooth devices, effectively causing Panther to forget about it.
- Disconnect—Disconnects a device but does not delete the pairing. Depending on the device (such as mouse), simply using it again causes it to reconnect.
- Pair New Device—Sets up a new device on your system.
- Set Up New Device—Does the same thing as Pair New Device but uses the Bluetooth Setup Assistant (path: `/Applications/Utilities/Bluetooth Setup Assistant`), which offers a "friendlier" approach to configuration.

Adding a New Device

To add a new device, you have two options: use the Setup Assistant, or click Pair New Device in the Devices pane of the Bluetooth System Preferences pane. Both setup processes are virtually identical. If you prefer the "wizard" approach to configuration, use the assistant; otherwise, you'll probably find that Pair New Device is slightly faster and more straightforward.

Clicking Pair New Device opens the Pair with Bluetooth Device window, shown in Figure 3.75.

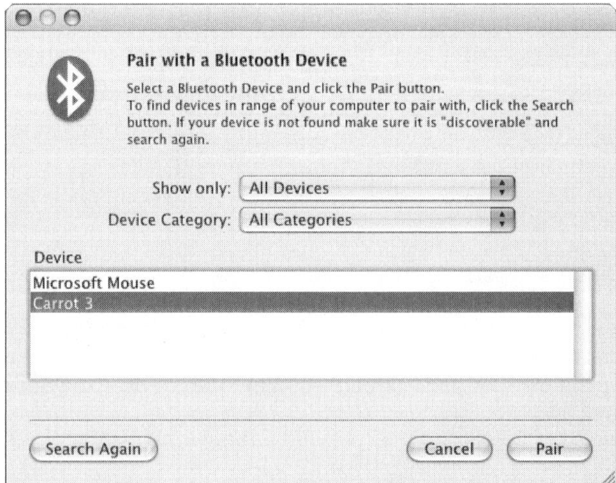

FIGURE 3.75 Set up new Bluetooth connections using the Pair New Device option.

Use the first pull-down menu to choose the type of device you're connecting to. If you aren't sure, it's safe just to leave All Devices selected. Next, choose the Device Category. You can choose to display only discovered devices, favorite devices, or devices you've used recently.

> **NOTE**
>
> Notice that you have the option of pairing with *favorite* devices. This means that you've previously used the device and marked it as a favorite. If this is the case, you can disable discoverability on the device and still pair with it.

If your Bluetooth devices are set as discoverable, or they match one of the other two categories (used recently or marked as a favorite), they appear in the list at the bottom of the window. If not, click the Search Again button.

Finally, choose the device you want to pair with; then click the Pair button.

Passkey

If prompted, enter a passkey to connect to the device, as shown in Figure 3.76. This is a key shared between your computer and the paired device. In many cases, you are prompted to enter this key on the device *after* you enter it on your computer.

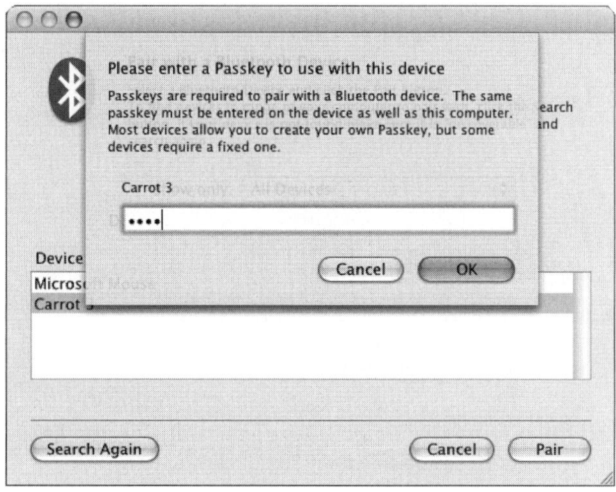

FIGURE 3.76 Passkeys are used to authoritatively pair two devices.

If the passkey is accepted, the device is considered paired and should be listed in the Devices pane of the Bluetooth System Preferences pane.

Bluetooth File Exchange

So, you've paired a device, now what can you do with it? If you've paired a phone, you can now use Address Book to make and receive phone calls directly from address cards. What the device does is, well, dependant on the device you're using! A common feature supported by PDAs and other computing devices is File Exchange. Using the File Exchange, you can browse and transfer files to a Bluetooth device, much like using a simple FTP client.

To use the Bluetooth File Exchange program (path: `/Applications/Utilities/BlueTooth File Exchange`), pair with the device you want to transfer files to/from; then start the File Exchange application either from the Utilities folder or from the Bluetooth menu extra.

Sending Files

To send a file to a device, use File, Send File (Command-O). Panther displays a dialog box enabling you to choose a file; then prompts you for the device that the file should be sent to, as shown in Figure 3.77.

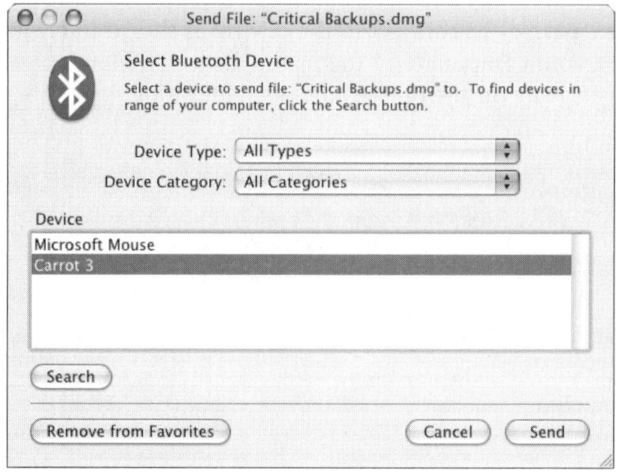

FIGURE 3.77 Choose the device that will receive the file.

Finally, click Send. If the remote device authorizes the transfer, the file will be sent.

Browsing Files

Another option for transferring files is to choose File, Browse files within the BlueTooth File Exchange application. Again you are prompted for the device you want to connect to (much like Figure 3.77). When selected, however, a file transfer screen appears, similar to Figure 3.78.

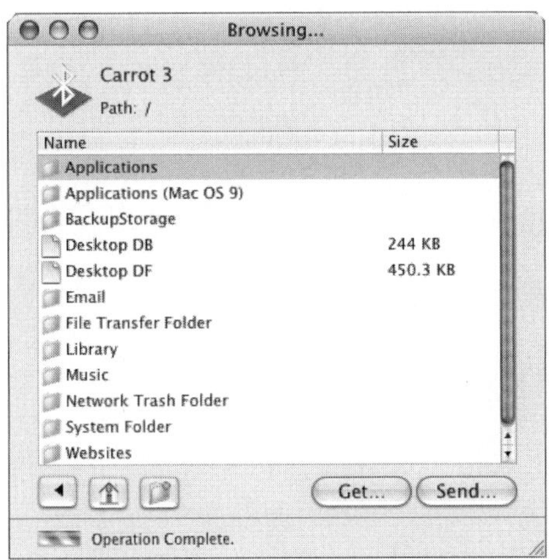

FIGURE 3.78 Use the file transfer window to get and send files to or from the remote device.

Navigate through the file listing as you would in the Finder. Using the three buttons in the lower-left corner of the window, you can move to previous folders, jump to the "top" level (the "house" icon), or create a new folder.

To retrieve a file, double-click it in the list, or highlight it and then click the Get button. You can select multiple files with Command or entire folders if you want.

To send a file, click the Send button; then choose the file you want to send.

To log off the device, simply close the file transfer window.

> **NOTE**
>
> If you commonly find yourself sending or browsing files, you can set Bluetooth File Exchange to default to one of these modes using the application preferences.

Bluetooth Keyboards and Mice

In the late betas of Panther (and presumably in the version you're using too), Apple has added a Bluetooth pane to the Keyboard and Mouse preferences pane. This pane, shown in Figure 3.79, provides status on the battery level of your Apple wireless keyboard and mouse.

Currently, this pane shows only the status for Apple devices, but this may change in the future. To set up a new device from this pane, click the Set Up New Device button. This launches the Bluetooth Setup Assistant.

FIGURE 3.79 Use the Bluetooth pane of the Keyboard and Mouse pane to monitor your Apple wireless device battery levels.

Bluetooth Serial Utility

Devices that require serial access, such as a PDA or cell phone require a Bluetooth serial port to be created to communicate with your system. The Bluetooth Serial Utility (path: `/Applications/Utilities/Bluetooth Serial Utility`) can be used to add a port to your system that is associated with a specific device.

The default Bluetooth Serial Utility opens to a list of the configured ports, as shown in Figure 3.80.

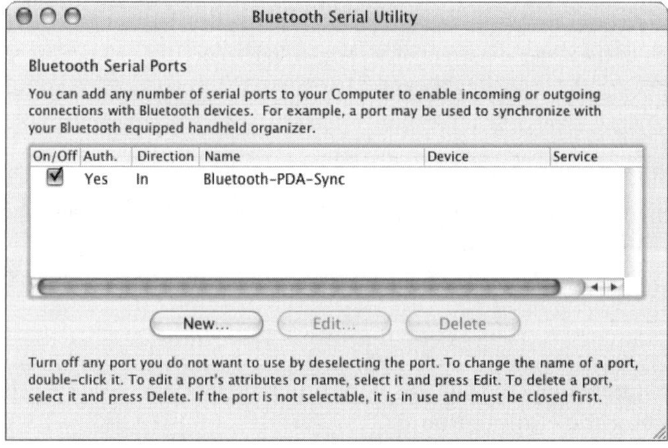

FIGURE 3.80 The Serial Utility displays the configured ports on your system.

Use the New, Edit, and Delete buttons to modify the ports configured on the machine. For example, to add a port for a cell phone that your computer will use as a modem, click the Add button. A configuration window appears, as in Figure 3.81.

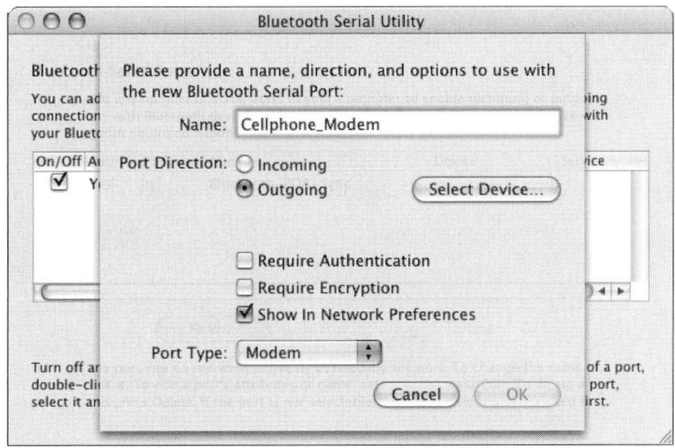

FIGURE 3.81 You can add serial ports associated with a given device.

Choose a name for the device, such as "Cellphone_modem"; next choose the port directory. The Incoming port is for connections being made *to* your computer, whereas Outgoing is used when your computer connects to the device. Because your computer needs to connect *to* the cell phone, choose Outgoing.

Next, click the Select Device button to choose the device you are connecting to. If you require authentication or encryption to use the port, use the check boxes to choose those options.

Because this example connection is for a modem, click the Show In Network Preferences, check box. This adds the port to your Network System Preferences pane, where it can be configured like any other modem.

Finally, choose the Modem port type. If the device is *not* a modem, you would simply choose RS 232—an industry standard serial port.

Finally, click OK, and your serial port will be configured.

Other Tools and Utilities

Mac OS X includes a few other tools and toys that you might be interested in using. These aren't covered in detail because of the nature of the tools. If you've used a computer, you'll be familiar enough with these applications that you'll be right at home.

- Calculator (path: `/Applications/Calculator`)—The Mac OS X calculator has both simple and scientific modes, a paper-tape display, and numerous conversion features, including a currency converter that updates exchange rates via the Internet.

- Stickies (path: `/Applications/Stickies`)—The classic Stickies application allows you to jot down brief notes and "attach" them to your screen.
- TextEdit (path: `/Applications/TextEdit`)—TextEdit is a styled text editor capable of opening, editing, and saving RTF and Word documents. TextEdit is also capable of plain text editing, so it can be used to modify Unix configuration files.
- Grab (path: `/Applications/Utilities/Grab`)—A screenshot utility that allows users to take timed screenshots.
- DigitalColor Meter (path: `/Applications/Utilities/DigitalColor Meter`)—The DigitalColor Meter utility allows you to sample onscreen colors and display their representation in a variety of color spaces, including HTML-ready Hex RGB.
- Chess (path: `/Applications/Chess`)—Last but not least, the 3D Chess application, shown in Figure 3.82 provides an intellectually stimulating gaming experience on your Mac. When your Windows friends are playing Solitaire, show them a real game. Although based on GNUChess, Apple provides a beautiful 3D interface to the classic Unix game.

FIGURE 3.82 Panther's Chess application is a thing of beauty.

Summary

This chapter covered the applications and utilities in Mac OS X that, although useful, are difficult to catalog into a specific category and too small to warrant a chapter of their own. There's plenty here to keep you busy—from building your contact library in Address Book to connecting Bluetooth devices to your computer. The applications and utilities contained in this chapter will be useful as you make your way through the rest of the book.

CHAPTER 4

Internet Applications

IN THIS CHAPTER

- Safari
- Mail
- Importing Mailboxes
- iChat AV
- Sherlock
- .Mac

The Mac OS has long been the leader in network connectivity among desktop operating systems. The Macintosh was using MacTCP and Open Transport while Windows 3.1 struggled to get online using third-party TCP stacks and DOS-based network card drivers. Although the playing field has mostly leveled, it's little surprise that Mac OS X includes a wide variety of Internet-related tools. Users who are interested in getting online, finding old friends, chatting with others, sending email, and surfing the Internet will be happy to find many applications to get them online in a matter of minutes.

Mac OS X comes with a number of network-enabled programs. This chapter covers the applications that work specifically with the Internet to gather information, send and receive messages, and make your online life easier:

- Safari (path: `/Applications/Safari`)—Apple's new Web browser based on open source technologies.
- Mail (path: `/Applications/Mail`)—Apple's first email offering since the delightful (and deceased) Cyberdog project (unless you count Claris Emailer). This email application features IMAP/POP3 support, HTML/RTF email, dynamic filtering, spam protection, and a frightfully modern interface.
- iChat AV (path: `/Applications/iChat`)—A chat program compatible with AOL Instant Messenger (AIM), provides Audio and Video conferences, and integrates with .Mac, Mail, and Address Book.
- Sherlock (path: `/Applications/Sherlock`)—Sherlock provides multisearch engine queries on popular e-commerce, news, and entertainment sites and returns results without the need for a Web browser.
- .Mac—Apple's pay-for Internet service for bringing Mac OS X with you, wherever you may be.

As with the previous chapters, the applications discussed here are presented with basic use information, followed by configuration and menu options. The goal is to provide information for beginners as well as useful reference for advanced users.

TIP

The assumption is that you already have a working network connection configured at installation or in your previous version of Mac OS X. For information on setting up an Internet connection, see Chapter 9, "Network Setup."

Safari

Many people purchase computers just to access information over the Internet. The iMac, in fact, was introduced as the "Internet" Mac. Although it has taken its place as a valuable home computer, the target audience was originally those who wanted to get online in two easy steps (there is no step three!).

Unfortunately, Apple's "Internet Experience" has been tied to Internet Explorer for the last few years. Although a capable browser, IE is *not* fast, sports a less-than-beautiful user interface, and has this annoying habit of not actually drawing Web pages until you resize the window.

In January 2003, Apple introduced Safari, a new, *fast* browser for Mac OS X. Safari is based on the `khtml` engine—part of the popular KDE (usually associated with Linux) project. Safari is fast, simple, Mac-like, and not a product of Microsoft.

The Safari Interface

Figure 4.1 shows the Safari interface, with all available interface options "on" (this is *not* the default state.). Most interface elements are turned on and off under the View menu with the exception of Tabs—a popular feature in alternative Web browsers (such as Safari) that allow multiple Web pages to be viewed in single window. If you've used a Web browser before, you might want to skip this section because it will likely be review. We've had many readers ask for a more tutorial approach for Mac OS X novices, however, so the information is included for their benefit.

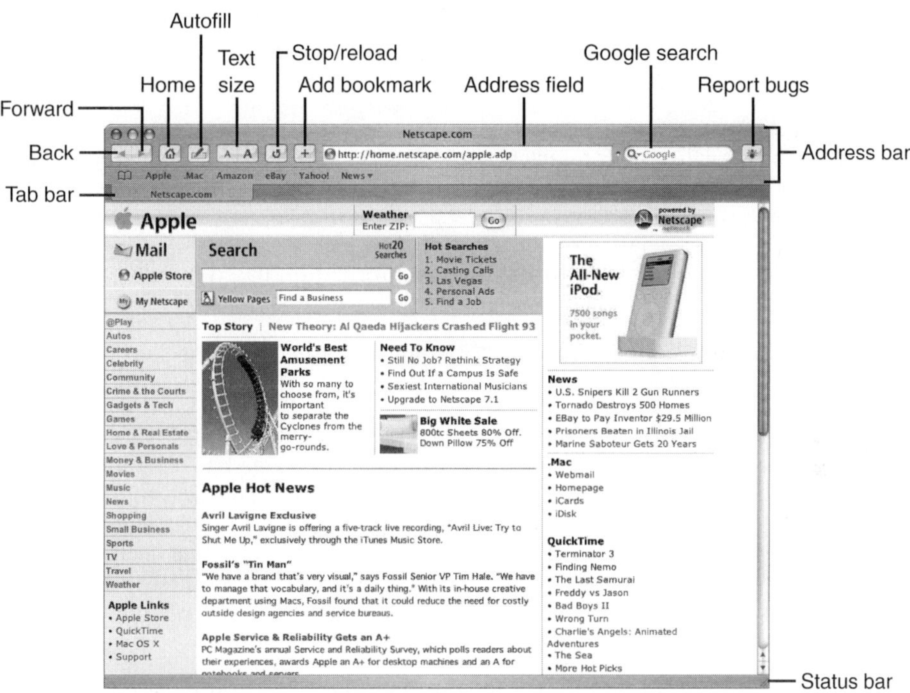

FIGURE 4.1 Apple's Safari Web browser with a "typical" set of interface options.

Address Bar

The top row of controls in the Safari window is the address bar. It contains the controls you use to navigate Web sites.

- The Back and Forward buttons work together. Use the Back button to return to the Web page you viewed previously. After you've gone back, you can use the Forward button to move ahead to where you were. If you haven't gone back through any pages you've already viewed, the Forward button is grayed out to show that it is not an active option at the current time.

> **TIP**
>
> Clicking and holding on a forward or backward arrow shows a list of pages that you've visited either in "front" of (since) or behind (before) your current page.

- The Home button returns you to the page set as your default startup page. Think of it as a shortcut for connecting to a site you visit frequently.

NOTE

To change the page that comes up automatically when Safari is launched, use the General pane of the Application preferences.

- The Autofill button attempts to fill in form information based on your Address Book entries and forms that you've completed previously in Safari.
- The Text Size button allows you to easily increase or decrease the font size in the current page.
- The Stop/Reload button changes depending on whether the current page identified in the address field has been loaded, or is loading. If a page has been loaded, you see the Reload button, which allows you to refresh the page. The Stop button appears as a page is loading to allow you to stop retrieving the current page.
- Clicking the Add Bookmark button, which looks like a "+", adds the current page to your bookmark list so that you can easily visit it again without writing down the address. We'll discuss Bookmarks more later in this section.
- The address field is where you provide the URL of the site you want to browse. Safari also uses the address field as a status bar to indicate how much of a page has loaded. As a page is read into Safari, a blue-shaded bar moves from left to right across the address field as information is received.
- The Google Search field allows you to type a word or phrase of interest and search the Google search engine for relevant sites. The results listing appears in your browser window. This is simply a shortcut for visiting `http://www.google.com/`.
- The Bug button was included to allow people to report any problems they experience in viewing pages. If a page fails to load in Safari, clicking this button allows you to submit an error report to Apple.

Bookmarks Bar

The Bookmarks bar holds shortcuts to sites you want to keep close at hand—think of it as a Dock for bookmarks.

You can add sites to the Bookmarks bar by dragging the icon in front of the URL in the address field into the Bookmarks bar. A dialog appears, allowing you to enter a more intelligible name than "eBay item #442231." Remove Bookmarks bar shortcuts by Command-dragging them outside the Safari window. If you drag within the Bookmarks bar area, you can rearrange them.

As the Bookmarks bar grows beyond the size of the Safari window (trust me, it will) or the window is resized so that your existing bookmarks don't fit, Safari adds the ">>" icon to the end of the Bookmarks bar (just like the Finder and other applications). Clicking and holding on this icon displays the hidden shortcuts in a list.

A special "permanent" and nonmovable shortcut called Show All Bookmarks within the Bookmarks bar resembles a book. This icon opens the Bookmark Manager, which provides *extensive* control over your Safari bookmarks.

TIP

In some of the Apple-supplied default Bookmarks bar shortcuts you may notice entries with a down arrow after their name. These are called *collections* and can only be added to the Bookmarks bar through the Bookmarks Library.

Tab Bar

Tabs are an option in Safari that allows you to have several Web pages open at one time without all the clutter of extra browser windows. Tabs have become a popular feature largely through the development of the Mozilla and Opera browsers. Safari borrows a page from both of these popular alternative browser platforms. Tabs must be activated through the Tabs pane of the application preferences.

Status Bar

The status bar, located at the bottom of the Safari window, displays information about a page as it loads—whether it has contacted the remote host, how many elements (such as images) of the page have been retrieved, and so on.

The status bar also provides information about hyperlinked elements on a page as you move your mouse cursor across them. For example, if you run your mouse across a text link or a linked image, the address of the link appears.

A Browsing Session in Safari

Now that you know what the parts of the Safari interface can do, let's do some Web browsing.

Loading and Navigating a Site

To visit a Web site for which you know the address, type the address in the address field in the Address bar and press Return on your keyboard. You see a blue-shaded bar move across the address field as the page loads and, if you've chosen to view the Status Bar, a count-down of the page elements that are loading.

NOTE

Web pages aren't a single object. Typically, they are composed of a page file and separate image files. (In some cases, there may be additional supporting files containing page content or formatting information as well.) The countdown in the status bar as a page loads tells you just how many files it requires!

When a page has loaded, you can click text links or linked images or buttons to move to other pages, or click in the address field to type a new address.

TIP

Web sites don't always work. If you try to visit a site and receive a "Server Not Found" message, the problem is not likely to be Safari. Such a message occurs when there are technical difficulties for the computer hosting the Web site or when a site is no longer available. Your best option is to double-check the address you've entered. If the address is correct, you may need to wait before trying the site again, in case there's some kind of temporary site outage. If the site doesn't return, you may want to try a Google search on the name of the site to see whether a "cached" version of the content is still available.

If you're looking for a site that you know was available at *some* time but appears to have vanished off the face of the earth, you may want to try the WayBack Machine at `http://www.archive.org` to retrieve an archived copy.

Address Autocompletion

If you begin to type in an address you've visited recently, Safari tries to autocomplete it. A drop-down menu of addresses for pages you've been to that match what you've typed so far appears; Safari's best guess of which address you're typing is highlighted in blue. If the page you want to view is listed in the drop-down menu, use your arrow keys or mouse cursor to select it. If it isn't listed, continue to type the rest of the address in the address field.

Form AutoFill

As you enter data in forms within Safari, you're creating a database that can be used to automatically fill in the contents of similar forms, hopefully saving you some typing.

By default, Safari completes a form if it is recognized. To control Form AutoFill for unknown forms, enable the AutoFill button in the address bar. Clicking the AutoFill button (Shift-Command-A) forces Safari to fill in a form to the best of its ability. You'll also notice that much like address autocompletion, Safari attempts to fill in individual form fields as you type.

If you resubmit a form that Safari has already stored, Safari may prompt you whether to keep the old values or replace them with the new entries—or do nothing at all.

To control where Safari pulls the data for Form AutoFill, open the application preferences and click the AutoFill icon to open the AutoFill preferences pane, shown in Figure 4.2.

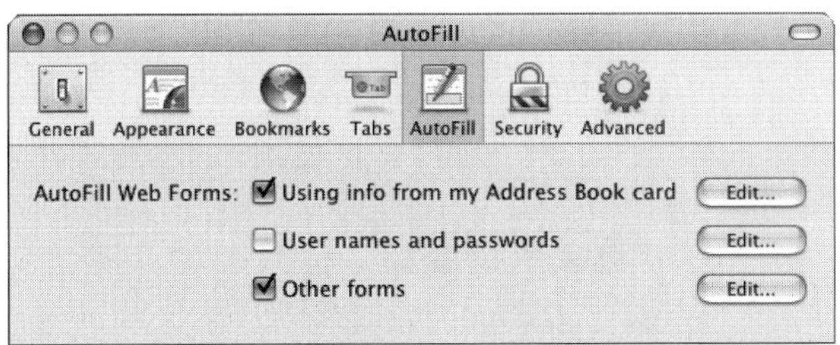

FIGURE 4.2 Choose where Safari AutoFill data comes from.

There are three sources for AutoFill data: Address Book (addresses, phone numbers, and such), usernames and passwords (names and passwords you've used to log in to Web sites), and other forms (any form you've filled in on a Web site).

Beside each of these options is an Edit button. Clicking Edit opens a window to display what username/passwords have been stored and what Web domains have forms saved (or, in the case of the Address Book, it opens the Address Book). You can select elements in these lists and remove them if they contain elements that you'd rather not use for AutoFill or that contain inaccurate data.

SnapBack

As you use Safari, you may notice an icon displaying a "return" arrow in an orange circle at the far-right side of the address field and Google field. Apple has dubbed this the "SnapBack" button. It appears in any page you navigate to through links within other Web pages. If clicked (or Option-Command-P is pressed), the SnapBack button takes you back to the last address you physically typed in the address field.

You can also manually set a page to be the one to which Snap-Back returns. Choose History, Mark Page for SnapBack from the menu (Command-Option-M). This is a convenient way to mark a specific page while you continue to following links.

NOTE

Google searches executed using the Google field in Safari automatically enable SnapBack. Just click the Snap-Back icon at the right end of the Google field or press (Option-Command-S)

Tabs

Tabs allow you to have several Web pages open at one time without the clutter of extra browser windows.

If you want to use tabs, open the Safari application preferences and then choose the Tabs pane (shown in Figure 4.3). Check the box for Enable Tabbed Browsing. You can also choose whether tabs containing freshly loaded pages are automatically selected (brought to the front) or whether they wait for you to click them. Finally, you can choose whether to show the Tab bar even when only one tab exists.

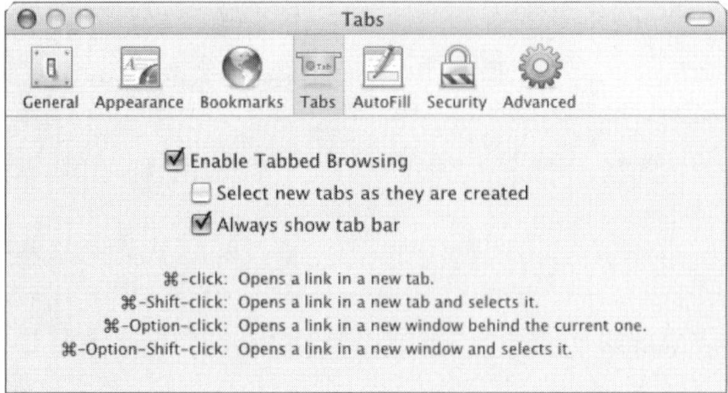

FIGURE 4.3 The Tabs preferences pane contains a few options as well as a list of keyboard shortcuts.

Tabs are easy to use. When you want one, simply choose File, New Tab from the menu (Command-T). You then see a row of boxlike buttons, or *tabs* just below the Address bar. Each Tab is labeled with the name of the Web page it contains, as shown in Figure 4.4, so you can easily click between them. If you want to close a tab, click the close icon on its far-left side.

CAUTION

If tabbed browsing isn't enabled in the Safari preferences, you will not see the option to open a tab under the File menu!

FIGURE 4.4 A row of tabs—each representing a Web page ready for viewing.

TIP

If you want to open a link in a new tab, hold down the Command key while clicking the link.

A unique feature of Apple's tab implementation is the ability to open any bookmark collection in tabs—all at once. When tabs are active, an extra option, Open in Tabs, appears within the submenu of any collection shown in the Bookmark menu. Choosing this loads all the pages in the collection in your current window—one in each tab. We'll look at how to create collections with the Bookmarks Library shortly.

TIP

If you want links clicked in external applications (such as Mail) to automatically open in a new tab, use the General application preferences pane to choose Open Links from Applications in the Current Window. You will *not* lose the page you were currently viewing.

Downloading Files

In addition to viewing Web pages with Safari, you can also use it to download files linked from Web pages.

NOTE

Safari only handles `http` protocol downloads. FTP downloads are handed off to the Finder. So, if you click an FTP link and Safari appears to do nothing, check the Finder.

When you click a link for a downloadable document, Safari automatically opens a Downloads window, as shown in Figure 4.5. Depending on your preference settings, this window may list other files you've downloaded as well as show status of the current download. You can clear the download list by clicking the Clear button.

TIP

If Safari does not recognize the document as something to download and instead starts to display it on the screen, you can force a link to download by holding down Option when clicking it.

Incidentally, this is not usually a failing of Safari, but a mistake in the MIME-type mapping of the remote server.

By default, Safari stores downloaded files on your desktop and attempts to post-process "safe" files by decompressing archives and opening common file formats such as PDFs, QuickTime media, and so on. These settings can be adjusted through the General pane of the application preferences.

FIGURE 4.5 See the progress of a file as it downloads.

CAUTION

There is a potential for downloaded files to contain malicious code. Be sure to "know your source" before downloading.

NOTE

Apple recently introduced Internet-enabled Disk Images that copy the software they contain to your desktop and then remove themselves without a trace. Be aware that if you're downloading a `.dmg` file, you *may* not see the image on your desktop after downloading. If it is an Internet-enabled disk image, and processing of "safe" files is turned on in Safari (the default), you will be left with only the files the image contained. For more information on these special new images, see `http://developer.apple.com/ue/files/iedi.html`.

Security and Privacy

Protecting your identity online and your browsing experience in general is key to the Safari experience. Safari offers several options to control cookies, pop-up windows, and more. To access the security features, open the Security pane of the Safari preferences pane, shown in Figure 4.6.

The Web content options choose what Safari allows on a Web page:

- Enable Plug-ins—Additional software components that allow the display of alternative media—such as QuickTime movies, Flash animation, and so on.
- Enable Java—Enables Java applications (using by-products such as TurboTax Online) to run within your browser.
- Enable JavaScript—A scripting language that enables your browser to perform basic computing functions on a Web page. Often used to verify form field contents before submitting them back to a server or to create rollover image effects on Web pages.
- Block Pop-up Windows—You know what they are. You hate them. Now block them!

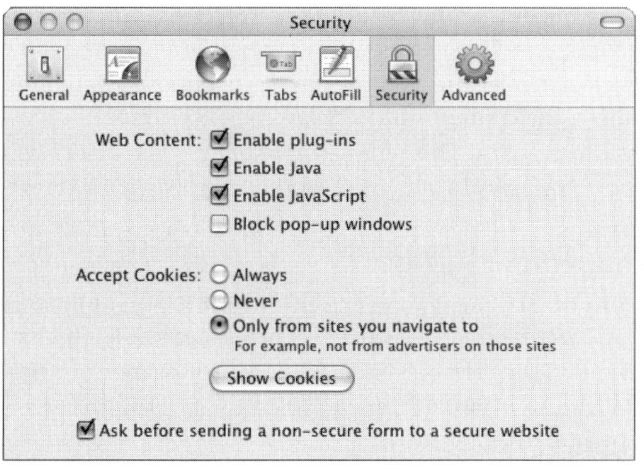

FIGURE 4.6 Protect yourself online.

TIP

Block Pop-up Windows can also be toggled on and off from the Safari application menu (Command-K).

Additionally, you can set when your browser will accept cookies from Web sites. Choose Always to allow *any* cookie to be set, Never to never allow any cookies, or Only from Sites You Navigate To to block cookies from advertisers and others not directly associated with the sites you are browsing.

Clicking the Show Cookies button displays a list of cookies stored on your machine and gives you the option to remove those you don't want stored.

NOTE

Cookies are a valuable tool for Web developers and are used extensively on major consumer sites. Disabling cookies completely is likely to result in sites that can no longer successfully be navigated.

It's important to note that much of the "controversy" surrounding cookies is purely hype. Cookies are sent to your browser by a remote site. They cannot be retrieved by any arbitrary Web site. In fact, cookies are not retrieved at all; they are sent voluntarily by the Safari browser on returning to a site that stored a cookie.

Finally, if you want to be prompted before sending information over the Internet in an insecure manger, click the Ask Before Sending a Non-Secure Form to a Secure Website check box.

Although these are the majority of the security controls, two other options may be of interest if you want Safari to dump any content that it may have cached while online, or if you want to reset Safari completely. Under the application menu, choose Safari, Empty Cache (Option-Command-E) to remove the contents of the Safari cache. To reset Safari to its default configuration, choose Safari, Reset Safari. This removes *everything*—your tracks will be wiped clean. No one will ever know you spend your entire workday browsing the PowerPuff Girls Web site.

Bookmark Management

Earlier, you learned to drag a Web address from the address field into the Bookmarks bar to quickly store it for later reference. As useful as that feature is, there's limited space for all the pages you want to keep. However, there is plenty of room in the Bookmarks window, shown in Figure 4.7, which you can open by clicking the Show All Bookmarks button in the Bookmarks bar.

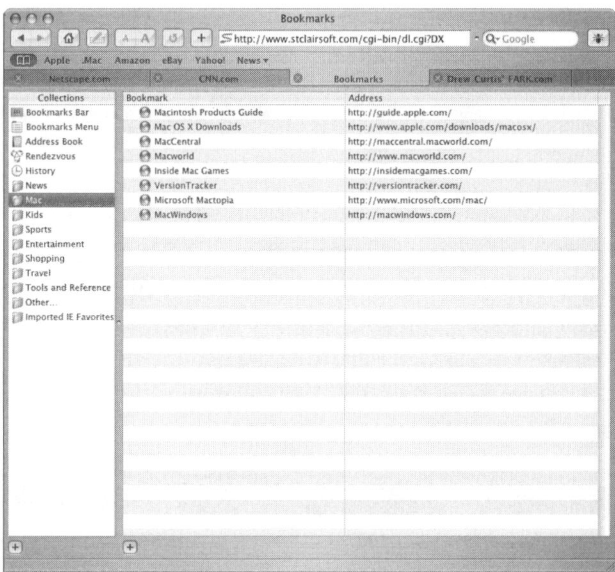

FIGURE 4.7 A special window to view and organize lists of your favorite Web sites. (When opened, it displays the last collection you visited.)

Collections

The Bookmarks Library offers a simple view of your URLs. Along the left side of the window is a list of collections—these are categories that you define (except for a few built-in collections) to help better organize bookmarks. There are five special categories, and the rest are entirely up to you:

- Bookmarks Bar—Bookmarks stored in the Bookmarks bar.

- Bookmarks Menu—Bookmarks stored in the Bookmarks menu.
- Address Book—URLs found within your Address Book entries.
- Rendezvous—Web sites located on your local network that are advertised via Rendezvous. (See Chapter 27, "Web Serving," for information on advertising Web sites via Rendezvous.)
- History—A list of Web sites that you've visited over the past week. These are also accessible through the History menu.

To view the contents of a collection, select it in the left-hand collection list. The content area to the right of the collections refreshes to display the bookmarks of sites stored in that collection.

Working with Bookmarks and Collections

Drag URLs in the Bookmark listing up or down to change their ordering (this makes a difference if you display the collections in the Bookmarks menu, which we'll discuss shortly) or drag them to the folders in the collection listing to add them to a collection. To add a new bookmark, drag its icon from the address field to the Bookmark listing (just as you did to add to the Bookmarks bar). To delete a bookmark, drag it to the trash or select it and press Delete. If you want to edit a bookmark name or URL, Control-click on the entry and choose Edit Name or Edit Address. Double-clicking on the fields opens the URL; it does not allow you to edit the field values, as you might expect.

To add new collections, click the "+" button below the collection list in the Bookmark Manager. A new untitled folder icon appears. Type a name for the new collection, or double-click its label at any time to edit it. Like bookmarks, collections can be rearranged by dragging within the list or deleted by dragging to the trash or selecting and pressing the Delete button.

CAUTION

At the time of this writing Safari does not prompt to make sure that you want to delete a collection or bookmark. You can quickly wipe out your bookmarks if you aren't careful and have a tendency to push the Delete key frequently.

NOTE

If you had another Web browser, such as Internet Explorer, on your computer at the time that Safari was installed, Safari may have created a folder of the bookmarks saved for its use.

You can add folders to a collection (think of it as a collection within a collection) by using the "+" button under the Bookmark listing. This adds a new folder to the Bookmark list (not the collection list). Drag bookmark entries into these folders to further refine your collection.

TIP

Both Collection folders and subfolders can be dragged from the Bookmarks Library into the Bookmarks bar to add a drop-down collection menu to the Bookmarks bar.

When adding bookmarks to the Bookmarks bar collection, you are also given an extra field called Auto-Tab in the bookmark listing. This field is active for subfolders within the Bookmarks bar and, when checked, makes the entry in the Bookmarks bar open *all* bookmarks within that subfolder in Tabs.

NOTE

Control-clicking on a bookmark in the library provides an option for opening that bookmark in a tab. Control-clicking on a subfolder within a collection shows an option for opening *all* bookmarks in that subfolder within tabs.

Adding Bookmarks with the Add Bookmark Button

Although the Bookmarks Library is great for arranging your URL shortcuts, opening it each time you want to add a site isn't necessarily efficient. Thankfully, Safari provides a quick solution. Clicking the Add Bookmark button in the address bar when you are viewing a page you want to add displays a dialog, shown in Figure 4.8, where you can name your bookmark and select a collection in which to store it.

FIGURE 4.8 Name and categorize the site.

Bookmark Display and Synchronization Options

Finally, Safari gives you several options on how you access bookmark collections. Obviously, you can always open the Bookmark Manager and see everything. Likewise, the Bookmarks Bar and Bookmark Menu collections are easy to find. However, it would be convenient if you could access *all* your collections through a single menu? Furthermore, it would be great to access all your bookmarks on *all* of your machines, or even over the Web. Well, Apple didn't *quite* come through on all of it, but you can at least get part of the way there.

To fine-tune the Bookmark display, open the Bookmarks pane of the application preferences pane, shown in Figure 4.9.

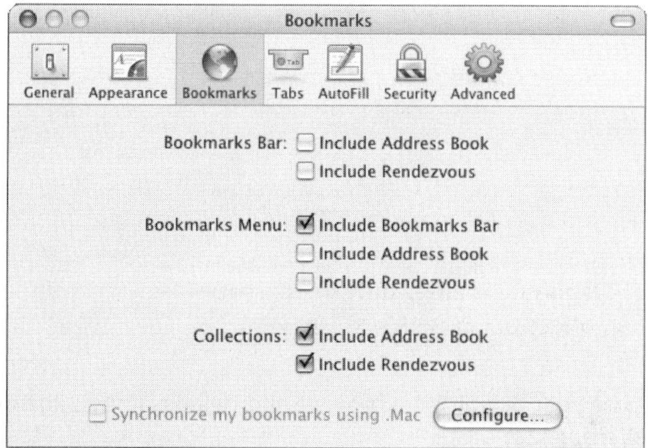

FIGURE 4.9 Fine-tune your bookmark settings.

Here you can choose whether the Bookmarks bar should display Address Book and Rendezvous entries (as drop-down collections) and, likewise, which entries should be shown in the Bookmark menu.

You can also click the Synchronize My Bookmarks Using .Mac check box to use .Mac (discussed shortly) to create a central library of bookmarks that all your computers can use *and* an online Bookmark Manager that enables you to view your bookmarks from anywhere. Clicking the Configure button launches iSync, which controls the .Mac bookmark synchronization. See Chapter 3, "Applications and Utilities," for information on setting up iSync.

Safari Preferences

Although we've already covered the Bookmarks, Tabs, AutoFill, and Security preferences panes within the discussion of Safari, there are several more esoteric settings that you might want to change to suit your browsing needs. Let's take a look at the remaining panes: General, Appearance, and Advanced.

General

Options under the General pane, shown in Figure 4.10, include many common settings related to how a Safari window is opened and how pages and files are accessed.

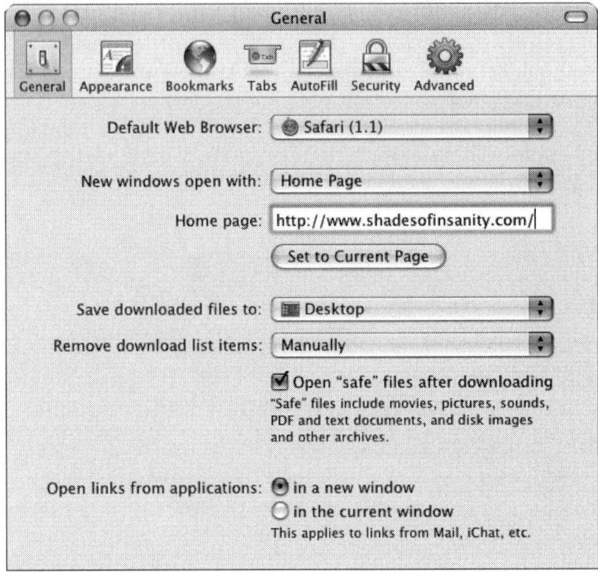

FIGURE 4.10 Choose your default Web browser and default home page in the General preferences pane.

The first option is the choice of your default Web browser (the Web browser that automatically launches whenever you click a link received in email or through another program). The drop-down menu lists any application recognized as a Web browser by your system.

You also have the option of choosing whether new windows that open come up with a specific home page that you've chosen, as an empty page, with any page that's currently open, or in Bookmarks mode.

The next three options pertain to downloading files. You have the option to save downloaded files to the desktop or to choose another location using the standard OS X file browser. You can also decide how items will be removed from your download list: manually, when Safari quits, or upon successful download. If you like to keep a record of what you've downloaded, set it at Manual; if you prefer a clean slate, choose one of the other options.

The third download-related preference is a check box for Open "Safe" Files After Downloading. Safe files, by Safari's definition, are files unlikely to cause harm to your system, including media files, such as images and sounds, PDF or text files, and disk images. If this option is checked, any "safe" files are processed automatically when they are downloaded; otherwise, you need to double-click downloaded files to launch or to uncompress them.

The final setting relates back to how Safari reacts to links you open from other applications. Decide whether to open links in a new window or in the current window. When using tabs, opening a link in the current window creates a new tab; it doesn't replace the contents of the existing tab.

Appearance

The Appearance pane, shown in Figure 4.11, contains the Web page display settings over which the viewer can have some input. You can choose any font on the system to be used on Web pages where another font is not specified. You can also choose a *fixed-width* font, a font for which all letters take up the same area in a line of text, to be used when the specified font needs to align in a specific way.

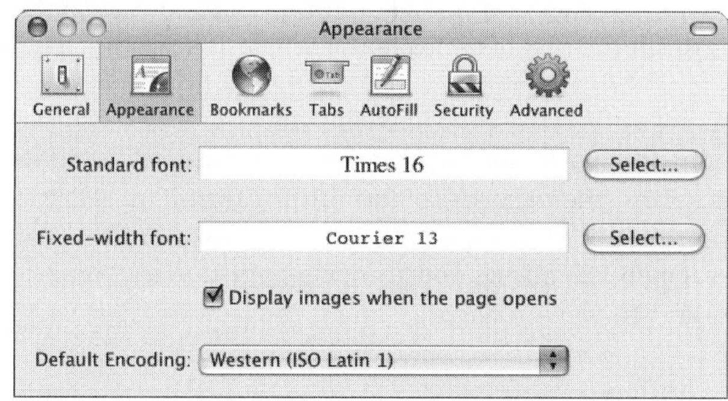

FIGURE 4.11 Choose fonts and character encoding preferences.

You can also decide whether to load images in a Web page, in case you'd rather not wait for them to download. Finally, you can set a default character encoding, which tells your browser how to interpret characters in a Web page. For example, if you regularly read Japanese Web sites, you would only be able to see the correct characters if your character encoding and the Web page used the same setting.

Advanced

The Advanced preferences pane allows you to set your own Style Sheet (Cascading Style Sheet or CSS), which is a specially formatted description of how text on a page should be displayed. For example, with a carefully written style sheet, you could have text in a Web page that is coded as a heading appear in extremely large type or change its color, or you could reset the background of a page to another color to increase or reduce contrast. (Although this feature can be useful, writing style sheets is outside the scope of this book. You might want to visit `http://www.blooberry.com/` for reference to the style sheet syntax.)

In addition, if you need to set a Proxy server for your Web connection, click the Change Settings button. This launches the System Preferences Network pane, which is where *all* proxy settings are configured.

The Safari Menu

Several features we've discussed previously in this chapter can be accessed through the Safari menu bar, but there are additional features available that you might want to use. Let's briefly review the menu options.

Safari Application Menu

The application menu contains the typical application options, as well as a few Safari specific entries.

From the Safari menu, you can report bugs to Apple or easily activate and deactivate the option to block pop-up windows. To keep others from using or viewing your settings, choose Reset Safari from the Safari menu to erase your browsing history, cached files, list of downloads, Google search entries, any cookies set on your computer, and all the data saved for use by the Autofill feature. Choose Empty Cache to delete the Web pages and images saved by Safari.

File

The File menu contains the basic options to open new windows or tabs or close them. As in most other applications, the page setup and print features are also located here. The Open Location option simply places the mouse cursor in the address field, ready for you to enter a Web address. Open File allows you to navigate to a Web page or image files on your computer that you want to view in Safari.

Edit

The Edit menu contains the standard Copy, Cut, and Paste commands as well as Select All and Delete.

Undo and Redo options are also found under the Edit menu, but they pertain not to moving between pages—we have Forward and Back buttons for that—but rather to changes you make to your bookmarks. Find can be used to quickly locate a word or phrase of interest on a page. For example, in a long list of names and addresses, you can use Find to go immediately to the entry for the person you want to contact.

Autofill, like the Autofill button mentioned earlier, helps you fill in online information.

The Spelling option won't check the spelling in Web sites that so you can recognize when they are poorly proofread. Rather, it allows you to check any text you enter in a text field on a page. For example, if you type a search term in the search field on the Google Web page or in the Google field in the Safari address bar, you can check the spelling before running a search. If you choose the Check Spelling as You Type option, you see a wavy red underline for any term your system doesn't recognize.

View

Choose which interface options appear in the Safari window in the View menu. You can also control the more advanced options for text encoding and view source. You may recall from earlier in the chapter that Web pages are written in HTML. View source allows you to see the HTML that the browser is using to display a given Web page.

The Text Encoding option lets you tell Safari in which format to display character sets used in Web pages. There is a default setting in the Appearance pane of the Safari preferences, but you can make temporary changes using this Text Encoding menu option.

History

The History menu contains duplicates of the basic controls for moving through pages: the Back, Forward, and Home items work the same as the buttons typically found in the address bar. Also in the History menu are the settings to mark a page for snap back and to snap back to the currently set page. Finally, the History menu displays a list of addresses for pages visited in the past week and the option to clear the history.

Bookmarks

The Bookmarks menu provides an alternative way to view and add bookmarks in Safari. (See "Managing Bookmarks" earlier in this chapter.)

Window

The Window menu contains options related to viewing Safari windows, including the download manager and tabs. It also includes the standard "minimize" and "zoom" window controls for covering or uncovering your desktop.

Help

The Help menu gives you access to Apple-created instructions for using Safari and to the acknowledgements and user license agreement for the software. It also allows you to view which plug-ins recognized by Safari are installed on your system.

Mail

The Mac OS X Mail application started as a reasonably straightforward port of NeXT Computer's Mail.app for NeXTStep/OpenStep. It had sloppy HTML rendering, and was really, really slow. In Panther, Mail finally reaches maturity by speeding up mail reading and rendering by an order of magnitude over the previous releases and by standardizing on the Safari HTML engine. If you've missed Outlook Express, this should finally appease your desire for a simple and fast mail client. Oh, and it also makes cool noises.

Setup

During the Mac OS X setup procedure (assuming that you've installed from scratch or purchased a new machine with OS X), the installer prompts for a default email account. Although this creates a single account for a single person, additional users and multiple accounts must be configured within Mail itself. For many people, the first task will be setting up a new account—this provides a perfect place to start.

Using Mail for the first time on a new user account opens a setup window to configure a new email account, as shown in Figure 4.12. If you're adding a second account, skip ahead to "Adding and Modifying Accounts and Settings."

FIGURE 4.12 The first time Mail is run, it forces an email account to be configured.

Seven pieces of information are required to set up an email account:

- Full Name—That thing that people call you by.
- Email Address—Your email address (for example, `jray@mymailmachine.com`).
- Incoming Mail Server—The server that stores your email. If you're using a .Mac account, use `mail.mac.com`.
- Account Type—Most ISPs support the POP3 protocol for accessing email. Apple's .Mac servers include support for IMAP. Read further for more information on both POP3 and IMAP and the differences between them.
- User Name—The username used to access an email account. This is the text that comes before the `@` in your email address (that is, `jray` is the username for `jray@mymailmachine.com`).
- Password—The password required to retrieve mail. Leaving this field blank prompts the user to enter the password when needed.
- Outgoing Mail Server (SMTP)—The server required to send messages. Users of .Mac email accounts can use `smtp.mac.com`.

If you are unsure of any of these fields, contact your ISP or network administrator. Do not attempt to use the mac.com hostnames unless you are using a .Mac email address. These are members-only servers and will deny access to those without an account. Click OK to save your account and start using Mail.

POP3 Versus IMAP

If your email provider supports both the POP3 and IMAP protocols, you're in luck! The POP3 protocol, although extremely popular, is not practical for people with multiple computers. I access the same email account from a number of different computers: one at work, one at home, and another while on the road. Keeping all these machines in sync is virtually impossible with POP3.

POP3 (Post Office Protocol v.3) works much as it sounds: Email is "popped" from a remote server. Incoming messages are stored on the remote server, which in turn waits for a connection from a POP3 client. The client connects only long enough to download all the messages and save them to the local hard drive. Unfortunately, after a message transfers from the server, it's gone. If you go to another computer to check your mail, it won't be there.

IMAP takes a different approach. Rather than relying on the client for message storage, IMAP servers keep everything on the server. Messages and mail folders remain on the server unless explicitly deleted by the client. When new messages arrive, the IMAP client application downloads either the message body or header from the server, but the server contents remain the same. If multiple computers are configured to access the same email account, the email appears identical between the machines—the same folders, messages, and message flags are maintained. In addition, the IMAP protocol supports shared folders between different user accounts and server-based content searches.

If your ISP does not support IMAP, you can sign up for a .Mac account. Apple's POP and IMAP service provides everything you need, along with exclusive Mac OS X downloads and online services.

Importing Mailboxes

After entering your basic account information, Mail immediately starts downloading your messages in the background and, at the same time, prompts you to import mailboxes from another email client such as Entourage or Eudora. This provides a convenient way to migrate to Mail without having to launch your old mail application to read past messages. Click Yes if you want to pull your old messages into Mail. You are then prompted for the mail client that you will be importing from, as shown in Figure 4.13.

NOTE

You can import legacy mail at any time (not just during the initial setup) by choosing File, Import Mailboxes from the menu.

Choose your legacy email application; then click the forward arrow in the bottom-right corner of the window. If you have mail stored in the Unix `mbox` format, use the selection Other.

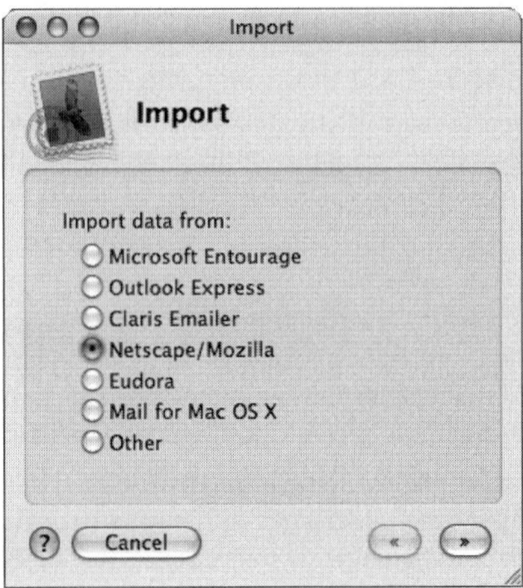

FIGURE 4.13 Choose the mail application that you want to import from.

Next you are prompted for *what* you want to import. Although it appears that Apple is preparing to provide support for importing addresses along with mail, the only available option at the time of this writing is Mailboxes. Make sure that Mailboxes is checked; then click the forward arrow again.

Mail displays a message that describes where your old mail files and folders are located. Read this screen carefully; then click the forward arrow.

Finally, select the location of the old files and click Choose. Mail reads your existing files and makes them available in your local Mail mailboxes.

TIP

There are two problems with importing legacy mail with Mail.app. First, not all email clients are supported. Popular emailers such as Opera and Mulberry are nowhere to be found. If you find yourself not being able to migrate to Mail, Emailchemy—a universal email converter (`http://www.weirdkid.com/products/emailchemy/index.html`)—may be able to save the day.

The second problem with migrating to Mail is that your contacts (and filters) are not preserved. Unfortunately, there is no clean way to handle this issue for every email client. If you're a Eudora user, you'll be interested in Andreas Amann's Eudora Mailbox Cleaner. EMC can completely migrate your Eudora contacts, filters, and messages to Mail and Address Book in a single pass—`http://homepage.mac.com/aamann/`.

Entourage users can drag and drop vCards (see Chapter 3 for more information) from Entourage to Address Book to transfer contacts. Or use Paul Berkowitz's Sync Entourage-Address Book to perform the action en bulk—`http://scriptbuilders.net/category.php?search=sync+entourage`.

You might also want to try the Import Addresses option found under the Script Menu. This AppleScript does a decent job of importing from several popular email clients.

Adding and Modifying Accounts and Settings

Mail supports multiple email accounts for a single user. After setting up the initial account, you can add other email accounts through the Accounts pane of the Application Preferences pane. Choose Mail, Preferences; then click the Accounts icon. Figure 4.14 shows the Accounts pane of the Preferences pane. Existing email accounts are listed on the left.

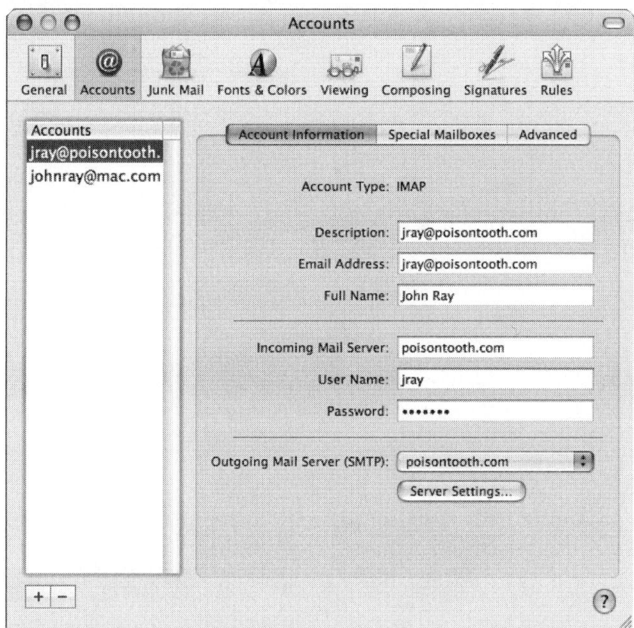

FIGURE 4.14 Multiple email accounts can be added through the Application preferences Accounts pane.

To add a new account to the list, click the "+" button. An account information dialog appears. This window is divided into three panes: Account Information, Special Mailboxes, and Advanced.

The general Account Information pane can be seen in Figure 4.15.

Use the Account Type pop-up menu to set the account type; then fill in the fields as you did when creating the initial account during the install process. Instead of just IMAP or POP accounts, there are four options:

- .Mac—Configures a Mac.com IMAP account with the appropriate Apple defaults.
- POP—Creates a POP3 account.
- IMAP—Creates an IMAP account.
- Exchange—Creates a Microsoft Exchange-ready account. Exchange integration and other Microsoft Windows compatibility topics are discussed in Chapter 30, "Windows Interoperability."

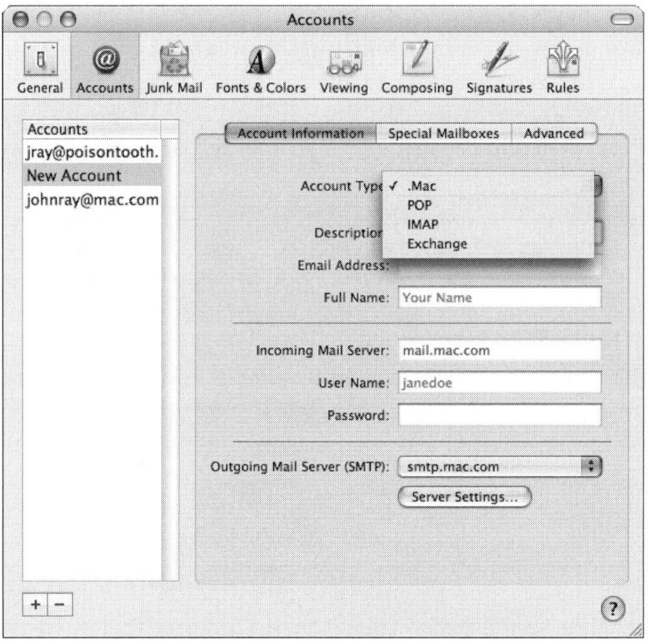

FIGURE 4.15 Enter the new email account information into this pane.

TIP

If you have multiple email return addresses and you want to be able to choose which address shows up in the From field on the final message, enter multiple addresses separated by commas in the Email Address field on the Account Information pane. This adds a pop-up menu to the message composition window where you can choose from the listed addresses.

Near the bottom of the Account Information pane are options for setting your SMTP servers. If you're using POP or IMAP, choose Add Server from the Outgoing Mail Server pop-up menu to add a new SMTP server, or choose to use one that you've already configured. The Server Settings button edits the currently selected SMTP server. Choosing Edit Server List displays a list of *all* SMTP servers and shows which accounts are using which servers.

NOTE

.Mac accounts use the `smtp.mac.com` server. This is set up automatically for you if you're adding a .Mac account. In this case, there is no reason to add your own SMTP server.

When adding or editing an SMTP server, you are prompted for the server name, port (if different from 25), and security information. If you are accessing an SSL-protected mail server (IMAPS, POPS), click the Use Secure Sockets Layer (SSL) check box. In addition, if your server uses authenticated SMTP, choose the authentication method and provide a username and password.

WHAT IS AUTHENTICATED SMTP?

The original SMTP protocol requires no authentication to send a message. Anyone could use any SMTP server to send any message (the origin of spam). Over time, servers developed advanced techniques to prohibit unauthorized use of the SMTP protocol, such as blocking by subnet or allowing users who have successfully checked mail to send mail from their IP address for a certain length of time.

This works, but it places some unreasonable restrictions on the user. Luckily, extensions have been made to the SMTP protocol that allow a username and password to be transmitted to the SMTP server when a connection is made. The server can then authenticate the user and allow unfettered access regardless of where or how the user is connecting.

The Special Mailboxes tab controls what and where Mail does with Draft, Sent, Junk, and Trash messages. When configuring an IMAP account, as shown in Figure 4.16, you can choose whether these "special" types of mailboxes are stored on the server, and when mail should be deleted from the server-based boxes.

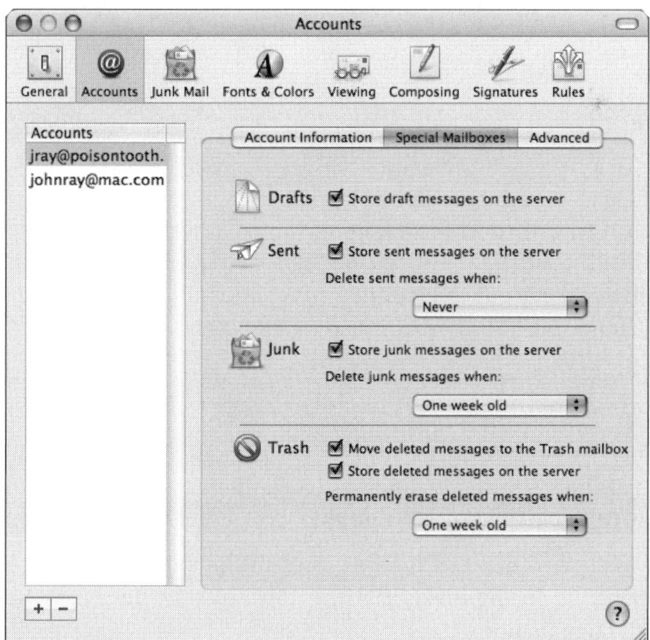

FIGURE 4.16 Special Mailboxes store Drafts, Junk, and other types of messages.

POP accounts are not given the option of storing special messages on the server. Instead, POP users can only choose when messages in any of the special mailboxes are erased.

Click the Advanced tab to fine-tune your account settings. Depending on the account type that you've chosen, the available options will change. Figure 4.17 displays the Advanced tab for IMAP (or Mac.com) accounts.

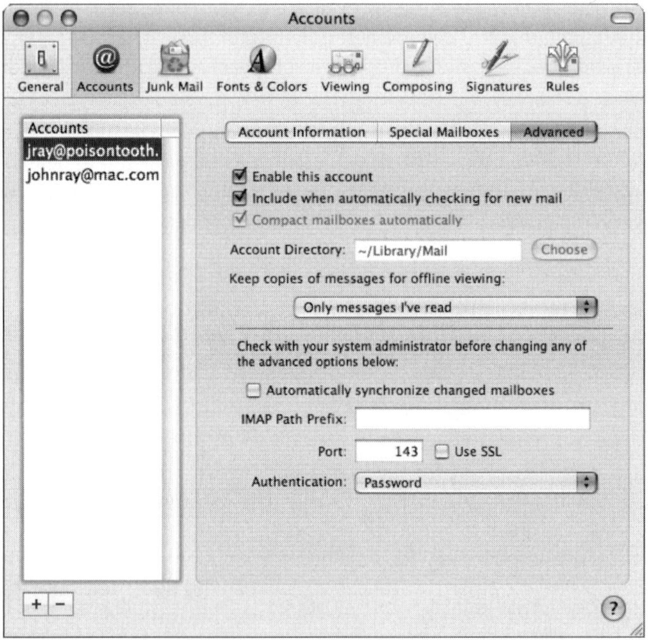

FIGURE 4.17 Each type of email account has different available options.

Each of the different mail account types has different available options. Choices available on the Advanced tab when using IMAP (or .Mac) include

- Enable This Account—Includes the account in the available account listing. If not enabled, it is ignored.
- Include When Automatically Checking for New Mail—If selected, the account will be polled for new messages at the interval set on the Preferences Account pane. If not, the account will be polled only when the user manually checks his mail.
- Compact Mailboxes Automatically—Cleans up the local mailbox files when exiting Mail. The benefit of using this is slight, and it can slow down the system when dealing with large mailbox files.
- Account Directory—The local directory where the Mail application stores your messages.

- Keep Copies of Messages for Offline Viewing—After a message is received on the server, the IMAP client has the option of immediately caching the text of the message on the local machine (cache all messages locally), caching read messages (cache messages when read), or never caching messages on the local drive (don't cache any messages). If you want to be able to read your mail while offline, you probably want the default setting of synchronizing all messages and their attachments.
- Automatically Synchronize Changed Mailboxes—When Mail notices a change in a mailbox and this option is selected, it automatically downloads the changes instead of waiting for the mailbox to be opened or manually synchronized.
- IMAP Path Prefix—The IMAP prefix required to access your mailbox. This field is normally left blank unless a value is specified by your mail server administrator.
- Port—The default IMAP port is 143. If your server uses a different access port, enter it here.
- Use SSL—Enable SSL encryption (IMAPS) of the email traffic. This setting must be supported by the server to be used.
- Authentication—Choose how you will authenticate with the remote server. Most ISPs use a plain password; special server configurations may require Kerberos or MD5.

NOTE

The default account directories are stored in `~/Library/Mail`. POP accounts store incoming messages in a flat Unix `mbox` format, so command-line applications such as Mail can read downloaded messages. IMAP accounts, however, do not use this format and instead store each message as a separate file.

If you are using a POP account, you can control how messages are retrieved and when they are deleted from your account, among other things:

- Enable This Account—Include the account in the available account listing. If not enabled, it is ignored.
- Include This Account When Checking for New Mail—If selected, the account will be polled for new messages at the interval set on the Mail Preferences Account pane. If not, the account will be polled only when the user manually checks his mail.
- Remove Copy from Server After Retrieving a Message—Choose the length of time (if any) messages should remain on the server after downloading. By leaving the messages on the server, you can create an IMAP-like environment where multiple computers can download the same messages. This is a "poor-man's" IMAP and does not support multiple server-based folders, shared folders, and so on. Click Remove Now to remove downloaded messages manually.

- Prompt Me to Skip Messages over <#> KB—Automatically skips messages over a set number of kilobytes. This setting is useful for keeping attachments from being downloaded.
- Account Directory—The local directory where the Mail application stores your messages.
- Port—The default POP port is 110. If your server uses a different access port, enter it here.
- Use SSL—Enable SSL encryption (POPS) of the email traffic. This must be supported by the server to be used.
- Authentication—Choose how you will authenticate with the remote server. Most ISPs use a plain password; special server configurations may require Kerberos or MD5.

After setting your account information, mailboxes, and options, click OK to save your account information.

NOTE

Whenever possible, use SSL encryption for POP and IMAP traffic. By default, these protocols transmit passwords in cleartext, making them highly interceptable.

The Mail Interface

Mail uses the special Mac OS X interface elements to create a unique and streamlined user experience. Figure 4.18 shows the Mail application, ready for action.

NOTE

If Mail opens to a screen asking for keychain access, click Allow Once to continue. Mail will start, but ask for the password each time it is run. Click Always Allow to eliminate the prompt altogether.

The keychain stores multiple passwords under a single master password. This allows you to unlock many resources just by remembering a single password.

The keychain access message might appear on recently upgraded systems, or if changes are made to the Mail application. It is not an error.

If you've used an email program such as Eudora or Outlook Express, you'll be completely comfortable with Mail's interface. The toolbar at the top of the window holds commonly used functions for creating, responding to, and searching for messages.

FIGURE 4.18 Mail has a modern interface that takes advantage of Mac OS X's special features.

Checking/Reading Mail

To check your account for messages, choose Mailbox, Get New Mail. If you have multiple accounts, choose the account you want to check, or choose All to query all configured accounts. You can set up how frequently Mail checks for new messages within the General pane of the application preferences, discussed later. Mail downloads your messages/message headers, and display the new email in the message list.

The list columns display the default columns' read/unread status, iChat status, subject, and day/time sent. Additional columns can be accessed under the View, Columns submenu. As with most list views, the columns can be sorted by clicking their headings.

> **TIP**
>
> You might want to enable the Message Number column under the View, Columns menu.
>
> Sorting by the message number is the best way to keep track of new messages as they come in. If a client includes incorrect time or time zone information when sending a message, it will probably be sorted incorrectly when you use Date and Time as the sort field.
>
> Unfortunately, Mail numbers different accounts using different numbers, so this works best on a single account, or when viewing one account at a time.

You can quickly hide the message by double-clicking the divider bar between the message list and the message text. This instantly drops the bar to the bottom of the Mail window filling the window with *just* the message list. Double-clicking the bar again returns it to its original position.

To read a message, highlight it in the list; the bottom of the window refreshes to contain a condensed view of the message headers along with the message content. If the message contains an attachment, an expandable list of files appears following the headers. When expanded, you can drag the attachment icons to your desktop, or, alternatively, click the Save All button to save all the attachments to a given location.

NOTE

Message attachments also show up as icons within the text of the message itself. You can drag these icons to your desktop as (yet another) way to access the attachments.

NOTE

If you receive a message that displays a header "Security" with a lock icon and the word "Encrypted", you're reading a message that has been encrypted using S/MIME (see `http://www.imc.org/ietf-smime/index.html` for details) and your public key (which can be automatically attached to messages you send).

If the message is unreadable, you do not have the proper certificate installed on your system; see the message composition section for more information.

Pressing the Delete key, or choosing Message, Delete from the menu, removes the active message or selected group of messages from the listing. Deleted messages are not immediately removed from the system; they are transferred to a Trash mailbox. What happens from there can be configured from the Viewing pane of the Mail Preferences pane.

Searching for Messages

To search for a piece of mail, use the Search field built into the toolbar. First access the search drop-down menu by clicking the magnifying glass. This allows you to choose what portion of the messages are being searched—the entire message, from, to, or subject headers and whether to search only the active mailbox or *all* mailboxes.

Next, start typing into the Search field. As you type, the search is carried out with only the matching items displayed in the message list. The matching string is highlighted in each message as you read it.

To reset the search results, click the "X" button at the end of the search field.

Working with Addresses

Panther treats every email address it sees as an object. When viewing a message, you can click on the addresses in the header to select them. When selected, a drop-down menu can be accessed at the right side of the contact, as shown in Figure 4.19.

FIGURE 4.19 Addresses are recognized and can be acted on as objects.

Depending on the context in which you display the menu, you can do everything from adding the address immediately to your Address Book, creating a new message to the person, or starting an iChat. When an address is added to your Address Book, the "email" portion of the address disappears from Mail, and only the contact's full name is shown.

If an address has been used to send email but isn't in your Address Book, you may see the option to Remove from Address History when you activate the address object's menu. Using this option removes the email address from Mail's "short-term memory" and keeps it from being autocompleted as you type in addresses.

NOTE

If you don't like this new form of addressing, you can shut it off by selecting Show Name and Address instead of Use Smart Addresses from the View, Addresses menu.

Threaded Browsing

In Panther, Mail adds full threaded browsing of your email. That's nice; what is a thread? A *thread* is a "conversation" you've had with someone over the span of several messages. Usually these are treated like separate emails (because they are) and are scattered throughout your other spam. With the Panther version of Mail, you can choose to browse your email in threaded mode, making it easy to follow the course of a conversation. To enable threads, choose View, Organize by Thread. Figure 4.20 demonstrates threaded mail browsing.

FIGURE 4.20 Organize your messages into threads.

Threads are identified by a blue highlight and the presence of an arrow in front of the initial message subject that started the thread and a number in the status field showing how many unread messages are in the thread, if any. Highlighting the initial message subject line displays information about the thread in the message content pane, such as who started the thread, when, how many messages it contains, which contain attachments, and how many of them are unread. Clicking a line within the content pane list jumps immediately to the chosen message.

NOTE

When Mail is in threaded mode, the threads are represented by a *virtual message* with the subject of the initial message. It isn't until you've opened the thread that can you choose and view the contents of the original message.

NOTE

Mail bases threads on a message's subject. If you have multiple messages with the same subject that *aren't* a thread, they will still be displayed as a thread.

To browse the thread within the message list, click the arrow at the front of the thread subject line. The message thread expands to show all the available emails within the thread and immediately jumps you to the first unread message. To collapse the thread, click in the first column (down and up opposing arrows) of any message within the thread or on the arrow in front of the initial thread subject line. The thread immediately collapses back to a single line.

The View menu's Expand/Collapse All Threads options can be used to quickly open and close all threads in your mailbox.

TIP

Previous versions of Mail identified threads by highlighting all the messages in a thread in a specific color wherever they appear in the message listing. To reenable this behavior (regardless of whether your email is organized by thread), use the option When Not Grouping Messages by Thread, Highlight Thread Instead found under the Viewing application preferences pane.

Dealing with Spam

Mail includes a built-in feature to help you manage the ever-increasing sea of spam that threatens to overtake your mailbox. When Mail thinks it's found a piece of spam, it highlights the item in brown in the message listing and displays a "spam" warning when you view the message, as shown (quite appropriately) in Figure 4.21.

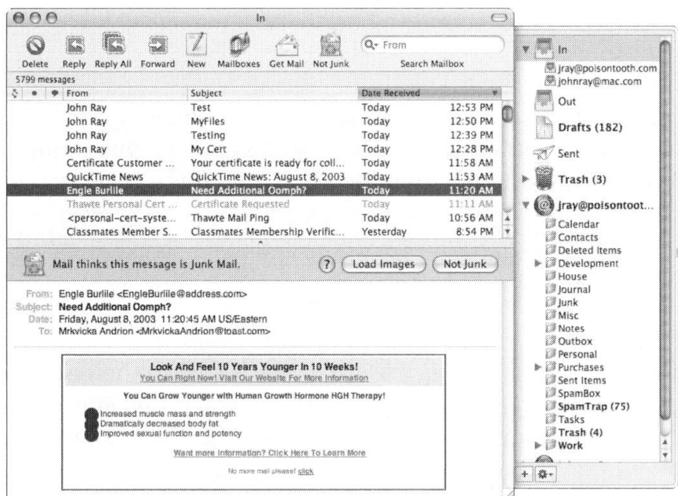

FIGURE 4.21 Mail provides built-in spam sensing heuristics.

Click the Not Junk button in the warning to tell Mail that it incorrectly labeled the message as spam. You can also use the Junk/Not Junk toolbar buttons to flag (or unflag) the currently selected messages(s) in the message listing as spam. The more you "train" Mail, the better it gets at identifying good and bad email.

When Mail has gotten to the point where it is consistently identifying spam, you can use the Junk Mail application preferences pane to automatically move messages to a special Junk mailbox rather than leave them in your inbox.

More Anti-Spam Features

Spammers are nasty. They use special tricks such as identifying whether your email account is active by sending HTML messages with dynamic image links to your address. If your email reader loads the images, the spammer immediately knows that the email account is active and capable of viewing HTML mail—even if you never click a link in the message! Mail understands this and provides the option of disabling the display of inline images and attachments. Under the Viewing application preferences pane, you can enable or disable the option to Display Images and Embedded Objects in HTML Messages. When images are disabled, Mail automatically displays a Load Images button at the top of the message content area. Only after the button is clicked does Mail load inline content—preventing the spammers from getting any feedback from your computer.

Another method of defeating spam is to bounce mail back to them. This creates the appearance that your account doesn't exist and, if you're lucky, results in having your name removed from their lists. To bounce a message, highlight the email in your list and then choose Message, Bounce (Shift-Command-B). Alternatively, you can add a Bounce icon to your Mail toolbar for fast access. Unfortunately, most spammers use fake reply-to addresses, which simply bounce your own bounce back to you.

iChat AV Integration

Mail integrates with iChat such that any message from a contact who is also on your buddy list displays that person's instant message status in a column within Mail if the Buddy Availability option is selected from the View, Columns submenu.

To launch an iChat AV session with an online buddy, highlight the message they've sent in your message list; then choose Message, Reply with iChat (Command-Option-I).

Mailboxes/Folders

To display the accounts and mailboxes that have been added to the system, click the Mailbox toolbar button, or choose View, Show Mailboxes (Shift-Command-M). The mailbox drawer slides out from the side of the mail window. You can use the disclosure arrows to collapse and expand the hierarchy of mailboxes. The number of unread messages is displayed in parentheses to the right of each mailbox.

> **NOTE**
>
> The default Mailbox/folder icons are *huge*. If you have a few dozen like me, you'll want to choose View, Use Small Mailbox Icons.

To file a message within a mailbox, click and drag it from the list view to the mailbox into which you want to transfer the message. If the mailbox drawer isn't open, it automatically pops open as the mouse approaches the edge of the window. Alternatively, you can use the Move To or Copy To options from the Message menu. Control-clicking or right-clicking a line in the message opens a contextual menu from which Transfer can also be accessed as well as most other options from the main Message menu.

NOTE

Apple refers to mailboxes as either *mailboxes* or *folders* apparently depending on the developers' moods as they created the interface. You can use these terms interchangeably when working with Mail.

Certain mailboxes, such as In, Out, Drafts, and Trash, are "special" in that they contain all of a specific type of mailbox for each account and are filled automatically:

- In—Contains all the Inboxes for all your accounts. You can either expand the master Inbox to pick a specific account's Inbox, or use the top-level Inbox to show all incoming messages in all your accounts, be they POP3, IMAP, or .Mac accounts.
- Out—Messages that are *going* to be sent but have not yet left your system.
- Sent—Messages that have already been sent from your computer.
- Trash—Like the Inbox, the Trash is a collection of messages—in this case, all messages that have been marked for deletion but are not yet deleted.
- Drafts—Messages that you are working on but have not yet sent.

NOTE

The Mail icon displays the total number of unread messages in *all* the Inbox folders. Unfortunately, there is currently no way to change the mailboxes it monitors for the unread count.

Another special mailbox category is On My Mac. This category contains all the mailboxes stored locally on your computer. This is of most interest to POP3 users who cannot create mailboxes on their remote mail server.

To create new mailboxes, choose Mailbox, New from the menu, or click the "+" button at the bottom of the Mail window drawer. You are prompted for where the Mailbox will be created, and what it should be called, as demonstrated in Figure 4.22.

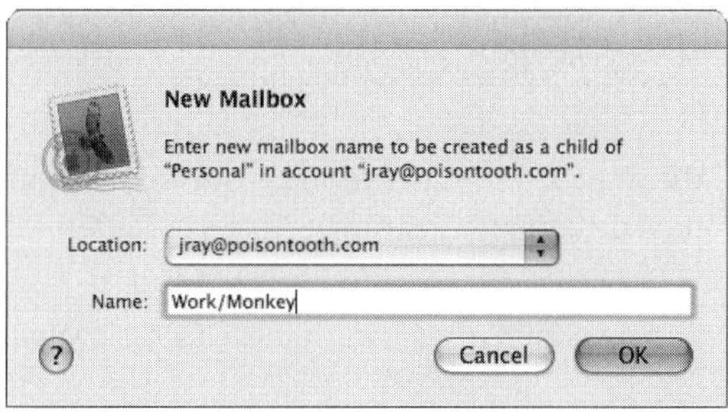

FIGURE 4.22 Choose where to create the new mailbox and what it should be called.

IMAP/Mac.com users can choose an email account from the Location pop-up menu. This stores the mailbox on the remote server. To create a mailbox inside another mailbox, type the full path of the mailbox you want to create. For example, if you already have a mailbox called `Work` and you want to make the mailbox `Monkey` inside it, type `Work/Monkey` in the Name field.

TIP

As a shortcut for creating mailboxes within mailboxes, highlight the "parent" mailbox that you want to create another mailbox inside of; then click "+" or choose the New mailbox option.

Also, notice that, like the Finder, the mailbox drawer has an action button. This button can be used to access the same functions as under the Mailbox menu bar.

To delete or rename a mailbox, highlight it in the mailbox list; then use Rename or Delete from the Mailbox menu.

Assigning Special Mailboxes

Mail automatically creates mailboxes for storing Sent items, Trash, Drafts, and Junk mail. If you'd rather use your own mailboxes for those purposes, highlight the mailbox you want to use; then choose the purpose with the Mailbox, Use This Mailbox For menu.

Synchronizing Mailboxes for Offline Reading

If you're using IMAP or .Mac, you may want to read your mail offline. This isn't a problem if you're using POP3, but IMAP and .Mac store messages on the server. To synchronize IMAP/.Mac messages for offline reading, highlight a mailbox in the account you want to sync and then select Mailbox, Synchronize or use the Mailbox action button.

Rebuilding Mailboxes

There may be times that Mail gets "out of sync" with your IMAP/.Mac mail server. The symptoms are usually missing messages or messages with the wrong content.

From my experience, this happens most often when accessing the mail server from another client and renaming/moving mailboxes. To rebuild the contents of any mailbox, choose Mailbox, Rebuild from the menu. Mail redownloads the contents of the mailbox and (hopefully) corrects the problem.

Toolbar Options

Like other applications, the Mail application supports toolbar customization. Open the customization sheet by choosing View, Customize Toolbar. Figure 4.23 shows the available customizations.

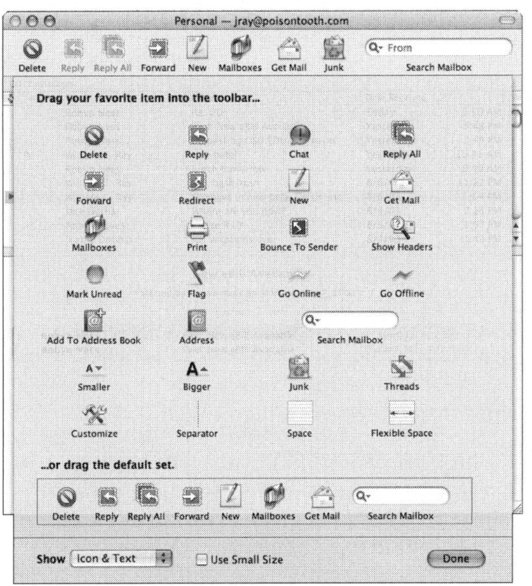

FIGURE 4.23 Customize the mail toolbar with your favorite buttons.

From the top left to bottom right, the available buttons are

- Delete—Delete the selected message(s).
- Reply—Reply to the author of the current message.
- Chat—Launch an iChat session with the sender of the selected message, if she is online. The iChat application is discussed later in this chapter in the section "iChat A/V."
- Reply All—Reply to all recipients of the current message.
- Forward—Forward the current message (and its attachments) to additional recipients.
- Redirect—Redirect the selected message; does not quote the original message's text.
- New—Type a new message.
- Get Mail—Retrieve new messages from available accounts.
- Mailboxes—Open the Mailbox drawer.
- Print—Send the active message to the printer.
- Bounce to Sender—Bounce the selected message. To the original sender, it appears that the message never reached you! The original message is automatically removed after bouncing.

- Show Headers—Display all the message headers, including the relay path in the message body.
- Mark Read/Unread—Toggle the read/unread state on a message.
- Flag—Toggle the flagged/unflagged state message.
- Go Online—Take the active email account offline. No further attempts to connect to the server will be made while in this mode.
- Go Offline—Take an offline email account back online.
- Add to Address Book—Add the sender of the selected message to the Address Book application.
- Address—Open the Address Book application.
- Search Mailbox—Search the open mailbox's To, From, or Subject field by choosing it from the pop-up menu and then entering the search text in the field.
- Smaller—Shrink the text size in the open message.
- Bigger—Enlarge the text in the open message.
- Junk—Toggle a message as being junk or not junk.
- Threads—Toggle thread viewing mode.
- Customize—Customize the toolbar.
- Separator—Add a vertical separator bar to the toolbar. This is for visual purposes only.
- Space—Add an icon-sized space to the toolbar.
- Flexible Space—Add a space to the toolbar that grows and shrinks with the size of the window.
- Default Set—Reset to the default set of toolbar icons.

Click Done to save the changes to the toolbar.

TIP

When a message is opened in its own window by double-clicking in the message list, that toolbar can also be customized. The only difference is that shortcuts related to the message list and mailboxes are not included in the toolbar customization choices.

Composing Messages

To write an email, click the New button or choose File, New Message (Command-N). To reply to an existing message, select that message in the list view; then click Reply to start a new message or choose Message, Reply (Command-R). The composition window appears, as shown in Figure 4.24.

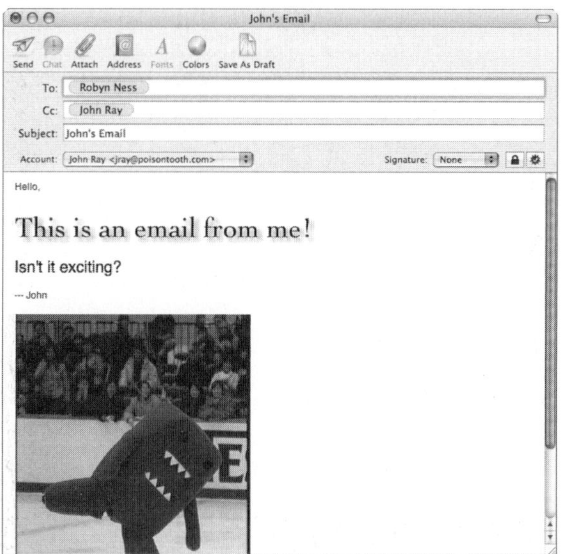

FIGURE 4.24 Mail supports styled messages and drag-and-drop attachments.

> **TIP**
>
> If text from the original message is selected when you choose to reply, it is included in the new message as a quote from the original message.

Message Addressing

Two fields are initially provided for addressing the message. Use the To line for single or multiple addresses that serve as the primary recipients of the message. A comma should separate multiple addresses. The Cc: line adds additional recipients who are not part of the main list. The primary recipients can see these addresses. The Subject line is used to set the subject or the title of the email.

Additional fields are accessible from the View menu. Choose Bcc Header (Option-Command-B) to add a Bcc header, or Reply-To Header (Option-Command-R) to add an alternative reply address. A Bcc (Blind Carbon Copy) works like a normal carbon copy but does not allow the recipients to view each other's email address or name. The Reply-To header is used to provide an alternative address for replying. For example, if I'm sending email from my `jray@poisontooth.com` account and want replies to go to `johnray@mac.com` instead, I'd enter the Mac.com address in the Reply-To Header field.

To enter an address in a field, simply start typing the contact's name or email address. As you're typing into any of the available fields, Mail attempts to recognize the address either from your Address Book or from other addresses you've used recently and "auto-complete" the address as you type. If it gets the correct address, press Tab or click outside the area where you are typing, and the address is entered as an object. If you've entered multiple email addresses for a single contact (home and work addresses, for example), click on the object; then use the drop-down menu on the right to choose from the different addresses available for that person, as shown in Figure 4.25.

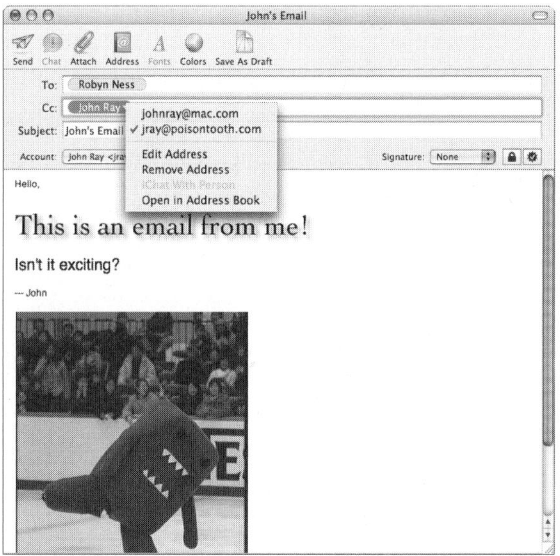

FIGURE 4.25 Choose which address you want to use for a given person.

From the same pop-up menu, you can also choose Edit Address to enter and edit the address manually, Remove Address to delete the address object from the field, iChat with Person (to start an iChat session if available), or Open in Address book to open the Address Book application and display the appropriate record.

Previous Recipients If Mail doesn't recognize an address or name as being in your Address Book, it might still autocomplete it if it happens to be an address stored in the Address History. The Previous Recipients list is much like a browser's page history. It is a record of addresses you've used (either through direct emails or by replying to messages) that are not part of your Address Book. You can display the stored list by choosing Window, Previous Recipients, as shown in Figure 4.26.

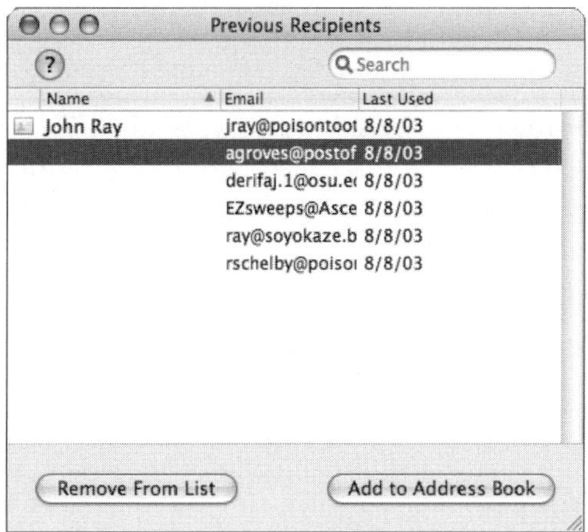

FIGURE 4.26 The Address History is a list of addresses used but not stored.

Use the buttons Remove from List to remove a selected address from the history list and Add to Address Book to move the address to your Address Book. The Search field can be used to search the list.

Address Panel To access the Address Book, click the Address button in the toolbar or choose Window, Address Panel (Option-Command-A), and an Address Book window appears. From the window, drag individual addresses, multiple addresses, or address groups, to the To/Cc/Bcc fields in the message composition window.

Protecting Against Sending Accidental Email Its surprisingly easy to find yourself in a ton of trouble (or an embarrassing situation) by including the wrong addresses on a piece of mail—such as sending private corporate secrets to your gossipy arch enemy. To help guard against this, Mail can be configured so that mail addressed to domains outside a given "safe" domain are highlighted in red as they are entered. To activate this feature, choose Mark Addresses Not in This Domain and fill in the appropriate domain in accompanying field within the Composing pane of the application preferences.

Message Composition

To create the message itself, input the text into the content area of the window. The toolbar can be used to attach files or pick fonts and colors. These options are also available from the Message and Format menus.

To add attachments, drag images and files (and even folders!) directly into the message. Depending on the type of file, it is added to the message as an icon (application, archive, and so on) or shown within the body (picture, movie).

Be aware that to receive rich-text email, the remote user must have a modern email program such as Outlook Express (or, better yet, Mail!). To create a message that anyone can receive, compose the content in Plain Text mode, selectable from the Format menu.

If you commonly use signatures with your messages, you can add signatures automatically to your message composition window through the Signatures preferences pane discussed later.

To send, click Send in the toolbar, or choose Message, Send (Shift-Command-D). If you want to save the message and work on it later, use File, Save as Draft (Command-S). This saves the message to your Drafts mailbox where you can open it and resume work at a later date.

TIP

When replying to a message, it is common to quote another message. As mentioned previously, you can quote a specific portion of a message by highlighting the appropriate message content before choosing Reply. Sometimes, however the "quote" level of the message isn't what you want—something you want to be quoted *isn't*, whereas something you don't want quoted is. To adjust the "levels" of quoting, select the text to change and use the Increase or Decrease options under Quote Level within the Format menu to change the quoting.

Message Encryption

Panther supports automatic encryption/decryption of email messages if you have a digital certificate for your email identity installed in your keychain (see Chapter 3 for details). The S/MIME standard used within Mail is a public/private key encryption system. Messages are encrypted using the *public* key of a recipient. Only the recipient's *private* key can decrypt an encrypted message, and only the recipient should ever have access to the private key.

To use mail encryption, you must install a digital certificate that contains your private key and public key. After doing this, you can add a "digital signature" containing your public key to your emails. This signature is subsequently stored automatically by other popular mail applications (including Panther's Mail) and can be used by other people to send you encrypted messages.

Similarly, your friends/coworkers can send you *their* public keys, which are automatically added to your keychain and can be used to send *them* encrypted messages.

While all this sounds confusing, you only need to worry about two actions: signing a message with your public key and encrypting a message with another user's public key. Both of these actions are easy in Mail:

1. First, make sure that you and the people you want to communicate with have obtained and installed certificates with your private keys. This is discussed in Chapter 3.

2. Next, send each other email that is signed with your public keys. This is as easy as clicking on the stamp/check mark icon button in the lower-right corner of the addressing area of your message (refer to Figure 4.24). If the icon is highlighted, the message automatically is signed. Exchanging signed emails adds your friend's public keys to your keychain.
3. Finally, after you've collected the public keys of your friends, you can send encrypted messages by clicking the "lock" icon (again refer to Figure 4.24) so that it is highlighted. The message is encrypted using the appropriate public keys before it is sent—virtually eliminating the threat of interception.

NOTE

If you do not see these icons in your window, you do not have the correct certificates installed on your system. A certificate is specific to a given email account, so you must make sure that you're using the same "From" address that you provided when applying for a certificate.

Toolbar Options

The message composition window can be customized just like the main mailbox view. When writing a message, choose View, Customize Toolbar from the menu. Figure 4.27 shows the customizations.

FIGURE 4.27 Customize the New Message toolbar with your favorite shortcuts.

From the top left to bottom right, the available shortcuts are

- Send—Send the current message.
- Chat—Open an iChat session with the message addressee (if he's been added to your iChat Buddy List).
- Attach—Choose a file to attach to the current message.
- Address—Open the Address Book window.
- Print—Print the open window.
- Append—Append the messages selected in the mailbox view to the contents of the current message.
- Colors—Open the Colors pane.
- Fonts—Open the Fonts pane.
- Save as Draft—Save the message to the Drafts folder; it is not sent.
- Smaller—Shrink the text size in the open message.
- Bigger—Enlarge the text in the open message.
- Make Rich Text—Toggle the current message to rich text mode.
- Make Plain Text—Toggle the current message to plain text mode. Note that doing this removes all message formatting.
- Customize—Customize the toolbar.
- Separator—Add a vertical separator bar to the toolbar. This is for visual purposes only.
- Space—Add an icon-sized space to the toolbar.
- Flexible Space—Add a space to the toolbar that grows and shrinks with the size of the window.
- Default Set—Reset to the default set of toolbar icons.

Click Done to save the changes to the toolbar.

Preferences

Mail's preferences pane of Mail help weed through the hellish reality of junk mail. The Junk Mail preferences pane, shown in Figure 4.28, is your control center for managing how Mail handles messages identified as junk.

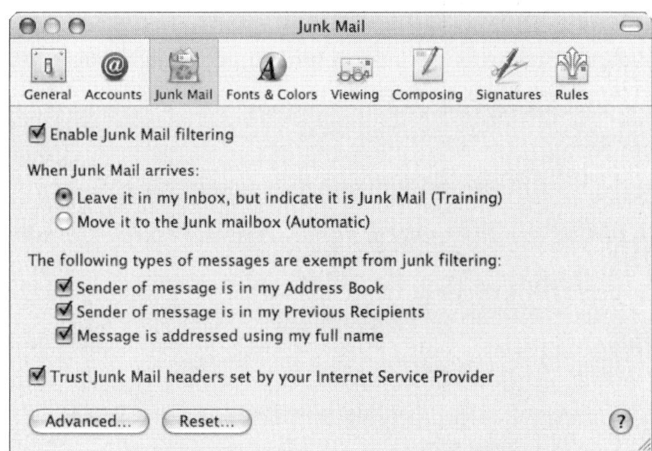

FIGURE 4.28 Control your spam from the Junk Mail application preferences pane.

Use these settings to control how Mail reacts to spam:

- Enable Junk Mail Filtering—Enable spam filtering.
- When Junk Mail Arrives—Choose to leave mail in the inbox (but highlighted as junk) or move it to the Junk mailbox.
- The Following Types of Messages Are Exempt from Junk Filtering—To help eliminate false positives, Mail automatically exempts spam status for messages from senders in your Address Book or Address History or messages addressed using your full name. Because it's unlikely that you communicate regularly with spammers, leaving these options checked is a pretty reasonable assumption.
- Trust Junk Mail Headers Set By Your Internet Service Provider—Mail servers have the capability to add spam headers (`X-Spam: yes`) to messages that the *server* feels is spam. If checked, Mail assumes that the mail headers are correct and treats the message as spam, even if other criteria are not met.
- Advanced—Allows you to configure how Mail recognizes and treats Junk mail by customizing the internal "Junk" rule. This is identical to other filters (see Rules, discussed shortly) but is specific to junk mail handling.
- Reset—Reset the junk mail database kept by Mail. If used, Mail forgets everything it has learned about what is/isn't spam on your system.

Fonts and Colors

The Fonts & Colors pane controls the default fonts used in the message list and message bodies. This pane is shown in Figure 4.29.

Options in the Fonts & Colors pane include

- Message List Font—Choose the Font and Size used in the listing of active messages.
- Message Font—Choose the Font and Size used in the body of messages.
- Used Fixed-Width Font for Plain Text Messages—If this option is checked, the system uses a monospace ("typewriter") font for unstyled messages.
- Plain Text Font—The font to use for plain text messages.
- Color Quoted Text—Text included when replying is automatically quoted and colored. If there are multiple levels of replies, each level can be set to a different color.

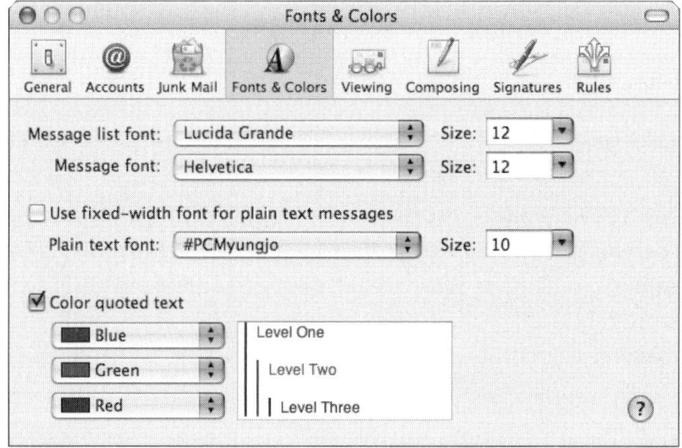

FIGURE 4.29 Choose the default message fonts and quote colors.

TIP

Using a fixed-width font is recommended for plain text messages. Many plain text messages are formatted using spaces for positioning elements—using a proportional font results in a skewed or sometimes unreadable display.

Viewing

The Viewing preferences control shows a contact's instant message status, the amount of header detail that should be displayed, and the downloading of attachments. Figure 4.30 shows the Viewing pane.

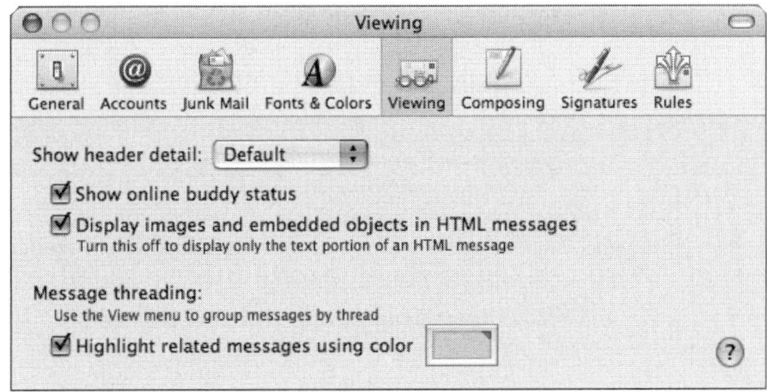

FIGURE 4.30 Control what you see when viewing messages.

Options in the Viewing pane include

- Show Header Detail—By default, only a few headers (From, Date, To, Subject) are shown. Using this pop-up menu, you can choose to hide all headers, show everything, or create a custom list of headers.
- Show Online Buddy Status—If a sender has a valid iChat buddy-list entry and this option is checked, her online status is displayed in the Buddy Availability field of the message listing.
- Display Images and Embedded Objects in HTML Messages—If this option is checked, HTML messages download all embedded images and movies, and display them within the message body.
- Highlight Related Messages Using Color—Choose the color used to highlight message threads when not organizing messages by thread.

Composing

Choose the default message format used when creating messages. The Composing pane includes a variety of esoteric settings, displayed in Figure 4.31.

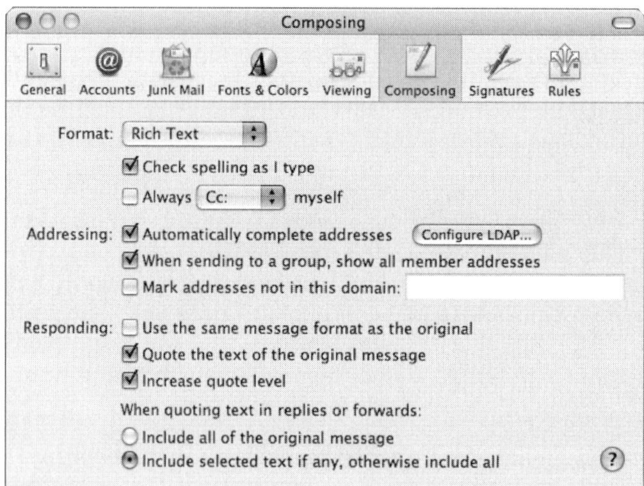

FIGURE 4.31 Choose the format for outgoing messages.

Options in the Composing pane include

- Format—Select between Rich Text and Plain Text as the default new message format. If you are communicating with a wide variety of people on unknown operating systems, it's best to stick to plain text.
- Check Spelling as I Type—When this option is checked, misspelled words are underlined in red in the message composition window. Control-click (or right-click) the word to display a list of suggestions.
- Always cc/Bcc Myself—If this option is checked, you receive a copy of any message you send. This is often used to verify (for your own peace of mind) that a message you sent *really* was sent.
- Automatically Complete Addresses—If this option is checked, Mail attempts to complete email addresses as you type using the Address Book entries, Address History, and configured LDAP servers.
- Configure LDAP—Set up LDAP servers for address searches. Mail uses the same servers as configured in Address Book. See the Address Book section of this chapter for more information.
- When Sending to a Group, Show All Member Addresses—If you are including a group from the Address Book application and this option is checked, the members of the group are listed in the message header separately.
- Mark Addresses Not in This Domain—Set a domain name that is considered "safe." Addresses not in this domain are highlighted in red.

- Use the Same Message Format as the Original—When replying to messages, use the same format (rich/plain) in the reply.
- Quote the Text of the Original Message—Display the text from the original message as indented quoted text when replying.
- Increase Quote Level—When replying, increase the quote level, meaning text that has already been quoted will be quoted again, and text that hasn't been quoted at all will become quoted.
- Include All of the Original Message—When replying, include the contents of the original message in the reply. The original message is quoted.
- Include Selected Text, If Any, Otherwise Include All—When replying, include only the selected portion of the original message. If nothing is selected, the entire message is included in the reply.

To use LDAP servers for address completion, first obtain the appropriate LDAP server information from your network administrator; then click the Configure LDAP button. A dialog appears listing all configured servers. Click the "+" button to add a new server, "-" to subtract an existing server, or Edit to reconfigure the highlighted server. Figure 4.32 shows a sample (nonworking) entry.

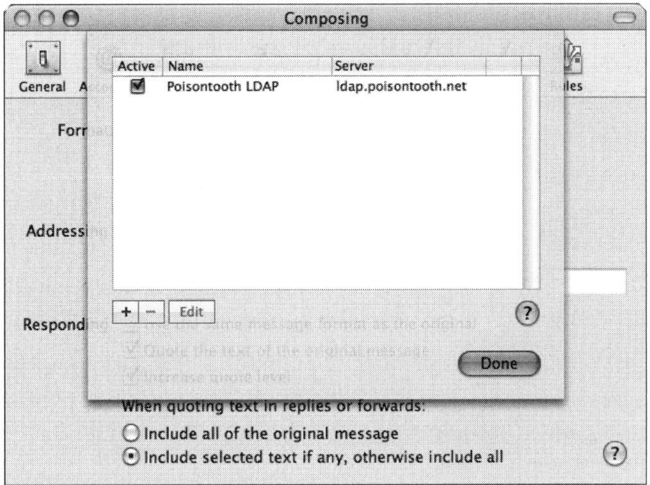

FIGURE 4.32 LDAP servers, if available, can be used to automatically complete email addresses from a centralized directory server.

Signatures

Everyone needs a signature—something to identify them as individuals or at least to tell others who you are! The Mail application handles multiple different signatures with ease. Figure 4.33 shows the Signatures pane. The available signatures are listed on the left side of the pane.

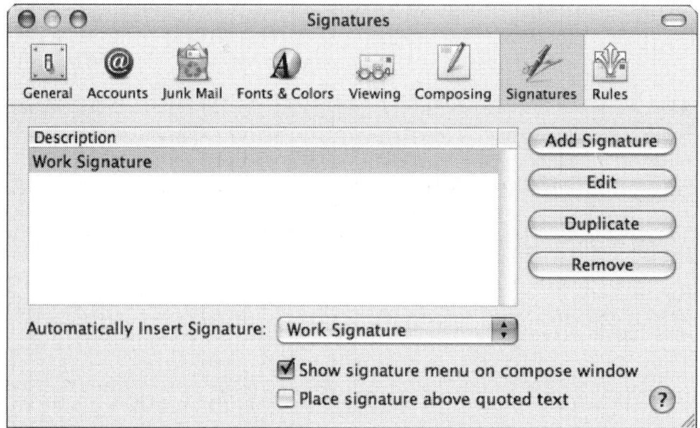

FIGURE 4.33 Create multiple signatures within the Mail application.

Options in the Signatures pane include

- Add Signature—Create a new signature. A text-entry pane appears to type or paste a new signature. If you paste in a rich-text clipping, click the Make Plain Text button to convert it to plain text.
- Edit—Edit an existing signature.
- Duplicate—Duplicate an existing signature.
- Remove—Delete a signature.
- Automatically Insert Signature—Choose the signature you want to use by default, or choose to insert them randomly or in sequential order.
- Show Signature Menu on Compose Window—If this option is checked, a Signature pop-up menu is added to the message composition window. From this pop-up, you can add all the stored signatures.
- Place Signature Above Quoted Text—Position the signature in message replies so that it falls above any quoted text.

Rules

Rules (filters) can perform actions on incoming messages, such as highlighting them in the message listing, moving them to other folders, or playing special sounds. Figure 4.34 shows the Rules pane.

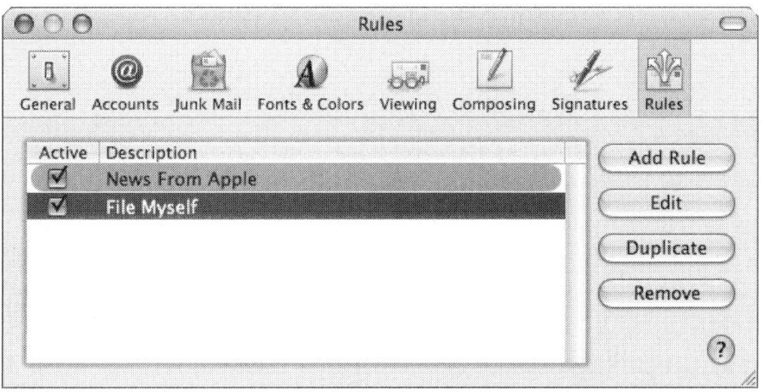

FIGURE 4.34 Rules can automate the process of going through your messages.

Each rule in the list is evaluated once per incoming message (unless the Active box is unchecked). In fact, multiple rules can act on a single message. To change the order in which the rules are applied, drag rule entries in the list to the order you want.

NOTE

Apple includes a default rule for dealing with Apple mailings. If you aren't subscribed to any Apple lists (or if you are and don't want them to be highlighted), you can delete or uncheck this rule.

There are four options for manipulating the rule list: Add Rule, Edit, Duplicate, and Remove. The function of each option is self-explanatory.

Rule creation is simple. Each rule consists of *conditions* that look at portions of the incoming message to determine what *actions* to perform. Figure 4.35 demonstrates the rule creation process.

When creating a new rule, first enter a description—this is used to identify the rule in the listing. Next, decide whether the rule you're creating will require *all* of a series of conditions to be met (such as 'from `"blah@emailaddress.com"` *and* containing the subject "Lottery"') or *any* of the conditions to be matched (an *or* condition such as 'from `"blah@emailaddress.com"` or `"blah2@emailaddress.com"`'). Use the pop-up menu following If to choose "any" or "all" condition matching.

Next, compose the conditions. The Rule starts with a single condition; additional conditions can be added by clicking the "+" button at the end of the condition line. Conditions can be deleted with the "-" button. In Figure 4.35, I'm matching any message where the From address contains either `jray@poisontooth.com` or `johnray@mac.com`.

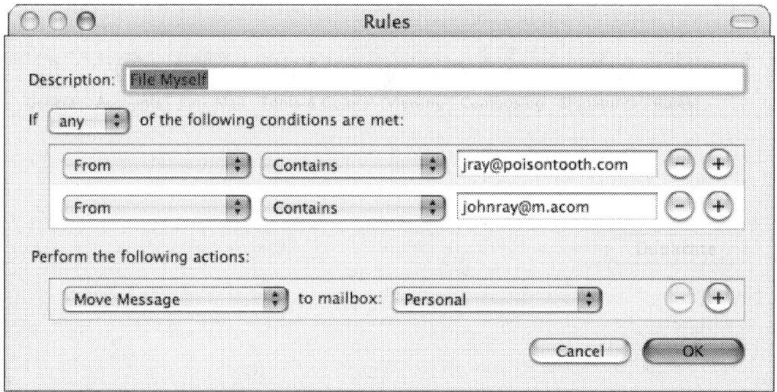

FIGURE 4.35 Unlike other email programs, Mail's rules are simple to create.

Finally, choose the actions; again using the "+" and "-" buttons to add and delete as many actions as you want. In this example, I've chosen to move any messages that match my conditions to the mailbox named Personal."

The conditions and actions are extremely flexible and allow you to match against your Address Book entries and the message content itself. Likewise, the actions give you complete control over the message:

- Move Message—Move the message to another mailbox.
- Copy Message—Copy the message to another mailbox, leaving a copy in the default mailbox.
- Set the Color—Set the highlight color for the message.
- Play Sound—Play a system (or custom) beep sound.
- Bounce Icon in Dock—Bounce the Mail icon in the Dock.
- Forward/Redirect/Reply To—Send the message to another email address. Click the Message button to enter text that will be included with the message being sent.
- Delete the Message—Delete the message. Useful for automatically getting rid of common spam messages.
- Mark as Read—Mark the message as read.
- Mark as Flagged—Flag the message.
- Run AppleScript—Run an AppleScript for advanced processing.
- Stop Evaluating Rules—Stop processing any further rules in the filter.

Click OK to set and activate the rule.

Menus

Wrapping up our Mail application overview, we'll look at the menu options. Most of these options have already been covered somewhere in the chapter, but there are a few obscure options you might be interested in.

File

The File menu is used to create a new message, or multiple "views" into your mailboxes. It can also be used to save a message as a draft before sending.

- New Message (Command-N)—Create a new message.
- New Viewer Window (Option-Command-N)—Open another mailbox viewer. The main Mail window is called the Viewer window.
- Close—Close the frontmost window.
- Save As (Shift-Command-S)—Save the current message in an external file.
- Save as Draft (Command-S)—Save the current message as a draft.
- Attach File (Shift-Command-A)—Attach a file to the message you are composing.
- Save Attachments—Save the message's attachments.
- Import Mailboxes—Launch an assistant to import mailbox files from Outlook Express, Netscape, Emailer, or other applications.
- Page Setup (Shift-Command-P)—Configure the printer.
- Print (Command-P)—Print the frontmost document.

Edit

The Edit menu performs as you would expect. Besides the usual Paste selection, it also offers the capability to Paste as Quotation, Paste with Current Style (maintains the text style of you document), automatically quoting the text in the clipboard. The menu also includes spell checking and search-and-replace options.

Use these Edit menu items when composing messages:

- Append Selected Messages (Shift-Command-I)—Add selected messages to the end of the message being written.
- Attach File (Shift-Command-A)—Attach a file to the message in the composition window.
- Remove Attachments—Remove any attachments in the message being composed.
- Attachments, Include Original Attachments—Include the attachments in a reply that were part of the original message.
- Attachments, Send Windows Friendly Attachments—Create attachments that will be "friendly" to Windows systems and not include Macintosh specific meta-information.

View

The View menu changes the way in which messages are listed in the mail program. Users can sort, display message sizes, and display messages marked for deletion.

- Columns—Select the columns displayed in the message listing.
- Sort By—Choose the column by which the mailbox viewer window is open.
- Organize By Thread—Enter threaded message browsing mode.
- Expand All Threads—Show the contents of all threads.
- Collapse All Threads—Reduce all threads to a single message listing line.
- Show Bcc (Option-Command-B)—Add a Blind Carbon Copy field to the composition window.
- Show Reply-To (Option-Command-R)—Add a Reply-To field to the composition window.
- Display Selected Messages Only—Focus hides all messages except those selected in the mailbox viewer. To restore the view of *all* messages, choose Show All Messages.
- Message—Choose to view the raw source of the message, complete headers, or the decoding type.
- Addresses—When Use Smart Addresses is selected in the Addresses submenu, Mail uses the "address objects" described in this chapter. To revert to the older addressing style choose Show Name and Address.
- Hide/Show Mailboxes (Shift-Command-M)—Show the mailbox tray.
- Show Deleted Messages (Command-L)—Show messages that are marked as deleted. When you're not using a Trash folder, messages are hidden from view after being marked as deleted.
- Hide/Show Status Bar (Command-Option-S)—Hide/Show the message count status bar directly under the toolbar.
- Hide Toolbar—Hide the toolbar in the active window.
- Customize Toolbar—Customize the toolbar for the frontmost window type.

Mailbox

The Mailbox menu is used to create or modify local or IMAP-based mailboxes. Mac OS X automatically switches between local and remote mailboxes depending on your account configuration.

- Online Status, Go Offline/Online—Log off all email accounts and do not attempt to check for mail.
- Online Status, Take <*account name*> Offline—Log out of a specific email account.

- Get New Mail, In all Accounts (Shift-Command-N)—Check for new mail in all accounts.
- Get New Mail, *<account>*—Get new messages from a specific account.
- Synchronize—Synchronize local mailbox with remote server for offline reading.
- Erase Deleted Messages—Choose to erase messages that have been moved to the trash for all your accounts, or a specific server.
- Erase Junk Mail (Option-Command-J)—Delete any messages stored in the Junk mailbox.
- New—Create a new mailbox. If an IMAP account is selected, the mailbox is created on the server.
- Rename—Rename the selected mailbox.
- Delete—Delete the selected mailbox.
- Go To—Show the contents of one of the default (In, Out, Trash, Drafts, Junk) mailboxes.
- Use This Mailbox For—Set the highlighted mailbox (for IMAP servers) so that it will be used to hold Drafts, Sent messages, and so on.
- Rebuild—Reloads the current mailbox. Occasionally, Mail gets out of sync and the message list is displayed incorrectly. Choose this option to fix the problem.

Message

Use the Message menu to operate on the message currently highlighted or being displayed. This menu can be used to clean up replies by removing attachments or appending additional messages.

- Send (Shift-Command-D)—Send the current message.
- Reply (Command-R)—Reply to the current message. If you have text selected when choosing this option, only that text is quoted.
- Reply All (Shift-Command-R)—Reply to everyone who received the original message.
- Reply with iChat (Option-Command-I)—Open an iChat session with the highlighted message's sender, if possible.
- Forward (Shift-Command-F)—Forward an existing message to another address.
- Redirect (Shift-Command-E)—Redirect an existing message to another address. Similar to Forward Message, but does not quote the original message.
- Bounce (Option-Command-B)—Bounce the message to the sender and remove it from the mailbox.

- Mark—Toggle Read, Flagged, and Junk mail status for the message.
- Move To—Transfer the message to another mailbox.
- Copy To—Copy the message to another mailbox.
- Move Again (Option-Command-T)—Transfer a message to the last mailbox accessed.
- Apply Rules (Option-Command-L)—Apply Mail rules (filters) to the selected message or messages.
- Add Sender to Address Book (Command-Y)—Add the sender to the Address Book application.
- Remove Attachments—Remove any attachments to the message before sending. Useful for stripping replies of their attachments.
- Text Encoding—Choose the text encoding for the message. This is usually determined automatically by your system language settings; used for international/cross-platform communication.

Format

The Format menu is used to change to the text style within a message you are composing. The following options are available for your use:

- Show Fonts—Choose a font for message composition.
- Show Colors—Choose a color to use with your font.
- Style—Set font sizes and basic styling (bold, italic, and so on).
- Alignment—Set the text alignment (left, right, center) for the active message.
- Make Plain/Rich Text (Shift-Command-T)—Toggle between plain and rich text modes. Remember, toggling a rich text message to plain text mode removes all formatting information.
- Quote Level, Increase (Command+')—Add a level of quotes (>) to the selection.
- Quote Level, Decrease (Option-Command-')—Remove one level of quoting (>) from the selection.

Window

The Window menu operates as it does in other applications—providing quick access to open windows. In addition, it provides an Address's selection for quick access to the Address Book window (Option-Command-A), Previous Recipients, as well as an Activity Viewer (Option-Command-V). The Activity Viewer shows task Mail is completing, along with a description of the action that is taking place. To cancel or stop an action, click the Stop button.

iChat AV

In the mid-1990s, Apple provided a fast and easy-to-use videoconferencing solution for its AV line of computers. The software, as nice as it was, saw a halt in its development during Apple's troubled search for a valid business model and a new operating system.

There are shareware/freeware conferencing solutions—Apple's own QuickTime Broadcaster can even be coaxed into filling the niche—but none approach the ease-of-use of Apple's other consumer-level software. With the release of Panther and iChat AV, ordinary users can once again hold high-quality full-motion videoconferences with their friends and colleagues.

iChat AV combines AOL compatible instant messaging with computer-to-computer video and audio chats. Figure 4.36 shows an example of a video chat session in progress.

FIGURE 4.36 Videoconferencing is simple and fun with iChat AV.

iChat AV allows you to communicate in real-time with people who use `Mac.com` or have an AOL Instant Messenger (AIM) account. Even if you have no intention of using the instant messaging capabilities, you'll still need one of these accounts because they are used to establish the initial audio or video connection. You can sign up for a free AOL Instant Messenger (AIM) account at `http://www.aim.com` or an iChat-only (free) .Mac username at `http://www.mac.com`.

NOTE

If other users on your local network use iChat AV, you don't need to use an AIM or `Mac.com` account to chat with them. Rendezvous has been incorporated into iChat so that it can automatically generate a buddy list of "nearby" users. Rendezvous is discussed further in Chapter 9.

NOTE

Apple has chosen to use SIP (Session Initiation Protocol, RFC 2543, `http://www.zvon.org/tmRFC/RFC2543/Output/frontpage.html`) and RTP (Real Time Protocol, RFC 1889, `http://www.zvon.org/tmRFC/RFC1889/Output/index.html`) along with well-known compression codecs for initiating and transmitting audio and video.

Unfortunately, it is incompatible with other similar implementations of conferencing software. If you want to try a cross-platform video-only solution, Yahoo's IM client for Mac OS X supports (and *has* supported) video for some time. Download the Yahoo client from `http://messenger.yahoo.com/messenger/download/mac.html`.

Conferencing Hardware

iChat AV works with recognized Mac OS X video sources—FireWire camcorders, Webcams, and analog A/V conversion devices, such as the Dazzle FireWire Bridge. Apple's own iSight camera (`http://www.apple.com/isight/`) is cost effective and produces high-quality images. If the $150 price tag is within range, I recommend the iSight purchase. If not, the iBot camera is available for the $50–75 range on eBay and works fine with iChat AV.

NOTE

Apple's iChat AV package includes drivers for popular cameras, including the iBot. If you've already installed third-party camera drivers, you may see the message "Your camera is in use by another application." Removing the third-party drivers and rebooting seems to solve the problem.

Of course, if you get the error message and *are* using the camera in another application, you may just need to quit the application.

CAUTION

It should be pointed out that iChat AV requires *at least* a 600MHz G3 for videoconferencing. If you attempt to use video on a slower machine, it reports that video is not available on your computer; other video chat software provides similar functionality with much less restrictive processor requirements.

Thankfully, Ecamm Network has provided a hack to get around both the 600Mhz and FireWire requirements. iChatUSBCam (`http://www.ecamm.com/mac/ichatusbcam/`) enables you to use USB cameras and low-end systems to run iChat A/V.

If you do not have a video camera, you can use iChat AV as an audioconferencing solution with any system-recognized microphone.

Finally, no matter what high-end CPU platform or video hardware you may own, you'll need network bandwidth to accommodate audio or video streams. The low-end requirements are 56kbps for audio, and 128kbps for video.

Realistically, 56k modem users may be able to audioconference if they have a stable and noise-free connection, but the best experience comes from a dedicated digital connection. xDSL, Cable, and LAN users should be able to carry high-quality audio/video streams easily.

Setup

The first time you start iChat AV, you are prompted for either your AIM or .Mac iChat username, as shown in Figure 4.37. To register for a free .Mac username, click the Get an iChat Account button.

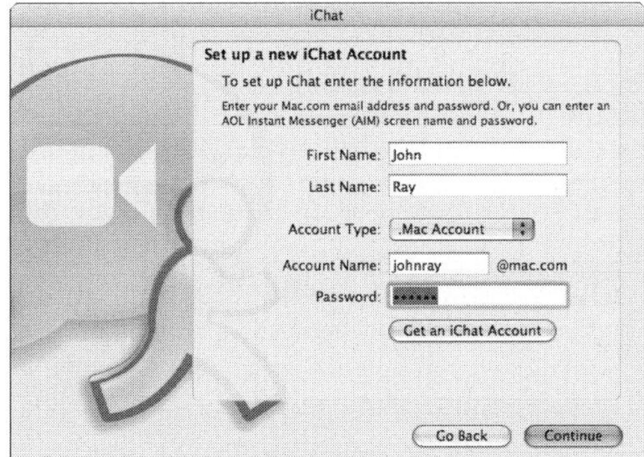

FIGURE 4.37 Enter your account information.

Next, you are prompted for whether you want to use Rendezvous for messaging. If you have a relatively contained local network, turning on Rendezvous probably isn't an issue. If you're part of a subnet with hundreds of clients, however, Rendezvous is probably going to overwhelm your buddy list.

Finally, iChat provides a preview of your audio and video input. Make sure that if you have a camera and a microphone attached the inputs are visible before continuing.

To access these settings after the initial iChat AV run, choose iChat, Preferences from the menu, and click the Accounts icon, as shown in Figure 4.38. Enter your AIM screen name or your full .Mac account (including the `@mac.com`) in the AIM Screen Name field, and enter your password in the Password field. You can quickly populate the fields with your system-stored .Mac preferences by choosing Use my .Mac Account from the AIM Screen Name field's pop-up menu.

If you're using an alternative AIM server or require a proxy, click the Server Options button to provide connection or proxy information for iChat AV.

Rendezvous messaging can be enabled or disabled by clicking the Enable Local Rendezvous Messaging check box.

FIGURE 4.38 Configure iChat for use with your .Mac or AIM account.

After configuring iChat AV, you can log into AIM or Rendezvous using the Log Into menu options found in the iChat AV application menu, or by setting your availability in the buddy list window (there's a pop-up menu directly under your username) or the iChat AV menu extra to anything but Offline.

NOTE

The iChat AV menu extra is displayed as a "speech bubble" on the right side of your menu bar. You do *not* have to have iChat AV open to log in to or out of AIM, or to initiate a chat session. This menu is always active and can be used to set your availability or choose a buddy to start a conversation.

Setting Your iChat AV Buddy Icon

A unique feature of the AIM service is the capability to set custom thumbnails of all your contacts and yourself—these are known as *buddy icons* (or *buddy pictures* depending on what label Apple decided to use where). Your buddy icon is automatically transmitted to your friends so that they can see whatever you've set your icon to be. Similarly, if they've set custom icons, they will automatically show up on your system.

By default your personal AIM buddy icon is the image set in the Address Book application or the icon used for your account image. To replace it with one of your choosing, drag a new image into the image well beside your name at the top of the Buddy List window. An editing window appears to allow you to position and scale the image, as shown in Figure 4.39. Drag the image so that the section you want to use as an icon is centered in the bright square in the middle of the window; then use the zoom slider underneath the image to zoom in and out. The center square shows the icon that will be set—albeit larger than its final size in iChat AV. When you're satisfied with the image, click Set.

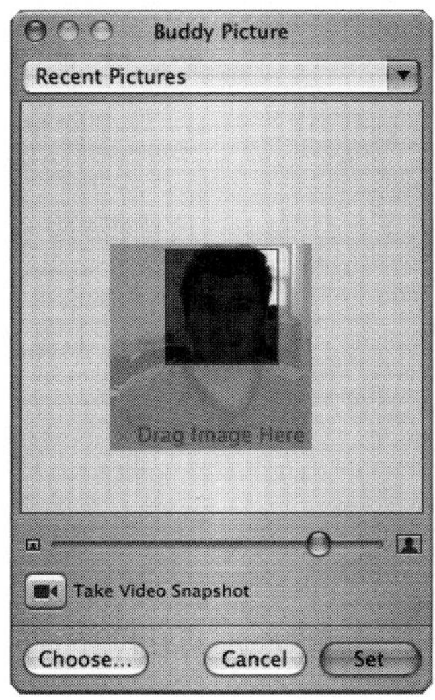

FIGURE 4.39 Position and crop your image.

If you want to choose another image from a file, click the Choose button, and you are presented with a standard file selection dialog box. Users with a camera attached will notice the Take Video Snapshot button at the bottom of their window. Clicking this button displays a live video preview, gives you roughly 3 seconds to primp and preen, and then automatically takes a snapshot that you can use as a buddy icon. This provides an easy way to create a new icon for your mood du jour.

Given that it is so easy to create and switch button icons, starting in iChat AV, you now have the ability to switch to any icon you've used recently by clicking your thumbnail image in the Buddy List window. A palette of frequently used icons displays, enabling you to quickly switch to icons to match your mood, as shown in Figure 4.40.

FIGURE 4.40 Jump to any of your frequently used icons.

Use the Edit Picture selection within the pop-up palette to reposition or recrop the selected icon.

> **TIP**
>
> If you *really* want to keep your buddy icon updated, consider iChat Streaming Icon (`http://ichat.twosailors.com/`). This unique application uses your camera to capture a new buddy icon as quickly as once every half second. Best of all, *any* AIM client can see the changes making it a means of transmitting video (albeit small and jerky video) to your non-Mac friends.

Status Settings

When you are logged in to iChat AV, other members can see whether you are available for a chat. By default there are just two states you can set your account to use: Available and Away—accessed from either the iChat AV menu extra or the drop-down menu under your name at the top of the Buddy List window. If your machine has been idle for several minutes, it automatically kicks into an "idle" state to show that you haven't been using your computer.

To create additional states, use the two Custom options found under the Buddy List availability menu. You are allowed to type your own custom label to be displayed in your buddies' chat clients.

> **NOTE**
>
> Your status, as well as the status of your buddies, is typically indicated by green (available), red (away), and orange (idle) dots next to each name (including yours) in the Buddy List window and iChat AV menu extra.
>
> If you have trouble differentiating between the colors or just want a change of pace, the availability "dots" can be changed to shapes using the General pane within the iChat AV preferences panes.

Buddy Controls

When you log in to AIM through iChat, the full Buddy List window appears onscreen to show whether your friends are online (not grayed out), whether they're available to chat, and what conferencing capabilities (Audio/Video) are available to them, as demonstrated in Figure 4.41. The video camera icon shows video availability, whereas the telephone represents an audio-chat ready contact. You can customize what details are displayed in the Buddy List and sort it by different criteria using the iChat AV View menu.

Rendezvous chatting, if active, opens a virtually identical window displaying the active iChat users on your local subnet.

FIGURE 4.41 You can easily see who's available to chat and their capabilities using the Buddy List; the listings for people who aren't connected to the AIM server are dimmed.

Adding Buddies

Because your buddy list is stored on the AIM servers, you must be logged in to manage the list. To add a buddy, click the "+" button at the bottom of the iChat Buddy List window.

A dialog containing your Address Book entries appears, as shown in Figure 4.42. If the person you want to add to your Buddy List has an AIM or `Mac.com` listing, highlight the person and click Select Buddy.

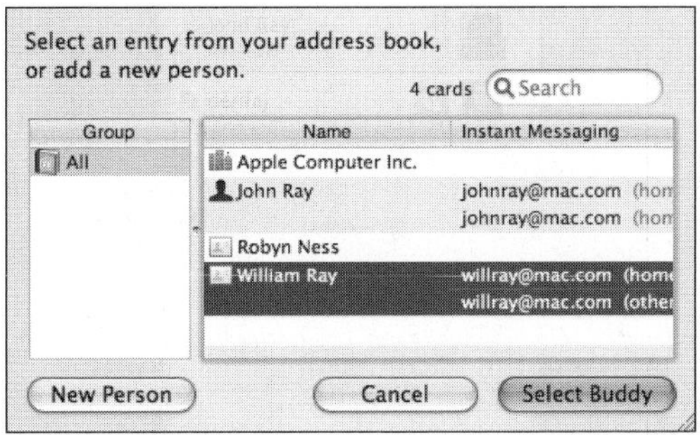

FIGURE 4.42 Add your AIM and .Mac buddies to your list.

If the person doesn't show an instant messaging name, you are prompted for the information. If the buddy-to-be isn't currently in your Address Book at all, click the New Person button to create a new entry. Enter the person's AIM or .Mac screen name, as well as his real name and email address in the window that appears. You can drag an image file (if available) into the image well to set a custom buddy icon. Click the Add button to save your new Buddy.

NOTE

Address Book and iChat are integrated such that adding a new buddy to iChat automatically adds a new card in Address Book. However, because your buddy list is stored on the Instant Messenger server, you can't remove a buddy simply by deleting an Address Book card. Instead, you must select the buddy in the Buddy List and choose Edit, Delete.

Also, keep in mind that deleting a buddy from the Buddy List does not remove the person's card from the Address Book.

Editing Buddy Info

To edit any information for a buddy that is already stored, select the buddy in the list; then choose Buddies, Get Info, or Control-click on the buddy herself and select Get Info. The Buddy Info, shown in Figure 4.43, provides quick access to your Address Book buddy information.

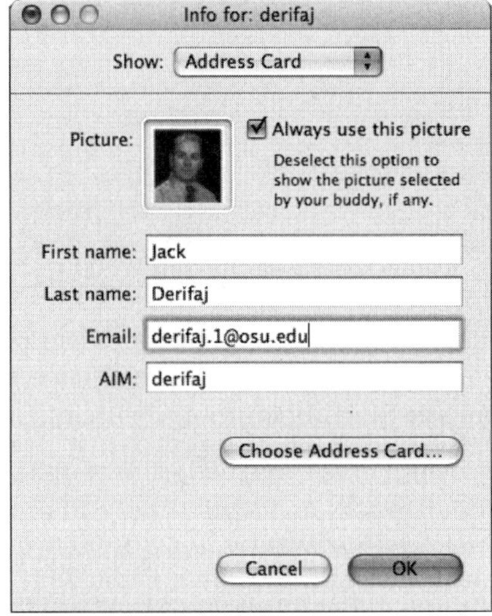

FIGURE 4.43 Edit your buddies and override their ugly and/or horrifying icons.

As with the initial setup, here you can set all the contact information for your buddy, as well as a custom buddy icon. If you *do* set a custom icon, you can choose to always use it in your buddy list. If this option is not set, your buddy icon can be overridden by any custom icon set on the remote system. Depending on how well you know your friends, this could lead to some embarrassment in the workplace.

Buddy Actions

From the Get Info window, you can also access Buddy Actions by choosing Actions from the Show pop-up menu. A Buddy Action, displayed in Figure 4.44, is simply something that "happens" when one of your contacts becomes available or does something interesting.

FIGURE 4.44 Buddy actions automatically react when your contacts do something.

In this example, I've chosen to speak the text "Anne is here!" and bounce the Dock item repeatedly when my buddy becomes available. Additionally, by checking the box Perform Actions Only Next Time Event Occurs, the action automatically is removed after the first time it is used. I have something very important to say to Anne, but usually could care less whether she is online, thus the setting. (No, Anne, that isn't true, I'm simply putting on airs for the reader.)

Seven possible events can be used to trigger a buddy action:

- Buddy Becomes Available—Your buddy has become available for IM'ing.
- Buddy Becomes Unavailable—Your buddy is no longer available for IM'ing.
- Message received—Your buddy has received an IM that you sent.
- Text Invitation—Your buddy has sent you a text chat invitation.
- Audio Invitation—Your buddy has sent you an audio chat invitation.
- Video Invitation—Your buddy has sent you a video chat invitation.
- Buddy Accepted A/V Invitation—Your buddy has accepted an A/V chat invitation that *you* have sent.

As you set actions for events, a megaphone icon appears beside the event that contains an action. This lets you keep track of what events trigger actions without having to select and inspect each one.

Before you ask, no, in the current shipping release of iChat AV, there is no action for speaking the contents of the messages sent to you.

Buddy Groups

If you're the sort who actually has friends, you may quickly find youself with a long-scrolling list of buddies in your window. To better manage your buddy list, you can arrange them into groups such as "People I know," "People who are stalking me," and "People I am stalking." After creating the groups, you can choose which group (or groups) are displayed at once.

To access the groups feature of iChat AV choose View, Show Groups. A window drawer appears, as shown in Figure 4.45. A default group Buddies contains all your buddies.

FIGURE 4.45 Arrange buddies into groups.

To add a new group, click the "+" button at the bottom of the group drawer and type a name for the group. Group names can be edited at any time by double-clicking its name in the list. Groups (and the buddies they contain) can be removed by selecting their name and choosing Edit, Delete (or pressing the Delete button on your keyboard).

After adding a group, populate it with buddies by dragging their names in the Buddy List onto the group names. To remove a buddy from a group, make sure that the group name is highlighted in the drawer; then drag the buddy back into the default Buddies group.

To only show the buddies within a specific group or set of groups, use the check boxes to the left of the group names to select which groups are displayed in your buddy list at a given time. The All Groupscheck box is a shortcut for selecting all the groups simultaneously.

To close the group drawer, click the arrow in the upper-right corner of the drawer, or choose View, Hide Groups from the menu.

TIP

If this seems like an awkward way to display groups, I agree. Thankfully, Apple added a hard-to-find preference that makes groups much more manageable. To add a permanent drop-down group menu to the Buddy List window, visit the General pane of the application preferences and click the Use Groups in Buddy List check box.

Instant Messaging

In iChat AV, there are three types of "messaging" that you can choose to use to communicate with your friends: text, audio, and video—represented by the "A", Phone, and Video camera icons at the bottom of your buddy list. To start a messaging session with one of your buddies, just select her name in the list and click the appropriate icon at the bottom of the Buddy List.

Alternatively, you can double-click your buddy's name to start a text chat, or click the telephone or video icon by her buddy picture to start an audio or video chat.

> **NOTE**
>
> The iChat AV menu extra can also be used to start a chat session by choosing a buddy name from the menu. If the buddy has multiple means of communicating (besides simple text), iChat displays a window with three buttons (Text, Audio, Video) and allows you to choose your prefered chat method.

For those who want to mouse around and use their menus, the Buddies menu also allows you to initiate a chat session, including two "special" chat types—one-way audio and one-way video. These are useful if you want to send audio or video to someone without a camera. They can type their responses to you and watch/hear your audio/video stream.

Text Messaging

Starting a text messaging session opens an empty chat window. Type your message in the message field at the bottom of the window and press Return on your keyboard. If you're into sending "emoticons" (smiley faces) there is a convenient pull-down smiley menu on the right side of the input field. Basic formatting controls (Bold, Underline, Font, and so on) are found under the Format menu and can be used to style your text on-the-fly.

After sending your message, it appears in the upper portion of the window, along with whatever reply the other person sends. The text of a conversation can be saved by choosing File, Save a Copy As.

If you receive a message while not already engaged in a chat session with the sender, you are alerted, and a message window appears. If you click on the window, it displays an area for you to type a response (immediately accepting the invitation) or provides you the option of clicking Block to block the request and further messages from the buddy, Decline to turn down the chat with your buddy, or Accept to start chatting. Again, if you enter a response and press Return, it is assumed that you have accepted the chat.

You can add the person you're currently chatting with to your Buddy list using Buddies, Add Buddy.

TIP

If you find the conversation bubbles "cute" but overwhelming (or perhaps just downright annoying), you can use View, Show as Text to disable them (and Show as Balloons to turn them back on when your Windows friends are over).

Further chat window View settings include the option to choose how buddies are identified in a chat (using their pictures, names, or both), the capability to set a customized picture as the chat background, and finally the option to clear the background picture after you've decided that it is way too silly a feature to enable.

NOTE

If, during the course of a conversation, the remote party closes the connection or gets bumped offline, the chat window stays open. If they come back, a message to that effect appears in the already open window, and you can resume the conversation where you left off.

HyperLinks and Files In addition to sending ordinary text messages, iChat allows you to send files. To send a file, drag its icon into the message area of a chat window and press Return on your keyboard. The recipient can then drag the file onto his desktop. If you send image files, they appear inside the chat window as part of the conversation. (For maximum compatibility with people using AIM programs other than iChat, it's recommended that you stick with JPEG and GIF image formats.)

Hyperlinks can also be sent as a special iChat object. To send a hyperlink, drag the bookmark from your browser, use the Edit, Attach Hyperlink option to enter in a clickable URL, or just type or paste it in, and it will automatically be recognized.

Private Messages AIM messages are not (usually) a direct line of communication between people. Instead, all IM traffic is routed through instant messaging servers, in the case of AIM, AOL's servers. Although this conveniently avoids many connection problems with firewalls and inbound traffic, it also leads to privacy concerns about who could potentially be watching your chat. In addition, the extra time required to transmit through a central server can slow file transfers between individuals. To avoid this, users can activate a direct instant messaging session where all information is passed directly between the participants' computers.

To do this, choose the buddy to send a direct IM to, and choose Buddies, Send Direct Message (Command-Option-Shift-M). If both you and the recipient are connected directly to the Internet, an IM session starts, exactly as it would through the AOL servers.

Group Chat Sessions You can participate in chats with different people simultaneously, each contained in its own separate window (the default). You can also start a chat session with multiple people where all participants can see messages and type simultaneously.

To start a group chat:

1. Highlight the buddies you want to invite to chat; then Control-click on any of the names and choose Invite To Chat.

2. Type a message inviting the participants. When the invited buddies receive the chat request, they can choose to accept or decline. If they accept, they can send and receive messages as part of the group.

If you start a multiperson chat, shown in Figure 4.46, and want to switch to a single-user IM or Direct IM, you can use the View, Chat Options menu selection. You are prompted for what type of IM session you want to switch to.

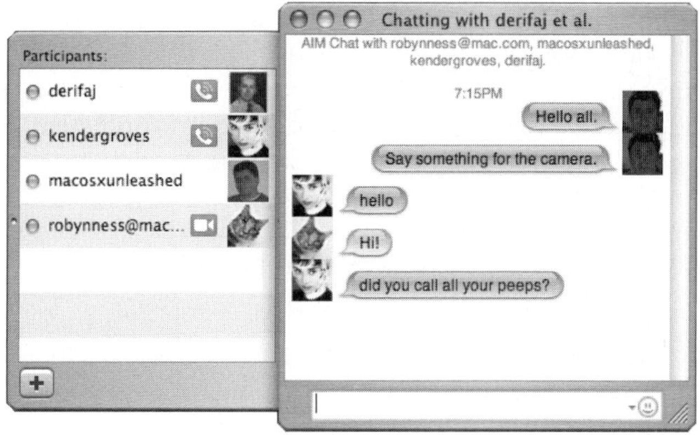

FIGURE 4.46 Start multiperson chats in iChat AV.

The chat options can also be used to view the Chat Name, which, in turn, can be used by any AIM user to join the chat, even if they aren't on your buddy list. In iChat AV, the File, Go To Chat selection allows any iChat user to enter the chat name and join your chat. Other AIM clients should offer the same feature, but how it is accessed obviously will vary.

Creating or Joining a Persistent Chat Room To start a group chat that remains open and allows others to join whenever they want, use File, Go To Chat (Command-G). When prompted, type the name of an existing chat room (if you want to join a chat someone else has created), or make up your own name. The iChat AV chat window appears with *no* participants. Others can join your chat room using the Go To Chat feature on their copy of iChat AV.

NOTE

Some chat names (including those with punctuation) are unacceptable when creating a chat room. If iChat AV does not return a chat window immediately on using Go To Chat, the name you typed is invalid.

Audio Chats

Surprisingly, it's actually *easier* to describe the options for audio and video chats than it is for text messaging. After an audio chat has been initiated, a small window, shown in Figure 4.47 appears.

FIGURE 4.47 The audio chat window displays input level, mute, and volume controls.

The input level meter can be used to gauge whether your microphone is positioned correctly, or whether you need to adjust the input level (gain) within the Sound System Preferences Pane. An iSight user in an average office environment should see 1/8-1/4-inch of "flicker" (background noise) on the left side of the bar. If background noise approaches 1/3-inch or 1/2-inch of the bar length, you may need to reduce the gain or find a quieter place to chat.

During a chat, you can adjust the volume using the chat window's volume slider, or quickly mute the conversation so that you can swear loudly by clicking the "crossed out" microphone button.

NOTE

If the volume is too high, you may experience feedback as the microphone starts to pick up the speaker sounds. You can fix this by lowering your gain, lowering the volume, or positioning the microphone farther away from your speaker.

Laptop users may notice that only a single speaker is active during A/V chats in iChat AV. This is a purposeful attempt to reduce feedback by disabling the speaker closest to the microphone.

If you are on the receiving end of an audio chat request, you are prompted with an incoming chat alert (similar to an incoming text message) and, after the alert window is clicked, given the option of accepting or declining the chat—or making a *text* reply. If you choose a text reply, you effectively open a new text chat with the remote party, and the audio chat is canceled.

TIP

Even if your buddy doesn't have an audio input source, you can still have a one-sided audio rant at him. Use the Buddies, Invite to One-Way Audio Chat option to start a one-way chat. Great for setting things straight with your significant other.

Video Chats

A video chat works virtually identically to an audio chat but with the added bonus of being able to *see* as well as hear the remote person. When a video chat is initiated, you see a preview of yourself until the chat is accepted. At that point, your image shrinks to the lower-right corner of the window, and your buddy's smiling face fills the rest, as shown in Figure 4.48. You can resize your mini preview by moving your cursor over it and then dragging the resize handle that appears. You can also click and drag the mini preview to any of the four corners of the window.

FIGURE 4.48 Video chats—be seen and heard.

At the bottom of the video chat window is a microphone button for muting the audio portion of chat and a button with two opposing arrows for expanding the view to fill the whole screen.

NOTE

Apple has done an excellent job of smoothing the scaled video when in full-screen mode or when the video window is enlarged. If you haven't tried scaling the video because you're not a fan of pixelized images, give it a try anyway—it's impressive.

When in full-screen mode, moving the mouse displays several button controls above your preview image: an "X" to close the chat, a microphone to mute, and double arrows to shrink back to a windowed view. Again, use the drag handle that appears in the upper-left corner of the preview to resize your own image onscreen or click and drag the entire mini preview window to move it to another corner.

To pause the video display at any time, use Video, Pause Video.

When recieving a video chat request, clicking the alert window gives you a preview of your own video feed so that you can make sure that you've dressed yourself properly before clicking the Accept button to start the chat. Like the audio chat, you can also decline a chat request or send a text reply instead of video.

If your friend has no video camera connected, you can still give her the pleasure of watching you by starting a One-Way Video Chat using the Buddies menu.

Video Bandwidth and Settings

Depending on you and your buddies' connections, video and audio chats may be a bit choppy or sporadic. To get an idea of the throughput of your connection, choose Video, Connection Doctor. The Connection Doctor (which doesn't really make anything better) is displayed in Figure 4.49.

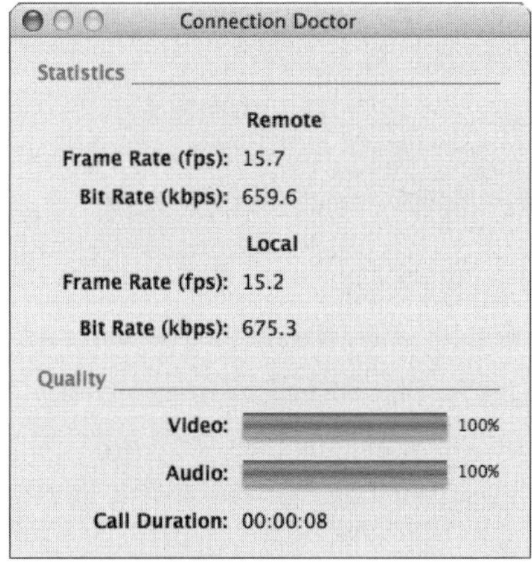

FIGURE 4.49 The Connection Doctor displays stats on your current A/V connection.

Some choppiness problems can be rectified by limiting the amount of data being streamed to your chat partner. Usually iChat AV determines the proper streaming rate automatically, but in some cases you may want to try setting the value yourself. To do this, use the Video preferences pane within the iChat AV preferences, shown in Figure 4.50.

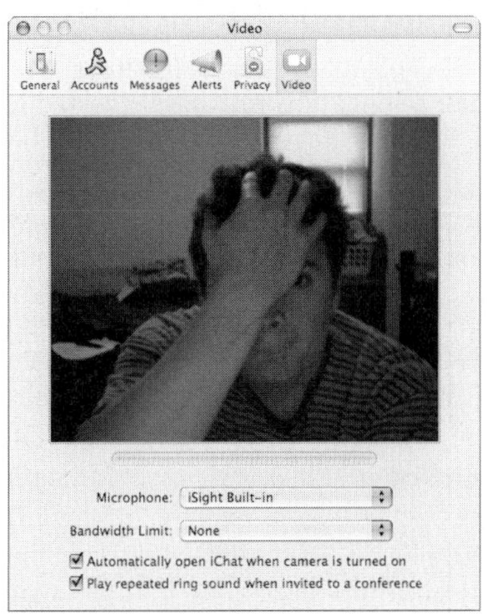

FIGURE 4.50 Adjust your iChat AV preferences

The bandwidth limit is initially set to *none*, meaning that iChat attempts to stream data as quickly as possible to the remote site. You can limit the bandwidth to anywhere from 100kbps to 2Mbps. Low-end (ISDN) connections should restrict the bandwidth to 100kbps, whereas cable and xDSL users may be able to get away with 200kbps or possibily 500kbps. (For those saying "hey, my cable modem can max out at 3Mbps!"—that's true but is almost always the *downstream* speed. Upstream rates usually range from 192kbps to 500kbps.) Only local or high bandwidth (T1/T3/ATM) connections should attempt the higher settings.

In addition to the bandwidth settings, the Video preferences pane gives you access to a preview of your video and audio input and lets you choose which of your audio input sources will be used as the microphone.

Users with an iSight will appreciate the option to Automatically Open iChat When Camera Is Turned On. This launches iChat when the iSight iris is opened.

Finally, there is a check box to repeatedly play a ringing sound when you're invited to an A/V chat. Why this isn't located under the Alerts preferences pane is beyond me.

Firewalls

iChat A/V's video features work well as long as *one side* of a connection is not behind a firewall or connection sharing device. To use video/audio conferencing behind a firewall, you must enable ports 5060 UDP (conference notifications) and 16384-16403 UDP (audio and video) to be passed through to the iChat AV computer. To read Apple's tech note on this topic, visit `http://docs.info.apple.com/article.html?artnum=93208`.

Additional Preferences and Application Settings

Although most of the iChat AV options can be controlled from the Buddy List or menu bar, few options for fine-tuning the application must be accessed from the preferences.

General

Use the General control pane to enable or disable the iChat menu extra (Show Status in Menu Bar), switch to shape-based status, and control what happens (login/logout) when you start and quit iChat AV.

A nice feature found in the General pane is the option to control what your computer does when you return to it after it has been set to Away status. Rather than automatically make you available, you can choose to remain away (and not be bothered by your friends), or have it prompt you to ask whether it should change your status.

Accounts

The Accounts pane is used to fill in the username and password for your .Mac or AIM account. If there are special proxy or login host requirements, the Server Options button can be used to set them.

Messages

You can make additional changes to the appearance of the chat windows under the Messages pane of the iChat preferences, shown in Figure 4.51, including font color and balloon color. Because remote users have control over the fonts and colors that appear in your window, iChat AV gives you the option of reformatting incoming messages to a specific balloon and font color.

FIGURE 4.51 Change your balloon colors, fonts, and so on.

Rendezvous users can choose to show messages as they're being typed (after a short delay) by clicking the Send Text As I Type check box. You can also choose to confirm file transfers, and save chat transcripts for blackmailing your friends later.

Alerts

Under the Actions preferences, choose what iChat does when you or your buddies log in or out. Use the Event pop-up menu to choose an event to modify; then click the check boxes for the actions you want to apply, such as playing sounds, speaking text, and bouncing icons. This is similar to the individual Buddy Actions discussed earlier but applies to *everyone* not just a specific person.

Privacy

The Privacy preferences allow you to choose who in the AIM/.Mac community can send you messages. Choose categories of users, such as those in your buddy list, or name individual users using the Edit List buttons who can or cannot contact you.

If you don't want other people to know that you're idle and that your computer is available for stealing, click the Block Others from Seeing That I Am Idle check box.

Menus

The iChat menus can be used to access a few additional features.

iChat Application Menu

The iChat Application menu can be used to access the application preferences as well as to log in and out of AIM and Rendezvous.

View

The View menu can sort your buddy list based on availability or other attributes, and can even set/clear a background image used in all your chat windows.

Buddies

Under the Buddies menu, you'll find all the actions you can perform when you've selected a person on your buddy list, such as sending messages, emailing, getting info about, or even ignoring.

Video/Audio

The Video (or Audio if you don't have a camera) menu provides quick access to full-screen video, sound muting, video pausing, and the Connection Doctor bandwidth statistics.

Format

Use the Format menu as you would with a word processor to control the font, color, and style of outgoing text messages.

Window

Finally, the Window menu is used to open the AIM Buddy List (Command-1) or Rendezvous Buddy List (Command-2) if you've closed the windows on your computer. Address Book can also be launched by choosing it from this menu.

Sherlock

As its name implies, the Sherlock application is something of a detective, tracking down information on the Internet based on the information you provide. Sherlock is *not* a search engine but an application that provides a common interface to many different types of searches. With specialized categories including yellow pages and a dictionary, Sherlock will quickly become your one-stop reference tool.

Channels

Sherlock packages an Internet search as an element called a *channel*. The default channels are listed in the Channels menu of the Channels pane. They're also listed in the toolbar at the top of the Sherlock window, as shown in Figure 4.52. Choosing a channel refreshes the screen to display the search options appropriate for that channel.

NOTE

Keep in mind that Apple *does not* generate the information returned by Sherlock. If there are inconsistencies in the results, they are the product of the search provider, usually displayed at the bottom of each search channel pane.

Let's take a look at each default channel's use and special features.

FIGURE 4.52 Several search channels are ready-to-use in Sherlock.

Internet

The Internet channel compiles search results from popular Internet search sites, such as Ask Jeeves and Lycos. As shown in Figure 4.53, each search result lists the title and address of a Web page, a relevance rating, and the search site or sites that provided the entry.

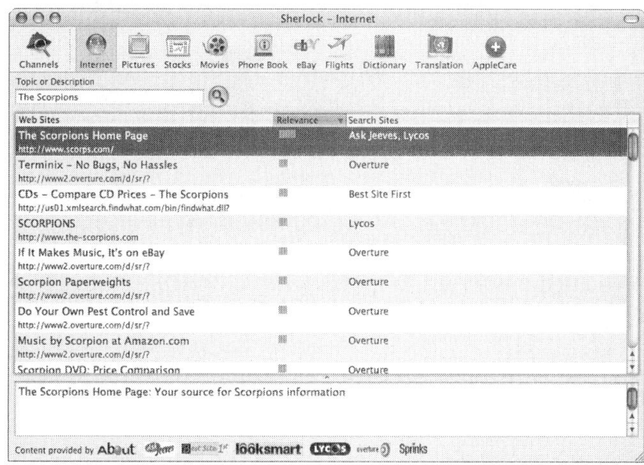

FIGURE 4.53 Searching the Internet from a variety of search engines is simplified by Sherlock.

To perform an Internet search, simply type your search terms into the text entry field at the top of the Internet channel pane and click the green search button or press Return. When the results listing appears, you can select an entry with a single click to see a site description if one is available. Double-clicking launches your default Web browser and opens the page you requested.

Pictures

Similar to searches using the Internet channel, the Pictures channel queries image databases for digital pictures based on your search terms. Thumbnail images of the results are displayed in the results pane, as shown in Figure 4.54. Double-click a thumbnail image in the results to open a Web page displaying the full-sized picture.

> **CAUTION**
>
> The photos displayed in the Pictures channel searches might not be free for commercial use. Read the terms of service from the originating site if you have any questions about what's allowed.

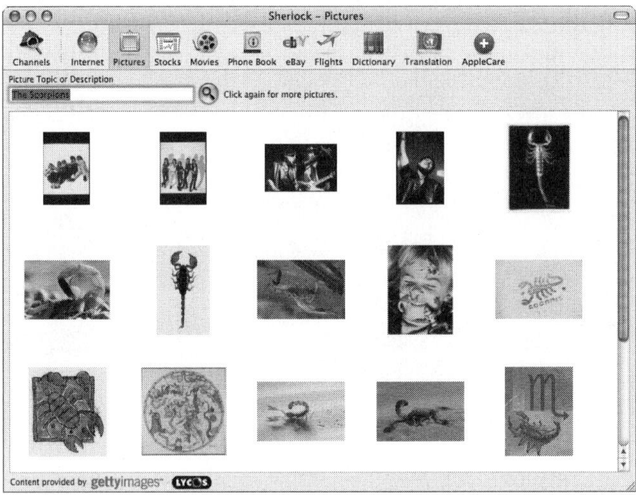

FIGURE 4.54 Results appear as thumbnail images—double-click one to see the original.

Stocks

The Stocks channel, shown in Figure 4.55, provides details about the market performance of publicly traded companies. The information shown includes the stock price at last trade, price change, price range over the course of the day, and the volume of shares traded. You can also view charts of a company's performance over the past year or week or for the current day.

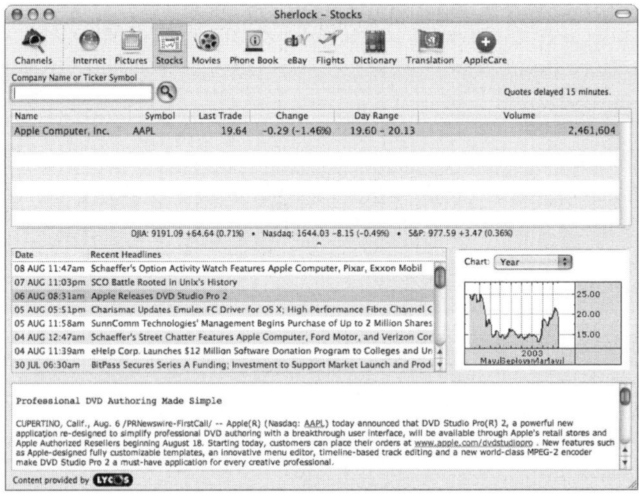

FIGURE 4.55 Enter a company's name or market symbol to see information about it, including recent news stories.

To find information about a company, enter its name or market symbol. Market symbols are unique identifiers, but many companies have similar names or several separate divisions. If you enter a name, you might see a sheet asking you to choose the company you're interested in, as shown Figure 4.56. When the correct name or symbol appears in the text entry field, click the green search button or press the Return key.

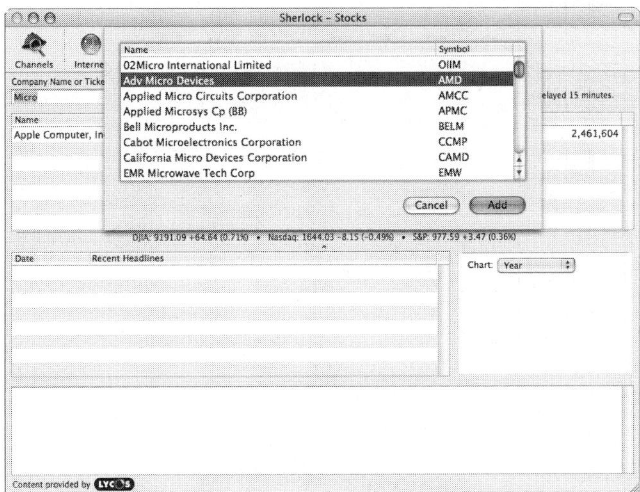

FIGURE 4.56 If you enter a string of letters that appears in more than one company name, a dialog appears where you can choose the company you're interested in.

> **CAUTION**
>
> Market symbols and companies with similar names can make it difficult to ask for the listing you really want. If you don't enter the exact market symbol, some guesswork might be involved for Sherlock to return any results. Always check to make sure that the displayed information is for the company you thought you requested!

As you view information for different companies, they are added to the list in the middle of the Stocks pane so that you can easily return to them. If you want to remove a listing, simply select it and press the Delete key on your keyboard.

In addition to providing stock quotes, Sherlock also displays recent news articles pertaining to the selected company. To read a story, select its headline from the left of the chart, and the bottom pane displays the full text.

Movies

Sherlock's Movies channel, shown in Figure 4.57, pulls together all the information you need to choose a movie and a theater where you can watch it.

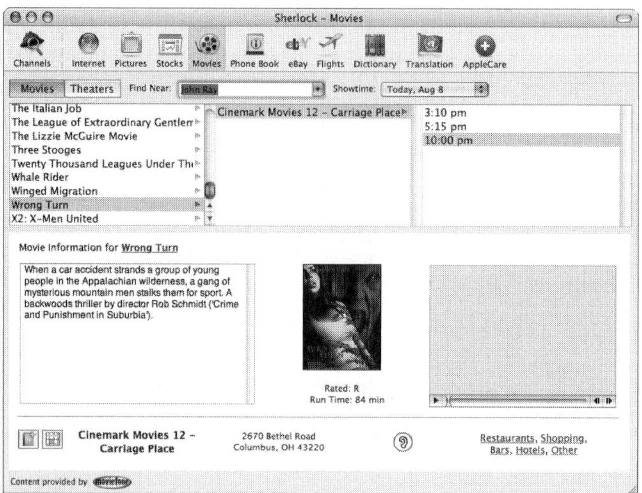

FIGURE 4.57 The Movies channel displays a QuickTime preview of the selected movie as well as theater addresses.

To use the Movies channel, you must enter either your city and state or your ZIP Code in the Find Near field, or just use the default Address Book entry denoted by your name. Then you can choose to search either Movies or Theaters in your area. The Showtime pop-up menu enables you to choose the date of interest to you.

Choose the movie and theater listings at the top of the pane that are of interest to you, and the bottom of the window fills with theater and movie information. In addition to a text summary of the movie, you can watch a preview for the selected option in QuickTime.

NOTE

To play the QuickTime preview, you might be prompted to set your network connection information in QuickTime Preferences if you haven't already done so. Refer to the section on QuickTime in Chapter 8, "Digital Video," for more details.

At the bottom left of the Movies channel you may see two additional buttons: the first adds the theater to your Address Book; the second uses the Phone Book channel (discussed next) to map the theater location.

Phone Book

The Phone Book channel has two modes: a person search (a la White Pages) and a business search (a la Yellow Pages).

The person search mode, shown in Figure 4.58, allows you to find a phone number and address by entering a person's name and a general location. To perform a person search, click the information button at the upper left (the one with an "i" in a white circle). Enter a last name, a first name, and either the city and state or the ZIP Code of the area to search. Then click the green search button. In the middle pane, choose from among the list of potential matches to see detailed information, including a map.

NOTE

As you type in the Find Near field, Sherlock attempts to autocomplete the city, state, and ZIP Code for you.

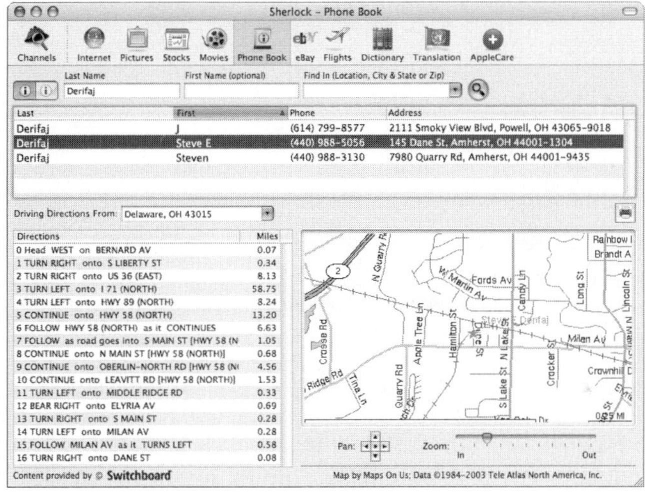

FIGURE 4.58 Locate a person by name and location.

Use the business search to obtain the phone number and address for businesses and to view a map of to their locations. Simply click the information button on the right (the one with an "i" in a yellow circle), enter the business name and either the city and state or the ZIP Code of the area to search, and click the green search button. In the middle pane, choose from among the list of potential matches to see detailed information.

NOTE

To receive driving directions to addresses retrieved in either the person or business search, you need to enter an address in text field labeled Driving Directions From, or choose your name for your Address Book address. The Directions pane fills with step-by-step instructions.

eBay

From the eBay channel, you can search active eBay auctions and track those of interest to you. To search, enter keywords in the Item Title text entry field and set your other parameters, such as product category, region, and price range, and then click the search button. When you choose a result from the search, its details are displayed in the bottom of the window, as shown in Figure 4.59.

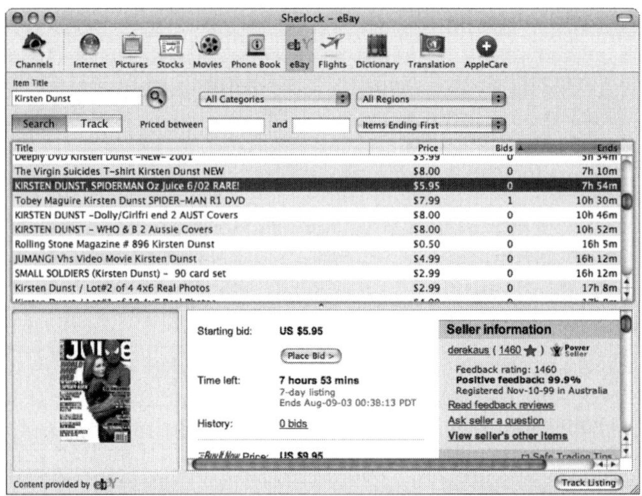

FIGURE 4.59 If you enjoy online auctions, the eBay channel will feed your addiction.

To track an item, highlight it in the results listing and click the Track Listing button at lower right. Changing to Track mode using the button just below the search field reveals a list of only those items you're tracking. To remove an item, select it and press the Delete key on your keyboard.

Flights

For information on current flights, go to the Flights channel. Here you can view flight status by route or by airline and flight number. Select a specific flight for details about the aircraft and flight. For some entries, you can also view a chart depicting the plane's position en route, as shown in the lower-right corner of Figure 4.60.

You can click the small switchlike button at the bottom right of the Flights pane to set preferences for the Flights channel. As shown in Figure 4.61, you can choose airlines and airports by continent on which to focus your searches.

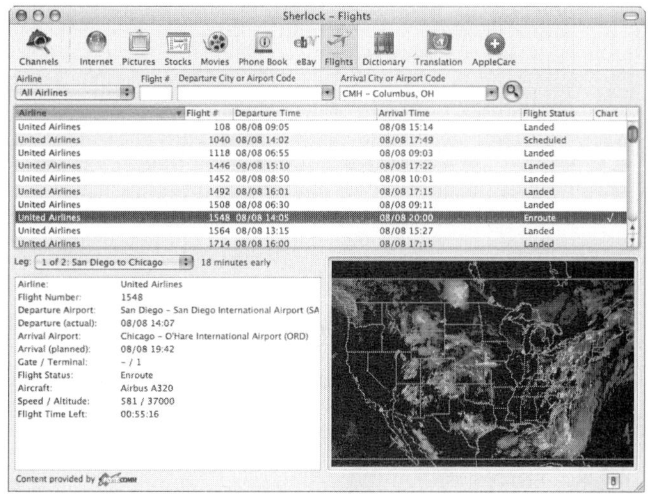

FIGURE 4.60 View the status of specific flights, including a chart of the flight path.

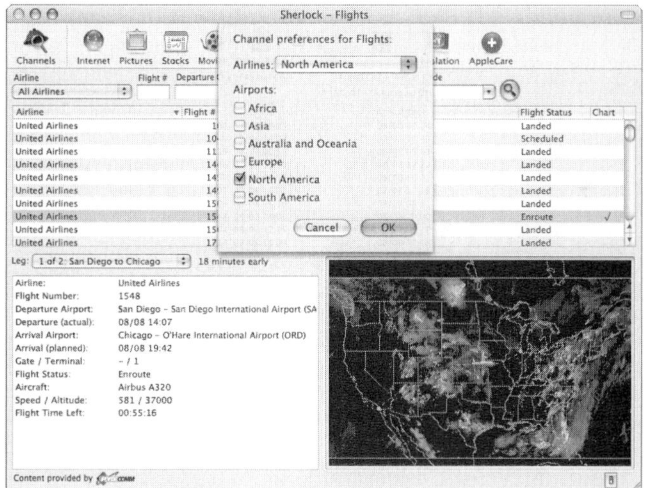

FIGURE 4.61 Choose a continent to select all airlines flying in a region, or check boxes for all continents whose airports you want to include in your search.

Dictionary

As you might expect, you look up definitions in the Dictionary channel (shown in Figure 4.62). For some words, you also see a list of phrases in the lower half of the pane that contain that word or relate to it. (Clicking the Pronunciation Key link opens Dictionary.com's pronunciation symbol key in your default browser.)

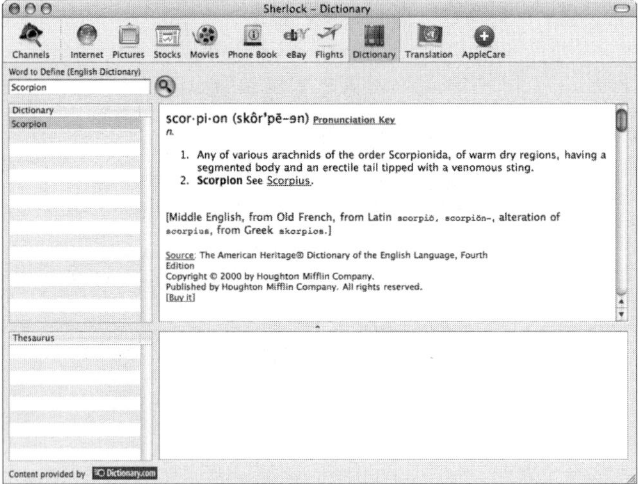

FIGURE 4.62 Expand your vocabulary with help from the Dictionary channel.

Translation

The Translation channel, shown in Figure 4.63, performs rough translations between different languages. English speakers can translate into simplified and traditional Chinese, Dutch, French, German, Greek, Italian, Japanese, Korean, Portuguese, Russian, and Spanish, and then back to English.

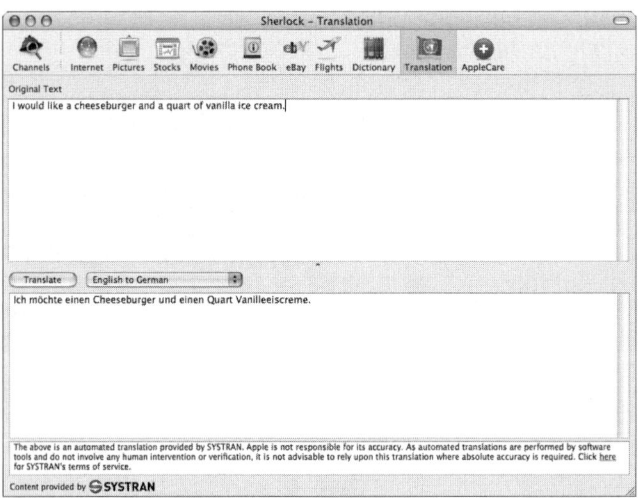

FIGURE 4.63 Translate between languages with ease.

To translate text, type or paste the original text into the top text field, choose an option for translating the original language into another language, and click the Translate button.

When using this service, keep in mind that computer-generated translations do not match the output of a skilled human translator.

AppleCare

If you have a specific technical question about Apple software or hardware that OS X's Help Viewer can't resolve, use the AppleCare channel, shown in Figure 4.64, to search the AppleCare Knowledge Base for reports about Apple products and issues.

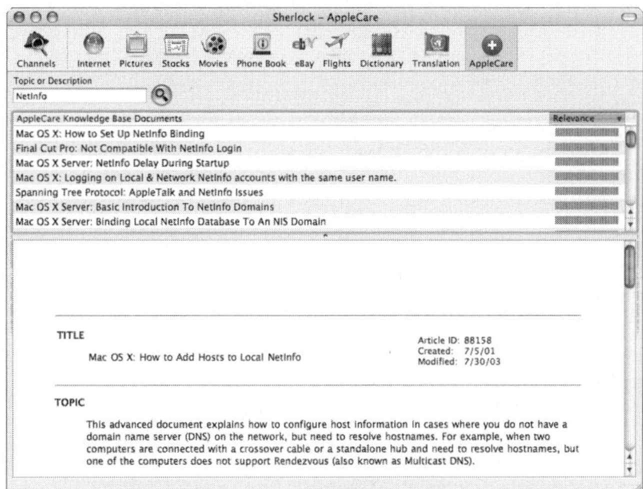

FIGURE 4.64 A quick search of the AppleCare Knowledge Base can answer many of your questions about Apple products.

Now that we have explored the default channels, let's take a quick look at some channels written outside Apple.

Third-Party Channels

In addition to the channels you've seen so far in this chapter, which are maintained by Apple, many channels are written by others to view information on topics ranging from news to astrology and song lyrics to television listings.

To access third-party channels, click the Channels button at the upper left of the Sherlock toolbar to open the Channels Collection pane. Note that this is *very* similar to the Bookmarks Library in Safari. Next, choose Other Channels from the Collection list along the left-hand side of the window. As shown in Figure 4.65, a plethora of channels appears in the right-hand column along with the countries to which they apply and a brief description.

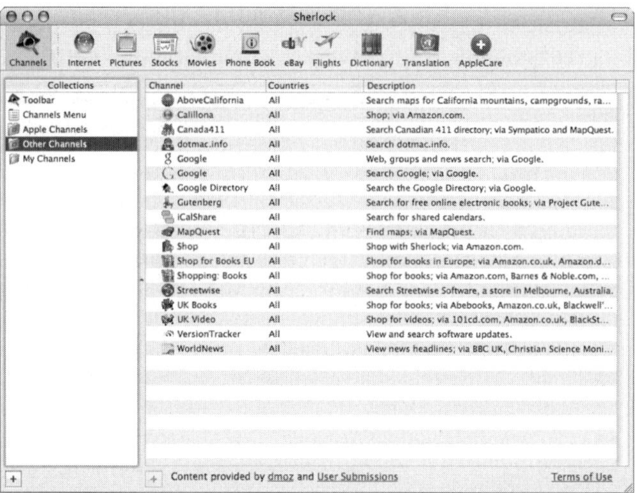

FIGURE 4.65 The list of channels created outside Apple.

To open one of these channels, simply double-click its entry in the listing. Each channel has its own interface to support the information it displays; you have to follow the cues in the channel's interface to figure out what information is provided and how to perform a search.

CAUTION

The quality of third-party channels varies greatly. Some are very helpful, whereas others merely frustrate. They're *all* free, however, so it doesn't hurt to try.

The Channels Collection

The method used in the preceding section to access the third-party channels provides a glimpse at how you can manage a collection of Sherlock channels, much as you manage bookmarks in Safari. Clicking the Channels icon in the upper-left corner of the Sherlock window opens the Channels Collection, shown previously in Figure 4.65.

Along the left side of the window are channel collections. Each collection contains one or more Sherlock channels, viewed by highlighting the collection name in the Collections list. There are four collections by default:

- Toolbar—Channels displayed in the Sherlock toolbar
- Channels Menu—Channels displayed in the Channels menu
- Apple Channels—Channels provided by Apple
- Other Channels—Third-party channels
- My Channels—An empty collection ready for your use

To create a new custom collection, click the "+" button at the bottom of the collection list. A new "untitled" collection folder appears. You can change the name immediately or double-click it at any time to provide a new label.

To add channels to the collection drag the channel icons from one of the channel collections (such as Other Channels) to your custom collection folder. After organizing the collection the way you want, you can even drag the collection folders themselves to the Toolbar collection to add them directly to the Sherlock toolbar, or to the Channels Menu collection to add them as a submenu of the Channels menu.

Again, like Safari, Sherlock also supports subfolders within a collection. The "+" button below the channel listing can be used to add a subfolder window a collection. Channels can be dragged to the subfolder to further organize your searches.

Sherlock Preferences

Sherlock preferences, accessible from the application menu, contain the option to accept or deny cookies as well as manage cookies already on your system. Because many channels rely on cookies to work, disabling cookies may effectively disable Sherlock's functionality.

Sherlock Menus

The Sherlock menus are the standard fare—not hiding many options not already covered in this section. There are two features you may find useful, however. First, File, New can be used to create a new Sherlock window, allowing you to have multiple searches in progress at a time. Second, the Channel, Make a Shortcut (Command-L) option allows you to save a double-clickable shortcut to a channel that you can save on your desktop, or send to a friend to try.

.Mac

Completing the Mac OS X Internet access suite is .Mac—Apple's $100 subscription-based Mac OS X "add on." Apple has had a reasonably difficult time selling .Mac as being a necessary part of Mac OS X. They've integrated the operating system with some of its features (as we'll see shortly) but haven't done a good job of convincing users that they need it.

Defining .Mac

Part of Apple's problem is that .Mac is not well defined. If you don't subscribe to the service, yet use a Mac on a daily basis, you're probably not feeling like there's anything missing from your operating system (except perhaps Windowshades, tabbed Finder windows, and so on). Apple itself doesn't seem to know what .Mac is, other than a potentially renewable revenue stream.

The easiest way to define .Mac is to enumerate the features it offers:

- Network storage (iDisk)—The .Mac iDisk offers 100MB of network-accessible storage. Using your iDisk, you can access your files from other machines or even share them with friends. Based on the lightweight WebDAV protocol (which runs over HTTP), iDisk is fast, cross-platform, and less susceptible to network "issues" such as firewalls.

TIP

See Chapter 27 for information on setting up Apache to act as your own WebDAV server.

- Synchronization services—.Mac, in conjunction with iSync, provides a means for all your Macs to share the same bookmarks, Address Book information, and calendars. Instead of maintaining two sets of bookmarks on your desktop and laptop, a single global set of bookmarks is maintained and synchronized through .Mac.
- Network-based Mac OS X information—A .Mac account can hold information that you normally access through applications on your computer and make it available to you through a network connection wherever you are. Calendars, Contacts, and Bookmarks are currently available with additional "access it anywhere" services in development. The .Mac screensaver (discussed shortly) even allows you to view slideshows stored on remote users' iDisks.
- .Mac email—Apple-hosted email services, including a nice Web interface, are included as part of the subscription. Additional accounts with a 5MB mail quota can be added to a .Mac account for a small fee.
- Exclusive software—Although not earth-shattering, Apple is currently offering two pieces of .Mac "members only" software: Virex (virus protection) and Apple's own Backup (personal document backups). These pieces of software are actually a good value if you need the functionality they offer. (See Chapter 32, "System Maintenance," for more information on Backup). If you were, for example, planning to buy a Virus protection package for $50 already, that's half the cost of a .Mac subscription.
- Family-oriented Web services—The .Mac Web site makes it easy to create custom Web sites—either using files from your iDisk, or simply by exporting them from within iPhoto. Users can also send iCards created with your own or professionally photographed images.
- Training—Basic Macintosh tutorials and training materials are available online for common family/consumer activities such as using iTunes, creating Web pages, and so on. These features are definitely geared toward beginners.
- Software discounts—Special software discounts are offered for select packages, such as children's games. Again, this feature of Mac.com is offered primarily for the benefit of home users. Power users expecting to find a 50% discount on Doom 3 are going to be sorely disappointed (prove me wrong Apple, please).

TIP

Apple lists iChat as one of the .Mac features. iChat, however, is available for anyone's use. A .Mac account gets you the ability to use your .Mac email address as your buddy name; however, even if you just sign up for a demo account, you get to keep the account name indefinitely and can use it with iChat as you want.

Because describing how to use a Web site (`http//www.mac.com`) is not the purpose of this book (and the information contained on the site is variable in nature), we won't attempt to document the features that you access through your Web browser. Instead, we'll look at how .Mac's Panther-integrated features are used in Mac OS X; then take a brief walk-through of the Web services so that you can make the decision of whether you want to join the .Mac club.

NOTE

If you intend to rely on .Mac for mission critical (or life critical) email, check around to make sure that it offers the availability and reliability that you need. Although I personally have experienced .Mac outages rarely throughout my use (which is extremely light), they do happen. Some users have experienced email outages that last for days. At present, Apple does not provide the support or status reporting features common to ISPs offering email and Web hosting services.

Setting Up .Mac Service

To set up your .Mac services, open the System Preferences application and click the .Mac pane. Your screen should resemble Figure 4.66.

FIGURE 4.66 Configure or create .Mac services in the .Mac preferences pane.

Your choices are limited: Either enter your existing .Mac member name and password, or click the Sign Up button to create a new account. If signing up for the first time, your Web browser is launched, and you are taken to the `http://www.mac.com` signup page. Keep in mind that you don't need to commit to a full account immediately. You can apply for a 60-day free trial and try the members-only features (except for the exclusive software) before you buy.

If you already have a .Mac account, enter your information in the appropriate fields; then either close the pane or click the iDisk button to view the status of your iDisk (this is a quick way to verify that the account information is entered correctly and everything is working as it should).

Using the iDisk

The Apple iDisk is really just a WebDAV share that your system automatically "knows" how to connect to without additional information. If you're used to working with AppleShare, NFS, or CIFS servers and you connect to network resources regularly, there are few surprises. iDisk requires a network connection and is *barely* usable on dial-in lines. Cable and DSL should be considered the minimum tolerable network requirement for making a connection.

Starting in Panther, iDisk does have one feature that sets it apart from a normal network share—the capability to keep a local copy of its contents that are synchronized automatically when you connect to the Internet. This means that you always have an up-to-date offline copy of the files in case you don't have Internet access.

From the perspective of the end user, iDisk synchronization is entirely transparent—your iDisk appears like any other disk whether working with the contents online or using the local copy. As you make changes to the files, they are noted and automatically uploaded to the .Mac server in the background. You can also choose to manually synchronize files if you want.

iDisk Storage Space and Settings

You can customize how your iDisk works and view a quick status of how much space is available by clicking the iDisk button within the .Mac system preferences pane. The pane shown in Figure 4.67 is displayed.

At the top of the pane is the amount of storage currently in use and the total available. You can buy additional iDisk storage space by clicking the Buy More button. Additional iDisk space is sold, like .Mac, on a subscription basis. The storage pricing is currently set at these prices (not including the base $100/year membership fee):

$60/200MB

$100/300MB

$180/500MB

$350/1GB

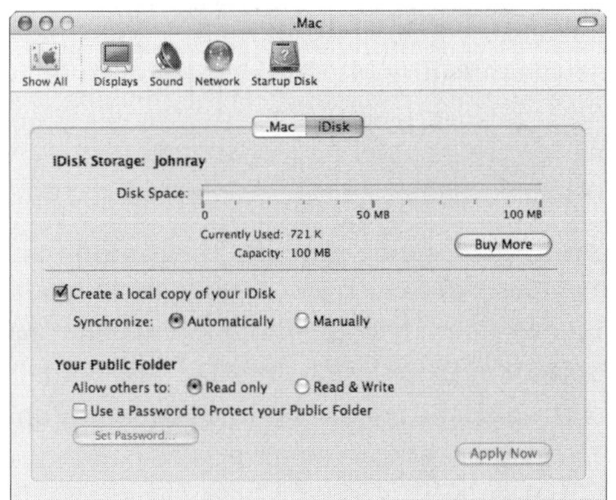

FIGURE 4.67 Configure your iDisk and view the space available.

Here you can also choose how and whether the iDisk is synchronized: either automatically when you connect to the Internet, manually, or not at all. If you do *not* check the Create a Local Copy of Your iDisk check box, the iDisk will only be accessible over the Internet (as it was in previous versions of Mac OS X). You cannot work with the contents without an active network connection.

If you do choose to synchronize your iDisk, choose whether it will happen automatically or manually using the radio buttons.

NOTE

If you ever choose to shut off synchronization after it has been running, Mac OS X will move the disk image file it has been using as the local iDisk copy to your desktop. You can mount it to get at the contents or throw it away if you want.

TIP

The default iDisk sync settings (keep a local copy of the iDisk and synchronize automatically) make the following two assumptions: You have a reasonably fast Internet connection, and you make small changes to the contents of your iDisk. If you find yourself replacing 100MB of files daily, synchronization is just going to eat up time and network bandwidth.

If you *always* have a fast connection and don't access your iDisk files that much anyway, not using the local iDisk option might be the most efficient options.

If synchronization takes a *long* time each time you use it (dial-in users), you might want to set it to "manually" and only start a synchronize when you aren't going to be using your computer heavily.

Also in the iDisk pane are controls for determining how your public folder is accessed. The iDisk public folder is a special directory on the iDisk that can be read by other Mac OS X users without needing your .Mac login information. You can use the Public folder as a place to exchange files with a few people, or perhaps release a new piece of software you've written to the world.

To keep things under your control, Apple provides the option of choosing whether other users (that is, not you) have read-only or read-write access to your folder, and whether the folder should be password protected. If you choose to password protect the folder, you are prompted to set a new password; *do not* use your .Mac password. This is a password that you give out to your friends so that they can connect to your Public folder.

Click Apply Now to activate your iDisk settings.

CAUTION

First and foremost, do *not* store copyrighted/pirated material in your Public folder; this should be obvious.

Second, if you enable read/write access to your Public folder, be aware that you've turned over a portion of your iDisk storage space to the public. If your public folder is filled, it counts against your 100MB iDisk total.

Accessing and Synchronizing Your iDisk

After entering the membership information needed to connect to your iDisk, you can immediately start using the service by opening a Finder window and then clicking the iDisk icon in the shortcut list or by choosing Go, iDisk, My iDisk from the Finder menu (Shift-Command-I). After a few seconds, the iDisk icon (a blue orb) appears on your desktop and/or in your Finder Sidebar.

If this is the first time that you've used your iDisk (and you haven't configured it otherwise), Mac OS X prompts you to synchronize the entire contents of your iDisk before going any further. If you intend to keep the disk synchronized, allowing the initial synchronization is a good idea. It may take a while at first, but subsequent syncs will only need to copy the data that has changed, if any.

You can force a synchronization at any time by clicking the chasing arrow (circular arrows) icon to the right of the iDisk icon in the Finder. If you've chosen to have your Mac automatically synchronize the iDisk, you can tell when the synchronization is in progress by watching the icon to the right of the iDisk in your Finder window; it spins while synchronizing.

Open the iDisk like you would any other disk. If you clicked the iDisk icon in the Finder shortcut bar, the Finder window refreshes to show its contents. If you mounted it from the Go menu, you can double-click the iDisk icon on the desktop.

An iDisk contains nine folders:

- Backup—If you've used the Apple Backup utility, this folder contains the data that has been stored. It is created and maintained automatically.
- Documents—Your personal storage space for "stuff"; no one has access to these files but you.
- Library—Data storage for applications such as iSync. Again, these files are maintained automatically and probably shouldn't be touched.
- Movies—A place to store your (Webified) Movie files. Movies placed in this location are available for use within the .Mac HomePage Web site builder utility.
- Music—A place for you to store your music files. With the advent of the Apple Music Store, I'd venture a guess that Apple will be adding the capability to download song purchases to this folder in the future.
- Pictures—Like Music and Movies, Pictures provides a content-specific place for you to drop your image files. Images placed in the Pictures folder are available within HomePage and the Apple's iCard builder.
- Public—Your online folder that can be opened to the public. Files stored here can be accessed (if you choose) by friends, or anyone in the world.
- Sites—The files for your Apple-hosted mac.com Web site are stored in the Sites folder. Files placed here are accessible via the URL `http://homepage.mac.com/<mac.com username>/<filename>`.
- Software—Apple's collection of freeware and demo Mac OS X software and music. If you need a quick software fix, this is where you can find it.

Work with iDisk as you would a hard drive or network share, but be aware that copying files to or from the iDisk takes time. If you are configured to maintain a local copy of the iDisk, transfers will be nearly instantaneous, but the actual transfer occurring in the background may take minutes or hours, depending on the quality of your connection.

Accessing Other User's iDisks

To access the iDisks of other users (or their public folders) in pre-Panther Mac OS X, you either needed to use the .Mac Web site, or type a URL that mapped to the iDisk within the Mac OS X Connect To Server dialog box.

In Panther, simply choose Go, iDisk, Other User's iDisk from the Finder menu. You are prompted for the user's membership name and password, as shown in Figure 4.68.

To mount a user's Public folder, choose Go, iDisk, Other User's Public Folder. In this case, you are prompted for the member name, but you do not need to supply a password unless one has been set by the owner of the remote iDisk account.

4

FIGURE 4.68 Mount another user's iDisk

TIP

You can still mount the iDisk volume with Connect To Server by supplying the URL `http://idisk.apple.com/`*`<mac.com username>`*.

If you prefer the command line, `mount_webdav` *`<webDAV URL> <mount point>`* will work nicely. (For example, to mount my `johnray` account at the directory `/Users/jray/myiDisk`, I'd type `mount_webdav http://idisk.mac.com/johnray /Users/jray/myiDisk`.

See Chapter 12, "Introducing the BSD Subsystem," for more information about accessing the Mac OS X command line.

iDisks are the cornerstone of the .Mac service and are what make most of the other services possible. Without, for example, a central storage place to keep iSync information, there would be no means of synchronizing multiple computers on different networks.

.Mac Screensaver

Trying to fit a .Mac topic area within *Mac OS X Panther Unleashed* has proven to be difficult. What applications should be included under .Mac, and which stand alone? In Chapter 3 we discussed iSync, iCal, and Address Book, in this chapter we covered Safari, and in future chapters we'll discuss additional software that interacts with .Mac. The determination of what falls under .Mac has boiled down to "what Panther software wouldn't work at all if .Mac didn't exist?" iDisk is one component, and the second (perhaps unlikely) feature is a screensaver.

The .Mac screensaver enables a user to view slideshows that they (or someone else) have created and saved to their .Mac accounts using iPhoto (discussed in Chapter 6, "Photography and Imaging").

To use the screensaver, open the Desktop and Screen Saver System Preferences pane. Choose .Mac from the list of available Screen Savers and then click the Configure button. A dialog appears, as shown in Figure 4.69, that contains all slideshows that you've subscribed to.

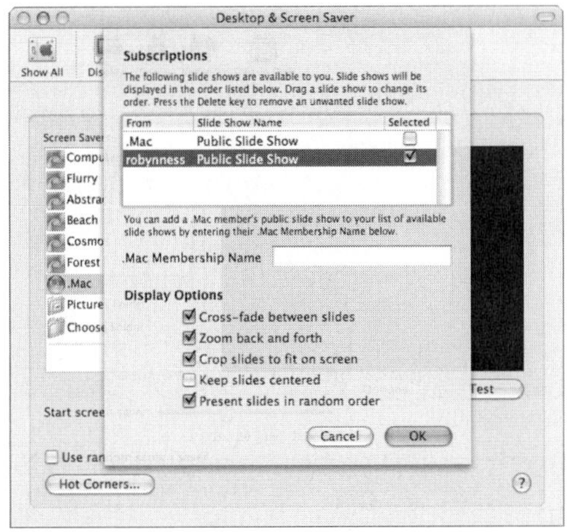

FIGURE 4.69 Create a slideshow that any Internet-connected Mac can view.

To add a new show, enter the name of the .Mac account (such as `robynness`) in the .Mac membership name field, choose the display options you want used during the presentation, and then click OK. The next time your screensaver is activated, you see the photographs you added with iPhoto.

To remove or disable subscriptions, you must click Configure again, select the slideshow, and then press your Delete key, or use the Selected check box to simply disable it.

.Mac Screensavers on Non-.Mac Servers

Even though it doesn't appear in the System Preferences pane, the .Mac screen effect is actually capable of displaying pictures from any source. The preferences file `~/Library/Preferences/ByHost/com.apple.iToolsSlideSubscriptions..` (the ending varies based on your computer) contains entries for each of slideshows that look something like this:

```
<dict>
        <key>ConfigURL</key>
        <string>http://homepage.Mac.com/johnray/.Pictures/
        Slide Shows/Public/config.plist</string>
        <key>Selected</key>
        <false/>
        <key>ShowName</key>
        <string>Public Slide Show</string>
        <key>UserName</key>
        <string>johnray</string>
</dict>
```

The key component is the ConfigURL string. This URL points to an XML formatted list of the images in the slideshow and their URL (which doesn't have to be a .Mac account). The format of the config file resembles the following:

```
<?xml version="1.0" encoding="UTF-8"?>
<!DOCTYPE plist PUBLIC "-//Apple Computer//DTD PLIST 1.0//EN"
"http://www.apple.com/DTDs/PropertyList-1.0.dtd">
<plist version="1.0">
<dict>
    <key>BaseURL</key>
    <string>http://homepage.Mac.com/robynness/.Pictures/
    Slide Shows/Public/</string>
    <key>Images</key>
    <array>
        <string>Image-001.jpg</string>
        <string>Image-002.jpg</string>
        <string>Image-003.jpg</string>
        <string>Image-004.jpg</string>
        <string>Image-005.jpg</string>
        <string>Image-006.jpg</string>
        <string>Image-007.jpg</string>
        <string>Image-008.jpg</string>
        <string>Image-009.jpg</string>
    </array>
    <key>SizeOfSlideshowInBytes</key>
    <integer>423560</integer>
</dict>
</plist>
```

Here the BaseURL specifies the Web server that holds the images, whereas the Images array contains the names of the images in the slideshow.

To manually create a slideshow on another server, you must edit the preferences file to point to another valid ConfigURL and then place a valid XML configuration file in that location, which, in turn, must point to a Web server containing the pictures.

If this doesn't make sense, don't worry; you're under no obligation to try it. It's simply a way for the adventurous sorts to replicate a .Mac feature on their own. For information on XML (as it pertains to plists) and creating your own Web server, see Chapter 20, "Command-Line Configuration and Administration," and Chapter 27, "Web Serving."

The .Mac Web Services

The final .Mac features we'll look at are the Web services. Accessed with a Web browser through `http://www.mac.com`, these features are aimed at families and those on-the-go types who frequently have to access the Internet or send email through computers that aren't their own.

Web Sites

The HomePage Web site builder, shown in Figure 4.70, allows anyone to create Web pages without any knowledge of HTML. Simply copy images and movies to your iDisk (in the appropriate folders, of course), choose a HomePage template, and then add your own narrative content.

FIGURE 4.70 Use the HomePage builder to create instant Web sites.

Apple provides templates for photo albums, resumes, iMovies, and more. If you're an advanced user, you can always add your own content directly to the iDisk Sites folder and create any site you want.

iCards

The Apple iCards are a collection of elegant photographs that you can add a message to and forward to your friends, demonstrated in Figure 4.71. Images that you've placed in your iDisk Pictures folder are also available for use.

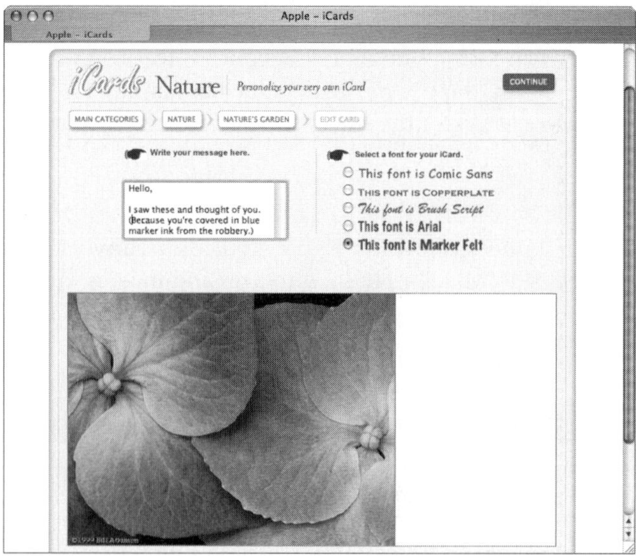

FIGURE 4.71 Create your own iCards to send to friends.

Even if you aren't exactly thrilled by the idea of sending iCards, you may enjoy looking through the iCard photograph library. Apple's selection of photographs is excellent.

Access on the Go

Probably the most compelling Web service for advanced users is the access to traditionally "desktop" information while on the go. ISync keeps everything "connected" so that what you see on your desktop is what you see online, and vice versa. Figure 4.72, for example, shows the Safari Bookmark browser.

Likewise, .Mac email and Address Book entries are also accessed through a Web interface and carry the feel of a native Mac OS X application along with them. Figure 4.73 shows the .Mac Web-based email.

Because we've already covered the iCal Web calendars earlier (see Chapter 3 for details), there's very little left to say.

As of the time of this writing, this *is* .Mac. The direction Apple seems to be heading in is providing ways of taking your data with you. The synchronization of desktop applications with Web services is likely to be the focus of future developments. As you've seen, and will continue to see throughout the book, certain applications provide support for saving information to .Mac—either through iSync, or as a direct function of the application.

If you're an enterprising user with your own server, yes, you can probably replicate many, if not all, of these services for free. The benefit of .Mac is that it is already in place, is centralized, and works (at least usually).

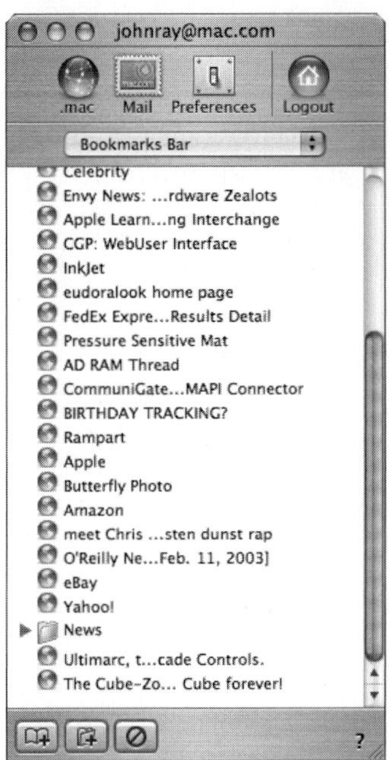

FIGURE 4.72 The Safari Bookmark browser allows you to access and update bookmarks from anywhere.

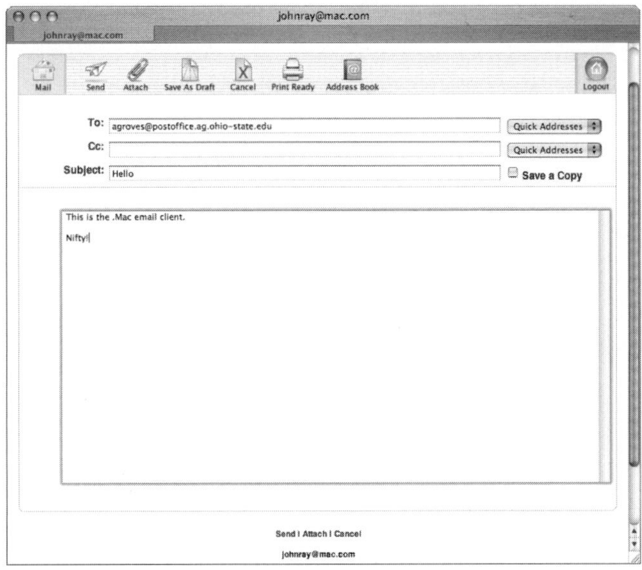

FIGURE 4.73 It's like your Mac OS X email application—in a Web browser.

Summary

This chapter covered a lot of ground—everything from searching the Internet with Sherlock and sending email to videoconferencing with iChat AV. The Internet applications provided with Mac OS X can get anyone up and running online in a matter of minutes.

CHAPTER 5

Installing Third-Party Applications

IN THIS CHAPTER

- Software Sources and Formats
- Using StuffIt Expander
- Installing Software
- Interesting Software

Mac OS X comes with enough software and tools to keep an avid email reader or Web browser happy for quite a while. For the rest of us, however, it is lacking in many of the creative tools that have made the Macintosh platform so appealing. This chapter covers the basics of installing your own applications and points out a few that you might want to try.

This chapter serves as a point of demarcation within the contents of this book. It effectively ends the coverage of basic Mac OS X applications. Subsequent chapters focus on the Apple iLife suite and associated software. If you aren't yet comfortable with using the operating system, I recommend spending some time getting to know your system before continuing.

Software Sources and Formats

Before you can use software, you must first download and unarchive it. The process of downloading software with Safari is not covered here because it is (I hope) a commonplace activity, although a few additional applications will be introduced to make downloads easier.

TIP

For those with a fast connection, try accessing your iDisk from Mac OS X. Apple has done a good job of keeping an up-to-date software library on the network disks, making installs as easy as a drag-and-drop. No—your local iDisk copy does not contain the software library.

There are a number of good online libraries of Mac OS X software. The following sites are the best places to look for the latest and greatest downloads:

- VersionTracker—`http://www.versiontracker.com/`. Updated continuously throughout the day, VersionTracker's Web site tracks Classic Mac OS, Mac OS X, and Windows applications.
- MacUpdate—http://www.macupdate.com/. Like VersionTracker, MacUpdate provides a continuously updated software listing for Macintosh applications but surpasses VT in speed.
- Mac OS X Apps—`http://www.macosxapps.com/`. This site features in-depth discussions on new software and uses a Slashdot-like interface for posting and discussion.
- Useful Mac—`http://www.usefulmac.com/`. Useful Mac features Macintosh news and links to essential (and just plain cool) utilities.
- Apple's Mac OS X Downloads—`http://www.apple.com/downloads/macosx/`. Although not always updated as quickly as the other two sites, Apple's collection is well documented and easily navigated.

Legacy Encoding Formats

Mac OS X, although commercially available for several years now, is still in a state of transition. The HFS filesystem that has been the cornerstone of Macintosh storage for more than a decade poses part of the problem. HFS/HFS+ support the traditional Macintosh resource forks, and, for compatibility, so does Mac OS X. Unfortunately, resource forks do *not* translate directly to a flat file format, making storage and transmission of "resource-laden" files impossible on non-HFS (Unix, Windows, and so on) filesystems—impossible without an additional level of encoding.

MacBinary takes into account the Macintosh-specific features of the HFS/HFS+ filesystem and provides a method of representing both the data and resource fork within a single binary data stream. MacBinary files can be identified by the `.bin` suffix. You're most likely to find Carbon applications using MacBinary.

Another legacy distribution format is BinHex. BinHex is similar to the output of the Unix `uuencode` command—it enables the transfer of binary files using a 7-bit text encoding. BinHex files can be recognized by the `.hqx` suffix. Because most Internet connections are capable of full binary transfers, `.hqx` usage is largely on the decline. You're most likely to encounter these files as email or newsgroup attachments, or if you frequent the Info-Mac HyperArchive (`http://hyperarchive.lcs.mit.edu/HyperArchive.html`).

Common Archive Formats

Neither MacBinary nor BinHex is an archive format—they are common Macintosh file encodings but are not capable of packaging software for installation. Five archive methods are common to Mac OS X software distributions:

- `.dmg`/`.img`—Apple's preferred distribution format, the Disk Image is a double-clickable file that mounts a virtual disk image on your desktop. The `.dmg` file format is often combined with one of the other two archive types.
- `.pkg`/`.mpkg`—Package and multipackage files—another archive format unique to Mac OS X, `.pkgs` bundle an entire software distribution within a single folder (which appears as a single file within Mac OS X). The `.mpkg` format is used in conjunction with multiple `.pkg` files to install several related packages simultaneously. Apple's Installer application is used to install package files.
- `.sit`—The StuffIt archive is the most popular format for Carbon and Classic applications. Mac OS X ships with StuffIt Expander, an application capable of unarchiving `.sit` files and decoding `.hqx`/`.bin`-encoded distributions.
- `.tar.gz` or `.tgz`—Gzipped tarfile. This is actually a combination of the gzip (compression) and tar (archiving) utilities of the BSD subsystem. These files can be unarchived from the command line using `tar zxf` *<archive name>* or using StuffIt Expander.
- `.jar`—Java archive. Although not OS X–specific, a Java archive is a completely packaged and ready-to-run application. You can launch Java `.jar` apps by double-clicking their icon—no other processing is necessary.

When encountering a file that needs unarchiving or decompressing, most likely you'll turn to StuffIt Expander. StuffIt Expander can handle almost any format you give it, including popular "alternative" archive formats such as Bzip and Rar.

Using StuffIt Expander

The quick-and-dirty instructions for using StuffIt Expander (path: `Applications/Utilities/StuffIt Expander`) are as follows: Drag your archive file(s) (`.hqx`, `.bin`, `.sit`, `.tar.gz`, and so on) on top of the StuffIt Expander archive. StuffIt will launch and decode and unarchive the selections.

Alternatively, start the Expander application; then use File, Expand (Command-O) from the menu to choose the files to expand or drag your files into the StuffIt window.

TIP

I recommend adding StuffIt Expander to the Finder Sidebar for access from any folder. Alternatively, add the icon to the Dock for systemwide accessibility.

A number of settings can fine-tune how StuffIt Expander deals with archive files after they have been extracted, and the text files within. If you use StuffIt archives in a cross-platform environment, these options can help reformat files for better viewing on the Macintosh. Improper use can also corrupt source code files.

Preferences

Open the StuffIt Expander preferences from the application menu. Eight categories of options can be set. Switch between each area by clicking the appropriate icon on the left side of the preferences window.

Expanding

The Expanding preferences, displayed in Figure 5.1, control what happens to archives as they are being extracted and after the extraction has completed.

FIGURE 5.1 The Expanding pane controls the unarchiving process.

Adjust the process of expanding archives with the following settings:

- Expand Archives and Compressed Files—Checked by default. If this setting is deselected, StuffIt Expander will not decompress archived files. Click the Delete After Expanding check box to automatically remove archives after successfully expanding.
- Expanded Encoded Files—Selected by default, this setting ensures that StuffIt decodes MacBinary, BinHex, and other encoded files. The Delete After Expanding check box enables automatic removal of encoded files as they've been decoded.

- Continue to Expand—If this setting is checked, StuffIt attempts to expand archives it finds inside a given archive.
- Ignore Return Receipt Requests—Some StuffIt archives may request that a notification be sent upon expanding the file. Selecting this check box ignores the notification requests.
- Scan for Viruses Using—Use this setting and the associated pop-up menu to choose a virus-scan utility to automatically check files processed by StuffIt Expander. Remember, Virex is included in the .Mac subscription.
- Open Palm `.prc` and `.pdb` Files—Expand Palm Pilot archive files.
- Show Drag Window on Launch—Display the StuffIt Expander window for accepting dragged files on launch.

Joining

The Joining pane controls how split archives are handled. By default, StuffIt Expander attempts to join segmented files and then automatically expands the completed archive. Use the check boxes on this screen to alter these settings or configure StuffIt Expander to automatically remove individual segment files after they are joined (the complete file will remain).

TIP

If you happen to encounter a segmented disk image, it does *not* need to be joined to be used. Mounting/using any segment of the image automatically includes the rest of the segments. This can be a bit disconcerting, but it actually *does* work.

Disk Images

The Disk Images pane controls what StuffIt does when it encounters a disk image. The default is to mount disk images on the desktop by way of the Apple Disk Copy utility. It is best not to check Mount Images Unlocked by Default. When a disk image is mounted unlocked, it can be modified inadvertently and may not function properly. This is typically a problem with bootable images, so it may not affect you anyway.

Destination

As the pane name suggests, Destination sets the location where unarchived files will be stored.

The following options are available under the Destination pane:

- Destination—Set the destination where the unarchived files and folders are saved. The default setting, Same as Original, creates expanded items in the same volume/folder as the archive itself. Choose Ask to prompt for a destination each time the expansion begins, or click Use to pick a specific path for all unarchived files.

- Create Surrounding Folder—When an archive is expanded, it usually results in one or more files and folders. Create Surrounding Folder places these items into a single folder depending on the chosen condition: When the archive contains multiple items, Never, or Always.

Watch Folder

Setting up a Watch Folder can be useful if you've created a drop box for other users or simply want a place to put files and have them automatically expanded as they arrive. Figure 5.2 shows the Watch Folder pane.

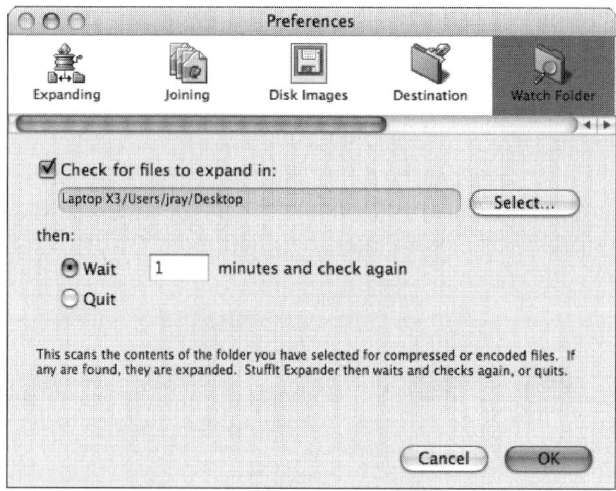

FIGURE 5.2 Set up a Watch Folder to look for incoming archives.

Control the functionality of your Watch Folder with these settings:

- Check for Files to Expand In—When this box is checked, StuffIt Expander monitors the selected folder for new archives or encoded files.
- Wait—Choose the length of time (in minutes) Expander waits before rechecking the folder.
- Quit—Choose Quit if you want StuffIt to exit after expanding files.

NOTE

StuffIt Expander does not install a system-level service—the Expander application itself must remain active for the Watch Folder feature to work.

Error Reporting

Choose whether StuffIt Expander displays errors in an alert window, ignores errors, or logs errors to a user-specified file. If you're mass-expanding StuffIt files, reporting errors via Alert window may disrupt processing. Ignoring or logging errors allows all archives to be processed regardless of any issues that occur along the way.

Version Check

Use the check box on the Version Check pane to enable StuffIt Expander to check online for new versions. This feature is on by default and is not at all intrusive. Uncheck the feature to prevent your system from contacting Aladdin Systems.

Internet

The final configuration pane, Internet, is used to set the file types that StuffIt Expander is registered to handle on the Mac OS X system. As shown in Figure 5.3, you can mix and match among the 18 available archive and encoding types. Click the Use StuffIt Expander for All Available Types button as a shortcut for clicking all the check boxes.

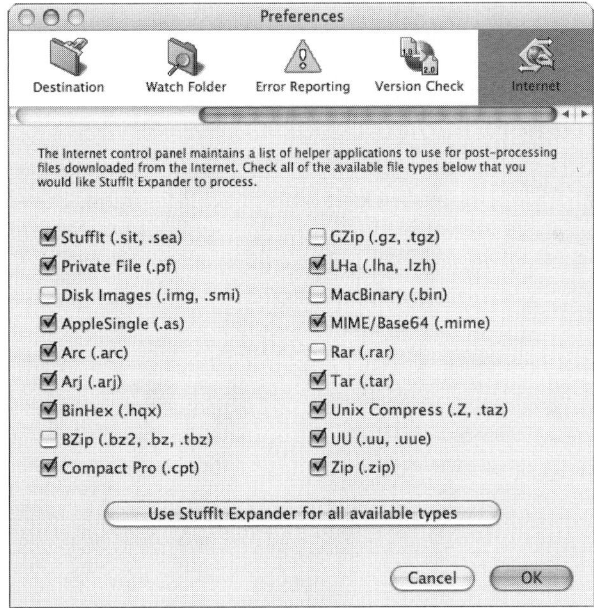

FIGURE 5.3 The Internet pane registers the file types that StuffIt Expander will handle.

Installing Software

Although there is no definitive installation technique used by all software on Mac OS X, there are two common methods that you will use repeatedly. Obviously, for any software, you should read the documentation that comes with it; but for those who are anxious to double-click, it's good to know what to expect.

Keep in mind when installing applications that other users on the computer do not implicitly have access to your home directory. If you install a large application in your home directory, it will be accessible only by you. This can lead to multiple users installing copies of the same application throughout the system. To best utilize disk space and resource sharing, applications should be installed in the `/Applications` directory or within a subdirectory of `Applications`.

CAUTION

Be sure to read your software license agreements regarding operation by multiple users. If an application is only licensed for a single user (rather than a single computer), it should not be placed where any Mac OS X user can have access. If it is placed there, you should adjust its access permissions appropriately.

Disk Images/Internet-Enabled Disk Images

The vast majority of Mac OS X applications use the `.dmg/img` file format and a simple drag-and-drop installation. Double-clicking a disk image launches the Disk Utility application (see Chapter 3, "Applications and Utilities") and mounts the virtual disk on your computer. Some disk images contain a double-clickable installer, but most enable the user to drag the application from the image directly to the location where the user wants to store it.

NOTE

To copy all the files in a disk image, select the mounted image on the desktop, hold down Option, and drag the image wherever you want (even the desktop). A complete duplicate of the contents of the image is created.

A new twist to disk image installations is Apple's Internet-enabled disk image, described fully here: `http://developer.apple.com/ue/files/iedi.html`. An Internet-enabled disk image is a standard disk image that behaves a bit "differently" when it is mounted. Instead of requiring the user to remove the files from the disk, an Internet-enabled disk image mounts invisibly and then automatically copies the files out of the image to the same location on the drive as where the image was stored (usually the desktop). If multiple files are present, a folder with the same name as the disk image is created, and all the files are copied to that folder. The image itself is moved to the trash after the process is complete.

NOTE

After an Internet-enabled disk image has been used, it is moved to the trash and "disabled." If you move the image out of the trash, it will mount and behave like any other disk image.

Apple's Installer (`.mpkg/.pkg` Files)

The Apple installer provides a simple step-by-step installation system for installing package and multipackage files (`.pkg/.mpkg`)—in fact, it is the same installation application used to set up the Mac OS X operating system itself.

NOTE

Packages can be installed from the command line using the installer utility. Use this syntax to install a package on your system:

```
installer -pkg <package name> -target <target path>
```

In most cases, the target path will be / (your main system drive). For more information on accessing the command line, see Chapter 12, "Introducing the BSD Subsystem."

The Apple Installer is invoked by double-clicking a `.pkg` or `.mpkg` file. The installer process, shown in Figure 5.4, typically, walks the user through six steps on six different screens:

- Introduction—Describes the software you are installing. Presumably you already *know* what you're adding to your system, but you may find additional "breaking news" information on this screen.
- License—Displays the license agreement for the software. At this stage you must either agree or disagree with the text of the license. Remember, Mac OS X can be shared by multiple users, so be sure that your license is valid for multiple people on a single machine before continuing. (I write this just as the organization I work for is undergoing a license audit by one of the big developers.)
- Select Destination—Choose the target hard drive for the installation. Available and required space is displayed on this screen.
- Installation Type—Customize installation options on the Installation Type screen.
- Installing—Software installation on Mac OS X can take a bit "longer" than you might expect. Although copying the files is generally fast, the process of "optimizing" can take a virtual eternity.
- Finish Up—Cleans up after itself and reboots the system if necessary.

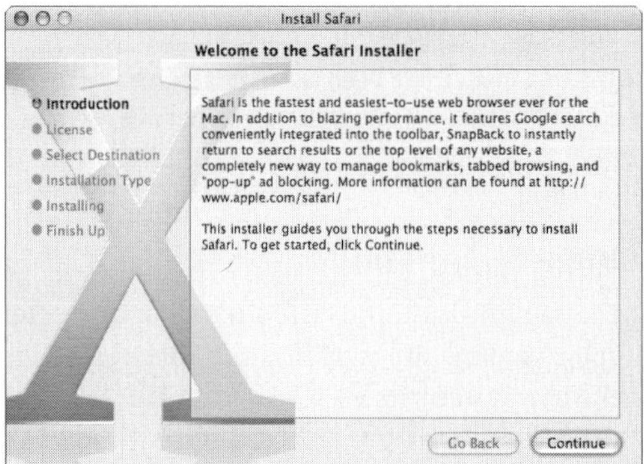

FIGURE 5.4 The Mac OS X installer walks you through the installation process.

Starting in Panther, you can now load multiple packages and start several installations simultaneously, saving you a bit of time. Unfortunately, although almost all areas of Mac OS X have been improved since the initial release, the installer has remained relatively static. Other Unix-like operating systems such as Debian and Red Hat Linux offer the ability to track dependencies between software components and uninstall packages.

Apple's Installer application does not offer an uninstall option but does save a Bill of Materials (BOM) that can be used to determine what files were modified during installation. See Chapter 32, "System Maintenance," for more information on viewing BOM files.

NOTE

There are a number of packages for creating software installers under Mac OS X. The operation of these applications is usually similar to Apple's installer—read a license, choose a destination, and install.

If you encounter `.tar`, `.Z`, or `.gz` files that do not unarchive correctly with StuffIt Expander or do not contain a GUI installer, turn to Chapter 12 for information on working with Unix applications within the BSD subsystem. If you're interested in installing Unix applications, these are discussed in Chapter 16, "Command-Line Software Installation."

Java

Not quite "Unix" software, not quite Mac OS X native, Java applications fall into the difficult category of not being quite Mac-like but definitely worth checking out. Although some Java applications have already been packaged for Mac OS X and modified to take advantage of Mac user interface elements (such as the menu bar, Application menu, and so on), the vast majority of Java applications are platform neutral (as they should be) and may be visually "awkward."

Regardless, thousands of Java applications are freely available for download that can run directly on Mac OS X. Most of the time, you'll start Java within Mac OS X either by visiting a Web page in your browser, or by double-clicking a `.jar` file.

In the event that you want to launch Java applets outside a Web browser, or use `.jnlp` files (Java Network Launching Protocol), you'll need some additional tools. Three GUI Java utilities are included with your system that you may (at some time) need: Applet Launcher, Java Plug-in Settings, and Java Web Start.

TIP

Mac OS X allows you to double-click `.jar` files to launch them. You can also use the command-line Java suite to launch or compile Java applications.

Most typically, you'll be interacting with a `.jar` file, which can be started with `java -jar` *<filename.jar>*. In some special cases, the Java application may not be packaged as a `.jar` and will be a set of unarchived `.class` files. In this case, use `java` *<classname>*.

If you're a Java developer, you can use `javac`, `jar`, `javadoc`, and `jdb` to compile, debug, and prepare your own applications. Sun provides extensive J2SE documentation at `http://java.sun.com/docs/index.html`.

Applet Launcher

The Applet Launcher (path: `/Applications/Utilities/Java/Applet Launcher`) provides a simple method of launching an applet that is located at a Web (`http://`) or file (`file://`) URL.

The Launcher opens windows with a URL field at startup, as shown in Figure 5.5. To launch an Applet, enter a URL to the containing HTML page within the field and then click the Launch button. For local applets, click the Open button, or choose File, Open (Command-O) from the menu.

FIGURE 5.5 Enter a URL and click Launch to start an applet.

The History menu contains a list of recently visited URLs. You can choose one from the list to quickly jump to it.

Very little configuration can be performed on Applet Launcher. If you want to clear the history of recent applets, use the Clear History button in the application preferences.

Quitting the Applet Viewer quits all open applets.

Java Plug-in Settings

The Java Plug-in Control Panel sets attributes of the Mac OS X Java Plug-in Engine. Any applets using the Java plug-in inherit these settings. You can view the official Sun documentation for this application at `http://java.sun.com/j2se/1.4.1/docs/guide/plugin/developer_guide/control_panel.html`.

Java Web Start

Java Web Start is Sun's attempt to provide a single-click "no-install" means of launching Java applications from a Web page. The key behind Java Web Start is a `.jnlp` file, which contains information required to download, store, and execute a given application. Mac OS X even prompts you to save commonly used Web Start applications as a double-clickable Mac OS X application (although `.jnlp` files themselves are double-clickable and launched via Java Web Start).

The idea behind Web Start is that you can browse libraries of JNLP applications; click a single link in your browser; download, install, and be using the application in seconds—without any additional configuration. Downloaded applications are automatically added to the Web Start window, as seen in Figure 5.6 and can be run by selecting their icon and clicking Start.

FIGURE 5.6 Java Web Start stores applications you've started previously.

Unfortunately, the actual practice of publishing software via JNLP is pretty rare. Sun has placed demos (and product information) at `http://java.sun.com/products/javawebstart/`, but if you want to test a few third-party applications, visit `http://www.chemaxon.com/marvin/jnlp/`.

NOTE

Java Plug-in Settings and Java Web Start are both Java applications from Sun Microsystems; they are not Apple products, and this is definitely reflected in their interface design.

Interesting Software

For those coming to the Macintosh platform from Mac OS 8/9 and Windows, there are probably a handful of applications you know about and need (Office, Photoshop, Filemaker) and plenty of software already included in Mac OS X to handle basic day to day tasks such as email and Web browsing. Although this software is great, not exploring additional offerings would be a mistake. The shareware/freeware scene is alive and well on Mac OS X. What follows is a short list of some useful or, if nothing else, amusing applications.

Internet Software

Although Mac OS X provides a great suite of connectivity apps, it doesn't have the tools necessary to make everyone happy. The following applications can be downloaded to expand your library and Internet arsenal.

- OmniWeb—The "prettiest" and most feature-full Mac OS X Web browser. OmniWeb has been in development since the days of OpenStep and uses just about every interface feature that Mac OS X has to offer. `http://www.omnigroup.com`
- Chimera—Using the Mozilla engine, Chimera presents an entirely Mac OS X native appearance and user experience. *This* is the application that users felt should become Apple's branded browser. `http://www.mozilla.org/projects/camino/`
- iChat Streaming Icon—If you use iChat AV and have a video camera (such as the iSight) connected, this application turns your AIM icon into a live video feed! `http://ichat.pardeike.net/`
- Proteus—An all-in-one instant messaging client with an excellent aqua interface, Proteus has a number of features found nowhere else, such as the ability to execute shell scripts on incoming messages. `http://www.indigofield.com/about_proteus.php`
- RBrowser—A GUI SSH/FTP/SFTP client with more features than most users will ever need. RBrowser is patterned after the NeXT file browser and includes security options not found in other applications. `http://www.rbrowser.com`
- Transmit—An FTP client that focuses on functionality and ease of use. A single-window control transfers to and from remote hosts. `http://www.panic.com/transmit/download.html`
- Thunderbird—Although very early in the development stages, the Mozilla project's email application Thunderbird shows great promise. It's fast, supports POP/IMAP, and has an attractive skinnable interface. `http://www.mozilla.org/projects/thunderbird/release-notes.html`
- Watson—The "inspiration" (either intentionally or unintentionally) for Sherlock 3, Watson provides a GUI front-end to otherwise complex Web services. It continues to draw rave reviews and provides an arguably better user experience than Sherlock. `http://www.karelia.com/watson/`

Applications and Utilities

Occasionally we all need to do some work. You can choose from a growing number of productivity applications and useful utilities. These are some of the highlights available:

- Can Combine Icons—An amazing icon compositing tool that can be used to create your own custom Mac OS X icons. By compositing two images or icons (such as a folder icon and an application icon), you can create custom folders for storing your documents. `http://ittpoi.com/`
- Audio Hijack—Can modify any Macintosh audio output—applying special effects, such as echoes, filters, reverb, and so on, in *real-time*. In addition, AH can record *any* audio output—including Internet audio streams. `http://www.rogueamoeba.com/audiohijack/`
- SoundHack—Designed for digitally processing sounds to obtain unique results, SoundHack is both fun for hobbyists and useful for musicians. It's definitely worth a download. `http://www.soundhack.com/`
- REALbasic—The Macintosh equivalent of Visual Basic. The REALbasic environment uses an object-oriented model and graphical interface design tools to get up and running in no time. Users can create software ranging from games to client/server applications. `http://www.realbasic.com/`
- ColdStone—Want to write your own role-playing games for the Mac and Windows? Ambrosia's ColdStone development environment makes it easy for anyone—even those with no programming experience at all. `http://www.ambrosiaSW.com/games/coldstone/`
- Revolution X—A cross-platform (Windows/Mac/Linux) Hypercard-like development system. Create applications that run on the top three platforms from within Mac OS X. `http://www.runrev.com/`
- StoneStudio—A suite of applications developed for designers interested in publishing to paper or the Web. The collection of applications is authored in Cocoa, giving you full access to many of the advanced features of Mac OS X. StoneStudio goes head-to-head with applications such as Macromedia FreeHand and includes additional features such as animated GIF creation and AppleScripting. `http://www.stone.com/StoneStudio/StoneStudio.html`
- PixelNhance—A simple (and free) application that exists for the sole purpose of adjusting attributes (contrast, saturation, and so on) of existing images. This is a must-have for iPhoto users. `http://www.caffeinesoft.com/`
- GraphicConverter—Although the name implies that this software package is good at converting between image formats (and it is), it also has the capability to manipulate photos. Despite its small size, the base feature set of GraphicConverter should be enough for most common image editing functions. `http://www.graphicconverter.net`

- OmniGraffle—Although somewhat difficult to describe, OmniGraffle is *not* difficult to use. OmniGraffle is a flow-charting, object-oriented drawing/task management/just-plain-cool application. `http://www.omnigroup.com`
- Nisus Writer Express—In the mid-1990s, an *amazing* word processor named Nisus appeared on the Macintosh platform. Sadly, over the years it fell into software disrepair and was not made available for Mac OS X. Now, Nisus is back as Nisus Writer Express with the features you *need* and some unique options such as noncontiguous selections. If you *don't* need the bloat of Word, Nisus is a great and inexpensive alternative. `http://www.nisus.com/`
- JbidWatcher—If you use eBay frequently, you've probably experienced "sniping" where a user grabs your prized trinket away at the last second. JbidWatcher gives you the power to do the same and provides excellent auction tracking services as well. JbidWatcher is written in Java but runs great on Mac OS X. `http://jbidwatcher.sourceforge.net`
- Enigmo—Not much for productivity? Enigmo is possibly the most fun I've had since Lemmings and The Incredible Machine. It is a fully 3D puzzle game with the objective of redirecting dripping liquids into their allotted containers. No, really...it's fun! `http://www.macplay.com/games/enigmo.php`
- MacMAME—If you're a child of the '80s (or just like classic arcade games), the Macintosh port of MAME (Multi Arcade Machine Emulator) should grace your desktop. Capable of playing thousands of classic games (with the appropriate ROM files), MacMAME is free and an almost endless source of entertainment. `http://www.macmame.org/`

TIP

If you download MAME and find yourself wondering *how* you actually get ROMs, visit `http://www.mame.dk/` for more information.

If you're interested in emulation on the Mac in general, visit `http://www.emulation.net` for links to every emulator available for Mac OS X.

System Additions

The default Mac OS X GUI and associated widgets are nice but barely scratch the surface of what is possible. Third-party developers have been hard at work creating their own additions, and the results are great.

- ASM—Miss the application switcher menu in the upper-right corner of your screen (Mac OS 8/9)? Bring it back with ASM for Mac OS X. `http://www.vercruesse.de/software`

- CandyBar—Brings drag-and-drop icon customization to Mac OS X. Within a few seconds, you can completely customize all the Mac OS X icons without needing to know where or how the images are stored in the system. `http://www.iconfactory.com/cb_home.asp`
- DragonDrop—Miss pop-up tabbed windows? If you find it difficult to get over the lack of tabbed windows in Mac OS X, download DragonDrop—a reimplementation of the Classic feature. `http://cs.oberlin.edu/~dadamson/DragonDrop/`
- FruitMenu—Adds the traditional Apple menu to the Mac OS X system: `http://www.unsanity.com/haxies/fruitmenu/`
- Fireflies—An OpenGL screensaver that simulates flocking behavior and implements unique Matrix-like spinning effects. `http://s.sudre.free.fr/Software/Fireflies.html`
- Konfabulator—A Javascript engine and interface API that enable users to write and run dozens of Mac OS X additions. Even if you aren't a programmer, there are many applications written for Konfabulator and ready for your free use. `http://www.konfabulator.com/downloads/`
- Marine Aquarium—Even though a version of this screensaver ships with Windows XP, it's still a thing of beauty. Marine Aquarium features 3D photo-realistic animated fish in a high-resolution marine aquarium. `http://www.serenescreen.com/product/maquariumx/`.
- Metallifizer—Enjoy the metallic appearance of tools such as iChat? Want to "metallize" applications such as Mail? Hate the metallic appearance of tools such as iChat? Want to remove it? Do both with Metallifizer from Unsanity. `http://www.unsanity.com/haxies/`
- Paint Effects—The Paint Effects saver is a demonstration of the power of Maya 3D. One of the first screensavers available for Mac OS X, it still shines three years later. Regardless of your interest in 3D modeling, download this screensaver. You're guaranteed to spend numerous hours gawking at the scenes it creates. `ftp://ftp.aliaswavefront.com/pub/ScreenSaver/Macintosh/`
- Plasma Tunnel—A screensaver that takes you through a glowing twisting and winding texture-mapped tunnel. Not for the easily dizzied. `http://www.fruitz-of-dojo.de/php/download.php4`
- SharePoints—If you want to use AppleShare to share something other than your "Public" directory, the SharePoints system preferences pane can do just that. `http://www.hornware.com/sharepoints.html`
- Meteorologist—A free weather display for your Dock and menu. Keep track of the weather forecasts for multiple cities within a non-intrusive interface. `http://sourceforge.net/projects/heat-meteo`.

- WebDesktop—Overlays a live Web page on your desktop using the Safari SDK and Mac OS X transparency effects. A great way to keep track of Fark.com—use it as your background! `http://www.stevenf.com/index.php?node=WebDesktop`
- WindowShade X—Missing the Windowshade feature popular in Mac OS 9? Bring it back with this "haxie" from Unsanity. (Unsanity puts out some great little utilities, if you haven't guessed by now.) `http://www.unsanity.com/haxies/`
- Alfred—A manager for items in the System Library and user Library folders (screensavers and such). This is roughly the equivalent of the old Mac OS Extension manager. `http://www.inferiis.com/products/alfred/`

Summary

Mac OS X uses the same compression and encoding methods that have been widespread on the Macintosh system for the last decade. In addition, it also supports Unix standards such as `.tar` and `.gz`. The included StuffIt Expander application can deal with most common archive types and makes it simple for even the first-time user to start downloading software for his library.

Although a new operating system, Mac OS X already has many applications that utilize its cutting-edge graphics capabilities in ways never seen before on a desktop computer. Although this chapter contains a list of interesting software, it should serve only as a starting point for exploring the possibilities of the operating system.

PART II

Mac OS X Media Tools

IN THIS PART

CHAPTER 6

Photography and Imaging

IN THIS CHAPTER

- iPhoto
- The iPhoto Interface
- Image Capture

Kicking off our coverage of the Mac OS X Media tools, we'll start with our first look at a member of the Apple iLife Suite, iPhoto, and follow up with iPhoto's older, less flashy cousin, Image Capture. Between these two applications, you can import and manage hundreds of photographs, order hardcover photo albums, create digital copies of your existing photos on your flatbed scanner, and share your camera or scanner with your office or roommate. Working with digital images has never been easier.

iPhoto

Have a digital camera? If so, you've probably struggled to keep track of image files with names such as 200324057. With Mac OS X, there's an easy way to store, organize, edit, and even share your photographs. It's called iPhoto (path: `/Applications/iPhoto`). iPhoto connects directly to many cameras, so you can skip loading special software, download your pictures, and share them with others quickly and painlessly.

NOTE

Most modern digital cameras and media readers are compatible with iPhoto. To view Apple's compatibility list, visit `http://www.apple.com/iphoto/compatibility/camera.html`.

Those without a compatible media device can still use iPhoto to organize digital images by importing the files into iPhoto after they have been transferred to your computer using the manufacturers' software.

CAUTION

Before we get started, be aware that iPhoto (in its current form) does not handle extremely large volumes of image files well, nor does it allow multiple users to access the same image library. Scrolling through libraries containing more than 1,000 images is painfully slow, even on hardware less than a year old. (G5 owners can disregard that comment!)

If you're looking for an alternative, iView Media Pro is an excellent choice (`http://www.iview-multimedia.com/`). Those in need of a photo tool that can handle 20,000 images without skipping a beat might want to look into Extensis Portfolio (`http://www.extensis.com/portfolio`), which comes in standalone and server versions.

The iPhoto Interface

Apple's iPhoto, like much of the iLife suite (as you'll see in subsequent chapters), is contained within a single window, shown in Figure 6.1.

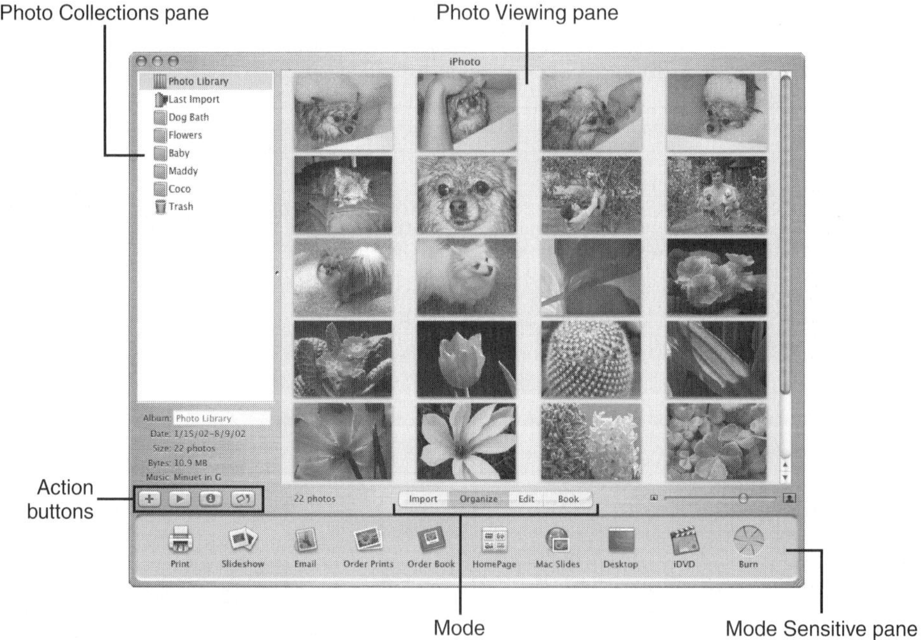

FIGURE 6.1 The iPhoto interface—simple and elegant.

NOTE

The first time you start iPhoto on your computer, it asks what you want to happen when a camera is connected to your system. You can choose to ignore, launch iPhoto, or launch another application, such as Image Capture, discussed in the "Image Capture" section later in this chapter.

iPhoto operates in one of four modes, selectable using the mode button bar near the bottom of the window:

- Import—Download pictures from your camera or media reader into iPhoto.
- Organize—Print, email, burn CD/DVDs, and otherwise display your photographs.
- Edit—Apply simple photo-editing tools to clean up your less-than-perfect images.
- Book—Create a made-to-order book based on a photo album.

Within the iPhoto interface are several distinct areas—or panes. These are context-sensitive and change depending on what features of the software you're using. The bottom pane contains mode-specific functions, the left-hand side holds collections ("albums") of pictures, and the upper-right viewing area displays the actual images, either in thumbnail or full frame. You can resize the contents of the viewing area using the slider to the right of the mode buttons.

TIP

To jump between the smallest and the largest possible display sizes, click on the small and large image icons at either end of the resize slider.

Photo Collections and Information

The left-hand pane remains static regardless of the mode iPhoto is operating in. It contains collections of photographs—referred to by iPhoto as, surprise, *albums*. In addition to the albums you create, it holds three "special" photo collections called Photo Library, Last Import, and Trash.

The Photo Library contains all the images imported by iPhoto. Last Import is a special collection containing the most recent pictures imported from your camera. Trash contains any images that you've decided you want to delete. Like the Finder, images first go into the trash and then are removed by choosing File, Empty Trash from the menu.

Selecting any of the collections refreshes the viewing area with thumbnail images of its contents.

Below the photo collections is a section containing information about the selected item. For example, in Figure 6.1, Photo Library is selected, so the information section displays the name of the selection, the range of dates for the images it contains, the number of images it contains, and the total file size of its contents. It also displays the music currently selected to accompany slideshows, which we will discuss shortly. If a specific thumbnail image were selected, the given information would be the image title, date imported, size of image in pixels, file size, and current slideshow music. You can change the title or the date by typing directly into the appropriate field.

TIP

Additional details about a selected image can be accessed by choosing File, Show Photo Info from the menu. This opens a window containing information about the image, file, and originating camera. If your camera supports it, the window also contains technical details such as shutter speed, aperture, and use of a flash for the photograph.

Action Buttons

Directly below the Photo Collections in the static left-hand pane are four iPhoto action buttons. These buttons provide quick access to features that you might need regardless of the iPhoto mode you are in:

- Create a New Album—Enables you to create a special group of chosen photos that you can arrange in any way or export as a unit. We'll talk more about albums later.
- Play the Slideshow—Plays a full-screen slideshow, complete with music, of all the photos currently displayed in the viewing area—starting with the first selected photo (if any). You can alter the slideshow settings under the Slideshow option of the Organize mode, including the length of time each slide plays and the song to accompany the slide show—you can even choose a song from your iTunes folder.
- Show Information About the Selected Photos—Toggles the information area through three different display modes—normal, extended (includes a field for entering comments about the selected photo), and hidden (the info area is hidden entirely).
- Rotate the Selected Photos—Rotates the selected items. You can set the rotation direction to clockwise or counterclockwise in the iPhoto application preferences.

Now that you know where to find the basic components of iPhoto (the mode buttons, image viewing pane, photo collections, action buttons, and mode-sensitive area), let's start using the application.

Importing Image Files

The first time you connect a supported camera to your computer and set the camera to its playback or transfer mode, iPhoto opens automatically. If it doesn't, you can manually launch iPhoto either from the Dock or the Applications folder. The iPhoto window launches in Import mode.

The Import pane, shown in Figure 6.2, displays the camera status, Import button, and an option to delete images from the camera after they're stored in iPhoto.

To import the photos on your camera, click the Import button in the lower-right corner of the window. If the box for Erase Camera Contents After Transfer is checked, the Confirm Move dialog, shown in Figure 6.3, appears and prompts you to approve deletion of the original photo from the camera. Thumbnails of the transferring images appear in the image well of the Import pane along with the number of photos remaining to be transferred.

When the import is complete, the new images appear in the photo viewing area along with any other images you've imported.

FIGURE 6.2 The Import mode enables you to follow the progress of your photos as they're transferred from the camera to your computer.

FIGURE 6.3 Confirm that you want to delete the photos from the camera after they've been imported.

NOTE

By default, new *rolls* (groups of pictures imported at one time) are added to the bottom of the viewing area, but you can change that to order with the most recent at the top inside the application preferences pane.

To import images already stored on your hard drive or other media, simply select them and drag them onto the Photo Library icon at the upper left. Thumbnails appear as if the images were another "roll" of film. If you already have images organized into folders, you can drag the folders (or the groups of images themselves) into the collection pane, and they will be added as individual albums.

Organizing Images

After you've imported some image files into iPhoto, switch to the Organize mode to work with your images.

While in the Organize mode, you can choose to display the images in your viewing area with additional information, including their titles, keywords, and film rolls, by using the View menu.

Viewing Options

The Keywords option shows any keywords you've attached to an image file to the right of its thumbnail image. We'll look further at applying keywords in just a moment.

Displaying by Film Rolls divides the photos in the viewing area into sections labeled with roll number, date of import, and number of photos imported, as shown in Figure 6.4.

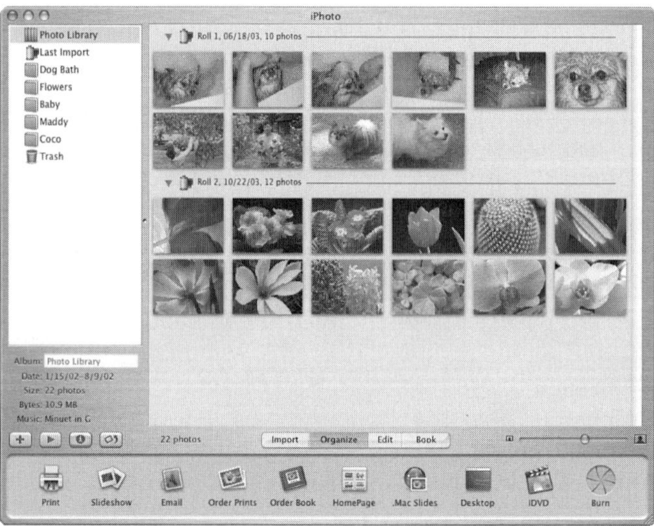

FIGURE 6.4 The Roll view shows photos divided into virtual rolls based on when they were imported.

To order the images in your Photo Library by film roll, date, or title, select the appropriate option in the Arrange Photos submenu of the View menu.

Selecting Images

You can select an image in the viewing area by single-clicking it. You can select a group of consecutive pictures by clicking just outside the edge of the first photo and dragging to create a box connecting all the photos that you want to select, or select a group of nonconsecutive pictures by holding down the Command key as you click the desired images.

Setting Image Titles

Selecting Titles in the View menu displays the title of each image beneath its thumbnail in the viewing area. The default titles of images imported by iPhoto aren't extremely useful. You can give them more meaningful titles by selecting the image, clicking on the information action button until the title field is visible, and editing the field to reflect a more appropriate title.

Deleting Images

If you want to delete a photo or several photos visible in the viewing area, highlight the photos you don't want to keep and then press the Delete key on your keyboard. In the original version of iPhoto, when you deleted a photo it was truly gone forever. In more recent versions, deleted photos are stored in a special Trash area, much like the one for your entire system.

You can view the contents of the Trash by selecting its icon on the left side of the iPhoto window. If you decide to save a photo that you sent to the Trash, you can drag it back to your Photo Library. When you are positive that you don't want to see any of the items in the Trash again, choose File, Empty Trash from the menu.

Applying Keywords

A good way to organize your photo collection is with keywords. When applied, keywords appear next to the image thumbnails in the viewing area whenever the Keywords option is highlighted within the View menu.

To assign Keywords, open the Keywords/Search window, shown in Figure 6.5, by choosing Edit, Keywords from the menu (Command-K).

You can use iPhoto's default keywords or create your own custom keywords. To write your own, choose New from the Keywords pop-up menu at the top of the Keywords/Search window. Then, in the line that appears, type your new keyword.

To change an existing keyword, select it in the keyword list and choose Rename from the Keywords pop-down menu at the top of the Keywords window. Keep in mind that the change cascades to any photos assigned the previous keyword.

To delete a keyword, click to highlight it in the keyword list, and choose Delete from the Keywords pop-down menu.

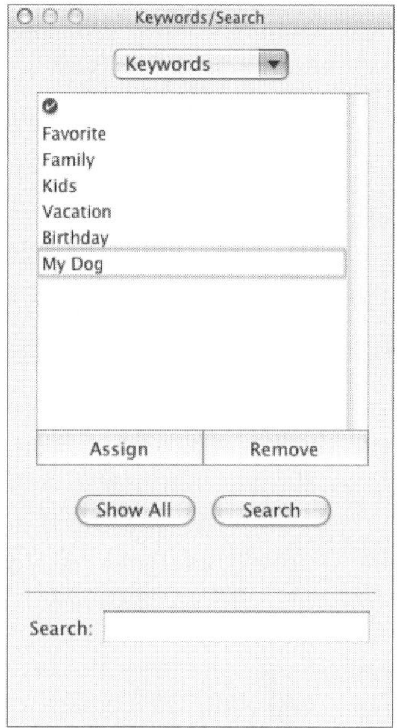

FIGURE 6.5 The Keywords window allows you to assign and search by keywords.

To apply keywords to a photo, select one or more image thumbnails in the viewing area and highlight the keyword you want to apply by clicking it. Then, click the Assign button below the keyword list. In Figure 6.5, two pictures are being assigned the keyword "Sage."

To remove a keyword, select the image and click back into the Keywords/Search menu. All the keywords you've added to the selected photo will be highlighted in the list so that you can remove them all, or click on the one you want to remove. Click the Remove button to remove the highlighted keywords.

NOTE

Included in the keyword list is a check mark symbol, which acts somewhat differently than the other keywords. Whereas other keywords are visible only when you've chosen to display them in the View menu, the check mark is always visible in the lower-right corner of the thumbnails it has been applied to. Also, the check box cannot be renamed or deleted as the other keywords can.

Searching by Keyword, Title, or Comment

After you've applied keywords, you can search your image collection for photos labeled with a specific keyword or combination of keywords. Open the Keywords/Search window, select the keyword you want to target from the keyword list, and click the Search button near the middle of the window. Only those pictures that match your search appear in the viewing area. Click the Show All button to return to the full photo listing.

In addition to searching by assigned keywords, you can also search for words in your image titles or comments. Just type the word in the Search field at the bottom of the Keywords/Search window. You don't need to click the search button, or even finish typing the word, before iPhoto attempts to match your search criteria. Delete the search term or click Show All to return to the full photo listing.

Creating an Album

Life happens in a sequence and often we want to organize our photos to tell a story in sequence. To choose the sequence of a set of images, you must create an album and add the photos you want to work with. (Keep in mind, that every photo imported into iPhoto will appear in your Photo Library; adding photos to albums doesn't move them out of the Photo Library.)

TIP

You can choose whether to arrange the photos in an album by film roll, date, or title by choosing View, Arrange Photos in the menu, just as you can for your Photo Library. However, for albums there's a fourth option that lets you arrange your images manually by dragging and dropping. This gives you the power to order them in any way you see fit.

Albums are especially useful if you have many photos—attempting to view several thousand photos all at once can bring iPhoto to a crawl. Albums are also a basic unit in iPhoto that can be used when creating books, slideshows, and Web pages, coming up later.

The option to make a new album is available from any mode in iPhoto but is most useful in Organize modes because it allows you to drag images to the album. To create a new album, perform the following steps:

1. Click the button showing a + sign near the left edge of the iPhoto window, or choose File, New Album from the menu.
2. A dialog box (shown in Figure 6.6) appears, prompting for a name for your album. (If you change your mind later, you can double-click the name of the album in the album list to change it.)
3. When you've named your album, click OK.

The album you created appears at the bottom of the collection list (but above Trash) at the left of the iPhoto interface. If you want to change the order of your albums, select the one you want to move and drag it to a new position. A black bar indicates where the album will be inserted, as shown in Figure 6.7. If you want to remove an album, select it and press the Delete key on your keyboard. You will see an alert asking you to confirm deletion.

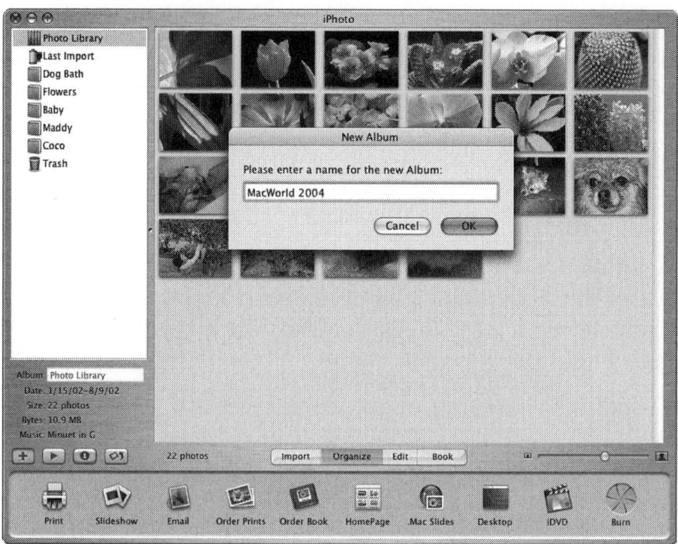

FIGURE 6.6 Enter a name for your album.

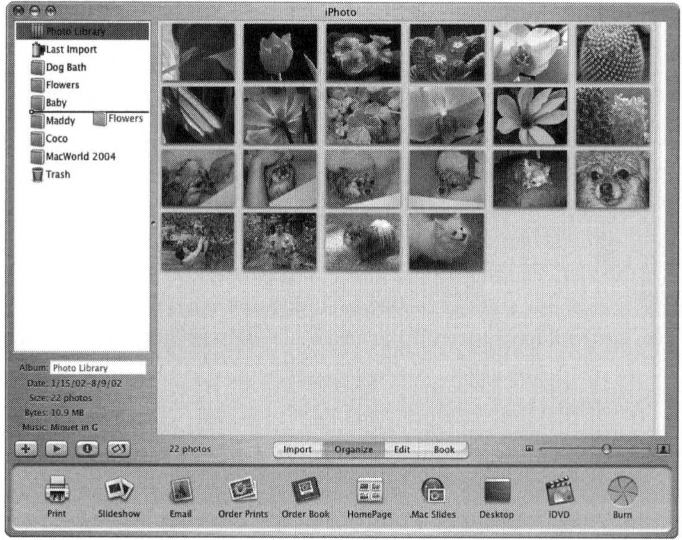

FIGURE 6.7 Reorder your albums by dragging them around in the list.

TIP

Remember, as mentioned earlier, if you already have images arranged in folders on your computer, dragging a folder into the collection pane area adds the folder as a new album with all the images it contains.

Adding Images to an Album

To add images to your album, make sure that you're in Organize mode and select the images you want from the viewing area. You can select them one at a time or in groups. Drag your selection to your album name until a black border appears around it. As you drag, a faded version of one of the selected images appears behind your cursor, along with a red seal showing how many items you're dragging, as shown in Figure 6.8.

FIGURE 6.8 Drag one or more photos into your album.

NOTE

The images within albums are something like aliases on your desktop—you can delete a photo from an album without affecting the original file. However, when you delete an image from the Photo Library, it goes into the Trash and also disappears from any albums to which it has been added. Choosing Empty Trash would then permanently remove the image from your system.

After you've created an album and added images, you can open the album and drag the contents into any order you want. If you start to rearrange your photos and the View is not set to Manually, iPhoto switches for you automatically. You can also remove images from the album by selecting them and pressing the Delete key on your keyboard.

NOTE

Dragging photos from an album or any collection to the Finder creates a copy of that image file at the location you placed it (such as your desktop).

Editing Photos

iPhoto's Edit mode enables you to improve your existing photos by resizing them, adjusting their coloration, and performing simple retouching. To edit a photo, select it in Organize mode; then click the Edit mode button or double-click a thumbnail image. You'll see a screen similar to that shown in Figure 6.9, with a large view of the photo and a number of editing tools in the bottom page. While in Edit mode, you can use the Prev and Next buttons at bottom right to move through a group of images without going back into Organize mode.

NOTE

When editing a photo that's been added to an album, bear in mind that any changes appear in both the Photo Library and the album.

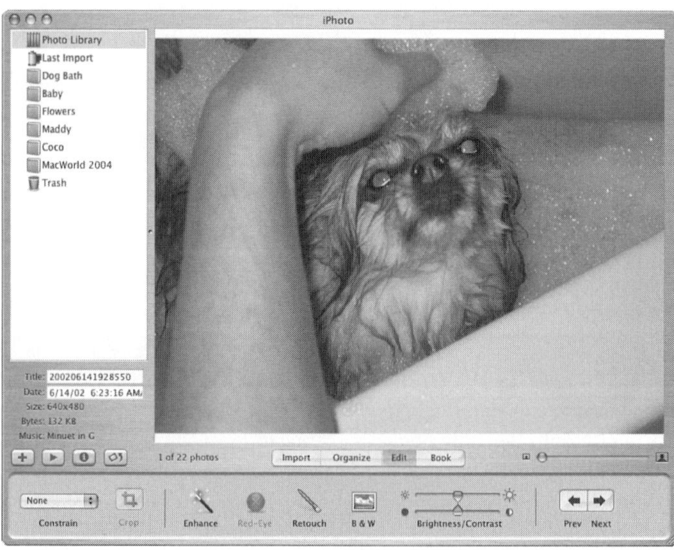

FIGURE 6.9 In Edit mode, you can crop your images or change their appearance by altering color, contrast, brightness, and so on.

Cropping

A major function available in Edit mode is *cropping* to remove extraneous photo details such as your thumb or your cousin's inappropriate hand gesture. iPhoto enables you to constrain the size of your cropped images to fit the common photos sizes 4×6, 5×7, and 8×10, as well as ratios such as square, 4×3, and a size to fit the resolution of your monitor.

> **NOTE**
>
> Depending on the resolution of the images produced by your digital camera, you might not be able to crop to a small section of a photo without the resulting image becoming grainy or fuzzy. This is a problem if you plan to order prints from your photos because although the images might look okay onscreen, they could be unsuitable for printing. When ordering prints or books, watch out for the low-resolution warning symbol, which looks like a yellow traffic sign (see Figure 6.12 later in the chapter for an example). It appears when creating a book or ordering prints if iPhoto determines that an image's resolution is not sufficient for the requested size of the finished image.

To crop an image, open it in Edit mode and follow these steps:

1. Set a Constrain option if you want to maintain a specific width-to-height ratio.
2. In the viewing area, place your mouse pointer at one corner of the object or scene you want to select. Click and drag to form a selection box around it, as shown in Figure 6.10. To reposition the selection box, move your mouse pointer towards the center of the selected area until it changes to a hand and then drag the box where you want it.

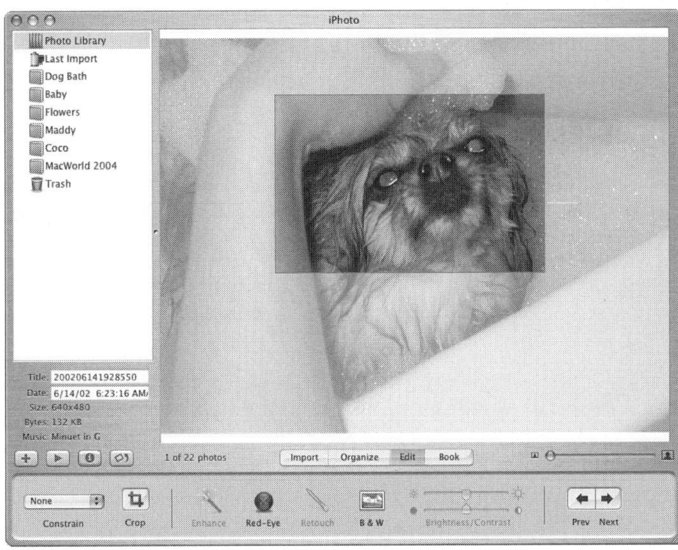

FIGURE 6.10 Drag your cursor to create a box containing the part of the photo you want to keep.

3. Click the Crop button to apply your change and see the result in the viewing area.

If you don't like the look of the cropped image as well as you liked the original, you can undo your most recent edit by choosing Edit, Undo from the menu.

TIP

After you make changes to images in iPhoto, you can always revert to the image as it was first imported by choosing File, Revert to Original from the menu. This enables you to make changes freely without fear of losing your original. However, if you achieve an effect you like, you might want to duplicate the photo in that state before trying additional edits. To do so, select the desired photo and choose File, Duplicate. That way, choosing File, Revert to Original after further editing returns you to that state instead of the original form of the image.

Brightness/Contrast

In addition to cropping, you can edit your images with the Brightness and Contrast sliders. The brightness control can fix minor problems from under- or overexposure. Contrast increases the difference between light and dark elements by making lighter areas lighter and darker areas darker. Contrast also increases the saturation of colors. Although these settings are good for small corrections, they can't save a photograph shot in really poor light conditions.

Red-Eye and Black & White

The Red-Eye and Black & White tools change the coloration of entire photos or the area within a selection box. The Red-Eye option reduces red tint from the eyes of people and pets who are possessed by demons.

Use the Black & White option to convert an entire image to black-and-white or create interesting effects by converting only selected portions of the image. To correct red-eye, mark a crop selection box as tightly around the red eyes as possible and then click the Red-Eye button.

NOTE

iPhoto's Red-Eye tool leaves a lot to be desired. For one thing, most red-eye regions are round, but iPhoto's cropping tool can only make rectangular selections. If you happen to select a portion of anything with red tones in it that lies outside the red-eye region you want to correct, you will also remove the red from that area.

Enhance

The Enhance tool changes the coloration of the selected image. This is a "magic" tool—it decides what it feels are the best tonal changes to apply to the image and then makes them. If you don't like the results, there are no controls to adjust its performance. To use it, simply click the Enhance button. If you don't like the results, you can always choose Edit, Undo from the menu.

Retouch

The Retouch tool is used to blend specks and imperfections in your photos into the areas surrounding them. This tool is different from what we've already discussed, all of which either work on the entire image or a preselected area. When using Retouch, your mouse cursor appears as a set of crosshairs as it does when you are cropping a photo. You use these crosshairs to target image flaws. It may help to use the size slider to magnify the image so that you can see the area you want to retouch, as shown in Figure 6.11. When you have this cursor positioned near a discolored spot, click your mouse button and watch the color in the region around your cursor even out.

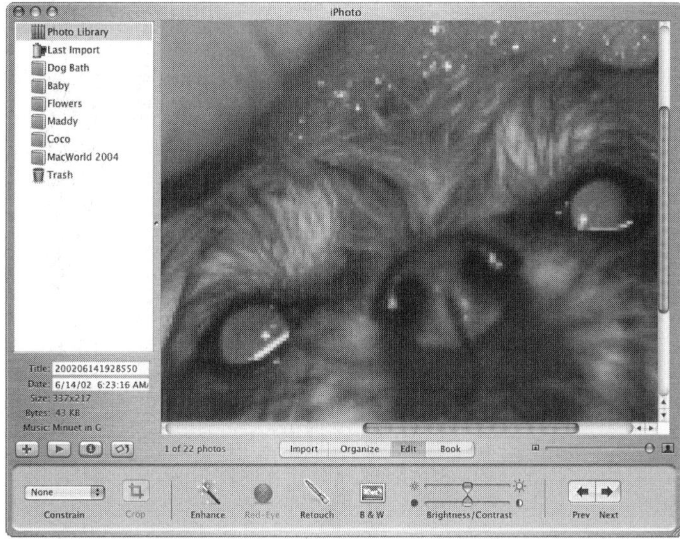

FIGURE 6.11 An enlarged view of the problem area makes retouching more precise.

> **TIP**
>
> When using the Retouch tool, be patient. Changes are made slowly so as to blend seamlessly into the picture.

Using Other Photo-Editing Software with iPhoto

Although iPhoto is a fantastic tool for organizing photos and performing simple cropping, you may want to perform your serious editing in a separate image editing program. A few popular examples are

- PixelNHance (`http://www.caffeinesoft.com/`)—Free and excellent for simple color correction and enhancement. An absolute "must-have" for iPhoto users.

- GraphicConverter (`http://www.graphicconverter.net/`)—A popular shareware application bundled with Apple's high-end machines. Offering many image manipulation and drawing tools, GraphicConverter is an excellent value, but may be overly complex for beginning users.
- Photoshop/Photoshop Elements (`http://www.adobe.com/`)—Adobe's venerable Photoshop application is the leading photo manipulation software available. Providing high-end editing and filtering features, Adobe Photoshop requires an additional reference or training to be used to its full potential. Two versions are available: Photoshop and its slightly simpler (and lower priced) alternative, Photoshop Elements.

To open an iPhoto image file in another image editing program, click and drag an image thumbnail from the Organize view onto the icon for the photo-editing program. If you plan to edit with an outside program frequently, you can go into the iPhoto Preferences and set images to open automatically in the outside program when double-clicked.

If you do choose to edit your photos in a program other than iPhoto, keep in mind that changes saved to an original image from an outside program replace the original file in iPhoto's folders, so you cannot revert to the original image as you normally would. It might be best to make a duplicate before you begin editing.

If you choose to further edit an image that has already been altered from within iPhoto, the image is already a copy, so you will be able to revert to the original version. To check whether a file is an original or a copy before you begin editing, look at the File menu to see whether Revert to Original is an available option or is grayed out. If it is grayed out, the photo you're working with is the original.

Designing a Photo Book

Book mode, shown in Figure 6.12, is a specialized option used to arrange an album's photos into a book format, including any supporting text. You can then order copies of your book in the Organize mode, as we'll discuss later in the section "Sharing Your Photos."

In the Book options pane, the Theme pop-up menu enables you to choose a basic style, including Story Book, Picture Book, and Catalog. The options differ in their picture layouts and built-in text areas, and how the photos are arranged on the page. When you choose a theme, the photos in the selected album are placed in a basic template in the order they appear in the album. The individual pages appear in a row at the bottom of the photo viewing area.

TIP

It's best to choose the look you want for your book carefully before you start customizing it. If you change from one theme to another, you lose any text (except photo titles and comments) or special page formatting you've made.

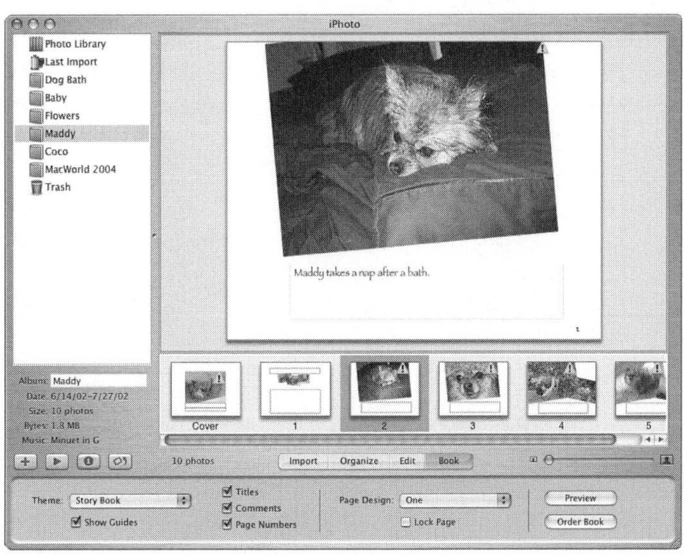

FIGURE 6.12 Book mode enables you to lay out the photos in an album as a book.

> **NOTE**
>
> Earlier we mentioned that when iPhoto attempts to use an image that isn't of a sufficiently high resolution for printing (in this case printing a book) it flags the problem with a yellow warning icon. You can see this in action on the cover, and pages 2, 3, 4, and 5 of the sample book shown previously in Figure 6.12.

Check boxes in the Book options pane allow you to choose whether to show image Titles, Comments, and book Page Numbers on the pages (if the theme you've chosen includes space for them).

You can also choose whether to show guides for the text boxes by click the Show Guides check box. If you're planning to edit/add text, you'll want to enable Show Guides so that the text areas are defined onscreen (otherwise, you might not know where to type!). To edit text within a text area, select a page; then click and type in the area. To check your spelling for a given page, choose Check Spelling from the Spelling submenu of the Edit menu. You can also change the font of an entire book in the Font submenu of the Edit menu.

When you choose a theme, an album's photos are inserted into the page template in the order in which they appear in your album. The first image in the album, for example, is the default cover shot. The Page Design pop-up menu enables you to adjust the templates to show more or fewer images on a selected page. If you like the composition of some of the pages and don't want them to be shifted when you apply new templates or move other pages around, you must select the pages and activate the Lock Page check box. You can alter the layout of any page except the cover.

NOTE

You can change the order of entire pages by dragging them to a new position in the scrolling page list. However, to change the cover photo, you must go into Organize mode and rearrange the images in your album to place another photo first. Any changes made to page order in your book are reflected in the order of images in the album.

To get a better feel for the chosen layout, use the Preview button to page through your book in a separate window, as shown in Figure 6.13. When you are satisfied with your book, click the Order Book button to open a window with purchasing details.

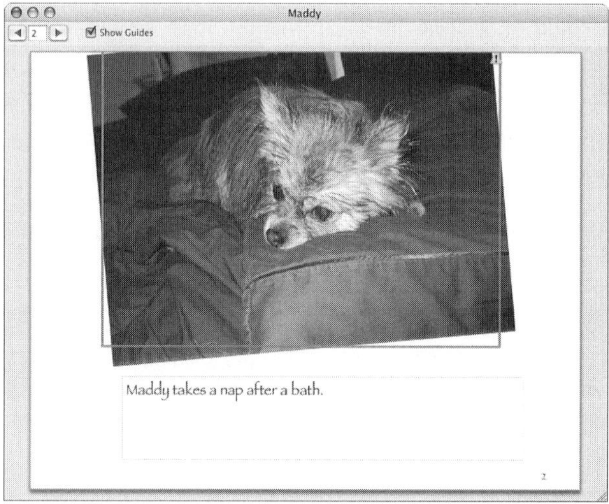

FIGURE 6.13 View your book in a separate window using the Preview button.

Sharing Your Photos

iPhoto offers a variety of ways for you to share your photos with others, both in print and onscreen. They are located along the bottom of the iPhoto window when in Organize mode.

Printed Photos

For those who want to share their photos the traditional way, in print format, iPhoto offers three button choices: Print, Order Prints, or Order Book.

Clicking the Print button enables you make print settings for the selected item, including Style (how the page is laid out) and the number of copies. Use the Style pop-up menu to choose between common layout types such as Greeting Card and Contact Sheet. Each style has additional settings that appear after it is selected. Use these to fine-tune the appearance of your printed page.

Many additional print settings, including special instructions for paper type, are revealed by clicking the advanced button at the bottom of the print window.

The Order Prints and Order Book buttons connect you to remote Web sites where you can choose what to order and supply your billing information.

NOTE

If an Internet connection is not available, the ordering functions do not work correctly on your computer.

You can order prints of your pictures just as you would with pictures captured on film, or you can order a bound book of an album as you designed it using the Book mode. If you order a book, be aware that the base size is 10 pages. If your book has fewer than 10 pages, several pages at the end are left blank. Also, additional charges are made on a page-by-page basis for books of more than 10 pages.

Digital Sharing

To share your photos digitally with others, you can use the Email option. The Email option enables you to easily email a photo stored in iPhoto. Clicking the Email button brings up a dialog box in which you can choose the size of the image and whether to include the image title and comments. Click the Compose button to open a mail window containing the selected photograph and then add the email address of the recipient.

If you are a . Mac member (see Chapter 4, "Internet Applications") you can also use the HomePage and .Mac Slides options. Clicking the HomePage button enables you to select up to 48 images from your Photo Library or a specific album to insert into a basic Web page layout that will be stored in your .Mac account. You can view a sample page at `http://homepage.mac.com/robynness/PhotoAlbum1.html`.

Choosing the .Mac Slides option lets you upload the currently selected album to your .Mac server space, or iDisk, that can be used as a screensaver by anyone running version 10.1.5 or later of Mac OS X. You can only offer one slideshow at a time, but this is a fun way to share pictures with friends and family. When you update the slides, your friends' screensavers are automatically updated the next time they connect to the Internet.

NOTE

After you upload a .Mac slideshow, how can you share it with your family and friends? Tell them to go to the Desktop & Screen Saver pane of System Preferences and choose .Mac from the list in the Screen Saver pane. Then, they need to click the Configure button and, in the Subscription window that opens, type your .Mac membership name and click OK. It takes a few moments for the images to be downloaded from the Internet to their computers.

If you want to test drive a .Mac slideshow, enter **`robynness`** as the .Mac membership name in the Subscribe window.

For more information on .Mac and the .Mac screensaver, see Chapter 4.

If your Mac has a CD burner or a DVD burner, you have the additional option of burning an album, or your entire library, to a CD or DVD. Click the Burn button and insert a blank disc when prompted. Click the Burn button a second time to write the disc.

The iDVD option, available to those with computers equipped with Apple's SuperDrive and with iDVD installed, exports your iPhoto slideshows—including music choice and slide timing—into iDVD. All that's left is to use iDVD to choose a background image for the main title page and burn your DVD. (You learn more about iDVD in Chapter 8, "Digital Video.")

Viewing Your Own Digital Photos

In addition to sharing your photos with others, you can also enjoy them at your own computer with the iPhoto Slide Show and the Desktop options.

The Slide Show option brings up a dialog box, shown in Figure 6.14, with options for setting the duration each image stays onscreen, whether the slides are displayed randomly and whether they repeat, and which music accompanies the show. The music listing comes directly from your iTunes music library (discussed in Chapter 7, "Audio"). The pop-up menu at the top of the music list can be used to choose any custom playlist you've created in iTunes, or the entire iTunes Library. If you don't have an iTunes library yet, choose Sample Music for a few built-in tunes. The search field and Play button at the bottom of the window can be used to search for a specific song or listen to the currently selected track.

When you've made your settings, click Save Settings to save your choices as the default and click Play Slideshow to start the iPhoto slideshow.

The Desktop option enables you to choose a single photo from your collection for use as a desktop background. To set a desktop, simply select the image you want and click Desktop. Your desktop background is immediately replaced with the selected image. To change your background back to a non-iPhoto background, open the Desktop & Screen Saver pane of System Preferences and choose a different image.

TIP

The iPhoto albums are automatically displayed in the Desktop & Screen Savers System Preferences pane enabling you to set desktop images and slideshow screensavers directly from the preferences pane without opening iPhoto.

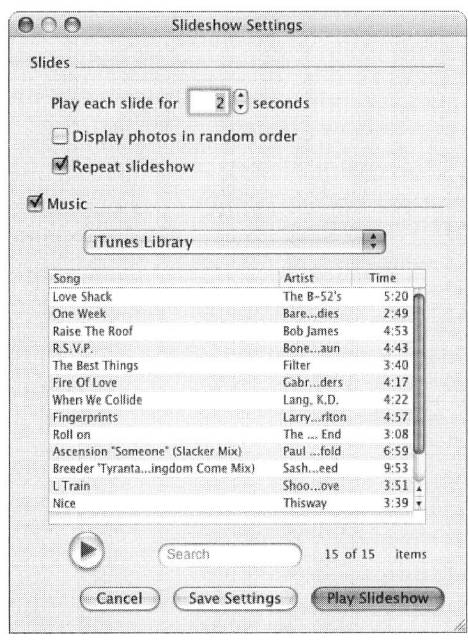

FIGURE 6.14 Customize your onscreen slideshows by choosing music and setting slide duration.

Preferences

The iPhoto application preferences, shown in Figure 6.15, allow you to customize several functions of the program.

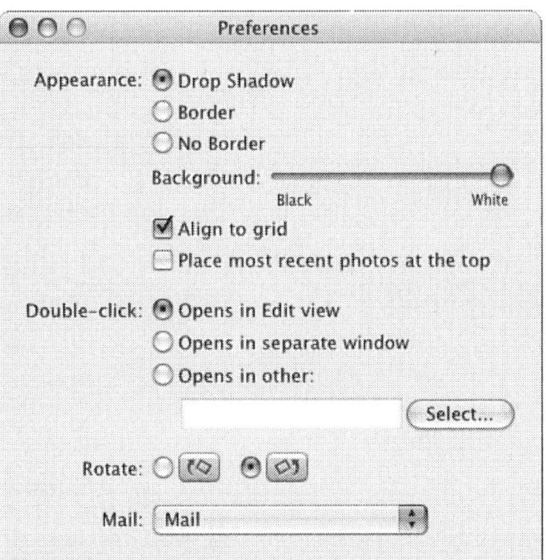

FIGURE 6.15 Customize the appearance of the iPhoto viewing area, the action associated with double-clicking a photo, the direction of image rotation, and your default email program.

Appearance

The first preference options alter the appearance of the iPhoto viewing area. Here, you can choose whether a drop shadow, a border, or no adornment appears around thumbnails and full images. You can also choose a background shade for the viewing area by positioning the slider at white, black, or anywhere between for shades of gray.

The Align to Grid check box alters how thumbnails are positioned. It doesn't make much difference if all the images in your library have the same dimensions. However, if some are horizontal and others vertical, alignment keeps the same number of pictures per row instead of squeezing in however many will fit.

The Place Most Recent Photos at the Top option does exactly as it says; if left unchecked, the most recent photos are added to the end (or bottom) in the rows making up your Photo Library.

Double-Click

Double-Click refers to the action that occurs when you double-click on a thumbnail image in your Photo Library or an album. The default setting is to open in iPhoto's Edit mode, but those who want to edit with an external program may like to select the Opens in Other radio button and then select an application on their hard drive.

Rotate

The Rotate options simply let you choose whether to rotate images clockwise or counterclockwise. You may find that you tend to turn your camera consistently to one side to capture vertical shots. Setting the rotate option to your liking can save you from having to rotate 270 degrees (three clicks of the rotate button) to get to the point of view you want.

Mail

Mail allows you to choose which installed email program is used when you select Email from the Organize pane. By default, it is set to Mail, which was installed with OS X. If you've installed another email program (such as Entourage), you will have the option to select it.

Additional Software

To supplement the features of iPhoto, you might want to consider checking out these third-party applications. They provide some interesting options not currently available in iPhoto:

- ExhibitionX (`http://www.davidahmed.com/exhibitionx.html`)—Creates a 3D gallery of your iPhoto albums. Although the long-term usefulness is debatable, it's definitely a crowd-pleaser and provides plenty of iPhoto-compatible eye-candy.
- myPhoto (`http://agent0068.dyndns.org/~mike/projects/myPhoto/index.php`)—A PHP script for dynamically displaying/searching iPhoto albums online. For more information on PHP, see Chapter 28, "Web Programming."

- iPhoto Library Manager (`http://homepage.mac.com/bwebster/iphotolibrarymanager.html`)—For some reason Apple has chosen to allow only a single iPhoto Library per user (the Library being the collection of all photos and albums). Thankfully, third-party solutions, such as iPhoto Library Manager, make it possible to have as many libraries as you want and switch between them effortlessly.
- Image in a Hurry (`http://www.sentman.com/imageinahurry/`)—Unless you're on a dual G4 or a new G5, iPhoto can get a bit "clunky" when browsing a few thousand images. If you just want to find an image and start working with it, Image in a Hurry provides fast photo album browsing and exporting.

Image Capture

Have a digital camera? a digital media reader? a flatbed scanner? What? It's connected to your *coworker's* machine? That's fine—in Panther you can just share.

Although iPhoto is great for personal photo libraries, sometimes you just want to download images from your capture device, a media reader, or maybe scan a few images on a flatbed scanner—and sometimes the device you want to use might not be connected to the computer you want to use it on.

The Mac OS X Image Capture application (path: `/Applications/Image Capture`) enables you to connect a digital camera, media reader (USB/FireWire), or flatbed scanner to your Mac and import images, or even share the device to a remote computer. The remote machine accesses the device as if it were connected locally.

The first time you use Image Capture, start the application by hand. Using the Image Capture preferences, you can choose to start the application automatically when your camera, media reader, or scanner is plugged in and activated (placed into connect mode or scanning is started).

When started, Image Capture displays a control window for each of the capture devices that you've connected. The digital camera/media reader controls provide the ability to download pictures, whereas the scanner controls allow a user to preview and scan images.

All functions of the Image Capture application are carried out through the control windows—even closing the application is just a matter of closing the windows; it quits automatically.

Cameras and Media Readers

The camera/media reader control window should resemble that of Figure 6.16. The type of camera or media reader and number of images available for download are displayed. Note that the camera icon itself resembles the actual device connected.

FIGURE 6.16 The Image Capture application can be used to download images outside iPhoto.

> **TIP**
>
> Although most popular cameras are now supported by Mac OS X, I recommend investing in a digital media reader. These devices cost between $20–$50, are well supported in Mac OS X, and transfer much faster than most computer-to-camera connections.

To control where images are stored after downloading and what (if any) post processing is performed, used the Download To and Automatic Task pop-up menus.

Download To

The default location for camera downloads is the Pictures, Movies, and Music folders in the current user's home directory (some digital cameras support basic audio and video recording). To change the directory, use the Download To pop-up menu to choose Other and then select the directory to hold the files.

Automatic Task

After a Hot-Plug action is executed, Mac OS X can automatically use one of eight different AppleScripts to format and arrange your photos. The AppleScripts are located in the `/System/Library/Image Capture/Automatic Tasks` folder and can be modified (or added to). You can learn more about AppleScript in Chapter 21, "Scripting Languages."

The eleven available default scripts are

- Build Slide Show—Displays a slideshow of the downloaded photos after retrieving them from the camera.
- Build Web Page—Builds a complete Web page, with thumbnails, for the downloaded images. The Web page is stored in a folder named `Index` in the same location as the images used
- Crop to 3×5—Creates a PDF of the image(s) in your `Pictures` directory where each is cropped to 3×5.

- Crop to 4×6—Creates a PDF of the image(s) in your `Pictures` directory where each is cropped to 4×6.
- Crop to 5×7—Creates a PDF of the image(s) in your `Pictures` directory where each is cropped to 5×7.
- Crop to 8×10—Creates a PDF of the image(s) in your `Pictures` directory where each is cropped to 8×10.
- Fit in 3×5—Creates a PDF of the image(s) in your `Pictures` directory where each is scaled to 3×5.
- Fit in 4×6—Creates a PDF of the image(s) in your `Pictures` directory where each is scaled to 4×6.
- Fit in 5×7—Creates a PDF of the image(s) in your `Pictures` directory where each is scaled to 5×7.
- Fit in 8×10—Creates a PDF of the image(s) in your `Pictures` directory where each is scaled to 8×10.
- Preview—Displays the images in the Preview application.

To choose another script or application, use the Other pop-up menu selection to browse the filesystem and select an alternative.

Downloading All/Some Images

When you're ready to download images, you can choose all the pictures, or select from thumbnails of the images stored on the camera. If you choose Download All, Image Capture downloads the files from your camera.

After the download is complete, Image Capture performs your selected Automatic Task, if any.

To download only certain images from your device, click the Download Some button. After a brief delay, thumbnails appear, as shown in Figure 6.17.

Click a thumbnail to select it; then, if necessary, use the Rotate Left/Right and Delete buttons to fix the photo orientation or remove it completely from the device. The view button can be used to toggle between the thumbnail view and a Finder-like list view with extended image information (size, resolution, and so on).

If you didn't get it right on the initial control screen, you can reassign the Download folder and Automatic Tasks using the pop-up menus at the top of the screen.

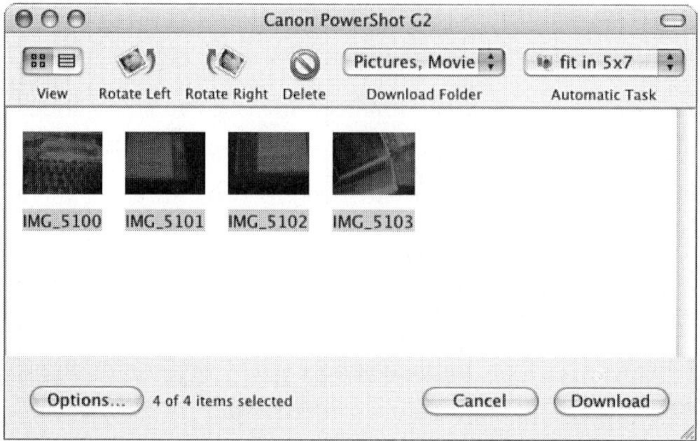

FIGURE 6.17 Choose the images to download.

TIP

If you have a supported camera that allows the computer to trigger a snapshot, you can add a Take Picture toolbar button to the image download window.

Another useful feature missing from the default toolbar is the Thumbnail Size slider, which allows you to scale the preview thumbnails much as you can within iPhoto.

Use the Customize Toolbar option under the View menu or Command-Option-Click on the window's toolbar button.

Camera Options

The Image Capture Options button controls what happens when images are downloaded from a camera or media reader and how they appear within the image file browser. There are three panes within the preferences: Download Options, View Options, and Device Options.

The Download Options pane, shown in Figure 6.18, customizes the image download process.

Choose from these available settings:

- Delete Items from Camera After Downloading—Removes all image files from the camera or media reader on download.
- Create Custom Icons—Automatically generates custom thumbnail icons for each of the downloaded images.
- Add Item Info to Finder File Comments—Uses the Finder's comment field (accessible from Show Info) to store information (size, name, and so on) about each camera file.
- Embed ColorSync Profile—Adds a ColorSync profile to each image file to ensure consistency across output devices.

- Automatically Download All Items—Automatically starts the download process as soon as a camera or media reader is connected.
- Set Camera's Date and Time—Synchronizes the camera's time to the time of the Mac OS X host computer.

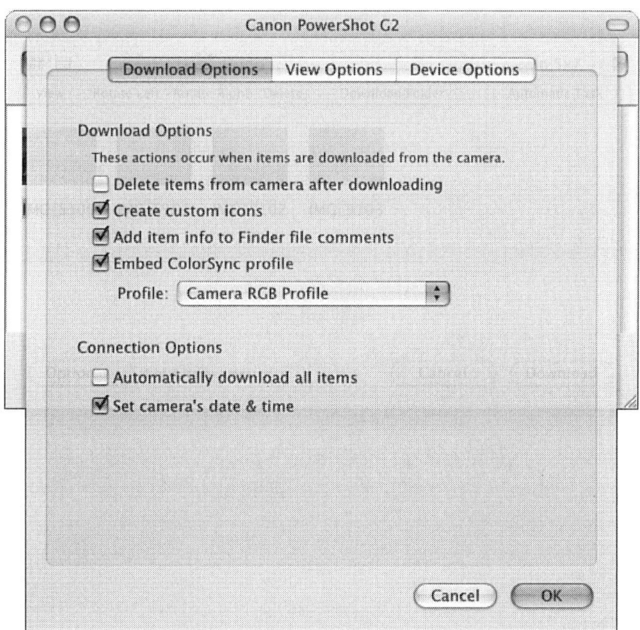

FIGURE 6.18 Download options are used to fine-tune image transfers.

The second pane, View Options, is used to configure how the image listing appears within the Image Capture application.

These settings are similar to those of the Finder views:

- Icon Size—Use the slider to control the size of the preview icons when viewing images in Icon View mode.
- Columns—Pick and choose the columns to display within the image List view. Not all the available options are supported by all cameras, so don't be surprised if some fields are left blank.
- Icon Size—There are two sizes for the icons shown within the List view. Pick your size here.

Finally, the Device Options pane lists the connected device and any available options that can be set for it (usually none).

Flatbed Scanners

Flatbed scanners work a bit differently from digital cameras. When the Image Capture senses that a supported scanner (that is, many Epsons) has been attached and the scanner's Scan button clicked, it automatically launches into Scan mode, shown in Figure 6.19, and scans a preview into the Image Capture window.

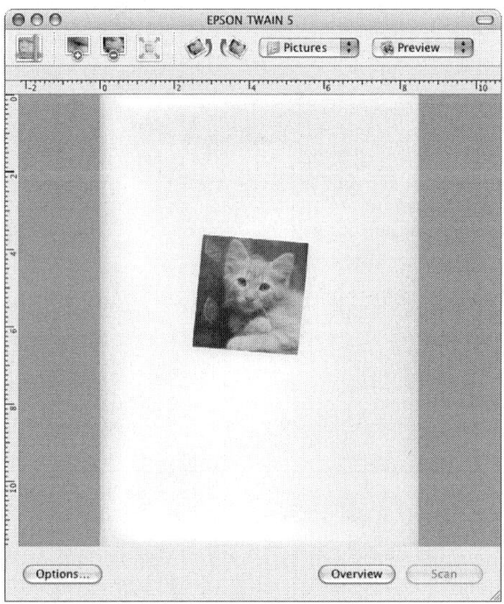

FIGURE 6.19 Image Capture can work with flatbed scanners.

The scanner mode of Image Capture is controlled by the toolbar buttons along the top of the window. From left to right, these are

- Scan Setup Drawer—Opens a window drawer containing settings for the document type, source, resolution (dpi), source size, and percentage scaling, demonstrated in Figure 6.20. Of these, you're likely to want to adjust the document type to match your source material and the resolution to something appropriate for your scanner.
- Zoom In—Zooms in on Page view in the Image Capture window.
- Zoom Out—Zooms out on Page view in the Image Capture window.
- Size to Fit—Sizes the Image Capture's Page view to fit the window.
- Rotate Left—Rotates the page to the left.
- Rotate Right—Rotates the page to the right.
- Download Folder—The location where scanned images are stored.
- Automatic Task—What to do after an image is scanned. By default, Image Capture launches Preview.

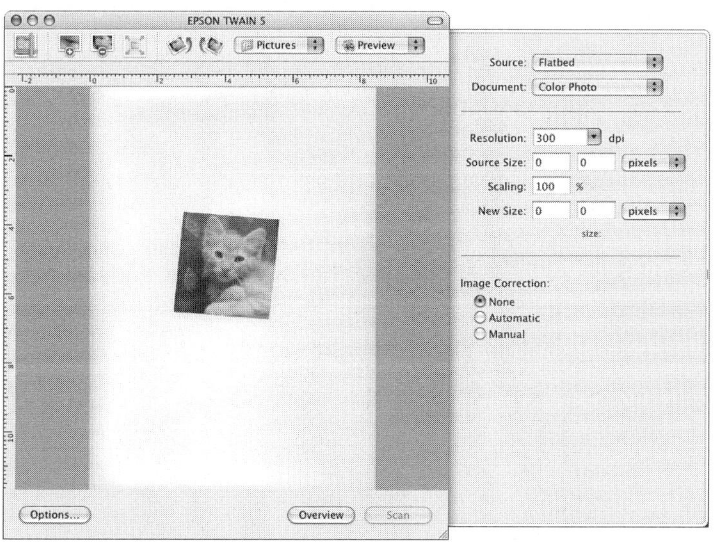

FIGURE 6.20 Use the Scan Geometry button to set up the scan type, dimensions, and resolution.

In the lower-right corner of the window are the scan "action" buttons: Overview and Scan.

The Overview button creates a quick preview scan that is displayed in the Image Capture window (the default action when you click your scanner's Scan button). After an overview has been created, you must draw a crop region around what is "important" on the page. Click and drag within the page to create a rectangle that will be the focus of your detailed scan. Areas of the image outside this crop area will not be included in the final image. You can reposition the crop rectangle by clicking and dragging inside it, or resize it using the handles on the rectangle's sides.

The Scan button creates a detailed scan at the resolution specified in the Scan Geometry drawer—saving it to the Download Folder and processing it with the Automatic Task setting.

TIP

If your scanner is incompatible with Mac OS X and the manufacturer hasn't made a solution available, your best bet is VueScan (`http://www.hamrick.com/index.html`). VueScan is an excellent flatbed/film scanner that produces amazing results on a wide variety of hardware. The only drawback is the interface, which, although not nearly as elegant as Image Capture, offers control over the finest details.

Options

As with the digital camera and media reader functions, scanning options are set by clicking the Options button. Image Capture options for scanners differ slightly from the other devices. The Settings options, shown in Figure 6.21, provide the capability to create custom icons for scanned images as well as store information about the scan in the Finder's comment field and to embed ColorSync profiles in each image.

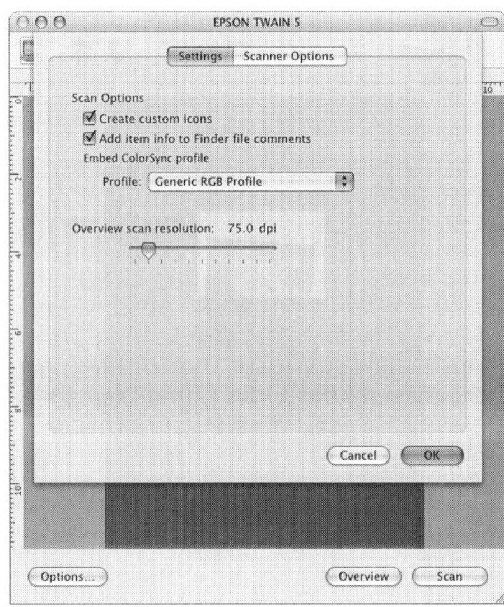

FIGURE 6.21 Set your scanner options; then scan away.

Additionally, the Overview Scan Resolution slider allows you to choose the resolution at which the overview (preview) scan is created.

The Scanner Options button, like Device Options for cameras and media readers, provides information about the connected scanner and any additional device-specific options that are configured.

Sharing Devices

Starting with the release of Panther, Mac OS X can share the devices that Image Capture recognizes. Continuing its tradition of refining poorly placed interface elements only to introduce more, Apple has added these sharing features *not* to the Sharing System Preferences pane but to the Image Capture application preferences.

There are two functions you'll use when sharing devices: sharing and browsing. Sharing allows you to share your scanners and cameras, whereas browsing serves to find and connect shared devices. Sharing is enabled through the Sharing pane of the application preferences, as is browsing. The browsing feature, however, when enabled, is accessed from the Devices menu.

To set up sharing, open the Image Capture application preferences and switch to the Sharing pane. A screen similar to that shown in Figure 6.22 appears.

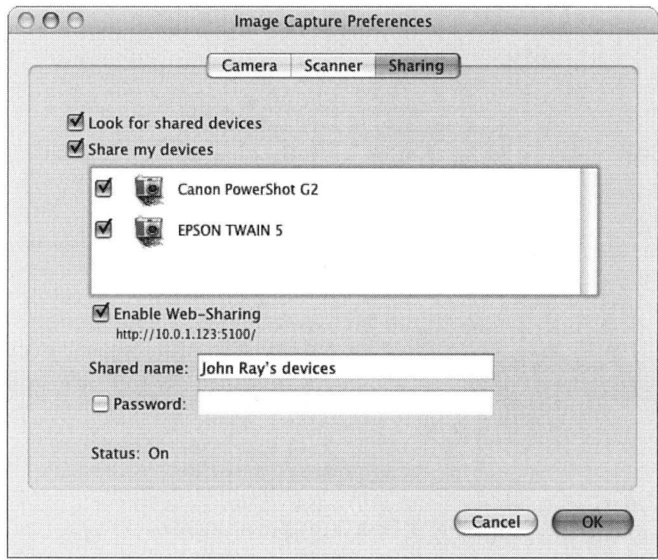

FIGURE 6.22 Configure sharing (and browsing) of image capture devices on Panther.

The Look for Shared Devices check box enables the Browse Shared Devices option in the Devices menu. Make sure that this is checked if you have any intention of using a shared scanner or camera.

Next, configure the sharing options. Click the Share My Devices check box and the check boxes in front of the devices you want to make available. The sharing setup is complete and active.

Decide whether you want to enable Web-sharing of your digital camera (scanners currently aren't supported). If so, click the Enable Web-Sharing button—we'll get to exactly what this does shortly.

If you want to change the name that your shared devices appear under, enter a new Shared Name, and (if desired) a password the will be required to access the resources.

NOTE

After sharing is enabled, it is active even after you exit Image Capture.

Browsing and Using Shared Devices

To browse and connect to shared devices (assuming that you've enabled browsing) choose File, Browse from the menu. A window appears listing each device source, which can subsequently be expanded to show the shared capture devices, as shown in Figure 6.23.

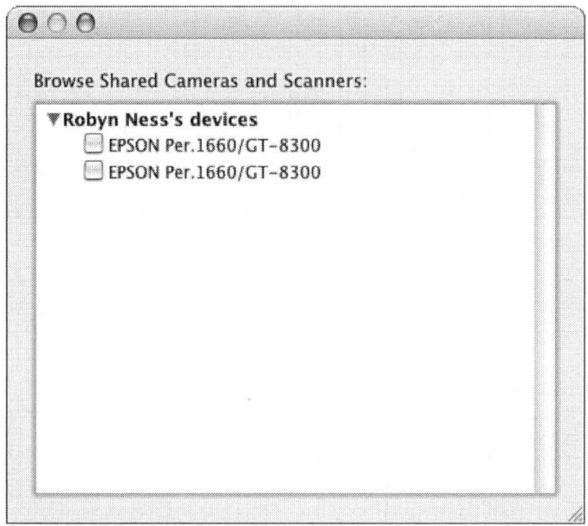

FIGURE 6.23 Find and connect to shared devices.

Click the check box in front of each device you want to use; then close the Browse window. Within a few seconds, Image Capture displays control windows for each of the devices exactly as if they were directly connected to your computer. Interact with the devices exactly as if they were local. Unfortunately, this may mean having to get up and actually *walk* to swap photos in and out of the office flatbed scanner.

Web-Sharing of Digital Cameras

Your mind says "what?" and, well, so does mine. Although this might be a feature that Apple drops from the shipping version of Panther, it *is* intriguing. If you enable Web-Sharing (the - is Apple's not mine), you'll notice that the Sharing setup window (see Figure 6.22) refreshes to display a Web-Sharing URL. The URL should be the same as your machine hostname/IP and the port 5100—that is, `http://<machine name>:5100`.

Visiting the URL from another computer displays a page, shown in Figure 6.24 with controls similar to Image Capture's image download window.

Use your mouse to highlight images just as you would locally (try it—it actually *feels* like an application, not a Web page); then click the controls along the top of the window to perform those actions on the selected image.

If your camera supports it, you can use the Take Picture and Remote Monitor features to take an instant snapshot or view the current image through your camera's viewfinder.

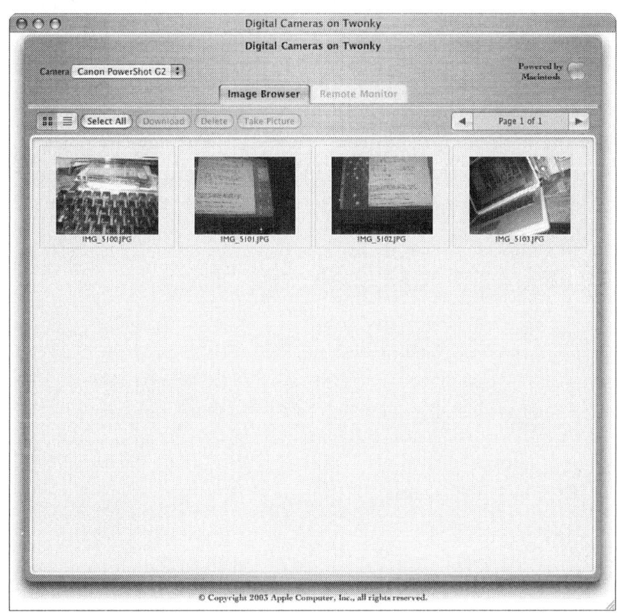

FIGURE 6.24 Control your digital camera over the Web.

Although this is certainly a cool gee-whiz feature, we can only guess as to how many people will be racing to access their digital cameras across the Internet, and our initial guess is "not many."

Preferences

Wrapping things up, the remaining Image Capture preferences are easy to understand and indicative of its "split camera/scanner personality." The camera preferences consist of a single pop-up menu where you can choose what application to launch when a camera is connected.

The scanner preferences provide the same choice—what to do when Mac OS X senses that a scanner button has been clicked. For scanners that come with their own TWAIN-compliant drivers, you can select the Use TWAIN Software Whenever Possible check box to force Image Capture to scan via the manufacturer's drivers.

Summary

This chapter provided an introduction to the first of Apple's "Digital Hub" iLife tools—iPhoto, along with the lesser-known (but strangely functional) Image Capture.

iPhoto provides excellent image manipulation and organization tools that take the monotony out of downloading and storing digital photos. It also breaks the digital/paper boundary by providing a number of easy-to-use methods of ordering prints and bound hardcover albums of your pictures.

Image Capture overlaps with some of the iPhoto feature set but also includes the ability to drive compatible flatbed scanners, and even share scanners and cameras over the network. Although the interface for sharing is a bit clunky in the current release, these features show just how strongly Apple is pushing to make Mac OS X as robust as possible.

CHAPTER 7
Audio

IN THIS CHAPTER

- Sound Preferences
- iTunes
- Recording Audio in Panther
- Audio MIDI Tool

In Chapter 6, "Photography and Imaging," you were introduced to the first of Apple's iLife Suite—the photo management tool iPhoto and the image import software Image Capture. In this chapter, we continue our look at the iLife applications by learning about iTunes—Apple's free music management software (which should be available for Windows just about the time you read this) that includes tight integration with the online Apple Music Store and the portable iPod music player. In addition, you'll be introduced to a few applications that can provide audio input features strangely absent from Apple's current system release.

Sound Preferences

Mac OS X sound input and output are controlled primarily through the Sound System Preferences pane. Advanced controls are available in the Audio Midi Setup application, discussed later in this chapter. The three subpanes within the Sound preferences are Sound Effects, Input, and Output. These control alert sounds, audio input, and audio output as you would expect.

Sound Effects

The Sound Effects pane provides access to the system alert sounds and other "effect" sounds that play while you use your computer, as shown in Figure 7.1. Choose the alert sound that you want your computer to play when it needs to get your attention. System sounds are stored in `/System/Library/Sounds`. You can add your own systemwide sounds to the directory `/Library/Sounds`, or personal sounds to `~/Library/Sounds`. These directories probably don't exist on your system, so you might need to create them.

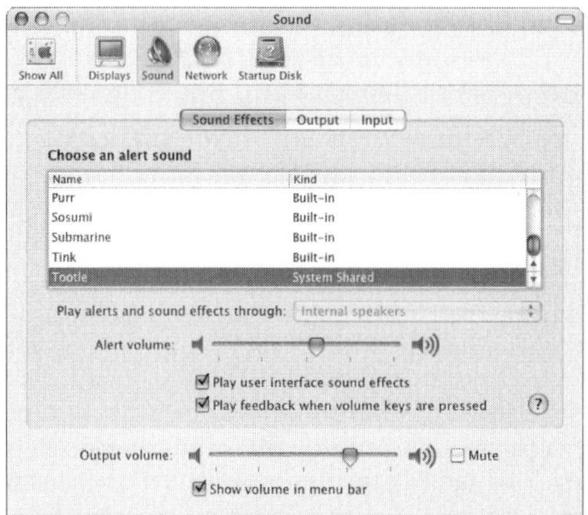

FIGURE 7.1 Choose your system alert sound and output levels.

If there are multiple output devices to your machine, use the Play Through pop-up menu to choose which device alert sounds will play through. Two sliders are provided for controlling output volume. The first controls the output volume of alert sounds, whereas the second determines overall system volume and is available on all the Sound subpanes. Click the Show Volume in Menu Bar check box to add a volume control menu extra to your menu bar. The Mute check box completely disables sound output, if desired.

TIP

Your keyboard also provides volume control and mute capabilities. Use the speaker buttons to raise, lower, or silence your speakers. To play feedback while raising or lowering volume from the keyboard, make sure that the Play feedback check box is selected; otherwise, you might not be able to determine the volume level unless a sound is playing during the adjustment.

Finally, if you want more than an alert sound to enhance your Mac OS X experience. Click the Play User Interface Sound Effects check box. When active, you'll hear a few additional noises when you perform actions such as emptying the trash or removing items from the Dock.

Output

The Output subpane enables you to choose which output device your computer uses if multiple devices are connected, as well balance control over the speaker output. If you have a 5.1 sound output system, you'll have additional controls beyond the standard stereo speakers, shown in Figure 7.2.

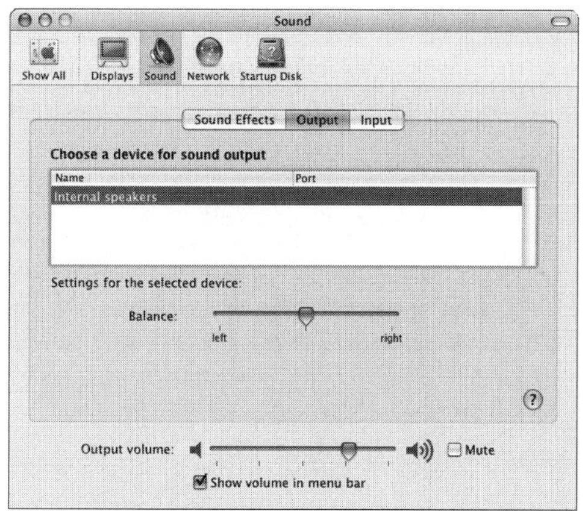

FIGURE 7.2 Choose and configure your output device.

Input

On the third pane, Input, displayed in Figure 7.3, you can pick between the available input devices as well as adjust the gain (Input Volume) for your the chosen source. The Input Level meter is used to help adjust the input volume. This meter displays the current level of sound input. The highest level that has been reached is highlighted within the graph for easy reference.

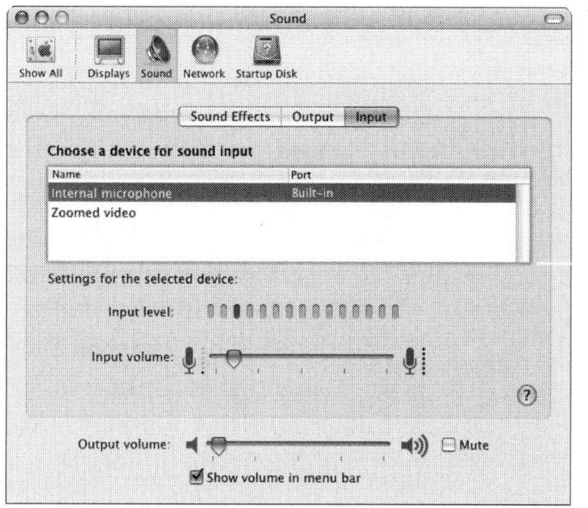

FIGURE 7.3 Choose an input source and adjust the gain.

TIP

The last section of this chapter deals with actual sound input, which you can use to record your own alert sounds. Strangely enough, Apple does not provide its own tool for simple audio recording...yet.

iTunes

If you like music, iTunes can serve as your CD player, MP3 ripper, song organizer, jukebox, eye candy, and CD burner. And, amazingly, it's simple enough to use that even if you've never burned a CD, ripped an MP3, or listened to Internet radio, you can be doing all three within 5 minutes—tops.

First Run Setup

The first time you launch iTunes, it runs through a setup assistant to locate AACs/MP3s and configure Internet playback. At any time during the setup procedure, click Next to go to the next step, or Previous to return to the preceding step. Clicking Cancel exits the setup utility and starts iTunes.

The first step of the setup process, displayed in Figure 7.4, allows you to set Internet access options.

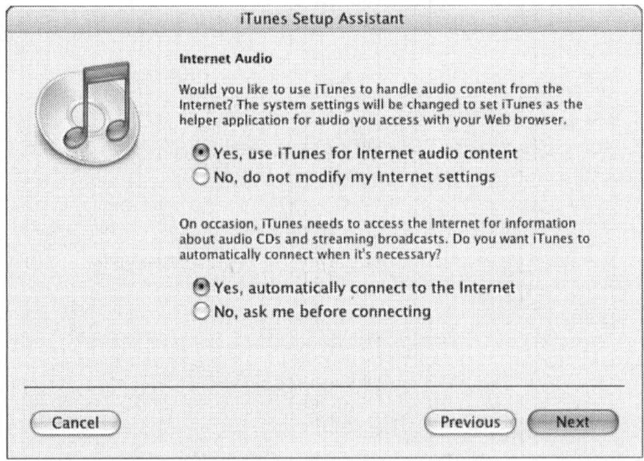

FIGURE 7.4 Choose how iTunes works with your Internet applications.

iTunes is perfectly suited for handling streaming audio. If you've never listened to Internet radio before, you'll appreciate how quickly and easily iTunes enables you to find the type of music you want to hear and start listening. If you already have a streaming music player, such as Audion (`http://www.panic.com/audion/`), tell iTunes not to modify your Internet settings.

iTunes also works with Gracenote's CDDB (`http://www.gracenote.com`) to look up information about your CDs, such as the artist and song title. The Yes, Automatically Connect to the Internet radio button, selected by default, enables this feature. To force iTunes to prompt you before connecting to the Internet, click No, Ask Me Before Connecting. Click Next when you're satisfied with your responses.

Next you are prompted to decide how iTunes will find music files on your computer. By default, iTunes locates all the MP3 and AAC files in your home directory and *copies* them to the music library. To disable this feature, click No, I'll Add Them Myself Later. The process of searching the drive for files can take a while, so I prefer to add content when *I* want to. If you're accustomed to horror stories about services such as Kazaa or GNUtella, don't worry: iTunes is *not* sharing the files it finds; it is simply adding them to your music library.

Finally, iTunes asks whether you want to be taken to the iTunes Music Store or to your central music library. Unless you feel like immediately spending some cash, have it take you to your library—we'll get to the Music Store soon enough.

Click Done to begin using iTunes.

The iTunes Interface

Everything you need to do anything in iTunes is found in the main window, pictured in Figure 7.5. The five main control areas are

- Source—Lists the available MP3 sources. Attached MP3 players, such as your iPod, CDs, playlists, the central music library (labeled Library), Radio, and Apple Music Store, make up the available sources.
- Song list—The list of music contained on the selected source. When viewing your own MP3 and AAC libraries, the song list can be browsed in a normal List view or in a columned Browse mode (Command-B)—similar to the Finder's List and Column views. The Browse mode is only available when viewing the Library and Music Store sources.
- Player controls—Allow you to skip between different songs, play, pause, and adjust the output volume of the currently playing track. Clicking directly on the sound slider moves the volume adjustment immediately to that level.
- Status—Displays information about the currently playing song. The top line displays the artist, the name of the song, and the name of the album.
- Album artwork—Displays a picture of the album cover of the currently playing song *if* it has been enabled in the song file.

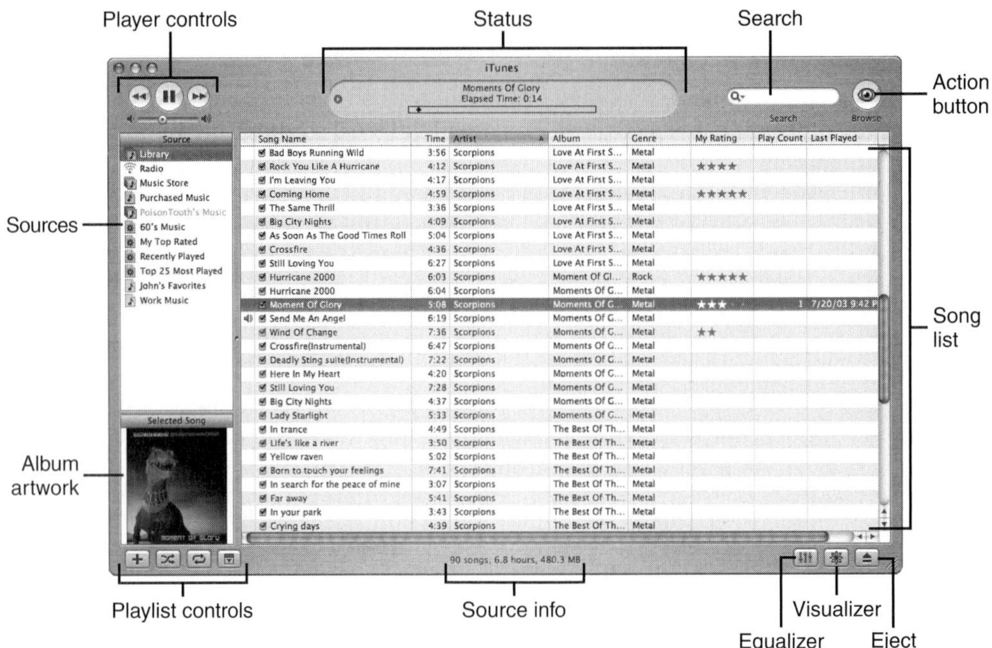

FIGURE 7.5 A single iTunes window provides access to almost all application functions.

Supporting these areas are a plethora of buttons that help you organize your music, modify how it is played, or sometimes just make pretty pictures. Don't worry; we'll discuss these later. For now it's just a matter of locating them in the interface.

- Search—Typing a few letters into the iTunes Search field immediately displays all audio tracks in the current playlist or library that match the string in any way (artist, song, or album).
- Action button—The action button performs a different function depending on what source is currently being viewed.
- Playlist controls—Three playlist controls are available: Create Playlist, Shuffle Order, and Loop. As their names suggest, these buttons can be used to create new playlists and control the order in which the audio tracks are played back.
- Source Info—At the bottom of the iTunes window is information about the contents, playing time, and total file size of the currently selected source. The default mode displays approximate time—clicking on the text toggles to precise playing time.
- Equalizer (Command-2)—The Equalizer allows you to choose preset frequency levels by musical genre, or to set them manually by dragging the sliders. The mode defaults to "Flat" where all the controls are set in the middle of their range.

- Visualizer—Turns the visualization effects ("music for the eyes") on and off.
- Eject—Ejects the currently inserted CD.

So, now that you know what the controls are called and where they're located, let's take a look at how iTunes is used.

The Library Music Source and Song List

The central repository for all your songs is the Library item listed in the Source pane. If there is a song file on your computer that iTunes knows about, you can find it by selecting the Library source item. The song list displays the stored songs in a simple list. Each audio track is listed on its own line with Name, Time, Artist, Album, Genre, My Rating, Play Count, and Last Played (these can be seen in Figure 7.5). You can modify the displayed columns by choosing Edit, View Options from the menu. As always, the listing can be sorted by clicking on a column heading.

NOTE

The information that can be displayed for a given song is dependent on what information is stored with the song file. If the Artist's name was never stored, for example, iTunes simply shows a blank in that field.

If you'd prefer to browse by Genre, Album, and Artist rather than a single huge list, you can. A column mode allows you to drill down through Genre, Artist, and Album, and then finally view the matching list of songs in a list. Click between the normal List and Browse modes using the action button (labeled Browse when viewing the Library), or choose Edit, Show/Hide Browser (Command-B) from the menu. Figure 7.6 shows the iTunes Library in Browse mode.

FIGURE 7.6 Browse the iTunes Library in columns.

TIP

When in Browse mode, you can select all the elements in a column by choosing the special All item from the top of the column listing. If you want to pick and choose between multiple items within a column, hold down Shift and click to make contiguous selections, or Command-click to select noncontiguous items.

Although most of the columns in both List and Browse modes (for example, Album, Artist) are self-explanatory, a few conceal some of the special features of iTunes:

- Equalizer—Choose one of the Equalizer presets for each song. The Equalizer is discussed later in the chapter.
- Last Played—The last time the song was played.
- My Rating—A listener-supplied rating of a song—from zero (anything on the radio today) to five stars (The Scorpions).
- Play Count—The number of times a given song has been played in iTunes.

You'll also notice that each song has a check box in front of its name. You can uncheck a song to keep it from being played.

A listing of the iTunes music library can be exported as an XML file for use in other applications by choosing File, Export Library.

Playing a Song in the Song List

Double-clicking the space directly in front of the check box in the song list starts playing the chosen song. Alternatively, you can use player control buttons to skip forward or back in the list and play or pause the selected song.

As the song plays the status area updates with a progress bar that shows how far the playback of the current song has progressed. Dragging the progress bar handle can move the playback back or forward in the audio track.

Clicking each of the text lines in the status area toggles between different types of information. The song title toggles between title, artist, and album. Likewise, the Elapsed Time line can be toggled to display remaining time and total time. To display a stereo frequency response monitor, click the arrow on the left of the status display.

Searching the Library

The Search field in the upper right corner of the iTunes window enables you to quickly find a song by typing in a piece of information (name, artist, album, and so on) into the field. As you type, the contents of the song list refresh to show songs that match. To match only against a specific field, click the magnifying glass to show a drop-down menu that allows you to choose between searching all fields, or just a specific piece of information.

To clear a search, either remove the search text from the field or click the "X" icon at the end of the search field.

Editing Song Information, Artwork, and Ratings

As mentioned earlier, if iTunes doesn't "know" something about a song, such as the artist, it can't display or organize the music by that field. If you own the song, however, presumably *you* know the artist, album, and so on information and can add it yourself.

To edit or add information directly within the song listing, make sure that the song is selected in the listing; then double-click the field you want to edit and start typing. In some fields (such as Artist), iTunes automatically tries to autocomplete the artist name from artists it has previously cataloged, saving you typing time if it guesses correctly.

The Ratings field works a bit differently. To set a rating for a song, click and drag in the field until the number of starts you want to add are displayed. This is a *completely* arbitrary value and is only useful when sorting or organizing your music. iTunes does not use the information internally in any way.

One last piece of information that can be edited for the selected song is the album artwork (found in the lower left corner of the iTunes window). This is usually the album cover or something else to distinguish the track and is automatically displayed when the song is playing. To add artwork for the selected song, drag an image into the image well that subtly says Drag Album Artwork Here. To view the "large" version of a piece of album art, click the image well, and a window appears with the full-size image. You can hide or show the album artwork by clicking the Hide/Show Artwork button in the lower-left corner of the iTunes window (fourth from the left) or by choosing Edit, Hide/Show Artwork (Command-G).

NOTE

Album artwork doesn't come "for free"; it adds to the size of your music files (and, obviously, your library). If you're trying to pack as much music as possible on your MP3 player, adding images might not be the best idea.

7

The editing features of the song list are mostly useful for adding a few missing pieces of information. It is awkward to use if you have to add *all* the fields for a piece of music. A better idea is to use the Get Info window, discussed later in the section "Get Info."

Adding Audio to the iTunes Library

Obviously, knowing how to use your iTunes Library isn't going to be of much use unless you can actually fill it with music. There are four primary ways to do this—either by encoding music from a CD, adding existing music files, using Audible.com content, or purchasing songs online from the iTunes Music Store.

Ripping CDs

Encoding, or *ripping*, CDs lets you take the tracks from a CD and save them in the AAC (Advanced Audio Coding) or MP3 formats. MP3s are a highly compressed lossy audio format that has become popular in recent years—much to the dismay of the recording industry, whereas AACs are the new "up and comer" format supported by Apple's iTunes Music Store. AAC purports to produce higher quality files than MP3 at the same bit rate.

This means that you can encode at lower bit rates, have the same quality sound as MP3, and save significant drive space at the same time. The "big" draw to AAC, however, is that it supports digital rights management, meaning that AAC files can be protected so that they only play on properly authorized computers. This protection is the only reason that the Apple Music Store can exist with the blessing of the RIAA. Unfortunately, Apple's protected AAC files are not universally supported by all operating systems and playback devices. Windows users can rely on QuickTime for Windows and (hopefully) iTunes for Windows by the time you read this.

TIP

The iTunes default import format is now AAC. If you would rather use the more universal MP3 format, you can change the encoder under the Import application preferences pane.

To encode your own MP3/AAC files from a CD, find the CD you want to use and then follow these steps:

1. Insert the CD into your Macintosh.
2. iTunes queries an Internet CD database to get the names of all the tracks on your disk. If, during setup, you chose to not have this happen automatically, select Get CD Track Names from the menu.
3. The CD appears within the Source pane. Click the name to display all the tracks within the song list pane.

Pause for a moment to make sure that iTunes has found the right names for the CD and its tracks. In the unlikely event that no CD information could be located, it will appear as Untitled in the Source pane. Remember, if iTunes couldn't find your song information, or you aren't connected to the Internet, you can edit each MP3 file's stored artist/title information by double-clicking its fields within the song listing, or by using the Get Info feature, discussed in the section "Get Info."

If the information for the CD was not found online and you must enter it by hand, you can be a good "netizen" by submitting your updated information back to the Internet CD database by choosing Advanced, Submit CD Track Names from the menu.

After you're satisfied with how the tracks appear, continue the import process:

1. Select the tracks you want to encode. If no tracks are selected, the entire CD will be imported.
2. Click the action button (now labeled Import) to encode the selected tracks. As they are importing, the CD plays, and a small graphic appears to show whether it has been imported or is currently being imported. You can disable playback while importing using the Importing pane of the application preferences.

By default, the encoded songs are stored in `~/Music/iTunes/iTunes Music`. An entire CD can take from 5–80 minutes to process, depending on the speed of your CD-ROM drive. To pass the time, you can continue to use iTunes while the tracks are imported. When the import is finished, your computer will chime, and the songs will be available under the Library source.

To eject the CD, click the Eject button in the lower-right corner of the iTunes window.

Adding Existing Song Files

If you're working with an existing library of songs rather than a CD, you can easily add them to your library. Choose File, Add To Library (Command-O) from the menu to choose the folder that contains the music. Alternatively, you can simply drag a folder of songs from the Finder into the library song list. By default, iTunes copies the files from wherever they are to your iTunes Library.

TIP

The process of importing MP3s takes time. Each MP3 is examined for ID3 tags and is cataloged in the iTunes database. If you're adding iTunes from a network drive, be prepared to take a quick lunch break.

If you'd prefer that iTunes doesn't copy your song files to the central `~/Music/iTunes/iTunes Music` storage location, you can modify this behavior in the Advanced iTunes application preferences pane by unchecking Copy Files to iTunes Music Folder When Adding to Library. Doing this, although preventing your computer from having multiple copies of your songs, ultimately leads to a disjointed music collection. If you move some of the song files on your drive, iTunes will no longer be able to find them. If you've taken this route and want to reintegrate your songs into a single library, choose Advanced, Consolidate Library from the menu.

In addition to MP3 and AAC files, iTunes is capable of importing any QuickTime audio formats and can convert these files to ACC/MP3 format using Convert Selection to ACC/MP3 under the Advanced menu.

NOTE

iTunes converts only to the current default file format. Use the Importing application preferences pane to change this setting.

The iTunes Music Store

The "big" new feature .of iTunes that is getting a lot of attention is the iTunes Music Store, which allows you to browse available songs and albums, listen to short samples, and then purchase song files online. To access the Music Store, click Music Store in the iTunes Source list. While in the Music Store, the area that typically displays your local music files is replaced by a list that you can navigate as you would a Web page, as shown in Figure 7.7.

FIGURE 7.7 The "home page" of iTunes Music Store.

In the Music Store, you can view lists of today's top songs and top albums; look through new releases; browse by genre; or perform searches by song, artist, album, or composer name. When you find something that interests you, you can use the standard iTunes player controls to listen to a short clip of the song to see whether you want to purchase the full version—at the time of the this writing, individual songs cost 99 cents, and full albums were around $10.

Browsing the iTunes store is a bit like exploring a Web site. You may find yourself watching an exclusive artist video or linking to the artist's Web site. There isn't a cut-and-dry way to describe the experience; you just have to try it.

As you click links to move around in the store, path buttons at the top of the window, as shown in Figure 7.8, tell you where you are, and arrow buttons allow you to move back and forward and to return to the "home page."

Search, Browse, and Requests Although some people may enjoy browsing the iTunes Music Store in the Web browserlike interface, others may find other options easier to use. At the top of the left-hand column on the iTunes Music Store home page are options for Power Search, Browse, and Requests & Feedback, which provide more structured interfaces for targeted searches.

TIP

While the iTunes Music Store is "active" in iTunes, the search box at the top right can be used to search the store instead of your local files.

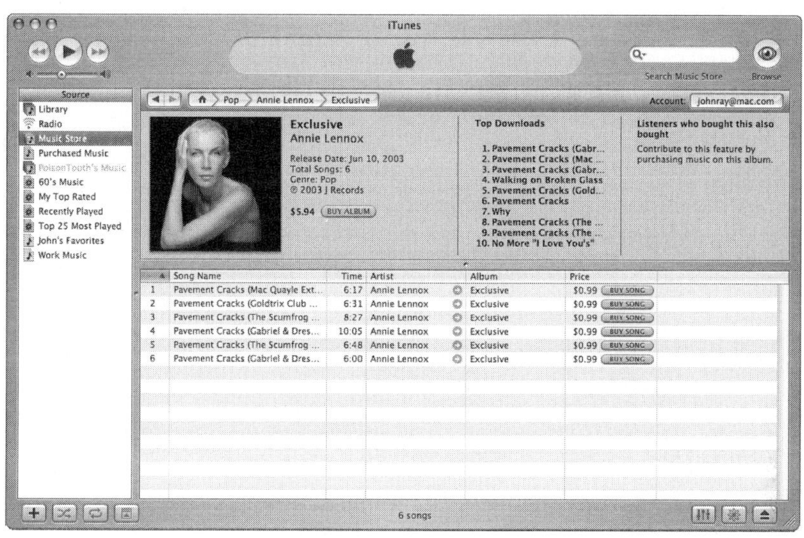

FIGURE 7.8 As you browse, use the buttons above the main content area to keep track of where you are.

Power Search, as shown in Figure 7.9, provides fields for Song, Artist, Album, Genre, and Composer. This allows people who know precisely what they're looking for to locate it efficiently. However, be a bit cautious about using this search if you aren't certain how to spell the name of something—the Power Search doesn't show close matches.

FIGURE 7.9 Enter any information you are sure of to see whether the Power Search can help you find it.

The results for the Power Search can be sorted by song name, time (or length of track), artist, album, or relevance. (You can also sort by price, but at this time all prices for individual songs are the same!)

The Browse option, demonstrated in Figure 7.10, is similar to the Browse feature of the main music library. When you choose a genre in the left-hand column, artists for that genre appear in the middle column. Choosing an artist displays albums in the right-hand column. Selecting an album displays the song tracks in the album in the bottom pane, where you can listen to a sample or make a purchase.

FIGURE 7.10 Browsing is a powerful way to search for specific songs, or to locate unfamiliar artists in a favorite genre.

Although the Power Search and Browse option are effective ways to locate songs you want, there will probably be times when a song you desperately want to buy isn't available from the Music Store. If that happens, you can select the option Requests & Feedback from the main iTunes Music Store pane. In the window that appears, type a short message about what you're looking for so that Apple knows what artists and/or songs it should try to include. You can also use this section to send feedback about errors you come across, such as misspellings or miscategorizations.

Making a Purchase After finding a song, the next step is to buy! To do this, you must first create an account, which you initiate by clicking the Sign In button at the upper left of the Music Store pane. This opens the window shown in Figure 7.11, where you can create an account from scratch or simply use your .Mac account (if you set up one).

FIGURE 7.11 Create an iTunes account or sign in through .Mac.

To create an account, you need to fill out a form with your email address, a password you want to use, and your credit card information. When you are finished creating your account, you can sign in to make your purchase.

NOTE

For those who don't like the idea of anyone sitting in front of your computer purchasing music with your account, you can click the account Sign Out button to deactivate purchasing privileges.

If you or (someone else) should happen to attempt a Sign In and mistype your password three times in a row, your account will have to be reset before login can continue.

When you are logged in to the Music Store, you can locate a song or album you want to purchase and click the Buy Song/Album button at the end of the row. To ensure that you haven't accidentally clicked the Buy button for the wrong song, you see a message asking you to confirm that you want to buy and download the selected song, as shown in Figure 7.12. You have the option to check a box not to be warned about buying songs in the future—but, remember, if you accidentally choose the wrong item, this message is your chance to correct your mistake.

TIP

If you want, iTunes can operate in a "Shopping Cart" mode that allows you to add items to your cart without downloading them and then "Checkout" to purchase and download them all at once. This feature is enabled through the Store application preferences pane.

FIGURE 7.12 You can confirm your intention to buy before the download begins.

When you confirm your purchase, the file begins to download, and its status appears in the Status area at the top of the iTunes window.

NOTE

If your download is interrupted or you accidentally cancel it, don't worry—iTunes knows. Choose Advanced, Check for Purchased Music from the menu, and, after you enter your account information, iTunes resumes any incomplete downloads.

After you've downloaded your first song, a playlist appears in the Source pane. Called Purchased Music, this playlist is just like any other playlist—songs purchased from the Music Store appear in it, but you can delete them from the playlist, and they will still remain in your library.

Authorizing Purchased Music AAC files from the iTunes Music Store behave a bit differently than other song files in iTunes. Songs purchased by each iTunes Music Store account can only be authorized to play on three computers at any time.

The first time you try to play a purchased music file you will have to authorize the current computer as one of those three. (This is a measure taken to make sure that the files are not traded widely among users, which would deprive artists and record company of revenue from the works they release.) The Authorize Computer window, shown in Figure 7.13, automatically appears when playing purchased music on an unauthorized computer. You are required to enter the password of the iTunes Music Store account that purchased the song.

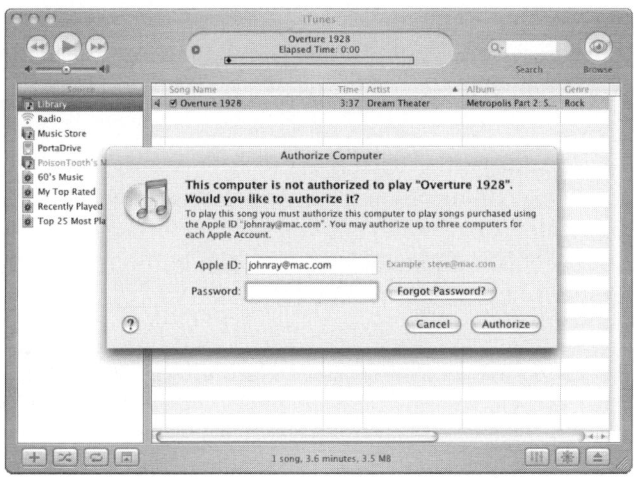

FIGURE 7.13 You must formally authorize a computer for it to be able to play music downloaded from the iTunes Music Store.

NOTE

Songs purchased from the Music Store can only be shared with other authorized computers on your local network through the Sharing options discussed later in the section "Sharing Music on Your Local Network with Rendezvous."

If you decide that you don't want to play your songs on a given computer anymore, you must choose Advanced, Deauthorize Computer; then choose Deauthorize Computer for Apple Account from the window that appears. This "frees up" a spot in your authorization count and allows you to authorize another machine for playback.

In addition to the restriction of three playback machines, when burning music to CD (discussed later in the chapter) you can only burn 10 CDs in a row of a single playlist composed of purchased songs.

Audible.com Content

In addition to song files, iTunes can now handle Audible.com's spoken word files. To use audible audio files (`.aa` files), you must first sign up for an account at `http://www.audible.com/`. There is a free Robin Williams interview with John Lasseter of Pixar fame that's worth a listen even if you don't want to pay money for anything else.

To add audible content to iTunes, follow the same procedure as with an MP3. The first time you add Audible content, you are prompted for your username and password to unlock the file. This will be stored in iTunes to verify that you have rights to play a given file—much the same as when using Apple Music Store purchases. You can remove the username and password from iTunes (if you feel uncomfortable with it being stored, or change your account information) by choosing Advanced, Deauthorize Computer; then selecting Deauthorize Computer for Audible Account.

Playlists

The key to many of the remaining iTunes features lies in creating a playlist. A *playlist* is nothing more than a list of songs from your library that is arranged in a way that you like to listen to them. Think of it as choosing songs to listen to from a jukebox and actually getting to hear the ones you want *when* you want.

> **NOTE**
>
> Playlists are used in the other iLife applications to provide access to your music collection.

There are two types of playlists—simple and smart. A *simple playlist* contains a group of songs in the order you've chosen. A *smart playlist*, however, dynamically chooses music based on criteria you give it. You can differentiate between the two in your Source pane by their icons. Simple playlists are light blue with a "note," whereas smart playlists are purple with a "gear" icon.

Simple Playlists

To create a new simple playlist from a group of songs in the library:

1. Select the Library in the Source pane.
2. Choose one or more songs in the song list.
3. Choose File, New Playlist from Selection (Shift-Command-N).

Alternatively, you can create a new empty playlist by clicking the "+" icon in the bottom-left corner of the iTunes window (Command-N). Next, drag songs from the library onto its icon in the Source page. Playlists can be renamed by double-clicking their names in the Source pane, or by selecting them and pressing the Return key.

To remove songs from a simple playlist, select them in the song list; then press the Delete key. This removes them only from the playlist, not from your library.

Smart Playlists

Using the Smart Playlist option, you can create ever-changing playlists based on criteria such as genre or your personal song ratings. Choose File, New Smart Playlist (Option-Command-N) from the menu, and set your criteria in either the Simple or Advanced tabs, as shown in Figure 7.14.

Use the criteria to match between the different song attributes and a value, such as "My Rating" and five-star songs. To add multiple criteria, click the "+" button at the end of the selection criteria line. Use the "-" button to remove criteria.

You can also choose to limit the playlist to a certain number of songs, based either on a random selection or other attributes.

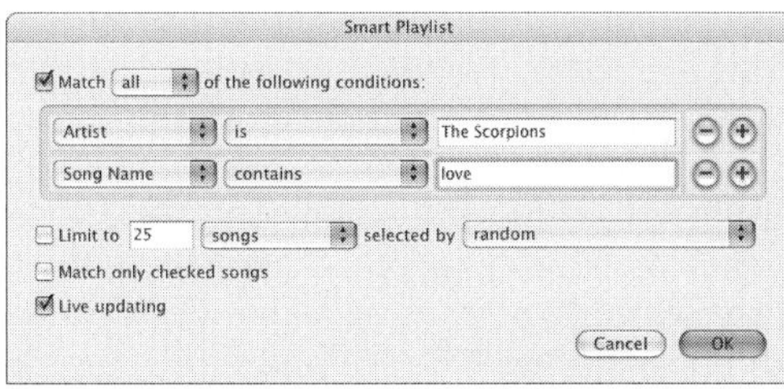

FIGURE 7.14 Smart playlists are based on a dynamic search of your library contents. These criteria create a playlist of songs by The Scorpions with the word "Love" in the title.

Check the Live Updating check box to force iTunes to keep the smart playlist up-to-date at all times. Click OK to save the playlist.

You can edit smart playlists by selecting them in the Source pane, and then choosing File, Edit Smart Playlist from the menu.

NOTE

Unlike simple playlists, you cannot delete songs from the listing. The list is generated automatically, and, to remove a song, you must modify the criteria for the playlist so that the song is no longer selected.

Working with Playlists

After you've created a playlist, you can work with it in exactly the same manner as the main library source. The only difference is that the songs that appear are only those contained in the playlist.

Playback, browse, and search features all work identically. The benefit, however, is that you can more easily choose what you want to hear, when you want to hear it. You can queue up some of your favorite party music (The Scorpions) for your next big get-together, or maybe create a collection of love music (The Scorpions) for a big date.

Song lists can be exported to text or XML format for use in other applications or databases by choosing File, Export Songlist.

TIP

Double-clicking a playlist icon (or any source icon) opens a new window with only the contents of that source. This is a nice way to create a cleaner view of your audio files.

In addition, playlists allow you to work with the size constraints of MP3 players and CDs so that you can take your music with you rather than lug around your entire library on a portable hard drive.

NOTE

Yes, I know, the latest iPods can easily hold most users' entire iTunes libraries. There are still, however, dozens of iTunes compatible MP3 devices that cannot.

Let's take a look at how playlists are used with MP3 players and CDs now.

Burning a Playlist to CD

If you have a Mac with a supported CD burner, you can use a playlist to burn an audio CD laid out exactly like the playlist. Highlight the playlist in the Source pane, click the Burn CD action button in the upper-right corner of the iTunes window, and then follow the onscreen instructions, inserting a recordable CD when prompted. The process, you'll find, is similar to burning CDs from the Finder.

By default, iTunes will burn an audio CD that you can play on any consumer CD player—meaning that you can fit roughly 74 minutes of music on a CD. Recently, however, CD players have been coming out that support the MP3 format—meaning that you can burn MP3 files directly to CD in their compressed format. This means that you can fit several *hours* of music on a CD. To change the format iTunes uses when creating a CD, use the Burning pane of the application preferences.

NOTE

At present, iTunes has no support for printing CD labels. For those who like to know which Scorpions compilation they're about to play, you might want to check out Discus (`http://www.magicmouse.com/_discus.html`), a full-featured CD labeling solution, or disc-label, (`http://www.disclabel.com/`), which integrates with iTunes and iPhoto to make label printing a breeze.

Copying Playlists to MP3 Players (and the iPod)

After a playlist has been built, you can drag its name from the Source pane to any listed MP3 player source. The files are automatically copied to the connected player. If the player does not have enough available space, you need to remove files from your playlist or select the external player and remove tracks from its memory. After you've copied the songs to your player, click the Eject button in the lower-right corner of the iTunes window, disconnect your player, and be off!

If you're the lucky owner of an iPod, things are a bit nicer for you. Apple has engineered iTunes with iPod-specific features.

The first time an iPod is plugged in to your Mac, Panther automatically launches iTunes and (if it isn't already) asks whether you want to link your iPod to the collection of music in iTunes. An iPod can be linked only to a single music collection. This prevents you from accidentally copying copyrighted material from place to place.

By default, iTunes attempts to synchronize your entire music collection with your iPod each time it is plugged in. This, as you might guess, can take a while the first time it is performed or after making significant additions to your iTunes Library. During the process of synching with your music library, your iPod will display a Do Not Disconnect warning message. After the synchronization has completed, it will automatically be unmounted ("ejected") by default. If it is *not* unmounted, you can eject it manually by clicking the iTunes Eject button in the lower-right corner of the iTunes window.

You can change the syncing options by clicking the iPod icon that appears in the lower-right corner of the iTunes window (fourth from the right). This displays the iTunes iPod preferences, as shown in Figure 7.15.

FIGURE 7.15 Choose your iPod preferences and be merry.

Use the first three radio buttons to choose whether to automatically update all songs and playlists or only selected playlists, or whether to manually manage songs and playlists (by dragging a dropping on the iPod).

The last three check boxes control whether connecting the iPod autolaunches iTunes, whether the iPod can be used as a FireWire disk, and whether only songs with their check boxes checked in the song list will be updated during a synchronization.

NOTE

If you do *not* have Enable FireWire disk mode enabled and you try to use the iPod as a disk, you'll drive yourself insane. The iPod icon will appear on your desktop when it is connected, yet will disappear when you are finished using iTunes. Leaving this item checked only means that you will manually have to unmount the iPod when you're finished using it instead of iTunes doing it automatically.

Listening to Internet Radio

Depending on your connection speed, Internet radio could be your ticket to high-quality commercial-free music. Unfortunately, most dial-in modems have poor sound quality, but DSL and cable modem users can listen to much higher quality streams. To see what's available and start listening requires only a few clicks:

1. To display a list of the available streaming stations, click Radio in the Source pane. After a few seconds querying a station server, a list of available music genres is displayed.
2. Each genre can be expanded to show the stations in that group by clicking its disclosure triangle. Stations are listed with a Stream (station) Name, Bit Rate, and Comment (description). The bit rate determines the quality of the streamed audio—the higher the bit rate, the higher the quality—and the higher the bandwidth requirements.
3. Double-click a station to begin playing, or select it and then click the Play button. iTunes buffers a few seconds of audio, and then starts playing the streaming audio. If iTunes stutters while playing, look for a similar station that uses a lower bit rate.

TIP

Conversely to what seems logical, you can drag stations from the Radio Tuner source and play them in a playlist. The playlist plays as it normally would, but starts playing streaming audio when it gets to the added Internet radio station.

You cannot burn a radio station to a CD or store it on an external MP3 device.

Sharing Music on Your Local Network with Rendezvous

After you've added music and created playlists, you may want to share your music with others on your local network using Rendezvous. You can share your entire library or selected playlists. You can even share but require a password to limit listeners to those you invite. The settings for these options are located under the Sharing pane of the iTunes application preferences, shown in Figure 7.16.

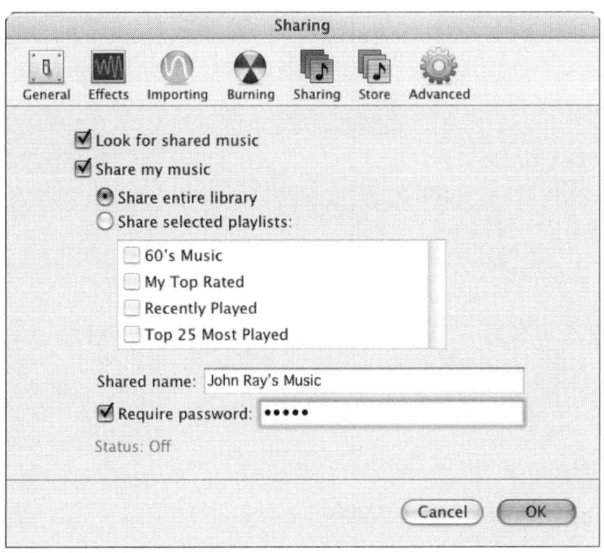

FIGURE 7.16 The Sharing preferences allow you to let others listen to your music library.

The first of the Sharing options is a check box for your computer to look for music shared by other iTunes 4.0 (or later) users on your local network. If checked, any libraries or playlists located will appear in blue in the iTunes Source pane.

If you want to share your music, you can choose to share the entire library or specific playlists. You can also give your collection a catchy name or leave it as the default, as shown previously in Figure 7.16.

If you want to share with only those who have a password, check the Require Password box, type the word or phrase you want to require, and click OK at the bottom of the preferences window to activate. Now, those who try to access your music will see a pop-up password prompt when trying to connect.

iTunes sharing is active only *while iTunes is running*. Quitting iTunes stops your library from being shared.

TIP

In the original release of iTunes 4.0, Apple provided the option of sharing your iTunes Library over the Internet. As of iTunes 4.0.1, this has been removed. For more information on how to implement this feature via other (free) software, check out the `mod_mp3` section of Chapter 27, "Web Serving."

If you're adventurous, you might want to try the hack iCommune 401(ok) to reenable Internet sharing in later versions of iTunes (`http://icommune.sourceforge.net/401ok/`), or use the standalone iCommune application (`http://icommune.sourceforge.net/`) to do share iTunes music collections without iTunes.

Additional Playback Features

iTunes has several additional features besides the simple playback controls that can be used to enhance your audio experience.

Keyboard and Dock Control

To make playback as easy to manage as possible, Apple provides extensive keyboard shortcuts for controlling iTunes:

- Play/Stop—Spacebar
- Next Song—Command-right-arrow
- Previous Song—Command-left-arrow
- Volume Up—Command-up-arrow
- Volume Down—Command-down-arrow
- Mute—Open-Command-down-arrow

In addition, the Dock icon can be used while iTunes is hidden or in the background to move between songs, play, pause, or change the playing order.

Shuffle and Repeat

To randomize the play order for the selected source, click the Shuffle button (second from the left) in the lower-left of the iTunes window. If you want to repeat the tracks, use the Loop button to toggle between Repeat Off, Repeat Once, and Repeat All.

Playback Window Size

The iTunes window is a bit large to conveniently leave onscreen during playback. Luckily, two other window modes take up far less space. Quite illogically, you access these smaller modes by clicking the window's Zoom (maximize) button.

After you click Zoom, the window is reduced to the player controls and status window. Even this window is a bit large for some monitors, though. To collapse it even more, use the resize handle in the lower-right corner of the window.

To restore iTunes to its original state, click the Zoom button again.

Equalizer

The Equalizer can adjust the frequency amplification on a per-song basis. Use the Equalizer by selecting a song in the library and then clicking the Equalizer button at the bottom of the iTunes window, or by choosing Window, Equalizer (Command-2) from the menu. Figure 7.17 shows the iTunes Equalizer.

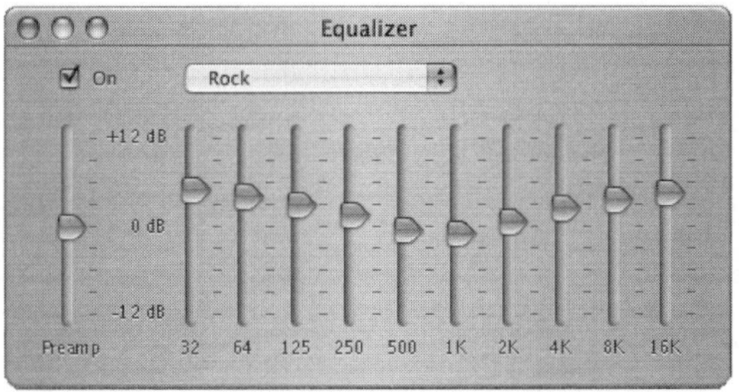

FIGURE 7.17 Adjust your songs for the best output.

Use the Preamp slider to increase or decrease overall song volume, and the individual frequency sliders to change the tonal qualities of the sound. The pop-up menu at the top of the window toggles between different equalizer presets and can save your current custom settings.

TIP

Remember that any saved equalizer settings can be applied to a song directly in the song list by adjusting the view options to show the Equalizer column and then clicking on the equalizer pop-up button for a given song to choose a setting.

Visualizer

The iTunes Visualizer creates a graphical visualization of your music as it plays. While playing a song, click the Visualizer button (second from the right) in the lower-right corner of the iTunes window, or choose Visuals, Turn Visualizer On (Command-T) from the menu to activate the display. Figure 7.18 shows the Visualizer in action.

The Visuals menu can control the size of the generated graphics as well as toggle between full-screen (Command-F) and window modes. To exit full-screen mode, press Esc.

While the windowed Visualizer display is active, the Options action button in the upper-right corner of the window becomes active. Click this button to fine-tune your Visualizer settings—including pixel doubling ("rougher but faster display") to speed up the display.

NOTE

Several third-party visualizer plug-ins are available that you can use in place of iTune's built-in visualizer. To add a new visualizer, download it and then place the plug-in file in `~/Library/iTunes/iTunes Plug-ins` for your own personal use, or `/Library/iTunes/iTunes Plug-ins` for use by anyone with an account on the machine.

Additional visualizers will be displayed at the bottom of the iTunes Visualizer menu.

Check the "Additional Software" section for download information for several nice Visualizers.

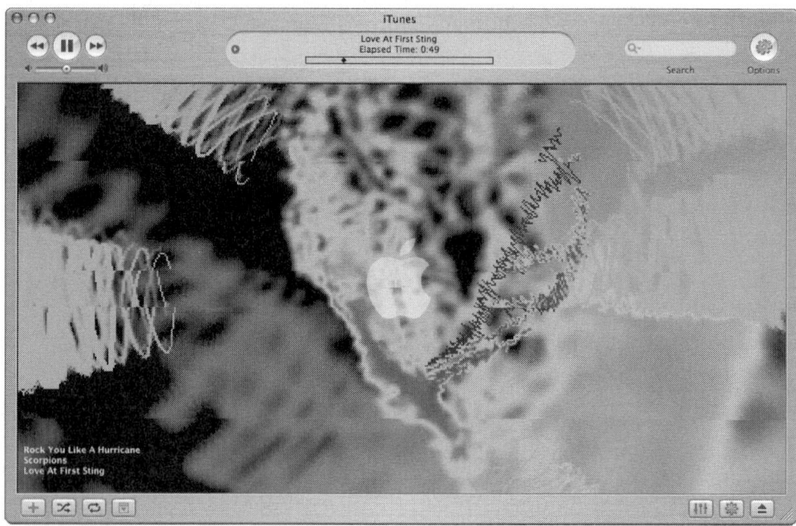

FIGURE 7.18 The Visualizer displays images to match your music.

Get Info

As mentioned earlier in the chapter, you can edit information for songs by double-clicking their field entries within the song listing. That, however, isn't necessarily the easiest way.

To edit the information for a song, select it in the song list and choose File, Get Info (Command-I). iTunes displays a summary window similar to that shown in Figure 7.19.

Use the buttons at the top of the window to navigate between the Summary, Info, Options, and Artwork panes.

The Info pane is used to assign or edit Artist, Year, Composer, Album, Genre, and other song attributes. These will immediately be available for sorting within the Library song listing.

The Options pane enables you to set a volume adjustment for the song if it is either too loud or soft, as well as a preset equalizer setting, rating, and start/stop time.

Finally, the Artwork pane can be used to add one or more images to a song file. Click the Add button to add an image, or select an existing image and click Delete to remove it. The slider to the right of the Add and Delete buttons is used to scale the image thumbnails, much like the thumbnail size control in iPhoto.

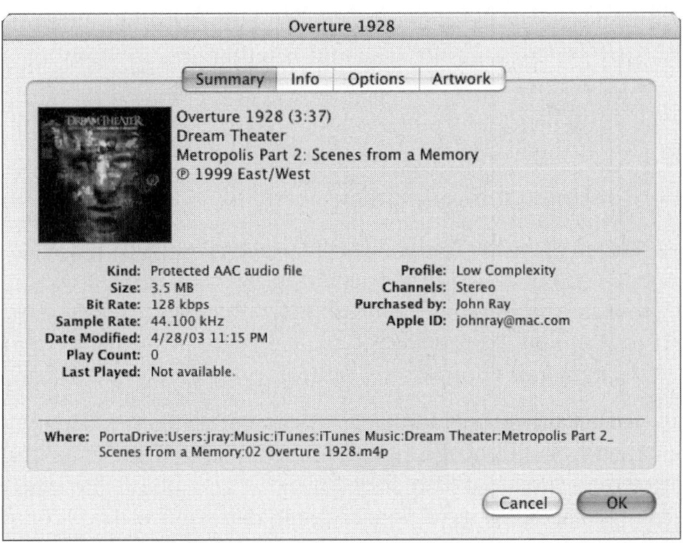

FIGURE 7.19 Use iTunes to view and edit song information.

Preferences

The iTunes Preferences provide control over the interface, sound effects, importing, burning, and file organization:

- General—Choose the size of the text in the Source and Song listing panes and whether to show Genre as a third column in Browse mode. Pick what iTunes will do when a CD is inserted (including Import songs and Eject for fast ripping), and whether iTunes should connect to the Internet as necessary and register itself as your streaming MP3 playback application. If another application has already registered itself, click the Set button to re-register iTunes.
- Effects—Enable crossfade (the fade-in of a sound file as another is fading out), the iTunes Sound Enhancer, which increases the stereo separation effect, and Sound Check, a feature that keeps your song playback level constant, regardless of how the song has been encoded.
- Importing—Choose whether to import in AAC, MP3, AIFF, or WAV format, the import bit rate, whether songs should be played while importing, and whether iTunes should add CD track numbers to song names. Advanced users can choose Custom from the bit rate Configuration pop-up menu. This opens an additional window enabling you to choose VBR recording, sample rates, and other encoding options.

- Burning—Choose the CD Recorder to use with iTunes (if more than one is connected); the preferred Burn speed; and whether you are burning an MP3 Music CD, Audio CD, or Data CD as well as the track gap length (in seconds) for audio discs. Clicking the Use Sound Check button adjusts the volume of all songs written to the CD so that they are played at the same volume level.
- Sharing—We discussed this earlier, remember?
- Store—Choose whether the Music Store is displayed within iTunes, and whether to use 1-Click shopping (the default) or a Shopping Cart. Additionally, choose whether you want to hear your purchases immediately after they've been downloaded, and whether iTunes should load the Music Store previews completely before playing them. If you experience choppy song samples, you should enable this option.
- Advanced—Advanced settings allow you to change the iTunes Library location, the streaming buffer size, and how songs are shuffled, as well as decide whether iTunes should keep your music folder organized by artist and album and whether files should automatically be copied to the iTunes Music folder when you add them to the library.

NOTE

If you choose to organize by artist and album, iTunes creates a folder for each artist and then album names within each folder. This is great *if* all your song files have the correct information tags. Unfortunately, you might end up with multiple folders for the same band. If, for example, one song was labeled as being by "Scorpions" and another "The Scorpions," two separate artist folders would be created, even though it is the same band.

Additional Software

Third-party developers and enamored users of iTunes have created numerous additions to the iTunes application that can make your music-listening life even better. From new visual plug-ins to controlling your iTunes playback with a cell phone, it's been done.

- Get Artwork (`http://homepage.mac.com/gklein1`)—The Get Artwork iTunes AppleScript attempts to download album artwork for your existing songs by querying `allmusic.com`. This is a bit easier than hunting down the images on your own.
- Fetch Art (`http://staff.washington.edu/yoel/fetchart/`)—Like Get Artwork, Fetch Art retrieves artwork for your albums automatically. Fetch Art uses Amazon.com as its image source.
- Salling Clicker (`http://homepage.mac.com/jonassalling/Shareware/Clicker/index.html`)—Amazing remote control software uses your Sony Ericsson phone to control iTunes (amongst other things!). If you have a Sony phone, buy this software!
- G-Force (`http://www.55ware.com/gforce/index.html`)—G-Force is a popular third-party visualizer plug-in for iTunes.

- Volcano Kit (http://www.volcanokit.com/volcanokit2/iTunesVis/index.php)—The Volcano Kit iTunes Visualizer provides an interesting display of waveform frequency and amplitude while your songs play.
- iTunes Reports (http://www.scruffyware.com/products/digilifereports/iTunesReports.html)—Interested in a clean and configurable way to output information about your iTunes Library? The iTunes Reports software creates attractive customized listings of your music library.
- netTunes (http://www.shirt-pocket.com/netTunes/netTunesDescription.html)—Excellent iTunes remote network control software that features the full native iTunes interface in a scalable window.
- launchTunes (http://www.shirt-pocket.com/launchTunes/launchTunesDescription.html)—launchTunes overcomes one of the biggest problems with Rendezvous song sharing—starting iTunes on your remote Macs. With launchTunes installed, when iTunes starts locally, it also launches iTunes on any remote server.
- ltjBPM (https://mail.oatbit.com/~jared/ltjbpm.html)—Probably only useful for musicians or deejays, ltjBPM is a simple beats-per-minute calculator that integrates with iTunes for adding BPM field information.

Recording Audio in Panther

Apple has done an excellent job of providing a clean and easy way for you, the user, to get songs from your CDs onto your computer. But what about sounds themselves? Applications such as Mail and iChat provide the capability for you to choose your own custom notification sounds—heck, Mail on the NeXT and OpenStep platforms allowed you to attach voicemail to outgoing email (this was called LipService, by the way).

So, why, 10 years later, does Apple expect us to get a recording contract, have a studio record our sounds to CD, get the CD pressed and placed in stores, and then purchase our own CD via the Music Store just to get a few sounds recorded onto our desktops? (This is sarcasm folks, I don't *really* think Apple expects that.)

Unfortunately, there *isn't* a basic sound editing application in Mac OS X. To create your own audio, you'll have to either purchase a commercial application such as Apple's SoundTrack (http://www.apple.com/soundtrack/) or look into a more affordable alternative.

TIP

If your computer is audo-input challenged and has no microphone port (as is my cube), Griffin Technologies' iMic ($39.99) offers audio input at an affordable cost (http://www.griffintechnology.com/products/imic/index.html). In addition, Griffin's Final Vinyl application offers an excellent sound input solution for iMic customers (http://www.griffintechnology.com/software/software_imic.html).

NOTE

The "lite" version of Peak (Peak LE) is priced at $99, which is a great deal for what the program *does*, but perhaps a bit more than what someone who just wants to record "I love peas!" as his new system beep is likely to want to pay.

Audio In

At the top of the affordable list is the freeware Audio In (`http://home3.swipnet.se/~w-34826/`; click the Soft button in the lower-right corner). Audio In has a delightfully simple interface that does *exactly* what its name implies. It gives you a simple means of getting audio into your Mac. Figure 7.20 displays the main Audio In window.

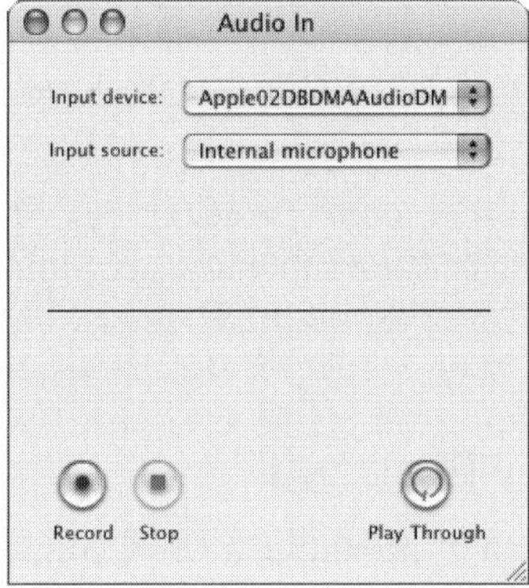

FIGURE 7.20 Audio In brings audio…in.

Use the input source pop-up menu to choose what device will be capturing the audio recording. It is unlikely that you'll need to adjust the input device unless you have third-party audio input hardware connected to your Mac.

If you want to hear the audio coming from your input source, click and drag on the Playthrough button. As you drag, a small indicator rotates around the circle to display the current playthrough volume level—beware of the potential for feedback!

Finally, click Record (Command-R) to start recording. As you record, the audio waveform will be displayed in the center of the Audio In window, as shown in Figure 7.21.

When finished recording, click the Stop button (Command-.). Audio In will have saved the file Recording 1.AIFF to your desktop. To change the name and location where a file is recorded, choose File, Save Recording As (Shift-Command-A) *before* starting to record audio.

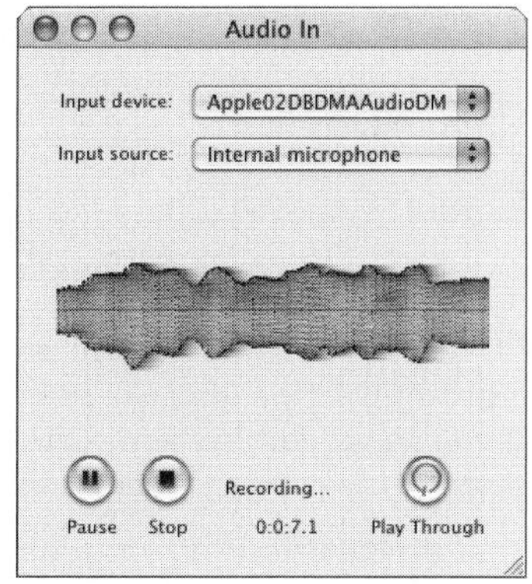

FIGURE 7.21 The waveform is displayed as it is recorded.

> **NOTE**
>
> If you know how long the audio segment you want to record is before you start, you can record for a specified duration by choosing File, Record for Duration (Shift-Command-R).

Remember, personalized sounds should be placed in the `~/Library/Sounds` folder to be automatically recognized by Mac OS X for use in other applications.

Volume Operated Recording

Audio In offers two additional features that make it worth every cent you paid for it. The first, voice-operated recording, is revealed by choosing View, Show Vox Settings from the menu. The Voice Operated Recording preferences appear in a drawer as shown in Figure 7.22.

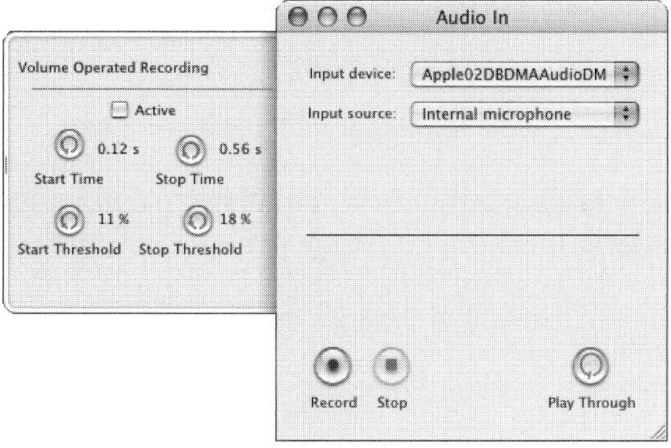

FIGURE 7.22 Set the voice-operated recording options.

Voice-operated recording starts recording when it "hears" a sound, and stops when the sound stops. You can use this for recording what goes on in your office while you're away or just to take notes at an important meeting. Because "silence" isn't recorded, you don't waste drive space or have to spend hours reviewing the recording to find where people were talking.

To activate voice-operated recording, click the Active check box at the top of the drawer. Next, choose the Start and Stop times if you aren't comfortable with the defaults. The Start Time is the amount of continuous sound that triggers Audio In to start recording, whereas the Stop Time is the amount of silence required for it to stop. Similarly, the Start Threshold and Stop Threshold are the percentage of the maximum input volume required to trigger a recording and the percentage it must drop to for recording to stop. These four controls operate like the playthrough control—you must click and drag left or right on the button to change the values.

Scheduled Recording

The second nifty Audio In feature is scheduled recording. Choosing View, Show Schedule from the menu displays a schedule listing in a window drawer, as shown in Figure 7.23.

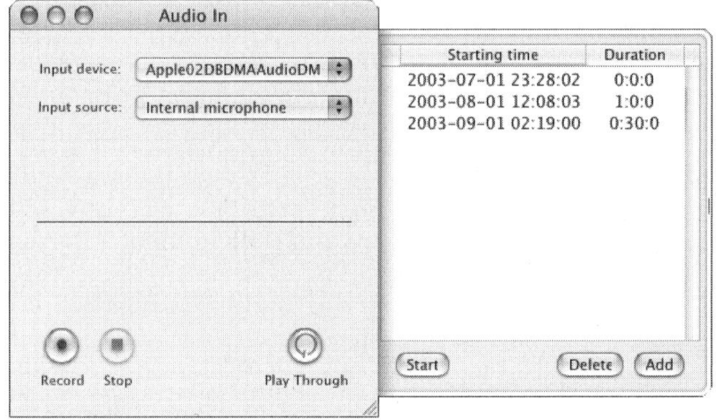

FIGURE 7.23 Schedule your audio recordings into the distant future.

You can schedule a recording for any future date and time provided that Audio In remains running on your computer. To schedule a recording time, click the Add button, and a new date and time are added to the schedule list. Double-click the fields in the schedule to set a start date and time and the duration (in hours:minutes:seconds format) for the recording.

After scheduling the events you want, click Start in the drawer to use the schedule. Audio In displays a Waiting message in its main window. Click Stop in the main Audio In window to cancel the schedule.

Within the schedule listing, Audio In can display three status icons to indicate how the schedule is progressing: an exclamation mark, a large brown dot, and a smaller green dot. The green dot indicates that a scheduled item has been recorded successfully, the brown dot shows that an item is being recorded currently, and finally, the exclamation mark shows an entry with either a zero-length duration or a date/time that has already passed.

NOTE

You can see a log of all recording by choosing File, Show Log from the menu.

Overall, Audio In is a great solution for the lack of an Apple-supplied audio input products. Although it doesn't provide audio editing features, it is more than enough to start playing with the audio input capabilities of your Mac.

Amadeus II: A Walkthrough

A nice, inexpensive alternative to Peak with far more features than Audio In is the application Amadeus II from HairerSoft (`http://www.hairersoft.com/Amadeus.html`). Amadeus, shown in Figure 7.24, sports a simple interface with easy-to-use controls and waveform editor.

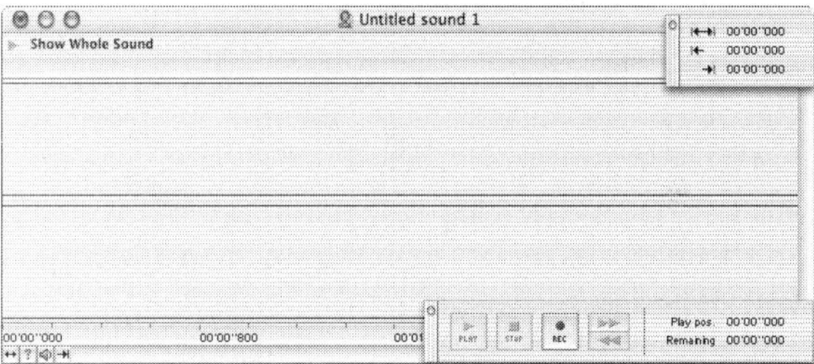

FIGURE 7.24 Amadeus II is an inexpensive means of adding "audio-in" features to Mac OS X.

To record audio, simply click the Record button in the tape recorder-like Navigator window. This brings up the Record session window, shown in Figure 7.25.

In this window, the same tape player controls are used to start a recording session, pause or stop a recording session, play back the current contents of the session, or even set up a timed session that starts and ends at a later date. The sliders at the bottom of the window control the left and right input gain. The Input button at the top of the window allows you to choose your input source (Microphone, iSight, and so on).

After recording your sounds, click OK to open them in the waveform editor, as shown in Figure 7.26. You can now use the playback controls in the Navigator window to listen to the recorded audio.

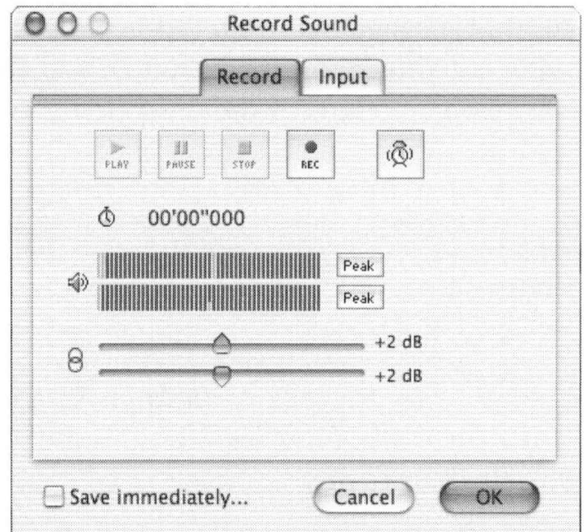

FIGURE 7.25 Use Amadeus to record and edit stereo audio.

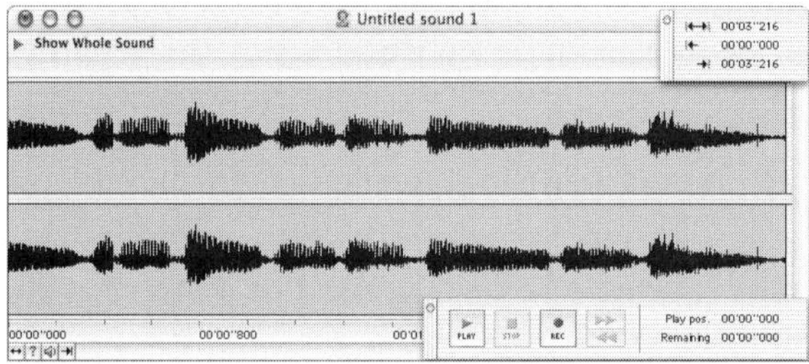

FIGURE 7.26 Captured sounds can be edited in the waveform window.

There are two tracks in the waveform window. The first is the captured waveform for the right stereo channel; the second is the left channel. Along the bottom of the window is the time base for the recording. You can "zoom" in or out of the waveform (effectively showing a smaller or larger segment of time, respectively) by clicking on the double arrow icon in the lower-left corner of the Amadeus window.

Alternatively, click the Show Whole Sound disclosure arrow at the top of the window to show an overview of the entire recorded sound. Clicking and dragging in the overview draws a box around a portion of the recording, which, in turn, expands to fit within the right and left waveform tracks.

Surprisingly enough, sound recordings can be edited much like text in a word processor. A vertical insertion line in the waveforms is similar to the insertion point in a text document. Clicking and dragging across a portion of the waveform selects it. Pressing Delete removes it. You can use the Cut, Copy, and Paste commands to move portions of audio around just as you would a chunk of text.

To record additional audio within an existing waveform, simply click to position the vertical insertion line (our insertion point), wherever you want the new recording to be inserted; then click the Record button and record a new session. The waveform for the new recording is inserted directly into the existing sound.

Effects can be applied to the waveform to improve the quality or just to make it more interesting. To apply an effect, select a portion of the waveform that you want to alter; then choose an effect (Amplify, Echo, Change Speed and Pitch) from the Effects menu. Figure 7.27 demonstrates the Echo effect being applied.

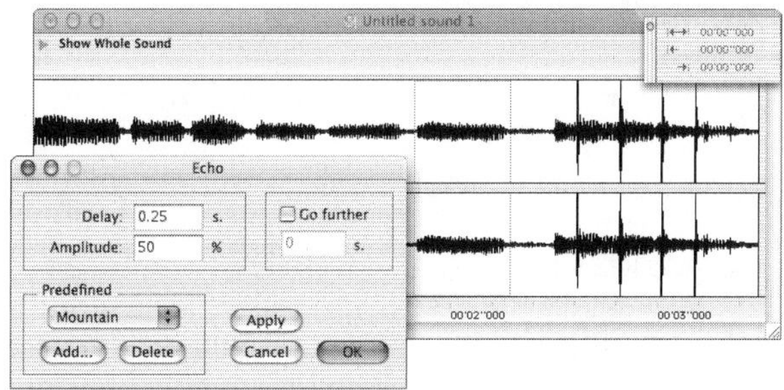

FIGURE 7.27 Apply special effects to your audio recordings.

When you're satisfied with the results, choose File, Save As from the menu. Amadeus can save to a variety of formats, including MP3, and the Mac OS X native sound file format AIFF.

With luck, Apple will add a few basic audio features of its own to Mac OS X—at least offering a convenient way to create new system beeps. For now, the third-party offers do a great job in their own right.

Audio MIDI Tool

The Apple Audio MIDI tool (`/Applications/Utilities/Audio MIDI Setup`) is included with Mac OS X but is mainly targeted at individuals using third-party audio hardware with their Macintosh. Shown in Figure 7.28, the Audio Devices pane of the tool allows you to configure your audio input and output settings for a given sound device.

The Audio Devices pane can be considered an "expanded" version of the Sound System preferences pane (see Chapter 11, "Additional System Components," for details) that includes the capability to increase input and output volume on a per-channel basis, enables per-channel muting and playthrough, and a offers variety of other pro-audio features. A number of the settings are grayed out on a stock Macintosh because they are not supported by the Apple sound hardware.

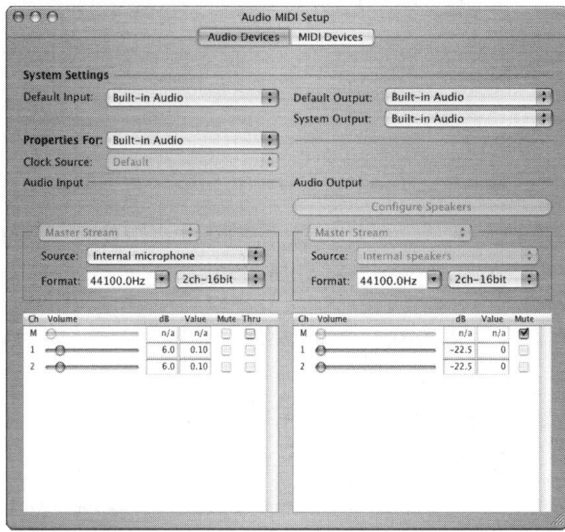

FIGURE 7.28 Use the Audio MIDI Tool to configure the audio I/O for third-party sound hardware.

The MIDI (Musical Instrument Digital Interface) pane of the Audio MIDI Tool is used by musicians to create and map interdevice connections between MIDI devices. Elements such as keyboards and sequencers can be added to the MIDI control view or detected automatically and displayed with a full graphical representation of their physical cabling.

Summary

Mac OS X shines as an audio library platform with excellent integration of the iTunes music software and Apple-created technologies such as the iPod and Rendezvous. Surprisingly, Apple has neglected to include basic audio input facilities for creating system sounds or just recording memos.

This chapter provided coverage of the venerable iTunes application, as well as introduced a few solutions for filling in the gaps in Apple's audio input void.

CHAPTER 8

Digital Video

IN THIS CHAPTER

- Multimedia Software
- QuickTime 6
- iMovie
- iDVD

Rumor has it that Mac users are creative types. Mac OS X provides the tools that users need to work with movies, images, DVDs, video cameras, scanners, MP3 players, and more. This chapter looks at the remaining elements of Apple's iLife Suite (iMovie, iDVD) along with the QuickTime Player. If you want to make a movie, this is the chapter that will satisfy your crave.

Multimedia Software

The Mac OS X multimedia software we're going to look at in this chapter ranges from movie creation to DVD playback:

- iMovie (path: `/Applications/iMovie`)—iMovie is a movie creation tool for users with FireWire cameras. Featuring a simple project-oriented interface, it can be used to create digital movies with professional-level effects.
- iDVD (path: `/Applications/iDVD`)—After building your productions with iMovie, burn them to a DVD with iDVD. The iDVD software can create complete DVD products with menus, animation, and other advanced features.
- QuickTime (path: `/Applications/QuickTime Player`)—Apple's flagship multimedia software is pervasive throughout the Mac OS X operating system. The QuickTime player provides a simple playback interface for viewing static or streaming media.

The applications discussed here are presented with basic use information, covering as many features as possible. Some people have written complete books on iMovie and iDVD, but we'll do our best to be direct and to the point.

QuickTime 6

What would an Internet experience be like without streaming sound and video? If you have a dial-up connection, the answer is enjoyable; but for those of us lucky enough to have broadband access, streaming media is reasonably feasible through the use of the QuickTime Player provided with Mac OS X. QuickTime is Apple's digital media engine that processes everything from MIDI to movies and still images.

In this chapter, we're interested in QuickTime's streaming capabilities. QuickTime uses the Internet standard, RTSP (Real-Time Streaming Protocol), to deliver high-quality streams based on any of the QuickTime codecs. In addition, QuickTime can use traditional protocols such as FTP and HTTP.

The difference between FTP/HTTP streaming and RTSP is the TCP/IP transport used to deliver the data. FTP and HTTP are known as *reliable* protocols. When a server transmits using HTTP or FTP, it must carry on a conversation with the remote client. For each piece (packet) of information that is sent, the remote machine must reply with an acknowledgement (ACK). If the client does not reply, the server resends the data, or, after enough time passes, closes the connection.

RTSP, on the other hand, uses the UDP protocol (a different component of the TCP/IP protocol suite) to deliver unreliable data streams. Although the term *unreliable* might not sound appealing, in the case of streamed video, it is. RTSP (via UDP) sends data out as quickly as it can. If there is a glitch in the connection, it doesn't have to wait for the remote computer to respond, and it doesn't have to resend data—it just keeps going. The result is a video feed that can recover from errors and doesn't slow down. When watching live video presentations, UDP is the only way to go.

Unfortunately, UDP tends to break behind firewalls or masqueraded connections. To get around this, Apple has provided the capability to stream over HTTP. RTSP is recommended when possible; HTTP provides a comparable streaming experience, although it is susceptible to more hiccups than the UDP-based protocol.

Setting Up QuickTime

There are two places you're most likely to run into QuickTime media—through the QuickTime player and via a Web browser. Before you can use either, you must first configure QuickTime through its System Preferences pane. Failing to do so displays the lowest-quality stream. Open System Preferences (path: `/Applications/System Preferences`) and click the QuickTime icon to configure your QuickTime settings.

NOTE

QuickTime settings are made on a per-user basis. This includes registration. Each user of the system needs to license QuickTime Pro separately if he wants to access its advanced features.

Plug-In

The Plug-In preferences pane is shown in Figure 8.1. At the bottom of each QuickTime preferences pane are the About QuickTime and Registration buttons. Clicking the About QuickTime button displays information on the version of QuickTime installed and provides a link to Apple's QuickTime Web site. Choosing Registration allows you to enter registration information for QuickTime Pro. The QuickTime Pro software adds additional features to the Player application—we'll look at these a little later.

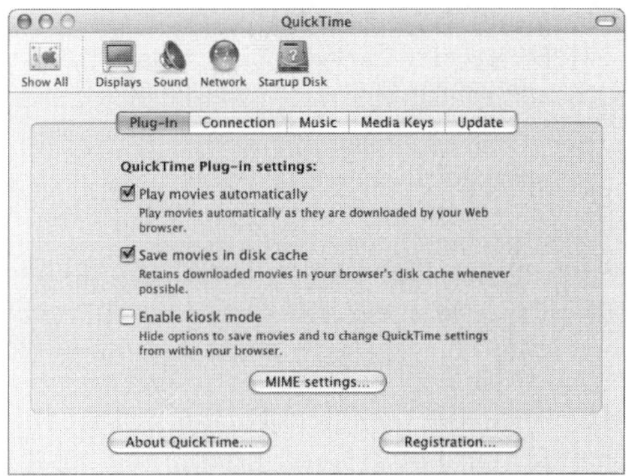

FIGURE 8.1 The Plug-In pane controls how the QuickTime browser plug-in works.

The QuickTime plug-in is used when movies are viewed in a browser. There are four configurable options: Play Movies Automatically, Save Movies in Disk Cache, Enable Kiosk Mode, and MIME Settings.

If you've checked Play Movies Automatically, QuickTime starts playing a movie after enough of it has been buffered. This applies to nonstreamed movies. If this option is not selected, you must click the Play button to start viewing a movie. If you want to save movies that have played in your browser, click the Save Movies in Disk Cache check box. This speeds up commonly accessed movies and is great for those days when you repeatedly keep pulling up the one funny video clip to show your coworkers.

Users interested in using QuickTime in kiosks can limit the end user's access to QuickTime controls by clicking the Enable Kiosk Mode check box. This isn't needed for normal use.

The final available preference, the MIME Settings button, opens a list of all the MIME types that QuickTime can handle and everything it is currently configured to display. Some items are intentionally disabled (such as Flash) because they are better handled by other browser plug-ins.

Connection

The Connection pane, shown in Figure 8.2, configures the type of network access QuickTime can expect your computer to have.

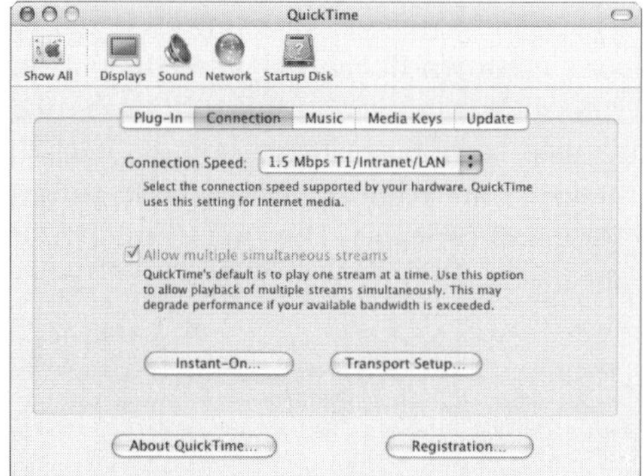

FIGURE 8.2 Choose your connection speed and transport type for best movie quality.

Choose your network speed from the Connection Speed pop-up menu. This is not the speed you *wish* you had, but rather the actual speed of your line. This choice helps QuickTime choose the appropriate type of media to display depending on how fast it can be received.

Click the Instant-On button to enable the QuickTime 6 Instant On feature and choose how long QuickTime should wait for (and buffer) information before it starts playing a stream.

Click the Transport Setup button to choose the protocol used for streaming. By default, QuickTime attempts to choose the best transport based on your network topology. It's best not to change these settings unless you know your network supports them. Users behind a firewall can choose the ports used for either HTTP or UDP transports. It's best to talk to your network administrator before changing anything.

NOTE

If your computer is connected directly to the Internet via a DSL/cable modem or you are on a network without a firewall, either of the transports should work fine for you. Try each to see which displays faster and cleaner streams on your system.

By default, QuickTime allows only a single media stream. If your bandwidth allows, click the Allow Multiple Simultaneous Streams option to stream many sources at once. This option is automatically selected when selecting a high-speed network.

Music

QuickTime supports multiple plug-in synthesizers when playing MIDI music. By default, it uses the QuickTime Music Synthesizer.

If you install software that offers another synthesizer plug-in, you can select it from the list in this preferences pane. Highlight the item you want to use by default and click Make Default. This sets it as the default synthesizer used by any application playing QuickTime MIDI files.

Media Keys

Some media files can be secured with an access key. The Media Keys pane allows you to enter keys directly into the QuickTime preferences so that the files can be accessed transparently at any time. Use the Delete, Edit, and Add buttons to modify your access keys.

Update

QuickTime supports automatic updating in much the same way as the Mac OS X operating system (see Chapter 32, "System Maintenance," for more information). Unlike the operating system, however, QuickTime checks for updates outside the normal system updater context. When you're using QuickTime, it occasionally scans for updates and additions that can be downloaded.

The QuickTime updater can also be used to add third-party software, such as new codecs, to the system.

Click the Update or Install QuickTime Software or Install New Third-Party QuickTime Software radio buttons, and then click Update Now to start. Follow the onscreen instructions to complete the installation.

NOTE

The actual installation is performed using the Software Update utility built into the system, although the process is controlled by QuickTime's own update application. For more information on Software Update, see Chapter 32.

To toggle the QuickTime auto-update feature, click the Check for Updates Automatically check box.

When you're finished setting up QuickTime, close the System Preferences application.

Browser Plug-in

Many QuickTime movies play from within your browser window. This is probably the most common place you'll view streaming media, so let's take a look at the controls of the QuickTime browser plug-in. Figure 8.3 shows a QuickTime movie playing in the Safari browser.

The movie controls are located across the bottom of the video. If you've used a VCR or other media player, you've certainly seen these before. There are, however, a few shortcuts you might want to know.

The volume control, for example, can be instantly muted by Option-clicking the speaker icon. You can also control the volume level using the up arrow and down arrow keys on the keyboard. To increase the volume beyond its normal limit, hold down the Shift key while dragging the volume control.

FIGURE 8.3 Most users experience QuickTime through their browser.

Playback controls can be activated from the keyboard, saving the need to mouse around on your screen. To toggle between playing and pausing, press the spacebar. To rewind or fast forward, use the left arrow and right arrow keys, respectively.

At the lower far-right of the control bar area is the QuickTime menu. This provides quick access to QuickTime settings. QuickTime Pro users can use this menu to save movies to their hard drive. (Note: Saving a streaming movie saves a reference to the movie, not the actual contents of the movie.)

If the movie being played is streaming from the remote server, some of these controls might not be available. For example, live streams can't be fast-forwarded or rewound, but streamed files can be. The available controls depend entirely on the movie you're viewing.

The QuickTime Player

The QuickTime Player application (path: `/Applications/QuickTime Player`) provides another means of viewing movies and streams. In fact, many users might be surprised to find that they can use the player application to tune in a variety of interesting streams—ranging from news to entertainment—without the need for a Web browser.

Apple has been working with entertainment and news outlets for the past few years to develop QuickTime "stations" for your listening and watching enjoyment. Don't have a good source for NPR in your neighborhood? Use QuickTime TV to play a high-quality NPR stream, anytime, anywhere.

QuickTime Content

To start using the QuickTime player, open it from its default home in the Dock, or from the System Applications folder. The QuickTime window should open directly to a featured "Hot Pick"—something Apple thinks you should be interested in, but you probably aren't.

The "Q" button in the lower-right corner of the Player window provides a shortcut to the different available media sources. Simply click the button and navigate to the content you want, from choices such as entertainment, news, and music, as shown in Figure 8.4. Some sources launch your Web browser to make additional selections—just follow your onscreen instructions and all will be well.

FIGURE 8.4 Click "Q" to view QuickTime content featured by Apple.

When QuickTime starts to load a streaming video clip, it goes through four steps before displaying the video:

- Connecting—Connection is made to the streaming server.
- Requesting data—Waits for acknowledgement from remote server.
- Getting info—Retrieves information about the QuickTime movie.
- Buffering—QuickTime buffers several seconds of video to eliminate stuttering from the playback.

If the player stalls during any of these steps, it might be a problem with the remote server or your transport setting. Try another streaming source, and if it still fails, use the QuickTime Preferences pane to select an alternative transport.

Other QuickTime Sources

You can use the QuickTime Player to play information from other sources in addition to the Apple-linked content. You can open local movie files by choosing File, Open Movie (Command-O) or by dragging a movie file onto the QuickTime Dock icon. If you have a streaming server URL, you can select File, Open URL in New Player (Command-U) to directly open the stream.

QuickTime refers to any media type as a movie. For example, you can open and play CD audio tracks and MP3s using the Open Movie command. Even though there aren't any visuals, these media types are still referred to as *movies* in QuickTime's vocabulary.

TIP

An interesting example of QuickTime Streaming in action is the Race Rocks Web site. Race Rocks is an inside view of an ecological preserve being transmitted 24 hours a day using Macintosh and AirPort technology: `http://www.racerocks.com/`. To immediately view streaming video from the Race Rocks island, enter the URL `http://stream.qtv.apple.com/channels/ali/racerocks/racerocks_camera1_ref.mov` into the QuickTime Player application. Open a URL in QuickTime Player by choosing File, Open URL in New Player from the menu (Command-U).

QuickTime Player Controls

The QuickTime Player, shown in Figure 8.5, works much like a VCR. The top of the window holds the video pane. Directly below the video is a status bar to display the progress of the player and any feedback it needs to provide to the user.

FIGURE 8.5 If you've used a VCR, you can control the QuickTime Player.

The status bar has three components: the elapsed time, the playback progress, and a miniature frequency monitor. Dragging the arrow above the progress bar quickly moves the current position in the movie (except in the cases of live streams, for reasons that should be obvious).

TIP

QuickTime Pro users might notice that directly below the progress bar are two selection triangles. Use these triangles to select start and end points for the video clip. The selection can then be copied or pasted into other movies.

Although the frequency monitor is of little value as-is, clicking it toggles the status bar to and from basic sound controls—balance, bass, and treble control. Use the + and - buttons to adjust the values of these settings.

Below the status bar are the main playback controls that provide the basic control over movie playback.

Because many video clips are small, the QuickTime Player window can be resized by using the window resize handle in the lower-right corner. By default, QuickTime Player resizes the window to maintain the same aspect ratio. To squeeze or stretch the window, hold down Shift while resizing. To switch between common sizes, use the Movie menu to select from Half Size (Command-0), Normal Size (Command-1), Double Size (Command-2), and Fill Screen (Command-3).

TIP

Minimizing a QuickTime Player movie while it is playing adds a live icon to the Dock. The movie (with sound) continues to play in the minimized Dock icon. Even if you don't have a use for this, give it a try—it's extremely cool!

NOTE

QuickTime Pro users have an additional option to present the movie on the screen. This clears all other information from the monitor and plays the full-screen video (Command-F).

QuickTime Favorites

To keep track of your favorite movies (either local files or streaming), you can use the QuickTime Favorites menu, which works just like a lame version of your favorite browser's bookmark menu.

When viewing a movie that you want to bookmark as a favorite, choose Favorites, Add Movie as Favorite (Command-D). You can now select the movie from the Favorites menu itself.

To remove a favorite item, choose Favorites, Show Favorites. A window with a list of all the favorite movies appears. Highlight the item to remove and press your Backspace key. If you'd rather organize than delete, dragging the items in the Favorites window reorders them.

Getting Movie Information

There are two ways to get extended information about a movie, including the codecs used, FPS, duration, and other useful tidbits. For a summary of information, choose Window, Show Movie Info (Command-I).

The collapsed Movie Info window displays only the title and copyright information. Click the disclosure arrow to display additional data. Figure 8.6 shows the expanded Movie Info window.

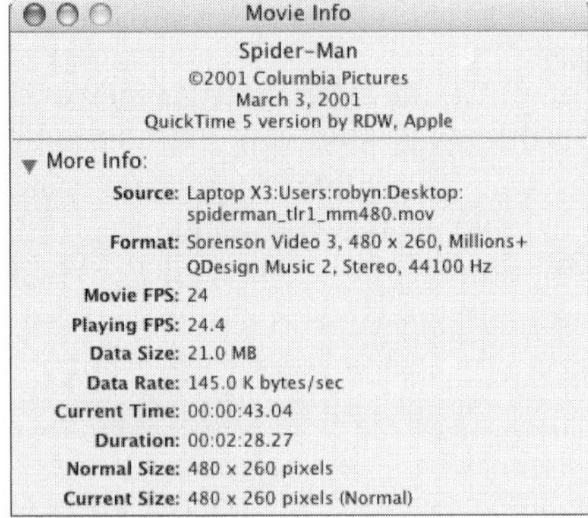

FIGURE 8.6 The expanded Movie Info window contains summary data on the currently playing file.

The type of information shown depends on the type of movie being played. Streaming video, for example, includes network data such as bit rate and quality.

To view even more detailed information, choose Movie, Get Movie Properties (Command-J).

Movie properties, shown in Figure 8.7, can be used to view information about every component of a video file or stream.

At the top of the Properties window are two pop-up menus. The menu on the left selects the object to examine—video tracks, audio tracks, or the movie as a whole. The pop-up menu on the right selects between the different properties that can be viewed. Common properties include Annotations, such as author, title, and copyright, Format, Size, and Bit Rate (streaming transmission rate).

NOTE

QuickTime Pro users can view a much larger number of movie properties as well as set information about a movie, such as its color palette, graphics mode, and mask.

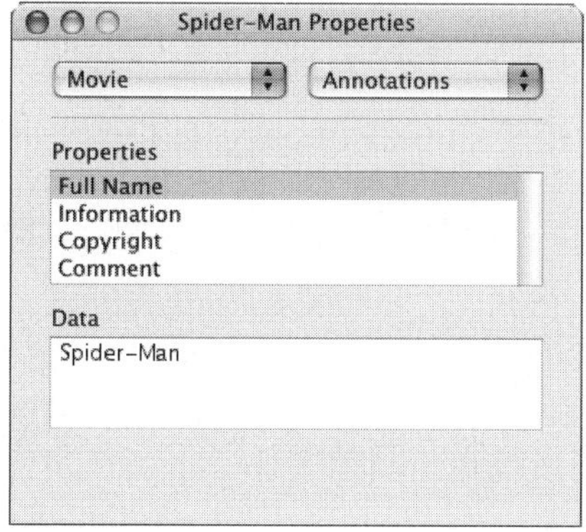

FIGURE 8.7 Use movie properties to view detailed information about the components of a QuickTime movie.

QuickTime Preferences

The application Preferences menu actually contains three different choices: Player Preferences, QuickTime Preferences, and Registration.

The Player Preferences set preferences for the Player application itself, whereas the QuickTime Preferences refer to the QuickTime System Preferences pane discussed earlier. If you're interested in registering QuickTime (which we highly suggest), the Registration option provides an input area for entering your registration code.

Figure 8.8 shows the Player preferences.

Use the following options in the Player Preferences to control how the application handles multiple movies and playback:

- Open Movies in New Players—By default, QuickTime Player reuses existing windows when opening new movies. To open new movies in new windows, check this option.
- Automatically Play Movies When Opened—Does what it says! When this option is checked, the player starts playing a movie immediately after it is opened.
- Play Sound in Frontmost Player Only—By default, sound is played only in the front-most player window. To hear sound from all playing movies simultaneously, uncheck this option.
- Play Sound When Application Is in Background—If this option is checked, sound continues to play even when QuickTime Player isn't the frontmost application.
- Show Equalizer—Displays the onscreen equalizer.

- Show Hot Picks Movie Automatically—When this option is checked, QuickTime player displays Apple's Hot Pick movie each time it launches.
- Pause Movies When Logged Out—If you have fast user switching enabled (see Chapter 2, "Managing the Panther Workspace," for details), checking this option pauses any QuickTime movies that are playing when a user-switch occurs.

Click OK to save the application preferences.

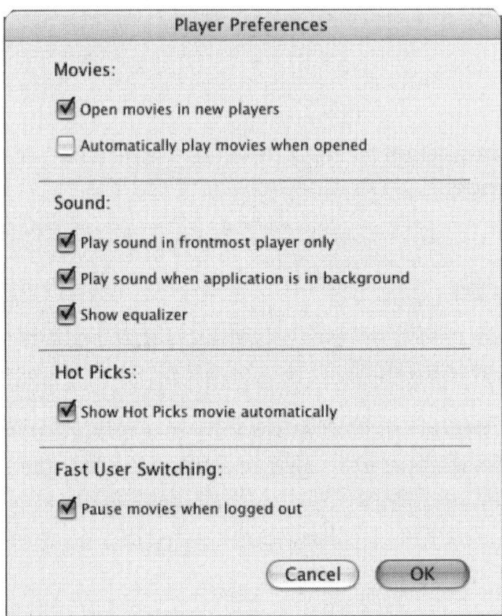

FIGURE 8.8 Choose how QuickTime Player reacts to opening and playing movies.

QuickTime Pro Features

For most users, the standard version of QuickTime is probably more than enough to handle their media needs. If you're interested in creating or editing digital movies, you can upgrade to QuickTime Pro and gain access to some interesting new features. There isn't anything additional to install, just a registration code to enter, so it's easy to get up and running with QuickTime Pro.

Upgrading gives you access to a number of video editing functions, such as copying and pasting portions of video tracks, applying effects filters, altering video codecs, and working with the new Internet standard MPEG 4. Users can extract and convert audio and video tracks—even export video tracks as image sequences.

Basic playback features are also improved. Users can present a movie on the entire screen, rather than just a window, as well as control contrast, tint, and brightness on a per-movie basis. If you've ever played a movie with improper gamma settings (way too dark), you'll greatly appreciate these features.

iMovie

For those with digital video cameras, Apple's iMovie software (path: /Applications/iMovie) can provide a simple creative outlet, or a means of making production quality video shorts. iMovie allows you to combine video clips, add sound effects and voiceovers, create title text, and export your final work into formats others can view.

Required Equipment

A large part of what makes iMovie work so well is FireWire. Developed by Apple, FireWire is a high-speed peripheral data transmission standard ideal for working with information-dense content, such as audio and video. It works so well, in fact, that Apple won a Primetime Emmy award in 2001 for its contributions to the television industry.

FireWire transfers video and audio digitally, requiring no encoding or decoding on the part of the computer. However, this does mean that you'll need a computer with a FireWire port and a digital video camera that supports FireWire and the DV codec standard. The Web site http://www.apple.com/imovie/compatibility/camcorder.html lists many compatible video cameras.

NOTE

Not all compatible cameras refer to this technology as FireWire. Depending on the manufacturer, it might also be known as IEEE 1394 or i.Link, but they work just the same.

Using USB and Nonsupported FireWire Devices

Unfortunately, many FireWire and USB camera devices are not compatible, including Apple's iSight. USB and FireWire Webcams do not natively support the DV standard required by iMovie and, to be used, must be compressed and saved using the DV codec. If you can save the video using a standard QuickTime video codec, iMovie can import it, but it takes awhile.

You can, however, use a third-party application to record and save to a DV compressed file all at once. Several applications can do this, but one of the best is uGrabIt (http://www.derbrill.de/ugrabit/content/e_index.html). uGrabIt enables you to choose an NTSC or PAL DV standard, pick any recognized video input device, and start recording. Movie files that are captured with uGrabIt can be imported instantly into iMovie and be fully usable within the application.

Using Analog Equipment

Posing another compatibility problem are users who need to transfer footage from analog camcorders. If you find yourself in this situation, consider purchasing an analog to DV bridge. These devices provide standard RCA-style video/audio inputs and output a FireWire DV stream.

Be warned, in this area you seemingly get what you pay for. The Formac Studio DV (`http://www.formac.com/p_bin/?cid=solutions_converters_studiodv`) is a little more expensive, but far more Mac-like than solutions from other companies. I have had rather unpleasant video-syncing experiences with the Hollywood-DV bridge (`http://www.dazzle.com`), but at around $240, it may be suited for small conversions from time to time.

Given the price of the DV-analog conversion equipment, it might be worthwhile to simply look into what digital camcorders are available in your price range. Many modern cameras offer DV-analog transcoding that allows you to plug an analog device into the camera and output DV through the camera's FireWire port.

The iMovie Interface

When you first open iMovie, it gives you the options to create a new project, open a project, or quit. click Create Project and choose where to save it. The next time you use iMovie, the last project you worked on is opened automatically. To create a new project or open another project, you can then select those options from the File menu.

> **NOTE**
>
> iMovie defaults to NTSC operation. To change to the PAL format, using the application preferences. You *cannot* convert a project that is already created.

Before you start using the application, let's take a look at the interface. It is composed of three panes, as shown in Figure 8.9. At upper left is the iMovie monitor, where clips, other elements, and the project-in-progress can be viewed. The iMovie monitor is typically controlled by three buttons—rewind to beginning, playback, and playback full screen—along with a volume slider. Although these controls may seem a bit "sparse," you can quickly navigate your clips and movie by dragging the Playhead (the little blue slider arrow) within the blue scrubber bar back and forth.

A control pane containing clips and effects controls is in the upper right. A row of buttons below this pane (including Clips, Photos, Audio, Titles, Transitions, Effects, and iDVD) control its contents.

Along the bottom of the screen is the Project View pane representing video and sounds of the project-in-progress. This pane can operate in one of two modes: Clip Viewer or Timeline Viewer. The Clip Viewer displays a thumbnail of each of the video clips used to build your movie. The Timeline Viewer, on the other hand, shows each clip against a ruler-like timeline. This allows you to see how long your movie is and adjust clip durations and so on. The Timeline Viewer also includes a Playhead marker that you can drag along the timeline to view portions of your project. This is the mode visible within Figure 8.9.

FIGURE 8.9 The iMovie interface shows previews on the left, the element shelf on the right, and a project view (consisting of either the Clip Viewer or Timeline Viewer) along the bottom.

We'll now walk through each of the control areas on the button bar to show you how to use the features within iMovie.

Clips

By default, the ..Clips button should be selected in the iMovie controls button bar. When Clips is selected, the Controls pane displays the iMovie shelf. The shelf is used to store all the video clips used to make your movie.

Transferring Clips from a Camera

Before starting transfers from your camera, make sure that iMovie is toggled to "camera" mode using the switch directly to the left of the iMovie playback controls. When the switch is toggled in the direction of the camera icon, iMovie is in camera mode and can interact with your FireWire device. When it is toggled toward the scissors, it is in editing mode. The exact terms your camera uses may be different from what is presented here, but the process should be almost identical:

1. Insert the tape containing the footage you want to edit into the camcorder.

2. Connect the camcorder to the computer via the FireWire port, using the FireWire cable that came with the camera. Turn on the camera and set it to playback mode.
3. In the iMovie monitor of the iMovie interface, slide the switch toward the DV camera icon.
4. Set the camera to play. As the tape runs, recorded images appear in the iMovie monitor, and the accompanying sound track is played. You may want to play back in slow motion (if your camera supports it) to better judge where you want to start importing video.
5. When you reach the approximate section that you want to use in your movie, click the Import button at the bottom of the iMovie video window—the clip will be recorded. Click Import again to stop gathering the clip. (Remember that you can edit clips after they are saved in iMovie, but that means you should leave a little bit of extra space at the beginning and ending of your chosen clips.) If you stopped/started the camera when making your video, iMovie senses these transitions and adds each part as a separate clip. You can adjust this behavior with the Automatically Start New Clip at Scene Break application preference.

Repeat this process to import more clips until you have enough to begin the editing process. As you add clips, the spaces in the shelf show them as numbered items, as shown in Figure 8.9. If you want to give them text labels, click the bottom of the slide until the .title area turns gray and then change the label

CAUTION

Video clips take up a lot of drive space. Keep an eye on the Free Space status bar in the lower-right corner of the window so that you don't run out of room.

Importing Video Clips

If you're working with movies captured outside iMovie, you can import them into the application by dragging them directly from the Finder into the Clips shelf. Alternatively, use File, Import to choose a clip and add it to your project. Be aware that the process of converting existing movies *is* time consuming unless they are already in the DV format.

Cropping Video Clips

After you've imported clips, you can begin making your movie. The first thing you'll want to do is refine the cropping you performed when transferring clips from the camera. The most important control in cropping is the scrubber bar—the blue bar that .appears below the iMovie monitor to represent the duration of the clip.

To crop a clip, follow these steps:

1. Select a clip from the Clips shelf. Your chosen clip is highlighted in blue and appears in the iMovie monitor.
2. In the IMovie monitor, find the split arrow below the scrubber bar. The right side of the arrow marks the *end* of the clip, and the left side marks the start.
3. To choose your segment, drag each side of the arrow to set the start and stop points for the clip. This produces a yellow bar representing your cropped clip, as shown in Figure 8.10.

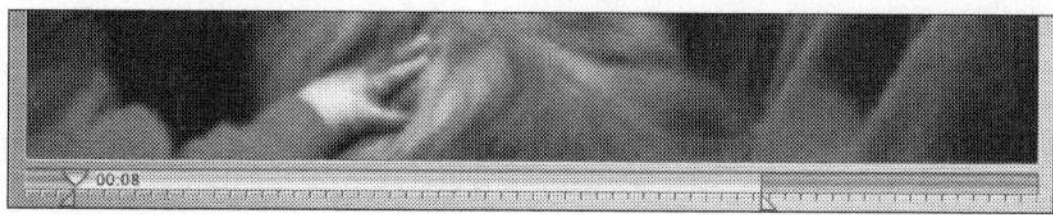

FIGURE 8.10 To crop footage, drag the arrows to the appropriate start and end points.

4. When you are happy with your clip, choose Edit, Crop from the menu to trim the parts you didn't select from that item on the Clips shelf.

Repeat this cropping procedure for all your clips, saving the good parts and leaving out the rest.

Should you want to use multiple segments from a single clip, you must first copy it. To do this, select the clip and choose Copy and then Paste from the Edit menu. A duplicate appears in the Clips shelf, allowing you to preserve the original in its entirety.

Splitting Clips

Sometimes you might find that you want to break an existing clip into multiple pieces. To do this, you *split* the clip into two parts, and then, if desired, split the parts again, and so on. To split a clip, use the Playhead in the IMovie monitor to choose a break point; then select Edit, Split Video Clip at Playhead (Command-T). The. clip is split, and both parts appear in the Clips shelf.

Assembling Your Movie (Clip Viewer/Timeline Viewer)

After you've prepared your clips, you can begin assembling your movie. Drag the clips from the Clips shelf into Project View pane along the bottom of the window (as shown in Figure 8.11). It doesn't matter whether you're in the Clip Viewer mode or Timeline Viewer Mode, although the Clip Viewer may prove easier to use for developing the basic structure of your movie.

In the Clip Viewer, you can edit your movie by dragging clips into the order you want them. You can preview your work at any time by clicking the Play button in the IMovie monitor; however, if you want to preview the entire project, make sure that no clip is selected in the Project View pane, or only the selected clip will play.

The Project View pane can also be used in Timeline view by clicking the clock icon. In the Timeline view, there are three bars, the first representing the video track of your project (anything that shows onscreen), and two audio tracks for adding and mixing sound (we'll get to that later). The length of each element is represented by the length of the item in the track, as shown in Figure 8.12 (note that no audio is present in Figure 8.12.)

FIGURE 8.11 Drag chosen clips to the Clip Viewer.

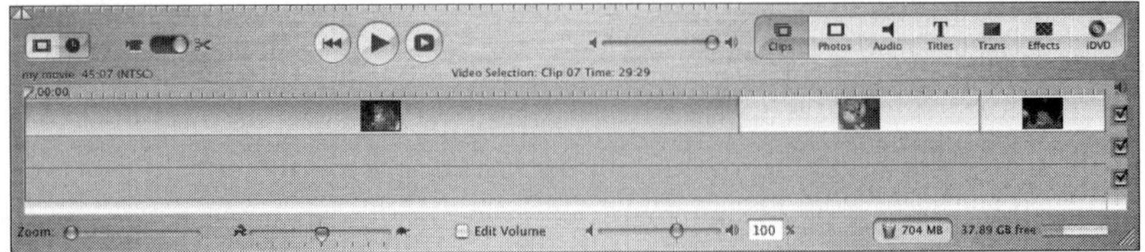

FIGURE 8.12 The Timeline view shows the video and audio elements as well as their duration.

When in the Timeline view a few special controls are visible at the bottom of the window that are not available anywhere else in iMovie. The first, Zoom, controls the *time resolution* of the Timeline Viewer. The farther in you zoom, the more space on the bar a second occupies. The farther out you zoom, the less space it takes up. The second control—speed (denoted by a bunny and a tortoise)—sets the speed at which a selected clip plays. To speed up or slow down a video clip, select it in the Timeline Viewer and then use this slider. The third control, sound editing, is discussed later.

Photos

Photographs can be worked with much like video clips—you can apply the same effects and transitions, as well as use a special effect designed specifically for digital photographs—an effect dubbed the *Ken Burns Effect*. This effect, which we'll discuss later, can add motion and depth to otherwise still images. To access the Photo features of iMovie, click the Photos button in the Controls button bar. The Photo palette appear, as shown in Figure 8.13.

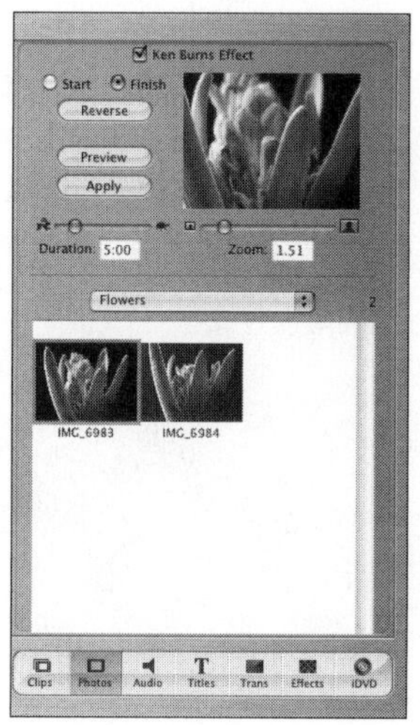

FIGURE 8.13 The Photos pane provides direct access to iPhoto images.

iPhoto Integration

To add a photograph that you've previously stored within your iPhoto library, click the Photos button in the icon bar in the lower-right portion of the iMovie window. At the top of the pane are the controls for the Ken Burns Effect, followed by the library of available iPhoto images. The pop-up menu at the top of the image catalog can be used to limit the images being displayed to any of the iPhoto albums you've created, or two special categories:

- iPhoto Library——-All images in the iPhoto library.
- Last Import—The last group of images you imported into iPhoto.

Choose the album or category that contains the image you want to use; then scroll through the image catalog to find the exact picture you want to add.

Finally, drag the image to the Timeline or Clip View at the bottom of the iMovie window. iMovie behaves exactly as if you are adding a video clip with a five second duration. Figure 8.14 shows a collection of three images that have been added to the Clip View in iMovie.

By default, iMovie attempts to apply the Ken Burns Effect to your photo. Because we haven't discussed this yet, you can press Command-. to cancel the effect. To stop this from being the default action, uncheck the Ken Burns Effect check box at the top of the Photos pane.

FIGURE 8.14 Just think of still images as video clips without much video.

The Ken Burns Effect

So... what is this thing that Apple so desperately wants us to use? The Ken Burns Effect is a method of bringing life to still images that was pioneered by the filmmaker Ken Burns, who has created many award-winning documentaries, and whose work has even been nominated for an Academy Award.

NOTE

For a complete background on Ken Burns and his work, visit `http://www.pbs.org/kenburns/`.

The effect is really quite simple. Rather than just putting a photograph onscreen while someone narrates, a virtual "camera" pans over the image, zooming in or out as it goes. A photograph of a bouquet of flowers, for example, could start zoomed in on one particular flower and then zoom out, centering the bouquet on the screen as it goes. When the effect is used properly, the end result is stunning and can make the viewer forget that he or she is not watching live video.

To use the Ken Burns Effect in iMovie, first make sure that you are in the Photos pane; then click to activate the Ken Burns Effect check box. Select the image that you want to apply the effect to. At the top of the Photos pane are the controls that you will use to determine the path that the virtual camera will take, how long the resulting video clip will be, and how far in or out the virtual camera is zoomed.

For example, I've chosen a picture of a flower bud to apply the effect to. I want to start out zoomed in on the bud and then zoom out to show the entire plant. To do this, I click the Start button and then click and drag the image within the Ken Burns Effect image well. This allows me to center where the camera starts when the effect is applied. Next, I adjust the Zoom level either using the slider control or by directly typing in the Zoom field. Figure 8.15 shows the start settings of my Ken Burns Effect.

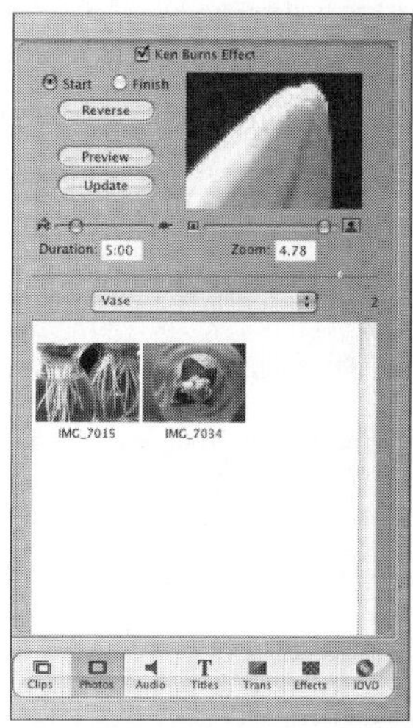

FIGURE 8.15 Choose the starting location and zoom for the image.

To complete the effect, I need to repeat the same process for the finish point of the effect. This time, I click the Finish button, click and drag the image so that it appears as I want it in the image well, and then adjust the zoom so that I can see the whole picture, as shown in Figure 8.16.

To preview the Ken Burns Effect before you actually apply it to an image, click the Preview button. To reverse the path that the virtual camera takes (effectively switching the Start and Finish points), click the Reverse button. If you want the total time the transition takes to last longer (or shorter) than five seconds, adjust the duration slider, or type directly into the Duration time field. Finally, to add the image with the Ken Burns Effect to the timeline or clip view, click the Apply button. The effect make take several minutes to apply (watch the little progress bar that appears above the image in the Clip View or Timeline).

NOTE

The settings you choose when adding the Ken Burns Effect to a photograph are used as the default for subsequent images you add. Because iMovie, by default, attempts to apply the Ken Burns Effect to everything, make sure that what it's doing is really what you want.

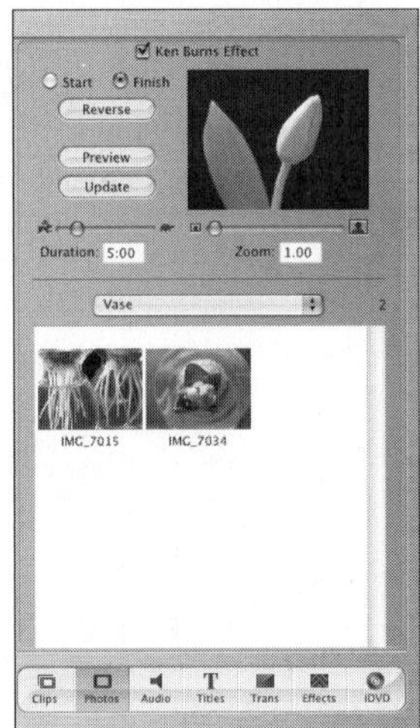

FIGURE 8.16 Set the finish point and zoom level to complete the transition.

Adding Photos Directly

You can easily add photos directly to iMovie by dragging the image files from your desktop into either the Clips shelf, the Clip View, or the Timeline.

So, what if you want to add photos directly, *and* use the Ken Burns Effect? If the settings for the Ken Burns Effect are already configured the way you want before you add your picture, you literally don't have to do anything. Just add your image and allow the Ken Burns Effect to automatically be applied. If, however, you want to customize the effect for the image you're adding, you must follow these steps:

1. Add the image by dragging it into iMovie.
2. Cancel the automatic application of the Ken Burns Effect by pressing Escape (Esc) or Command-..
3. Click on the image in the Clip Viewer or the Timeline to select it.
4. Switch to the Photos pane by clicking the Photos icon in the icon bar in the lower-right portion of the iMovie window.
5. The selected image appears in the Ken Burns Effect pane.
6. Choose the effect settings you want; then click Apply.
7. The Ken Burns Effect with your custom settings is applied to the image you've added to iMovie directly.

As you can see, working with the iPhoto integration is a much more straightforward means to managing images and applying the Ken Burns Effect. Hopefully Apple will clean up this process in the future and add a preference for the automatic application of the Ken Burns Effect. For now, however, you have to make sure that iMovie doesn't start adding effects where you don't want them.

Still Images from Video

One final source for still images is a video clip itself. iMovie makes it easy to create a still image from any frame in a video file. To do this, switch to the Timeline Viewer and drag the Playhead until the image that you want to use as a still appears within the main viewer. Next, choose Edit, Create Still Frame. iMovie adds a still image with a five second duration to the available iMovie Clips.

Still Images and Duration

A point of confusion when working with still images is the duration, and how duration can be changed. A still image that does not have the Ken Burns Effect applied is, by default, treated as a five second video clip. To change the length of time that it is displayed onscreen, simply double-click it within the Timeline or Clip View. A window, as shown in Figure 8.17, appears where you can manually enter how long the clip should last.

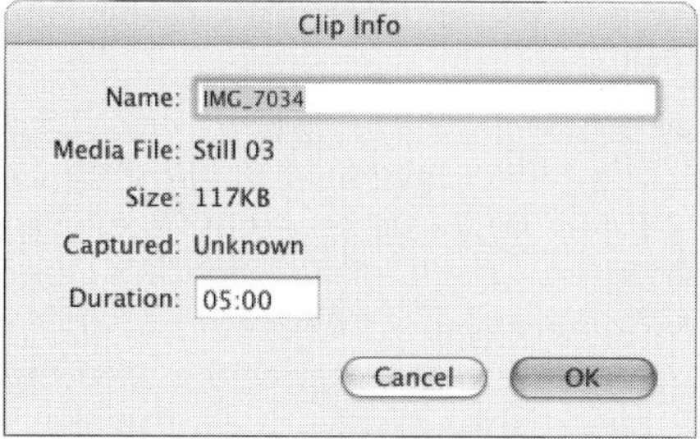

FIGURE 8.17 Change how long a still image is displayed.

The same, however, cannot be said for an image that has had the Ken Burns Effect applied. Double-clicking a Ken Burns image shows a noneditable duration.

The reason for this difference is that an image that has had the Ken Burns Effect applied to it is effectively a piece of video. It has different frames that iMovie calculated based on the settings you gave it. A "real" still image is just a single frame that iMovie understands it should display for a set length of time.

To change the duration of a Ken Burns Effect image, select the image within the Timeline or Clip View; then click the Photos button to switch to the Photos pane. The selected image is shown in the Ken Burns preview, and the settings used to create the image are loaded. Adjust the duration using the duration slider; then click the Update button to re-render the effect with the new duration.

Still Images, Effects, and Transitions

iMovie makes it simple to apply effects and transitions to images that you've added to your project. In fact, there is virtually no difference between working with still or Ken Burns Effect image clips and video clips. There are two specific situations, however, when you may be prompted to do something that isn't clear:

- Increase clip duration—Sometimes the length of a still image clip isn't long enough for a given transition (a wipe, fade, and so on) to be applied. In this case, iMovie tells you that the clip must be longer. All you need to do is adjust the duration (as discussed previously).
- Convert still clip to regular clips—Sometimes, when you apply an effect that changes over time—such as Earthquake, which makes each frame shift slightly to create a "shaking" appearance—iMovie states "This effect generates different results for each frame, which will not show up on Still Clips."

To apply the effect, iMovie must effectively change the still image into a video clip. Click the Convert button when prompted, and iMovie renders the effect. The only drawback to this is that, like an image with the Ken Burns Effect added, you won't be able to change the duration as you would with a normal still image. To revert to a normal still clip, you need to delete the converted clip and re-add the original image.

Audio

In an iMovie project, sound often plays almost as important a part as video. Sound and music can set the stage for a romance, suspense, comedy, or thriller. It can help create pacing for the movie and smooth through otherwise troublesome video transitions. When using iMovie to import and arrange movies from your camera, you've already got audio in your projects. Movie clips themselves can contain embedded sounds, and these are usually transferred and saved along with the movie files. Although this is convenient if you only want to use the sounds you've recorded with your camera, it doesn't give you the flexibility to mix sounds or add additional sounds to your movie.

Audio Tracks

To accommodate additional sound effects, iMovie includes two sound tracks that can hold any sound, music, or audio that want. There are a total of three available iMovie tracks: Video/Audio, Audio Track 1, and Audio Track 2. These are visible only in the Timeline Viewer.

There is no difference in functionality between the Audio 1 and 2 tracks. You can use one track to hold sound effects, the other for background music, or mix and match them as you choose. In addition, each track can overlap audio clips, allowing you almost limitless layers of audio. You could, for example, have a base piece of background music in Audio Track 1 and then perhaps an environment sound track layered on top of it, and, finally, sound effects layered on top of that in Audio Track 2. Figure 8.18 shows a layering possibility much like this scenario.

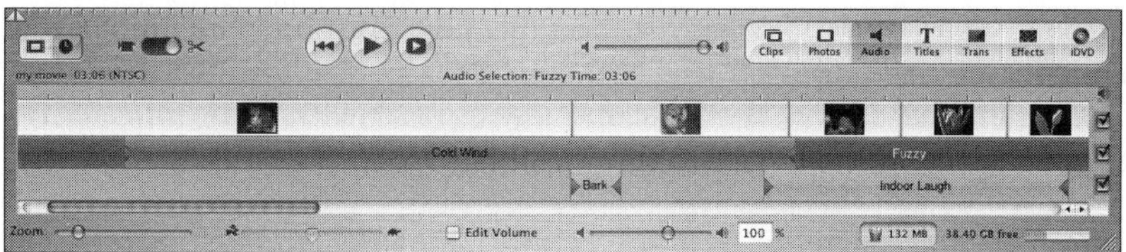

FIGURE 8.18 Audio can be layered via the different audio tracks, or within a single audio track.

NOTE

You've probably figured this out, but you must be in the Timeline view rather than the Clip View to see the available audio tracks.

Sounds that are added to either of the audio tracks can be moved to the other track by clicking and dragging between the tracks in the timeline. No matter what type of sound you're adding, it is referred to within iMovie as an "Audio Clip."

Audio Playback

However you've decided to layer your audio, iMovie automatically composites it correctly when you play back your movie project. If you've included audio clips in all the tracks, they'll automatically all play back when you play the movie.

Sometimes this can get to be a bit of a pain as you try to fine-tune your special effect sounds and don't want to hear the dialog from your video tracks, or the background music you've added. To enable you to focus on a single set of audio, Apple has provided the ability to control audio playback using the three check boxes to the right of the video and audio tracks, shown in Figure 8.19.

FIGURE 8.19 Turn on and off audio tracks to focus on a particular part of your sound editing.

You can also control the overall volume of the movie using the volume control slider to the right of the main playback controls.

Accessing the iTunes Music Library

There are a number of different ways to add audio to a project, so we'll start with one of the most common (and useful), then discuss how to work with audio clips that have been added to a timeline, and, finally, examine other means of importing audio.

Adding audio to an iMovie project takes place through the Audio pane, accessed by clicking the Audio button in the icon bar on the lower-right half of the screen. Figure 8.19 shows the iMovie window with the iTunes Audio pane active.

Your iTunes library is the default source for audio added to the project. You can use the pull-down menu at the top of the iTunes listing to choose between your iTunes playlists or type a few characters into the search field at the bottom of the song list to filter the songs that are shown.

TIP

When using the Search field to find your iTunes music, you'll notice that an "X" appears at the end of the field after you've typed in a few characters. Clicking the "X" clears out the search results and returns to the full list.

If you have a library of thousands of songs and can't remember which one you're looking for, you can choose a song from the list and then click the Play button underneath the list to listen to the song.

CAUTION

You must remember that using copyrighted material is *against the law*. Make sure that any songs you're using on a movie are public domain or properly licensed. If you're making the movie just for yourself, you can use music you own, but if the final product might be seen by others, you cannot distribute the copyrighted material.

After you've located the song file that you want to add to the iMovie project, position the Playhead where you want the sound to be inserted, click within the audio track that should receive the sound file, and then click the Place at Playhead button in the Audio pane. iMovie takes a few seconds (or minutes, depending on the length of the file), and then the corresponding audio clip appears in the selected audio track as a colored bar labeled with the name of the audio file.

TIP

In the shipping version of iMovie, there is no obvious means of telling which audio track is currently selected. The last track you clicked on is the one used for inserting audio.

If you happen to end up with audio inserted in the wrong track, simply click and drag the audio from one track to another.

Another, perhaps more elegant, way to add audio clips to the project is to drag a name from the list in the Audio pane to the audio track where it should be inserted. As you drag the name into the timeline, a yellow "insert" bar appears to show you where the audio will be inserted when you stop dragging.

You can even extend this technique to the Finder by dragging audio files directly from your desktop into the Timeline.

Manipulating Audio Within the iMovie

Sometimes you place a sound in a movie and it "just doesn't fit," or doesn't sync up with the video. To move an audio clip, click and drag it horizontally within the Timeline. The audio segment moves to any position you want within the project. While you are dragging, the Playhead automatically tracks the start position of the audio, enabling you to position it perfectly within the project.

TIP

For extremely fine control of audio positioning, click to select the audio clip in the Timeline (it darkens in color to show that it is selected), and then use the left and right arrow keys to move it frame by frame along the Timeline. Holding down the Shift key increases the movement to 10 frames at a time.

If you decide that you want to remove an audio clip from the project, simply click on it; then press Delete or choose Edit, Clear.

Locking Audio to a Video Clip Often the act of moving audio around is an attempt to synchronize it with a piece of video. iMovie's capability to position on a frame-by-frame basis makes this simple, but what if you decide later that you want to reposition the video clip? If you drag the video, all your hard work synchronizing the audio is lost.

To "lock" a piece of audio to the video track, select the audio that you've positioned where you want it; then choose Advanced, Lock Audio Clip at Playhead. The audio track is then "attached" to the video that occurs at the same place as the audio. Moving the video track within the timeline moves the audio as well, keeping your synchronization intact. You can tell that a lock is in place by graphical "pushpins" that appear on the audio and video tracks, as shown in Figure 8.20.

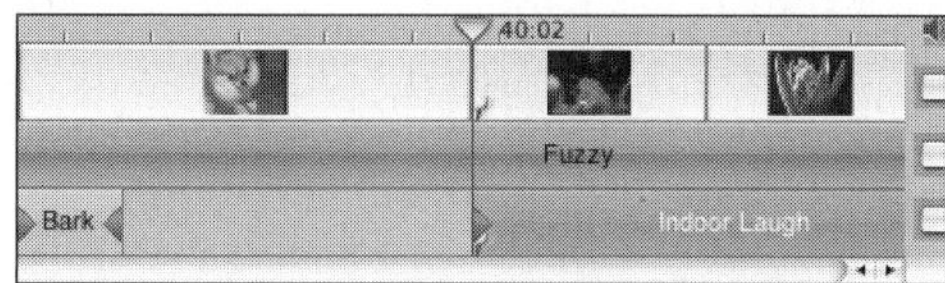

FIGURE 8.20 Pushpins denote an audio track that is locked to a video track.

To unlock an audio clip, select it within the audio track; then choose Advanced, Unlock Audio Clip.

CAUTION

Locking audio to a video clip works one way. It does not lock the video to audio. If you drag the video clip, the audio moves with it, but not vice versa. Dragging the audio simply repositions the lock to the video, potentially losing any synchronizing work you've done.

By default, all locked audio clips are displayed with the pushpins all the time. To change the display so that the pushpins are shown only when the audio clip is selected, check the Show Locked Audio Only When Selected option within the iMovie preferences.

Using Crop Markers Like video, audio clips also have crop markers that can be used to choose how much, or how little of a clip is played. These two arrows appear at the ends of an audio clip and can be dragged with the mouse to limit audio playback to a certain part of a sound, as demonstrated in Figure 8.21.

FIGURE 8.21 Drag the crop markers to limit what parts of the sound are played.

To completely crop (remove) the portions of the audio clip that aren't being played, mark off the appropriate portions with the crop markers and then choose Edit, Crop.

Adjusting Volume Suppose that you want soft background music in one portion of your movie, but want it to slowly build to a blaring orchestra in another? Before iMovie 3, the only way to do this was to edit the sound files in another audio program. Now, adjusting the volume is as simple as clicking and dragging.

To edit the volume editing mode, click the Edit Volume check box at the bottom of the iMovie window. Within a few seconds, all the audio clips (and the video clips that contain audio) display little lines through them. These lines represent the volume level of the clips.

To change the volume level of a clip, highlight the clip within any of the tracks (remember, even the video track's audio can be adjusted here); then click and drag the volume adjustment at the bottom of the iTunes window, or type a new volume level (100% being the "default" volume) into the field beside the volume slider. As you change the volume level, the line raises or lowers within the clip. Multiple clips can even be selected at once (Shift-click) and simultaneously be adjusted with this control.

You're thinking, "Okay, that's nice; but it still doesn't get me the fine-tuned control I need to really mix different audio clips together." Don't worry; volume adjustment can be as simple (as you've seen) or as complex (as you're about to see) as you want.

To alter the volume level within a specific part of an audio or video clip, click and drag the volume line within the clip. As you drag, an adjustment "handle" (a big yellow dot) appears. Dragging this dot up or down raises or lowers the volume at that point. To carry the volume change through to a different part of the clip, simply click wherever you want another volume adjustment handle to be added, and the level changes are carried through to that point.

Each handle that is added also carries with it a transition point that determines how the audio clip transitions to the new volume level (will it happen abruptly? smoothly?). The transition point is displayed as a small red/orange square to the right of the adjustment handle. The point can be dragged so that it is right above or below an adjustment handle, making for an immediate transition in volume, as shown in the Indoor Laugh sound in Figure 8.22.

FIGURE 8.22 Moving the transition point directly above or below the adjustment handle causes an immediate volume transition.

To smooth things out a bit, the transition point can be dragged all the way along the volume line up to another adjustment point. The transition then occurs all the way between these two points. For example, Figure 8.23 shows the same volume adjustment being made as in Figure 8.22, but the transition takes place over a much larger span of the audio clip.

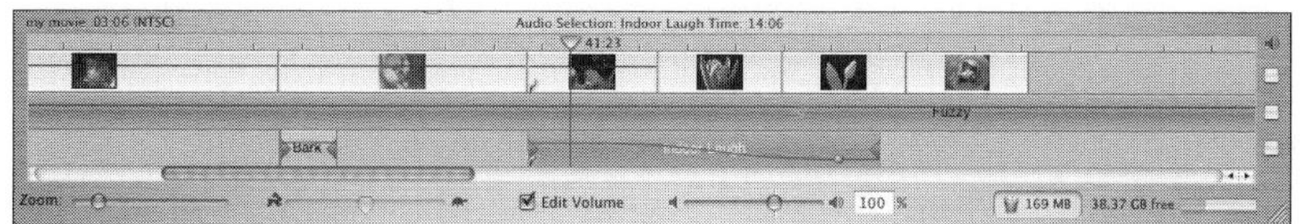

FIGURE 8.23 The transition point can be used to spread the volume transition out over a long span of the audio clip.

Volume adjustment can be used to ramp down an audio clip while ramping up another (similar to video transitions that blend the end of one clip with the beginning of another; this is called a *cross-fade*), or to create any number of other effects within your project.

Splitting Audio If you have a sound or song that you want to play part of at one time, and another part at another time, you have two choices: You can import the audio clip twice, or you can simply "split" the existing clip into different pieces and use them wherever you want. To split an audio clip, position the Playhead where you want the clip to break; then choose Edit, Split Audio Clip at Playhead.

New crop marks appear at the location of the split within the audio clip. You can use these markers to fine-tune the split location, as shown in the Indoor Laugh sound in Figure 8.24.

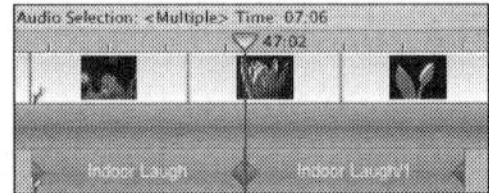

FIGURE 8.24 Using the split feature adds crop markers at the location of the Playhead.

To "finish" the split, you must choose Edit, Crop; otherwise, the split audio segments will still be attached to one another and won't be able to be moved separately.

Other iMovie Audio Sources

Now that you've learned how to work with audio clips in iMovie, let's take a quick look at the other sources of audio available for adding audio clips to your project. At the top of the Audio pane is a pop-up menu with additional choices for importing audio clips. As you've already seen, the iTunes Library and playlists are available .

iMovie Sound Effects A great source for canned sound effects is the included iMovie sound effects library, accessed by choosing iMovie Sound Effects from the top of the Audio pane in iMovie. The iMovie sound effects, shown in Figure 8.25, encompass a wide range of environmental and special effect sounds. The Skywalker Sound Effects (from George Lucas's Skywalker ranch) are high-quality effects that can be used to create an impressive sound track.

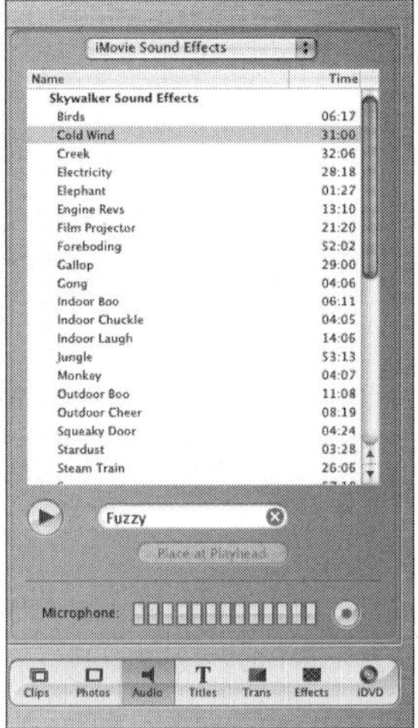

FIGURE 8.25 Choose from dozens of built-in sound effects.

Unlike iMovie music, you cannot click the Place at Playhead button to insert a selected sound effect (I can't imagine why not, but it doesn't work!). Instead, you must click and drag the name of an effect into your audio track. After it is added, it behaves like any other audio clip.

Audio CDs To add a sound track from an audio CD, put the CD in your computer's CD-ROM drive and then wait a few seconds. iMovie automatically switches to Audio CD mode, queries the Internet CD database to get a list of track names, and then displays the contents of the CD in the Audio palette.

Choose the song you want to add to one of your iMovie audio tracks; then either use the Place at Playhead button or drag the song to the Timeline to add it to the project.

Recording a Voice Track If you want to narrate a portion of the video, position the Playhead where you want to start recording from your computer's microphone and then click in the audio track that should receive the audio. Finally, click the red Record button to the right of the Microphone label at the bottom of the Audio pane. A graph of the level of sound input is shown beside the label as it records. To stop recording live audio, click the Record button again.

The new audio clips are added to your project with the sequential labels "Voice 1", "Voice 2", and so on.

Extracting Audio from Video Clips As already mentioned, the video track often also contains audio that accompanies a video clip. When adjusting volume, you can adjust the volume of a video clip just as you would an audio clip in an audio track.

Having video so closely tied to audio, however, has its disadvantages—you cannot manipulate the audio and video independently of one another. Thankfully, iMovie allows you to "decouple" the audio and video from one another. To do this, select a video clip with audio; then choose Advanced, Extract Audio. After a few seconds, the audio from the video clip appears in the audio track below the video clip. Figure 8.26 shows a video clip in the timeline before audio extraction, and Figure 8.27 shows the same clip after extraction.

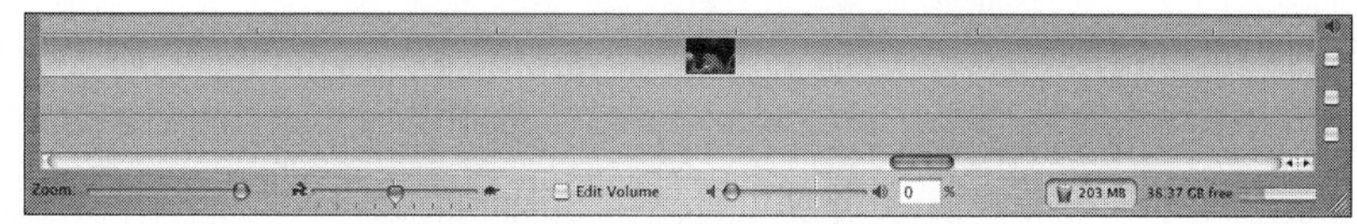

FIGURE 8.26 Normally, audio is embedded in the video clip...

FIGURE 8.27 ...but it can easily be extracted.

After audio is extracted from a video file, it can be manipulated like any other audio clip.

In some cases, audio extraction happens automatically. If, for example, you cut and paste a video clip using the Advanced, Paste Over at Playhead option, iMovie automatically extracts the audio of the original clip and moves it to an audio track so that it is not replaced by the paste over. The video clip that is pasted over is lost, but the audio remains.

This feature can be disabled by deselecting Extract Audio in Paste Over within the iMovie preferences .

TIP

iMovie has the capability to speed up or slow down video clips, as well as reverse their playback. These features do not work on audio clips. You can, however, apply the transformations to a video clip and then extract the audio, and the changes will carry with it.

Titles

The next pane, Titles (shown in Figure 8.28), is used to add text effects to your project. If you're looking for a way to add credits or an attractive animated splash screen to your project, this is where you'll get it done.

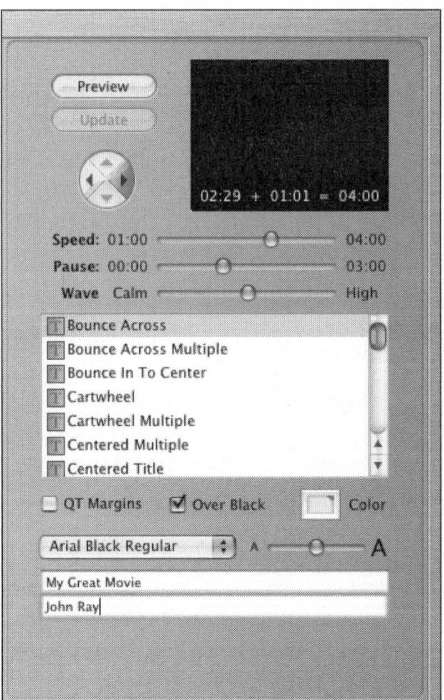

FIGURE 8.28 The Titles pane.

The Titles pane contains a scrolling list of text effects; controls for setting the text font, color, and size; and for adjusting the effects applied to the text.

There are two types of text effects you can add: normal and multiple. Normal effects operate on one or two lines of text—usually the title of your movie or some other single piece of information. Multiple-style effects allow you to set multiple pieces of information (such as all the actresses starring in your movie) to display on the screen. Obviously, if you're doing the credits to a movie with 100 stars, you would want to use a multiple effect rather than a set up different text effects for every single person.

NOTE

Some title effects support multiple pieces of information but aren't labeled with "Multiple" in their name. You'll just have to click through them to see.

Adding a Title

To add a title effect to a movie, first choose from the list of effects. In Figure 8.29, Gravity Multiple is selected. Next, enter your text in the fields at the bottom of the pane. Because this is a Multiple-style effect, "+" and "-" buttons can be used to add fields for more lines of text. You can adjust the text appearance using the font menu, font size slider, and color well.

FIGURE 8.29 A sample title.

Now use the circular arrow buttons at the top of the pane to choose which direction (if any) the title moves. Most effects feature motion—the Gravity effect, for example, has the letters appear to "fall" into place. Using the arrow buttons, you can choose whether they fall down, up, left, or right onto the screen. Use the Speed, Pause, and other sliders that may appear to adjust how fast the title effect plays and the length of time it pauses on your screen. Not all the sliders show for all of the effects, so it's likely that your screen will vary from what is shown here.

As you make changes to the title effect, the results are displayed repeatedly in the small preview area in the upper-right corner of the pane. The preview also displays a calculation of how long the title effect plays. To see a full-sized preview of the effect, click the Preview button.

Before adding the title to your project, you need to make two more choices: whether to use QT Margins and whether the title plays Over Black.

- Over Black—Controls whether the title effect is superimposed over video, or over a black background. If *unchecked,* the title appears over the video clip it precedes.
- QT Margins—When this is selected, it is assumed that QuickTime is the mode of playback—*not* a television. In this case, some of the text might not be visible on your TV screen. It's best just to leave this unchecked at all times.

Finally, after setting up your title effect, drag it from the scrolling list of effects to the Clip Viewer or Timeline Viewer to add it to your project. The title may take a few minutes to render, denoted by a small progress bar in the lower part of its block in the Clip/Timeline Viewer.

To update a title later, select it in one of the Project Viewers; then open the Titles pane. Choose your new settings and click Update. The title will need to re-render, but after it does, the new settings will be active.

Transitions

Transitions, the next action to explore, are one of the more "fun" aspects of iMovie. Transitions give you the ability to seamlessly blend one clip into another using fade-out/fade-in effects, dissolves, and more. Figure 8.30 shows the Transitions pane in iMovie.

Adding Transitions

Adding a transition is virtually identical to adding a title. Choose the effect from the scrolling list, choose a direction (if available) with the circular arrow controller, and set a speed. The preview in the upper-right corner of the pane refreshes with a demonstration of the transition as you make your selections. Click the Preview button to see a large preview of the transition effect.

Finally, drag the transition to a point between two clips in one of the Project Viewer panes. After a short rendering process, it will be visible within your movie.

FIGURE 8.30 The Transitions pane can be used to blend one clip into another.

> **NOTE**
>
> Transitions can also be applied to the beginning or end of your movie to provide a smooth transition from the black background.

Like titles, transitions can be updated by selecting them in the Project Viewer, opening the Transitions pane, making your changes, and then clicking the Update button.

Effects

Effects are exactly what you'd expect—special effects that you can add to your movie. Rather than moving to someplace where you suspect there will be an earthquake and repeatedly filming your scene trying to capture a shaking effect, you can simply apply an Earthquake effect using the Effects controls, shown in Figure 8.31.

Unlike titles and transitions, effects are applied to an entire clip. If you want to apply an effect to only a portion of a clip, you must use the Timeline Viewer and position the Playhead where you want the effect to start, and choose Edit, Split Video Clip at Playhead (Command-T). Next, position the Playhead where you want the effect to stop and repeat the split. This creates three separate clips from the original; you can safely apply the effect to the clip in the middle without modifying the other two.

Adding an Effect

To add an effect, select it from the list; then use the sliders at the bottom of the Effects pane to adjust the appearance. Unlike titles and transitions, almost every effect has slightly different configuration parameters. Fog, for instance, has sliders for controlling Amount, Wind, and Color, whereas Earthquake has settings for Sideways and Vertical shaking.

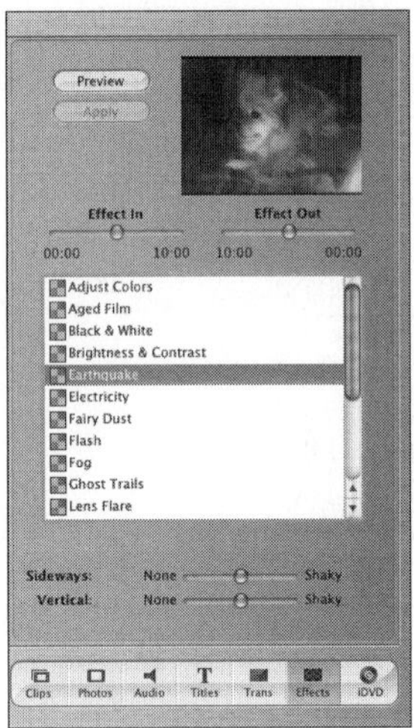

FIGURE 8.31 Apply special effects to your movies.

Some effects allow you to position them within the preview area in the upper-right corner of the pane. The lens flare, for instance, centers on wherever you click your mouse in the preview. Because it's easy to preview effects, you should click through the available options to get a feel for what they do and how they can be controlled.

When you've fine-tuned the effect to your liking, you can use the Effect In and Effect Out sliders to adjust how long it takes the effect to "fade in" and subsequently "fade out" of the clip. If both sliders are set to "00:00", for example, the effect appears instantly and disappears instantly at the end of the clip. By adjusting the sliders, you can more smoothly transition the effect into the clip.

Finally, click the Apply button to render the effect onto your video clip. Effects can take a long time to render, so be patient during this process.

iDVD

Distributing your iMovies on DVD is the ultimate goal of most users. You start by recording your footage digitally, editing in iMovie, and retaining the digital quality by going directly to DVD. iMovie makes creating DVDs simple by linking up with iDVD.

Although there is an Export To iDVD option in the File, Export dialog box, it is no longer necessary to export to iDVD because iMovie prepares projects for iDVD every time they are saved. You can still choose to "export" your project this way.

More directly, click the iDVD control button to open the iDVD pane, shown in Figure 8.32. Then click the Create iDVD Project button. It takes a moment for your movie to open in iDVD where you can customize the menus and add additional movies.

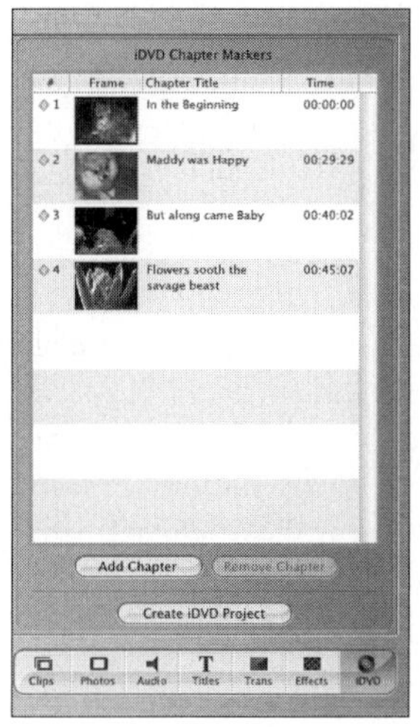

FIGURE 8.32 The iDVD controls link iMovie with iDVD.

Adding Chapter Markers Also within the iDVD pane is the option to add chapter markers to your project. Chapters allow you to segment your video project so that people viewing the completed DVD can skip straight to the part they want to see, just like on a commercial DVD. You know...like the scene where Free Willy jumps over the rock barrier...or maybe not.

Follow these steps to add chapters to an existing iMovie.

1. Open a finished iMovie project and make sure that you are in Timeline view.
2. Click on the iDVD button in the main iMovie window to display the iDVD palette.
3. In the Timeline Viewer, move the Playhead to the point in your movie at which you want to start a new chapter.
4. In the iDVD palette, click the Add Chapter button.
5. A row for the newly created chapter appears in the iDVD palette, where you can type in a Chapter Title.
6. A small yellow diamond appears in the Timeline Viewer to mark the location of chapters, as shown in Figure 8.33.

FIGURE 8.33 Chapter markers appear as yellow diamonds at the top of the Timeline.

7. You can repeat steps 4 through 6 until you've added up to 36 chapters to your iMovie.
8. Export the project to iDVD. Chapter markers are automatically retained.

Finishing Up

When you're satisfied with your movie (and assuming that you haven't used the iDVD Controls to open it in iDVD), you can prepare it for viewing in several different formats using File, Export. In addition to exporting it back to your camera, you can choose from several QuickTime options such as Email (small, high compression), CD-ROM (large, low compression), and Web Streaming (a "hinted" QuickTime movie ready to be streamed by Apple's QuickTime Streaming Server—`http://www.apple.com/quicktime/products/qtss/`).

Preferences

The iMovie preferences offer three areas to tweak the application:

- General—Choose whether you want iMovie to make a noise when it is finished exporting, whether it should use only short time codes, and whether new projects are created in the NTSC or PAL formats.
- Import—Choose to automatically start new clips at scene breaks (the default). This forces the start of a new clip when iMovie detects that the camera had started and stopped recording at a point on the videotape. Also choose where imported clips are added and the duration of any still clips. You can also choose whether clips are added only to the Clips pane (The clips "shelf"), or also to the Timeline Viewer—effectively building the movie as it is imported.
- Advanced—By default, pasting a video clip over another replaces the audio. Choose Extract Audio in Paste Over to keep the original clip's audio. You can also choose to Filter Audio from the camera and play back video clips on the Camera display as well as the iMovie window.

iDVD

High-end DVD authoring systems, such as Apple's DVD Studio Pro, can embed programmatic logic within DVD menus and adjust video stream encoding endlessly. For personal users, however, iDVD takes a more simplified approach to DVD creation that will seem immediately familiar to anyone who has created Web pages, used the old Apple HyperCard system, or even just filed documents in the Finder. There are four potential components to an iDVD-authored DVD:

- Folders (menu)—An iDVD folder (or "menu" in traditional DVD lingo) holds the different components that a user can access visually through his DVD player. If you have four different movies of your puppy chasing butterflies, you can create a folder with four buttons for each of the movies. You can also create additional folder items that lead to other video clips, and even other folders. Much as folders can be used to categorize documents on your computer, they can be used to organize the movies and images on your DVD.
- Movies—Most DVDs contain video—and presumably yours will too. iDVD can use almost any QuickTime movie on a DVD, except those in the MPEG1 format, or QuickTime VR and Flash animations. For the best results, however, you should use DV format video from a digital video camera. DV encoded files are produced by iMovie 2, so any iMovie 2 production is immediately iDVD-ready.
- Slideshows—iDVD contains a unique slideshow feature that enables users to add still images to their finished product. Slideshows can be driven automatically or manually, and can include an accompanying sound track.
- DVD-ROM files—Though not part of what most of us think of when we hear "DVD," DVD-ROM files can be included as a value-added feature of any iDVD production. DVD-ROM files are simply files that you can use on your computer, rather than watch on a DVD player. For example, you can include the actual images that make up an iDVD slideshow so that someone watching the DVD could pop it into his computer and copy the image files directly off for use as Desktop backgrounds, and so on.

Using these four iDVD components, you can create a home-grown DVD that rivals those that you can buy shrink-wrapped from your local video store.

Collecting Your Resources

To get started using iDVD, you first need a compatible Macintosh. At the time of this writing, a "compatible Macintosh" means a Mac with an Apple-supplied SuperDrive. Next, you need iDVD source material. This includes any images you want to use for slideshows, your DV movie files, and any files that you want to include on your DVD-ROM.

NOTE

As you'll learn shortly, iDVD allows you to change the backgrounds (and background sounds) of the different folders (menus) and buttons on your DVD. If you have additional movie, image, or sound files that you want to use to customize your iDVD project, you should collect them before starting.

iDVD automatically looks for audio in your iTunes library, photos in your iPhoto library, and movies in your home directory's Movies folder (`~/Movies`). If you already have your resources in these locations, you're in good shape.

NOTE

If you've exported from iMovie to iDVD, iDVD opens with all of your movie components already added. You can simply customize the appearance of the DVD (as described shortly) and burn.

Using iDVD

When you've found the components that you'll be using to build your DVD, open the iDVD application (path: `/Applications/iDVD 3/iDVD`). If this is the first time you've opened the application, it immediately prompts you to open an existing project, create a new project, or open the tutorial. If you have an existing project (including the tutorial) "in progress," it automatically opens that project—you must choose File, New Project (Command-N) from the menu to save the current project and start fresh.

Click the New Project button, choose a name and a location for your iDVD project, and finally, click Create. This remains the "active" iDVD project (even if you exit the application) until you manually start a new project.

CAUTION

The project name is used as the default label for the DVD that you create. Although it might seem appropriate to name the project file "My stupid client's DVD," keep in mind that unless you manually change the DVD label, the name might bite you later. The DVD's Disc name can be changed at any time by choosing Project, Project Info from the menu.

After your new project is started, the iDVD workspace appears as shown in Figure 8.34. This window provides a view of what will appear on your television screen when the DVD plays. If it doesn't look right here, it's not going to look right on the finished product.

Along the bottom of the window are the six primary controls that you'll use throughout creating your DVD:

- Customize—A DVD is more than just a collection of video clips; it is also an artistic medium for presenting those clips. Your DVD can have animated backgrounds that appear on the menu screens, animated buttons to play your video clips, and even a sound track that plays while the person viewing the CD navigates the menu options. Apple calls the collection of backgrounds, sounds, and buttons that you can use to customize your DVD a *theme*. The Customize button activates a Window tray containing the tools for selecting one of more than a dozen Apple-supplied themes, or customizing the DVD using your own media files. The theme, Theater, can be seen in Figure 8.34.
- Folder—Creates a new folder (or menu) on the DVD. After a folder is added, double-clicking it in the DVD workspace window takes you "inside" that folder, where you can then add other folders, video clips, slideshows, and so on.
- Slideshow—Adds a slideshow of your favorite image files to the current DVD menu.

- Motion—Many themes contain motion, such as animated folder backgrounds or animated buttons. Displaying all these animated items at once can slow down your computer. Click the Motion button to toggle Motion on and off within the iDVD workspace or choose Advanced, Motion (Command-M) from the menu.
- Preview—View the current DVD project as it will appear on your DVD player. The Preview button even opens a small DVD "remote" for controlling the DVD.
- Burn—Finalizes your iDVD project by burning it to a DVD-R. This is the last step you'll take in creating your DVD.

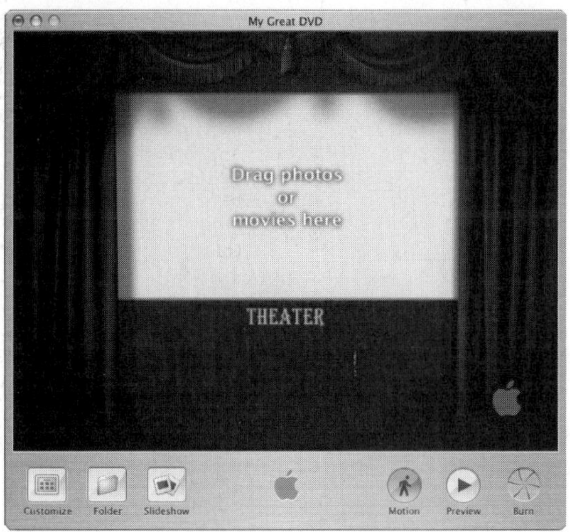

FIGURE 8.34 The iDVD workspace is surprisingly simple.

Adding to the iDVD Workspace

Your DVD project starts with a blank workspace. This is the top-level folder (menu) of your DVD—what the people viewing your DVD see when they first put the Disc into their player. Let's see what you can do to customize the workspace and how you can add your media elements to it.

Setting Screen (Menu) Titles and Backgrounds

Each folder has a title that is displayed as part of the screen background. The default title is set by the theme that you currently have selected. Figure 8.34 shows the Theater theme, and the default title is "Theater." To change the title, simply click the default text to select it and then start typing. Figure 8.35 shows the title editor in action.

At this point, you might be thinking, "Hey, I don't want a theater as my background; why bother editing the title if I don't like this theme?" Don't worry; the title is an element of the current folder (menu). No matter what theme you choose, it will still be there. It will change its size and appearance, but always be present (unless you remove all the title text!).

Many of Apple's newer themes, including Theater, include an area that prompts you to drag an image or movie to the area. This is called the *drop zone* and can be used to integrate your photo or movie into the background. To add an image/movie to this area, either drag a file from the Finder into the drop zone, or click the Customize button and use the button bar at the top of the window drawer to choose Photos or Movies. The Movies pane is active in Figure 8.36.

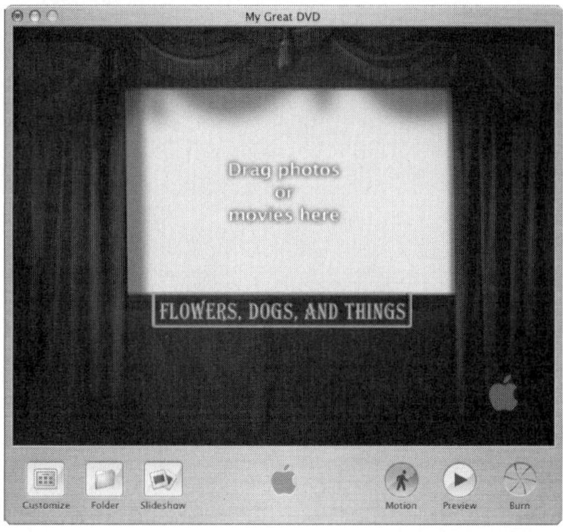

FIGURE 8.35 Click the title to select and edit it.

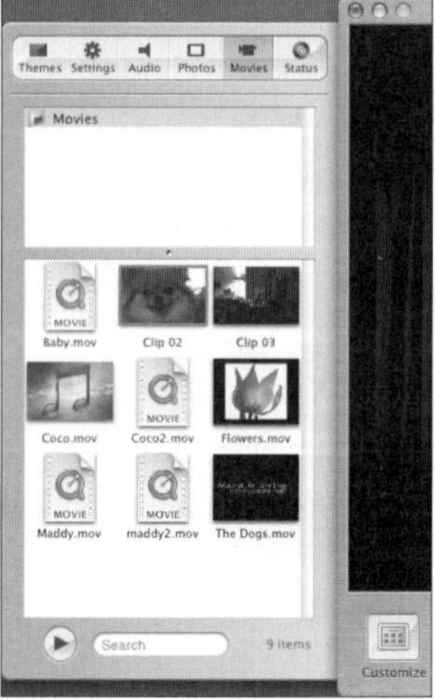

FIGURE 8.36 Choose a photo for the background.

TIP

By default, iDVD only searches for movies in the user's Movies folder. Additional folders can be added using the Movies pane of the application preferences.

Drag the thumbnail of the movie into the drop zone, and it is added to the background. If the movie or image is larger than the drop zone, you can click and drag inside the drop zone to move the visible area until what you want to see is onscreen.

You'll see more customization features shortly. This is just a taste.

TIP

You can hide the drop zones using the General pane of the application preferences.

Adding Movies

To add a movie to the current iDVD folder, drag its icon from your Finder window into the iDVD workspace, or from the Movies pane within the Customize drawer. iDVD adds a new movie button to your current folder (menu). When you're viewing your DVD, this is the button you click to watch your movie clip. The button is labeled with the same name as the movie file stored on your computer. To change the label, click the text in the workspace and then start typing.

In addition to changing a button's label, you can also change the background image of the button. Button backgrounds are only visible on some themes by default; this can be customized using the Settings pane in the customize drawer, which we'll see shortly. By default, any movie button that *does* have a background automatically plays the movie itself within the button! (You must have the Motion button enabled to see this effect.)

If you find this distracting, you can change the background to any still frame within the movie or to a shorter sequence of the video click. To do this, click the button in the workspace to highlight it. This displays a control area above the selected button, as shown in Figure 8.37.

FIGURE 8.37 Select a button to control its background.

Drag the slider handle from left to right to choose the "start point" for where the button motion will begin within the video clip. If you want to remove the motion altogether, uncheck the Movie check box. The video freezes, and you can use the slider to control the frame displayed in the button background.

You can add up to six buttons in a given folder including the default "parent" folder. If you want to add more, you must create folders (menus) to hold them.

Folders

Additional folders can be added to a DVD by clicking the Folder button at the bottom of the workspace, or by choosing Project, Add Folder (Shift-Command-N) from the menu. A new folder button named My Folder is added to the current workspace folder. Edit the folder button's label using the same technique as for a movie button. Figure 8.38 shows the iDVD workspace with two folders added—Coco and Maddy—and a movie button named My Two Dogs.

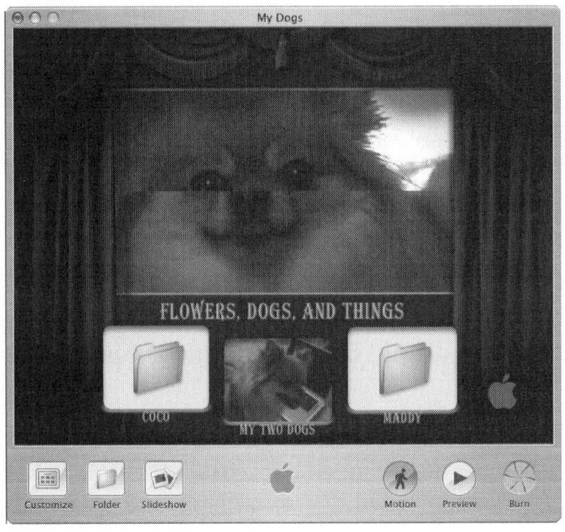

FIGURE 8.38 Folder buttons add new levels to your DVD.

You can immediately "open" a new folder by double-clicking its icon in the workspace. When you're inside a new folder, your screen shows a new empty workspace. You can edit the screen title of your new folder, drag new movie files into the workspace, or add more folders or slideshows. You'll also notice a small "return" arrow in the lower-left corner of the workspace. This arrow, shown in Figure 8.39, is an automatically added control that, when clicked either by you (in the workspace) or by your viewers (watching the DVD on their television), takes you to the previous folder. Think of it as providing the same function as the "back" arrow within the Finder window toolbars.

Like the movie buttons, folder buttons can also be customized. Clicking a folder button image selects the button and displays a control similar to the movie button, but without the movie check box. Dragging the slider switches the button's background between the first frame of all the movies that it contains.

FIGURE 8.39 Additional folder levels contain a "back" arrow to move to the previously visited folder (menu).

Slideshows

One final element that you can add to the iDVD workspace is a slideshow. Slideshows are exactly what they sound like—a group of still images that can be either manually or automatically viewed. To add a slideshow, click the Slideshow button at the bottom of the workspace window or choose Project, Add Slideshow (Command-L) from the menu. A new slideshow button named My Slideshow appears. You can customize the name of the slideshow button in the same manner as the folder and movie buttons.

To create the actual contents of the slideshow, double-click its button. The slideshow creation screen, shown in Figure 8.40, appears.

You can add images to the slideshow by selecting and dragging them to the slideshow editor window from either the Finder or the Photos pane in the Customize drawer. The easiest way is to use the Photos pane and drag in a specific photo album from the top of the pane. This adds the photos in the same order that you've arranged them in iPhoto, as shown in Figure 8.41.

You can rearrange photo ordering by click-dragging the entries within the list.

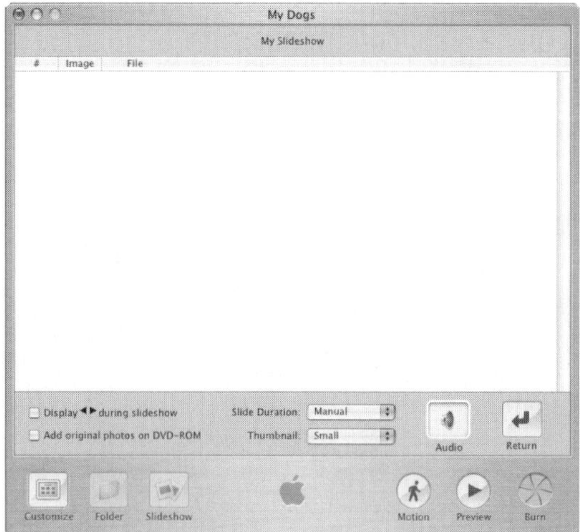

FIGURE 8.40 The slideshow features its own editor.

FIGURE 8.41 The easiest way to add photos is using the Photos pane.

TIP

Images are scaled to fit the resolution. For best results, make sure that your images are sized to 640×480 before adding them to the slideshow.

Near the bottom of the slideshow editor are a few options that you can use to customize how the slideshow will run and control the editor:

- Display <> During Slideshow—If this option is selected, iDVD adds arrow controls to move forward and backward during the slideshow. The arrows are superimposed over each of the slideshow icons in the editor window.
- Add Original Photos on DVD-ROM—Adds the actual photo files to the DVD so that they can be read on a computer.
- Audio—To add background music to the slideshow, drag a sound file from the Audio pane of the Customize drawer to the Audio well. If you want to use the audio from a movie, you can also drag movie files to the well and iDVD uses the first audio track from the movie as its sound track.
- Slide Duration—The length of time the slide is displayed onscreen. If this option is set to manual, the person viewing the slides must manually page between them. If you're accompanying your slideshow with music, choose the Fit to Audio option to time the slideshow to end with the sound track.
- Thumbnail—Choose the size of the image thumbnails that appear in the slideshow list.

After customizing your slideshow, click the Return button to return to the main iDVD workspace view. As a final step, you may want to change your slideshow button background. As with the other buttons we've looked at, just select the slideshow button and then use the slider to change the background to one of the images within the slideshow.

Button Backgrounds and Arrangement

You've seen three types of iDVD buttons (movies, folders, and slideshows) and three unique ways they can be customized, but iDVD's button background customization doesn't stop there: You can also add a static image as a button background by dragging an image from the Finder onto the button in the Workspace mode. Or, if you prefer, use a video clip as your button's background by dragging the movie file onto the button. This works for all three types of buttons and doesn't change what the button does when it is clicked. (That is, if you have an existing movie button playing its own video clip, dragging a new video clip to the button does not change what happens when the button is clicked, only what background the button displays.)

By default, the iDVD buttons arrange themselves (you can customize this with Themes, which you'll learn about in a few minutes). To change the position of a button, drag it on the screen. It will "snap to" one of the Theme's predetermined locations. To remove an existing button, highlight it and press the Delete key. The remaining buttons automatically rearrange to fill the empty space.

If you find that you've built a portion of your DVD (a folder containing movies, a movie, a slideshow, and so on), and you want to move it somewhere else on your DVD (into another folder), just use the Edit menu to cut the button from the existing location and paste it wherever you want. Cutting and pasting folders move the contents of the folder along with them.

Previewing

To preview how a DVD will look when it is finished, click the Preview button in the lower-right corner of the workspace. The workspace will "lock" and not allow any further changes until the Preview button is clicked again. At the same time, a DVD controller appears, as shown in Figure 8.42.

FIGURE 8.42 Use the iDVD controller to interact with the DVD.

Click the Menu button while playing a video clip to return to the current iDVD folder, or the Title button to move to the top folder.

The circular control in the button of the iDVD controller can be used to highlight and select buttons on the DVD, just like on a real DVD controller. Finally, the volume slider sets the sound level for the preview.

TIP

If you don't like using the controller, you can simply click the buttons within the iDVD window itself to navigate your project.

Click the Exit button on the controller or the Preview button in the iDVD window to exit preview mode.

Burning

The final step of creating a DVD is burning. To burn a DVD, click the Burn button and insert a DVD when prompted. Be sure to enable motion prior to clicking the Burn button. If motion is not enabled in iDVD, it will not be enabled in your final DVD product.

In some cases, you might notice that your DVD cannot be burned immediately. All video tracks on a DVD must first be encoded in the MPEG2 format. This is a processor-intensive activity that is likely to take a while. iDVD automatically starts encoding your movies as soon as they are added to the project, but if you're a fast worker, you might finish your project before it finishes encoding. If this happens, just wait, and it will quickly catch up.

NOTE

You can check on the encoding status of any video track using the Status pane of the Customize drawer. We'll take a look at this feature shortly.

After burning, your DVD is ready to use in your Macintosh, or a consumer DVD player. Almost all current DVD players support DVD-R playback, but if you're making a new DVD player purchase, you might want to check to be sure. Check `http://www.apple.com/dvd/compatibility/` for more information.

Advanced Customization

The iDVD application is so easy to use that even its advanced features are a breeze to master. There are a few more options that we'll take a look at now—most notably customizing themes. If you don't like your DVD's interface, this is where you can learn how to change it.

Choosing Themes

Themes can make a generic DVD into something that looks as if it came out of a professional development studio. Each folder within a DVD can contain its own theme. Apple ships iDVD with a number of predesigned themes that you can use "out of the box" or customize with your own graphics, fonts, and sounds. To switch to a new theme, click the Customize button at the bottom of the iDVD workspace. A window drawer appears with all your customization options. Click the Themes button to display the prebuilt themes, as shown in Figure 8.43.

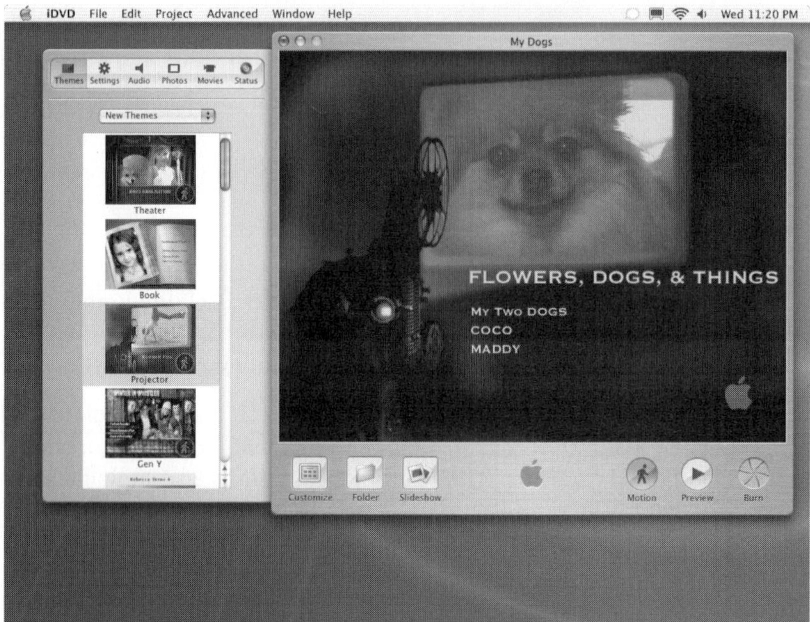

FIGURE 8.43 Choose from one of Apple's predesigned themes.

Use the menu at the top of the theme list to choose between displaying New, Old, All, or any Favorite customized themes you may have created. Some themes are denoted as Motion Themes because they contain background motion while waiting for the user to make a selection. Motion themes are set off in the theme list by a little "person" (motion) icon in the lower-right corner of the theme thumbnail. Clicking a theme thumbnail applies that theme to the current folder that you're viewing in the iDVD workspace—it does not change the themes of other folders. To change all the themes within folders under the current folder, choose Advanced, Apply Theme to Folders. To apply a theme to the entire project, use Advanced, Apply Theme.

Customizing Themes

If you don't like any of Apple's built-in themes, you can easily create one of your own. First, choose the theme that you like most from the theme list, and click the Settings button. Your screen refreshes and displays the theme Settings pane, as demonstrated in Figure 8.44. Here you can change almost all the attributes of a given theme.

Change any of the following settings to customize the appearance of the theme:

- Motion Duration—If you're using a theme with a motion background or animated (video clip) buttons, use the Motion Duration setting to choose how long the motion lasts (from 0 to 30 seconds) before it starts repeating. If your clips are longer than 30 seconds, they are truncated to this setting. This affects all onscreen motion, both background and buttons—they cannot be set separately.

- Background—Use the Background Image/Movie and Audio wells to customize the theme background. Drag a new movie to the well to create a new motion background, or an image to set a still background. Drag any audio file (including a movie with an audio track) to the audio well to set the background sound track. Because you can't have this pane *and* the Photos or Movies pane active simultaneously, it's easier to just use the drop zone discussed earlier in the chapter.
- Title—Control the positioning, font, color, and size of the theme's title text. The Font, Color, and Size attributes work as you would expect. The position setting provides several aesthetically pleasing presets, and a Custom option, which allows you to drag the title text anywhere you want within the screen.
- Button—The Button settings change the appearance (border, labels, and so on) of the onscreen folder, slideshow, and movie buttons. By default, the large rectangular button selector (at the top left of the button controls) is set to From Theme, which uses the button style from the theme you are customizing. Click the button selector to choose from several other button shapes and sizes. Use the Snap to Grid and Free Position settings to choose how the buttons are positioned onscreen. Finally, use the Position, Font, Color, and Size settings to control how the button labels are drawn onscreen.

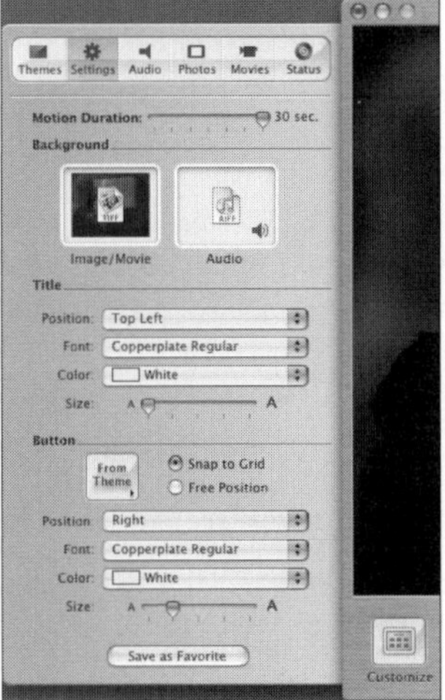

FIGURE 8.44 Use the Customize option to change a theme to your liking.

TIP

If you want no-text buttons, this option is available from the Position settings within the button customization controls.

When you've created a theme that you want to save, click the Save in Favorites button. iDVD prompts you for a theme name and gives you the option of sharing your theme with all iDVD users.

To apply the theme to your project, choose Advanced, Apply from the menu.

TIP

An easier way to customize the background audio for a theme is to drag a song file from the Audio pane of the Customize window drawer into the DVD preview screen—much like dragging an image into the drop zone. The background music changes instantly.

Status

The final element of the Customize drawer is the Status pane. This provides control over your DVD-ROM contents and lets you view how your movie encoding is progressing. At the top of the Status window is a display of how much time/space you have left on your DVD. As you add more files and movies to the DVD, the DVD icon fills to show your usage.

NOTE

By default, iDVD provides 60 minutes of recordable space per DVD. If you exceed this amount, it automatically switches to a lower quality (lower bit-rate) recording to fit up to 90 minutes of video.

The default status view is Encoder Status, set using the pop-up menu at the top of the display. The encoder status shows how far along each video clip is in MPEG2 encoding. A DVD cannot be burned until all video tracks are successfully encoded. Figure 8.45 shows the encoder status.

The second status display, DVD-ROM Contents, shown in Figure 8.46, is a display of all the files that will be added as DVD-ROM material to your finished DVD. You can drag and drop files and folders to the list to add them to the DVD-ROM. If you created a slideshow and used the Add to DVD-ROM option, it automatically appears in this pane.

To remove existing files, highlight them in the list and press the Delete key, or drag them to the Mac OS X trash. New folders can be created using the New Folder button at the bottom of the display. Folders can be renamed by double-clicking their name in the list; filenames cannot be changed after they have been added.

Project Info

If you move files around, iDVD may lose track of them. The Project Info window, accessed by choosing Project, Project Info from the menu (Command-I), displays a complete list of the files in use by your project, their paths, and a file status indicating whether there were any problems reading the file. In addition, the Project Info window provides the only place where you can change your DVD Disc's label. Be aware that no spaces are allowed in DVD volume names—any that you enter are converted to the underscore (_) character automatically by iDVD.

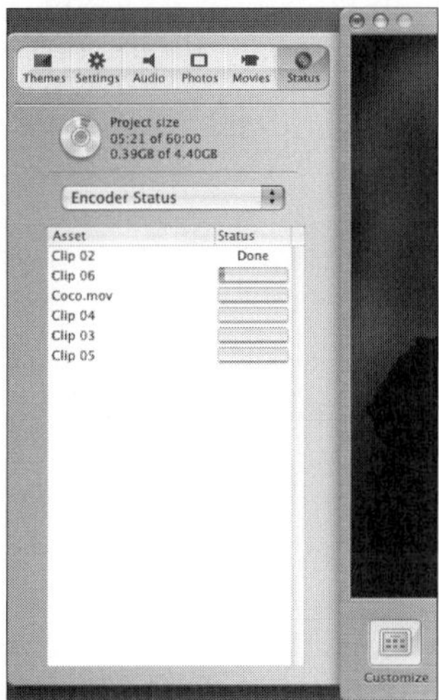

FIGURE 8.45 Check the encoding status of your video clips.

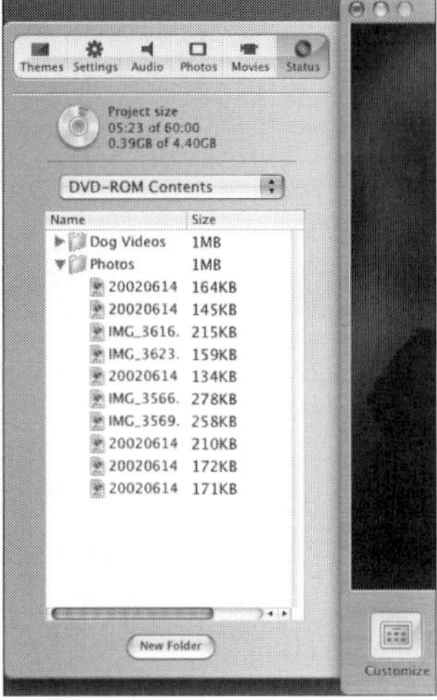

FIGURE 8.46 Add or remove DVD-ROM contents in the status area.

TV Safe Area

Not all TVs are created equal. Many conventional televisions (nondigital) suffer from overscan, in which portions of the image are "lost" off the edges of the screen. iDVD can provide a visual representation of what "may be lost" from your DVD by turning on the Show TV Safe Area (Command-T) in the Advanced menu. This drags a border around the workspace that should be considered "unsafe" for important content. If, for example, you've customized a theme, and your buttons and title fall within the bordered area, you might want to reconsider the positioning.

NOTE

Apple has been liberal with its TV Safe Area. It should be considered a worst-case display of your DVD. Most modern televisions do not suffer from the same overscan issues as older sets and provide controls for positioning onscreen images.

Preferences

The final controls for iDVD are the preferences, found under the iDVD application menu. Use the General Settings, shown in Figure 8.47, to control whether drop zones are visible onscreen, whether an Apple logo is superimposed on the project, whether MPEG2 encoding should take place in the background, and, finally, whether the MPEG2 encoded ("rendered") files are deleted after a project is closed.

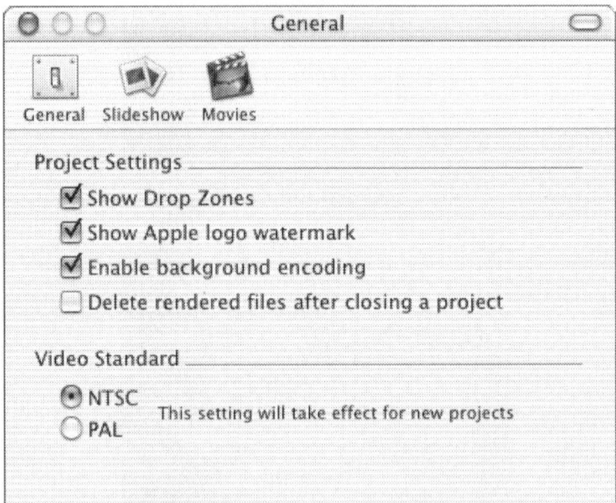

FIGURE 8.47 A few final settings for iDVD can be found in the preferences.

The Video Standard setting can be used to choose NTSC or PAL output for the final DVD. You must choose between NTSC or PAL before starting a project—you cannot convert your project on-the-fly.

The Slideshow Settings pane provides global control over whether slideshows are always added to the DVD-ROM (remember, you can choose this on a per-slideshow basis when setting up your show) and whether slides should be scaled to the TV-safe area.

Finally, the Movies pane allows you to shut off chapter marker submenus (automatically added by iDVD when importing an iMovie with chapter markers), or have iDVD prompt to confirm that it should import the markers. In this pane you can also set the location where iDVD searches for movie files to be added to the Movies pane of the Customize drawer.

Summary

This chapter covered a lot of ground, from viewing online movies with QuickTime to using iMovie to create movies, complete with special effects, to creating your own DVDs. All this functionality is included with your Mac OS X computer, or available as a free download from Apple's Web site. Mac OS X is fully equipped to be a multimedia powerhouse without needing to spend a dime on additional software.

PART III

User-Level OS X Configuration

IN THIS PART

CHAPTER 9

Network Setup

IN THIS CHAPTER

- TCP/IP
- The Network Preferences Pane
- AppleTalk
- The Sharing Control Pane
- Connecting to Remote Servers
- Managing Locations
- Testing Network Settings

Unix, as a rule, is happiest when it gets to run as an always-on, always-network-connected operating system. Unix machines tend to run continuously (talking to other machines via the network) for months or years at a time, and the underpinnings of the networking system are designed for this mode of operation. Surprisingly, Apple has managed to pin a reasonable facsimile of the Mac OS as-needed picture of networking at the user level, onto the Unix networking framework. You already learned how to set up basic networking functions during the install process. In later chapters, you'll learn how this was accomplished at the Unix level, and how to perform even more sophisticated network tricks at the command line. In this chapter, we'll cover some of the networking technologies available, the GUI network controls, and, as a bit of network troubleshooting, we'll use the Network Utility tool.

TCP/IP

TCP/IP, the acronym that has become a de facto name for a network communications protocol, stands for Transmission Control Protocol/Internet Protocol. TCP/IP has become so ubiquitous that many think of it, not just as a communications protocol, but as the *only* network communications protocol. Although not the only protocol out there (AppleTalk, covered later in this chapter is one of the others), TCP/IP has proven flexible enough to support different types of data with a large range of requirements for delivery, timing, and reliability.

Basically, the TCP/IP protocol can be thought of as specifying the manner in which pieces of data should be transferred between two machines. This protocol includes the notion that the transmission of data can be broken down into a number of separate and abstract layers. Figure 9.1 shows the

TCP/IP protocol stack, the conceptual breakdown of the protocol into layers. This is commonly referred to as the OSI (Open Systems Interconnect) model of networking. Because the functions of the layers are conceptually separate, the manner in which the function of any layer is accomplished does not matter, as long as it cooperates with the layers above and below it in the manners that they expect.

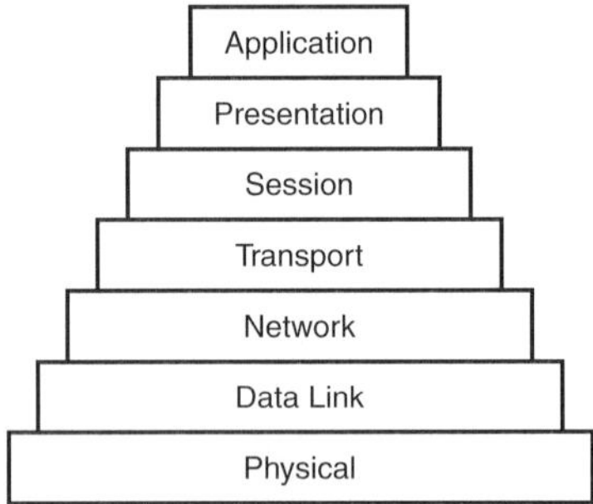

FIGURE 9.1 The OSI network model, on which the TCP/IP stack is built.

For example, it doesn't matter whether the physical layer is carried by twisted-pair Ethernet cabling, radio waves, or even with data written on slips of paper and handed back-and-forth between people sitting at terminals. As long as the data transmitted by the Physical layer gets retrieved from or inserted into data structures correctly at the Data Link layer, the rest of the TCP/IP stack functions identically.

This separation of functionality into independent and abstract pieces is typical of Unix technologies and allows the TCP/IP protocol to handle the transmission of a wide range of data types. Whether the data is equipment control where real-time transmission is critically important, or financial transactions where security and error-free transmissions are more important than speed, it is likely that the data can be fit into the TCP/IP model.

Going forward in the chapter, there are several TCP/IP-related terms you should be familiar with. These items define your connection to the Internet:

- IP address—The address that uniquely identifies your computer on the Internet. An IP address is typically represented in the form `###.###.###.###`, such as `192.168.0.1`. An IP address is assigned either by your network administrator or automatically via a DHCP or BOOTP server.

  The IP address shown in the preceding paragraph is for the IPv4 protocol (Internet Protocol Version 4). This protocol uses a 32-bit address space and has been around for the last 20 years. As the popularity of the Internet increases, the number of addresses available in the IPv4 address space decreases. To address the impending address shortage, NAT (Network Address Translation) is regularly implemented in businesses and at home. This creates a private internal network that uses addresses that the IPv4 protocol has already specified are acceptable to use for this purpose, whereas another machine with NAT software, or a NAT hardware device, has a unique IP that the outside world recognizes and handles the negotiations between the outside world and the private network. The dynamic IP addresses that your ISP serves also assist with coping with the address shortage, by providing addresses for machines as they need them, rather than uniquely assigning an IP address for each customer's machine.

To also help fix this address space shortage, the IETF (Internet Engineering Task Force) has introduced the next version of the Internet Protocol, IPv6 (Internet Protocol Version 6). IPv6 uses a 128-bit address space, vastly increasing the number of addresses available. Additionally, it provides some improvements in routing and network configuration. It is expected that IPv4 and IPv6 will coexist for many years as the Internet transitions from one protocol to the other.

- Hostname—Typically, a hostname simply refers to the network name of your computer. Some people might use the term hostname to refer to the FQDN (fully qualified domain name) as well. This is the entire Internet name of your machine as registered with a DNS server, such as `www.poisontooth.com`. If you have a name registered with a DNS, your machine will use this as the hostname; otherwise, it will use the name configured as your Computer Name (from Sharing Preferences) by default. The default can be overridden by changing the *`HOSTNAME`* entry in `/etc/hostconfig` to whatever name you'd prefer your machine to use. If you have a name registered with a DNS, this name should be used because a number of important networking features will not work properly if this value appears to be misconfigured.
- Subnet mask—Similar in appearance to an IP address, a subnet mask tells your computer which part of the IP address identifies the network it is on, and which is the individual computer. Most users will be part of a class C network with the subnet mask `255.255.255.0`. The last segment of the IP address identifies the computer, whereas the first three segments identify the network.
- Gateway/router address—The gateway address is an IP address of a network device that connects your local network to the rest of the Internet. A gateway handles any necessary translation between different types of networking media.
- DNS—Domain Name Servers are Internet servers that provide translation between IP addresses and fully qualified domain names. Each request for a machine using its FQDN requires an interaction with a DNS before a connection can take place.
- Network interface—The device that connects your computer to the network. This can be an Ethernet port, AirPort card, and so on. Some computers might have multiple network interfaces. Mac OS X names its interfaces sequentially. The `en0` interface is built-in Ethernet, and `en1` is typically AirPort.

In addition to the canonical TCP/IP terms common to all Unix networking configurations, it will be helpful to know a few Apple-specific networking terms for discussion and comparison:

- AppleTalk—AppleTalk is a network protocol with goals similar to those of TCP/IP but designed for less general-use applications, and with features to make it more friendly to nonexpert users. Instead of requiring each computer to have an assigned, distinct identification number, AppleTalk was designed to allow each computer to independently choose its own identification number, and to advertise its identification, and services that it provided to the network. With only normal TCP/IP network methods, there is no convenient way for one computer to discover that another provides a service (such as a shared printer). The reason is that, although the service may be provided, there isn't any networkwide broadcast of this information. To use a remote printer in this networking model, you need to know the TCP/IP address of the machine to contact regarding the use of the printer. AppleTalk overcame this problem by each computer continuously and repeatedly advertising all the services it provided, but this results in continuous traffic on your network. Because of this, it is usually limited to local networks only, because you probably don't want to know about all the printers available on Macs all across the country.
- Computer Name—In the AppleTalk world, each computer can claim a name for itself and advertise this on the network. The names do not have to be different. This value is configured through the Sharing control pane, or manually through the `/etc/hostconfig` file.
- Rendezvous—Rendezvous is an Apple product based on the Zeroconf project (`http://www.zeroconf.org`, a project of the Internet Engineering Task Force, `http://www.ietf.org`). Zeroconf is an attempt to provide AppleTalk-like networking simplicity with TCP/IP networking services. Although the ultimate goal of Zeroconf is fully automated network configuration, with Mac OS 10.2, Apple began promoting Rendezvous (née Zeroconf) as a service-discovery protocol carried over TCP/IP. This provides an open-API method for computers to communicate in a manufacturer-agnostic manner about services that they provide or require. Using Rendezvous services is as simple as using the Rendezvous Computer Name as an URL in a Web browser.
- Rendezvous Computer Name—Yet another name for your computer. This parameter, also configurable through the Sharing pane, defaults to a value similar (excluding illegal characters) to your Computer Name, with `.local` appended. The Rendezvous Computer Name, also called your Local Hostname is used by your computer when advertising services to the network, and when trying to connect to your computer from others that want to use services you provide. The Rendezvous Computer Name is also used, possibly incorrectly, in a number of other networking contexts, such as the name that Postfix (see Chapter 29, "Creating a Mail Server")attempts to report for the machine. See Chapter 29 for more information on Sendmail.

Using these pieces of information, you can configure your computer to access the Internet. Although most dial-in accounts automatically set these parameters for you, users connecting directly to a network via Ethernet or AirPort need to know the appropriate settings for their network to continue.

If you want more information on the TCP/IP protocol and its use, I recommend *Special Edition Using TCP/IP* (ISBN: 0789718979).

The Network Preferences Pane

The Network control pane, already introduced during the installation, is the GUI brain center of the OS X interface to TCP/IP. This control pane, in actuality, just provides a series of hints to the underlying Unix TCP/IP control software, but it does so in a much prettier, and often more convenient, fashion than twiddling configuration parameters at the command line. The primary control with which you should familiarize yourself is the Configuration menu. In previous versions of Mac OS, various portions of the networking software were configured by separate control panes, and each pane was controlled by its own independent saved configuration setting. Mac OS X has instead placed all network configurations under a single parent control pane, with an umbrella configuration setting that covers TCP/IP, modem control, AppleTalk, and location settings.

The two main options in this pane are the Location and Show options. Location can be set to Automatic, New Location, Edit Locations, and any locations that you've already created. What appears by default under the Show menu varies with your system's hardware. Options include Network Status, Internal Modem (dial-up connection, if you have a modem), IrDA modem (infrared port, if you have this interface), Built-in Ethernet, AirPort (if your machine has an AirPort), and Network Port Configurations. The collection of these that are visible to you may also be modified by enabling and disabling each connection type on a per-location basis.

Available to each subpane are Assist Me and Apply Now options as well as the Help Viewer. The Assist Me option takes you directly to the Network Assistant. In the expectation that the Network Status pane is one that you will want to regularly access, it appears at the top row of the System Preferences. Also note that this System Preference requires administrative access to change.

The Network Status Subpane

This subpane shows you the status of your network ports. For an active network port, you can see such information as your machine's current IP address. Additionally you can select a network port here, and configure it or connect using it. Figure 9.2 shows the Network Status subpane for a PowerBook. The appearance of this subpane varies with your hardware and what hardware you have disabled.

FIGURE 9.2 The Network Status subpane of the Network control pane.

The Network Port Configurations Subpane

Most of the available selections in the Show menu switch between subpane groups specifying configurations for particular network interfaces. The Network Port Configurations subpane doesn't provide network configuration but allows you to enable and disable already existing configurations for the interfaces and create new configuration sets. Figure 9.3 shows the Network Port Configurations subpane of the Network control pane. OS X, to make network configuration as easy as possible, attempts to automatically detect and select the correct network configuration for any given situation. This convenience comes at a slight cost in startup time, so unless you actually intend to use all the available configurations, we don't recommend leaving all the configurations enabled as shown in Figure 9.3.

If you've already experimented enough to find the location settings and mastered the ability to switch between them, the capability to save multiple configurations for a single interface assigned to the same "location" might seem redundant. It becomes useful, however, in situations where you have multiple IP addresses at the same conceptual location, on a single network interface. Without requiring you to iterate through different location settings, setting up several different configurations would allow the system to automatically search through each until it found a working set of parameters. This might occur if you have multiple in-building networks with different IP ranges on each, but with each connected to share resources.

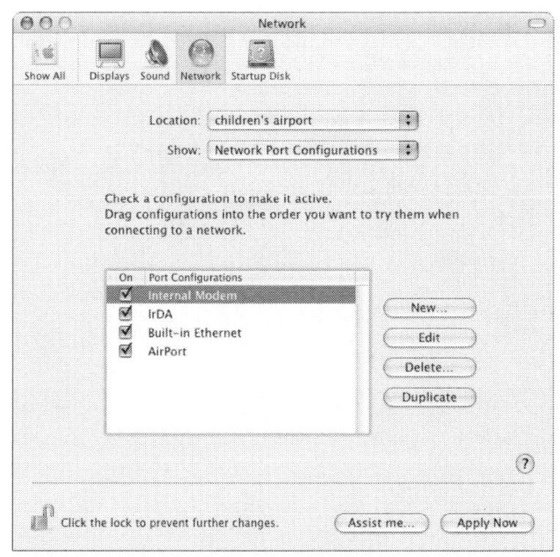

FIGURE 9.3 The Network Port Configurations subpane of the Network control pane.

Another possible use is if you have a number of different dial-up service providers and want your machine to try each until it finds an open one.

Ethernet

If you are connected to your network via an Ethernet connection (a physical chunk of wire, typically twisted pair, which looks like a bulky phone cable), you need to configure your connection under the Ethernet configuration option. Because switching from one physical transport to another requires only changing a little bit in a few protocol layers, it's similar to dial-up configurations you've already seen.

Under the TCP/IP subpane, by default you have the option to configure IPv4 and/or IPv6. Generally, you have the option of providing manual configuration settings or of getting your configuration parameters from a server. For IPv4, what you will most likely be using, you can configure your Ethernet port manually, using DHCP with a manual address, using DHCP, or using BootP, or you can turn it off. For IPv6, you can configure automatically or manually, or you can turn it off.

Under the TCP/IP subpane, shown in Figure 9.4, you can configure how your TCP/IP stack gets its control and configuration information. The manual configuration settings for IPv4, shown in Figure 9.4, allow you to configure individual options by hand.

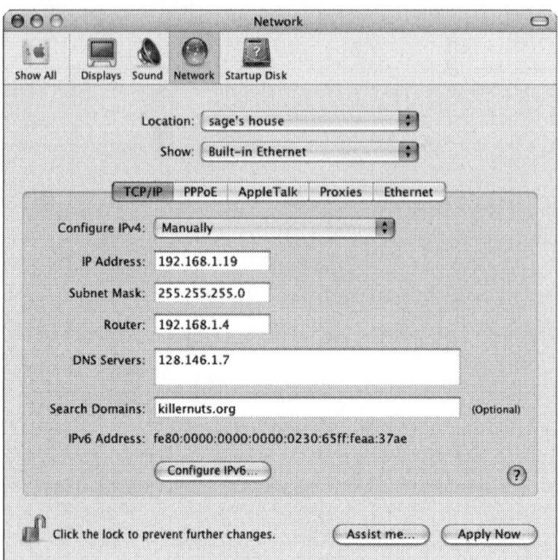

FIGURE 9.4 The TCP/IP subpane, showing available options for the Built-in Ethernet configuration set.

If you need to provide manual configuration information for IPv4, you need to know and fill in the following information—you should be able to get this information from your network administrator:

- IP Address—Your computer's IP address. This should be four sets of digits, separated by periods, such as `192.168.1.19`.
- Subnet Mask—This should be four sets of numbers separated by periods, as well. Most likely it will be `255.255.255.0` or `255.255.0.0`.
- Router—The machine that your machine must contact to reach the outside network world. This will frequently (but not always) be similar to your IP address, only with the final number replaced by a `1`. Your network administrator might also call this machine a gateway.
- DNS— (Domain Name Servers) The IP addresses of machines that translate between IP addresses and fully qualified domain names (FQDNs), such as `www.apple.com`.
- Search Domains—Partial domain names to append to machine names, if you give less than an FQDN. For example, you might frequently work with machines on the domains `macosxunleashed.com` and `apple.com`. If you want your machine to try to connect to `info.macosxunleashed.com` or `info.apple.com` whenever you ask it to connect to `info`, you can enter the domains here. Your machine will try them both when it discovers that you've asked for a name that does not resolve as an FQDN.

This section automatically displays an IPv6 address for your machine, but you can choose to automatically or manually configure it. If you need to provide manual information for

IPv6, you need to be able to manually fill in the IP address, the router, and the prefix. Get this information from your network administrator and write it down carefully.

TIP

Although essentially identical TCP/IP and other subpanes are available under this and other configurations, the settings entered in each are specific to the interface configuration set in which they are entered. Information entered in one interface configuration set does not automatically become the default information for any other interface. Therefore, you might need to enter such things as proxies, for example, in more than one place, depending on how your network is set up.

As mentioned earlier, TCP/IP is just one of a number of communications protocols. It's actually possible to run multiple communications protocols over the same piece of wire at the same time. In a clever use of this capability, it's possible to establish a PPP connection via Ethernet wiring rather than a phone line. If your service provider gives you this option, you can configure it with the subpane shown in Figure 9.5. The options available in this subpane are exactly analogous to the options under the dial-in PPP configuration. Here you can also choose to show the PPPoE status in the menu bar.

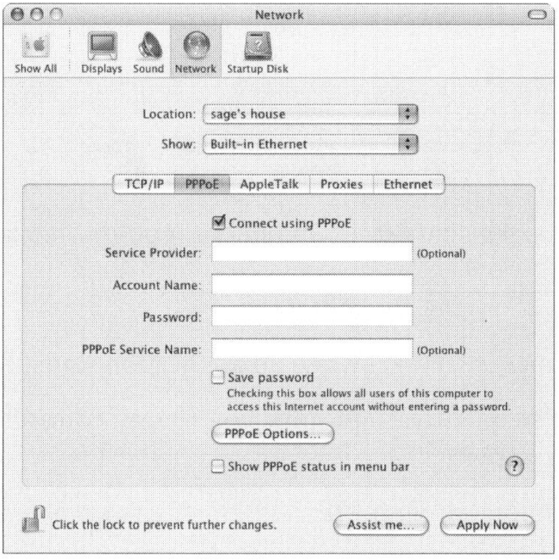

FIGURE 9.5 The PPPoE subpane of the Ethernet configuration set.

In this subpane, you have the following fields to fill in:

- Service Provider—An informational field similar to the service provider field for a dial-in connection.
- Account Name—The user or account name for your PPPoE ISP.
- Password—The password for your account.

- PPPoE Service Name—Another informational field.
- Save Password—Again, if you want this account to function automatically without needing to specify a password at each network connection, select this option.

The PPPoE subpane has a number of advanced options that can be configured from a drop-down pane that appears when the PPPoE Options button is clicked. Shown in Figure 9.6, these options allow you to configure the behavior of your PPPoE connection.

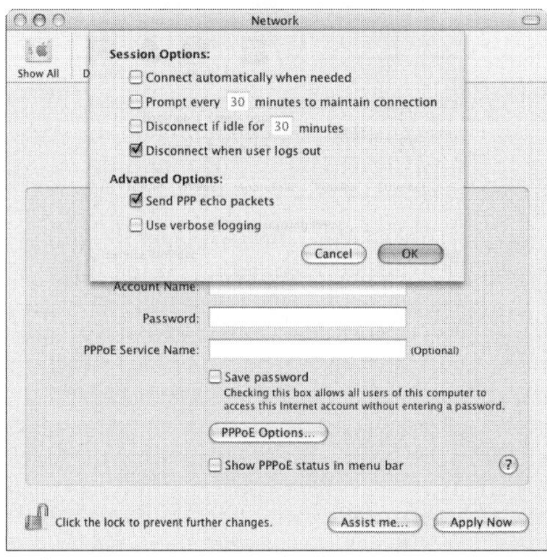

FIGURE 9.6 The PPPoE Session and Advanced options drop-down pane for the PPPoE subpane.

The pane enables you to configure the following:

- Whether to automatically connect when an application starts that needs TCP/IP services.
- Whether, and how frequently, to prompt you to stay connected, if there hasn't been any recent network activity.
- How long to wait before disconnecting when there's no network activity.
- Whether to disconnect when there's no user logged in on the console.
- Whether to send PPP echo packets. Some ISPs periodically send little "are you really there?" messages to connected computers to make sure that everything is working properly—this option controls whether to respond. Unless you have been told by your ISP to do otherwise, leave this option checked.
- The verbose logging option increases the amount of information regarding dial-up connections stored in the system logs.

If you're on a network segment where you must connect to proxy servers instead of directly to outside services such as FTP and Web servers, the Proxies subpane is the place to tell the system about the proxies. Shown in Figure 9.7, the Proxies subpane allows you to select what is needed and how to contact the proxy types. This pane is identical to the Modem, Ethernet, and AirPort configuration sets.

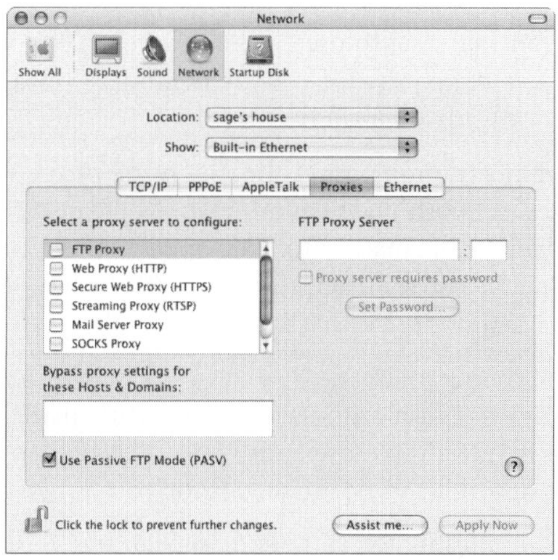

FIGURE 9.7 The Proxies subpane of the Ethernet configuration option.

The Proxies submenu proxy types are

- FTP Proxy—If you need to contact a proxy to use FTP, enter its IP address and the proxy port here.
- Web Proxy (HTTP)—Configure this if you need to go through a proxy to access the Web. There are occasions where you might want to use a Web proxy even if you don't have to. For example, if you want to make your server connections anonymous by going through one of the Web's anonymous proxy servers.
- Secure Web Proxy (HTTPS)—If you need to go through a secure proxy to access the Web, configure this option.
- Streaming Proxy (RTSP)—Most types of proxy setups are designed to prevent a remote host from having any chance of connecting back to your machine. This makes it difficult for streaming services that need to send a lot of data as quickly as possible; hence, a specific proxy type for streaming data. If you're behind a firewall, you probably need to configure this—if your network services allow streaming data through at all.

- Mail Server Proxy—If your ISP provides a proxy server for mail access, configure this option.
- SOCKS Firewall—The SOCKS firewall system can be used to proxy for a number of different network services. If your network uses a SOCKS-type firewall, enter its information here.

You can also configure your machine to use PASV (passive) FTP mode for transferring data, an option that will probably be required if you are behind a firewall, or on a NAT (network address translation) private local network.

Finally, you can configure hosts and domains in which the proxy settings should be ignored. If you contact servers both inside and outside your local firewall, you might want to provide your local network information for this option. Therefore, your machine doesn't need to contact the proxy and then reconnect inside your local network for interior connections.

Shown in Figure 9.8, the Ethernet subpane displays your machine's Ethernet ID and allows you to configure the hardware either automatically or manually. Unless told otherwise by your network administrator, always choose automatically. Choosing the wrong settings manually can cause a lot of unnecessary headaches for you.

As mentioned previously, AppleTalk is a different communications protocol that is independent of TCP/IP, so this pane will be covered in a section dedicated to AppleTalk later in this chapter.

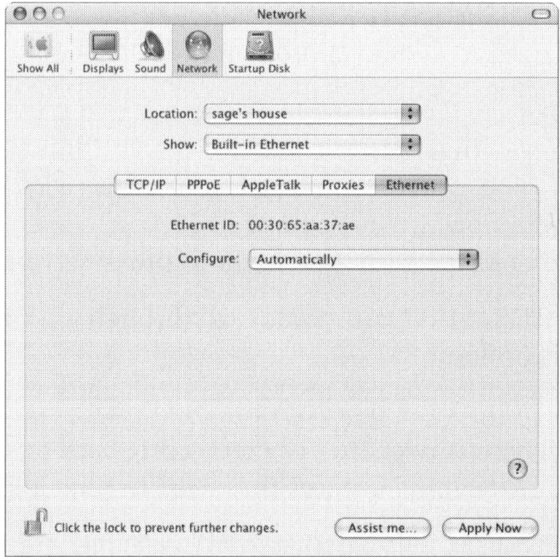

FIGURE 9.8 The Ethernet subpane of the Ethernet configuration option.

Internal Modem

Under the Internal Modem option of the Show menu, you can configure the settings required to establish a dial-up connection. The subpanes available enable the configuration of how TCP/IP gets its settings, the PPP (Point-to-Point Protocol, carried over a dial-up connection) configuration parameters, modem settings, and network proxy server settings.

For TCP/IP, you have essentially the same options available as you do for Ethernet. Figure 9.9 shows the options available for TCP/IP setup under a modem connection. Most dial-up Internet service providers use PPP to service connections, so you'll probably be selecting the Using PPP option. Under this pane, you have partial manual configuration of the network parameters, but it would be unusual if an ISP (Internet service provider) did not provide the information for these settings automatically, using PPP.

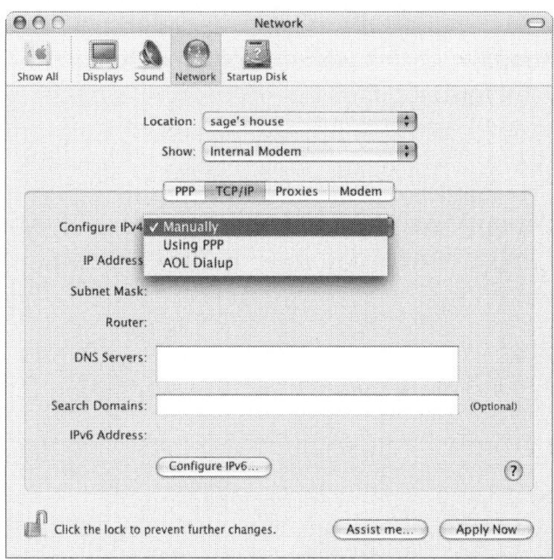

FIGURE 9.9 The TCP/IP options for the Modem configuration are essentially identical to those for the Ethernet configuration.

Under the PPP subpane, shown in Figure 9.10, you can configure how to connect to your ISP. Almost all ISPs use PPP to provide TCP/IP over dial-up connections. If yours does not, you will need to follow its instructions, which will probably include installation of some custom software.

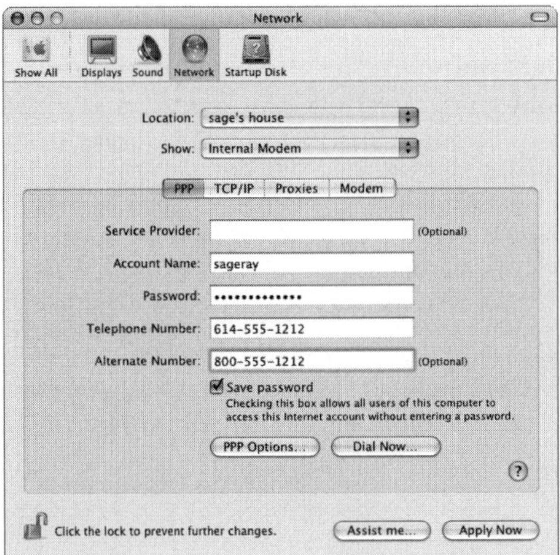

FIGURE 9.10 The PPP subpane of the Modem configuration allows you to specify your dial-up account information.

The PPP subpane has the following fields:

- Service Provider—An optional field where you can specify a name for the service provider. This option is useful if you have multiple providers that your machine needs to dial, and you need a better way to keep track of them than just by phone number.
- Account Name—The username or account name that you have with this ISP.
- Password—The password for this account and ISP.
- Telephone Number—The telephone number to dial.
- Alternate Number—An alternative number to dial for the same service provider. If your ISP doesn't have alternative dial-in numbers, leave this blank.
- Save Password—If your machine is going to be used by multiple users, and you don't want them to be able to connect to the Internet using your account information and password, don't check this box.

The PPP pane also has a PPP Options button and corresponding drop-down pane that enables you to configure several other options with respect to the dial-up connection, as shown in Figure 9.11.

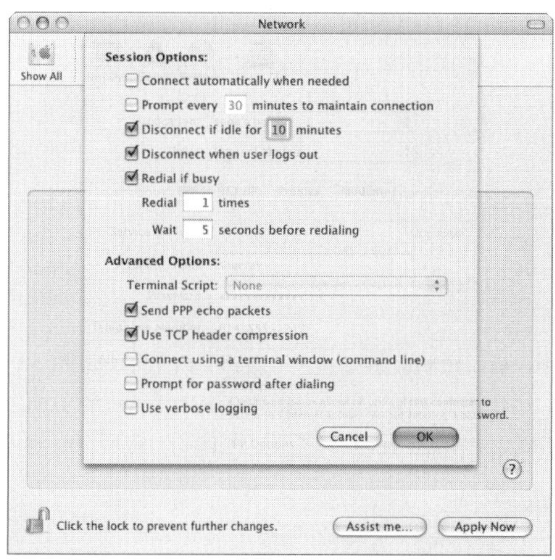

FIGURE 9.11 The Session and Advanced dial-up options drop-down pane for dial-up connections.

The pane enables you to configure the following:

- Whether to automatically dial and make a connection when an application starts that needs TCP/IP services.
- Whether, and how frequently, to prompt you to stay connected, if there hasn't been any recent network activity.
- How long to wait before disconnecting when there's no network activity.
- Whether to disconnect when there's no user logged in on the console.
- Whether to, how many times to, and how rapidly to redial the phone if the ISP is busy.
- Whether to send PPP echo packets. Some ISPs periodically send little "are you really there?" messages to connected computers to make sure that everything is working properly—this option controls whether to respond. Unless you have been told by your ISP to do otherwise, leave this option checked.
- Whether to compress TCP header information. TCP/IP information is carried in packets, with a significant amount of meta-information about the contents of the packet. Compressing this information can speed your network connection but requires processor power. On a fast machine, you'll probably get a network speedup from compressing headers, unless your ISP is using some ancient hardware that takes more time to perform the compression/decompression than the savings in transmission time.

- Whether to use a manual terminal window for connection. If your ISP doesn't use a standard PPP server, you might need to carry on some textual dialog with the server during connection. Selecting this option opens a terminal for you to interact with the host during connection.
- Whether to prompt for a password after dialing.
- The verbose logging option increases the amount of information regarding dial-up connections stored in the system logs.

The Modem subpane, shown in Figure 9.12, allows you to select your modem, configure the dialing type, and determine whether you want to hear your connections as they progress. Additionally, here you can choose to display modem status in the menu bar.

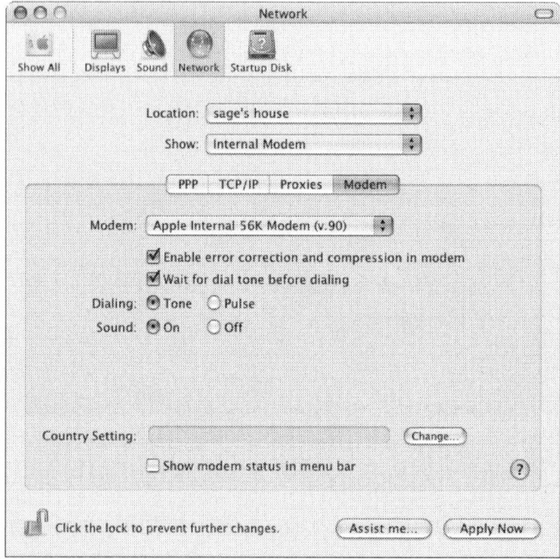

FIGURE 9.12 The Modem subpane of the Modem configuration.

The Internal Modem setting set also includes a Proxies subpane identical to that under the Built-in Ethernet configuration.

AirPort

An AirPort connection is logically almost identical to a hardwired TCP/IP connection, so the configuration options are almost identical to those for Ethernet. This configuration has TCP/IP and Proxies subpanes with options identical to the Ethernet configuration settings. It also includes an AirPort subpane, shown in Figure 9.13, wherein you can choose your default AirPort network either automatically or by specifying one, and enter your network password if one is required.

FIGURE 9.13 The AirPort subpane of the AirPort configuration set.

If you select the Show AirPort Status in the Menu Bar check box, an AirPort menu extra appears in your menu bar. The AirPort menu extra provides a continuous display of your signal strength and access to basic AirPort functionality such as disabling the card, choosing the network to connect to, or creating an AirPort network using your computer as a basestation. Selecting the Allow This Computer to Create Networks check box enables Software AirPort Basestation capabilities on your machine—you need to enable Internet Sharing from the Sharing control pane if you want machines using your AirPort card as a basestation to also be able to connect through your machine to the Internet.

IrDA

If your computer (such as a PowerBook) includes an infrared interface, you will also have an IrDA Modem option available under your Show pop-up menu. IrDA is most useful for direct computer-to-computer connections when a quick expedient connection is necessary and you don't have an Ethernet cable or AirPort connection available. It's also possible, if you have a modem that supports IrDA connections (such as a cell phone with an IrDA port), to use the external Ir-capable device to create your network connection. Figure 9.14 shows the IrDA Modem configuration pane, where you can configure your connection to an external IrDA device. The other network configuration subpanes are identical to the configuration subpanes you've seen previously in this chapter.

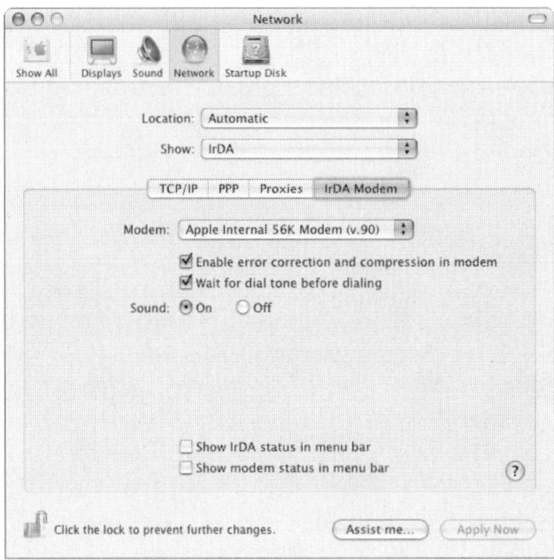

FIGURE 9.14 The IrDA Modem subpane of the IrDA configuration.

AppleTalk

AppleTalk is a communications protocol pioneered by Apple in the era of the Macintosh Plus. This protocol was designed for networking small collections of computers on relatively small networks. Because it was designed to facilitate network-building by people with no interest in being network designers or administrators, AppleTalk is a rather chatty and inefficient protocol. Because of its ease of use, it has survived the transition to a mostly Ethernet-based world and prospered in environments where its inefficiencies do not impair other network services.

Because of its intimate association with Apple's printing and file-sharing software, AppleTalk is sometimes thought of as actually being disk services and print services. In reality, it's a communications protocol, over which disk, print, and other services can be delivered. Because of this, like TCP/IP, AppleTalk connectivity is configured from the Network control pane, and services that need to use AppleTalk are configured elsewhere.

Setting Up

AppleTalk is enabled and configured from the AppleTalk subpanes of the Ethernet and AirPort configuration sets.

TIP

Remember that these subpanes, although they contain identical options, are configurations for two different interfaces. You can configure different parameters for each, to be used with each of the interfaces as appropriate.

Figure 9.15 shows the AppleTalk subpane for the AirPort configuration (the Ethernet version looks identical). The AppleTalk settings configured here are specific for the interface configuration set that you're editing. You can choose to configure AppleTalk automatically or manually. Unless otherwise directed, automatic is probably sufficient.

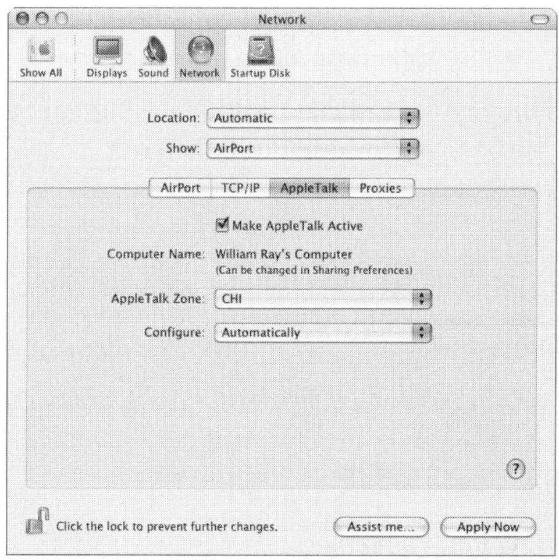

FIGURE 9.15 The AppleTalk subpane of the Network control pane.

In the AppleTalk subpane, the following options can be configured:

- Make AppleTalk Active—Activate AppleTalk for this interface. AppleTalk must be activated for an interface if you need to share your files via AppleShare on that interface.
- Computer Name—This is your AppleTalk Computer Name, which is distinct from your Hostname and from your Rendezvous Computer Name. This parameter is configured from the Sharing control pane. It's stored in and configurable via editing the `APPLETALK_HOSTNAME` parameter in `/etc/hostconfig`, but this is not recommended because services that use this value are not notified of changes to the file. If you want to change this value by editing the `/etc/hostconfig` file (for example in a script), you need to restart your machine after the change, or restart any individual services (see the command-line documentation for the command `kill` and the section on system startup scripts) that you need to be current.
- AppleTalk Zone—If your AppleTalk network has multiple zones, you can select the zone you want your computer to join from this menu. If you're on a network with multiple zones, your network administrator should be able to tell you what the proper setting is for your computer.

- Configure—Gives you the option of manually configuring your AppleTalk network parameters, or automatically determining the information. The AppleTalk Network ID and Node ID are similar to a TCP/IP subnet and IP address. The difference is AppleTalk is designed so that the computers in a network can cooperatively and automatically work out this information for themselves, without needing it to be specified by the users or administrators. There are very few instances in which you should need to set up the system for manual configuration.
- Node ID—If your network administrator tells you that you need to configure your machine for fixed, rather than automatically determined, AppleTalk network information, the node ID goes here.
- Network ID—If your network administrator tells you that you need to configure your machine for fixed AppleTalk network information, the Network ID goes here. If your network administrator gives you the network ID as ###.###, instead of a number between 1 and 65534, multiply the first by 256 and add the second to it. If you are given the number as ##.##.##, multiply the first by 256, the second by 16, and then add the those two results with the third number.

The Sharing Control Pane

As of OS 10.2, Apple has consolidated the GUI-based ability to enable or disable all standard information-sharing type services into a single list of selectable check boxes. They also provide a simple GUI interface to the built-in firewall. Internet connection sharing is also controlled through this pane. Changing settings in this pane requires administrative access.

The Services Subpane

Figure 9.16 shows the Services subpane of the Sharing control pane. Select the services you want running on your machine—they'll be available on all configured interfaces. Checking the check box for a particular sharing type enables that information-sharing service for all configured interfaces. Selecting or deselecting these options does nothing more than make a few configuration changes in textual configuration files. It's possible to make much more fine-grained configuration choices by modifying these files by hand, or by automated scripts, but simply enabling or disabling these services here will be sufficient for many users. If you need a more sophisticated configuration, see Chapter 20, "Command-Line Configuration and Administration," and Chapter 31, "Server Security and Advanced Network Configuration."

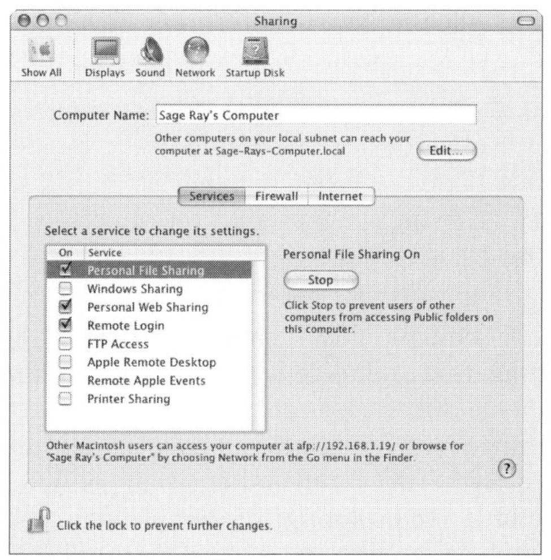

FIGURE 9.16 The Services subpane of the Sharing control pane.

Under the Services subpane, you can configure the following services:

- Personal File Sharing—Share your files via AppleShare, including AppleShare over TCP/IP. This does not enable NFS file sharing, the normal Unix file sharing method.
- Windows Sharing—Share your files via SAMBA, the open-source implementation of Microsoft's SMB file-sharing protocol. More configuration options for SAMBA are covered in Chapter 30, "Windows Interoperability."
- Personal Web Sharing—Turn on the Apache Web server, to serve Web pages from your computers. More configuration options for Apache are covered in Chapter 27, "Web Serving."
- Remote Login—Allow Secure Shell (SSH) access so that you can work on the command line of your machine from remote machines. More configuration options for SSH are covered in Chapter 26, "Remote Access and Control."
- FTP Access—Allow access to your machine via FTP, the File Transfer Protocol. More configuration options for FTP are covered in Chapter 25, "FTP Serving and Alternatives."
- Apple Remote Desktop—Allow others to manage your computer via Apple Remote Desktop. When you select this option the first time, a sheet appears to allow you to set up access privileges. You can modify these settings through the Access Privileges button that appears when you select Apple Remote Desktop. Additionally, you can choose to show the Apple Remote Desktop status in the menu bar.

- Remote Apple Events—Allow software running on other machines to communicate AppleEvents (a feature of AppleScript) to software on your machine.
- Printer Sharing—Share printers connected to this machine so that other machines can print to them. When you select this option in this pane, it is also automatically selected in the Print & Fax pane. When you deselect it in this pane, it is also deselected in Print & Fax. Likewise, whichever action you choose in Print & Fax carries over automatically here.

With OS X, Apple has made some significant changes to the way AppleTalk works both when sharing and mounting disks and folders. Some of these changes make good sense—for example, the Unix-side file ownerships control what can be accessed from remote—no more sharing settings for drives and folders. If you have permission to use it locally, you have permission to access it remotely. On the other hand, the new model of browsing the AppleTalk network feels a little like exploring an alien planet, compared to the comfortable and convenient network-world view we've come to expect from the Chooser.

To share files under AppleTalk in OS X, you have to do two things—turn on AppleTalk from the AppleTalk pane of the network interface you want to configure, and turn on Personal File Sharing from the Sharing control pane.

Unlike the way file sharing worked in pre-10 versions of Mac OS, you don't enable and disable sharing for individual devices or folders. Instead, the new model shares everything, and the user ID with which remote machines connect, controls which volumes or folders appear to be available for that connection. Regardless of other permissions, the contents of each user's Public folder are shared with guest-read permission to the world.

The Firewall Subpane

A firewall is something interposed between the stuff that's important, and the stuff that's dangerous. In a vehicle, this is the bit of the car that separates the passenger compartment from the engine, protecting the riders from dangers that might occur under the hood. In the world of computers, it's something that sits between the outside network and network services on your computer, to protect the computer from network-based attacks. Not that long ago, firewalls were seldom seen, annoying things that got in your way, hindered your work, and generally annoyed everyone, including the seemingly dictatorial network administrators who imposed them upon their users. Now, everyone wants one.

The most effective firewalls are completely separate devices, physically separating the protected network from the exterior network and its dangers. Much less expensive, and somewhat less effective, is firewall software that lives on the same machine it's protecting. Although a hardware firewall can interrupt network traffic upstream of the protected computer, and prevent the traffic from ever reaching the protected machines, a software firewall must transparently intercept traffic as it reaches the machine, determine whether to accept it, and then hand it to the service for which it was destined. This method doesn't prevent the traffic from reaching the machine, but rather tries to prevent the traffic from reaching the services it was headed for. It's not always a successful way of trying to do things, as demonstrated by the fact that there have been a number of commercial software firewalls for a certain other operating system that provide less than complete protection. The firewall software running under OS X's Firewall pane (ipfirewall, sometimes called ipfw), is well respected, however, and although not conceptually as secure as a separate firewall device, it's quite powerful and provides a good level of protection.

Like many of the more powerful aspects of the Unix underpinnings of OS X, the GUI interface to the firewall provides access to only the simplest functionality of the software. The ipfirewall software is capable of considerable sophistication in its control of your network connection, but it requires manual editing of configuration files. More sophisticated configuration than can be accomplished through the GUI is covered in Chapter 31.

Under the Firewall subpane of the Sharing control pane, shown in Figure 9.17, you can enable OS X's built-in firewall software and perform simple configuration and control. You can't actually select the check boxes for services that are enabled/enabled via the Services subpane—they're automatically checked if you enable the service.

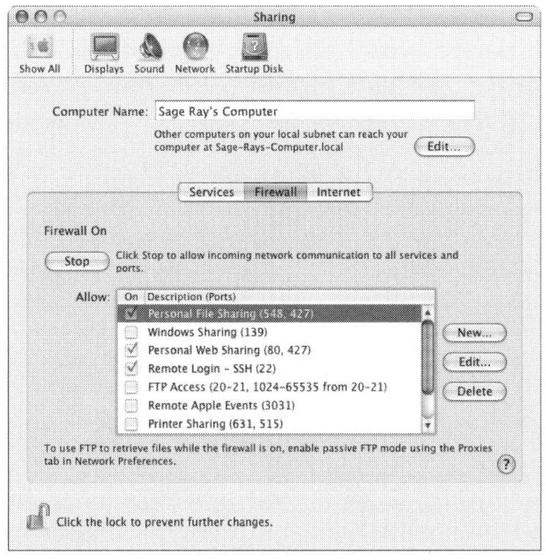

FIGURE 9.17 The Firewall subpane of the Sharing control pane.

Click the Start (or Stop) button to enable (disable) the firewall. If the firewall is disabled, all services on your machine are on their own (though potentially protected by TCP Wrapper or `xinetd` configuration parameters; see Chapters 20 and 31) as far as network security goes, and all ports on your machine can be reached from the network. When enabled, the firewall prevents network clients from accessing any port that it isn't explicitly configured to allow. This can protect your machine against compromise by malicious software that might open a port and allow access without your knowledge (though again, much more sophisticated configuration is possible from the command line). The check boxes shown in the scrolling list activate and disable access for certain services or port ranges. Those for known services enabled through the Services subpane, however, are automatically checked when the service is enabled, and unchecked when the service is disabled, and cannot be edited through the Firewall subpane. These entries for known services also cannot be edited.

If you click the New button, you are presented with a dialog like that shown in Figure 9.18, where you can configure other services that you want the firewall to allow connections to. Either select a known service-type entry from the shown pop-up list, or select the Other entry to configure for unknown services. There's a text-entry box hiding under the menu where you can enter a port number if needed.

NOTE

Remember, if you've enabled the firewall and haven't added an entry to pass traffic for a network client type, that traffic will be blocked by the firewall, and the client may not work. Put another way, if you're trying to use a new network client, and it's not working, check whether your firewall is enabled!

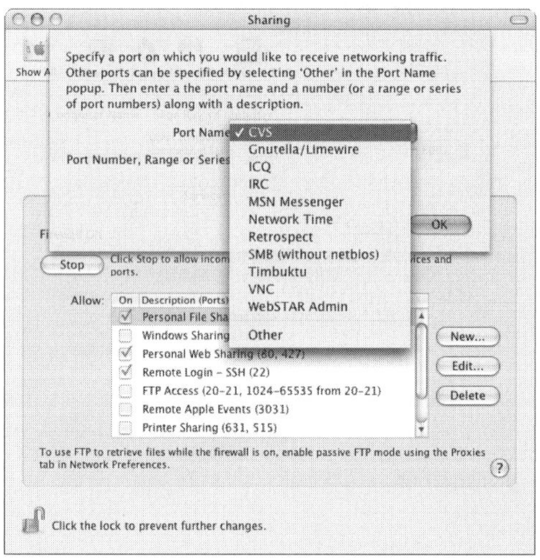

FIGURE 9.18 Adding a new service to those passed by the firewall.

The Internet Subpane

If you have multiple computers on which you want to be able to access the Internet, and only one convenient connection to the Internet itself, you can now easily configure OS X to share the connection it has to the Internet with other machines connected to it on other interfaces. Yet again, more sophisticated options are available at the command line, but being able to just click a button and turn your machine into an AirPort Basestation, or allow all your local machines to communicate with the Internet through your modem is wonderfully convenient. Figure 9.19 shows the Internet subpane of the Sharing control pane. Clicking the Start button enables a number of things under OS X's hood and makes useful automatic configuration choices based on the rest of your Network preferences. When enabled, Internet connection sharing allows any computers connected to this one, to use this machine's primary connection to connect to the Internet. If your primary connection is via AirPort, any machines connected to this one via Ethernet can connect to the Internet, using this machine's AirPort connection. If your primary connection is an Ethernet connection, your machine becomes an AirPort Basestation, and shares its connection to others using AirPort, as well as allowing others on the same Ethernet network to connect through it. You can configure typical AirPort Basestation options, such as the name, a password, whether to enable WEP encryption, and, if enabled, whether to use 40-bit or 128-bit encryption. If your connection is a modem, your machine becomes an AirPort Basestation, as well as shares the modem connection through the Ethernet.

CAUTION

You have limited configuration options here. You can't enable or disable DHCP services for the shared connection, and you can't configure what interfaces you want to allow sharing on, or through. DHCP runs by default when you enable Internet connection sharing, and DHCP IP-address service is provided on any interfaces where your machine hasn't made a DHCP connection itself. This can cause problems, if you're using a fixed IP address on a network where there is also a DHCP server providing addresses for transient clients. Enabling connection sharing when using such a network causes your machine to also become a DHCP server to the network, competing with the legitimate DHCP server. This can cause confusing results and possible network errors.

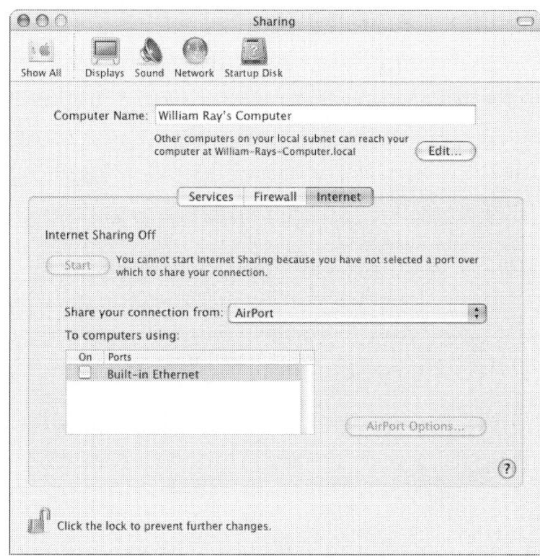

FIGURE 9.19 Sharing your network connection has never been easier.

Connecting to Remote Servers

To access a filesystem or folder from a machine, browse to the machine on which you're interested in using the Network Finder volume, as described in Chapter 2, "Managing the Panther Workspace," in the section "Browsing Network Volumes"; then double-click the icon to open a connection dialog, as shown in Figure 9.20.

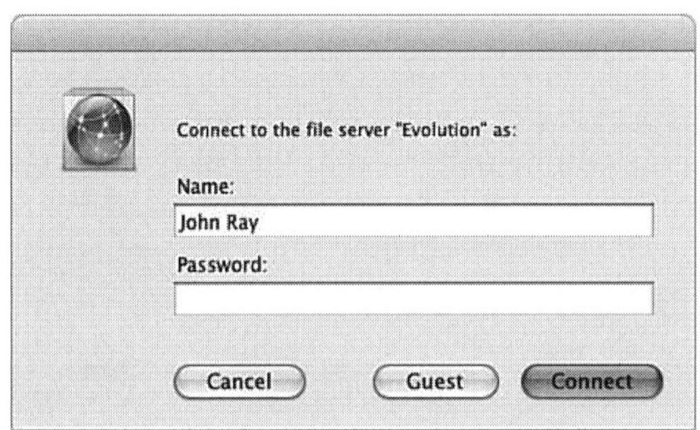

FIGURE 9.20 When connecting to a remote server, you must do so either as a guest, for access to Public folders, or as a user to access files that require read permission.

Authenticate with your user ID and password to access the folders and filesystems on the remote machine where the user ID has read permission, or click the Guest button to access any available guest shares. You may notice in Panther that you do not have as many options in the connect dialog box as you did in previous versions of Mac OS X. This is because you are not mounting the volume in the traditional Mac sense but connecting to it within the Network Volume hierarchy. After entering a username and password, you can browse further into the files and folders on the volume that have the appropriate permissions set. Servers that you've successfully authenticated with appear a slightly darker tint in the Finder than those that you haven't passed credentials to. You can browse to and access files on any server that you've authenticated with at any time during a single Mac OS X login session.

Volumes you access using this "browsing" method are not "mounted" and do not appear as volumes on your desktop or in the Finder sidebar. To "mount" a volume in the traditional sense, you must use the Finder Connect to Server (Command-K) feature discussed, again, in Chapter 2's section "Browsing Network Volumes." When connecting to a volume in this fashion, you are prompted with a more familiar connection dialog, as shown in Figure 9.21.

Again, enter the login information for the server, or click "guest" to connect to any guest shares, such as a user's public folder. You'll also notice the return of the Options dialog box, shown in Figure 9.22.

Here you can elect to add the user ID and password information to a keychain. The Options dialog also enables you to send your password in clear text—that is, unprotected and visible to anyone watching your network. We strongly recommend that you not enable the Clear Text option. A nice new feature is the ability to secure the connection with SSH (Secure Shell, see Chapter 26 for a complete discussion), which uses strong encryption to protect your entire data stream. We recommend you use this wherever possible unless you have a known-secure network, or would be severely impacted by the small time penalty that the encryption/decryption cycle costs.

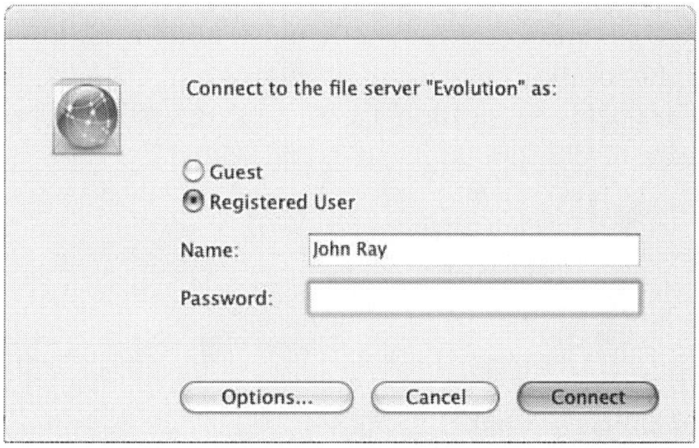

FIGURE 9.21 Using Connect to Server gives a more traditional connection dialog.

Disks and folders that you mount via the Connect to Server dialog appear on your desktop or in the Finder sidebar as described in Chapter 2. Conveniently, this is even true of services such as FTP. They also appear at the top level of the Finder hierarchy, with the other drive resources.

FIGURE 9.22 The options available when connecting to an AppleShare server. Do not enable clear text passwords unless you have a good reason to do so and are secure against the significant risks. Selecting secure connections through SSH is a good idea if available.

Mounted network volumes can be accessed like any other filesystem, with the exception of FTP, which remains a read-only mount.

Managing Locations

With OS X, Apple has made location management considerably easier than it was with previous versions of the Macintosh operating system (though somewhat less powerful). Instead of managing configurations for each protocol in its own pane and then switching between different collections of the configurations with the Location Manager tool, interface configurations in OS X are accessed directly under the location setting. Figure 9.23 shows the entirety of the location management interface in OS X. Selecting a location from this menu switches between location-specific settings in the subpanes below it. From this menu, locations can be chosen, duplicated, and edited.

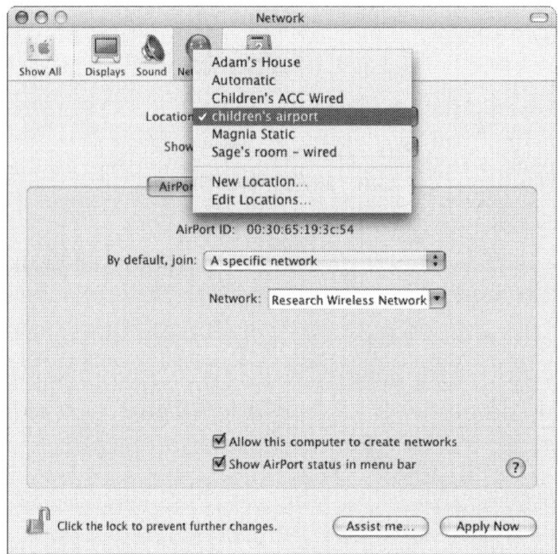

FIGURE 9.23 The location management menu in the Network control pane.

Each location in the Locations menu carries with it settings for the Configure menu and the subpanes that it switches through. That is, when you are entering information into the specific interface configuration panes, it is assigned to the currently displayed location. If you switch to a new location, you get new information and configurations in the interface configuration panes.

If you set the location setting to Automatic, the system attempts to guess the correct location information and switches between locations, based on what it can determine regarding its network environment.

TIP

You can switch between locations that you've configured through the Network control pane, using the Location submenu from the Apple menu.

Testing Network Settings

Unix-based operating systems are inherently networked operating systems from the original design, so they have a rather complete suite of network diagnostic software that comes with the basic operating system by default. We cover interaction with the command-line versions of these tools in several chapters to come. Apple has also provided a convenient GUI tool that functions as a front end to many of the diagnostics that the command-line tools can perform. Although it doesn't provide access to the complete range of options for each of the commands, the Network Utility application (path: `/Applications/Utilities/Network Utility`) is convenient for those who don't care to remember the syntax of command-line tools. The drawback is the need to navigate multiple windows to access the tool, and the requirement for a graphical interface, whereas the command-line tools can be accessed to determine the health of your network from any machine with a network connection. The unexpectedly poor performance of the GUI tools from previous versions of OS X appears to have been resolved in 10.2. The Network Utility application provides access to network diagnostics, which are described in the following sections:

- Info
- Netstat
- AppleTalk
- Ping
- Lookup
- Traceroute
- Whois
- Finger
- Port Scan

Info

The Interface Information (command-line command `ifconfig`) diagnostic gives you configuration information about your network interface. Shown in Figure 9.24, this diagnostic provides information regarding the traffic and error rate of the interface, as well as speed, hardware address, and vendor information.

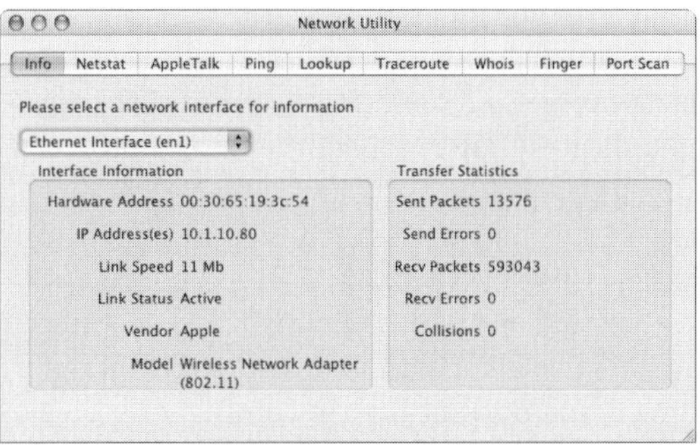

FIGURE 9.24 The Info pane of the Network utility provides information regarding the network interface and its performance.

Netstat

The Network statistics (command-line command `netstat`) diagnostic gives you statistical information regarding your network. It can provide four types of network information—routing tables, by-protocol comprehensive statistics, multicast statistics, and curent socket statistics. The information that's provided is extremely terse and dense, but with experience, it can prove invaluable in diagnosing network problems. Figure 9.25 shows the routing information display.

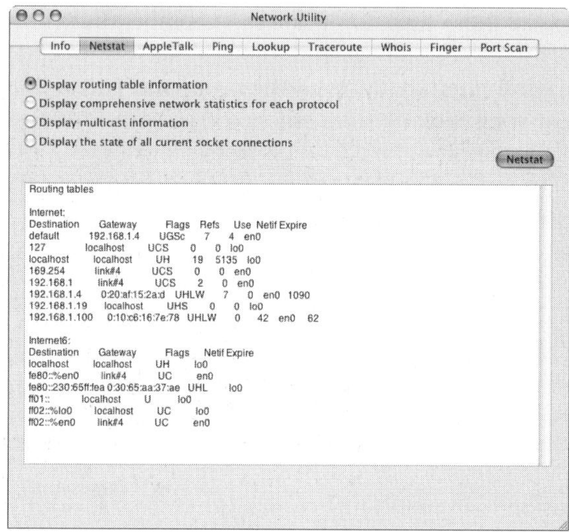

FIGURE 9.25 Click the Netstat button on the Netstat pane to look up connection information, but don't be surprised if you have to wait a while.

To get this information takes the GUI client some time, and you might have to wait for several minutes before the utility responds. The routing information specifies what your computer knows about how to get information to remote locations. The IPv4 information displayed in Figure 9.25 indicates that the machine knows how to send information to three machines (`192.168.1.4`, `192.168.1.19`, and `192.168.1.100`), directly to an entire C-class network (`192.168.1.`) by one route, directly to an automatically configured B-class network (`169.254.`, a network used by Rendezvous/Zeroconf), and to all other locations (`default`), by going through `192.168.1.4`, which is this machine's default router. The comprehensive network statistics display includes considerably more information than fits in the display in Figure 9.26. Included is a fairly complete listing of every type of network connection and traffic that your machine has engaged in, and any problems or abnormalities that have been observed with the data transmissions for that traffic.

TIP

This information is formatted in such a way that it would be much easier to read and understand in a fixed-pitch font than in the font that Apple's used for this display. Copying the data out and viewing it in a fixed font in TextEdit or your favorite text editor will make it easier on the eyes.

The multicast information display provides information regarding multicast broadcast network information. If you are using your machine to stream QuickTime video, or for other multicast applications, this display might provide useful information. Otherwise, expect it to remain essentially empty, as shown in Figure 9.27.

The socket connection section displays information on all current Internet and local (Unix) domain socket connections. The information displayed in this section is much larger than what is shown in Figure 9.28. The active Internet connections portion shows the local addresses and remote addresses involved in the connections as well as the state of the connection. Common states you'll see are established, closed, and listen. In the local (Unix) domain socket connections portion, the listing includes a connection type of stream or dgram, inode numbers, and occasionally a filename identifier.

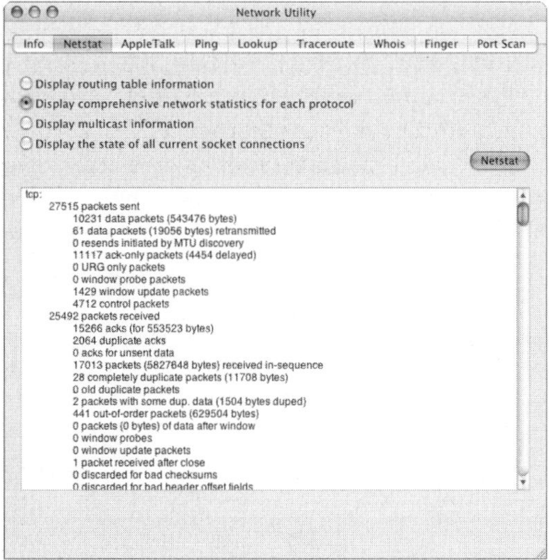

FIGURE 9.26 A portion of the comprehensive network statistics display of the Network Utility.

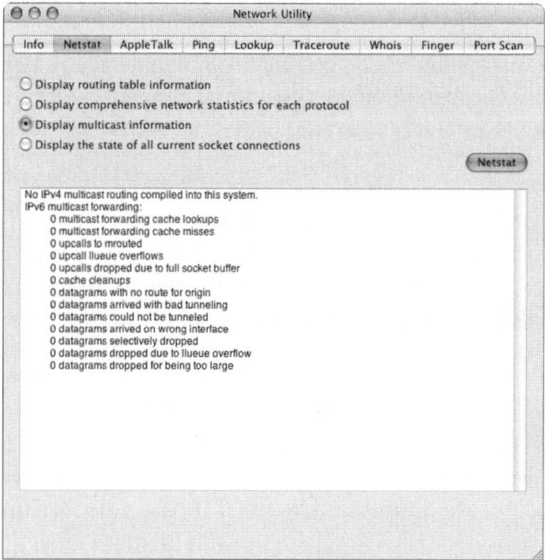

FIGURE 9.27 The multicast information display of the Network Utility. If you do not use multicast services, expect this display to remain essentially empty.

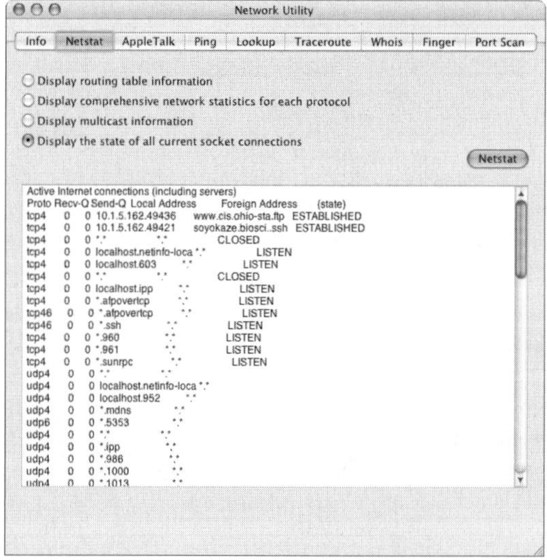

FIGURE 9.28 The active sockets connection information display of the Network Utility.

AppleTalk

The AppleTalk (various command-line utilities) pane provides information on the AppleTalk network. Four types of information are available: AppleTalk statistics and error counts, saved PRAM AppleTalk information, available AppleTalk zones on the network, and information on a specific AppleTalk node. Of these four, the AppleTalk statistics and error counts display and the available AppleTalk zone information are probably the most interesting.

The AppleTalk statistics and error counts display, shown in Figure 9.29, can provide information on how healthy your AppleTalk network is at the given moment. If you have been having a lot of trouble and discover from this that many errors are occurring, let your network administrator know.

Figure 9.30 shows the AppleTalk zones display, which displays the available AppleTalk zones for your network. If you see many more zones than you ought to, let your network administrator know.

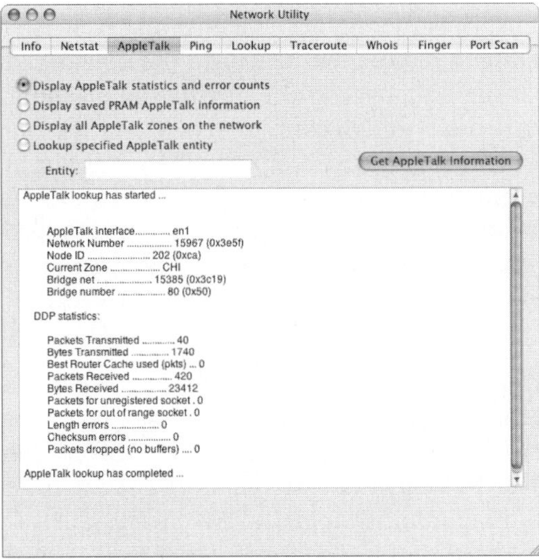

FIGURE 9.29 The AppleTalk statistics and error counts information display of the Network Utility.

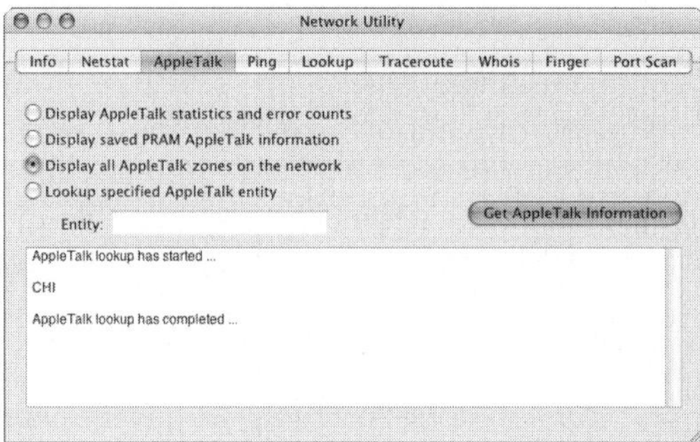

FIGURE 9.30 The AppleTalk zones information display of the Network Utility.

Ping

The Ping pane provides network connection/traffic testing (command-line program `ping`), as shown in Figure 9.31. It enables you to ping a remote machine to determine whether it, and the network between your machine and it, is alive. The `ping` program injects packets destined for a remote machine into the network, destined for a mandatory service that echoes the ping back to the originating machine. Usually, 10 packets are injected into the network at one-second intervals, and the round-trip time, as well as information regarding any packets that don't complete the trip, is reported back. You have the option of continuously sending packets to the remote host, but unless you have permission and a good reason to do so, this is usually considered, at the minimum, to be rude. The `icmp_seq` value increases by one for every packet sent, so if you see a gap in the values displayed, you know that one (or more) packets did not complete their round-trips.

Also displayed is a TTL (Time To Live) value, which starts at 255 and decreases for every machine that reroutes the packet. Usually, all these values will be the same, but if network trouble causes packets to take alternative routes between the machines, differing TTL values might be reflected. To keep errant packets from circling the Internet forever, each packet is restricted to a finite number of machines—usually 255—that can touch it before it dies. Packets that get lost in routing loops and never make it to their destination quickly run out of TTL counts and are discarded. Finally, the time each packet took to traverse the network is displayed in milliseconds (thousandths of a second).

A number of modern firewalls optionally reject ping requests. Consequently, you may run into times when a ping request makes it seem like a host is unreachable when it really is not.

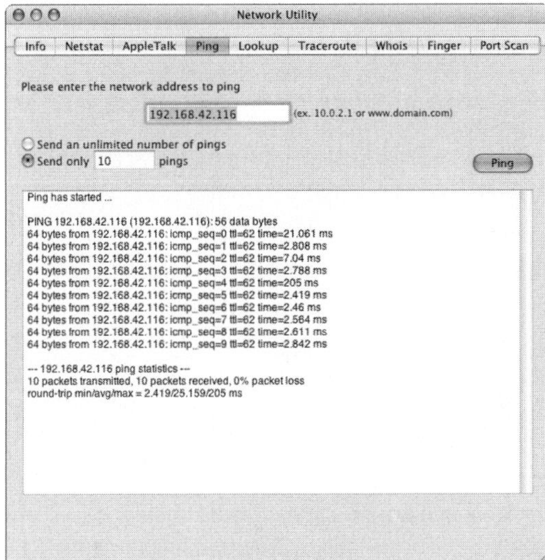

FIGURE 9.31 The Ping pane of the Network Utility allows you to determine whether a remote host can be reached, and how the network between the machines is performing.

Lookup

The Lookup (command-line command `nslookup` [deprecated] or `dig`) diagnostic enables you to query the DNS (Domain Name Service) information for a machine. This includes information that maps the fully qualified domain name (FQDN), such as `www.killernuts.org`, to an IP address, and considerable additional information as well. The default operation of the diagnostic is to look up IP addresses for an FQDN, as shown in Figure 9.32.

The diagnostic can also look up other types of information out of the DNS, such as what machine handles the email for a host, and the canonical names (aliases) by which it might be known. Figure 9.33 shows the range of options for the lookup diagnostic. We recommend the use of the `dig` version because `nslookup` is deprecated and can't be guaranteed to return complete information in the future.

9

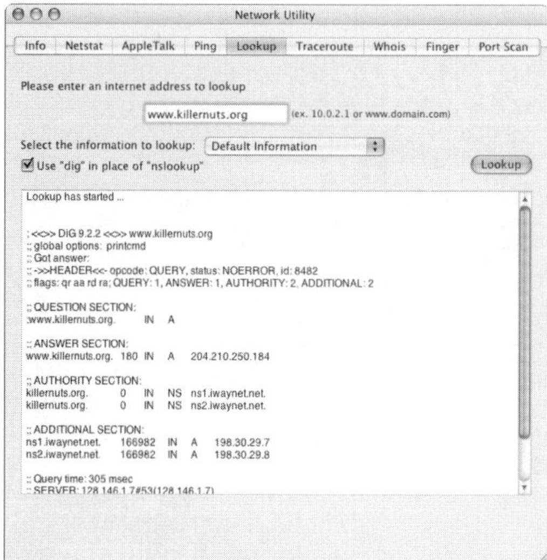

FIGURE 9.32 The results of a default search for *`www.killernuts.org`* with the Lookup tool of the Network Utility application.

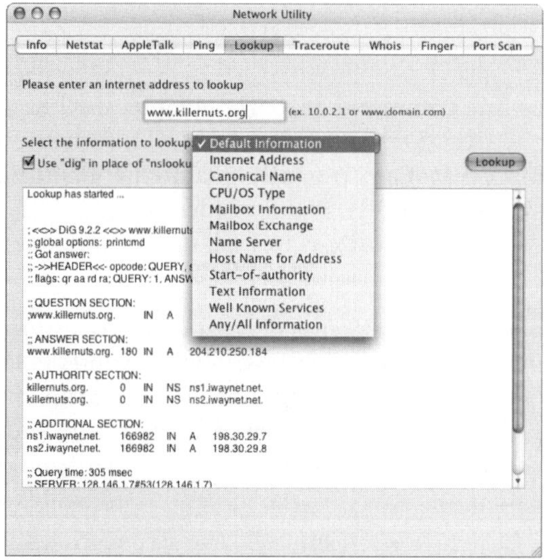

FIGURE 9.33 The Lookup type options for the Lookup tool of the Network Utility application set the amount of data that will be queried from the remote server.

The information that the Lookup tool can provide includes the following:

- Default Information—The default information returned by the DNS server in response to a query: typically, the IP address to hostname mapping, the Start of Authority (SOA) record holders for the domain name, and the authoritative DNS servers for the domain.
- Internet Address—The IP address associated with a host name.
- Canonical Name—An IP address can have both a proper name and potentially multiple alias names that point to it. The canonical name lookup provides information on the proper name that is equivalent to an alias.
- CPU/OS Type—Attempts to get operating system and CPU information for a remote host, but this is not a mandatory item for the host to provide to the world.
- Mailbox Information —Mailbox or mailing list information. There is no requirement that this information be maintained correctly on the DNS host, so the results of a query for this information should not be considered definitive.
- Mailbox Exchange—MX (Mail Exchanger) record information. It is frequently impractical to have every host in a domain manage its own incoming email. For this reason, a DNS record might specify that mail appearing to be destined for one particular host be routed instead to an alternative destination. This allows, for example, mail to `ray@calvin.biosci.ohio-state.edu`, `ray@suzie.biosci.ohio-state.edu`, and `ray@waashu.biosci.ohio-state.edu` to all be routed to, and received by, the mail server machine `ryoko.biosci.ohio-state.edu`.
- Name Server—Returns the list of authoritative name servers for a domain.
- Host Name for Address—Reverse lookup of an FQDN for a particular IP address.
- Start-of-Authority—A particular DNS server must be specified as the authoritative server for a particular IP-to-domain name mapping. An additional piece of information, known as the Start of Authority (SOA) record, specifies a host that is authoritative for other information, such as contact information for problems with the domain. Frequently these are the same, but it is possible that DNS information may be delegated to servers that do not have all the same information stored as the SOA records—for example, when DNS information is maintained internally by a domain but a parent organization keeps administrative control. In this case, the SOA records should be consulted for all information other than IP-to-hostname mapping.
- Text Information—Any optionally registered textual information regarding the queried host. Few domains register anything interesting in this field.
- Well Known Services—Return information regarding well-known service types that the host might be providing. This is intended to give information regarding such things as whether the host is running FTP services, or HTTPD services, and so on. This is not a required piece of information for a host to provide to its DNS server, so few bother to provide correct or interesting information here.

- Any/All Information—Investigate and return all known information regarding the host. The actual information returned depends on the configuration of the server queried and the information it contains. Typically, a query for All information returns something similar to the default information.

Traceroute

The Traceroute (command-line program `traceroute`) diagnostic provides information on the route that a packet must travel between your machine and a remote machine. When the network is working properly, this information will usually be of little interest to you. If you can't reach a remote machine, however, it is sometimes useful to see this information so that you can tell whether the problem is with only a segment of the network, or if it's with the remote machine itself. Figure 9.34 shows the result of a successful Traceroute to the host `www.tcp.com`. Each line of the output indicates a machine through which the traffic to `www.tcp.com` had to be routed, and the time it took for that particular router to respond. The trace ends at the host `www.tcp.com`, indicating that the network is successful at transmitting data between the querying host and `www.tcp.com`.

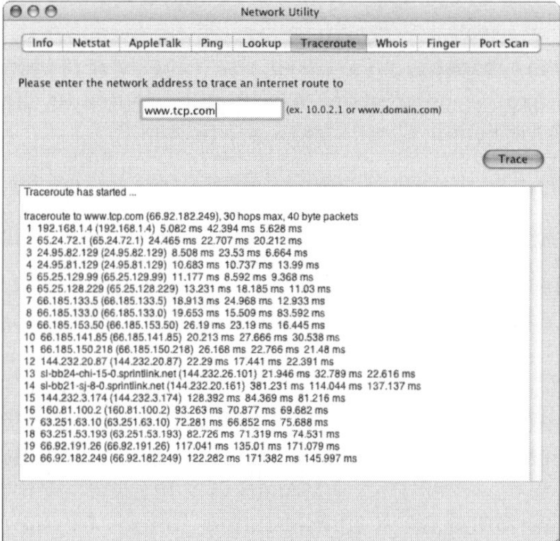

FIGURE 9.34 The Traceroute output includes diagnostic information regarding each router that the packet needed to traverse to reach the remote host.

Figure 9.35 shows the result of an attempt to trace the route to a host that is down, on the same subnet as `www.tcp.com`. The traffic in this case manages to make it almost all the way to its final destination, but cannot reach the requested final host. If we know that the host is not, in fact, the next machine along the network (that is, the Traceroute fails somewhere between you and the target, rather than at the target), we can infer that the problem is actually a network problem. Therefore, the routing of traffic between your machine and the remote machine is currently defective.

If a transient failure were occurring in the Internet and the trace stopped well before reaching the target host's subnet, we could determine that problems reaching the host were because of something other than the host itself being down.

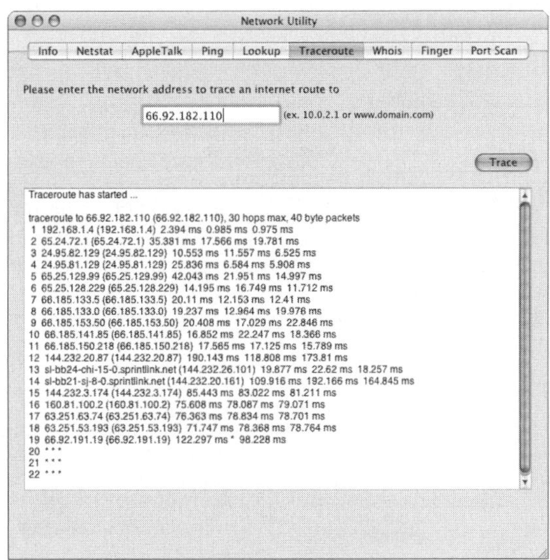

FIGURE 9.35 The output from a Traceroute showing an unsuccessful attempt to reach a remote host on the same subnet as `www.tcp.com`.

Whois

The Whois (command-line program `whois`) program actually has a more flexible use than is presented by this tool. It is designed to talk to remote servers that provide a sort of phone directory function. Apple has pointed the Whois tool of the Network Utility application to a subset of `whois` servers that provide directory information regarding the ownership and management of hostnames and domains, but you can also specify a `whois` server that is not already on the list. Figure 9.36 shows the results of trying to use the Whois tool to look up `itchysweater.com`. The `whois` server selected, `whois.internic.net`, machine knows only that another server, `whois.godaddy.com`, should know the complete information for this host. Figure 9.37 shows a portion of the results of specifying `whois.godaddy.com` as the `whois` server and reissuing the `whois` query for `itchysweater.com`.

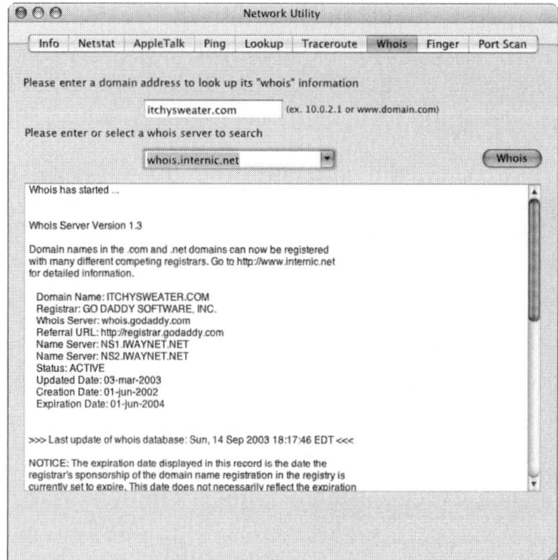

FIGURE 9.36 The output from *`whois`* for *`itchysweater.com`* at *`whois.internic.net`*.

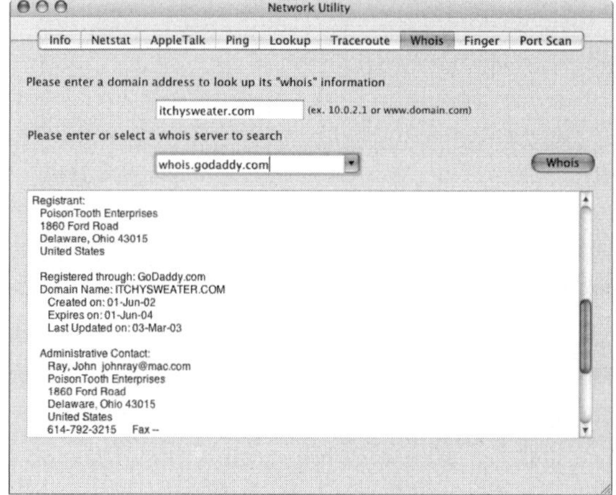

FIGURE 9.37 The output from *`whois`* for *`itchysweater.com`* at *`whois.godaddy.com`*. This server knows considerably more about the domain.

If you're willing to ignore the sample text in Apple's dialog box, you can also use the Whois tool from the Network Utility application to make other types of queries to `whois` servers. For example, if you point the `whois` server to `osu.edu`, you can find out everyone who has "ness" in their name by searching for `ness` in the domain address box. Figure 9.38 shows a portion of the results of this search. In this case, it's a listing of people and email addresses that the server knows about at the institution that match the query "ness". This particular Whois server also enables you to get more specific information regarding the people identified and gives instructions at the bottom of the listing of names. Other `whois` servers can be contacted similarly and can be used to obtain a range of types of information.

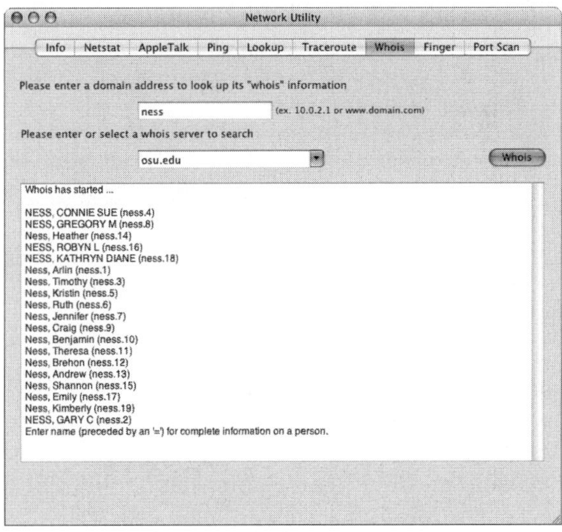

FIGURE 9.38 The output from a "misuse" of the Whois tool of the Network Utility application to query a *whois* server that doesn't provide domain name information.

Finger

The Finger (command-line program `finger`) tool of the Network Utility application gives you the ability to query the `finger` server of a host. This server, if enabled, provides information regarding who a user is (full name and so on) and when the user was most recently logged in. It is generally considered to be a minor security risk to run the `finger` server, because it lets crackers know whether it's safe to break into a system. But, if you know of a machine that has the service enabled, you can use this tool to access it. Figure 9.39 shows the results of using the `finger` tool to finger `ray@rosalyn.biosci.ohio-state.edu`. Notice that the server returns information about all known users with `ray` in their names. Different `finger` servers return different information about users. This one is rather sparse, leaving out most of the users' personal information but still indicates whether the users are logged in.

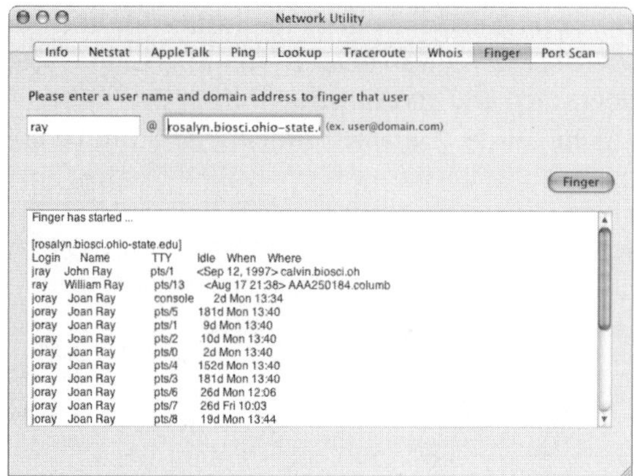

FIGURE 9.39 The output of a Finger tool lookup of `ray@rosalyn.biosci.ohio-state.edu`.

Port Scan

Port Scan (various command-line programs) examines a host for available opportunities to access it via the network. Conceptually, TCP/IP networking is accomplished by establishing connections between logical constructs, known as ports, created by the networking software of each machine. These ports can be thought of as analogous to a series of numbered sockets into which a network connection can be plugged. The network connection must be plugged into one socket on each communicating machine; hence, it has an originating port and a destination port. Some network services always exist at particular fixed ports and are connected to based on the knowledge that they exist at these known locations. Other applications attempt to generate a small level of security by opening a randomly numbered port and not advertising its presence. Connections then require that a connecting machine know where to look to find them. This isn't a particularly useful way of establishing security, but it does turn out to be a reasonably decent way for a cracker to hide the fact that he or she has broken into your machine. After the system has been compromised, many crackers will install a backdoor on an unknown port so that they can come and go undetected, instead of connecting to the normal known ports, and thereby incurring a noticeable connection to a known service.

The Port Scan tool of the Network Utility application causes your machine to examine all the ports on a remote machine and tell you which of them appear to have software listening to them. If the monitored ports don't correspond to known services, it's possible that there's been a network break-in. Figure 9.40 shows the Port Scan tool results for a machine running FTP, Sendmail, SSH, a POPmail server, and a Web server. I can account for ports 21, 22, 25, 31, 80, and 110 from the services I know I'm running. A few of the others I can account for in additional bits of software that could be running, but the others? Maybe it's time for me to check my machine's security. (On the other hand, when I wrote about the Port Scan tool for this section under 10.0, it produced verifiably wrong results, not showing ports I could prove were open, and showing others I was certain weren't open, so maybe I don't really have a problem.) There are better ways of examining your own machine (see Chapter 31, `netstat` at the command line, for one). Additionally, it is considered to be excruciatingly bad form to `portscan` someone else's computer. This is exactly the methodology that crackers use to examine a machine for known vulnerabilities. We'd go so far as to say that it is a bit irresponsible of Apple to have put this tool in a user-level GUI application, and we recommend that you not use it, except on your own devices.

CAUTION

Think carefully before you use the Port Scan tool on a machine that you're not the owner or administrator of. Scanning a host without permission can be considered an attempted break-in and could result in legal action against you. Think carefully before you use it on one that you do own as well. Make a typo in your IP address, and it's probably someone else's machine that your Mac will be nosing through.

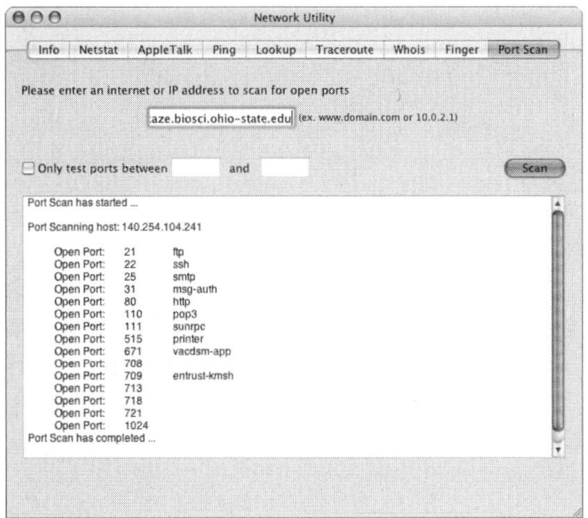

FIGURE 9.40 The output of the Port Scan tool of the Network Utility application.

Summary

Linux and Unix operating systems have a history of being difficult to configure for online use. Users must often understand the complexities of TCP/IP to correctly set up their devices. Mac OS X puts a clean, user-friendly interface on network setup and enables the user to get online without ever seeing a command line.

This chapter covered the Mac OS X network configuration utilities, and how they can be used to create a connection through modem, Ethernet, and wireless interfaces. Macintosh users are accustomed to quickly and easily finding and connecting to network resources. Although the interface has changed, the process is just as easy.

In addition to network setup, we covered enabling information sharing through the Sharing control pane and protecting your information with Apple's new firewall. We also took an in-depth look at the Mac OS X Network Utility, which provides a suite of diagnostic tools for a Mac user to test his connections. Macintosh networking has never had a more solid and stable base than it does in Mac OS X.

CHAPTER **10**

Printer, Fax, and Font Management

IN THIS CHAPTER

In this chapter, we look at basic printer and font management in OS X. First, you see how to add a local or network printer. Then you learn more about your printer and its queue, as well as selecting settings for your print job and sending it to a printer. After a brief examination of the printer, we look at font management. You see how to manage your font collections, add a new font, and manipulate the keyboard inputs available in OS X.

One of the neatest additions Apple put into OS X with the release of 10.2 was the CUPS (Common Unix Printing System) printing system. With 10.3, Apple expands support for more CUPS features. With almost any other printing system you might have encountered, support for a printer depends on whether the printer manufacturer decides to write a driver for your machine, and whether the output you get from one printer looks similar to that from another depends on how the different manufacturers have implemented their drivers. CUPS is different. CUPS is a system that makes every printer look like a PostScript printer from the application's point of view, completely eliminating all the weirdness that has long been associated with using PostScript or TrueType (scalable) fonts, or natively vector graphics from programs such as Illustrator, on inherently bitmapped printing devices such as ink-jet printers. "Drivers" for CUPS can be written by interested users, manufacturers, or third-party retailers, and are relatively simple modules that plug into the main printing system and instruct it in how to talk to a particular type of printer. Between the various sources of printer descriptions for CUPS, more than 3,000 different models of printers are supported.

NOTE

Complete and complex configurations of CUPS are covered in considerable detail by Michael Sweet in *CUPS: Common Unix Printing System*, ISBN 0-672-32196-3, from Sams Publishing. What we cover here should be sufficient for most users setting up systems with a few printers. CUPS is capable, however, of so much more. If you've a complicated printing setup, want to exert more control over your print jobs than is clear from these details, or need to manage a printing network involving many printers, this book can help.

Apple has neatly wrapped the CUPS system into both its GUI and command-line printing environment. Where Apple's tools stop and CUPS begins is completely hidden to the user and really of no consequence. The integration is sufficiently seamless that unless you really want to dig around in its guts, you'll never have to even know that CUPS exists—printing simply works much better now.

Print Center

The familiar Chooser is not a part of OS X. Instead, the heart of the OS X GUI environment printing system is the Printer Setup Utility, which also appears as the Print Center. The Print Center/Printer Setup Utility is used for adding and deleting printers, setting the default printer, and interacting with the queues. The Print Center combines the printer tasks it once took both the Chooser and a desktop printer icon to accomplish. Desktop printer icons, however, are once again supported, as a sort of a limited view into the Printer List of the Printer Setup Utility. The rest of the familiar printing activities are available under the File menu of each application. The Print Center/Printer Setup Utility is located in `/Applications/Utilities`.

Note that just adding a printer in the Print Center is sufficient to enable both GUI and command-line printing under modern versions of OS X. Under the original releases, this was not true, and information needed to be added to the NetInfo database as well. Now, if you want, you can still enable some printing capabilities through NetInfo (which you learn about in Chapter 11, "Additional System Components"), but most any configuration you could want can be handled through the Print Center and an auxiliary configuration interface accessed via a Web page. A small amount of Print and Page Setup dialog preferences can also be configured via the Print & Fax control pane.

Local USB or FireWire Printer

Because all modern Macintosh hardware comes with USB and FireWire ports, a local USB or FireWire printer is easy to add. Talking to printers on either of these local interfaces is conceptually similar, so the same instructions apply to either connection type.

When you open the Print Center or Printer Setup Utility, if no Printer List window appears, you can select Show Printer List from the View menu to check for your USB printer (or the Printers menu, in previous versions). Your printer, if plugged in, turned on and supported, should appear in the Printer List window. If you don't see your printer listed, or if it is listed as unsupported, check the software CD that came with your printer for OS X drivers. If it does not have any, check the manufacturer's Web site for the latest drivers and instructions. OS X comes with some third-party USB printer drivers. If the drivers that come with OS X work with your printer, you should be ready to print. If none of these sources have driver modules available, there are still a few other possibilities, but they're a bit more complicated, so we'll cover them later in the section on installing CUPS modules.

After the drivers are properly installed, your local USB printer should be available for printing. Click the Add icon in the Printer List, and it brings up a dialog allowing you to select among printer connections and types. In the upper pop-up menu, select USB (or a manufacturer's typed USB, such as Epson USB, if this matches your printer) as the connection type. Your USB printer should then appear in the dialog, and you should have the opportunity to select the printer type from the Printer Model pop-up at the bottom of the dialog.

As of 10.2, OS X allows you to share your printer via the network. This capability is enabled via selection of the Printer Sharing check box under the Services pane of the System Preferences Sharing pane. If you share your printer, it appears in other local network users' Printer Setup Utility Printer lists automatically.

Network Printers

If you do not have a local USB printer, or if network printers also are available, you might want to add a network printer to your Printer List. Due to the way CUPS works, you won't need to do anything to add some network printers to your Printer List. Similar to the way the Chooser used to discover AppleTalk printers on your network, the CUPS system automatically knows about shared printers available through the CUPS system on other local machines. Unlike the Chooser, the CUPS system also knows and shares the configuration information for those printers, so you've no need to select printer models or configure CUPS printers; they are simply available as already-configured printer choices whenever they can be found on the local network.

To add a network printer that's not already visible in the Printer List to your system:

1. Select Printers, Add Printer from the menu, or click Add Printer directly from the Printer List.

2. Select the connection type. Available connection types for network printers include IP Printing, Open Directory, Rendezvous and traditional AppleTalk, and Windows Printing via SAMBA:

    - IP Printing is for LPR and distant (as opposed to local to your machine, or local network) CUPS and IPP (Internet Printing Protocol—the printing information language that CUPS speaks) printers shared using a traditional Unix printer-sharing scheme. It also supports HP JetDirect network printing access. The Print Center can provide connectivity for both the GUI and command-line aspects of OSX to these well-established types of printing resources.

- Open Directory is for printers advertised via NetInfo or other directory information service types such as LDAP or NIS. In Chapter 11, we look at adding a network printer via the Open Directory connection.
- Rendezvous and AppleTalk are Apple's modern and legacy methods of automatically discovering and configuring local resources. The functions of both are analogous, in that they both provide a simple listing of network resources that they can observe in the immediate network vicinity.
- Windows Printing allows access to printing resources being shared through the Windows SAMBA resource-sharing scheme. To use this resource, you need to know a user ID and password that are allowed to access a local Windows Workgroup printing resource.

Figure 10.1 shows the IP Printing dialog. In the window you specify the following:

- The IP printing connection type—LPD/LPR is for classic Unix Line Printer Daemon resources. Internet Printing Protocol is for IPP printers (typically served by CUPS) at remote sites too distant on the network for their services to be automatically discovered. HP JetDirect is for Hewlett Packard printers with JetDirect printing interfaces. Rendezvous, although currently an option as an IP printing type, probably doesn't really belong here, because it's also its own printing type in the higher-level connection type menu. Because it's an autodiscovery mechanism, you don't get to enter parameters for things such as the IP address of the printer host when Rendezvous is selected. You can, however, see the IP connection types available for each Rendezvous printer from the pop-open menus attached to each field.
- The IP address or name of the printer or host. Printing via the network requires some means of identification of the target, and without a locally discovered name (via AppleTalk or Rendezvous), an IP address can get you to just about anywhere on the planet.
- The queue—The default is to use the default printer queue. An alternative queue name can be specified instead.
- The printer model—Here you can select a specific LaserWriter model, a generic PostScript printer, or a specific PPD for your printer model. Finding your exact printer model for network printers is usually not necessary. Unlike for local printers such as USB printers, this model information isn't used to determine how to actually connect and print to the printer. For network printers, the remote host running the printer needs to know that. Your machine only needs to know the specific model of the printer so that programs know about page margins and similar configuration options.

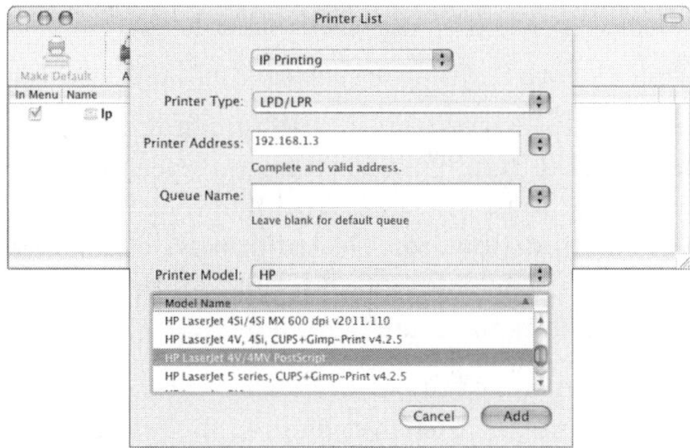

FIGURE 10.1 Fill in information at the IP Printing dialog to select that connection type, select your printer model if a PPD is available for it, or simply use Generic as the Printer Model. Other possible connection dialogs require similar information.

Selecting an AppleTalk printer is much like selecting an AppleTalk printer in the venerable Chooser. If you are on a multizone AppleTalk network, you have the option of choosing among the available zones. Printers registered as available in each zone are automatically discovered and displayed for you to choose from. You should see a selection of familiar AppleTalk printers. Make sure that you have turned on AppleTalk in the System Preferences Network pane.

Selecting a Rendezvous printer is like selecting an AppleTalk printer, only there's no zone setting to fiddle with.

If you select the Open Directory connection type, you are presented with list of printers registered with known Directory Services. For example, NetInfo printers can be added to your local NetInfo database (covered in Chapter 11), or discovered through information passed in NetInfo databases to which your machine may be subscribed (also Chapter 11). If you have printers being advertised through Directory Services, they appear here, and you may select among them. Selection of a printer and model is as for other printing types.

3. Click Add. Based on the selections you've made previously, a printer is set up, enabled, and listed in the Printer List.

Examining Printers

The Printer Setup Utility's Printer List itself is the place to examine known, available printers. Each entry in the Printer List shows, by default, the printer name and its status. Under the View menu of the Print Center, the Columns sub-menu allows you to select from other information to display in the list. The available columns are as follows—optional columns are marked with an *:

- In Menu (previously called Favorites)—A column allowing you to enable and disable printer availability without removing them from the Printer List. Checked printers are available for printing to in the pop-up printer-selection menu in the Print dialog. Unchecked printers do not show up. Selected printers can be sorted to the top of the list for your convenience. The check box for one will be grayed out because you can't disable the display of your default printer.
- Name—The configured name of the printer. For printers you control, you can edit this value under the Name and Location pane of the Show Info option of the Printers menu.
- *Status—The status information the printer reports.
- *Jobs—The number of current print jobs waiting on the printer.
- *Kind—The printer model as configured.
- *Host—The host serving the printer, or local, if the printer is directly connected to your machine.
- *Location—The location information reported by either the machine serving the printer, or the directory service describing the printer. If the printer is local to your machine (including network printers incorrectly identified as local), you can edit the location information by using Get Info from the Printer List, selecting the Name and Location pane, and changing the location.

Figure 10.2 shows a sample Printer List. In this Printer List, five printers are shown. One (`lp`) is an Apple LaserWriter Select 360 that's attached through the Directory Services (NetInfo) method of specifying network resources (we'll show how this printer gets created in Chapter 11). One is an HP Color LaserJet connected via AppleTalk. One (`192.168.1.3`) is an HP LaserJet 4MV connected via direct IP printing (LPR/LPD). In 10.3 (or at least the current beta), these have no host information at all, even though all three are network printers, two having a fixed IP and the other having a fixed AppleTalk ID. In 10.2, these show `local` as their host, despite the fact that they're network printers. In earlier versions of OS X, these would identify themselves as being served via NetInfo, AppleTalk, and from a particular IP address, respectively. The fact that this information is not correctly displayed is probably a bug. Based on the ongoing changes to the printing system interface, this area is probably under active development, and you should expect to eventually start seeing more useful information regarding the printers and their current states in this window.

The other two printers are CUPS printers that are shared from `ori.pediatrics.ohio-state.edu`. Under OS X 10.2, these would have shaded entries to indicate that they're automatically discovered printers. Under 10.3, the Printer List is currently displaying their *descriptions*, rather than their *names* (they're actually named `jiji` and `makoto`). If you want to access them from the command line, you have to know the proper names, but the Print dialog in applications is currently (release 7b44) displaying the description information as well. This is probably also a bug; previous versions of OS X displayed the name here properly, so we expect that the exact information displayed here might change by the time you're reading this.

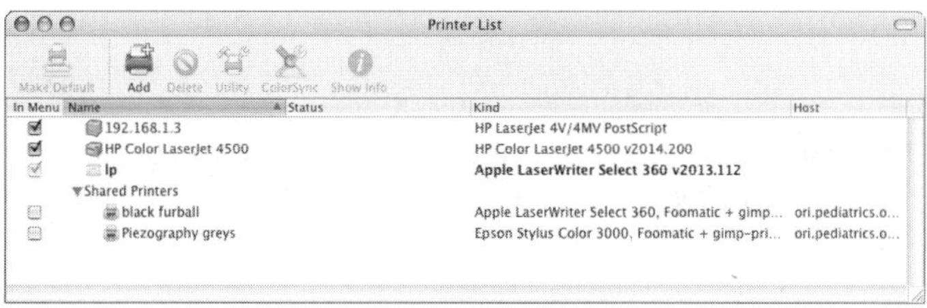

FIGURE 10.2 This Printer List shows five printers, three of which are configured locally, and two of which are discovered from other computers on the network.

The bolded line indicates that printer `lp` is currently my default printer. Each time you add a printer, the newly added one automatically becomes the default. To make a specific printer your default, select the printer in the Printer List and then choose the Make Default icon, or choose Printers, Make Default from the menu. Selecting a printer as a destination in an application's Print dialog also currently changes the default. To delete a printer, select it in the Printer List and click Delete.

To see a printer's job list, or queue, select Printers, Show Jobs from the menu. Figure 10.3 shows a sample print queue that has experienced an error and is retrying the send. According to the status entry, it hasn't yet given up. If the job had experienced a serious error, the Stop Jobs button would have changed to Retry, and there would be a more serious-sounding error report displayed in the window. Some print configurations will never give up, even if they can't contact the printer or remote host at all. Others will error out and give you potentially useful diagnostics in this window. When a job gets stuck, as this one has, you can either delete the job, or pause it by selecting the print job and clicking the appropriate button. If something happens and the printer or CUPS thinks that the job is completely broken, your options change to deleting it, or retrying the job. If there's a known printer problem that will take some time to fix, you can stop the printer, or put the job on hold, and reenable the job after the printer's working properly again.

When the printer is stopped, a Start Jobs icon appears as well. While a successful job is printing, the status bar is blue and alternately flashes Processing Job and Preparing Data for the duration of the print time. The buttons at the bottom of the status window are grayed out while the print job is processing, unless you select the print job. Figure 10.4 shows a sample status window for a normal print job. The status entry for a printer that is printing becomes Printing, and during this time the Print Center appears in the Dock, where you could also click to get this information. In some versions of OS X, the Print Center icon shows pages remaining to be printed and has a pop-up menu with queues and active/waiting jobs.

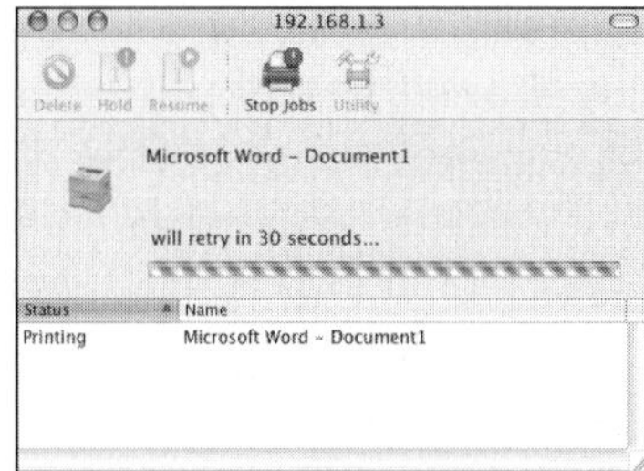

FIGURE 10.3 The print queue for printer 192.168.1.3 shows that the current print job has encountered an error in communications but is still retrying the connection. You could choose to delete the job or put it on hold. If it had fully errored out, you could retry it.

FIGURE 10.4 The print queue for printer `lp` shows that the current print job is proceeding normally.

At the top of each printer's window, you can choose to stop the jobs for a printer. When you do that, the status entry for the printer in the Printer List reflects that the queue has stopped by listing the status as Stopped. After you have stopped a printer queue, the option available becomes Start Jobs. Hold and Delete also appear, allowing you to place an individual job on hold, or delete it entirely.

Printer Classes

New with 10.3, Apple has added support for CUPS printer classes. Printer classes are user-created groupings of printers that can be treated like a single printer from the perspective of applications that want to print output. Classes appear in the Print dialog's list of printers just like any other individual printer. When selected and a print job sent to a printer class, CUPS delivers the print job to the first available printer in the class.

This capability to group printers might sound unimportant from the perspective of a home user with only a few printers, but it can be a real time and labor saver for a business with many shared networked printers.

To place printers into a class, select all of them that you want to put into the class in the Printer Setup Utility and then select the Printers, Pool Printers. You are presented with a dialog where you can confirm the printer selections you've made and give the class a name. You can create multiple printer classes and place any printer into any number of classes as well, allowing flexible groupings of your printing resources.

When created, printer classes look to the rest of the system like individual printers but are handled by CUPS by load-sharing the print jobs across the available printers. In any place that the system expects to see a specific printer name (including command-line commands such as `lpr`—see Chapter 15, "Command-Line Applications and Application Suites"—that don't document this feature), you can substitute a printer class, and CUPS manages the actual destination in the background.

The CUPS System Interface

Most of the software acting as glue between the Print Center interface, the command line, and GUI applications is based on or related to CUPS. CUPS is a general printing solution that's been being developed on other Unix variants for several years, and now is available on OS X. Because one of the goals of CUPS is to bring AppleTalk-like printing simplicity to Unix, and because the other Unix systems don't have the Print Center built in, CUPS itself has a nice configuration and control system of its own. This system is accessed through a Web-page interface that you should be able to find via the URL `http://127.0.0.1:631/`. As the Print Center/Printer Setup Utility matures, this interface becomes more and more redundant. It still, however, presents a few capabilities not available through the Print Center, and it allows GUI-based remote configuration and administration of printers through CUPS, so it's worth being familiar with, even if you don't use it regularly.

As mentioned previously, one really nice feature of CUPS is the availability of an enormous number of printer drivers through a range of sources. Installation and configuration aren't exactly as friendly as Mac users will prefer, but the steps necessary to install an incredible number of printing devices under OS X should be comfortable actions to you by the time you've completed a few more chapters. Here, we'll show you how to extend the range of your system's printing capabilities by using some of the publicly available tools, and how to configure the CUPS printing system through the Web interface. Specifically, we'll carry out some of the one-time setup necessary to use the full power of

CUPS. (Apple leaves out a few important bits, apparently assuming that all you're interested in printing with, is relatively recent printers.) The following procedure really isn't overly complex even without reading ahead, so if you're mildly adventurous and have a printer that you can't configure through the Print Center that you want to see printing, have at it.

In the following example, I'll install the components necessary to get a 1984 Apple ImageWriter I dot-matrix, serial-interface printer to function as a USB-connected PostScript printer. Yes, this is a ludicrous printing combination. It reaches somewhere around a roaring four pages per hour, but it demonstrates just how flexible CUPS really is as a printing environment, and it covers each of the steps necessary to get any other CUPS-supported printer up and running on your system. If you have a different model printer, the only substantial change in the following instructions is to substitute your printer type at the step where you create the PPD file.

NOTE

The automated printer-driver filter and the database that provides it with printer configuration information are undergoing a significant redesign as we write this book. There are currently two ways in which you can install the driver software, and they're not entirely compatible with each other. The more recent is backward compatible with the older, but the older does not work well with the newer database files. There are some pregenerated Mac OS X installers that just take a double-click to get everything we describe here installed and working, but they're unfortunately part of the older system and don't support the newer printer descriptions. It's your choice whether you want to install the older style (`cupsomatic`) drivers, or newer style (`foomatic`) drivers. We recommend the newer `foomatic` drivers because these support more printers, but the older `cupsomatic` drivers are currently easier to install.

Installing CUPS/`foomatic`/`cupsomatic` Drivers and Support Software

(Option 1) Download the foomatic-rip filter set from `http://www.linuxprinting.org/foomatic.html`. The current version as we're writing lives at `http://www.linuxprinting.org/download/foomatic/foomatic-filters-3.0.0.tar.gz`. The goal is to get a script that lives in this file (`foomatic-rip`) into the directory `/usr/libexec/cups/filter/`. At this point, the authors haven't made this easy. Hopefully, that'll change by the time you're reading this, but if it doesn't, follow these instructions:

1. Open a Terminal window (that's the `Terminal` program in Applications/Utilities, if you haven't worked with it before). You're about to use the command line, but you don't need to know what any of this means right now; you'll learn about it all in a few chapters.

2. In the terminal window, type **`cd`** and then press the spacebar. In a Finder window, drag the folder that *contains* the `foomatic-filters...gz` file and drop it into the terminal window. Press the Return key.

3. In the terminal window, type **`gunzip foomatic-filters-3.0.0.tar.gz`** and press the Return key (if the version's changed, replace `foomatic-filters-3.0.0.tar.gz` with the name of the `foomatic-filters` file you've downloaded). Now type **`tar -xf foomatic-filters-3.0.0.tar`** and press the Return key. Give your password when asked.

4. In the terminal window, type **`cd foomatic-filters-3.0.0`** and press the Return key. Now type **`ls`** and press the Return key. You should see a list of files that looks something like this:

```
COPYING        config.cache             foomatic-rip
CVS            config.log               foomatic-rip.1
ChangeLog      config.status            foomatic-rip.1.in
Makefile       configure                foomatic-rip.in
Makefile.in    configure.in             install-sh
README         filter.conf              makeMan
TODO           foomatic-gswrapper       makeMan.in
USAGE          foomatic-gswrapper.1     make_configure
acinclude.m4   foomatic-gswrapper.1.in
aclocal.m4     foomatic-gswrapper.in
```

   In the terminal window, type **`./configure`** and press the Return key. Next type **`make`** and press Return, and finally type **`sudo make install`** and press the Return key. (You've just built a piece of Unix software—a subject you'll learn much more about in the chapters to come.)

   To finish up, type **`cd /usr/libexec/cups/filter/`** into the terminal and press Return. Then type **`sudo ln -s /usr/local/bin/foomatic-rip ./`** and press Return. You're now finished with the terminal for a while.

(Option 2) Download the `cupsomatic` filter and any of the collected printing driver files from `http://www.linuxprinting.org/macosx/`, and install the package. This installs `/usr/libexec/cups/filter/cupsomatic`, which is an older version of the `foomatic-rip` program, as well as some collection of printer description (PPD) files. You can install multiple printer driver collections from this page if you need printers that aren't all available in a single package. The `cupsomatic` software you've just installed is compatible with any of the drivers shown on the `http://www.linuxprinting.org/macosx/` page, and with minor editing (edit the driver [PPD] file and change all occurrences of the text `foomatic-rip` to read `cupsomatic`) with some of the drivers available from the driver database, but it is generally now unsupported software.

1. If you went with option 2 and will not have Windows systems trying to print through your CUPS-served printers, skip ahead to step 4. If you will have Windows clients, you need to install another bit of software to help them out a bit: `http://www.linuxprinting.org/foomatic-gswrapper` is necessary—see the instructions at `http://www.linuxprinting.org/gswrapper.html`; then skip ahead to step 4.

2. If you used option 1, point your browser at `http://www.linuxprinting.org/printer_list.cgi`. Select an appropriate PPD file for your printer. This PPD contains not only information on the details of printer capabilities but also the information necessary to have CUPS translate into the language that this printer understands.

   For example, `http://www.linuxprinting.org/show_printer.cgi?recnum=23776` points to a printer definition to feed into CUPS and the `foomatic-rip/cupsomatic` driver to allow you to print PostScript to the ancient but indestructible Apple ImageWriter I dot-matrix printer. If you were installing this, you'd follow the link, for example, to the `iwhi` driver, and select the Download PPD file option from the Recommended driver section of the page.

3. Wherever this file lands on your machine, you need to copy it to `/usr/share/cups/model/<filename>`, where *<filename>* is the PPD file that you downloaded. In my case (for the ImageWriter I), the file is `Apple-ImageWriter-iwhi.ppd`. After you have the PPD file in the `/usr/share/cups/model` directory, you're almost finished with the installation.

3a. Some printers require a separate, printer-specific filter installation in addition to the `cupsomatic` filter and the PPD. The same page that points to the PPD contains instructions on downloading and installing this filter. Follow these if necessary for your printer.

4. Install Ghostscript. Ghostscript is a software PostScript and PDF interpreter that also contains an amazing number of output drivers for assorted printers. For many printers, it can convert directly from PostScript to the printer's natural binary language. For others, it can be used to convert from PostScript into a generic intermediate image format that can be used as input by a printer-specific driver. Ghostscript, compiled with almost every supported printer type enabled, as well as some special printer-driver software is available from the GIMP-Print project at `http://gimp-print.sourceforge.net/MacOSX.php3`. With 10.3, Apple provides most of the GIMP-Print software, but as of this writing, not the crucial Ghostscript module. Download and install the most recent version of EPS Ghostscript that the GIMP-Print folks have listed. If you're running 10.2, or want more recent GIMP-Print drivers than Apple makes available, it won't hurt to download and install the GIMP-Print driver collection either. Installation is via a simple Apple `.dmg` installer for both Ghostscript and GIMP-Print.

5. If your system does not include back-end files named `serial` and `file` in `/usr/libexec/cups/backend/`, download the `serial` and `file` CUPS drivers from `http://www.macosxunleashed.com/downloads/` and install them in this location. Make sure that the files have execute permission (`chmod 755 /usr/libexec/cups/backend/file; chmod 755 /usr/libexec/cups/backend/serial`, or use the Finder's Get Info permissions dialog). If we've gotten a working `parallel` driver by the time you read this, it will be available from the same location.

6. All that now remains to do is restart the `cups` daemon (`sudo killall -HUP cupsd`, or just restart your machine if that doesn't make sense), and you should be able to add a printer using this new information.

CAUTION

You may find it necessary to restart your machine regardless of whether you're comfortable restarting the daemon. We've experienced some erratic behavior when restarting the CUPS daemon both through the simple `kill` statement, and through the `StartupItems` script.

Now you have CUPS installed and printer drivers for a number of printers available as well. If you need additional drivers for other printers, you can continue creating PPDs at `http://www.linuxprinting.org/` and installing them on your system, or you can wait until later; you can always add others whenever you need them.

Configuring Printers Through the CUPS Administrative Web Interface

After the `cupsomatic/foomatic-rip` drivers and support software are installed and a proper driver for your printer is available, setting up the printer requires a number of steps through the CUPS administration Web interface, accessed through `http://127.0.0.1:631/`:

1. The first is adding a few identifying bits of information to the system. Figure 10.5 shows the first step reached under the CUPS Add Printer item. This item is linked from a number of places in the CUPS administrative Web pages. The easiest to access is under the Do Administration Tasks item from the main `http://127.0.0.1:631/` page.

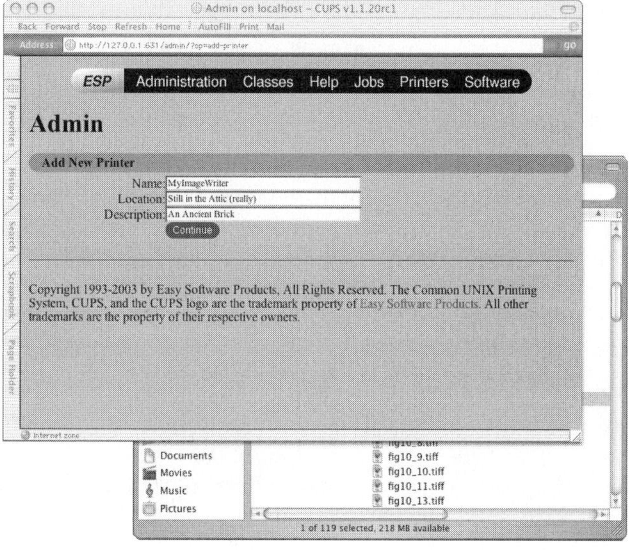

FIGURE 10.5 The first step of setting up a printer under CUPS is defining a name, location, and description.

2. The next step is selecting the type of connection, as shown in Figure 10.6. This is moderately cryptic, because several connection types seem to overlap. For my printer, I'm going to use the `file` connection type, because on Unix systems, serial devices just look like files that you can write data into. The following list details the known printer connection types that CUPS can use. Not all these may be available on your system, and what you can use depends on a number of configuration choices you make and optional software that you may have installed.

    - Laser is for AppleTalk LaserWriter printers—you can add any of these through the Print Center, so there's no need to fiddle with them here.
    - AppleTalk Printer Access Protocol is standard AppleTalk printing, which should also include LaserWriter printers. Most of these can probably also be added through the Print Center.
    - AppSocket/HP JetDirect is an option to talk to HP JetDirect servers. Most of these support AppleTalk or LPR printing, so there's little reason to use this option.
    - Internet Printing Protocol (http) is for IPP printers accessible via HTTP. Currently, CUPS is about the only system you'll see using IPP, and your local CUPS printers will appear in the Print Center. Remote ones you can configure here using this option.
    - Internet Printing Protocol (ipp) is for IPP printers accessible through IPP's own protocol. Again, CUPS will be hosting most of these, and you can access them through the Print Center if they're local, or set them up here if you need to provide a remote address.
    - LPD/LPR Host or Printer is for Line Printer Daemon printers accessible via TCP/IP. You can configure these in the Print Center, or via NetInfo as shown in Chapter 11 as well.
    - USB Printer covers directly connected USB devices. The USB driver seems moderately functional for serial and file printing types, but this isn't how they're supposed to be done.
    - Serial is for printers attached to serial ports. You may not have this option unless you've downloaded the serial driver from `http://www.macosxunleashed.com/downloads/`. Apple's started including it in the distribution again. In some versions of OS X it's there; in some it's missing. This driver should work with real serial ports, and with USB-adapter serial ports, if your USB port reports the existence of a serial port in a syntax that the driver understands (as of August, 2003, at least some do not).

- Parallel is for printers attached to parallel ports. This is the choice if you have a USB-to-parallel adapter being used to hook up your printer.
- FAX and Modem are a CUPS interface into the OS X print-to-FAX system.
- Depending on the version of OS X you're running, you may have an option labeled either ZeroConf or Rendezvous, which configures the system to automatically discover available printers being shared by other ZeroConf-capable systems.
- Windows Printer via Samba is for network printers attached to Microsoft Windows machines and served via the SAMBA resource sharing protocol.
- File is a catch-all last-ditch option to be used for printing to printers that can be accessed by writing data to a named file (this isn't as weird as it sounds—most peripherals in Unix can be accessed by reading from, or writing to, specific files in the `/dev/` directory. When the OS recognizes the existence of a peripheral—a printer, for example—a special file is created in `/dev/` that is connected to the printer. Read from the file, and you'll get any status information the printer cares to share. Write to it, and what you put in it, gets printed.

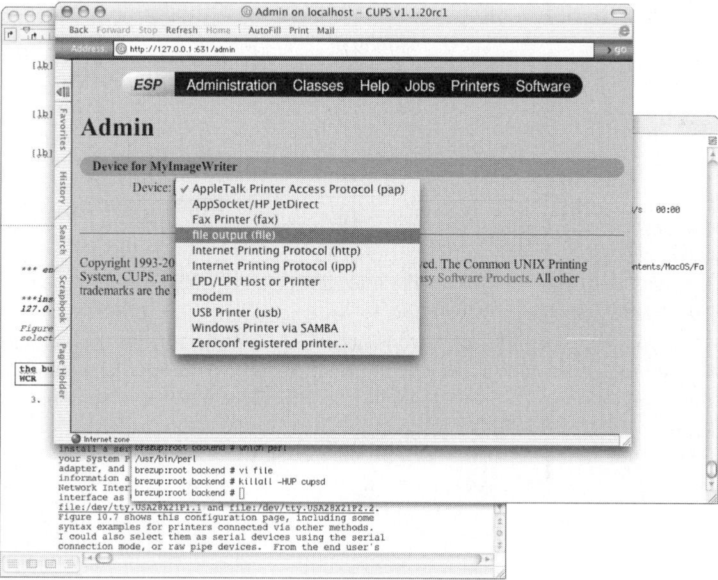

FIGURE 10.6 The second step in configuring the printer is selecting the type of connection being used.

3. Next you need to provide distinct connection information for the printer. In my case, I'm using a USB serial adapter, which appears as `/dev/tty.USA28X21P1.1` and `/dev/tty.USA28X21P2.2`. (Try checking your network pane to see what your serial ports are named. If you're trying to install a serial printer, you may need to quit and restart your System Preferences utility to get it to detect the adapter, and the name might be incomplete—missing the information after the second decimal—as shown in the Network Interfaces pane.) These can be selected in the Web interface as USB type devices, with the URIs `file:/dev/tty.USA28X21P1.1` and `file:/dev/tty.USA28X21P2.2`.

   Figure 10.7 shows this configuration page, including some syntax examples for printers connected via other methods. I could also select them as serial devices using the serial connection mode, or raw pipe devices. From the end user's perspective, there's little difference between these options, but from someone inclined to poke at the system's guts, the ability to treat the printer either as a file that can be written to, a "pipe" into which data can be pumped (more on this in Chapter 15), or as a serial communications device, gives great power and flexibility for sophisticated control.

   To enable file-type output, you need to edit `/etc/cups/cupsd.conf` and change the line that reads

   ```
   #FileDevice No
   ```

   so that it reads

   ```
   FileDevice Yes
   ```

CAUTION

This change could incur some security problems. For example, it potentially allows users to write into any file that the CUPS system can write into. It's the most debuggable of the interfaces, however, and we're going to show you how to write your own, basic printer driver in a few chapters, so if you're inclined to hack at your system, or want to get a freaky old printer to work, you might need to temporarily enable it. Unfortunately, the pipe-output back-end type, which is almost as nice for debugging, doesn't seem to currently be supported, or straightforward to hack into working condition.

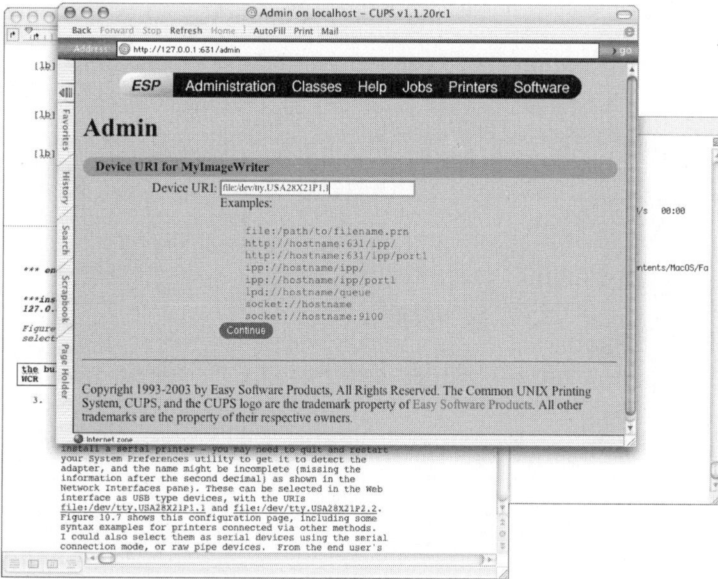

FIGURE 10.7 The third step is providing a rather cryptic definition of how the software can contact and interact with the printer description. In this case, it's an URI for a file, where the Unix side of OS X can write directly to the serial interface.

4. The fourth step is selecting the printer's manufacturer, as shown in Figure 10.8. If the manufacturer of your printer isn't shown, either you haven't downloaded and installed the PPD properly, or your PPD doesn't report the correct information to CUPS.

NOTE

Don't expect your list of available manufacturers or printers to look like mine. The PPDs that you configure and install from `linuxprinting.org`, or from GIMP-Print, control the options you see on your system.

5. Given a manufacturer, the interface constructs a list of printers, from which you can choose your specific printer, as shown in Figure 10.9. Hopefully, after you click Continue at this step, you'll get a page saying your printer has been installed and configured properly. At this point, your printer should be available in the Print Center for printing in both GUI and command-line applications.

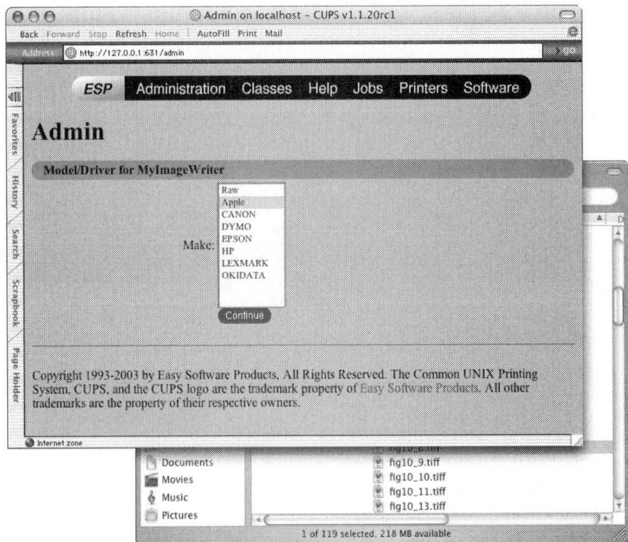

FIGURE 10.8 The fourth step is selecting the printer's manufacturer. This selection modifies the list of printers available on the next page.

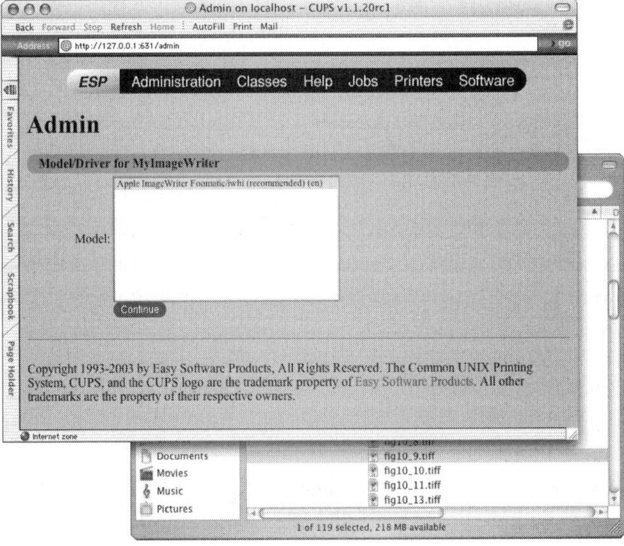

FIGURE 10.9 Finally, you can select the specific printer type you're installing. The Foomatic part of the name is generated by the Foomatic PPD generator.

After you have configured a printer, you can visit its configuration page to make modifications to the printer's connection, location, and description; turn the queue for it on and off; and manage jobs on it. Figure 10.10 shows the Web interface to this functionality. The Print Center can make most of these modifications as well, when the printer is visible to it.

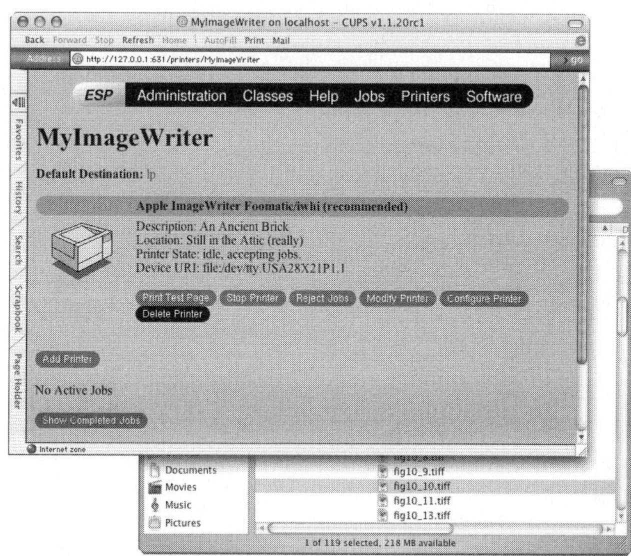

FIGURE 10.10 The printer status page for MyImageWriter, under the CUPS Web interface. You can start and stop the printer queue, send test pages, reconfigure the printer's connection, and make some modifications to the printer's behavior from this page.

Under the Configure Printer option shown in the previous Admin page, you have control over a number of simple options regarding the printer. For the ImageWriter, a page like that shown in Figure 10.11 appears, with settings to control the default printing resolution, default page size, and whether to print banners or trailer pages for each job. The banners and footers are contained in PostScript files stored in the directory `/usr/share/cups/banners`.

Figure 10.12 shows the output printed through the driver set up in this example. As you can see, a printer with 120×144 resolution and dot-gain approaching 100%, is not the most beautiful output device for printing PostScript data. However, it *does work*. Other, more capable printers work better, and there is active development in the GIMP-Print community of quite high-quality drivers for a number of high-resolution ink-jet devices. With CUPS, PostScript printing support for the modern photo-quality ink-jet printers is only a few open-source mouse-clicks away.

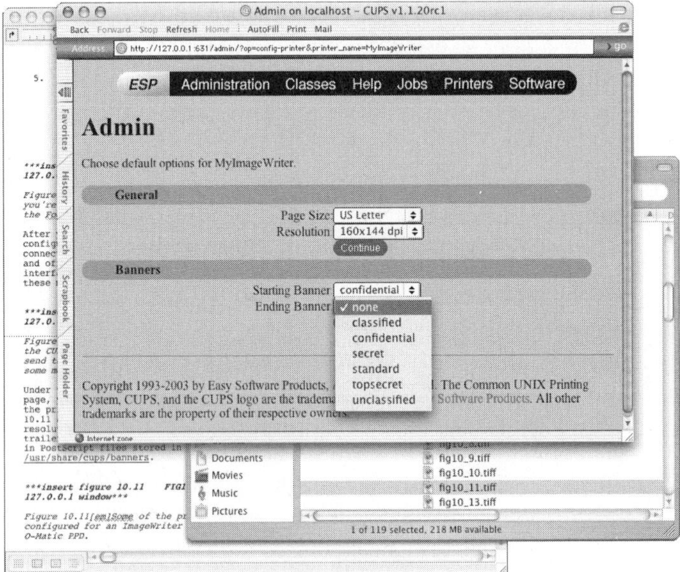

FIGURE 10.11 Some of the printing options that can be configured for an ImageWriter type printer, according to the PPD-O-Matic PPD.

FIGURE 10.12 PostScript printed output, from an iMac 17-inch (2002), printed on an Apple ImageWriter I (1984).

NOTE

Most of the same configuration options for CUPS printers specified by URI connection are also available under a hidden Advanced dialog option in the Print Center. If you hold down the Option key while clicking Add, to add a new printer, you have the option of choosing Advanced from the list of printer connection types. The dialog that appears gives you access to the same installation and configuration options as adding a printer through the CUPS administrative interface, though it provides much less hinting as to what valid responses are.

These same options, and a few more, are available via the command-line interface to CUPS administration, which is covered in Chapter 15.

Administrating CUPS Printers from Remote Locations

One of the nice things about having a Web-based interface to the CUPS printing system, is that if you configure the server to allow it, you can check on your printers and perform any administration tasks from any location just as easily as you can from the console of your machine. All that is required to enable remote administration is to modify the CUPS configuration file that tells it what machines it should allow to connect to the administrative Web interface. This file lives in `/etc/cups/` and is named `cupsd.conf`. The syntax is identical to normal Apache Web server configuration syntax, so you'll learn considerably more about things you can do to customize its operation when Apache is covered in Chapter 27, "Web Serving." For now, the options you're interested in examining are the `Listen` option, by default set to `127.0.0.1:631`, the `BrowseAllow` option, by default set to `127.0.0.1`, and the `Allow From` option (which occurs twice in the file) which also is `127.0.0.1` by default.

If you want to allow another specific machine to connect, you can extend the access to the administrative Web interface by adding `<your ip address>:631` as an additional `Listen` option, and adding `BrowseAllow` and `Allow From` lines for the IP address of the specific machine you want to allow to connect. You can set up considerably more sophisticated access restrictions and allowances, such as password-restricted access, and selective access to different parts of the Web interface if you explore the full options available for Apache Web server configuration.

CAUTION

Changes to this file can break printing if you move your machine from network to network!

If you enter your machine's IP as an IP to `Listen` at, and your machine's IP address changes, the `cupsd` server won't be able to bind that network address, and it will quit. This will leave your machine without printing services. Usually though, there's little reason to want to enable remote printer administration on a machine that's moved from place to place, so this is really only likely to be a problem for the experimenter and not a practical limitation.

Printing

Sending a job to the printer from an application in OS X works as it did in previous versions of the operating system. Choose File, Page Setup to set basic page settings. Choose File, Print to send your job to the printer and specify additional characteristics for the print job.

If you installed separate printer drivers from your manufacturer, your printing dialogs may have additional custom options not covered here.

Page Setup

Under the File menu of an application, choose Page Setup to set the basic settings. Figure 10.13 shows what Page Setup looks like in OS X. Page Setup appears as either a sheet or a window, depending on the application. Sometimes it can be accessed only from the File menu, and in other applications it is available through an icon-bar selection, or with Shift-Command-P. The Settings option has the major choices of Page Attributes, Custom Page Size, application-specific options (varies by application), and Summary. The menus in the middle of the dialog change based on the choice under the Settings menu. At the bottom of Page Setup, there is a button for direct access to the Help Center, as well as buttons for Cancel and OK. We will break down our examination of Page Setup according to the Settings choices.

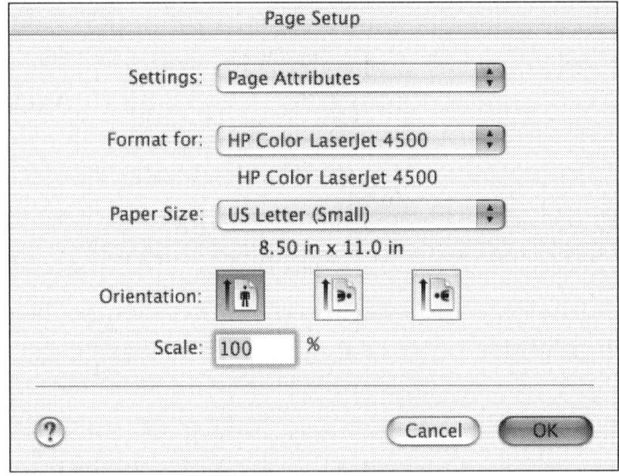

FIGURE 10.13 Page Setup can still be found under the File menu in OS X. The page settings are almost identical to previous versions of the operating system.

Page Attributes

The Settings option is set to Page Attributes by default. The Page Attributes that can be specified are the printer, page size, orientation, and scale.

Format For Under the Page Attributes section of Page Setup, you can select which printer to format for. The available printer choices are Any Printer and whatever printers are included as part of your Printer List. Page Setup formats for Any Printer by default, and Any Printer has an additional description of Generic Printer. When you select a printer in your Printer List, a more specific description appears. Note that in our example, the Page Setup describes printer jiji as an Apple Personal LaserWriter.

Paper Size Page size is also specified in Page Setup. The available paper sizes vary with the selected printer. The default page sizes available for Any Printer range from 3×5 to 16×24—obviously not all of which are possible on some printers. So although Any Printer is fine to use as a general default, don't be surprised if its settings don't literally work for any printer. Whenever you select a paper size, its dimensions appear as an additional description. For Any Printer, US Letter, 8.5"×11", is the default paper size. Keep an eye on the setting that this option comes up with. Some specific printers seem to default to US Letter Small as their default paper size, which can wreak havoc with page layouts that you've constructed for full-size US Letter paper.

Orientation The Orientation setting controls which edge of the paper is "up" with respect to the print. Portrait, the norm for written-text type output, is available as well as two forms of Landscape (more commonly used for photographs). For Landscape, you can specify whether the top of the printout should be at the right or left side of the paper. Simply select the appropriate icon to suit your needs. Portrait is the default orientation.

Scale Scale is a box where you can input the desired scaling. The default is 100%.

Custom Paper Size

The Custom paper size dialog allows you to create your own special paper sizes if the printer's description does not already include a page size you want to work with. You are prompted for page height and width, and all four margins. You can save your favorite custom page sizes for later reuse.

Page Summary

The Summary option of Page Setup displays a summary of the settings you have selected for all the Page Attributes categories. Figure 10.14 shows a sample summary.

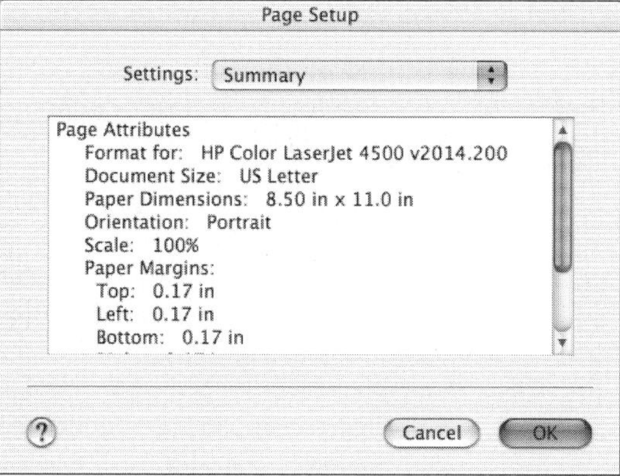

FIGURE 10.14 The Summary section of Page Setup summarizes the information from each of the Page Setup subpanes.

Application Specific

Page setup dialogs may also include application-specific entries in the Settings menu. These can include almost any configuration option and can override the settings in other panes of the Print Setup dialog, if the application-specific and normal options overlap. Microsoft Word, for example, duplicates almost all the regular page-setup options in its own application-specific pane. It further allows the page setup options configured there to apply to sections of the document, and to have different page setup options for different sections of a document.

Print

The Print control is located under the File menu, typically attached to the Command-P keystroke. Select this menu option to print a file. Choosing Print opens the Print dialog box, as shown in Figure 10.15. Depending on the application, the Print dialog box appears either as a sheet or as a separate, movable window.

In the top part of the Print dialog, using the Printer pop-up menu, you can select what printer you want to route the printout to (or edit the Printer List to include it, if it's not available for selection). Using the Presets pop-up, you can select among (or save) collections of Print configuration settings.

The options necessary to configure a number of Printing preferences appear in the middle part of the Print dialog box. From a pop-up menu, you can select among the options you want to configure (not all of which will be available for every printer): Copies & Pages, Layout, Output Options, (print) Scheduling, Paper Handling, ColorSync, Cover Page, Error Handling, Printer Features, Application Specific, and Summary can all be configured or viewed here. Settings that you make here can be saved by under the Presets pop-up menu.

The bottom section of the Print dialog box has buttons for Help, Preview, Cancel, and Print, as well as the options to save the printout as a PDF instead of printing it, and to send it via FAX to a remote FAX machine. Preview is sometimes available under the File menu of an application, but it always appears as a button in the Print dialog box.

Note that the Print dialog box that is used by the Terminal application varies from the more traditional Print dialog box described in this section. Other applications may make custom Print dialogs available as well.

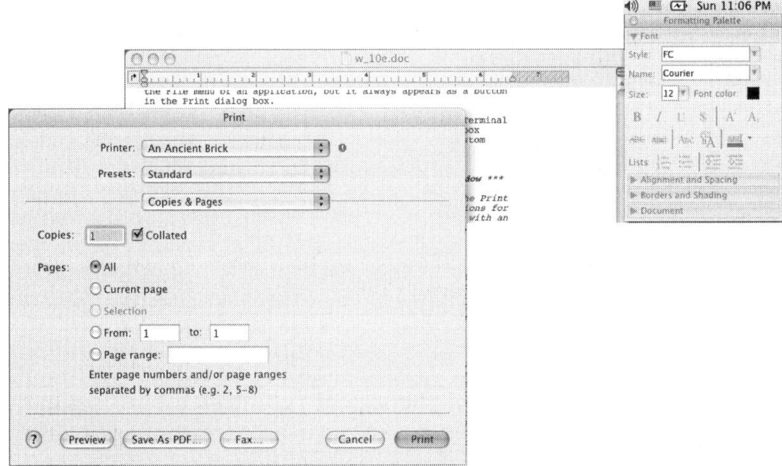

FIGURE 10.15 Choosing File, Print opens the Print dialog box, where you can select a printer and various options for your print job. Note the small stop sign (the tiny octagon with an exclamation point in it) to the right of my chosen printer, indicating that this print queue is currently stopped.

Printer

Whichever printer is listed in your Printer List as your default printer appears here initially. You can also select from any of the other printers available in your Printer List, or you can choose Edit Printer List at the bottom of the menu of available printers, to add to or modify your Printer List. This option immediately takes you to the Printer Setup Utility, where you can add or delete printers.

Presets

Presets are collections of print-option settings that you've saved. The default is Standard, which is your plain-vanilla one-copy, all pages, no special options setting. After you have saved a customized setting, you can select Standard or any of your customized setting collections by name. The Save, Save As, Rename, and Delete options available under the Presets menu allow you to manage the presets you have constructed. Custom presets that you construct are available from all applications, though application-specific options for seemingly identical preferences may not be transferred between different applications.

Copies & Pages

Copies & Pages, the first item in a pop-up menu of many items, is the default pane in the Print dialog. Here you specify the number of copies you want to print, whether the pages should be collated, and a page range. For the page range, you can select either All, to print the entire document, or Current, to print the currently visible page, or you can specify an actual range of page numbers.

Layout

Layout, shown in Figure 10.16, is where you select layout settings. The first available option is Pages Per Sheet, where you can select 1, 2, 4, 6, 9, or 16 pages per sheet. The next option is Layout Direction. There are four layout direction options: horizontally from left to right, horizontally from right to left, vertically from left to right, and vertically from right to left. The available layout directions are indicated with helpful icons. The final layout option is Border. Available options for Border are None, Single hairline, Single thin line, Double hairline, and Double thin line.

If you have a printer that can print both sides of the page (called duplex printing), you may be able to set that print option in the Layout pane under Two Sided Printing, or you may have a separate configuration pane for duplex printing. The duplex options allow you to select between binding edges for the prints. This controls which way the two-sided prints "flip" so that you can turn the page either at the top, or at the side.

Output Options

The Output Options pane, shown in Figure 10.17, allows you to save your print job to a file instead. Currently, the available output options are PDF and PostScript. The Print button becomes a Save button, allowing you to select a location where your file should be saved.

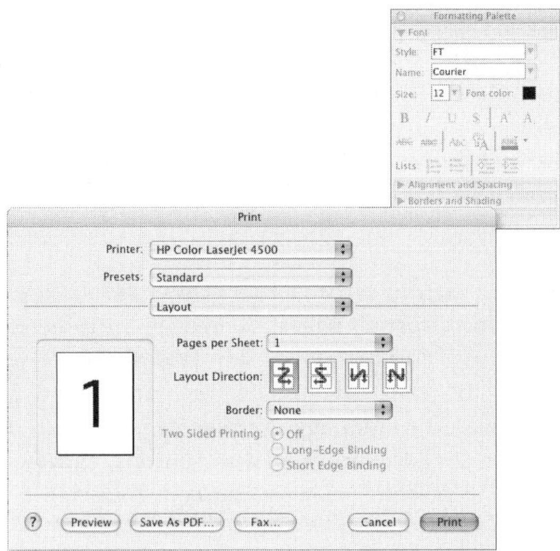

FIGURE 10.16 The Layout section of Print is where you specify the number of pages per sheet, layout direction, border, and duplexing options.

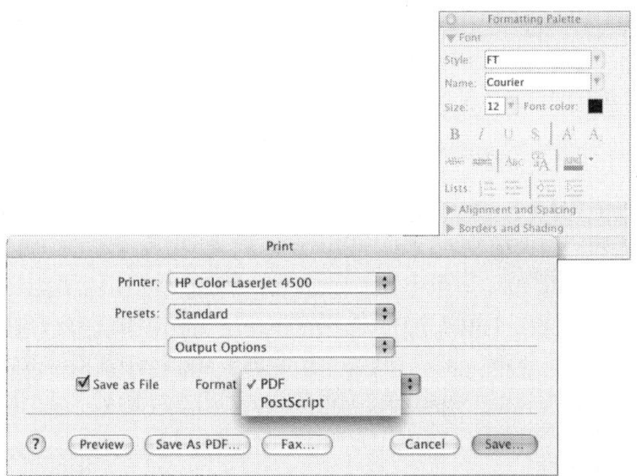

FIGURE 10.17 In the Output Options section of the Print dialog box, you can save your Print job as a PDF file or PostScript file.

Paper Handling

The Paper Handling section, shown in Figure 10.18, allows you to specify whether to print all, or just even or odd pages, or to reverse the printing order. This may not seem a particularly useful collection of options, but in fact it's a convenient way to get two-sided printing out of a printer that can only print on one side of the page. Using the options here, you can print first the odd pages, take the stack of paper directly out of your printer's output stack, put it back in the input tray, and then print the even pages onto the other side of the stack. We strongly suspect that the name of this menu choice may change in the future.

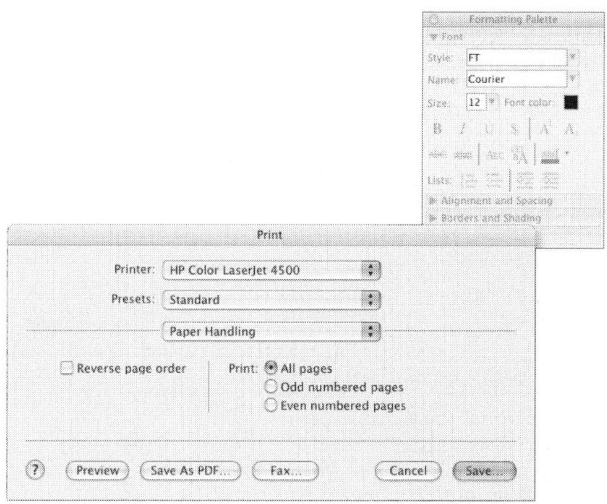

FIGURE 10.18 The options necessary to perform "manual duplex printing" are available in the Paper Handling section of the Print dialog.

Scheduler

The Scheduler option, shown in Figure 10.19, allows you to control when your printout gets printed. It also lets you set a print priority for the printout. These settings interact in such a way as to make the when portion of the setting mostly a suggestion, and the priority portion of the setting a control as to how serious the timing suggestion actually is. The higher the priority you set, the stronger the time portion of the suggestion and the closer to the set time that your printout is likely to appear. The lower the priority, the less important your time suggestion becomes (subject to the fact that it won't ever print *before* you set the time to print), and the more subject to being delayed by other printouts it becomes. You could, for example, set the printout to be printed Now and set the priority to Low, and end up with your printout not appearing for several hours, as other more important print jobs repeatedly bump it out of the way in the queue.

ColorSync

Figure 10.20 shows the ColorSync options available in MS Word. Other ColorSync options appear contextually in other applications. In addition to a number of Quartz filters that can generate subtly different output presentations by filtering the input, if you have a monochrome printer, the pane gives you the ability to choose between having colors mapped to grays in software, or directly in the printer's hardware. It might seem that there's little difference in where one discards the color information to create a grayscale print from a color image, but in fact there are sometimes significant visual consequences—instances where an image would be simply unusable printed one way, and acceptable when printed the other. A distinct example of this occurs with Hewlett-Packard color LaserJet printers. HP's internal conversion from color to grayscale works much better for many purposes than converting the data externally and printing directly in grayscale mode. It appears that this is due to the HP LaserJet using color toners to mix gray shades in certain areas of the image where subtle shading is necessary, and where its black toner would create a too-contrasty effect. We can't guarantee that either setting of this option is always the right one for every job, but we can guarantee that there will be some differences on some jobs—experiment and pick the one that works best for you.

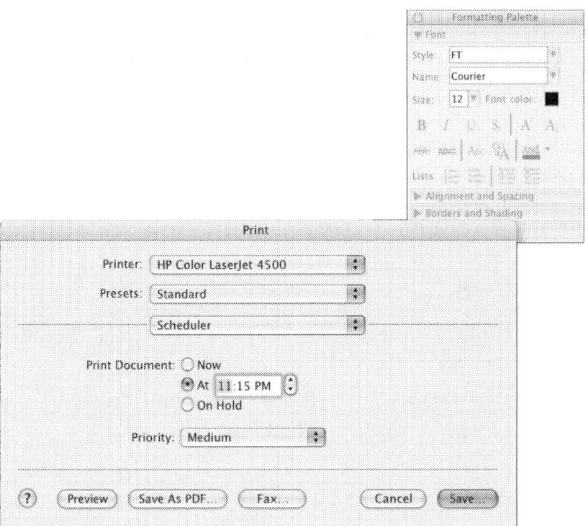

FIGURE 10.19 The controls available for scheduling your printout. Think of the time setting as a suggestion, and the priority setting as an "importance of obeying the suggestion" setting.

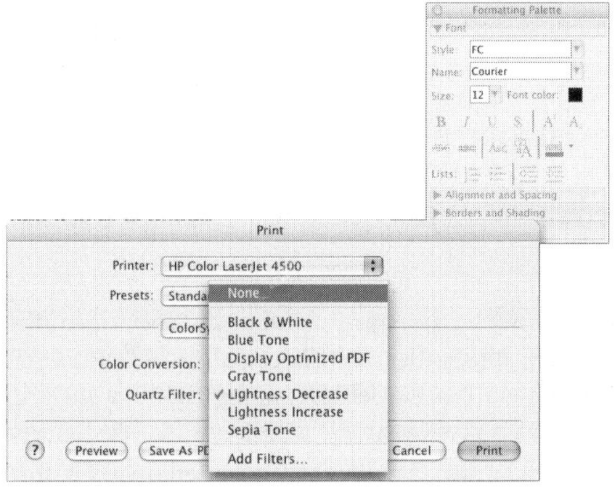

FIGURE 10.20 The ColorSync options allow the user to apply some Quartz-layer filtering to the output, and to hint about where certain data conversions should occur in the print processing stream.

Cover Page

Figure 10.21 shows the Cover Page option set. Some printers and printer configuration sets won't support this option. Currently there are only the options of setting some banner text regarding the document's confidentiality, of placing the banner page before or after your printout, and of adding some text to the cover page regarding appropriate billing. We expect this page to mature over time, as many print systems allow the cover page to be printed from a separate paper bin (letterhead for example), and other useful manipulations of that type.

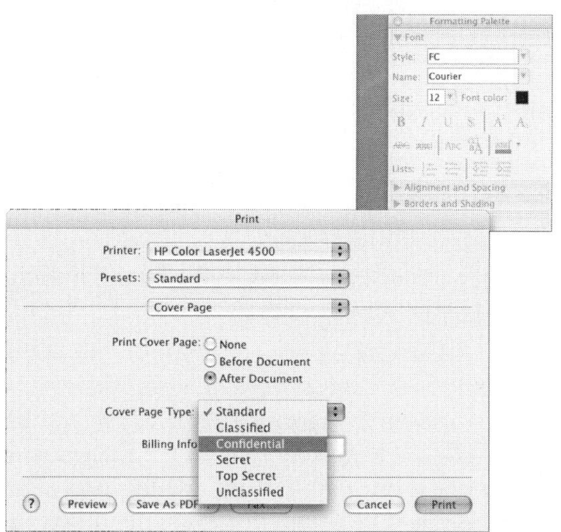

FIGURE 10.21 The Cover Page options allow you to specify an extra identifier page to be layered with your printout so that when people are pulling it from the printer, they know who it belongs to.

Error Handling

Figure 10.22 shows the default Error Handling options for a PostScript printer that can have multiple trays (Many inkjet printers won't provide this dialog). The Error Handling options that appear for this printer are for PostScript Errors and Tray Switching. The PostScript error choices are to either have No Special Reporting, which is the default, or to Print Detailed Report. The Tray Switching error options are Use Printer's Default, Switch to Another Cassette with the Same Paper Size, or Display Alert. Unfortunately, because the authors have only PostScript printers readily available to test, we can't tell you whether another error handling option might appear in place of the PostScript Errors option, or whether that option is simply grayed out for non-PostScript printers. CUPS-served printers by the way, should universally function as PostScript printers for this option, regardless of the actual printer type.

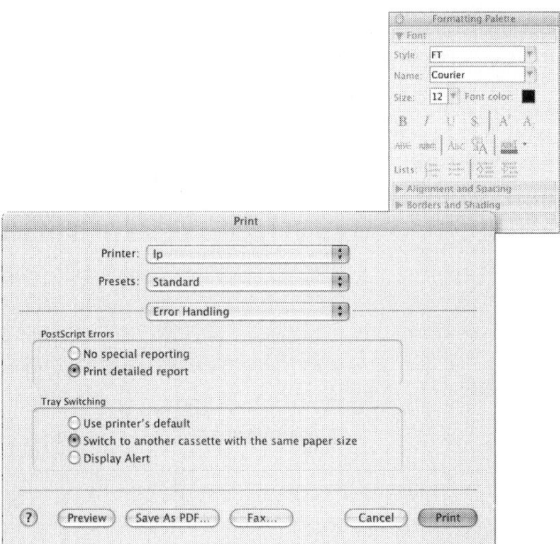

FIGURE 10.22 Error handling options can be set in the Error Handling section of the Print dialog box.

Paper Feed

The Paper Feed option group, shown in Figure 10.23, is where you set any special paper feed options. You can either choose to specify that all your pages come from a particular paper feed option, or that the first one comes from one location and the remaining pages from a different location. This could be useful, for example, if you have a tray dedicated to letterhead. The actual paper feed choices available for the different categories vary with the printer.

If you want to print your job on special paper, either the first page, or all of it, the manual feed for the first page option can be a useful tool to have in your bag of tricks. More than once, we've sent a print job down to the networked color laser to be printed on a batch of high-quality stock for publication, only to find that some grad student's print job has gotten in ahead of ours and eaten up a bunch of our high-quality paper. If your printer supports it, you can use the first-page-manual option to delay your print job until you're actually at the printer and can make sure that it's going through under your control, on your desired paper.

This works because most printers will pause indefinitely waiting for a piece of paper to be dropped in the manual feed slot. If you select manual for the first page, the effect then is not only that you get to feed it your first page separate from the cassette (allowing you to use letterhead if you choose), but that the printer waits to grab that page out of the manual feeder before it starts loading pages from the normal tray for the rest of your job. This makes for a nice pause in the process during which you can load whatever special paper you want to use, drop your manual-feed page in the manual feed tray, slap in the cassette of special paper that you don't want to lose to someone else's printouts of email messages and Web funny pages, and be relatively certain that your job is going to proceed immediately and with no break in the middle for someone else to use the paper you've loaded.

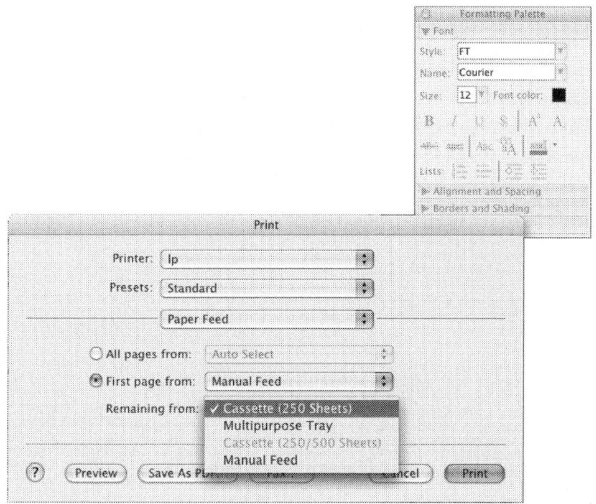

FIGURE 10.23 The print job can be configured to select its first page from one source and the remaining pages from a different paper tray. This lets you conveniently use letterhead for lead pages, or otherwise segregate your leading and body pages by paper type.

Application-Specific

Sometimes an application will have a category for additional special options unique to it. This is always a good place to check if you find that your print results are a bit unexpected. For example, if you print something created in color to a color printer, but it prints in grayscale, you would want to check here for additional options for your particular application because it might have some default control that forces grayscale output, despite the other printing settings. Figure 10.24 shows some of the options that MS Word registers with the Print dialog.

Printer-Specific

Printers with special capabilities may register printer-specific menu items and panes as well. These can include anything from special handling for different paper stocks, to control of built-in color profiles. Figures 10.25 and 10.26 show two different subpanes, Color Options and Printer Features. These both contain assorted options specific to the selected printer. These options range from a number of ways of suggesting what you want the output print to look like (vivid, subdued, monotone, and so on), as well as special handling for different media types.

On other printers, different options appear: Some have more color controls, others have resolution controls, and so on.

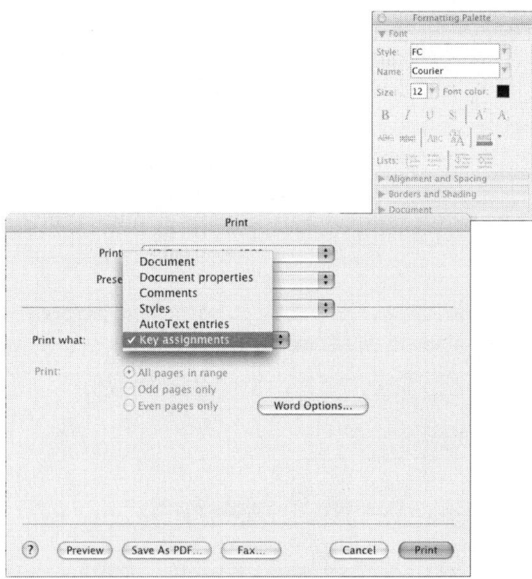

FIGURE 10.24 Applications can add specific options to the Print dialog under application-specific menus.

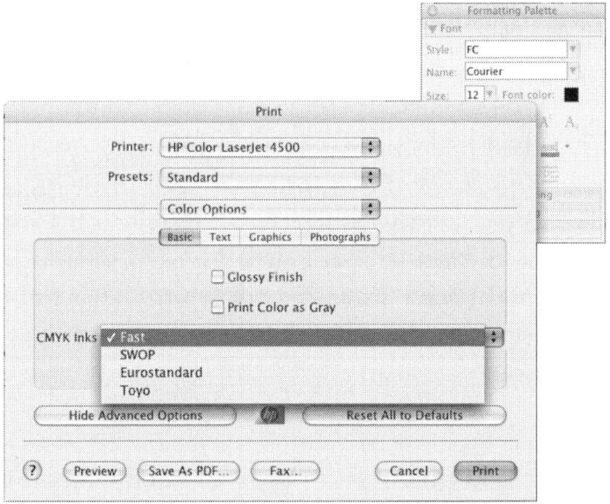

FIGURE 10.25 The HP LaserJet 4500 printer is a color laser printer, but it allows you to print color documents in grayscale, with the conversion being done at the printer. Other options for printer-specific color capabilities, such as ironing a glossy surface onto the image, are available from this dialog as well.

FIGURE 10.26 Specifying the media type for the printer. Among other things, it knows that if it's printing transparencies, it needs to lay down less toner so that the transparency won't be too opaque.

Print Summary

The Summary option displays a summary of all the settings that you specified with Print. A sample Print Summary is shown in Figure 10.27.

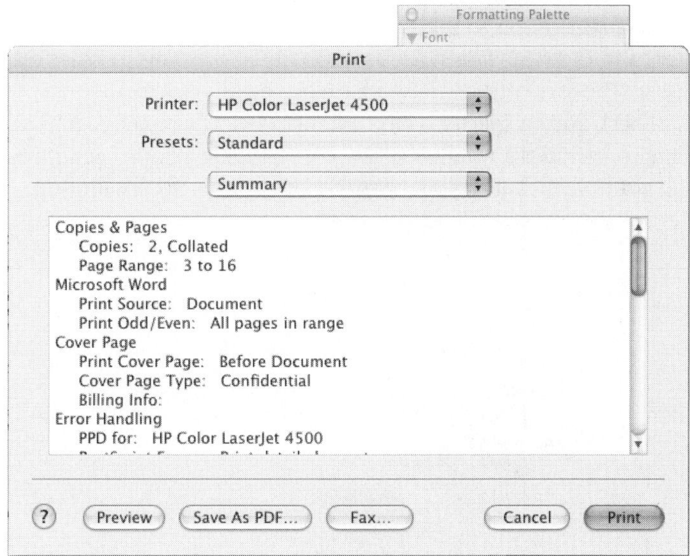

FIGURE 10.27 The Summary section of the Print dialog box displays a summary of the settings for the current print job.

Preview

The behavior of the Preview button of the Print dialog box varies with the application. In some applications, the Preview button calls the Preview application. From the Preview application itself, you can then choose such options as Save as PDF, Page Setup, or Print.

In other applications, the Preview button launches a customized Preview option, where you can also choose Page Setup or Print. In either case, it is expected that you should be able to print directly from the Preview option, no matter how Preview is handled.

Save As PDF

The Save As PDF button brings up a dialog allowing you to enter a filename and select a directory in which to save. The PDF that is saved is the same as the one saved through the Output Options pane.

Fax

The Fax button in the Print dialog allows you to send your print job off to a fax machine and have it printed there. If the receiving machine is actually a Macintosh, it could well be automatically saving an electronic copy of the data when it's received, but there is nothing that forces the transaction to be with another computer. You have effectively acquired the ability to treat any fax machine that you can find a phone number for, as a printer for your system. When you click the Fax button, the Print dialog changes subtly to present more options required for faxing. Where previously you could select a printer, there is now a "To" line, where the fax system wants you to enter a phone number. This field is tied directly to the Address Book, through the icon/button that looks like a person's head and shoulders. Clicking this button allows you to select from your known contacts and have their fax information automatically inserted. The form additionally allows you to specify a prefix that you need to dial out on the local phone network (many businesses require that you dial 9 before an outgoing number), and to specify text to be included as a cover page. The dialog, shown in Figure 10.28, also includes a number of the configurable option panes available for the general printing control, such as layout, number of copies, and scheduling.

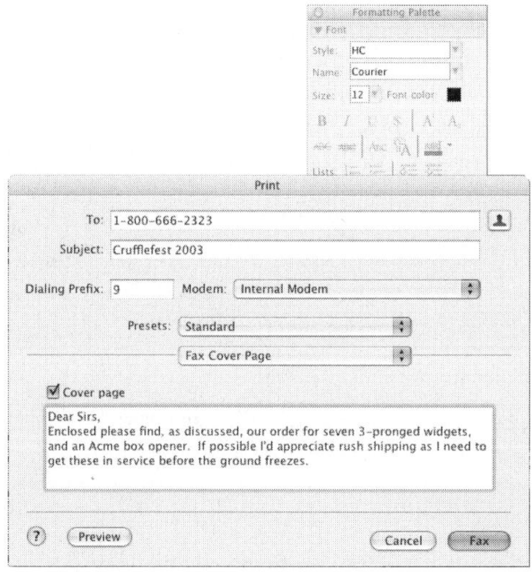

FIGURE 10.28 The Print dialog changes into a Fax dialog if you click the Fax button at the bottom.

Managing Fonts

With the initial releases of OS X, Apple introduced a new type of font suitcase designed to reduce the incompatibilities between the many different font systems available for different computers. With 10.3, Apple has continued to upgrade the font system and has added a convenient new font manager: Font Book. Font Book gives you a simple and intuitive way to preview what fonts you have installed, group your installed fonts into useful collections, and to install new fonts into your system. In addition to using the new font format, OS X supports these Windows font formats: TrueType fonts with extension `.ttf`, TrueType collections with extension `.ttc`, and OpenType fonts with extension `.otf`. OS X also supports PostScript Type 1, legacy bitmap fonts, and Unicode. Unicode is a universal character-encoding standard for multilingual text support across multiple platforms. Supporting Unicode enhances OS X's multilingual support. OS X's multilingual support is most clearly seen in the available keyboards in the International System preferences pane. At this point, though, you might wonder if your old collection of fonts will work in OS X. Fortunately, OS X also supports older font suitcases used in earlier versions of the operating system without any conversion.

Installing a New Font

Installing a new font on your system is not difficult. For example, to install the Pushkin handwriting font from the ParaType free fonts page (`http://www.paratype.com/shop/`), download the following file to your drive:

```
http://www.fontstock.com/softdl/PushkinTT.zip
```

This is actually a Windows TrueType font, but as we know, OS X conveniently understands these, as well as many traditional Mac OS font types. You can uncompress the zip file by double-clicking on it, dropping it on StuffIt Expander, or, if you're inclined to manage your system from the command line, you can use the `unzip` command:

```
unzip PushkinTT.zip
Archive: PushkinTT.zip
 inflating: Pushkin.ttf
```

The first line shown here is the command you type. The next two lines are lines of output that the command produces as it unzips the file. You can then install it from the command line by copying it into the appropriate directory on your system. If you want this font to be available to all users on your machine (our recommended configuration), copy it to the `/Library/Fonts/` directory. If you want the font to be available for your use only, copy it to your `~/Library/Fonts/` directory. Alternatively, you can simply double-click the `Pushkin.ttf` file, and Apple's new Font Book application opens, shows you a sample of the font, and allows you to install it with a simple button click.

If you want to use the command line to copy the file, use the following syntax:

```
ditto Pushkin.ttf /Library/Fonts/
```

If you've only ever worked in a graphical user environment and have never used a command line, you might not see much point to being able to do something like install a font from a command line. After all, it's much easier to just double-click the font file, right? Consider the situation where you want to install dozens, or even hundreds of fonts that you've accumulated. Suddenly you're faced with double-clicking a multitude of files, or, if you select them all and open them simultaneously, at least clicking Install in a great number of font-sample windows. As you will learn in the coming chapters, telling the command line to execute the appropriate commands over and over, for each font you're interested in, takes only slightly more effort than telling it to do a single file. For one or two fonts, working through the Finder and Font Book may indeed be faster, but at the command line, there is only a keystroke or two difference between installing 2 fonts, and installing 200. For large administrative tasks, the command line quickly takes the lead.

NOTE

You will find some online Mac OS X references that indicate that you can or should install fonts into the `/System/Library/Fonts` folder. These are antiquated instructions generated during the earliest releases of Mac OS X. At the time, Apple's filesystem layout was not well understood, and almost everyone was writing instructions and documentation based on what worked, as determined by experimentation. Now we know that the `/System` folder is intended for Apple's use alone, whereas the `/Library` folder is intended to be an area where you as an administrator can add files that should be available systemwide.

If you installed the font by dragging and dropping in the Finder, or by clicking Install in Font Book, that's it; you're finished with the install. You'll need to restart some applications that you want to be able to use the font, but you shouldn't need to restart your machine, or even log out. Unfortunately, as of the current version of 10.3, if you install from the command line, things aren't so nice, and you need to restart the machine before the new fonts will be recognized. Because this is a step backward from the convenience of font installation under prior versions of OS X, it wouldn't be surprising to find this fixed again in some future version. Figure 10.29 shows what the terminal looks like in the Pushkin handwriting font.

CAUTION

Macintosh suitcases and PostScript fonts need to be copied into the `/Library/Fonts/` or `~/Library/Fonts/` directory by using the `ditto` command, by dragging and dropping in the Finder, or by using Font Book to do the install, rather than using the `cp` command, because these fonts can contain resource-fork data, which is not correctly handled by the `cp` command.

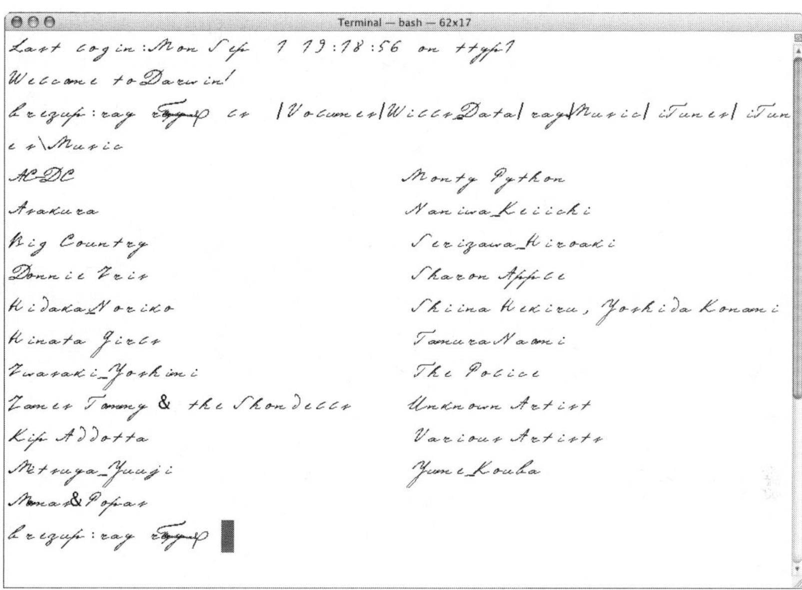

FIGURE 10.29 A terminal window set to use the Pushkin handwriting font. Although this is an amusing change for a terminal, it is perhaps not the best font choice for regular terminal usage.

Using Font Book

Figure 10.30 shows the Font Book application's interface. If you've already used the font selection interface in previous versions of OS X, the Font Book application's interface will be very familiar. Like many OS X information-navigation interfaces, it consists of a set of vertically scrolling panes proceeding from the most general information in the leftmost pane to the most specific in the rightmost. In Font Book's case, the leftmost pane contains a list of font collections, the middle pane lists individual fonts that are members of the collection selected in the left pane, and the right pane shows a sample of a particular selected font and the font's associated information. As seen from Figure 10.30, a given font can contain a number of font styles (typefaces), and some information regarding these styles can be seen by mousing over the listed fonts. Likewise, the number of fonts and typefaces in a collection can be browsed by mousing over the listed collections.

The + buttons under the column of collections and under the column of fonts allow you to add new collections or fonts, respectively. Fonts can be added to a collection (and can be members of multiple collections) by selecting them and dragging them from the font list into the desired target collection. Collections and fonts can be deleted by selecting them and pressing the Delete key on the keyboard. You can also disable fonts and collections without deleting them. This is useful if you find that some of your fonts are cluttering up your font menus and interfering with work, but you still need them for specific uses and don't want to delete them.

Under the Preview menu, you have the option of choosing to preview fonts in a number of ways. The Sample option is essentially the collection of upper- and lowercase letters and numerals available in the font. The font's Repertoire is the complete collection of characters available in the font. Custom Display allows you to set the text displayed for the preview. Custom defaults to an upper/lower/numerals lists but can be edited by clicking in the font-preview window.

About the only thing confusing about the interface is the slider at the right-hand side of the page, which, if you look, is clearly not a vertical-scroll slider. Yet in practice, many users seem to click on it and drag it up and down expecting the preview display to scroll. In actuality, it's a size slider, controlling the displayed size of the font in the preview. If you adjust it until your font preview doesn't all fit in the window, a vertical (and/or horizontal) scrollbar appears as needed.

Under the Edit menu there is an option to Resolve Duplicates. This option only becomes enabled if you have fonts or typefaces selected that contain duplications. Unfortunately, it won't (currently) resolve duplicates across your entire set of fonts and faces, and instead requires that you select only the fonts that are duplicates of each other. This is facilitated by Font Book placing a dot to the right of any font or typeface that appears to contain duplicates. In the case of Figure 10.30, the font Verdana is indicated to contain duplicates, and in it, apparently each of the typefaces has been duplicated.

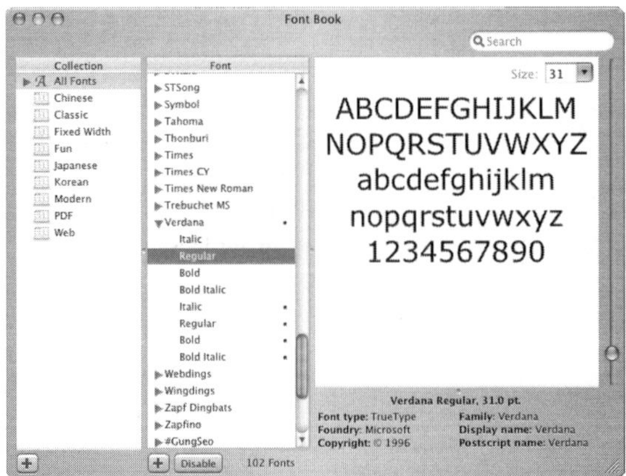

FIGURE 10.30 The Font Book application, browsing the Verdana font. Font Book allows you to organize and preview fonts in an interface similar to the Font selection pane.

Using the Font Pane

You can access your fonts in the Font pane, which is available in many of the typical OS X applications. The location of the Font pane varies with the application. For example, some applications include Fonts as a menu bar item, and you select Show Fonts under that menu or a hierarchical submenu of it. Other applications include the Font pane as an option, although it might be a nested option, under another menu bar category, such as Format. The Font pane has divisions for Collections, Family, Typeface, and Size. Because the default collection is All Fonts, you can indeed see your entire collection of available fonts with ease. However, the Fonts pane also displays the collections you've created through Font Book, so you can group your fonts together, as well as use some precreated groupings that Apple provides.

The Font pane also includes a number of font display and rendering options and some styling options such as colors, strikethrough and underline, and character spacing options. Sometimes these options get a little confusing because there can be application-specific additions to this pane, yet the applications don't necessarily obey all the options that are set. For example, the Terminal includes a pane containing Character Spacing options (to spread the characters apart, or condense them closer together) at the bottom of the Font pane. It, however, doesn't obey any of the character rendering options that create drop-shadows or even the font color setting from the Font pane (this might be a bug?). In general, however, in most applications these options control the onscreen selection and rendering of fonts, and are primarily available for the purpose of customizing your display and making information easier (or at least more enjoyable) to read.

Applications that are more typesetting, or graphics/layout oriented have their own way of specifying font rendering options. Figure 10.31 shows the Font pane interacting with TextEdit. In this figure, different drop-shadow rendering options have been applied to different portions of the text. We've included snapshots of the drop-shadow rendering controls from the Font pane directly above each quote on which they were used.

To switch between collections, just click the desired collection in the Collections column. Although this sounds obvious, it is not so obvious if you don't see the Collections column. If you shrink the Font pane horizontally too far, the similarity to Finder multicolumn view disappears, and the Collections column does too. You don't get a horizontal scrollbar with which to browse the different levels of the hierarchy. If your view of the Font pane starts with the Family column, widen the pane by dragging it at the bottom right.

The little "gear wheel" (Apple calls it an action button) icon at the bottom left of the Font pane gets you to a menu with a number of useful settings. Hiding the preview and/or effects (or showing them if they're hidden) has exactly the expected effect: the font sample at the top of the Font pane, or the rendering controls are hidden (or shown).

The Add to Favorites option under the pop-up enables you to add fonts directly to a collection of favorite fonts, without having to go through Font Book. Actually, because Favorites doesn't appear as a collection in Font Book, the Add to Favorites option is your only route to adding fonts to this collection. When you select a font from the Favorites collection, the Add to Favorites pop-up menu button becomes Remove from Favorites, allowing editing of your Favorites list.

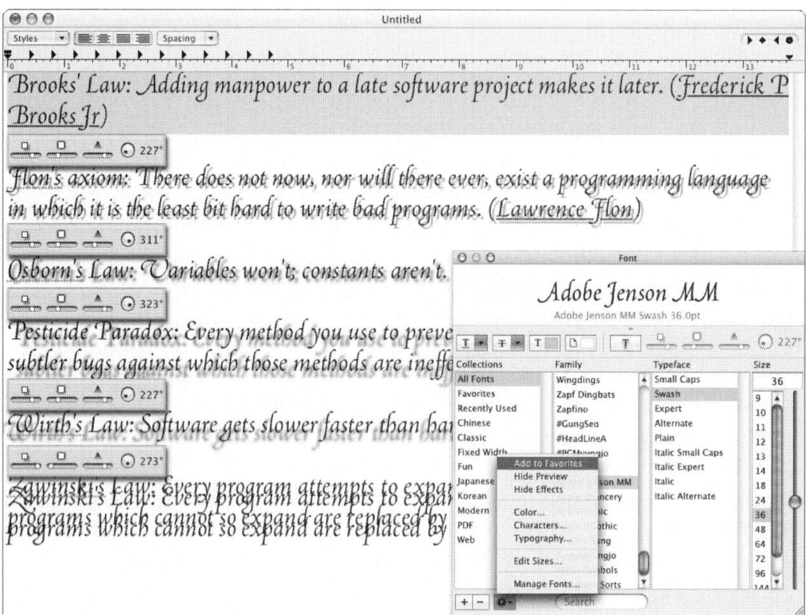

FIGURE 10.31 The Font pane is your interface to selecting fonts and onscreen rendering options.

The Edit Sizes option under the action section of the Font pane enables you to choose whether you want to see font sizes listed as fixed sizes, a size slider, or as both. It also enables you to edit the available sizes. For a fixed view, you can add or delete a specific size from the fixed list. For a sliding scale, you can edit the minimum and maximum font sizes. Figure 10.32 shows the Font - Sizes window that first appears for editing sizes. It changes slightly to enable you to adjust the minimum and maximum available font sizes on the slider.

The Color option under the action button pop-up, as well as the button in the rendering options with the pea-soup yellow-green box on it, opens a standard color browser where you can specify, by a wheel, spectrum, color scales, and so on, a color for the font you are using.

In earlier versions of OS X, there used to be an Extras section to the Font pane, with a Get Fonts option that took you to `http://www.apple.com/fonts/buy/`, which appeared to be a site where Apple was intending to sell additional fonts. This option no longer appears, and the Web site was offline during the 10.2 release, but it's back again with a "Coming Soon" banner, so perhaps Apple is once again hoping to implement this option.

As you shrink the Font pane by dragging the bottom-right corner inward, it selectively shrinks various elements, hides others, and also changes elements into more compact forms such as pop-up menus instead of scrolling lists. This can be very convenient if you need some settings visible for working in your document but don't want to waste all the screen real-estate that would be lost to the full-sized pane. This can also be really annoying if you can't get to the Action pop-up menu because it has decided to disappear, and the only solution is dragging the window out to a large size to convince the interface that it'll fit again.

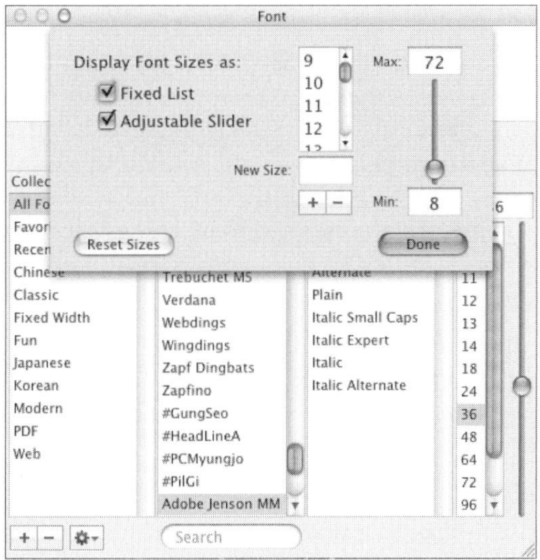

FIGURE 10.32 The Font – Sizes window, which appears when you select Edit Sizes under the Extras section in the Font pane, is where you select how the font size options will be displayed.

The appearance of the font pane is saved on a per-application basis, so you can have it customized in size to what you need in each application, and when you use it from that application again, it will appear as you last left it. When you quit the application associated with a particular Font pane, that Fonts pane also closes.

As for actually using a font in your application, select the font you want to use from the Fonts pane and start typing. If you need to switch the font of a section of text, select the text you want to change, and select the desired font. The font switches to what you want, and you can continue typing. If you want to see the Fonts pane in action, although the presentation is a little dated, check the QuickTime movie at `http://www.apple.com/macosx/theater/fonts.html`.

Using the Keyboard Menu and Alternative Input Scripts

Apple has, for several generations of Mac OS, made a clever feature available as an optional part of the operating system. This software, WorldScript and the various language kits it supported, was a way of putting a layer of abstraction between what you type on the keyboard, and what is actually entered into a document that you are working with. The system was modeled on the notion that a computer might have only one physical keyboard, but a knowledge of the language and locale in which the user is working would enable a translation between what keys are physically pressed and contextually correct data output. This functionality is now a default part of OS X and is embodied in a two-part system comprised of key-mapping tables called keyboards and locale-sensitive processing software known as input scripts.

Keyboard mapping tables are used to map between a particular key that is pressed and an output symbol that is generated. For example, you might have heard of the Dvorak keyboard, a more efficient alternative to the QWERTY keyboard that you are probably already familiar with. A keyboard mapping might be used to remap the keys on your QWERTY keyboard, so that they function as though your keyboard was a Dvorak keyboard instead. A keyboard mapping can also be used to do things such as change the currency indicator to the appropriate currency for the locale—British pounds for U.K. English and American dollars for American English, for example.

Input scripts, on the other hand, can perform more sophisticated, context-sensitive alterations of data as it is entered. This modification can be anything from changing the font used to display all or certain characters, to providing phonetic ways of entering symbols not directly available from the keyboard.

These two pieces of functionality, accessed jointly through the Keyboard menu (discussed in the following section) and the International pane of the system controls, give you the ability to enter data in character sets appropriate for other languages, whether they are English-like languages or languages with completely different symbol sets and entry needs.

The use and utility of this are probably not immediately apparent from just a description, but working through the following example should give you an idea of just how powerful the keyboard tables and input scripts can be.

The first place to examine when configuring or customizing your input environment is the International pane. Figure 10.33 shows the Language tab of the International pane. In the bottom portion, there is an option to select the default behavior of scripts. The "fine print" explanation in the tab tells us that what we select here affects sort order, case conversion, and word definitions. From the perspective of a user with an American English keyboard, nothing obvious happens, even if I switch to one of the other choices in the Roman script. This is because the Roman script is used for Roman-like language input styles. Most European languages use an alphabet, character ordering, and display styles that have significant similarities. The number of characters is roughly the same, text flows from left to right on the page, there are uppercase and lowercase letters, and so on. On the other hand, languages such as Arabic, Hebrew, Chinese, and Japanese have very different symbol sets, character ordering, and display styles that are unlike each other and the majority of European languages. By convention, therefore, languages with Roman-like characteristics use the Roman input script.

Other languages might use their own particular input scripts, which can provide language-specific input functionality, or they might use the Unicode input script. Unicode is an internationally standardized way of providing input in a number of symbol sets that cannot be conveniently represented on a standard keyboard. The Unicode input script cannot provide customized input processing in a language-contextual manner but does provide a standardized way to input many characters from a keyboard with only a limited number of keys. To use Unicode, therefore, you need to have a mapping between keyboard sequences and output symbols. As a demonstration of the power available in other input scripts, we'll take a look at the Japanese input script, and how it maps from phonetic keyboard input in Romanji, into natural Japanese Katakana, Hiragana, and Kanji.

When looking through the International pane's Language tab, click the Customize Sorting button (it's called Customize Sorting, because the language behavior selected for a particular script affects things such as the alphabetic sort order) and browse the choices under Roman and Japanese. You will note that Roman has many choices, whereas Japanese has only Japanese. (Japanese, on some systems, will be displayed in Japanese—if you don't read Japanese, it's the one with characters that look like a chest of drawers, a strange telephone pole with slanty bars, and an indescribable pictogram.) Now pick an appropriate default for yourself. Note that the available selection on your machine might differ from what is shown here.

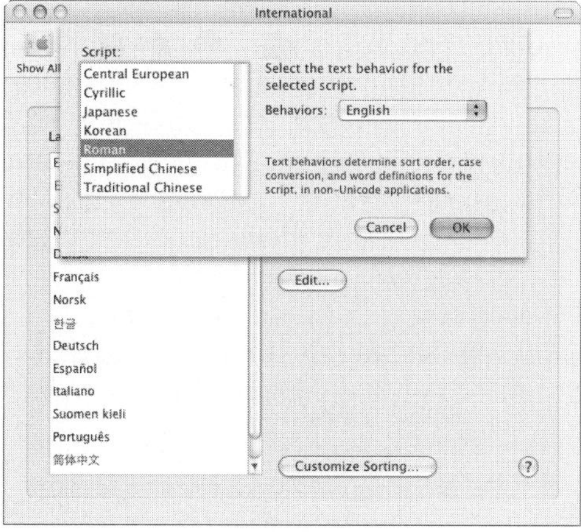

FIGURE 10.33 The Language tab of the International pane is where you select a default script.

Figure 10.34 shows the more interesting tab for our purposes, the Input Menu tab. The Input Menu tab enables you to pick various types of keyboardlike layouts and associated input methods. Browse through the Input Menu options in this section. Note that many are in the Roman script and in the Unicode script, and a few are in several other variants. As a user, you'll want to select your most native language type as an input script. For the examples in the following section, select a few that use the Roman script. Also select the Character Palette input option. Finally, if you want to follow our example of how an input script can interact with a keyboard layout in a sophisticated manner, select the Japanese layout, which is the one that looks like a red ball with a little red Apple logo on a white flag, and the Hiragana and Katakana keyboards for it.

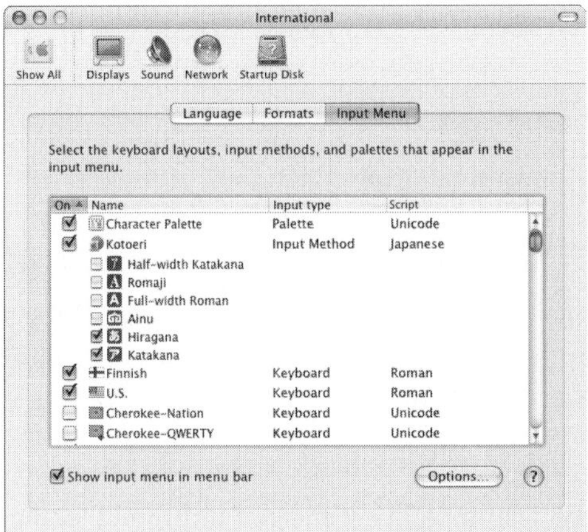

FIGURE 10.34 You can select any keyboard layouts that might be of interest to you in the Input Menu tab of the International pane.

With previous versions of the system, when you select more than one keyboard, a little menu consisting of flags signifying your chosen script and keyboard appeared automatically. Now you need to select the Show Input Menu in Menu Bar option in the International pane, to get this menu to appear. This little "flag menu" is the Keyboard menu, which shows which keyboard layouts are available, and which is chosen. The Open International option takes you to the Input Menu tab of the International pane. The most obvious way to switch between keyboard layouts is to select the one you want from the Keyboard menu itself. However, if you check the Options section of the Input Menu tab of the International pane, you see that you can also use Command-Option-Space to rotate to the next keyboard in the Input menu. Command-Space swaps keyboards with the previously most recently used keyboard.

CAUTION

This feature now works subtly differently than it previously did. Earlier versions used Command-Option-Space to switch to the next keyboard available *in the currently active script*. In other words, if you were in a keyboard that used the Roman script interface, the key combination rotated to the next Roman keyboard in your menu. You could use Command-Space to rotate to the default keyboard of the *next* script. Currently (release 7b44), Command-Option-Space rotates to the top keyboard of the top script of your input menu and then rotates sequentially through the keyboards available in the menu. Command-Space rotates between the most recently used keyboard of the *previous* most recently used script—that is, if you've been using Roman-script keyboards for a while and have switched between a number of them, Command-Space swaps you to whatever (not Roman) script you used before the Roman script, and into the keyboard you were using in it. Personally, I think this is confusing—I hope they switch back.

FIGURE 10.35 This is the Keyboard menu that appears in the Finder when you have enabled more than one keyboard layout under the Input Menu tab of the International pane and made the Input menu visible in the Finder.

Take a few moments to play with the Roman script keyboard layouts in an application such as TextEdit. A simple example to check is the British keyboard. If you switch to it and type **#**, you will discover that you get £, the British pound. Switch to the French keyboard and start pressing the number keys. You get many characters with accents instead. To get a number, hold down the Shift key while pressing a number key.

Hopefully, you have gotten used to the idea of the script interpreting your input as appropriate for the keyboard layout you have selected. Although these modifications of your input might seem relatively simple, this is because you've been working in your already familiar Roman input script.

Now, let's take a look at a more interesting keyboard layout and input script—the one for Japanese. As you go through the example, notice where the input script is interpreting the input that you type, and attempting to produce contextually correct output for you. Apple has historically produced some fantastic software for mapping between QWERTY-type keyboards and non-romance languages. These software packages were once priced outside the range of students of the languages, and often many professional users, predominantly because they included enormously expensive fonts as a part of the package. Now, through marketing magic we won't pretend to understand, Apple is providing an ever-expanding collection of these language kits as well as the associated fonts as a standard part of OS X. We'll use Japanese as an example of how these input scripts and keyboards interact, primarily because as authors we understand a bit about how this language works with the system, but please feel free to experiment in whatever language you're comfortable with.

Figure 10.36 shows a Japanese phrase. For those who don't read Japanese, the pronunciation is (as close as we can represent in English) Kazenotaninonaushika, which translates as "Nausicaä of the Valley of the Wind," the title of a popular Japanese children's film.

Without the functionality available in the language kit, typesetting this phrase from the keyboard would be very difficult. It contains characters from three different Japanese alphabets—one of which contains thousands of characters. Entering this without a language kit would entail finding the right keys to produce the characters from the two small phonetic alphabets, all the while switching between fonts and picking from a huge list of characters in the thousand-plus character alphabet. With the Japanese kit, typesetting this is only a little more complex than typing the phrase phonetically as it is pronounced in English.

風の谷のナウシカ

FIGURE 10.36 The Japanese phrase Kaze no tani no Nausicaä serves as our example of using the input system.

Using TextEdit and the Japanese language kit, we can easily reproduce the text shown in Figure 10.36. Although this example is in Japanese, the same steps can be used for any language you use. From within the application where you want to use an alternative input script, choose the keyboard layout from the Input menu. The input script for that keyboard takes over the input for the application.

CAUTION

This functionality is now even enabled in the Finder and the Terminal. Be careful if you're working in an alternative keyboard and input script, and switch between applications, because the language you're working in will follow you around the system. This can produce unexpected results, especially in applications that have traditionally been ASCII/English alphabet based, such as the Terminal.

OS X 10.3 has changed the way that some language kits interoperate with the system in some significant ways. Primarily among these, some input scripts and keyboards carried along with them language-specific interfaces to the system. These could be accessed from a little floating Operations Palette that appeared when in a language that provided them. 10.3 no longer has an Operations Palette, and instead adds various language-specific options to the Input menu when in the associated keyboard. Because of this, you can expect new Input menu options to appear when working in different languages. The proper use of these is beyond the scope of this book, but hopefully the in-language Help sections that Apple provides for each will be sufficient for users who want to use these features. Given that Apple keeps expanding the capabilities of OS X, we strongly suspect that all the language-specific features such as in-language file management that used to exist under the Operations Palette are still hidden in here somewhere!

To reproduce the Japanese phrase in our example, all we need is to make sure that the appropriate keyboard is selected, and that we know how to say (phonetically) what we want to type. The one you want is the Hiragana keyboard, which puts the input script in a mood to accept phonetic input in an English-like form, converts it to "Native" Japanese phonetics if possible, and "Foreign" Japanese phonetics if not. Further it converts appropriate groupings of native phonetics into pictogram/ideogram characters if there are pictograms with the appropriate composite pronunciation.

For the sample phrase, the characters we are looking for break up partly as words and partly as phonetics (words for the pictogram-based parts of the phrase, and phonetics for the phonetic character parts), as follows

```
kaze no tani no na u shi ka
```

In the Font pane, pick a fairly large size for the font so that you can easily read what you are typing. Then type the letter **k**. So far, nothing unexpected happens. Type the letter **a**. As soon as you type this, the input script recognizes that you have entered a phoneme and replaces it with the appropriate phonetic character for the selected alphabet. The character for the sound `ka` has appeared and replaced the `k` and `a` characters. Type the letter **z**. Now you have a Hiragana character and the letter `z`, as shown in Figure 10.37. Now type the letter `e`. Again, the input script recognizes a phoneme. The character for the `ze` sound has appeared. Note the characters have an underscore. This means that the input script recognizes that other possible representations in the language could also be appropriate and is prompting that we might want to change the current representation—in this case, from a phonetic representation to a pictographic representation.

To select from possible representations that fit the current input, press the spacebar. The input system selects a character for you. If the character is not correct, press the spacebar again. This opens a little window, as shown in Figure 10.38, from which you can manually select a character. You can scroll the selection up and down in the list by using the arrow keys on your keyboard, and you can select a character by clicking on it. You can accept the current selected character or characters by pressing the Return key, and select and exit the menu by double-clicking your desired character. When you have the character that you want and are back to the TextEdit window, just start typing from the example again.

If the scrolling list of alternative representations doesn't provide what you're looking for, you can also bring up the Character Palette. This appears in many applications as an option labeled Special Characters that appears under the Edit menu but is also universally available through the Input menu itself, if you have it selected as a Keyboard/Input method via the International pane.

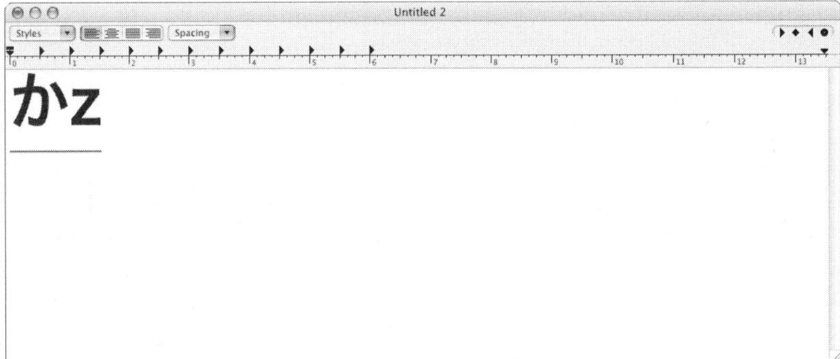

FIGURE 10.37 The Japanese character for *ka* followed by the letter *z* are showing after typing *ka*, and then *z*. The underscore means that we have not picked any final representations yet.

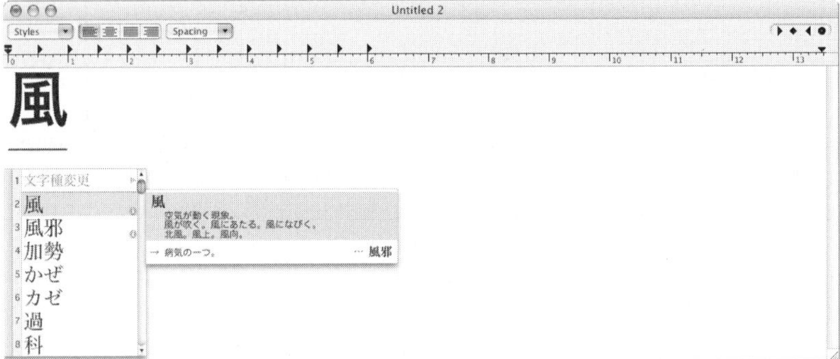

FIGURE 10.38 Press the spacebar twice to get a menu that enables you to choose another character.

The Character Palette provides access to a large selection of characters in a number of fonts, styles, and groups. If you needed a Kanji numeral for example, you'd select Japanese from the View pop-up menu, and then select from either categorized input (By Category pane), as shown in Figure 10.39, or if you're a dedicated user of Kanji, by stroke and radical (shapes and styles of the lines that make up the characters) from the by Radical pane.

> **NOTE**
>
> The Kanji items in the by Radical pane of the Character Palette are listed by radical (base character) in increasing stroke order. These characteristics are specific to a traditional method of characterizing and specifying Japanese Kanji characters. If your language kit uses a similar method of characterizing pictogram or other characters, you can expect a similar presentation in the Character Palette. Otherwise, expect the ordering to be as the characters would be traditionally alphabetized in the language.

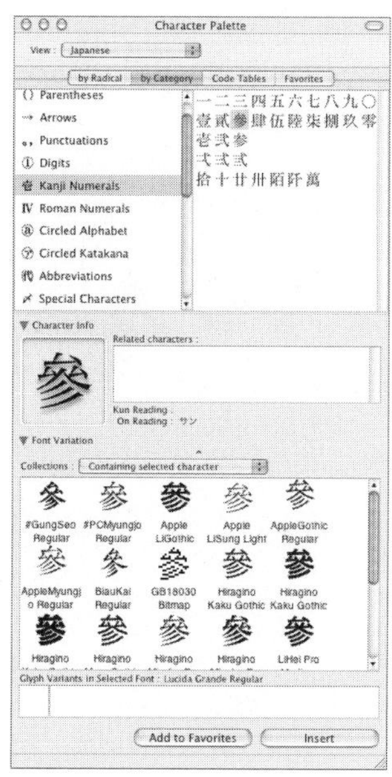

FIGURE 10.39 The Character Palette provides categorized access to a great number of characters in useful groupings.

To select an item from the Character Palette, select the desired character in the grid and drag it into your document, or double-click the character, and it will be inserted automatically.

The Character Palette has more than just Japanese language items, so you might be interested in playing with it more later. These currently include Cyrillic, Greek, and a number of pictorial symbols such as boxes and lines. The available categories and even the available panes from which to select categories, vary depending on the language view type you've selected. This palette provides access to an immense number of character types and manipulations. You can access categorized characters in areas as diverse as the symbols used for marking up dental x-rays and charts regarding treatments, to characters for drawing in-text boxes and grids, and from fractions to alphabets or numerals drawn in circles or squares.

A particularly nice feature of the Character Palette is the ability to view what a particular character looks like in all the fonts that have it available. This can be useful for selecting the best font from which to get selected special characters to put into a presentation or chart.

The example we're working on can be successfully completed without the help of the Character Palette, so continue through the rest of the phrase, picking and choosing characters using the spacebar as you go. The final part of the title we're working on, Nausicaä, is written in the other Japanese phonetic alphabet, Katakana. To work in this character system, select the Katakana keyboard type from the Input menu. Now type **`na`** and press Return. Next, type **`u`** and press Return. Then type **`shi`** and press Return. Finally, type **`ka`** and press Return. Pressing Return after each indicates to the input script that you're finished entering a phonetic equivalent, and that you want to accept the symbol that it has chosen. Now you have finished typing the title. What you have typed should match what is shown in Figure 10.40.

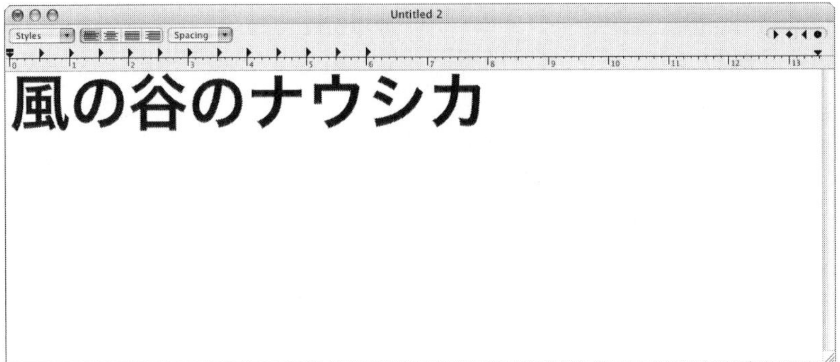

FIGURE 10.40 Now we have successfully converted `kazenotaninonaushika` into correctly written Japanese.

This particular title was a convenient example for you to try because it uses characters from all three Japanese alphabets, giving you the opportunity to see examples of each of the input script methods and the way they interact. Even if you're interested in working in a different language kit, we hope you find this information useful. If you understand the functionality we've presented here, you should be able to find similar functions in the language kit of your choice.

NOTE

After having spent the time to type the Japanese for the Nausicaä title, you might be interested in learning more about the animated film. Check `http://www.nausicaa.net/` to learn more about this and other films by the same studio.

Finally, Figure 10.41 shows just a small sampling of the types of characters available in the Character Palette, with some of these entered into the TextEdit application. This palette provides a significant resource for picking and choosing characters appropriate to different languages, even if you don't know how to pronounce the symbol phonetically.

Hopefully, this section has provided a fun way to learn about the way different keyboard inputs can work under OS X. If you want to watch your system type right-to-left instead, enable the Hebrew input method and experiment with it.

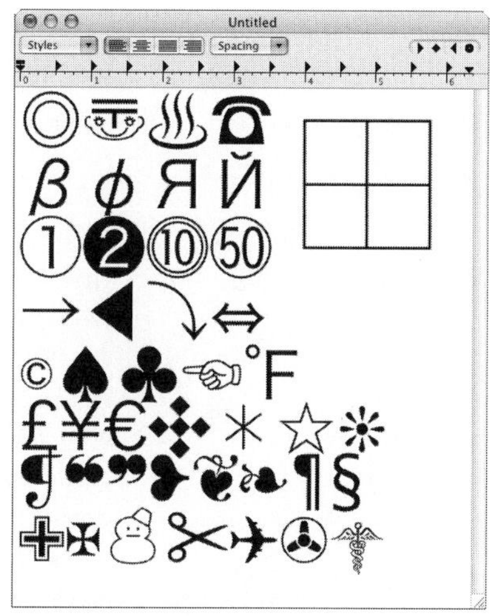

FIGURE 10.41 The Character Palette provides access to many additional characters through a number of categorized lists.

When you have multiple enabled keyboards, the Input (sometimes called Keyboard) menu appears in the menu bar. You can easily select a desired keyboard by selecting it from the Input menu. For keyboards that belong to the Roman script input, the changes in the behavior of your keyboard might be subtle. With the Japanese script input keyboard, however, the input method is far more interactive than the Roman script input keyboards. Other input scripts and keyboards are available, and we hope that the techniques you've learned in experimenting with the Japanese system will help you to work in any other input systems that you need.

Font Web Sites

There are many places that you can download fonts, including free fonts. Just do a search on your favorite Web search site, and you should be pleased with the results, perhaps even overwhelmed. Table 10.1 includes a few sites here to get you started. However, for your reference, we include sites other than ones with just downloadable fonts.

TABLE 10.1 Font-Related Web Sites

Web Site	URL	Content
iFree Top Font Sites	`http://www.ifree.com.au/top/fonts/index.html`	Lists many links to font sites.
WebFontList	`http://www.webfontlist.com/`	Lists many links to font sites, both free and shareware.
Karen's Koncepts Free Fonts Resources	`http://www.netmegs.com/koncepts/freefont.htm`	Lists many links to sites with fonts, both free and shareware.

TABLE 10.1 Continued

Web Site	URL	Content
MyFonts.com	`http://www.myfonts.com/`	A site where you can buy fonts through participating foundries. Provides some font utilities to help you find the right font. Has links to other font sites and font utility sites.
MyFonts.com: WhatTheFont	`http://www.myfonts.com/WhatTheFont/`	The direct link to MyFonts.com's WhatTheFont utility. This interesting utility can be used to try to identify a font from a scanned image.
Identifont—identify fonts and typefaces	`http://www.identifont.com/identify.html`	A site that helps you identify a font by asking a series of questions about the font.
Apple—Fonts/Tools	`http://fonts.apple.com/`	Apple's technical site on fonts and font development.
TrueType Typography: TTF fonts & technology	`http://www.truetype.demon.co.uk/index.htm`	An informative site on TrueType typography. Includes info about history and specification.
Adobe Solutions Network: OpenType Specification	`http://partners.adobe.com/asn/tech/type/`	Lists the Adobe type specification, including OpenType.
Free Fonts, TrueType, OpenType, ClearType Microsoft Typography	`http://www.microsoft.com/typography/default.asp`	Microsoft's Typography site. Includes technical information as well as a link to Microsoft's free fonts.
Microsoft Typography Fonts and products	`http://www.microsoft.com/typography/fonts/default.asp`	Provides a listing of what fonts come in what Microsoft products. Does not include images of the fonts.
Unicode Home Page	`http://www.unicode.org/`	Includes information on Unicode and the Unicode standard.

Summary

In this chapter, you learned a variety of basics involving printer and font management. You learned about the Print Center, which enables you to add and delete printers, select a default printer, and work with the print queues. You learned that printing from an application works the same as in traditional Mac OS. Under the File menu, Page Setup enables you to set the attributes for your page or view a summary of the attributes. Also under the File menu, Print enables you to send a job to the printer. You can also specify further options about your printout, including an output option to print to a PDF file. After learning basics about the printer, you learned how to manage fonts. You learned how to install a new font and how to use the Font pane, including using it to manage font collections. Finally, you enhanced your font experience by learning about input methods that use multilingual characters. You experimented with switching between various Roman script inputs as well as the Japanese script input.

CHAPTER 11

Additional System Components

IN THIS CHAPTER

- User Account Creation
- Using NetInfo Manager
- Using the NetInfo Database to Customize a User
- Enabling the `root` Account
- Groups
- System Preferences: Personal
- System Preferences: Hardware
- System Preferences: System

Mac users wouldn't be happy without the ability to customize their systems. Although Mac OS X is a secure multiuser operating system, it gives individuals a great deal of freedom to customize their settings. Even though some restrictions might initially seem odd to users more familiar with a single-user OS, in some ways, Mac OS X users have considerably more freedom than was available in the past. As in versions of the Mac OS before Mac OS X, different desktop backgrounds, screen savers, color profiles, and even speech recognition settings can be customized. However, with Mac OS X, these settings can be customized on a per-user basis so that from any individual's point of view, the machine appears to be configured to exactly his favorite state. What's more, with the proper additional configuration, much of the personalization of a machine can be shared among a group of machines, enabling (if desired) every machine in the group to be personalized identically. The mechanics of doing so are covered in Chapters 23, "File and Resource Sharing with NFS and NetInfo," and 24, "User Management and Machine Clustering."

As in previous versions of the Mac OS, a large portion of a user's personalization of his environment is stored in preference files. Under Mac OS X, these files are stored in the user's home directory, which enables each user to personalize his own settings. This also provides a very useful service in allowing those customizations to be shared across multiple machines, although the details of this are a topic for a later chapter. The notion of control panels has given way to the Mac OS X System Preferences panel, but the idea is still very much the same. Using System Preferences, users can choose an individual panel to change a series of related configuration options. Unlike previous versions of Mac OS, however, some user settings and preferences are stored in a network-accessible database. This database (NetInfo) enables certain user settings to be more easily shared among groups of machines.

This chapter covers the available System Preferences panels, as well as an introduction to the NetInfo database. You learn how to interact with the NetInfo database, how System Preferences controls work, and what they change on your system. If you want to fine-tune any areas of the operating system, this is the first place to look.

User Account Creation

In this section, we touch on some of the basics involved in user account creation. Later in this chapter, we look at some ways we can customize user account creation, and Chapter 24 looks at user management in detail.

Introduction to Multiuser Systems

Mac OS X is a Unix-based operating system. As such, it's a multiuser operating system; that is, everyone who uses the machine may do so by having an account on the machine. A user can use his account on the machine either at the console or via a network connection—if you choose to enable remote login from the sharing pane of System Preferences, which we discuss in further detail in Chapter 26, "Remote Access and Control."

A particularly nice feature of a multiuser system is that multiple users can use the machine at the same time. While each user is using the system, it seems to each user as if he's the only user on the system.

Each user has a home directory where he stores his files. In Mac OS X, the users' home directories are located in the `/Users` directory. Figure 11.1 shows the `/Users` directory on a sample Mac OS X client.

NOTE

Although the text of this book often shows directories using their full pathname (such as /Users), the Mac OS X Finder shows only the name of the directory at the end of the path. In the case of /Users, this would simply be Users. The shortening of pathnames isn't critical, but to successfully interact with the system, it's important to understand how the Mac OS X directory structure looks and works.

When a user logs in to the system, the default area where he is logged in is his home directory; hence, the use of the house as an icon in the Finder window. Additionally, you see the same icon in Figure 11.1 among the user directories. Users can still see most areas on the machine, although they might not necessarily be able to see all of another user's files. In a multiuser system, users can set permissions on their files to allow different types of access. Even if other users can see your files, they can't modify them unless you've set permissions to allow them to do so. For example, Figure 11.2 shows how the home directory for user `nermal` looks to another user. A number of folders have a white minus in a red circle on them. Directories so marked aren't viewable by this user. The other files and directories, however, can be viewed by this user

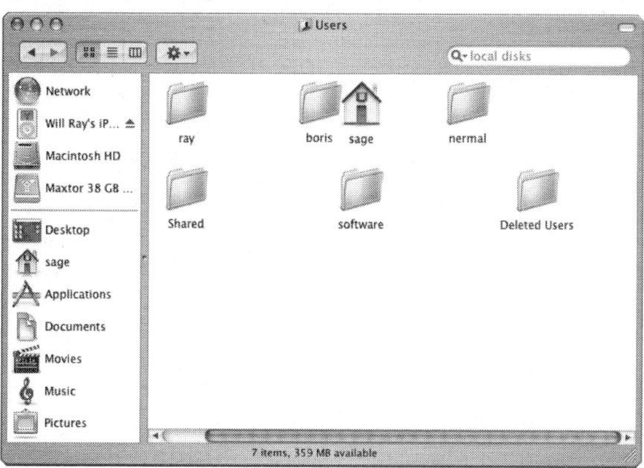

FIGURE 11.1 You can get to the /Users directory by clicking on your OS X drive in your finder view and opening the Users folder.

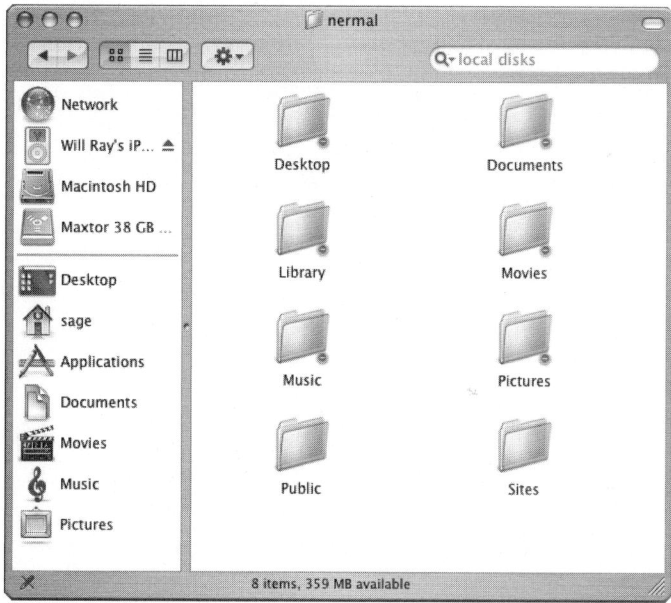

FIGURE 11.2 Depending on how the owner grants permissions on his files and directories, other users might not be able to view them.

Adding a New User

When you install Mac OS X, you're asked to provide your name and a short name that can be used as your login name. During the installation process, you create an account. Specifically, you create an administrator account. Adding another user account is much like creating the original administrator account that you create at installation time.

Because it can be used to modify the machine settings or install software, the administrator account is a rather powerful account. When you add a new user, you have the choice of adding a regular user or adding one with administrator capabilities. Although it's helpful to have more than one user with administrator capabilities, don't give administrator access to every user account that you create. Otherwise, every user on the machine can modify your system.

You create a new user account using the Accounts pane in the System section of System Preferences as follows:

1. Open the Accounts pane in System Preferences.
2. Click the make changes lock icon if it's set not to allow changes, and enter your administrator username and password. Click the plus sign in the lower left. This adds a user in the Other Accounts section along the left whose privileges are automatically listed as Standard. Figure 11.3 shows the Accounts pane as it appears before starting to add a new user.

FIGURE 11.3 The Accounts pane, where you can create and delete users, or edit user information.

The first section for adding a new user, the Password section, shown in Figure 11.4, has the following fields:

- **Name**—This is where you enter your user's name. In Mac OS X, this is a name that the user can use to log in to the machine.
- **Short Name**—The short name is the username; that is, the name of the account. This is also a name that the user can use to log in to the machine. This name can be up to eight characters in length, must have no spaces, and must be in lowercase letters. This name is used by some of the network services.
- **New Password**—The password should be at least four characters. Many systems recommend at least six characters with a variety of character types included in the password.
- **Verify**—This is where you reenter the password for verification purposes.
- **Password Hint**—This is an optional field. The password hint is displayed if the user enters an incorrect password three times. If you include a hint, make sure that the hint is not so obvious that other users can guess the password.

FIGURE 11.4 Complete the fields in the Password section to start to create a new user.

When you have entered the information for the Password section, continue to the next section, Picture. When you complete the Password section and continue to another section, your new user's identification as shown in the left column is updated to include the user's name. In the section on customizing a user, you learn how to create a specific user called `software` with a specific user ID and group ID.

The Picture section, shown in Figure 11.5, is where you select a picture for the new user. This picture is used in the login window, in the My Card in the Address Book, and as the default iChat picture. Either select one of the default images, choose a custom picture elsewhere on your machine, or choose to take a video snapshot by selecting Edit..., if you have a camera, such as iSight, attached.

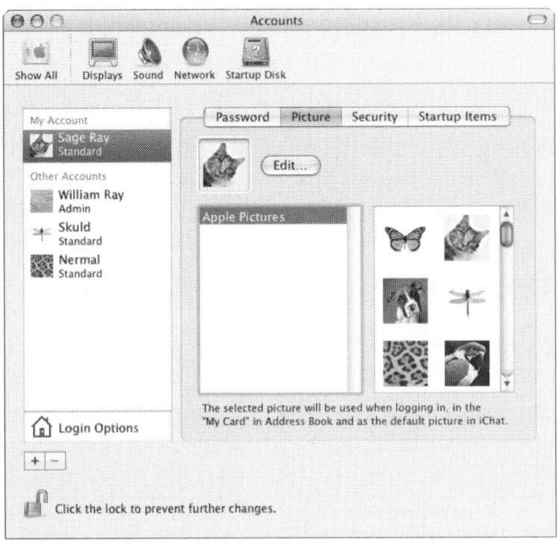

FIGURE 11.5 Select a picture for the new user in the Picture section.

The Security section is shown in Figure 11.6. In this section, you can choose whether to use FileVault. FileVault encrypts the contents of the user's home directory by using the user's login password. You can also set a master password for FileVault. The master password allows you to unlock any user's FileVault protection. This can be useful if a user forgets his login password. FileVault can't be turned on for the new account until a master password has been set. A user cannot turn on FileVault security for his account, even if a master password has been set. Rather, an administrative user must turn on the FileVault protection for a user. Finally, in this section you can decide whether to grant the user to have administrative privileges.

The Limitations section enables you to configure some of the actions the user is allowed to perform. You can select No Limits, Some Limits, or Simple Finder. No Limits places no limits on the account. Some Limits, shown in Figure 11.7, enables you to specify whether the user can open all of system preferences, modify the dock, change his password, or burn CDs and DVDs. Additionally, the user can be restricted to use only certain applications. The Simple Finder option restricts the user to a simplified dock and allows him to use only those applications showing in the My Applications folder in the Dock. If you choose to place limitations on the user, the user's description in the left column changes from Standard to Managed.

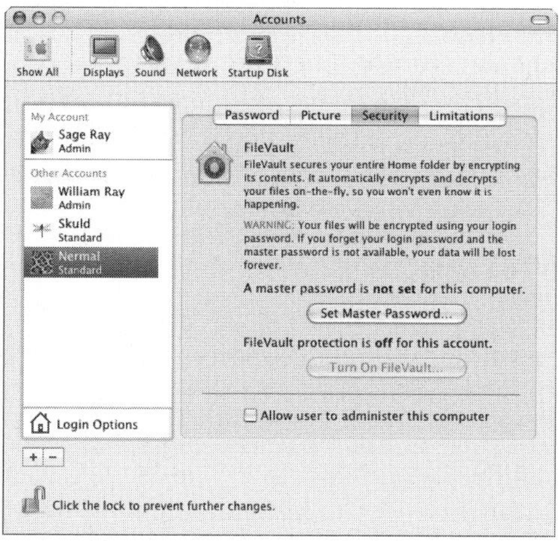

FIGURE 11.6 FileVault protection and administrative privileges can be set in the Security section.

FIGURE 11.7 Place the appropriate restrictions, if any, on a user's account in the Limitations section. The Some Limits option is shown here.

You can also edit user information, such as the login password. Click on the account to be edited, and change whatever needs to be changed. For a login password, this involves entering a new password and entering that password at the verification step. You will probably see a message about not being able to change the user's Keychain password, but this doesn't affect your ability to change the user's login password. To delete a user account, simply select the account to be deleted and click the minus sign at the lower left corner of the pane. A sheet appears, asking you to confirm the action and telling you that the contents of user's home directory will be stored as a file in the Deleted Users folder. The deleted account is stored as a disk image. If you do not want to keep the contents of the user's directory, you can also select the Delete Immediately... option. The Accounts pane does not allow you to delete the original administrator user account.

Using NetInfo Manager

The Accounts pane is intended to be a simple interface to the user accounts of the system and doesn't provide access to more complex aspects of user's accounts nor to more sophisticated configuration options. For this, you need to use NetInfo Manager. The principles behind the use of NetInfo Manager are very Unix-like, but the NetInfo database itself is unfamiliar to most traditional Unix users. NetInfo is a vestige of Mac OS X's NeXTStep heritage that has been integrated into the more traditional Unix underpinnings of Mac OS X because it's a considerably more powerful information sharing system than its traditional Unix counterparts. The NetInfo database is a hierarchical database that stores information on your machine's configuration and resources.

The NetInfo hierarchy is composed of directories. Each directory has properties. Each property has a name and value. The main directory on a given machine is the root directory, represented by `/`. Each machine has a local database with information about the machine's local resources.

The NetInfo hierarchy can extend beyond your local machine. As you might have guessed, your machine can be part of a NetInfo network. A NetInfo network is a hierarchical collection of domains, where each domain has a corresponding NetInfo database. A NetInfo network could have an unlimited number of domains, but up to three domains is most common. Your machine has its own local domain, but it could belong to a domain comprised of it and other machines. That domain could describe resources available to your local cluster of machines, it could also belong to another domain that might include information on yet another level of resources available, and so on.

Your machine could be part of a larger NetInfo network. However, because NetInfo isn't a widespread network type, it's more likely your machine is using its NetInfo database either as a standalone machine or, possibly, as part of a Unix cluster (a cooperating group of machines).

This chapter examines the NetInfo database using the graphical interface, NetInfo Manager, as well as a few command-line tools. Don't be concerned if you're unfamiliar with the terminal and command line at this point. You don't need to know anything more than how to type a few short commands. You'll learn how to work with the NetInfo database by customizing several aspects of your system, modifying a local user, and adding arbitrary data structures into the NetInfo database. Chapter 23 covers some more advanced NetInfo topics that require a bit more familiarity with the command line.

Using NetInfo Manager to Examine the NetInfo Database

NetInfo Manager (path: `/Applications/Utilities/NetInfo Manager`) is the graphical interface to the NetInfo database. Using NetInfo Manager to examine some of the contents of your NetInfo database is the easiest way to see the hierarchical arrangement of the database.

When you first start NetInfo Manager, it should open to the local domain `/`. If it doesn't, open the NetInfo database on your machine by choosing Open under the Domain menu and selecting the domain `/`. This opens a window from which you can select a domain. If your machine is using the default configuration, the `/` domain is your only choice, as shown in Figure 11.8.

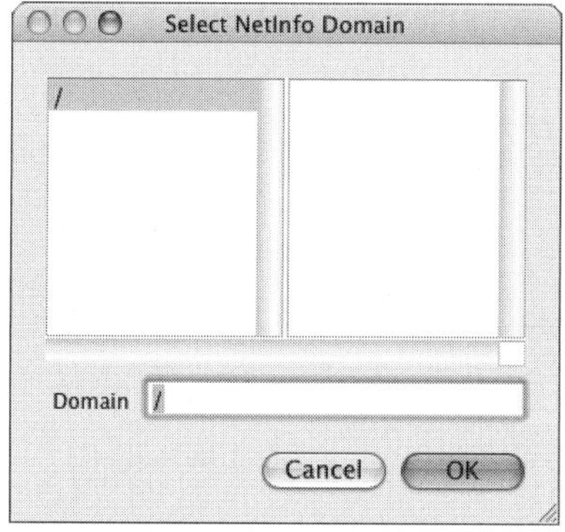

FIGURE 11.8 Opening your machine's NetInfo database from the top level.

Your machine's local NetInfo database also has the name, or tag, `local`. When you looked at the Domain menu, you might have noticed the option to Open by Tag. If you try to Open by Tag rather than Open, the dialog box shown in Figure 11.9 asks for the hostname or IP address and the NetInfo database tag. Possible entries you can use for your own host include its IP address or 127.0.0.1 or localhost. For the tag, enter `local`.

NOTE

If you are trying to serve a NetInfo domain to other machines in addition to your local domain, the NetInfo server should start automatically using the automatic configuration. If it does not, you can override this by changing `NETINFOSERVER=-AUTOMATIC-` to `NETINFOSERVER=-YES-` in `/etc/hostconfig`.

No matter which way you choose to open your NetInfo database, after you have it open, the result is the same except that how the name of the local database is displayed might vary. Figure 11.10 shows what you get if you choose to open NetInfo database using Open and selecting the default domain. Here the name is displayed as `local@localhost - /`. In our case, the Open by Tag window displays the database as `local@127.0.0.1`.

FIGURE 11.9 Opening your machine's NetInfo database by tag.

FIGURE 11.10 The top level of your NetInfo database as seen in NetInfo Manager.

As you can see in Figure 11.10, the hierarchical nature of the NetInfo database is immediately apparent. Immediately you see a directory browser in the top portion of a splitview and a properties table in the bottom portion. In the leftmost column, it's in the top level, /. In the second column is a list of directories. If you scroll through the list, you'll see some of the types of information that the NetInfo database stores. In the bottom portion, the properties table shows properties for a given directory. Figure 11.10 shows the properties for the / directory. We see that our machine is the master of its local database and that we could add a list of trusted networks.

Let's examine the NetInfo database using NetInfo Manager. If we click the aliases directory in the second column, more data appears in the third column. In the properties table, we see the property values for the aliases directory. It has only a property called name with a value of aliases. Yes, the name property is indeed the name of the directory. The third column displays the actual contents of the aliases directory. The hierarchical information appears directly above the directory browser.

Figure 11.11 shows where we are at this point. Note that above the second column, the one that shows the contents of `/`, is a `/`, and that above the third column, which shows the contents of aliases, is aliases.

FIGURE 11.11 The third column shows the contents of the aliases directory. The bottom properties table shows any properties associated with the aliases directory.

If we click the postmaster directory in the third column, we see that we have reached the end of the hierarchy. What was the third column is now the second column. The third column has no data. The labels above the directory browser also show where we are in the hierarchy in addition to labeling the contents of a column. The bottom splitview shows the properties of the postmaster directory. In addition to the name property, we see that the postmaster directory also has a members property with a value of root. What we learn from Figure 11.12 is that postmaster is aliased to root. The portion of the NetInfo database that we just looked at is what, in Unix machines, is usually stored in the file `/etc/aliases` or `/etc/mail/aliases`, depending on the system.

Let's look at something else in the NetInfo database. If we click groups in the left column, we see the same behavior we saw with the aliases directory. It has only a `name` property. Similar to the aliases directory, it has additional directories under it, as displayed in the third column. The third column has enough directories to have to scroll through the listing. If you scroll to the sshd group and click it, you'll see what's shown in Figure 11.13.

In Figure 11.13, we see that the `/groups/sshd` directory of the NetInfo database contains a name property with the value `sshd`, a `passwd` property with the value `*` and a `gid` property with the value `75`. As you might have guessed, this is NetInfo's way of displaying information that would normally be stored in a file, `/etc/group`, on a typical Unix machine.

FIGURE 11.12 The bottom properties table shows the contents of the postmaster directory. The lack of data in the third column shows that we've reached the end of the hierarchy.

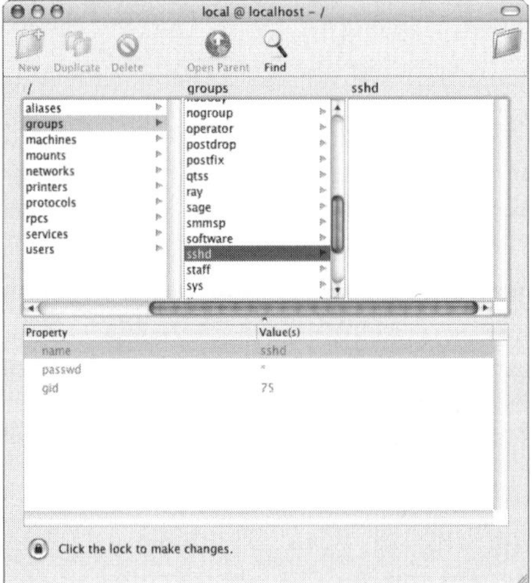

FIGURE 11.13 The contents of the `/groups/sshd` directory of the NetInfo database.

As you've have seen in your brief tour of the NetInfo database, the hierarchical nature of the database indeed becomes apparent when viewed in the NetInfo Manager.

Creating a Backup of the Local NetInfo Database Using NetInfo Manager

Because the NetInfo database is so important to maintaining the machine's internal world view, it's important for you to make backups of it periodically—especially if you're going to be doing experiments that you might not be able to back out of neatly. In Mac OS X 10.2 and earlier, the NetInfo Manager provided a graphical way to make a backup of the database. However, Mac OS X 10.3 does not seem to include this feature at this time. If you are going to make any major changes to your NetInfo database, check Chapter 23 for command line instructions.

Modifying the NetInfo Database

We'll use the addition of a printer definition to the `printers` directory as our example of modifying the NetInfo database. If you are also going to make any changes and are concerned about losing NetInfo data, check Chapter 23 before continuing. You already know some easier ways to add printers, but this makes good practice because it gives us an opportunity to show several representative techniques of working with the NetInfo database, including one that imports traditional Unix configuration files.

Modifying the NetInfo Database Using NetInfo Manager: Adding a Printer Definition in the GUI NetInfo Manager Tool

To make adding a printer definition easier through the NetInfo Manager, we've widened the view a bit and increased the amount of space available for the values section.

As we observed in the previous section, the NetInfo database is the information warehouse used by your Mac OS X machine. It's used in many instances in which plain text files would ordinarily be used on other Unix systems. For printers, the equivalent file on some Unix systems is `/etc/printcap`. You might want to take a look at the man page for `printcap` to familiarize yourself with some of the values we'll enter. Because Mac OS X now uses the CUPS printing system, it doesn't make use of `printcap` and its convoluted but highly specific configuration options. Sometimes printing under a system such as CUPS can seem a bit like voodoo because it automates so many things that seem like they *should* require specific configuration, but when the magic is working, it's considerably more pleasant than working with `printcap` files!

To add a PostScript printer definition served by another Unix machine, do the following:

1. If you're not already in NetInfo Manager, start it up, and open your local database.
2. As you probably noticed in the previous section, the values shown in the bottom properties table of NetInfo Manager were grayed out, and therefore couldn't be edited. To make changes to the NetInfo database, click the lock in the bottom-left side of the window. Enter the administrator username and password and click OK. If you just backed up your NetInfo database using NetInfo Manager, this step is unnecessary.

3. Click the printers directory. In the bottom splitview, you will see that the printers directory has only a name property with a value of printers. In the right column, you'll see nothing. At this time, we're at the end of the hierarchy.

4. Under the Directory menu, select New Subdirectory. Notice that a directory, called new_directory, appears in the column to the right of where printers is located. Notice also that, in the bottom splitview, the new_directory has only a name property with the value new_directory, as shown in Figure 11.14.

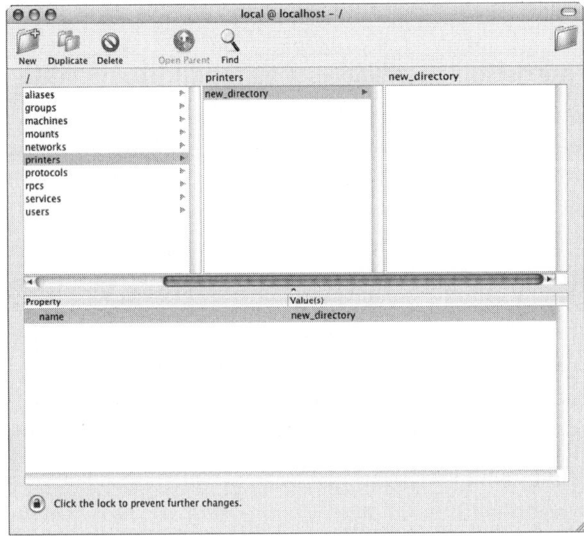

FIGURE 11.14 To add a printer definition to the printers directory, select New Subdirectory under the Directory menu. A new directory called new_directory is created.

5. Change the name of new_directory to the name that we want to call our printer—lp. Double-click new_directory in the bottom window, and change the name to lp. You might have to wait a couple seconds before you can edit the value.

6. Now new_directory has one property called name with a value of lp. We need more values than that to define our printer, however. Under the Directory menu, select Insert Property or New Property. Insert Property and New Property both add a new property above the name line. Some versions of NetInfo Manager include an Append Property option that adds a new line following the name line. For this example, it shouldn't matter which you select. Now a new line with a new_property with a grayed-out value of <new_value> is added, as shown in Figure 11.15. It doesn't matter where in the list the new_property lands. The NetInfo database sorts everything to the way it wants it.

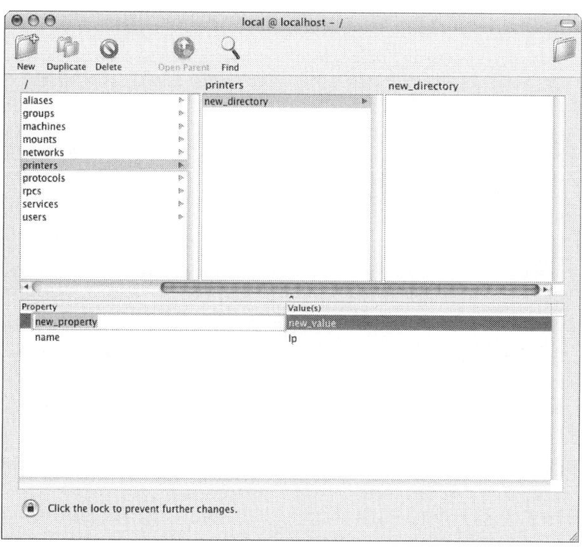

FIGURE 11.15 Under the Directory menu, select either Insert Property or New Property to add a new property. A new property called new_property with a grayed-out value of <new_value> is added.

7. As you did before for the lp value, double-click new_property. Change the property to lo. To change the value, double click on it, and change it to lock. If it's not editable (shows <no value> instead of new value or is missing or grayed out), select New Value or Insert Value under the Directory menu. Now <no_value> becomes an editable new value. Change it to lock. You should have two lines that resemble the ones shown in Figure 11.16.

8. Using the techniques described in the previous steps, add the following lines to further define lp:

Property	Value(s)
rp	<name of the remote printer as it's known to the remote host>
rm	<IP address or name of the remote machine>
lp	/dev/null
sd	/var/spool/lpd/lp
LPR_PRINTER	1

You'll need to click off of the subdirectory you're editing into a different NetInfo subdirectory and answer "yes" to saving changes, or specifically select Domain->Save Changes to get the modifications you make to the directory properties to take hold.

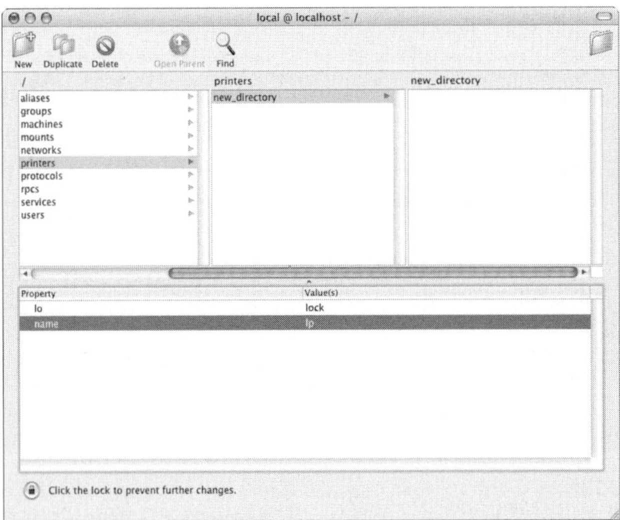

FIGURE 11.16 After adding a new property and editing its values, we now have two lines in our printer definition.

9. In a Terminal window or using the Finder's Go To Folder menu option, look at this directory: `/System/Library/Printers/PPDs/Contents/Resources`. You should see a listing of directories of the form *<language>*.lproj. Here's what the en.lproj (english) directory looks like:

```
brezup:sage Resources $ ls en.lproj
LaserWriter 12_640 PS.gz             LaserWriter IIg v2010.130.gz
LaserWriter 16_600 PS Fax.gz         LaserWriter Personal 320.gz
LaserWriter 16_600 PS-J.gz           LaserWriter Personal NTR.gz
LaserWriter 16_600 PS.gz             LaserWriter Pro 400 v2011.110.gz
LaserWriter 4_600 PS.gz              LaserWriter Pro 405 v2011.110.gz
LaserWriter 8500 PPD v1.2.gz         LaserWriter Pro 600 v2010.130.gz
LaserWriter Color 12_600 PS-J.gz     LaserWriter Pro 630 v2010.130.gz
LaserWriter Color 12_600 PS.gz       LaserWriter Pro 810.gz
LaserWriter Color 12_660 PS.gz       LaserWriter Pro 810f.gz
LaserWriter IIf v2010.113.gz         LaserWriter Select 360.gz
LaserWriter IIf v2010.130.gz         LaserWriter Select 360f.gz
LaserWriter IIg v2010.113.gz         LaserWriter Select 610.gz
```

Another place to look is in `/Library/Printers/PPDs/Contents/Resources/en.lproj`. This directory contains the default English PPDs that come with Mac OS X. If you see a PPD for your remote printer, add a property to the `lp` definition that follows the form shown here for a LaserWriter Select 360:

```
ppdurl    file://localhost/System/Library/Printers/PPDs
➥/Contents/Resources/en.lproj/LaserWriter Select 360
```

NOTE

Spaces in the name might need to be URL encoded by a substitution of %20 in their place. Note also that the `.gz` appendix has been dropped. The PPD specified here doesn't seem to be used in the CUPS printing system, so it probably isn't an issue if you're using OS X 10.2 or newer, but this line must be entered correctly for previous versions of Mac OS X to print properly.

CAUTION

We've had a few problems with various parts of Mac OS X wanting the PPD file to be in gnuzip (`.gz`) compressed format and other parts seemingly wanting it uncompressed. If you get odd errors that appear to relate to your PPD, try uncompressing the PPD. StuffIt Expander will do, or you can use command-line gunzip as detailed in Chapter 13, "Common Unix Shell Commands: File Operations."

If your printer could be described as a generic PostScript printer, create a property for `ppdurl` and then delete the value (Delete Value under the Directory menu of NetInfo Manager) so that the entry shows

```
ppdurl  <no_value>
```

If you have another PPD file for your printer on the system, specify its location. To enable Delete Value, you might need to double-click on the value field of the item you're trying to modify. Note that deleting the value is different than simply erasing the contents of the value field.

10. Now you've entered all the values to define a PostScript printer attached to a remote host. Figure 11.17 shows what values for a remote LaserWriter 360 attached to another Unix system would look like.

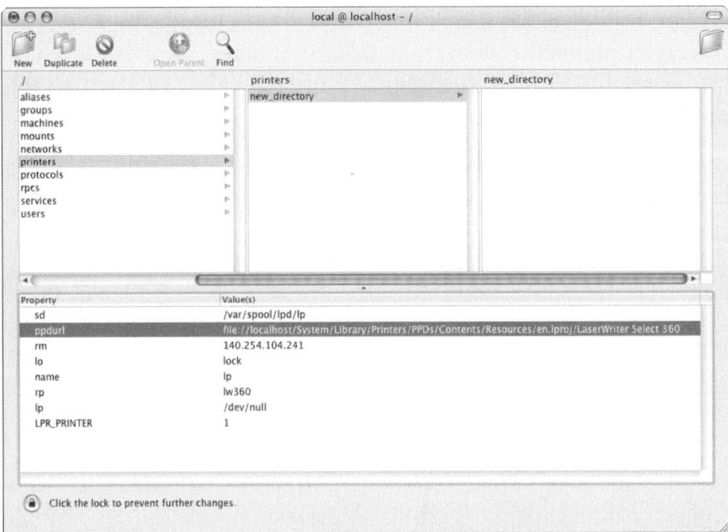

FIGURE 11.17 Completed values for the definition of a remote PostScript printer. In this case, we know that the remote PostScript printer is a LaserWriter Select 360.

11. To save our changes to the NetInfo database, select Save Changes from the Domain menu.

12. A request to Confirm Modification appears. Click Update this copy. Now the new_directory has been changed to lp, as shown in Figure 11.18.

13. Under the Management menu, select Restart Local NetInfo Domains. (This used to be Restart all NetInfo Domains on Local Host, which is actually a much better name because the intent isn't just to restart the local domain, but it seems that was a bit wordy for a menu item.) An alert asks whether you really want to restart the machine's NetInfo servers. Click Yes. Restarting the NetInfo domains shouldn't strictly be necessary, but we've seen occasional problems in which restarting the domain was necessary to propagate changes.

14. Click the lock at the bottom-left side of the window to end your ability to make changes at this time, and then close NetInfo Manager. You might find it sufficient to just click on the lock to save your changes.

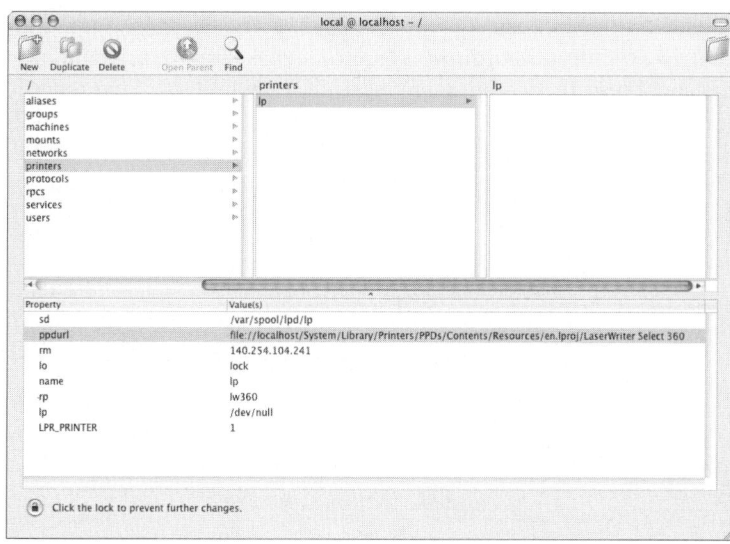

FIGURE 11.18 After saving our changes to the NetInfo database, we see that the directory called new_directory has become lp, and NetInfo has sorted the directories to reflect its desired ordering. We've successfully added a new hierarchy level to the NetInfo database.

Adding a Printer to Print Center We've updated the NetInfo database, but because the CUPS printing system doesn't directly use `printcap` or its equivalent NetInfo directory as Mac OS X version 10.1 and earlier did, to be able to use this printer in GUI applications or at the command line, we must add the printer to the Printer List in Print Center:

1. Start Print Center (path: `/Applications/Utilities/Print Center`). Either select Add Printer from the Printers menu or click the Add icon in the Printer list.
2. Select the Open Directory connection type. You should see lp listed as shown in Figure 11.19. In some versions of the Print Center, this dialog knows that the printer information is coming from NetInfo and the host that's serving the print queue. Use the Printer Model pop-up to select the correct PPD as you did for printers configured directly through the Print Center in Chapter 10, "Printer, Fax, and Font Management." Click Add.
3. You're almost ready to try printing. The spool directory (the sd property) doesn't yet exist. If you try to print via the command line using `lpr`, you *should* get an error at this point, but you won't because CUPS spools for itself and ignores this value. Still, we're not quite certain what will happen if you're trying to set up a heterogeneous collection of mixed LPR and CUPS printing services, and it won't hurt anything to

have a few extra directories if they're not used. If the directories are used under some circumstances, creating them now saves headaches later. In a Terminal window, make the spool directory, `/var/spool/lpd/lp`. The directory `/var/spool/lpd` probably doesn't exist, so you must create it first. Unless you enabled the root account (covered later in this chapter), you must use the `sudo` command (and be an Admin user) to execute these commands. Enter your administrator password when asked.

```
brezup:ray ray $ sudo mkdir /var/spool/lpd
Password:
brezup:ray ray $ sudo mkdir /var/spool/lpd/lp
brezup:ray ray $ sudo chmod 770 /var/spool/lpd/lp
brezup:ray ray $ sudo chown daemon:daemon /var/spool/lpd/lp
```

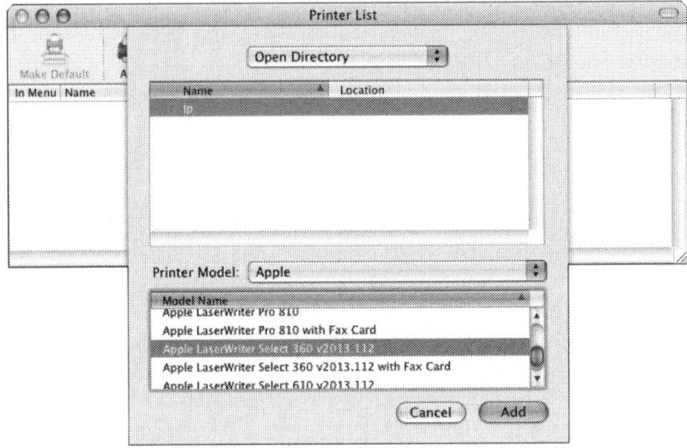

FIGURE 11.19 When we add our printer lp to the list of printers in the Print Center, lp appears as a choice under the NetInfo Network type Directory Services.

4. Test your printer from the command line by running lpr:

   ```
   brezup:ray ray $ lpr file2
   ```

   To see your print job in the queue, check the queue:

   ```
   brezup:ray ray $ lpq
   lp is ready and printing
   Rank   Owner  Job   File(s)              Total Size
   active ray    1     file2                2048 bytes
   ```

5. Test `lp` from a Mac OS X application such as Internet Explorer.

Modifying the NetInfo Database from the Command Line: Using the Command Line to Add a Printer

If you were to flip forward to Chapter 23 and look at the documentation for the tool we use to add a NetInfo printer at the command line, you might think that performing this task from the command line would be especially painful. However, this method can actually be easier than the method we've just described.

Loading Traditional Unix Flat-File Databases As we mentioned, Mac OS X uses the NetInfo database to store information about printers, whereas some versions of Unix store this information in a file called `/etc/printcap`. Mac OS X has a nice command-line tool available that understands certain typical Unix flat-file databases and can convert them to NetInfo data. One of the flat-file formats that the `niload` tool understands is the `printcap` format.

To add a PostScript printer served by a remote Unix host using primarily command-line tools, do the following:

1. Make a backup of the NetInfo database.
2. Look at the man page for printcap in Appendix A and study the following example to familiarize yourself with the basic format of the printcap file.
3. Using your favorite text editor, create a printcap-test file in some location such as your home directory. Pay no attention to, and especially do not overwrite, any printcap file that that might already exist in /etc/ on your system. That file is part of the CUPS system.
4. Add a line of this form to your printcap-test file:

```
lp2:\
:lp=/dev/null:rm=192.168.1.5:rp=lw360:\
:sd=/var/spool/lpd/lp:
```

> **NOTE**
>
> This file is a virtual single line, even though it is entered on three lines. The \ at the end of each displayed line tells the software that the current line continues to the next line in the file.

These values should already look familiar. The lp2 on the first line is the name of our printer. The lp on the second line becomes the lp property with the value /dev/null. (Remember to use the name or IP address of the machine that serves your remote printer; my settings probably won't work on your network!) The rm on the second line becomes the rm property with the value of the IP address or name of the remote machine. The rp on the second line becomes the rp property with the value of the name of the printer as it's known on the remote host. The sd on the third line becomes the sd property with a value of the spool directory, /var/spool/lpd/lp. You could continue to extend this with similar lines for the other properties you want to enter (such as custom lock file names, and so on) simply by adding more lines of the same format to your file. Always remember to end internal lines with \ so that the software knows to continue reading on the next line. Remember also not to put a \ on the last line so that the software knows it's reached the end of the definition.

NOTE

Notice that we used the name lp2 here because you might already have defined lp as a printer name from the first example in this chapter. You can enter any name value you like as the item before the first colon so long as it doesn't overlap with an already existing printer name definition.

5. Use the niload command to load the flat file you made into the NetInfo database. Complete documentation for these command-line NetInfo utilities is covered in Chapter 23.

   The basic form of the command we will use is niload *<format>* *<domain>* < *<filename>*.

   ```
   brezup:sage sage $ sudo niload printcap . < printcap-test
   ```

   Look at the results of what you just did using NetInfo Manager. In our command-line result, both lp from our first installation and lp2 appear.

   ```
   brezup:sage sage $ niutil -list . /printers
   70     lp
   78     lp2
   brezup:sage sage $ niutil -read . /printers/lp2
   lp: /dev/null
   name: lp2
   rm: 192.168.1.5
   rp: lw360
   sd: /var/spool/lpd/lp
   ```

   Figure 11.20 shows an example of what the niload version of the printcap data looks like in NetInfo Manager.

   Notice that the printcap entry does not necessarily use all the values that previous versions of Print Center generated into NetInfo. The minimum values that can be defined in a typical printcap file are acceptable to the NetInfo database.

6. Create the spool directory. In a Terminal window, create the spool directory, /var/spool/lpd/lp2. The directory /var/spool/lpd should already exist.

   ```
   brezup:sage sage $ sudo mkdir -p /var/spool/lpd/lp2
   brezup:sage sage $ sudo chmod 770 /var/spool/lpd/lp2
   brezup:sage sage $ sudo chown daemon:daemon /var/spool/lpd/lp2
   ```

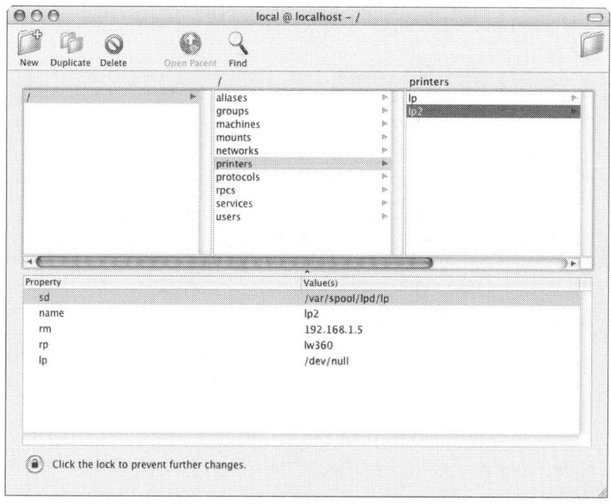

FIGURE 11.20 niload has been successfully used to load printcap information into the NetInfo database.

7. Start the Print Center, and add lp2 via the Directory Services, NetInfo Network type, as you added lp previously.

8. Test printing via lpr in the command line as well as through the normal print menu of a Mac OS X application.

Loading Arbitrary Data from Files Finally, let's look at loading arbitrary data into the NetInfo database for those cases in which there might not be a predefined flat file format to load from. In this example, we take one step over in addition to those previously shown: We create a directory into which to load the information as a separate step. Interestingly, we must include the `name` parameter in the text file specification of the data we're loading. If the name we place in the file is different from what we specify via the command-line parameter, the directory specified at the command line is renamed to the name specified in the file. This should give you an idea of how you can update or modify already existing NetInfo directories as well. We use loading another printer definition as our example so that you can more easily compare each method. By now you're getting to be an old hand at adding printers, so we keep this description short.

1. As previously, make a backup of the NetInfo database.

2. Using your favorite text editor, make another plain-text data file to load into NetInfo. In this file, enter your information corresponding to the following in exactly this form:

```
{
 "name" = ("lp3");
 "rm" = ( "192.168.1.3" );
```

```
    "lo" = ( "lock" );
    "rp" = ( "remoteprint" );
    "lp" = ( "/dev/null" );
    "sd" = ( "/var/spool/lpd/lp3" );
}
```

Remember to change the name value to match the directory you've created, and change the rm and rp values to their appropriate values for your network.

3. Create the appropriate directory into which to load these values in NetInfo. I'm calling mine `lp3`.

```
sudo niutil -p -create -t localhost/local /name=printers/name=lp3
```

4. Load the file into NetInfo with niload. I named my file `niload_printer_test` in this example.

```
sudo niload -r /name=printers/name=lp3 . < niload_printer_test
```

5. Add the printer at Print Center and test as previously. We leave it up to you to check what the data looks like in NetInfo Manager or at the command line.

The NetInfo Manager Interface

Now that you've had a chance to use NetInfo Manager, let's take a brief look at the NetInfo Manager interface itself. NetInfo Manager and the NetInfo database can seem so overwhelming at first that now is a good time to take a step back and look at the interface itself.

As you've seen throughout this chapter, many options are available under the menu items of NetInfo Manager. Because there are so many options, it can be easy to overlook the buttons that are included in the upper left of the NetInfo Manager window.

The buttons provide some useful shortcuts for some actions. Here are descriptions for the buttons, from left to right:

- **Create New Directory**, the button with a folder and a plus sign, is used to add a new subdirectory to the NetInfo database.
- **Duplicate Selected Directory**, the button with two folders, causes the selected folder to be duplicated. You might find this button particularly useful as you create more groups and some types of users.
- **Delete Selected Directory**, the button showing a circle with a slash in the middle, deletes the selected directory when clicked.

- **Open Parent Domain**, the button with an earth and an up arrow, causes NetInfo to move to the parent domain of the current domain. If your machine isn't part of a complicated network, you might not find much use for this button. For the typical user whose machine is only a part of its own local NetInfo domain, this button is grayed out.
- **Show Find Panel**, represented by button containing a magnifying glass, is used to open the Find dialog box. You might find this button useful for searching the NetInfo database. Figure 11.21 shows the results of using Find on lp in our NetInfo database.

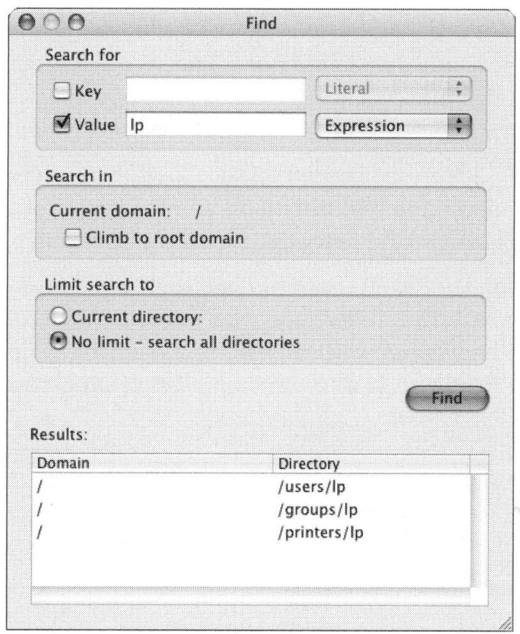

FIGURE 11.21 The Find button can be used to search the NetInfo database.

In addition to the buttons is the folder at the right that we mentioned earlier. The folder was originally used to indicate your present location in the NetInfo database. However, starting with the Mac OS X 10.2 release, that information is displayed above the directory browser in the upper splitview. The folder can be used to drag and drop directories for copying or moving them. The upper splitview is where you navigate through the NetInfo database. The lower splitview is where you view the contents of a specific directory in the NetInfo database.

Using the NetInfo Database to Customize a User

Now you've had the opportunity to examine the NetInfo database, back it up, and use several tools to modify it. In the previous section, you saw that changes could be made in the NetInfo database and a small sampling of how these changes interact with and provide information to other tools. We make use of that idea in this section, in which you learn how to customize a user account. We use the Accounts control panel to create a user, but we customize our user by editing information in the NetInfo database.

In our example, we make a user who we want to use as our general software user. This is a specialized user whose account we want to use when compiling software for the system, but we do not want this user to be one of the administrators for the machine. We want our user to belong to a group called `tire` with group ID `100`. We'd also like to have a specific user ID, `502`, for our user, whose account we intend to call `software`. To create this user, do the following:

1. Open the Accounts control pane in System Preferences. Click the lock icon if it's set not to allow changes. Add a new user with a short name of software. Our software user's display name is skuld. Choose whatever password you prefer. Don't give your software user admin privileges.

2. Open NetInfo Manager and select the local domain if it's not already selected. Click the lock to make changes and enter the administrator username and password.

3. Click the groups directory and scroll through the list. Because tire is not a default group that comes with the system, you should not see a group called tire. Therefore, you must make a new group. Click any group to see what values are typically included in a group. Figure 11.22 shows the types of properties that belong to a group.

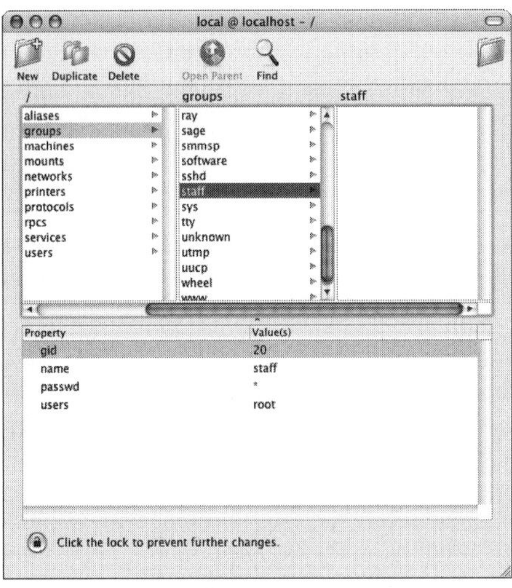

FIGURE 11.22 Looking at the staff directory, we see that the typical properties for a group are passwd, name, gid, and users.

4. Click groups. From the Directory menu, select New Subdirectory. A new directory called new_directory appears. Edit the name property and add other properties as follows:

Property	Value
name	tire
passwd	*
gid	100
users	software

The * in the password field means that a group password is not being assigned. So far, we have only one user in our group: the user named software. As the term *group* implies, we can have more than one user in a group.

5. Select Save Changes from the Domain menu. A question to Confirm Modification appears. Click Update this copy. Now new_directory has become tire, as shown in Figure 11.23.

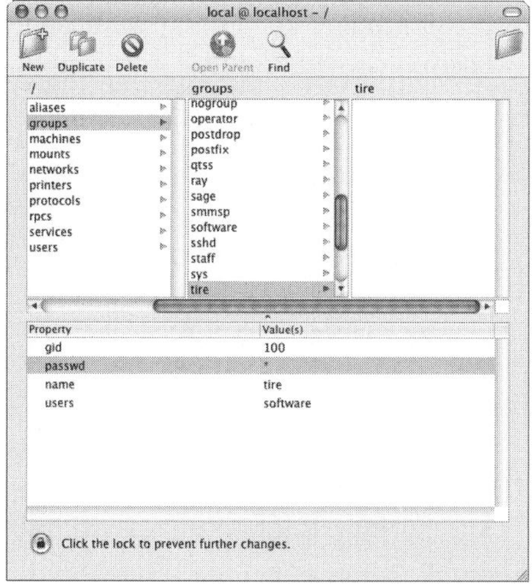

FIGURE 11.23 We now have a new group called tire with GID 100. At this time, only one user, software, belongs to the group.

6. Click users and then click software. Now the default information about user software appears in the properties table. If this is one of your first users, UID 502 might already be the user ID; otherwise, you can change software's UID shortly. A group ID that is the same as the UID is probably what was made. If you look at the values section for software, you can see that the Accounts pane added quite a bit of information about software to the NetInfo database.

If software were not one of the first users on my system, I would already have a user with UID 502. Because of this, I would have to either change the UID of my original user or delete the user. If the original user were not an important user, such as a user created to run demonstration commands, rather than a real user who is using the machine, I would just delete the user. If I wanted to keep my user, I could change the UID of the original user to one that wasn't already taken, and then change the UID of software to 502.

NOTE

If I decided to rearrange UIDs instead of simply deleting the user, I would also have to change the ownership of all the files that belonged to my previous user to belong to their new UID. File ownerships are stored based on numeric UID. Changing a user to a previously used UID gives that user access to and ownership of any files that still belong to that numeric UID.

For your purposes, the user ID for software might not be important. Because we want to share some of our resources with another machine that also has a user called software and whose UID is 502, it's important for us to make software's UID 502 for compatibility purposes. In both cases, we want the user software to belong to group tire. Change the GID to 100. Change the UID as appropriate for your situation. Select Save Changes from the Domain menu, and click Update this copy in the Confirm Modification box. Figure 11.24 shows the updated information for our user software.

FIGURE 11.24 Now our user software has UID 502 and GID 100. We can see from this information that user software has been assigned a password, a home directory in `/Users/software`, and a default shell of /bin/bash.

7. Click the lock to save your changes and end your ability to make further changes.
8. Open a Terminal window, go to software's home directory, and look at the directory's contents. Take note that the directory was created by the Users pane with the default values. The update to the information in the NetInfo database, however, was not entirely reflected in the system. So, you must manually implement those changes. First, here's the default information for the software user that was created on our system:

```
brezup:sage software $ ls -al
total 24
drwxr-xr-x 13 software software  442 27 Aug 20:49 .
drwxrwxr-t 11 root    admin      374 27 Aug 23:00 ..
-rw-r--r--  1 software software  3 25 Aug 23:18 .CFUserTextEncoding
-rw-r--r--  1 software software  6148 27 Aug 20:49 .DS_Store
drwx------  2 software software  68 27 Aug 20:47 .Trash
drwx------  3 software software  102 25 Aug 23:18 Desktop
drwx------  3 software software  102 25 Aug 23:18 Documents
drwx------ 18 software software  612 27 Aug 20:46 Library
drwx------  3 software software  102 25 Aug 23:18 Movies
drwx------  3 software software  102 25 Aug 23:18 Music
drwx------  3 software software  102 25 Aug 23:18 Pictures
drwxr-xr-x  4 software software  136 25 Aug 23:18 Public
drwxr-xr-x  4 software software  136 25 Aug 23:18 Sites
```

In our example, `software`'s original `UID` was `502`, which is still `software`'s `UID`. Depending on what changes you had to make in the NetInfo database to get the desired UID, you would probably see the original UID number that belonged to `software` here rather than the username. If you didn't change your `software` user's `UID`, you should see `software` in that column, as we see here. The default `GID` that the Accounts pane used for creating `software` was `GID 502`, the same number as the UID, and has the same groupname, `software`, as well. So, the information that we see for `software`'s home directory is the information that was originally assigned to `software`. We have to update the information to `software`'s directory to reflect the new information.

As `root`, or using `sudo`, in the `/Users` directory, change the ownership of `software`'s directory to the `software` user in group `tire`:

```
brezup:sage Users $ sudo chown -R software:tire software
Password:
```

Check the results:

```
brezup:sage Users $ ls -ld software
drwxr-xr-x 13 software tire 442 27 Aug 20:49 software
brezup:sage Users $ ls -l software
```

```
total 0
drwx------  3 software tire 102 25 Aug 23:18 Desktop
drwx------  3 software tire 102 25 Aug 23:18 Documents
drwx------ 18 software tire 612 27 Aug 20:46 Library
drwx------  3 software tire 102 25 Aug 23:18 Movies
drwx------  3 software tire 102 25 Aug 23:18 Music
drwx------  3 software tire 102 25 Aug 23:18 Pictures
drwxr-xr-x  4 software tire 136 25 Aug 23:18 Public
drwxr-xr-x  4 software tire 136 25 Aug 23:18 Sites
```

If you changed the `UID` of a user who was originally assigned `UID 502`, look at that user's home directory and make the appropriate ownership changes.

Sane User Account Management

Like the creation of our `tire` group in which we're housing non-administrative users who are still used for system maintenance, it's very useful to add groups to your system for any logically collected groups of users on your system. The Unix privilege system underlying Mac OS X contains a mechanism to allow groups of users to mutually share access to files within their group, while protecting those files from other users on the same system.

To enable this capability, you must create groups for those users to belong to, and you must add their usernames to the `users` value list of the group. A single user can be a member of an arbitrary number of groups and can assign files that he owns to be visible to any one of (or none of) the groups to which he belongs. To make use of this capability, the user must use the command-line group ownership tools discussed in Chapter 14, "Advanced Shell Concepts and Commands."

With the release of 10.3, Apple has chosen to follow an administrative philosophy that believes it's easiest to create a new group for each and every user created and to assign each user to belong, by default, to his own group. This has the advantage that it's easy to assign a small group of users to belong to the same group as some user `jim` by simply assigning them to the group `jim`. In other words, it makes management of groups that relate to individuals relatively easy—all of `jim`'s friends belong to group `jim`, and he can easily allow them privleged access to some of his files (though the administrator still must do the work of adding users to group `jim`—there's no current way for `jim` to do this himself).

Unfortunately, this administrative philosophy works well for managing a bunch of individuals, but it doesn't work well for managing things such as project groups or users who are otherwise logically grouped on the system into large "classes" of some sort. For this sort of system use, it's more convenient to have all users who belong to some project, or who have some grouped privelege class, to have the same default group. If an individual wants to have a group-of-friends type group, `root` can always create an individual group for them as well as the general-class groups. Because `root` has to manually add "`jims` friends" to group `jim` in the new-group-for-each-user design, it's not really any more inconvenient to create additional per-user groups for those individuals who might want to have them when using the general-class group paradigm.

If you decide to dispose of Apple's new-group-for-each-user paradigm for management of your system, you'll want to create at least one general-user group in NetInfo, typically called `users`, into which you can assign users who don't logically seem like `staff` users. Apple's Accounts pane now creates users as members of their own individual groups, and you're welcome to leave them with these default groups, but we'll also show you how you can automate the creation of users, and take control of the group assignment process in Chapter 23.

On the other systems we run, we have a logical distinction between `staff` users and normal users, so we find it convenient to mirror this with our OS-X installations by creating a group to assign new, nonstaff users to. On our Mac OS X machines, we created this as `GID 99`, with group name `users`. We assume this value as a default in various other locations in this book.

NOTE

In more than a few years of managing clusters of Unix machines with aggregate hundreds of users, I don't think I've come across more than a handful of situations in which using Apple's current new-group-per-user paradigm would have been helpful in managing users and groups. I've come across many more instances in which using the old-style paradigm of assigning all non-administrative users to the same `users` group, and then creating new specific groups as needed, was a better solution. If you're only going to be housing a small number of users on your system, Apple's method is probably fine, but if you'll have many users, I expect that you'd find limiting things to a smaller number of user groups to be beneficial.

Enabling the `root` Account

As mentioned earlier, the administrator account is a powerful account. But the most powerful account on a Unix machine is the account called `root`. People also refer to `root` as the super user, but the account name itself is `root`. On most Unix systems, the first available account is the `root` account. In Mac OS X, however, the `root` account is disabled by default as a security precaution.

At some time, however, you might find it necessary to enable the `root` account. The `root` account can modify system settings, modify files it does not own, modify files that can't be written to by default, modify a user's password, install software, become another user without having to know the password of that account, and so on. In other words, `root` can do anything anywhere, making the power of `root` immense. Because `root` has so much power, the only users who can become `root` are users with administrative privileges. Because a user with administrative privileges can become the `root` user, you should assign these capabilities to only completely trusted individuals.

If you choose to enable the root account, remember to use it with caution. Although the root account might provide some extra utility, you could accidentally wipe out your system if you don't pay careful attention to what you type. In addition, the root password you choose should be difficult to guess. Finally, become the root user only for as long as necessary to complete the task at hand.

With the presence of an administrative user, it might be a long time, if ever, before you discover a need to enable the root user. You can take many approaches for dealing with the root user—from ways to use root without enabling the root account to actually enabling the root account.

Let's take a look at four different ways to gain root access to your system. Although you can choose whichever method you like, it's useful to understand that even though some of these methods appear to work magic, they all accomplish very much the same thing.

The root user is disabled because it does not have a valid password set. Because there are a number of ways to set a password, there are also several ways to enable root, including one method (the first method we'll look at) that was designed specifically for assigning the root account password and *only* the root password. In addition, you'll see how the sudo command can provide root-level access even when the root password is disabled. We recommend that users access the root account only when absolutely necessary.

Using the NetInfo Manager Utility

The NetInfo Manager Utility provides a graphical method for enabling the root user.

1. Start the NetInfo Manager utility and click the lock to make changes.
2. For Mac OS X 10.2 and later, select Enable Root User from the Security menu. For Mac OS 10.1 and 10.0, select Security from the Domain menu. Then choose Enable Root User from the submenu. Unless you've previously set a root password, a message appears with a NetInfo error indicating that the password is blank. Click OK.
3. Enter the root password you want to use, and then click Set. Remember that the root password should not be easily guessable.
4. Enter the password again for verification and then click Verify.
5. Click the lock button again to prevent any further changes. Then close NetInfo Manager.

Figure 11.25 shows an example of what an enabled root account looks like in NetInfo Manager. Note that the password field no longer has a single * in it; instead it has a string of *s.

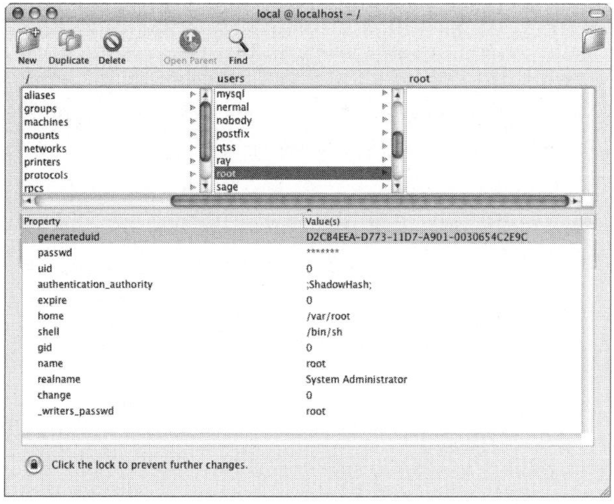

FIGURE 11.25 The root account has been enabled on this machine. Note the * that was in the password field has been replaced with several *s.

Using the Mac OS X Installation CD

Because the Mac OS X installation CD comes with an option to reset a user's password, you could use the installation CD itself to enable the `root` user.

To enable the `root` account using the Mac OS X installation CD, do the following:

1. Insert the Mac OS X CD.
2. With the CD in the CD-ROM drive, reboot the machine. Hold the C key while the machine reboots.
3. Wait for the Installer to appear and then select the Reset Password option under the Installer menu.
4. Select the Mac OS X disk that contains the root account you want to enable. If a spinning CD icon appears after you've chosen the Reset Password option, don't wait for the spinning to end to select your Mac OS X disk.

   The System Administrator (`root`) user appears as the default user in a pop-up menu that lists all the users.
5. Enter a new password and then reenter the password for verification. Click Save.

   Click OK when the Password Saved box appears.
6. Quit the Password Reset application, quit the Installer, and click Restart.

Using sudo at the Command Line

Although we don't start looking at the command-line utilities in depth until later, let's take this opportunity to demonstrate some ways to accomplish tasks that root might do by using the sudo command-line utility. It's all right if you don't feel comfortable trying anything you see in this section at this time. When you are more familiar with working with the command line, you can return to this section. If you want to try anything in this section, you can run the commands in a Terminal window. Just open the Terminal application in the Utilities folder in the Applications folder.

Using sudo to Run Commands as root

sudo is a command-line utility that enables the use of the root account without necessarily enabling root.

For example, in a Terminal window, you could use sudo to reboot the machine now:

```
brezup:sage sage $ sudo shutdown -r now
```

The most common way to use sudo is to preface each command that you want root to perform with the sudo utility. If you're asked for a password, use the password of the user who is executing the sudo command. If the user isn't eligible to execute sudo, the command isn't executed, and the attempt is recorded in /var/log/system.log. The /etc/sudoers file stores the information on which users are eligible to execute which commands. The default /etc/sudoers file in Mac OS X enables the root user and any user who belongs to group admin to execute all commands. In other words, any administrative user is eligible to execute sudo.

If you need to execute a few commands in a row as root, you could try a couple alternative uses of sudo. When you're done with the tasks for root, type **exit** at the end of your session.

In this example, your shell is elevated to that of root until you exit the session:

```
brezup:sage sage $ sudo -s

We trust you have received the usual lecture from the local System
Administrator. It usually boils down to these two things:

    #1) Respect the privacy of others.
    #2) Think before you type.

Password:
brezup:root sage #
```

Notice that in this instance the prompt changes to include root and # as a reminder that you now have the power of root. The message that sudo shows is shown only the first time that you run sudo.

In this example, sudo is used to run su to become root until you exit the session. When root is enabled, su can be used to switch to the root user. When using su by itself, the password you enter to become root is that of root, rather than yours, as you do with sudo.

```
brezup:sage sage $ sudo su
Password:
brezup:root sage #
```

To return to the status of a regular user, type **exit** when you're done with your root session.

Using sudo to Enable the root Account

Recall that the sudo command is used to execute a command that root might execute. One way to enable the root account is to use sudo to execute passwd, which is a command used to change passwords.

Here's an example:

```
brezup:sage sage $ sudo passwd root
Password:
Changing password for root.
New password:
Retype new password:
brezup:sage sage $
```

The password that you initially enter is your password. Then you supply a password for root and reenter it for verification. If you mistype the password, you're prompted again, as shown in this example:

```
brezup:sage sage $ sudo passwd root
Password:
Changing password for root.
New password:
Retype new password:
Mismatch; try again, EOF to quit.
New password:
Retype new password:
brezup:sage sage $
```

Groups

As mentioned earlier, a multiuser environment allows many users to be logged on to the same machine at the same time. The users' files, as well as the rest of the files in the system, have associated permissions. These permissions are specified for the owner of the file, the group to which the user belongs, and all users. It's the group concept that we'd like to briefly look at now. In later chapters, we look at working with groups.

A group can have a group password, although the use of a group password is uncommon. Additionally, a group has a group ID number, name, and members. As you saw when we created a user, the default group ID for a user created by using the Accounts pane is the same as the new user's UID, and the groupname to which the user belongs is the same as the username.

A user can belong to more than one group. This could be useful for a specific project, for example. You immediately see its usefulness, however, with administrative privileges. Users who have administrative privileges also belong to the group called `admin`, which has group ID `80`. The `root` user also belongs to the group `admin`. Although being in this group gives an administrative user a lot of power, `root` is still the most powerful user. Figure 11.26 shows how a typical administrative user might appear in NetInfo Manager. Note that the administrative user's primary group ID is listed as being the group number identical to her UID. Chapter 24 covers the creation and modification of users and groups in depth, so don't worry if you still have questions.

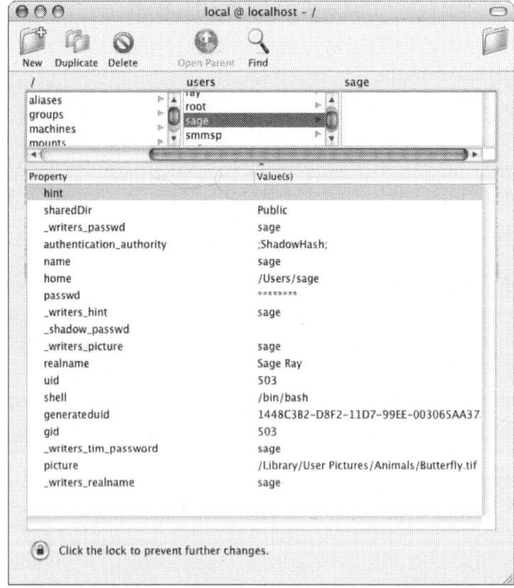

FIGURE 11.26 A typical administrative user, as shown in NetInfo Manager.

In Figure 11.27, you can see that our sample administrative user, `sage`, also belongs to group `admin`, which is group ID `80`.

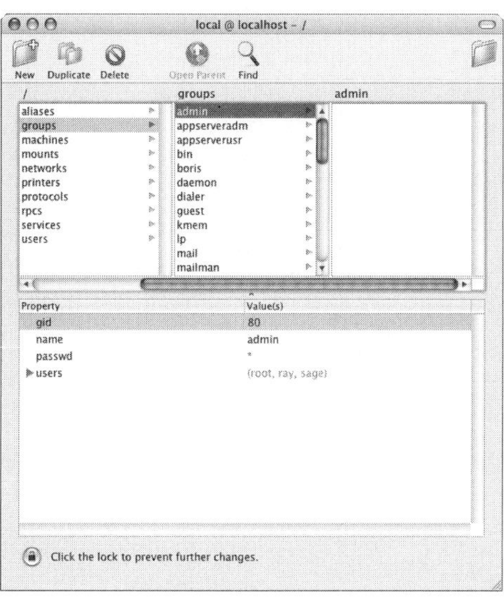

FIGURE 11.27 Administrative users also belong to the group `admin`.

To see permissions on a file in the Finder, select Show Info (Command+I) from the File menu. In the window that pops up, click the Ownership & Permissions section. Permissions can also be changed in this same window. Figure 11.28 shows the permissions on the `/System/Library/Fonts/` directory. As you can see, system (`root`) has read and write permissions, group `wheel` has read-only permission, and others have read-only permission. To copy fonts into that directory, you have to become `root`. If you're interested in more permissions controls in a GUI application, check `http://www.gideonsoftworks.com/filexaminer.html` for an application called FileXaminer. It enables you to change many attributes of a file, including permissions, ownership, and group. The Finder includes options to do this as well.

If you look at the permissions on the `/Library/Fonts/` directory, you'll see that users in `admin` have permission to read and write. That's why an administrative user can copy fonts to that directory.

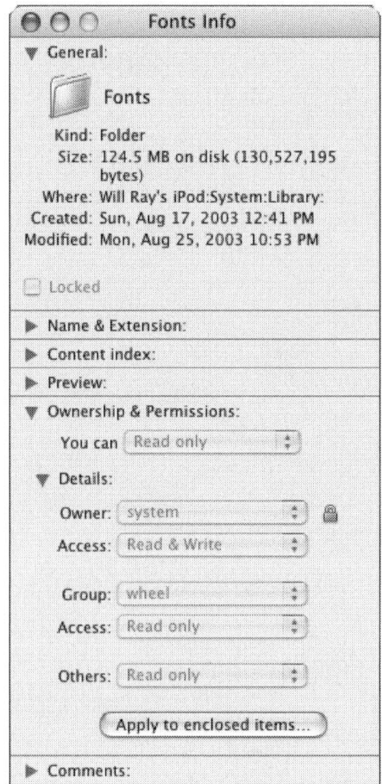

FIGURE 11.28 The permissions on the `/System/Library/Fonts/` directory show that members of group `admin` have no write permission. Therefore, an administrative user cannot copy anything to that directory.

System Preferences: Personal

So far in this chapter, we have looked at quite a few additional system components, including user account creation, using the NetInfo Manager, enabling the `root` account, and briefly looking at the concept of groups. In the remainder of the chapter, we concentrate on the System Preferences. System Preferences replaces the control panels of traditional Mac OS. Although the arrangement of the System Preferences is not exactly like that of the control panels of traditional Mac OS, the remainder of the chapter should seem a bit friendlier than the material we looked at in the earlier sections.

System Preferences is divided into four major sections: Personal, Hardware, Internet & Network, and System. Some applications also have a preference pane, which appears in a fifth category called Other. Figure 11.29 shows a sample System Preferences with all these categories. However, some applications install a System Preferences pane in one of the major categories. Firewalk X, which installs a System Preferences pane under the Internet & Networking category, is one such application. Likewise, the Ink and BlueTooth panes only appear if you have the appropriate peripherals attached to your machine.

In this section, we cover System Preferences panes that aren't covered elsewhere in the book. Consequently, we don't cover any of the preferences in the Internet & Network category because they're covered in other chapters.

The Personal section of System Preferences includes panes for customizing your personal desktop experience. With the controls in this section, you can customize such settings as desktop backgrounds, highlight color, and language preferences. In this section, we specifically look at the Appearance, International and Security.

FIGURE 11.29 System Preferences in Mac OS X 10.3.

Appearance

The Appearance pane, shown in Figure 11.30, enables you to set some general behaviors, which can be grouped as appearance, scroll behavior, number of recent items, and font smoothing.

In the first section of the pane, a general color scheme for the overall appearance of the menus, buttons, and windows is set. The choice is between blue and graphite. In addition, you can set the highlight color for selected text and lists. A few more choices are available for highlight color: graphite, silver, blue, gold, red, orange, green, purple, or other, which brings up a standard color browser from which you can select any color you want.

In the next section, you can select where scroll arrows are placed and the resulting behavior of clicking in the scrollbar. Scroll arrows can be placed either at the top and bottom or together. The resulting behavior of clicking in the scrollbar can be set either to jump to the next page or to scroll to a specific point. You can also set whether smooth scrolling is used and whether double-clicking in a window title bar minimizes the window.

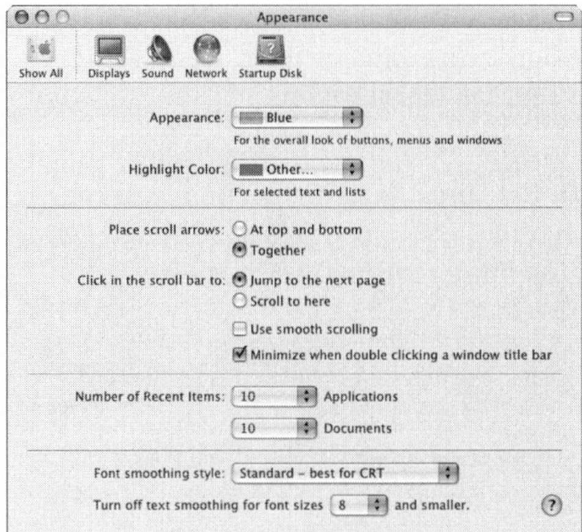

FIGURE 11.30 The Appearance pane controls settings for overall appearance, highlight color, scrollbar behavior, and font smoothing.

The next section is where you set the number of recent items for applications and documents. For both types, the choices are None, 5, 10, 15, 20, 30, or 50.

In the final section of the pane, you can turn off smoothing for fonts smaller than size 8, 9, 10, or 12. Here you also select a font-smoothing style from among these choices: Standard—best for CRT—Light, Medium—best for Flat Panel, and Strong.

International

Settings involving language, date format, keyboard layouts, and so on are set in the International pane.

Language

Figure 11.31 shows the Language section. This is where you set your preferred language order to use for application menus and dialogs. Just drag the languages around until you've achieved the desired order. If not all the languages you want to rank are shown, click the Edit button to edit the language listing. Select the languages of interest and then rank their order.

In the bottom portion of the Language section, at the Customize Sorting... button, select a default set of behaviors for scripts. The behaviors affect sort order, case conversion, and word definition. The Roman script has many options available to choose as the default.

FIGURE 11.31 The preferred language order for application menus and dialogs is set in the Language section of the International pane.

Formats

The Formats section enables you to set preferences involving dates, times, and numbers displays. First select a region. If you don't initially see your desired region, try checking the Show All Regions box. Some regions will display a note that they are only available in Unicode applications. This sets defaults for the Dates, Times, and Numbers categories. The long date and short date format can be set in the Date section under Customize... You can set such items as the date separator, whether to use a leading zero, and the preferred order of month, day, and year. In the Times section, you can customize such items as whether to use a 12-hour or a 24-hour clock, the separator, and whether to use a leading zero for the hour. In the Numbers section, you can customize such settings as the separator used for decimal and thousands and the symbol used for currency and where it is placed. Finally, you can select either U.S. or metric measurement units. Figure 11.32 shows the Formats section set for the defaults for the Austria (German) region.

Input Menu

In the Input Menu section shown in Figure 11.33, you can turn on multiple keyboard layouts. When more than one keyboard layout is selected, they appear in an Input menu and you can rotate through the choices. Mac OS X has an interface layer that attempts to map input to an equivalent appropriate to the script. For the Roman script, many keyboard layouts are available. For example, if you select the U.S., British, and French keyboards, you see slightly different behaviors in the interpretation of the underlying Roman script for them. For example, the pound sign (#) is interpreted on the British keyboard layout as £ instead. The French keyboard layout interprets many numbers as lowercase accented characters. To get numbers in that layout, you use the Shift key. More information on the Input Menu can be found in Chapter 10.

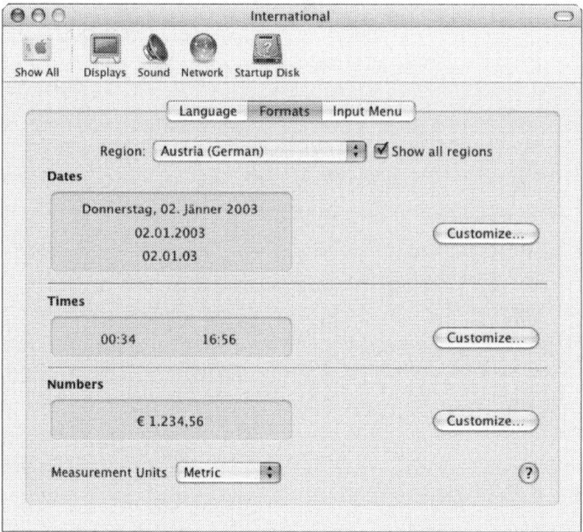

FIGURE 11.32 The Formats section of the International pane is where you set your preferences for dates, times, and number displays.

FIGURE 11.33 Multiple keyboard layouts can be specified in the Input Menu section of the International pane.

Security

The Security preference pane (see Figure 11.34) allows you to set FileVault protection in addition to other settings. FileVault encrypts your home directory using your login password. Also in the Security pane, you can set whether a password is required to wake the computer from sleep or a screen saver. If you are running a truly multiuser machine, or if your machine is located in a rather public place, this option is recommended. In addition, for all accounts on the computer, you can decide to disable automatic login, require a password to unlock each secure system preference pane, or set an automatic logout after a specified number of minutes of inactivity.

Note that this system preference pane requires administrative privileges.

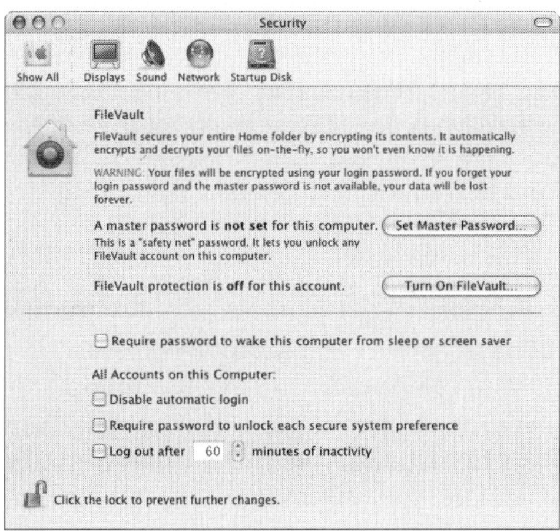

FIGURE 11.34 In the Security pane, you can turn on FileVault protection and set other basic security preferences.

System Preferences: Hardware

The Hardware section of System Preferences includes panes for customizing hardware settings. With the controls in this section, you can customize such items as display and sound settings. In this section, we look specifically at the CDs & DVDs, Displays, Energy Saver, Keyboard & Mouse, and Print & Fax panes.

CDs & DVDs

In the CDs & DVDs pane, shown in Figure 11.35, you set how the system responds when you insert different types of CDs and DVDs. For blank CDs and DVDs, you can set the system to ask you what to do, open the Finder, open iTunes or iDVD, as appropriate, open another application, run a script, or simply ignore. For a music CD, you can set it to open iTunes or another application, run a script, or ignore. For a picture CD, you can set it to open iPhoto or another application, run a script, or ignore. For a video DVD, you can set it to open DVD Player or another application, run a script, or ignore.

FIGURE 11.35 Set what action occurs when you insert a CD or DVD in the CDs & DVDs pane.

Displays

The Displays pane in System Preferences functions in a way that's similar to the Monitors control panel or the Monitors portion of the Monitors & Sound control panel of traditional Mac OS. As you might have noticed, Displays is also located in the System Preferences toolbar. Some versions of Mac OS X also contain a Displays Dockling. The options available in the Displays pane vary with the type of display. For example, for a laptop with no other displays attached, expect only the Display and Color sections to be available. For an older iMac, expect to also have a Geometry section. Your system may have options not shown here.

Display

As you might expect, in the Display section, shown in Figure 11.36, you can set the resolution, the number of colors displayed, and the refresh rate. There's an option to make the Displays information available in the menu bar and an option to ask the pane to list only modes that the display recommends. You'll probably see some of the options gray out on checking the box. A slider scale adjuster for brightness may also be available as well as one for contrast. Or your Display section might not have any sliders here. This section may also contain a button to allow you to detect displays. The option to show recent modes may also be available. The Display section in Figure 11.36 is from a laptop.

Geometry

The Geometry section, shown in Figure 11.37, is where you can set typical monitor geometry settings: position, height/width, pincushion, rotate, keystone, and parallelogram. The buttons surrounding the display depicted in the Geometry tab changes with each option. Click on the buttons to make your adjustments. You can also select the factory defaults. Not all monitors have this section. The Geometry example shown in Figure 11.37 comes from an older iMac.

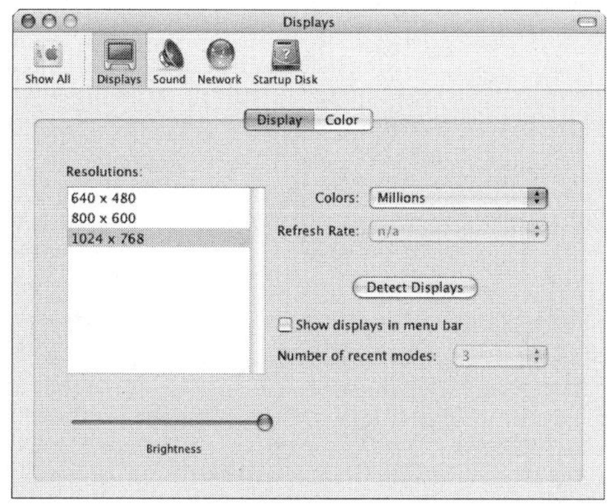

FIGURE 11.36 The Display section of the Displays pane is where you set resolution and color depth.

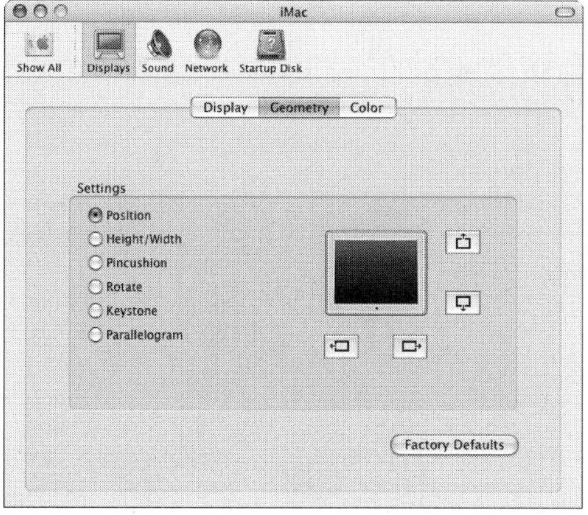

FIGURE 11.37 The Geometry section of the Displays pane is where you set typical monitor geometry settings.

Color

In the Color section, shown in Figure 11.38, you select a color profile for your monitor. If no ColorSync profile is available for your monitor, you can create a custom profile by clicking the Calibrate option. The Calibrate option starts Display Calibrator, which guides you through the calibration of your monitor. If you have calibrated your monitor, the resulting profile appears as one of your choices here. The exact choices also vary with the display type. Figure 11.38 shows an example of the Color section from a laptop.

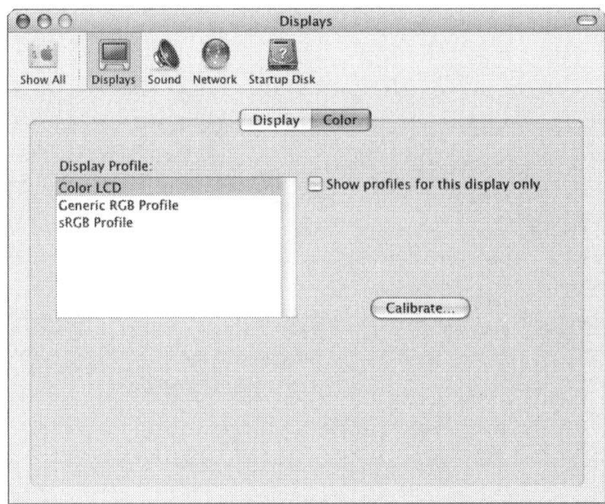

FIGURE 11.38 The Color section of the Displays pane is where you select a color profile for your monitor.

Arrangement

When multiple monitors are attached, the main monitor has an extra tab called Arrangement, shown in Figure 11.39.

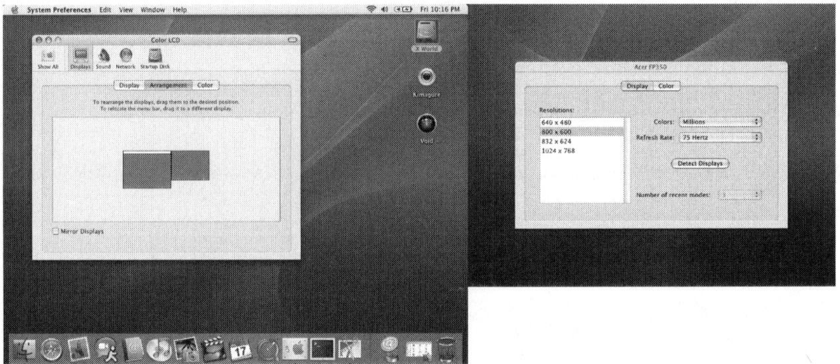

FIGURE 11.39 When you select the Displays pane while multiple monitors are attached, the Displays pane of the main monitor includes an Arrangement section.

When you open the Displays pane while multiple monitors are attached, the controlling monitor has the extra Arrangement section. At the same time, the other monitors display the normal Displays pane without any additional sections. In this area of the Displays pane, you can Geometry section select how the monitors are arranged.

Figure 11.40 shows two monitors running something other than the Displays pane.

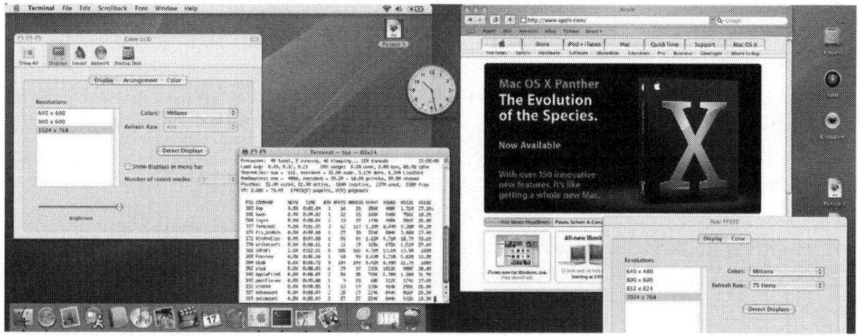

FIGURE 11.40 Here you can see the multiple monitors in active use. Notice that a clock window is stretched across both windows as well as some of a terminal window.

Display Calibrator

Display Calibrator, as mentioned earlier, is the utility that creates a ColorSync profile specific to your monitor. The utility is located in `/System/Library/ColorSync/Calibrators`.

Figure 11.41 shows the introductory screen for Display Calibrator. As you can see, the calibrator guides you through adjusting your brightness, contrast, luminance response, gamma, and white point. The calibrator has an expert mode available, which you can select by checking the Expert Mode box. Previously, expert mode did not necessarily provide more steps, only more options with some of the steps. Currently, you might expect to perform extra steps in expert mode. Depending on your monitor, you might not have to perform all the steps shown here, or you might have additional steps not shown here. To provide some experience with the different modes, we vary the modes shown and try to provide examples of as many of the steps as possible.

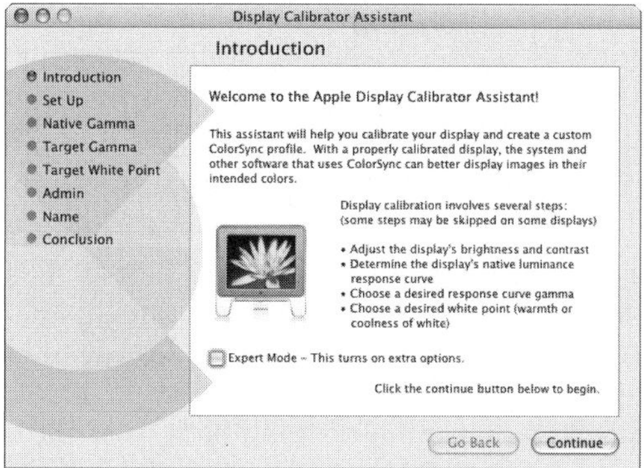

FIGURE 11.41 The introductory screen of Display Calibrator. Here you can choose whether to be in expert mode.

NOTE

Depending on your monitor and the settings you normally worked with, you might be pleasantly surprised, or surprisingly dismayed, at the results of putting together a calibration for your monitor. Calibrating your monitor enables you to see image files and online content as they were intended to be seen, assuming that the person creating the original file had her display calibrated as well. Unfortunately, many users don't have their monitors calibrated, and although the monitors provided by Apple have historically been well behaved with respect to their color response curves, this is by no means a universal constant among all monitor manufacturers. The end result is that if you calibrate your monitor, you see all the errors in everyone else's monitor calibrations in the files they create. Carefully created content looks wonderful, and less carefully created content looks, well...we'll leave that to you to judge.

Overall, we recommend using a carefully and correctly calibrated monitor so that content you create is correct even though much Web content created on inexpensive hardware might look better if browsed with an incorrect setting.

The next step may vary. Some monitors may go through the Set Up step, shown in Figure 11.42. In this step, you adjust the display's brightness and contrast. The Display Calibrator assistant instructs you to set your contrast to the highest setting and to adjust your brightness until the oval in the dark square is barely visible. This step is the same in the expert and normal modes.

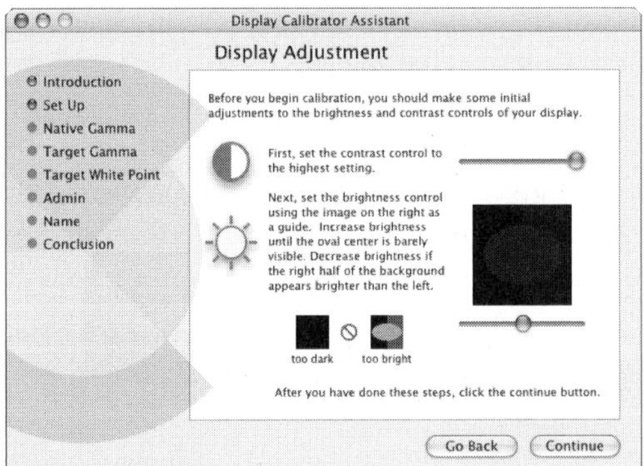

FIGURE 11.42 In the Set Up step, you adjust the contrast and brightness of your display.

The next step for your monitor can be the Native Gamma step in which you determine your display's native luminance response curves. For some displays, the normal mode may not exist, but the expert mode may consist of five separate steps. For other displays, the normal mode may be a one-step version of the expert mode. For both modes, the utility suggests that it might be helpful to squint or stand back from the display to accomplish this task. Figure 11.43 shows the Native Gamma step in normal mode.

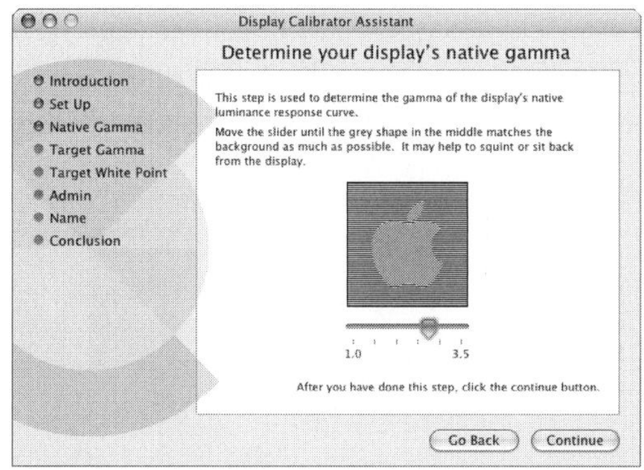

FIGURE 11.43 In the Native Gamma step, shown here in normal mode, you determine the native gamma of your display.

The next step is the Target Gamma step, in which you select a target gamma for your display. Figure 11.44 shows this step in normal mode. In this mode, you select from standard Macintosh gamma, standard PC gamma, or native gamma. The target gamma is selected in expert mode on a slider, which has the Macintosh and PC gammas marked. You'll find that your monitor displays a broader and smoother color palette if you choose the Macintosh default gamma of 1.8. If you do a lot of image creation for the Web, you might find it useful to create two ColorSync profiles: one for a standard Macintosh display and one for a standard PC display. Two such profiles would give you the ability to see approximately how your images appear on each of these common display types.

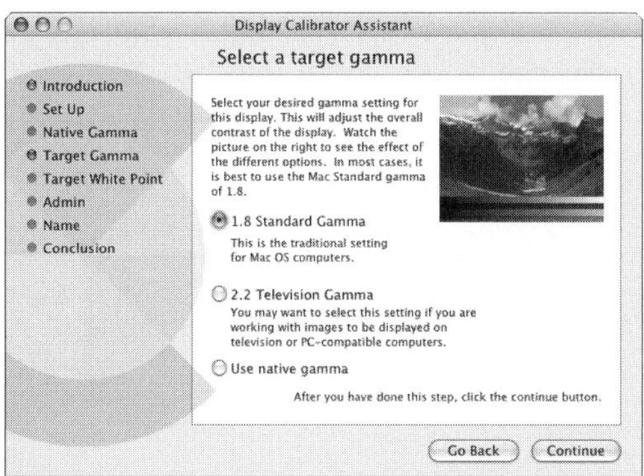

FIGURE 11.44 In the Target Gamma step, shown here in normal mode, you select the target gamma of your display.

In the next step, the Target White Point step, you select a target white point setting for your display. Figure 11.45 shows this step for the normal mode, which provides three basic choices with comments on the choices, as well as a choice for no white point correction. The expert mode provides a slider interface for these choices, but no comments on possibly pertinent choices.

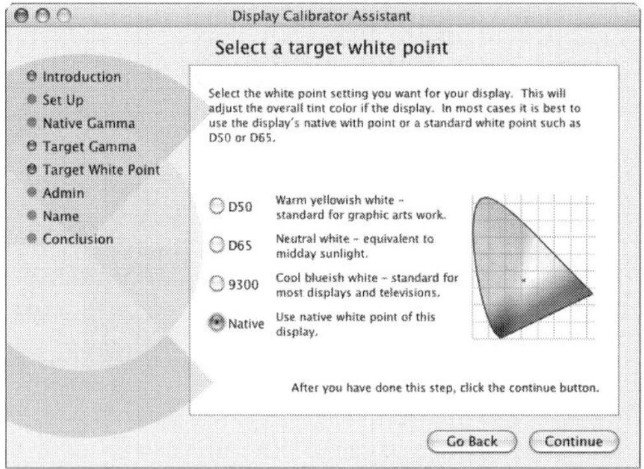

FIGURE 11.45 Select a target white point setting for your display in the Target White Point step, shown here in normal mode.

The next step in expert mode is the Administrator Options step, shown in Figure 11.46. You might not experience this step in normal mode. In this step, you can choose to make this color profile available as a possible default for every user on the system. Normally, the profile becomes available as a possible default only for the user who created it, and is placed in `~/Library/ColorSync/Profiles`. This step, though, puts the profile in `/Library/ColorSync/Profiles/Displays/`. If you set up a profile in normal mode and decide later that you would like to make it available to all users, as an administrative user, copy the profile that was created in your home directory to the systemwide location. If you don't like a profile you created, simply delete it.

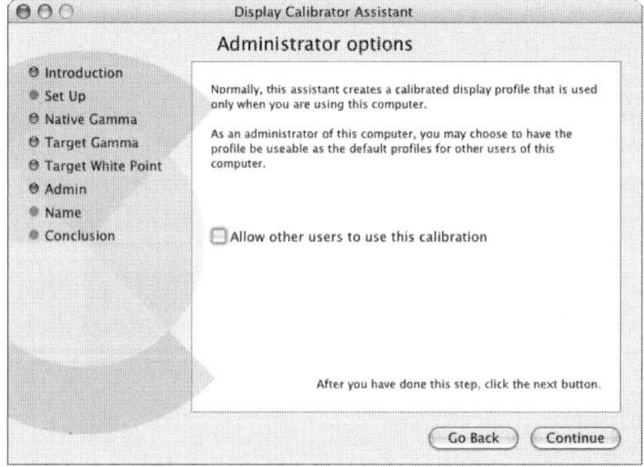

FIGURE 11.46 In expert mode, the Administrator Options step enables you to provide this profile as a possible default to any user on the system.

Figure 11.47 shows the next step, the Name step, which is the same in both expert and normal modes. Here you provide a name for your profile. If you created a profile for a special purpose, such as creating a profile with PC contrast, you might consider including something about the purpose in the name.

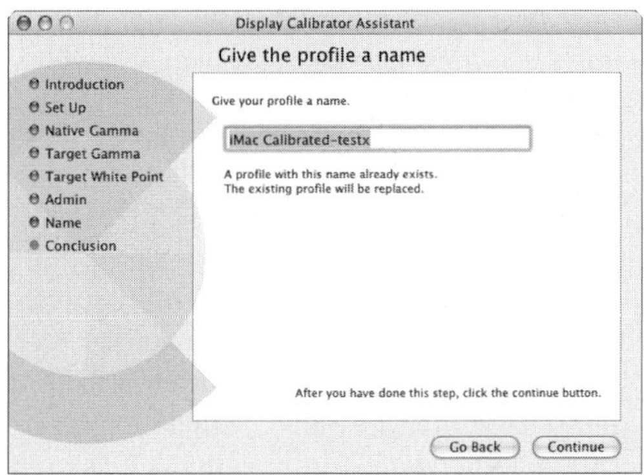

FIGURE 11.47 Provide a name for your new ColorSync profile in the Name step.

The final step, aptly named Conclusion, is shown in expert mode in Figure 11.48. This step is an informational step. In normal mode, the utility indicates that the new profile has been created and set as the default profile, and it provides information on changing your current profile. Changing your current profile can be done either in the Color section of the Displays system preferences pane, or in the devices section of the ColorSync utility. Expert mode not only provides this information, but also provides a basic summary of the profile you created.

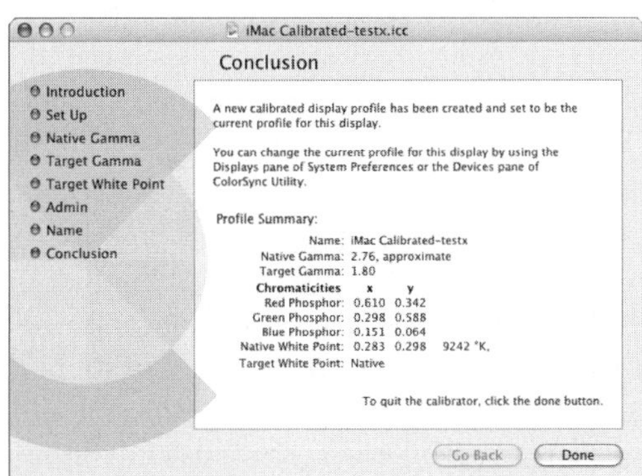

FIGURE 11.48 In the final step, shown here in expert mode, you see comments on the new profile and changing your current profile, as well as a summary of the new profile.

Energy Saver

The Energy Saver pane is where you set sleep and wake options for your machine, as well as whether it should automatically restart after power failure. The options available in the Energy Saver pane vary with the type of computer you have.

In the pane, for a laptop you select a certain energy optimization setting. The available choices are Automatic, Highest Performance, Longest Battery Life, DVD Playback, Presentations, and Custom. The Automatic option sets options for highest performance when the laptop is plugged in, and sets options for longest battery life when the battery is in use. The pane also provides the option to display the battery status in the menu bar. You can further choose to show details. If you do so, for a laptop, you'll have the option to change which settings are viewed in the Settings for pop-up menu. Additionally, for a desktop or laptop, you'll see the Sleep, Schedule, and Options sections. In the Details section for a laptop, you can also set the settings for Power Adapter and Battery Power. Which setting is displayed by default depends on which power source the laptop is currently using. For a desktop machine, the Sleep, Schedule, and Options sections are available without any additional energy customizations necessary. The basic Energy Saver pane for a laptop is shown in Figure 11.49. A desktop machine's Energy Saver pane always shows details and does not have a hide details option.

Note that administrative privileges are required to make changes to this pane.

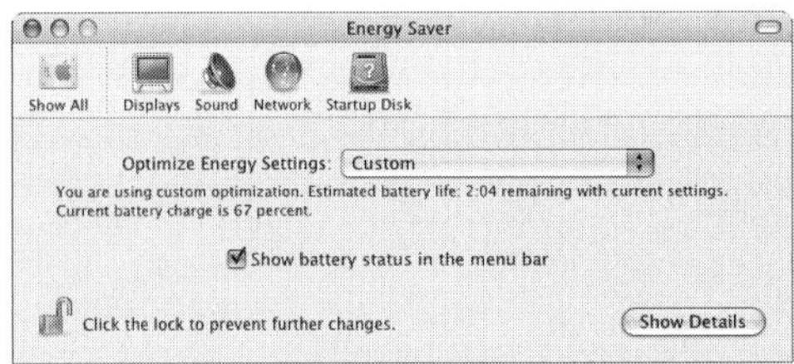

FIGURE 11.49 The Energy Saver pane for a laptop with details hidden.

Sleep

The Sleep section of the Energy Saver pane, shown in Figure 11.50, is where you set the sleep options for your machine. Sleep is a low-power mode for the machine and is especially useful for laptops. Using a slider, you specify how long your machine should be inactive before it sleeps. If your display is set to sleep before your screen saver activates, a button that takes you directly to the Desktop/Screen Savers system preference is made available so that you can change your screen saver setting if you want. Apple recommends that you set this option to Never whenever you're burning CDs in iTunes. The Energy Saver pane further enables you to specify separate sleep timing for the display and the hard disk.

On a note related to energy, in some versions of Mac OS X, the PowerBook has a Dockling that looks like a battery and indicates the charge level of the battery. This Dockling is located in the `/Applications/Dock Extras` folder. In other versions, you can find this Dockling in the menu bar. The sample Energy Saver pane shows the option to include battery status in the menu bar.

Although the Energy Saver pane includes additional options for a laptop, the actual choices under the Sleep section itself are the same for a laptop or desktop machine.

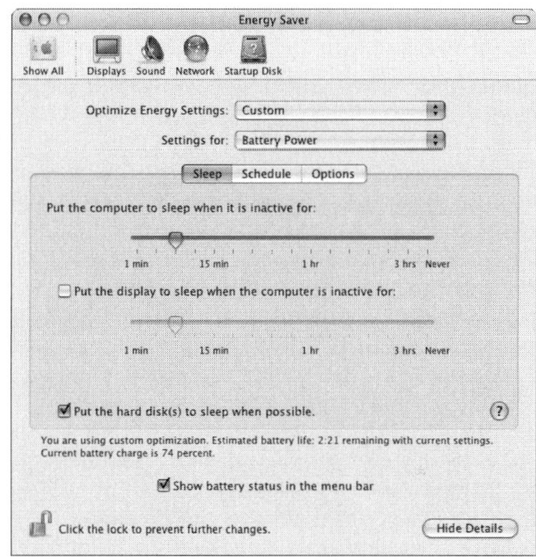

FIGURE 11.50 Sleep time and sleep timing options are specified in the Sleep section of the Energy Saver pane.

Schedule

The Schedule section of the Energy Saver pane, shown in Figure 11.51, enables you to specify startup, sleep, and shutdown times for the machine. You can set times for weekends, weekdays, every day, or specific days of the week. The options in this section are the same for desktop machines.

Options

The Options section of the Energy Saver pane, shown in Figure 11.52, is where you set the wake options for your machine. You can set the machine to wake when the modem detects a ring or to wake for network administrative access. Additionally, you can set your machine to automatically restart after a power failure.

As with the other sections, the options available under the Options section itself are the same for a laptop or desktop machine.

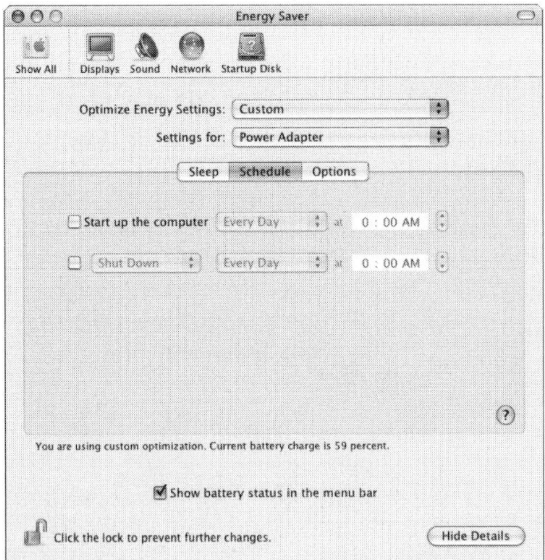

FIGURE 11.51 Regular startup and shutdown times can be specified in the Schedule section of the Energy Saver pane.

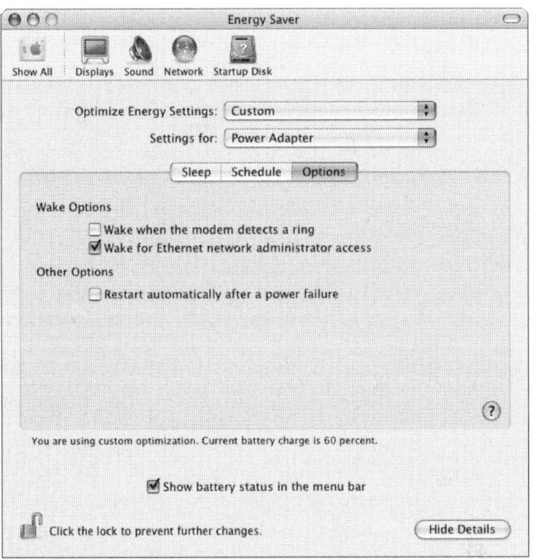

FIGURE 11.52 Wake options and whether the machine should automatically restart after a power failure are specified in the Options tab of the Energy Saver pane.

Keyboard & Mouse

As with many of the Hardware system preferences, the sections available in the Keyboard & Mouse pane vary with your hardware. Nonetheless, this is the pane in which you specify settings for your keyboard and mouse and/or trackpad, as well as keyboard shortcuts.

Settings

The Settings section of the Keyboard pane, shown in Figure 11.53, controls the key repeat rate and the amount of delay until repeat. You can test the rate and delay in a test space within the pane itself. If it takes your fingers some time to release the keys as you're typing, you might want to try some longer settings here. In this day of word processing rather than typing at the typewriter, these controls might not seem important. At the very least, we can reduce Mr. Kitty's typing speed.

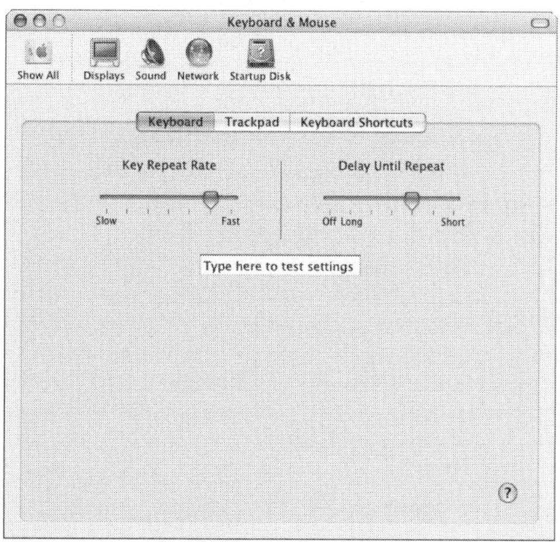

FIGURE 11.53 The key repeat rate and the amount of delay until repeat are set in the Keyboard section of the Keyboard pane.

Mouse

If you are using a mouse on your computer, you'll have a Mouse section in this pane, shown in Figure 11.54. The tracking, scrolling, and double-click speeds are set here. The pane itself also provides a space in which you can test the double-click speed.

Trackpad

If you are using a laptop, you'll have a Trackpad section in the Keyboard pane, shown in Figure 11.55. Here you can control tracking speed and the double-click speed. The pane itself has a space in which you can test the double-click speed.

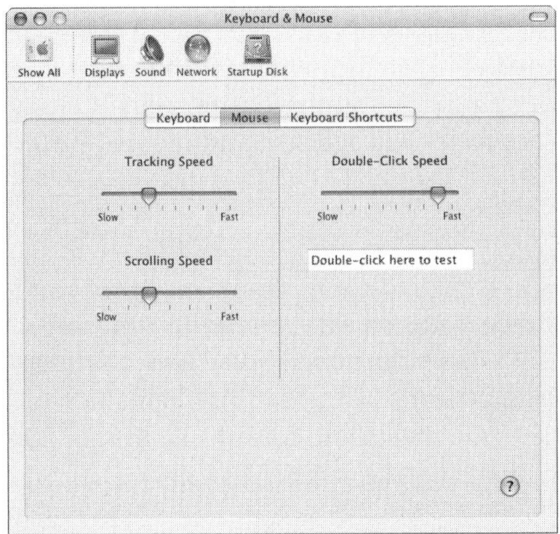

FIGURE 11.54 Mouse behavior is set in the Mouse section of the Keyboard & Mouse pane.

Additionally, the pane enables you to specify settings involving trackpad use. You can decide to use the trackpad for clicking and dragging. Additionally, you can set the trackpad to ignore accidental trackpad input or to ignore the trackpad completely when a mouse is present.

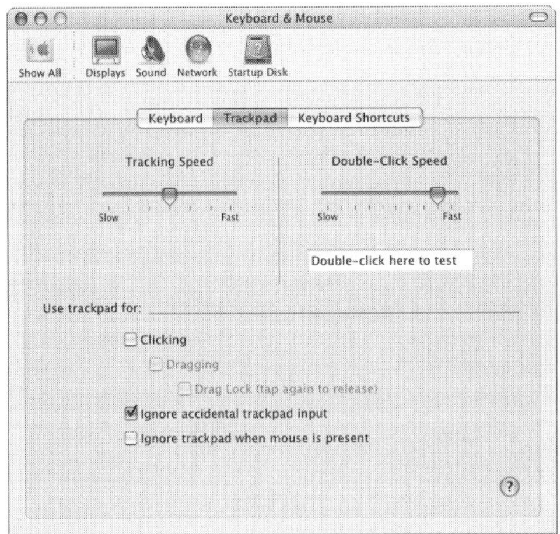

FIGURE 11.55 Trackpad behavior is set in the Trackpad section of the Keyboard & Mouse pane.

Keyboard Shortcuts

In the Keyboard Shortcuts section of the Keyboard pane, shown in Figure 11.56, you can choose to use a number of default keyboard shortcuts, or you can change default keyboard shortcuts to shortcuts that you might find more useful. Default keyboard shortcuts are readily available for Screen Capture, Universal Access, Keyboard Navigation, and the Dock. You can also specify keyboard shortcuts for specific applications. The plus and minus signs enable you to add to and delete items from the list. You can create shortcuts that apply globally to all applications, or you can create shortcuts for specific applications. If you don't like what you've done, you can always choose to restore the default settings. Last, in this section, you can turn on full keyboard access. With full keyboard access on, you can use keyboard controls in conjunction with typical navigation methods. Full keyboard access is available for activating access to the menu, dock and other screen areas, for highlighting items, and for selecting an action. Check the available help via the provided question mark for keyboard equivalencies. Some are also listed in the Keyboard Navigation section of the shortcuts listing.

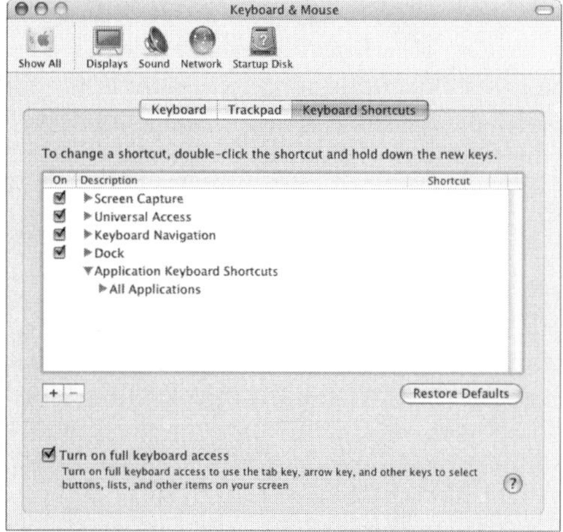

FIGURE 11.56 You can set keyboard shortcuts in the Keyboard Shortcuts section of the Keyboard pane.

Print & Fax

The Print & Fax preferences pane is where you specify basic settings involving printing and faxing. Note that this system preference requires administrative privileges to make changes.

Printing

Figure 11.57 shows the Printing section of the Print & Fax pane. In this section, you can set up printers by clicking the Set Up Printers... button, which automatically opens the Print Setup Utility for you. You can also set which printer is listed as the selected printer in the Print Dialog. Choices include the last printer used, any printer you've set up in the

Printer Setup Utility, or the option to edit your list of printers. You can also set the default paper size for Page Setup here from a wide selection of paper sizes. Last, you can choose to printers connected to your machine with other machines.

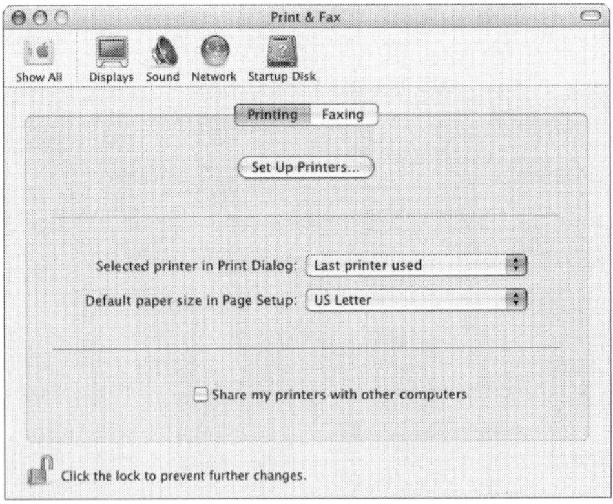

FIGURE 11.57 Many basic settings for printing can be set in the Printing section of the Print & Fax pane, including the ability to share your printers.

Faxing

The Faxing section of the Print & Fax pane, shown in Figure 11.58, enables you to set your machine up to receive faxes. If you want this capability, provide your phone number and specify how the fax should be handled. You can specify after how many rings a fax should be answered, a location for the fax to be saved, an email address to which the fax should be sent, and/or a printer where the fax should be printed.

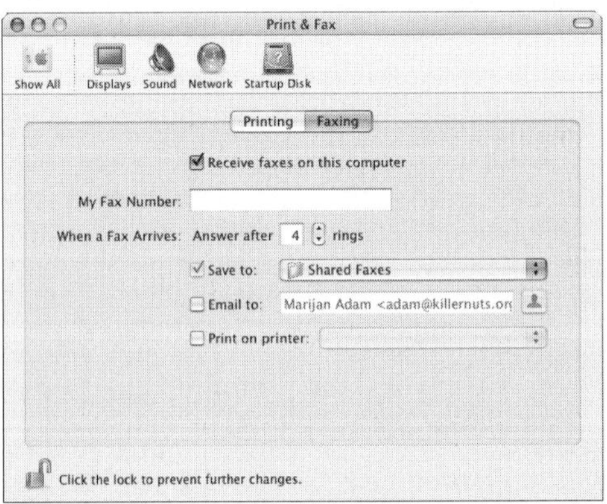

FIGURE 11.58 Set up parameters for allowing your machine to receive faxes in the Faxing section of the Print & Fax pane.

System Preferences: System

The System section of System Preferences includes panes for customizing system settings. With the controls in this section, you can customize such settings as the date and time display, the startup disk, and a software update schedule. In this section, we look at the rest of the Accounts pane and the Date & Time, Speech, and Universal Access panes.

As you have seen in this chapter, most of the System Preferences are stored on a per-user basis. However, some affect the entire system, and therefore, require administrative access to update, as the lock in the lower left corner of those panes indicates. So far in this chapter the Accounts, Security, Energy Saver, Print & Fax panes are such preferences. The Network and Sharing preferences, covered in Chapter 9, "Network Setup," also require administrative access. The remaining panes that require administrative access are Date & Time and Startup Disk.

Accounts

The Accounts pane has three sections: My Account, Other Accounts and Login Options. Earlier in the chapter, we looked at the Other Accounts portion, where you can create, modify, and delete user accounts. Now let's look at the My Account and Login Options sections.

My Account

The My Account section allows a user to change his password in the Password section, change his picture in the Picture section, and edit his startup items in the Startup Items section, shown in Figure 11.59. Drag any applications that you would like to open at login to the pane, and they will be added to the list of applications that start at login. You can further choose to have a startup application hide upon login. Startup order is determined by the order of the applications in the list. Simply drag the applications to adjust the order.

FIGURE 11.59 The Startup Items section of the Accounts pane is where you specify what applications, if any, you would like to start at login.

Login Options

The Login Options section in the Accounts pane, shown in Figure 11.60, is available toward the bottom left of the pane. In this section, you can select whether to display the Login Window as a list of users, the default, or as a window that requires the user to enter both username and password. In this section, you can also set a user to automatically log in. This option is not recommended if your machine is truly serving as a multiuser machine, as anyone can easily modify the automatically logged in account without having to know anything about the username or password for the account. In this section, you can choose to hide the Sleep, Restart, and Shut Down buttons. If your machine is serving as a multiuser machine, especially in a public location, this option is recommended. This provides you a little more control over the machine's uptime, but does not prevent anyone from turning the machine off at the power button. Finally, in this section, you can enable fast user switching, a feature discussed in Chapter 2, "Managing the Panther Workspace."

FIGURE 11.60 You can configure the behavior of the login window in the Login Options section of the Accounts pane.

Date & Time

Various aspects of the date and time are specified in the Date & Time pane of System Preferences.

Date & Time

In the Date & Time section of the Date & Time pane, you actually set the date and time. If your computer gets time from a network time server, you don't need to set the time, but you do need to set the server. Select one of Apple's network time servers, or provide an address for another one. If you set the time manually, you can also access the

International pane from here to set date and time formats. Figure 11.61 shows the Date & Time section. Note that if you receive your time setting from a network time server, you might have trouble when your machine boots up if it can't find the network time server.

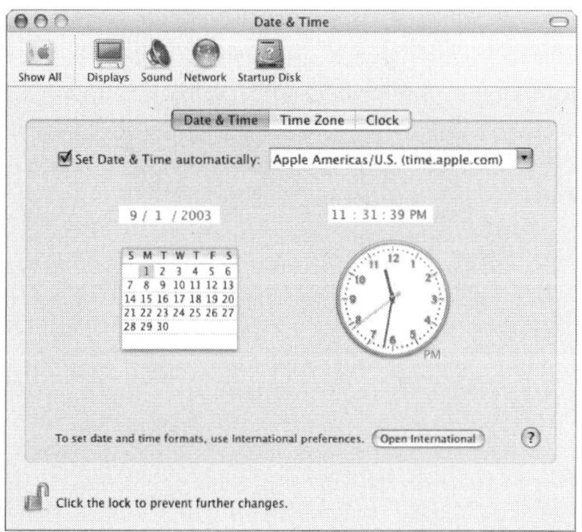

FIGURE 11.61 The current date and time are set in the Date & Time section of the Date & Time pane.

Time Zone

The Time Zone section, shown in Figure 11.62, is where the time zone is set. You just click on your approximate area on the map, and select a nearby city from the pop-up window. If you don't like scrolling through the list of cities, you can also type in nearby cities. If a city is recognized, the time zone information is filled in and the time changes to the time for that city. This method can be useful if you are having trouble determining what the correct time zone is.

Setting the time zone is useful for providing a meaningful time stamp on files. The time stamp is especially meaningful for data which is transferred, such as mail.

Clock

Figure 11.63 shows the Clock section, where you set specifics about displaying and announcing date and time. You can choose to have date and time displayed. If you choose this option, you can select various ways they are displayed. The date and time can be displayed in the menu bar or in a window. If you choose to display date and time in a window, you can set the window's transparency using the Transparency slider. You can also choose whether the display is digital or analog. If you choose a digital display, you can select various options for how it is displayed.

In this section, you can also choose to have the time announced, and you can select an interval of on the hour, half hour, or quarter hour for the announcement, as well as an announcement voice. For the voice, you can select the default voice or various other voices. You can set a custom rate and volume for the voice and play the settings until you find something you like.

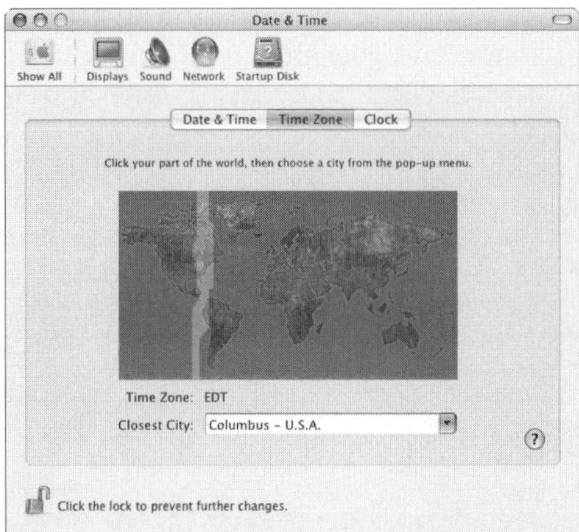

FIGURE 11.62 Select your time zone in the Time Zone section of the Date & Time pane.

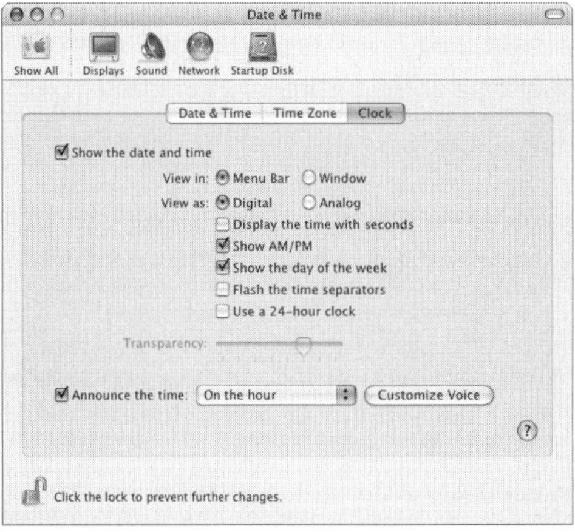

FIGURE 11.63 Preferences involving displaying and announcing date and time are set in the Clock section of the Date & Time pane.

Speech

The Speech pane under System Preferences controls speech recognition, the default voice, and the spoken user interface.

Speech Recognition

The Speech Recognition portion of the Speech pane has sections called On/Off, shown in Figure 11.64, Listening, shown in Figure 11.65, and Commands, shown in Figure 11.66, for the Apple Speakable Items recognition system. The Apple Speakable Items recognition system is the system that enables you to interact with the computer by speaking certain commands to it.

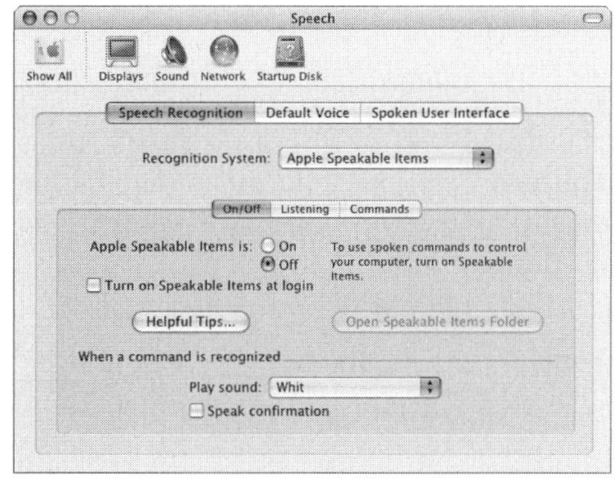

FIGURE 11.64 The On/Off section of the Speech Recognition section of the Speech pane.

In the On/Off section, you can

- Turn speech recognition on or off.
- View some helpful hints on getting started with speech recognition.
- View the Speakable Items folder.
- Choose to open Speakable Items at login.
- Select a sound that the computer plays when it understands your spoken command. If you added a new sound to the system, the sound appears here as one of your choices.
- Choose to enable speak confirmation.

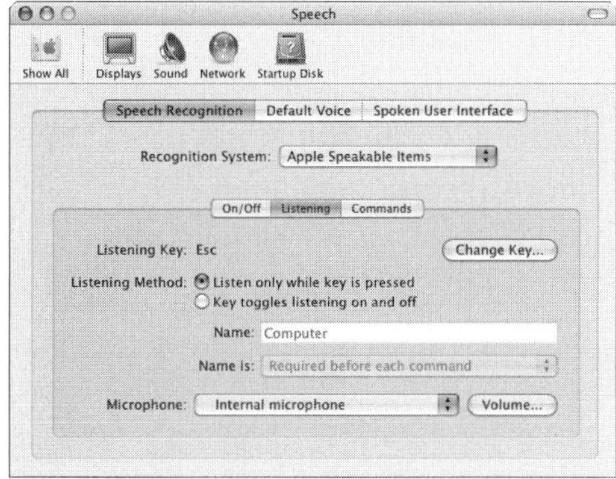

FIGURE 11.65 The Listening section of the Speech Recognition section of the Speech pane.

In the Listening section, you can

- Set which key is used as the listening key. The default is the Escape key.
- Set the listening method. The default is to have the machine listen when the listening key is pressed. The listening key can be set to toggle listening on and off. You can then preface a command, if you so choose, with whatever name you list here. We got a response once from the computer when prefacing commands with Hello Computer, but we still find the default method to work better at this time.
- Set the volume for a given microphone. When you're setting the volume, you read a set of statements that appears after clicking the Volume button.

In the Commands section of the Speech Recognition section, shown in Figure 11.66, you can select which commands are available when Speakable Items is by selecting command sets. Available command sets currently are: Address Book, Global Speakable Items, Application Specific Items, Application Switching, Front Window, and Menu Bar. Each set may also include a configure option. The Address Book set provides access to names contained in your address book, and the configure option allows you to set which names are speakable. The Global Speakable Items provides access to commands that may be spoken in any application, and the configure option allows you to choose whether exact wording is required for the speakable items. The Application Specific Items set allows you to access commands that may be spoken when an application is in the front, but there is no configure option at this time. The Application Switching set allows you to switch between running applications or to launch a recently run application, and does not have a configure option at this time. The Front Window set allows you to speak front window controls, such as push button names and radio names. The pane notes that this option requires that access for assistive devices must be set in the Universal Access pane. This command set does not have a configure option at this time. The Menu Bar set enables you to speak names of any menu or menu item. Like the Front Window set, this command set also requires that access for assistive devices is set in the Universal Access pane.

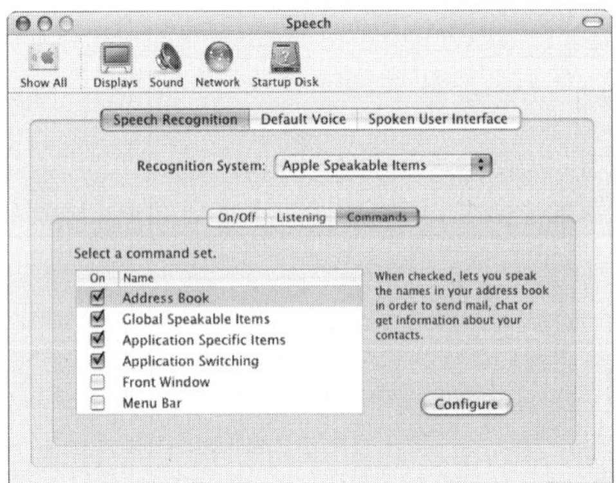

FIGURE 11.66 The Commands section of the Speech Recognition section of the Speech pane.

Default Voice

In the Default Voice tab of the Speech pane, shown in Figure 11.67, you set the voice used by applications that speak. You can select the voice and rate of speech and test the settings.

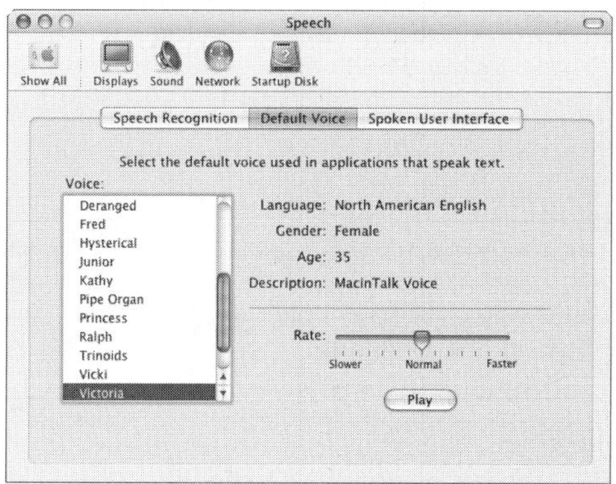

FIGURE 11.67 The Default Voice recognition of the Speech pane.

Spoken User Interface

In the Spoken User Interface tab of the Speech pane, shown in Figure 11.68, you can select settings for the behavior of talking alerts and other spoken items.

For talking alerts, you can select which phrase is spoken. Your choices are Alert!, Attention!, Pardon me!, Excuse me!, Next in the list, Random from the list, or you can edit the phrase list. You can add and remove phrases from the list. You can also select whether the alert text itself should be spoken. Here you also set which voice is used for the talking alerts voice, as well as how many seconds the alerts voice should wait before speaking. Finally, you can test the settings until you like them.

For other spoken items, you can choose to have the computer announce when an application requires your attention, speak whatever text is under the mouse, or speak selected text whenever a key or key combination that you specify is pressed. If the computer is already speaking, that key combination causes the computer to stop speaking instead. If you choose to have text under the mouse spoken, you're directed to the Universal Access pane to set the option to enable access for assistive devices.

Speech Feedback

When you turn on speech recognition, the Speech Feedback window appears, as shown in Figure 11.69. The Speech Feedback window, a small round window, shows the microphone level. Additionally, when you aren't speaking, it shows what key to press so that the computer listens. If you've chosen to use the key toggle method, it shows what phrase you intend to speak before issuing a command to the computer.

FIGURE 11.68 Set characteristics for the spoken user interface under the Spoken User Interface section of the Speech pane.

When you're speaking, the microphone image changes and the horizontal lines, which start as gray lines, display the microphone level (as shown in Figure 11.70), and the feedback on what key to press or phrase to speak to cause the computer to listen disappears. The bottom line is a blue color. The next two lines are green, and the top line is red. The Helpful Hints recommends that you try to speak in the green levels. The arrow at the bottom of the window has links to the Speech Commands window and the Speech Preferences pane. You can open the Speech Commands window by either saying "Open Speech Commands window," or clicking on the arrow. The Speech Commands window shows the commands that you may speak to the computer in the bottom portion. This is updated as you change which application you're using.

FIGURE 11.69 The Speech Feedback window as it is shown when speech recognition is first turned on.

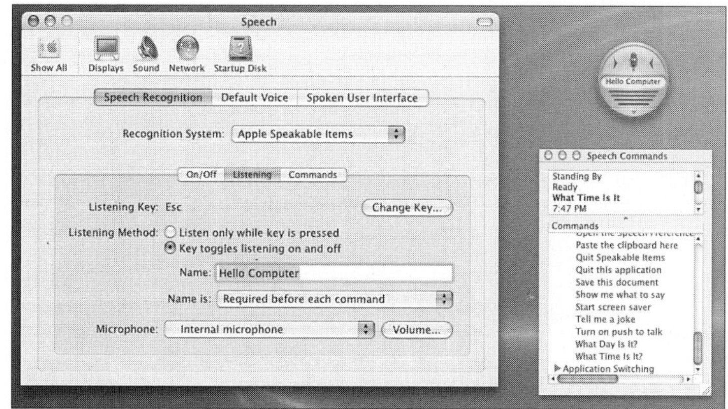

FIGURE 11.70 The Speech Commands window as it appears when you're speaking to the computer.

Figure 11.71 shows what to expect when Speech Recognition works for you. The Speech Commands window shows not only which commands you may speak to the computer, but also which commands you have spoken so far.

FIGURE 11.71 Here Speakable Items was used to open and control Internet Explorer. Note that the Speech Commands window shows which commands have been spoken so far.

Universal Access

The Universal Access pane is where you can customize the computer to assist you with any difficulties that you have in seeing or hearing the computer, as well as set some keyboard and mouse behaviors to assist with any difficulties you experience with those devices.

All the subdivisions of the Universal Access pane include the ability to enable access for assistive devices and to enable text-to-speech for the Universal Access preferences pane. Because text-to-speech for the Universal Access pane is enabled by default, the computer speaks the text to you on mouseover. Depending on the volume settings for your machine, this could be rather startling initially.

Seeing

In the Seeing tab of the Universal Access pane, shown in Figure 11.72, you can set options for zooming in and out. You can also set your monitor to display white on black or to display in grayscale. The Option+Command+= combination zooms in, whereas Option+Command+- zooms out. You might find it easier to think of the zoom in option as Option+Command++, which was the original notation that Apple used for zooming in, but please note that the + in that notation is not literally a +. The combination does not and never did require a shift to literally get the +, but was simply used to depict the key that contains the +, which is a more intuitive symbol for zooming in than the =. After you're zoomed, you can navigate. Figure 11.73 shows a zoomed-in example of the Seeing tab.

FIGURE 11.72 Select settings to help you see your display better under the Seeing section of the Universal Access pane.

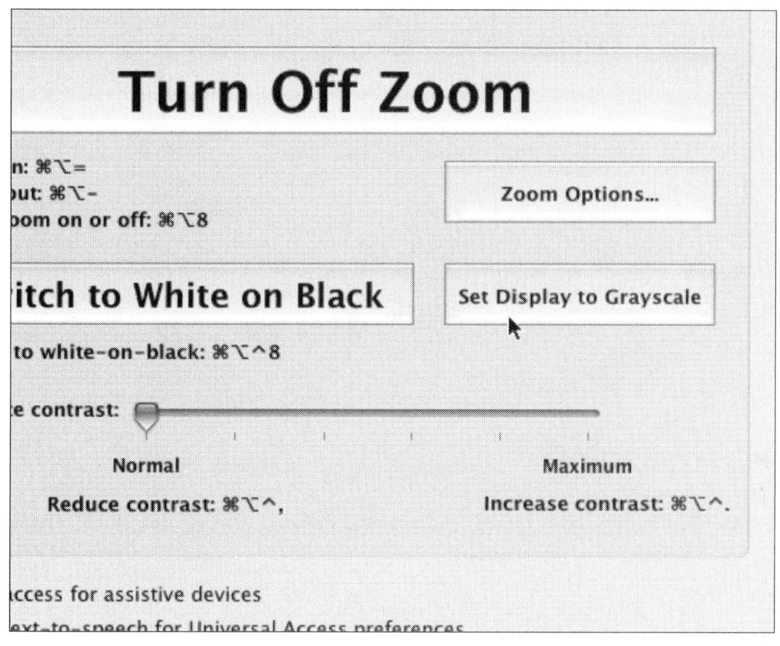

FIGURE 11.73 Zooming in on the Seeing section of the Universal Access pane.

Hearing

In the Hearing section, shown in Figure 11.74, you can set the screen to flash whenever a sound occurs. To get an idea of what to expect, you can test the behavior with the Flash Screen button. Finally, you can adjust the volume with the Adjust Sound button, which opens the Input section of the Sound pane for you.

Keyboard

In the Keyboard section, shown in Figure 11.75, you can set the Sticky Keys on or off. If you set the Sticky Keys on, you can also choose to have the machine beep when a modifier key is set and to show pressed keys onscreen. The Sticky Keys option is useful if you have trouble executing multiple key combinations, such as Command+I. The keys are displayed in the same fashion as the keyboard volume controls. Note that you can also press the Shift key five times as the way to toggle on and off the Sticky Keys behavior.

From the Keyboard section, you can also adjust settings for difficulties with keystrokes being repeated. You can turn Slow Keys on or off here. If Slow Keys is on, there's a delay between when the key is pressed and when it's accepted. This delay time is set in the Acceptance Delay slider scale. Additionally, you can choose to enable click key sounds while you're typing or otherwise interacting with the keyboard. It sounds much like you're typing at a typewriter when that option is enabled. Finally, you can adjust repeat timing through the Set Key Repeat button, which brings up the Keyboard section of the Keyboard & Mouse pane.

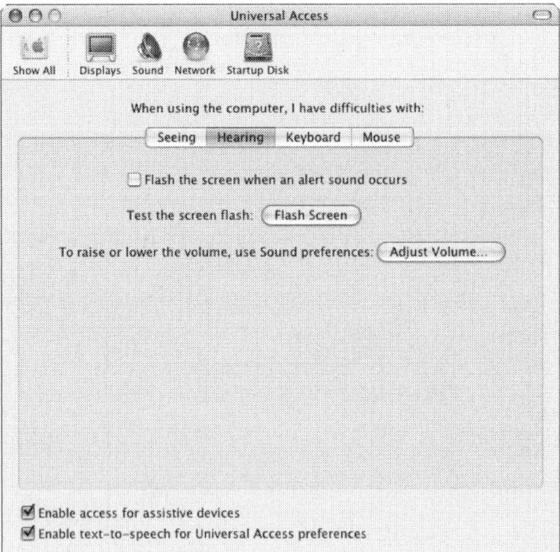

FIGURE 11.74 Set the screen to flash whenever an alert sound occurs in the Hearing section of the Universal Access pane.

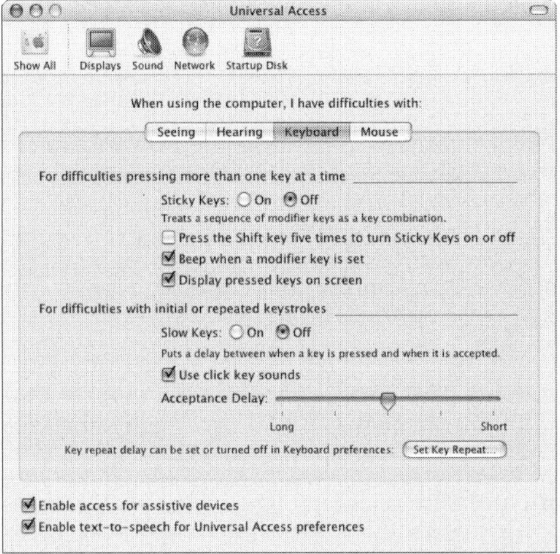

FIGURE 11.75 If you have difficulties pressing more than one key at a time or with keystrokes being repeated, make keyboard adjustments to assist you under the Keyboard section of the Universal Access pane.

Mouse

If you have difficulties using the mouse, you can set Mouse Keys on in the Mouse section, shown in Figure 11.76. When you turn Mouse Keys on, the numeric keypad is what you use to move the cursor around. The Mouse section also enables you to customize mouse pointer movement by setting a preferred initial delay and maximum speed using slider controls. Note that you can also press the option key five times as a way to toggle on and off Mouse Keys. In this section, you can also enable full keyboard access by clicking on the Open Keyboard Preferences, which takes you to the Keyboard pane.

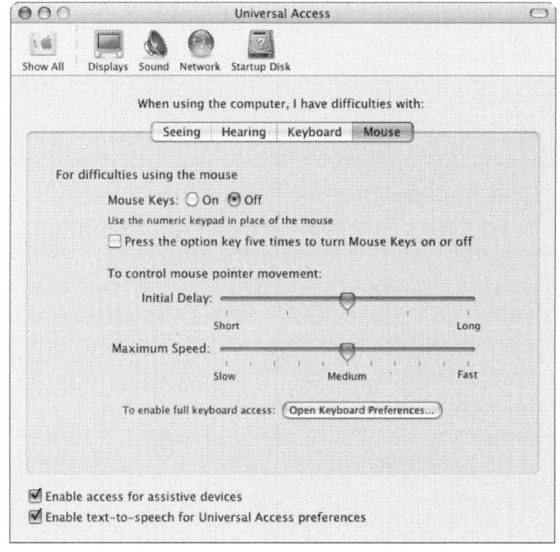

FIGURE 11.76 Set the Mouse Keys on in the Mouse section of the Universal Access pane if you have difficulties with the mouse.

Summary

This chapter rounded out the user configuration options for Mac OS X. The Apple-supplied System Preferences panels give user-friendly control over a wide variety of system functions. These panels can be thought of as analogous to the older control panels of Mac OS 9.*x*. This chapter covered the System Preferences panels that control each user's desktop environment.

There are additional panels, and more coverage is provided in other chapters where appropriate. If you didn't find the information you're looking for here, it's likely covered in greater detail elsewhere. We apologize that all System Preferences couldn't be covered completely in one area, but the size and complexity of Mac OS X results in trade-offs of where to place content. We chose to keep similar topics together. Because of this,

Desktop/Screen Saver, Dock, and Expose are covered in Chapter 2, "Managing the Panther Workspace"; Ink, BlueTooth, Classic, and Startup Disk are covered in Chapter 3, "Applications and Utilities"; .Mac is covered in Chapter 4, "Internet Applications"; Sound is covered in Chapter 7, "Audio"; QuickTime is covered in Chapter 8, "Digital Video"; and Network and Sharing are covered in Chapter 9, "Network Setup".

PART IV

Introduction to BSD Applications

IN THIS PART

CHAPTER 12

Introducing the BSD Subsystem

IN THIS CHAPTER

- Unix-Based Mac OS
- BSD Philosophy
- Using Terminal
- Interacting with Unix: Basic Unix Commands
- The Unix Filesystem
- Basic Filesystem Navigation

In this chapter, we finally reach the topic of the underlying Unix subsystem, something for which some readers have been waiting years, some have been dreading since they heard about the underpinnings of OS X, and hopefully a good number of you have been living happily with for going on three years now. We start conversing directly with the BSD-5-derived Unix implementation that underlies Mac OS X. Berkeley Software Distribution (BSD) is one of the two major philosophical variants of Unix. Apple has named its version Darwin, so you'll see this term used frequently to refer to both the Open-Source effort Apple has underway to further develop the base of OS X, and the underlying system as accessed at the command line.

If you're a longtime Unix user, you'll probably find much of the rest of this book familiar, and you should consider it a reference to those places where the Apple implementation differs from what you're already familiar with. If, on the other hand, you're new to Unix, you'll soon have to decide whether you're satisfied with Mac OS X as simply a more stable, more powerful flavor of the Mac OS you've grown to know and love, or whether you want to learn even more. In this chapter, we cover the primary concepts that you need to understand to use the BSD subsystem and introduce some of the most important command-line programs.

Unix-Based Mac OS

If you're not familiar with Unix, you've probably heard and read enough to have developed any number of preconceptions regarding what using it will be like. Almost all of them are probably at least a bit intimidating. You've probably heard that Unix commands are cryptic and that the learning curve is steep. Even worse, it uses a command-line interface—you've actually got to *type* at the thing to tell it what to do, and we all know how archaic that mode of controlling a machine is.

It might be archaic, but that does not mean that there's anything wrong with it or that it's not the best way to accomplish certain tasks. We know—many of you have been poking fun at that *other* OS for years because its unfortunate users had to type to make it work. Don't worry; we've laughed, too. You're just going to have to be courageous and admit that you've used the keyboard in the Mac OS Finder to do things such as jump a Finder window to a file with a particular name. The mouse is a wonderful tool for doing things where the brain's visual processing machinery can come into play. The keyboard is also a powerful tool for other types of interaction, and it would be silly to intentionally restrict yourself to only one type of interface when other complementary interfaces are available. In many ways, what Apple has given you is analogous to being provided with a high-end sports car, and a fully equipped machine shop and garage to work on it. If buzzing around in the fancy car is your pleasure, you are free to do so without ever opening the hood. On the other hand, if you feel like working on the engine, all the tools are there to allow you to further customize and enhance your ride to your heart's content.

Regardless of what you've heard, the idea that learning and using Unix will be fun and rewarding is likely to be furthest from your mind. We hope that in this and upcoming chapters, we'll be able to convince you differently. If we can't, don't worry. Nothing about Mac OS X requires you to learn and use anything other than the graphical interface that we've already covered. You can live with your Mac OS X machine, use it for the same type of applications you always have, and love it in all its "nontypishness," without ever having to learn any of this Unix stuff. However, if you want to learn how to make your machine even more powerful, make yourself more productive, and customize everything to an exquisite extent, give this command-line stuff a try.

CAUTION

Having just told you that we think you'll like the Unix side of your machine if you give it a fair chance, and encouraged you to try it out, we'll turn around and caution you about its use. Unix is not for everyone. Although we'd love to see every Macintosh user graduate to the power available in the BSD subsystem, we can't avoid the reality that Unix is more complicated and powerful than some users will ever want to use. Just as some of us are safer not owning super-fast sports cars, some are less a threat to ourselves and others if we don't have a big box of firecrackers, and some would be better off if we couldn't buy donuts by the dozen, Unix is just too much for some people. It might be too much power, or too much flexibility, or too much information to remember, but Unix seems specially designed to create a user who epitomizes the phrase "knows just enough to be dangerous."

Evaluate your needs honestly. We're firmly convinced that everyone can learn Unix, and everyone can use it safely, but the reality is that not everyone will. If you're hesitant about trying out the Unix side of your new OS because you think it might be too difficult, we suggest that you give it a try because we think we can convince you that it's not as tough as you think. If you're not sure that Unix is a good match for what you do, you might be right: It might be better if you use OS X as the super-stable, more flexible OS on which to run your GUI-based programs, and leave the BSD subsystem alone.

BSD Philosophy

One of the complaints you might have heard from people regarding Apple's new OS is that it is based on immensely old operating system technology. They're right! The roots of Unix lie almost in the roots of modern computing itself. The thing that they're wrong about is their claim that this is a Bad Thing. Unix development started more than three decades ago, and the operating system that you can use today is the product of the work and improvements of thousands upon thousands of developers. Along the way, Unix has picked up some powerful design concepts and some wonderful solutions to problems common in the computing world.

Much of the "Unix way" is based on the idea of abstracting interfaces into the simplest possible terms. Initially, this was simply because the OS was experimental, and the simplest possible interface—one that wouldn't need to be fiddled with later—was the most expedient to construct. Over time, this "do it the easy way" methodology has evolved into a powerful design concept: abstraction. This concept will be mentioned time and again as it makes its appearance in different topics throughout the book.

As an initial explanation, though, an example provides immediate understanding. Among many other concepts, Unix abstracts the notion of things that can be read from, or written to, as files. To Unix, everything from which data can be read is treated as though it were a file, and everything to which data can be written is treated as though it were also a file. Why? Because after you've developed an in-OS methodology to control reading and writing to files, it's a nuisance to have to implement almost identical methodologies for reading and writing to the network, or writing data to printers, or reading data from the keyboard. Instead, it's considerably easier to write an abstraction layer that talks to the particular device and makes it appear to the OS as just another file. If you make your printer look like a file, printing is simply "writing to a file" for any application. If you make your keyboard input look like it's coming from a file, any application can automagically accept input from either the keyboard or an actual on-disk file, without knowing the difference.

What starts as a time-saving implementation turns into a powerful interface feature, allowing the addition of arbitrary devices, without needing to implement new OS features—just write something that makes the device "look like a file," and suddenly the OS can use it. This notion of abstraction ends up being powerful for the end user, and similar abstractions are pointed out in the sections to come.

More information on Unix and its role in computing can be found at `http://www.macosx-unleashed.com/unixhistory.html`.

Using Terminal

The Terminal program, found in the Utilities subfolder of the Applications folder, is the primary method for communicating with the BSD subsystem of the OS X installation, via the Unix command line. Some tricks and nifty applications are already appearing to insulate you from the need to work with the command line for some applications. We cover these as well, but the terminal itself will probably be your primary mode of interaction.

Simply put, `Terminal`, which appears to the Finder as simply Terminal, and being an application bundle, to the command line as a directory named `Terminal`, is the "terminal" by which you can type commands to your machine. It's the software version of what used to be implemented as a dedicated hardware device, one that understood how to display data and put it in specific positions on a screen. A terminal itself isn't particularly interesting but provides the mechanism for communication between you and programs that are more interesting to talk to.

Terminal itself has a number of useful preferences that you can set that modify how several things in this and subsequent chapters work, but before we go into those details, let's see just what Terminal can do for you. The preferences for Terminal, as well as some of the additional functionality available through the menus, are covered at the end of this chapter.

Interacting with Unix: Basic Unix Commands

You've already learned how to interact with Unix using OS X's Aqua interface and the GUI tools discussed throughout the first 11 chapters of this book. Much of the rest of the book provides the information you need to interact with Unix textually, through the command line. Although there are no sharp dividing lines between Unix commands, Unix programs, and Unix applications, there is some benefit in making at least a fuzzy semantic distinction between them.

The Unix design philosophy drives programs that are used in day-to-day interaction with a Unix machine to be small, single-purpose, and nonoverlapping in functionality. The presence of a vast array of these single-purpose programs, designed so that they can be combined in near-infinite combinations, allows the user to construct customized solutions for most any problem. The necessity for some programs to provide more complicated functionality, requires them to be less-single purpose, and to allow somewhat more overlap. Finally, just as in other operating systems that you're used to, there are programs that are large, multifunctional, and monolithic. Typically, Unix users think of the small, single-purpose programs as *commands*, and the large, multifunctional programs as *applications*. Although they're all programs, the term *program* is frequently reserved for a program that doesn't fit the description of a command or an application. This somewhat muddy semantic distinction between types of programs might seem confusing at first, but as you become more comfortable using Unix, it will make more sense to you. As an example to get you started, you can think of a Unix command as a small program with a single function such as listing files. A Unix application is typically a much larger program, perhaps something like a word processor or a Web browser. Moreover, although both are programs, the term *program* itself is infrequently used to describe anything that falls into either of these categories.

Thankfully for the beginning Unix user, making complete sense of the semantic distinctions isn't necessary for anything other than conversing with other Unix users. Unix commands, programs, and applications are all run by typing their names at the command line. The remainder of this chapter covers what you need to know to start interacting with the command line, and the most basic Unix commands needed for day-to-day use.

Introduction to the Unix Shell

As mentioned previously, a terminal alone isn't sufficient to allow you to interact with your machine. The terminal needs something to talk to, and that thing is usually a program called a *shell*. Unix shells provide text-based interaction between the user and the rest of the operating system. For those who have experience with the DOS environment, you can think of a Unix shell as similar to a very powerful version of COMMAND.COM. Please don't let that put you off. COMMAND.COM does not approach being a fair comparison for a Unix shell, but both do let you type commands to the computer.

Although it is text-based, you can think of a shell running in a terminal as sharing a few conceptual similarities with a Finder window.

Any running shell can be thought of as "being in a place" in the filesystem, just as a Finder window is open to a certain folder in the system. This place is the *current working directory*.

Each shell can navigate through the filesystem by moving to parent or higher-level directories, or by moving to child or lower-level directories. Again, this is much like the functionality provided by the folder menu in each Finder window and the folders displayed in the window.

Unlike a Finder window, a shell in a terminal is not restricted to running a command that is present in the same directory that the terminal is "at"—it can run commands located anywhere on the machine.

Also unlike Finder windows, shell commands that you execute in terminal windows (usually) run within the terminal window, and they (usually) consume the resources of the shell such that the shell becomes "preoccupied" and can't run another command until the current one finishes.

Most flavors of Unix come with a number of different shells from which the user can choose, and the BSD version underlying OS X is no exception. With OS X, you can choose from the following five shells, or possibly more, if Apple or another source makes them available.

- `sh`—The Bourne shell. The Bourne shell is ubiquitously available on Unix, but does not have syntax or features particularly friendly to the user. It is most frequently used for writing shell scripts (programs written to run using the shell language itself, rather than a more traditional programming language; how to write them is covered in Chapter 18, "Advanced Unix Shell Use: Configuration and Programming (Shell Scripting)") that are expected to run on any version of Unix. Sometimes it is used for the login shell of particularly important accounts, such as `root`.
- `csh`—The C shell (yes, it's pronounced *seashell*). The `csh` shell is a more user-friendly shell that takes its name from the C programming language. `csh` syntax is similar to the C language, and it provides significant power for both shell programming and for users. `csh` is almost as omnipresent as `sh`.

- `tcsh`—Enhanced C shell. Many people considered `csh` to have been a botched implementation in a number of ways and wanted something with similar syntax, but less broken. `tcsh` was born to fix the bugs, and extend the functionality, of `csh` and includes nice features such as automatic command completion and a command history. `tcsh` is appearing as a standard available on more and more distributions, but although it's a frequent favorite for day-to-day use as a login shell, many traditional Unix users are still shy of using it for writing shell scripts that they might want to distribute widely.
- `bash`—The Bourne again shell (and yes, Unix programmers frequently have a twisted sense of humor). The Bourne again shell is a modern shell that takes the enhancements that make `csh` and `tcsh` more useful for user interaction and implements them in a shell with the `sh` syntax. `bash` is popular among Linux users because it's the default login shell for many Linux distributions. `bash` users and `tcsh` users tend to engage in heated and sometimes hostile debate over their shells of choice; `bash` users tend to think of `tcsh` as an undisciplined and poorly arranged set of hacks that is unsuited for any but the most trivial day-to-day tasks, and `tcsh` users tend to think of `bash` as a product of zealots who are unable to see the utter misanthropy of the interface they've designed.
- `zsh`—`zsh` is designed to be an interactive user shell that incorporates powerful programming features. The intent in its creation seems to have been to build an amalgam of the most powerful features of the other shells, and to introduce a number of new features as well. The shell has been described as suffering from "feeping creaturism" (see the Jargon File, sometimes called the "Hacker's Dictionary"—available at `http://www.catb.org/jargon/html/F/feeping-creaturism.html`, among a plethora of other locations), and of having a few more features than even the author knows about.

Despite the fact that you'll find references and diatribes on the Internet that make the issue seem to take on almost religious significance, shell preference is just that, personal preference. There are well-considered reasons for picking any of them, and a user's personality as well as the type of work that he is doing ultimately dictates the shell environment in which he'll be most effective and happy. Starting with 10.3, Apple has chosen to make `bash` the standard shell for OS X. The previous default was `tcsh`, and the change will aggravate a great many users because many do not like the syntax of `sh`. Thankfully, if you have a preference for a different shell, changing yours is a simple matter of resetting a terminal preference or a NetInfo setting. On the other hand, being forced to perform day-to-day work in the same shell language that you'll need to use for the most widely useable distribution (if you plan to use scripts you write anywhere other than on your machine) is a strong plus for `bash`.

Examples in this book are shown using the default `bash` shell in most places, with `tcsh` samples where the usage diverges significantly., Regardless of what shell you choose, interaction with each is similar. To issue a command to the computer using a shell, you type the name of the command and press the Return key. In general, the command you requested will be executed by the shell and will occupy the shell until it finishes, at which time you'll be returned to the shell prompt. If the command requires additional information, it might be required on the command line in the form of flags or arguments. *Flags* are usually individual letters or words preceded by a dash (-) that indicate the turning on or off of an option; *arguments* are words or data provided on the command line for the command to process. Some commands also require that data be provided at internal prompts or data entry areas created by the command when it is run. As mentioned previously, we'll discuss more complex programs and applications in following chapters.

NOTE

When documenting commands throughout the book, we will use the following syntax:

```
commandname <required options> [optional options] <arg1> <arg2>
```

and

```
commandname <required> [optional] <arg1> <arg2> ...
```

These mean that you type `commandname` at the prompt, must choose one or more entries from the <required options>, and may choose one or more options from the [optional options]. In the first invocation form, two additional required arguments are expected on the command line; in the second, the command accepts a variable number of arguments. In general, single-letter options, usually preceded by a - (minus) sign, when enclosed in <> brackets are required, and when enclosed in [] brackets are optional. The brackets shown in the syntax examples are not actually entered on the command line—they are shown only to distinguish required and optional options. Arguments are required if shown, and an alternative form of the command is displayed with no options if this is also an allowable syntax. Options separated by a vertical bar, ¦, are exclusive; you must, or may, pick one or the other (depending on whether they're required or optional), but you cannot specify both.

For example, the fictitious command documentation shown in Table 12.1 indicates that a command named `silly` can be invoked as `silly`, `silly -L`, and `silly -P`. Invoked as `silly`, it does the same thing as `silly -L`; that is, it makes a silly laugh. Invoked as `silly -P`, it makes a silly picture. Each form also can be called with an arbitrary number of filenames following the command, in which case `silly` will place its output in the specified files.

TABLE 12.1 Command Documentation Table for the Fictitious `silly` Command

silly	Does something silly, optionally into files.
silly [-L¦P] <filename> <filename2> ...	
silly [-L¦P]	
-L	Default: Makes a silly laugh.
-P	Makes a silly picture.

Shell Rules and Conventions

In dealing with the shell, it helps to remember a few rules. The first rule you need to know is that things that you type in Unix are case sensitive. This includes commands. Unlike with Mac OS and Windows, you cannot mix case and still have a command function. You must type the name exactly as it is stored on the system. Mac OS X has the option (the default, actually) of using HFS+, which isn't case sensitive, but this creates some odd behavior in its interaction with the BSD subsystem. There are classical Unix commands included in the BSD subsystem that have names that differ only by capitalization and that normally do different things. For example, `Mail` and `mail` are two different traditional Unix programs, and they traditionally have different functionality (both deal with email, but do different things). On OS X installed over an HFS+ filesystem, it is indeterminate which program runs when you type `mail` (or `Mail`) at the command line. Apple has gone a long way to making the capitalization issue transparent to the user, but there are still places where capitalization sensitivity (or lack thereof) comes back to bite people. Because there's no obligation for OS X to be running on HFS+, and it's quite possible that you will be mounting drives from other machines that aren't running OS X at all, you really should treat everything in the BSD subsystem as though it were case sensitive, even if your installation actually isn't. It may seem initially inconvenient to remember the exact capitalization that's been used for various commands (really, they're *almost* all lowercase, so it's not that difficult), but with time it will become second nature to you. Regularly practicing good form with respect to case specificity will almost certainly save you considerable headaches eventually.

Next, when you type at the command line, characters that you type become part of the command. Most alphanumeric characters, as well as underlines and hyphens, are valid parts of commands. Most symbols aren't valid parts of commands, and some have special meanings to the command line. Table 12.2 shows some of the symbols with special meaning to the command line.

TABLE 12.2 Command-Line Symbols

Symbol	Meaning
*	When used as part of a filename, the * character substitutes for zero or more characters in a filename. This is called a *wildcard.* For example, specifying a filename of `*.gif` as an argument to a command-line program tells the shell to search the current directory for all files that have names ending in `.gif` and substitute all these filenames on the command line at this point in the command.
?	A single-character wildcard. Functions like *, except that it substitutes for a single character in filenames, instead of any number of characters. If you need some specific number of wildcarded positions, you can use multiple ? characters, one for each.
Tab	If you press the Tab key at the command line, the shell attempts to complete the command for you. If the portion of the command or filename that you've typed is unique, the shell fills in the rest of the information for you. For example, if you're in your home directory, and you want to specify the `Documents` directory on the command line, typing `Docu` and then pressing the Tab key will most likely fill out the command line to include the full `Documents` name.

TABLE 12.2 Continued

Symbol	Meaning
space	Unix interprets a space between words on the command line as a separator between parts of the command. This is not always what you want because Macintosh filenames can have spaces. The Unix command line usually interprets the space in a Mac filename such as `My File` as indicating two different files: one named `My` and one named `File`.
\	The shell escape character. If you need to insert a character into a Unix command or filename that is usually interpreted by the shell (such as a space or `*` character), you can place the `\` character before the character that would usually be interpreted by the shell. This is called *escaping* the special character. You frequently see this on the command line to specify Mac filenames such as `My File`, which in Unix must be specified as `My\ File`.

NOTE

Note that you can use the shell escape character `\` to allow inclusion of usually special characters into a single command argument, or, alternatively, you can often place the argument in quotes. Therefore, if you wanted to list the directory *`My Big Directory`*, you could either specify it as *`My\ Big\ Directory`*, or as *`"My Big Directory"`* when used in a command. Although the quoted version is a little easier to read, we recommend familiarizing yourself with the escaped version because this is what the shell will use when automatically expanding arguments when you press the Tab key.

Most useful shells provide a history mechanism whereby previous commands can be recalled and reused. Previous commands may be recalled to the command line by use of the up arrow key. If you need the last command you typed, just press the up arrow key, and it will be recalled to the command line. You can rotate through the command history with the up arrow and down arrow keys to pick the command you need.

The command line also provides editing capabilities. You can use the left arrow and right arrow keys to move around in the command line currently displayed, and edit it by typing new characters or deleting existing characters with the Delete key. This also applies to commands that you've recalled via the command history with the arrow keys.

When you type a command, the system searches for a command with that name in the list of directories known as the `PATH`. This is done because a complete search of the entire filesystem could take a long time, and restricting the portions of the filesystem examined to only a small subset speeds up things significantly. Unfortunately, the current directory, where the shell "is," isn't necessarily in the `PATH`. Because of this, you might be in a directory named `/Users/wizbot/spin/`, and there might be a command named `spinnin` in the directory, but typing `spinnin` produces only the error `command not found`. In this case, you can run the command by specifying either the full name of the path to the command (`/Users/wizbot/spin/spinnin`), or by specifying the relative path to the command (`./spinnin`). You can also solve the problem by adding the path to the directory holding spinnin to the PATH list, or by adding the current directory to the PATH. You learn about this and more in Chapter 18. You also learn considerably more about paths in the immediately following sections, covering the filesystem and basic navigation.

Occasionally, you might do something that leaves your shell in an apparently unusable state. Frequently, this is because you've started a process that is expecting input from you. You can try several key combinations that might help you regain control of your shell:

- Ctrl-D—This key combination sends an End Of File (EOF) signal to the current process, usually terminating input. If the process is designed to continuously accept data until reaching the EOF, sending it this key combination causes it to stop accepting input and go about whatever it was designed to do next.

CAUTION

Be careful with Ctrl-D. If you're not currently running a process in the shell, you'll send the EOF to the shell itself, which tells it that you're finished sending input (typing commands to it) and it will summarily stop. If you've set your Terminal preferences to close the window when the last process running in it stops, that Terminal window goes away as well.

- Ctrl-Z—This key combination suspends the current foreground process (more on foreground and background processes in the "Process Management" section of Chapter 14, "Advanced Shell Concepts and Commands"). The process won't continue to run; it simply sits there in suspended animation until you either close the shell (perhaps by logging out), thereby killing it, or until you reenable it using one of the techniques discussed in "Process Management."
- Ctrl-C—This key combination is the Unix break character. This usually (you can configure the behavior) kills the current process and returns you to the shell prompt.

Don't be afraid to test the commands shown in this book. The system can do a pretty good job of protecting itself from anything a normal user can type, and we'll be sure to place conspicuous warnings with any commands capable of causing mischief in any case. With a little experimenting, we think you'll find that you can do a surprising number of things with only a few keystrokes.

Getting Started

So, now that we've taken all that time to provide background on using the shell, you might think that this is going to be confusing, intimidating, or difficult. It's not. It might seem confusing for a bit, but it's not difficult, and if you don't let it become intimidating, you'll find that you can quickly pick up techniques that make day-to-day use of your machine more convenient and productive. There's absolutely no need for you to learn everything that you can do with the shell all at once. As a matter of fact, there's no need to learn more than a handful of commands and techniques at any one time. We've written this section of the book as though you were going to start it as a shell novice, and graduate after six chapters as an experienced shell programmer. Next to nobody is going to follow that path. This, however, isn't a bad thing; almost nobody follows anybody else's path with learning to use the command line.

You start off doing a few things that are useful to you, and as you become proficient with those, it's natural to start adding new abilities and knowledge to your repertoire. Exactly what you learn when isn't really at all important. We've presented the material in an order that we think makes learning to use most commands and utilities (including ones that we haven't room to cover in this book) straightforward, but don't feel that you need to learn it all before you can start utilizing what you've learned. Unless you really want to, don't even try to learn it all, before you become comfortable with the parts that help you right now, with whatever you're regularly doing.

That being said, what exactly does this Terminal and shell thing do? It gives you a place to type things, and a place for the machine to respond. Before we get started on specifics, let's look at the sorts of things you can do in a shell running in Terminal. First, when you start Terminal, it gives you a friendly message and a prompt indicating that it's time for you to type something:

```
Last login: Sat Sep 20 22:50:19 on console
Welcome to Darwin!
/Volumes/Wills_Data/ray
bash-2.05a$
```

That's not too interesting. What's the point of telling me what version of `bash` I'm running. If I cared, I could probably ask it, right? Let's make that prompt into something more useful. How about our machine name, our username, and the directory we're currently in:

```
bash-2.05a$ PS1='\h:\u \W \$ '
brezup:ray ray $
```

Well, that's a little better, at least now I know who and where I am when I look at the terminal. `PS1` is a shell variable that customizes your prompt. `\h` calls out your machine name, `\u` calls out your username, `\W` (capitalization is important) calls out the name of the current directory, and `\$` places the traditional `bash $` character at the end of the prompts. If you're following along, believe it or not, you're customizing your shell environment already. It's not quite the same type of tweaks that you can get out of the Appearance control pane, but this is exactly the sort of small utility command that makes your life easier. And you don't need to read all the way up to Chapter 18 where we cover many other variables like `PS1` that can be set to make your life easier, for you to start making productive use of what you know now. We use this prompt (and a slight variation on it) throughout the book.

So now you've customized a bit of your environment. What sort of useful things can you do now? How about a calendar?

```
brezup:ray ray $ cal 2003
                                2003

        January                 February                 March
 S  M Tu  W Th  F  S     S  M Tu  W Th  F  S     S  M Tu  W Th  F  S
          1  2  3  4                       1                       1
 5  6  7  8  9 10 11     2  3  4  5  6  7  8     2  3  4  5  6  7  8
12 13 14 15 16 17 18     9 10 11 12 13 14 15     9 10 11 12 13 14 15
19 20 21 22 23 24 25    16 17 18 19 20 21 22    16 17 18 19 20 21 22
26 27 28 29 30 31       23 24 25 26 27 28       23 24 25 26 27 28 29
                                                30 31
         April                    May                    June
 S  M Tu  W Th  F  S     S  M Tu  W Th  F  S     S  M Tu  W Th  F  S
       1  2  3  4  5                 1  2  3     1  2  3  4  5  6  7
 6  7  8  9 10 11 12     4  5  6  7  8  9 10     8  9 10 11 12 13 14
13 14 15 16 17 18 19    11 12 13 14 15 16 17    15 16 17 18 19 20 21
20 21 22 23 24 25 26    18 19 20 21 22 23 24    22 23 24 25 26 27 28
27 28 29 30             25 26 27 28 29 30 31    29 30

         July                   August                 September
 S  M Tu  W Th  F  S     S  M Tu  W Th  F  S     S  M Tu  W Th  F  S
       1  2  3  4  5                    1  2        1  2  3  4  5  6
 6  7  8  9 10 11 12     3  4  5  6  7  8  9     7  8  9 10 11 12 13
13 14 15 16 17 18 19    10 11 12 13 14 15 16    14 15 16 17 18 19 20
20 21 22 23 24 25 26    17 18 19 20 21 22 23    21 22 23 24 25 26 27
27 28 29 30 31          24 25 26 27 28 29 30    28 29 30
                        31
        October                 November                December
 S  M Tu  W Th  F  S     S  M Tu  W Th  F  S     S  M Tu  W Th  F  S
          1  2  3  4                       1        1  2  3  4  5  6
 5  6  7  8  9 10 11     2  3  4  5  6  7  8     7  8  9 10 11 12 13
12 13 14 15 16 17 18     9 10 11 12 13 14 15    14 15 16 17 18 19 20
19 20 21 22 23 24 25    16 17 18 19 20 21 22    21 22 23 24 25 26 27
26 27 28 29 30 31       23 24 25 26 27 28 29    28 29 30 31
                        30
```

Know another quick way to get a calendar for all of any year with only eight keystrokes?

How about a peek at how long your machine's been running?

```
brezup:ray ray $ uptime
11:51PM up 1:02, 2 users, load averages: 0.16, 0.24, 0.16
```

Not only does it tell me how long it's been booted this time around (only 1 hour, 2 minutes right now), but also how many users are using the system, the time, and how hard the processor's working (.16 processes running during the command's averaging period, which is not working too hard at all).

How about what your current IP address is and the state of your network?

```
brezup:sageray Documents $ ifconfig -a
lo0: flags=8049<UP,LOOPBACK,RUNNING,MULTICAST> mtu 16384
        inet6 ::1 prefixlen 128
        inet6 fe80::1 prefixlen 64 scopeid 0x1
        inet 127.0.0.1 netmask 0xff000000
gif0: flags=8010<POINTOPOINT,MULTICAST> mtu 1280
stf0: flags=0<> mtu 1280
en0: flags=8863<UP,BROADCAST,SMART,RUNNING,SIMPLEX,MULTICAST> mtu 1500
        inet6 fe80::230:65ff:feaa:37ae prefixlen 64 scopeid 0x4
        inet 192.168.1.19 netmask 0xffffff00 broadcast 192.168.1.255
        ether 00:30:65:aa:37:ae
        media: autoselect (10baseT/UTP <half-duplex>) status: active
        supported media: none autoselect 10baseT/UTP <half-duplex>
➥10baseT/UTP <full-duplex> 10baseT/UTP <full-duplex,hw-loopback>
➥ 100baseTX <half-duplex> 100baseTX <full-duplex> 100baseTX
➥<full-duplex,hw-loopback>
fw0: flags=8822<BROADCAST,SMART,SIMPLEX,MULTICAST> mtu 2030
        tunnel inet -->
        lladdr 00:30:65:ff:fe:aa:37:ae
        media: autoselect <full-duplex> status: inactive
        supported media: autoselect <full-duplex>
```

Okay, so there's a bunch of information that you're not interested in there, but buried in the middle is a line that says `inet 192.168.1.19`, which is my current IP address. Actually, a couple of lines look like that, because those are all valid IP addresses by which this machine knows itself (127.0.0.1 exists on every machine, and always points back to itself). There's a 426Kilobyte application that you can find on the net that can retrieve this information and show it to you when you double click it. Is the convenience of double-clicking worth the difference between 11 keystrokes and 426Kb? Okay, so maybe the trouble of looking through that output is worth spending some disk space on. What if we add 15 more keystrokes (for a total of 26), and get the output down to only the IP address lines?

```
brezup:sageray Documents $ ifconfig -a | grep "inet "
    inet 127.0.0.1 netmask 0xff000000
    inet 192.168.1.19 netmask 0xffffff00 broadcast 192.168.1.255
    tunnel inet -->
```

Still worth nearly half a Megabyte of disk space? Well, the 426Kb application also can monitor your IP address and email you when it changes, but by the time you're finished with Chapter 18, you'll know how to add that capability to what you've seen here, and how to store it as your own little application that you can run with whatever name you care to call it. This'll cost you a one-time payment of another 100 or so keystrokes, depending on the length of your email address. It's rarely the functionality that takes up the room in these sorts of utility applications. Instead it's all the additional trimmings that must be layered around a simple utility to make it into a nice double-clickable GUI-driven application.

Hardly a day goes by when we don't see one or more utilities that someone's published for Mac OS X that aren't amazingly overcomplex and oversize for the capabilities that they bring to the end user. It's truly wonderful that people are willing to write little applications that perform useful actions and post news about them on macnn.com, and we wish their authors only the best. But it would often be of much more use for the author to just show the handful of lines of shell commands necessary to duplicate the effect. You can help change this landscape and further educate yourself at the same time, by learning how to construct simple utilities yourself (which you will be doing before you know it), and by urging utility authors to tell you how they did it, instead of just asking for impenetrable double-clickable applications.

Other command-line commands that you learn about in this and the following chapters are usually similarly designed. They do some small utility task, but they do it flexibly, and with a minimum of muss, fuss, or effort. By the end of Chapter 18 you will learn how to string them together into arbitrarily complex collections of commands that perform custom operations for you, and that can make use of your computer significantly more enjoyable and productive. Remember as you read through these chapters that it's not imperative for you to learn all the commands as you read about them. We've presented the commands in such an order that the topics build on each other, so paying attention to the general concepts helps a lot, but a multitude of commands are available in the shell, and even the most experienced Unix users rarely use more than a few percent on a regular basis.

The Online Manual Pages

The very first command that you should become familiar with is the `man` (manual) command. All good Unix systems provide an online collection of manual pages that detail almost every command available in the system. OS X is no exception. Simply type `man` <*commandname*> at any shell prompt, and if there is a manual page documenting the command, it will be shown to you. For example, to see the man pages for the `date` command (which tells you the date and time), you could type

```
brezup:sage Documents $ man date
DATE(1)       System General Commands Manual         DATE(1)


NAME
   date - display or set date and time
```

```
SYNOPSIS
   date [-nu] [-r seconds] [+format]
   [[[[[cc]yy]mm]dd]hh]mm[.ss]

DESCRIPTION
   date displays the current date and time when invoked without arguments.
   Providing arguments will format the date and time in a user-defined way
   or set the date. Only the superuser may set the date.

   The options are as follows:

   -n   The utility timed(8) is used to synchronize the clocks on groups
        of machines. By default, if timed is running, date will setthe
        time on all of the machines in the local group. The -n option
        stops date from setting the time for other than the current
        machine.

   -r   Print out the date and time that is seconds from the Epoch.

   -u   Display or set the date in UTC (universal) time.

   An operand with a leading plus (``+'') sign signals a user-defined format
   string which specifies the format in which to display the date and time.
   The format string may contain any of the conversion specifications
   described in the strftime(3) manual page, as well as any arbitrary text.
:
```

TIP

If your terminal shows you a line that says `more` at the bottom of the window, a pathname and a percentage figure, or :, it means that there is more output to be seen. Simply press the spacebar and the next page of output scrolls into view. Which of the options displayed depends on what pager is being used. The first two are displayed when the pager is `more`, but : is displayed when the pager is `less`. If `less` is used as the pager, you will be able to search the man pages. As of Mac OS X 10.3, `more` is no longer included, but for more information on `less`, see Chapter 13, "Common Unix Shell Commands: File Operations."

A vast quantity of information is available in the `man` pages, books and books worth of it. In 1993, I had a complete printed set of the `man` pages that were shipped with an early version of Sun Microsystems' flavor of Unix. These manuals completely filled a 4-foot by 6-foot bookcase of 8.5×11 three-ring binders, and the quantity of information provided in the man pages has only been expanding. Once upon a time, this quantity of information was actually a significant burden to store on expensive and scarce disk space, and so it was stored in a mildly compressed format that wasn't easily human-readable, and the man man page reading software was written to unpack this data and display it as necessary. Processors weren't so fast back then either, so the unpack and display step made the process a little slower than most people liked. To accommodate, the system was also designed to allow a duplicate set of man pages, in an unpacked format as well, which could be transparently (and more quickly) pulled up if they were available on the system.

For reasons seemingly lost in the depths of time, someone also made the decision that the creation of a searchable database for the man pages would be left to the same process as the act of unpacking (known as "formatting") the man pages. The result of this is that now, even as machines have become fast enough that on-the-fly formatting is an imperceptible delay, and the disk space occupied by uncompressed (formatted) copies is insignificant, we're still saddled with a man system where man pages are typically delivered in a file format in which they can't be easily read or searched, and where creating a searchable version usually requires an additional step beyond what comes native on your machine.

By default, Mac OS X is delivered without formatted man pages, but Apple's XCode (Developer Tools) installer now takes the initiative to run the formatting commands when it finishes the install process. Unfortunately, this doesn't mean that you no longer need to know about the formatting process because other software that you might install on the system may come without preformatted man pages. Because of this, you can end up in a situation where some of your man page system is searchable, and some invisible to the search software, if you don't run the formatting commands manually yourself when you install new software that adds pages to the man page system.

If you needed to format your Apple-supplied man page collection, either because you haven't installed the XCode distribution, or because you want to update the formatted pages with additional information that has been installed, you can do it like this:

```
brezup:ray Documents $ sudo catman -M /usr/share/man
Password:
catman: can't open /usr/share/man/man/: No such file or directory
catman: can't open /usr/share/man/manu: No such file or directory
catman: can't open /usr/share/man/mans: No such file or directory
.
<lots of errors deleted>
.
nroff -mandoc /usr/share/man/man1/[.1 > /usr/share/man/cat1/[.0
nroff -mandoc /usr/share/man/man1/a2p.1 > /usr/share/man/cat1/a2p.0
nroff -mandoc /usr/share/man/man1/addftinfo.1 >
➥/usr/share/man/cat1/addftinfo.0
nroff -mandoc /usr/share/man/man1/afmtodit.1 >
➥/usr/share/man/cat1/afmtodit.0
nroff -mandoc /usr/share/man/man1/alias.1 > /usr/share/man/cat1/alias.0
/usr/share/man/man1/alias.1:1: can't open `man1/tcsh.1':
➥No such file or directory
```

```
nroff -mandoc /usr/share/man/man1/alloc.1 > /usr/share/man/cat1/alloc.0
/usr/share/man/man1/alloc.1:1: can't open `man1/tcsh.1':
➥No such file or directory
nroff -mandoc /usr/share/man/man1/appleping.1 >
➥/usr/share/man/cat1/appleping.0
nroff -mandoc /usr/share/man/man1/appletviewer.1 >
➥/usr/share/man/cat1/appletviewer.0
nroff -mandoc /usr/share/man/man1/apply.1 > /usr/share/man/cat1/apply.0
nroff -mandoc /usr/share/man/man1/apropos.1 > /usr/share/man/cat1/apropos.0
nroff -mandoc /usr/share/man/man1/ar.1 > /usr/share/man/cat1/ar.0
nroff -mandoc /usr/share/man/man1/arch.1 > /usr/share/man/cat1/arch.0
nroff -mandoc /usr/share/man/man1/as.1 > /usr/share/man/cat1/as.0
nroff -mandoc /usr/share/man/man1/asa.1 > /usr/share/man/cat1/asa.0
nroff -mandoc /usr/share/man/man1/asn1parse.1 >
➥/usr/share/man/cat1/asn1parse.0
nroff -mandoc /usr/share/man/man1/at.1 > /usr/share/man/cat1/at.0
mdoc warning: list open at EOF! A .Bl directive has no matching .El
nroff -mandoc /usr/share/man/man1/atlookup.1 >
➥/usr/share/man/cat1/atlookup.0
.
<lots of output nroff lines>
.
mkdir /usr/share/man/cat2
nroff -mandoc /usr/share/man/man2/__syscall.2 >
➥/usr/share/man/cat2/__syscall.0
/usr/share/man/man2/__syscall.2:1: can't open `man2/syscall.2':
➥No such file or directory
nroff -mandoc /usr/share/man/man2/_exit.2 > /usr/share/man/cat2/_exit.0
nroff -mandoc /usr/share/man/man2/accept.2 > /usr/share/man/cat2/accept.0
nroff -mandoc /usr/share/man/man2/access.2 > /usr/share/man/cat2/access.0
nroff -mandoc /usr/share/man/man2/acct.2 > /usr/share/man/cat2/acct.0
nroff -mandoc /usr/share/man/man2/adjtime.2 > /usr/share/man/cat2/adjtime.0
nroff -mandoc /usr/share/man/man2/bind.2 > /usr/share/man/cat2/bind.0
nroff -mandoc /usr/share/man/man2/brk.2 > /usr/share/man/cat2/brk.0
nroff -mandoc /usr/share/man/man2/chdir.2 > /usr/share/man/cat2/chdir.0
nroff -mandoc /usr/share/man/man2/chflags.2 > /usr/share/man/cat2/chflags.0
Usage: .Fd function_declaration -- Fd is not callable (#137)
nroff -mandoc /usr/share/man/man2/chmod.2 > /usr/share/man/cat2/chmod.0
.
<lots of output nroff lines>
.
/usr/libexec/makewhatis /usr/share/man
```

Even if Apple's XCode install has already run the catman formatting step for you on the man page set they've provided, you won't hurt anything if you decide you want to run it again yourself. You'll eventually want to run catman on the /usr/local/man directory (into which most third-party Unix applications will install their man pages) so that non-Apple man page information is searchable as well. When you run catman, don't worry too much about the warning messages that you see. So long as the warning messages look similar to what is shown here, everything is working okay.

NOTE

For the inquisitive, the sudo command used at the beginning of the examples here is used to cause the command that follows it to run with root (Administrative) privileges. If you have enabled the root account, you could also do this by using the su command to switch to a shell running as the root user, which is an even more powerful administrative user than the normal OS X Admin user group. We don't recommend that you spend much time in an sued shell because you can do a lot of damage in this mode, but some way to run commands as root is required for doing certain sorts of maintenance like this. We cover the advantages and disadvantages of sudo and su, and the intricacies and requirements for their use, in later chapters.

The catman command that follows the sudo command uncompresses, indexes, and formats the contents of the compressed man page data files.

After you have a formatted man page set (the default for Apple's man pages, but remember you'll need to format your own for other software you install), you can use the -k option to man. (This is equivalent to the apropos command; wherever you see man -k, you can substitute apropos, if that's easier for you to remember. There's also a similar program, whatis, that works just like these, only constrains the results to only whole-word matches of the query.) This option searches the man pages for pages with keywords matching what you've entered. For example, if you want to know which man pages might have information on the subject of time, you could issue a man command like this:

```
brezup:ray Documents $ man -k time
BIO_f_ssl(3o), BIO_set_ssl(3o), BIO_get_ssl(3o), BIO_set_ssl_mode(3o),
.
Benchmark(3)          - benchmark running times of Perl code
CPAN::FirstTime(3), s-1CPAN:s0 - Util for s-1CPAN:s0:Config file Initialization
.
Time::localtime(3)
➥- by-name interface to Perl's built-in localtime() function
Time::tm(3)
➥- internal object used by Time::gmtime and Time::localtime
ac(8)                 - display connect time accounting
adjtime(2)
➥- correct the time to allow synchronization of the system clock
alarm(3)              - set signal timer alarm
```

```
.
.
sleep(1)          - suspend execution for an interval of time
.
strftime(3)       - format date and time
time(1)           - time command execution
time(3)           - get time of day
time2posix(3), posix2time(3) - convert seconds since the Epoch
times(3)          - process times
timezone(3)       - return the timezone abbreviation
touch(1)          - change file access and modification times
tzfile(5)         - time zone information
tzset(3)          - initialize time conversion information
ualarm(3)         - schedule signal after specified time
uptime(1)         - show how long system has been running
utime(3)          - set file times
utimes(2)         - set file access and modification times
vtimes(3)         - get information about resource utilization
zdump(8)          - time zone dumper
zic(8)            - time zone compiler
```

This command lists each of the man pages that the system knows about that match the keyword (in this case, `time`) that you've requested.

Finally, it's important to know that the man page system has several sections into which the content is divided. Because of this, there might be commands that have multiple man pages, each in a different section. The system is divided into sections roughly segregated into the following topics:

- `Man1`—Typical user commands. Documentation of commands that can be executed by the normal user at the command line.
- `Man2`—System calls. Documentation of routines internal to the system that programmers can use in programs.
- `Man3`—User-level library calls. Documentation of C and other library functions for programmers.
- `Man4`—Device drivers, protocols, and network interfaces. Documentation of the internals of hardware support and software APIs for these items.
- `Man5`—File formats. Documentation of file format details for both system control files and certain program data files.
- `Man6`—Games and demos. Documentation for amusement software.
- `Man7`—Miscellaneous. Various tables of useful information, such as ASCII tables.

- Man8—Maintenance commands. Documentation for maintenance and system administration commands.
- Man9—System Kernel Developer's commands. Documentation for system kernel developer commands.

CAUTION

The segregation of the man pages into the directories Man1–Man9 is not absolute. Third-party software providers have a bad habit of breaking convention and placing their man pages in inappropriate sections.

If you look at the earlier listing for the `man -k time` command, you will notice that each topic listed includes a number or letter in parentheses after the name of the topic. This is the man page section in which the item occurs.

NOTE

Your system might not show exactly these same items. The available man pages depend on whether you've installed the developer toolkit and on any other software installed on the system. If the following examples using manual section 3 do not work for you, read through them now, and try them again after you've installed the developer tools. We're including them here because we expect that many users will have "installed ahead," or are reading this book while trying to learn on a completely configured machine at work or school. If you're following along in a from-the-ground-up installation, bookmark this section on man pages, and try it out again after finishing the developer tools install, which is necessary for the next chapter.

To look at man pages in other sections of the manual, specify the numeric or character identifier for the section between the `man` command and the item you want to look up. For example, the system includes man pages for both the `time` command and the `time()` C library function. `man time` defaults to showing you the man page for the command-line–related item, if one exists, so both `man time` and `man 1 time` show you the man page for the `time` command:

```
brezup:ray Documents $ man time

TIME(1)      System General Commands Manual         TIME(1)

NAME
   time - time command execution

SYNOPSIS
   time [-lp] utility
```

```
DESCRIPTION
   The time utility executes and times utility. After the utility finishes,
   time writes the total time elapsed, the time consumed by system overhead,
   and the time used to execute utility to the standard error stream. Times
   are reported in seconds.

   Available options:

   -l   The contents of the rusage structure are printed.

   -p   The output is formatted as specified by IEEE Std 1003.2-1992
        (``POSIX.2'').

   The csh(1) has its own and syntactically different builtin version of.
   The utility described here is available as /usr/bin/time to csh users.
:
```

The following man command produces identical results:

```
brezup:ray Documents $ man time
```

If you want to know about the C library function named `time()`, however, you will need to look in the program-functions–related section of the man pages, using `man 3 time` as your command:

```
brezup:ray Documents $ man 3 time

TIME(3)       System Library Functions Manual        TIME(3)

NAME
   time - get time of day

LIBRARY
   Standard C Library (libc, -lc)

SYNOPSIS
   #include <time.h>

   time_t
   time(time_t *tloc);

DESCRIPTION
   The time() function returns the value of time in seconds since 0 hours, 0
   minutes, 0 seconds, January 1, 1970, Coordinated Universal Time.
```

```
A copy of the time value may be saved to the area indicated by the
pointer tloc. If tloc is a NULL pointer, no value is stored.

Upon successful completion, time() returns the value of time. Otherwise
a value of ((time_t) -1) is returned and the global variable errno is set
:
```

NOTE

If you add any software to the system, it may place man pages into the system man directories (located in /usr/share/man on OS X), or into the local man directories (located in either /opt/man or /usr/local/man, or both). If you do this, you will need to rebuild the catman database before the new manual pages will show up when you use the man -k option.

The man system is self-documenting, of course, so if you want to read further about the man command, simply type **man man**.

A command documentation table (our revised and sometimes corrected version of the man pages, with most esoteric or uninteresting options pared out) for man is shown in Table 12.3, which lists the syntax and selected options for man. The complete documentation table is located in Appendix A.

TABLE 12.3 Syntax and Selected Options for man

man	Formats and displays online manual pages.
man [-adfhktw] [<*section*>] [-M <*path*>] [-P <*pager*>] [-S <*list*>] [-m <*machine*>] [-p <*string*>] <*name1*> <*name2*> ...	
-a	Displays all the manual pages for a specified section and name combination. (The default is to display only the first page found.)
-d	Displays debugging information, rather than manual pages.
-f <*keyword*>	Displays a list of manual pages that contain complete word matches to the <*keyword*>. Same as whatis.
-h	Displays the help for man.
-k <*keyword*>	Displays a list of manual pages that contain the <*keyword*>. Same as apropos.
-w	Lists the pathnames of manual pages that would be displayed for the specified section and name combination.
-S <*list*>	Searches the specified colon-separated sections in <*list*>. Overrides MANSECT environment variable.

The optional <*section*> argument restricts man's search to the specified section.

The Unix Filesystem

To the novice Unix user—especially one coming from a GUI environment as nice as the Mac's—venturing into the Unix filesystem will probably feel like a journey back to the Stone Age. Files upon files, nothing to indicate what any of them do, and not a friendly icon in sight. Although the filesystem might initially appear cryptic and primitive, you will find that with experience, it actually affords you considerable sophistication and control. This sophistication comes from the ability to combine the functions of many small programs into larger programs with arbitrarily complex functions.

Before the use of most Unix commands will make sense, you need to understand a few things about the design of the Unix filesystem. The Mac OS X HFS+ filesystem doesn't strictly adhere to the model that most forms of Unix use, but from the point of view of the BSD subsystem, it functions in an analogous manner. You'll find a number of differences between the way Unix thinks of files, and what you're probably used to, but after you get used to them, you'll probably find these differences are to your liking.

Basic Unix File Principles

Unix filesystems have a single root directory. Unlike Macintosh filesystems with their multiple drive icons on the desktop, and Windows machines with their ABCs, Unix filesystems have only a single top-level designator for the filesystem. This is the root directory named `/`. Unix considers all its files to belong to a tree-shaped structure, with the root directory at its base and files as the leaves. Directories are the branching points between the branches. Unix trees are upside down with respect to real trees, as the root directory is at the top of the tree. Any directory can contain files and other directories.

NOTE

The term `root` is used for multiple meanings in Unix. The `root` user is the most authoritative user of the system, with essentially absolute control over any process or configuration. The root of the filesystem is the top directory of the filesystem, beneath which all other files and directories occur.

Every file in the Unix filesystem has a unique and unambiguous name that points to it. This complete name is known as the "full path" to the file and can be specified from any directory in the filesystem to indicate any file in the filesystem. The full path to a file always starts with the root directory and ends in the filename, indicating directory names along the way, separated by the separator character `/`. A full path may be thought of as the shortest list of directories that must be traversed from the root to reach the file. A file with the full path `/home/wizbot/spin/spinnin` is named `spinnin` and is located in the directory `spin`, which is located in the directory `wizbot`, which is located in the directory `home`, which is located in the root directory `/`.

Files have both full paths and relative paths. A *relative path* is a path from the current directory, instead of from the root directory. There are two special relative directory names. One of these is `.`, which indicates the current directory; the other is `..`, which indicates the directory that is the parent of this directory. For example, assume that there is a directory named `spun` in the same directory as the directory named `spin` in the earlier path (it would have a full path of `/home/wizbot/spun`). If we are in the directory `spun` and want to specify the relative path to `spinnin`, we can do so with the relative path `../spin/spinnin`.

TIP

Full paths always start with `/`; relative paths never do.

Not only don't you have multiple drives at the top level of the system, but you, as the user, don't need to know what drives are where. Additional drives (or, more properly, *partitions*) appear as directories and can be mounted at any point in the filesystem to appear as an extended branch in the system. Sound strange? After a while it won't. In one of the nice feats of Unix abstraction, the system removes from the user's sphere of concern what hardware devices actually exist, and where they are or how they're connected. After you get used to this system, you'll see that it makes good sense. So long as you can uniquely identify a file by name in the filesystem, why would you care which spinning chunk of metal it lives on? This system has additional nice features. If you find one day that you've run out of space to put files in some particular location, you can simply add a drive to the system and mount it—that is, make it appear as the directory—where you need space. There's no need to reconfigure things or move files around, because the additional space will simply appear as new space in whatever directory you mount it as.

If the importance of that isn't clear, imagine the situation where you've been downloading a lot of information from the Internet. You've been storing everything in a directory named `Macintosh HD/Web Stuff/Downloads`, and you've just run out of space on Macintosh HD. In other operating systems, including the old familiar pre-OS X Mac OS, even if you had another disk available and ready to add to the system, you would need to rearrange things, perhaps creating `Macintosh HD2/Web Stuff/Downloads` and moving everything from the original directory over to the new one. With Unix based OSes, including OS X, this is unnecessary. You would still need to move your files, but you could add the new drive and make it appear (mount it) as the directory `Macintosh HD/Web Stuff/Downloads`. Suddenly, that directory would have plenty of space, and you wouldn't need to rearrange the filesystem, reconfigure your Internet applications to download to a new location, or develop a new set of downloading habits.

As a matter of fact, you don't even need to know what country your files physically reside in. Again, Unix abstraction comes into play, and a remote file server is mounted as a directory under the local filesystem just as additional physical storage is. From your point of view, a remote file server is just another directory; the only difference between accessing files on it and on local storage is the possible network delay associated with transporting the files.

Regardless of whether you know where your files actually are, the shell, as previously mentioned, is always somewhere in the filesystem structure. Just like a Finder window that is showing what file icons are open, and currently displaying, some particular location on your system, a shell displaying a prompt is in some specific location. Commands that use files reference files from the point of view of being "in" that directory. The `pwd` command causes the shell to tell you what directory it's currently in.

Also as previously mentioned, Unix is a case-sensitive system, and Unix filenames are case sensitive from the command line. From OS X, this isn't necessarily the case (depending on which base disk format you chose for your installation), but when you're working from the command line, remember that what you type must have the correct capitalization.

A file has three attributes that control who can access the file. These attributes control access at the level of whether the file can be read, written to, and executed. Additionally, these attributes can be specified separately for the user who owns the file, a group of selected users, and everybody on the system. These attributes can be set to any combination of values, although some combinations do not make much sense. For example, you would expect an application to be executable, a configuration file for a program to be readable, and something like your daily schedule to be both readable and writable. Unix, however, will do whatever you tell it to with the file permissions. If you make your daily schedule executable, Unix will do its best to execute it, which most likely will result in an error message and no damage done. If you tell Unix that an application is writable, it will be happy to let you edit it in a word processor, which will probably make the application useless. We cover file permissions in more detail later in the "Introduction to File Permissions" section of Chapter 14.

Everything in the filesystem has an owner. Every file and directory in the Unix filesystem has auxiliary information attached to it that specifies the individual user who owns it, and also the group of users that it belongs to (also known as *group ownership*). Depending on the permissions, this user or group of users can access the file. The individual owner of the file can control its group ownership and the access privileges that the group, and all other users on the system, can use in accessing the file.

Each user has a home directory. This is one special directory in the filesystem that is owned by the user and is used to contain configuration files and other content specific to the user. From the point of view of the filesystem, the user's home directory is no different than any other directory, but it is significant in that it is the directory where you start when you open a terminal and shell on the system. To make things simpler for you, Unix doesn't require that you remember the path to your directory; it can always be specified by the special full path `~<username>`.

Keep these basic principles in mind when reading about the commands to work within the filesystem. We cover some of them in more detail later in this chapter, but it helps to have a basic understanding of them as we move to the explanations and examples of commands.

NOTE

When discussing your interaction with the shell, we frequently use "you" interchangeably with the shell. It's much shorter to write "in the directory where you type the command" than "in the current working directory of the shell that you're interacting with when you type the command."

Basic Filesystem Navigation

The most basic commands for dealing with the Unix filesystem are those for moving around the filesystem (changing that "somewhere" that the shell always is) and for listing the contents of directories (finding out what's in the same location as the shell or in some other directory). Before you start moving around, however, it's a good idea to be able to find out where you are.

Where Are You? pwd

The `pwd` command (print working directory) prints the full path to the current working directory—the location where you "are" at the moment in this particular shell.

```
brezup:nermal Documents $ pwd
/Users/nermal/Documents
```

Table 12.4 shows the complete command documentation table for `pwd`.

TABLE 12.4 The Command Documentation Table for `pwd`

`pwd`	Prints current working directory.
`pwd [-L¦P]`	
`-L`	Prints the logical path to the current working directory, as defined by the shell in the environment variable `PWD`.
`-P`	Default. Prints the physical path to the current working directory, with symbolic links resolved.

NOTE

Sometimes `pwd` doesn't respond with identical information to what we expect. For example, if we `cd` (change directory—a command covered shortly) to the directory named `/var/tmp`, and issue the `pwd` command, we get `/private/var/tmp` as an answer. This is because Apple has put some of the normal Unix directories in weird places and pulled some trickery to get them to appear as though they're where they should be. This is a compromise forced on the system because it must be able to coexist with Mac OS on the same drive. If you want to see `pwd` return the same information as where you `cd`ed to, use `pwd -L`.

Listing Files in Various Locations: ls

The ls command lists files in the directory where you currently are. More properly, the ls command lists files anywhere in the filesystem, presuming that you have permissions with which to do so. If you don't specify any other directory for it to list, ls defaults to listing the files in the current working directory.

For example, to list the files in the current working directory, simply type ls.

```
brezup:nermal Documents $ cd /
brezup:nermal / $ pwd
/
brezup:nermal / $ ls
AppleShare PDS            Network                  etc
Applications              System                   mach
Applications (Mac OS 9)   System Folder            mach.sym
Cleanup At Startup        TheFindByContentFolder   mach_kernel
Desktop DB                TheVolumeSettingsFolder  private
Desktop DF                Trash                    sbin
Desktop Folder            Users                    tmp
Developer                 Volumes                  usr
Documents                 bin                      var
Late Breaking News        cores                    vol.tar
Library                   dev                      ???T+???Blank1
```

This example shows that the directory / contains 33 things. From this listing, you can't tell which of those things are directories and which of those things are files.

There's really no need to issue the pwd command as shown in the preceding example. If you don't know where you are in the filesystem, pwd tells you. If you already know, there's no need to ask the computer to tell you.

NOTE

Many of the command listings shown here are based on a user account we've created for demo purposes, with the username nermal. You're welcome to use your own account instead of nermal for the examples.

If you want to list the files in a directory other than the one that you are currently in, simply specify the path to the directory after the ls command. The path to specify can be either a relative or an absolute path. For example, to list the files in a directory named /Users/nermal/ if you're in the directory /Users/, simply type ls nermal/.

```
brezup:nermal / $ cd /Users/
brezup:nermal /Users $ ls
Shared joray miwa  nermal
```

```
brezup:nermal /Users $ ls nermal/
Desktop          Network Trash Folder      chown-output
Documents        Pictures                  myfile
Library          Public                    output-sample6
Movies           Sites                     su-output
Music            TheVolumeSettingsFolder   typescripts
```

You could also produce this same output by using the absolute path. Instead of the relative path `nermal/` from the current directory `/Users/`, you could look explicitly in `/Users/nermal/`:

```
brezup:nermal / $ cd /Users/
brezup:nermal /Users $ ls
Shared joray miwa  nermal
brezup:nermal /Users $ ls /Users/nermal/
Desktop          Network Trash Folder      chown-output
Documents        Pictures                  myfile
Library          Public                    output-sample6
Movies           Sites                     su-output
Music            TheVolumeSettingsFolder   typescripts
```

Or, if you're in the directory `/Users/nermal/Documents/` and want to list the files in the directory that is the parent of this directory (`/Users/nermal/`), you can use the relative path `.` (the parent directory) to access it. To do this, use `ls ../`.

```
brezup:nermal nermal $ cd /Users/nermal/Documents
brezup:nermal Documents $ ls ../
Desktop          Network Trash Folder   chown-output
...looks the same, still!
```

Likewise, if you want to list the contents of `/Users/nermal/typescripts/`, and you're in `/Users/nermal/Documents/`, you could type

```
brezup:nermal nermal $ cd /Users/nermal/Documents
brezup:nermal Documents $ ls ../typescripts/
typescript        typescript-copy-2    typescript2     typescript5
typescript-copy   typescript-copy-3    typescript4
```

Like most Unix commands, the `ls` command has a plethora of options from which to choose. These options allow you to specify which files you want to list and what information you want to list about them. Table 12.5 shows the syntax for `ls` as well as some common and interesting options. The complete documentation table can be found in Appendix A.

TABLE 12.5 Syntax and Selected Options for `ls`

`ls`	Lists directory contents.
`ls [-ABCFGHLPRTWZabcdfghiklmnopqrstuwx1] [<file1> <file2> ...]`	
	For each operand that names a file of a type other than directory, `ls` displays its name as well as any requested, associated information.
	If no operands are given, the contents of the current directory are displayed. If more than one operand is given, nondirectory operands are displayed first; directory and nondirectory operands are sorted separately and in lexicographical order.
`-A`	List all entries except for `.` and `..` Always set for superuser.
`-C`	Force multicolumn output. This is the default when output is to a terminal.
`-F`	Display a slash (/) immediately after each pathname that is a directory, an asterisk (*) after each that is executable, an at sign (@) after each symbolic link, an equals sign (=) after each socket, a percent sign (%) after each whiteout, and a vertical bar (¦) after each that is a FIFO.
`-G`	Enables colorized output. Equivalent to defining `CLICOLOR` in the environment.
`-R`	Recursively lists subdirectories encountered.
`-T`	When used with the `-l` option, displays complete time information for the file, including month, day, hour, minute, second, and year.
`-a`	Includes directory entries whose names begin with a dot (`.`).
`-c`	Uses time when file status was last changed for sorting or printing.
`-d`	Directories are listed as plain files (not searched recursively).
`-h`	When used with the `-l` option, uses unit suffixes: Byte, Kilobyte, Megabyte, Gigabyte, Terabyte, and Petabyte to reduce the number of digits to three or less using base 2 for sizes.
`-l`	Lists in long format. Long format lists the following: file mode, number of links, owner name, group name, number of bytes in the file, abbreviated month, day-of-month file was last modified, hour file last modified, minute file last modified, and the pathname.
`-r`	Reverses the order of the sort to get reverse lexicographical order or the oldest entries first.
`-t`	Sorts by time modified (most recently modified first) before sorting the operands by lexicographical order.
`-u`	Uses time of last access, instead of last modification of the file for sorting (`-t`) or printing (`-l`).
`-x`	The same as `-C`, except that the multicolumn output is produced with entries sorted across, rather than down, the columns.

You can use an `ls` command like this to produce a listing that shows the contents of the root directory and indicates the following for each file (or directory): who the owner of the file is, what group the file belongs to, and the size of files.

```
brezup:nermal / $ ls -l
total 13232
-rwxrwxrwx  1 root wheel   106496 Apr 20 14:59 AppleShare PDS
drwxrwxrwx 25 root admin   806 Apr 18 11:05 Applications
drwxrwxrwx 18 root wheel   568 Apr 20 14:54 Applications (Mac OS 9)
drwxrwxrwx  2 root wheel   264 Apr 6 12:24 Cleanup At Startup
-rwxrwxrwx  1 root wheel   212992 Apr 20 14:59 Desktop DB
```

```
-rwxrwxrwx  1 root wheel   1432466 Apr 20 14:57 Desktop DF
drwxrwxrwx  6 root staff   264 Apr 4 11:51 Desktop Folder
drwxrwxr-x 12 root admin   364 Mar 1 20:29 Developer
drwxrwxrwx  6 ray  staff   264 Apr 4 14:20 Documents
-rwxrwxrwx  1 root wheel   0 Apr 4 14:11 Late Breaking News
drwxrwxr-x 21 root admin   670 Apr 18 11:04 Library
drwxr-xr-x  6 root wheel   264 Apr 4 12:47 Network
drwxr-xr-x  3 root wheel   58 Apr 12 00:51 System
drwxrwxrwx 40 root wheel   1316 Apr 20 14:50 System Folder
drwxrwxrwx  2 ray  staff   264 Mar 23 14:59 TheFindByContentFolder
drwxrwxrwx  4 ray  staff   264 Mar 23 14:46 TheVolumeSettingsFolder
drwxrwxrwx  2 ray  staff   264 Apr 20 14:58 Trash
drwxr-xr-x  6 root wheel   160 Apr 16 12:37 Users
drwxrwxrwt  6 root wheel   264 Apr 20 15:00 Volumes
drwxr-xr-x 33 root wheel   1078 Apr 16 09:40 bin
lrwxrwxr-t  1 root admin   13 Apr 20 15:00 cores -> private/cores
dr-xr-xr-x  2 root wheel   512 Apr 20 15:00 dev
lrwxrwxr-t  1 root admin   11 Apr 20 15:00 etc -> private/etc
lrwxrwxr-t  1 root admin   9 Apr 20 15:00 mach -> /mach.sym
-r--r--r--  1 root admin   652352 Apr 20 15:00 mach.sym
-rw-r--r--  1 root wheel   4039744 Mar 30 23:46 mach_kernel
drwxr-xr-x  7 root wheel   264 Apr 20 15:00 private
drwxr-xr-x 56 root wheel   1860 Apr 16 09:41 sbin
lrwxrwxr-t  1 root admin   11 Apr 20 15:00 tmp -> private/tmp
drwxr-xr-x 10 root wheel   296 Apr 12 14:45 usr
lrwxrwxr-t  1 root admin   11 Apr 20 15:00 var -> private/var
-rw-r--r--  1 root admin   10240 Apr 16 09:35 vol.tar
-rwxrwxrwx  1 root wheel   221696 Apr 4 13:57 ???T+???Blank1
```

The output might look a little confusing at first, but it breaks down into parts that are easy to understand.

The first line contains information telling you the total sum for all the file (not including directories) sizes contained in the directory. The total is in 512-byte blocks—divide by 2 if you prefer your answer in kilobytes.

Next come lines detailing the contents of the directory, one file or directory listed per line.

At the beginning of each line are 10 characters. These indicate the values of 10 flags that belong to the file. The first flag indicates whether the file is a directory, a symbolic link (Unix for *alias*), or just a plain normal file. If the first flag is a `d`, the indicated item is a directory. If it is an `l`, the item is a link. If it is only a `-`, the item is a file. Next is a set of three values, `r`, `w`, and `x`, repeated three times. These three values specify the read flag, the write flag, and the execute flag for each user who owns the file, the group that owns the file, and all other users on the system. If a - is shown instead of an r, w, or x, the user, the group, or everybody on the system is not allowed to perform whatever action—read, write, or execute—that the flag is missing for.

Shortly following the 10 flag characters, each line contains an entry indicating the user who owns the file; in this case, root owns many of the files shown. The user ray owns a few.

Following the information indicating the owner of the file is another entry indicating the group that owns the file. Group ownership of a file is not as stringent as the user ownership of a file. The individual owner of a file is the only user allowed to modify the permissions of a file. So, although a user who belongs to the group that owns the file may be able to write to the file, he or she cannot modify the flags indicating what the permissions are for the file.

Next is an entry indicating the size of the file in bytes. Entries for files indicate the full size of the file on disk. Entries for directories indicate another value loosely associated with the number of entries that the directory contains.

Following the size of the file comes an entry indicating the date of the most recent modification of the file. If the file was modified within the last year, the date and time are given; otherwise, the month, day, and year are given.

Finally, each entry lists the filename. Note that the filenames are identical to the name shown by the use of ls from our first example, with the exception of core, etc, tmp, mach, and var. Each of these entries is followed by an odd arrow that points to a path. Note that the file type for these is indicated by ls as a symbolic link. Just as a Mac OS alias points to a file or directory in another location, a symbolic link also points to a file or directory in another location. The information shown following the arrow is the path to which each particular entry points.

To prevent clutter, the ls command, by default, does not show certain files and directories that are expected to be configuration files or to contain maintenance or control information. Specifically, files or directories whose names begin with a dot (.) are not shown. Still, if you want to see them, there is an ls option that will allow this. If you want to see absolutely everything in the directory, add the -a option to the ls command; for example, ls -la (or ls -al, the order of options doesn't typically matter in most commands).

```
brezup:nermal / $ ls -al
total 13264
drwxrwxr-t 39 root admin   1282 Apr 20 15:00 .
drwxrwxr-t 39 root admin   1282 Apr 20 15:00 ..
-rwxrwxrwx  1 root admin   8208 Apr 18 11:05 .DS_Store
d-wx-wx-wx  2 root admin   264 Apr 4 12:20 .Trashes
-r--r--r--  1 root wheel   142 Feb 25 03:05 .hidden
dr--r--r--  2 root wheel   224 Apr 20 15:00 .vol
-rwxrwxrwx  1 root wheel   106496 Apr 20 14:59 AppleShare PDS
```

```
drwxrwxrwx 25 root admin  806 Apr 18 11:05 Applications
drwxrwxrwx 18 root wheel  568 Apr 20 14:54 Applications (Mac OS 9)
drwxrwxrwx  2 root wheel  264 Apr 6 12:24 Cleanup At Startup
-rwxrwxrwx  1 root wheel  212992 Apr 20 14:59 Desktop DB
-rwxrwxrwx  1 root wheel  1432466 Apr 20 14:57 Desktop DF
drwxrwxrwx  6 root staff  264 Apr 4 11:51 Desktop Folder
drwxrwxr-x 12 root admin  364 Mar 1 20:29 Developer
drwxrwxrwx  6 ray  staff  264 Apr 4 14:20 Documents
-rwxrwxrwx  1 root wheel  0 Apr 4 14:11 Late Breaking News
drwxrwxr-x 21 root admin  670 Apr 18 11:04 Library
drwxr-xr-x  6 root wheel  264 Apr 4 12:47 Network
drwxr-xr-x  3 root wheel  58 Apr 12 00:51 System
drwxrwxrwx 40 root wheel  1316 Apr 20 14:50 System Folder
drwxrwxrwx  2 ray  staff  264 Mar 23 14:59 TheFindByContentFolder
drwxrwxrwx  4 ray  staff  264 Mar 23 14:46 TheVolumeSettingsFolder
drwxrwxrwx  2 ray  staff  264 Apr 20 14:58 Trash
drwxr-xr-x  6 root wheel  160 Apr 16 12:37 Users
drwxrwxrwt  6 root wheel  264 Apr 20 15:00 Volumes
drwxr-xr-x 33 root wheel  1078 Apr 16 09:40 bin
drwxrwxrwt  1 root admin  68 Jun 28 23:09 cores
dr-xr-xr-x  2 root wheel  512 Apr 20 15:00 dev
lrwxrwxr-t  1 root admin  11 Apr 20 15:00 etc -> private/etc
lrwxrwxr-t  1 root admin  9 Apr 20 15:00 mach -> /mach.sym
-r--r--r--  1 root admin  652352 Apr 20 15:00 mach.sym
-rw-r--r--  1 root wheel  4039744 Mar 30 23:46 mach_kernel
drwxr-xr-x  7 root wheel  264 Apr 20 15:00 private
drwxr-xr-x 56 root wheel  1860 Apr 16 09:41 sbin
lrwxrwxr-t  1 root admin  11 Apr 20 15:00 tmp -> private/tmp
drwxr-xr-x 10 root wheel  296 Apr 12 14:45 usr
lrwxrwxr-t  1 root admin  11 Apr 20 15:00 var -> private/var
-rw-r--r--  1 root admin  10240 Apr 16 09:35 vol.tar
-rwxrwxrwx  1 root wheel  221696 Apr 4 13:57 ???T+???Blank1
```

Notice that several new files have appeared at the top of the listing relative to our previous output. These all start with `.` characters at the beginnings of their filenames. They aren't shown in the normal `-l` listing, because files that start with `.` are understood by convention to be configuration files, and other types of content that the average user doesn't want to be troubled with seeing on a day-to-day basis when looking at the directory contents. You can make any file "slightly invisible" at the command line by adding a `.` to the beginning of its name.

Moving Around the Filesystem: cd, pushd, popd

Now that you know how to determine where you are in the filesystem and how to list the files in a particular location, it's time to learn how to change your location. Unix provides two primary mechanisms by which you can do this. The first of these is the cd (change directory) command. This command does exactly what you would expect from its name: It changes your location in the filesystem to whatever location you ask it. If you want to change the current working directory from /var to /var/log/, you can type cd /var/log/. Because cd, like most Unix commands, accepts either relative or absolute paths, you can also make this change by typing cd log/, as shown here:

```
brezup:nermal var $ cd /var/log
brezup:nermal log $
```

or:

```
brezup:nermal var $ cd log
brezup:nermal log $
```

TIP

Remember that you can always use ~ as a quick absolute path to your home directory. You can also use ~ to construct absolute paths to directories or files beneath your home directory. If you want to change into the directory named fizbin located in your home directory, you can use the cd command cd ~/fizbin.

The cd command can also be used without an argument, in which case it assumes that you want to go to your home directory, and takes you to that location:

```
brezup:nermal log $ cd
brezup:nermal nermal $
```

Table 12.6 shows the command documentation table for cd.

TABLE 12.6 The Command Documentation Table for cd

cd	Changes working directory.
cd [-L¦-P] [<*dir*>]	
cd	
<*dir*> is an absolute or relative pathname. The interpretation of the relative pathname depends on the CDPATH environment variable.	
-L	Forces symbolic links to be followed.
-P	Uses physical directory structure instead of following symbolic links.
An argument of - is equivalent to $OLDPWD.	

The bash and tcsh shells (similar to most others) also support a considerably more powerful way of navigating through the filesystem. This method, accessed through the pushd and popd commands, uses a computer structure called a *stack*. Using a stack allows you to go to another location and return to wherever you came from, without needing to remember the location and cd back.

NOTE

Computer scientists use the term *stack* as a friendly term for a data structure also known as a Last In, First Out (LIFO) structure. A classical LIFO structure has one place into which data can be put or retrieved from the structure. If you put one piece of data into the structure, and then put in a second, you can't get the first back out again until you remove the second. See? The last thing you put in must be the first thing you take out. It's also called a stack because it works just like a stack of plates at a cafeteria. The last plate put on the stack (the one at the top of the stack) is the one that you take off first.

The pushd and popd commands work in concert. pushd puts the current directory on the stack and takes you to whatever directory you tell it to. popd takes you to whatever directory is on top of the stack and removes that directory from the stack.

For example, if you're in /var/tmp/ and you want to temporarily change to the directory /etc/httpd/, you could do so by issuing cd commands that you already know about, like so:

```
brezup:nermal tmp $ pwd
/private/var/tmp
brezup:nermal tmp $ cd /etc/httpd
brezup:nermal httpd $ pwd
/private/etc/httpd
...
(do some work here perhaps)
...
brezup:nermal httpd $ cd /var/tmp
brezup:nermal tmp $ pwd
/private/var/tmp
```

This works, but has the strong disadvantage that you need to use the wetware in your head to remember where you were, and how to get back. It's also tedious if you're doing something that requires you to make this flip back and forth between the directories frequently. It seems like there should be a way to let the computer leave a trail of breadcrumbs for you, marking the waypoints of your travels about the directories as it were, and then to use this information to be able to automatically backtrack whenever needed. There is—the solution is the pushd and popd commands.

As mentioned previously when discussing pwd, the results of looking at where you are, may not agree entirely with where you think you've gone. This is the cause of the discrepancy seen between the locations cd'ed to, and the results of the pwd location checks shown here.

To do the same thing using pushd and popd is easier:

```
brezup:nermal tmp $ pwd -L
/var/tmp
brezup:nermal tmp $ pushd /etc/httpd
/etc/httpd /var/tmp
brezup:nermal httpd $ pwd -L
/etc/httpd
brezup:nermal httpd $ popd
/var/tmp
brezup:nermal tmp $ pwd -L
/var/tmp
```

Because the stack of directories is arbitrarily deep, you can push multiple items on before you start popping them off. For example:

```
brezup:nermal tmp $ pushd /etc/httpd
/etc/httpd /var/tmp
brezup:nermal httpd $ pwd -L
/etc/httpd
brezup:nermal httpd $ pushd /Users
/Users /etc/httpd /var/tmp
brezup:nermal Users $ pwd -L
/Users
brezup:nermal Users $ popd
/etc/httpd /var/tmp
brezup:nermal httpd $ pwd -L
/etc/httpd
brezup:nermal httpd $ popd
/var/tmp
brezup:nermal tmp $ pwd -L
/var/tmp
```

To be able to switch back and forth between a pair of directories, simply don't give an argument to pushd. It will pop the directory on top of the stack, push the current directory on, and switch you to the directory that it popped off. If that's a little confusing, just remember that if you've just come from somewhere using pushd, you can get back again using pushd with no arguments. When you're back, you've again just come from somewhere using pushd, so to get back to where you came from you just pushd... For example, you might do something like this:

```
brezup:nermal tmp $ pushd /etc/httpd
/etc/httpd /var/tmp
brezup:nermal httpd $ pwd -L
/etc/httpd
brezup:nermal httpd $ pushd
/var/tmp /etc/httpd
brezup:nermal tmp $ pwd -L
/var/tmp
brezup:nermal tmp $ pushd
/etc/httpd /var/tmp
brezup:nermal httpd $ pwd -L
/etc/httpd
( And this can go on forever)
```

Finally, note that the stack used by tcsh isn't technically a classical LIFO structure because it has a side door. You might have noticed that pushd prints out the stack of directories after it's used each time. If you need to switch to a directory that's not at the top, issue pushd +*n*, where *n* is the depth of the directory you want to go to. Doing so shuffles that directory out to the top of the stack, and switches you to it.

Table 12.7 shows the complete command documentation table for pushd.

TABLE 12.7 The Command Documentation Table for pushd

Pushd	Pushes a directory onto the directory stack.
pushd [-**n**] [dir]	
pushd [-**n**] [+n] [-n]	
Adds a directory to the top of the directory stack, or rotates the stack, making the new top of the stack the current working directory. With no arguments, exchanges the top two directories and returns 0, unless the directory stack is empty.	
-**n**	Suppresses the normal change of directory when adding directories to the stack, so that only the stack is manipulated.
+n	Rotates the stack so that the *n*th directory (counting from the left of the list shown by dirs, starting with zero) is at the top.
-n	Rotates the stack so that the *n*th directory (counting from the right of the list shown by dirs, starting with zero) is at the top.
<dir>	Adds *<dir>* to the directory stack at the top, making it the new current working directory.

Table 12.8 shows the complete command documentation table for popd.

TABLE 12.8 The Command Documentation Table for popd

popd	Removes entries from the directory stack.
popd [**-n**] [+n] [-n]	
With no arguments, removes the top directory from the stack, and performs a cd to the new top directory.	
-n	Suppresses the normal change of directory when removing directories from the stack so that only the stack is manipulated.
+n	Removes the *n*th entry counting from the left of the list shown by dirs, starting with zero. For example: popd +0 removes the first directory; popd +1, the second.
-n	Removes the *n*th entry counting from the right of the list shown by dirs, starting with zero. For example: popd -0 removes the last directory; popd -1, the next to last.

Terminal Preferences and Configuration

As with most OS X GUI tools, a number of things about Terminal can be customized. Because you're probably familiar with configuring GUI apps by now, we'll just hit the highlights and give you an overview of what is configured where.

In Preferences under Terminal, shown in Figure 12.1, you configure the shell to use for interaction in the terminal. Because everything we show in this book is in bash, we recommend that you keep the default setting, `Execute the default login shell using /usr/bin/login`, rather than specifying another shell. If you do decide to specify another shell, you may find that you have to set it, close the Terminal Preferences, and try opening a new terminal window a few times. Also, here you can set Terminal to open a saved terminal settings file upon launching. You can also configure the type of terminal that Terminal claims to be. If you remember, we said that Terminal is a software version of what used to be hardware devices used to talk to machines. There were many different hardware terminal types, and they all spoke their own hardware-specific languages. This setting in the Terminal's preferences allows you to tell Terminal what type of hardware appliance to claim to be, in case the software at the other end of the communications pipe wants to take advantage of special features that a given hardware terminal appliance may have had. We recommend that you leave this with Apple's default setting unless you meet a system that claims to not know how to speak to your Terminal. A setting of VT100 or VT52 is also likely to be widely compatible.

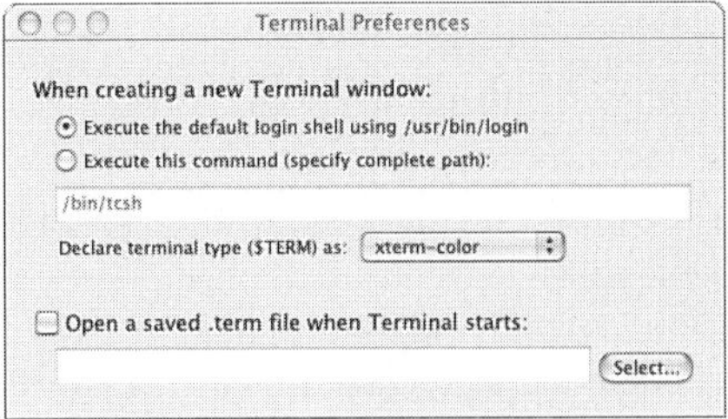

FIGURE 12.1 The shell is configured in the Terminal Preferences, located under Preferences under the Application (Terminal) menu.

Additional preferences can be chosen by selecting Window Settings under the Terminal menu, or by selecting File, Show Info under the File menu. This brings up the Terminal Inspector, where you can set the following settings via a pop-up menu:

- Shell, shown in Figure 12.2, lets you configure the behavior of the terminal window when the shell or application running in it exits. You can choose to close the window, not close the window, or only close the window if the shell exited cleanly. If you change your shell in Terminal Preferences, you see that shell listed rather than `bash`.

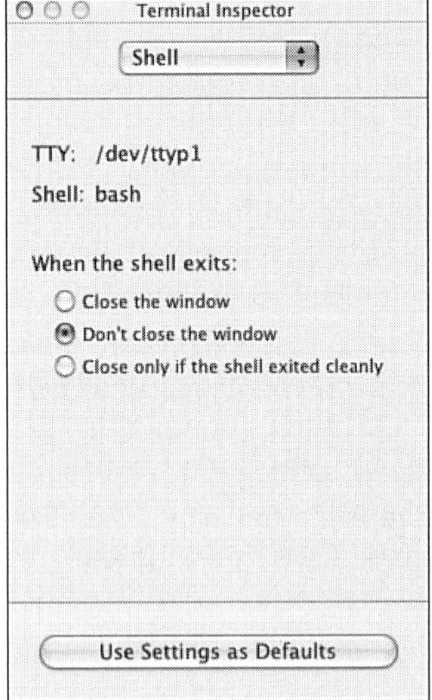

FIGURE 12.2 Under the Shell pop-up of the Terminal Inspector, the terminal's behavior upon exiting is specified.

- Processes, shown in Figure 12.3, shows you any current processes that that terminal is the parent of. As you'll learn later in this chapter, Unix commands run "in" terminals. If you were to run `ls`, which we will also see later in this chapter, `ls` would be added to the current process listing for that terminal window. Here you can also specify the behavior of a terminal window upon closing it. Because Unix commands run "in" terminals, closing a terminal when an application running "in" it is still active can have undesirable results. You can choose to have Terminal prompt you always, never, or only if commands other than the ones listed are running. You can also modify that command list.

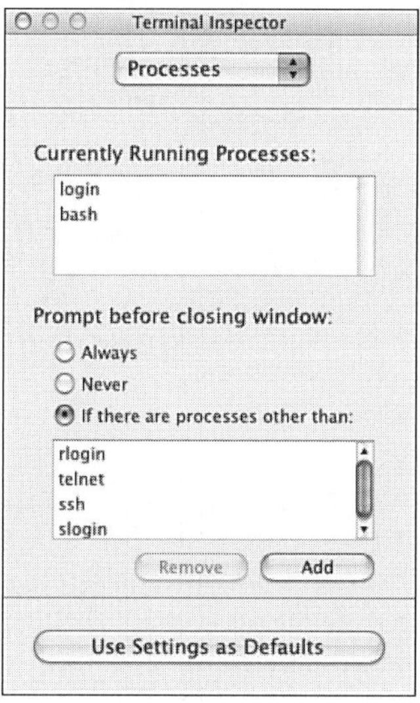

FIGURE 12.3 The Processes section of the Terminal Inspector.

- Emulation, shown in Figure 12.4, allows you to configure input and output options. You can configure a number of input options. Here you can translate between Unix newline only and Macintosh carriage return when pasting between Terminal and other applications, as well as configure several other features of the way that the Terminal emulates hardware devices. If your text gets pasted as all one line rather than multiple lines, you probably need to change the newline pasting setting. Another input option is to use Escape Non-ASCII Characters in the stream, which is to say, cause the Terminal to specially mark nonprinting characters. Whether you need to enable or disable this depends on the applications you're trying to run in the Terminal. If you get weird characters being displayed instead of formatted text, or your Terminal output is positioned oddly around the screen instead of some characters appearing, try toggling this setting. Reverse Linewrap allows you to travel back up a wrapped line, instead of backspace stopping at the left edge of the window.

Strict VT-100 Keypad Behavior emulation configures whether your numeric keypad behaves as defined for the VT-100 terminal, or whether it makes some common, but nonconforming changes in the behavior. Again, the setting you need depends on the software you run. If you get odd behavior from your keypad keys in the software you need, toggle this setting. The Audible Bell setting, as you might expect, causes "bell" events in the terminal to make a sound. The video bell flashes the terminal when the terminal bell would ring.

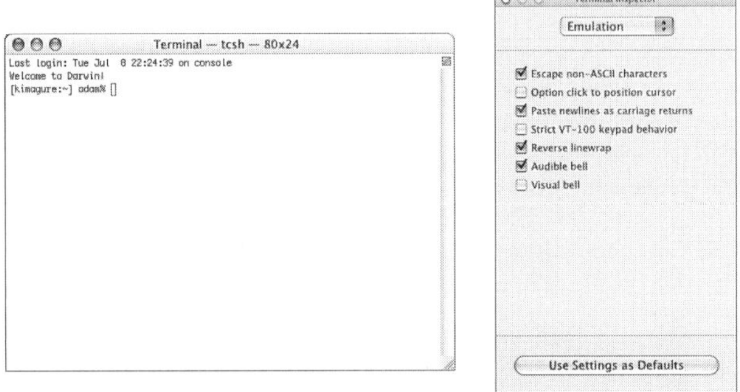

FIGURE 12.4 The Emulation section allows you to configure input and output options.

- The Buffer section of the Terminal Inspector, shown in Figure 12.5, lets you disable the scrollback buffer, or set how many lines to keep in the buffer. We suggest you use many, many lines! We couldn't live with less than a 3000-line scrollback buffer. As memory and disk space become cheaper every day, you'll probably find that you want, and can use, even more. Whether to wrap lines is your choice, as is whether you want the terminal to scroll to the bottom when you enter data into it. You can also choose whether to rewrap lines when resizing a window.
- The Display section of the Terminal Inspector, shown in Figure 12.6, lets you specify the type of cursor you want and whether it blinks. Additionally, you can configure the font. Be sure to pick a monospace font, such as Monaco or Courier, because the formatting you see in the terminal is typically based on spaces. Output, documentation, and so on will look better in the terminal. Proportional fonts are better suited for applications such as word processors. Character set encoding is also configured here. We recommend you leave it at `Unicode (UTF-8)`, because some applications require it. With the Unicode setting, however, you might see some characters translated as question marks in a diamond. For those applications, you might want to experiment with other character encoding sets. Drag and drop copy/pasting allows the terminal to interact conveniently with more traditional Macintosh programs but causes some interesting effects if you drop in text that you couldn't have typed in the Terminal.

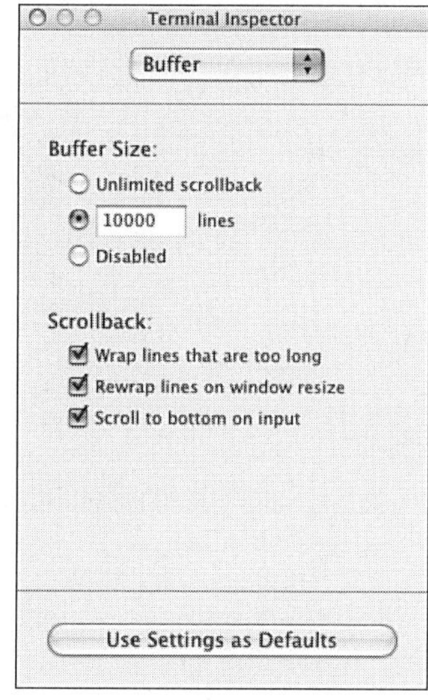

FIGURE 12.5 The Buffer section allows you to configure the scrollback buffer.

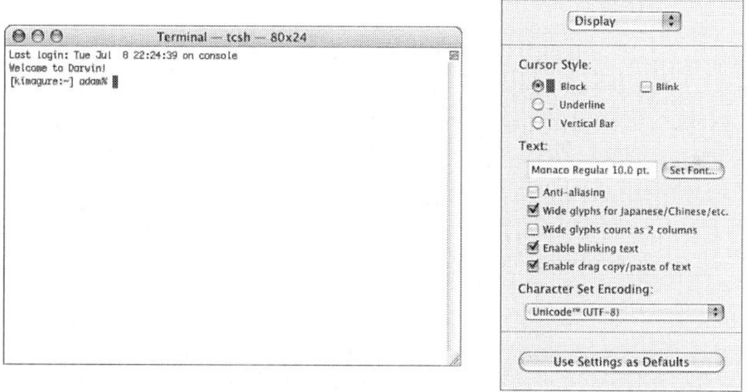

FIGURE 12.6 In the Display section you can set the cursor style, text, and character set encoding.

- The Color section, shown in Figure 12.7, lets you configure the colors of many features of the terminal, including the background and selection. Additionally, you can set a transparency level for the background and/or an image to use as the terminal background. If you find the colors that some command-line software chooses to use for its text to be annoying or unreadable, you can disable the color and force it all to nice clean black by disabling ANSI color here.

  If you want to quickly change colors in the terminal, in addition to the custom option, preset options are available: Black on white, White on black, Green on black, Black on light yellow, White on blue, or Blue on white. One of those preset color selections might bring back fond memories of your Apple IIe, or other computer.

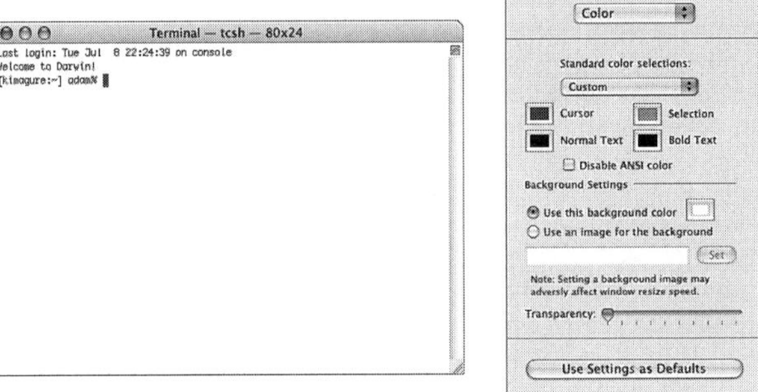

FIGURE 12.7 The Color section of the Terminal Inspector.

- The Window section, shown in Figure 12.8, lets you configure the window's dimensions by specifying the number of columns and rows displayed. You can also customize what is displayed in the title bar by giving a custom name and checking boxes for what additional data you want to have displayed, such as the shell command name, the window's dimensions, or the current process running in the terminal window.

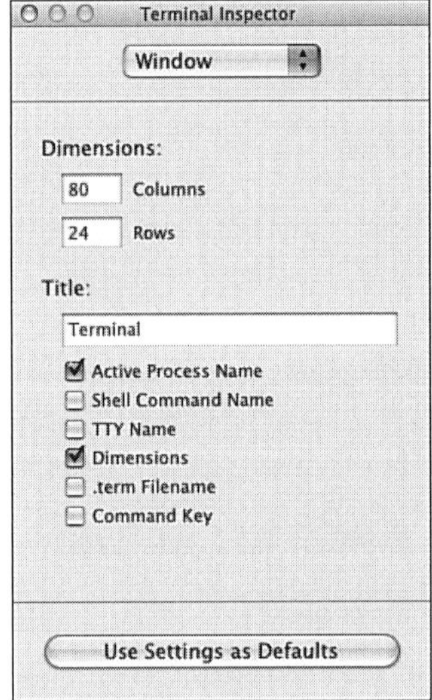

FIGURE 12.8 In the Window section you can set window dimensions and the title bar display.

- The Keyboard section, shown in Figure 12.9, lets you configure the actual data sent when you press almost any key or key combination on the keyboard. This can be handy both for customizing the keyboard to work with your software, and for finding out just what the keyboard is doing for certain key combinations when you're trying to customize other software to match it. You can also configure whether the Delete key sends Backspace (in Unix, typically deletes to the left of the cursor) or Delete (typically deletes to the right of the cursor). If you have software that requires a meta key (a virtually obsolete keyboard key once popular on some terminals), you can set the option to send the meta sequence. Typically this is not needed because almost all software that expected to see meta as a character sent from the keyboard now uses the escape key instead.

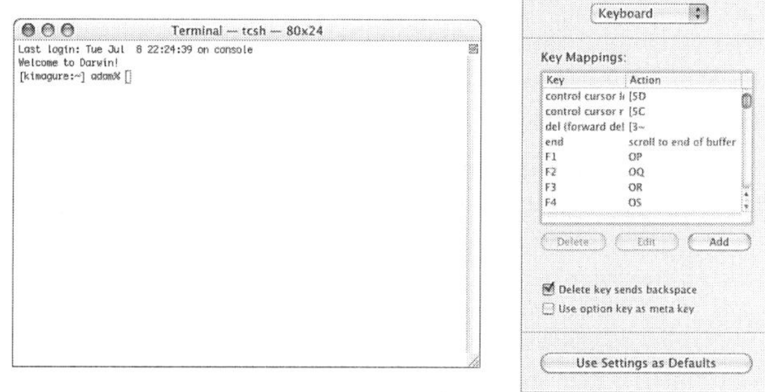

FIGURE 12.9 In the Keyboard section, you can set keyboard mappings and the behavior of Delete and Option keys in the Terminal.

The Use Settings as Default button that appears at the bottom of each item in the Terminal Inspector allows you to save those settings as your default settings, so that whenever you open a terminal, it opens with those saved settings.

The Save and Save As items are accessible from the File menu. These allow you to save the preferences of a Terminal window or window set. This could be useful, for example, for saving different colored terminals that you use for different purposes.

Open allows you to open a terminal window using settings that you saved to a `.term` file.

Also accessible are the Save Text As and Save Selected Text As items. These allow you to save the complete text buffer of the terminal, or whatever text you have selected in the terminal.

The New Command item of the File menu produces a dialog box in which you can enter a command to run in a new terminal window. If the command doesn't produce an interactive environment, the new window just tells you that the command ran, which isn't very useful. If the command is an interactive one such as `emacs` (`emacs` is a powerful text editor that you'll learn about in Chapter 15, "Command-Line Applications and Application Suites"), it produces a new window and runs the specified command in that window.

TIP

Although the New Command item might not sound particularly useful at first, this is actually a powerful tool. The point isn't to give you yet another way of running a program in a terminal, but rather to give you a way to save a preference for what program is running in a terminal. If you use the New Command to start a program in a terminal, and then Save that terminal from the File menu, you'll get a Terminal document that you can double-click and have that command executed for you. If you're constantly using a terminal to log in to another system, or to run an editor, and so on, you can save Terminal documents for each, and just double-click the saved document to launch each application in its own terminal as necessary. This becomes a real time-saver when the commands you run have many command-line options and take a long time to type without errors.

The File menu item Set Title is another way to bring up the Terminal Inspector. Of course, the Terminal Inspector comes up with the pop-up menu set to Window, but you can still navigate through the inspector.

Additionally, the File menu includes the option to send a Break signal to the terminal, which can be invaluable for stopping a program that has gone awry without taking the drastic step of closing the terminal.

Most of the items in the Edit menu are familiar. The Find item, however, leads to an option to bring up the Find panel, from which you can search for data in the Terminal's buffer.

The Font and Windows menus have the properties you already expect.

Each terminal window itself has an option to view it as a split window. Click on the icon (little square with a squiggle in it) at the upper right of the terminal window. You can adjust the vertical height of the resulting split window sections by dragging the bar. The top section stores your buffer, and the lower window generally contains your current activity. The split window may be especially useful for running an editor and using the scrollback buffer for items to copy and paste into the editor. Figure 12.10 shows an example of the split window.

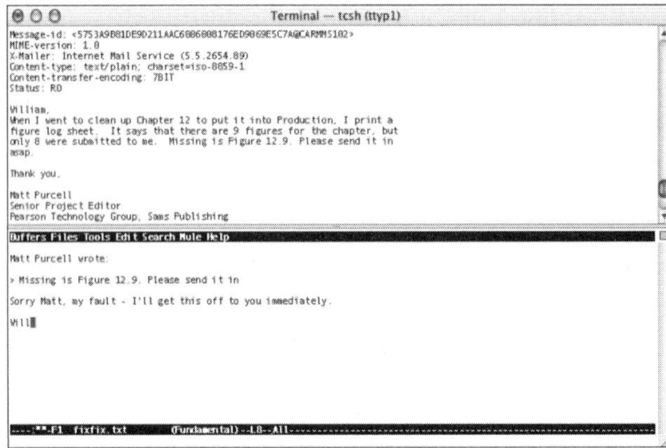

FIGURE 12.10 The Terminal window includes an option to be displayed as a split window.

Summary

In this chapter, we began the introduction to what is, for most practical purposes, a second operating system living under the hood of your OS X computer. The BSD Unix variant underlying the graphical interface to OS X is a fully featured Unix and provides a command-line interface to your operating system.

This chapter covered some of the background information that you need to know for interacting with the command line, as well as a few commands for getting around the filesystem. However, the most important thing to remember from this chapter is not the particular commands or syntax detailed here, but rather the general way that these commands work and feel. The most powerful tool in a Unix user's toolbox is an understanding of "The Unix Way." The best method of learning about Unix is by experience and experimentation. You will soon find that you can use your understanding of the way things work in Unix to rearrange and recombine examples that we've shown to synthesize new solutions.

CHAPTER 13

Common Unix Shell Commands: File Operations

IN THIS CHAPTER

- Researching Files
- Examining File Contents
- Deleting Files
- Searching for Files, Directories, and More
- File Compression and Archiving
- Summary

Having mastered navigating about the filesystem, it's now time to learn how to interact with some of the files. We'll start with basic file manipulation commands that do things such as rename files and make copies of them, and then cover more complicated things such as finding files, extracting portions of their contents, and archiving them.

As mentioned previously, Unix commands tend to be small, single-function commands that can be combined to form more complex functionality. You see this demonstrated by many commands in this chapter; their functionality might seem oddly limited, if you're not used to the Unix command philosophy. By the time you're finished with this chapter, however, you should begin to see how the commands could be fit together, and you should be able to abstract what you learn here to most Unix commands.

Rearranging Files

If you're a long-time Macintosh user, you are probably familiar with the notion of moving files about by way of the Macintosh's drag-and-drop formalism. Unix and its command line might not seem like a particularly appealing way to deal with moving files—having to type the names and paths to directories can't possibly be much fun! There's no denying that there are certain tasks for which the drag-and-drop way works much better than the command line. But, although you might not have thought about it, there are also situations in which drag-and-drop makes your life much more difficult. Interestingly, these are frequently situations in which the command line works particularly well; for example, when a folder contains many files of the same type, and you're interested in using a number of them that are related by name rather than by icon position. In a situation such as this, rearranging things in the Finder, or Shift-clicking your way through the list of files to pick the ones you want, is usually less efficient than choosing them from the command line by using a shell filename wildcard. Similarly, it's frequently faster to type a filename, if you know it, than to scroll around in a Finder window looking for the file. For these reasons, as well as conveniences that really become apparent only from experience rather than explanation, the command line makes for a useful complement to the Finder for certain operations.

Moving and Renaming Files: `mv`

Renaming files in Unix is accomplished with the `mv` (move) command. It might seem odd at first that renaming a file is accomplished by moving it, but it makes sense in the Unix philosophy of accomplishing things in simple, abstract ways. Why create two commands that do essentially the same thing, when one command can do both with the same syntax, the same way? To rename a file from one name to another, simply use `mv` *`<oldfilename> <newfilename>`*. For example, if you're in a directory with a file named `mynewfile`, and you want to rename it as `myoldfile`, you might do something like this:

```
brezup:nermal Documents $ ls
lynx    lynx.cfg  mynewfile test
brezup:nermal Documents $ mv mynewfile myoldfile
brezup:nermal Documents $ ls
lynx    lynx.cfg  myoldfile test
```

Remember that most commands can take absolute paths or relative paths to files? Well, being in the same directory and using just the filenames is using the relative paths. On the other hand, you can accomplish the same thing using the absolute paths to the files. Starting from where we left off in the previous example, this might look like the following:

```
brezup:nermal Documents $ pwd
/Users/nermal/Documents
brezup:nermal Documents $ mv /Users/nermal/Documents/myoldfile
➥/Users/nermal/Documents/myevenolderfile
brezup:nermal Documents $ ls
lynx    lynx.cfg  myevenolderfile test
```

Because you can do that, why should you need to be in the same directory as the files at all? As a matter of fact, because you can specify the full paths to the files, what is to stop you from changing something other than the filename when you use the `mv` command? What if you decide to change one of the directories in the full path while you're at it? For example, let's look at what happens if you move a file from the `Documents` directory at the same time that you change its name:

```
brezup:nermal Documents $ cd ~
brezup:nermal nermal $ ls
Desktop          Network Trash Folder   chown-output
Documents         Pictures         myfile
Library          Public          output-sample6
Movies          Sites           su-output
Music           TheVolumeSettingsFolder  typescripts
brezup:nermal nermal $ ls Documents
lynx    lynx.cfg  myevenolderfile test
brezup:nermal nermal $ mv /Users/nermal/Documents/myevenolderfile
➥/Users/nermal/Public/myolderfile
brezup:nermal nermal $ ls Documents/
lynx   lynx.cfg test
brezup:nermal nermal $ ls Public/
Drop Box  myolderfile
```


The end result is that Unix's abstraction of file access and naming causes the full path to the file to be, essentially, the full proper name of the file. "Renaming" it using the `mv` command can result in a change to any part of that name, including the parts that indicate the directory in which the file exists. See? Nothing odd about using the same syntax to rename files as used to move them about at all.

NOTE

Moving or renaming directories is exactly the same as moving or renaming files, with the exception of trying to move a directory from physical media that belongs to one disk partition or network device to media belonging to another. If you try to do this, the system warns you that you're trying to move a directory across partition boundaries and disallows the action. There's no simple way around this, so we'll cover a trick that you can use to get around this limitation of the filesystem in the section on `tar` later in the chapter. The obvious, and somewhat brute-force solution, is to do it the way it's always been done on the Mac: Copy the directory to the location on the other drive or partition and then delete the original. But this changes the modification times of the files, and you might not want that.

CAUTION

You can't create a directory structure by the action of a move command. If you try to move `/usr/local/wizbot` to `/usr/remote/wizbot`, and the directory `/usr/remote/` does not exist, the `mv` command exits and notifies you of the error.

Table 13.1 lists the syntax and primary options for mv.

TABLE 13.1 The Syntax and Primary Options for mv

mv	Moves files.
mv [-f¦-i¦-n] [-v] *<source> <target>*	
mv [-f¦-i¦-n] [-v] *<source1> <source2> <source3>* .. *<directory>*	
In the first form, mv renames *<source>* to the name provided by *<target>*. If *<source>* is a file, a file is renamed. Likewise, if *<source>* is a directory, a directory is renamed.	
In the second form, mv moves the list enumerated by *<source1> <source2> <source3>* .. to the directory named by *<directory>*.	
-f	Forces an existing file to be overwritten.
-i	Invokes an interactive mode that prompts for a confirmation before overwriting an existing file.

Creating Directories: mkdir

The mkdir command is used to create directories. The usual syntax is simple, being most commonly used as

```
mkdir <new directory name>
```

This creates a new directory named *<new directory name>* in the current directory. Full and relative paths are allowed to the new directory being specified. If the path to the directory that you are attempting to create does not completely exist, mkdir does not (by default) create the entire directory structure. For example, if you want to create /usr/local/tmp/testing/morefiles/, and the directory /usr/local/tmp/testing/ does not exist, you either have to create it before you can create /usr/local/tmp/testing/morefiles/ or use the -p option to mkdir. The -p option causes mkdir to create the entire path (if any of it's missing), as well as the final directory. This can be both a great convenience and a real nuisance. If you're an accurate typist, you don't need to issue multiple mkdir commands to create a deep directory hierarchy. On the other hand, because it creates directories that don't exist, a typo in a higher-level directory name just causes the mistyped name to be created, making typing errors annoyingly invisible when they're committed. Users new to Unix might like to add the -v flag as well so that mkdir reports what it's doing as it goes. Table 13.2 shows the syntax and primary options for mkdir.

TABLE 13.2 The Syntax and Primary Options for mkdir

mkdir	Makes directories.
mkdir [-pv] [-m *<mode>*] *<dir1> <dir2>* ...	
mkdir creates the named directories in the order specified. The permissions on the directories are controlled by the current umask.	
The user must have write permission in the parent directory.	

TABLE 13.2 Continued

`-p`	Creates all nonexistent parent directories first. If this option is not specified, the full path prefix of each operand must already exist. Intermediate directories are created with permission bits `rwxrwxrwx` (`0777`) as modified by the current `umask (2)`, plus write and execute permission for the owner.
`-m <mode>`	Sets the permission bits of the created directory to *<mode>*. *<mode>* can be in any formats specified to the `chmod (1)` utility. If a symbolic mode is specified, the operation characters + and - are interpreted relative to an initial mode of `a=rwx`.
`-v`	Be verbose about what `mkdir` is doing.

Copying Files: cp

The `cp` (copy) command functions similarly to the `mv` command, but instead of renaming a file between two locations, the `cp` command creates a duplicate of the file. The syntax is also similar, copying a file from one location to another or copying a number of files into a directory.

If our user `nermal` wants to copy some images to the `/Users/shared` directory so that all users can conveniently find the images without having to remember which user has the images, she can copy them with the `cp` command to the desired location.

Because `nermal` is new to Unix, she first decides to double-check that the images are located where she thinks they ought to be with the following:

```
brezup:nermal Documents $ ls -l Public/Drop\ Box/shar*tiff
-rw-r--r-- 1 nermal staff 872714 Apr 16 16:17 Public/Drop Box/sharing-1.tiff
-rw-r--r-- 1 nermal staff 873174 Apr 16 16:17 Public/Drop Box/sharing-2.tiff
```

Then she actually copies them and verifies that they copied:

```
brezup:nermal Documents $ cp Public/Drop\ Box/shar*tiff /Users/shared/
brezup:nermal Documents $ ls -l /Users/shared
total 3424
-rw-r--r-- 1 nermal wheel 872714 Apr 23 11:08 sharing-1.tiff
-rw-r--r-- 1 nermal wheel 873174 Apr 23 11:08 sharing-2.tiff
```

She could have copied each file individually, but `cp` can fortunately take multiple files in its arguments, so she can use `shar*tiff` to refer to both files. Note that the copies in the `/Users/shared` directory show the date that they were copied, rather than the original date. If everyone knows that the images from April 16 are the ones they need to use, they might be confused by the April 23 date. `nermal` could remove this confusion by specifying the `-p` option, which preserves as much as possible of the original modification time, user information, and so on:

```
brezup:nermal Documents $ cp -p Public/Drop\ Box/shar*tiff /Users/shared/
brezup:nermal Documents $ ls -l /Users/shared
total 3424
-rw-r--r-- 1 nermal staff 872714 Apr 16 16:17 sharing-1.tiff
-rw-r--r-- 1 nermal staff 873174 Apr 16 16:17 sharing-2.tiff
```

Note the use of the \ character to escape the space in the folder named `Drop Box` so that the shell doesn't interpret `Public/Drop` as one argument and `Box/shar*.tiff` as another.

If user `joray` has promised `nermal` some test data in a subdirectory named `tests-for-nermal` in `joray`'s home directory, `nermal` can recursively copy the test directory to her own home directory as follows:

```
brezup:nermal Documents $ cp -R ~joray/tests-for-nermal ./
```

A check shows that a directory was indeed copied:

```
brezup:nermal Documents $ ls -ld tests-for-nermal
drwxr-xr-x 9 nermal staff 262 Apr 23 11:29 tests-for-nermal
```

Not only that, but there was a directory under that directory, and `cp` copied it:

```
brezup:nermal Documents $ ls -l tests-for-nermal
total 48
-rw-r--r-- 1 nermal staff  15 Apr 23 11:29 broken
-rw-r--r-- 1 nermal staff  20 Apr 23 11:29 broken-again
-rw-r--r-- 1 nermal staff  23 Apr 23 11:29 fix
-rw-r--r-- 1 nermal staff  17 Apr 23 11:29 fix2
-rw-r--r-- 1 nermal staff 848 Apr 23 11:29 test
drwxr-xr-x 4 nermal staff  92 Apr 23 11:29 test-data
-rw-r--r-- 1 nermal staff 848 Apr 23 11:29 test2
```

You have seen just some of what you can do with `cp`. The complete syntax and options for `cp` are shown in Table 13.3, the command documentation table.

TABLE 13.3 The Command Documentation Table for `cp`

`cp`	Copies files.

`cp [-R [-H ¦ -L ¦ -P]] [-f ¦ -i] [-pv] <source> <target>`

`cp [-R [-H ¦ -L ¦ -P]] [-f ¦ -i] [-pv] <source1> <source2> .. <directory>`

In its first form, `cp` copies the contents of *<source>* to *<target>*.

In its second form, `cp` copies the contents of the list enumerated by *<source1>* *<source2>* .. to the directory named by *<directory>*. The names of the files themselves are not changed. If `cp` detects an attempt to copy to itself, that attempt fails.

TABLE 13.3 Continued

`-R`	If <*source*> is a directory, `cp` recursively copies the directory. This option also causes symbolic links to be copied, rather than indirected through. Created directories have the same mode as the corresponding source directory.
`-H`	If `-R` is specified, symbolic links on the command line are followed, but symbolic links in the tree traversal are not.
`-L`	If `-R` is specified, all symbolic links are followed.
`-P`	If `-R` is specified, no symbolic links are followed.
`-f`	Forces an existing file to be overwritten.
`-i`	Invokes an interactive mode that prompts for a confirmation before overwriting an existing file.
`-p`	Causes `cp` to retain as much of the modification time, access time, file flags, file mode, user ID, and group ID information as permissions allow.
`-v`	Be verbose about the copy process and the results.

NOTE

Apple added a bit of Apple flavor to a number of Unix command-line utilities and created a few of its own that merge the world of Apple's GUI and HFS+ filesystem with traditional Unix command-line functionality. If you've a need to copy files with resource forks (such as Classic Mac OS applications and similar files), see Chapter 32, "System Maintenance," for documentation on the *`ditto`* command. If you've installed the developer tools and have added the path `/Developer/Tools/` to your path, you also have access to `CpMac` and `MvMac`, which are Mac-resource-fork-aware versions of `cp` and `mv`, as well as a number of other resource-fork-related command-line tools.

Creating Symbolic Links: `ln`

Sometimes it is useful to link a name with a particular file or directory. This can be done with the `ln` command. It is especially useful for administrative purposes, but even a regular user might need to link a filename or directory name to some other particular name. The best way to do this is to use a symbolic link. The simplest syntax for making a symbolic link is

```
ln -s <source> <target>
```

Because the syntax is similar to the basic `cp` syntax, you won't have much trouble remembering it.

You might be wondering just what sort of use you might have for symbolic links. An instance in which you might use a symbolic link is for your Web site. Suppose that you are using a Web editing suite that uses `home.html` for the default name for the main page of your Web site. Suppose, however, that your Web server is set to read only files named `index.html` as the default page for a directory. If you use `home.html`, you might have to give out something like `http://ryoohki.biosci.ohio-state.edu/~nermal/home.html` as your URL. If, on the other hand, your `home.html` file were really called `index.html`, you could give out a slightly shorter URL instead: `http://ryoohki.biosci.ohio-state.edu/~nermal/`.

What could you do to get an `index.html` file in your directory if your Web editing suite won't create one? And how could you keep it conveniently updated to match `home.html`? Well, as you just saw, you could copy `home.html` to `index.html`. But the next time you edited `home.html`, you would then have to remember to copy `home.html` to `index.html` when you were finished. Although you might be good about remembering to do that, you undoubtedly will eventually forget, probably when it matters most. If you simply link `index.html` to `home.html`, every time you update `home.html`, you don't have to remember to do anything else! To create the symbolic link, do the following:

```
brezup:nermal public_html $ ln -s home.html index.html
```

A quick check shows us that `index.html` is now a link to `home.html`.

```
brezup:nermal public_html $ ls -l
total 16
-rw-r--r-- 1 nermal staff 52 Apr 23 11:56 home.html
lrwxr-xr-x 1 nermal staff  9 Apr 23 11:56 index.html -> home.html
```

NOTE

You need to set your Apache Web server `followsymlinks` option for symbolic links to work properly as shown. See Chapter 27, "Web Serving," for information on how to do this.

A common administrative use for symbolic links is to move a directory from one partition to another, while leaving the path that a user would use to get to the directory the same. This makes the change that the administrator has made transparent to the user for most purposes. An example of this follows. On this machine, `obup`, the `/usr` partition was getting full, so the local directory of `/usr/local` was moved to a partition named `/home`. After the directory was moved, the `/usr/local` directory was replaced with a symbolic link that points to `/home/local`.

```
obup:joray / $ ls -l /usr/local
lrwxrwxrwx  1 root   other  11 Mar 20 1997 /usr/local -> /home/local
```

If a user changes to the `/usr/local` directory and then checks her location with `pwd`, she finds the following:

```
obup:joray / $ cd /usr/local
obup:joray local $ pwd
/home/local
```

So, as the user might have grown to expect, she can still cd to /usr/local but without having to know any of the "administrivia" behind its actual location.

Table 13.4 shows the syntax and primary options for ln.

TABLE 13.4 The Syntax and Primary Options for ln

ln	Makes links.
ln [-fhinsv] *<source>* *<target>*	
ln [-fhinsv] *<source1>* *<source2>* *<source3>* .. *<directory>*	
In the first form, ln links *<source>* to *<target>*. If *<target>* is a directory, a link named *<source>* is placed in *<target>*.	
In the second form, ln makes links to the files enumerated by <source1> *<source2>* *<source3>* .. in *<directory>*. The links have the same names as the sources in the list.	
There are two types of links: hard links and symbolic links. The default is hard links. A hard link to a file is indistinguishable from the original entry. Hard links may not normally refer to directories and may not span filesystems. Although infrequently necessary, hard link properties make them ideal for creating what are essentially duplicate "real" names for a given file, where the properties of an "alias-like" name are not sufficient.	
A symbolic link refers by name to the file to which it is linked. Symbolic links may refer to directories and may span filesystems.	
-f	Forces the link to occur by unlinking any already existing links.
-h	If *<target>* or *<directory>* is a symbolic link, it is not followed.
-s	Creates a symbolic link—this is most like the idea of aliases, with which you're already familiar.

Changing Modification Times and Creating Empty Files: touch

The touch command is used to update the last-modified time for a file. This command also has the side effect of creating a new, empty file, if the file that you attempt to touch does not exist.

Neither of these functionalities probably sounds particularly interesting at the outset, but, in fact, they both have good uses. For example, most archiving and backup software is frequently configured to back up only files that have changed since the last backup. Using touch on a file makes it appear to have been changed, which results in it being flagged for backup. Because the touch command can be quickly applied from the command line to a large number of files, it allows you to conveniently force some files to be backed up without having to open and resave each in its parent applications.

Creating empty files doesn't have much use at the command line but turns out to be useful when you start writing programs in the shell scripting language (see Chapter 18, "Advanced Unix Shell Use: Configuration and Programming (Shell Scripting)"). In this case, multiple simultaneously running scripts can be made to talk to each other by the creation of empty files known as *flag files*—essentially the electronic equivalent of a script raising a flag to tell another script that something has happened.

To create a new (empty) file with touch, or to update the modification date of the file to the current time, the syntax for the touch command is simply

```
touch <filename to modify>
```

The touch command can actually update files to have any modification time that you want, although the preceding is by far the most common usage. Table 13.5 shows the syntax and options for touch.

TABLE 13.5 The Command Documentation Table for touch

touch	Changes file access and modification times.
touch [-acfhm] [-r <file>] [-t [[CC]YY]MMDDhhmm[.SS]] <file> ...	
touch sets modification and access times of files to the current time of day. If the file does not exist, it is created with default permissions.	
-a	Changes the access time of the file.
-c	Does not create the file if it does not exist.
-f	Attempts to force the update, even if file permissions do not currently permit it.
-h	If <file> is a symbolic link, changes access and/or modification time of the link.
-m	Changes the modification time of the file.
-r <file>	Replaces access and modification time with that of <file> instead of using the current time.
-t	Changes the access and modification time to the specified time.

Examining File Contents

Moving around the filesystem, and moving files around the filesystem, isn't all that interesting if you can't look at what's in the files. Unix provides a number of facilities for examining the contents of files, and frequently these are more convenient to use than their graphical counterparts. BBEdit, for example, is a wonderful text editor, and it's light enough in memory footprint to load quickly. However, if you want to see whether the file you're thinking about deleting is really the file you mean to delete, and the information is readily apparent by looking at the beginning of the text, there are much more efficient ways to examine the contents from the command line than starting up a GUI program just to glance at the file.

Looking at the Contents of Files: cat, more, less

Now that you have learned a little bit about how to list and copy your files, it is time to learn how to examine the contents of your files.

`cat` reads files and displays their contents. In this example, you see that `myfile` is short.

```
brezup:nermal Documents $ cat myfile
Hi. this is nermal.

I hope you enjoyed myfile.
```

If the file were longer, it would keep scrolling by on the screen either until you pressed Ctrl-C to break the process or the file came to an end.

It might seem odd that anyone would want a program that just dumped all the output to the terminal, with no convenient way to slow it down or page through it. However, this is part of the Unix philosophy. The `cat` command reads files and sends their contents to the terminal. (Actually, `cat` sends their contents to `STDOUT`, a way of connecting commands that you'll learn more about in Chapter 18. `STDOUT` just happens to be connected to the terminal, unless you tell the command line otherwise.) In the Unix way of doing things, it is the job of some other program to provide a paged display of data.

Table 13.6 shows the complete syntax and primary options for `cat`.

TABLE 13.6 The Syntax and Primary Options for `cat`

`cat`	Concatenates and prints files.
`cat [-nbsvetu] <file1> <file2> ...`	
`cat [-nbsvetu] [-]`	
`cat` reads files in sequential, command-line order and writes them to standard output. A single dash represents standard input.	
`-n`	Numbers all output lines.
`-b`	Numbers all output lines, except blank lines.
`-s`	Squeezes multiple adjacent empty lines, causing single-spaced output.
`-v`	Displays nonprinting characters. Control characters print as `^X` for Control-X; delete prints as `^?`; non-ASCII characters with the high bit set are printed as `M-` (for meta) followed by the character for the low 7 bits.

You could also use `cat` to read the contents of longer files. However, the contents of your file scroll quickly. If you hope to read the contents as they appear, it would be better to use `more`, which also reads and displays files, but it pauses the display after a screenful.

The contents of `nermal`'s short file look the same when viewed with `more`:

```
brezup:nermal Documents $ more myfile
Hi. this is nermal.

I hope you enjoyed myfile.
```

With a longer file, though, more pauses after a screenful:

```
brezup:nermal Documents $ more /var/log/system.log
Sep 11 16:00:54 localhost syslogd: restart
Sep 11 16:00:54 localhost syslogd: kernel boot file is /mach_kernel
Sep 11 16:00:54 localhost kernel: /IOFireWireSBP2LUN/com_apple_driver_LSI_FW_
➥500/IOSCSIPeripheralDeviceNub/IOSCSIPeripheralDeviceType00/I
OBlockStorageServices/IOBlockStorageDriver/Maxtor
➥1394 storage Media/IOApplePartitionScheme/untitled@3
Sep 11 16:00:54 localhost kernel: BSD root: disk1s3, major 14, minor 9
Sep 11 16:00:54 localhost kernel: HFS: created HFBT on Maxtor 38 GB HD
Sep 11 16:00:56 localhost kernel: Jettisoning kernel linker.
.
.
.
Sep 11 16:01:13 localhost kernel: obtaining ID
Sep 11 16:01:13 localhost kernel: from Registry
Sep 11 16:01:13 localhost kernel: ATIRage128: using AGP
Sep 11 16:01:15 localhost lookupd[136]: lookupd
➥(version 322) starting - Thu Sep 11 16:01:15 2003
Sep 11 16:01:17 localhost diskarbitrationd[106]:
➥disk1s3 hfs  E14C9FFC-2328-3ACB-98DC-EA27AD8B1880 Maxtor 38 GB HD   /
Sep 11 16:01:17 localhost SystemStarter: Welcome to Macintosh.
Sep 11 16:01:17 localhost kernel: UniNEnet: Ethernet address 00:30:65:aa:37:ae
Sep 11 16:01:17 localhost kernel: IOFireWireIP:
➥FireWire address 00:30:65:ff:fe:aa:37:ae
/var/log/system.log (3%)
```

In this display, we can see at the bottom of the screen that we are looking at a file called system.log, and that we have viewed about 3% of the file. After we are finished looking at that screenful, we can press the spacebar and look at the next screenful of text. The most common syntax you will use for more is

```
more <filename>
```

Another way of looking at files with a paged view is by using the command less. less started off live as a more advanced pager that was named as a Unix-style pun on more. Now, more is actually just an alternative functionality of the less executable, and traditional more isn't included as an independent application. more and less have traditionally had several differences in their behaviors, and the new less appliction preserves these differences when it's invoked under each name.

For example, more traditionally scrolls data off the top of the screen when you press the spacebar to move to the next page, and less traditionaly erases the screen and repaints it with the new page of data. This difference may not seem significant at first, but it means that in `more`, you can scroll back to something that's earlier in the file by using Terminal's scrollbar. In `less` on the other hand, things don't accumulate in the scroll buffer. If your terminal type supports it, though, `less` erasees the screen back to what it was before you ran `less`, when it exits, leaving no mess from the pager in your Terminal window or buffer at all.

Another difference is that `more` traditionally exits after hitting the bottom of the file, whereas `less` traditionally remains in the pager, allowing you to issue in-pager searches and move throughout the file even after it's hit bottom.

`less`'s commands are based both on traditional `more` and `vi`, a text editor examined in Chapter 15, "Command-Line Applications and Application Suites." Although `less` is frequently thought of as a command, it has enough complex functionality for the user who wants it, that `less` might be better called an *application*. The fact that it is most frequently used for its command-like capabilities leads to its inclusion here.

The appearance of `less` output is similar to that from `more`:

```
brezup:nermal Documents $ less system.log
Sep 11 16:00:54 localhost syslogd: restart
Sep 11 16:00:54 localhost syslogd: kernel boot file is /mach_kernel
Sep 11 16:00:54 localhost kernel: /IOFireWireSBP2LUN/com_apple_driver_LSI_FW_
➥500/IOSCSIPeripheralDeviceNub/IOSCSIPeripheralDeviceType00/I
OBlockStorageServices/IOBlockStorageDriver/Maxtor
➥1394 storage Media/IOApplePartitionScheme/untitled@3
Sep 11 16:00:54 localhost kernel: BSD root: disk1s3, major 14, minor 9
Sep 11 16:00:54 localhost kernel: HFS: created HFBT on Maxtor 38 GB HD
Sep 11 16:00:56 localhost kernel: Jettisoning kernel linker.
.
.
.
Sep 11 16:01:13 localhost kernel: obtaining ID
Sep 11 16:01:13 localhost kernel: from Registry
Sep 11 16:01:13 localhost kernel: ATIRage128: using AGP
Sep 11 16:01:15 localhost lookupd[136]: lookupd
➥(version 322) starting - Thu Sep 11 16:01:15 2003
Sep 11 16:01:17 localhost diskarbitrationd[106]:
➥disk1s3  hfs   E14C9FFC-2328-3ACB-98DC-EA27AD8B1880 Maxtor 38 GB HD     /
Sep 11 16:01:17 localhost SystemStarter: Welcome to Macintosh.
Sep 11 16:01:17 localhost kernel: UniNEnet: Ethernet address 00:30:65:aa:37:ae
Sep 11 16:01:17 localhost kernel: IOFireWireIP:
➥FireWire address 00:30:65:ff:fe:aa:37:ae/var/log/system.log
```

Like `more`, `less` pauses after a screenful. At the bottom, we also see that the file is called `system.log`, but it is not displaying the percentage of the file that we have examined.

The most common syntax you will use for `less` is

```
less <filename>
```

`less` is powerful. The most important thing to remember about `less` is how to invoke help, which can be done by issuing either `less -?` or `less --help`. Depending on how your shell interprets a question mark, you might have to try `-\?` or `"-\?"` for help. The man page is overwhelming, but the `--help` option is easy to read and organized nicely. Some of the highlights from the output of the `--help` option are included in Table 13.7.

Many options are available in `less`, and there is much that you can do after you are in `less`. Table 13.7 shows the syntax for `less`, as well as some basic information on movement and pattern searching in `less`. More detailed documentation is available in Appendix A.

TABLE 13.7 The Command Documentation Table for `less`

`less` Opposite of `more`.

Pages through data or text files.

```
less -?
less --help
less -V
less --version
less [-[+]aBcCdeEfFgGiIJmMnNqQRrsSuUVvwX~][-b <space>][-h <lines>][-j <line>] [-k
<keyfile>] [--{oO} <logfile>] [-p <pattern>][-t <tag>] [-T <tagsfile>] [-x <tab,...>]
[-y <lines>] [-[-z] <lines>][-# <shift>][+[+]<cmd>] [--] [<file1>...]
```

Summary of `less` Commands

Commands marked with * may be preceded by a number, *N*.

Notes in parentheses indicate the behavior if *N* is given.

h	H					Display this help.
q	:q	Q	:Q	ZZ		Exit.

MOVING

e	^E	j	^N	CR	*	Forward one line (or *N* lines).
y	^Y	k	^K	^P	*	Backward one line (or *N* lines).
f	^F	^V	SPACE		*	Forward one window (or *N* lines).
b	^B	ESC-v			*	Backward one window (or *N* lines).
z					*	Forward one window (and set window to *N*).
w					*	Backward one window (and set window to *N*).
ESC-SPACE					*	Forward one window, but don't stop at end-of- file.

TABLE 13.7 Continued

d	^D		* Forward one half-window (and set half-window to *N*).
u	^U		* Backward one half-window (and set half-window to *N*).
ESC-(	RightArrow		* Left 8 character positions (or *N* positions).
ESC-)	LeftArrow		* Right 8 character positions (or *N* positions).
F			Forward forever; like "tail -f".
r	^R	^L	Repaint screen.
R			Repaint screen, discarding buffered input.

Default "window" is the screen height.
Default "half-window" is half of the screen height.

SEARCHING

/pattern	* Search forward for (*N*-th) matching line.
?pattern	* Search backward for (*N*-th) matching line.
n	* Repeat previous search (for *N*-th occurrence).
N	* Repeat previous search in reverse direction.

JUMPING

g	<	ESC-<	* Go to first line in file (or line *N*).
G	>	ESC->	* Go to last line in file (or line *N*).
p	%		* Go to beginning of file (or *N* percent into file).

13

Looking at Portions of the Contents of Files: head, tail

Sometimes, however, you need to see only a portion of a file, rather than the entire contents. To see only portions of a file, use either head or tail. As the names suggest, head displays the first few lines of a file, whereas tail displays the last few lines of a file.

Let's look at the first few lines of system.log:

```
brezup:joray log $ head system.log
Sep 11 16:00:54 localhost syslogd: restart
Sep 11 16:00:54 localhost syslogd: kernel boot file is /mach_kernel
Sep 11 16:00:54 localhost kernel: /IOFireWireSBP2LUN/com_apple_driver_LSI_FW_
➥500/IOSCSIPeripheralDeviceNub/IOSCSIPeripheralDeviceType00/
➥IOBlockStorageServices/IOBlockStorageDriver/Maxtor 1394 storage ➥Media/IOAp-
plePartitionScheme/untitled@3
Sep 11 16:00:54 localhost kernel: BSD root: disk1s3, major 14, minor 9
Sep 11 16:00:54 localhost kernel: HFS: created HFBT on Maxtor 38 GB HD
```

```
Sep 11 16:00:56 localhost kernel: Jettisoning kernel linker.
Sep 11 16:01:02 localhost kextd[86]: registering service
➥"com.apple.KernelExtensionServer"
Sep 11 16:01:03 localhost kernel: Resetting IOCatalogue.
Sep 11 16:01:04 localhost kernel: Matching service count = 0
Sep 11 16:01:08 localhost kernel: AppleRS232Serial:
➥0    0 AppleRS232Serial::start - returning false early, Connector or
➥machine incorrect
brezup:joray log $
```

Nothing other than the first few lines of the file is displayed. Because head is not a pager, we do not see the name of the file displayed at the bottom of the screen, and the system prompt returns immediately when head is finished displaying its output. Table 13.8 shows the complete syntax and options for head.

TABLE 13.8 The Syntax and Options for head

head	Displays the first lines of a file.
head [-n *<number>*] *<file1> <file2>* ...	
head [-n *<number>*]	
-n <number>	Displays the first *<number>* of lines. If *n* is not specified, the default is 10.

tail behaves in the same way as head, except that only the last few lines of a file are displayed, as you see in this sample:

```
brezup:joray log $ tail system.log
Sep 16 11:31:32 localhost sshd[891]:
➥Accepted password for sageray from 192.168.1.4 port 2260 ssh2
Sep 16 22:58:32 localhost xinetd[329]:
➥service ssh, IPV6_ADDRFORM setsockopt() failed: Protocol not available
➥(errno = 42)
Sep 16 22:58:32 localhost xinetd[329]:
➥START: ssh pid=906 from=192.168.1.4
Sep 16 22:58:52 localhost sshd[906]:
➥Accepted password for sageray from 192.168.1.4 port 2272 ssh2
Sep 16 23:54:18 localhost xinetd[329]:
➥service ssh, IPV6_ADDRFORM setsockopt() failed: Protocol not available
➥(errno = 42)
Sep 16 23:54:18 localhost xinetd[329]:
➥START: ssh pid=1004 from=192.168.1.4
Sep 16 23:54:25 localhost sshd[1004]:
➥Accepted password for sageray from 192.168.1.4 port 2274 ssh2
Sep 16 23:58:42 localhost xinetd[329]:
➥service ssh, IPV6_ADDRFORM setsockopt() failed: Protocol not available
➥(errno = 42)
```

```
Sep 16 23:58:42 localhost xinetd[329]:
➥START: ssh pid=1010 from=192.168.1.4
Sep 16 23:58:49 localhost sshd[1010]:
➥Accepted password for sageray from 192.168.1.4 port 2275 ssh2
```

Table 13.9 shows the complete syntax and options for `tail`.

TABLE 13.9 The Syntax and Options for `tail`

`tail`	Displays the last part of a file.
`tail [-f ¦ -F ¦ -r] [-b <number> ¦ -c <number> ¦ -n <number>] <file>`	
`-f`	Waits for and displays additional data that `<file>` receives, instead of stopping at the end of the file.
`-F`	Similar to `-f`, except that every five seconds, `tail` checks whether `<file>` has been shortened or moved.
`-r`	Displays the file in reverse order, by line. This option also modifies the `-b`, `-c`, and `-n` options to specify the number of units to be displayed, rather than the number of units to display from the beginning or end of the input.
`-b <number>`	Specifies location in number of 512-byte blocks.
`-c <number>`	Specifies location in number of bytes.
`-n <number>`	Specifies location in number of lines.

If *<number>* begins with +, it refers to the number of units (512-byte blocks, bytes, or lines) from the beginning of the input. If *<number>* begins with – or no explicit sign, it refers to the number of units from the end of the input.

Deleting Files

Removing files and removing directories with Unix are fairly straightforward tasks, so you need to know only two commands to accomplish them.

Removing Files and Directories: `rm`, `rmdir`

Now that you have filled up your directory with many files, it is time to learn how to clean it up a bit. You can remove a file with `rm`.

Our user `nermal` has decided that her file called `myfile` is no longer needed. To remove it, she does the following:

```
brezup:nermal Documents $ ls -l myfile
-rw-r--r-- 1 nermal staff 51 Apr 12 15:11 myfile
brezup:nermal Documents $ rm myfile
remove myfile? Y
```

As you notice in this example, `rm` prompts for confirmation before removing the file. Your system might not be configured to make `rm` prompt you for the removal of files. You can cause `rm` to ask for confirmation by aliasing `rm` to `rm -i`. Aliasing is a technique covered in more depth in Chapter 18. For now, you want to add either the first or second lines that follow to the `.bashrc` file or `.cshrc` file in your home directory (the first if you're using `bash`, and the second if you're using `tcsh`). Alternatively, you could add them to `/etc/bashrc` or `/etc/csh.cshrc` to make the change for all users of your system.

For `bash`:

```
alias rm='rm -i'
```

For `tcsh`:

```
alias rm 'rm -i'
```

We highly recommend that you follow these instructions to make your `rm` command interactive at the first possible opportunity. After you're a seasoned Unix user, you're welcome to run with `rm` in noninteractive mode by default; but until you've been sure that you're ready a long, long time, it's probably safest to have it operate interactively by default.

CAUTION

Okay, so perhaps suggesting that you put something like a few years of Unix experience under your belt before using `rm` in the noninteractive mode is a bit facetious and silly. On the other hand, I don't think I know a single long-time Unix user who *hasn't* entered an `rm` command, pressed Return, and then felt his stomach bounce off the floor as he realized that the reason the command didn't return immediately was because it was currently deleting his entire filesystem. I've seen this happen to seasoned system administrators, so I really do want to stress that with `rm`, overconfidence can be deadly.

Our user `nermal` has also decided that she is finished with the data that she copied from user `joray`'s directory and that she wants to remove the entire directory. The easiest way to do this is to force `rm` to recursively remove the directory, using options `-r` for recursive, and `-f` to override the interactive mode she has enabled by default, as shown here:

```
brezup:nermal Documents $ ls -ld tests-for-nermal
drwxr-xr-x 9 nermal staff 262 Apr 23 11:29 tests-for-nermal
brezup:nermal Documents $ rm -rf tests-for-nermal
[localhost:~] nermal% ls -ld tests-for-nermal
ls: tests-for-nermal: No such file or directory
```

Removing a directory and all its contents using the recursive and force options to `rm` is easy, but it is also silent and very fast. Remember to use those options only when you really mean it. Double-check everything before you run it. As you can see in the example, there is no recourse if you type the wrong thing.

Table 13.10 shows the syntax and primary options for `rm`.

TABLE 13.10 The Syntax and Primary Options for `rm`

`rm`	Removes directory entries.
`rm [-dfiPRrvW] <file1> <file2> ...`	
`-f`	Forces the removal of files without prompting the user for confirmation. The `-f` option overrides any previous `-i` options.
`-i`	Invokes an interactive mode that prompts for confirmation before removing a file. The `-i` option overrides any previous `-f` options.
`-d`	Attempts to remove directories as well as other types of files.
`-R`	Attempts to recursively remove files. Implies `-d` option.
`-W`	Attempts to undelete files. This option can be used to recover only files covered by whiteouts.

`rm` removes symbolic links, but not the files referenced by the links.

Attempting to remove the files (directories) `.` and `.` is an error, though you can remove the directory that you're currently in by using other valid names for it. If you do this, you'll find that many shell commands suddenly don't work. You can usually rescue the situation by issuing a `cd ~/` command.

There is also a command available for removing directories: `rmdir`. Unfortunately, it is only useful for removing empty directories. Table 13.11 shows its complete syntax and options.

TABLE 13.11 The Command Documentation Table for `rmdir`

`rmdir`	Removes directories.
`rmdir [-p] <directory1> <directory2> ...`	
`rmdir` removes each `<directory>` argument specified, provided it is empty. Arguments are processed in the order listed on the command line. To remove a parent directory and subdirectories of the parent directory, the subdirectories must be listed first.	
`-p`	Attempts to remove the specified directory and its parent directories, if they are empty.

Searching for Files, Directories, and More

Unix traditionally has provided useful tools for searching for files by name and content, and Apple has expanded on these by making available a command-line interface into the same databases that the Finder uses to locate files. Unix's traditional tools don't work from a database like the Finder's file searching function does, so they run more slowly. On the other hand, they aren't hampered by needing a database to run, or by being only as current in their results as the last database update.

Finding Files: `locate`, `find`

Sometimes you want to find some files, but you are not sure where they are. Two tools are available to search for files: `locate` and `find`. If you know some of the name of a file, you can use the `locate` utility to try to find it.

For example, our user `nermal` looked earlier at a file called `system.log`. Does our machine have other files that have `log` in their name? You bet! The syntax for `locate` is

```
locate <pattern>
```

We encourage you to try the `locate` command for files with `log` in them (`locate log`) to see the output, but it is much too long to include here. `locate` searches a database of pathnames on the machine.

> **NOTE**
>
> If you try `locate log` and produce no output, it's because your machine hasn't generated the database of paths yet. This database starts off empty and is automatically rebuilt once a week. We've provided an example of how to force the database to be built in Chapter 1, "Panther System Elements." Also, if you're particularly adventurous, you will find what you need to know to build it by hand in the `/etc/weekly` script, but this is a bit more complex than a novice will want to face.

Further information on `locate` is shown in the command documentation table, Table 13.12.

TABLE 13.12 The Command Documentation Table for `locate`

`locate`	Finds files.
`locate` *<pattern>*	
Searches a database for all pathnames that match *<pattern>*. The database is rebuilt periodically and contains the names of all publicly accessible files.	
Shell and globbing characters (`*`, `?`, `\`, `[`, and `]`) may be used in *<pattern>*, although they must be escaped. Preceding a character by `\` eliminates any special meaning for it. No characters must be explicitly matched, including `/`.	
As a special case, a pattern with no globbing characters (`foo`) is matched as (`*foo*`).	
Useful files:	
`/var/db/locate.database`	Database
`/usr/libexec/locate.updatedb`	Script to update database

A more powerful and more ubiquitous tool for finding files is `find`. It is much slower than the `locate` command because it actually searches the filesystem every time it's used instead of consulting a database, but that also means that it doesn't depend on a database for its information and the information is always completely up-to-date.

After running her search for files containing `log` in the name, our sample user `nermal` was overwhelmed by the results. However, she thinks that she might have heard that general system log files might be located in `/usr` or `/var`. To check whether what she recalls is correct, she decides to run `find`:

```
brezup:nermal Documents $ find /var /usr -name \*log\* -print
/usr/bin/grep-changelog
/usr/bin/logger
/usr/bin/login
/usr/bin/logname
/usr/bin/rcs2log
/usr/bin/rlog
/usr/bin/rlogin
/usr/bin/slogin
/usr/bin/xmlcatalog
/usr/include/httpd/http_log.h
/usr/include/libxml2/libxml/catalog.h
/usr/include/php/ext/standard/php_ext_syslog.h
/usr/include/php/main/logos.h
/usr/include/php/main/php_logos.h
/usr/include/php/main/php_syslog.h
/usr/include/sys/syslog.h
/usr/include/syslog.h
/usr/lib/pam/pam_nologin.so
/usr/lib/ruby/1.6/tkdialog.rb
.. there's a mess o' files in the middle here,
.. none of which are system.log, trust us!
/usr/share/vim/vim62/syntax/catalog.vim
/usr/share/vim/vim62/syntax/changelog.vim
/usr/share/vim/vim62/syntax/debchangelog.vim
/usr/share/vim/vim62/syntax/logtalk.vim
/usr/share/vim/vim62/syntax/lprolog.vim
/usr/share/vim/vim62/syntax/prolog.vim
/usr/share/vim/vim62/syntax/purifylog.vim
/usr/share/vim/vim62/syntax/rcslog.vim
/usr/share/vim/vim62/syntax/verilog.vim
/usr/share/zsh/4.1.1/functions/_logical_volumes
/usr/share/zsh/4.1.1/functions/_rlogin
/usr/X11R6/bin/xlogo
```

```
/usr/X11R6/include/X11/bitmaps/xlogo11
/usr/X11R6/include/X11/bitmaps/xlogo16
/usr/X11R6/include/X11/bitmaps/xlogo32
/usr/X11R6/include/X11/bitmaps/xlogo64
/usr/X11R6/lib/X11/doc/html/xlogo.1.html
/usr/X11R6/lib/X11/xedit/lisp/progmodes/xlog.lsp
/usr/X11R6/man/man1/xlogo.1
brezup:nermal Docuements $
```

In the preceding statement, `nermal` searches `/usr` and `/var`. The results, though, do not include the `system.log` file that `nermal` knows user `joray` was looking at earlier. According to these results, many files in `/usr` contain `log`, but nothing in `/var`. This seems slightly odd—so many files (some of them not even really "log" files, but just containing "log" in their names) in the filesystem below one directory, but nothing in the other. `nermal` is sure that `/var` is the other possibility she has heard for a location for the file, so perhaps there's something about `/var` that's different, and the reason nothing at all shows up isn't because nothing's there, but rather because it isn't being searched. It turns out that if you look

```
brezup:nermal Documents $ ls -l /var
lrwxrwxr-t 1 root admin 11 Sep 17 23:47 /var -> private/var
```

`/var` is actually a symbolic link to another directory. If you read `find`'s man page, you'll discover that in its default behavior, `find` won't traverse symbolic links. Adding `-H`, as one of the options for `find` causes it to return information on the referenced file (target of the link), rather than for the link itself:

```
brezup:nermal Documents $ find -H /var -name \*log\* -print
find: /var/backups: Permission denied
find: /var/cron: Permission denied
find: /var/db/dhcpclient: Permission denied
find: /var/db/netinfo/local.nidb: Permission denied
find: /var/db/openldap/openldap-data: Permission denied
find: /var/db/openldap/openldap-slurp: Permission denied
find: /var/db/shadow: Permission denied
/var/log
/var/log/cups/access_log
/var/log/cups/error_log
/var/log/ftp.log
/var/log/httpd/access_log
/var/log/httpd/error_log
/var/log/install.log
/var/log/ipfw.log
/var/log/lastlog
```

```
/var/log/lookupd.log
/var/log/lpr.log
/var/log/mail.log
/var/log/netinfo.log
/var/log/secure.log
/var/log/system.log
/var/log/windowserver.log
find: /var/root: Permission denied
find: /var/run/sudo: Permission denied
/var/run/syslog
/var/run/syslog.pid
find: /var/spool/cups: Permission denied
find: /var/spool/mqueue: Permission denied
find: /var/spool/postfix/active: Permission denied
find: /var/spool/postfix/bounce: Permission denied
find: /var/spool/postfix/corrupt: Permission denied
find: /var/spool/postfix/defer: Permission denied
find: /var/spool/postfix/deferred: Permission denied
find: /var/spool/postfix/flush: Permission denied
find: /var/spool/postfix/hold: Permission denied
find: /var/spool/postfix/incoming: Permission denied
find: /var/spool/postfix/maildrop: Permission denied
find: /var/spool/postfix/private: Permission denied
find: /var/spool/postfix/public: Permission denied
find: /var/vm/app_profile: Permission denied
```

There, in the middle of that output, is the `system.log` file, as well as some additional files with `system.log` in their name. As we see from the output, `nermal` does not have permission to search everywhere, but `find` responds with information for areas where permissions permit it. `nermal` was lucky that her machine's logs appear to include `log` in the name. That is not the case on all systems.

Numerous options are available in `find`. In addition to being able to search on a pattern, `find` can also run searches based on ownership, file modification times, file access times, and much more. Table 13.13 shows the complete syntax and some useful options for `find`. Complete documentation is available in Appendix A.

TABLE 13.13 The Syntax and Primary Options for `find`

`find`	Finds files.

`find [-H ¦ -L ¦ -P] [-EXdsx] [-f` *<file>*`]` *<file>* `...` *<expression>*

`find` recursively descends the directory tree of each file listing, evaluating an *<expression>* composed of primaries and operands.

TABLE 13.13 Continued

Options	
-E	Causes find to interpret regular expression patterns specified with -regex or -iregex as standard modern regular expressions, rather than as basic regular expressions (BREs). See re_format(7) manual page for a description of each format.
-P	Causes the file information and file type returned for each symbolic link to be those of the link itself. This is the default.
-d	Causes a depth-first traversal of the hierarchy. In other words, directory contents are visited before the directory itself. The default is for a directory to be visited before its contents.
-x	Excludes find from traversing directories that have a device number different from that of the file from which the descent began.
-f	Specifies a file hierarchy for find to traverse. File hierarchies may also be specified as operands immediately following the options listing.
Primaries (Expressions)	
All primaries that can take a numeric argument allow the number to be preceded by +, -, or nothing. *n* takes on the following meanings: +*n* More than *n* -*n* Less than *n* n Exactly *n*	
-atime *n*	True if the file was last accessed *n* days ago. Note that find itself changes the access time.
-ctime *n*	True if the file's status was changed *n* days ago.
-mtime *n*	True if the file was last modified *n* days ago.
-newer *XY* <*file*>	True if the current file has a more recent last access time (X=a), change time (X=c), or modification time (X=m) than the last access time (Y=a), change time (Y=c), or modification time (Y=m) of file. In addition, if Y=t, then file is instead interpreted as a direct date specification of the form understood by cvs(1).
-name <*pattern*>	True if the file or directory name matches <*pattern*>. Pattern may include standard shell globbing wildcards such as *, but the shell gets to expand these characters before find gets a hold of them. This means that if you find / -name *.log, the search will actually be for all files beneath the root directory that have the *same name as* files in your *current* directory that end in .log. If you want to find all files that end in .log, not just ones that also occur in your current directory, you need to escape the wildcard so that it isn't interpreted by the shell, and so that it gets passed on for find to work with when it searches. This can be accomplished as shown in the earlier examples by preceding characters that the shell would expand with a \ character (that is, -name *.log would search for all files ending in .log). It is also possible in recent versions of the bash shell and find to use double quotes around a wildcarded string to keep it from expanding in the shell (that is, -name "*.log" should be equivalent to -name *.log).

TABLE 13.13 Continued

`-iname <pattern>`	True if the filename or directory name matches `<pattern>` in a case-insensitive way.
`-exec <command> [<argument> ...];`	True if `<command>` returns a zero-value exit status. Optional arguments may be passed to `<command>`. The expression must be terminated by a semicolon. If `{}` appear anywhere in the command name or arguments, they are replaced by the current pathname.
`-fstype`	True if the file is contained in a filesystem specified by `-fstype`.

Finding Files with Specific Contents: grep

Trying to remember what you've named a file that you need can sometimes be a real chore, especially if you haven't used the file for a long time, or its name is similar to many other files on your system. For situations such as these, it is useful to be able to search for files based on patterns contained within the contents of the files themselves, rather than just the filenames. The basic syntax for grep is

```
grep <pattern> <files>
```

Here is a sample of using grep:

```
brezup:joray Documents $ grep me file*
grep: file1: Permission denied
file2:It's me. Doing some
file3:Yep, me again..
file4:me again
file5:Another test by me...
```

In the preceding statement, we see that grep provides output as permissions permit. We also see that the default output lists only the file, the filename, and lines containing the searched pattern. A number of options are available in grep. For example, we could ask grep to list the line numbers on which our pattern, me, appears in the files:

```
brezup:joray Documents $ grep -n me file*
grep: file1: Permission denied
file2:2:It's me. Doing some
file3:2:Yep, me again..
file4:6:me again
file5:1:Another test by me...
```

Another available option is the recursive option, for descending a directory tree searching all the contents.

The grep command is even more powerful than might be immediately apparent because it is also useful for searching for patterns in the output of other commands. It could, for example, have been used to filter the rather verbose output from the preceding finds, to print out only the specific lines containing exact matches to the filename of interest. Although we haven't gotten to the syntax of the more complex matter of chaining Unix commands together to make sophisticated commands, keep `grep` in mind as a building block, and consider its possible uses when you reach the end of Chapter 14, "Advanced Shell Concepts and Commands."

Table 13.14 shows the syntax and primary options for `grep`.

TABLE 13.14 The Syntax and Primary Options for `grep`

`grep`
`egrep`
`fgrep`
	Prints line matching a pattern.

`grep [options] <pattern> <file1> <file2> ...`	
`grep [options] [-e <pattern> ¦ -f <file>] <file1> <file2> ...`	
`grep` searches the list of files enumerated by `<file1> <file2> ...`, or standard input if no file is specified or if `-` is specified. By default, the matching lines are printed.	
Two additional variants of the program are available as `egrep` (same as `grep -E`) or fgrep (same as `grep -F`).	

`-C <num>`
`-<num>`
`--context[=<num>]`
	Prints <*num*> lines of output context. Default is 2.

`--binary-files=<type>`	Assumes a file is type <*type*> if the first few bytes of a file contain binary data. Default <*type*> is binary, and `grep` normally outputs a one-line message indicating the file is binary, or nothing if there is no match. If <*type*> is without-match, it is assumed that a binary file does not match. Equivalent to `-I` option. If <*type*> is text, it processes the file as though it were a text file. Equivalent to `-a` option. Warning: Using this option could result in binary garbage being output to a terminal, some of which could be interpreted by the terminal as commands, resulting in unwanted side effects.
`-c` `--count`	Prints a count of matching lines for each file. Combined with `-v`, counts nonmatching lines.
`-v` `--invert-match`	Inverts matching to select nonmatching lines.
`-r` `--recursive`	Recursively reads files under directories. Equivalent to `-d` recurse option.
`-f <file>` `--file=<file>`	Reads a list of patterns from `<file>`, which contains one pattern per line. An empty file has no patterns and matches nothing.
`-e <pattern>` `-regexp=<pattern>`	Uses `<pattern>` as the pattern. Useful for protecting patterns beginning with `-`.

TABLE 13.14 Continued

`-G` `--basic-regexp`	Interprets *<pattern>* as a basic regular expression. This is the default behavior.
`-E` `-extended-regexp`	Interprets *<pattern>* as an extended regular expression. Equivalent to `egrep`.
`-F` `--fixed-strings`	Interprets *<pattern>* as a list of fixed strings, separated by newlines, any of which is to be matched. Equivalent to `fgrep`.
`-i` `--ignore-case`	Ignores case in *<pattern>* and input files.
`-n` `--line-number`	Output includes the line number where the match occurs.
`-s` `--no-messages`	Suppresses error messages about nonexistent or unreadable files.
`-w` `--word-regexp`	Selects only lines that have matches that form whole words.
`-x` `--line-regexp`	Selects only those matches that exactly match the whole line.

File Compression and Archiving

As in the Macintosh world, a number of standards have arisen in the Unix world for compressing and archiving files. Unlike the Mac world, however, these programs don't tend to be do-all programs such as StuffIt that can archive, compress, password-protect, and perform a wealth of other useful file archive functions. Following the Unix tradition, software that compresses files mostly just compresses files. Software that collects many files together into a single-file archive mostly just collects many files together into a single-file archive. There are a few exceptions, and some more recent (and some would say misquided) implementations of Unix utilities try to stuff everything but the kitchen sink into their functionality. Primarily though, functions are kept usefully separated into distinct commands and their functionality combined when needed. For example, the functions of file collection and file compression are used together to collect files into an archive (uncompressed) and then subsequently used to compress the files into a compressed archive. Likewise, the analogous procedure to "UnStuffIting" a file traditionally requires two steps in Unix because decompression of the archive and unpacking of its contents are two separate steps.

TIP

For those looking for a more seamless solution than the Unix way, take heart. The newer versions of BSD's`tar` program also include compression/decompression facilities. It's not an awfully Unix-like way to do things, but if you insist on the convenience, we won't hold it against you.

NOTE

Every now and then, you'll find a tar file that won't untar properly, complaining of permission errors writing files, or just plain refusing to read properly. This is sometimes caused by incompatibility between some special features available in the GNU (GNU stands for GNU's Not Unix, and is the operating moniker for software developed or supported by the Free Software Foundation—the pioneers of the Open Source movement) version of tar (now found on OS X 10.3), and the BSD version of tar (found on earlier versions of OS X, and many other Unix platforms).

Your best course of action is to complain to the package's author and get them to tar the data up without using either the BSDtar or GNUtar special options. Alternatively, you could choose to install BSDtar on your machine, but if you do, make sure that you install it as bsdtar, or some other name that won't conflict with the default system tar. Each flavor is unique enough that it will cause problems with software installations if an installer script thinks it's talking to one flavor tar, and it's really the other that's assumed its name.

This, by the way, is a perfect example of why it's a bad idea to start adding "special functionality" routines to a program with a simple purpose such as tar. The result is files that are no longer universally exchangeable, and software versions that are a nightmare to try to keep in sync.

Compressing and Decompressing Files: compress, gzip, uncompress, gunzip, zcat, bzip2, bunzip2, bzcat, bzip2recover

Unix has various tools available for compressing and decompressing files. Compressing files, of course, causes them to take up less space. As drive space becomes cheaper, this is perhaps not as great a concern. However, if you will be transferring files over the network, smaller files transfer faster. In addition, you might find it useful to compress files—especially archives of software packages you have installed—for writing to CD-ROM, where space is limited.

compress and gzip are the compressing tools available on your system; uncompress and gunzip are the decompression tools. compress and uncompress are more widely available by default on systems. The gzip tool, however, can compress further than compress.

Software packages that you download are frequently distributed as files compressed by compress or gzip. Files that you download ending in .Z are files compressed with compress. Files ending in .gz are compressed with gzip. Decompress files ending in .Z with uncompress; decompress files ending in .gz with gunzip. You also occasionally see files ending in .tgz, which is the result of shoehorning .tar.gz (for tar archive, compressed with gzip) into a three-letter file extension). There's also a zcat utility that performs a function analogous to cat, only it decompresses the files before writing them to standard output (STDOUT). zcat operates on both gzip .gz and compress .Z files.

Here is a sample of compressing a file using gzip:

```
brezup:miwa source $ ls -l sendmail-src.tar
-rw-r--r--  1 miwa class 4454400 Jul 6 2000 sendmail-src.tar
brezup:miwa source $ gzip -9 sendmail.8.10.2-src.tar
```

```
brezup:miwa source $ ls -l sendmail.8.10.2-src.tar*
-rw-r--r--  1 miwa class 1250050 Jul 6 2000 sendmail-src.tar.gz
```

As we see from the preceding `ls` listing, the size of the file has been reduced, and `.gz` has been appended to the filename. Table 13.15 shows the syntax and options for `compress` and `uncompress`. Table 13.16 shows the syntax and primary options for `gzip` and `gunzip`.

TABLE 13.15 The Command Documentation Table for `compress` and `uncompress`

`compress`	Compresses data.
`uncompress`	Expands data.
`compress [-cfv] [-b <bits>] <file1> <file2> ...`	
`uncompress [-cfv] <file1> <file2> ...`	
`compress` reduces the size of a file and renames the file by adding the `.Z` extension. As many of the original file characteristics (modification time, access time, file flags, file mode, user ID, and group ID) are retained as permissions allow. If compression would not reduce a file's size, the file is ignored. `uncompress` restores a file reduced by `compress` to its original form and renames the file by removing the `.Z` extension.	
`-c`	Writes compressed or uncompressed output to standard output without modifying any files.
`-f`	Forces compression of a file, even when compression would not reduce its size. Additionally, forces files to be overwritten without prompting for confirmation.
`-v`	Prints the percentage reduction of each file.
`-b <bits>`	Specifies the upper-bit code limit. Default is `16`. Bits must be between `9` and `16`. Lowering the limit results in larger, less compressed files.

TABLE 13.16 The Command Documentation Table for `gzip`, `gunzip`, and `zcat`

`gzip`	Compresses or expands files.
`gunzip`	
`zcat`	
`gzip [-acdfhlLnNrtvV19] [-S <suffix>] <file1> <file2> ...`	
`gunzip [-acfhlLnNrtvV] [-S <suffix>] <file1> <file2> ...`	
`zcat [-fhLV] <file1> <file2> ...`	
`gzip` reduces the size of a file and renames the file by adding the `.gz` extension. It keeps the same ownership modes and access and modification times. If no files are specified, or if the filename is specified, standard input is compressed to standard output. `Gzip` compresses regular files but ignores symbolic links.	
Compressed files can be restored to their original form by using `gunzip`, `gzip -d`, or `zcat`.	
`gunzip` takes a list of files from the command line, whose names end in `.gz`, `-gz`, `.z`, `-z`, `_z`, or `.Z`, and which also begin with the correct magic number, and replaces them with expanded files without the original extension. `gunzip` also recognizes the extensions `.tgz` and `.taz` as short versions of `.tar.gz` and `.tar.Z`, respectively. If necessary, `gzip` uses the `.tgz` extension to compress a `.tar` file.	

TABLE 13.16 Continued

zcat is equivalent to gunzip -c. It uncompresses either a list of files on the command line or from standard input and writes uncompressed data to standard output. Zcat uncompresses files that have the right magic number, whether or not they end in .gz.

Compression is always formed, even if the compressed file is slightly larger than the original file.

-d	Decompresses.
--decompress	
--uncompress	
-f	Forces compression or decompression, even if the file has multiple links, if the corresponding file already exists, or if the compressed data is read from or written to a terminal. If -f is not used, and gzip is not working in the background, the user is prompted before a file is overwritten.
-h	Displays a help screen and quits.
--help	
-r	Traverses the directory structure recursively.
--recursive	If a filename specified on the command line is a directory, gzip/gunzip descends into the directory and compresses/decompresses the files in that directory.
-S <*suffix*>	Uses <*suffix*> instead of .gz. Any suffix can be used, but we recommend that suffixes other than .z and .gz be avoided to avoid confusion when transferring the file to another system.
--suffix <*suffix*>	A null suffix (-S ") forces gunzip to try decompression on all listed files, regardless of suffix.
-t	Test. Checks the integrity of the compressed file.
--test	
-<*n*>	Regulates the speed of compression as specified by -<*n*>, where -1 (or --fast) is the fastest compression method (least compression) and -9 (or --best) is the slowest compression method (most compression). Default compression option is -6.
--fast	
--best	

A relatively recent compression utility is the bzip2 package, developed to provide better compression, data protection, and recovery capabilities, and to eliminate patent and licensing conflicts that have arisen over some aspects of other compression utilities. The bzip2 package is used much like gzip and gunzip, compressing with bzip2, and decompressing with bunzip2, and typically using files suffixed with .bz2. There is also a bzcat (nope, no 2) utility that is the equivalent of cat, only uncompressing the file as it is catted. Because the bzip2 compression standard compresses data into independent blocks, partial data can be recovered from bzip2 files that have been corrupted or truncated. The bzip2recover program is used to read damaged .bz2 files and recover what data is still extractable from them. The command documentation table for bzip2, bunzip2, bzcat, and bzip2recover is shown in Table 13.17.

TABLE 13.17 The Command Documentation Table for bzip2 and bunzip2

bzip2, bunzip2	Block-sorting file compressor, v1.0.2
bzcat	Decompresses files to stdout.
bzip2recover	Recovers data from damaged bzip2 files.
bzip2 [-hcdfkqstvzVL123456789] [*<filename1>* *<filename2>* ...]	
bunzip2 [-fkvsVL] [*<filename1>* *<filename2>* ...]	
bzcat [-s] [*<filename1>* *<filename2>* ...]	
bzip2recover *<filename>*	
bzip2, bunzip2, and bzcat are really the same program. The decision about what actions to take is done on the basis of which name is used.	
bzip2 compresses files using the Burrows-Wheeler block sorting text compression algorithm and Huffman coding.	
bzip2 expects a list of filenames to accompany the command-line flags. Each file is replaced by a compressed version of itself, with the name *<original_name>*.bz2. Each compressed file has the same modification date, permissions, and, when possible, ownership as the corresponding original so that these properties can be correctly restored at decompression time.	
If no filenames are specified, bzip2 compresses from standard input to standard output.	
bzip2 reads arguments from the environment variables BZIP2 and BZIP, in that order, and processes them before reading any arguments from the command line. Chapter 18 provides an in-depth discussion of how to set and use environment variables to control your software.	
Compression is always performed, even if the compressed file is slightly larger than the original.	
bunzip2 (or bzip2 -d) decompresses files. Files not created by bzip2 are detected and ignored, and a warning is issued. Filenames are restored as follows:	
<filename>.bz2 *<filename>*	
<filename>.bz *<filename>*	
<filename>.tbz2 *<filename>*.tar	
<filename>.tbz *<filename>*.tar	
<anyothername> *<anyothername>*.out	
Supplying no filenames causes decompression from standard input to standard output.	
bzcat (or bzip2 -dc) decompresses all specified files to standard output.	
bzip2recover is a simple program whose purpose is to search for blocks in .bz2 files and write each block out into its own .bz2 file. You can then use bzip2 -t to test the integrity of the resulting files and decompress those that are undamaged.	
Bzip2recover takes a single argument, the name of the damaged file, and writes a number of files, rec00001file.bz2, rec00002file.bz2, and so on, containing the extracted blocks. The output filenames are designed so that the use of wildcards in subsequent processing—for example, bzip2 -dc rec*file.bz2 > recovered_data—processes the files in the correct order.	
-h	Displays a help menu.
--help	
-d	Forces bzip2 to compress.
--decompress	
-f	Forces overwrite of output files. Normally, bzip2 does not over-

TABLE 13.17 Continued

`--force`	write existing output files. Also forces `bzip2` to break hard links to files, which it otherwise doesn't do. `bzip2` normally declines to decompress files that don't have the correct magic header bytes. If forced (`-f`), however, it passes such files through unmodified. This is how GNU `gzip` behaves.
`-k` `--keep`	Keeps (doesn't delete) input files during compression or decompression.
`-t` `--test`	Checks integrity of the specified file(s), but doesn't decompress them.
`-z` `--compress`	Forces compression, regardless of the invocation name.
`-1 (or --fast) . -9 (or --best)`	Sets block size to `100k . 900k`. The `--fast` and `--best` aliases are primarily for GNU `gzip` compatibility. In particular, `--fast` doesn't make things significantly faster. `--best` merely selects the default behavior.

Archiving Files: tar

`tar` is a useful tool for archiving files. Although originally intended for archiving to tape, `tar` is commonly used for archiving files or directories of files to a single file. After you have the archive file, it is common to compress it for further storage or distribution.

The most common options that you will probably use with `tar` are `-c` for creating a file, `-t` for getting a listing of the contents, `-x` for extracting the file, `-f` for specifying a file to create or act on, and `-v` for verbose output.

Here is an example of looking at the contents of a `tar` file. It is often useful to look at the contents of a `tar` file before extracting it. Because a `tar` file can be an archive of files rather than an archive of a directory of files, it is helpful to see the contents. That way, you know whether you should create a separate directory for extracting the file so that you have its contents in one place, or whether it will create a directory into which the files will be extracted.

Although not all the output is shown in this example, you can see nonetheless that the archive creates a directory into which the files are extracted:

```
brezup:nermal source $ tar -tvf sendmail.8.10.2-src.tar

drwxr-xr-x 103/700     0 2000-06-07 13:01 sendmail-8.10.2/
-rw-r--r-- 103/700   795 1999-09-27 17:39 sendmail-8.10.2/Makefile
-rwxr-xr-x 103/700   327 1999-09-23 17:31 sendmail-8.10.2/Build
-rw-r--r-- 103/700   321 1999-02-06 22:21 sendmail-8.10.2/FAQ
-rw-r--r-- 103/700  1396 1999-04-04 03:01 sendmail-8.10.2/INSTALL
```

```
-rw-r--r-- 103/700  8923 1999-11-17 13:56 sendmail-8.10.2/KNOWNBUGS
-rw-r--r-- 103/700  4116 2000-03-03 14:24 sendmail-8.10.2/LICENSE
-rw-r--r-- 103/700  23017 1999-11-23 14:08 sendmail-8.10.2/PGPKEYS
-rw-r--r-- 103/700  13703 2000-03-16 18:46 sendmail-8.10.2/README
-rw-r--r-- 103/700 348392 2000-06-07 03:39 sendmail-8.10.2/RELEASE_NOTES
drwxr-xr-x 103/700     0 2000-06-07 13:00 sendmail-8.10.2/devtools/
...
```

Table 13.18 shows the syntax and options for `tar`.

TABLE 13.18 The Command Documentation Table for `tar`

`gnutar` `tar`	Tape archiver; manipulates "`tar`" archive files

`gnutar [[-]bundled-options Args] [gnu-style-flags] [filenames ¦ -C directory-name] ...`

`tar` is short for "tape archiver," so named for historical reasons; the `gnutar` program creates, adds files to, or extracts files from an archive file in `gnutar` format, called a tarfile. A tarfile is often a magnetic tape but can be a floppy diskette or any regular disk file.

The first argument word of the `gnutar` command line is usually a command word of bundled function and modifier letters, optionally preceded by a dash; it must contain exactly one function letter from the set A, c, d, r, t, u, x, for append, create, difference, replace, table of contents, update, and extract. The command word can also contain other function modifiers, some of which take arguments from the command line in the order they are specified in the command word. Functions and function modifiers can also be specified with the GNU argument convention (preceded by two dashes, one function or modifier per word). Command-line arguments that specify files to add to, extract from, or list from an archive may be given as shell pattern matching strings.

Functions (Exactly one of the following must be specified)

`-A`
`--catenate`
`--concatenate`
	Appends the contents of named file, which must itself be a `gnutar` archive, to the end of the archive (erasing the old end-of-archive block). This has the effect of adding the files contained in the named file to the first archive, rather than adding the second archive as an element of the first.

`-c` `--create`	Creates a new archive (or truncates an old one) and writes the named files to it.

`-d`
`--diff`
`--compare`
	Finds differences between files in the archive and corresponding files in the filesystem.

`-r` `--append`	Appends files to the end of an archive.
`-t` `--list`	Lists the contents of an archive.

TABLE 13.18 Continued

-u --update	Appends the named files if the on-disk version has a modification date more recent than their copy in the archive (if any).
-x --extract --get	Extracts files from an archive. The owner, modification time, and file permissions are restored, if possible.
Selected Options	
--overwrite	Overwrites existing files when extracting.
-O --to-stdout	Extracts files to standard output.
--owner=<*name*>	Forces <*name*> as owner for added files.
--group=<*name*>	Forces <*name*> as group for added files.
--atime-preserve	Doesn't change access times on dumped files.
-m --modification-time	Doesn't extract file modified time.
--same-owner	Tries extracting files with the same ownership.
--no-same-owner	Extracts files as yourself.
-f *[<hostname>:]<file>* --file=*[<hostname>:]<file>*	Read or write the specified file (default is /dev/sa0). If a hostname is specified, gnutar uses rmt(8) to read or write the specified file on a remote machine. - may be used as a filename, for reading or writing to/from stdin/stdout.
-[0-7][lmh]	Specifies drive and density.
-M --multi-volume	Creates/lists/extracts multivolume archive.
-L <*num*> --tape-length=<*num*>	Changes tape after writing <*num*> x 1024 bytes.
-F <file> --info-script=<*file*> --new-volume-script=<*file*>	Runs script at end of each tape (implies -M).
-X <*file*> --exclude-from=<*file*>	Excludes patterns listed in <*file*>.
-N <*date*> --newer=<*date*> --after-date=<*date*>	Only stores files newer than <*date*>.
--newer-mtime=<*date*>	Only stores files with modification time newer than <*date*>.
--help	Prints help information; then exits.

TIP

StuffIt Expander can decompress/unzip/ungzip a file and then untar it for you, if you prefer to drag and drop your file archiving tasks. It's not as flexible with respect to what it extracts from an archive, and there are some problems with long filenames, but it's quick and convenient in some situations.

Summary

This chapter introduced the most common Unix command-line file manipulation commands. Commands to copy, move, delete, search, and display files, as well as archive and compress files were covered. You will most likely type at least one command from this chapter, or the Chapter 12, "Introducing the BSD Subsystem," for every other command or application that you invoke from the Unix command line.

These commands also provide a good introduction to the Unix concept of small, single-function commands. What you've learned here about how a task can be accomplished the Unix way should serve you well in determining how to use other Unix commands that we don't have the time to cover in such depth.

PART V

Advanced Command-Line Concepts

IN THIS PART

CHAPTER 14

Advanced Shell Concepts and Commands

IN THIS CHAPTER

- Introduction to File Permissions
- Process Management
- Communication Between Processes: Redirection, Pipes

Now that we've covered the use of some of the most common Unix commands and their individual options and quirks, it's time to step back and examine some of the factors that affect the use of all shell commands.

In this chapter, we'll cover the Unix permission system, whereby you can control who is allowed to access your files, and what access rights they have.

We'll also cover process management from the command line, including how to identify and terminate processes that are causing problems for you.

Finally, we'll cover one of the most powerful shell formalisms, the notion of input and output redirection. This formalism is the root of much of the real power of the Unix command line. You should think about how commands that you've already learned might be enhanced by what you learn in that section.

Because process management and input/output control are intimately linked to the shell itself, there are some differences between how you do these things that depend on the shell you've picked. Fortunately, the capabilities of both `csh` and `sh`-type shells are similar with respect to basic process and input/output control, so the differences are mostly cosmetic.

Introduction to File Permissions

This section expands on the topic of file permissions, which was introduced in the section on the `ls` command in Chapter 12, "Introducing the BSD Subsystem." It's likely that you won't have an immediate use for modifying file permissions, and it's possible that you'll never need to deal with them at all. However, if you want to work with other users on the same system, or decide to start writing your own programs, understanding the permission system will be necessary.

NOTE

A subset of the Unix file permission system can be accessed from the OS X Finder. These are controlled from the `Get Info` window `permissions` tab, as detailed in Chapter 3, "Applications and Utilities."

Read, Write, and Execute

Permissions are specified as a collection of three flags. These flags (also called *bits*) control whether data in the file may be read, written, and executed. Unix takes these flags literally. So, if you have a program and you unset its execute flag, you won't be able to run the program—the system simply won't understand that the program is executable. Likewise, if you set the execute flag for a file containing a word processor document, Unix will assume that the file contents are a program and try its best to run the file. This is unlikely to do anything but produce an error message.

In the case of directories, the same bits apply, but the meanings are slightly different. The read and write bits control whether the contents of the directory may be read, and whether the directory can be written to, respectively. The execute bit, however, controls whether the directory can be `cd`ed to, or otherwise moved into by a shell or program.

The permissions for whether a directory listing can be read or written to are separate from the permission that controls whether you, or programs, can move into it. Also, the permissions for files contained in the directory do not necessarily need to agree with the permissions of the directory. The significance of this might not be immediately apparent, but the meaning is literal. If you have files that have world read permission turned on, you can put them in a directory and set the bits on the directory so that the files in it can be read, but the files can't be listed. Likewise, you can set the permissions so that the directory allows anyone on the system to write files into it, but nobody can read the files or list the contents.

The execute permission for directories interacts with the read and write permission for files in it, in a slightly nonintuitive fashion. Read permission for the directory allows you to read the directory listing but not the files. Read permission for a file in the directory allows you to read the file but not list the directory. However, to be able to read the file, you—or rather the software you're using to read the file—need to be able to go into the directory. Because of this, if you turn on read permission for a directory and not execute permission, you can list the directory but not read the files, no matter what the permissions on the files are. Likewise, you (or software under your control) can't write into a directory with only write permission turned on; execute permission must be enabled as well.

If you know that the file `fizbin` exists in the directory `thozbot`, but read permission is turned off for `thozbot` and execute permission is turned on, you can still read `fizbin` (assuming that you have read permission on `fizbin` itself) by using its full or relative path from outside the `thozbot` directory. If you don't know that `fizbin` exists in the directory, there's no way for you to find out because you can't enter the directory or list the contents.

NOTE

Interesting applications for separated directory/file permissions immediately spring to mind. For example, perhaps you want to have a "drop box" directory where people could leave you files, but could not snoop around and see or read what anyone else had written. A directory with permissions set to write and execute only would accomplish this.

Alternatively, a directory set to execute permission only, containing files with read permission enabled, would allow you to distribute files privately from a directory. With this setup, you could use one directory to distribute different files to a number of people privately, by giving each person only the filenames of the files he is allowed to read. Nobody can list the contents of the directory, but a person can read files from it, if he knows the correct filenames.

Owner, Group, and World

Adding a layer of complexity to the permission system, the read, write, and execute permissions detailed earlier can be specified separately for three subsets of users. They can be set for each owner of the file, the group owner of the file, and the world.

The owner of a file is, as the name implies, the user who owns the file. Each file on a Unix system has information stored about it that indicates to which user account the file belongs. Files that you create automatically belong to your user ID. Other files on the system belong to other users, or to one of the system accounts that exist to help the operating system keep its processes sorted out and secure.

Files have an additional piece of ownership information: the group ownership of the file. The group ownership specifies, by group name, a collection of users who share the group permissions to the file. This additional information facilitates the sharing of information among more than one user. Creating groups and controlling their membership are covered in Chapter 11, "Additional System Components."

Finally, there is a set of permission bits that control the access level enjoyed by the world, or at least all the other users on the system. If you provide any sort of guest access to your machine, it's best to assume that the file's world permissions do in fact apply to just about everyone, independent of location.

TIP

Remember that the permissions allowed each type of user, owner, group, and world do not need to be the same. If you want to allow your friends to look at the data in your daily calendar file and the correlated data in your address/contacts file, you can set permissions on these files so that you (the user) can read and write them, but the group to which your friends belong can only read them. You might even want to let the world read the contents of your schedule, so you could turn on read access for the world for it. However, you probably don't want the world picking through your personal address book, so you could shut off all access from the world by turning off all three flags for the world on that file.

Extended Bits

In addition to the read, write, and execute bits for each file and directory, a few additional bits exist as well. These bits are typically used by system administrators, but they occasionally come in handy for other users.

The complete set of bits, including the extended bits, that control the permissions and properties of a file or directory are called the *mode bits* for the file.

Special Flags

Further extending the classical set of mode bits is a set of special flags. These are definitely not for use by anyone but the administrator, but are mentioned here because one particular bit can sneak up and bite you.

The most important of these for you to watch out for is the immutable flag. This flag is set by the Finder's locked status for a file. It's not currently clear why Apple chose this particular flag to map to the Finder's locked status, but it causes a few problems on the Unix side. Specifically, if you set a file's immutable flag, it becomes almost impossible to change that file in any way. It can't be modified, it can't be overwritten, it can't be deleted—it becomes, as the name implies, immutable. Although Apple's tech notes indicate that there is a way to override the immutable flag and remove the file, as of this writing, this does not seem to work for system immutable flags set through the `chflags` command (detailed later in this chapter).

Checking the Permissions: `ls -l`

Remember that the `ls -l` command shows you the permissions associated with files. To find out the permissions associated with a single file, give it a filename to list:

```
brezup:ray testing $ ls -l /etc/passwd
-rw-r--r-- 1 root wheel 1374 29 Jul 14:15 /etc/passwd
```

Controlling Permissions: `chmod`

After you are comfortable examining the permissions of files, you'll probably want to be able to change them. This is accomplished with the `chmod` (change mode) command. This command operates in either a "fully specified mode bits" manner, or in a "change this specific mode bit" manner, depending on the arguments you give it on the command line.

The "change this specific mode bit" form is the more friendly of the two, and works by allowing you to specify a bit to change, how to change it, and which type of user to change it for. The complete syntax for this form of the command is

```
chmod <u|g|o|a><+|-><r|w|x> <filename> ...
```

To use it, simply do the following:

1. Choose whether you want to change the permissions for the user (yourself), the group, or the world. If you want to change the user, the first argument is u; g is for group; and o is for other (world).
2. Choose whether you want to add, delete, or absolutely specify a permission. If you want to add a permission, follow your first argument with a + sign; if you want to remove a permission, follow it with a - sign; otherwise, to set the permissions to an absolute value, use a = sign.
3. Indicate the permission or permissions you want to add, delete, or set, using r for read, w for write, and x for execute. Follow these by the names of the files or directories for which you want to change the permissions.

You might also use an a to indicate all, in place of the u, g, or o argument, if you want to make the change for the file to all three user types.

For example, consider a file named fizbin with the current permission set so that the user has full read, write, and execute permission, and the group and world have no permissions at all.

```
brezup:ray testing $ ls -l
total 0
-rwx------ 1 ray staff 0 Apr 22 23:32 fizbin
```

Perhaps this file is not actually a program, and to prevent yourself from accidentally trying to run it, you want to remove the execute permission from the user.

```
brezup:ray testing $ chmod u-x fizbin
brezup:ray testing $ ls -l
total 0
-rw------- 1 ray staff 0 Apr 22 23:32 fizbin
```

Now you want to make it readable by both the group and the world.

```
brezup:ray testing $ chmod g+r fizbin
brezup:ray testing $ chmod o+r fizbin
brezup:ray testing $ ls -l
total 0
-rw-r--r-- 1 ray staff 0 Apr 22 23:32 fizbin
brezup:ray testing $ chmod u+x,g=rx,o=rx fizbin
brezup:ray testing $ ls -l
total 0
-rwxr-xr-x 1 ray staff 0 Apr 22 23:32 fizbin
```

As you can see, this method of changing file permissions is fairly simple, but it does not lend itself to setting many permissions at once. Although it's possible to say `chmod u=rwx,g=xr,o=xr <filename>` to set all the permission bits at once to force the file's mode bits into some particular pattern in a single command, this is a bit cumbersome. To solve this, the `chmod` command also includes an "all at once" option, whereby you can specify the full complement of mode bits simultaneously in a more compact form.

This form of the command can appear to be slightly less clear because it requires you to do a little math, but in reality it's no more complicated. In this form, the `chmod` command considers the mode bits for the file to be binary bits. To use the command, you need to specify which bits to set and which to unset.

Unfortunately, you can't do this in a manner as nice as just giving `chmod` a set of nine `rwxrwxrwx` characters, or ones and zeros. Instead, you must break up the nine bits of the mode bit set into three sets of three bits (`rwx rwx rwx`), and calculate the decimal equivalent of the bits that you want set.

Put another way, you could think of the elements in `rwx` as specifying where, in a binary string, a `1` occurs. This is done as shown following:

```
100 - read permission.  100 in binary = 4 in decimal.
010 - write permission.  010 in binary = 2 in decimal.
001 - execute permission. 001 in binary = 1 in decimal.
```

To find the decimal value equivalent of a particular combination of `r`, `w`, and `x` bits, you sum the decimal values that correspond to the bit patterns that represent them. So, if you wanted read and execute permission, with no write permission, you would add `4 + 1 = 5`, and for user, group, or world, you would put a `5` in the pattern where needed.

A full example should help to explain this. Let's again consider the `fizbin` file, which, due to the use of `chmod` previously, has mode bits of `rw-r--r--`. That is to say, the user can read and write, and both the group and world can read. If you wanted to change this to mode bits `r-xr-x--x`, the syntax shown for the friendlier mode of `chmod` would require several commands. Instead, you could make this change in a single command by using the "all at once" form. To do so, follow these steps:

1. Split the desired permissions into user, group, and world bits. This results in `r-x` belonging to the user, `r-x` belonging to the group, and `--x` belonging to the world.
2. Calculate the decimal values for each: `r-x` is read permission and execute permission, which is `4+1 = 5`. `r-x` for the group is the same. `--x` for the world is execute permission alone, which is simply `1`.
3. Put these together with the `chmod` command and the filename to change the mode bits for the file. In this case, `chmod 551 fizbin`.

Let's see whether it works:

```
brezup:ray testing $ ls -l
total 0
-rw-r--r-- 1 ray staff 0 Apr 22 23:32 fizbin
brezup:ray testing $ chmod 551 fizbin
brezup:ray testing $ ls -l
total 0
-r-xr-x--x 1 ray staff 0 Apr 22 23:32 fizbin
```

> **NOTE**
>
> Most people simply get the most useful permission numbers stuck in their heads after a few uses: 7 = read/write/execute, 5 = read/write, 4 = read. 755 is "I get to do everything, everyone else can read and execute it, but not modify it." 700 is "I get to do everything, but nobody else can do anything," and so on. After a while, these become second nature and are much shorter to type than the letter-specified permissions of the first form shown.

Table 14.1 shows the command syntax and the most interesting options for `chmod`. The complete documentation is available in Appendix A.

TABLE 14.1 The Command Syntax and Most Interesting Options for `chmod`

`chmod`	Changes file modes
	`chmod [-R [-H ¦ -L ¦ -P]] [-fvh]` *<absolute_mode>* *<file1>* *<file2>* ...
	`chmod [-R [-H ¦ -L ¦ -P]] [-fvh]` *<symbolic_mode>* *<file1>* *<file2>* ...
`-R`	Recursively descends through directory arguments to change file modes.
`-H`	If `-R` is specified, symbolic links on the command line are followed. Symbolic links encountered in tree traversal are not followed.
`-L`	If `-R` is specified, all symbolic links are followed.
`-P`	If `-R` is specified, no symbolic links are followed.
-h	If the *<file>* is a symbolic link, change the mode for the link rather than for the file that is the target of the link.

Unless `-H` or `-L` is specified, `chmod` on a symbolic link always succeeds and has no effect. The `-H`, `-L`, and `-P` options are ignored unless `-R` is specified. Furthermore, `-H`, `-L`, and `-P` override each other. The last option specified determines the action taken.

Permissions are described by three sequences of letters in the order listed here. Each sequence describes the permissions for user, group, and other. If a certain permission has not been granted, a `-` (dash) appears in its place.

User	Group	Other
`rwx`	`rwx`	`rwx`

The permissions on a file can be viewed using `ls -l` and changed using `chmod`.

TABLE 14.1 Continued

Absolute Mode

Absolute mode is constructed by `OR`ing any of the following modes:

`4000`	Sets user ID on execution—If this is a program, cause it to run as though the user who owns it is actually running it, regardless of who executes it.
`2000`	Sets group ID on execution—If this is a program, cause it to run with the group ID of the program, regardless of group memberships of the user who executes it.
`1000`	Turns on sticky bit—Has different meanings in different contexts: for directories, protect files from modification by other than owner, even if the user has permissions to write in the directory—overridden by directory ownership.
`0400`	Allows read by owner.
`0200`	Allows write by owner.
`0100`	Allows execute (search in a directory) by owner.
`0600`	Allows read, write by owner.
`0500`	Allows read, execute by owner.
`0300`	Allows write, execute by owner.
`0700`	Allows read, write, execute by owner.
`0040`	Allows read by group.
`0020`	Allows write by group.
`0010`	Allows execute (search in a directory) by group.
`0060`	Allows read, write by group.
`0050`	Allows read, execute by group.
`0030`	Allows write, execute by group.
`0070`	Allows read, write, execute by group.
`0004`	Allows read by other.
`0002`	Allows write by other.
`0001`	Allows execute (search in a directory) by other.
`0006`	Allows read, write by other.
`0005`	Allows read, execute by other.
`0003`	Allows write, execute by other
`0007`	Allows read, write, execute by other.

Symbolic Mode

Symbolic mode is a comma-separated list, with no intervening white space, of the form:

`[<who>]<operator>[<permissions>]`

<who> has the following form:

< u ¦ g ¦ o ¦ a>

u	User's permissions.
g	Group's permissions.
o	Other's permissions.
a	All permissions (user, group, other); equivalent to ugo.

TABLE 14.1 Continued

<*operator*> has the following form:	
`< + ¦ - ¦ = >`	
+	Adds <*permissions*>.
If <*permissions*> is not specified, no changes occur.	
If <*who*> is not specified, <*who*> defaults to a, and <*permissions*> are added as specified, except that `chmod` does not override the file mode creation mask.	
If <*who*> is specified, <*permissions*> are added as specified.	
-	Removes <*permissions*>.
If <*permissions*> is not specified, no changes occur.	
If <*who*> is not specified, <*who*> defaults to a, and <*permissions*> are removed as specified, except that `chmod` does not override the file mode creation mask.	
If <*who*> is specified, <*permissions*> are removed as specified.	
=	Assigns the absolute <*permissions*> specified.
<*permissions*> has the following form:	
`<r ¦ w ¦ x ¦ X ¦ s ¦ t ¦ u ¦ g ¦ o>`	
`r`	Sets read bits.
`w`	Sets write bits.
`x`	Sets execute/search bits.
`X`	Sets execute/search bits if the file is a directory, or if any execution/search bits are already set in the file before `X` would act on the file. `X` is used only with + and is ignored in all other cases.
`s`	Sets the `set-user-ID-on-execution` and `set-group-ID-on-execution` bits. A process runs as the user or group specified by `s`.
`t`	Sets the sticky bit.
`u`	User permission bit in the mode of the original file.
`g`	Group permission bits in the mode of the original file.
`o`	Other permission bits in the mode of the original file.
Operations with <*who*>=o in combination with <*permissions*> `s` or `t` are ignored.	

Controlling a File's Group Ownership: `chgrp`

As covered in Chapter 11, a user may belong to multiple different groups. Each of those groups may have different purposes on the system, for example, allowing groups of individual users to collaborate on projects, and allowing some users to belong to multiple different project groups.

A user who is a member of a group can access files that have that same group as their group owner. Unlike with some real-life groups of people, each user can simultaneously participate in all groups of which they are a member, no matter how many groups that may be. This makes perfect sense for accessing files—you can access a file that belongs to any group of which you are a member at any time.

Creating new files is a little more confusing. A file has only one group ownership, so there's got to be some way of determining which of the many groups you belong to the new file gets created as belonging to. In current BSD-derived versions of Unix, this determination is based on the group ownership of the directory you're in. Whatever group owns the directory you're working in, this is the group to which any files you create in the directory will have their group ownership set. This is true regardless of whether you are actually a member of this group.

In addition to being created as belonging to the group owner of the current directory, group ownership of a file can be further controlled by the file's owner. The owner of a file has the ability to change the group ownership of a file to any group to which the owner belongs. Issuing `chgrp` *<groupname> <filename>* switches the group ownership of *<filename>* to *<groupname>*, assuming that you are a member of *<groupname>*. Table 14.2 shows the command syntax and most interesting options for `chgrp`. The complete documentation is shown in Appendix A.

TABLE 14.2 The Command Syntax and Most Interesting Options for `chgrp`

`chgrp`	Changes group ownership for a file or directory.
`chgrp [-R [-H ¦ -L ¦ -P]] [-fhv]` *<group> <file1> <file2>* `...`	
`-R`	Recursively descends through directory arguments to change the group ID.
`-H`	If `-R` is specified, symbolic links on the command line are followed. Symbolic links encountered in tree traversal are not followed.
`-L`	If `-R` is specified, all symbolic links are followed.
`-P`	If `-R` is specified, no symbolic links are followed.
`-h`	If the *<file>* is a symbolic link, change the group ID of the link instead of the target file.

Unless `-h`, `-H`, or `-L` is specified, `chgrp` on symbolic links exits with no error and has no effect.

The `-H`, `-L`, and `-P` options are ignored unless `-R` is specified. These options also override each other, so the last one specified on the command line determines the action taken by the command.

The group may be either a numeric group ID or a group name. If a group name exists for a group ID, the associated group name is used for the group.

The user invoking `chgrp` must belong to the specified group and be the owner of the file, or be the superuser.

Unless invoked by the superuser, `chgrp` clears the `set-user-id` and `set-group-id` bits.

Controlling the Special Flags: `chflags`

To modify the special flags, you use the `chflags` command. It's not at all clear what Apple is using the special flags for at the moment, although we do know that the Finder's locked status of a file sets the immutable bit on the Unix side. For example:

```
brezup:ray testing 141$ ls -l
total 0
-rw-r--r-- 1 ray staff -  0 Jun 27 14:22 test
```

```
-rw-r--r-- 1 ray staff -  0 Jun 27 14:22 test2
brezup:ray testing 142$ su
Pcxassword:
```

NOTE

Note the use of the su command here to switch user IDs to become root. By default, the prompt changes to include a trailing # rather than the normal $, %, or > character when you're working as root. Also notice that the history command number switches from the command number in my history, to the command number for root's command history when I'm working as the root user.

Always remember to exit from the root subshell when you're finished working as root. If you prefer, you could use sudo to execute these commands instead of switching user IDs to the root user. There are arguments for and against either method, which are discussed in more detail directly following this section.


```
brezup:root testing 21# chflags schg test
brezup:root testing 22# ls -ol
total 0
-rw-r--r-- 1 ray staff schg 0 Jun 27 14:22 test
-rw-r--r-- 1 ray staff -  0 Jun 27 14:22 test2
brezup:root testing 23# chflags noschg test
chflags: test: Operation not permitted
brezup:root testing 24# rm test
override rw-r--r-- ray/staff for test? y
rm: test: Operation not permitted
brezup:root testing 25# exit
brezup:ray testing 143$
```

The immutable flag is a relatively recent Unix invention and indicates that the file *cannot* be changed. It's clear from the example that *immutable* really means just that: Even root can't delete the file, and what's more, root can't even remove the system immutable flag after it has been set. If a user sets a user immutable flag (uchg instead of schg), the user can neither unset nor remove the flag, but root can remove the file using rm.

Even booting back into Mac OS 9.2 and trying to unlock the file from a Get Info dialog in the Finder turns out to be insufficient. The only successful route that we've found thus far is to remove the locked flag by using the venerable ResEdit program!

We don't really recommend experimenting with the chflags command much because it has the potential to make a real mess of things, and there's no documentation of what Apple is using the rest of the flags for. We've included the syntax and more interesting options in Table 14.3, in case you should run across command examples using this in the future, as adventurous hackers pry the secrets out of OS X.

TABLE 14.3 The Command Syntax and Most Interesting Options for `chflags`

`chflags`	Changes file flags.
`chflags [-R [-H ¦ -L ¦ -P]] <flags> <file1> <file2> ...`	
`-R`	Recursively descends through directory arguments to change file flags.
`-H`	If `-R` is specified, symbolic links on the command line are followed. Symbolic links encountered in tree traversal are not followed.
`-L`	If `-R` is specified, all symbolic links are followed.
`-P`	If `-R` is specified, no symbolic links are followed.
Symbolic links do not have flags. Unless `-H` or `-L` is specified, `chflags` on a symbolic link always succeeds and has no effect. `-H`, `-L`, and `-P` options are ignored unless `-R` is specified. Furthermore, `-H`, `-L`, and `-P` override each other. The last option specified determines the action taken.	
`<flags>` is a comma-separated list of keywords. Currently available keywords are as follows:	
`arch`	Sets the `archived` flag (superuser only).
`opaque`	Sets the `opaque` flag (owner or superuser only).
`nodump`	Sets the `nodump` flag (owner or superuser only).
`sappnd`	Sets the system `append-only` flag (superuser only).
`schg`	Sets the system `immutable` flag (superuser only).
`uappnd`	Sets the user `append-only` flag (owner or superuser only).
`uchg`	Sets the user `immutable` flag (owner or superuser only).
Prepending the letters `no` to a flag turns off the flag.	

Being Someone Else: `su`, `sudo`

Because Unix is a multiple user operating system, it's sometimes convenient to be able to momentarily switch user IDs so that you can do something as a different user than the one you're currently logged in as. To eliminate the need to log out and log back in under an alternative ID, Unix provides the `su` command (meaning switch user), which allows you to briefly act as another user for whom you know the login password. The `su` command is often used to switch to the `root` user ID, for the purpose of performing system maintenance, but it can also be used to switch to any other user ID on the system.

The `su` command can be dangerous. When you are running as another user, you have all the permissions that the other user has and all of that user's capabilities. If this is another normal user on the system, you can just as easily damage his files as you can your own. If you've `su`'ed to the `root` user, you can, with a single typo of an `rm` command, delete every file on your drive. Table 14.4 shows the command syntax and options for the `su` command.

CAUTION

This does not mean that you should never use the `su` command. There are operations that you must perform as the `root` user, and you're just as likely to make some terrible mistake and mess up another user's files if you'd logged out and logged in as the other user. Respect the `su` command, be aware of the extra responsibility you have if you're working in someone else's account, realize the danger of careless operation as `root`, and you'll be fine.

TABLE 14.4 The Command Syntax and Most Interesting Options for su

`su`	Substitute user identity
`su [-flm] [<login>] [-c <shell arguments>]`	
su requests the password for login and switches to that user and group ID after obtaining proper authentication. A shell is then executed, and any additional shell arguments after the login name are passed to the shell.	
If su is executed with no username as an argument, `root` is assumed.	
If su is executed by `root`, no password is requested, and a shell with the appropriate user ID is executed.	
`-c`	Invoke the following command in a subshell as the specified user.
`-f`	If the invoked shell is `csh` or `tcsh`, this option prevents it from reading the `.cshrc` file. This both prevents items in the `.cshrc` from overriding current environment settings and can be useful if execution of the `.cshrc` is resource intensive or otherwise would interfere with a proper login.
`-l`	Simulate a full login. The environment is discarded except for HOME, SHELL, PATH, TERM, and USER. USER is set to the target login. PATH is set to `"/bin:/usr/bin"`. TERM is imported from your current environment. The invoked shell is the target login's, and su changes directory to the target login's home directory. The `-l` option is synonymous with "`-`", as in `su -`.
`-m`	Leave the environment unmodified. The invoked shell is your login shell; the current directory is not changed. As a security precaution, if the target user's shell is a nonstandard shell (not listed in `/etc/shells`), and the caller is not `root`, su will fail. This option is useful and is the default in many (but apparently not the OS X 10.3) versions of su. Unfortunately, there are some inconsistencies in the way that this currently works. Some of the environment (your prompt, for example) is maintained unchanged without this option and changed with it, whereas other parts are maintained unchanged when `-m` is set and are overridden without it. Usually, we'd recommend aliasing su to `su -m` as the best option, but the current behavior is confusing.
The `-l` and `-m` options are mutually exclusive; the last one specified overrides any previous ones. Only users in group `"wheel"` (normally `gid 0`) or group `"admin"` (normally `gid 20`) can su to `"root"`.	
By default (unless the prompt is reset by a startup file), the superuser prompt will self-modify to end with a # character to remind you of the awesome power of the `root` shell.	

Similar to the su command, the sudo command allows you to execute a single command as another user. Instead of switching user IDs and working as the other user, sudo executes a single command and returns you to working under your own ID. A particularly useful feature of sudo is that it can be configured to allow you to operate as another user without knowing that user's password. Apple has used it this way to allow Admin-group users to run commands as `root` by using their own passwords. To make this happen, sudo's configuration is somewhat complex, requiring a complete specification of what users are allowed to run what commands, under what circumstances, and which user IDs they should appear to run these commands as when they're using them. Table 14.5 shows the command syntax and most interesting options for sudo. More documentation is available in Appendix A.

TABLE 14.5 The Command Syntax and Most Interesting Options for sudo

sudo	Execute a command as another user.

sudo -V|-h|-l|-L|-v|-k|-K|[-H][-P][-S][-b] | [-p *<prompt>*] [-u *<username>*|<#uid>] *<command>*

sudo -V|-h|-l|-L|-v|-k|-K|[-H][-P][-S][-b] | [-p *<prompt>*] [-u *<username>*|*<#uid>*] -s

sudo allows a permitted user to execute a *<command>* as root or another user, as specified in /etc/sudoers. The real and effective uid and gid are set to match those of the target user as specified in the passwd file or Netinfo map. By default, sudo requires that users authenticate themselves with a password. (Note: By default this is the user's password, not the root password.) After a user has been authenticated, a time stamp is updated, and the user may then use sudo without a password for a short period of time after the time stamp (5 minutes unless overridden in sudoers). The time stamp is updated every time a command is executed through sudo, providing a sliding window during which the user may use commands as the alternative user without re-entering the required password. sudo determines who is an authorized user by consulting the file /etc/sudoers. By giving sudo the -v flag, a user can update the time stamp without running a command.

If a user who is not listed in /etc/sudoers tries to run a command via sudo, mail is sent to the proper authorities, as defined at configure time or /etc/sudoers. Note that the mail will not be sent if an unauthorized user tries to run sudo with the -l or -v flags. This allows users to determine for themselves whether they are allowed to use sudo.

sudo can log attempted sudo sessions as well as errors to syslog(3), a log file, or both. By default, sudo logs via syslog(3).

When used with the -s option instead of a *<command>*, sudo executes the target user's shell in a manner similar to the su command. The change of effective user, and executing of the shell are logged, but commands executed while in that shell are not recorded.

-l	List out the allowed (and forbidden) commands for the user on the current host.
-v	Update the user's time stamp, prompting for the user's password if necessary. This extends the sudo timeout for another 5 minutes (or whatever the timeout is set to in sudoers).
-k	Invalidates the user's time stamp by setting the time on it to the epoch. The next time sudo is run, a password will be required. This option does not require a password and was added to allow a user to revoke sudo permissions from a .logout file.
-b	Tells sudo to run the given command in the background. Note that if you use the -b option you cannot use shell job control to manipulate the process.
-S	Causes sudo to read the password from standard input instead of the terminal device.

TABLE 14.5 Continued

-H	Sets the `$HOME` environment variable to the `homedir` of the target user (`root` by default) as specified in `/etc/passwd` or NetInfo. By default, `sudo` does not modify `$HOME`.

`sudo` tries to be safe when executing commands. To accomplish this, most shell variables specifying load paths for dynamically loaded libraries, user paths and similar routes by which commands may be spoofed, are ignored when searching for commands and when loading dynamic modules. This will not affect general use of the `sudo` command, but may result in unexpected behavior in some situations. Carefully read Apple's `man` page for `sudo` (which is not quite in sync with the version of the command provided) if you experience difficulty with more sophisticated configurations.

Proper attention to configuration of the `/etc/sudoers` file is outside the scope of this book, but we've tried to cover the basics of the configuration in Chapter 31, "Server Security and Advanced Network Configuration," where we introduce advanced security concepts. If you need to set up your machine with a sophisticated multiuser configuration that allows for cross-user sudoing, see Chapter 31, and then check out the `sudoers` `man` page. You also might want to look for *Maximum Mac OS X Security*, also by Will, John, and Joan Ray from Sams Publishing.

14

SU OR SUDO?

You will see numerous examples of people using the `sudo` command to run commands as the `root` user in documentation and suggestions floating around the Internet. In general, I disagree with this practice on a number of levels. The most fundamental of these is that the `sudo` command was not really intended to work the way people are using it under OS X. The `sudo` command is intended to give the `root` user a way to allow nonprivileged users limited access to run very specific commands with `root` permissions—for example, to allow the person who's the Web master to restart the Web server (which starts as `root`). Instead, Apple has used it as a way to allow Admin users to run all commands as `root`. This is okay for users who are only going to do one or two things as `root` ever in their use of the machine, but I don't think that the use of `sudo` inspires the same care as using `su`, where you take a separate action to actually *be* another user.

Another problem with using `sudo` this way is that as a single-command-line command way of doing things as `root`, it's much too easy to embed dangerous uses in muscle memory. If you're working for a while on something that requires `root` privileges and are, for example, regularly issuing `sudo rm <filename>` commands to accomplish some task, it's likely that the next time you want to remove a file (even not intending to be `root`), what will appear at the command line is `sudo rm <filename>`. This is when a simple typo can sneak up and bite you really hard. If you consciously `su` to `root` when you need to operate as `root`, and conscientiously exit the `root` login when you're finished, you can't accidentally develop bad muscle-memory habits.

On the other hand, using `su` instead of `sudo` is no panacea either. It's extremely easy to forget to log out of the `root` shell when you're finished with the parts that necessitate `root` access. Likewise, it's tempting to just stay in a `root` shell for tangential operations that don't really require `root`, if you think you might need the `root` privileges again soon. Both of these are also dangerous behaviors. The first at least can be somewhat mitigated by configuring your shell to visibly distinguish when you're running as `root`. The second, however, requires that you consistently place security and safety before convenience at the command line. This is not always easy to do, even for the most conscientious users. But for me at least, it's easier than overcoming muscle-memory habits.

Process Management

In Chapter 3, you were introduced to the way that OS X is composed of many different cooperating processes. This is not particular to OS X, but instead is also the norm for Unix. Instead of a monolithic OS and user interface environment, Unix and (even more so) the Mach kernel on which OS X is based both operate as collections of a large number of cooperating programs. These programs create the illusion and functional experience of a seamless interface but provide considerably more flexibility in the user's ability to modify things to suit his particular needs.

For example, with (the old, now "Classic") Mac OS, you're used to having a clock in the menu bar, and having the option to turn it on or off and perhaps set the font. This functionality is a built-in part of the OS and user interface. With Unix, if you want a clock, you run a separate program that displays a clock. Because the clock is a program and not an integral part of the OS, it can be any program. By selecting different programs, the clock can be made to appear as any type that you choose, anywhere on the screen that you choose.

It might take a while for you to come to appreciate the flexibility that this "everything is a process" idea of building operating systems provides for you. Monolithic OS and user interface environments have the advantage of being able to guide the user somewhat more strictly. They also are able to "guarantee" some types of responsiveness in ways that can't be done when all the user interface components are controlled by separate programs. Many of the things we will say are advantages of the new Unix environment—such as processes that run and provide some sort of functionality with no user interface (background processes), or programs that start at some prespecified time—you might think are not so impressive because they were available in earlier versions of Mac OS. It is true that these advantages have been available. But as much as we love the Mac OS, we have to admit that they have been, at best, hacks; attempts to implement what you now have available to you, the Unix way of managing processes.

Listing Processes: ps

The ps command is used for listing the process status report. This is the command-line version of the Process View utility. There are many options to ps, but you will probably find issuing ps with the a, u, and x options to be most useful (this combination produces one of the more complete and informative, yet relatively concise displays):

```
ps -aux
```

The following provides a sample of what to expect the output to look like:

```
brezup:ray testing $ ps -aux

USER     PID %CPU %MEM   VSZ  RSS TT STAT STARTED   TIME COMMAND
williamr  483 11.4 4.2  349852 43580 ?? S   11:40PM  1:21.21 /Volumes/S
williamr  451 10.2 0.5  94172  4892 ?? S  11:29PM  0:03.09 /Applicati
williamr  186  0.1 1.5  66904 15228 ?? Ss  11:26PM  0:23.20 /System/Li
root     82  0.0 0.1  28304  1264 ?? Ss  11:26PM  0:02.10 kextd
```

```
root     104  0.0 0.2  29820  1872 ?? Ss  11:26PM  0:01.47 /usr/sbin/
root     105  0.0 0.1  27852  876 ?? Ss  11:26PM  0:00.61 /usr/sbin/
root     107  0.0 0.0  18064  104 ?? Ss  11:26PM  0:00.58 update
.
.
.
williamr  453  0.0 0.1  18648  760 std S  11:29PM  0:00.08 -bash
williamr  480  0.0 0.4  29908  4000 ?? S  11:32PM  0:00.12 /System/Li
williamr  484  0.0 1.1  92732 11156 ?? S  11:40PM  0:00.62 /Volumes/S
root     488  0.0 0.0  18108  336 std R+  11:44PM  0:00.00 ps -aux
root      1  0.0 0.0  18080  300 ?? Ss  11:25PM  0:00.06 /sbin/init
root      2  0.0 0.0  18616  200 ?? Ss  11:25PM  0:00.11 /sbin/mach
root     76  0.0 0.0  18096  200 ?? Ss  11:26PM  0:00.07 /usr/sbin/
```


If your terminal window is narrower than the complete width of the output, it will be truncated on the right edge of your terminal. This is apparent in the previous output on most lines. If you want to see more of the command, you can add the `w` flag to `ps`, to cause it to ignore your terminal width and output 132 columns of information regardless of wrapping:

```
brezup:ray testing $ ps -auxw

USER     PID %CPU %MEM   VSZ  RSS TT STAT STARTED   TIME COMMAND

williamr  483 16.0 4.5  326612 46884 ?? S  11:40PM  1:56.68
➥ /Volumes/Software/Work_Software/Microsoft Office X/Microsoft W
williamr  451  9.5 0.5  94628  5540 ?? S  11:29PM  0:06.90
➥ /Applications/Utilities/Terminal.app/Contents/MacOS/Terminal -
root     489  6.0 0.0  18108  336 std R+  11:47PM  0:00.02
➥ ps -auxw
williamr  186  3.0 1.5  67108 15364 ?? Ss  11:26PM  0:26.99
➥ /System/Library/Frameworks/ApplicationServices.framework/Frame
root     307  1.1 0.0  18328  268 ?? Ss  11:26PM  0:00.13
➥ ntpd -f /var/run/ntp.drift -p /var/run/ntpd.pid
root     105  0.0 0.1  27852  876 ?? Ss  11:26PM  0:00.61
➥ /usr/sbin/diskarbitrationd
root     107  0.0 0.0  18064  104 ?? Ss  11:26PM  0:00.66
➥ update
.
.
.
williamr  480  0.0 0.4  29908  3996 ?? S  11:32PM  0:00.12
➥ /System/Library/Services/AppleSpell.service/Contents/MacOS/App
williamr  484  0.0 1.1  92732 11220 ?? S  11:40PM  0:00.62
➥ /Volumes/Software/Work_Software/Microsoft Office X/Office/Micr
root     452  0.0 0.0  27544  508 std Ss  11:29PM  0:00.03
```

```
➥ login -pf williamray
root      1  0.0 0.0  18080  300 ?? Ss  11:25PM  0:00.06
➥ /sbin/init
root      2  0.0 0.0  18616  200 ?? Ss  11:25PM  0:00.11
➥ /sbin/mach_init
root     76  0.0 0.0  18096  200 ?? Ss  11:26PM  0:00.07
➥ /usr/sbin/syslogd -s -m 0
root     82  0.0 0.1  28304  1264 ?? Ss  11:26PM  0:02.10
➥ kextd
root     104  0.0 0.2  29820  1872 ?? Ss  11:26PM  0:01.47
➥ /usr/sbin/configd
```

If you have more wordy commands in deeper directories that need even more than 132 columns to display, the w flag can be specified twice (as in ps -auxww), causing ps to completely ignore column-width issues.

The output from ps using these flags includes the owner of the process (USER), the process ID (PID), the percentage of the CPU (%CPU) and memory (%MEM) being consumed by the process, the virtual size of the memory space used by the program (VSZ) as well as the amount of that size that's resident in main memory (RSS), the controlling terminal (TT = ?? for no terminal), the run state of the process (STAT = R for running, S for short sleep, others), the time the process started (STARTED), the accumulated CPU time (TIME), and the command that is running (COMMAND). The output is sorted by the percentage of the CPU that's being used for each command. More display options and orderings are available with the ps command, and command options, syntax, and keyword definitions for ps are included in the command documentation table—Table 14.6.

TABLE 14.6 The Command Syntax and Most Interesting Options for ps

ps	Displays process status report.
ps [-aCcefhjlMmrSTuvwx] [-O *<fmt>*] [-o *<fmt>*] [-p *<pid>*] [-t *<tty>*] [-U *<username>*]	
ps [-L]	
-a	Includes information about processes owned by others in addition to yours.
-c	Changes the command column output to contain just the executable name rather than the full command line.
-f	Shows command line and environment information about swapped-out processes. This is honored only if the user's user ID is 0.
-j	Prints information associated with the following keywords: user, pid, ppid, pgid, sess, jobc, state, tt, time, and command.
-l	Displays information associated with the following keywords: uid, pid, ppid, cpu, pri, nice, vsz, rss, wchan, state, tt, time, and command.
-M	Prints the threads corresponding with each task.
-m	Sorts by memory usage, rather than by process ID.
-r	Sorts by current CPU usage, rather than by process ID.
-T	Displays information about processes attached to the device associated with standard output.

TABLE 14.6 Continued

`-u`	Displays information associated with the following keywords: `user`, `pid`, `%cpu`, `%mem`, `vsz`, `rss`, `tt`, `state`, `start`, `time`, and `command`. The `-u` option implies the `-r` option.
`-v`	Displays information associated with the following keywords: `pid`, `state`, `time`, `sl`, `re`, `pagein`, `vsz`, `rss`, `lim`, `tsiz`, `%cpu`, `%mem`, and `command`. The `-v` option implies the `-m` option.
`-w`	Uses 132 columns to display information, instead of the default, which is your window size. If the `-w` option is specified more than once, `ps` uses as many columns as necessary, regardless of your window size.
`-x`	Displays information about processes without controlling terminals.
`-p` *<pid>*	Displays information associated with the specified process ID *<pid>*.
`-t` *<tty>*	Displays information about processes attached to the specified terminal device *<tty>*.
`-U` *<username>*	Displays information about processes belonging to the specified *<username>*.

The following is a list of the definitions of the keywords that some of the options already include. More keywords are available than are defined here.

`%cpu`	Percentage CPU usage (alias `pcpu`).
`%mem`	Percentage memory usage (alias `pmem`).
`command`	Command and arguments.
`cpu`	Short-term CPU usage factor (for scheduling).
`jobc`	Job control count.
`lim`	Memory use limit.
`nice`	Nice value (alias to `ni`).
`pagein`	Pageins (total page faults).
`pgid`	Process group number.
`pid`	Process ID.
`ppid`	Parent process ID.
`pri`	Scheduling priority.
`re`	Core residency time (in seconds; 127 = infinity).
`rss`	Resident set size (real memory).
`rsz`	Resident set size + (text size/text use count) (alias `rs-size`).
`sess`	Session pointer.
`sl`	Sleep time (in seconds; 127 = infinity).
`start`	Time started.
`state`	Symbolic process state (alias `stat`).
`tsiz`	Text size (in kilobytes).
`tt`	Control terminal name (two-letter abbreviation).
`uid`	Effective user ID.
`user`	Username (from `uid`).
`vsz`	Size of process in virtual memory in kilobytes (alias `vsize`).
`wchan`	Wait channel (as a symbolic name).

Listing Shell Child Processes: `jobs`

The term *jobs* and the term *processes* are frequently used interchangeably when discussing programs running on a Unix machine. But there is also a more specific meaning of jobs that has to do with processes that are run within, or by, a shell process.

Unix processes have the notion of parent and child processes. For example, consider `Terminal.app`. If you run a shell in a terminal window (which is what you most frequently will do to get access to a shell), the running process that is that shell will be a child of `Terminal.app`. If you run a process in the shell, such as `ls`, or any other commands we discuss in this book, the process that is that command will be a child of the shell. Likewise, the shell will be the parent of the `ls` command run in it, and `Terminal.app` will be the parent of the shell. `Terminal.app` itself in this case will most likely be the child of the OS X Finder, and the Finder will be the child of whatever process controls OS X logins. Every process in this way can trace its execution lineage back to the ancestor of all executing programs, `/sbin/init`, which will have process ID `1`.

Therefore, a *user's jobs* refers to all processes running on a machine that belong to a particular user. *Shell jobs*, on the other hand, refers to processes that are children of (that is, were run by) a particular running instance of a shell.

The `jobs` command displays current processes that are children of the shell where the command is issued. This might not make much sense just yet because we haven't introduced any way for you to run a command and have it execute to completion before returning to the command prompt, but we will cover this material shortly. The `jobs` command gives you the ability to find out what jobs are present and what state they are in. For example, the shell shown in the following output has three jobs running in the background, and one job that is stopped:

```
brezup:ray testing $ jobs
[1]   Running              ./aaa.csh &
[2] -  Running              ./bbbb.csh &
[3]   Running              ./test.csh &
[4] +  Stopped              ./test2.csh
```

`Stopped` (`tcsh` uses the label `Suspended` instead of `Stopped`) jobs are jobs that are not executing for one reason or another. In this case, the suspended job was stopped with the Ctrl+Z shell key sequence discussed in Chapter 12 and is waiting for the user to resume it, send it to the background, or kill it off.

The `+` and `-` characters between the job number and the status indicate the most current job, and the previously most current job, respectively. "Most current" in this case means either the most recent job stopped that had been running in the foreground, or the most recent job that was started into the background.

The command documentation for `jobs` in Table 14.7 also includes information on how a job may be referenced, based on the output of `jobs`, for use in other job-control commands.

TABLE 14.7 The Command Syntax and Most Interesting Options for `jobs`

`jobs`	Displays the table of current jobs.
`jobs [-lnprs] [<jobspec>]`	
`jobs -x <command> [<args>]`	
`-l`	Lists jobs in long format. This includes the job number and its associated process ID, in case, for example, you want to use various `kill` signals, discussed in the following section, against jobs you have running in the shell.
`-p`	`bash/sh` specific: Lists the process ID of the job's process group leader.
`-n`	`bash/sh` specific: Only list information for jobs whose status has changed since the last time the user has queried the status.
`-r`	`bash/sh` specific: Only list running jobs.
`-s`	`bash/sh` specific: Only list stopped jobs.

After you know what jobs belong to the current shell, there are several ways to construct a proper *<jobspec>* to refer to a job. `%` introduces a job name. Job number `1` is `%1`. An unambiguous string of characters at the beginning of the name can be used to refer to a job; the form is `%`*<first-few-characters-of-job>*. An unambiguous string of characters in the job name can also be used to refer to a job; for example, the form `%?`*<text-string>* specifies a job whose name contains *<text-string>*. These *<jobspec>* references can be used with a number of commands that interact with running processes to specify which, out of a collection of running jobs, the command needs to work with.

If *<jobspec>* is supplied, the output is restricted to only that job.

With the `-x` *<command>* option, `jobs` functions as a meta-command, and rewrites, and then executes *<command>* such that any *<jobspec>* that appears in *<command>* or *<args>* is first replaced by the appropriate process ID. This gives you an easy way to use commands that want to work on process IDs with shell-job *<jobspec>*s. This usage is particularly useful with commands such as `kill` (discussed later in this chapter), which can be issued as `jobs -x kill` *<jobspec>* to execute `kill` against a particular job, instead of requiring the job's process ID.

Output pertaining to the current job is marked with `+`; output from a previous job, `-`. `%+`, `%`, and `%%` refer to the current job. `%-` refers to the previous job.

NOTE

In `tcsh` the `jobs` command provides only the `-l` option. The syntax for job listings and *<jobspec>* references, however, is similar.

Backgrounding Processes: `bg`

The `bg` command backgrounds a suspended job. The process continues, only in the background. The most noticeable effect for the user is the return of the command prompt. Backgrounding processes is particularly useful for commands and programs that do not produce command-line output. Although the user's prompt returns, the process continues.

It does not make sense to background something like `ls`, which is trying to show you output to the terminal. On the other hand, backgrounding the process responsible for a long `cp` or `compress` can be very convenient. The usual method for suspending a running process is to press Ctrl+Z, which stops, but does not kill, the process. For example:

```
brezup:ray testing $ jobs
[1] - Running              ./aaa.csh &
[4] + Running              ./test.csh &
brezup:ray testing $ ./test2.csh
^Z
[5] + Stopped              ./test2.csh
brezup:ray testing $ jobs
[1]  Running              ./aaa.csh &
[4] - Running              ./test.csh &
[5] + Stopped              ./test2.csh
brezup:ray testing $ bg
[5]  ./test2.csh &
brezup:ray testing $ jobs
[1] - Running              ./aaa.csh &
[4] + Running              ./test.csh &
[5]  Running              ./test2.csh &
```

When stopped with Ctrl+Z, `bash` automatically lists the job you've just stopped, whereas `tcsh` provides the complete current list of jobs.

CAUTION

If you're running multiple jobs in a single terminal, there's only one place (that terminal) for them, and any job-control software you're using, to display output. The result is that the output from the programs living in the terminal all get interleaved into the same display. This can occasionally produce some confusing-looking output. It's not so bad when you have a bunch of programs all babbling at the same time, and you know that it's all jibberish. Sometimes, however, it can be insidiously confusing. For example, output-timing issues sometimes result in the shell displaying its prompt just before another command prints information to the terminal. This causes the information to be printed as though it were a command, sitting after the prompt at the command line.

For example, in the case of the previous `bg` command, with certain shell configurations, running `bg` produces not only a line detailing the job that's just been put in the background but also a line telling you what directory you're currently working in. This directory display has an annoying habit of landing at the (empty) command-line prompt when it appears. The result is output that looks like this:

```
localhost ray 188> bg
[5]  ./test2.csh &
localhost ray 189> /Users/ray
```

This looks, on the screen as though I'd typed /Users/ray at the prompt for command number 189, but in fact that's just output from the bg command, and there is currently nothing on the command line for command number 189. Pressing Return if this happens will not harm anything, and you'll just get your prompt back, safe and ready to work again.

If there were multiple suspended jobs, I could pick which one to send to the background by the use of a job specifier `<jobspec>` (as defined in the discussion of the `jobs` command), using the syntax `bg <jobspec>`. Table 14.8 shows the `bg` command syntax.

TABLE 14.8 The bg Command

`bg`	Backgrounds a job
`bg [<jobspec> ...]`	
`<jobspec> &`	
`bg`	

`bg` backgrounds the jobs specified by the given *<jobspecs>*, or if no argument is given, the current job. `<jobspec>` may be any acceptable form described in `jobs`. A job that is currently a foreground job may be backgrounded simply by referring to it using the `%` notation—that is, `%1 &` backgrounds job `1`.

Backgrounding Processes with &

Processes can also be put in the background by using the & symbol at the end of the command line. Simply add this symbol to the end of any command line, and the resulting process will be run in the background automatically.

```
brezup:ray testing 190$ jobs
[1] - Running              ./aaa.csh &
[4] + Running              ./test.csh &
[5]   Running             ./test2.csh &
brezup:ray testing 191$ ./bbbb.csh &
[6] 691
brezup:ray testing 192$ jobs
[1] - Running              ./aaa.csh &
[4]   Running             ./test.csh &
[5]   Running             ./test2.csh &
[6] + Running              ./bbbb.csh &
```

When a job is put into the background using the & suffix for a command line, it automatically prints out its job number and process ID.

This syntax is also an abbreviation for the bg command as used on stopped jobs.

```
brezup:ray testing 193$ ./ccc.csh
^Z
[7] + Stopped             ./ccc.csh
brezup:ray testing 194$ jobs
[1]  Running             ./aaa.csh &
[4]  Running             ./test.csh &
[5]  Running             ./test2.csh &
[6] - Running             ./bbbb.csh &
[7] + Stopped             ./ccc.csh
brezup:ray testing 195$ %7 &
[2]+ ./ccc.csh &
brezup:ray testing 196$ jobs
[1]  Running             ./aaa.csh &
[4]  Running             ./test.csh &
[5]  Running             ./test2.csh &
[6] + Running             ./bbbb.csh &
[7] - Running             ./ccc.csh
```

Foregrounding Processes: fg

The command fg returns a job to the foreground, where it continues to run. The command may be either a background job or a suspended job. If you don't specify a *<jobspec>*, the current job (the one indicated by the + in the jobs listing) is brought to the foreground.

```
brezup:ray testing 207$ jobs
[1] - Running             ./aaa.csh &
[5] + Running             ./test2.csh &
brezup:ray testing 208$ fg %1
./aaa.csh
```

Table 14.9 shows the documentation for fg.

TABLE 14.9 The Command Syntax and Most Interesting Options for fg

fg	Foregrounds a job.
fg [*<jobspec>*...]	
<jobspec>	
fg	

Brings the specified jobs (or, if no argument is given, the current job) to the foreground. *<jobspec>* may be any acceptable form as described in jobs. Like backgrounding jobs, referring to a backgrounded or stopped job in % notation (that is, simply referencing its *<jobspec>*) brings it to the foreground—that is, entering %1 on the command line foregrounds background job 1.

Stopping Processes, Sending Signals: `kill`, `killall`

The `kill` command sends a signal to a process or terminates a process. It is most commonly used in conjunction with `ps`, which provides the process ID of the process to which you want to send a signal.

You will probably most often use this command either to terminate a process, or to send a hang up signal (HUP) to force a process to reread its configuration file.

The syntax that you will probably most often use is one of the following forms:

```
kill -9 <pid>
kill -HUP <pid>
```

In the first example, the `-9` sends an explicit termination (`KILL`) signal to the process specified. This is a request that the OS cause the process to stop, now, no questions asked. Unless the process is in such a state that it cannot be terminated (certain types of operations cannot be interrupted by design), it will cease to execute immediately. Effectively, this is much like pulling the power-plug for the process. In the second example, the `-HUP` sends a hangup signal to a process. This signal is frequently used by the OS to indicate to programs that some other piece of software to which they've been speaking, has, so to speak, hung up the phone. Some programs interpret this as a sign that they should tidy up whatever they've been doing and then quit, whereas others have been designed to interpret HUP as an indication that they should reread their configuration files and restart themselves. You will see at least one example of this second behavior later in the book.

Table 14.10 shows the command syntax and options for `kill`.

TABLE 14.10 The Command Syntax for `kill`

`kill`	Sends a signal to a process or terminates a process.
`kill [-`*<signal>*`] %`*<job>* ¦ *<pid>*	
`kill -l [exit-status]`	
`-l [exit-status]`	With no argument, lists the all the signal names; otherwise, lists the signal associated with the status `exit-status`.
<signal>	Specifies which signal to send to a process. If *<signal>* is not specified, the `TERM` (terminate) signal is sent. *<signal>* may be a signal number or signal name.
`%`*<job>*	`csh/tcsh` specific: Specifies the job that should receive a signal. In `bash`, use `jobs -x kill` *<jobspec>* to cause `jobs` to rewrite the argument to `kill` from a *<jobspec>* to a *<pid>*.
<pid>	Specifies the process ID that should receive a signal. The process ID can be determined by running `ps`.

Signal `KILL (9)` is a sure way to kill a process. Signal `HUP` is another common signal to send to a process. You often can send a `HUP` signal to a process to get it to reread its configuration file. It's also sometimes a useful signal to send to programs that haven't noticed that a connection was broken because it will induce those that have been designed to do so, to clean up after themselves, and then cleanly exit, rather than either hanging forever waiting for the other end of the communication to resume, or to crash inelegantly.

The `killall` command is similar to the `kill` command, except that it `kill`s (or sends various signals to) processes by name, instead of by process ID. This can be considerably more convenient if you want to `kill` the execution of a command you've just run, or if you want to wipe all copies of some server running on your machine simultaneously. However, although it's usually more convenient for you to remember a command name than to look up a process number, `killall` is less specific than `kill`, in that it has no way to differentiate between multiple running copies of the same program. Instead, when you `killall mail`, you `kill` all running copies of `mail` owned by your user ID. If you're currently operating as `root`, you `kill` all copies of `mail` that anyone's running on the machine. Table 14.11 shows the command syntax and most interesting options for `killall`.

TABLE 14.11 The Command Syntax and Most Interesting Options for `killall`

`killall`	Kills processes by name
`killall [-d ¦ -v] [-help] [-l] [-m] [-s] [-u` *<user>*`] [-t` *<tty>*`] [-c` *<procname>*`] [-`*<SIGNAL>*`] [`*<procname>* `...]`	
`Killall` kills processes selected by name, as opposed to the selection by `pid` as done by `kill`. By default, it sends a `TERM` signal to all processes with a real UID identical to the caller of `killall` that match the name *<procname>*. The `root` user is allowed to kill any process.	
`-l`	Lists the names of the available signals and exits, like in `kill`.
`-m`	Matches the argument *<procname>* as a (case-insensitive) regular expression against the names of processes found. CAUTION! This is dangerous; a single dot matches any process running under the real UID of the caller.
`-`*<SIGNAL>*	Sends the specified *<SIGNAL>* instead of the default `TERM`. The signal may be specified either as a name (with or without a leading SIG), or numerically.
`-u` *<user>*	Limits potentially matching processes to those belonging to the specified *<user>*.
`-t` *<tty>*	Limits potentially matching processes to those running on the specified *<tty>*.
`-c` *<procname>*	When used with the `-u` or `-t` flags, limits potentially matching processes to those matching the specified *<procname>*.

Listing Resource-Consuming Processes: `top`

The `top` command displays system usage statistics, particularly of those processes making the most use of system resources. Processes are displayed at one-second intervals. The `top` command can be useful for diagnosing unusual behavior with a process. It is worthwhile to run `top` from time to time so that you learn what the typical behavior for your system is.

When `top` is displaying processes, it takes over your screen. You can quit the display by pressing the Q key. The following is a sample of what `top` output looks like:

```
Processes: 49 total, 2 running, 47 sleeping.. 112 threads      22:00:10
Load Avg: 1.14, 0.96, 1.07   CPU usage: 74.8% user, 15.5% sys, 9.7% idle
SharedLibs: num = 107, resident = 24.5M code, 2.80M data, 7.56M LinkEdit
```

```
MemRegions: num = 3665, resident = 50.9M + 7.60M private, 69.7M shared
PhysMem: 56.3M wired, 70.9M active, 132M inactive, 259M used, 764M free
VM: 2.36G + 72.3M  18452(0) pageins, 0(0) pageouts

 PID COMMAND    %CPU  TIME   #TH #PRTS #MREGS RPRVT RSHRD RSIZE VSIZE
 990 top      3.8% 0:00.61  1  15  24  240K  428K  604K 26.9M
 989 bash      0.0% 0:00.02  1  12  15  172K  880K  780K 18.2M
 988 login     0.0% 0:00.05  1  12  35  140K  420K  508K 26.9M
 963 pickup     0.0% 0:00.03  1  12  19  132K  512K  580K 26.9M
 904 bash      0.0% 0:00.09  1  12  16  180K  880K  796K 18.2M
 903 login     0.0% 0:00.05  1  12  35  140K  420K  508K 26.9M
 878 sleep     0.0% 0:00.01  1  11  15  72K  340K  276K 17.6M
 877 tcsh      0.0% 0:00.02  1  12  18  180K  644K  648K 22.1M
 864 sleep     0.0% 0:00.00  1  11  15  72K  340K  276K 17.6M
 863 tcsh      0.0% 0:00.03  1  12  18  180K  644K  648K 22.1M
 848 Terminal  45.0% 0:35.40  4  70  156 1.94M+ 10.1M 7.39M+ 95.3M+
 668 lookupd   0.0% 0:01.16  2  33  55  340K  956K 1.11M 28.5M
 596 Microsoft  0.7% 0:02.77  1  68  97 1.81M 7.90M 4.41M 90.5M
 595 Microsoft  26.9% 24:30.31  4  89  240 25.2M 40.9M 40.5M  146M
 396 Finder    0.0% 0:14.44  1  80  133 3.48M 15.2M 12.3M  112M
 395 SystemUISe  0.0% 0:05.96  1  192  191 1.57M 8.48M 5.38M 93.3M
```

Table 14.12 shows the command syntax and most interesting options for `top`.

TABLE 14.12 The Command Syntax and Most Interesting Options for top

`top`	Displays system usage statistics.
`top [-u] [-w] [-k] [-s <interval>] [-e ¦ -d ¦ -a] [-l <samples>] [<number>]`	
`top`	
`-u`	Sorts by CPU usage and displays usage starting with the highest usage.
`-s <interval>`	Samples processes at the specified `<interval>`. Default is one-second intervals.
`-e`	Switches to event-counting mode where counts reported are absolute counters. Options `-w` and `-k` are ignored.
`-d`	Switches to an event-counting mode where counts are reported as differences relative to the previous sample. Options `-w` and `-k` are ignored.
`-a`	Switches to an event-counting mode where counts are reported as cumulative counters relative to when `top` was launched. Options `-w` and `-k` are ignored.
`-l <samples>`	Switches from default screen mode to a logging mode suitable for saving the output to a file. If `<samples>` is specified, `top` samples the number of samples specified before exiting. The default is `1`.
`<number>`	Limits the number of processes displayed to `<number>`.

TABLE 14.12 Continued

Pressing the Q key causes top to exit immediately.	
Columns displayed in default data mode:	
PID	Unix process ID.
COMMAND	Unix command name.
%CPU	Percentage of CPU used (kernel and user).
TIME	Absolute CPU consumption (min:secs.hundredths).
#TH	Number of threads.
#PRTS (delta)	Number of MACH ports.
#MERG	Number of memory regions.
VPRVT (-w only)	Private address space currently allocated.
RPRVT (delta)	Resident shared memory (as represented by the resident page count of each shared memory object).
RSHRD (delta)	Total resident memory (real pages that this process currently has associated with it; some may be shared by other processes).
VSIZE (delta)	Total address space currently allocated (including shared).
Columns displayed in event-counting modes:	
PID	Unix process ID.
COMMAND	Unix command name.
%CPU	Percentage of CPU used (kernel and user).
TIME	Absolute CPU consumption (min:secs.hundredths).
FAULTS	Number of page faults.
PAGEINS	Number of requests for pages from a pager.
COW_FAULTS	Number of faults that caused a page to be copied.
MSGS_SENT	Number of mach messages sent by the process.
MSGS_RCVD	Number of mach messages received by the process.
BSDSYSCALL	Number of BSD system calls made by the process.
MACHSYSCALL	Number of MACH system calls made by the process.
CSWITCH	Number of context switches to this process.

Communication Between Processes: Redirection, Pipes

Building an operating system out of a multitude of small, cooperating processes would not provide such flexibility and power to the user were it not for a simple method of making all of these processes speak to each other. At the heart of the interprocess communications model of Unix is a simple but amazingly effective abstraction of the idea of input and output.

To paraphrase the model on which Unix bases input and output, you can imagine that Unix thinks of user input to a program as a stream—a stream of information. Output from the program back to the user can be thought of in the same way. A stream of information is simply a collection of information that flows in or out of the program in a serial (ordered) fashion. A user can't send two pieces of information to a program at the same time—two key presses, no matter how closely they occur, are ordered, one first and one second. A cursor moving across a screen provides information serially as to where it is now, and where it was then. Even if two events manage to occur simultaneously, the electronics of the machine can't really deal with simultaneous events, and so they end up being registered as separate events occurring very close in time. Output must be similarly serially ordered. Whether you are drawing data to the screen or sending data over an Internet connection, no two data items leave a program at exactly the same time; therefore, they are also a serial stream of information.

Because both input and output from processes are streams of information, and every function of the system from user programs to reading files to parts of the OS is a running process, Unix models the implementation of communication between the processes as simply tying the output stream of one process to another's input stream. Tying the standard output stream (named `STDOUT`) from one process to the standard input stream (named `STDIN`) of another is called *creating a pipe* between them. When you understand the view of data moving into or out of a process as being a data stream, it is immediately obvious that there is no need for the system to concern itself over the endpoints of the stream. Data simply moves about the system between programs in streams, as though each program had input and output spigots, and someone had connected garden hoses between them. The input spigots all look the same, and the output spigots all look the same, so the OS can tie any output into any input, and let the programs worry about whether they know what to do with the data in the stream.

For example, one endpoint of a stream might be connected to the output (`STDOUT`) of a process that is taking input from a user at a keyboard, and the other endpoint might be connected to the input (`STDIN`) of a process manipulating that information and writing it into a file. On the other hand, the same information could be placed in a file, and we could replace the user entering information with a process that could read the file and write the same information onto its `STDOUT`. If we tie the stream created in this fashion into the `STDIN` of the same manipulation program, there would be absolutely no difference between these two situations from the OS's point of view.

In short, this abstraction provides that so long as the input coming to a process "looks like" the input the process expects; it does not matter to the process or the OS where that input comes from. Likewise, provided that the destination of the output from the process "acts as expected," it does not matter where the output is actually going.

Redirection: `STDIN`, `STDOUT`, `STDERR`

Unix makes this input/output model available to the user through a concept known as *redirection*. This is implemented as a requirement that all processes adhere to certain conventions regarding input and output.

At the base is the notion that input and output from programs is generally from, and to, a user typing information at the command line. Even programs that are not intended to be used by a person at a command line are expected to adhere to the model that input comes from a user, and output goes to a user.

This might seem counterintuitive, but further conventions are required that allow this seeming restriction to be less restrictive, while generalizing the input/output model sufficiently that it can be applied to almost any need. Two of these are the idea of input arriving in a program through a virtual interface known as `STDIN` (standard input), and output leaving the program through a virtual interface known as `STDOUT` (standard output). It also requires the convention of a third virtual interface by which error messages can be conveyed, which is `STDERR` (standard error).

Redirection is accomplished by attaching these virtual interfaces to each other in various combinations—essentially redirecting the input or output from a process to a different location than to a user or from a user.

Standard In: `STDIN`

The virtual input interface to programs is called `STDIN`, for standard input. A program can expect the incoming data stream from the user (or any other source) to arrive at `STDIN`.

When you interact with a command-line program, the program is reading the data you are entering from `STDIN`. If you prefer not to enter the data by hand, you can put it in a file and redirect the contents of the file into the program's `STDIN`—the program will not know the difference.

A program that you can use for an example is the `spell` program. Apple hasn't distributed `spell` with OS X as of this writing, but we've provided instructions on how to install it in Chapter 15, "Command-Line Applications and Application Suites." If you're using a system on which it's already been installed, follow along here. Also, the installation's not too difficult if you care to glance ahead and just trust us on the commands you don't recognize yet to perform the install. If not, `spell` still makes a good program for explanation because it has exactly the features we want to exhibit—just read along and imagine that it's really working until you get to Chapter 15.

The `spell` command finds misspellings. Given input from `STDIN`, `spell` parses through it, checks the input against a dictionary, and returns any misspellings it finds. To issue the `spell` command from the command line, you might type something like the following:

```
brezup:ray testing $ spell
Now is the tyem for all good authors to come to thie ayde of some very
good Unix users
Ctrl+D
```

Pressing Ctrl+D finishes the input, sending an end-of-data signal into `STDIN`, effectively telling the program that no further information is to come. The `spell` program goes to work, and returns the following:

```
tyem
thie
ayde
```

Each of the misspelled words (or at least words that aren't in the dictionary) is displayed, exactly as expected.

This might not seem to be a particularly useful program at first glance—how often do you want to type a sentence, just to find out what words are misspelled in it? The key to its usefulness, however, is that the `spell` program does not care whether you typed the input, or whether the input came from a file.

NOTE

Actually, it's more proper to think of `spell` as not caring whether the input comes from a file or from you instead. The `spell` program is designed to work with input coming from a file or a program. It just happens that because of the input/output model abstracting all system input and output as from/to a userlike interface, in operation, `spell` doesn't care whether the input comes from a user, or from a file instead. Many programs you'll find available for Unix fall into this category—they are designed to take input or provide output to or from other programs or files rather than from users. The input/output model, however, allows a user to interact with the software anyway. Because of this, you might occasionally find the syntax in which these programs converse to be slightly odd. Just remember, they weren't really designed to talk directly to you.

Now try it with data from a file. Fire up your favorite text editor, and create a file containing the same text you typed to spell previously. Then try `spell` by redirecting this file into its `STDIN` interface. If you named your file `reallydumbfile`, you can run `spell` on it by typing the following:

```
brezup:ray testing $ spell < reallydumbfile
tyme
thie
ayde
```

This looks a little more useful. The < character redirects `STDIN` for the program to its left to come from the file named to its right. Here, it redirects `STDIN` for the `spell` program so that it comes from the file `reallydumbfile` rather than from your keyboard.

Standard Out: `STDOUT`

The virtual output interface that Unix provides to programs is called `STDOUT`, for standard output. Just as you can redirect `STDIN` from a file, if you want to store the output of a command in a file, you can redirect `STDOUT` from the program into the file. The > character directs the `STDOUT` of the program to its left into the file named to its right. For example, if you want to collect the last few lines of `/var/log/system.log` into a file in your home directory, you could type

```
brezup:ray testing $ tail -20 /etc/services > ~/my-output
```

This command directs the shell to create a file named my-output in your home directory, and to redirect STDOUT from the tail command (that is, the data tail would print if you just issued the command tail -20 /etc/services) into the file. If my-output already exists in your home directory, it will be overwritten by the output from tail.

If you want to collect and archive the data, by appending it to my-output instead of overwriting it, the shell can be directed to append rather than replace the data. In this case, STDOUT is redirected with >> rather than the single >. The >> character pair appends the STDOUT of the program to the left into the file named on its right.

You can also simultaneously redirect STDOUT and STDIN, like this:

```
[localhost:~/Documents] nermal% spell < reallydumbfile > reallydumbspelling
[localhost:~/Documents] nermal% ls
get_termcap      lynx.cfg       reallydumbspelling termcap-1.3.tar
lynx         reallydumbfile   termcap-1.3      test
[localhost:~/Documents] nermal% cat reallydumbspelling
tyem
thie
ayde
```

Standard Error: STDERR

To make your life easier, Unix actually has two different output interfaces that it defines for programs. The first, STDOUT, has just been covered. The second, STDERR, is used to allow the program to provide error and diagnostic information to the user. This is done for two reasons. First, it allows error information to be reported in such a way that it does not interfere with data on the STDOUT interface. Second, if you are redirecting STDOUT from a program to another program or to a file, you would not see error messages if they were carried on STDOUT. By providing a separate error channel, Unix gives the user the choice of how and where error and diagnostic information should be displayed, independent of information that is actually correct output data.

tcsh and bash syntax disagree rather significantly here. In tcsh if you want to redirect STDERR into the same stream as STDOUT, effectively combining these two different pieces of information, you can do so by using the character pair >& to indicate redirection in the command, instead of >. bash allows this syntax for combining the streams (though it prefers the use of &>), but in bash you also have the option of redirecting STDERR independently of STDOUT. To redirect just STDERR, use 2> as the redirection specifier rather than >.

As mentioned earlier, both bash and tcsh are vastly more complex than can be completely covered in a book of this size, and input/output redirection is one of the principal areas of complexity. If you want to perform more complex manipulations of your command's input and output, see your online man pages to learn how the shell of your preference behaves.

Pipes

Finally, there is nothing in the input/output model that restricts redirection to coming from or going into files/users (if everything looks like a user/looks like a file, then letting software talk to anything else is just as good). `STDIN` and `STDOUT` can just as easily be tied together instead of being tied into files or the command line.

Perhaps more correctly, the OS never really redirects to or from files. What the OS is really doing when you redirect into a file is invisibly creating a process that writes into a file, and redirecting your output to the `STDIN` of the process writing the file. Likewise, when you redirect a file into a program's `STDIN`, the OS is invisibly creating a process that opens and reads the file, and is tying the `STDOUT` from this process into your process's `STDIN` (and now you see why we said the model was based on input and output being attached to users, rather than to files). For the user's convenience, these common actions are abbreviated into the < and > redirection characters.

Programs, on the other hand, are connected by directly redirecting their `STDOUT` and `STDIN` interfaces with a pipe. To create a pipe in Unix, you simply use a ¦ character between the programs on the command line.

Again, an example is more illustrative than a considerable amount of explanation. Consider a situation in which you want to examine the content of a file that is larger than will fit on one screen. You can accomplish this easily by piping the output from the `cat` command into a pager, such as the `more` command.

```
brezup:ray testing $ cat /usr/share/file/magic ¦ more
# Magic
# Magic data for file(1) command.
# Machine-generated from src/cmd/file/magdir/*; edit there only!
# Format is described in magic(files), where:
# files is 5 on V7 and BSD, 4 on SV, and ?? in the SVID.

#------------------------------------------------------------------------------
# Localstuff: file(1) magic for locally observed files
#
# $Id: Localstuff,v 1.1 2003/07/02 18:00:17 eseidel Exp $
# Add any locally observed files here. Remember:
# text if readable, executable if runnable binary, data if unreadable.
#------------------------------------------------------------------------------
# acorn: file(1) magic for files found on Acorn systems
#

# RISC OS Chunk File Format
# From RISC OS Programmer's Reference Manual, Appendix D
```

```
# We guess the file type from the type of the first chunk.
0     lelong      0xc3cbc6c5   RISC OS Chunk data
>12   string      OBJ_        \b, AOF object
>12   string      LIB_        \b, ALF library

byte 920
```

Of course, you already know that you could have accomplished this by just using `more /usr/share/file/magic`. The point, though, is that although we told you how to use `more` to read a file before, `more` *actually* wants to take its input from `STDIN` and uses a file specified as an argument only as a last resort.

Knowing this, you now know how to make any other output from any other program viewable with the `more` pager. This lets you do things such as look at the full contents of your filesystem, without needing an immensely large scroll buffer in your terminal:

```
brezup:ray testing $ ls -lRaF / ¦ more
ls: .Trashes: Permission denied
total 8721
drwxrwxr-t 39 root wheel    1326 16 Aug 17:16 ./
drwxrwxr-t 39 root wheel    1326 16 Aug 17:16 ../
-rwxrwxr-x  1 ray  unknown   6148 16 Aug 17:15 .DS_Store*
d-wx-wx-wt  4 ray  admin    136 12 Aug 01:09 .Trashes/
-rw-r--r--  1 ray  admin   39568 11 Aug 22:42 .VolumeIcon.icns
-r--r--r--  1 root wheel    156 29 Jul 14:15 .hidden
dr--r--r--  2 root wheel    256 16 Aug 17:16 .vol/
drwxrwxr-x 28 root admin    952 11 Aug 23:50 Applications/
drwxr-xr-x  2 ray  unknown    68 11 Aug 23:54 Calendars/
drwxr-xr-x  4 ray  unknown   136 11 Aug 23:54 Contacts/
-rw-r--r--  1 root admin    1024 11 Aug 23:50 Desktop DB
-rw-r--r--  1 root admin     2 11 Aug 22:43 Desktop DF
drwxr-xr-x  2 ray  unknown    68 13 Aug 10:58 Desktop Folder/
drwxrwxr-x 13 root wheel    442 2 Jul 17:22 Developer/
-rw-r--r--  1 ray  admin     0 11 Aug 22:42 Icon
drwxrwxr-x 35 root wheel    1190 13 Aug 20:45 Library/
drwxr-xr-x  1 root wheel    512 16 Aug 23:19 Network/
drwxr-xr-x  5 root wheel    170 2 Jul 17:22 System/
drwxr-xr-x  3 ray  unknown   102 13 Aug 10:58 TheVolumeSettingsFolder/
drwxr-xr-x  2 ray  unknown    68 13 Aug 10:58 Trash/
drwxrwxr-t  9 root admin    306 16 Aug 16:28 Users/
drwxrwxrwt  8 root admin    272 16 Aug 17:16 Volumes/
byte 1356
```

One particularly useful use of such piping of commands together comes when you want to filter the output of a command so that you only see the most interesting parts. For example, if you want to find files in your current directory that were edited in August, you could turn to Chapter 12 or to Appendix A and look up how to filter dates in `ls`, or you could use what you probably already remember about `grep`. Adding a pipe from `ls -l`, into a `grep` command looking for the string `Aug` is as simple as entering both commands on the command line, separated by a ¦ character.

```
brezup:ray Documents $ ls -l
total 16456
-rw-r--r--   1 ray staff 4925440 Jun 11 00:11 BTS.tar
drwxr-xr-x  17 ray staff    578 Jun 13 08:57 BTS_folder
drwxr-xr-x  28 ray staff    952 Jun 12 11:27 Core
drwxr-xr-x   4 ray staff    136 Mar 9 02:13 DnD_data
drwxr-xr-x  10 ray staff    340 Jul 2 10:43 Mailsmith User Data Backup
drwxr-xr-x  17 ray staff    578 Aug 15 23:58 Microsoft User Data
drwxr-xr-x   7 ray staff    238 Jul 16 2002 Software_Docs
drwxr-xr-x  48 ray staff   1632 Aug 15 00:19 buying_the_farm
drwxrwxrwx  39 ray staff   1326 Apr 24 19:02 dna_demos_2002
drwxr-xr-x   4 ray staff    136 May 29 13:12 games
-rw-r--r--   1 ray staff  610678 Aug 15 02:24 hd_genes_aa.fa
-rw-r--r--   1 ray staff 1645031 Aug 15 02:24 hd_genes_nt.fa
-rw-r--r--   1 ray staff  609071 Jun 9 21:06 lumberjk.mp3
drwxr-xr-x  17 ray staff    578 May 21 16:56 openGL
drwxr-xr-x  36 ray staff   1224 Aug 15 00:19 research
drwxr-xr-x 104 ray staff   3536 Jun 26 10:39 security
drwxr-xr-x   5 ray staff    170 Dec 27 2002 source
-rw-r--r--   1 ray staff  623484 Jan 18 2002 squirrel.mpg
drwxrwxrwx  16 ray staff    544 Sep 16 2002 stylewriter
drwxrwxrwx   7 ray staff    238 Aug 16 15:56 unleashed

brezup:ray Documents $ ls -l ¦ grep "Aug"
drwxr-xr-x  17 ray staff    578 Aug 15 23:58 Microsoft User Data
drwxr-xr-x  48 ray staff   1632 Aug 15 00:19 buying_the_farm
-rw-r--r--   1 ray staff  610678 Aug 15 02:24 hd_genes_aa.fa
-rw-r--r--   1 ray staff 1645031 Aug 15 02:24 hd_genes_nt.fa
drwxr-xr-x  36 ray staff   1224 Aug 15 00:19 research
drwxrwxrwx   7 ray staff    238 Aug 16 15:56 unleashed
```

Sometimes, you want to filter both `STDOUT` from the command and `STDERR`. `find`, for example, has an annoying tendency to report all manner of errors about directories that you're not allowed to look in. This often clutters up the output such that you can't actually find what it was that you wanted to find. Here, redirecting STDOUT using only the ¦ character is insufficient, because find helpfully puts the error messages on STDERR, where they won't be captured by the ¦ pipe (which only works on STDIN).

In tcsh, redirecting both STDIN and STDERR simultaneously is simply a matter of using the ¦& pipe combination instead of the single ¦ character. In bash, it's just slightly more complex. bash can't redirect both at once, but it can redirect STDERR into STDOUT. The syntax for that looks like 2>&1. After STDERR has been redirected into STDOUT, the combined stream can then be redirected into grep with the ¦ character.

```
brezup:ray testing $ find / -name 702_fall_grades -print
find: cannot read dir /lost+found: Permission denied
find: cannot read dir /usr/lost+found: Permission denied
find: cannot read dir /usr/local/lost+found: Permission denied.
.
.
.
^C
brezup:ray testing $ find / -name grades1 -print 2>&1 ¦ grep "702_fall_grades"
/Users/ray/Biophysics/702_fall_grades
```

These are, of course, simplistic examples of connecting programs, but keep an eye out for how pipes are used throughout the rest of the book. The ability to create small programs with small functions and to tie these together into arbitrarily large programs with arbitrarily complex behaviors is powerful. This is one of the main reasons that having access to the BSD half of your new OS is so valuable.

Think back to programs such as grep, and you can probably begin to see how you could apply this to creating custom solutions to problems that you might have encountered. You should also begin to see why this functionality cannot be conveniently duplicated with a GUI-only interface.

Joints in Pipes: tee

On occasion, you might want to redirect STDOUT to both a file and another program at the same time. In such a case, you can use the tee command. This command accepts data on STDIN, writes it to a filename specified on the command line, and continues to send the data, unaltered on STDOUT.

Consider an example in which you want to search through your files, looking for files that match a particular name pattern. You want to both browse the found names as they appear, and collect the names into a log file so that you can use the information again later. In this example, we will look in a rather inefficient fashion for files with names that contain java. Because many of them are probably on the system, we want the output piped through a pager (more). We also want to collect the filenames into a file in our home directory named my_output.

```
brezup:ray testing $ find / -name \*java\* -print ¦ tee ~/my_output ¦ more
find: /.Trashes: Permission denied
/Applications/Internet Explorer.app/Contents/Resources/Spanish.lproj/Ayuda/➥Con-
tents/java.htm
/Applications/Utilities/Java/Java Web Start.app/Contents/MacOS/javaws.cfg
/Applications/Utilities/Java/Java Web Start.app/Contents/MacOS/javaws.jar
/Applications/Utilities/Java/Java Web Start.app/Contents/MacOS/javaws.policy
.
.
.
```

It might take a while for this to start printing output to the screen because it could take `find` a while to start finding appropriately named files. If you let this run to completion, you can then look at the file `my_output`, and it will have all the stuff you just scrolled through with `more`. If you press Ctrl+C to stop the find and the listing, you'll kill the `tee` process, and it won't write its output. Because this isn't a valuable listing, you might prefer to kill it off rather than actually wait for this to finish just to see the output, but you wouldn't want to do this if it was important to capture the output.

DIFFICULTIES WITH RUNNING FIND

If you haven't upgraded to at least OS X 10.2, there's a chance you can't run `find` from the root directory as anything other than the `root` user. This appears to be a bug on Apple's part and seems to be fixed in 10.2. If you've got a single, single-partition drive, it seems to work okay; if you don't, `find` dies with a permission denied at the root level. We've worked out a fix for this, but we can't guarantee that our fix doesn't break something else. If you want to try it, do exactly the following:

```
su
umount /.vol
chmod 555 /.vol
sync;sync;sync;reboot
```

At this point, your machine should reboot. If you typed everything properly, after your machine comes back up, `find` will work from the root directory. Be patient if it seems that your machine is not responding immediately.

The `tee` command is invaluable if you need to split one `STDOUT` stream to be used by multiple different processes, or if you need to collect logging or partial output from intermediate steps in a large, multiprogram piped command. Table 14.13 shows syntax and options for `tee`.

TABLE 14.13 The tee Command

tee	A pipe fitting
tee [-ai] <file>	
-a	Causes tee to append to <file> rather than overwriting it
-i	Causes tee to ignore SIGINT signals

The tee command accepts input on STDIN and writes the same output to both STDOUT and to a <file>.

Summary

This chapter detailed some of the general concepts and commands that can be used to interact with and control the behavior of other shell commands. File permissions, process management, and output redirection are all fundamental Unix concepts, although ones that many Unix users frequently choose to ignore.

Most anything that you can do with Unix, you can do without paying particularly close attention to this chapter, although the process might be many times as hard and take many times as long to accomplish. For this reason, we recommend that you familiarize yourself with these ideas and commands—they are fundamental to using Unix effectively, if not to simply using it.

CHAPTER 15

Command-Line Applications and Application Suites

IN THIS CHAPTER

- Networking Applications
- Mail Clients
- Text Editors
- Printing Tools
- Bridging the GUI to Command Line Gap: Hybrid Software

In the last few chapters, we covered what you need to know to get around in the command-line–based BSD environment. We also introduced you to the use of simple programs. In this chapter, we cover command-line programs with more complex interfaces. If you're from a classic Mac background, the previous chapters' small building block–type programs are probably a slightly foreign concept because most Mac applications have historically been self-contained. The Unix applications introduced in this chapter will be somewhat more familiar because they are more similar to the functionally complete programs you're used to.

Networking Applications

Many of the command-line network applications are simply textual equivalents of graphical network applications with which you're likely to be already familiar. There are command-line applications for browsing the Web, transferring files over the Internet, reading your email, and most other network functions you're familiar with. Most of these have both advantages and disadvantages with respect to their graphical counterparts. The mouse has proven to be an efficient tool for tasks involving complex selections, and the command-line applications fail in situations that would require fast and furious mousing. On the other hand, if you're using a terminal and at a command-line prompt, it's almost always faster to use a textual tool to do something quick, such as transfer a file via FTP, than it is to start a graphical client. An additional difference is that some command-line applications can function in both an interactive fashion and as a building-block program.

This allows many of them to be used in shell scripts or other programs to provide their functionality to a more complex program that needs to use it.

NOTE

URLs are one of the most ubiquitous formalized ways of specifying the place a program should look for a particular network resource. You're almost certainly familiar with URLs in a practical sense—many of them look like `http://www.apple.com/`. What you might not be aware of is that this string `http://www.apple.com/` has meaning beyond simply specifying the name of a machine, `www.apple.com`, to which software should connect. The `http://` part of the expression is also used, and specifies the connection protocol, which should be used for accessing this resource. Other connection protocols can be specified by the use of other prefixes before the machine name, such as `ftp://`.Technically, the URL actually has three parts, a protocol specifier (`http`, `ftp`, `gopher`, and so on), followed by a host specification, followed by a path, with the syntax *`<protocol>`*`://`*`<host><absolute path>`*. It is technically an error for the path to be empty, and as an absolute path, it must begin with a `/`. This means that URLs that you occasionally see as `http://www.someplace.com` are actually incorrect, and properly should be specified as `http://www.someplace.com/`. As a matter of fact, when you enter a URL that's missing the trailing `/` character into your Web browser, the result is an error from the server—browsers have just been written to disguise this fact from the casual computer user. Instead of returning the top of the Web site directory as you might have come to expect when using a URL such as `http://www.someplace.com`, the Web server returns an error, indicating that your Web browser might want to try a syntactically correct URL, and your browser is obliged to try again. This costs extra load on the server, extra data transmitted, and extra time—all of which are annoying to someone at some level.

As we've pointed out previously, Unix is a particular and precise environment. Specifying `www.apple.com` as a URL to a Web browser is sloppy and imprecise, and works only in certain cases in which the browser manufacturer has decided to write its software to try to compensate for poor habits on the part of the user.

A considerable amount of Unix software isn't written to support sloppy usage on the part of the user and requires that you enter complete and correct URLs, including the `http://`, or other prefix, part of the URL to function correctly.

Some recent Unix software is starting to go the route of the large browsers and support the sloppy usage without a specified protocol, but much still does not, and we don't believe this is a positive trend. We've made every effort to provide complete and correct URLs in the text here, and we hope that you'll get used to using them properly—it will eventually save you a considerable headache when you meet an application that requires you to be as precise as it is.

Browsing the Web: `lynx`

`lynx` is a command-line Web client. Surprising as it might seem, many people prefer browsing the Web in a text-only application. There are, of course, many pages that simply can't be browsed without a graphics-capable application, but those pages are written by people who aren't concerned with making their information as widely available as possible and don't seem to be of interest to people who prefer to browse in text only.

TIP

For more information on why you might want, or not want, to make your pages available as plain text, see Chapter 27, "Web Serving."

NOTE

There's a reasonable chance that `lynx` isn't installed on your system. It's currently not distributed by Apple. It's a favorite, however, among command-line aficionados, so you might find it already installed at work or school. We're going to use it for a few things later in the chapter, so if you don't have it, you'll be installing it in Chapter 16, "Command-Line Software Installation." The install we do for `lynx` will be of the easiest possible command-line install style, so you might even want to flip forward a few pages and do the install now.

The basic syntax of `lynx` is `lynx` *<URL>*. This gives you a textual representation of the page, and a few lines of prompting information as to what you can do from there. For example, looking at `http://www.apple.com/`, `lynx` produces the following output:

```
brezup:ray ray $ lynx http://www.apple.com/
#                                      Apple

  #home index

  Apple The Apple Store Music .Mac QuickTime Apple Support Mac OS X
   Hot News Switch Hardware Software Made4Mac Education Pro business
             Developer Where to Buy

         Office:mac v.X boxes Office:mac v.X boxes
            Good things come in threes.

          Hot News Headlines Hot News Ticker

  Power Mac G5. The world's fastest personal computer. DVD Studio Pro 2.
  Professional DVD authoring made easy. Order now. Soundtrack. Produce
  music with thousands of loops and effects. iSight. The eyes and ears
                of iChat AV.

     Important update for Power Macs and iMacs with SuperDrive.

            _________________________ Go
             Site Map ¦ Search Tips
```

15

```
          Visit the Apple Store online or at retail locations.
                    1-800-MY-APPLE
               Find Job Opportunities at Apple.

             Visit other Apple sites around the world:
                   [Choose...____]

             Contact Us ¦ Terms of Use ¦ Privacy Policy
         Copyright ? 2003 Apple Computer, Inc. All rights reserved.

                 Powered by MacOSXServer

(NORMAL LINK)  Use right-arrow or <return> to activate.
 Arrow keys: Up and Down to move. Right to follow a link; Left to go back.
 H)elp O)ptions P)rint G)o M)ain screen Q)uit /=search [delete]=history list
```

Not bad; it's useable, and it sure loads faster than all those fancy graphics if you've got a slow connection!

If you want to move down the page, you can press the spacebar. Use the up and down arrow keys to move from link to link. Use the right-arrow key or press Return to select a link. The right-arrow and left-arrow keys take you, somewhat predictably, to the target of the currently selected link, or back to the previous page. As you might have noticed, some of the comments we have made here appear at the bottom of the screen output. As you use `lynx`, it provides helpful hints on what you might want to do. These appear near the bottom of the screen and contain helpful information such as how to enter text in a text entry field, or move to the next page using the spacebar.

TIP

I mentioned that `lynx` provides helpful hints on what to do because a significant amount of human-computer-interface research indicates that to many people, omnipresent onscreen help is almost invisible. Keep your eye on the onscreen hints—even if it's not the best user interface design, it is there to help, and it's a lot faster than searching the help pages.

Because you don't have a mouse and cursor with which to navigate pages being displayed in `lynx`, a number of keyboard commands are available to perform various actions. Table 15.1 shows common one-key commands within `lynx`.

TABLE 15.1 Common One-Key Commands Within the lynx Interactive Web Browser

Key	Action
+	Move up the page.
-	Move down the page.
b	Move up the page.
<space bar>	Move down the page.
<right arrow>, <return>	Go to selected link.
<left arrow>	Go back.
<up arrow>	Select previous link, downloadable element, or form field.
<down arrow>	Select next link, downloadable element, or form field.
d	Download the target of the currently selected link or downloadable element.
H	Go to the lynx help pages. These pages are implemented as HTML pages, so you can go forward and back in them with the forward and back arrows.
O	Go to the lynx Options page. Here you can set an assortment of internal parameters such as where your lynx bookmarks are stored.
P	Print the current page.
G	Go to a new URL.
M	Go back to the Main page, by which lynx means the page that you first started on.
Q	Quit the program.
/	Search in the page.
<delete>	Show the history for the current browser window.

A veritable plethora of additional one-key options are explained in the lynx help, under the Key-stroke Commands heading.

The lynx browser also sports a wide range of command-line options that enable or modify advanced behaviors. These include items such as sending the data to STDOUT, or collecting a list of the URLs contained in the document.

Finally, it should be mentioned that lynx, like much Unix software, works great as a command-line building-block utility. Ever wanted to process the contents of a Web page, perhaps to do something such as collect all the links from someone's page of interesting links, without having to dig through the source by hand? Using the -dump option causes lynx to send the target document of the URL to STDOUT, followed by a list of the URLs in the document. For example, if you wanted to collect a list of URLs to the files available on http://www.macosxunleashed.com/ (specifically, the stuff in the downloads subdirectory), you could use lynx like this:

```
brezup:sage Documents $ lynx -dump http://www.macosxunleashed.com/downloads

Index of /downloads

   * [1]Parent Directory
   * [2]26FIG112.gif
   * [3]26FIG133.gif
   * [4]CGvirusscan.tgz
   * [5]Python-2.2.tgz
   * [6]gdbm-1.8.0.tar.gz
   * [7]ispell-3.1.20.tar.gz
   * [8]ispell-english.zip
   * [9]jpegsrc.v6b.tar.gz
   * [10]libpng-1.0.10.tar.gz
   * [11]lynx.cfg
   * [12]lynx.gz
   * [13]netpbm-9.12.tgz
   * [14]nmap-2.54BETA25.tar.gz
   * [15]page1440.pdf
   * [16]pine4.43.tar.Z
   * [17]portsentry-1.0.tar.gz
   * [18]spell-1.0.tar.gz
   * [19]termcap-1.3.tar.gz


   Apache/1.3.26 Server at www.macosxunleashed.com Port 80

References

   1. http://www.macosxunleashed.com/
   2. http://www.macosxunleashed.com/downloads/26FIG112.gif
   3. http://www.macosxunleashed.com/downloads/26FIG133.gif
   4. http://www.macosxunleashed.com/downloads/CGvirusscan.tgz
   5. http://www.macosxunleashed.com/downloads/Python-2.2.tgz
   6. http://www.macosxunleashed.com/downloads/gdbm-1.8.0.tar.gz
   7. http://www.macosxunleashed.com/downloads/ispell-3.1.20.tar.gz
   8. http://www.macosxunleashed.com/downloads/ispell-english.zip
   9. http://www.macosxunleashed.com/downloads/jpegsrc.v6b.tar.gz
  10. http://www.macosxunleashed.com/downloads/libpng-1.0.10.tar.gz
  11. http://www.macosxunleashed.com/downloads/lynx.cfg
  12. http://www.macosxunleashed.com/downloads/lynx.gz
  13. http://www.macosxunleashed.com/downloads/netpbm-9.12.tgz
```

```
14. http://www.macosxunleashed.com/downloads/nmap-2.54BETA25.tar.gz
15. http://www.macosxunleashed.com/downloads/page1440.pdf
16. http://www.macosxunleashed.com/downloads/pine4.43.tar.Z
17. http://www.macosxunleashed.com/downloads/portsentry-1.0.tar.gz
18. http://www.macosxunleashed.com/downloads/spell-1.0.tar.gz
19. http://www.macosxunleashed.com/downloads/termcap-1.3.tar.gz
```

If you wanted to parse just the URLs out of this output, you could simply run `lynx` and pipe the output though `grep` looking for URL patterns. Something like `lynx -dump http://www.macosxunleashed.com/downloads/ | grep "http:"` will do the trick and produces the following output:

```
brezup:sage Documents $ lynx -dump http://www.macosxunleashed.com/downloads

 | grep "http:"

  1. http://www.macosxunleashed.com/
  2. http://www.macosxunleashed.com/downloads/26FIG112.gif
  3. http://www.macosxunleashed.com/downloads/26FIG133.gif
  4. http://www.macosxunleashed.com/downloads/CGvirusscan.tgz
  5. http://www.macosxunleashed.com/downloads/Python-2.2.tgz
  6. http://www.macosxunleashed.com/downloads/gdbm-1.8.0.tar.gz
  7. http://www.macosxunleashed.com/downloads/ispell-3.1.20.tar.gz
  8. http://www.macosxunleashed.com/downloads/ispell-english.zip
  9. http://www.macosxunleashed.com/downloads/jpegsrc.v6b.tar.gz
 10. http://www.macosxunleashed.com/downloads/libpng-1.0.10.tar.gz
 11. http://www.macosxunleashed.com/downloads/lynx.cfg
 12. http://www.macosxunleashed.com/downloads/lynx.gz
 13. http://www.macosxunleashed.com/downloads/netpbm-9.12.tgz
 14. http://www.macosxunleashed.com/downloads/nmap-2.54BETA25.tar.gz
 15. http://www.macosxunleashed.com/downloads/page1440.pdf
 16. http://www.macosxunleashed.com/downloads/pine4.43.tar.Z
 17. http://www.macosxunleashed.com/downloads/portsentry-1.0.tar.gz
 18. http://www.macosxunleashed.com/downloads/spell-1.0.tar.gz
 19. http://www.macosxunleashed.com/downloads/termcap-1.3.tar.gz
```

The `-dump` option turns out to be useful for doing things that don't relate to processing the URLs as well, such as downloading files from FTP or HTTPD servers. You see examples of this use of `lynx` during the software installs in Chapter 16.

Table 15.2 shows the `lynx` syntax and most interesting options. More documentation is available in Appendix A.

TABLE 15.2 The Command Documentation Table for `lynx`

`lynx`	Textual Web browser
`lynx [options] [<file>]`	

You can find out which options are available by running `lynx -help`. Here is the listing of command-line options for the current version of `lynx`:

`-`	Receive options and arguments from `STDIN`.
`-accept_all_cookies`	Accept cookies without prompting if `Set-Cookie` handling is on (off).
`-auth=<id>:<pw>`	Authentication information for protected documents.
`-base`	Prepend a request URL comment and BASE tag to `text/html` for `-source` dumps.
`-book`	Use the bookmark page as the start file (off).
`-cache=<NUMBER>`	<NUMBER> of documents cached in memory.
`-cfg=<FILENAME>`	Specify a `lynx.cfg` file other than the default.
`-cmd_log=<FILENAME>`	Log keystroke commands to the given file.
`-cmd_script=<FILENAME>`	Read keystroke commands from the given file.
`-connect_timeout=<N>`	Set the <N>-second connection timeout (`18000`).
`-cookie_file=<FILENAME>`	Specify a file to use to read cookies.
`-cookie_save_file=<FILENAME>`	Specify a file to use to store cookies.
`-cookies`	Toggle handling of `Set-Cookie` headers (on).
`-core`	Toggle forced core dumps on fatal errors (off).
`-crawl`	With `-traversal`, output each page to a file. With `-dump`, format output as with `-traversal`, but to `STDOUT`.
`-dont_wrap_pre`	Inhibit wrapping of text in `<pre>` when `-dump`ing and `-crawl`ing, mark wrapped lines in interactive session (off).
`-dump`	Dump the first file to `STDOUT` and exit.
`-from`	Toggle transmission of From headers (on).
`-get_data`	User data for `get` forms, read from `STDIN`, terminated by `'---'` on a line.
`-help`	Print this usage message.
`-homepage=<URL>`	Set home page separate from start page.
`-image_links`	Toggles inclusion of links for all images (off).
`-index=<URL>`	Set the default index file to <URL>.
`-localhost`	Disable URLs that point to remote hosts (off).
`-mime_header`	Include MIME headers and force source dump.
`-nobold`	Disable bold video attribute.
`-nobrowse`	Disable directory browsing.
`-nocolor`	Turn off color support.
`-nofilereferer`	Disable transmission of Referer headers for file URLs (on).
`-nolist`	Disable the link list feature in dumps (off).
`-noredir`	Don't follow Location: redirection (off).
`-noreferer`	Disable transmission of Referer headers (off).
`-noreverse`	Disable reverse video attribute.

TABLE 15.2 Continued

`-nostatus`	Disable the miscellaneous information messages (off).
`-nounderline`	Disable underline video attribute.
`-number_fields`	Force numbering of links as well as form input fields (off).
`-number_links`	Force numbering of links (off).
`-pauth=<id>:<pw>`	Authentication information for protected proxy server.
`-popup`	Toggle handling of single-choice `SELECT` options via pop-up windows or as lists of radio buttons (off).
`-post_data`	User data for `post` forms, read from `STDIN`, terminated by `'---'` on a line.
`-pseudo_inlines`	Toggle pseudo-`ALT`s for inlines with no `ALT` string (on).
`-realm`	Restrict access to URLs in the starting realm (off).
`-reload`	Flush the cache on a proxy server (only the first document affected) (off).
`-source`	Dump the source of the first file to `STDOUT` and exit.
`-traversal`	Traverse all HTTP links derived from start file.
`-useragent=<Name>`	Set alternative Lynx User-Agent header.
`-verbose`	Toggle `[LINK]`, `[IMAGE]`, and `[INLINE]` comments with filenames of these images (on).
`-width=<Number>`	Screen width for formatting of dumps (default is 80).
`-with_backspaces`	Omit backspaces in output if `-dumping` or `-crawling` (like `man` does) (off).

Accessing FTP Servers: `ftp`

`ftp` is the command name for the program that implements the FTP protocol (creative, no?). Historically on the Macintosh, the `Anarchie` and `Fetch` programs have been the FTP clients of preference, and both of these provide features sadly lacking in the default command-line `ftp` interface. The command-line interface, however, is again a quick and convenient way to get or put a file or three, without needing to launch a graphical client. It also tends to be better for diagnosis purposes when an FTP transfer fails, or when a file can't be found. All the messages from the server can be seen immediately and are directly in response to the commands you issue, so if something's wrong, it's much clearer at what point it goes that way.

To connect to a remote site using `ftp`, simply issue the command as `ftp <ftp site>`. This, presuming all goes well, connects you to the remote site and requests your user ID and password. If you're trying to connect to a public site, the default guest user ID is `anonymous`. After that, the site asks you for a password, which if you're connecting as an anonymous user, should be given as your email address. Responding properly to both these queries (anonymous and your email address, or your correct user ID and password) takes you to an internal prompt in the `ftp` program from where you can traverse the site's directories and upload or download files.

Following is a sample of what you might see after connecting to a site that doesn't really want you there. This sort of information is largely hidden in the graphical FTP clients, frequently leaving you clicking Retry indefinitely; in reality, the site is trying to give you some helpful information.

```
brezup:ray testing $ ftp ftp.cis.ohio-state.edu
Connected to www.cis.ohio-state.edu.
220 www.cis.ohio-state.edu FTP server (Version wu-2.6.1(1)
Tue Nov 6 12:29:49 EST 2001) ready.

Name (ftp.cis.ohio-state.edu:nermal): anonymous
331 Guest login ok, send your complete e-mail address as password.
Password:
530-Sorry, the limit of 20 users logged in has been exceeded (20).
530-We've had to cut back to avoid swamping our outside link.
530-
530-Please try again later.
530-
530-To report problems, please contact ftp@cis.ohio-state.edu.
530 Login incorrect.
```

And this is an example of what you might see if you have connected properly:

```
brezup:ray testing $ ftp ftp.cis.ohio-state.edu
Connected to www.cis.ohio-state.edu.
220 www.cis.ohio-state.edu FTP server (Version wu-2.6.1(1)
Tue Nov 6 12:29:49 EST 2001) ready.
Name (ftp.cis.ohio-state.edu:nermal): anonymous
331 Guest login ok, send your complete e-mail address as password.
Password:
230-Hello [unknown]@ryoohki.biosci.ohio-state.edu.
230-
230-This is the anonymous FTP archive of the Computer and Information
230-Science Department and The Ohio State University.
230-
230-You are user 5 out of 20 users currently allowed in.
230-
230 Guest login ok, access restrictions apply.
Remote system type is UNIX.
Using binary mode to transfer files.
ftp>
```

NOTE

If you attempt to access these servers and get different results, don't be alarmed. These are simply examples of various results that can occur, and your results might be different depending on when you connect, where you're connecting from, and whether the site has changed its configuration since these dialogs were captured.

From this `ftp>` prompt, you can issue commands, such as `help`, `rhelp`, `get`, `put`, `cd`, `ls`, `pwd`, and potentially others, depending on the server configuration. The output from the `help` command gives you a list of commands available to you in your client (don't worry if this looks like a long list; we cover the good ones in the following text and in Appendix A), and the output of `rhelp` tells you about commands on the server:

```
ftp> help
Commands may be abbreviated. Commands are:

!         features    mls       proxy     size
$         fget      mlsd      put       sndbuf
account     form      mlst      pwd       status
append     ftp       mode      quit      struct
ascii      gate      modtime     quote      sunique
bell      get       more      rate      system
binary     glob      mput      rcvbuf     tenex
bye       hash      msend     recv      throttle
case      help      newer     reget      trace
cd        idle      nlist     remopts     type
cdup      image      nmap      rename     umask
chmod      lcd       ntrans     reset      unset
close      less      open      restart     usage
cr        lpage      page      rhelp      user
debug      lpwd      passive     rmdir      verbose
delete     ls       pdir      rstatus     xferbuf
dir       macdef     pls       runique     ?
disconnect    mdelete     pmlsd      send
edit      mdir      preserve    sendport
epsv4      mget      progress    set
exit      mkdir      prompt     site

ftp> rhelp
214-The following commands are recognized (* =>'s unimplemented).
  USER  PORT  STOR  MSAM*  RNTO  NLST  MKD   CDUP
  PASS  PASV  APPE  MRSQ*  ABOR  SITE  XMKD  XCUP
```

```
  ACCT*  TYPE  MLFL*  MRCP*  DELE  SYST  RMD   STOU
  SMNT*  STRU  MAIL*  ALLO  CWD   STAT  XRMD  SIZE
  REIN*  MODE  MSND*  REST  XCWD  HELP  PWD   MDTM
  QUIT   RETR  MSOM*  RNFR  LIST  NOOP  XPWD
214 Direct comments to ftp@cis.ohio-state.edu.
```

Usually, the commands you'll be most interested in are the ones for moving around the filesystem, and retrieving and sending files. The commands you're most likely to use frequently are the `cd` and `lcd` commands, which are analogous to the command-line `cd` command for the remote and local directories, respectively, and the `get` and `put` commands, which retrieve files from the server and send files to it.

Additionally, you can ask for help on specific commands—one of the more interesting ones to ask about in the listing shown is the `site` command:

```
ftp> rhelp site
214-The following SITE commands are recognized (* =>'s unimplemented).
  UMASK       GROUP       INDEX       GROUPS
  IDLE        GPASS       EXEC        CHECKMETHOD
  CHMOD       NEWER       ALIAS       CHECKSUM
  HELP        MINFO       CDPATH
```

The `site` command implements FTP-site-specific command options, and you would need to contact the administrator to find out exactly what the command options are and which you are allowed to use.

Files that you get from the FTP server are placed (unless you specify otherwise by giving a download path along with the `get` command at the prompt) into the same directory from which you issued the `ftp` command.

Another thing that the command-line `ftp` client does much better than the graphical clients is let you know and access special features that the server has available for your use. Because the command-line client can't recursively download directories as the graphical clients can, and because it predates the graphical clients by many years, the most popular Unix FTP servers provide facilities to compensate. For example, many sites provide automatic `tar`ring and `compress`ing of directories, so that even though you can't recursively download a directory, you can still retrieve it all, conveniently `tar`red and `compress`ed with a single command. To access these special facilities, though, you have to `get` files that don't exist—typically named `<directoryname>.tar` or `<directoryname>.tar.gz`. The server intercepts the request for the nonexistent name and dynamically creates the tarfile or compressed tarfile. This facility could be accessed, even with graphical clients, but because the clients by default hide the server messages, the user rarely knows they're available, and the nonexistent filenames are notoriously difficult to click on.

The following is an example of interaction with a server that provides this sort of special facilities to the user.

NOTE

Not all servers provide this sort of special functionality. Many of the best do, but a good number of sites have dropped many functions designed to help the online visitor. This is largely due to the significant cost of providing resources of this nature, the fact that every feature designed to assist the visitor increases the resource cost, and a massive level of abuse of FTP sites by users who behave in antisocial fashions.

If you want to see resources remain available, don't abuse the sites that provide them. If an FTP server says it's at its user limit, don't just keep reconnecting every two seconds. This constant reconnection and rejection cycle actually costs the server a significant amount of load, and it annoys the administrators and makes them even more likely reduce the number of available user slots and convenience features in the future.

```
brezup:ray testing $ ftp ftp.cpan.org

Trying 142.132.1.82...
Connected to ftp.cpan.ddns.develooper.com.
220 theoryx5.uwinnipeg.ca FTP server
➥(Version wu-2.6.2(1) Thu Jul 11 15:44:16 CD
T 2002) ready.
Name (ftp.cpan.org:sage): anonymous
331 Guest login ok, send your complete e-mail address as password.
Password:
.
.
.
230-You are currently user # 2 out of a maximum of 20 users. The current
230-local time is Mon Aug 5 21:48:46 2002.
230-
230-This server supports on-the-fly
➥decompression of files (for file.gz, use
230-the command `get file`), compression
➥of files (for file, use the command
230-`get file.gz`), and creation of tar and zip archives of directories:
230-for directory "package", cd to the parent directory and use one of
230-  get package.tar
230-  get package.tar.Z
230-  get package.tar.gz
230-  get package.zip
230-Remember to transfer such files in binary mode.
```

```
230-
230-If you have problems listing files with the 'ls' command,
230-try using 'dir' instead.
230-
230 Guest login ok, access restrictions apply.
Remote system type is UNIX.
Using binary mode to transfer files.

ftp> cd /pub/CPAN/authors/id/W/WI

250 CWD command successful.

ftp> ls -l

227 Entering Passive Mode (142,132,1,82,230,163)
150 Opening ASCII mode data connection for /bin/ls.
total 24
-r--r--r--  1 8129   200      452 Mar 26 13:53 CHECKSUMS
drwxrwxr-x  2 8129   200     4096 Jun 11 2001 WICKLINE
drwxrwxr-x  2 8129   200     4096 Mar 26 13:39 WIHAA
drwxrwxr-x  2 8129   200     4096 Jan 25 2002 WILSONPM
drwxrwxr-x  2 8129   200     4096 Oct 31 2001 WIMV
drwxr-xr-x  2 8129   200     4096 Dec 20 1998 WINKO
226 Transfer complete.

ftp> cd WINKO

250 CWD command successful.

ftp> ls -l

227 Entering Passive Mode (142,132,1,82,236,51)
150 Opening ASCII mode data connection for /bin/ls.
total 20
-r--r--r--  1 8129   200      548 Dec 13 2000 CHECKSUMS
-rw-r--r--  1 8129   200      965 Dec 11 1996
➥String-BitCount-1.11.readme
-rw-r--r--  1 8129   200     2316 Dec 11 1996
➥String-BitCount-1.11.tar.gz
-rw-r--r--  1 8129   200      925 Dec 10 1996
➥String-Parity-1.31.readme
-rw-r--r--  1 8129   200     3586 Dec 11 1996
➥String-Parity-1.31.tar.gz
```

```
226 Transfer complete.

ftp> cd ..

250 CWD command successful.

ftp> binary

200 Type set to I.

ftp> get WINKO.tar.gz

local: WINKO.tar.gz remote: WINKO.tar.gz
227 Entering Passive Mode (142,132,1,82,207,26)
150 Opening BINARY mode data connection for /bin/tar.
226 Transfer complete.
10240 bytes received in 00:00 (73.63 KB/s)

ftp> quit

221-You have transferred 7375 bytes in 1 files.
221-Total traffic for this session was 10107 bytes in 3 transfers.
221-Thank you for using the FTP service on onion.valueclick.com.
221 Goodbye.

[Sage-Rays-Computer:~/osx-test] sage% ls

WINKO.tar.gz

[Sage-Rays-Computer:~/osx-test] sage% gunzip WINKO.tar.gz
[Sage-Rays-Computer:~/osx-test] sage% tar -tvf WINKO.tar

drwxr-xr-x 2 1001   1001      0 Dec 20 1998 WINKO
-r--r--r-- 1 1001   1001     548 Dec 13 13:31 WINKO/CHECKSUMS
-rw-r--r-- 1 1001   1001     965 Dec 10 1996➥
WINKO/String-BitCount-1.11.readme
-rw-r--r-- 1 1001   1001    2316 Dec 11 1996➥
WINKO/String-BitCount-1.11.tar.gz
-rw-r--r-- 1 1001   1001     925 Dec 10 1996➥
WINKO/String-Parity-1.31.readme
-rw-r--r-- 1 1001   1001    3586 Dec 11 1996➥
WINKO/String-Parity-1.31.tar.gz
```

NOTE

Don't be surprise if you try this with CPAN and don't get these results. CPAN uses some tricks to load-balance, and not all the servers that they distribute the load over support these functions.

In this example, we retrieved a `tar`red and `gzip`ped copy of the `WINKO` directory, with a single command, even though that `.tar.gz` file doesn't exist on the system. As shown, it arrives on our local machine with the contents expected.

NOTE

Even more sophisticated things can be done with the servers, but their implementation tends to be site specific. Pay attention to the introductory and help messages presented by servers that you connect to. The site administrators often use these messages to inform you of any special capabilities, as well as how you can use them.

Table 15.3 shows the syntax and most interesting options for `ftp`. More documentation is available in Appendix A.

TABLE 15.3 The `ftp` Command Syntax and Useful Options

`ftp` File transfer program.

```
ftp [-AadefginpRtvV] [-o <outfile>] [-P <port>] [-r <seconds>]
      [-T <dir>,<max>[,<inc>][[<user>@]<host> [<port>]]] [<host>:<path>[/]]
      [file:///<file>] [ftp://[<user>[:<pass>]@]<host>[:<port>]/<path>[/]]
      [http://[<user>[:<pass>]@]<host>[:<port>]/<path>] [...]
ftp -u <url> <file> [...]
```

The remote host with which `ftp` is to communicate can be specified on the command line. Done this way, `ftp` immediately tries to establish a connection with the remote host. Otherwise, `ftp` enters its command interpreter mode, awaits commands from the user, and displays the prompt `ftp>`.

Option	Description
`-A`	Forces active mode `ftp`. By default, `ftp` tries to use passive mode `ftp` and falls back to active mode if passive is not supported by the server.
`-a`	Causes `ftp` to bypass normal login procedure and use an anonymous login instead.
`-f`	Forces a cache reload for transfers that go through the FTP or HTTP proxies.
`-g`	Disables filename globbing (that is to say, don't allow wildcard filename expansions).
`-i`	Turns off interactive mode when transferring multiple files.

TABLE 15.3 Continued

-n	Does not attempt auto-login on initial connection. If auto-login is not disabled, ftp checks for a .netrc file in the user's directory for an entry describing an account on the remote machine. If no entry is available, ftp prompts for the login name on the remote machine (defaults to the login name on the local machine), and if necessary, prompts for a password.
-p	Enables passive mode operation for use behind connection filtering firewalls. This option has been deprecated as ftp now tries to use passive mode by default, falling back to active mode if the server does not support passive connections.
-v	Enables verbose and progress. Default if output is to a terminal (and for progress, if ftp is in the foreground). Shows all responses from the remote server as well as transfer statistics.
-V	Disables verbose and progress, overriding the default of enabled when output is to a terminal.
-o *<output>*	When auto-fetching files, saves the contents in output. If output is not - or doesn't start with ¦, only the first file specified is retrieved into output; all other files are retrieved into the basename of their remote name.
-P *<port>*	Sets the port number to *<port>*.
-r *<seconds>*	Retries the connection attempt if it failed, pausing for *<seconds>* seconds. Please be kind to the FTP servers and don't set this to a value smaller than 20 seconds or so—larger would be better.
-T *<direction>*,*<maximum>* [,*<increment>*]	Sets the maximum transfer rate for *<direction>* to *<maximum>* bytes/second, and if specified, the *<increment>* to *<increment>* bytes/second.
-u *<url>* *<file>*	Uploads files on the command line to *<url>* where *<url>* is one of the ftp URL types as supported by auto-fetch (with an optional target filename for single file uploads), and *<file>* is one or more local files to be uploaded.

When ftp is in its command interpreter mode awaiting instructions from the user, there are many commands that the user might issue. Some of them include

ascii	Sets the file transfer type to network ASCII. Although this is supposed to be the default, it is not uncommon for an FTP server to indicate that binary is its default.
binary	Sets the file transfer type to support binary image transfer.
image	Same as binary.
quit	Terminates the ftp session and exits ftp. An end of file also terminates the session and exits.
cd *<remote_directory>*	Changes the current working directory on the remote host to *<remote_directory>*.
cdup	Changes the current working directory on the remote host to the parent directory (same as cd ../)

TABLE 15.3 Continued

`lcd` *<directory>*	Changes the working directory on the local machine. If no directory is specified, the user's home directory is used.
`close`	Terminates the `ftp` session with the remote host and returns to the command interpreter.
`dir [`*<remote-directory>* `[`*<local_file>*`]]`	Prints a listing of the directory on the remote machine. Most Unix systems produce an `ls -l` output. If *<remote_directory>* is not specified, the current directory is assumed. If *<local_file>* is not specified, or is `-`, the output is sent to the terminal.
`open` *<hostname>* `[`*<port>*`]`	Attempts to establish an `ftp` connection on *<hostname>* at *<port>*, if *<port>* is specified.
`glob`	Toggles filename expansion for `mdelete`, `mget`, and `mput`. If globbing is turned off, filename arguments are taken literally and not expanded.
`delete` *<remote_file>*	Deletes the specified *<remote_file>* on the remote machine.
`mdelete` *<remote_files>*	Deletes the specified *<remote_files>* on the remote machine.
`get` *<remote_file>* `[`*<local-file>*`]`	Downloads *<remote_file>* from the remote machine to the local machine. If *<local_file>* is not specified, the file is also saved on the local machine with the name *<remote_file>*.
`mget` *<remote_files>*	Downloads the specified *<remote_files>*.
`put` *<local_file>* `[`*<remote_file>*`]`	Uploads the specified *<local_file>* to the remote host. If *<remote_file>* is not , specified, the file is saved on the remote host with the name *<local_file>*.
`mput` *<local_files>*	Uploads the specified *<local_files>*.
`help [`*<command>*`]`	Displays a message describing *<command>*. If *<command>* is not specified, a listing of known commands is displayed.
`ls [`*<remote_directory>* `[`*<local_file>*`]]`	Prints a list of the files in a directory on the remote machine. If *<remote_directory>* is not specified, the current working directory is assumed.If *<local_file>* is not specified, or is `-`, the output is printed to a terminal. Note that if nothing is listed, the directory might only have directories in it. Try `ls -l` or `dir` for a complete listing.
`mkdir` *<directory>*	Makes the specified *<directory>* on the remote machine.
`rmdir` *<directory>*	Removes the specified *<directory>* from the remote machine.
`passive [auto]`	Toggles passive mode if no argument is given. If `auto` is given, acts as if `FTPMODE` is set to `auto`. If passive mode is turned on (default), the `ftp` client sends a `PASV` command for data connections rather than a `PORT` command. `PASV` command requests that the remote server open a port for the data connection and return the address of that port. The remote server listens on that port, and the client then sends data to it. With the `PORT` command, the client listens on a port and sends that address to the remote host, who connects back to it. Passive mode is useful when FTPing through a firewall. Not all `ftp` servers are required to support passive mode.

TABLE 15.3 Continued

`progress`	Displays a status bar indicating the progress of each transfer as it occurs. Seeing that something is actually happening can be a real comfort when doing large transfers over slow lines.
`pwd`	Prints the current working directory on the remote host.
`rate` *`<direction>`* `[`*`<maximum>`* `[`*`<increment>`*`]]`	Throttles the maximum transfer rate to *`<maximum>`* bytes/second. If *`<maximum>`* is 0, disables the throttle. Not yet implemented for `ascii` mode. *`<direction>`* may be any one of: `get` (incoming transfers); `put` (outgoing transfers); `all` (both). *`<maximum>`* can be modified on-the-fly by *`<increment>`* bytes (default: 1024) each time a given signal is received: `SIGUSR1` (increments *`<maximum>`* by *`<increment>`* bytes; `SIGUSR2` (decrements *`<maximum>`* by *`<increment>`* bytes—result must be a positive number). If *`<maximum>`* is not supplied, displays current throttle rates.

Terminals in Terminals: `telnet`, `rlogin`, `ssh`

Because one of the primary methods for interacting with a Unix machine that you're sitting in front of is via a textual terminal, it should come as no surprise that a number of network tools are available to allow you to access remote machines through that same interface. The three primary examples of these are the `telnet`, `rlogin`, and `ssh`/`slogin` (secure shell) clients. Each of these provides a connection to a remote machine that is analogous to the one that `Terminal.app` provides to your local machine—you get access to a command prompt and can run software on the remote machine just like software in `Terminal.app` on the local machine.

The `telnet` Program

`telnet` is a venerable connection program that speaks a language compatible with the over-the-wire communication protocol used by many Internet services. The protocol is a fundamental building block of much of the Internet and has been used to provide everything from Web services to file transfer services to terminal services. It is, unfortunately, as trivial as it is ubiquitous and provides almost no built-in security. Because of this, terminal services implemented directly in the protocol are inherently insecure, and the `telnet` client and server fall into this category.

The syntax of the `telnet` command is `telnet` *`<host>`* `[`*`port number`*`]`.

If you're communicating with a system that's either not connected to the Internet or run by a particularly non-security-conscious system administrator, you might actually be able to use it as a terminal application. In that case, if you issue the `telnet` command, you might see something like the following:

```
brezup:ray testing $ telnet krpan.killernuts.org
Trying 192.168.1.10...
Connected to krpan.killernuts.org (192.168.1.10).
Escape character is '^]'.

Red Hat Linux release 7.0 (Guinness)
Kernel 2.4.2 on a 2-processor i686
login: adam
Password:
Last login: Thu Apr 19 19:36:23 on vc/1
You have mail.

Terminal: vt100.
Printer set to newsioux

krpan adam %
```

At that point, you're at a shell prompt on the remote machine and can interact with it just as you interact with your local machine via its shell prompt in the terminal.

NOTE

Don't expect to actually be able to `telnet` to `krpan.killernuts.org` to test this. We don't know any system administrators who leave `telnet` available on their machine, and we had to enable it specifically for the example.

If everyone you know is concerned about security and has their `telnet` daemons disabled, there are still a number of interesting uses for the `telnet` client. Because many servers for other Internet applications speak the same protocol, you can use the `telnet` protocol to talk to them as well. It might not seem like a useful idea to be able to talk to a Web server with a terminal program that doesn't understand anything about the HTTP language and can't display the data properly, but it turns out to have a number of interesting applications.

For example, your Web browser tells you that a server isn't responding—can you tell whether it's the Web server software that's not responding, or the machine that hosts it that's not responding? `telnet` to the HTTP port (port 80) on the server, and see what the response is. If the Web server software and machine are both okay, your session should look something like this:

```
brezup:ray testing $ telnet www.biosci.ohio-state.edu 80
Trying 140.254.12.240...
Connected to ryoko.biosci.ohio-state.edu.
Escape character is '^]'.
```

If the machine is okay, but the Web server software isn't speaking, the session might instead look more like this:

```
brezup:ray testing $ telnet rosalyn.biosci.ohio-state.edu 80
Trying 140.254.12.151...
telnet: connect to address 140.254.12.151: Connection refused
telnet: Unable to connect to remote host
```

If the machine is completely absent from the network, such as `catbert` in the following example, the response gets only to the `Trying` line and hangs there, well, trying—I pressed Ctrl-C in the example to convince it to give up.

```
[localhost:~] nermal% telnet catbert.biosci.ohio-state.edu 80
Trying 140.254.12.236...
^C
```

Finally, if there really isn't a machine by that name at all, you'll see

```
[localhost:~] nermal% telnet dingbat.biosci.ohio-state.edu 80
dingbat.biosci.ohio-state.edu: No address associated with nodename
```


CAUTION

Please don't use the `telnet` program as a terminal program unless you are connecting to a machine that has no connection to the Internet. The program transfers all data in plain text, and anyone with physical access to any of the communication hardware involved in the connection (such as the phone lines, ethernet wiring, the air, if you're using AirPort) can read everything you type, including user IDs and passwords out of the data stream. There are better alternatives that we'll cover shortly.

The `rlogin` Program

Whereas the `telnet` communication package was conceived with hardly any concern for security, the `rlogin` communications package was developed under the seemingly quaint notion that certain connections could be trusted, based only on their self-proclaimed credentials. Passing its data using the same unprotected protocol as `telnet`, `rlogin` is supposed to give the administrator some confidence in the identity of a connecting visitor by virtue of the fact that the connection came from a trusted port. Using it is similar to `telnet`, except that it doesn't accept an optional connection port, and it automatically fills in your user ID on the remote system based on your local system user ID. The syntax is simply `rlogin` *<remotehost>*.

NOTE

A long, long time ago, in a decade almost two removed, the Internet and the perceptions regarding users who could connect to it were very different. Along with the lack of `this.dot.that.dot.coms` all over the place, and the lack of spam in your email, Unix was an expensive commercial operating system. Machines that ran it were expensive, and the people who ran them, even people on different ends of the earth who had never met each other, thought of each other as fellow members of a professional fraternity. Professional courtesies were extended, and if you were a system administrator, a concern about another's security was the same as a concern about your own security.

Because of this expectation that any person running a Unix machine was another security-conscious professional, early security measures were based on utilizing this trust as a form of security credential. Security-conscious professionals were as worried about allowing security risks on others' machines as incurring security risks on their own. A security-conscious professional would never let a "bad" user use his system. The only people who could connect using the `rlogin` client were users on some Unix machine somewhere. Taken together, any user with valid credentials on a Unix machine, verified by their being allowed to run the `rlogin` program, must, by association, be a trustable user.

Taken in the context of today's rampant attacks against system security, this might sound like a naively bad security method, but until the advent of "personal Unixes" such as Linux, it worked surprisingly well. Given that much of today's data is passed around with equally insecure connections, without even a trust-based attempt to verify the authenticity of the content, we probably shouldn't poke too much fun at the naiveté of the early communication packages.

As you are coming into the world of having your own personal Unix machine connected to the Internet, we encourage you to adopt some of the historic notions regarding administrator responsibility and fraternity, but not their naive notions regarding security.

As with the `telnet` program, if you're connecting to machines that aren't connected to the Internet, the `rlogin` client is just as good as any. If you're connecting to machines that are connected to the Internet, please don't use the `rlogin` program, even if the remote machine makes it available. Doing so only risks your accounts and data on both local and remote machines, and the security of both machines as well.

The Secure-Shell Software Suite: `slogin`, `scp`, `sftp`, and Others

The Secure Shell collection of programs provides strongly encrypted communications between your machine and a remote server. The implementation that Apple has chosen to provide is based on the OpenSSH (`http://www.openssh.org/`) distribution of the protocols. The protocol requires both client software, which we cover in this chapter, and server software, which is covered in Chapter 26, "Remote Access and Control." Here, we assume that you already have a server to talk to and detail the use of the client software on the Unix side of your OS X machine to talk to your remote server.

`slogin`

The starting point for use of the Secure Shell client is the `slogin` (also available under the name `ssh`) program. This program replaces the functionality of the `telnet` and `rlogin` programs, and provides some additional capabilities as well. Unlike `telnet` and `rlogin`, `slogin` passes all information between the machines as encrypted data, using a public-key encryption method.

NOTE

Public-key encryption is a clever method of encrypting data. Basically, in public-key encryption schemes, every person interested in exchanging encrypted information creates two keys. One of the created keys is the person's private key, and the other is the person's public key. These keys are mathematically related, but one cannot be derived from the other. The cleverness resides in the mathematical relationship between the keys. When you encrypt data, you encrypt it using two keys: your private key and the public key of the message's intended recipient. The keys are related in such a fashion that data encrypted with your private key, and another's public key, can be decrypted only with a combination of your public key and the other person's private key. This encryption method is used in both systems such as the PGP (Pretty Good Privacy) email encryption software and in data transmission software such as `ssh`. In email encryption, you use your private key, and the email recipient's public key, to encrypt mail destined for them, and they use your public key and their private key to encrypt mail destined for you. In the encryption of data transmission in software such as `ssh`, the system again uses your private and public keys, and a pair of private and public keys belonging to the remote system to which you are connecting.

The basic use of `slogin` is much like that for `rlogin`—simply issue the command `slogin` *<machinename>*, where *<machinename>* is the name or IP address of the remote machine to which you want to connect. If the remote machine is running a Secure Shell server and it is configured to allow you to connect, the server responds by asking for your password. If you respond correctly, you are left at a shell prompt on the remote machine and can type into it and execute commands, just as though you were in a `Terminal.app` window typing to your local machine.

TIP

The command `ssh` is equivalent to the command `slogin`. We use `slogin` in our examples and discussion here to make it clear where we're talking about `slogin` the program, and SSH the acronym for the Secure Shell package, but you can substitute the command `ssh` wherever you see `slogin` used here.

A successful `slogin` attempt might look something like this:

```
brezup:ray testing $ slogin rosalyn.biosci.ohio-state.edu
ray@rosalyn.biosci.ohio-state.edu's password:
Last login: Tue May 13 2003 01:16:06 -0500 from dhcp065-024-074-
```

```
You have new mail.

...Remote login...

Rosalyn ray 1 >
```

Again, at this point we're at a shell prompt on the remote machine `rosalyn.biosci.ohio-state.edu`.

If you don't want to log in to the remote machine as the same user ID as you are on the current machine, you can specify a user ID using `-l` *<username>* after the hostname. Alternatively, you can use *<username>*@*<hostname>* to specify the user and host. If I wanted to log in to rosalyn as user `testing` (regardless of what user I am on my local machine), I could use this syntax:

```
brezup:ray testing $ slogin testing@rosalyn.biosci.ohio-state.edu
testing@rosalyn.biosci.ohio-state.edu's password:
Last login: Tue Jun 24 2003 15:30:04 -0500
You have new mail.

...Remote login...

Rosalyn testing 1 >
```

Some system administrators choose not to allow remote logins through simple password authentication. Passwords are generally too short to be difficult for a computer to guess by simple brute-force methods. Instead, the Secure Shell suite allows the use of arbitrarily long, multiword passphrases. An `slogin` connection requiring this type of login looks like this:

```
brezup:ray testing $ slogin rosalyn.biosci.ohio-state.edu -l joray
Enter passphrase for key '/Users/ray/.ssh/id_dsa':
Last login: Tue Aug 06 2003 14:39:47 -0500 from cvl232015.columb
You have new mail.

...Remote login...

Rosalyn joray 1 >
```

If the remote machine is running this more restrictive security (and we recommend that you do so, if you choose to enable remote connections to your machine when we get to Chapter 26), you will be asked, not for your password, but for your passphrase if you have created one. The connection will be refused if you have not created a passphrase.

Creating a passphrase involves a bit of work on your part. This is because if you really want security, you can't allow the encrypted keys that identify you to be seen on the network. Therefore, after the key is created, you need to transfer it to the remote machine via some old-fashioned, physical method, such as writing it on a floppy disk and taking this directly to the remote machine.

TIP

If you're in charge of setting up both machines, you could leave password access under Secure Shell on long enough for you to copy the keys back and forth on the encrypted channel, and then turn off password access to tighten security.

Creating a passphrase for yourself involves the following:

On your OS X machine, generate a key pair by running

```
ssh-keygen -t <type>
```

The `-t` option specifies the key type to be generated. This can be `rsa` for RSA or `dsa` for DSA (isn't case-sensitivity fun?) RSA is used in SSH1 servers, whereas either RSA or DSA can be used with SSH2 servers. RSA, Rivest-Shamir-Adelman, named for its developers, is the most commonly used public key algorithm. DSA, Digital Signature Algorithm, is a signature-only algorithm, based on the Diffie-Hellman discrete logarithm problem.

When you run `ssh-keygen`, you are asked for a passphrase to protect the private key. It is recommended that the passphrase be at least 11 characters long and include as many character types as possible: uppercase letters, lowercase letters, numbers, and special characters. Spaces may be included as part of the passphrase.

Here is a sample run:

```
brezup:miwa miwa $ ssh-keygen -t dsa
Generating public/private dsa key pair.
Enter file in which to save the key (/Users/miwa/.ssh/id_dsa):
Enter passphrase (empty for no passphrase):
Enter same passphrase again:
Your identification has been saved in /Users/miwa/.ssh/id_dsa.
Your public key has been saved in /Users/miwa/.ssh/id_dsa.pub.
The key fingerprint is:
7d:25:3e:87:3b:25:24:cf:5a:05:0e:1d:19:ad:67:10 miwa@brezup
```

As `ssh-keygen` tells us, user `miwa` does indeed have the promised keys, as shown in the following output. The private key was saved as `id_dsa`, and the public key was saved as `id_dsa.pub`; both are stored in the directory `~/.ssh/`.

15

```
brezup:miwa miwa $ ls -al ~/.ssh
total 16
drwx------  4 miwa miwa 136 17 Aug 22:09 .
drwxr-xr-x 12 miwa miwa 408 17 Aug 22:08 ..
-rw-------  1 miwa miwa 744 17 Aug 22:09 id_dsa
-rw-r--r--  1 miwa miwa 601 17 Aug 22:09 id_dsa.pub
```

Next, we need to transfer the file `id_dsa.pub` to the remote host. Because you might be generating different keys for different hosts, it's most convenient if you rename the file first—this also helps prevent you from overwriting it the next time you create a key, or overwriting the key on the remote host when you transfer it. You might also want to consider using the `-f` option to specify a different filename when you generate your public key. However, we wanted to show you what to expect by default. Because it's your public key, it doesn't matter whether the world can see it—you can copy it to your remote host via FTP, move it there with a floppy, or paste it across a logged-in terminal session.

On the remote host, in the `.ssh` directory in your home directory (`~/.ssh/`), the public key you just created needs to be added to the file `authorized_keys` (`~/.ssh/authorized_keys`). If the file does not exist, it must be created. If you copied the key over in a file, you can do this by simply using the `cat` command:

```
cat <mynewkeyfile> >> ~/.ssh/authorized_keys
```

When adding the new key to the file, make sure that the key is added as a single long line of data. If your key arrived in one long line of data in a file, the `cat` command shown will work fine. Otherwise, if you're pasting the key in via the terminal, or aren't sure it's in a single long line in the file, it's best to check `~/.ssh/authorized_keys` to make sure that it arrived correctly.

TIP

Many terminals will be friendly and line-wrap the key, if you try to paste it through a logged-in terminal window. If your passphrase refuses to work, make sure that there are no extra blank lines in your `~/.ssh/authorized_keys` file, that the key is on a line by itself (rather than attached to the backside of another key), and that the key hasn't accidentally accumulated any line breaks.

Having done all this, if you now try to `slogin` to the remote host where you just added your key (and assuming that the remote host is running `sshd2`!), you should be greeted with a login process asking for your passphrase rather than your password. Enter the passphrase exactly as you did to create the keys, and you will enjoy a data connection that is almost impossible to decrypt, and an access code (your passphrase) that is much more secure than a simple password.

> **NOTE**
> There are a number of variations on the movement of the public key and its installation on the remote host. These revolve around the version of server running on the remote machine. Considerably more detail and examples of these options are given in Chapter 26, where we cover getting these outside machines to talk to your OS X box.

The slogin program also provides a neat method for protecting data transmissions other than terminals. This is implemented as an encrypted tunnel between the two machines connected by the slogin terminal connection. Essentially, slogin can be instructed to watch for connections that come to your local machine, package the data from these connections up, encrypt it, ship it off to the other end of the tunnel, and unpackage it again. You then use your ftp, or any other network connection program, to connect to your local machine (not the remote machine!), and slogin tunnels that connection to the remote machine and makes the connection at the other end. Because your user ID and password for the FTP server are carried over the encrypted tunnel, they're never in clear text on the network, and your login information and any data you transmit are protected.

To demonstrate this, the following slogin connection sets up a tunnel from the local machine to a remote machine named waashu, over which ftp connections can be carried.

```
brezup:root testing # slogin waashu.biosci.ohio-state.edu
➥-l testing -L21:waashu:21
The authenticity of host 'waashu.biosci.ohio-state.edu
➥(140.254.104.239)' can't be established.
DSA key fingerprint is 3d:1d:6b:78:c9:7e:63:b9:8b:6d:13:5f:e5:3b:f1:20.
Are you sure you want to continue connecting (yes/no)? yes
Warning: Permanently added 'waashu.biosci.ohio-state.edu,140.254.104.239'
➥(DSA) to the list of known hosts.
testing@waashu.biosci.ohio-state.edu's password:
Last login: Tue Jul 15 2003 15:37:15
You have new mail.

/usr/local/testing

WAASHU testing 1 >
```

In this case, we've never connected waashu before, so slogin asks whether we really believe that we're making a connection to the right host and that it's really giving us valid credentials (this is the one point in all our communications where an imposter in the middle of the communication could easily insert false information and fool us into transmitting our information insecurely). Again, this leaves the terminal connected to the remote machine, and sitting at a shell prompt on the remote machine. The -L21:waashu:21

part of the command sets up the tunneling magic. It tells `slogin` to start listening on port 21 (which is the port that the FTP server would usually listen to), capture anything it sees, package it up securely, and transmit it to waashu, where it is to be unpackaged and sent to waashu's port 21 (thereby connecting to waashu's FTP server).

> **NOTE**
>
> Note that only the `root` user can map to ports numbered lower than 1024. For this reason, the `slogin` forwarding as shown here isn't quite what you want to do for day-to-day use. It's the easiest for basic illustration, though—a more practical example comes a little later.

After `slogin` is connected like this, it is connecting port 21, the normal `ftp` port on our machine (`localhost`), to port 21 on the remote host we're logged in to. Fire up another terminal window. The second terminal window is used to invoke `ftp` to connect over the tunnel (by connecting to our local machine, usually available as `localhost` and always available as 127.0.0.1) like so:

```
brezup:miwa miwa $ ftp localhost
Connected to localhost.biosci.ohio-state.edu.
220 waashu.biosci.ohio-state.edu FTP server ready.
Name (localhost:joray): joray
331 Password required for joray.
Password:
230 User joray logged in.
Remote system type is UNIX.
Using binary mode to transfer files.
ftp> passive
Passive mode on.
ftp> cd osx-misc
250 CWD command successful.
ftp> binary
200 Type set to I.
ftp> put developer-1.tiff
local: developer-1.tiff remote: developer-1.tiff
227 Entering Passive Mode (140,254,12,239,60,59)
150 Opening BINARY mode data connection for 'developer-1.tiff'.
226 Transfer complete.
1255376 bytes sent in 16.2 seconds (77490 bytes/s)
ftp> quit
221 Goodbye.
```

To check whether it arrived okay, we go to the waashu terminal:

```
WAASHU osx-misc 203 > ls -l dev*tiff
-rw-r--r--  1 joray  user  1255376 Apr 21 20:35 developer-1.tiff
```

Note that when we `ftp` to `localhost`, `ftp` reports that we're connected to `localhost`, but `waashu` responds. The tunnel is working as expected.

As noted earlier, use of port `21` is restricted to the `root` user, but for your first introduction, it made sense to direct the `ftp` port to the `ftp` port. There is nothing that limits the forwarding to connecting identically numbered ports, though, and `ftp` can also connect to ports other than the usual port `21`. For use on a day-to-day basis, a normal user can replace the `-L21:`*`<machinename>`*`:21` section of the command with `-L2000:`*`<machine-name>`*`:21`. The `ftp` command then is extended by adding the port number for the local connection, as `ftp localhost 2000`. This probably sounds more complicated than it really is. It really doesn't look much different than just directing the `ftp` port to the `ftp` port. In one window, run this:

```
brezup:miwa Documents $ slogin waashu.biosci.ohio-state.edu
➥-l testing -L2000:waashu:21
```

And in another, run the `ftp` command as like so:

```
brezup:miwa Documents $ ftp localhost 2000
```

This works identically to having `root` route the tunnel as shown in the first example.

If your machine doesn't know the target by a short name (such as <waashu>), you need to use an IP address or fully qualified hostname for the `-L<sourceport>:<target host-name>:<targetport>` part of the command as well as the base `slogin` itself.

Also an option, if all you want to do is forward a port without receiving a shell prompt on the remote host, use the `-N` option to `slogin`. This doesn't cause it to return to the command line but is useful in stored terminal scripts if you're not interested in leaving a prompt open and unused (usually a good idea for security purposes).

Table 15.4 shows the syntax and additional options for the operation of `slogin`. Complete documentation is available in Appendix A.

TABLE 15.4 The Syntax and Some Interesting Options for `ssh` and `slogin`

`ssh`	
`slogin`	Secure shell remote login client.
`ssh [-l <login_name>] <hostname> ¦ <user>@<hostname> [<command>]`	
`ssh [-aAfgknqtTvxXCNP1246] [-b <bind_address>] [-c <cipher_spec>] [-e <escap_char>] [-i <identity_file>] [-l <login_name>] [-m <mac_spec>] [-o <option>] [-p <port>] [-F <configfile>] [-L <port>:<host>:<hostport>] [-R <port>:<host>:<hostport>] [-D <port>] [<hostname> ¦ <user>@<hostname>] [<command>]`	
`-a`	Disables forwarding of the authentication agent connection.
`-A`	Enables forwarding of the authentication agent connection. This can also be specified on a per-host basis in a configuration file.

TABLE 15.4 Continued

`-f`	Requests `ssh` to go to background just before command execution. Implies `-n`. The recommended way to start X11 programs at a remote site is `ssh -f` *<host>* `xterm`.
`-v`	Verbose mode. Causes debugging messages to be printed.
`-x`	Disables X11 forwarding.
`-X`	Enables X11 forwarding. This can also be specified on a per-host basis in a configuration file.
`-C`	Requests compression of all data.
`-N`	Does not execute a remote command. Useful for just forwarding ports. SSH2 only.
`-P`	Uses a nonprivileged port for outgoing connections. Useful if your firewall does not permit connections from privileged ports. Turns off RhostsAuthentication and RhostsRSAAuthentication.
`-1`	Forces SSH1 protocol only.
`-2`	Forces SSH2 protocol only.
`-e ch¦^ch¦none`	Sets escape character for sessions with a `pty` (default: ~). The escape character is only recognized at the beginning of a line. Followed by a `.` closes the connection; followed by `^Z` suspends the connection; followed by itself sends the escape character once. Setting it to none disables any escapes and makes the session fully transparent. You might want to set this to something other than the default if you find that you're using `Mail`, and the ~ command in `Mail` keeps being absorbed by the `slogin` client.
`-i` *<identity_file>*	Specifies the file from which the identity (private key) for RSA authentication is read. Default is `$HOME/.ssh/identity`.
`-l` *<login_name>*	Specifies the user to log in as on the remote machine. This may also be specified on a per-host basis in a configuration file.
`-o` *<option>*	Can be used for giving options in the format used in the configuration file. Useful for specifying options that have no separate command-line flag. Option has the same format as a line in the configuration file.
`-p` *<port>*	Specifies the port to connect to on the remote host. This can be specified on a per-host basis in the configuration file.
`-F` *<configfile>*	Specifies an alternative per-user configuration file. If a configuration file is given on the command line, the systemwide configuration file (`/etc/ssh_config`) is ignored. Default per-user configuration file is `$HOME/.ssh/config`.
`-L` *<port>*`:`*<host>*`:`*<hostport>*	Specifies that the given port on the client (local) host is to be forwarded to the given host and port on the remote side.
`-R` *<port>*`:`*<host>*`:`*<hostport>*	Specifies that the given port on the remote (server) host is to be forwarded to the given host and port on the local side.

scp, sftp, and Others

In addition to the slogin program, the Secure Shell suite of programs provides additional data encryption and protection functions to the user. There are components that function analogously to the cp command that you learned about in Chapter 14 (scp), and to the ftp command that you learned about earlier in this chapter (sftp).

The scp command can copy a file either from, or to, a Secure Shell remote host. The syntax, like cp, is scp *<from>* *<to>*. Either *<from>* or *<to>* can be specified as a remote machine and file, in the syntax of [*<username>*@]*<remotemachine>*:*<pathtofile>*. For example, the following command copies ~ray/public_html/my_bookmarks.html from the machine soyokaze (soyokaze is a host alias to soyokaze.biosci.ohio-state.edu on this machine) to a file by the same name in the local folder ~/Documents/.

```
brezup:ray testing $ scp ray@soyokaze:public_html/my_bookmarks.html
➥~/Documents/
ray@soyokaze.biosci.ohio-state.edu's password:
warning: Executing scp1 compatibility.
my_bookmarks.html               100% 271KB 45.4KB/s  00:05
```

Likewise, the following copies the file myfile from the current directory to the directory /tmp on the machine known as soyokaze (again, you will need a long name here if your local machine doesn't know the target machine by a short alias) and names it yourfile on the remote machine soyokaze, again logging in using the user ID ray.

```
brezup:ray testing $ scp ./myfile
➥ray@soyokaze.biosci.ohio-state.edu:/tmp/yourfile
ray@soyokaze.biosci.ohio-state.edu's password:
scp: warning: Executing scp1.
myfile                       37% 208KB 20.6KB/s  00:17 ETA
```

Note that scp doesn't make complaints about the host key the second time because it has already accepted and stored it.

Table 15.5 shows the syntax and interesting options for scp.

TABLE 15.5 The Syntax and Interesting Options for scp

scp	Secure remote copy.
scp [-pqrvBC46] [-F *<ssh_config>*] [-S *<program>*] [-P *<port>*] [-c *<cipher>*] [-i *<identity_file>*] [-o *<ssh_option>*] [[*<user>*@]*<host1>*:]*<file1>* [...] [[*<user>*@]*<host2>*:]*<file2>*	
-p	Preserves modification times, access times, and modes from the original file.
-r	Recursively copies entire directories.
-C	Enables compression. Passes the flag to ssh(1) to enable compression.
-F *<ssh_config>*	Specifies an alternative per-user configuration file for ssh. Option is directly passed to ssh(1).

TABLE 15.5 Continued

`-P <port>`	Specifies the port to connect to on the remote host.
`-i <identity_file>`	Specifies the file from which the identity (private key) for RSA authentication is read.
`-o <ssh_option>`	Passes specified options to `ssh` in the format used in `ssh_config(5)`.

The `sftp` command can also be used to securely transfer files. It was not available in the original OS X 10.0 distribution but was included in a later update.

The basic syntax for using `sftp` is

```
sftp [<username>@]<host>
```

This syntax opens an interactive `sftp` session, which works much like a typical interactive `ftp` session, as shown here:

```
brezup:sage Documents $ sftp miwa@rosalyn.biosci.ohio-state.edu
Connecting to rosalyn.biosci.ohio-state.edu...
miwa@rosalyn.biosci.ohio-state.edu's password:
sftp> lcd terminal
sftp> cd terminal-misc
sftp> put term-display-1.tiff
Uploading term-display-1.tiff to
➥/home/miwa/terminal-misc/term-display-1.tiff
sftp> ls
drwxr-xr-x  2 miwa   class     512 Aug 6 20:56 ./
drwxr-xr-x 21 miwa   class    1024 Aug 6 20:53 ../
-rw-r--r--  1 miwa   class  921862 Aug 6 20:57 term-display-1.tiff
sftp> quit
```

In this example, an interactive `sftp` session was used by user `sage` to transfer the file `term-display-1.tiff` to user `miwa`'s `terminal-misc` directory on the remote host `rosalyn.biosci.ohio-state.edu`. The `lcd` command was used to change to `sage`'s `terminal` directory on the local machine, `brezup`, and `cd` was used on the remote host to change to `miwa`'s `terminal-misc` directory. Of course, the `sftp` command could have been issued directly in `sage`'s `terminal` directory. Like an interactive `ftp` session, the interactive `sftp` session can take commands such as `cd`, `ls`, and `put`. As is the case with `scp`, if you have the same username on both machines, it is not necessary to supply a *<username>* because the current username is assumed by default.

Table 15.6 shows the syntax and some of the useful options for `sftp`. Complete documentation is available in Appendix A.

TABLE 15.6 The Syntax and Some Interesting Options for `sftp`

`sftp`	Secure file transfer program.
`sftp [-vC1] [-b <batchfile>] [-o <ssh_option>] [-s <subsystem> ¦ <sftp_server>] [-B <buffer_size>] [-F <ssh_config>] [-P <sftp_server path>] [-R <num_requests>] [-S <program>] <host>`	
`sftp [[<user>@]<host>[:<file1> [<file2>]]]`	
`sftp [[<user>@]<host>[:<dir>[/]]]`	
The first usage initiates an interactive session.	
The second usage retrieves files automatically if a noninteractive authentication is used. Otherwise, it retrieves the specified files after interactive authentication.	
The third usage causes `sftp` to start in an interactive session in the specified directory.	
`-b <batchfile>`	Batch mode. Reads a series of commands from an input batch file instead of `stdin`. Because it lacks user interaction, it should be used in conjunction with noninteractive authentication. `sftp` aborts if any of the following commands fail: `get`, `put`, `rename`, `ln`, `rm`, `mkdir`, `chdir`, `lchdir`, and `lmkdir`.
`-o <ssh_option>`	Passes options to `ssh` in the format used in the `ssh` configuration file. Useful for specifying options for which there is no separate `sftp` command-line flag. For example, to specify an alternative port use: `sftp -oPort=24`.
`-C`	Enables compression (via `ssh`'s `-C` flag) .
`-F <ssh_config>`	Specifies an alternative per-user configuration file for `ssh`. Option is passed directly to `ssh`.
`-1`	Specifies the use of protocol version 1.
Interactive Commands	
`cd <path>`	Changes remote directory to `<path>`.
`lcd <path>`	Changes local directory to `<path>`.
`chgrp <grp> <path>`	Changes group of file `<path>` to `<grp>`.
`chmod <mode> <path>`	Changes permissions of file `<path>` to `<mode>`.
`chown <owner> <path>`	Changes owner of file `<path>` to `<owner>`.
`get [<flags>] <remote-path> [<local-path>]`	Retrieves the `<remote-path>` and stores it on the local machine. If the local pathname is not specified, it is given the same name it has on the remote machine. If the `-P` flag is specified, the file's full permission and access time are copied too.
`help`	Displays help text.
`lls [<ls-options> [<path>]]`	Displays local directory listing of either `<path>` or current directory if `<path>` is not specified.
`lmkdir <path>`	Creates local directory specified by `<path>`.
`ln <oldpath> <newpath>`	Creates a symbolic link from `<oldpath>` to `<newpath>`.
`lpwd`	Prints local working directory.

TABLE 15.6 Continued

ls [<*path*>]	Displays remote directory listing of either <*path*> or current directory if <*path*> is not specified.
mkdir <*path*>	Creates remote directory specified by <*path*>.
put [<*flags*>] <*local-path*> [<*remote-path*>]	Uploads <*local-path*> and stores it on the remote machine. If the remote pathname is not specified, it is given the same name it has on the local machine. If the -P flag is specified, the file's full permission and access time are copied too.
pwd	Displays remote working directory.
quit	Quits sftp.
rename <*oldpath*> <*newpath*>	Renames remote file from <*oldpath*> to <*newpath*>.
rmdir <*path*>	Removes remote directory specified by <*path*>.
rm <*path*>	Deletes remote file specified by <*path*>.
symlink <*oldpath*> <*newpath*>	Creates a symbolic link from <*oldpath*> to <*newpath*>.
! <*command*>	Executes command in local shell.

The "Busload of Useful Tricks" Network Client: cURL

cURL, more commonly known simply as curl, is a command-line tool for getting or sending data to network services using URL syntax. The name is a bit of a play on words, being pronounced either as one word as in "kurl," or as two as in "see URL" (implying the unspoken "do URL" to those with a Unix sense of humor). curl is based on the libcurl library, which has the goal of bringing convenient URL-type data access and transfers to software that needs it.

Philosophically, curl is a very Unix-friendly program, providing a very specific function, while trying not to overlap the functionality of other programs. We are including it among these other more applicationlike programs because curl makes an excellent assistant program for almost any software that needs network access. As such, it might not fit our definition of an application or application suite, but it does integrate well as a network-access partner for other applications and application suites.

At its simplest, curl syntax is curl [options] <*URL*>. The complexity and power come from the range of available options. For example, to retrieve the Web page http://www.biosci.ohio-state.edu/ using curl, the syntax is simply:

```
curl http://www.biosci.ohio-state.edu/
```

The output of this is identical to using lynx -dump -source http://www.biosci.ohio-state.edu/. curl, however, can grab the name of the remote file from the remote server and write the data into a file by that name locally for you, without you having to do a redirect as you would with lynx. Therefore, you could use

```
curl -O http://www.biosci.ohio-state.edu/index.html
```

instead of

```
lynx -dump -source http://www.biosci.ohio-state.edu/index.html > index.html"
```

`curl` isn't a replacement for `lynx` because it isn't a Web-browser, but, on the other hand, `curl` is bidirectional and can send data as well as receive it. The `-T <file>` option directs that the local file named `<file>` be sent to the remote machine and file or directory name as specified in `<URL>`.

```
brezup:ray Unleashed $ curl -T fig18_.gif ftp://192.168.1.143/incoming/
 % Total    % Received % Xferd  Average Speed          Time             Curr.
                                Dload  Upload  Total    Current  Left     Speed
 52  763k    0      0  52  402k    0  27744  0:00:28  0:00:14  0:00:14  34526
```

This results in `fig18_.gif` being `ftp`ed from the current directory to the machine located at `192.168.1.143` and placed in the `incoming` subdirectory of the `ftp` directory on that machine. Speed and progress statistics are displayed as the file is transmitted.

These are the variations on `curl` that most people will use, most frequently, but the range of available options is truly diverse. Table 15.7 shows the syntax and some of the more useful options for `curl`, including hints on how to access secure servers, track cookie contents, and other useful trivia. Complete documentation for `curl` is available in Appendix A.

15

TABLE 15.7 The Syntax and Some Interesting Options for `curl`

`curl`	A utility for getting a URL with FTP, TELNET, LDAP, GOPHER, DICT, FILE, HTTP or HTTPS syntax.
`curl [<options>] [<URL>...]`	
`-a`	
`--append`	(FTP) When used in an `ftp` upload, this tells `curl` to append to the target file instead of overwriting it. If the file doesn't exist, it is created.
`-A <agent string>`	
`--user-agent <agent string>`	(HTTP) Specifies the User-Agent string to send to the HTTP server. Some badly done CGIs fail if it's not set to "Mozilla/4.0". To encode blanks in the string, surround the string with single quote marks. This can also be set with the `-H/--header` flag of course.
`-b <name=data>`	
`--cookie <name=data>`	(HTTP) Passes the data to the HTTP server as a cookie. The data is supposedly the data previously received from the server in a `Set-Cookie:` line. The data should be in the format `NAME1=VALUE1; NAME2=VALUE2`, but there's nothing to say you can't change it. If no = is used in the line, it is treated as a filename to use to read previously stored cookie lines from, which should be used in this session if they match. Using this method also activates the cookie

TABLE 15.7 Continued

	parser, which makes `curl` record incoming cookies too, which may be handy for using this in combination with the `-L/--location` option. The file format of the file to read cookies from should be plain HTTP headers or the netscape cookie file format. Note that the file specified with `-b/--cookie` is only used as input. No cookies are stored in the file. To store cookies, save the HTTP headers to a file using `-D/--dump-header`.
`-B` `--use-ascii`	Uses ASCII transfer when getting an FTP file or LDAP info. For FTP, this can also be enforced by using a URL that ends with `;type=A`.
`--connect-timeout <seconds>`	How long to wait for a server before giving up.
`-c` `--cookie-jar <file name>`	Specifies a file where `curl` should store any cookies it receives. If you set the `<file name>` to a single `-` (dash), the cookies are written to `STDOUT`.
`-C <offset>` `--continue-at <offset>`	Continues/resumes a previous file transfer at the given offset. The given offset is the exact number of bytes skipped, counted from the beginning of the source file before it is transferred to the destination. If used with uploads, the `ftp` server command `SIZE` is not used by `curl`. Upload resume is for FTP only. HTTP resume is only possible with HTTP/1.1 or later servers.
`--crlf`	Cause `CR` (carriage return) characters to be converted to `CRLF` (carriage return/line feed) on upload. Specifying `--crlf` twice forces this option off.
`-d <data>` `--data <data>`	(HTTP) Sends the specified data in a `POST` request to the HTTP server (can be changed to `GET` by the `-G/--get` option), in a way that can emulate as if a user has filled in an HTML form and clicked the Submit button. Note that the data is sent exactly as specified with no extra processing (with all newlines cut off). The data is expected to be `url-encoded`. This causes `curl` to pass the data to the server using the content-type `application/x-www-form-urlencoded`. Compare to `-F`. If more than one `-d/--data` option is used on the same command line, the data pieces specified are merged together with a separating `&`-letter. Thus, using `-d name=daniel -d skill=lousy` generates a `post` chunk that looks like `name=daniel&skill=lousy`. If this option is used several times, the ones following the first append data.

TABLE 15.7 Continued

`--data-binary <data>`	(HTTP) Posts data in a similar manner as `--data-ascii` does, although when using this option the entire context of the posted data is kept as-is. If you want to post a binary file without the strip-newlines feature of the `--data-ascii` option, this is for you.
`-D <file>` `--dump-header <file>`	(HTTP/FTP) Writes the HTTP headers to this `<file>`. Writes the FTP file info to this `<file>` if `-I/--head` is used. Handy for storing the cookies that anHTTP site sends to you. The cookies could then be read in a second `curl` invoke by using the `-b/--cookie` option.
`-e <URL>` `--referer <URL>`	(HTTP) Sends the Referer Page information to the HTTP server. This can also be set with the `-H/--header` flag, of course. When used with `-L/--location` you can append `;auto` to the referer URL to make `curl` automatically set the previous URL when it follows a `Location:` header. The `;auto` string can be used alone, even if you don't set an initial referer. This option lets you lie to servers about the page that directed you to a particular link, potentially bypassing "deep linking" safeguards.
`-F` `--form <name=content>`	(HTTP) This lets `curl` emulate a filled-in form in which a user has clicked the Submit button. This causes `curl` to `POST` data using the content-type multipart/form-data according to RFC1867. This enables uploading of binary files and so on. To force the content part to be a file, prefix the filename with an @ sign. To just get the content part from a file, prefix the filename with the character <. The difference between @ and < is that @ makes a file get attached in the post as a file upload, whereas the < makes a text field and just gets the contents for that text field from a file.
`-G/--get`	Use the HTTP `GET` protocol rather than the `POST` protocol for sending data.
`-h` `--help`	Displays help.
`-H` `--header <header>`	(HTTP) Extra header to use when getting a Web page. You may specify any number of extra headers. Note that if you should add a custom header that has the same name as one of the internal ones `curl` would use, your externally set header will be used instead of the internal one. This allows you to make even trickier stuff than `curl` would normally do. Do not replace internally set headers without knowing perfectly well what you're doing. Replacing an internal header with one without content on the right side of the colon prevents that header from appearing.

TABLE 15.7 Continued

`-I` `--include`	(HTTP) Includes the HTTP-header in the output. The HTTP-header includes things such as server name, date of the document, HTTP version, and more.
`-j` `--junk-session-cookies`	Discard session cookies from any cookie data read from a cookie file. This has the effect of starting a new session. Browsers typically discard session cookies when they quit, but it's useful to keep them around until you want to discard them with `curl` because it's a single-command, single-connection program.
`-k` `--insecure`	Allows `curl` to perform insecure connections. If this option is not specified, connections to servers with apparently incorrect security certificates will be barred.
`-K` `--config` *<config file>*	Specifies which *<config file>* to read `curl` arguments from. The *<config file>* is a text file in which command-line arguments can be written that then will be used as if they were written on the actual command line. Options and their parameters must be specified on the same line in the file. If the parameter is to contain whitespace, the parameter must be enclosed within quotes. If the first column of a `config` line is a `#` character, the rest of the line will be treated as a comment. Specify the filename as `-` to make `curl` read the file from `stdin`.
`-l` `--list-only`	(FTP) When listing an FTP directory, this switch forces a name-only view. Especially useful if you want to machine-parse the contents of an FTP directory because the normal directory view doesn't use a standard look or format.
`--limit-rate` *<speed>*	Throttle the data connection to a maximum of *<speed>* bytes per second. The transfer speed may also be given in *<speed>*`K` to specify kilobytes/second or *<speed>*`M` to specify megabytes/second. If you're really optimistic, *<speed>*`G` asks for gigabytes/second transfer rates.
`-L` `--location`	(HTTP/HTTPS) If the server reports that the requested page has a different location (indicated with the header line `Location:`) this flag instructs `curl` to reattempt the get on the new location. If used together with `-i` or `-I`, headers from all requested pages are shown. If this flag is used when making an HTTP `POST`, `curl` automatically switches to `GET` after the initial POST is done.

TABLE 15.7 Continued

Option	Description
`-m` `--max-time <seconds>`	Maximum time in seconds that you allow the whole operation to take. This is useful for preventing your batch jobs from hanging for hours due to slow networks or links going down. See also the `--connect-timeout` option.
`-M` `--manual`	Manual. Displays the `curl` man page.
`-n` `--netrc`	Makes `curl` scan the `.netrc` file in the user's home directory for login name and password. This is typically used for `ftp` on Unix. If used with `http`, `curl` enables user authentication. See `netrc(4)` for details on the file format. `curl` does not complain if that file hasn't the right permissions (it should not be world nor group readable). The environment variable `HOME` is used to find the home directory. The basic `.netrc` file syntax looks like: `machine <host.domain.com> login <myname> password <mysecret>`
`-o` `--output <file>`	Writes output to `<file>` rather than to `stdout`. If you are using `{}` or `[]` to fetch multiple documents, you can use # followed by a number in the `<file>` specifier. That variable is replaced with the current string for the URL being fetched.
`-O` `--remote-name`	Writes output to a local file named like the remote file we get. (Only the file part of the remote file is used; the path is cut off.) You may use this option as many times as you have number of URLs.
`-q`	If used as the first parameter on the command line, the `$HOME/.curlrc` file will not be read and used as a config file.
`-R` `--remote-time`	Attempts to determine the timestamp on the remote file and use that on the local copy.
`-s` `--silent`	Silent mode. Doesn't show progress meter or error messages.
`-S` `--show-error`	When used with `-s`, it makes `curl` show error messages if it fails.
`-T` `--upload-file <file>`	Transfers the specified local `<file>` to the remote server at `<URL>`. If there is no file part in the specified URL, `curl` appends the local filename. Note that you must use a trailing / on the last directory to really prove to `curl` that you aren't providing a filename, or `curl` thinks that your last directory name is the remote filename to use. That will most likely cause the upload operation to fail. If this is used on an http(s) server, the `PUT` command is used.

TABLE 15.7 Continued

`--trace <file>`	Output a full diagnostic trace of all data exchanged between the local and remote hosts. A single `-` (dash) as `<file>` sends the output to `STDOUT`.
`--trace-ascii <file>`	Output a diagnostic trace of all information in ASCII format. `curl` claims this is easier for humans to read.
`-u` `--user <user:password>`	Specifies user and password to use when fetching. See `README.curl` for detailed examples of how to use this. If no password is specified, `curl` asks for it interactively.
`-x` `--proxy <proxyhost[:port]>`	Uses specified proxy. If the port number is not specified, it is assumed at port 1080.
`-y` `--speed-time <time>`	If a download is slower than `speed-limit` bytes per second during a `speed-time` period, the download gets aborted. If `speed-time` is used, the default `speed-limit` will be 1 unless set with `-y`.
`-Y` `--speed-limit <speed>`	Apply a lower-limit to the download speed. If a download is slower than this given speed, in bytes per second, for `speed-time` seconds, it gets aborted. `speed-time` is set with `-Y` and defaults to `30` if not set.
`-z` `--max-redirs <num>`	Set the maximum number of server redirections to follow before giving up.
`-3` `--sslv3`	(HTTPS) Forces curl to use SSL version 3 when negotiating with a remote SSL server.
`-2` `--sslv2`	(HTTPS) Forces curl to use SSL version 2 when negotiating with a remote SSL server.
`-#` `--progress-bar`	Displays progress information as a progress bar instead of the default statistics.

Mail Clients

Depending on how your machine is configured, you might not have a use for the first email reading command discussed in this chapter. It is detailed here partly for historical completeness, and partly because it is an excellent utility for your use, if you have the opportunity.

The `mail` program is an email reading and sending program that works on email that is actually received and managed by your local machine. If all you've ever used is a POPmail or IMAP client, such as Eudora or Mailsmith, you're probably unfamiliar with the idea of your local machine being its own email server. Unix machines have, since the dawn of email, been part of the backbone by which email makes its way around the Internet. Configured properly, they don't need POPmail servers—they *are* POPmail (and IMAP) servers. Email gets around between them by way of the SMTP (Simple Mail Transfer Protocol) and is delivered (with a few minor exceptions) directly from the sender's machine to the receiver's machine.

What does this mean to you? If your machine is set up to receive and deliver mail itself, mail doesn't arrive at 10-minute intervals (or however frequently you have your POPmail client configured to connect). It arrives as instantaneously as it can make its way across the Internet—usually within a few seconds of being sent. It doesn't require your ISP's mail service to be up and running for you to receive mail because you (for email purposes) are your own ISP. Old-time Unix users are frequently amused by the instant messaging services that seem to be all the rage as the hot new Internet technology. Unfettered by the POPmail and IMAP protocols, plain old email *is* an instant messaging technology.

Building Block Simplicity: `mail`

The `mail` program is a simple command-line program for sending and reading email. Invoked with no arguments, its default behavior is to display the list of messages in your system mailbox and provide a prompt from which further interaction can occur. Used in this fashion, `mail` produces output similar to the following:

> **NOTE**
>
> If you're just setting up your system, you're unlikely to have any mail and will probably get only a message that says No `mail for` *`<username>`*. If you never set up your machine as its own mail server, you'll have no reason to read your mail this way. You might still want to set up your machine to do its own mail delivery, which allows you to use the `mail` command as a building block application for shell scripts. We'll talk more about this in Chapter 18, "Advanced Unix Shell Use: Configuration and Programming (Shell Scripting)."

```
[ryoohki:~] sage% mail
Mail version 8.1 6/6/93. Type ? for help.
"/var/mail/sage": 10 messages 10 unread
>U 1 jason@animedownload. Fri Jun 28 23:09 36/1465 "Re: VCD/SVCD"
 U 2 udayrao@yahoo.com   Sat Jun 29 07:07 20/684
➥"Hi,mboy-trans,japanese"
 U 3 derik@pobox.com    Fri Jul 5 07:24 34/951  "Re: VCD/SVCD"
 U 4 flyer0@yahoo.com   Sat Aug 3 20:52 2027/146273
➥"Nothing down here!!"
 U 5 laurent@ohmforce.com Sun Aug 4 21:34 2041/147189 "A humour game"
 U 6 ray.3@osu.edu     Mon Aug 5 11:22 36/1504 "welcome week..."
```

```
 U 7 vulstyle@hotmail.com Mon Aug 5 20:14 1892/136421
➥"Introduction on ADSL"
 U 8 fyrclwn@adelphia.net Mon Aug 5 20:17 64/2429
➥"I WannaJoin the Mailin"
 U 9 walker.591@osu.edu  Mon Aug 5 21:38 34/1030
➥"Re: welcome week..."
 U 10 enews@mcad.edu    Tue Aug 6 17:52 115/7041
➥"MCAD Anime & Manga Wor"
&
```

The & on the last line is the internal `mail` prompt from which you can enter commands.

At the & prompt internal to `mail`, you have a number of options. These include the expected functions of reading, sending, and deleting messages, as well as a few others. Table 15.8 details the syntax and some useful options in the `mail` program. Complete documentation is available in Appendix A.

TABLE 15.8 The `mail` Program Syntax and Useful Options

`mail`	Sends and receives mail.
`mail [-iInv] [-s` *<subject>*`] [-c` *<cc-addr>*`] [-b` *<bcc-addr>*`]` *<to-addr>*`...`	
`mail [-iInNv] -f [`*<name>*`]`	
`mail [-iInNv] [-u` *<user>*`]`	
`mail`	
`-i`	Ignores `tty` interrupt signals. Especially useful for communication on noisy phone lines.
`-n`	Ignores `/etc/mail.rc` on startup.
`-s` *<subject>*	Specifies the subject. Uses only the first argument after the flag. Be sure to use quotes for any subjects with spaces.
`-c` *<cc-addr>*	Sends a carbon copy to the users specified in *<cc-addr>*.
`-b` *<bcc-addr>*	Sends a blind copy to the users specified in *<bcc-addr>*. The list should be a comma-separated list.
`-f [`*<name>*`]`	Reads the contents of your `mbox` or the file specified by *<name>*. When you quit, `mail` writes undeleted messages back to this file.
`-u` *<user>*	Equivalent to `-f /usr/mail/`*<user>*.
Here are some of the useful options available within `mail`:	
`-`*<n>*	Displays the previous message, if *<n>* is not specified; otherwise, displays the *<n>*th previous message.
`?`	Displays a brief summary of commands.
`^D`	Sends the composed message.
`!`*<shell_command>*	Executes the shell command that follows.
`<return>`	
n	
`+`	Goes to the next message in sequence.

TABLE 15.8 Continued

R	Replies to the sender of the message. Does not reply to any other recipients of the message.
r	Replies to the sender and all other recipients of the message.
mail *<user>*	
m	Sends mail to the *<user>* specified. Takes login names and distribution group names as arguments.
d	Takes as its argument a list of messages and marks them to be deleted. Messages marked for deletion are not available for most other commands.
dp	Deletes the current message and prints the next message.
u *<messages>*	Takes a message list as its argument and unmarks the messages for deletion. A message list is a series of space-separated message numbers.
e	Takes as its argument a list of messages and points a text editor at each one in turn.
inc	Checks for any new incoming messages that have arrived since the session began and adds those to the message list.
s	Takes as its argument a list of messages and a filename and saves the messages to the filename. Each message is appended to the file. If no message is given, saves the current message.
w	Similar to save, except saves only the body of messages.
U	Takes as its argument a list of messages and marks them as not read.
a	With no arguments, prints out the list of currently defined aliases. With one argument, prints out the specified alias. With multiple arguments, creates a new alias or edits an old one.
unalias	Takes as its argument a list of names defined by alias commands and discards the remembered groups of users.
x	Exits mail without making any changes to the user's mbox, system mailbox, or the -f file that was being read.
q	Terminates the session, saving all undeleted messages in the user's mbox.

CAUTION

Under some versions of OS X, Apple has provided a program named Mail, as well as a program named mail. (Remember, capitalization makes a difference in the Unix world; these programs have different capitalization and therefore are not the same thing.) This does not seem to be the case with a fresh install of 10.3, but we can't be sure of the results of every possible upgrade path. In most Unixes, there is a difference in functionality between Mail and mail. Specifically, mail is usually a simple application mostly useful for quick shell-scripting applications—it usually produces a dump of all new messages as its default action. Mail, on the other hand, usually provides the interface discussed here. Intentionally or unintentionally, Apple's mail acts like the traditional Mail. As of this writing, the versions of Mail that we can find also act like the traditional Mail, but that has not always been the case with OS X. Apple's mail program is also the one that is documented.

Full-Featured Power: `pine`

`pine` is a command-line-based modern email client. It provides access to system mailboxes, as well as remote (or local if you choose) POPmail and IMAP servers. The `pine` email client provides an interface that will be much more familiar to users of applications such as Eudora. Although text-based, it provides a menu-driven interface with multiple mailboxes, sophisticated filtering, and other friendly conveniences. As of this writing, Apple doesn't distribute `pine` as a default application with OS X, but it's a popular enough mail client that many sites will have it installed. If you're playing system administrator for your own machine, the installation of `pine` is covered in Chapter 16.

`pine`, being a menu-driven, windowed system, doesn't lend itself to command documentation tables, so we give you a pair of screenshots from the running program. Figure 15.1 shows the first `pine` screen you'll see when you start it up. Unless you have `sendmail` working properly, *don't* press the Return key to send the requested statistic information!

FIGURE 15.1 The initial pine window. From this window, you can choose from any of the keys shown at the bottom to start using the program.

Figure 15.2 shows the more typical `pine` screen from which you'll work. You can choose items from the textual menu shown on the screen, and also choose commands from those shown at the bottom of the screen. One thing that you should be aware of is that `pine` usually expects you to "go back" to get out of any particular situation or location you've gotten to in the program. It's sort of like wandering around on the Web—there isn't necessarily a link back to the first page from any subpages several layers down in the system. Look for options that take you to the previous screen and so on to assist in navigating the system.

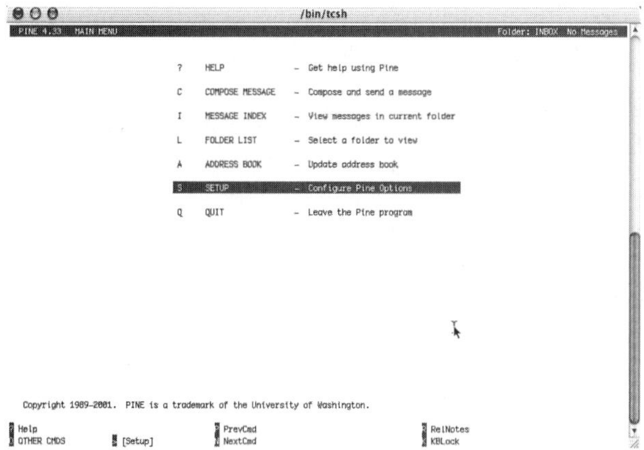

FIGURE 15.2 The normal top-level window for the `pine` email reading program.

Text Editors

Even though you might think that you'll never have a reason to use anything other than a GUI text editor such as `Alpha`, `Pepper` or `BBEdit`, there are a few arguments to be made for text-only mode editing in a terminal. Among them are that the text-only editors can even be used when the system can't display a GUI interface, and that an editor in a terminal can start much faster than most GUI editors. There's also the advantage that if you have occasion to work on Unix machines other than OS X boxes, the command-line editors are what you will have available.

Finally, at this point, the GUI clients available currently seem to have a bit of a problem figuring out whether they should convert a file that they load into Mac-style text (for newlines), or Unix-style text. The Unix command-line editors are a bit more predictable in preferring Unix-format text. Because of this, if you're working with files in the traditional-Unix side of the system, you're probably safer sticking to the command-line editors.

When it comes to editing text on the Unix side, you'll find that many Unix programs use text files as input, create text files as output, or are configured using commands and variables set up in text files. To change the contents of these files, you'll need to use a text editor.

As a matter of fact, most Unix software doesn't know the difference between a text file and any other file. Unlike in Mac OS, from the point of view of OS X's underlying Unix system, files are files are files. If the user chooses to view some of them as containing text, and some as containing programs, that's the user's business. An interesting consequence of this lack of concern about a file's contents is that the operating system is just as happy to allow you to use a text editor to edit the contents of your spreadsheet program itself as it is to enable you to attempt to run your email mailbox. Of course, if you actually have execute permission turned on for your email and try to run it, it's almost certainly going to result in nothing more interesting than a Bus Error and an immediate exit of the command—but the OS will try.

TIP

If you are a programmer, you might find this lack of distinction (yet another example of Unix abstraction at work) to be useful. On occasion, you might find a program that needs a minor change, such as the correction of a misspelling or a change of wording. In these instances, it is sometimes more convenient to simply load the executable file into a text editor and make the correction directly into the binary. This isn't a trick for the faint of heart, but sometimes it's the quick fix you need, and occasionally it's the only fix available for software for which you don't have access to the source.

If you spend much time discussing Unix editors with longtime Unix users, you'll find that there is a disagreement of warlike proportions between the users of the two most common editors: `vi` and `emacs`. Although these editors are actually rather complementary in their functions and are both useful tools to have in your toolbox, chances are that you will run into many users who insist that one or the other editor is completely useless. If you listen to them, instead of keeping both tools handy, you'll be depriving yourself of the better solution to at least some tasks.

Many Unix editors have immense power. `emacs`, for example, not only contains its own built-in programming language but can also function as a complete windowing system, a compiler/debugger interface, a news reader, and many other things. Even with a book of this size, however, there isn't space to do more than address the basics of using these editors. After you've mastered the basics, if you're interested in learning more, we encourage you to stop by your local bookstore or library and choose from among the several books available on each of the major Unix editors.

Quick, Dirty, and Omnipresent: `vi`

The `vi` editor is Unix's most universal editor. Some users pronounce it *vee-eye*, and some pronounce it *vye*, and a growing contingent claim it's pronounced *six*, when used on OS X. There seems to be no concrete consensus which pronunciation is correct (but the people who say *vye* are still wrong). `vi` isn't an easy editor, and it isn't friendly. It is, however, a quick-starting editor with a small memory footprint, which you will find on every Unix machine you encounter, regardless of flavor. `vi`, although annoying to learn, is frequently the most convenient editor to use for doing things such as making single-line changes to configuration files.

NOTE

Apple now provides `vim` "Vi IMproved" as a `vi`-replacement. `vim` provides some useful enhancements that are well beyond the design intent of `vi`. Historically `vi` has eschewed fancy features such as syntax highlighting and multilevel undo, in favor of speed of use and ubiquity. Although it does have a sophisticated search-and-replace facility, some of `vi`'s strongest points are that it's small, fast, and available everywhere. These features have made `vi` a favorite of system administrators the world over because they know, with almost certainty, that even if all they have to work with on a machine is a paper-terminal (a thing that's much like a printer with a keyboard—no screen, just input on one line, output on the next, repeat…), `vi` will be there and work just like it does everywhere else. `vim` doesn't share these characteristics. It's reasonably fast on today's gigahertz processors, but it's about 20x the size of `vi` in terms of disk and memory footprint, and it's by no means universally installed on all Unix systems. The improved features available in `vim` allow it to compete with some of the more complex `emacs` features, so you might find that it suits your needs as your day-to-day "power" editor, but we also recommend learning to operate comfortably within the `vi` subset of commands, just in case you ever need to work with the real thing.

When trying to use `vi` (or `vim`), there are a number of things you need to know to make it useful.

`vi` operates in one of two modes: command mode or insert mode. In command mode, you have control over things such as cursor position, deleting characters, and saving files. In command mode, every keyboard character you type will be interpreted as part of a command of some sort. In insert mode, every keyboard key you type is inserted into the file you are editing. This distinction is bound to be confusing at first, but if you use `vi`, you'll find that its speed makes it a preferred editor for quick changes to files. Also, you will find the Return key included in the explanations here, because some commands take effect immediately, and some require you to press Return after you enter them.

Table 15.9 shows some of the most used keys and tasks. If you're just coming to `vi` for the first time, *don't look too long at this table yet*; it will just look confusing! Flip past it to the short example of how to use `vi` and then turn back here and see whether, following the table, you understand what each keypress did and why.

NOTE

Despite what anyone tells you, `vi`'s not difficult to use; it just looks that way. It looks that way because any way of presenting the separate command and editing interface in a discussion, or at least any way we've ever seen or come up with, looks confusing. Try it. It's not difficult; it *will* make sense.

TABLE 15.9 Common Keypresses and the Resultant Actions in `vi`

Mode	Key(s)/Key Combination(s)	Action
Command	`l`	Move right
	`h`	Move left
	`j`	Move to next line
	`k`	Move to previous line

TABLE 15.9 Continued

Mode	Key(s)/Key Combination(s)	Action
	Put cursor on character and press `x` key	Delete character under cursor
	Press `d` key twice	Delete an entire line, including an empty line
	`A`	Enter insert mode at end of current line
	`i`	Enter insert mode before the character under the cursor
	`a`	Enter insert mode after the character under the cursor
	`:w Return`	Save the file
	`:w <filename> Return`	Save the file to *<filename>*
	`:q Return`	Quit
	`:q! Return`	Quit without saving
	`:wq!`	Save file and exit
Insert Mode	`Esc` key	Switch to command mode
	`Backspace` or `Delete` key	Backspaces or deletes, but only for data entered in current insert mode session on the current line
	Any printable keyboard	Insert the character at the cursor character

Instead of trying to walk through a screenshot-by-screenshot example of using `vi`, try typing the following example. Remember to compare what you're typing to the commands in Table 15.9, and watch what happens. Although the finer details are not revealed by this example, you will pick up enough to get you started doing useful work, and to get out of any sticky situations you might find yourself in while editing a file.

Try typing the following exactly as it appears here, and observe what happens. Where a new line appears in the text, press Return. Remember that `<esc>` is the Escape key.

```
brezup:ray testing $ vi mynewfile
iThis is my new file
This is line one of my new file
This is a test
This is line four of my new file<esc>kddkA
This is line three of my new file<esc>khhhhhhhhhhhhhhhhhxxxitwo<esc>:wq!
```

Your machine should respond

```
"mynewfile" [New file] 4 lines, 119 characters
```

Although, you might not be able to see that because it flashes off the screen pretty quickly. Now look at what you have:

```
% cat mynewfile
This is my new file
This is line two of my new file
This is line three of my new file
This is line four of my new file
```

Table 15.10 shows the syntax and common options for the `vi(vim)` command.

TABLE 15.10 The Syntax and Common Useful Options for `vi (vim)`

`vi`	
`ex`	
`view`	Screen-oriented text editor
Line-oriented screen editor	
Read-only version of `vi`	
`vi [-eFlRrSv] [-c <cmd>] [-t <tag>] [-w <size>] [<file1> <file2> ...]`	
`ex [-eFlRrSsv] [-c <cmd>] [-t <tag>] [-w <size>] [<file1> <file2> ...]`	
`view [-eFlRrSv] [-c <cmd>] [-t <tag>] [-w <size>] [<file1> <file2> ...]`	
`vi/vim` is a screen-oriented text editor; `ex` is a line-oriented editor. `vi` and `ex` are different interfaces to the same program. `view` is equivalent to `vi -R`, the read-only option to `vi`.	
`vim` has many more options than `vi`, but the following are the common ones you'll probably be most interested in:	
`-e`	Starts to edit in `ex` mode—that is, act like the line-mode `ex` editor. Few people like it when they land in `ex`; entering `q` at the prompt gets you out.
`-R`	Starts editing in read-only mode.
`-r <recoveryfile>`	Recovers the specified `<recoveryfile>`. If no file is specified, it lists the files that could be recovered. If no recoverable files with the specified name exist, `vi` starts editing as if the option has not been issued.
`-c <cmd>`	Executes `<cmd>` immediately after starting the edit session. It is especially useful for initial positioning in the file but is not limited to positioning commands.
`-t <tag>`	Starts editing at the specified `<tag>`.
`-`	Use `STDIN` as the source of the data to edit. Commands come from `STDERR`.
`vi` has two modes: command mode and input mode. Command mode is the initial and normal mode. Exiting from input mode (by pressing the `Esc` key) returns the user to command mode. Pressing the `Esc` key while in command mode aborts a partial command.	
Some commands for moving around in a file:	
`h`	Moves the cursor one character to the left.

TABLE 15.10 Continued

l	Moves the cursor one character to the right.
j	Moves the cursor one line down.
k	Moves the cursor one line up.
<arrow keys>	The arrow keys often also function properly for moving around in a file. Most seasoned users find the h/l/j/k keys faster for navigation.
<*num*>G	Moves the cursor to the line number specified by <*num*>. If <*num*> is not specified, the cursor moves to the last line of the file.
<*num*><*key1*>[<*key2*>...]	If <*key1*> is a single-key command, act as though the user had pressed the <*key1*> <*num*> times. If pressing <*key1*> would switch from command to editing mode, collect <*key2*>...<*keyN*> until the user presses <esc>; then act as though the user had typed these keys <*num*> times in editing mode.
Some commands for inputting text (input mode):	
i	Inserts text before the cursor.
a	Appends new text after the cursor.
A	Appends new text at the end of the line where the cursor is.
o	Opens a new line below the line where the cursor is and allows the user to start entering text on the new line.
O	Opens a new line above the line where the cursor is, and allows the user to start entering text on that new line.
Some commands for copying text:	
yy	Copies the line the cursor is on.
p	Appends the copied line after the line the cursor is on.
Some commands for deleting text:	
dd	Deletes the line the cursor is on.
<*num*>dd	Deletes <*num*> lines, starting with the line the cursor is on.
dw	Deletes the word the cursor is on.
x	Deletes the character the cursor is on.
Some other useful text manipulation:	
r<*x*>	Replaces the character the cursor is on with <*x*>.
J	Joins the line the cursor is on with the line below.
Some commands for pattern searching:	
/<*pattern*>	Searches forward in the file for <*pattern*>, starting with the location of the cursor.
?<*pattern*>	Searches backward in the file for <*pattern*>, starting with the location of the cursor.
n	Repeats the last / or ? pattern search.
N	Repeats the last / or ? pattern search in reverse.
Some commands to write the file:	
:w<return>	Writes the file back to the filename originally specified when vi was started.
:w <*filename*><return>	Writes the file to the filename specified by <*filename*>.

TABLE 15.10 Continued

Some commands to quit editing and exit `vi`:	
`:q<return>`	Exits vi. Refuses to quit if there are any unsaved modifications, or if the file is read-only.
`:q!`	Exits `vi`, even if there are any unsaved modifications.
`ZZ`	Exits `vi`, saving changes.
Miscellaneous functionality:	
`:next`	Switch editing to the next file specified on the command-line.

Everything and the Kitchen Sink: emacs

On the other end of the spectrum from vi's odd syntax and tiny footprint is emacs. In certain circles, it is thought that emacs is an acronym for **E**macs **M**akes a **C**omputer **S**low because emacs epitomizes the notion of an everything package and has the memory footprint to prove it. Including a windowing system, an email reading client, a news reading client, a programming language, and an online help database, to name only a few of its features, emacs can almost certainly do anything you want a plain text editor to do.

NOTE

Don't believe me? emacs also includes an implementation of the aged Eliza psychoanalyst and a Zippy the Pinhead quote generator. Do you really think there's anything that's *not* in there? If you're creative, you can convince Zippy to have a conversation with Eliza inside emacs. Alternatively, you can play the pong video game, convert text to morse code, manage your PIM schedule, or automatically insert keywords into your email to cause it to be flagged by the FBI's Carnivore mail-scanner as a possible terrorist threat. Browsing the categorized packages listing by entering `Esc-x help<CR> p` in a fresh emacs window should get you started on finding a wealth of interesting features you might never have imagined possible in a text editor.

With today's fast machines and nearly unlimited memory, the major complaints against emacs (it's a gargantuan application with a legendary hunger for computer resources—hey it's not all bad—people write haiku about it too!) aren't a significant impediment to its use.

From the point of view of the average user, emacs has a much more intuitive interface than vi. You're always in insert mode, just as you're used to in GUI-based word processors. Commands are handled by the use of `Control+`*<key>* combinations, instead of the use of a separate mode.

To use emacs, there are some basics that you need to know—you can get more information from the online tutorial mentioned at the end of this section. In the following list, whenever you see `Ctrl+` preceding a character, it means that you need to hold down the Control key and type that character. Whenever you see `Esc-` preceding a character, it means to press the `Esc` key, and then the character.

- The emacs editor doesn't have a separate mode for entering commands. You are always either typing a command or typing text—no switching between modes for them. This is just like most word processors that you are probably familiar with. To enter text, just type what you want to appear. To enter a command (usually Ctrl+<*key*> or Esc-x <*somecommand*>), just type the command as shown.
- You can position the cursor keys in emacs by using the arrow keys. If you're working across a network connection, the arrow keys might not work, but you can also position the cursor with Ctrl+<*key*> combinations. Ctrl+f moves the cursor forward. Ctrl+b moves it back. Ctrl+n moves to the next line. Ctrl+p moves up one line.
- You can delete everything from the cursor to the end of the line with Ctrl+k. A second Ctrl+k deletes the now blank line.
- Ctrl+g is the emacs "quit what you're doing" command. If you've started typing a command and change your mind, press Ctrl+g to abort.
- If you use Ctrl+k to delete a line or lines, you can use Ctrl+y to yank it (them) back. You don't have to yank them to the same location from which you deleted them.
- To save the file you're working on, press Ctrl+x Ctrl+s.
- To save the file to a new name, press Ctrl+x Ctrl+w <*filename*> Return.
- To exit emacs, press Ctrl+x Ctrl+c. If emacs proceeds to ask you about unsaved buffers, it's because you have unsaved work. You can either answer no, and save your work, or answer yes to the "quit anyway?" questions and exit without saving.

Beyond the Ctrl+ commands available in emacs, an amazingly extensible set of commands also come into play if you use the Escape (Esc) key. These commands are usually known as emacs "meta" commands, even though the machines with the meta key from which the commands draw their name have long since faded into history. These commands, even though they're initiated by pressing the Escape key, are usually abbreviated in the documentation with a leading M, for meta. The complete set of these commands is the subject of more than one book, and we recommend that you investigate your library or bookstore options, if you really want to understand the inner workings. If you're a puzzle solver, some of the interesting items are documented in Table 15.10. A good place to start on meta commands will be with testing out the emacs online help system. Start emacs by simply typing emacs at the prompt. After it starts, press Esc-x, and then type help- and press the spacebar. You will be presented with a list of emacs commands starting with help-, including useful things such as help-for-help, a good place to start.

Instead of a quick example like the one we used for vi, we suggest you take the emacs tutorial. To enter the emacs tutorial, all you need to do is start emacs and press Ctrl+h t (hold the Ctrl key, press the h key, release them both, and press the t key). If you type a ? after the Ctrl+h instead of the t, you'll see that there is actually a whole world of alternatives to the t (Ctrl+h i is another good place to look). These alternatives give you access to a range of different types of helpful information. For now, take the tutorial. If you're curious, you can probably spend almost eternity exploring the rest of the options available.

Table 15.11 shows a portion of the command documentation table for `emacs`, as well as a listing of some of the help topics detailing a number of the available meta commands. The synopses of the help topic areas should give you an idea of some of the things that you can do, and some of the information that you can look for in the online documentation. A vastly more detailed list of capabilities can be accessed in `emacs` itself by typing `M-x info`, and selecting the `emacs` documentation line. It should be clear even from this highly abridged listing that the complete documentation for `emacs` is voluminous.

TABLE 15.11 The Syntax and Some Useful Options for `emacs`

`emacs`	Editor
`emacs [`*`<command-line switches>`*`] [`*`<file1> <file2>`*`...]`	
`emacs` is a powerful editor that can actually do more than edit files. It has an extensive information system, which can be accessed in `emacs` with the key sequence `<Ctrl+h i>` (holding down the Control key and h and then i). The information system can be navigated using the arrow keys to move around and pressing the Return key to make a selection.	
`emacs` has an interactive help facility, `<Ctrl+h>`. The interactive "Info" information facility, which is a hierarchically organized, (usually) searchable collection of informative "topic related" documents, is one type of help available. A help tutorial is available with `<Ctrl+h t>`. Help Apropos `<Ctrl+h a>` helps the user find a command given its functionality. Help Character `<Ctrl+h c>` describes a given character's effect.	
The following are `emacs` options of general interest:	
`<file>`	Edits the specified *`<file>`*.
`+`*`<number>`*	Moves the cursor to the line number specified by *`<number>`*. (Do not include a space between + and *`<number>`*.)
`-q`	Does not load an init file.
`-u `*`<user>`*	Loads the init file of the specified *`<user>`*.
`-t `*`<file>`*	Uses the specified *`<file>`* as the terminal instead of using `stdin/stdout`. This must be the first argument specified in the command line.
`-nw`	Tells `emacs` not to use its special X interface. When running under X11, some versions of `emacs` default to building a menued interface that interacts (some say poorly) with the X11 cursor, allowing it to act a bit more like the traditional point-and-click editors with which you're familiar. This is sometimes convenient but can also be incredibly annoying at times. If the `-nw` option is given when invoking `emacs` in an `xterm(1)` window, the `emacs` display is done in that window, and `emacs` won't build its special interface. This must be the first option specified in the command line. This is useful if you're running an X server but want `emacs` to display in a terminal rather than X-windows `xterm`, or just plain don't want the special X11 interface.

15

TABLE 15.11 Continued

The following are basic emacs key sequences. Remember that two keys pressed simultaneously have a plus sign between them, and a space indicates pressing them sequentially. Most Unix documentation, including the online man pages and info pages will document `Esc-x` as `M-x`, for the Meta key:

Up Arrow	Move cursor up one line.
Left Arrow	Move cursor to the left one character, to end of previous line if at left side of current line.
Right Arrow	Move cursor to the right one character; move to the beginning of the next line if at the right side of the current line.
Down Arrow	Move cursor down one line. Adds a new line to the file, if currently on the last line of the file.
`Ctrl+p`	Move cursor up one line.
`Ctrl+b`	Move cursor to the left one character, to end of previous line if at left side of current line.
`Ctrl+f`	Move cursor to the right one character, move to the beginning of the next line if at the right side of the current line.
`Ctrl+n`	Move cursor down one line. Adds a new line to the file, if currently on the last line of the file.
`Ctrl+v`	Move down one page in file.
`Esc-v`	Move up one page in file.
`Ctrl+l`	Move current line to the center of the page.
`Ctrl+a`	Move cursor to the beginning of the current line.
`Ctrl+e`	Move cursor to the end of the current line.
`Esc-a`	Move cursor to the beginning of the current sentence.
`Esc-e`	Move cursor to the end of the current sentence.
`Ctrl+x Ctrl+h`	Bring up list of `Ctrl+x` prefixed commands. (If you do this, you will see that this table is a *very* abbreviated list!)
`Ctrl+x Ctrl+s`	Save the file.
`Ctrl+x Ctrl+w`	Prompt for new name to save file.
`Ctrl+x Ctrl+c`	Exits `emacs`.
`Ctrl+x Ctrl+f`	Prompt to open file.
`Ctrl+x Ctrl+b`	List current file buffers.
`Ctrl+x b`	Prompt to switch to another buffer.
`Esc-x`	Prompt to open file in literal `find-file-literally` mode—no Mac/Unix linefeed interpretation and so on. This is an important option for Mac users wanting to use `emacs` to convert Mac files to the Unix line-ending style.
`Ctrl+x Ctrl+d`	List directory in `emacs` buffer (allows opening files by browsing directory rather than by typing name).
`Ctrl+x Ctrl+o`	Delete blank lines in file.
`Ctrl+x Ctrl+t`	Transpose lines.
`Ctrl+spacebar`	Set mark at the current cursor position.

TABLE 15.11 Continued

`Ctrl+x Ctrl+l`	Downcase region. The region is the area between the cursor, and where the current mark is set.
`Ctrl+x Ctrl+u`	Upcase region. The region is the area between the cursor, and where the current mark is set.
`Ctrl+w`	Delete from mark to cursor. Deleted text goes to kill-ring buffer.
`Ctrl+s`	Enter incremental search mode. Any characters typed after `Ctrl+s` are searched for. Pressing `Ctrl+s` again searches for the next instance of the current search term. Use `Ctrl+g`, or a navigation key such as the forward/backward arrows or `Ctrl+f`/`Ctrl+b` to get out of this mode.
`Ctrl+r`	Enter incremental search mode, searching backward in the file.
`Esc-w`	Copy from mark to cursor into kill-ring buffer.
`Ctrl+k`	Delete from cursor to end of line. Place deleted text in kill-ring buffer.
`Ctrl+y`	Yank top data from kill-ring buffer into the text at the current cursor position.
`Ctrl+x 2`	Split current window vertically into two editing windows (two full-width windows, half the previous height).
`Ctrl+x 3`	Split current window horizontally into two editing windows (two full-height windows, half the previous width).
`Ctrl+x o`	Switch to next editing window in split-window mode.
`Ctrl+x 1`	Switch to single-window mode, keeping the current window open.
`Ctrl+x 0`	Remove current editing window, keeping others.
`Ctrl+x (`	Start recording keyboard macro.
`Ctrl+x )`	Stop recording keyboard macro.
`Ctrl+x e`	Execute recorded keyboard macro.
`Ctrl+u <####>`	Creates a numeric argument for the next command.
`Ctrl+u <####>` *<keyseq>*	Execute *<keyseq>* #### times.
`Ctrl+x f`	Set fill column for word wrap. Requires a numeric argument set with `Ctrl+u <####>`.
`Esc-x fill-region`	Word wrap region between cursor and mark.
`Ctrl+h Ctrl+h`	Bring up menu of help subjects.
`Ctrl+h t`	Bring up `emacs` tutorial.
`Ctrl+h i`	Bring up `emacs` info-mode manual browser. Browsing through the `emacs` info through this interface is recommended.
`Esc-x info`	Bring up `emacs` info-mode manual browser.
`Esc-x apropos`	Prompt for command or key sequence to document.
`Ctrl+h h`	Bring up list of ways to say hello in 34 different languages—we told you emacs had *everything* in it!

The following is a listing of some of the interesting parts of the information system's main menu for `emacs`. You're supposed to be able to find these and search the subtopics in them by using `Esc-x Index-info` and entering a search, but there's currently no index distributed for you to search in. Because of this, if you want more information on these topics (there are actually many more than listed

TABLE 15.11 Continued

here), you'll need to bring up the Info system with `Ctrl+h i`, navigate (using the down-arrow) to the `Emacs` section, and then browse the topics included there. We wish we had the space to discuss and document even a fraction of the power that `emacs` provides, but lacking space, a back-of-the-dustjacket listing of the features we think are most interesting will have to suffice. Think of this listing as a jumping-off place for finding your way to `emacs` information, and a whirlwind tour of some of the options you might never have known were available in a text editor:

Basic Interest	
Distrib	How to get the latest Emacs distribution.
Copying	The GNU General Public License gives you permission to redistribute GNU Emacs on certain terms; it also explains that there is no warranty.
Intro	An introduction to Emacs concepts.
Glossary	The glossary.
Mac OS	Using Emacs in the Mac.
Manifesto	What's GNU? Gnu's Not Unix!
Indexes (nodes containing large menus)	
Key Index	An item for each standard Emacs key sequence.
Command Index	An item for each command name.
Variable Index	An item for each documented variable.
Concept Index	An item for each concept.
Option Index	An item for every command-line option.
Important General Concepts	
Screen	How to interpret what you see on the screen.
User Input	Kinds of input events (characters, buttons, function keys).
Keys	Key sequences: what you type to request one editing action.
Commands	Named functions run by key sequences to do editing.
Entering Emacs	Starting Emacs from the shell.
Exiting	Stopping or killing Emacs.
Command Arguments	Hairy startup options.
Fundamental Editing Commands and Concepts	
Basic	The most basic editing commands.
Minibuffer	Entering arguments that are prompted for.
M-x	Invoking commands by their names.
Help	Commands for asking Emacs about its commands.
Important Text-Changing Commands and Concepts	
Mark	The mark: how to delimit a "region" of text.
Killing	Killing text.
Yanking	Recovering killed text. Moving text.
Accumulating Text	Other ways of copying text.
Rectangles:	Operating on the text inside a rectangle on the screen.
Search	Finding or replacing occurrences of a string.
Fixit	Commands especially useful for fixing typos.

TABLE 15.11 Continued

Major Structures of Emacs	
Files	All about handling files.
Buffers	Multiple buffers; editing several files at once.
Windows	Viewing two pieces of text at once.
Advanced Features	
Major Modes	Text mode versus Lisp mode versus C mode.
Indentation	Editing the whitespace at the beginnings of lines.
Text	Commands and modes for editing English.
Programs	Commands and modes for editing programs.
Building	Compiling, running, and debugging programs.
Maintaining	Features for maintaining large programs.
Abbrevs	How to define text abbreviations to reduce the number of characters you must type.
Picture	Editing pictures made up of characters using the quarter-plane screen model.
Dired	You can "edit" a directory to manage files in it.
Calendar/Diary	The calendar and diary facilities.
Shell	Executing shell commands from Emacs.
Hardcopy	Printing buffers or regions.
PostScript	Printing buffers or regions as PostScript.
Sorting	Sorting lines, paragraphs, or pages within Emacs.
Two-Column	Splitting apart columns to edit them in side-by-side windows.
Editing Binary Files	Using Hexl mode to edit binary files.
Saving Emacs Sessions	Saving Emacs state from one session to the next.
Emulation	Emulating some other editors with Emacs.
Hyperlinking	Following links in buffers.
Dissociated Press	Dissociating text for fun.
Amusements	Various games and hacks.
Customization	Modifying the behavior of Emacs.
The deeper levels of the documentation include topics covering the following (and many more) useful areas:	
The Organization of the Screen	
Point	The place in the text where editing commands operate.
Echo Area	Short messages appear at the bottom of the screen.
Mode Line	Interpreting the mode line.
Menu Bar	How to use the menu bar.
Basic Editing Commands	
Inserting Text	Inserting text by simply typing it.
Moving Point	How to move the cursor to the place where you want to change something.
Erasing	Deleting and killing text.
Undo	Undoing recent changes in the text.

15

TABLE 15.11 Continued

Files:Basic Files	Visiting, creating, and saving files.
Continuation Lines	Lines too wide for the screen.
Position Info	What page, line, row, or column is point on?
Arguments	Numeric arguments for repeating a command.
The Minibuffer	
Minibuffer File	Entering filenames with the minibuffer.
Minibuffer Edit	How to edit in the minibuffer.
Completion	An abbreviation facility for minibuffer input.
Minibuffer History	Reusing recent minibuffer arguments.
Repetition	Re-executing commands that used the minibuffer.
Help	
Help Summary	Brief list of all Help commands.
Key Help	Asking what a key does in Emacs.
Name Help	Asking about a command, variable, or function name.
Apropos	Asking what pertains to a given topic.
The Mark and the Region	
Setting Mark	Commands to set the mark.
Transient Mark	How to make Emacs highlight the region—when there is one.
Using Region	Summary of ways to operate on contents of the region.
Mark Ring	Previous mark positions saved so you can go back there.
Global Mark Ring	Previous mark positions in various buffers.
Deletion and Killing	
Deletion	Commands for deleting small amounts of text and blank areas.
Killing by Lines	How to kill entire lines of text at one time.
Other Kill Commands	Commands to kill large regions of text and syntactic units such as words and sentences.
Yanking (that is, pasting, for Mac folks)	
Kill Ring	Where killed text is stored. Basic yanking.
Appending Kills	Several kills in a row all yanked together.
Earlier Kills	Yanking something killed some time ago.
Controlling the Display	
Scrolling	Moving text up and down in a window.
Horizontal Scrolling	Moving text left and right in a window.
Follow Mode	Lets two windows scroll as one.
Selective Display	Hiding lines with a lot of indentation.
Searching and Replacement	
Incremental Search	Search happens as you type the string.
Nonincremental Search	Specify entire string and then search.
Word Search	Search for sequence of words.
Regexp Search	Search for match for a regexp.
Regexps	Syntax of regular expressions.
Replace	Search, and replace some or all matches.

TABLE 15.11 Continued

Replacement Commands	
Unconditional Replace	Replacing all matches for a string.
Regexp Replace	Replacing all matches for a regexp.
Replacement and Case	How replacements preserve case of letters.
Query Replace	How to use querying.
Commands for Fixing Typos	
Kill Errors	Commands to kill a batch of recently entered text.
Transpose	Exchanging two characters, words, lines, lists.
Fixing Case	Correcting case of last word entered.
Spelling	Apply spelling checker to a word or a whole buffer.
Using Multiple Buffers	
Select Buffer	Creating a new buffer or reselecting an old one.
List Buffers	Getting a list of buffers that exist.
Kill Buffer	Killing buffers you no longer need.
Several Buffers	How to go through the list of all buffers and operate variously on several of them.
Multiple Windows	
Basic Window	Introduction to Emacs windows.
Split Window	New windows are made by splitting existing windows.
Other Window	Moving to another window or doing something to it.
Pop Up Window	Finding a file or buffer in another window.
Force Same Window	Forcing certain buffers to appear in the selected window rather than in another window.
Change Window	Deleting windows and changing their sizes.
Major Modes	
Choosing Modes	How major modes are specified or chosen.
Commands for Human Languages	
Words	Moving over and killing words.
Sentences	Moving over and killing sentences.
Paragraphs	Moving over paragraphs.
Pages	Moving over pages.
Filling	Filling or justifying text.
Case	Changing the case of text.
Text Mode	The major modes for editing text files.
Outline Mode	Editing outlines.
TeX Mode	Editing input to the formatter TeX.
Nroff Mode	Editing input to the formatter nroff.
Formatted Text	Editing formatted text directly in WYSIWYG fashion.
Filling (that is, automatically rewrapping) Text	
Auto Fill	Auto Fill mode breaks long lines automatically.
Fill Commands	Commands to refill paragraphs and center lines.

TABLE 15.11 Continued

Editing Programs	
Program Modes	Major modes for editing programs.
Defuns	Commands to operate on major top-level parts of a program.
Program Indent	Adjusting indentation to show the nesting.
Comments	Inserting, killing, and aligning comments.
Parentheses	Commands that operate on parentheses.
Documentation	Getting documentation of functions you plan to call.
Hideshow	Displaying blocks selectively.
Symbol Completion	Completion on symbol names of your program or language.
Misc for Programs	Other Emacs features useful for editing programs.
C Modes	Special commands of C, C++, Objective-C, Java, and Pike modes.
Fortran	Fortran mode and its special features.
Indentation for Programs	
Basic Indent	Indenting a single line.
Multi-line Indent	Commands to reindent many lines at once.
Lisp Indent	Specifying how each Lisp function should be indented.
C Indent	Extra features for indenting C and related modes.
Custom C Indent	Controlling indentation style for C and related modes.
Documentation Lookup	
Info Lookup	Looking up library functions and commands in Info files.
Man Page	Looking up man pages of library functions and commands.
Lisp Doc	Looking up Emacs Lisp functions, and so on.
C and Related Modes	
Motion in C	Commands to move by C statements, and so on.
Electric C	Colon and other chars can automatically reindent.
Hungry Delete	A more powerful DEL command.
Other C Commands	Filling comments, viewing expansion of macros, and other neat features.
Comments in C	Options for customizing comment style.
Fortran Mode	
Motion: Fortran Motion.	Moving point by statements or subprograms.
Indent: Fortran Indent.	Indentation commands for Fortran.
Comments: Fortran Comments.	Inserting and aligning comments.
Autofill: Fortran Autofill	Auto fill minor mode for Fortran.
Columns: Fortran Columns.	Measuring columns for valid Fortran.
Abbrev: Fortran Abbrev.	Built-in abbrevs for Fortran keywords.
Compiling and Testing Programs	
Compilation	Compiling programs in languages other than Lisp (C, Pascal, and so on.).
Compilation Mode	The mode for visiting compiler errors.
Compilation Shell	Customizing your shell properly for use in the compilation buffer.
Debuggers	Running symbolic debuggers for non-Lisp programs.

TABLE 15.11 Continued

Executing Lisp	Various modes for editing Lisp programs, with different facilities for running
Lisp Eval	Executing a single Lisp expression in Emacs.
Running Debuggers Under Emacs	
Starting GUD	How to start a debugger subprocess.
Debugger Operation	Connection between the debugger and source buffers.
Commands of GUD	Key bindings for common commands.
GUD Customization	Defining your own commands for GUD.
Dired, the Directory Editor	
Dired Enter	How to invoke Dired.
Dired Navigation	How to move in the Dired buffer.
Dired Deletion	Deleting files with Dired.
Flagging Many Files	Flagging files based on their names.
Marks vs Flags	Flagging for deletion versus marking.
Operating on Files	How to copy, rename, print, compress, and so on, either one file or several files.
Shell Commands in Dired	Running a shell command on the marked files.
Transforming File Names	Using patterns to rename multiple files.
Comparison in Dired	Running `diff` by way of Dired.
Subdirectories in Dired	Adding subdirectories to the Dired buffer.
Subdirectory Motion	Moving across subdirectories, and up and down.
Dired and Find	Using `find` to choose the files for Dired.
Customization	
Minor Modes	Each minor mode is one feature you can turn on independently of any others.
Variables	Many Emacs commands examine Emacs variables to decide what to do; by setting variables, you can control their functioning.
Keyboard Macros	A keyboard macro records a sequence of keystrokes to be replayed with a single command.
Key Bindings	The keymaps say what command each key runs. By changing them, you can "redefine keys".
Keyboard Translations	If your keyboard passes an undesired code for a key, you can tell Emacs to substitute another code.
Syntax	The syntax table controls how words and expressions are parsed.
Init File	How to write common customizations in the `.emacs` file.
Variables	
Examining	Examining or setting one variable's value.
Easy Customization	Convenient and easy customization of variables.
Hooks	Let you specify programs for parts of Emacs to run on particular occasions.
Locals	Per-buffer values of variables.
File Variables	How files can specify variable values.

TABLE 15.11 Continued

Keyboard Macros	
Basic Kbd Macro	Defining and running keyboard macros.
Save Kbd Macro	Giving keyboard macros names; saving them in files.
Kbd Macro Query	Making keyboard macros do different things each time.
Customizing Key Bindings	
Keymaps	Generalities. The global keymap.
Prefix Keymaps	Keymaps for prefix keys.
Local Keymaps	Major and minor modes have their own keymaps.
Minibuffer Maps	The minibuffer uses its own local keymaps.
Rebinding	How to redefine one key's meaning conveniently.
Init Rebinding	Rebinding keys with your init file, `.emacs`.
Function Keys	Rebinding terminal function keys.
Named ASCII Chars	Distinguishing <TAB> from Ctrl+i, and so on.
Mouse Buttons	Rebinding mouse buttons in Emacs.
Disabling	Disabling a command means confirmation is required before it can be executed. This is done to protect beginners from surprises.
The Init File, `~/.emacs`	
Init Syntax	Syntax of constants in Emacs Lisp.
Init Examples	How to do some things with an init file.
Terminal Init	Each terminal type can have an init file.
Find Init	How Emacs finds the init file.
Dealing with Emacs Trouble	
DEL Does Not Delete	What to do if <DEL> doesn't delete.
Stuck Recursive	`[...]` in mode line around the parentheses.
Screen Garbled	Garbage on the screen.
Text Garbled	Garbage in the text.
Unasked-for Search	Spontaneous entry to incremental search.
Memory Full	How to cope when you run out of memory.
Emergency Escape	Emergency escape—What to do if Emacs stops responding.
Total Frustration	When you are at your wits' end.
Command-Line Options and Arguments	
Action Arguments	Arguments to visit files, load libraries, and call functions.
Initial Options	Arguments that take effect while starting Emacs.
Command Example	Examples of using command-line arguments.
Environment	Environment variables that Emacs uses.
Environment Variables	
General Variables	Environment variables that all versions of Emacs use.
Misc Variables	Certain system-specific variables.

Printing Tools

You already have some printing capability from the Terminal's printing menu options and built in to the rest of your OS X system. The command line, however, has its own printing facility, allowing you to direct the output of commands to a printer, without having to select that output in the terminal and use the menu options to print. These command-line tools are actually fairly sophisticated, although they provide only a minimalist interface to the printing architecture. Print queuing, job-status notification, and print-job logging are all part of the standard Unix `lpr` printing system.

Since Mac OS X 10.2, OS X includes Common Unix Printing System (CUPS) software. This package includes versions of print commands traditionally found on BSD systems as well as versions of print commands traditionally found on System V machines. Mac OS X 10.1 and earlier include only versions of BSD print commands. If you are running Mac OS X 10.1 or earlier, you do not have all the commands listed in this section. The first command listed in each subsection is the BSD-compatible command, and the one that you can find in Mac OS X 10.2 as well as earlier versions. The second command listed in each subsection is the System V-compatible command and is found only in the 10.2 and more recent distributions of OS X.

15

Sending Jobs to the Printer: `lpr`

The command to send a job to the printer is `lpr`. Although there are a number of options to `lpr`, the most common forms that you will probably use are

```
lpr <filename>
lpr -P<printer> <filename>
```

The first example sends `<filename>` to the system's default printer. The second example sends `<filename>` to an alternative printer named `<printer>`. If your system has more than one printer available to it at the command line, the second form might be of use. Note that there is no space between the `-P` and `<printer>`. This is an example of traditional `lpr` syntax, which we are mentioning in case you encounter this on another system. The `lpr` that ships with Mac OS X 10.2 documents a space between the `-P` and `<printer>`, but the traditional syntax also works. If you are using Mac OS X 10.0 or 10.1, the `lpr` that ships with it only documents the traditional syntax; however, the nontraditional syntax also works. You can send multiple jobs to the printer at once, and they will be queued and printed in sequence.

The command provides no feedback other than a return to your prompt:

```
brezup:ray testing $ lpr my-test
brezup:ray testing $
```

Despite this, it's sent the file `my-test` off to be printed on my default printer. If I wanted to send the file to a printer other than my default printer, the `-P <printername>` option allows me to specify any printer configured on my system by name. Table 15.12 shows the syntax and important options for `lpr`.

TABLE 15.12 The Syntax and Important Options for `lpr`

`lpr`	Sends a job to the printer.
`lpr [ -E ] [ -P <printer> ] [ -# <num-copies> [ -l ] [ -o <option> ] [ -p] [ -r ] [ -C/J/T <title> ] [ <file1> <file2> .. ]`	
`lpr` submits files for printing. Files named on the command line are sent to the specified printer (or the default system printer if none is specified). If no files are listed on the command line, `lpr` reads the print file from the standard input.	
`-P <printer>`	Specifies *<printer>* as the printer. Otherwise, the site's default printer is used.
`-# <num-copies>`	Sets the number of copies to print from 1 to 100.
`-r`	Removes the named print files after printing them.
`-T <title>`	Sets the job name.

The other command that you can use to send a job to the printer is `lp`. The syntax that you will most commonly use is similar to that of `lpr`, but it supports a number of additional options:

```
lp <filename>
lp -d <printer> <filename>
```

Here is a sample of the command in use:

```
brezup:ray testing $ lp term-window-1.tiff
request id is HP_Color_LaserJet_4550-4 (1 file(s))
```

Notice that the command responds by providing the job number, `HP_Color_LaserJet_4550-4`, in this case. The job number consists of the printer name and a number.

Table 15.13 shows the syntax and important options for `lp`.

TABLE 15.13 The Syntax and Important Options for `lp`

`lp`	Sends a job to the printer.
`lp [ -E ] [ -c ] [ -d <printer> ] [ -h <hostname> ] [ -m ] [-n <num-copies>] [ -o <option> ] [ -q <priority> ] [ -s ] [ -t <title> ] [ -H <handling> ] [ -P <page-list> ] [ <file1> <file2> .. ]`	
`lp [ -E ] [ -c ] [ -h <server> ] [ -i <job-id> ] [ -n <num-copies>] [ -o <option> ] [ -q <priority> ] [ -t <title> ] [ -H <handling> ] [ -P <page-list> ]`	

TABLE 15.13 Continued

`-d <printer>`	Prints to the specified *<printer>*.
`-h <server>`	Specifies the print server hostname. The default is localhost or the value of the `CUPS_SERVER` environment variable.
`-i <job-id>`	Specifies an existing job to modify.
`-m`	Sends email when the job is completed.
`-n <num-copies>`	Sets the number of copies to print from 1 to 100.
`-t <title>`	Sets the job name.
`-H <handling>`	Specifies when the job should be printed. A value of immediate prints the file immediately, a value of hold holds the job indefinitely, and a time value (`HH:MM`) holds the job until the specified time. Use a value of resume with the `-i` option to resume a held job.
`-P <page-list>`	Specifies which pages to print in the document. The list can contain a list of numbers and ranges (#-#) separated by commas (for example, 1,3-5,16).

Checking the Print Queue: `lpq`

Because `lpr` provides no feedback other than a return to your prompt, you might sometimes find it useful to check the print queue to check on the status of your print job. The `lpq` command displays the print queue:

```
brezup:ray testing $ lpq
HP_Color_LaserJet_4550 is ready and printing
Rank   Owner  Job   File(s)              Total Size
active ray    4    term-window-1.tiff        921600 bytes
```

This actually provides quite a bit of information. From the `HP_Color_LaserJet_4550` line we get the printer's name. You might see anything here, depending on how the printer has been named. For example, you might even see location and printer model number here.

The output displays each print job on one line. In this example, there is only one print job. The line describing the print job includes a print job number and the filename, size, and owner. If multiple jobs were queued on the printer, however, each would be listed here, along with the job owner, making it convenient to track down who's hogging all the printer time!

Table 15.14 is the command documentation table for `lpq`.

TABLE 15.14 The Command Documentation Table for `lpq`

`lpq`	Displays the queue of print jobs.
`lpq [ -E ] [ -P <printer> ] [ -a ] [ -l ] [ +<interval> ]`	
`-E`	Forces encryption when connecting to the server.
`-P <printer>`	Specifies *<printer>* as the printer. Otherwise, the site's default printer is used.

TABLE 15.14 Continued

`-a`	Displays the queues for all printers.
`-l`	Displays the queue information in long format. Includes the name of the host from which the job originated.
`+<interval>`	Displays a continuous report of the jobs in the queue once every `<interval>` seconds until the queue is empty.

The other command that you can use to check the print queue is `lpstat`:

```
brezup:ray testing $ lpstat
HP_Color_LaserJet_4550-4     ray     1080320  Thu Aug 8 17:23:24 2003
```

The output of `lpstat` is similar to that of `lpq`. It includes the job number, owner, file size, and date.

Table 15.15 shows the syntax and important options for `lpstat`.

TABLE 15.15 Command Documentation Table for `lpstat`

`lpstat`	Prints CUPS status information.

`lpstat [ -E ] [-a [<printer(s)>]] [-c [<class(es)>]] [ -d ] [ -h <server> ] [ -l ] [-o [<destination(s)>]] [ -p [<printer(s)>]] [ -r ] [ -R ] [ -s ] [ -t ] [ -u [<user(s)>]] [ -v [<printer(s)>]]`

`-a [<printer(s)>]`	Shows the accepting state of printer queues. If no printers are specified, all printers are listed.
`-d`	Shows the current default destination.
`-h <server>`	Specifies the CUPS server to communicate with.
`-l`	Shows a long listing of printers, classes, or jobs.
`-o [<destination(s)>]`	Shows the jobs queue on the specified destinations. If no destinations are specified, all jobs are shown.
`-p [<printer(s)>]`	Shows the printers and whether they are enabled for printing. If no printers are specified, all printers are listed.
`-r`	Shows whether the CUPS server is running.
`-R`	Shows the ranking of print jobs.
`-s`	Shows a status summary, including the default destination, a list of classes and their member printers, and a list of printers and their associated `-d`, `-c`, and `-p` options.
`-t`	Shows all status information. This is equivalent to using the `-r`, `-d`, `-c`, `-d`, `-v`, `-a`, `-p`, and `-o` options.
`-u [<user(s)>]`	Shows a list of print jobs queued by the specified users. If no users are specified, lists the jobs queued by the current user.
`-v [<printer(s)>]`	Shows the printers and what device they are attached to. If no printers are specified, all printers are listed.

TABLE 15.15 Continued

`-W [`*<which jobs>*`]`	Shows the current status of jobs that are waiting or being processed, or the completion status of jobs that have finished (or at least it's supposed to; it's not clear whether this works as of 2003/08/17). *<which jobs>* may be `completed` or `not-completed`. This option must appear before `-o` for it to take effect.

Removing Printer Jobs: `lprm`

If you decide that you want to remove a print job from the queue, use the `lprm` command. You might find it useful to use in conjunction with `lpq`.

Here is an example of using `lprm`:

```
brezup:sage Documents $ lpq
_192_168_1_3 is ready and printing
Rank  Owner  Job   File(s)             Total Size
active sage  27    view8.tiff          472064 bytes
1st    sage  28   view9.tiff          422912 bytes
2nd    sage  29   view7.tiff          424960 bytes

brezup:sage Documents $ lprm 28
brezup:sage Documents $ lpq
_192_168_1_3 is ready and printing
Rank  Owner  Job   File(s)             Total Size
active sage  27    view8.tiff          472064 bytes
1st    sage  29   view7.tiff          424960 bytes
```

In this example, we used `lpq` to get a print job number and then used `lprm` to cancel a specific job number. Because this version of `lprm` does not provide feedback on the job cancellation, we again used `lpq` to verify the job's cancellation.

Table 15.16 is the command documentation table for `lprm`.

TABLE 15.16 The Command Documentation Table for `lprm`

`lprm`	Removes print jobs from the queue.
`lprm [ -E ] [ - ] [ -P` *<printer>* `] [` *<job#1> <job#2>* `.. ]`	
`-E`	Forces encryption when connecting to the server.
`-`	Removes all print jobs in the queue.
`-P` *<printer>*	Specifies *<printer>* as the printer. Otherwise, the site's default is used.
<job#>	Removes from the queue the print job specified by *<job#>*. The *<job#>* can be determined by using `lpq(1)`.

The other command that you can use to remove a print job from the queue is `cancel`. Because the `lp` command provides the print job name when you issue the command, you might not necessarily need to check the queue. However, the `cancel` command does not provide output, so you may want to use `cancel` in conjunction with `lpstat` to verify the job cancellation, as shown in the following example:

```
brezup:sage Documents $ lpstat
_192_168_1_3-31     sage     424960  Thu Aug 8 17:36:35 2002
_192_168_1_3-32     sage     472064  Thu Aug 8 17:36:40 2002
_192_168_1_3-33     sage     422912  Thu Aug 8 17:36:46 2002
brezup:sage Documents $ cancel _192_168_1_3-32
brezup:sage Documents $ lpstat
_192_168_1_3-31     sage     424960  Thu Aug 8 17:36:35 2002
_192_168_1_3-33     sage     422912  Thu Aug 8 17:36:46 2002
```

Table 15.17 is the command documentation table for `cancel`.

TABLE 15.17 The Command Documentation Table for `cancel`

cancel Removes print jobs from the queue.	
`cancel [ -a ] [ -h <server> ] [ <id> ] [ <destination> ] [ <destination-id> ]`	
`-a`	Removes all jobs from the specified destination.
`-h <server>`	Specifies the print server hostname. The default is `localhost` or the value of the `CUPS_SERVER` environment variable.

Controlling CUPS from the command line: `lpoptions`, `lpadmin`, `lpinfo`

Although not strictly part of the command line suite of printing tools, the CUPS system includes command-line management software that provides administration and control capabilities far beyond what is currently available from either Apple's Print Center or the CUPS Web interface. The most important of these, `lpadmin`, `lpoptions`, and `lpinfo`, allow you to create, configure, examine, and delete printers that can be accessed through the standard command-line printing interface (`lpr`), and through GUI applications via the Print dialog.

Configuring a CUPS Printer from the Command Line

Here we will duplicate our example of adding a serial port based Apple ImageWriter printer that we used in Chapter 10, "Printer, Fax, and Font Management." It's assumed that the correct PPD file has been downloaded and placed in `/usr/share/cups/model/`, and that the `cupsomatic` filter is installed in `/usr/libexec/cups/filter/`. The `file` type dummy backend shouldn't be needed, but it shouldn't hurt anything by being present either. (It's necessary for the GUI interface because it generates the list of "valid" device URIs from the output from the collection of `backend` scripts. If there isn't a `file` script, the

GUI doesn't know that it can do `file` printing. But the CUPS printing system knows about file output innately, so the command-line tools simply believe whatever you tell them and don't look in the `backend` directory to determine what's available.)

TIP

To better understand some of the command-line options, look back to Chapter 10 for more in-depth explanations of the concepts.

In Chapter 10, we specified the printer as printer name "test"; gave it a location and description; and then picked a connection type for it, specified the device URI, and finally selected a PPD. These are exactly the same steps we'll take here, only we aren't going to take them on five separate Web pages, or via dialog box entries. Instead, all this goes onto a single command line.

NOTE

If you didn't do it in Chapter 10, and Apple hasn't started distributing everything necessary to use CUPS and Gimp-Print, you'll need to install the ESP Ghostscript version available from `http://gimp-print.sourceforge.net/MacOSX.php3`.

Specifying, with the `-p` option, a printer that doesn't already exist, causes `lpadmin` to create it. Using the `-D` option allows the provision of a description. The `-L` option allows the provision of a location. The `-v` specification of a device URI provides both the connection type and the specific connection location information. The `-m` option allows you to pick a PPD from the `model` directory, and finally, the `-E` option enables the printer for access. The command needs to be run as `root`.

```
lpadmin -p test_again -D "My ImageWriter Again" ➥-L "Still in the Attic" ➥-v
file:/dev/tty.USA28X21P1.1 ➥-m Imagewriter.ppd -E
```

It might look a bit long, but it's really no more than a compound of what we did via the GUI into a single command. After executing this command, you could check your Print Center application, and you would see that a new printer had been added and activated. It will appear in the Print Center as `My ImageWriter Again` and be available from the command line as printer `test_again`.

Writing Your Own Simple Printer Driver for CUPS

As a matter of fact, from the command line we've got considerably more power available in configuring the printer. From the Apple Print Center interface, and from the CUPS administration Web pages, we've only basic options available as to how to get data to the printer. I actually had to cheat a tiny bit in constructing the Chapter 10 demonstration for how to use the Print Center and CUPS interface with my ImageWriter. My serial interface currently refuses to accept any sort of flow control, and it's much faster than my poor old

ImageWriter. Because of this, on large pages and images, the end of the page gets garbled because the printer can't keep up with the data stream.

I cheated by making a small modification to the `cupsomatic` Perl script to throttle the speed down to something my printer can handle. Still, this is inelegant because I might have several printers that use the `cupsomatic` filter, and I won't necessarily want to throttle them all down to ImageWriter speeds. The command line `lpadmin` tool, however, gives me the option of saying "chuck all that automagic stuff; I'll run my printer myself, thank you very much," and allows me to specify a driver of my own creation. This comes at the cost of me having to write code to pass my data through Ghostscript (`gs`) for PostScript processing, if I want that functionality, and having to handle spooling the data to the printer myself.

This isn't a particularly appealing portion of the OS to be diddling about with, but still, it's not that difficult either, and it means that if you have any command-line software that can be made to speak to your printer, you can use it as glue between your printer and the CUPS system. For example, although only a basic vestige of a print spooler, the following code works nicely for passing PostScript code through Ghostscript (a PostScript interpreter) to format it for my ImageWriter, and for spooling the data to the serial port slowly enough that it doesn't overrun the printer's buffer.

```
#!/usr/local/bin/perl
use Time::HiRes qw ( time alarm sleep );
$thispid = $$;
open devfile, (">"."/dev/tty.USA28X21P1.1");

while(<>)
{
 $infile .= $_;
}

$tmppsname = "/tmp/tempps".$thispid.".ps";
$tmpprnname = "/tmp/tempprint".$thispid.".prn";
open temppsfile, (">".$tmppsname);
print temppsfile $infile;
close temppsfile;

system "/usr/local/bin/gs -q -dNOPAUSE -dBATCH -sDEVICE=iwhi
➥-sOutputFile=$tmpprnname $tmppsname";

open tempprnfile, ("<",$tmpprnname);
while(read(tempprnfile,$line,128))
{
 print devfile $line;
```

```
 $line = '';
 sleep(.4);
}

close tmpprnfile;
close devfile;
system "rm -f $tmppsname";
system "rm -f $tmpprnname";
exit;
```

If I've named it `/usr/local/bin/myspooler.pl`, I can load it up as the driver for a CUPS printer named `testsomemore` by using the command line:

```
lpadmin -p testsomemore -D "Ye Olde Printer" -L "Cobweb City"
➥-i /usr/local/bin/myspooler.pl -E
```

The script isn't smart enough to handle data types other than PostScript, and some data streams have sections that still overrun the buffer even with a .4 second sleep embedded between every 128 characters (for example, the printer can't feed 128 blank lines in .4 seconds), but it's a solid beginning on which you could build a driver for any printer that you know how to access through the command line. If your serial interface (or other printing interface to which your printer is connected) handles flow control, you can safely do away with the kludgy `sleep` command and let the printer worry about pausing the interface when it needs time to catch up.

Don't struggle too hard trying to understand what that code does right now. You'll learn everything you need to know to modify it for your purposes in Chapter 21, "Scripting Languages," in the section on Perl programming. For now, simply understand that it does the following:

1. Captures data that software hands to it through CUPS.
2. Writes that to a temporary file with what should be a unique name.
3. Uses ghostscript (`gs` at the command line) to process the first temporary file into the language supported by my ImageWriter.
4. Writes the result of this processing into a second temporary file with a unique name.
5. Reads that file in, 128 bytes at a time.
6. Sends each 128-byte chunk to the `/dev/` device associated with my serial port.
7. Cleans up after itself by closing connections to the open files and deleting the temporary files it has used.

This method (using `-i` scripts to process data) is unfortunately not entirely satisfactory for all users at this time because it appears that GUI printing does not interact cleanly with printers specified in this fashion. The `testsomemore` printer created in the previous example is completely functional at the command line. Under some versions of OS X it's an apparent black hole for data printed by GUI applications. Under 10.3, it appears to work, but on versions where it's a problem, GUI applications think that they're printing, but the printer spool never sees the data. I suspect that this is a symptom of some portion of the CUPS system being misconfigured on older versions of OS X, and it deciding that the target printer does not know how to handle the data type output by the application (as in, CUPS doesn't understand that the printer can handle PostScript, and so trashes the printing job rather than passing it on to the printing script). Lack of documentation prevents a complete diagnosis and correction for 10.2 versions, but Apple seems to have corrected the problem in 10.3.

If you wanted to extend a script like this to non-PostScript data, a possible solution would be to hack on a PPD like the `Imagewriter.ppd` file and on the `cupsomatic.pl` script. Duplicating the `cupsomatic.pl` script and adding the spooling functionality from this script should be fairly simple. Because `cupsomatic.pl` already understands how to properly convert each input data format into PostScript for output, this is an easier solution than trying to write our own processing filters around the minimal spooler we've constructed here. A more complex printing script might not be so easy to integrate. We leave the investigation of both of these solutions, should anyone other than myself be interested in whether a 1984 ImageWriter works with a 2002 iMac while using a buggy serial driver that doesn't understand flow control, to the creativity of the reader.

Although `lpadmin` is useful for creating and managing printers at the command line, `lpoptions` is useful for examining and setting print configurations. For example, `lpoptions -d testsomemore` sets the default printer for command line `lp` and `lpr` printing requests to the `testsomemore` printer configured in the previous example. This command does *not* affect the default printer for GUI printing.

Finally, `lpinfo` is useful for querying the CUPS system about currently installed printing devices and drivers. `lpinfo -m` is particularly useful for determining the correct model information to hand to the `-m` option of the `lpadmin` command.

The syntax and important options for `lpadmin`, `lpoptions`, and `lpinfo` are shown in Tables 15.18, 15.19, and 15.20, respectively. Complete documentation listings are available in Appendix A.

TABLE 15.18 The Syntax and Important Options for `lpadmin`

`lpadmin`	Configures CUPS printers and classes.
`lpadmin [ -E ] [ -h` *<server>* `] -d` *<destination>*	
`lpadmin [ -E ] [ -h` *<server>* `] -p` *<printer> <option(s)>*	
`lpadmin [ -E ] [ -h` *<server>* `] -x` *<destination>*	

TABLE 15.18 Continued

`lpadmin` configures printer and class queues provided by CUPS. It can also be used to set the system default printer or class.

When specified before the `-d`, `-p`, or `-x` options, the `-E` option forces encryption when connecting to the server.

The first form of the command sets the default printer or class to *<destination>*. Subsequent print jobs submitted via the `lp(1)` or `lpr(1)` commands use this destination unless the user specifies otherwise.

The second form of the command configures the named *<printer>*.

The third form of the command deletes the printer or class *<destination>*. Any jobs that are pending for the *<destination>* are removed, and any job that is currently printing is aborted.

Printer queue configuration options:

`-c` *<class>*	Adds the named printer to *<class>*. If *<class>* doesn't exist, it is created automatically.
`-i` *<interface>*	Sets a System V style interface script for the printer. This option cannot be specified with the `-P` option (PPD file) and is intended for providing support for legacy printer drivers.
`-o` *<name>*=*<value>*	Sets a PPD or server option for the printer. PPD options can be listed using the `-l` option with the `lpoptions(1)` command.
`-o job-k-limit=`*<value>*	Sets the kilobyte limit for per-user quotas. The *<value>* is an integer number of kilobytes; one kilobyte is 1024 bytes.
`-o job-page-limit=`*<value>*	Sets the page limit for per-user quotas. The *<value>* is the integer number of pages that can be printed; double-sided pages are counted as two pages.
`-o job-quota-period=`*<value>*	Sets the accounting period for per-user quotas. The *<value>* is an integer number of seconds; 86,400 seconds are in one day.
`-r` *<class>*	Removes the named printer from *<class>*. If *<class>* becomes empty as a result, it is deleted.

`-u allow:`*<user>*,*<user>*
`-u deny:`*<user>*,*<user>*
`-u allow:all`
`-u deny:none`
	Sets user-level access control on a printer. The latter two forms turn user-level access control off.

`-v` *<device-uri>*	Sets the *`device-uri`* attribute of the printer queue. If *<device-uri>* is a filename, it is automatically converted to the form file:/file/name.
`-D` *<info>*	Provides a textual description of the printer.
`-E`	Enables the printer and accepts jobs; this is the same as running the accept(8) and enable(8) programs on the printer.
`-L` *<location>*	Provides a textual location of the printer.
`-P` *<ppd-file>*	Specifies a PostScript Printer Description file to use with the printer. If specified, this option overrides the `-i` option (interface script).

TABLE 15.19 The Syntax and Important Options for lpoptions

lpoptions	Displays or sets printer options and defaults.
lpoptions -d <*printer*>	
lpoptions [-p <*printer*>] -l	
lpoptions -p <*printer*> -o <*option*>[=<*value*>] ...	
lpoptions -x <*printer*>	
-d <*printer*>	Sets the default printer to <*printer*>. Overrides the system default printer for the current user.
-h <*server*>	Specify the CUPS server to talk to.
-l	Lists the printer specific options and their current settings.
-o <*option*>=<*value*>	Specifies a new option for the named destination (available options can be seen with -l).
-p <*printer*>	Sets the destination to <*printer*>.
-x <*printer*>/<*instance*>	Removes the options for the named destination. This option is useful for a CUPS feature that Apple has apparently not-yet implemented—management of multiple queues with different defaults on the same printer.

If no options are specified using the -o option, the current options for the named printer are reported on the standard output.

Options set with the lpoptions command are used by the lp(1) and lpr(1) commands when submitting jobs.

TABLE 15.20 The Syntax and Important Options for lpinfo

lpinfo	Shows available printing devices and drivers.
lpinfo [-E] [-l] [-m] [-v]	
-E	Forces encryption when connecting to the server.
-l	Shows a "long" listing of devices or drivers.
-m	Shows the available printer drivers on the system. This option is useful for discovering what -m models are available for use with the lpadmin command.
-v	Shows the available printer devices on the system.

Bridging the GUI to Command Line Gap: Hybrid Software

One final class of software we'll touch on in this chapter is a diverse group of commands, programs, and applications that we've taken to calling *hybrid software*. These programs bridge the gulf between the GUI and command line, bringing GUI interfaces to command-line tools, or command-line access to traditionally GUI features. Hybrid software is one of the most interesting and potentially enabling aspects of OS X, and currently seems to be one of the most overlooked as well. We hope we've convinced you by now that command-line software can be incredibly powerful, even if you might still have reservations regarding how user friendly it may be. Many hybrid applications bring the user-friendly graphical mode of interaction you're accustomed to under classic Mac OS, and under OS X Aqua, to command-line power and flexibility. Others bring "Mac OS" accessibility to the command line.

The range of applications possible is limited only by the combinations of command-line software that might be composed, which as you will continue to find throughout this book, is nearly endless. Because we can't hope to document everything available, we'll introduce you to the general concepts by covering the simple tools Apple has made available, an interesting application that lets you put a GUI interface on any command-line tool, and a large suite of tools that blend an old-favorite Mac OS text editor with a traditional Unix text-processing and publication system. The general concepts used in these pieces of software, such as the simple extension of functionality by adding additional command-line parameters to configuration files, should be of general use when you find software of this nature.

The Command Line and the Pasteboard (Clipboard): `pbcopy`, `pbpaste`

Of the tools that Apple has provided, `pbcopy` and `pbpaste` are two that are both subtle and interesting. These command-line tools interact with the same clipboard (or pasteboard, as it is being called under OS X), that the GUI Copy/Paste menu actions and keyboard equivalents do. This allows you to move data back and forth between GUI tools and command-line applications with ease. The data is currently limited to textual data types (including formatted text), and EPS, which restricts the utility somewhat, but these commands still play an important role that cannot be accomplished by the traditional Copy and Paste menu actions. Specifically, these commands accept input on the command line's Standard Input, or write their output to the command line's Standard out, allowing them to be used in the construction of small automated programs (you'll learn more about scripting the shell in Chapter 18). The command documentation tables for `pbcopy` and `pbpaste` are shown in Tables 15.21 and 15.22, respectively.

TABLE 15.21 The Command Documentation Table for `pbcopy`

`pbcopy`	Copies data from `STDIN` into the clipboard/pasteboard.
`pbcopy [-help] [-pboard <general¦ruler¦find¦font>]`	
pbcopy places data from its standard input (`STDIN`) into the Mac OS X clipboard/pasteboard. OS X supports multiple pasteboards (clipboards) for different data types, though the use of the ones other than `general` are as yet poorly documented by Apple.	
`-help`	Displays its only option, `-help`.
`-pboard` *<board>*	Specify the pasteboard to use. Options for *<board>* are `general`, `ruler`, `find`, and `font`.

TABLE 15.22 The Command Documentation Table for `pbpaste`.

`pbpaste`	Writes textual data from the Mac OS X clipboard/pasteboard to `STDOUT`.
`pbpaste -help`	
`pbpaste [-P rtf¦ps¦ascii] [-pboard <general¦ruler¦find¦font>]`	
`pbpaste` pastes textual data from the clipboard/pasteboard to the command line via `STDOUT`. The `-P` option allows you to suggest a preferred output format but is not necessarily obeyed.	
`-P rtf`	Prefer output in Rich Text Format if available.
`-P ps`	Prefer output in Encapsulated PostScript format if available.
`-P ascii`	Prefer American Standard Code for Information Interchange (yes, that's what ascii stands for) plain text format.
`-pboard` *<board>*	Specify the pasteboard to use. Options for *<board>* are `general`, `ruler`, `find`, and `font`.

Integrating GUI Tools and Command-Line Programs: TurboTool

Until you're comfortable with the material in Chapter 18 and have started to write your own shell scripts that can make good use of these, you might find TurboTool from `http://www.turbotool.de/` to be more immediately gratifying (though it'll be more powerful too, after you master adding your own shell script functionality to it). This tool allows you to wrap GUI and drag-and-drop interfaces around a number of built-in functions, and even more powerfully, around command-line commands and scripts. Figures 15.3, 15.4, and 15.5 show the three components of a TurboTool action that extract image data from the clipboard, resize it 75%, and then write it to disk as a JPEG file.

The first component, shown in Figure 15.3 uses a built-in TurboTool action (TurboTool calls them "atomics") to read image data from the clipboard, using Mac OS's built-in clipboard-conversion capability to extract a TIFF if possible. The second component, shown in Figure 15.4, pulls up a file-request type dialog where you can enter a filename for the image and sets an internal TurboTool variable to the result so that the next step has a filename to save to. The final component, shown in Figure 15.5 is perhaps the most interesting. It executes a small shell script to perform the functionality of converting the data from the TIFF read from the clipboard into a JPEG and resizing it 75%.

FIGURE 15.3 The TurboTool Action Inspector allows you to examine or build small functional components into complex actions. Here, the acquisition of a TIFF format file from data in the clipboard is requested.

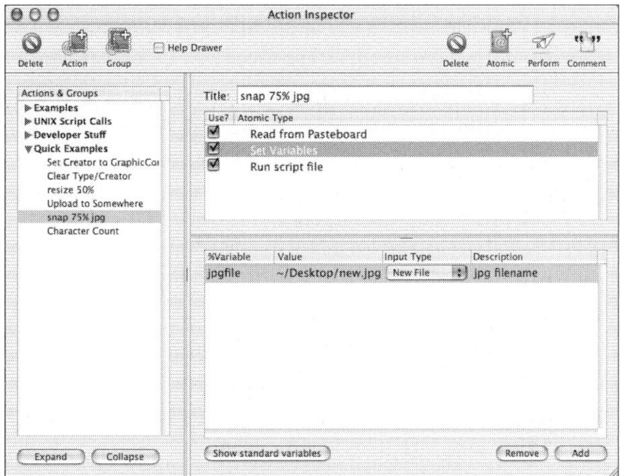

FIGURE 15.4 The second component of the resize to 75% and save as JPEG action, is to query the user for a filename with which to save the final image.

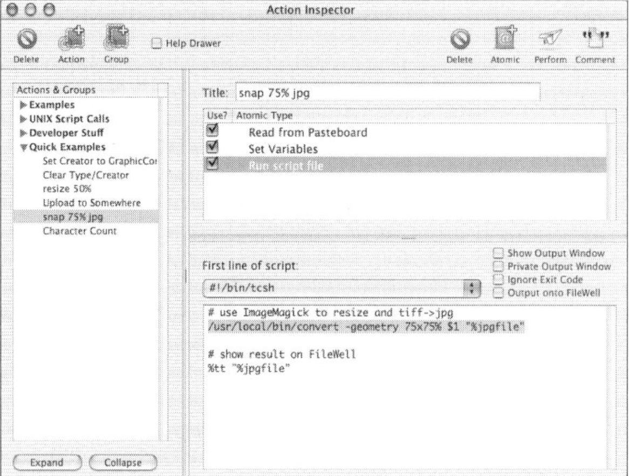

FIGURE 15.5 The third component uses a command-line tool to actually execute the requested resize and save actions.

Mixing and Matching to Text-Processing Perfection: AlphaX, OzTeX, and TeX

We've repeatedly written that one of the most significant benefits of the traditional Unix mindset and way of doing things is that it allows you to mix and match the components you need to suit the job you're doing, and your own personal way of working. As a final demonstration of how this benefit carries over to GUI applications in hybrid application suites, we want to mention the combination of AlphaX, OzTeX, and TeX, which together comprise what could be called a word processor.

Reading as far as you have in this book, you might find the notion of a word processor to be somewhat contrary to the "small programs, with specific functions" philosophy that we've been repeating with respect to Unix. In fact, this combination of software works unlike any other word processing application you're likely to be familiar with and fits the Unix philosophy quite well. It fits it so well in fact, that if you decide to try out this system, we almost guarantee that you'll experience some initial discomfort in trying to learn the new patterns of thinking required.

Perhaps the largest single item of culture shock that you'll find is that there is no WYSIWYG (What You See Is What You Get) interface to the formatting of your text. That's right—the wonderfully convenient and powerful paradigm for content editing that Apple brought to light in 1984 with MacWrite, that what you see on the screen as you're editing, is what appears on the page when you print, is conspicuously absent from this system. And, this is a *GOOD* thing! WYSIWYG editors revolutionized desktop document creation and turned an entire generation on to writing their own documents, creating their own content, and formatting it how they chose. It was a brilliant decision on Apple's part to foster this as the paradigm for the coming age of personal computing, and a wonderful enabling technology for those who want to create documents rich with personal style.

Unfortunately, we aren't all born to be brilliant document formatters, and personal expressions of style aren't always the best way to clearly convey information. Worse, it seems rare that those who have important information and content to convey, are also blessed with the necessary stylistic insights to convey that information clearly.

Working in the academic environments that we do, it's common for us to see people using traditional Macintosh or Windows word processors to write letters, papers, or books, who are expending as much effort on trying to format their document professionally as they are on writing the content of the document itself. This creates enormous inefficiency in the dissemination of knowledge. These people are students and faculty and are working hard to clearly and concisely capture their knowledge in written form, and simultaneously are being required by the WYSIWYG word processors to suddenly become professional typesetters if they want to have professional looking output. This is an unreasonable burden, and one that I believe we, as computer users, only willingly assume because we've become accustomed to the apparent freedom that WYSIWYG editors appear to give by allowing us to endlessly tweak the visual presentation until it is "just so."

As you might imagine, the traditional Unix way of approaching the problem is rather different. Instead of requiring the author to become an expert typesetter, "word processing" in the TeX sense is based on the use of a typesetting program. In this system, the typesetting program itself is the expert typesetter, and the author is free to concentrate on the content. Of course, TeX is also sensitive to the notion that users do desire and deserve significant control over the formatting of their documents. To facilitate this, the author can provide local and global suggestions regarding the formatting to the typesetting program. This system actually provides considerably more control over the final formatting than WYSIWYG word processors do, for the typesetter is in fact an interpreter for a programming language designed around the idea of formatting text, and the author has the option of exerting as much, or as little control over the system's automated choices as she wants.

Without a doubt, this method of work requires a significant rearrangement of the way one approaches writing problems, and the sense that you're "not in control" can be irrationally disturbing, especially for someone long-accustomed to the WYSIWYG way. Your humble author came to TeX after having worked in the Unix world for several years, and I still found the transition to be difficult. I spent a long time resisting everyone's suggestions to stop fighting with the system, concentrate on my writing, and "let go" so that the system could do what it was designed to do. It took probably a year of working in TeX on a daily basis before I discovered that I was no-longer fighting for control.

Having cleared that mental hurdle, however, I can safely say that I have no desire to ever return to WYSIWYG word processors for any serious writing. If clearly conveying information is the paramount concern for a document, I find it tremendously liberating to not have to worry about formatting, and to be able to concentrate on what I am writing rather than how it appears onscreen. The TeX system's expert typesetting rules almost always make good formatting choices, and I can override them in those specific instances where I am displeased with the final appearance of the result. Only if a document's physical layout is of similar importance to the content (such as with advertising, flyers, leaflets, and similar material), will I resort to a WYSIWYG editor (and even these documents could be accomplished with the TeX typesetting system if the investment in time to write the layout rules for an advertising flyer could be justified by its repeated use).

This having been explained, a short description is in order regarding how AlphaX, OzTeX, and TeX are interrelated in this Unix-style word processing suite.

- AlphaX is a text editor. That is, it edits text. Not styled text, not text in different fonts, not text in different colors or sizes, just "plain old text" text. It's an OS X incarnation of the venerable Alpha editor from the days of Mac OS. One of the neatest things about Alpha, which you'll learn more in Chapter 21, is that in spirit, it should have been a Unix application, all along. Alpha, available in a number of variations on a number of platforms, is a text editor built out of a graphics-enabled scripting language. When you run Alpha, what you run is essentially a collection of scripts that cooperatively create a text-editing interface. If you're so inclined, you can edit and add to the scripts, changing the functionality of the editor to suit your particular needs.

  As a text editor, Alpha is oriented toward the editing of various types of programming languages, including the TeX and LaTeX typesetting languages. Conveniently, it provides a multitude of options for syntax highlighting in different languages and automatic insertion of assorted syntactic constructs. This allows you to, in HTML language mode, do things such as select `HTML Menu->Lists->Unordered List`, and have Alpha automatically insert a syntactically correct `<UL>` item as a neat little form into which you can fill elements to create the unordered list you need. In TeX mode, it lets you do things such as select `TeX Menu->"Document->Insert Document->Letter"`, and it inserts all the necessary control code to define a business letter, into which you only need to fill your specific content.

  Perhaps more importantly, Alpha, through its intimate association with the scripting system, provides a high level of integration between content being edited in an Alpha window and a number of command line and Native OS X tools. If you're editing a Perl program, you can simply select Run Buffer and Alpha will start Perl and hand your code to it, retrieving the output into a new window. If you're writing C code, or working in any of a dozen other languages, similar integration is possible. This holds, of course, for TeX typesetting code as well, allowing you to conveniently edit your content in a plain text editor, and handing that content off to the typesetter as necessary for typesetting and display. You can learn more about AlphaX, which is currently in public beta-testing, at `http://www.maths.mq.edu.au/~steffen/Alpha/AlphaX/`.

- OzTeX is an implementation of the TeX typesetting system as a GUI application, but more importantly, it's a viewer for the results of TeX typesetting and a front-end application that integrates a number of different tools that must be run to handle all aspects of typesetting a document using the TeX system. OzTeX currently contains an internal implementation of the TeX system because of its heritage as a Mac OS application, and additionally can use command-line TeX tools. It is expected to eventually transition to a more Unix-like application where it will make full use of the command-line TeX tools and be relieved of the burden of the internal implementation. OzTeX is available from `http://www.trevorrow.com/oztex/`. Because all of TeX is community supported, many useful little packages are contributed by different authors, and it sometimes takes a while to accumulate all the useful bits that you might want for a project. On the OzTeX CD, Andrew Trevorrow distributes many useful TeX-related tools and auxiliary packages, so if you find TeX and LaTeX to be useful to your work, but find that you'd like more third-party utilities than you really want to install, Andrew's OzTeX CD is a great convenience.

- TeX, as has been previously explained, is an expert typesetting system embodied in a suite of several, traditionally command line, applications. The input that you provide to TeX is a plain text document containing the content you want to typeset and, optionally, small fragments of code in the typesetting language that TeX speaks, to describe to the system any nondefault formatting that you want to apply. You mark up your content, in plain text using a simple syntax to indicate the content's structure. TeX reads your marked-up text, applies either its default rules for formatting the structures you've marked up, or any variant formatting you've requested, and writes out a formatted version of the document in a `.dvi` (device independent) file. This file can then be read by dvi viewers (such as OxTeX) to show you what the formatted output will look like, or converted into any number of printer-driver languages (such as PostScript) for delivery to a hard copy output device.

  LaTeX is a macro package that lives on top of TeX and provides a number of advanced document formatting features to the author. All major TeX implementations include the LaTeX macro package as a standard component.

  Gerben Wierda's TeX implementation is a blend of a number of TeX distribution lineages, packaged as a convenient Mac OS X `.dmg` installer, or as a network-aware installation program that downloads and installs needed components when run. It is available from `http://www.rna.nl/tex.html` (and also on Andrew's OzTeX CD). The i-Installer version of the installation program is recommended.

Taken together, these packages allow the following chain of events to occur relatively seamlessly: You author TeX and LaTeX documents in AlphaX. When you're satisfied with the content (not the appearance—the content—what you have to say) you've created and want to see how it will look printed, you trigger AlphaX to hand off these documents to OzTeX by use of a menu selection, or a keypress combination. OzTeX determines the document type and invokes TeX, or the LaTeX macro package as appropriate. TeX formats the document and writes a `.dvi` file. OzTeX recognizes the creation of the `.dvi` file and opens a viewer showing you exactly what your document will look like when printed.

15

This might sound like a long and cumbersome sequence of events, but by now, it should seem like a perfectly logical Unix way of proceeding. Also by now, you should be getting the idea that Unix allows the programmer to hide many of these interactions from the user, if the user wants to ignore them. From the user's perspective, it turns out that this interaction is not particularly cumbersome at all. Instead, in practice, the process looks like you type some content into an AlphaX window and press Command-T. A second or two later (faster if you have a machine with more horsepower than my G4 PowerBook), a preview of your document, exactly as it will print, appears in a window. Note that this is actually much more WYSIWYG than what you get from a normal WYSIWYG word processor. With this system, what you see, is directly rendered from the code that will be used to drive your printer. If you've ever fought with the weird "What You See Is (Kind Of Like, But Not Quite) What You Get" problems some word processors seem to always have with font widths not being quite right and character alignments being ever so slightly off between the display and the printout, you'll find this display to be refreshingly accurate. Being derived from the code that drives the printer, it contains all the same positioning and formatting as what will print. Your display may not have the resolution of your printer, and so might not be able to display characters exactly identically, but they should be pixel-perfect in their formatting and alignment.

Figure 15.6 shows the code of a simple LaTeX document to construct a business letter, as shown by AlphaX. If this book were in color, you'd see the syntax coloring indicating that the editor knows which parts of the document are LaTeX commands, which are comments, and which are my actual content. The entire structure of this document was set up for me by AlphaX; all I've done is filled in my textual content where I needed it and a bit of code to pull in my digital signature file. It may be of interest to note that lines starting with `%` symbols are comments in TeX/LaTeX. Being a programming language, I can comment out parts of the document to keep them from displaying or printing, while still keeping them unaltered in the text document itself. This can be useful when working on multiple versions of the same document, or when making sweeping changes to a document where large sections need to be deleted or rearranged, but you don't want to lose track of important points made in the original.

Also remember, this is a plain text document. I can edit it at the command line with `vi` or `emacs`. I can typeset it at the command line using the command-line TeX tools. If I'm away from home and I need to edit it and print a copy for my secretary, my PCS-modem phone and my PDA are all I need to connect to my desktop machine, fire up a text editor, make the edits, typeset, and print a new copy. Editing the document is location and software independent, and because TeX runs on almost every hardware platform conceivable, if I want to take it with me, typesetting it is location and hardware independent as well.

Figure 15.7 shows OzTeX's view of the output from Figure 15.6's LaTeX code. If you have particularly good eyes, you'll notice that the text formatting displays the characteristics of text layout done by a typesetting professional. Character pairs such as fi show proper ligatures, and line lengths are massaged, by minute variation of intercharacter and interword spacing, to avoid widow words at the end of paragraphs. Considerably more is going on behind the scenes that isn't apparent from this partial-page display, such as paragraph balancing to avoid widow lines at the top of pages, proper formatting of oblique as well as italic typefaces, and too many more careful optimizations of the layout to name.

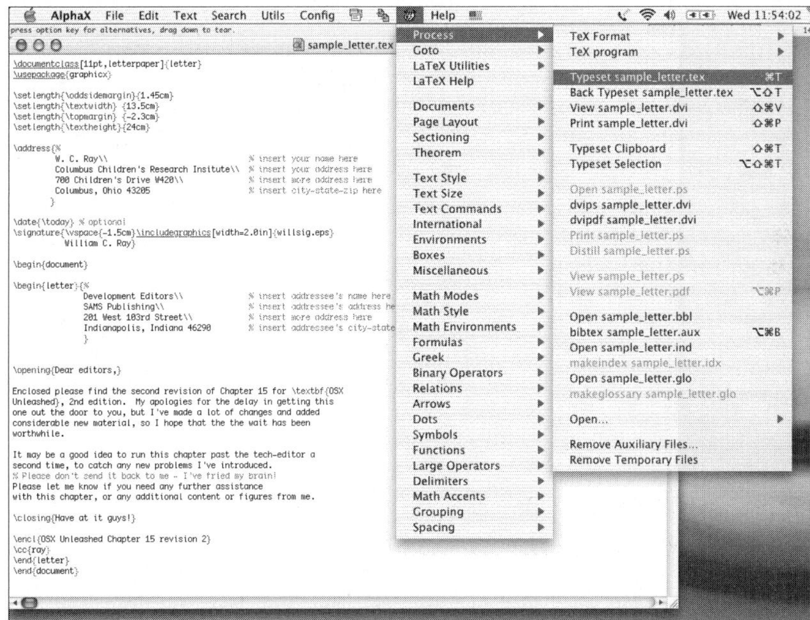

FIGURE 15.6 Editing a LaTeX document in AlphaX.

> **NOTE**
>
> If you've found this notion of a plain-text, programmatic typesetting language to be of interest, we encourage you to check out Donald Knuth's definitive work on TeX *The TeXbook* and Leslie Lamport's definitive work on LaTeX *LaTeX: A Document Preparation System.* Helmut Kopka's *A Guide to LATEX: Document Preparation for Beginners and Advanced Users* is also a good book that actually covers a fair bit of what you need to know about both LaTeX and the underlying TeX system. If you're tempted by the idea, think back to this system after you've read through Chapter 18 on shell scripting, and Chapter 21's section on Perl programming. The ability to automate changes to documents and build formatted text structures with software can be useful. The plain text nature of TeX's input lends itself nicely to such manipulation.

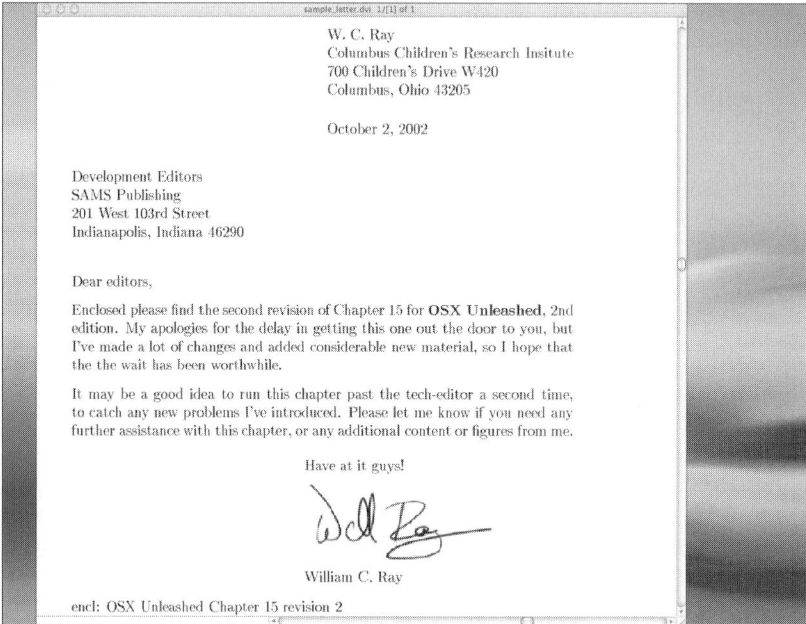
W. C. Ray
Columbus Children's Research Insitute
700 Children's Drive W420
Columbus, Ohio 43205

October 2, 2002

Development Editors
SAMS Publishing
201 West 103rd Street
Indianapolis, Indiana 46290

Dear editors,

Enclosed please find the second revision of Chapter 15 for **OSX Unleashed**, 2nd edition. My apologies for the delay in getting this one out the door to you, but I've made a lot of changes and added considerable new material, so I hope that the the wait has been worthwhile.

It may be a good idea to run this chapter past the tech-editor a second time, to catch any new problems I've introduced. Please let me know if you need any further assistance with this chapter, or any additional content or figures from me.

Have at it guys!

William C. Ray

encl: OSX Unleashed Chapter 15 revision 2

FIGURE 15.7 The result of LaTeX formatting the code shown in Figure 15.6.

We don't expect the majority of our readers to decide to become TeX hackers based on this short introduction, but even if it doesn't sound interesting enough to install the software to try it out, we hope you come away from this discussion with an idea of what is possible, if the power of the GUI, and the command line are taken together. Even if TeX just isn't your thing, understand that what this specific-programs-for-specific-functions system allows is complete customization of a word processor environment.

Due to the newness of OS X, you're currently rather limited in your choices for filling out this suite, but imagine if all word processing applications were handled in a similar fashion, instead of as monolithic applications like MS Word. If you didn't like a component, you could easily switch it out and use a different one that provided better functionality for your use in its place. In this instance, you can switch out AlphaX for BBedit, or any other command-line editor. It makes no difference to the system, choose whichever one you like. If you don't like OzTeX, there are a half dozen other TeX front ends (see Weirda's list at `http://www.rna.nl/tex.html` for details) that can sit between your editor of choice and the TeX command-line software. If you don't like LaTeX/TeX as a typesetter, you could use PDFTeX (typesets LaTeX directly to PDF files), or one of the *roff family of text formatters (an unpleasant group of text formatters primarily used for formatting Unix man pages these days; see the man page for `groff` if you want the gory details), or `txt2pdf` (`http://www.sanface.com/txt2pdf.html`). If the major software vendors get on board with this way of doing things, you'll suddenly be able to pick the best components from each, to meet your own personal working style and the requirements of the work you need to do.

Summary

In this chapter, you were introduced to command-line tools for accessing network resources of a number of types. The chapter also covered the two premier Unix text editors, the Unix printing environment that functions as a small suite of cooperating commands, and a sampling of tools that interoperate between the command line and other parts of OS X.

As of now, you have been introduced to a range of command-line programs representative of the types of interactions you will experience with almost any Unix software at the command line. Many of these commands and applications probably still seem cumbersome, and you will probably need to refer to the book frequently to remember an option. Don't be discouraged at this. There is probably not a single person alive who actually remembers all the possible commands in the `emacs` environment. Use the commands when the opportunity occurs, and reference the book or the man pages to help recall what you've forgotten. Even the best Unix users refer to the man pages or a book with considerably more frequency than Mac OS users look at their user manuals. Eventually the parts of the programs that you use with regularity will sink in to "muscle memory," and you'll be able to whiz around the command line doing what you do on an everyday basis, without needing to consult your references at all.

CHAPTER 16

Command-Line Software Installation

IN THIS CHAPTER

- Installing the Developer Tools
- Installing Software at the Command Line

This chapter introduces software installation at the command line. We focus specifically on command-line installs for command-line software because these are the variety that will be the least familiar. You should be aware, however, that some GUI software might require you to install it by using a command-line program such as `tar`.

Because of the long-standing position of Unix at the forefront of the Open Source software movement, the majority of traditional Unix programs are distributed as source code rather than as an executable application. If you're like most classic Macintosh users, you've probably never even looked at the code it takes to create a program, let alone tried to convince a machine to turn it into a fully functional application. As OS X becomes more popular and more prevalent in the market, we're seeing much more software distributed in precompiled form to satisfy those who really don't want to know this stuff. There are, however, still many useful applications that haven't been built into nice, neat, clickable OS X installers, and until they are, building your own really isn't that difficult.

The components needed to compile and install many pieces of Unix software right out of the box (or more accurately, right out of the `ftp` directory) are already located on your system. You need some support files that tell software how to interact with the hardware, the source for whatever application you want to build, and a compiler to build it with. In the good tradition of Unixes everywhere, Apple has provided the first and last of these for you; all that remains is for you to pick the software you want and issue a few fairly standard commands.

NOTE

Just so that you don't take this the wrong way—not all Unix software compiles as easily as what we demonstrate here. Apple has arranged some things in a sufficiently nonstandard fashion that some software seemed almost impossible to compile in Mac OS X version 10.0.4. Although things definitely got better in 10.2, and 10.3 is looking promising, it's still not as easy as using a Unix that's been around for 10 years. We expect that things will continue to improve over time, and that more software will compile cleanly. For the adventurous, Chapter 17, "Troubleshooting Software Installs, and Compiling and Debugging Manually," details some of the steps that can be taken if things shown in this chapter don't work properly for the software you want. Even if you're comfortable rolling up your sleeves and jumping into the code, we can't guarantee that everything you try can be compiled.

Installing the Developer Tools

The Mac OS X Developer Tools include compilers, libraries, and assorted programs. The parts that we're most interested in are the compilation and debugging tools. If you're interested in details regarding the libraries and so forth, remember those man commands, and spend some time digging around in the system man pages to learn what other neat things exist after the installation.

Installing

Installation of the Developer Tools is much like installing other software from the GUI. Insert the CD, and click the installer package. Be aware that the Developer Tools can only be installed on your startup volume, and that the installer, like the installer for the OS itself, has a rather poor notion of the amount of time the install will take. You also might be interested in installing the auxiliary CHUD tools (Computer Hardware Understanding Developer tools) package that's provided. We won't be using CHUD tools for anything in this book, but it's a potentially useful bit of software, and while you have the CD in the drive, you might as well install it too. The CHUD tools installation has changed a few times, from being an installer supplied on a self-mounting disk image that's on the developer CD, to being an optional install available from within the XCode/Developer Tools itself. The CHUD tools allow you to closely monitor your hardware's behavior, and to tweak some hardware performance options, such as the cache settings. The average user has little need to run the CHUD tools, but some of the information they can provide can be interesting nonetheless.

Installing Software at the Command Line

The majority of the Unix software you'll find that hasn't been specifically made for OS X is created by other users just like you. Some of them are professional programmers, but the vast majority of them are simply hobbyists who've put together an application because they wanted something that did what it does, and they've made it available for you to install out of the sense of "team spirit" that pervades the Unix and Open Source communities. Because of the wide range of individuals involved, the possibilities for how the software might be delivered and what you will need to do to install it are truly limitless. We'll do our best to give an overview of the techniques used, but pay attention to the author's instructions to see whether or where they differ from our suggestions. Also, don't be afraid to use your own common sense if you find something that doesn't have instructions and our samples don't appear to apply.

Regardless of the actual steps involved in the installation, there are some things to keep in mind if you want to keep your system in some semblance of order.

- You'll usually have as much flexibility, and often even more flexibility, about where you install software in Unix as you do in Mac OS. Unfortunately, although the Mac OS Finder invisibly and automatically updates the database of software that's installed for you, Unix doesn't. If you install command -line software in random places throughout the system, you will need to continuously update your `PATH` variable to reflect the changes. For this reason, despite having the option to install just about anywhere, you'll probably be happiest if you confine your installs to a few common and highly recommended locations. Specifically, those locations are the `/usr/local` and `/opt` directory trees. The popular Fink distribution installer also uses `/sw/`. These are the most common and best places to install software if you want convenience in your system.
- If you have multiple users on the system, even if you update your own `PATH`, other users' paths won't be updated, and, consequently, they might not be able to run the software. This can be an advantage, or disadvantage, depending on whether you want to hide the software from others or make it publicly available.
- If you decide to reconfigure your system or reinstall something, it will be much easier if you keep a complete copy of the distribution and any special options you picked to make it work. Use the `tar` command and `compress` or `gzip` commands (explained in Chapter 13, "Common Unix Shell Commands: File Operations"), after you've successfully managed to install it. You'll probably want to `make clean` the distribution first, if possible—that incantation will be explained shortly.
- If you want to maintain your sanity, it will help if you always download software packages into the same location, and do all your configuration and software building in subdirectories of the same directory.
- Never compile or install software as the `root` user. Some would suggest that we append *unless absolutely necessary* to that dictum, but we won't. We know, you're going to ignore that suggestion, and compile, install, and run random bits of software you've downloaded as `root`. Everybody ignores it—on occasion we do too. It'll come back and bite you. Trust us, we've been there. One day you'll run a poorly written (or maliciously written) install script, and it'll go off and damage your system. You'll think, "Why, oh, why did I just run that command as `root`? Nothing

about it required root privileges. If only I'd been a bit more careful." We won't tell you "we told you so," but we will tell you that a lot of the pain is avoidable, if you're willing to have some discipline about how you run your system.

Some software might insist that you install it as root, but the root user is the single user with the capacity to destroy your system with a single command. It might be preachy to suggest that you're probably better off without most software that requires you to be root to install it, but until you *know* when it's safe to ignore this suggestion, you'll be much safer following it.

NOTE

Some readers with Unix experience, and particularly those experienced in the Linux flavor, may find this caution peculiar, in that a considerable amount of third-party software ends up installed in privileged system directories these days. These users are accustomed to needing to be root to do simple installs. Fortunately, this is the wrong way to do things, and it's a rare Unix application that forces you to do things in a poorly thought-out fashion. Almost all non-OS-vendor (in this case non-Apple) software should be installed and owned by non-root users. Even vendor-supplied copies of third-party applications (such as the Apache Web server or the Perl programming language) are best owned and installed by non-root users.

This model makes life a bit more difficult than just having root own everything (and so the vendors of Unix-come-lately versions seem to be leaning toward making everything owned by root), but the benefits of behaving in a responsible and secure fashion far outweigh the minor inconvenience. If you conscientiously make sure that everything that's not distinctly part of the OS is owned by a nonprivileged user, you can allow nonprivileged users to modify and maintain those parts of the system with no fear that they are going to damage the OS itself. Even if you, as the person at the keyboard aren't different in any way, when you're operating as root, you're inherently putting your machine in more danger than when you're operating as a nonprivileged user. If non-OS-vendor software is installed and owned by a non-root user, time working with and installing that software, and any unfortunate things that may happen as a result of code that it runs, are done by a nonprivileged user. The machine is more secure, and the danger of a malicious script or an errant keystroke causing damage to the system is significantly reduced. If you have a true multiperson, multiuser system, the workload of managing software can be safely distributed, and users who need to be able to modify configurations (such as changing the Web server settings), can do so without having to annoy root, or develop the meticulous operating habits that someone running as root must conscientiously maintain.

Implementing this model on your system takes a little additional effort on your part. You won't be able to follow people's simple-minded instructions to "sudo make install" bits of software. But, your machine will be better managed, and more secure, and you'll be helping to keep mushy-headed thinking from taking hold of the Mac OS X platform if you just take the time to follow these suggestions and set up a nonprivileged software account to own and install the majority of your third-party software.

- Another useful trick for keeping your system in order is to create a special user ID that is used solely for software installations and management. The ownership of the /usr/local and /opt directories can be set to this user ID, as well as the ownership of wherever you download software and where you store it. This user ID does not need to have, (definitely should not have), administrator privileges on the system. This minimizes the risk of simply doing something wrong, or accidentally damaging the running system. It also minimizes the impact that a malicious user, distributing damaging scripts in the guise of useful software, can do to your system.

Downloading

You'll find Unix software being distributed in Usenet newsgroups, on Web pages, FTP servers, through email, and other mechanisms. No matter how it's distributed, you are going to need to transfer a copy of the software, from wherever it is stored, onto your local machine.

You've got all the tools necessary to accomplish any of these in both the command-line programs discussed here and in the previous chapter, as well as the GUI clients covered earlier.

Keep in mind while acquiring the software that things will go smoothest if the following things occur:

- The software is downloaded by the user who will be responsible for the installation.
- The software is downloaded into a directory where it can be unpackaged and compiled, if necessary. This includes the requirement for sufficient disk space, as well as the appropriate permissions for the user ID that will be doing the installation. If you have a tendency to download software as your primary logged-in userid and then try to manage it as a special, limited software-install user, the software user probably won't be able to read, or modify your downloaded copies, and you'll just get annoyed with the requirements to move everything around in circles so that both you and the software-install user can access the files. Learn to use `curl` or `lynx` for downloading your software so that you can paste links from a Web-browser that's running as you, to a terminal where you're logged in as the software user for downloads. Alternatively, make the directory where you download the software group-writeable and put yourself and the software-install user in the same group.
- If you're using `ftp`, remember use binary mode.
- Put StuffIt Expander in your Dock, so that you can drag and drop onto it conveniently. Usually, you'll want to use the command line `gunzip` and `tar` utilities, but sometimes StuffIt Expander is just the ticket for getting a packaged-up software distribution out of an archived newsgroup posting that you've found via Google.

Unarchiving

Some software comes as source code (the language that compilers read) that explains to the compiler how to create a finished program. Some comes as final executable programs.

Either way, most software comes as a tarfile compressed with either the compress program (usually denoted by a `.Z` file suffix), or the `gzip` program (usually denoted by a `.gz` suffix).

The first thing you'll need to do after downloading, therefore, is usually to `uncompress` or `gunzip` the tarfile.

Next you'll usually need to untar the tarfile (with `tar -xvf <tarfile>`). Before you do that, however, it's usually a good idea to make sure what's in the tarfile. You're interested in the contents, as well as where the tarfile wants to put the stuff that's in it. The second item is of particular importance—some software authors have the sloppy habit of letting their tarfiles place files in the current directory rather than a subdirectory (as mentioned in the section on `tar` in Chapter 13). Additionally, some packages are distributed as tarfiles that are designed to untar "in place" in the system. That is, they place files directly into their final locations (such as `/usr/local/bin`) rather than into a temporary subdirectory for subsequent installation.

Finally, keep in mind that if you download with a Web browser, it isn't unusual for the browser to remove the file suffix without actually doing anything to the file. This results in downloaded `gzip` files that are missing their `.gz` suffix and so on. This confuses the daylights out of some utilities designed to work with these files. If you have downloaded a piece of software with a Web browser that arrives as a `.tar` file but `tar` refuses to unpack it, try adding a `.Z` or `.gz` suffix and see whether `uncompress` or `gunzip` will process the renamed file.

If you've downloaded a precompiled application that only needs you to unpack it in place or put it in a final location after unpacking the distribution, you're all set. If you've downloaded a package that is distributed as source code, skip to the next section on compiling software.

Installing `lynx`

The `lynx` command-line Web browser is such a useful tool that we'll do a download and unarchive install right now. A precompiled version of `lynx` is available from `http://www.macosxunleashed.com/downloads/`.

Before you install `lynx`, we recommend that you make a change in your system's configuration that helps keep your system safe from malicious software and accidents during software installs. Use the Accounts control pane discussed in Chapter 11, "Additional System Components," to create a new user to own all your software. There we showed how to create the unprivileged `software` user with group `tire`. This is the user who will own and install our programs for us. Because `software` is not an administrative user and has privileges only in her home directory and in `/usr/local/`, `software` can't damage anything outside those locations. At worst, a malicious script or accident at the keyboard will just screw up what `software`'s already installed, leaving the rest of the machine safe.

Next, su to the root user. Finally, change the ownership of the directory /usr/local/ on your machine to belong to the software user and group. If you're using unprivileged user software, with group tire, from the command line, this looks like the following:

```
brezup:ray testing $ su
Password:
brezup:root testing # cd /usr
brezup:root usr # chown software.tire /usr/local
brezup:root usr # ls -ld local
drwxr-xr-x 4 software tire 92 Apr 21 22:00 local
```

1. Now, log out and log back in as the unprivileged software user that you created. Or, if you prefer, you can start multiple terminals, or use Apple's User Switching technology to flip between sessions logged in as yourself and the unprivileged software user.

2. Start a terminal and create the directories /usr/local/lib, /usr/local/man, /usr/local/man/man1, and /usr/local/bin (mkdir /usr/local/lib; mkdir /usr/local/man; mkdir /usr/local/man/man1; mkdir /usr/local/bin).

3. Next, point your browser at http://www.macosxunleashed.com/downloads/ and download the files lynx.gz, lynx.1, and lynx.cfg.

   Chances are if you're using Internet Explorer, it's going to insist on decompressing lynx.gz automatically. If not, you will need to find the file (double-click lynx.gz in the download manager, and click Reveal in Finder) and then drag it to your software user's Documents folder.

4. In the terminal, cd ~/Documents. Uncompress the lynx.gz archive with the command gunzip lynx.gz. If your browser already did this for you, a file named lynx might be in your Desktop folder.

5. Wherever the file lynx ends up, copy it to /usr/local/bin/. Use cp *<path to lynx>* /usr/local/bin/. *<path to lynx>* might just be lynx, or it might be ~/Desktop/lynx.

   In the same directory, you should find the lynx.1 file that you downloaded—this is the man page for lynx and belongs in /usr/local/man/man1; copy it there with cp lynx.1 /usr/local/man/man1/. If you want to be able to find it with the whatis command, you can catman -M /usr/local/man now as well.

6. Read the beginning of lynx.cfg. You can do this with less lynx.cfg. You can set a lot of configuration defaults in this file, but for now, leave the defaults as they are and copy the file to its intended destination. It should tell you that it belongs in /usr/local/lib/lynx.cfg, so cp *<path to lynx*.cfg> /usr/local/lib/lynx.cfg.

7. Just to make sure that the lynx file is executable, chmod 755 /usr/local/bin/lynx.

8. Log out and back in as your normal user. You might need to set your path to include `/usr/local/bin`, if it doesn't already. The easiest way to do this, as explained in Chapter 12, "Introducing the BSD Subsystem," is to extend your path with `PATH="$PATH:/usr/local/bin/"` in your `.bashrc` file, or `set path=($path /usr/local/bin)` placed in your `.cshrc` file, depending on which shell you're using. If you want this path to be available to everyone, all the time, you could put those statements in the systemwide `/etc/` versions of the files, `/etc/bashrc` and `/etc/csh.cshrc`.

The `lynx` application should now be executable and behave just as detailed in Chapter 15, "Command-Line Applications and Application Suites."

Before you go on, stop and think for a moment about what you've just done. If the terminal is still a strange place to you, you might be feeling as if you've just uttered some magic incantations and not be too sure you could do this again without the explicit instructions. Most things you come across will have instructions that are relatively explicit, but that's not the point. All that you've done is: Download the software—you're used to doing that in your Web browser, FTP client, or the like—you've done nothing different here. Then you unpackaged it—nothing new there either—you've used StuffIt Expander before, right? Finally, you made a few new directories and copied the software where you wanted it to go. None of this was difficult for you, and it won't be difficult for you in the future either. Don't let the fact that you're using unfamiliar tools now get in the way of the fact that you know what to do every step of the way. Soon you'll find this way of working to be just as second nature to you as double-clicking an "install" icon.

NOTE

Regarding `sudo`: You'll probably see many references all over the Internet to people doing this, that, or the other thing that requires `root` privileges, using of the `sudo` command instead of suing to `root`. It's okay to do this, if you want, but really, the `sudo` command wasn't intended, and isn't really an ideal solution for what people are using it for. This style of letting an administrative user use `sudo` to execute *any* command with `root` privileges is just sort of a kludge that Apple has made available to get around inexperienced users needing to wear the system-administrator hat.

The real purpose of the `sudo` command is to allow the `root` user to grant the ability to access *specific* `root`-privileged commands to users who don't have full `root` access. Typically, this is used to allow, for example, the person who maintains the Web server to restart that server, even though restarting the Web server requires `root` privileges. The person able to do this wouldn't be given the right to do anything else as `root`, just this. The `sudo` command isn't typically used to grant access to all commands as `root`, and for a user used to its traditional usage, this feels sort of sloppy. Feel free to do anything that we write as suing to `root`, by `sudo`ing every command, if you feel it makes you a safer user.

In a sense, you can't forget to log out of an sued shell if you're using `sudo`. This makes some users, particularly inexperienced users who aren't used to paying attention to security details, into safer administrators of their machines.

In a different sense, you simply can't log out of a sudoed session. For a period after you use sudo, it'll believe that the person at the keyboard has root permissions, whether it's you sitting there or not. Actually, there is a way to log out, but nobody ever shows it as part of their examples. Because of this, the normal reader is encouraged, by the uses that you'll see online and in documentation, to use sudo in an unsafe manner. The style of use that you'll see most often used and recommended for sudo is far less safe for the conscientious user than using su. (Proper use and configuration of the sudo command to limit user access to privileged commands is covered in Chapter 31, "Server Security and Advanced Network Configuration.")

The major difference for the conscientious user is that you know that you absolutely must log out of the sued shell as soon as you've accomplished what you need to do when using su. You can deauthenticate to sudo as well, but sudo deauthenticates itself after a while, and the perception, reinforced by almost all examples you'll see people giving, is that simply using the sudo command and allowing it to deauthenticate itself is a safe practice. This is not the case, or at least there is no reason to assume that the lack of exploits that have been reported will continue after Apple's non-canonical use of sudo becomes more widespread.

A secondary, but still significant difference is that it's easy to embed a short repetitive pattern into what is often called "muscle memory." Muscle memory isn't under direct conscious control, and this generates a risk. If you're confronted with commands that require frequent use of sudo, your fingers will eventually learn to type sudo automatically, and you will find that you start using sudo *<command>* any time *<command>* might even possibly need root permission for you to run it.

This gets especially risky if *<command>* is something like rm. If you're doing a bunch of drive cleanup and working between different users' directories, you might find that you're sudo rming many files. If your fingers learn to automatically type **sudo rm**, and you make a typo in what you planned to rm the next time around, you can end up doing a lot of damage to your system because the odds are good that you're going to run it sudoed, whether you intended to or not.

su doesn't cause similar problems (for conscientious users) because it requires considerably more typing than sudo and because a conscientious user becomes root, does what is necessary, and then gets back out. Even if the commands you're using get embedded in muscle memory, you're just running them as *<command>*, and you won't be running with root permissions if your fingertips happen to type one unrequested.

The sudo command works by initially authenticating that you really are who the shell thinks you are, and then (assuming that sudo believes your account has sufficient privileges), allowing you to run software as the root user. The sudo command then starts a timer, and if you use it again within some short time period of when you ran it last, it simply *assumes* that you still are who it thinks you are and doesn't ask for your password to authenticate again. This short time period (several minutes by default) during which you can run any command with root privileges, and without entering a validating password, provides the potential for a real security problem. This opens the door for malicious software writers to embed sudoed commands into their applications that can lay in wait for some unsuspecting user to run the software within the timeout window and then take advantage of the fact that the user has preauthenticated to run as root.

Because of this, although both operating as root with su and operating as root with sudo have risks, the risks are different, and for any given individual, either may be the safer option. sudo's safer for users who can't, or won't, be bothered by being security conscious, and who would end up opening the door to their machines and then never getting around to closing them if they were using su. sudo shuts the door for you; it just takes it some time.

su's safer for users who are security conscious and who close every door they open, every time. If you don't remember to log out from sued shells, and you aren't conscientious enough to never run an unknown/unverified command or program in an sued shell, you'll eventually get bitten either by malicious software, or by a mistake in typing. If you are conscientious, though, the su command will never be a door for a malicious software writer to attack your machine. On the other hand, if you use the sudo command frequently, and don't use the sudo -k command to deauthenticate after each and every use, your system is vulnerable to opportunistic malicious software that can slip through the crack during the period that sudo's holding the door open.

Right now, it probably comes down to personal preference. sudo's been around long enough, that if there were any major security concerns with the sudo program itself, someone would have probably found them by now. The potential exploit of malicious scripts taking advantage of the sudo timeout period is not something that we currently see affecting users. This lack of activity, however, doesn't imply that the exploit won't be used in the future.

Me, I'm extremely sensitive to muscle-memory issues, having had the occasion to train my fingers to type a similar incantation as a prefix to `rm` to get around the per-file prompting when I was first working with Unix in 1986. This bad habit bit me badly several years later, and since, I've become very fond of the # prompt for `root`. I see the # prompt, and I know I had better be darned careful about what I'm doing. I see the $ (or %, or > in other shells) prompt, and I know that I'm generally safe and can't do the system any great harm. It makes me happy and reduces my stress level. If you don't have fingers that type short commands faster than your brain can keep up, and you find worrying about logging out again when you're `root` more stressful, by all means, use sudo instead of suing to `root`. The potential problems with being sloppy with su are real and affect users who aren't paying enough attention every day. No one needs more stress, or more opportunities to do something to screw up our machines!

Compiling

Compilation is the process that a program-language compiler uses to take source code and convert it into an actual executable application. It is also used to describe running the compiler to perform the compilation. To those coming from a Macintosh or Windows background, the idea of having to cook your own software from the raw ingredients probably evokes images of impossibly cryptic commands and more headaches than you would ever want to deal with. Thankfully, compiling prepackaged source code isn't quite cooking from the raw ingredients—it's usually more like warming up a TV dinner. (If you're interested in learning to cook software from scratch, we recommend Kernigan and Ritchie's excellent *The C Programming Language*, and Donald Knuth's *The Art of Computer Programming* books on software architecture.)

It's still complicated enough—and there are plenty of places it can go wrong—that most users will at least initially find it less than fun. It'll be the last *scary* topic we introduce in this book, though—everything after this is applications of what you've learned in the last few chapters and this one, and the introduction of new programs for you to use. Actually, this stuff isn't that scary either. If you make it through this chapter and we haven't scared you away from the BSD subsystem, you're home free—we promise!

NOTE

In addition to installing software using GUI installers and compiling your own at the command line, there's a third major way of installing software under OS X. This method, using a software package management system, is covered in Chapter 19, "X Window System Applications," where we will use the Fink ports package management system to install some X11 software for the X Window system.

Much of what you can install at the command line in this chapter can be more easily installed using the Fink package manager, so if you find this chapter's manipulations to be more than you're willing to deal with, don't worry; there are easier ways to install most of this and other software. Think of this mostly as a practice and learning experience. We've selected some software that demonstrates many of the characteristics you'll find common among most manual software installs. If you think of building your system this way as an exciting challenge, you'll be able to go well beyond what's available from GUI or package-manager installations. If you look at playing with the guts of the system as an unpleasant exercise best avoided, you probably won't mind trading a bit of a wait, for someone else to do the "dirty work" of fitting new software into Fink.

Basic Steps: `configure`, `make`

Let's start with an example of a software install—things can get more complicated than this, but for many applications written by conscientious programmers, these steps will suffice. For now, read this with the assumption that the software package `pine4.56` has been successfully downloaded, uncompressed, and untarred. Installs shown here are also done assuming that you're logged in as your `software` user, and that you've downloaded software into the `Documents` directory. (Don't worry that you haven't done these things yet; we just want to outline and explain the important steps before we dig into a complete example.)

Almost universally, the first command you'll issue to compile software is either `./configure` (if it's present) or `make` (if `./configure` is not present). For `pine`, the only things you have to type are

```
make
build osx
cp bin/pine /usr/local/bin/
mkdir /usr/local/man/
mkdir /usr/local/man1/
cp docs/pine.1 /usr/local/man/man1/
```

That doesn't look too hard, does it? The basic operations are simply `make`, `build`, and copying some files into standard locations in the filesystem.

If you want to follow along with this example, the pine package shown here can be downloaded from ftp://ftp.cac.washington.edu/pine/pine.tar.gz. The simplest way to do this is with curl:

```
cd ~/Documents
curl -O ftp://ftp.cac.washington.edu/pine/pine.tar.gz
gunzip pine.tar.gz
tar -xf pine.tar
```

NOTE

If you prefer to use the command-line Internet client `lynx`, you could issue the same download request by using the following command in place of the `curl` command:

```
lynx -dump ftp://ftp.cac.washington.edu/pine/pine.tar.gz > pine.tar.gz
```

The developers of `lynx` are changing and rearranging the way that some of the download functions work in the program. If your version of `lynx` produces files that can't be `gunzip`ped as shown in the examples, you've been unlucky and gotten one of the versions that automatically uncompresses and `gunzip`s files on download, even when storing them to disk. In this case, remove the `gunzip` step from the process and start off with the file as a `.tar` file instead.

`ftp://ftp.cac.washington.edu/pine/pine.tar.gz` is always a link to the most recent version, so `pine` may have advanced beyond 4.56 by the time you're reading this. We know, `pine4.56` compiles okay, so if you download a more recent version and have problems, you should be able to get 4.56 from its `old` directory—most likely at the URL `ftp://ftp.cac.washington.edu/pine/old/pine4.56.tar.gz`.

After you've downloaded and unpacked your distribution, it's time to dig in and build some software.

```
brezup:software source $ cd pine4.56/
brezup:software pine4.56 $ ls -l
total 136
-rw-r--r--  1 software tire  2866 9 Jan 2003 CPYRIGHT
-rw-r--r--  1 software tire 12196 9 Jan 2003 README
-rwxr-xr-x  1 software tire 16490 9 Dec 2002 build
-rwxr-xr-x  1 software tire  6039 15 Mar 1996 build.cmd
-rwxr-xr-x  1 software tire 16871 9 Dec 2002 buildcyg
drwxr-xr-x 10 software tire  340 29 May 16:00 contrib
drwxr-xr-x 13 software tire  442 29 May 16:00 doc
drwxr-xr-x 16 software tire  544 29 May 16:00 imap
-rw-r--r--  1 software tire  1551 15 Mar 1996 makefile
drwxr-xr-x 84 software tire  2856 29 May 16:00 pico
drwxr-xr-x 99 software tire  3366 29 May 16:00 pine
```

There's no file named `configure`, so try `make`:

```
brezup:software pine4.56 $ make
Use the "build" command (shell script) to make Pine.
You can say "build help" for details on how it works.
```

So, this software install isn't quite standard—it doesn't use `make`, other than to tell us that it doesn't use `make`. If you read the `README`, and look at the output of build help, which points you to `docs/pine-ports`, you'll observe that an `osx` option already is available, so give that a try:

```
brezup:software pine4.56 $ ./build osx
make args are CC=cc osx

<much output deleted>

Building c-client for osx...
echo `cat SPECIALS` > c-client/SPECIALS
cd c-client;make osx EXTRACFLAGS='\
 EXTRALDFLAGS='\
 EXTRADRIVERS='mbox'\
.
.
.
Once-only environment setup...
echo cc > CCTYPE
echo -g -O ' > CFLAGS
echo -DCREATEPROTO=unixproto -DEMPTYPROTO=unixproto \
.
.
.
ln -s os_osx.h osdep.h
ln -s os_osx.c osdepbas.c
ln -s log_std.c osdeplog.c
.
.
.
Building OS-dependent module
If you get No such file error messages for files x509.h, ssl.h,
pem.h, buffer.h, bio.h, and crypto.h, that means that OpenSSL
is not installed on your system. Either install OpenSSL first
```

16

```
or build with command: make osx SSLTYPE=none
`cat CCTYPE` -c `cat CFLAGS` `cat OSCFLAGS` -c osdep.c
`cat CCTYPE` -c `cat CFLAGS` mail.c
.
.
.
Building bundled tools...
cd mtest;make
cc -I../c-client `cat ../c-client/CFLAGS`  -c -o mtest.o mtest.c
.
.
.
Making Pico and Pilot
make CC=cc -f makefile.osx
rm -f os.h
ln -s osdep/os-osx.h os.h
cc  -g -DDEBUG -Dbsd -DJOB_CONTROL  -c -o main.o main.c
cc  -g -DDEBUG -Dbsd -DJOB_CONTROL  -c -o attach.o attach.c
.
.
.
Making Pine and rpload/rpdump.
make CC=cc LDAPLIBS=-lldap LDAPCFLAGS=-DENABLE_LDAP -f makefile.osx
rm -f os.h
ln -s osdep/os-osx.h os.h
./cmplhlp2.sh < pine.hlp > helptext.h
cc  -g -DDEBUG -DDEBUGJOURNAL -DENABLE_LDAP -Dconst=
➥ -DSYSTYPE=\"OSX\"  -c -o addrbook.o addrbook.c
.
.
.
Links to executables are in bin directory:
__TEXT __DATA __OBJC others dec   hex
3989504 299008 0    3112960 7401472 70f000 bin/pine
659456 12288  0    663552 1335296 146000 bin/mtest
700416 77824  0    700416 1478656 169000 bin/imapd
266240 12288  0    274432 552960 87000  bin/pico
262144 12288  0    274432 548864 86000  bin/pilot
913408 20480  0    921600 1855488 1c5000 bin/rpdump
913408 20480  0    921600 1855488 1c5000 bin/rpload
659456 12288  0    663552 1335296 146000 bin/mailutil
659456 12288  0    659456 1331200 145000 bin/ipop2d
663552 12288  0    663552 1339392 147000 bin/ipop3d
Done
```

Wow, that's a lot of output! If you were watching closely, you'll have seen some warnings fly by in there, but as long as it didn't explicitly say "Error" in there, and, at the end, it tells you that there are executables in the bin directory, you're in good shape. Let's look in the bin directory and see what you've got.

```
brezup:software pine4.56 # ls -l bin
total 36848
-rwxr-xr-x 2 software tire 1408404 20 Aug 10:27 imapd
-rwxr-xr-x 2 software tire 1326092 20 Aug 10:27 ipop2d
-rwxr-xr-x 2 software tire 1333548 20 Aug 10:27 ipop3d
-rwxr-xr-x 2 software tire 1327524 20 Aug 10:27 mailutil
-rwxr-xr-x 2 software tire 1329184 20 Aug 10:27 mtest
-rwxr-xr-x 2 software tire  543636 20 Aug 10:28 pico
-rwxr-xr-x 2 software tire  536976 20 Aug 10:28 pilot
-rwxr-xr-x 2 software tire 7351192 20 Aug 10:31 pine
-rwxr-xr-x 2 software tire 1843356 20 Aug 10:31 rpdump
-rwxr-xr-x 2 software tire 1846852 20 Aug 10:31 rpload
```

We were building pine, and in fact there is an executable pine in the bin directory, as well as a number of other applications. Installing pine now is simply copying it to /usr/local/bin with cp bin/pine /usr/local/bin. After that, pine should function as shown earlier.

A number of other executable applications are in that bin directory, too. You might want to spend the time to find out whether they do anything that you'd find useful—for example, along with pine, you've just built pico, which is a popular text editor that's been gaining on emacs and vi for quite a while. If you check the version of pico, a fairly popular and friendly terminal-based text editor included with OS X 10.2 and 10.3, you'll find that it's version 2.5, and you've just built pico version 4.6, possibly a worthwhile upgrade. We'll leave the exercise of reading about the rest of the utilities you've just built up to you.

To make this a little easier, you might have noticed at the first listing of the directory, there is a doc directory. Things such as man pages are probably found there, so let's take a look:

```
brezup:software pine4.56 $ ls doc
brochure.txt  pico.1      pine.1      tech-notes
mailcap.unx   pilot.1     rpdump.1    tech-notes.txt
mime.types    pine-ports  rpload.1
```

Great! Things that end in .<#> are usually man pages that belong in the man# section of the manual. Let's put the pine.1 page for pine into the appropriate man1 directory in /usr/local/man. If you didn't already create the /usr/local/man/man1 directory when you installed lynx earlier, you'll get a response something like this:

```
brezup:software pine4.56 $ cp doc/pine.1 /usr/local/man/man1/
cp: /usr/local/man/man1: No such file or directory
```

In which case, you've just got to make the directory:

```
brezup:software pine4.56 $ mkdir /usr/local/man/man1
mkdir: /usr/local/man/man1: No such file or directory
```

Of course, if you didn't create them already, there's probably no `/usr/local/man` directory either. Thankfully, you only have to do these kinds of directory creation steps once—most other command-line software will want the same directory structure, and this will be the only time you have to create these directories.

```
brezup:software pine4.56 $ mkdir /usr/local/man
brezup:software pine4.56 $ mkdir /usr/local/man/man1
```

Alternatively, you could make both directories with the same command, by using the `-p` "make intermediate directories" option of `mkdir`:

```
brezup:software pine4.56 $ mkdir -p /usr/local/man/man1
```

If another application needs another directory, of course you'll need to create it, but you've got almost everything standard covered by now.

```
brezup:software pine4.56 $ cp doc/pine.1 /usr/local/man/man1
```

And now we can try looking at the man page. If you're using a version of OS X that doesn't include the `manpath` command (versions 10.3 and 10.2.6 both have it), or you don't have `/usr/local/bin` added to your executable search path, you'll see something like the following; otherwise, you should see the man page for `pine` appear, just like any other man page on your system:

```
brezup:software pine4.56 $ man pine
man: no entry for pine in the manual.
```

This error indicates that the `man` command doesn't know where to find the man page for `pine`—specifically, that it hasn't been informed of the `/usr/loca/man/man1` directory that you just put it in. On recent versions of OS X, all you need to do to make that directory visible to `man`, is to include the `/usr/local/bin` directory in your executable search path, and the `manpath` command will automatically provide `man` with likely sounding directory names that are near the executable directories. If for some reason you really want to stuff `man` pages off in weird corners where the `manpath` command can't find them automatically, you can always set the `MANPATH` environment variable as a way of explicitly telling `man` where to look.

NOTE

With bash, the shell is supposed to automatically discover new programs that have been added to directories in your PATH and let you immediately run them by name. This doesn't always work, and the only cure we're aware of is to quit the shell and start another one. With tcsh, you can tell the shell that it's time to refresh its list of available commands by running the rehash command.

In this case, I've deliberately forgotten to set the executable search path to include /usr/local/bin, so the manpath command doesn't know about /usr/local/man as a place to find man pages. Again, fixing these things is best done in your .bashrc or .cshrc file, or the system equivalents. Setting it by hand now can be accomplished as follows:

```
brezup:software pine4.56 $ echo $PATH
/bin:/sbin:/usr/bin:/usr/sbin
brezup:software pine4.56 $ PATH=$PATH:/usr/local/bin
brezup:software pine4.56 $ echo $PATH
/bin:/sbin:/usr/bin:/usr/sbin:/usr/local/bin
brezup:software pine4.56 $ man pine
pine(1)                                    pine(1)

NAME
    pine - a Program for Internet News and Email

SYNTAX
    pine [ options ] [ address , address ]
    pinef [ options ] [ address , address ]

DESCRIPTION
    Pine is a screen-oriented message-handling tool. In its default con-
    figuration, Pine offers an intentionally limited set of functions
    geared toward the novice user, but it also has a growing list of
    optional "power-user" and personal-preference features.  pinef is a
    variant of Pine that uses function keys rather than mnemonic single-
    letter commands. Pine's basic feature set includes:
.
.
.
```

If you install other programs from the bin directory, you'll want to copy their man pages over as well. Finally, clean up after yourself, and put the pine stuff into your installed software directory in case you need it again:

```
brezup:software pine4.56 $ make clean
make: *** No rule to make target `clean'. Stop.
```

Usually, there's a make clean command to remove all the large files created by the build process, but reading the help for pine says it wants build clean instead:

```
brezup:software pine4.56 $ ./build clean
make args are CC=cc clean
Cleaning c-client and imapd
Removing old processed sources and binaries...
<deletia>
Cleaning Pine
rm -f *.o os.h os.c helptext.c helptext.h pine pine.exe
➥ rpdump rpdump.exe rpload rpload.exe
<more deletia>
Cleaning pico
rm -f *.a *.o *~ pico_os.c os.h pico pico.exe pilot pilot.exe
<and more deletia>
Done
brezup:software pine4.56 $ cd ../
brezup:software source $ tar -cf installed_pine4.56.tar pine4.56/
brezup:software source $ gzip installed_pine4.56.tar
brezup:software source $ mkdir installed
brezup:software source $ mv installed_pine4.56.tar.gz installed/
brezup:software source $ \rm -rf pine4.56
brezup:software source $ \rm -rf pine.tar
```

That's it! If you've been following along, you've just compiled and installed a piece of software. Is your heart racing or are your palms sweaty? Do you feel like a different person? No? Didn't think so. Most software installations, by and large, are exactly this anticlimactic.

TIP

Curious about the \ before the rm in the last command of that example? Remember when we suggested aliasing rm to rm -i, to help avoid deleting things unintentionally? Remember also that the \ character escapes things in the shell? If you precede an aliased command with an \ escape character, the effect is that the command as the command line sees it, isn't exactly the same as the command that you set up the alias for. Effectively, for the execution of this command, the alias does not exist. In this case, it allows us to recursively delete the entire pine4.56 directory and all its contents without needing to repeatedly answer Y to delete each file.

TIP

Why did I throw away the tarfile that I downloaded, and create another one of the directory I was just working in for archiving in my installed directory? Because I have a terrible time remembering what installation options I might have used, files that I might have edited, and tweaks that I might have had to make to configure and install the software the way that I want it. By archiving a copy of the install directory in exactly the condition it is in when I run my final successful `make` (or in this case, `build`), I don't need to remember these things; they're preserved right there for me in the `tar` file.

Next, let's do a couple of quick installs that use a more standard installation protocol. They're a collection of steps to get you set up for a considerably more difficult install we'll do in the troubleshooting section of the next chapter. The first of these is `libjpeg`, and the second is `libpng`. These are library packages that will be needed later to support the `netpbm` package—an amazingly powerful command-line graphics processing program. The complete standard invocation for configuration and compiling is usually:

```
configure
make
make test
make install
```

If you read the `README` file for this software, you'll see it gets an additional `make install-lib` step—always read the `README` and `INSTALL` files if they are present!

1. Download both `libjpeg` and `libpng` with `lynx`:

   ```
   cd ~/Documents/
   curl -O ftp://ftp.uu.net/graphics/jpeg/jpegsrc.v6b.tar.gz
   curl -O ftp://swrinde.nde.swri.edu/pub/png/src/libpng-1.2.5.tar.gz
   ```

   If you browse around the `png/src` directory, you'll see that there's a `macosx` makefile available, so grab that too (the makefile is the thing that tells `make` how to build a piece of software for your particular platform—usually these are included with the source itself).

   ```
   curl -O ftp://swrinde.nde.swri.edu/pub/png/src/➥libpng-1.2.5-
   makefile.macosx.tar.gz
   ```

2. Uncompress and unarchive the `libjpeg` archive:

   ```
   brezup:software source $ gunzip jpegsrc.v6b.tar.gz
   brezup:software source $ tar -xf jpegsrc.v6b.tar
   ```

TIP

If you prefer to uncompress and untar the file in one step, you can use `tar -xvzf jpegsrc.v6b.tar.gz` instead. I habitually do this process as two separate steps because I work between a number of Unix-based platforms, and not all of them have `tar`s that include the uncompress option. Rather than be somewhere in the middle of typing `make` when I notice that the `tar` command returned an error, it's easier for me to simply always use two steps.

16

3. cd into the directory, check to see whether there's a configure file, or only a makefile, and either ./configure, or make, as appropriate:

```
brezup:software source $ cd jpeg-6b/
brezup:software jpeg-6b $ ls

README       jcmarker.c   jdhuff.h     jpegint.h    maktjpeg.st
ansi2knr.1   jcmaster.c   jdinput.c    jpeglib.h    makvms.opt
ansi2knr.c   jcomapi.c    jdmainct.c   jpegtran.1   rdbmp.c
cderror.h    jconfig.bcc  jdmarker.c   jpegtran.c   rdcolmap.c
cdjpeg.c     jconfig.cfg  jdmaster.c   jquant1.c    rdgif.c
cdjpeg.h     jconfig.dj   jdmerge.c    jquant2.c    rdjpgcom.1
change.log   jconfig.doc  jdphuff.c    jutils.c     rdjpgcom.c
cjpeg.1      jconfig.mac  jdpostct.c   jversion.h   rdppm.c
cjpeg.c      jconfig.manx jdsample.c   libjpeg.doc  rdrle.c
ckconfig.c   jconfig.mc6  jdtrans.c    ltconfig     rdswitch.c
coderules.doc jconfig.sas jerror.c     ltmain.sh    rdtarga.c
config.guess jconfig.st   jerror.h     makcjpeg.st  structure.doc
config.sub   jconfig.vc   jfdctflt.c   makdjpeg.st  testimg.bmp
configure    jconfig.vms  jfdctfst.c   makeapps.ds  testimg.jpg
djpeg.1      jconfig.wat  jfdctint.c   makefile.ansi testimg.ppm
djpeg.c      jcparam.c    jidctflt.c   makefile.bcc testimgp.jpg
example.c    jcphuff.c    jidctfst.c   makefile.cfg testorig.jpg
filelist.doc jcprepct.c   jidctint.c   makefile.dj  testprog.jpg
install-sh   jcsample.c   jidctred.c   makefile.manx transupp.c
install.doc  jctrans.c    jinclude.h   makefile.mc6 transupp.h
jcapimin.c   jdapimin.c   jmemansi.c   makefile.mms usage.doc
jcapistd.c   jdapistd.c   jmemdos.c    makefile.sas wizard.doc
jccoefct.c   jdatadst.c   jmemdosa.asm makefile.unix wrbmp.c
jccolor.c    jdatasrc.c   jmemmac.c    makefile.vc  wrgif.c
jcdctmgr.c   jdcoefct.c   jmemmgr.c    makefile.vms wrjpgcom.1
jchuff.c     jdcolor.c    jmemname.c   makefile.wat wrjpgcom.c
jchuff.h     jdct.h       jmemnobs.c   makelib.ds   wrppm.c
jcinit.c     jddctmgr.c   jmemsys.h    makeproj.mac wrrle.c
jcmainct.c   jdhuff.c     jmorecfg.h   makljpeg.st  wrtarga.c
```

Yes, that's a bunch of files—it's nothing to worry about though. The configuration and build scripts put together by the author will take care of the details; all you need to do is remember the general steps for building and respond as requested if there's something the software or READMEs ask you to do. There's a configure file, so call ./configure:

NOTE

Why ./configure instead of just configure? Because there might be many different executables named configure on your machine, and you want to be sure to run only this one in this directory. As a matter of fact, on most competent Unix installations, typing configure (or any program name) at the command line will most frequently *not* run a version of that command that's in the current directory. OS X seems currently to be reasonably well configured with respect to default paths, so if you want the command line to search the current directory for executables, you'll have to add it to your path.

```
brezup:software jpeg-6b $ ./configure
checking for gcc.. gcc
checking whether the C compiler (gcc ) works.. yes
checking whether the C compiler (gcc ) is a cross-compiler.. no
checking whether we are using GNU C.. yes
checking how to run the C preprocessor.. gcc -E
checking for function prototypes.. yes
checking for stddef.h.. yes
checking for stdlib.h.. yes
checking for string.h.. yes
checking for size_t.. yes
checking for type unsigned char.. yes
checking for type unsigned short.. yes
checking for type void.. yes
checking for working const.. yes
checking for inline.. __inline__
checking for broken incomplete types.. ok
checking for short external names.. ok
checking to see if char is signed.. yes
checking to see if right shift is signed.. yes
checking to see if fopen accepts b spec.. yes
checking for a BSD compatible install.. /usr/bin/install -c
checking for ranlib.. ranlib
checking libjpeg version number.. 62
creating ./config.status
creating Makefile
creating jconfig.h
```

configure runs and drops you back to the command line with no complaints, so now it's time to run make:

```
brezup:software jpeg-6b $ make
gcc -O2 -I.  -c -o jcapimin.o jcapimin.c
```

16

```
gcc -O2 -I.  -c -o jcapistd.o jcapistd.c
gcc -O2 -I.  -c -o jctrans.o jctrans.c
gcc -O2 -I.  -c -o jcparam.o jcparam.c
gcc -O2 -I.  -c -o jdatadst.o jdatadst.c
.
.
.
rm -f libjpeg.a
ar rc libjpeg.a jcapimin.o jcapistd.o jctrans.o jcparam.o jdatadst.o \
jcinit.o jcmaster.o jcmarker.o jcmainct.o
➥jcprepct.o jccoefct.ojccolor.o \
jcsample.o jchuff.o jcphuff.o jcdctmgr.o
➥jfdctfst.o jfdctflt.o jfdctint.o \
jdapimin.o jdapistd.o jdtrans.o jdatasrc.o
➥jdmaster.o jdinput.o jdmarker.o \
jdhuff.o jdphuff.o jdmainct.o jdcoefct.o
➥jdpostct.o jddctmgr.o jidctfst.o \
jidctflt.o jidctint.o jidctred.o jdsample.o
➥jdcolor.o jquant1.o jquant2.o \
jdmerge.o jcomapi.o jutils.o jerror.o jmemmgr.o jmemnobs.o
ranlib libjpeg.a
gcc -O2 -I.  -c -o cjpeg.o cjpeg.c
gcc -O2 -I.  -c -o rdppm.o rdppm.c
.
.
.
gcc -O2 -I.  -c -o wrjpgcom.o wrjpgcom.c
gcc -o wrjpgcom wrjpgcom.o
```

Again, you arrive back at the command line, so it's time to try `make test`:

```
brezup:software jpeg-6b $ make test
rm -f testout*
./djpeg -dct int -ppm -outfile testout.ppm ./testorig.jpg
./djpeg -dct int -bmp -colors 256 -outfile testout.bmp ./testorig.jpg
./cjpeg -dct int -outfile testout.jpg ./testimg.ppm
./djpeg -dct int -ppm -outfile testoutp.ppm ./testprog.jpg
./cjpeg -dct int -progressive -opt -outfile testoutp.jpg ./testimg.ppm
./jpegtran -outfile testoutt.jpg ./testprog.jpg
cmp ./testimg.ppm testout.ppm
cmp ./testimg.bmp testout.bmp
cmp ./testimg.jpg testout.jpg
cmp ./testimg.ppm testoutp.ppm
cmp ./testimgp.jpg testoutp.jpg
cmp ./testorig.jpg testoutt.jpg
```

If there was a problem, `make test` would have spit out some error diagnostics and told you that it had encountered trouble. Because it didn't, you're ready to move on to `make install`:

```
brezup:software jpeg-6b $make install
/usr/bin/install -c cjpeg /usr/local/bin/cjpeg
/usr/bin/install -c djpeg /usr/local/bin/djpeg
/usr/bin/install -c jpegtran /usr/local/bin/jpegtran
/usr/bin/install -c rdjpgcom /usr/local/bin/rdjpgcom
/usr/bin/install -c wrjpgcom /usr/local/bin/wrjpgcom
/usr/bin/install -c -m 644 ./cjpeg.1 /usr/local/man/man1/cjpeg.1
/usr/bin/install -c -m 644 ./djpeg.1 /usr/local/man/man1/djpeg.1
/usr/bin/install -c -m 644 ./jpegtran.1 /usr/local/man/man1/jpegtran.1
/usr/bin/install -c -m 644 ./rdjpgcom.1 /usr/local/man/man1/rdjpgcom.1
/usr/bin/install -c -m 644 ./wrjpgcom.1 /usr/local/man/man1/wrjpgcom.1
```

Notice that it's using the `/usr/local/man/man1` directory that you created earlier. If you hadn't done so, it would be complaining here.

NOTE

Sometimes `make install` rules automatically create directories needed for installation, but this particular install doesn't do this. Many authors assume that any sane version of Unix would already have directories such as `/usr/local/bin` and `/usr/local/man` and that creating them should never be necessary. Within a few installations, you'll have created all the directories that are customarily present, and then things should take care of themselves because authors tend to be more careful to explicitly create directories that aren't in the "normally present" tree.

Finally, if you read the `README`, you'd see that we need a `make install-lib` step here, too:

```
brezup:software jpeg-6b $ make install-lib
/usr/bin/install -c -m 644 jconfig.h /usr/local/include/jconfig.h
/usr/bin/install: /usr/local/include/jconfig.h: No such file or directory
make: *** [install-headers] Error 1
```

What did I say about that installer not creating directories? Now it needs a `/usr/local/include` directory as well:

```
brezup:software jpeg-6b $ mkdir /usr/local/include
brezup:software jpeg-6b $ make install-lib
/usr/bin/install -c -m 644 jconfig.h /usr/local/include/jconfig.h
/usr/bin/install -c -m 644 ./jpeglib.h /usr/local/include/jpeglib.h
/usr/bin/install -c -m 644 ./jmorecfg.h /usr/local/include/jmorecfg.h
/usr/bin/install -c -m 644 ./jerror.h /usr/local/include/jerror.h
/usr/bin/install -c -m 644 libjpeg.a /usr/local/lib/libjpeg.a
```

Then you're finished. To tidy things up, `make clean`, delete the original `tar` file, `tar` and then delete the directory you've been working in, `gzip` the new `tar` file, and store it in your `installed` directory.

Now let's take a look at what you just did. Other than creating a directory to fix the not-quite-functional installer, the entire process was: `./configure`, which guessed a few settings about your machine, and then a series of `make`, `make test`, `make install`, and `make install-lib`. Other than the `./configure`, the actual program called in each case was `make`, and it was directed to make different things with each call. The identities of these things are defined by the software author in a control file called a makefile and named, unsurprisingly, either `Makefile` or `makefile`. With any well-written software package, the makefile will direct `make` (called with no arguments) to compile the software with default settings. Frequently, but not always, a test suite is provided that can be invoked with `make test`.

Finally, an installer routine is invoked, by convention, with `make install`. In the case of `libjpeg`, the package provides both a few small executables and some library functions for other software, should you want them. The basic `make install` process puts the small executables in `/usr/local/bin` but doesn't install the libraries because not everyone wants them. Therefore, there's an optional `make install-lib` step to install the libraries and support files. If you've followed along this far, your `/usr/local` structure should be fairly mature, and most software won't need you to create any more directories for it.

NOTE

Some software that you try to install will want you to use the `bsdmake` version of the `make` program instead of just `make` (which in Apple's case is currently `GNUmake`). Apple has also provided a separate `gnumake` executable, should you find software that wants GNUmake to be named `gnumake` or `gmake`. If you find a request for `bsdmake` in a `README` file (or software that complains about syntax errors in the makefile), try substituting `bsdmake` or `gnumake` for `make` at the command line. If you find a program that outputs what seems to be incomprehensible gibberish when you type `make`, give the other versions a try and see whether they do any better.

The `configure` step is typical as well, although the mechanics vary depending on the application you're compiling. Most of the time, `configure` can either examine your system and determine, or make an educated guess about, configuration options. Occasionally, it requires you to provide it with some information, but in most cases it's all right to accept the default answers suggested by `configure` if you don't have a better answer or don't know the answer.

Finally, let's run through the install of `libpng` because without it, the broken `netpbm` we're going to fix in the next section is truly hopeless:

```
brezup:software source $ gunzip libpng-1.2.5.tar.gz
brezup:software source $ tar -xf libpng-1.2.5.tar
```

```
brezup:software source $ cd libpng-1.2.5
brezup:software libpng-1.2.5 $ ls
ANNOUNCE    contrib     pngbar.jpg   pngread.c    pngwio.c
CHANGES     example.c   pngbar.png   pngrio.c     pngwrite.c
INSTALL     libpng.3    pngconf.h    pngrtran.c   pngwtran.c
KNOWNBUG    libpng.txt  pngerror.c   pngrutil.c   pngwutil.c
LICENSE     libpngpf.3  pngggccrd.c  pngset.c     projects
README      png.5       pngget.c     pngtest.c    scripts
TODO        png.c       pngmem.c     pngtest.png
Y2KINFO     png.h       pngnow.png   pngtrans.c
configure   pngasmrd.h  pngpread.c   pngvcrd.c
```

It has a `configure`, so use it:

```
brezup:software libpng-1.2.5 $ ./configure

 There is no "configure" script for Libpng-1.2.5. Instead, please
 copy the appropriate makefile for your system from the "scripts"
 directory. Read the INSTALL file for more details.
```

Another nonstandard installation, so follow the instructions:

```
brezup:software libpng-1.2.5 $ ls scripts

SCOPTIONS.ppc          makefile.bd32     makefile.intel   makefile.so9
descrip.mms            makefile.beos     makefile.knr     makefile.solaris
libpng-config-body.in  makefile.bor      makefile.linux   makefile.std
libpng-config-head.in  makefile.cygwin   makefile.macosx  makefile.sunos
libpng.icc             makefile.darwin   makefile.mips    makefile.tc3
libpng.pc.in           makefile.dec      makefile.msc     makefile.vcawin32
makefile.32sunu        makefile.dj2      makefile.ne12bsd makefile.vcwin32
makefile.64sunu        makefile.freebsd  makefile.netbsd  makefile.watcom
makefile.acorn         makefile.gcc      makefile.openbsd makevms.com
makefile.aix           makefile.gcmmx    makefile.os2     pngdef.pas
makefile.amiga         makefile.hpgcc    makefile.sco     pngos2.def
makefile.atari         makefile.hpux     makefile.sggcc   smakefile.ppc
makefile.bc32          makefile.ibmc     makefile.sgi
```

Fantastic! A `macosx` file! Copy it to the `libpng` directory as `makefile` and run `make`, `make test` (the output of which we're omitting here), and `make install`:

```
brezup:software libpng-1.2.5 $ cp scripts/makefile.macosx ./makefile
brezup:software libpng-1.2.5 $ make
```

16

```
cc -fno-common -I../zlib -O  -c -o png.o png.c
cc -fno-common -I../zlib -O  -c -o pngset.o pngset.c
cc -fno-common -I../zlib -O  -c -o pngget.o pngget.c
.
.
.
ar rc libpng.a png.o pngset.o pngget.o pngrutil.o pngtrans.o pngwutil.o
➥ pngread.o pngrio.o pngwio.o pngwrite.o pngrtran.o pngwtran.o pngmem.o pngerror.o
pngpread.o
ranlib libpng.a
cc -fno-common -I../zlib -O  -c -o pngtest.o pngtest.c
cc -o pngtest -fno-common -I../zlib -O pngtest.o -L. -L../zlib -lpng
➥ -lz -current_version 0.1.2.5
cc: -current_version only allowed with -dynamiclib
make: *** [pngtest] Error 1
```

Oops. I bet I just stumbled across the reason for that macosx makefile provided on the ftp site.

```
brezup:software libpng-1.2.5 $ gunzip ../libpng-1.2.5-makefile.macosx.tar.gz
```

What's in the tar file?

```
brezup:software libpng-1.2.5 $ tar -tf ../libpng-1.2.5-makefile.macosx.tar
makefile.macosx
```

So it unpacks into the current directory, rather than a subdirectory.

```
brezup:software libpng-1.2.5 $ tar -xf ../libpng-1.2.5-makefile.macosx.tar
brezup:software libpng-1.2.5 $ mv makefile.macosx makefile
```

And I'm back to trying the make again:

```
brezup:software libpng-1.2.5 $ make
cc -o pngtest -fno-common -I../zlib -O pngtest.o -L. -L../zlib -lpng -lz
ld: warning -L: directory name (../zlib) does not exist
cc -dynamiclib -flat_namespace -undefined suppress -o libpng12.0.1.2.5.dylib
png.o pngset.o pngget.o pngrutil.o pngtrans.o pngwutil.o pngread.o pngrio.o
pngwio.o pngwrite.o pngrtran.o pngwtran.o pngmem.o pngerror.o pngpread.o
cat scripts/libpng.pc.in | sed -e s\!@PREFIX@!/usr/local! | \
  sed -e s/-lm// > libpng.pc
( cat scripts/libpng-config-head.in; \
echo prefix=\"/usr/local\"; \
echo I_opts=\"-I/usr/local/include/libpng12\"; \
echo L_opts=\"-L/usr/local/lib\"; \
echo libs=\"-lpng12 -lz\"; \
```

```
cat scripts/libpng-config-body.in ) > libpng-config
chmod +x libpng-config
```

It had a warning, but no errors! You can run `make test` here to verify that it works—we'll just show the output of `make install`:

```
brezup:software libpng-1.2.5 $ make install
cp png.h pngconf.h /usr/local/include/libpng12
chmod 644 /usr/local/include/libpng12/png.h
➥ /usr/local/include/libpng12/pngconf.h
(cd /usr/local/include; ln -f -s libpng12 libpng; ln -f -s libpng12/* .)
cp libpng.a /usr/local/lib/libpng12.a
chmod 644 /usr/local/lib/libpng12.a
(cd /usr/local/lib; ln -f -s libpng12.a libpng.a)
cc -dynamiclib -compatibility_version 3 -flat_namespace \
-undefined suppress -o libpng.3.1.2.5.dylib png.o pngset.o
➥ pngget.o pngrutil.o pngtrans.o pngwutil.o pngread.o
➥ pngrio.o pngwio.o pngwrite.o pngrtran.o pngwtran.o pngmem.o
➥ pngerror.o pngpread.o
cp libpng.3.1.2.5.dylib /usr/local/lib
cp libpng12.0.1.2.5.dylib /usr/local/lib
chmod 755 /usr/local/lib/libpng12.0.1.2.5.dylib
chmod 755 /usr/local/lib/libpng.3.1.2.5.dylib
(cd /usr/local/lib; \
ln -f -s libpng.3.1.2.5. \
libpng.3.; \
ln -f -s libpng.3. libpng.; \
ln -f -s libpng12.0.1.2.5. \
libpng.; \
ln -f -s libpng.3.1.2.5. \
libpng.3.; \
ln -f -s libpng12.0.1.2.5.dylib \
libpng12.0.dylib; \
ln -f -s libpng12.0.dylib \
libpng12.dylib)
cp libpng.pc /usr/local/lib/pkgconfig/libpng12.pc
chmod 644 /usr/local/lib/pkgconfig/libpng12.pc
(cd /usr/local/lib/pkgconfig; ln -f -s libpng12.pc libpng.pc)
cp libpng.3 /usr/local/man/man3
cp libpngpf.3 /usr/local/man/man3
cp png.5 /usr/local/man/man5
cp libpng-config /usr/local/bin/libpng12-config
chmod 755 /usr/local/bin/libpng12-config
(cd /usr/local/bin; ln -sf libpng12-config libpng-config)
```

16

All done. You've survived yet another software install. By now, this should be starting to look a bit more tedious than double-clicking an installer but no more threatening. Even though this install didn't go entirely as planned, you survived the whole thing without needing to do anything other than notice that there was an updated file provided by the authors and follow some simple instructions. The vast majority of Unix software installs are this easy (or even easier, because most wrap their updates in relatively quickly). Unfortunately, OS X isn't as well supported in the `configure` scripts as some major Unix flavors just yet, so there are a few rough spots like the `makefile` still. It's catching on quickly though, so soon, expect that 90% of all software will install with `./configure`, `make`, `make test`, and `make install`, and no further interaction from you.

> **NOTE**
>
> How can you enhance your chance of compilation success? You can make more installs work using the `configure` command by copying some files that Apple has provided into the software directory where you will be running `configure`. None of the installs shown here benefit from this, but copying `/usr/share/automake-1.6/config.guess` and `/usr/share/automake-1.6/config.sub` to the directory where you run `configure` might help with some compilations.

Summary

In this chapter, you did something the vast majority of Macintosh users have never done—compile and install your own software. We hope that you found this experience completely anticlimactic. OS X is still rough enough around the edges that if you try to install every program out there, you will run across some that raise your blood pressure. But on Unix flavors that have existed for a longer time, almost every piece of source can be compiled with the same standard installation procedure: `./configure`, `make`, `make test`, and `make install`. We expect that OS X will mature rapidly to the point that all installs are as simple as what we've gone through here.

CHAPTER 17

Troubleshooting Software Installs, and Compiling and Debugging Manually

IN THIS CHAPTER

- Common Sense and Configuration Options
- File Locations and Fighting with Installers
- Using the gdb Debugger
- Recommended Command-Line Software Installations
- Summary

Sometimes, when you try to compile and install a program, it won't work as easily as the examples in Chapter 16 "Command-Line Software Installation." Sometimes it's a matter of the program not being tweaked to run properly on OS X. Sometimes the program is just poorly written. Most often, however, it's because the vast majority of software written for Unix is in a constant state of revision, and minor bugs are introduced, squashed, and often re-created again in some other subroutine, on a regular basis. If you're in no hurry to use the software, don't worry that it doesn't compile. As long as you've paid attention to this suggestion: *Never compile or install software as a user with a privileged account*, the attempt to compile and run it has done nothing more than occupy some disk space and cause a little frustration. Write to the program's author, let him or her know that something's not right, and it will probably be fixed in a reasonable amount of time.

If you're in a hurry, or are either inquisitive or stubborn, there are some things that you can try to get the software working. A few of these involve updating certain parameters in your environment, and one involves rolling up your sleeves and digging around in the program's guts. If the latter is something you've never imagined doing, don't worry—it's your choice! Just remember that as long as you're working in a nonprivileged account, you can't really do much damage—the software is already broken; you can't hurt the system. The worst that will happen is you don't improve anything.

This chapter lays out a few common things to check when an install doesn't seem to work and takes you through an example of what is necessary to fix one particularly troublesome install. Because every problem install is different, we can't give you an exhaustive list of things to look for. Instead, we hope the tour of a problematic install and the example of using the GNU debugger gives you an idea of what to look for and how to solve the problem.

If you find this material too complicated, don't let it bother you. This chapter provides an example of the routes of attack that you can take if you choose to pursue the issue. If you aren't inclined to fight with a recalcitrant install, feel free to skip this chapter. Nothing in the rest of the book requires that you be comfortable with the troubleshooting material.

At the end of the chapter, we've provided a short section outlining a number of useful applications that you might like to install at the command line. Where possible, we've included copies of the source and compiled binaries of all that we can (copyright restrictions prevent us from distributing some packages because the authors prefer you to download the source from their sites only) at `http://www.macosxunleashed.com/downloads/`. In general, the precompiled software will work for you, but if you want the most current and complete version of a piece of software, it's always best to go to the source and build it yourself.

Common Sense and Configuration Options

A reasonable number of problems can be solved by a suitable application of common sense. The biggest problem with this is that users appear to have a difficult time figuring out what sense is common, and what is not. Repeatedly, I have seen users who were convinced their problems were the fault of a program or machine, and were hopping mad at the system for treating them poorly. Most frequently, however, it turns out that they've mistyped some command or entered an incorrect parameter, and fixing this also fixes the problem. Conversely, I've seen users who have spent hours fighting with a problem, firmly convinced that they were making some trivial error and were simply incapable of seeing it. Almost to the user, these cases turn out to be actual machine or software errors rather than user errors. If you're new to the Unix environment, watch for this tendency—if you think something is the system's fault, stop to consider whether you really have done everything properly. If you think you're doing something wrong but can't figure out what it is after suitable inspection, don't forget that the people who wrote the software are users too and could have made an error just as easily.

That being said, we'll provide a general list of things that might help you figure out what's going wrong with a piece of compiled software. There is no such thing as a complete list, but these are relatively good places to start.

- The absolute first thing to try, if software doesn't install, is reading the instructions. I know, you've already read the instructions. Read them again.

TIP

Try taking out a marker and highlighting the specific places where it says "type this" and "enter that." I've been coding on Unix machines for almost 18 years, and I still religiously highlight all relevant sections of installation and configuration instructions. Get into the habit—it's good for you.

- Make sure while reading the instructions that you've read any sections dealing specifically with OS X. If there's nothing that deals specifically with OS X or Darwin, the instructions for BSD, NextStep, or OpenStep installation might be of interest.
- Examine the evidence of a problem. Error messages are generally trying to tell you something beyond the simple fact that there was an error. They sometimes do an abysmally bad job of it, but the average error message contains at least some clues as to what the error is and how to fix it.
- If the error involves something going wrong well after the compile—for example, when the program is running—check whether the program outputs log files. Many programs write progress reports and debugging information into log files. The location of these files is frequently defined in the program's configuration options, but programs can also log via the SYSLOG facility and write log information into files in the `/var/log/` directory.

TIP

I can't stress strongly enough how important or useful log entries can be. I know, in the throes of fighting with an error it's difficult to remember to look at the logs, but at least 50% of the time I'm having a problem, if I remember to look, the logs have an answer for me.

- If the program doesn't have a log file, check to see whether it has a debug or verbose mode (usually invoked with `-d` or `--debug` and `-v` or `--verbose`, respectively). Adding these to the program's invocation either enables log output to a file or causes the program to produce useful output to the terminal.
- If the problem is that at the compilation step, the program makes a complaint that it can't find a library (typically a file ending in `.o` or `.so`), it might be because the compiler doesn't know where to find it, not because it doesn't exist. If you can find the file it's complaining about, you can attempt to fix the problem in one of two ways. The first involves editing the makefile. If you can find where the library is used in the makefile (look for the `<filename>.o` string in the makefile), you can try adding `-L<pathtodirectory>` to the makefile. `<pathtodirectory>` should be the full path to the directory that the library was found in.

- Similarly, at runtime, you may occasionally find programs that refuse to execute with errors that indicate an inability to find a dynamically loaded library (typically `<filename><revision>.dyld` or `<filename><revision>.so`). If you encounter this, you need to search your system (use `find` from the root directory) for a version of the missing library (anything with the same major version should work fine—dynamic and shared libraries have a number of revision levels, typically indicated by a triple of dot-separated numbers appended to the filename `<major>.<minor>.<bugfix>`). Add the path to the directory containing the library to your `DYLD_LIBRARY_PATH` and/or `LD_LIBRARY_PATH`. Typically, the `DYLD_LIBRARY_PATH` setting should be sufficient (set this to a colon-separated list of paths to the directories where you've found the missing files), but some software may require the `LD_LIBRARY_PATH` instead. At the command line, enter `DYLD_LIBRARY_PATH=<paths_to_libraries>`, or (`setenv DYLD_LIBRARY_PATH <paths_to_libraries>` if you're using `tcsh`) to make the setting.

- The configure script frequently pulls some options and makes some decisions based on the contents of two files in the current directory where it's run. Because not everyone has updated their scripts to correctly handle Darwin-based systems, sometimes it helps to copy the versions that Apple provides in `cp /usr/share/automake-1.6/config.*` into the current directory before running `configure`.

- A syntax error from the compiler that indicates a line number is a warning from the compiler that invalid code has been found in the file. This is an indication that there's something wrong with the program, or perhaps that you've downloaded it incorrectly, or that it has become corrupted on your local machine. Sometimes these are fixable without too much trouble—for example, something you can easily repair in the syntax is the damage that's done when a Mac-OS-side editor has saved a file with Macintosh end-of-line characters rather than Unix end-of-line characters (or has accumulated an assortment of each through the use of different editors).

- "Downloaded incorrectly" problems can frequently be traced to the fact that Unix and Macintosh applications use two different symbols to indicate the end of a line of text. Apple is trying to rewrite many command-line utilities so that they're platform agnostic with respect to the carriage-return versus linefeed issue, but Apple can't do it for every application that you might compile. If you use Macintosh applications such as text editors, or Web browsers to download or modify code or configuration files, expect to see the occasional compilation or execution error as a result of having the line endings changed (it happens to all of us, more frequently than we like to admit!)

  Similar problems pop up from time to time when you've used a text editor that saves "state" information along with the data. If you find yourself in a situation where a compiler or program complains that the syntax of a file is incorrect (or the software just plain dies while reading files), check your line endings. Pure plain text editors such as BBedit and Alpha both include the option to save files with Unix line endings in their Save As dialogs. Both also include the option to discard state information. The command-line `emacs` editor tells you whether your file has Macintosh line endings in its status line. If you use the `emacs` `M-x find-file-literally` option to load a file, it loads with the Mac's `control-M` line endings as `control-M`, and you can use `M-x replace-string` to switch them to Unix line endings (`control-J`).

- Apple has supplied `make` as a version of GNUmake. Some software makefiles are designed for the BSD version of `make` instead and break when GNU's `make` is used. If you get weird errors during compilations that seem to indicate a syntax error with the makefile itself, try using `bsdmake` rather than `make`.
- A number of the `configure` scripts and makefiles out there assume that if they're using GNU's `make`, it'll be named `gmake`, or `gnumake`, and that if `make` is named just plain `make`, it's a BSD derived version. Calling GNUmake `make` on OSX can cause problems with makefiles that are (poorly) designed to detect which `make` system they're running under, and that try to automatically use the correct syntax for the version of `make` that's in use. Sometimes it helps to put a `gmake` link in `/usr/local/bin` and point it to `/usr/bin/make`, or to invoke your compilations explicitly with `gmake`.
- Yet another inconsistency results in the occasional inability for `make` to proceed properly through the entire hierarchy of directories where it needs to be run. One of the first things to try, if you're seeing messages from `make` that say "`entering directory <dirname>`", followed shortly by a compilation error, is to manually `cd` to that directory and run `make` in it by hand. You might need to do this several times, with directories at each level in the hierarchy. If `make` turns out to work properly when manually run in the subdirectory where it was previously breaking, repeat this step as necessary throughout the directory structure of the program and then return to the top-level directory for the compile, and run `make` there again. This should use all the subparts you've assembled and correctly finish the process. Occasionally, it'll find yet something else wrong in a subdirectory due to some cross-dependency with another subdirectory. If that's the case, try stepping through the process again and see whether the final `make` at the top level gets further the next time. If it does, you're making progress. If it doesn't, it's time to look elsewhere for the source of the trouble.
- Due to differences between compiler and linker versions, and the fact that any given compilation process may have been designed for something other than what you've got on your system, it's sometimes necessary to add certain "flags" to compile and link steps. These are usually defined in the makefile as `CFLAGS` and `LDFLAGS` variables. The most common flags of interest are `-flat_namespace`, `-undefined suppress`, `-no-cpp-precomp`, and `-fno-common`. The exact combination of these that you may need to either add, or remove from the `CFLAGS` and `LDFLAGS` definitions varies from package to package. In general, if you get complaints regarding undefined symbols, try adding `-undefined suppress`, and potentially `-flat_namespace`. `-fno_common`

actually makes the compiler more strict about certain things but also makes it behave more like the default behavior on some other systems. Unless the software was designed for Darwin, `-no-cpp-precomp` is usually safe to add and is a good try if you're seeing complaints about syntax.

Cargo-Cult Compiling

Many of the recommendations we've made in this section amount to what a programmer would consider to be *cargo-cult compilation* (the uneducated application of various "magic" incantations to a problem, with no real understanding of what any of them do, in the hopes that one or more might solve the problem). The term comes from the story of primitive island cultures that supposedly picked up the habit of building mock airstrips, radio shacks, and barracks in an attempt to induce planes and ships to land there, having once seen planes and ships land near similar structures during wartime occupations.

In the world of real programmers, cargo-cult programming is generally looked down on. Programming is a precise art, and those who denigrate that art by cutting and pasting bits of code that they don't understand, but that they believe has some functionality, aren't real programmers regardless of what they've put on their resume.

You however, aren't expected to be a real programmer. It's great if you are, but if you're not, and you're not trying to be, using cargo-cult techniques to try to solve a compilation error is a valid approach to the problem. We've given you some of the best general-purpose incantations we know. If you're not trying to be a real programmer, and you have software that won't compile, try out some of them. The worst that can happen is that the compile still doesn't work. And never let a real programmer knock the result if you get something working. If he'd done his job, you wouldn't have had to fix it!

File Locations and Fighting with Installers

For this example, you need the `netpbm` package, available from `http://www.macosxunleashed.com/downloads/netpbm-9.12.tgz`, or from its original home at `http://download.sourceforge.net/netpbm/netpbm-9.12.tgz`. A more recent version of `netpbm` is available, and it's the one you'll actually want to install and use, but this older version makes for a nice tour through the underbelly of a software install. The easy download solution is

```
curl -O http://download.sourceforge.net/netpbm/netpbm-9.12.tgz
```

The file should be 2057293 bytes in length. Uncompress it, untar it, and check whether it wants `configure` or `make`:

```
brezup:software source $ gunzip netpbm-9.12.tgz
brezup:software source $ tar -xf netpbm-9.12.tar
brezup:software source $ cd netpbm-9.12
brezup:software netpbm-9.12 $ ls
```

```
COPYRIGHT.PATENT     README.VMS        pbmplus.h
GNUmakefile        amiga           pgm
GPL_LICENSE.txt      compile.h         pnm
HISTORY          configure         ppm
Makefile         empty_depend       scoptions
Makefile.common      installosf        shhopt
Makefile.config.djgpp   libopt.c          stamp-date
Makefile.config.in    libtiff          stamp-date.amiga
Makefile.depend      magic           testgrid.pbm
Netpbm.programming    make_merge.sh       testimg.ppm
README          mantocat         urt
README.CONFOCAL      mkinstalldirs       version.h
README.DJGPP       netpbm.lsm        vms
README.JPEG        pbm            zgv_bigmaxval.patch
```

There's a `configure` file, so run it. This one is going to make some guesses and ask you some questions. Pick the options shown in the following example because they're necessary to get the rest of the example to work:

```
brezup:software netpbm-9.12 $ ./configure
su: ./configure: /bin/perl: bad interpreter: No such file or directory
```

Hold on; problem number one—that wasn't the expected behavior. The file `configure` is right here in the directory with you; what's with this no such file business? Actually, it's complaining about something else, not the configure script itself. (If you are running `tcsh`, you get an even less useful error—simply `tcsh: ./configure: Command not found`!)

```
brezup:software netpbm-9.12 $ head ./configure
#!/bin/perl -w

use strict;

# This program generates Makefile.config, which is included by all of the
# Netpbm makefiles. You run this program as the first step in building
# Netpbm. (The second step is 'make').

# This program is only a convenience. It is supported to create
# Makefile.config any way you want. In fact, an easy way is to copy
.
.
.
```

The problem is that OS X doesn't have Perl as `/bin/perl`; it's `/usr/bin/perl`. Fire up `vi` (or your favorite text editor) and change that first line to `#!/usr/bin/perl -w`. A more permanent solution to the fact that different systems have Perl in `/bin/`, `/usr/bin/`, or

17

/usr/local/bin/ is to make a link in each of these places where it isn't, back to /usr/bin/perl, so that software written on other systems can run without modification. If you want, the following should fix Perl for most scripts:

```
brezup:root netpbm-9.12 # ln -s /usr/bin/perl /bin/perl
brezup:root netpbm-9.12 # ln -s /usr/bin/perl /usr/local/bin/perl
```

> **NOTE**
>
> Of course, you do need to be root, or sudo your way to the first of those commands, should you choose to make these links.

Because Perl is only the most common thing you'll find that might be affected by this type of configuration problem, and you're unlikely to want to use the link solution for all of them, here, we'll take the route of fixing the configure script instead.

```
brezup:software netpbm-9.12 $ head ./configure
#!/usr/bin/perl -w

use strict;
.
.
.
```

Now try again:

```
brezup:software netpbm-9.12 $ ./configure
Which of the following best describes your platform?
1) GNU/Linux
2) Solaris or SunOS
3) AIX
4) Tru64
5) Irix
6) Windows (Cygwin or DJGPP)
7) BeOS
8) NetBSD
9) none of these are even close

Your choice ==> 1

Enter the installation directory (the prefix on all installation
paths for 'make install'). This is not built into any programs;
It is used only by 'make install'.
```

```
install prefix (/usr/local/netpbm)=>

Do you want static-linked Netpbm libraries or shared?

static or shared (shared)=> static

Can't exec ""ginstall"": No such file or directory at ./configure line 195.

We have created the file 'Makefile.config'. You can now
proceed to enter the 'make' command.

Note, however, that we have only made a rough guess at your
configuration, and you may want to look at Makefile.config and
edit it to your requirements and taste before doing the make.
```

NOTE

By the way, we picked GNU/Linux even though OS X is a BSD flavor, because many of the tools are GNU tools. Still, this will cause problems later because Linux typically has things in nonstandard places with respect to BSD, and Apple has maintained a lot of the typical BSD filesystem structure.

The results of the configure are better, but there's an ominous complaint in there about `can't exec ginstall`. To get things working will take editing that `Makefile.config` and making a few changes—mostly to patch things back to standard locations, from where Linux tends to store them. Fire up `vi` and look through `Makefile.config` for lines that look similar to the following; then change them until they're exactly as shown in the following listings:

- It seems to have ignored the `static` option given to `configure`, so set it here, too.

```
# STATICLIB = N
STATICLIB = Y
```

- `ginstall` is GNU's installation program. Apple probably uses it, but has probably named it *install* instead, so comment out the `ginstall` line and uncomment the `install` line.

```
#INSTALL = ginstall
#Solaris:
#INSTALL = /usr/ucb/install
#Tru64:
#INSTALL = installbsd
```

```
#OSF1:
#INSTALL = installosf
#Red Hat Linux :
INSTALL = install
```

This version of the software and the current version of the C compiler don't quite get along. Adding `-no-cpp-precomp` and `-fno-common` to the arguments that get handed to the C compiler—usually via a `CFLAGS` variable—helps in many cases. The flag `-flat_namespace` helps with some things as well, and the flag `-undefined suppress`, which used to help make the linker happy for this software under 10.1, now seems to cause problems (though it's necessary for some other compiles). Add the `-no-cpp-precomp` and `-fno-common` for a first try. Add the `-flat_namespace` and the `-undefined_suppress` options if it still bombs.

```
CFLAGS = -pedantic -no-cpp-precomp -fno-common -O3 -Wall
➥-Wno-uninitialized $(CDEBUG)
```

Linux installations tend to have taken a wrong turn in filesystem design, and include the binaries, libraries, and headers for optional packages in the `/usr/bin/`, `/usr/lib/`, and `/usr/include` directories. This makes system maintenance a real problem because your unprivileged software management user would need `root` privileges to work in those directories. Fix the defaults so that the `jpeglib` stuff comes from `/usr/local`, where we put it not too long ago:

```
#JPEGLIB_DIR = /usr/lib/jpeg
#JPEGHDR_DIR = /usr/include/jpeg
# Netbsd:
#JPEGLIB_DIR = ${LOCALBASE}/lib
#JPEGHDR_DIR = ${LOCALBASE}/include
# OSF, Tru64:
#JPEGLIB_DIR = /usr/local1/DEC/lib
#JPEGHDR_DIR = /usr/local1/DEC/include
# Typical:
JPEGLIB_DIR = /usr/local/lib
JPEGHDR_DIR = /usr/local/include
# Don't build JPEG stuff:
#JPEGLIB_DIR = NONE
#JPEGHDR_DIR = NONE
```

Do the same for the `libpng` stuff:

```
#PNGLIB_DIR = /lib
#PNGHDR_DIR = /usr/include/png
# NetBSD:
#PNGLIB_DIR = $(LOCALBASE)/lib
```

```
#PNGHDR_DIR = $(LOCALBASE)/include
# OSF/Tru64:
#PNGLIB_DIR = /usr/local1/DEC/lib
#PNGHDR_DIR = /usr/local1/DEC/include
# Typical:
PNGLIB_DIR = /usr/local/lib
PNGHDR_DIR = /usr/local/include
# No PNG:
#PNGLIB_DIR = NONE
#PNGHDR_DIR = NONE
```

Now you're ready to try the make. If you're running an older version of OS X, and someone hasn't fixed this peculiar problem already, you'll run into a problem with the compiler. If you're running 10.2 or later, you can skip ahead a couple paragraphs to where it says to "try the make again":

```
[Racer-X:~/Documents/source/netpbm-9.12] software% make

make -C pbm -f /Users/software/Documents/source/netpbm-9.12/pbm/Makefile all
ln -s ../pbmplus.h pbmplus.h
ln -s ../version.h version.h
../stamp-date
gcc -c -I../shhopt -pedantic -O3 -Wall -Wno-uninitialized
➥-o atktopbm.o ../pbm/atktopbm.c
make[1]: gcc: Command not found
make[1]: *** [atktopbm.o] Error 127
make: *** [pbm] Error 2
```


This is not the output we wanted! If the results of your make are more voluminous, skip ahead to where we run make again; otherwise, you need to deal with this complaint that it can't find the compiler. cc is the standard name for a C compiler, but gcc is the GNU C Compiler, and many software packages are written to take advantage of special features that the GNU compiler provides. Apple has been nice enough to provide the GNU compiler with the development tools, but on some versions of OS X has named it cc, instead of gcc. This causes programs that try to accommodate the compiler to break, because they don't realize that they're working with gcc, and make the wrong assumptions about what the compiler wants. It also causes problems with software that simply assumes everyone out there has gcc installed. The error for this program could be fixed by modifying the Makefile.config file again to call cc instead of gcc, but a similar problem will crop up with installations wondering where gcc is frequently, and many installers won't know that they can use the special gcc features unless the compiler is called gcc. If your system is missing a properly named gcc, a better fix is to create an alias (symbolic link) named gcc instead and point it at the cc compiler:

```
[Racer-X:~/Documents/source/netpbm-9.12] software% pushd /usr/local/bin
/usr/local/bin ~/Documents/source/netpbm-9.12
[Racer-X:/usr/local/bin] software% which cc
/usr/bin/cc
[Racer-X:/usr/local/bin] software% ln -s /usr/bin/cc ./gcc
[Racer-X:/usr/local/bin] software% popd
~/Documents/source/netpbm-9.12
```

Try the make again:

```
brezup:software netpbm-9.12 $ make
make -C pbm -f /Users/software/Documents/source/netpbm-9.12/pbm/Makefile all
ln -s ../pbmplus.h pbmplus.h
ln -s ../version.h version.h
../stamp-date
gcc -c -I../shhopt -pedantic -no-cpp-precomp -fno-common -O3 -Wall
➥-Wno-uninitialized -o atktopbm.o ../pbm/atktopbm.c
../pbm/atktopbm.c: In function `ReadATKRaster':
../pbm/atktopbm.c:307: warning: unsigned int format, int arg (arg 3)
../pbm/atktopbm.c:314: warning: implicit declaration of function `strcmp'
gcc -c -I../shhopt -pedantic -no-cpp-precomp -fno-common -O3 -Wall
➥-Wno-uninitialized  -o libpbm1.o ../pbm/libpbm1.c
gcc -c -I../shhopt -pedantic -no-cpp-precomp -fno-common -O3 -Wall
➥-Wno-uninitialized  -o libpbm2.o ../pbm/libpbm2.c
gcc -c -I../shhopt -pedantic -no-cpp-precomp -fno-common -O3 -Wall
 ➥-Wno-uninitialized  -o libpbm3.o ../pbm/libpbm3.c
gcc -c -I../shhopt -pedantic -no-cpp-precomp -fno-common -O3 -Wall
➥-Wno-uninitialized  -o libpbm4.o ../pbm/libpbm4.c
gcc -c -I../shhopt -pedantic -no-cpp-precomp -fno-common -O3 -Wall
➥-Wno-uninitialized  -o libpbm5.o ../pbm/libpbm5.c
cd ../shhopt; make shhopt.o
gcc -o shhopt.o -c -pedantic -no-cpp-precomp -fno-common -O3 -Wall
➥-Wno-uninitialized  -I. shhopt.c
rm -f libpbm.a
ar rc libpbm.a libpbm1.o libpbm2.o libpbm3.o libpbm4.o libpbm5.o
➥../shhopt/shhopt.o
ranlib libpbm.a
make -C . libopt
.
.
.
ln -s ../../pbmplus.h pbmplus.h
ln -s ../../pbm/pbm.h pbm.h
```

```
gcc -pedantic -no-cpp-precomp -fno-common -O3 -Wall -Wno-uninitialized
➥-I../../shhopt -c pbmtoppa.c -o pbmtoppa.o
gcc -pedantic -no-cpp-precomp -fno-common -O3 -Wall -Wno-uninitialized
➥-I../../shhopt -c ppa.c -o ppa.o
gcc -pedantic -no-cpp-precomp -fno-common -O3 -Wall -Wno-uninitialized
➥-I../../shhopt -c pbm.c -o pbm.o
gcc -pedantic -no-cpp-precomp -fno-common -O3 -Wall -Wno-uninitialized
➥-I../../shhopt -c cutswath.c -o cutswath.o
cd ../../pbm ; make libpbm.a
make[3]: `libpbm.a' is up to date.
gcc -o pbmtoppa pbmtoppa.o ppa.o pbm.o cutswath.o \
 `../../libopt ../../pbm/libpbm.a`
make -C pgm -f /Users/software/Documents/source/netpbm-9.12/pgm/Makefile all
ln -s ../pbmplus.h pbmplus.h
ln -s ../pbm/pbm.h pbm.h
ln -s ../pbm/libpbm.h libpbm.h
gcc -c -I../shhopt -pedantic -no-cpp-precomp -fno-common -O3 -Wall
➥-Wno-uninitialized -o asciitopgm.o
➥/Users/software/Documents/source/netpbm-9.12/pgm/asciitopgm.c
gcc -c -I../shhopt -pedantic -no-cpp-precomp -fno-common -O3 -Wall
➥-Wno-uninitialized  -o libpgm1.o
➥/Users/software/Documents/source/netpbm-9.12/pgm/libpgm1.c
gcc -c -I../shhopt -pedantic -no-cpp-precomp -fno-common -O3 -Wall
➥-Wno-uninitialized  -o libpgm2.o
➥/Users/software/Documents/source/netpbm-9.12/pgm/libpgm2.c
rm -f libpgm.a
ar rc libpgm.a libpgm1.o libpgm2.o
ranlib libpgm.a
.
.
.
gcc -o pgmtexture pgmtexture.o -lm `../libopt libpgm.a ../pbm/libpbm.a`
gcc -c -I../shhopt -pedantic -no-cpp-precomp -fno-common -O3 -Wall
➥-Wno-uninitialized -o rawtopgm.o
➥/Users/software/Documents/source/netpbm-9.12/pgm/rawtopgm.c
gcc -o rawtopgm rawtopgm.o -lm `../libopt libpgm.a ../pbm/libpbm.a`
gcc -c -I../shhopt -pedantic -no-cpp-precomp -fno-common -O3 -Wall
➥-Wno-uninitialized -o pgmkernel.o
➥/Users/software/Documents/source/netpbm-9.12/pgm/pgmkernel.c
gcc -o pgmkernel pgmkernel.o -lm `../libopt libpgm.a ../pbm/libpbm.a`
make -C ppm -f /Users/software/Documents/source/netpbm-9.12/ppm/Makefile all
ln -s ../pbmplus.h pbmplus.h
ln -s ../pbm/pbm.h pbm.h
```

```
ln -s ../pbm/libpbm.h libpbm.h
ln -s ../pbm/pbmfont.h pbmfont.h
ln -s ../pgm/pgm.h pgm.h
ln -s ../pgm/libpgm.h libpgm.h
gcc -c -I../shhopt -I/usr/local/include -pedantic -no-cpp-precomp
➥-fno-common -O3 -Wall -Wno-uninitialized -o 411toppm.o
➥/Users/software/Documents/source/netpbm-9.12/ppm/411toppm.c
cc1: warning: changing search order for system directory "/usr/local/include"
cc1: warning:  as it has already been specified as a non-system directory
/Users/software/Documents/source/netpbm-9.12/ppm/411toppm.c:60:20: malloc.h:
➥No such file or directory
make[1]: *** [411toppm.o] Error 1
make: *** [ppm] Error 2
```

Did I mention that I chose this install because it wasn't easy? Those error messages are just gcc being pedantic about the code. The C programming language has gone through a few revisions, and some programs still don't adhere to the most recent standards. The warnings won't hurt anything, but the error at the bottom of the output will. A few lines above the error is the complaint `header file malloc.h not found`. This is the actual source of the error. If you were a programmer, you'd be expected to clean up all those warnings as well, but for your purposes, just fixing the error is enough. If you were to read the code looking for occurrences of `malloc.h` (`grep` might help with this), you'd find there are comments detailing the ambiguities of different Unix flavors and their oddball `malloc.h` implementations. In Apple's case, it's that `malloc.h` isn't where the source expects it to be. You've got a choice of fixing all the code to point to `/usr/include/sys/malloc.h`, instead of `/usr/include/malloc.h`, or cheating a little and making it available somewhere that the `makefile` already has the compiler looking. We're going to take the cheating route and make a link to `/usr/include/sys/malloc.h` in `/usr/local/include/malloc.h`, where the compiler should be able to find it. There's actually another option, adding a path to the places that the compiler will search for header files, but it turns out that fix will break something else later on, so stick with our cheat:

```
brezup:software netpbm-9.12 $ pushd /usr/include
/usr/include ~/Documents/source/netpbm-9.12
brezup:software include $ find ./ -name malloc.h -print
.//malloc/malloc.h
.//objc/malloc.h
.//sys/malloc.h
brezup:software include $ popd
~/Documents/source/netpbm-9.12
brezup:software netpbm-9.12 $ pushd /usr/local/include
/usr/local/include ~/Documents/source/netpbm-9.12
brezup:software include $ ln -s /usr/include/sys/malloc.h ./
brezup:software include $ popd
~/Documents/source/netpbm-9.12
```

CAUTION

Note that you might want to remove that link to `malloc.h` after you're finished with the compile. You can always put it back later if you need it, but there are many pieces of software out there that try to figure out what system they're being built on, by checking where various files appear to be located. This one doesn't know about Apple's locations, and other bits of the install will break if you make the build find `malloc.h` where Apple has it stored. Others will misidentify your system if they see a copy in `/usr/local/include`. Apparently, you simply can't win them all—at least not all simultaneously. Because such files only need to be in place while an application's being built, you can put any file anywhere to satisfy the `make` process and then remove it later, so at least you can win them one at a time.

And, back to `make` again:

```
brezup:software netpbm-9.12 $ make
make -C pbm -f /Users/software/Documents/source/netpbm-9.12/pbm/Makefile all
make -C pbmtoppa all
cd ../../pbm ; make libpbm.a
make[3]: `libpbm.a' is up to date.
make -C pgm -f /Users/software/Documents/source/netpbm-9.12/pgm/Makefile all
cd ../pbm ; make libpbm.a
make[2]: `libpbm.a' is up to date.
make -C ppm -f /Users/software/Documents/source/netpbm-9.12/ppm/Makefile all
gcc -c -I../shhopt -I/usr/local/include -pedantic -no-cpp-precomp
➥-fno-common -O3 -Wall -Wno-
.
.
.
gcc -o ppmtojpeg ppmtojpeg.o `../libopt libppm.a ../pbm/libpbm.a
➥../pgm/libpgm.a` \
 -L/usr/local/lib -ljpeg
/usr/bin/ld: table of contents for archive: /usr/local/lib/libjpeg.a
➥ is out of date; rerun ranlib(1) (can't load from it)
make[1]: *** [ppmtojpeg] Error 1
make: *** [ppm] Error 2
```

Well, at least this time it not only tells us what the error is but also how to fix it.

```
brezup:software netpbm-9.12 $ ranlib /usr/local/lib/libjpeg.a
```

NOTE

Your system may, or may not encounter the error with `libjpeg.a`—it depends on the order in which you've done a number of things on your system. If you do encounter complaints about library tables of contents being out of date, just follow the instruction given and `ranlib` it.

```
brezup:software netpbm-9.12 $ make
.
.
.
gcc -c parallel.c -o parallel.o -pedantic -no-cpp-precomp -fno-common -O3
➥-Wall -Wno-uninitialized -I. -Iheaders
➥-I../../shhopt -I/usr/local/include
cc1: warning: changing search order for system directory "/usr/local/include"
cc1: warning:  as it has already been specified as a non-system directory
In file included from parallel.c:89:
/usr/include/sys/socket.h:77: parse error before "sa_family_t"
/usr/include/sys/socket.h:77: ISO C forbids data definition with no type
➥or storage class
/usr/include/sys/socket.h:212: parse error before "u_char"
/usr/include/sys/socket.h:213: ISO C forbids data definition with no type
➥or storage class
/usr/include/sys/socket.h:215: parse error before '}' token
/usr/include/sys/socket.h:223: parse error before "u_short"
.
.
.
parallel.c:1764: storage size of `nameEntry' isn't known
parallel.c:1790: sizeof applied to an incomplete type
parallel.c:1764: warning: unused variable `nameEntry'
make[2]: *** [parallel.o] Error 1
make[1]: *** [all] Error 2
make: *** [ppm] Error 2
```

This one is tough—tough enough that this would be where most people would throw up their hands and decide they don't need the software that badly. It hasn't complained that there's a file missing, but it's making some noise about parse errors and undefined types. It's bad to have parse errors and undefined things in programs, and there doesn't seem to be anything missing to have caused things to be undefined. Still, it's not as if doing some poking around is going to do anything worse than waste a bit of time, and you never know when you might get lucky, so let's press ahead. First, find the file it's complaining about:

```
brezup:software netpbm-9.12 $ find ./ -name parallel.c -print
.//ppm/ppmtompeg/parallel.c
```

Looking at this file, we see

```
#include <sys/types.h>
#include <sys/socket.h>
```

```
#include <sys/times.h>
#include <time.h>
#include <netinet/in.h>
#include <unistd.h>
#include <netdb.h>
```

The make process complained that there were undefined things in socket.h, and the only thing included before socket.h that could have defined them is types.h. types.h almost certainly lives in /usr/include/sys, based on the angle brackets surrounding the include filename in parallel.c. Searching in /usr/include/sys/types.h for the undefined u_char type, we find

```
#ifndef _POSIX_SOURCE
typedef unsigned char  u_char;
typedef unsigned short u_short;
typedef unsigned int  u_int;
typedef unsigned long  u_long;
typedef unsigned short ushort;     /* Sys V compatibility */
typedef unsigned int  uint;      /* Sys V compatibility */
#endif
```

Interestingly, the type is defined, but there's a cryptic #ifndef POSIX_SOURCE .. #endif surrounding the definition. If you were a programmer, the problem would be almost immediately obvious at this point. Because you're probably not a programmer, the most information you can get is that if something named POSIX_SOURCE is *not* defined, the needed u_char type *is* defined. Presumably, if POSIX_SOURCE is defined, u_char doesn't get defined here. Armed with this knowledge, if you search in parallel.c again, you'll find the following lines:

```
#define _POSIX_SOURCE
#define _POSIX_C_SOURCE 2
```

What do you know! Right there in parallel.c, it's shooting itself in the foot. Let's see what happens if we just comment that out, and have at it again. It already doesn't work, so the most that can go wrong is that it still won't work, right? Fire up your editor again, and change those lines so that they look like this:

```
/* #define _POSIX_SOURCE */
/* #define _POSIX_C_SOURCE 2 */
```

NOTE

No, I'm not sure what the #define _POSIX_C_SOURCE 2 line is doing—I'm playing non-programming user here. If I were playing programmer, I'd spend the time to figure out what it's doing, and whether there's anything I can do to correct the particular condition we're seeing. You might

17

not want to be a programmer, so let's play around and see what a non-programmer can accomplish. I commented the `POSIX_SOURCE` lines out on a non-programmer-like hunch, and things seem to have worked. There are undoubtedly numerous other possible solutions. You're welcome to try it without commenting it out and see what happens. I can't guarantee that the rest of the install will follow the course shown if you do, but it's just as possible that it will work better.

And, `make` again:

```
brezup:software netpbm-9.12 $ make
.
.
.
/usr/include/ppc/ansi.h:94: warning: ISO C89 does not support `long long'
In file included from /Users/software/Documents/source/netpbm-
9.12/pnm/pbmplus.h:115,
         from /Users/software/Documents/source/netpbm-9.12/pnm/pbm.h:7,
         from /Users/software/Documents/source/netpbm-9.12/pnm/pgm.h:7,
         from /Users/software/Documents/source/netpbm-9.12/pnm/ppm.h:7,
         from /Users/software/Documents/source/netpbm-9.12/pnm/pnm.h:7,
         from /Users/software/Documents/source/netpbm-9.12/pnm/pnmtopng.c:58:
/usr/include/stdlib.h:206: warning: ISO C89 does not support `long long'
/usr/include/stdlib.h:208: warning: ISO C89 does not support `long long'
/usr/include/stdlib.h:210: warning: ISO C89 does not support `long long'
/usr/include/stdlib.h:212: warning: ISO C89 does not support `long long'
gcc -o pnmtopng pnmtopng.o `../libopt libpnm.a ../ppm/libppm.a
➥../pgm/libpgm.a ../pbm/libpbm.a ` \
 -L/lib, -lz -L/usr/local/lib -lpng -lm
ld: warning -L: directory name (/lib,) does not exist
ld: table of contents for archive: /usr/local/lib/libpng.a is out of date;
➥rerun ranlib(1) (can't load from it)
make[1]: *** [pnmtopng] Error 1
make: *** [pnm] Error 2
```

You've already seen that one before:

```
brezup:software netpbm-9.12 $ ranlib /usr/local/lib/libpng.a
brezup:software netpbm-9.12 $ make
.
.
.
ar -rc libfiasco_lib.a arith.o bit-io.o dither.o error.o image.o list.o
➥misc.o rpf.o
make -C ../../pnm libpnm.a
```

```
make[3]: `libpnm.a' is up to date.
make -C ../../ppm libppm.a
make[3]: `libppm.a' is up to date.
make -C ../../pgm libpgm.a
make[3]: `libpgm.a' is up to date.
make -C ../../pbm libpbm.a
make[3]: `libpbm.a' is up to date.
gcc -o pnmtofiasco binerror.o cwfa.o getopt.o getopt1.o params.o \
`../../libopt codec/libfiasco_codec.a input/libfiasco_input.a
➥output/libfiasco_output.a lib/libfiasco_lib.a ` \
 `../../libopt ../../pnm/libpnm.a ../../ppm/libppm.a ../../pgm/libpgm.a
➥../../pbm/libpbm.a ` -lm
ld: archive: codec/libfiasco_codec.a has no table of contents, add one with
➥ranlib(1) (can't load from it)
ld: archive: input/libfiasco_input.a has no table of contents, add one with
➥ranlib(1) (can't load from it)
ld: archive: output/libfiasco_output.a has no table of contents, add one with
➥ranlib(1) (can't load from it)
ld: archive: lib/libfiasco_lib.a has no table of contents, add one with
➥ranlib(1) (can't load from it)
make[2]: *** [pnmtofiasco] Error 1
make[1]: *** [all] Error 2
make: *** [pnm] Error 2
```

That's getting a little boring! Don't you wish it would just run `ranlib` for you, instead of telling you it needs to be run? Actually, the installers are supposed to take care of that stuff for you. Like one of the earlier installs not creating the needed directories, this one also seems to have trouble running `ranlib`, so for some things you have to do it by hand:


```
brezup:software netpbm-9.12 $ ranlib codec/libfiasco_codec.a
ranlib: can't open file: codec/libfiasco_codec.a (No such file or directory)
```

Oops! That wasn't expected. Something else you don't (usually) need to worry about is that `make` might be recursively making things in subdirectories. The path shown in an error might not be the relative path from your location, but rather the relative path from wherever `make` is currently operating. In this case, we can just find the directories by name, and `ranlib` them that way:

```
brezup:software netpbm-9.12 $ find ./ -name libfiasco_codec.a -print
.//pnm/fiasco/codec/libfiasco_codec.a
brezup:software netpbm-9.12 $ find ./ -name libfiasco_input.a -print
.//pnm/fiasco/input/libfiasco_input.a
brezup:software netpbm-9.12 $ find ./ -name libfiasco_output.a -print
.//pnm/fiasco/output/libfiasco_output.a
```

```
brezup:software netpbm-9.12 $ find ./ -name libfiasco_lib.a -print
.//pnm/fiasco/lib/libfiasco_lib.a
brezup:software netpbm-9.12 $ ranlib .//pnm/fiasco/codec/libfiasco_codec.a
brezup:software netpbm-9.12 $ ranlib .//pnm/fiasco/input/libfiasco_input.a
brezup:software netpbm-9.12 $ ranlib .//pnm/fiasco/output/libfiasco_output.a
brezup:software netpbm-9.12 $ ranlib .//pnm/fiasco/lib/libfiasco_lib.a
```

And, `make` again:

```
brezup:software netpbm-9.12 $ make

gcc -o pnmtofiasco binerror.o cwfa.o getopt.o getopt1.o params.o \
`../../libopt codec/libfiasco_codec.a input/libfiasco_input.a
➥output/libfiasco_output.a lib/libfiasco_lib.a ` \
 `../../libopt ../../pnm/libpnm.a ../../ppm/libppm.a ../../pgm/libpgm.a
➥../../pbm/libpbm.a ` -lm
ld: multiple definitions of symbol _mv_code_table
codec/libfiasco_codec.a(mwfa.o) definition of _mv_code_table in section
➥ (__DATA,__data)
output/libfiasco_output.a(mc.o) definition of _mv_code_table in section
➥ (__DATA,__common)
make[2]: *** [pnmtofiasco] Error 1
make[1]: *** [all] Error 2
make: *** [pnm] Error 2
```

And we encounter another new problem. Here, it complains that a variable, `mv_code_table`, has been defined in multiple places. Programs can't get built very cleanly when that happens because a specific memory location is used for each thing defined, and the system has no way of knowing which location is intended if a variable name is defined in multiple places. Again, this is a place where many would stop, but we intrepid few will forge ahead. Always remember—it's already broken, what more harm can you do? Note that the system's been nice enough to tell you the `.c` files where the multiple definitions occur, `mwfa.c` and `mc.c`. Apparently, there's a definition of `mv_code_table` in both. The codec (that stands for enCOder/DECoder) is probably the more important one to keep the value defined in, so let's dig around in the definition in the output module.

```
brezup:software netpbm-9.12 $ find ./ -name mc.c -print
.//pnm/fiasco/input/mc.c
.//pnm/fiasco/output/mc.c
```

If you look in the `input/mc.c` file, you'll see that `mv_code_table` is defined as a `static int` and has a bunch of data included in it. If you look in the `codec/mwfa.c` file, you'll see something similar (with a note that this variable is supposed to be local). The version in the output directory, however, just defines the variable and stores no data in it. The one that's different looks like fair game to me. Change the line for mv_code_table in mc.c of the output directory so that it reads:

```
extern int mv_code_table [33][2];   /* VLC table for coordinates, mwfa.c */
```

This tells the compiler "go look somewhere else for this data" It's already defined somewhere else; the compiler told you so. Somewhere else must be a good place to look, right? And try the make, yet again.

```
brezup:software netpbm-9.12 $ make
.
.
.
make -C output libfiasco_output.a
gcc -c -I. -I../lib -I../codec -pedantic -no-cpp-precomp -fno-common -O3 -Wall
-Wno-uninitialized -o mc.o /Users/software/Documents/source/netpbm-
9.12/pnm/fiasco/output/mc.c
ar -rc libfiasco_output.a matrices.o mc.o nd.o tree.o weights.o write.o
make -C lib libfiasco_lib.a
make[3]: `libfiasco_lib.a' is up to date.
make -C ../../pnm libpnm.a
make[3]: `libpnm.a' is up to date.
make -C ../../ppm libppm.a
make[3]: `libppm.a' is up to date.
make -C ../../pgm libpgm.a
make[3]: `libpgm.a' is up to date.
make -C ../../pbm libpbm.a
make[3]: `libpbm.a' is up to date.
gcc -o pnmtofiasco binerror.o cwfa.o getopt.o getopt1.o params.o \
`../../libopt codec/libfiasco_codec.a input/libfiasco_input.a
➥output/libfiasco_output.a lib/libfiasco_lib.a ` \
 `../../libopt ../../pnm/libpnm.a ../../ppm/libppm.a ../../pgm/libpgm.a
➥../../pbm/libpbm.a ` -lm
ld: table of contents for archive: output/libfiasco_output.a is out of date;
➥rerun ranlib(1) (can't load from it)
make[2]: *** [pnmtofiasco] Error 1
make[1]: *** [all] Error 2
make: *** [pnm] Error 2
```

You know what to do:

```
brezup:software netpbm-9.12 $ ranlib ./pnm/fiasco/output/libfiasco_output.a
```

and make again.

17

```
[Racer-X:~/Documents/source/netpbm-9.12] software% make
.
.
.
gcc -o palmtopnm palmtopnm.o palmcolormap.o `../../libopt ../../pnm/libpnm.a
➥../../ppm/libppm.a ../../pgm/libpgm.a ../../pbm/libpbm.a ` \
gcc -c -I../../shhopt -pedantic -no-cpp-precomp -fno-common -O3 -Wall
➥-Wno-uninitialized -o pnmtopalm.o ../../pnm/pnmtopalm/pnmtopalm.c
../../pnm/pnmtopalm/pnmtopalm.c: In function `main':
../../pnm/pnmtopalm/pnmtopalm.c:42: warning: implicit declaration of
➥function `strcmp'
../../pnm/pnmtopalm/pnmtopalm.c:220: warning: implicit declaration of
➥function `memset'
../../pnm/pnmtopalm/pnmtopalm.c:290: warning: implicit declaration of
➥function `memcpy'
gcc -o pnmtopalm pnmtopalm.o palmcolormap.o `../../libopt ../../pnm/libpnm.a
➥../../ppm/libppm.a ../../pgm/libpgm.a ../../pbm/libpbm.a ` \

[Racer-X:~/Documents/source/netpbm-9.12] software%
```

Hard to believe, but it just finished the compile. Now if you do a `make install`, you'll be all set. `netpbm` installs its applications into `/usr/local/netpbm/bin/`; its man pages and so on go into directories in `/usr/local/netpbm`. Because of this, you'll again need to extend your path: `PATH=$PATH:/usr/local/netpbm/bin` or `set path=($path /usr/local/netpbm/bin/)`, depending on whether you're using `bash` or `tcsh`, respectively.

Finally, if you want to see whether it works, find something like a JPEG file, and try out the following:

```
pnm/jpegtopnm < ~/Pictures/<oldfile>.jpg | pnm/pnminvert |
➥ppm/ppmtojpeg > ~/Pictures/<newfile>.jpg
```

If you've installed it, that'd be just:

```
jpegtopnm < ~/Pictures/<oldfile>.jpg | pnminvert |
➥ppmtojpeg > ~/Pictures/<newfile>.jpg
```

Now take a look at the new file in your `Pictures` directory. The `netpbm` package is a large collection of programs that perform specific graphics manipulations. They can be chained together in arbitrary combinations to create arbitrarily complex graphics manipulations. We'll cover a few of the things it can do in Chapter 18, "Advanced Unix Shell Use: Configuration and Programming (Shell Scripting)." The number of uses is almost unlimited, so you really should read through the man pages for more ideas.

Now that you've gone through all of that, remember that this is an older version of netpbm. Installing the most recent version is much easier, but rather than have you go through the compile, we've just provided a completely fixed installer that you can download, type make, and be done with it. Download a copy of netpbm-10.17 from http://www.macosxunleashed.com/downloads/netpbm-10.17.tar.gz, gunzip it, untar it, and you should be able to make and then make install.

Using the gdb Debugger

If thinking about the problem, trying to do things as correctly as possible, and examining all the debugging information yields only an application that doesn't run correctly, you still have the option of digging around in the code. Thankfully, Apple has provided the GNU debugger, gdb, as part of the development tools. The GNU debugger is to the Unix debugging world what the GNU compiler is to the Unix programming world—a flexible, community-supported, de facto standard for programmer productivity.

The easiest way to explain how to use gdb is to demonstrate its use. The program has copious online help, as well as man pages, and an INFO section available through the emacs M-x info command. Before the demonstration, however, Table 17.1 contains a summary of command-line options and common internal commands.

NOTE

When following this debugging example, an almost overwhelmingly large number of details appear in the output. These all have important meanings to someone studying the inner workings of the program, but for the purpose of just trying to see what might be wrong, and whether you understand enough to fix it, you really only need to follow along with the details discussed in the example.

Don't let the other details intimidate you and convince you to ignore the possibilities the debugger presents. Even accomplished programmers sometimes let the apparent complexity of debugging output sidetrack them into using less effective tools, and wasting time. You can learn an incredible amount and get good at cleaning up little software errors by starting from these humble beginnings. All it takes is a willingness to experiment and pay attention to more, deeper details each time you learn something new.

In light of this, don't consider or expect this example to be a comprehensive discussion of how you use gdb to debug software. It's designed to show you what real errors look like, and to demonstrate to you that if you pay attention, it really is within the grasp of ordinary, everyday users to go hunting for, and potentially to fix software errors.

TABLE 17.1 The Command Documentation Table for the gdb Debugger

gdb	GNU debugger.

gdb [-help] [-nx] [-q] [-batch] [-cd=*<dir>*] [-f] [-b *<bps>*] [-tty=*<dev>*] [-s *<symfile>*] [-e *<prog>*] [-se *<prog>*] [-c *<core>*] [-x *<cmds>*] [-d *<dir>*] [*<prog>* [*<core>* ¦ *<procID>*]]

TABLE 17.1 Continued

gdb can be used to debug programs written in C, C++, and Modula-2.

Arguments other than options specify an executable file and a core file or process ID. The first argument encountered with no associated option flag is equivalent to the -se option; the second, if any, is equivalent to the -c option, if it is a file. Options and command-line arguments are processed in sequential order. The order makes a difference when the -x option is specified.

-help -h	Lists all options with brief explanations.
-symbols=<*file*> -s <*file*>	Reads symbol table from file <*file*>.
-write	Enables writing into executable and core files.
-exec=<*file*> -e <*file*>	Uses <*file*> as the executable file to execute when appropriate, and for examining pure data in conjunction with a core dump.
-se=<*file*>	Reads symbol table from <*file*> and uses it as the executable file.
-core=<*file*> -c <*file*>	Uses <*file*> as a core dump to examine.
-command=<*file*> -x <*file*>	Executes gdb commands from <*file*>.
-directory=<*directory*> -d <*directory*>	Adds <*directory*> to the path to search for source files.
-nx -n	Does not execute commands from any .gdbinit files. Normally, commands in these files are executed after all the command options and arguments have been processed.
-quiet -q	Quiet mode. Does not print the introductory and copyright messages. Also suppresses them in batch mode.
-batch	Batch mode. Exits with status 0 after processing all the command files associated with the -x option (and .gdbinit, if not inhibited). Exits with nonzero status if an error occurs in executing the gdb commands in the command files.
-cd=<*directory*>	Runs gdb using <*directory*> as the working directory rather than using the current directory as the working directory.
-fullname -f	Outputs information used by emacs-gdb interface.
-b <*bps*>	Sets the line speed (baud rate or bits per second) of any serial interface used by gdb for remote debugging.
-tty=<*device*>	Runs using <*device*> for your program's standard input and output.

These are some of the more frequently needed gdb commands:

break [<*file*>]<*function*>	Sets a breakpoint at <*function*> (in <*file*>).
run [<*arglist*>]	Starts your program (with <*arglist*>, if specified).
bt	Backtrace. Displays the program stack.
print <*expr*>	Displays the value of an expression.
c	Continues running your program (after stopping, such as at a breakpoint).

TABLE 17.1 Continued

`next`	Executes the next program line (after stopping); steps over any function calls in the line.
`step`	Executes the next program line (after stopping); steps into any function calls in the line.
`help [<name>]`	Shows information about gdb command *<name>*, or general information about using gdb.
`quit`	Exits gdb.

To use gdb, you first need something on which to use it. Type in the little program shown in Listing 17.1, just as it appears here. Alternatively, you can download it from macosxunleashed.com's downloads directory:

```
curl -O http://www.macosxunleashed.com/downloads/addme.c
```

```
curl command and URL verified - TJTName the file addme.c.
```

LISTING 17.1 The Source for the addme.c Demo C Program

```
/* addme.c  A really silly C demo program */
/* 990325 WCR                 */
/* Usage is <progname> <filename>     */

#include <stdio.h>

int addem(a,b)
int a, b;
{
 return a+b;
}

void main(argc,argv)
int argc;
char *argv[];
{
 int i;
 char infilename[8];
 int j;
 FILE *infile;
 char number[100];
 char *infilename2=infilename;
 strcpy(infilename2,argv[1]);
 i=0; j=0;
 infile = fopen(infilename2,"r");
```

LISTING 17.1 Continued

```
 if(infile==NULL)
 {
   printf("couldn't open file %s please try again\n",infilename2);
   exit(1);
 }

 i=0;
 while (fgets(number,90,infile) != '\0')
 {
   sscanf(number,"%d",&j);
   i=addem(i,j);
 }
 printf("Your total is %d\n",i);
 exit(0);
}
```

This simple little C program takes a list of integers from a file, one per line, and adds them together. So that you'll have a file to work from, create a file named `numbers` with the following contents:

```
1
2
13
15
```

Make sure that there are no blank lines above or below the data.

Also create a file with a very long name, such as `supercalifragilisticzowie`, and put the same data in it.

Note there's a bit of trickery involved in the way this code is written that's specifically there to generate an error. Even though there are a few errors in this code, some systems are sloppy enough with memory management that the program might run intermittently. Also, if you rearrange the definition of the variables `i` and `j`, you decrease the likelihood of a crash. Weird, huh?

So, let's see what we have. Time to compile the program. We don't have a `makefile`, so we'll have to do it by hand. Issue the command

```
cc -g -o addemup addme.c
```

After a few seconds, your machine should return you to a command line. The compiler should respond with a warning similar to the following:

```
addme.c: In function `main':
addme.c:14: warning: return type of `main' is not `int'
```

It should return you to the command line. If it does anything else, for instance, outputs

```
addme.c: In function `main':
addme.c:15: parse error before `char'
addme.c:23: subscripted value is neither array nor pointer
```

that means you've typed the program in incorrectly. Specifically, if you got this error, in all likelihood you forgot the semicolon after the line that says `int argc;`. The warning is just that: a warning, not an error. The most recent revision of the C programming language has a preference for a particular return type for the main program, and the compiler is just being pedantic.

After you get the program to compile cleanly with no errors, you're ready for the next step—trying it out. Issue the command `./addemup` and see what happens. Note that the command is `addemup`, not something related to `addme`. I could actually have named it anything I wanted, simply by changing the `-o addemup` part of the `cc` command. If you don't specify any output filename, `cc` names the output file `a.out` by default. Also, just so that you know, the `-g` flag tells the compiler to turn on the debugging output. This slows the program but gives the debugger important information.

```
./addemup
Bus Error
```

Well, that doesn't sound good. What could be wrong? You can probably figure it out just by looking at the code at this point, but on a more complicated program, that would be impossible. Instead, let's start the gdb debugger and take a look.

```
brezup:software source $ gdb ./addemup
GNU gdb 5.3-20030128 (Apple version gdb-286) (Sun Jul 27 08:48:09 GMT 2003)
Copyright 2003 Free Software Foundation, Inc.
GDB is free software, covered by the GNU General Public License, and you are
welcome to change it and/or distribute copies of it under certain conditions.
Type "show copying" to see the conditions.
There is absolutely no warranty for GDB. Type "show warranty" for details.
This GDB was configured as "powerpc-apple-darwin".
Reading symbols for shared libraries
warning: Mapped symbol file "/usr/libexec/gdb/symfiles/dyld.syms"
uses a different prefix ("") than the one requested ("__dyld_"); ignoring
. done
(gdb)
```

17

Okay, we're at a prompt. What do we do? The gdb debugger actually has a complete selection of online help available. To access the help system, simply enter the command help.

```
(gdb) help
List of classes of commands:

aliases -- Aliases of other commands
breakpoints -- Making program stop at certain points
data -- Examining data
files -- Specifying and examining files
internals -- Maintenance commands
obscure -- Obscure features
running -- Running the program
stack -- Examining the stack
status -- Status inquiries
support -- Support facilities
tracepoints -- Tracing of program execution without stopping the program
user-defined -- User-defined commands

Type "help" followed by a class name for a list of commands in that class.
Type "help" followed by command name for full documentation.
Command name abbreviations are allowed if unambiguous.
(gdb)
```

I'll leave some of the interesting items here for you to explore, rather than walk you through them. Right now, let's get back to debugging our program. To start the program, simply issue the command r.

```
(gdb) r
Starting program: /Users/software/Documents/source/addemup
Reading symbols for shared libraries . done

Program received signal EXC_BAD_ACCESS, Could not access memory.
0x90003608 in strcpy ()
(gdb)
```

So, gdb knows something. Not a very intelligible something at this point, but something none the less. Let's see whether it can be a bit more informative.

```
(gdb) where
#0 0x90003608 in strcpy ()
#1 0x00001c5c in main (argc=1, argv=0xbffffe68) at addme.c:23
(gdb)
```

gdb says the program broke in a procedure named `strcpy`, which was called from a procedure named `main`, in line 23 of our file `addme.c`. Depending on the compiler version and gdb version, you might also see a line or two for `start()`, which is OS X and gdb initializing and starting the program. Let's take a look at the region of the code in your file (line 23) that gdb indicates was the last place that things were working.

```
(gdb) l 23
18     char infilename[8];
19     int j;
20     FILE *infile;
21     char number[100];
22     char *infilename2=&infilename;
23     strcpy(infilename2,argv[1]);
24     i=0; j=0;
25     infile = fopen(infilename2,""r"");
26
27     if(infile==NULL)
(gdb)
```

Line 23 has a function `strcpy` on it (this C function copies the contents of one character array variable to another). The debugger seems to be on to something here. Let's set a breakpoint (a place we want the program to stop running and wait for us) at line 23 and see what happens.

TIP

C functions have man page entries too. You can get documentation on most anything you see as a function in a C program like this. If you're not a programmer, the meat of the documentation might not be much use to you, but for something like `strcpy`, knowing that the function is supposed to copy the contents of one argument into the other can be useful when looking at debugging output.


```
(gdb) b 23
Breakpoint 1 at 0x2320: file addme.c, line 23.
(gdb)
```

So far, so good. Now let's run the program again and see where this takes us.

```
(gdb) r
The program being debugged has been started already.
Start it from the beginning? (y or n) y
Starting program: /Users/software/Documents/source/addemup numbers
[Switching to process 22268 thread 0xf07]
```

```
Breakpoint 1, main (argc=1, argv=0xbffffd48) at addme.c:23
23    strcpy(infilename2,argv[1]);
(gdb)
```

Note that gdb asked me whether I wanted to restart from the beginning, and I told it to go ahead. Now it has run up to our breakpoint and is waiting for me to do something. Even if I don't know what strcpy does, there's still something obviously wrong with this line. I know I've got a variable named infilename2 and a funny variable named argv[1]. Let's see what gdb has to say about them.

```
(gdb) p infilename2
$1 = 0xbffff99c ""L\000\000@""
(gdb)
```

The $1 indicates that it's telling us about the first variable we asked about. The 0xbfff99c is the memory location where it's stored. Don't be surprised if yours is different, or your version of gdb doesn't show it—the default behavior depends on a number of factors outside the scope of this discussion. If you use gdb much, you'll pick up how to set your configuration to display the data you like from the help system as you need it. The L\000\000@ is the current contents of that memory, which currently isn't too informative. (Don't be surprised if yours has something else in whatever memory location shows up on your machine.) What can we tell about this argv[1]?

```
(gdb) p argv[1]
$2 = 0xbffffba9 0x0
(gdb)
```

Hmmm... 0x0 is a hexadecimal 0, or NULL in the C world. Examining the code again certainly suggests that something useful should be happening here. It looks as if infilename2 gets used to open a file in just a few lines, and neither L\000\000@ nor NULL looks promising as a filename. Nulls get used in C, but frequently they're signs of a problem, so let's think about this.

The program is trying to do something with a variable named argv[1]. The only other place this variable (argv) appears is in the main statement, the statement that starts off the actual program execution. It certainly looks as if there should be something other than a NULL here. Wait a minute, what did it say in the comments at the top? It said I needed to give it a filename! I didn't give it a filename, and it's trying to copy something that doesn't exist to get one. Aren't programmers supposed to check for that?

Let's see whether I'm right. I'll rerun the program with a filename this time.

```
(gdb) r numbers
The program being debugged has been started already.
Start it from the beginning? (y or n) y
```

```
Starting program: /Users/software/Documents/source/addemup numbers
[Switching to process 22269 thread 0x2307]

Breakpoint 1, main (argc=2, argv=0xbffffd3c) at addme.c:23
23    strcpy(infilename2,argv[1]);
(gdb)
```

I started it over, but I forgot to turn off my breakpoint. Still, this is a good opportunity for me to check whether I was right.

```
(gdb) p infilename2
$3 = 0xf7fff200 ""\000\000\200\000\000\000 ""
(gdb)
```

That's just as useless as before.

```
(gdb) p argv[1]
$4 = 0xf7fff80f ""numbers""
(gdb)
```

Now we're getting somewhere! If we remember to give it a filename, it actually gets one! To continue past the breakpoint, I can enter `c`.

```
(gdb) c
Continuing.
Your total is 31

Program exited normally.
(gdb)
```

The program now does exactly what it should. If I want to test it again without stopping at the breakpoint, I can delete the breakpoint and run it again.

```
(gdb) d 1
(gdb) r
Starting program: /Users/software/Documents/source/addemup numbers
[Switching to process 22270 thread 0x2607]
Your total is 31

Program exited normally.
(gdb)
```

The command `d 1` deletes breakpoint 1 (you can have multiples if you need them). Note that I didn't have to give it the command-line argument `numbers` this time when I hit `r` because it conveniently remembered command-line arguments between runs. As you can see, it runs properly to completion.

Quitting gdb with the quit command and trying it on the command line produces the same results.

```
brezup:software source $ ./addemup numbers
Your total is 31
brezup:software source $
```

Now let's see whether we can demonstrate another type of error. Do you still remember what your very long filename is? Try using that filename instead of numbers and see what happens.

```
brezup:software source $ ./addemup supercalifragilisticzowie
couldn't open file supercal please try again
brezup:software source $
```

Huh? I didn't call it supercal. Something happened to my filename. Time to break out gdb again and have another look.

```
brezup:software source $ gdb ./addemup
GNU gdb 5.3-20030128 (Apple version gdb-286) (Sun Jul 27 08:48:09 GMT 2003)
Copyright 2003 Free Software Foundation, Inc.
GDB is free software, covered by the GNU General Public License, and you are
welcome to change it and/or distribute copies of it under certain conditions.
Type "show copying" to see the conditions.
There is absolutely no warranty for GDB. Type "show warranty" for details.
This GDB was configured as "powerpc-apple-darwin".
Reading symbols for shared libraries
warning: Mapped symbol file "/usr/libexec/gdb/symfiles/dyld.syms"
uses a different prefix ("") than the one requested ("__dyld_"); ignoring
. done
(gdb) r supercalifragilisticzowie
Starting program: /Users/software/Documents/source/addemup
➥supercalifragilisticzowie
[Switching to process 22275 thread 0xb03]
Reading symbols for shared libraries . done
couldn't open file supercal please try again

Program exited with code 01.
(gdb)
```

Basically, it says the same thing. There must be something more we can find out, though. Let's look at the code and see whether we can figure out where that weird truncation came from.

```
(gdb) l
14   int argc;
15   char *argv[];
16   {
17    int i;
18    char infilename[8];
19    int j;
20    FILE *infile;
21    char number[100];
22    char *infilename2=infilename;
23    strcpy(infilename2,argv[1]);
(gdb)
24    i=0; j=0;
25    infile = fopen(infilename2,""r"");
26
27    if(infile==NULL)
28    {
29      printf(""couldn't open file %s please try again\n"",infilename2);
30      exit(1);
31    }
32
33    i=0;
(gdb)
```

Line 29 seems to be where the error message is coming from. Let's set a breakpoint there and see what happens.

```
(gdb) b 29
Breakpoint 1 at 0x2374: file addme.c, line 29.
(gdb) r
Starting program: /Users/software/Documents/source/addemup
➥supercalifragilisticzowie
[Switching to process 22276 thread 0xf07]

Breakpoint 1, main (argc=2, argv=0xbffffd2c) at addme.c:29
29      printf("couldn't open file %s please try again\n",infilename2);
(gdb)
```

We're at our breakpoint. `infilename2` is supposed to be `supercalifragilisticzowie`, and it is

```
(gdb) p infilename2
$1 = 0xbffff99c ""supercal""
(gdb)
```

Something's wrong here! Time to back up to our trusty breakpoint at line 23 and watch what happens from the top down.

```
(gdb) b 23
Breakpoint 2 at 0x1c08: file addme.c, line 23.
(gdb) r
The program being debugged has been started already.
Start it from the beginning? (y or n) y
Starting program: /Users/software/Documents/source/addemup
➥supercalifragilisticzowie
[Switching to process 22277 thread 0x2307]

Breakpoint 2, main (argc=2, argv=0xbffffd2c) at addme.c:23
23      strcpy(infilename2,argv[1]);
(gdb) p argv[1]
$1 = 0xbffffdec "supercalifragilisticzowie"
(gdb) p infilename
$2 = 0xf7fff200 ""\000\000\200\000\000\000 ""
```

So, the previous culprit isn't a problem here.

```
(gdb) p infilename2
$2 = 0xf7fff6b0 ""\000\000\200\000\000\000 ""
(gdb)
```

There's nothing interesting there. Let's see what happens on the next line—use the gdb command n to step to the next line. When you step to the next line, this line executes, so you should expect to see the results of that strcpy after stepping forward.

```
(gdb) n
24      i=0; j=0;
(gdb) p infilename2
$1 = 0xf7fff6b0 ""supercalifragilisticzowie""
(gdb)
```

As expected, infilename2 contains our atrociously long filename. Nothing wrong here, but by the time it hit line 29, it was broken, so let's step forward again and see what happens.

```
(gdb) n
25      infile = fopen(infilename2,""r"");
(gdb) p
$3 = 0xf7fff6b0 ""supercal""
(gdb)
```

Wait a minute! Now it's wrong! What happened? All that the program did was assign both the variables `i` and `j` to be zero, and somehow it affected `infilename2`. You wouldn't think this could happen, variables just changing their values willy-nilly.

In fact, if the program were written properly, this wouldn't happen. As a non-programmer, this is where you usually give up. That isn't to say that the exercise has been useless. With this information, you can more easily explain to the author or online support community what problems you've observed, so they can fix it more easily and quickly. Program authors hate it when they get bug reports that say, "it didn't work." This doesn't mean anything to them because if they could duplicate the problem on their end, they'd probably have found and fixed it already.

By taking these extra steps, the information you can provide about the program's problems can mean the difference between a fix that takes a few minutes to appear and a fix that never appears.

NOTE

If you're curious, and keep a C handbook around, fixing this particular error isn't that difficult. The error here is that the variable `infilename` has been defined to hold only eight characters. `infilename2` is essentially an alias to `infilename1` and is needed to fool the debugger into not telling you about the problem immediately. The assignment of the very long filename to `infilename2` actually works most of the time. It works because there's enough slop in the assignment of memory space that it's not going to write over anything important, although the `supercalifragilisticzowie` value hangs out the end of it and into unknown memory space.

The thing that actually makes the error show up almost all the time is the placement of the definitions of `i` and `j` around the definition of `infilename`. Most compilers will order variables in memory in the same order they were defined in the program. Because the compiler doesn't know you're going to stuff a huge string into `infilename`, it chooses memory close to `infilename` for the storage of `i` and `j`. With optimization turned off, most compilers will place `i` and `j` flanking `infilename` in memory, and a sufficiently long value in `infilename` will overlap the memory used by `i` and `j`. By assigning both `i` and `j` to 0 after assigning `infilename`, it's almost guaranteed that part of `infilename` will be damaged and that the program will fail. To fix the program so that this can't occur with any reasonable filename, simply change the definition of `infilename` to something like `char infilename[256];` instead of `char infilename[8];`.

Debugging in Gory Detail

Although details of kernel process tracing are a subject for a book on advanced system programming, experienced programmers reading here might be interested in knowing that OS X 10.2 ships with kernel tracing enabled. The `ktrace` command writes kernel trace logs for processes, and the `kdump` command reads `ktrace` logs and formats them into human-readable output. For the non-programmer interested in seeing just what the operating system is doing when a program is running (as opposed to the program-centric view shown by `gdb`), run `ktrace` on a command such as `ls` (`ktrace ls; kdump | less`). Working through the meaning of each call used in a program such as `ls` by using the `man` pages to look up functions, is an excellent excercise if you're interested in really understanding how the system works.

17

Recommended Command-Line Software Installations

As mentioned several times previously, thousands of freely available Unix programs can be downloaded as source and compiled for your machine. We've included a small sample of these in this section—some that we've used in this book, and some that are simply useful utilities to have available. If you browse the FTP sites and Web directories where you can find these sources, you'll discover many more programs that might be of interest. If you want to practice on a few more, here are some examples, with brief compilation and installation instructions for you to try your hand at.

> **TIP**
>
> Remember! if you really don't like doing this, you can install much of this software using the `fink` package manager covered in Chapter 19, "X Window System Applications." I frequently find the task of troubleshooting software compilation and installation to be a fun exercise. It's kind of a giant logic puzzle. Some of you will enjoy the same type of challenge. If you simply aren't interested, or don't have the time, *don't* let that get in the way of you using the software that's available. `fink` can do almost all the work for you.

`libtiff`

You'll need `libtiff` to install the newest version of `netpbm`. As the name suggests, it's a library that knows how to read and write Tagged Image File Format (TIFF) images.

```
curl -O http://www.macosxunleashed.com/downloads/tiff-v3.5.7.tar.gz
gunzip tiff-v3.5.7.tar.gz
tar -xf tiff-v3.5.7.tar
cd tiff-v3.5.7
./configure
```

Answer yes to the defaults.

```
make
make install
```

If you get the file `http://www.libtiff.org/` (for example, if you decide to get a more recent version) instead of the version we've provided at `http://www.macosxunleashed.com/`, you'll need to remove the statement `-undefined suppress` from the `configure` file, and the file `libtiff/Makefile.in` for the Darwin configuration sections before you start the configure.

`netpbm`

We've probably already said that `netpbm` is a cool collection of programs a few too many times, but once more won't hurt. The `netpbm` package gives you the ability to do many image manipulations from the command line. It's a great program suite if you want to automate the same operations on many images and can do everything from format conversion to inserting text into images. If you've followed all the other installs as directed, you can install this version much more easily than the version we used as an example of a difficult install.

```
curl -O http://www.macosxunleashed.com/downloads/netpbm-10.17.tar.gz
gunzip netpbm-10.17.tar.gz
tar -xf netpbm-10.17.tar
cd netpbm-10.17
make
make package pkgdir=/tmp/netpbm
./installnetpbm
```

And then follow the directions—accepting the defaults should be fine, except where it wants to install stuff into `/etc/` and `/usr/man/`. You can answer `N` to those, or create the `/etc/manweb.conf` file as `root` and then change its ownership to `software`. Don't worry if the `./installnetpbm` step throws up some errors about missing files; it seems to have some minor bugs and doesn't always notice that the files have been installed. Try running it again, and it probably won't complain the second time through.

You won't get it to run `ldconfig`, so just add `/usr/local/netpbm/lib/` to your `LD_LIBRARY_PATH` environment variable, as mentioned earlier in this chapter.

You might need to `ranlib` a directory or two in the middle of the `make` process, but that should be it! If you've changed your installation and need to run the `configure` step before the `make`, just search in your `/usr/local/lib` and `/usr/lib` directories for the correct answers to the questions about the proper names for the libraries.

Finally, add `/usr/local/netpbm/bin/` to your `PATH` or `path` variable, `PATH=$PATH:/usr/local/netpbm/bin` if you're in `bash`, or `set path=($path, /usr/local/netpbm/bin/)` if you use `tcsh`, and you're all set to use this software.

17

libtermcap

Apple has included a shared-library version of `libtermcap`, but no static library version. For most purposes, the shared library will do just fine, but if you find a piece of software that insists on linking to a static `libtermcap.a`, building one of your own isn't difficult. This resource is required by programs so that they can look up, and use, the differing screen format controls that different types of terminals provide, so expect to see it crop up in places that want to interact with you at the command line or in a terminal window of some sort.

You can download a copy of the `libtermcap` source from any GNU mirror, such as `ftp.gnu.org`, although we strongly recommend that you follow the instructions provided immediately after connection, and use a local mirror of the FTP site rather than the parent GNU site. The source should be in `/pub/gnu/termcap/`.

Installation is straightforward: `gunzip`, `tar -xf termcap-1.3.1.tar`, `cd termcap-1.3.1`, `cp /usr/share/automake-1.6/config.* ./`, `./configure`, `make`, `make install`.

Be aware that installing this is going to result in Apple-supplied `libtermcap` files living in the `/usr/lib` and `/usr/include` directories, and your version living in `/usr/local/lib` and `/usr/local/include`. When compiling other software, keep an eye on things to make sure that the compile doesn't use a header file from one location, and the corresponding library from the other. This usually can be rectified by changing the order that directories are specified in, in the `makefile`. Look for places where `-I`*`<directory>`* and `-L`*`<directory>`* specifications don't follow the same order, and if you experience problems, try rearranging them.

`spell` and `ispell`

`spell` is the spelling checker program that we used as an example for the discussion of `STDIN/STDOUT` and pipes. The `ispell` program is actually the base driver for the `spell` program and can do a number of things that we didn't demonstrate in the pipes section of Chapter 14, "Advanced Shell Concepts and Commands." You're encouraged to check out the man pages for more information.

This software has a somewhat convoluted install, but not because it's inherently difficult to install. The problem exists because the dictionaries that it uses are copyrighted and can't be legally distributed by the author of the `spell` program. This necessitates a separate download for the dictionaries, and some fiddling with the source to point it at the downloaded dictionaries.

The `ispell` home page is located at `http://www.cs.hmc.edu/~geoff/ispell.html`.

```
ln -s /var/tmp /usr/tmp
```

(A lot of software expects `/usr/tmp` to exist; you'll need `root` permission to make that link.)

```
curl -O http://www.macosxunleashed.com/downloads/ispell-english.zip
curl -O http://www.macosxunleashed.com/downloads/ispell-3.1.20.tar.gz
curl -O http://www.ibiblio.org/pub/gnu/spell/spell-1.0.tar.gz
unzip ispell-english.zip
gunzip ispell-3.1.20.tar.gz
gunzip spell-1.0.tar.gz
tar -xf ispell-3.1.20.tar
tar -xf spell-1.0.tar
cd ispell-english
mv american.med+ american.med
mv british.med+ british.med
mv * ../ispell-3.1/languages/english/
cd ../ispell-3.1
make all
```

This compiles for a little while and then dies with errors. After it does, edit the file `local.h` and add the following lines on the first two empty lines (you can get hints about other possible options and their syntax by reading the `config.h` file):

```
#define LANGUAGES "{american,MASTERDICTS=american.med,
➥HASHFILES=americanmed.hash}"
#define MASTERHASH "americanmed.hash"

make all
make install
```

The `make install` step needs a number of directories, and permissions to write into them, in the `/usr/local` tree. If they don't all exist on your system, create them and rerun the `make install` step.

```
cd ../spell-1.0/
cp /usr/share/automake-1.6/config.* ./
./configure
make
make install
```

Now you can run both the `ispell` program and the `spell` program as shown in Chapter 14.

The spell utilities can be compiled so that they load a local dictionary as well as the default, allowing you to add words to the dictionary. Unfortunately, the script that builds the dictionaries requires that `sort` accept a different syntax than OS X's `sort`. The adventurous are encouraged to attempt the repair—it's not too difficult, but it requires either a number of brute-force changes, or a bit of trickery to accomplish.

17

gdbm

This is the GNU `dbm` (database management) library. Software authors have chosen at least three different `dbm` flavors to support their applications. `gdbm` is the GNU-supported variant. These libraries don't conflict with each other, so it doesn't hurt to have extras installed, and `gdbm` is required for some installs.

The source can be downloaded from any GNU mirror (see `libtermcap` for suggestions).

Read the `README`s.

```
cp /usr/share/automake-1.6/config.* ./
./configure
make
make progs
make install
```

The make progs step makes test and conversion programs. Among other things, this step makes comparisons between the behavior of the gdbm and other dbm libraries installed on your machine. It is expected to fail on systems that do not have dbm or ndbm libraries (currently, Apple doesn't provide these, but this could change in the future). As of OS X 10.2, the make install step breaks with a complaint "/usr/bin/install: unknown user bin". You can fix this by either adding a bin user to your system or changing the definitions in the makefile so that the installation will be owned by your software user. There are arguments for either solution. You'll find other software that expects to be owned by bin; on the other hand, your /usr/local/ tree is completely owned by your software user. bin was traditionally the owner of vendor-supplied executables, so I prefer switching this install to be owned by the software user.

Python

Python is a programming language designed for building "smart" applications. Apple provides a version of Python with OS X versions 10.2 and newer, so you don't need to do this install if you're just experimenting with the language, and you have no complaints about the version. Because Python is a relatively young language, however, new features are constantly cropping up, and occasionally the odd security problem as well. If you need to update your system's Python version, you can do it with the source from http://www.python.org/

Read the READMEs.

```
./configure --with-suffix=.exe --with-dyld
```

Be aware that the system Python is in /usr/bin, and you want to replace that. You'll either need to remove the /usr/bin/python executable and install yours into /usr/local/bin, or you'll need to target the install at /usr/bin/ and do the make install as root. Edit the Modules/Setup file if there are any modules that you know you want to use. For example, if you are thinking about installing HostSentry, you should uncomment the lines for gdbm and syslog. If you discover later that there are some modules you want to use, you can edit the Modules/Setup file as appropriate, recompile, and reinstall python.

```
make
```

If you edited Modules/Setup, you see a comment in the early make output that you might have to rerun make (that is, run it a second time). If you see the comment, rerun make. Otherwise, you can run make test next.

```
make test
```

You might find that the make test step fails, even though the make step does not. Try installing your compiled python anyway. So far, people are reporting success in using python on OS X anyway.

```
make install
```

PortSentry

PortSentry, available at http://sourceforge.net/projects/sentrytools/, is a connection-monitoring program that attempts to determine whether your machine is being attacked via the network, and blocks access from machines that appear to be attempting malicious connections. We cover the setup and monitoring of this program in Chapter 31, "Server Security and Advanced Network Configuration."

Read the READMEs.

Edit, if needed, the portsentry_config.h file for the following location definitions: CONFIG_FILE, WRAPPER_HOSTS_DENY, SYSLOG_FACILITY, SYSLOG_LEVEL. The software author recommends leaving the settings alone.

Edit portsentry.conf. This is the file you edit to set the scan and response level.

Edit portsentry.ignore. This is the file that contains a listing of hosts that portsentry should ignore.

```
make generic
```

As root, run make install.

Start portsentry for TCP and UDP:

```
/usr/local/psionic/portsentry/portsentry -tcp
/usr/local/psionic/portsentry/portsentry -udp
```

Adjust configuration settings until you are happy with them.

Add portsentry to the system's startup scripts if you want portsentry to start at boot.

17

nmap

nmap, available from http://www.insecure.com/, is a tool that can be used to scan ports on your machine or other machines. You may or may not be interested in nmap if you are already using some combination of ipfw and/or PortSentry. The latest version of nmap has an OS X port available. The config.guess and config.sub files that come with it are even more up-to-date than the OS X default config.guess and config.sub files.

Read the READMEs.

```
./configure
make
make install
```

Tripwire 1.3.1 (Academic Source Release)

Tripwire, available from http://www.tripwire.com/, monitors the integrity of whatever important directories or files you configure it to monitor. Regular use of Tripwire can alert you to any unauthorized changes that have been made to files on your system.

```
Download the academic source release by filling out the form available at
http://www.tripwire.com/downloads/tripwire_asr/. Or, if you're really serious about
security, consider the more up-to-date commercial release.
```

The source expects `malloc.h` to be found in `/usr/include/` instead of `/usr/include/sys/`. You can either link `malloc.h` out to somewhere that the compiler can find it, or search through the source and change any lines that say `#include <malloc.h>` to `#include<sys/malloc.h>`. For most problems of this type, I'd usually say that linking `/usr/include/sys/malloc.h` to `/usr/local/include/malloc.h` would be the best idea. Unfortunately, you'll occasionally find software that tries to guess the type of OS you have based on where `malloc.h` lives, and there's a good chance it'll guess wrong if it sees it somewhere other than `/usr/include/sys/malloc.h`. In this case, it's probably better if you just edit the files. Alternatively, if you're in a hackish mood, you could link `malloc.h` out, do the compile, and then remove the link.

Some `gcc` compiler versions don't like the compiler directive `#if (TW_TYPE32 == int)`. If you get complaints about this line, you can look for these and replace them with `#if (0)`. You'll need to do this for each of several subdirectories of the `sigs` subdirectory. You can quickly find them all with `grep`:

```
cd sigs
grep "TW_TYPE32 == int" */*

crc32/crc32.c:#if ( TW_TYPE32 == int )
md2/md2wrapper.c:#if (TW_TYPE32 == int)
md5/md5wrapper.c:#if (TW_TYPE32 == int)
sha/shawrapper.c:#if (TW_TYPE32 == int)
snefru/snefru.c:#if (TW_TYPE32 == int)
```

Changing all those `#if` statements to `#if (0)` should work.

There's a bizarre interaction between the OS X GNUmake version of `make`, and some makefiles. You might need to `cd` into the various subdirectories (`sigs`, `src`) and run `make` in each of them individually if the main `make` process dies. If this happens, after you've run the `make` in the subdirectories, go back to the main directory and run `make` again. This might take several cycles before all the dependencies are worked out. Eventually, you should get to a point that running `make` builds two executables: `tripwire` and `siggen`. `make install`, and if all goes well, it's time to read the instructions and learn how to use it (or, wait until Chapter 31, when we'll get you started on Tripwire configuration, along with a number of other network security topics). If the `make install` doesn't work, it'll be because of missing directories, or a need to create the `man` user for the installation to proceed.

Note that this `make install` moves files when it installs them, instead of copying them. If you need to reinstall, either to place it somewhere else or because the install didn't finish properly, you'll need to `make` it all again.

Edit `tw.config`. This is the file where you specify what files or directories you want Tripwire to monitor.

Initialize the Tripwire database:

```
tripwire -initialize
```

Run `tripwire`:

```
tripwire
```

Add `tripwire` to a daily `cron` job so that Tripwire regularly checks the integrity of your important files and sends you the results.

TIP

You can't currently install `tripwire` directly through `fink`, or other package managers that I'm aware of, because of the licensing requirements that the authors have used. The FreeBSD ports system, however, is being ported to Mac OS X, and this package manager at least tries to build `tripwire` (by having you personally comply with the licensing requirements, and then modifying and building the source you've downloaded). The last time I tried to make it work, it wasn't functional (the `tripwire` build, that is—the ports system mostly seemed to be working nicely), but by the time you read this, it might be working. Check out `http://www.freebsd.org/ports/security.html#tripwire-1.2` for more information.

Summary

This chapter took you through a tour of several types of installation, compilation, troubleshooting and debugging, as well as provided some suggestions for installing many useful command-line applications. We have found that a large percentage of Unix users, after they have developed the necessary mindset regarding software installation, can productively fight through troublesome installs such as this by successively attacking small parts of the problem as shown here. The keys to remember are that the messages output from the compilers and debuggers do have meaning, and the worst that can happen by attempting to logically determine the cause of an error is that it doesn't help. Surprisingly often, a problem in a programming language can be fixed by working with error messages and making logical guesses, even if you don't know the language in the slightest.

Always remember: it all looks more difficult than it really is, and if it's already broken, you can't make it work any worse.

CHAPTER 18

Advanced Unix Shell Use: Configuration and Programming (Shell Scripting)

IN THIS CHAPTER

- Customizing Your Shell Environment and Storing Data
- Automating Tasks with Shell Scripts
- Making Shell Scripts Start at Login or System Startup

In the preceding several chapters, we have introduced you to the wide range of possibilities inherent in being able to access the Unix subsystem at the command line. Although we've said that being able to type to the command line can give you the power to do things that you've never been able to do before, we've also repeatedly hinted that there were ways that you could automate much of the typing and build your own mini-programs. In this chapter, we'll cover the final things you need to know to make this a reality.

With OS X 10.3, Apple has changed the default user shell from `tcsh` to `bash`. Because of this, not all of you will be using the same shell. Unfortunately, the mechanical details of these shells are different enough that they can't both be easily covered in a single discussion without becoming confusing. The concept of shell scripting itself, and of automating your command-line tools, is universal, however, and does not depend on what shell you're using to work in. Therefore, this chapter is divided into sections that discuss scripting as a concept—and in which we'll use one shell or the other, whichever is most illustrative of the scripting point at hand, to generate our primary examples—and subsections that discuss the mechanistic and syntactic details of the `bash` and `tcsh` shells themselves, as well as how these relate to the general scripting concepts. When you come to one of these shell-specific sections, concentrate on the version that deals with your shell. We wish we could put enough pages in this book to provide identical coverage of both. Unfortunately, if our popular reviews are correct, we'd need to put wheels and a tow-handle on the book if we did. To cut down on the bulk and weight a little bit, we'll confine most extended discussions, examples, and listings to one, or the other shell sections (the bash section, whenever it's possible to make the point clearly in bash). Because of this, regardless of which shell you're using, you'll want to skim the other section after reading the specifics of yours to catch any places where the other goes into greater detail. You'll be able to generate the analogous examples for each by following along with what is done in the other shell and applying the details regarding differences that we've provided in the section specific to your shell.

If you're interested in using a different shell, you'll find that the concepts and capabilities we cover here are almost universal, though the syntax and advanced features of these and other shells will differ somewhat. Some shells, such as zsh, have so many additional features beyond what we can cover there that a complete description of their use is sufficient to fill a book or two of their own.

Don't let the idea of multiple differing shell syntaxes sound intimidating to you. Even if you don't realize it yet, for whatever shell you're working in, you already know shell syntax. It's what you've been using for the last six chapters. To make the best use of the command-line environment, you'll also need to know about shell variables, conditional statements, and looping structures. At this point in your command-line experience, these will not be difficult details to master.

Customizing Your Shell Environment and Storing Data

Variables are a way of addressing bits of the computer memory so that we can store random pieces of information in it. It would be difficult to do much productive work with a computer if all we could store in any location was one particular, predetermined piece of information. Variables give us the ability to name a region X, store whatever value we want in X, and change the value whenever we want. Variables in the shell are used both to hold data to be used in commands and programs written in the shell and to control the behavior of certain aspects of the shell. You've already been introduced peripherally to this second use by way of the PATH variable, which affects where the shell looks to find executable programs. We'll go into somewhat more detail on this use in the next section and cover the former later in this chapter.

Environment and Shell Variables

Many shells make a distinction between environment variables and shell variables in one way or another. Both are variables that you can set and use in a shell. The difference is that environment variables are inherited by any programs (such as subshells) that are children of (Unixism for "run by") that shell, whereas shell variables are not inherited. This might not seem a useful distinction, but there are significant uses for each type. Noninherited shell variables don't cost memory and startup time for subshells, and can be expected to be empty in any shell until they are used to store something. Inherited environment variables, on the other hand, must be copied into the memory space of child programs, taking room and time, and they can be used to pass information between a parent shell and programs that it executes.

NOTE

It is traditional to use uppercase variable names for environment variables and lowercase variable names for shell variables, although there is no requirement that this tradition must be followed in your own scripts.

Setting Variables in `bash`

In `bash`, all variables start out as shell variables, and then are "upgraded" to environment variable status using the `export` command. To set a shell variable, the syntax is as follows:

```
<shellvariablename>=<value>
```

TIP

There are no spaces between the `<shellvariablename>`, the = character, or the `<value>`. Spaces that creep unannounced and unwanted into statements that you're typing will be one of the most common problems you encounter when working in `bash`.

To set a shell variable named `x` to contain the value `7`, the `bash` shell expression is simply

```
x=7
```

To make a shell variable into an environmental variable, the syntax is

```
export <shellvariablename>
```

To make the shell variable `x` (that we previously set to contain the value `7`) into an environment variable, the shell expression is

```
export x
```

This makes the variable `x` available to other programs we start from within this shell.

Setting Variables in `tcsh`

In `tcsh` one uses an explicit command to tell the shell to put a value into a variable, instead of just an = sign. Setting shell variables uses a different command than setting an environment variable: Shell variables use the command `set`, and environment variables use the command `setenv`. To set a shell variable, the syntax is as follows:

```
set <shellvariablename> = <value>
```

To set a shell variable named x to contain the value 7, the shell expression is simply

```
set x=7
```

TIP

tcsh is not as particular as bash about spaces, but it does require that the spaces be balanced. That is, you can use either x=7 or x = 7, but not x= 7 or x =7. The error that tcsh reports if you use either of these latter two constructs is a seemingly irrelevant complaint about a variable name needing to start with a letter.

To set an environment variable to a particular value, the syntax is

```
setenv <environmentvariablename> <value>
```

To set an environment variable named Y to contain the value 8, the shell expression is

```
setenv Y 8
```

Note that with setenv, no = sign is used.

CAUTION

In tcsh it's quite possible for you to create a shell variable and an environment variable with the same name, each containing a distinct value. In this case, most shell commands will see the variable as having the value of the shell variable rather than the value of the environment variable.

Using Variables

Both shell and environment variables are addressed for use by the prepending of a $ sign before the variable names. A simple demonstration can be accomplished with the echo command, which prints to the STDOUT of the shell, the value of the expression following it.

NOTE

Observe the shell prompt in the command-line examples I'm displaying in this chapter. It's probably not what you're used to seeing as a shell prompt. The shell prompt can be customized to a significant extent. See Table 18.2 (bash) or 18.4 (tcsh) in this chapter, and the man pages for bash and tcsh for information on how you can customize your prompt to include the information you find most useful. For many of the examples in this chapter, I'm using a shell prompt that includes a sequentially increasing number. This number is useful not only for demonstrations such as are being done in this chapter, but also for access to the command history list, discussed later in this chapter.

Using Variables in bash

The shell use of variables is simultaneously both rather simple and often annoying in its requirement for attention to detail. Variables are case sensitive, and the spacing between variables and operators such as the = sign in assignment statements is critical to the correct functioning of the statement. The habits necessary to work with shell variables however aren't hard to develop, and it's easy enough to experiment and try again if something doesn't work:

```
brezup:ray Documents 351 $ echo "Hi There"
Hi There
brezup:ray Documents 352 $ echo x
x
brezup:ray Documents 353 $ echo $x

brezup:ray Documents 354 $ x=7
brezup:ray Documents 355 $ echo x
x
brezup:ray Documents 356 $ echo $x
7
brezup:ray Documents 357 $ Y=8
brezup:ray Documents 358 $ export Y
brezup:ray Documents 359 $ echo $y

brezup:ray Documents 360 $ echo $Y
8
brezup:ray Documents 361 $ z=$x+$Y
7+8
brezup:ray Documents 362 $ let z=$x+$Y
brezup:ray Documents 363 $ echo $z
15
```


Here, a shell variable x and an environment variable Y have been set to values 7 and 8, respectively, and their values have been printed to the terminal. There are a few lines of "mistakes" interspersed to demonstrate the behavior of the shell if you don't get your variable names quite right when you're trying to use them. It's important to note that bash doesn't provide error diagnostics for simple misuses like asking for the value of a variable that's never been set. This can make finding errors in scripts more challenging.

Notice the result of the command numbered 361? bash automatically expands variables to their values (that is, replaces them in the expression with whatever value they contain), but it doesn't automatically evaluate arithmetic expressions. Because of this, the assignment done in command 361, z=$x+$Y, is treated as a string assignment: $x and $Y are replaced by their values to the left and right of the + sign, and the resulting string is stored in z. To tell bash to treat the expression as an arithmetic expression instead, the let command is used. This signals bash that the following arguments should be expanded, and then evaluated arithmetically, rather than as a string.

bash also supports the notion of array variables. An array can be created simply by assigning values to subscripted variables:

```
brezup:ray Documents 364 $ z[3]=12
brezup:ray Documents 365 $ z[$x]=14
brezup:ray Documents 366 $ echo $z[3]
15[3]
```

NOTE

Remember, the values of $x and $z have been set earlier.

Unfortunately, the syntax for retrieving the values isn't quite what you'd probably like it to be. Command 366 reports 15[3] in the preceding example because $z has previously been set to the value 15, and bash (annoyingly) expands that value instead of noticing that the [3] calls up an array subscript of z.

```
brezup:ray Documents 367 $ echo ${z[3]}
12
brezup:ray Documents 368 $ echo $z
15
brezup:ray Documents 369 $ z[$x+Y]=2
brezup:ray Documents 370 $ echo ${z[15]}
2
```

When setting an array value, the variable may be specified as <varname>[<subscript>], but when using it, curly braces must be placed around the <varname>[<subscript>] portion to prevent the shell from interpreting it as $<varname> followed by the string [<subscript>]. Inside the square braces specifying the subscript, expressions are treated as arithmetic and evaluated to determine the final subscript value.

TIP

Peculiarly, the arithmetic expansion inside [] means that you don't need to use a $ in front of a variable name to use that variable's value inside the [] braces. This allows the expression z[$x+Y]=2 to be written as z[x+Y]=2 and z[$x+$Y]=2 as well. Leaving out the $ is a good way to make what you write visually confusing, so we recommend against this, even though it's valid syntax.

Accessing the zero'th value of an array variable is the same as accessing the variable without an array subscript:

```
brezup:ray Documents 371 $ echo ${z[0]}
15
brezup:ray Documents 372 $ z[0]=32
brezup:ray Documents 373 $ echo $z
32
```

Finally, you can force the shell to recognize a portion of a command line as some variable and a portion as some other information by insulating the variable name with curly braces. For example, if you have a variable named zz and a variable named zzygy, you'd have trouble printing the value of $zz, followed by the characters ygy without this facility:

```
brezup:ray Pictures 453 $ zz="howdy neighbor"
brezup:ray Pictures 454 $ zzygy="plonk"
brezup:ray Pictures 455 $ echo $zz
howdy neighbor
brezup:ray Pictures 456 $ echo $zzygy
plonk
brezup:ray Pictures 457 $ echo ${zz}ygy
howdy neighborygy
```

The most common ways of using shell and environment variables in bash command lines are shown in Table 18.1.

TABLE 18.1 Useful bash Syntax Options for Setting and Accessing Shell and Environment Variables

Expression Syntax	Effect
<word>	Used as a part of a command-line expression, *<word>* is a string of non-whitespace characters, or a quoted string that possibly contains spaces.
<variable>	The name of a variable. Variable names are composed of alphanumeric and underscore characters and begin with an alphabetic character or underscore.
$*<variable>*	Expands to the contents of *<variable>*. This will typically be a *<word>* or *<wordlist>*. A *<wordlist>* is a series of words separated (in the default case) by spaces.
${*<variable>*[*n*]}	Expands the *n*th value of the array-variable named *<variable>*. The curly braces are required.
<variable>=*<word>*	Sets the value of *<variable>* to *<word>*.
<variable>[*n*]=*<word>*	Treats *<variable>* as an array of words, and sets the *n*th value to *<word>*. This has the effect of setting the *n*th word of a wordlist to *<word>*.
<variable>[*<expression>*]=*<word>*	Treats *<variable>* as an array of words and *<expression>* as an arithmetic expression. Evaluates *<expression>* and sets the *<expression>*th value of *<variable>* to *<word>*.

TABLE 18.1 Continued

Expression Syntax	Effect
`export <variable>`	Makes `<variable>` available to other processes as an environment variable.
`let <variable>=<expression>`	Treats `<expression>` as a mathematical expression, attempts to evaluate it, and assigns the result to `<variable>`.
`let <variable>=( <expression> )`	Same as the previous item. Parentheses can be used to order the execution of parts of the expression, and it's frequently helpful to use them around any expression on general principles.
`let <variable>[n]=<expression>`	Treats `<variable>` as an array and sets the *n*th value of it to the value of `<expression>`.

CAUTION

The spacing between the parts of a command, like the `let z=$x+$Y` command in the example, is one of the largest sources of difficulty to the beginning shell programmer. Making matters worse, the spacing that's required is different between shells, and what's required in one, breaks others. In `bash`, the lack of spaces between "words" that are being operated on, for example the `z`, the `=`, `$x`, `$y`, and the `+` symbol, are critical to the command being understood properly. The only place where there's much leniency is between the let and the arithmetic expression part of the command. Inserting spaces in other places will cause the arithmetic expression to be evaluated differently than you intend or cause the entire command to fail.

To demonstrate the difference between shell and environment variables, you can create a subshell and test the variables you used in the previous example in it:

```
brezup:ray Documents 373 $ bash
brezup:ray Documents 151 $ echo $x

brezup:ray Documents 152 $ echo $Y
8
```

As you can see, after the subshell is started (notice that the command number in the prompt drops to `151`—the size of the retained history prior to the parent shell), the environment variable `Y` maintains its value and the shell value `x` goes back to being undefined.

Using Variables in `tcsh`

`tcsh` syntax for everything but the most basic variable operations is similar to `bash` syntax, but not quite identical.

```
brezup Documents 200> echo "Hi There"
Hi there
```

```
brezup Documents 201> echo $x
tcsh x: Undefined variable.
brezup Documents 202> set x=7
brezup Documents 203> echo $x
7
brezup Documents 204> setenv Y 8
brezup Documents 205> echo $y
tcsh y: Undefined variable.
brezup Documents 206> echo $Y
8
brezup Documents 207> @ z = ( $x + $Y )
brezup Documents 208> echo $z
15
```

Here, a shell variable x and an environment variable Y have been set to values 7 and 8, respectively, and their values have been printed to the terminal. tcsh is more strict about variable name use than bash, and complains when you try to access the value of a variable that hasn't previously been set. The @ command is a tcsh shell built-in command, similar to the set command. However, the set command treats all its arguments as strings, whereas the @ command treats them as numbers, allowing math operations such as +, -, /, and *. The @ command, like the set command, sets a shell variable (or creates it if it does not exist). The set and @ commands can also be used as [set or @] *<variablename>*[*n*] = *<expression>*. In this form, the command attempts to treat the variable *<variablename>* as an array and set item *n* (the *n*th word, if echoed) to the value of *<expression>*. Table 18.2 lists the most frequently used methods for setting variable values.

TABLE 18.2 tcsh Syntax Options for Setting Shell and Environment Variables

Expression Syntax	Effect
<word>	Used as a part of a command-line expression, *<word>* is a string of non-whitespace characters, or a quoted string that possibly contains spaces.
$*<variable>*	Expands to the contents of *<variable>*. This will typically be a *<word>* or *<wordlist>*. $*<variablename>* preferentially expands to the value of the shell variable by the name *<variablename>* if both shell and environment variables with this name exist.
set *<variable>* = *<word>*	Sets the value of *<variable>* to *<word>*.
set *<variable>*[*n*] = *<word>*	Treats *<variable>* as an array of words, and sets the *n*th value to *<word>*. This has the effect of setting the *n*th word of a wordlist to *<word>*.
setenv *<variable>* *<word>*	Sets the environment variable *<variable>* to contain the value *<word>*. Most variable manipulations must be done in shell variables, and the values transferred into environment variables if needed.

TABLE 18.2 Continued

Expression Syntax	Effect
`@ <variable> = <expression>`	Treats <*expression*> as a mathematical expression, attempts to evaluate it, and assigns the result to <*variable*>. Most forms of errors in attempts at this result in the response `@: Expression Syntax`.
`@ <variable> = ( <expression> )`	Same as the previous item. Parentheses can be used to order the execution of parts of the expression, and it's frequently helpful to use them around any expression on general principles.
`@ <variable>[n] = <expression>`	Treats <*variable*> as an array, and sets the *n*th value of it to the value of <*expression*>.

CAUTION

The spacing between the parts of a command, like the `@ z = ( $x + $Y )` command on line 207 of the preceding example, is one of the largest sources of difficulty to the beginning shell programmer. The spaces between "words" that are being operated on—here the `$x`, the `$y`, and the `+` symbol—are critical to the command being understood properly. You can have more spaces, but if you remove a space, the words become indistinct, and the shell becomes confused. For example, if you remove the space between the `$x` and the `+` sign, `tcsh` will no longer see a variable named `$x`, a `+` sign, and a variable named `$y`. Instead, it will see a variable named `$x+` and a variable named `$y`, with no mathematic operation between them. This turns out to be two errors because the `+` symbol isn't a valid part of a variable name, and some math operation is required in the expression.

Peculiarly, while `tcsh` requires balanced spaces around the `=` character in `set` and `setenv` statements, it does not require balanced spaces around the `=` in `@` statements. There must be a space between the `@` and the variable into which the value is being placed, but one can write `@ z=3`, `@ z = 3`, `@ z= 3`, and `@ z =3` to the same effect.

To demonstrate the difference between shell and environment variables, you can create a subshell and test the variables you used in the previous example in it:

```
localhost ray 210> tcsh
/Users/ray
localhost ray 151> echo $x
x: Undefined variable.
localhost ray 152> echo $Y
8
```

As you can see, after the subshell is started (notice that the command number in the prompt drops to 151—the size of my retained command history list), the environment variable `Y` maintains its value and the shell value `x` becomes undefined.

Reserved Variables in the Shell

As mentioned earlier, certain shell and environment variables are reserved by the shell and used to either report various values to the user or to control the behavior of some parts of the shell or of programs that run as children of the shell. Tables 18.3 and 18.4 list the bash and tcsh shell variables that affect the behavior of bash, tcsh, and a few intimately related programs. Remember that any program you run in a shell may be additionally affected by environment variables. For example, the man command determines where to look for man pages by examining the MANPATH environment variable. This variable isn't set or controlled by either bash or tcsh, but if you set this environment variable to some path in your shell, the man command will inherit it and search in that path for man pages. Because every program may independently choose to examine any environment variables it chooses, it's best to look at the man pages for any programs to determine whether there are environment variables with which you can affect the program's behavior.

TABLE 18.3 The bash Reserved Shell Variables

Shell Variable	Effects
BASH	Expands to the full filename used to invoke this instance of bash.
BASH_VERSINFO	A read-only array variable whose members hold version information for this instance of bash. The values assigned to the array members are as follows: BASH_VERSINFO[0] The major version number (the release) BASH_VERSINFO[1] The minor version number (the version) BASH_VERSINFO[2] The patch level BASH_VERSINFO[3] The build version BASH_VERSINFO[4] The release status (for example, beta1) BASH_VERSINFO[5] The value of MACHTYPE
BASH_VERSION	Expands to a string describing the version of this instance of bash.
COMP_CWORD	An index into ${COMP_WORDS} of the word containing the current cursor position. This variable is available only in shell functions invoked by the programmable completion facilities.
COMP_LINE	The current command line. This variable is available only in shell functions and external commands invoked by the programmable completion facilities.
COMP_POINT	The index of the current cursor position relative to the beginning of the current command. If the current cursor position is at the end of the current command, the value of this variable is equal to ${#COMP_LINE}. This variable is available only in shell functions and external commands invoked by the programmable completion facilities.
COMP_WORDS	An array variable consisting of the individual words in the current command line. This variable is available only in shell functions invoked by the programmable completion facilities.
DIRSTACK	An array variable containing the current contents of the directory stack. Directories appear in the stack in the order they are displayed by the dirs builtin. Assigning to members of this array variable may be used to modify directories already in the stack, but the pushd and popd builtins must be used to add and remove directories. Assignment to this variable will not change the current directory. If DIRSTACK is unset, it loses its special properties, even if it is subsequently reset.

TABLE 18.3 Continued

Shell Variable	Effects
EUID	Expands to the effective user ID of the current user, initialized at shell startup. This variable is read-only.
FUNCNAME	The name of any currently executing shell function. This variable exists only when a shell function is executing. Assignments to FUNCNAME have no effect and return an error status. If FUNCNAME is unset, it loses its special properties, even if it is subsequently reset.
GROUPS	An array variable containing the list of groups of which the current user is a member. Assignments to GROUPS have no effect and return an error status. If GROUPS is unset, it loses its special properties, even if it is subsequently reset.
HISTCMD	The history number, or index in the history list, of the current command. If HISTCMD is unset, it loses its special properties, even if it is subsequently reset.
HOSTNAME	Automatically set to the name of the current host.
HOSTTYPE	Automatically set to a string that uniquely describes the type of machine on which bash is executing.
LINENO	Each time this parameter is referenced, the shell substitutes a decimal number representing the current sequential line number (starting with 1) within a script or function. When not in a script or function, the value substituted is not guaranteed to be meaningful. If LINENO is unset, it loses its special properties, even if it is subsequently reset.
MACHTYPE	Automatically set to a string that fully describes the system type on which bash is executing, in the standard GNU cpu-company-system format.
OLDPWD	The previous working directory as set by the cd command.
OPTARG	The value of the last option argument processed by the getopts builtin command.
OPTIND	The index of the next argument to be processed by the getopts builtin command.
OSTYPE	Automatically set to a string that describes the operating system on which bash is executing.
PIPESTATUS	An array variable containing a list of exit status values from the processes in the most recently executed foreground pipeline (which may contain only a single command).
PPID	The process ID of the shell's parent. This variable is read-only.
PWD	The current working directory as set by the cd command.
RANDOM	Each time this parameter is referenced, a random integer between 0 and 32767 is generated. The sequence of random numbers may be initialized by assigning a value to RANDOM. If RANDOM is unset, it loses its special properties, even if it is subsequently reset.
REPLY	Set to the line of input read by the read builtin command when no arguments are supplied.

TABLE 18.3 Continued

Shell Variable	Effects
`SECONDS`	Each time this parameter is referenced, the number of seconds since shell invocation is returned. If a value is assigned to `SECONDS`, the value returned upon subsequent references is the number of seconds since the assignment plus the value assigned. If `SECONDS` is unset, it loses its special properties, even if it is subsequently reset.
`SHELLOPTS`	A colon-separated list of enabled shell options. Each word in the list is a valid argument for the `-o` option to the `set` builtin command. The options appearing in `SHELLOPTS` are those reported as being `on` by the command `set -o`. If this variable is in the environment when `bash` starts up, each shell option in the list will be enabled before reading any startup files. This variable is read-only.
`SHLVL`	Incremented by one each time an instance of `bash` is started.
`UID`	Expands to the user ID of the current user, initialized at shell startup. This variable is read-only.
`BASH_ENV`	If this parameter is set when `bash` is executing a shell script, its value is interpreted as a filename containing commands to initialize the shell, as in `~/.bashrc`. The value of `BASH_ENV` is subjected to parameter expansion, command substitution, and arithmetic expansion before being interpreted as a filename. `PATH` is not used to search for the resultant filename.
`CDPATH`	The search path for the `cd` command. This is a colon-separated list of directories in which the shell looks for destination directories specified by the `cd` command. A sample value is `".:~:/usr"`.
`COLUMNS`	Used by the `select` builtin command to determine the terminal width when printing selection lists. Automatically set upon receipt of a `SIGWINCH`.
`COMPREPLY`	An array variable from which `bash` reads the possible completions generated by a shell function invoked by the programmable completion facility.
`FCEDIT`	The default editor for the `fc` builtin command.
`FIGNORE`	A colon-separated list of suffixes to ignore when performing filename completion. A filename whose suffix matches one of the entries in `FIGNORE` is excluded from the list of matched filenames. A sample value is `".o:~"`.
`GLOBIGNORE`	A colon-separated list of patterns defining the set of filenames to be ignored by pathname expansion. If a filename matched by a pathname expansion pattern also matches one of the patterns in `GLOBIGNORE`, it is removed from the list of matches.
`HISTCONTROL`	If set to a value of `ignorespace`, lines which begin with a space character are not entered on the history list. If set to a value of `ignoredups`, lines matching the last history line are not entered. A value of `ignoreboth` combines the two options. If unset, or if set to any other value than those documented here, all lines read by the parser are saved on the history list, subject to the value of `HISTIGNORE`. This variable's function is superseded by `HISTIGNORE`. The second and subsequent lines of a multi-line compound command are not tested and are added to the history regardless of the value of `HISTCONTROL`.

TABLE 18.3 Continued

Shell Variable	Effects
HISTFILE	The name of the file in which command history is saved (see HISTORY variable). The default value is ~/.bash_history. If unset, the command history is not saved when an interactive shell exits.
HISTFILESIZE	The maximum number of lines contained in the history file. When this variable is assigned a value, the history file is truncated, if necessary, to contain no more than that number of lines. The default value is 500. The history file is also truncated to this size after writing it when an interactive shell exits.
HISTIGNORE	A colon-separated list of patterns used to decide which command lines should be saved on the history list. Each pattern is anchored at the beginning of the line and must match the complete line. (No implicit * is appended.) Each pattern is tested against the line after the checks specified by HISTCONTROL are applied. In addition to the normal shell pattern matching characters, & matches the previous history line. & may be escaped using a backslash (\); the backslash is removed before attempting a match. The second and subsequent lines of a multi-line compound command are not tested, and are added to the history regardless of the value of HISTIGNORE.
HISTSIZE	The number of commands to remember in the command history (see HISTORY variable). The default value is 500.
HOME	The home directory of the current user; the default argument for the cd builtin command. The value of this variable is also used when performing tilde expansion.
HOSTFILE	Contains the name of a file in the same format as /etc/hosts that should be read when the shell needs to complete a hostname. The list of possible hostname completions may be changed while the shell is running; the next time hostname completion is attempted after the value is changed, bash adds the contents of the new file to the existing list. If HOSTFILE is set, but has no value, bash attempts to read /etc/hosts to obtain the list of possible hostname completions. When HOSTFILE is unset, the hostname list is cleared.
IFS	The Internal Field Separator that is used for word splitting after expansion and to split lines into words with the read builtin command. The default value is "<space><tab><newline>".
IGNOREEOF	Controls the action of an interactive shell on receipt of an EOF character as the sole input. If set, the value is the number of consecutive EOF characters that must be typed as the first characters on an input line before bash exits. If the variable exists but does not have a numeric value, or has no value, the default value is 10. If it does not exist, EOF signifies the end of input to the shell.
INPUTRC	The filename for the readline startup file, overriding the default of ~/.inputrc.
LANG	Used to determine the locale category for any category not specifically selected with a variable starting with LC_.
LC_ALL	This variable overrides the value of LANG and any other LC_ variable specifying a locale category.

TABLE 18.3 Continued

Shell Variable	Effects
LC_COLLATE	This variable determines the collation order used when sorting the results of pathname expansion and the behavior of range expressions, equivalence classes, and collating sequences within pathname expansion and pattern matching.
LC_CTYPE	This variable determines the interpretation of characters and the behavior of character classes within pathname expansion and pattern matching.
LC_MESSAGES	This variable determines the locale used to translate doublequoted strings preceded by a `$`.
LC_NUMERIC	This variable determines the locale category used for number formatting.
LINES	Used by the `select` builtin command to determine the column length for printing selection lists. Automatically set upon receipt of a `SIGWINCH`.
MAIL	If this parameter is set to a filename and the `MAILPATH` variable is not set, `bash` informs the user of the arrival of mail in the specified file.
MAILCHECK	Specifies how often (in seconds) `bash` checks for mail. The default is `60` seconds. When it is time to check for mail, the shell does so before displaying the primary prompt. If this variable is unset or set to something other than a positive integer, the shell disables mail checking.
MAILPATH	A colon-separated list of file names to be checked for mail. The message to be printed when mail arrives in a particular file may be specified by separating the filename from the message with a `?`. When used in the text of the message, `$_` expands to the name of the current mailfile (for example: `MAILPATH='/var/mail/bfox?"You have mail":~/shell-mail?"$_ has mail!"'`.) `bash` supplies a default value for this variable.
OPTERR	If set to the value `1`, `bash` displays error messages generated by the `getopts` builtin command. `OPTERR` is initialized to `1` each time the shell is invoked or a shell script is executed.
PATH	The search path for commands. It is a colon-separated list of directories in which the shell looks for commands.
POSIXLY_CORRECT	If this variable is in the environment when `bash` starts, the shell enters posix mode before reading the startup files, as if the `--posix` invocation option had been supplied. If it is set while the shell is running, `bash` enables posix mode, as if the command `set -o posix` had been executed.
PROMPT_COMMAND	If set, the value is executed as a command prior to issuing each primary prompt.
PS1	The value of this parameter is expanded and used as the primary prompt string. The default value is `"\s-\v\$ "`. We use `"\h:\u \W \! \$ "` or `"\h:\u \W \$ "`.
PS2	The value of this parameter is expanded as with `PS1` and used as the secondary prompt string. The default is `"> "`.
PS3	The value of this parameter is used as the prompt for the `select` command.
PS4	The value of this parameter is expanded as with `PS1`, and the value is printed before each command `bash` displays during an execution trace. The first character of `PS4` is replicated multiple times, as necessary, to indicate multiple levels of indirection. The default is `"+ "`.

18

TABLE 18.3 Continued

Shell Variable	Effects
`TIMEFORMAT`	The value of this parameter is used as a format string specifying how the timing information for pipelines prefixed with the `time` reserved word should be displayed. The `%` character introduces an escape sequence that is expanded to a time value or other information. The escape sequences and their meanings are as follows; the braces denote optional portions. `%%` A literal `%`. `%[p][l]R` The elapsed time in seconds. `%[p][l]U` The number of CPU seconds spent in user mode. `%[p][l]S` The number of CPU seconds spent in system mode. `%P` The CPU percentage, computed as `(%U + %S) / %R`. The optional `p` is a digit specifying the precision, the number of digits after a decimal point. A value of `0` forces no decimal point or fraction to be output. At most, three places after the decimal point may be specified; values of `p` greater than `3` are changed to `3`. If `p` is not specified, the value `3` is used. The optional `l` specifies a longer format, including minutes, of the form `MMmSS.FFs`. The value of `p` determines whether the fraction is included. If this variable is not set, `bash` acts as if it had the value `$'\nreal\t%3lR\nuser\t%3lU\nsys%3lS'`. If the value is `null`, no timing information is displayed. A trailing newline is added when the format string is displayed.
`TMOUT`	If set to a value greater than zero, `TMOUT` is treated as the default timeout for the read builtin. The select command terminates if input does not arrive after `TMOUT` seconds when input is coming from a terminal. In an interactive shell, the value is interpreted as the number of seconds to wait for input after issuing the primary prompt. Bash terminates after waiting for that number of seconds if input does not arrive.
`auto_resume`	This variable controls how the shell interacts with the user and job control. If this variable is set, single word simple commands without redirections are treated as candidates for resumption of an existing stopped job. No ambiguity is allowed; if more than one job begins with the string typed, the job most recently accessed is selected. The name of a stopped job, in this context, is the command line used to start it. If set to the value `exact`, the string supplied must match the name of a stopped job exactly; if set to `substring`, the string supplied needs to match a substring of the name of a stopped job. The `substring` value provides functionality analogous to the `%?` job identifier. If set to any other value, the supplied string must be a prefix of a stopped job's name; this provides functionality analogous to the `%` job identifier.
`histchars`	Two or three characters that control history expansion and tokenization. The first character is the history expansion character, the character that signals the start of a history expansion; normally this is the character `!`. The second character is the quick substitution character, which is used as shorthand for rerunning the previous

TABLE 18.3 Continued

Shell Variable	Effects
	command entered, substituting one string for another in the command. The default is ^. The optional third character is the character that indicates that the remainder of the line is a comment when found as the first character of a word, normally #. The history comment character disables history substitution for the remaining words on the line. It does not necessarily cause the shell parser to treat the rest of the line as a comment.

TABLE 18.4 The `tcsh` Reserved Shell Variables

Shell Variable	Effects
`addsuffix`	Controls addition of / to the end of directory paths and spaces after normal filenames when expanded by shell filename autocompletion.
`afsuser`	If set, this is the username to autologout under Kerberos authentication.
`ampm`	If set, shows time in 12-hour AM/PM format.
`argv`	The list of arguments passed to the shell on startup.
`autocorrect`	If set, attempts to fix command misspellings.
`autoexpand`	If set, passes command completion attempts through the expand-history processor. (See the `tcsh` man page for more details.)
`autolist`	If set, lists possible expansions for autocompletion if the expansion is ambiguous. If the value is set to `ambiguous`, lists possibilities only when an autocompletion attempt does not add any new characters.
`autologout`	The number of minutes of inactivity before autologout. Optionally, the number of minutes before automatic locking of the terminal.
`backslash_quote`	If set, backslashes (\ characters) are automatically inserted before any backslash or quote character in a command completion.
`cdpath`	A list of directories in which `cd` should look for subdirectories if they aren't in the current working directory.
`color`	If set, enables color display for the `ls` command and shell built-in command `ls-F`.
`command`	If set, contains the command that was passed to the shell with a `-c` flag.
`complete`	If set to `enhance`, completion ignores filename case and considers periods, hyphens, and underscores to be word separators, and hyphens and underscores to be equivalent.
`correct`	If set to `cmd`, attempts automatic spelling correction for commands. If set to `complete`, commands are automatically completed. If set to `all`, the entire command line is corrected.
`cwd`	The full path of the current working directory.
`dextract`	If set, `pushd` *+n* extracts the *n*th subdirectory from the stack, rather than rotating it to the top.
`dirsfile`	The default location in which `dirs -S` and `dirs -L` look for their history.

18

TABLE 18.4 Continued

Shell Variable	Effects
dirstack	An array of all directories in the directory stack.
dspmbyte	If set to euc, enables display and editing of EUC-Kanji (Japanese) code. If set to sjis, enables display and editing of Shift-JIS (Japanese) code. Other options are available—see the tcsh man page for more details.
dunique	If set, pushd removes any instances of the pushed directory from the stack, before pushing it onto the top of the stack.
echo	If set, each command and its arguments are echoed to the terminal before being executed.
echo_style	The style of the echo built-in. May be set to bsd, sysv, both, or none to control the behavior of the echo command. See the tcsh man page for more details on behavior affected.
edit	If set, allow command-line editing.
ellipsis	If set, use an ellipsis to represent portions of the path that won't fit in the prompt.
fignore	List of filename suffixes to be ignored in completion attempts.
filec	An unused tcsh shell variable, included to maintain backward compatibility with csh, which used this variable to control whether completion should be used.
gid	The user owning the shell's real group ID.
group	The user owning the shell's group name.
histchars	A string determining the characters used in history substitution. The first character replaces the default ! character, and the second replaces the default ^ character.
histdup	Controls handling of duplicate entries in the history list. If set to all, only unique history events are entered into the history. If set to prev, a run of identical commands is reduced to a single entry in the history list. If set to erase, a repeat of a command already in the history list removes the previous occurrence from the history.
histfile	The default location in which history -S and history -L look for a history file. If unset, ~/.history is used.
histlit	If set, the shell built-in, editor commands, and history-saving mechanism use the literal (unexpanded) form of lines in the history list.
history	The first word indicates the number of history events to save. The optional second word indicates a format for printing the history. See the tcsh man page for more details on format control strings.
home	Initialized to the home directory of the user. Command-line expansion of ~ refers to this variable for its action.
ignoreeof	If set to the empty string or 0 and the input is a terminal, an end-of-file command sent to the terminal causes the shell to print an error rather than exit.
implicitcd	If set, the shell treats a directory name entered on the command line as though it were entered as the argument of a cd command.
inputmode	Can be set to insert or overwrite to control the behavior of command-line editing.
listflags	Contains command-line flags to include with any used when issuing the ls-F shell built-in.
listjobs	If set, all current jobs are listed when a running job is suspended.

TABLE 18.4 Continued

Shell Variable	Effects
listlinks	If set, the ls-F shell built-in command shows the time of file to which symbolic links point.
listmax	The maximum number of items that the list-choices command-line editor and autocompletion will list without prompting.
loginsh	Set by the shell if it is a login shell.
logout	Set by the shell to normal before a normal logout, automatic before an automatic logout, and hangup if the shell was killed by a hangup signal (typically generated by kill -HUP, or by a terminal connection being interrupted rather than cleanly exited).
mail	The name of the files or directories to check for incoming mail. See both the tcsh and mail man pages for more information on the behaviors controlled by this variable.
matchbeep	Controls whether and when command-line completion rings the bell. Setting it to never prevents all beeps. nomatch beeps when there is no current match. ambiguous beeps when there are multiple matches. notunique beeps when there is an exact match, as well as other longer matches. If unset, the behavior is the same as ambiguous.
nobeep	If set, beeping is completely disabled.
noclobber	If set, the shell attempts to prevent output redirection from overwriting existing files. See the tcsh man page for more details.
noglob	If set, filename substitution and directory substitution are inhibited. Normally used only as a performance enhancement for shell scripts where filenames are already known.
nokanji	If set, disables kanji support so that the meta key is used.
nonomatch	If set, a filename or directory substitution that doesn't match any files does not cause an error.
nostat	A list of directories, or patterns that match directories, that should not be examined for matches during completion attempts.
notify	If set, announces job completions immediately rather than waiting until just before the next command prompt appears.
owd	The previous working directory.
path	A list of directories in which to look for executable commands. The path shell variable is set at startup from the PATH environment variable.
printexitvalue	If set and a program exits with a non-zero status, prints the status.
prompt	The string that is printed as the prompt for command-line input. This can contain both literal strings for display as well as a number of special patterns indicating the substitution of everything from the current directory to the username. See the tcsh man page for the (rather extensive) list of options available.
prompt2	The string to use for the inner prompt in while and foreach loops. The same format sequences as used in the prompt variable may be used in prompt2.
prompt3	The string to use for prompting regarding automatic spelling corrections. The same format sequences as used in the prompt variable may be used in prompt2.

TABLE 18.4 Continued

Shell Variable	Effects
promptchars	If set, specifies a pair of characters to substitute between for a shell prompt when a normal user and when su-ed to the super user.
pushdtohome	If set, pushd without any arguments is equivalent to pushd ~.
pushdsilent	If set, pushd and popd don't print the directory stack.
recexact	If set, completion is finished with an exact match even if a longer one is available.
recognize_only_executables	If set, command listings display only files in the path that are executable.
rmstar	If set, the user is prompted before rm * is allowed to execute.
rprompt	The string to print on the right side of the screen when the prompt is displayed on the left. This prompt accepts the same formatting controls as the prompt variable. In my opinion, this is a bizarre shell capability.
savedires	If set, the shell does a dirs -S before exiting.
savehist	If set, the shell does a history -S before exiting.
sched	The format in which the sched built-in prints scheduled events. The string format is the same as that for prompt.
shell	The file in which the executable shell resides.
shlvl	The nested depth of the current shell beneath the login shell for this session.
status	The status returned by the last command to exit.
symlinks	Can be set to several different values to control the resolution of symbolic links. See the tcsh man page for more details.
tcsh	The version number of the tcsh shell.
term	The terminal type currently being used to work in the shell.
time	If set to a number, executes the time built-in after any command that takes longer than that number of seconds. Can also control the format of the output of the time commands so executed. See the tcsh man page for further information.
tperiod	The period, in minutes, between executions of the tcsh special alias, periodic.
tty	The name of the tty for the current terminal, or empty if the current shell is not attached to a terminal.
uid	The user's real numeric user ID.
user	The user's login name.
verbose	If set, causes the words of each command to be printed after any history substitution. Can be set on startup by executing the shell with the -v command.
version	The shell's version ID stamp, as well as a considerable amount of information regarding compile-time options that were specified when the shell was compiled. See the tcsh man page for more information on interpreting the output.
visiblebell	If set, flashes the screen instead of using an audible terminal bell.
watch	A list of user/terminal pairs to watch for logins and logouts.
who	The format string for watch messages. See the tcsh man page for specific format information.
wordchars	A list of nonalphanumeric characters to be considered part of a word by the command-line editor.

The use of bash and tcsh reserved environment variables is similar in each shell: values that the shells set may be read and used in commands, and the values that the user can specify may be set to control certain aspects of the operation of the shell. For example, in tcsh, we like to customize our command-line prompt using the prompt variable:

```
# pwd
/Users/ray/Documents
# set prompt="$HOST $cwd:t \! >"
brezup Documents 151 >
```

In bash, we use the PS1 variable:

```
bash-2.05b$ pwd
/Users/ray/Pictures
bash-2.05b$ PS1='\h:\u \W \! \$ '
brezup:ray Pictures 440 $
```

Some of the options that are controllable in the shells are incredibly specific and provide considerable power only to a subset of users who need their unique functionality. Others, such as the tcsh's visiblebell setting or bash's MAILCHECK variable, allow every user to exert a considerable amount of control and apply significant customizations to their command-line environments.

On the other hand, reserved variables that are automatically set by the shell provide values for you to feed into custom tools and commands that you construct at the command line. The availability of variables such as tcsh's $cwd and bash's $PWD are instrumental in automating repetitive tasks in your environment.

Alternate Variable Addressing Methods

Both bash and tcsh shell and environment variables can also be addressed in a number of ways other than with the simple $<*variablename*> method used to return the contents of the variable. These alternate addressing methods can provide a range of information about the variable, allowing you to access everything from its contents to a count of the number of characters that it contains. Table 18.5 provides bash alternatives for accessing other information in the shell or other information regarding the variable, such as the number of words in the variable or whether the variable actually has a value. Table 18.6 provides the analogous information for tcsh.

TABLE 18.5 Alternative Variable Addressing Methods for bash

Addressing a Variable As	Returns
$name	The value of the variable.
${name}	If the variable contains multiple words, each is separated by a blank. The braces insulate name from characters following it, causing ${zz}ygy to be distinct from $zzygy.

18

TABLE 18.5 Continued

Addressing a Variable As	Returns
`${name[selector]}`	Treats name as an array of words and returns only the selected element from the list of words.
`$0`	Substitutes the name of the shell or of the file from which command input is being read (used in shell scripts).
`$number` `${number}`	Expands to the `number`th argument on the commandline when the shell was invoked.
`$*`	Expands to the complete list of arguments passed to the shell/shell script, starting with argument `1`. If `IFS` is set, and the expansion occurs within double quotes (that is, `"$*"`), the arguments are separated by the first character of the value of the `IFS` variable.
`$@`	Expands to the complete list of arguments passed to the shell/shell script, starting with argument `1`. If the expansion occurs within double quotes, each command-line argument is output as a separate word, separated by spaces.
`$#`	Expands to the number of parameters supplied on the command line.
`$?`	Expands to the status of the most recent foreground command/pipeline.
`$~`	Expands to the current option flags, including both those set at shell invocation and those set by the `set builtin` command.
`$$`	Expands to the process ID of the running shell. In a subshell executed as part of a command by use of parenthesis on the command line, it expands to the process ID of the parent shell, not the subshell.
`$!`	Expands to the process ID of the most recently executed background job started by this shell.
`${#name}`	Expands to the length, in characters of the value of `name`.
`${#@}` `${#*}`	Expands to the number of command-line parameters passed to the shell.
`${#name[*]}` `${#name[@]}`	Expands to the number of elements in the array `name`. Note that this is not necessarily equal to the maximum array subscript, but instead counts only populated array positions.
`${name:-word}`	Expands to the value of `name` if `name` is set; otherwise expands to `word`.
`${name:-$name2}`	Expands to the value of `name` if `name` is set; otherwise expands to the value of `name2`.
`${name:=word}`	Expands to the value of `name` if `name` is set; otherwise sets `name=word` and expands to `word`.
`${name:?word}`	Expands to the value of `name` if `name` is set; otherwise writes `word` to `STDERR`. Causes non-interactive shells to exit if an error is generated.
`${name:+word}`	Expands to the value of `word` if `name` is set; otherwise expands to nothing.
`${name:offset:len}`	Expands to a substring of the value of `name`, starting from position `offset` and extending for `len` characters. If name is `@`, expands to `len` values from the command line parameters, starting with the `offset`th parameter.
`${name:offset}`	Expands to a substring of the value of `name`, starting from position `offset` and extending to the end of the value.

TABLE 18.6 Alternative Variable Addressing Methods for `tcsh`

Addressing a Variable As	Returns
`$name`	The value of the variable.
`${name}`	If the variable contains multiple words, each is separated by a blank. The braces insulate name from characters following it, causing `${zz}ygy` to be distinct from `$zzygy`.
`$name[selector]` `${name[selector]}`	Treats name as an array of words and returns only the selected element from the list of words.
`$0`	Substitutes the name of the file from which command input is being read (used in shell scripts).
`$number` `${number}`	Equivalent to `$argv[number]`. Remember that `argv` is a variable containing an array of command-line arguments passed to the shell.
`$*`	Equivalent to the `$argv` array.
`$?name` `${?name}`	Substitutes `1` if variable `name` is set; `0` if it is not (that is, true or false, depending on whether the variable exists).
`$?0`	Substitutes `1` if the name of the program running the shell is known. This is specifically applicable to shell scripts and is always `0` for interactive shells.
`$#name` `${#name}`	Substitutes the number of words in `name`.
`$#`	Equivalent to `$#argv`.
`$%name` `${%name}`	Substitutes the number of characters in `name`. `$?` Expands to the status of the most recent foreground command/pipeline. Equivalent to the `$status` variable.
`$$`	Substitutes the process number of the parent shell.
`$!`	Substitutes the process number of the most recent background process started by the shell.
`$<`	Substitutes a line from `STDIN`. This can be used to read input from the keyboard into a shell script.

Variable Substitution Modifiers

Along with the capability to set variables to specific values and to manipulate variable values by the use of external programs, the shell also contains some capability to modify variables internally as well. This capability is mainly targeted to modification of command, filename, and path-like contents in variables. For example, this allows you to parse the extension part of a filename off a file with a name such as `myfile.jpg`—keeping either the extension, `jpg`, or the main name, `myfile`.

In `tcsh` these manipulations are an independent mechanism layered on top of the assorted variable addressing methods and effected by appending to the variable one or more sets of a colon followed by a modifier string.

In `bash` these manipulations are handled by a set of substitution methods that are part of the variable addressing and expansion syntax. The `tcsh` way of doing it is much less powerful than the bash way, but it's also far more readable and easier to remember for the sorts of manipulations that you'd do at the command line or in simple shell scripts. This is one of the areas of difference in which tcsh fans typically feel that bash is a highly unfriendly user environment.

Because the tcsh syntax is easier to follow, we'll cover it first this time around. Table 18.7 shows the tcsh variable substitution modifiers and their effects. Table 18.8 shows bash equivalents where available and some of the syntax of bash's more general substitution methods.

TIP

If the contents of these tables look intimidating, read ahead to the examples, and then come back here to see more specifically what was done. These are really quite powerful capabilities of the shell and ones that you won't want to be without. They're also not nearly as confusing to use as they are to explain!

TABLE 18.7 Shell and Environment Variable Substitution :<modifier> Options

Modifier String	Effect
h	Removes a trailing pathname component, leaving the head.
t	Removes all leading path components, leaving only the trailing file component.
r	Removes a filename extension .xxx, leaving the head portion of the filename before this.
e	Removes everything from a filename except for the extension.
u	Changes the case of the first lowercase letter to uppercase.
l	Changes the case of the first uppercase letter to lowercase.
s/l/r/	Substitutes l for r. l can be any simple string, as can r.
g	Applies the next modifier to each word, rather than just to the first occurrence.
a	Applies the next modifier as many times as possible to a single word. Beware of creating modification loops with this option.

TABLE 18.8 bash Shell and Environment Variable Substitution :<modifier> Options

Modifier String	Effect
${name%/*}	Removes a trailing pathname component from name, leaving the head. This is equivalent to tcsh's <variable>:h.
${name##*/}	Removes all leading path components from name, leaving only the trailing file component. This is equivalent to tcsh's <variable>:t.
${name%.+([!/])}	Removes a filename extension such as .xxx from name, leaving the head portion of the filename that occurs before this. This is equivalent to tcsh's <variable>:r.

TABLE 18.8 Continued

Modifier String	Effect
${name##*.}	Removes everything from filename name except for the extension. This works, unless the filename has no extension, but was specified in a path format in which one or more directories have extensions (periods in their names). In this case, it will return the portion of the path after the right-most period in the full pathname. This is almost equivalent (with the exception of where it doesn't work) to tcsh's <variable>:e.
${name%pattern}	Expands to the value of name, with the shortest match to pattern removed from the right hand side. This substituion is how the head-of-a-path operator at the beginning of this table is constructed.
${name[@]%pattern}	Expands to a list of all values of the array name, with the shortest match to pattern removed from the right hand side of each.
${name%%pattern}	Expands to the value of name, with the longest match to pattern removed from the right hand side.
${name[@]%%pattern}	Expands to a list of all values of the array name, with the longest match to pattern removed from the right hand side of each.
${name#pattern}	Expands to the value of name, with the shortest match to pattern removed from the left hand side.
${name[@]#pattern}	Expands to a list of all values of the array name, with the shortest match to pattern removed from the left hand side of each.
${name##pattern}	Expands to the value of name, with the longest match to pattern removed from the left hand side.
${name[@]##pattern}	Expands to a list of all values of the array name, with the longest match to pattern removed from the left hand side of each.
${name/pat/repl}	Expands to the value of name, with the first occurrence of pat replaced by repl. If repl is ommitted, pat is replaced by nothingness, deleting the first occurrence of it from the value.
${name[@]/pat/repl}	Expands to a list of all values of the array name, with the first occurrence of pat replaced by repl in each.
${name//pat/repl}	Expands to the value of name, with all occurrences of pat replaced by repl.
${name[@]//pat/repl}	Expands to a list of all values of the array name, with all occurrences of pat replaced by repl in each.

NOTE

Some bash pattern matching expressions are disabled by default. For example the "remove a trailing file extension" syntax shown in Table 18.8 won't work in bash's default configuration because it uses a repeated character class pattern option. (A complete treatment of regular expressions is beyond the scope of this book—the bash man page provides some information, but a much better reference is *Mastering Regular Expressions* from O'Reilly Publishing.) To enable extended pattern options, you need to tell bash to turn on the extglob shell flag-variable by using the command shopt -s extglob.

A number of additional behaviors can be configured in bash using the shopt command, but these move into the realm of so bash specific that they're best left for a book specifically on bash. bash users might wonder why these aren't controlled by variables in the shell, as are many other shell behaviors and capabilities. We wonder this too.

As a simple example in tcsh, if the variable x contains /home/ray/testfile.jpg, we can extract and act upon several different parts of this variable by using the modifiers shown in Table 18.7.

```
brezup Documents ray 152> set x=/home/ray/testfile.jpg
brezup Documents ray 153> echo $x
/home/ray/testfile.jpg
brezup Documents ray 154> echo $x:h
/home/ray
brezup Documents ray 155> echo $x:t
testfile.jpg
brezup Documents ray 156> echo $x:r
/home/ray/testfile
brezup Documents ray 157> echo $x:e
jpg
brezup Documents ray 158> echo $x:u
/Home/ray/testfile.jpg
brezup Documents ray 159> echo $x:s/test/special/
/home/ray/specialfile.jpg
brezup Documents ray 171> set y=( /home/ray/testfile.jpg /home/ray/filetest.jpg )
brezup Documents ray 172> echo $y
/home/ray/testfile.jpg /home/ray/filetest.jpg
brezup Documents ray 173> echo $y:u
/Home/ray/testfile.jpg /home/ray/filetest.jpg
brezup Documents ray 174> echo $y:gu
/Home/ray/testfile.jpg /Home/ray/filetest.jpg
brezup Documents ray 175> echo $y:au
/HOME/RAY/TESTFILE.JPG /home/ray/filetest.jpg
```

In bash, the analogous commands look like this:

```
brezup:ray ray 499 $ x=/home/ray/testfile.jpg
brezup:ray ray 500 $ echo $x
/home/ray/testfile.jpg
brezup:ray ray 501 $ echo ${x%/*}
/home/ray
brezup:ray ray 502 $ echo ${x##*/}
testfile.jpg
brezup:ray ray 503 $ echo ${x%.+([!/])}
```

```
/home/ray/testfile.jpg
brezup:ray ray 504 $ shopt -s extglob
brezup:ray ray 505 $ echo ${x%.+([!/])}
/home/ray/testfile
brezup:ray ray 506 $ echo ${x##*.}
jpg
brezup:ray ray 507 $ echo ${x/test/special}
/home/ray/specialfile.jpg
brezup:ray ray 508 $ y=([0]="/home/ray/testfile.jpg"
➥[1]="/home/ray/filetest.jpg")
brezup:ray ray 509 $ echo ${y/test/special}
/home/ray/specialfile.jpg
brezup:ray ray 510 $ echo ${y[0]/test/special}
/home/ray/specialfile.jpg
brezup:ray ray 511 $ echo ${y[@]/test/special}
/home/ray/specialfile.jpg /home/ray/filespecial.jpg
```

bash doesn't include options analogous to tcsh's capitalization controls as built-in functions. To perform maniupulations like changing the case of a value in bash, one would pass the value to an external program such as sed or awk and retrieve the processed value back into a shell variable.

NOTE

The four most important things to remember for working with variables in the shell are how to put values into variables, how to make the variables accessible to other shells and programs, the special treatment necessary to use a variable expression as an arithmetic expression, and how to get values back out of the variables you've set.

In bash, putting values in just uses the = sign, making them available to other programs uses the export command, treating them as math requires the let command, and getting values back out uses $, with a number of optional extra syntax bits on the expression.

In tcsh, these are matched by the set command, the setenv command, the @ expression prefix, and the $ prefix for accessing variables.

Nearly everything you will want to do with variables will involve permutations of these.

Command History Substitution

As briefly mentioned earlier, good user shells maintain a history of commands that you have executed at the command line. Although we've only mentioned selecting previous commands out of the history by use of the arrow keys up to this point, both bash and tcsh actually provide a number of options for the use of previous commands from the history in more sophisticated ways. Primary among these is the ability to select among the previous commands and substitute new information for previous information in the commands.

In `tcsh`, the modification strings for variables detailed earlier can be applied to commands in the history, and some additional history-specific modifiers can be used as well.

In `bash`, the modification expressions for variables don't work on commands in the history, but instead, a set of history-modification commands almost identical to the `tcsh` universal (variable and history) modification set is available for use on the command history.

The basic form of history substitution in both shells is simply the exclamation point, which indicates that a history substitution is to take place at that point in the command line. The characters following the exclamation point specify which item from the history is to be used and, optionally, what modifications need to be made to it. Table 18.9 lists the history item specifiers that can follow the exclamation point history substitution indicator.

TABLE 18.9 History Substitution Options for Both `bash` and `tcsh`

Item Following `!` Character	Meaning to the History Mechanism
n (*n* is a number)	Executes the item with that number out of the history list.
-*n* (*n* is a number preceded by a minus sign)	Executes the command *n* items before the current one.
# (the pound sign)	The current command. This allows recursion, so be careful! To indicate a modification of the current event, the # sign indicating the current command can be omitted if a substitution modifier is used also.
!	The previous command (equivalent to -1).
s (*s* is a character)	Executes the most recent command whose first word begins with *s*.
?*s*? (*s* is a string)	The most recent event that contains the string *s*.
Quick substitution (do not prepend the ! character)	
`^pattern^replacement^`	Reissues the most recent command, replacing the first occurrence of `pattern` in the command with `replacement`.

For example, a user's command history (listable by use of the `history` command) is shown in part here:

```
brezup:ray Documents 543 $ history ¦ tail -5
 539 ls -l
 540 cp file1.ps file1.ps.bak
 541 cp /usr/test/storage/file1.ps ./
 542 lpr file1.ps
 543 history ¦ tail -5
```

We could execute another `lpr file1.ps` simply by typing **`!l`** on a command line. Alternatively, `!?ora?` would execute the copy from `/usr/test/storage` by matching the string `ora` from `storage`. `!!` would re-execute the most recent command, which is `history` at command number 544, but will be whatever I issue as command 544 when I'm at the 545 prompt. `!-4` would execute the command `4` prior to the current command, which is currently the copy to `file1.ps.bak`, but this also changes as more commands are issued. `!540` reissues the `cp` to `file1.ps.bak`, but this resolution doesn't change over time, and `!540` will always produce that result in this instance of the shell. These are shown here:

```
brezup:ray Documents 544 $ !l
lpr file1.ps
brezup:ray Documents 545 $ !?ora?
cp /usr/test/storage/file1.ps ./
brezup:ray Documents 546 $ !!
cp /usr/test/storage/file1.ps ./
brezup:ray Documents 547 $ !-4
history ¦ tail -5
 543 history ¦ tail -5
 544 lpr file1.ps
 545 cp /usr/test/storage/file1.ps ./
 546 cp /usr/test/storage/file1.ps ./
 547 history ¦ tail -5
brezup:ray Documents 548 $ !540
cp file1.ps file1.ps.bak
```

These commands can be combined with substitution modifiers as detailed earlier to further reduce the amount of typing effort needed. In the history, `bash` doesn't use its variable substitution syntax, and instead uses the same `:<modifier>` syntax that `tcsh` does. See the `tcsh` variable substitution modifiers in Table 18.7 for history substitution modifiers that work in `bash`:

```
brezup:ray Documents 549 $ !?ora?:s/1/2/
cp /usr/test/storage/file2.ps ./
brezup:ray Documents 550 $ !540:gs/1/2
cp file2.ps file2.ps.bak
brezup:ray Documents 551 $ !540:r.newbak
cp file1.ps file1.ps.newbak
```

Table 18.10 shows some `history`-specific `:`*`<modifier>`* strings that can be applied to history substitutions.

TABLE 18.10 History-Specific :<modifier> Options Available in both bash and tcsh

Modifier String	Action
&	Repeat the previous substitution in this position.
p	Print out a history substitution with expanded substitutions, rather than execute the command.
q	Quote the value after this modification, preventing further modifications.
0	The leftmost argument of the command (typically, the command itself).
n	The *n*th argument of the command.
^	The first argument, equivalent to 1. The colon can be omitted from before this modifier.
$	The last argument. The colon can be omitted from before this modifier.
%	The word matched by an ?*s*? search. The colon can be omitted from before this modifier.
x-*y*	A range of arguments from the *x*th to the *y*th.
-*y*	Equivalent to 0-*y*. In tcsh the colon can be omitted from before this modifier.
*	Equivalent to ^-$, but returns nothing if the command is the only argument. The colon can be omitted from before this modifier.
x*	Equivalent to x-$.
x-	Equivalent to x*, but omits the last word $.

NOTE

These tables and examples cover only the most commonly used history and variable modification options. The bash and tcsh man pages alone would occupy more than 200 pages of this book, and they are tersely written, to say the least. Entire books have been written on using shells effectively, and if you're interested in making the absolute best use of the shell, we really recommend that you pick up one or a handful. Don't let the volume of options available overwhelm you, though. Most people who use Unix don't make use of even 10% of the options shown in the abbreviated discussion here, and are perfectly happy with their productivity at that level. Be aware that these options exist; they can make your life much easier if you find that you need them, but don't feel obliged to try to actually learn them until you do find a need.

Aliases and Shell Functions

The alias command is a simple tool that can help you customize your environment. It is the textual equivalent of the graphical Mac OS icon aliases (or Windows shortcuts) that you're probably already familiar with. It lets you specify a new name by which you can refer to an existing command. If you don't like typing history to list your command history, you can use the alias command to make typing h equivalent to typing history. We could have introduced this command much earlier in the discussion, but the information you have just learned about history and variable substitution makes the alias command much more powerful. The alias command has an almost trivial syntax: In bash it's `alias <newname>=<definition>`, and in `tcsh` it's `alias <newname> <definition>`. It accepts no command-line options and has no arguments or flags to control it. To alias `h` so that it calls `history` as described earlier, simply use `alias h='history'` (or in `tcsh`, `alias h 'history'`).

TIP

Single quotes aren't absolutely necessary here, but they are generally used around the thing you want to make an alias to, to prevent variable and history expansion in the alias. You generally want an alias to use variables as they'd expand at the current command-line prompt, rather than as they'd expand when you type the alias command.

The real power of being able to compress a collection of typing down into a single manageable command however is in what you can do to customize and automate your shell by making use of variable substitutions in those commands. In `tcsh` this ability is built into the `alias` command itself, while `bash` makes it available through a separate ability to define functions that behave like (very powerful, but strangely limited in their ability to deal with the command history) `tcsh` aliases. `bash` functions are defined much like aliases, but have the syntax `<funcname>() { <commands>; }` instead of the simpler `alias` syntax.

For example, there are a number of machines in another domain that I access on a regular basis. It's inconvenient to type `slogin oak.cis.ohio-state.edu`, `slogin shoe.cis.ohio-state.edu`, and so on whenever I need to access one of these machines. Using the trivial application of `alias`, I could change `slogin` so that I could type something shorter, such as `scis`. This would still leave me typing `scis oak.cis.ohio-state.edu`, and so on. Using power of substitution, however, this can be made much more useful.

In `bash` I can use the shell's capability to parse out command-line parameters into variables name `$<num>` to get at values that I put on the command line after calling a function.

```
brezup:ray ray 506 $ scis() { slogin $1.cis.ohio-state.edu; }
brezup:ray ray 507 $ scis oak
ray@oak.cis.ohio-state.edu's password:
brezup:ray ray 507 $ scis pear
ray@pear.cis.ohio-state.edu's password:
```

The first line of this example defines a function that causes `bash` to execute a little program for me whenever I type `scis`. The program's extremely short and consists only of the following; parsing off the first argument after the `scis` command; building a new expression that consists of `slogin`, followed by the value of the first argument, with "`.cis.ohio-state.edu`" appended to the end; and finally executing the command it has built.

In tcsh I can use similar facilities to get to command-line arguments, or I can also access the command history. This can get a bit more convoluted visually, but allows you more flexibility in generating useful aliases on-the-fly as you're working in the shell. bash's function paradigm is quite a bit more powerful, but requires significantly more forethought to use. For example, in tcsh, I can use the * modifier to the history, executed against the current command in the history (#), to pass the arguments given to my alias to another command of my choice. Specifically, I could use an alias such as `alias scis 'slogin \!#:*.cis.ohio-state.edu'`. tcsh supports using the command-line parameters as bash does, but this example should give you an idea of how the command history might be used in constructing useful aliases. In this case, it's using the `!#` history expansion, which expands to the entire current command line as typed so far, and the `:*` modifier that pares off the command-word portion and returns the rest of the arguments. The backslash before the history expansion prevents it from being expanded immediately at the prompt when I entered the alias command. Now, all I have to do is type `scis oak`, and the alias command expands the command to `slogin !#:*.cis.ohio-state.edu`. The history substitution then replaces the `!#:*` with the argument given to the command, which in this case is oak. The final command executed is `slogin oak.cis.ohio-state.edu`.

NOTE

Several comments in the tables on history substitution and modifiers relate to the `!#:*` expression suggested here. Most notably, if a modifier is acting on the current history event, the # can be omitted, and the : can be omitted before *. This history substitution specifier therefore abbreviates to `!*`, and the alias could therefore be written `alias scis 'slogin \!*.cis.ohio-state.edu'`.

Also, the `!*` substitution specifier substitutes the entire remainder of the command line from the current command. This is fine as long as I type `scis oak`, but if I type `scis oak apple pear`, the expansion is probably not going to be what I want. I could limit it to the first argument to the command with the ^ modifier, or the last argument with the $ modifier, instead of the * all arguments modifier I have used. It's a little bit sloppy, but I normally find it sufficient to just use the all modifier and to remember to issue commands within the restrictions that doing so imposes. For me, this is easier than remembering to use the proper modifier, but you're welcome to use whatever you find easiest.

NOTE

Nothing in the bash documentation suggests that history substitution isn't possible inside functions, but there doesn't seem to be a way to make it work. If you try to build a history-substituting function in bash, you'll find that it either substitutes the history at the moment of the function creation rather than at the point when you invoke it, or that it escapes the special characters that should cause history substitution and just prints them out instead of expanding them to the proper substitution. Maybe it's a bug, or maybe we just can't figure out the proper syntax.

Because bash undergoes frequent revisions, it's not unusual for portions of the behavior to change between releases. By the time you're reading this, bash might support history substitution inside functions as well.

To remove an alias, simply use the `unalias` command on the `<newname>` that you've created for your command. `bash` doesn't seem to have the facility to undefine functions that you've created.

Automating Tasks with Shell Scripts

With as many times as we've mentioned how powerful shell scripting can be and how much time and effort it can save you, you might be expecting that writing shell scripts is going to require dealing with some additional level of complexity on top of what you've already learned. Shell scripts are simple programs that you write in the language of the shell, and if you've made it this far in the book, you've been learning and working in the language of the shell for a few chapters now. If you consider this fact, and the notion that Unix, by design, attempts to abstract the notion of input and output so that everything looks the same to the OS, you might have a good guess at what we'll say next: That's right—you *already know* how to write shell scripts. There are a few more shell techniques that you can learn to enhance your ability to program the shell, but Unix itself doesn't care whether it's you typing at a command prompt or commands being read out of a file on disk. Everything you've typed so far in working with the shell could have been put in a file, and the computer could have typed it to itself—voilá, a shell script.

At its most trivial, a shell script can be exactly what you type at a prompt to accomplish some set of tasks. If you find that you have a need to repeatedly execute the same commands, you can type them once into a file, make that file executable, and forever after execute them all just by typing the name of the file.

It really is as simple as it sounds, but just in case it's not quite clear yet, an example should help. Consider the following situation: Let's say that every day when you log in to your computer, you like to check the time (with `date`), check to see who's online (using the `who` command), check to see how much space is left on the drive with your home directory (with `df`), and finally check who's most recently sent you mail (with `from`).

You could type each of these things to a command prompt when you log in to your machine, or you could put them in a file, make it executable, and let the file "type" them for you.

18

```
brezup:ray Documents 165 $ date
Mon Jun 18 23:35:55 EDT 2003
brezup:ray Documents 166 $ who
joray   ttyp0  Jun 14 18:22  (140.254.12.151)
ray    ttyp1  Jun 18 21:49  (24.95.74.211)
ray    ttyp2  Jun 15 10:00  (rodan.chi.ohio-s)
radman  ttyp3  Jun 18 23:33  (ac9d3e22.ipt.aol)
brezup:ray Documents 167 $ df .
Filesystem  512-blocks   Used  Avail Capacity Mounted on
/dev/disk0s11  12581856 12224784  357072  97%  /Volumes/Wills_Data
brezup:ray Documents 168 $ from | tail -10
```

```
From vanbrink@home.ffni.com Mon Jun 18 16:20:23 2003
From billp@abraxis.com Mon Jun 18 17:28:33 2003
From douglas_mille70@hotmail.com Mon Jun 18 18:34:28 2003
From owner-c-r-ffl@serge.shelfspace.com Mon Jun 18 19:23:42 2003
From owner-c-r-ffl@serge.shelfspace.com Mon Jun 18 20:42:53 2003
From owner-c-r-ffl@serge.shelfspace.com Mon Jun 18 21:24:00 2003
From buckshot@wcoil.com Mon Jun 18 22:02:15 2003
From jray@poisontooth.com Mon Jun 18 22:28:56 2003
From jray@poisontooth.com Mon Jun 18 23:15:28 2003
From owner-c-r-ffl@serge.shelfspace.com Mon Jun 18 23:34:43 2003

brezup:ray Documents 169 $ cat > imhere
#!/bin/bash
date
who
df .
from | tail -10
^D


brezup:ray Documents 170 $ chmod 755 imhere
brezup:ray Documents 171 $ ./imhere
Mon Jun 18 23:36:51 EDT 2003
joray  ttyp0  Jun 14 18:22  (140.254.12.151)
ray    ttyp1  Jun 18 21:49  (24.95.74.211)
ray    ttyp2  Jun 15 10:00  (rodan.chi.ohio-s)
Filesystem  512-blocks   Used   Avail Capacity Mounted on
/dev/disk0s11  12581856 12224784  357072   97%  /Volumes/Wills_Data
From billp@abraxis.com Mon Jun 18 17:28:33 2003
From douglas_mille70@hotmail.com Mon Jun 18 18:34:28 2003
From owner-c-r-ffl@serge.shelfspace.com Mon Jun 18 19:23:42 2003
From owner-c-r-ffl@serge.shelfspace.com Mon Jun 18 20:42:53 2003
From owner-c-r-ffl@serge.shelfspace.com Mon Jun 18 21:24:00 2003
From buckshot@wcoil.com Mon Jun 18 22:02:15 2003
From jray@poisontooth.com Mon Jun 18 22:28:56 2003
From jray@poisontooth.com Mon Jun 18 23:15:28 2003
From owner-c-r-ffl@serge.shelfspace.com Mon Jun 18 23:34:43 2003
From owner-c-r-ffl@serge.shelfspace.com Mon Jun 18 23:36:48 2003
```

As you can see, executing the file `imhere`, containing my commands, produces essentially the same output with much less typing. (The output has a few changes because one user has left the system, and new mail has arrived between the by-hand runs and the execution of the shell script.)

The only part of the `imhere` script that might be confusing is the first line, `#!/bin/bash`. The shell interprets the first line of a shell script in a special manner. If a pattern such as this is found, `#!`*`<path to an executable file>`*, the executable file named in that line is used as the shell for executing the contents of the script.

NOTE

The C shell, `csh`, and the Bourne shell, `sh`, are probably the best shells for you to write shell scripts in if you think you might be trying to use those scripts on other machines or giving them to other people. Some shells offer somewhat more power in their scripting capability, but `csh` and `sh` are the only shells that can be considered ubiquitous. This might not be a concern if you never intend your scripts to run anywhere but on your own personal machine. But if you think you might ever use another machine, or are interested in distributing your scripts to other people, you can't rely on any specialty shells being available.

In the world of real programmers and writers of fancy shell scripts, we'd be considered heretical for including `csh` (or `tcsh`) as a potential shell you might want to script in. The Bourne shell is the shell of choice for tasks that truly must be able to be run anywhere, but it's not a particularly friendly shell language to live in for day to day shell use. Some might say it's downright ugly. Since Apple's changed the default user shell to `bash`, many users will want to use it for scripting anyway. If you have the patience to use its complicated variable substitution syntax and function definitions for your work, you'll definitely have quite powerful scripting capabilities at your disposal. If on the other hand you prefer `tcsh`'s less powerful, but considerably more user-friendly style, you're not alone. Some long-time Unix users are starting to call `bash` the least-standard shell because of the changes in behavior that occur between versions.

In the end, it all boils down to user preference—don't let anyone tell you that you shouldn't use `bash` because it's too complicated or that you shouldn't use `tcsh` because it isn't complicated enough. If it works for you, and you're comfortable with it, use it.

TIP

In many scripting languages—`tcsh`/`csh`/`bash` shell scripting being no exception—anywhere a `#` appears indicates that the rest of the line is a comment. A `#!` on the first line of a file being executed by the shell is a special comment to the system, indicating which program is the intended interpreter for the script contained in the file.

Single-Line Automation: Combining Commands on the Command Line

Before we go too far with the notion of storing collections of commands in files, however, let's look at what can be done at just the command-line level. You already know about using pipes and variables. These concepts can be combined to produce very powerful expressions directly at the command line, without any need to store the collection of commands in a file.

Consider for a moment the netpbm collection of graphics manipulation programs that was installed in Chapter 17, "Troubleshooting Software Installations, and Compiling and Debugging Manually." Included in the capabilities of the suite are a number of conversions among various file formats, as well as a range of manipulations of the image content itself. With Mac OS, if you want to convert a GIF file into a PICT file, and convert it to four-color grayscale along the way, you have a number of options. You could fire up PhotoShop or GraphicConverter, perform the changes there, and save the file. Alternatively, you could program a conversion filter in DeBabelizer to perform this manipulation for you. With netpbm, you can perform the manipulation from the command line:

NOTE

In the following examples, we're going to use tcsh syntax in the running text because it's much easier to read, and considerably easier to translate from, into the bash version than it is to go the other direction. bash equivalents of the code only will be called out in notes.

```
brezup Documents 277> ppmtogif < sage.ppm > sage.gif
ppmtogif: computing colormap...
ppmtogif: 192 colors found
brezup Documents 278> giftopnm < sage.gif > sage.pnm
brezup Documents 279> ppmtopgm < sage.pnm > sage.pgm
brezup Documents 280> ppmquant 4 < sage.pgm > sage.pgm2
ppmquant: making histogram...
ppmquant: 120 colors found
ppmquant: choosing 4 colors...
ppmquant: mapping image to new colors...
brezup Documents 281> ppmtopict < sage.pgm2 > sage.pict
ppmtopict: computing colormap...
ppmtopict: 4 colors found
```

Figure 18.1 shows a comparison of the original image sage.gif, and the four-color grayscale image, sage.pict.

NOTE

The netpbm suite provides most of its manipulation facilities on an internal format, variably named .ppm, .pgm, or .pnm. It provides a number of filters that can read data into this format, a number of filters that can act upon and modify the contents of files in this format, and a number of filters that can output into other file formats. Together, these facilities enable a wide range of image formats to be read, manipulated, and written. Additionally, the file format is well documented and simple for a programmer to write code to parse. This makes it easy for a programmer to write her own filters to perform any manipulations that the provided software cannot. See the netpbm man pages, if you've installed this suite, for considerably more information on the use of netpbm.

FIGURE 18.1 A comparison of an original file and the result of processing it through one of a number of different `netpbm` filters.

From the brief discussion at the beginning of this section, you should already have an idea of how you could combine all that into a single file, if for some reason you wanted to perform that conversion to the `sage.gif` file over and over and over.

This does not seem to be a very useful thing to automate, and takes quite a bit of typing to boot (although, frankly, not nearly as much work as starting up Photoshop to do something this simple). Let's see what we can do with pipes and shell variables though to cut down on the amount of typing.

First, observe that all the programs are taking the input files on `STDIN` and are producing output on `STDOUT`. Unix command-line programs are frequently like this, and it's a very good thing. Using the power of pipes to connect one program's `STDOUT` to another program's `STDIN`, we can shorten that collection of commands to a single command line:


```
brezup Documents 287> giftopnm < sage.gif | ppmtopgm | ppmquant 4 |
➥ ppmtopict > sage.pict
ppmquant: making histogram...
ppmquant: 120 colors found
ppmquant: choosing 4 colors...
ppmquant: mapping image to new colors...
ppmtopict: computing colormap...
ppmtopict: 4 colors found
```

I'll let you verify that the output is graphically identical on a file of your own.

You might think that it's probably not very likely that you'll want to perform this single manipulation repeatedly to the same image. However, there are many times when you'd like to be able to perform a collection of manipulations like that on a number of different images. With what you know about shell variables, you might be able to come up with a way to abstract that command line so that it could be reused for any GIF file. You might try something like this:

```
brezup Documents 288> set infile=sage.gif
brezup Documents 289> giftopnm < $infile ¦ ppmtopgm ¦ ppmquant 4 ¦
➥ ppmtopict > $infile:r.pict
ppmquant: making histogram...
ppmquant: 120 colors found
ppmquant: choosing 4 colors...
ppmquant: mapping image to new colors...
ppmtopict: computing colormap...
ppmtopict: 4 colors found
```

NOTE

Note how I used the `:r` modifier to the shell variable `$infile` to remove the `.gif` suffix and added text after it to replace it with my new `.pict` suffix.

NOTE

In bash, this looks like

```
shopt -s extglob
infile=sage.gif
giftopnm < $infile ¦ ppmtopgm ¦ ppmquant 4 ¦
➥ ppmtopict > ${infile%.+([!/])}.pict
```

Now, you could simply use new values for `$infile`, and you'd have a reusable command that could perform the same manipulation on any GIF image.

It's still too much work though, right? Well, remember aliases? We can further automate things by using an `alias` command to compact that large command-line expression into something more manageable.

```
brezup Documents 290> alias greyconvert 'set infile=\!#:* ; giftopnm < $infile ¦
➥ppmtopgm ¦ ppmquant 4 ¦ ppmtopict > $infile:r.pict '
brezup Documents 291> greyconvert sage.gif

ppmquant: making histogram...
ppmquant: 120 colors found
ppmquant: choosing 4 colors...
ppmquant: mapping image to new colors...
ppmtopict: computing colormap...
ppmtopict: 4 colors found
```

NOTE

Notice how I've used the history substitution `\!#:*` to get the arguments passed into the alias, and then put those arguments (although I only expect one, a filename) into `$infile`?

NOTE

In `bash` we can't do variable expansion in aliases. We also can't do history substitution in functions. To accomplish the `tcsh` equivalent, we've got to define a function for `greyconvert` and use the command-line parameters to capture the file to be converted:

```
shopt -s extglob
greyconvert() { infile=$1; giftopnm < $infile ¦ ppmtopgm ¦ ppmquant 4 ¦
➥ ppmtopict > ${infile%.+([!/])}.pict; }
greyconvert sage.gif
```

That command is getting pretty long, isn't it? The good news is that for almost any task in Unix, you can figure out how to build up to an expression like this, just as shown here. Start by figuring out how to do it one step at a time on the command line, and work your way up to an elegant solution that solves the problem for you with as little repetitive work as necessary.

After you've invented useful aliases or functions such as this one for yourself, remember to store them in your `.cshrc`, `.tcshrc`, or `.bashrc` file in your home directory so that you can use them again whenever you log in to your computer.

Multi-Line Automation: Looping at the Prompt

Creating customized commands that perform special functions such as the `greyconvert` command built in the previous sections is useful, but it still doesn't address the need to automate tasks. For that, we need some sort of looping command, and `bash` and `tcsh` both offer two basic types of loops: the `for` loop and the `while` loop. Both commands repeat a block of shell commands. The first executes it "for each" of its arguments, and the second executes it "while" some condition is true.

Looping in `tcsh`

The `foreach` and `while` commands of the shell are unlike other shell commands that you've become familiar with in that they require additional information beyond the first command line. For example, the syntax for the `foreach` command in `tcsh` is

```
foreach <variablename> ( <item list> )
 <first command to execute>
 <second command to execute>
 .
 .
 .
```

```
 <nth command to execute>
end
```

The tcsh while command, on the other hand, has the syntax

```
while ( <comparison> )
 <first command to execute>
 <second command to execute>
 .
 .
 .
 <nth command to execute>
end
```

In the foreach command, the <*item list*> can be a space-separated list of items, a command that produces a space-separated (or return-separated) list of items, or a command-line wildcard that matches a list of files. As a demonstration, consider a situation in which we want to execute our previous greyconvert command on every GIF file in a directory containing many files. This can be accomplished in several ways by the use of the foreach command.

Looping in bash

The syntax for the for command in bash is

```
for <variablename> in <words> ; do
 <first command to execute> ;
 <second command to execute> ;
 .
 .
 .
 <nth command to execute> ;
done
```

The bash while command, on the other hand, has the syntax

```
while <commands> ; do
 <first conditional command to execute> ;
 <second conditional command to execute> ;
 .
 .
 .
 <nth conditional command to execute> ;
done
```

In the `for` command, `bash` steps throught the list of <words> and sets the value of <variablename> sequentially to each. After <variablename> is set to any given value from <words>, the list of commands is executed. Once the final value is extracted from <words> and the commands run the final time, the `for` loop terminates.

In the `while` command, `bash` executes `<commands>` (which can be a single word command, or a parenthesized, colon-separated list of commands). If the final command in `<commands>` returns a `true` (1) value, the `while` loop executes the conditional commands in the loop. This repeats until the final command in `<commands>` evaluates to `false` (`0`).

Using Looping Constructs at the Command Line

Using looping constructs at the command line is relatively powerful and allows you to execute a collection of commands many times, for many files (again, `tcsh` examples are somewhat clearer to read). The following example uses a wildcard to match all of the files of interest in the current directory, and then runs our `greyconvert` alias on each of them:

```
brezup amg 246> ls
AMG_cal-cover.gif      AhMyGoddess-v05.gif     AhMyGoddess-v10-f1.gif
AhMyGoddess-v01-f1.gif  AhMyGoddess-v06-f1.gif  AhMyGoddess-v10-i1.gif
AhMyGoddess-v01.gif     AhMyGoddess-v06.gif     AhMyGoddess-v10-i2.gif
AhMyGoddess-v02-f1.gif  AhMyGoddess-v07-f1.gif  AhMyGoddess-v10-i3.gif
AhMyGoddess-v02.gif     AhMyGoddess-v07.gif     AhMyGoddess-v10.gif
AhMyGoddess-v03-f1.gif  AhMyGoddess-v08-f1.gif  amg-nt0694_cover.gif
AhMyGoddess-v03.gif     AhMyGoddess-v08.gif     amg-nt0694_i1.gif
AhMyGoddess-v04-f1.gif  AhMyGoddess-v09-f1.gif  amg-nt0694_i2.gif
AhMyGoddess-v04.gif     AhMyGoddess-v09.gif
AhMyGoddess-v05-f1.gif  AhMyGoddess-v10-b.gif
brezup amg 247> foreach testfile ( *.gif )
foreach -> greyconvert $testfile
foreach -> end
ppmquant: making histogram...
ppmquant: 165 colors found
ppmquant: choosing 4 colors...
ppmquant: mapping image to new colors...
ppmtopict: computing colormap...
ppmtopict: 4 colors found
ppmquant: making histogram...
ppmquant: 159 colors found
.
.
.
ppmquant: making histogram...
ppmquant: 163 colors found
ppmquant: choosing 4 colors...
ppmquant: mapping image to new colors...
```

```
ppmtopict: computing colormap...
ppmtopict: 4 colors found
brezup amg 248> ls
AMG_cal-cover.gif     AhMyGoddess-v05-f1.pict  AhMyGoddess-v10-b.gif
AMG_cal-cover.pict    AhMyGoddess-v05.gif     AhMyGoddess-v10-b.pict
AhMyGoddess-v01-f1.gif  AhMyGoddess-v05.pict    AhMyGoddess-v10-f1.gif
AhMyGoddess-v01-f1.pict  AhMyGoddess-v06-f1.gif  AhMyGoddess-v10-f1.pict
AhMyGoddess-v01.gif     AhMyGoddess-v06-f1.pict  AhMyGoddess-v10-i1.gif
.
.
.
AhMyGoddess-v04-f1.gif  AhMyGoddess-v08.pict    amg-nt0694_i1.gif
AhMyGoddess-v04-f1.pict  AhMyGoddess-v09-f1.gif  amg-nt0694_i1.pict
AhMyGoddess-v04.gif     AhMyGoddess-v09-f1.pict  amg-nt0694_i2.gif
AhMyGoddess-v04.pict    AhMyGoddess-v09.gif     amg-nt0694_i2.pict
AhMyGoddess-v05-f1.gif  AhMyGoddess-v09.pict
```

In this example, the `foreach testfile ( *.gif )` line could have been replaced, with the following variants, with identical results:

```
foreach testfile ( `ls *.gif` )

foreach testfile ( AMG_cal-cover.gif AhMyGoddess-v01-f1.gif ..
➥ amg-nt0694_i2.gif )
```

NOTE

The second variant should be understood to contain a list of *all* GIF files in the directory, not just the three shown. The presence and direction of the single back quotes in the first line are also critical. Single back quotes around a command on the command line, if you remember, cause that command to be executed and its results substituted into the current command line in the place of the quoted command.

NOTE

In `bash`, the `for` command looks much the same:

```
for testfile in *.gif ; do
greyconvert $testfile
done
```

In `bash`, other equivalent expressions are

```
for testfile in `ls *.gif` ; do greyconvert $testfile; done

for testfile in AMG_cal-cover.gif AhMyGoddess-v01-f1.gif ..
➥ amg-nt0694_i2.gif ; do greyconvert $testfile ; done
```

The `while` command works similarly, executing its code block while some *<condition>* holds:

```
brezup Documents 249> set x = 10
brezup Documents 250> while ( $x > 0 )
while -> echo $x
while -> @ x = ( $x - 1 )
while -> end
10
9
8
7
6
5
4
3
2
1
brezup Documents 251> echo $x
0
```

NOTE

In `bash`, this would be written as follows:

```
x=10
while (( $x > 0 )) ; do
echo $x ;
let x=$x-1 ;
done
```

The double-parentheses are required around the comparison portion of the `while` statement to cause `$x > 0` to be evaluated arithmetically and a `true` or `false` value to be returned. One or more commands could also be embedded in the `while` condition as well —for example, the following `while` command produces identical results to the preceding code:

```
x=10;
while ( echo $x ; (( $x > 0 )) ) ; do let x=$x-1; done
```

This example obviously doesn't have much day-to-day applicability. Most `while` expressions that are actually useful do things like watch for particular events to occur, such as the existence of temporary files or disk space usage of more or less than some value. None of these is particularly easy to demonstrate in a text-only format such as a book, but we expect that you'll get the idea fairly quickly. Table 18.11 shows the conditional operators that can be used to construct the *<condition>* part of `while` loops and `if` conditional statements.

TABLE 18.11 Logical, Arithmetical, and Comparison Operators

<table>
<tr><th>Operator or Symbol</th><th>Function</th></tr>
<tr><td>||</td><td>Boolean OR arguments.</td></tr>
<tr><td>&&</td><td>Boolean AND arguments.</td></tr>
<tr><td>|</td><td>Bitwise Boolean OR.</td></tr>
<tr><td>^</td><td>Bitwise Exclusive OR.</td></tr>
<tr><td>&</td><td>Bitwise Boolean AND.</td></tr>
<tr><td>==</td><td>Equality comparison of arguments ($x == $y is true if the value in $x equals the value in $y).
Compares arguments as strings.</td></tr>
<tr><td>!=</td><td>Negated equality comparison of arguments ($x != $y is true if the value in $x is not equal to the value in $y).
Compares arguments as strings.</td></tr>
<tr><td>=~</td><td>tcsh-only: Pattern-matching equality comparison (matches shell wildcards).
Compares arguments as strings.</td></tr>
<tr><td>!~</td><td>tcsh-only: Pattern-matching negated equality comparison.
Compares arguments as strings.</td></tr>
<tr><td><=</td><td>Less than or equal to.</td></tr>
<tr><td>>=</td><td>Greater than or equal to.</td></tr>
<tr><td><</td><td>Less than.</td></tr>
<tr><td>></td><td>Greater than.</td></tr>
<tr><td><<</td><td>Bitwise shift left. To avoid the shell interpreting this as redirection, it must be in a parenthesized subexpression.
For example,
set y = 32;
@ x = ($y << 2)</td></tr>
<tr><td>>></td><td>Bitwise shift right. See preceding comment.</td></tr>
<tr><td>+</td><td>Adds arguments.</td></tr>
<tr><td>-</td><td>Subtracts arguments.</td></tr>
<tr><td>*</td><td>Multiplies arguments.</td></tr>
<tr><td>/</td><td>Divides arguments.</td></tr>
<tr><td>%</td><td>Modulus operator (divides and reports remainder).</td></tr>
<tr><td>!</td><td>Negates argument.</td></tr>
<tr><td>~</td><td>Ones complement (bitwise negation) of argument.</td></tr>
<tr><td>(</td><td>Opens parenthesized subexpression for higher-order evaluation.</td></tr>
<tr><td>)</td><td>Closes parenthesized subexpression for higher-order evaluation.</td></tr>
</table>

Another common use for the while command is to create infinite loops in the shell. This is a way to do things such as cause a shell command to execute over and over, potentially creating something like a "drop directory" that automatically processes files that are copied to it. For example, if we want to create a directory into which we could copy GIF files, and any files copied into it would have the greyconvert process run on it automatically, and then the GIF files would be deleted, we might try something like the following:

```
brezup Documents 252> while (1)
while -> foreach testfile (*.gif)
while -> greyconvert $testfile
while -> rm $testfile
while -> end
while -> sleep 60
while -> end
```

NOTE

The first four lines, with the while-> prompt, are actually part of the foreach command, but it doesn't display its prompt while the while-> prompt is active.

This while command attempts to loop perpetually (the value of 1 is true for the purposes of a comparison expression) and to internally execute our previous foreach loop to convert any files that match the *.gif pattern in the current directory. An rm command has been added to the foreach loop to remove the GIF file after it has been converted. The sleep 60 command after the foreach command's end causes the while loop to pause for 60 seconds before going on to its end statement and re-looping to the top of the while.

Unfortunately, from the command line, this does not quite work properly in all cases; when there are no files that match *.gif, the foreach line fails without creating its loop, and the end on line 4 is mistaken as intended to end the while loop.

NOTE

In bash, the equivalent while loop looks like this:

```
while (( 1 )) ; do
> for testfile in `ls *.gif` ; do
> greyconvert $testfile ;
> rm $testfile ;
> done
> sleep 60 ;
> done
```

bash doesn't suffer from the same problem creating the inner for loop that tcsh has with the foreach, so this actually turns into a useful piece of command-line code.

Thankfully, even in tcsh you can work around this problem by applying the final topic in our discussion of shell scripts.

Storing Your Automation in Files: Proper Scripts

With all the power available to you directly at the command line, the move to putting shell scripts in files should seem almost anticlimactic in its lack of complexity. As mentioned at the beginning of this chapter, anything that you can type on the command line, you can put in a file, and the system will quite happily execute it for you if you make the file executable. It really is that simple. There is really little more to say, except that putting your script in a file allows you to conveniently separate parts of the execution into separate shells, preventing conflicts such as those just demonstrated earlier with the `while` and `foreach` loops.

Any script that is put in a file and directly executed (rather than `source`d, in your current shell) creates its own shell in which to execute. To use this to make the previous example function properly, we can put the `foreach` section of the command into its own file:

```
brezup Documents 253> cat > greyconv.csh
#!/bin/csh
foreach testfile (*.gif)
greyconvert $testfile
rm $testfile
end
brezup Documents 254> chmod 755 greyconv.csh
brezup Documents 255> ls -l greyconv.csh
-rwxr-xr-x 1 ray staff 75 Jun 23 01:58 greyconv.csh
brezup Documents 256> cat greyconv.csh
#!/bin/csh
foreach testfile (*.gif)
greyconvert $testfile
rm $testfile
end
```

Then our perpetual `while` command can be run as

```
brezup Documents 257> while (1)
while -> ./greyconv.csh
while -> sleep 60
while -> end
```

NOTE

Of course, these examples as written require the previous definition of the `greyconvert` alias, or function. If you're using `bash`, you'll additionally need to `export greyconvert` for the function to be visible in the subshell created when you run the script.

There's nothing to prevent you from embedding the alias in a tcsh version of this script, or the function in the bash version if you don't feel like having it defined in your command-line environment. If you go with the idea of embedding the definition, you can make the script truly portable so that it can be given to other users and executed in other environments.

As a matter of fact, there's no reason to leave the while at the command line either—it might as well be embedded in the script too. In bash, this might look something like this:

```
#!/bin/bash

greyconvert() {
infile=$1;
giftopnm < $infile ¦ ppmtopgm ¦ ppmquant 4 ¦
➥ ppmtopict > ${infile%.+([!/])}.pict; }

while (( 1 )) ; do
for testfile in `ls *.gif` ; do
greyconvert $testfile ;
rm $testfile ;
done
sleep 60 ;
done
```

It's important to note that the $1 used inside the greyconvert function defined in this script refers to the first argument passed to the greyconvert function, not to the first argument passed to the script.

NOTE

Remember to chmod the script file so that it's executable. The shell won't let you run the script if it's not set to be executable.

This command will loop perpetually in the current directory, executing the greyconv.csh shell script every 60 seconds. Any file with a .gif extension that is placed in the directory will be passed through the greyconvert alias that we created earlier, and then the original file will be deleted. This will run perpetually in the directory, enabling any file dropped in to be converted (within 60 seconds) automatically. Because the end of the foreach is in a completely separate shell, it can't accidentally end the while, and everything will work as expected. Of course, if there were a reason to do this on a regular basis, you could put that while loop into its own shell script file. It could be stored and executed as a single command from the command line just like any other command.

NOTE

Particularly astute readers will observe that the script does not attempt to make sure that the entire GIF file actually exists in the directory before the script executes upon it. You might also expect that the behavior of the script could be rather unpredictable if the `greyconv.csh` script takes longer than a minute to execute. Shell scripts are generally an exercise in successive refinement to eliminate potential problems such as these, and these examples should be considered nothing more than the first step to a final application. You can get quite a bit of functionality out of simple scripts such as this. But if you're inclined to tackle the more complicated "correct" solutions, **we can't recommend strongly enough that you read the man pages and check out some books specifically on shell scripting**.

Shell Parameters and Conditional Execution in the Shell

Two final things to note now that we've introduced independent shells invoked as the result of placing scripts in files: the `$argv[1]...$argv[`*n*`]` list and the corresponding `$1...$`*n* command-line argument variables. (Refer to the table of shell variables and the table of alternative variable addressing methods for a refresher on these.) These parameters that can be passed into a shell script by placing values on the command line after the script name also allow us to introduce the `if` shell command, allowing conditional execution of code blocks.

If we'd like to make the `greyconv.csh` script somewhat more general, we can make use of the ability to pass arguments into the script. For example, it would be nice to be able to use `greyconv.csh` on the GIF files in a directory without actually having to be in the directory when we run the `while` loop. Simultaneously, we might like to have the ability to convert all the files in the current directory without needing to specify a directory name. There is no need to write two different scripts to do this. One script can do both by using conditional statements and checking to see if a parameter has been passed on the command line. If there is a shell parameter, it can be taken as the directory name in which to work, and if there are no shell parameters, the script can operate in the current working directory. The modified version of `greyconv.csh` is as follows:

```
#!/bin/csh

if ( $?1 == 1 ) then
cd $1
endif

foreach testfile (*.gif)
greyconvert $testfile
rm $testfile
end
```

This version of `greyconv.csh` demonstrates both an `if` conditional expression and the use of a command-line argument. The `if` statement checks whether the variable `$1` is set (using the `$?`*`<variablename>`* alternative variable addressing to check for existence). If it is set, the script assumes that the value in `$1` is the name of a directory, and it `cd`s into that directory before executing the `foreach` loop to convert and delete the GIF files. `greyconv.csh` can now be called with a directory, to operate in that directory, or without a directory specified, to operate in the current directory.

> **NOTE**
>
> In `bash`, we would write a `greyconv.sh` script instead. It might look something like this:
>
> ```
> #!/bin/bash
>
> greyconvert() {
> infile=$1;
> giftopnm < $infile ¦ ppmtopgm ¦ ppmquant 4 ¦
> ➥ ppmtopict > ${infile%.+([!/])}.pict; }
>
> if (( $# == 1 )) ; then
> cd $1
> fi
>
> while (( 1 )) ; do
> for testfile in `ls *.gif` ; do
> greyconvert $testfile ;
> rm $testfile ;
> done
> sleep 60 ;
> done
> ```
>
> Here, it's even more important to keep the use of `$1` straight in your head because the `$1` that means the first command-line argument passed to the command is used inside the `if` conditional to `cd` into the directory named in `$1` if it's provided. The `$1` that means the first argument passed to the `greyconvert` function is also used inside the function to assign the value of `infile`. The portions of the script in which each definition apply are called the scope of that definition. Functions get their own definition scope and redefine the positional parameter variables `$1..$n` as the values of their arguments *only inside the commands contained in the function itself.*

We hope that gives you a few ideas for how powerful shell scripts can be, and how you can use them to make your use of OS X much more productive. We've only just scratched the surface in this chapter, and have trivialized some explanations to their simplest case to avoid a chapter that takes half the book. What's here can get you quite a way into shell scripting, and many Unix users with years of experience don't use more than a fraction of what we've covered. Still, if you're looking for more power and more capabilities, don't hesitate to go to the man pages and shell programming–specific reference books.

Making Shell Scripts Start at Login or System Startup

Now that you know how to write shell scripts and run them as commands, making them start when you log in to your account, or making them start when the system starts, is straightforward.

You're already familiar with the Login preferences settings, and your ability to customize what programs start when you log in from it. An executable shell script is just another program as far as Unix is concerned, so you can configure scripts to start on login from there. If you're going to be working from the command line with any frequency, you might want to consider adding a single shell script to your login preferences and using that script to execute other scripts as necessary.

To add a shell script as an item that starts at system startup is also quite simple. Create a subdirectory for the script you want to run in the `/Library/StartupItems/` folder and place the script or a link to the script in the directory, giving it the same name as the directory. When the system starts, the script will execute. Remember that it's not going to have a terminal attached, so if it does things such as `echo` data, the data will have nowhere to appear. In Chapter 20, "Command-Line Configuration and Administration," we'll cover the contents of the `plist` (properties list) file that you can add to the directory with your script to customize some of its behavior.

Summary

This chapter rounded out the remainder of the general topics you need to know to productively use the Unix command-line shell. We described environment variables and shell variables—both those that affect the behavior of the shell directly and those that can be used in scripts. The chapter also expanded on the use of `STDIN` and `STDOUT`, as well as pipes on the command line. Finally, the use of loops, conditional expressions, and the storage of your command-line expressions in executable files gives you the ability to create powerful and completely customized solutions to problems that you encounter.

PART VI

Server/Network Administration

IN THIS PART

CHAPTER 19

X Window System Applications

IN THIS CHAPTER

- Introduction to the X Window System
- Installing the XFree86 OS X Distribution
- Using X11
- Configuring the X Window System
- Installing Some Additional Interesting X11 Software

In this chapter, we introduce the X Window System, Unix's favored graphical user interface (GUI). If we haven't convinced you that this Unix stuff is too confusing (and we hope we haven't!), you shouldn't be bothered by the fact that the X Window System is rather different from both the Mac OS GUI and the Mac OS X Aqua GUI, and that frequently it exists best as a completely separate graphical interface.

NOTE

We have a few too many Xs to go around. The X Window System, though, has had its X for two decades longer than Mac OS X, so we have to get used to the nomenclature. The X Window System is usually referred to as X#, where # is the major revision number. Alternatively, you may see X#R*n*, where # is the major revision, and *n* is the minor revision. As of this writing, X11R6 is the current version, but it is generally referred to as X11, or more simply, just X. X for the X Window System is pronounced as the letter X, not the number 10, as OS X is supposed to be said.

Both a bit of a boon and a bane to the new Mac OS X user, the X Window System will be an important, if somewhat confusing, feature of Mac OS X for some time to come. As the de facto standard for Unix GUI applications, you'll find that a considerable amount of software has been written to use the X Window System. Much of this software will probably be slow in being ported to the Aqua GUI interface, and some might not be ported at all. Because of this, if you want to make the most use of the available Unix software, it's necessary for you to install the software to enable you to use the X Window System and get to know a little about the way that the interface works.

In earlier versions of OS X, if you wanted to use X11, you needed to invest a bit of effort in installing it, or purchase a commercial product that installed it and integrated it with Aqua. With OS X 10.3, Apple has started providing its own version of X11. Actually, it's a modified version of an open source X11 product, and, as an actively developed open source application, it's a convenient example of how to use the final method of software installation that we'll cover in this book—using a "ports system," in this case Fink, to automatically install large collections of applications. Apple's X11 version can be installed as a custom installation option, and either it, or the version that Fink provides, is necessary to use applications written for X11. The new Apple installer, combined with using Fink to install applications, makes installation and use of X11 software a completely painless experience.

This chapter provides a basic introduction to X11, an explanation of how the X Window System interacts with the Mac OS X Aqua interface, and also an introduction to the Fink ports system.

Fink is a ports collection (collection of applications that have been tweaked to make them work, or work better, with OS X), package manager and auto-installer that the open source community has been constructing for Mac OS X. Fink also happens to be a great source of applications to run at the command line or under X11.

Introduction to the X Window System

In many ways, it's easier to explain how the X Window System is different from the interface that you're accustomed to than it is to explain how it's similar. Whether you're from a Mac or a PC background, you're certainly used to a graphical user interface, and both the X Window System and the interface to which you're accustomed display windows with program content and information in them. But beyond this, the X Window System is fundamentally a different interface than the GUI present on either of the popular desktop operating systems.

At the most obvious level, the X Window System is not a built-in part of the operating system. Whereas the Mac OS and Windows graphical user interfaces are intimately tied to the underlying OS, the X Window System is a completely separate system with no real attachment to the operating system underneath it. This separation makes for inefficiencies in the way the window system interacts with the OS and is the cause of certain performance issues that are of some annoyance. As you'll see, however, this separation between display and OS also provides a level of flexibility that cannot be readily accomplished with integrated systems.

Also different is the fact that the X Window System functions as a client/server system. Unlike OSes with integrated GUI functionality, programs that use the X Window System interface functionality don't actually display GUI elements. Instead they contact a completely separate program, the X server, and request that the server perform whatever display functions they require. This might seem like a bizarre and inefficient way of handling GUI element display, but it leads to the abstraction that's another major difference, and one of the sources of the extreme flexibility of the system.

The client/server model utilized for X Window System communication is a network-capable system. Messages requesting display functionality can be passed from client to server over a network connection. In fact, even connections from a client application running on the same machine as the display server are processed as though the client were speaking to the server over the network. A benefit of this model that isn't immediately obvious is that to a user sitting in front of a machine running the X Window System, it's completely transparent whether the programs being displayed on the machine are actually running on that machine or on some other machine. Other than possible delays due to delays in the network, the X Window System server responds identically to programs running on other machines as it does to programs running on its own.

Still not sure what this means to you? It means that you can display programs running on any machine anywhere (well, any machine running a Unix-like OS) on any other machine running an X Window System server. Applications running on remote systems aren't trapped in their own view of another system's desktop, but instead are full peers on the desktop right beside applications running on the same machine as the X server. This intermingling of clients displayed from local and remote hosts also isn't limited to just one remote host at a time, but instead any X11 program from any remote host can be displayed and interacted with simultaneously with all the other client programs being displayed by the server. This doesn't require some high-priced and proprietary commercial application or an experimental program and protocol; it uses well-established and open source software that has been under development by the online community for decades.

An additional difference between personal computer windowing systems and the X Window System is that the interface's look and feel are controlled by yet another separate program, rather than by the X Window System server or the OS itself. In the X Window System model, the X server is responsible for handling client display requests for displaying windows. Unless a client specifically draws things such as title bars for itself, X doesn't give them to it. The convention with the X Window System is that a separate program is run to create title bars and to manage user interactions such as moving windows around, iconizing and minimizing windows, and providing an application dock or other similar functionality.

The X11 software based on the XFree86 that Apple currently provides contains both a completely separate interface to the X11/Unix side of Mac OS X and also a mode to commingle applications running X11 with Mac OS X–native Aqua interface applications. This mixed mode will be the most comfortable for many Mac users because it provides almost seamless integration of X11 clients into the Aqua interface. It does, however, mildly break the normal X11 paradigm because the window management is handled by

Aqua and isn't as accessible to the X11 software as a normal X11 window manager would be. Still, for many uses, the convenience of having your X11 windows available in your normal Aqua interface is probably well worth the small loss of control that comes with tying X11 to Aqua.

Client/Server System

As mentioned briefly earlier, the heart of the X Window System is a server that provides display functionality to client applications. In a slight twist on the terminology that you're used to, the X Window System server is the application that runs on your local machine and physically draws data to your screen, and clients are the programs that run anywhere, including on remote machines. When you consider the functionality, this makes sense because a server provides a service: displaying data locally to you. Clients request the service, which is the display of data regardless of where the clients are. Figure 19.1 shows a typical X11 session with several programs displaying themselves on the X server. Among them are a number of `xterms`—applications similar to Terminal in functionality—as well as a text editor, an application dock, a game, and a mail application. The icons that appear as small computer terminals in the upper left are iconized applications; where the Mac OS uses windowshade title bars or minimizes things into the dock, the X Window System collapses applications into representative icons.

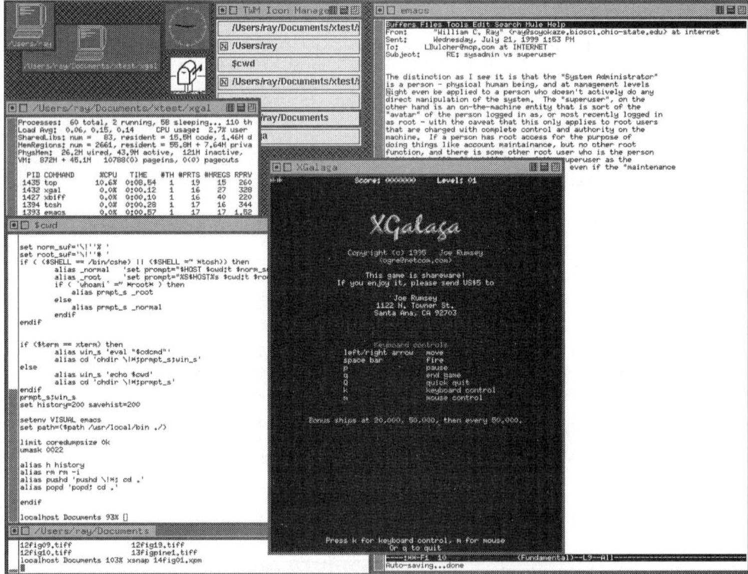

FIGURE 19.1 A typical X11 session with several programs running. The X Window System on a 1024×768 screen is a bit cramped but still usable.

Remote Application Display

Conveniently, this client/server model, like much of the software designed for Unix, is extremely abstract. Just as the input/output model abstracts the notion of where data comes from and goes to (to the point that it doesn't matter whether the data source is a program, user, or file), the X Window System client/server model doesn't care how the client and server are connected. This allows clients to connect to the server from any location and enables you to run software on remote machines and interact with its interface on your local machine.

In Figure 19.2, you again see the X Window System running on a machine. Other than the difference in a few running applications, there's little to distinguish it from Figure 19.1, which is exactly the point. In this screenshot, the Web browser, two of the Terminal windows (find the ones with host `soyokaze` in the command prompt), and the game are actually running on a machine on the other side of the city from the actual screen. Because the X11 client software creating these applications doesn't care what X11 server it's talking to, and the X11 server on my machine doesn't care whether the clients talking to it are running on the same machine, these applications function exactly as if they were running on my local machine instead of across the city. It wouldn't matter—outside possible slowdowns associated with network delays—whether the applications were running across the city or across the planet.

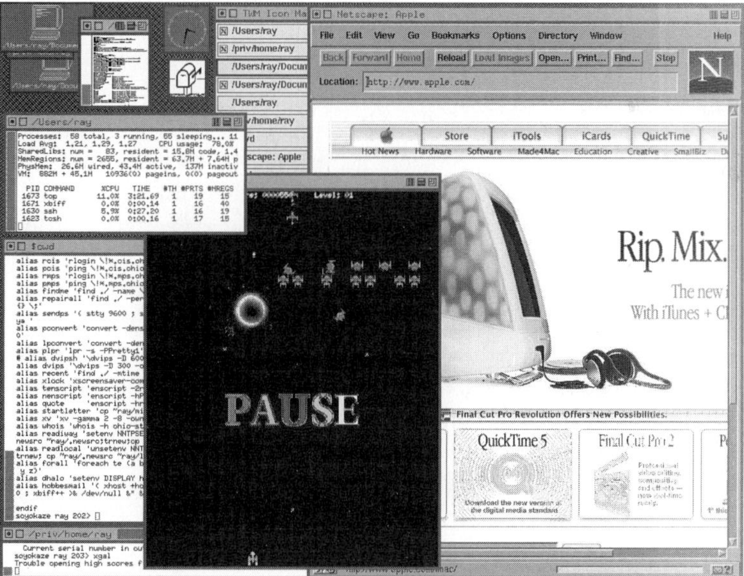

FIGURE 19.2 Another typical X11 session with several programs running. In this image, several of the windows actually belong to applications running on a remote machine.

The impact of this might not be obvious to you yet, but consider that with this capability, the following become possible:

- Have a document at home that you were supposed to edit and email to someone, but you forgot? Just connect to your home machine and fire up your editor with it displayed back to your local machine. Edit your document and send it on its way, all from your home machine, with the software displayed to wherever you are working. No need to transfer files, create multiple confusing versions, or work outside your favorite applications.
- Need to change something in a file and you don't have the software on the machine you're sitting at? No problem. Just connect over the network to a machine that has the software and use the software on it. No need to mount remote disks to run the application on your local machine. With X11 you get the ability to display the software's interface wherever you're sitting and run the software on the machine where it's stored.
- Stuck behind a firewall and can't get to eBay to submit a last-minute bid? Don't tell your boss about this, but using what you know about tunneling connections with `slogin` and a Web browser running on your home machine, you've got a recipe to browse from home, no matter where you're currently sitting.

Rooted Versus Nonrooted Displays

A quirk forced on the X Window System by attempts to get it to coexist with GUIs such as Aqua is the idea of rooted versus nonrooted displays. The X Window System has existed for years under the same impression that Mac OS has—that it's "the" windowing system running on any particular machine. As such, it includes the idea of a root window, much like the Mac OS desktop. The root window is assumed to be a full-screen window that exists behind all other windows in the system, and into which certain restricted types of information can be placed. To make the X Window System coexist with another windowing system that also wants to have a single whole-screen background window, only a few possible compromises can be made. To coexist, one of the systems has to give up its assumption of supremacy; one or the other could run entirely inside a window in the one that reigns supreme; or both could operate as usual, but display only one at a time, with the user toggling between them. If you've used `Timbuktu` or `VNC` before, you've used a system in which one display runs entirely inside a window on the other. There have been X11 implementations for Mac OS that have provided this option for X as well.

Displaying an entire windowing system rooted inside a window in another windowing system is a less than ideal solution. Outside the problem of not really integrating the functionality, and leaving the user with a poor workflow between applications in each of the environments, handling things such as mouse events destined for windows that are in the in-window system (as opposed to the window containing the system) is difficult.

Toggling back and forth between the systems has some advantages and some disadvantages. The confusion about the proper target for user events is eliminated, and each system can make full use of the hardware as it was intended to, but integration between the systems is even more difficult. The Apple/XFree86 X11 implementation provides one X Window System mode in which X11 exists as an entirely separate windowing system into which you can toggle. Figure 19.1 shows an X Window System session, and Figure 19.3 shows an Aqua session. These two are actually running on the same machine at the same time. The X Window System environment can be toggled to by clicking the X icon in the Aqua dock, and the Aqua environment can be toggled to by pressing Command-Option-A. Even when one of the environments isn't displayed, the applications in it keep on running. Although it's not convenient to interoperate between applications in one environment and applications running in the other, it's not a bad way to work, especially if you're mostly using Unix-side applications and not Aqua-native applications.

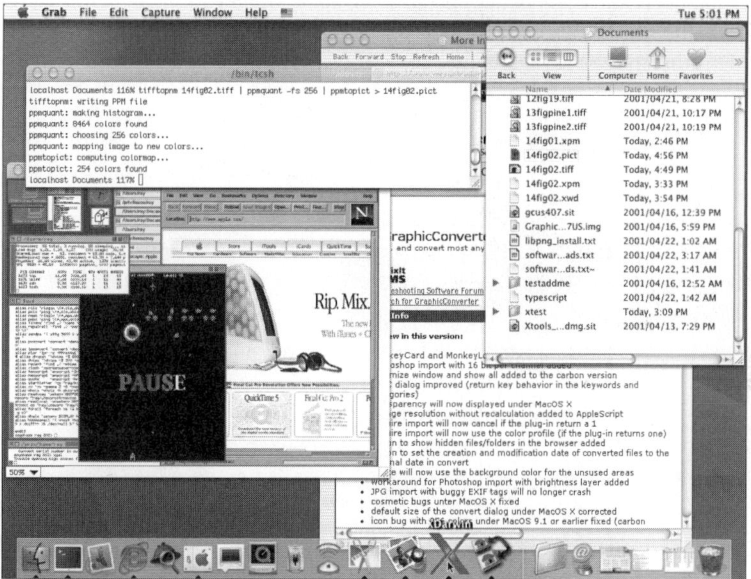

FIGURE 19.3 This Aqua session is running concurrently with the X11 session shown in Figure 19.1. The window containing what looks like an X11 session is the Preview application showing the screenshot for Figure 19.2.

The other available mode is a surprisingly successful implementation of nonrooted, or rootless, X11 environments. To produce such an environment, the X Window System model must be gutted of its notion of having a root window, and it isn't entirely clear how doing so might affect all possible X11 applications. However, it's clear that it works surprisingly well for at least most applications at this point. In addition, Apple's provided a way to wrap the X Window System applications with an Aqua interface manager, rather than a native X11 interface manager. Figure 19.4 shows an Aqua session with X11 applications running side by side with native Aqua applications. In fact, the Web browser in Figure 19.2 is running on a remote machine and is displaying happily integrated with Aqua applications on the local machine.

NOTE

It's not entirely clear what's been done with the root window in the rootless modes, or what the implications of the choice are for all X Window System applications. (For example, what happens to applications that display things in the root window?) The root window is an integral part of the X Window System philosophy, and it's a testimonial to both the creativity of the programmers and the power of Unix-like abstraction models that X11 still seems to work so well without it. There's a good chance that they've done something like implemented an X Window System server so that it displays the root window "somewhere else." *Somewhere else* is probably something like into an invisible and unused buffer in memory, and the programmers have fooled the applications into thinking that they're working in a normal X11 environment. We know it's geeky, but we think that the ability to do things like that with Unix applications is pretty cool.

FIGURE 19.4 X11 and Aqua applications can now coexist in the Aqua GUI, all managed by the Aqua user environment.

Installing the XFree86 OS X Distribution

The XFree86 distribution changes regularly, and the installation process for it is modified with almost the same regularity. Apple also now provides X11 as an optional install for OS X (under the Customize installation option) and an easy-installing distribution from the Mac OS X software Web site for updates. If you relish simplicity, you might want to work with Apple's distribution. Although we're saying that it's simple, we don't mean to demean it as lower performance, or less powerful. Apple's X11 is a full-featured X Window system, with some really nice tweaks thrown in by Apple to make it work and play better in the Aqua GUI environment. It provides all the functionality that the XFree86 version does, in better than 99.9% of all situations. The largest downside is that Apple's version of X11 has been so optimized to work with the Aqua GUI, that it's sometimes difficult to tear it away and get it to obey some traditional X11 configuration and setup rules.

If you're itching for the most recent features available, or you need an X11 that works identically (in terms of look and feel) to what you'll find on a traditional Unix or Linux box, you'll want to work with the distribution straight from XFree86. For the most current installation method, we suggest that you visit the SourceForge XonX site (go to `http://www.sourceforge.net` and search for `xonx`), read the documentation, and follow what SourceForge has to say. Alternatively, as of the most recent XonX project release, the XFree86 distribution itself has had Mac OS X/Darwin support rolled into it (but the XonX project might have more recent or experimental code available).

As of this writing, the XFree86 installation process involves downloading a number of files and running an installation script.

Plain Vanilla XFree86 Installation

The basic, straight-from-the-coding-projects-mouth XFree86 X Window System installation involves a number of steps, all fairly simple to accomplish:

1. Go to `http://www.xfree86.org/`.
2. Read the current release and installation notes, paying special attention to any specific OS X or Darwin information available. Go to the Support, Documentation and Resources page of the XFree86 site, and read the Current Release Documentation. Look for links to information on Mac OS X/Darwin.
3. Go to the Getting Started/Installation section of the documentation, and follow the directions for either installing by downloading and compiling the code or downloading the precompiled binaries.
4. Downloading the precompiled binaries involves following a link to an FTP server and downloading files as instructed by the documentation.
5. Execute the installation script as `root`.

After these are accomplished, XFree86 is ready to run, and you can run X11 applications on an X Window System server running in parallel with Aqua, or in rootless mode cooperating with Aqua.

TIP

If things are working the way they typically do, those instructions won't quite work, because someone will have updated the installer script or installer files so that they doen't match up properly, and something will complain that it can't be found or installed properly. Usually, fixing this is simply a matter of reading through the installation script in a text editor, observing where it's trying to install version 4.5 of a file, and you've downloaded 4.6, and making the appropriate changes by hand. By the time you're reading this, fixing the problem should not be difficult for you.

Installing `fink`

`fink` is a porting project and software package manager for Mac OS X. It's an open source community project intended to bring the wide wild world of Unix applications to Mac OS X at a level of difficulty that the average Macintosh user won't find frustrating or, hopefully, even annoying. Because this book is being written on the bleeding edge of the release of Mac OS X 10.3, `fink` itself hasn't been fully updated to work with 10.3 yet, and we'll have to show you how it works in 10.2 instead. Everything should be pretty much the same for 10.3, and hopefully will all be working smoothly by the time you're reading this.

When using `fink`, you have the choice of installing precompiled binary applications out of `fink`'s library or using `fink` as an automated system to work out and apply compilation details, building the software on your own system. Because the binary application library always lags a few versions behind what's available through the source distribution, and sometimes doesn't even provide versions of some software, we'll cover how to use the source distribution in this chapter. Using the source distribution is relatively easy—easier than any of the command-line software installations you've seen. Using the binary distribution is even easier, if you've a reason to prefer to work with it (for example, it doesn't require that you have the developer tools installed).

Because we seem to constantly be revising this book on the cusp of major operating system changes, we've gotten used to the fact that the corresponding `fink` version is rarely finished when we're writing. Because of this, you get to have the most grueling introduction possible to `fink`—pretty much building everything from scratch, straight from the command line. Don't let this bother you. The `fink` system is a study in automation—the "most grueling introduction possible" requires you to type about a half-dozen commands, press Return to accept a few default prompts, and go have dinner. After you do this, you can build entire applications with the simple command `fink install` *<packagename>*. The maintainers of `fink` application porting projects do all the hard work of figuring out the quirks of making software work with Mac OS X and then package it so that all the interdependencies are known and codified. When a package is made available, all you need to do is ask `fink` to install it, and, along with any other required software, it'll be automatically downloaded, configured, and installed.

NOTE

`fink` (`http://fink.sourceforge.net/`) isn't the only package system being promoted for Mac OS X, but it's one of the best supported and one of the most honest. The `gnu-darwin` group (`http://www.gnu-darwin.org/`) is also doing very nice work. There's also a collaboration going on between a number of the porting projects, with news and links maintained at `http://www.metapkg.org/`. There are, however, other groups out there operating less from a desire to help further open source computing and Mac OS X than from a desire to line their own pockets by preying on the fact that many traditional Macintosh users find the command line intimidating.

If you're really willing to pay $30 to avoid having to type one single line at the command prompt, these people provide the service you're looking for. If you're not too intimidated by the command line, however, be mildly suspicious of people who want to sell you ported Unix software. Some of them are doing a fine job of providing ported software and additional value-added features or documentation that make their commercial distribution of free software well worth the money. However, the migration of Mac users to a Unix-based OS has brought a whole crowd of vultures out of the woods hoping to make a quick buck. If it's a Unix application, there's a good chance you can find it for free from `fink`, `gnu-darwin`, or another porting group on the Net. This isn't to say that `gnu-darwin`'s ports CD is not a great deal at $30—that's only five cents per megabyte that you don't have to download and install. But when someone tries to charge you $30 for 5MB or is downloading and selling Web access to packages compiled and provided for free by `fink` and `gnu-darwin`, it should raise some eyebrows.

The first step in using `fink` to install software is to install `fink` itself. You only need to do this once, and despite the large volume of interaction we show here, it's really a simple process.

```
brezup:ray Software $ mkdir finkcvs
brezup:ray Software $ cd finkcvs
brezup:ray finkcvs $ cvs -
d:pserver:anonymous@➥cvs.fink.sourceforge.net:/cvsroot/fink login

(Logging in to anonymous@cvs.fink.sourceforge.net)
CVS password:
```

The CVS password for anonymous, download-only access is empty, so just press Return at the password prompt.

```
brezup:ray finkcvs $ cvs -d:pserver:anonymous@
➥cvs.fink.sourceforge.net:/cvsroot/fink checkout fink
cvs server: Updating fink
U fink/.cvsignore
U fink/AUTHORS
U fink/COPYING
U fink/ChangeLog
U fink/INSTALL
U fink/INSTALL.html
.
.
.
cvs server: Updating fink/update
U fink/update/ChangeLog
U fink/update/Makefile.in.in
U fink/update/config.guess
U fink/update/config.sub
U fink/update/ltconfig
U fink/update/ltmain.sh
brezup:ray finkcvs $ cd fink
brezup:ray fink $ ./bootstrap.sh
Welcome to Fink.

This script will install Fink into a directory of your choice,
setup a configuration file and conduct a bootstrap of the installation.

perl: warning: Setting locale failed.
perl: warning: Please check that your locale settings:
    LC_ALL = (unset),
    LANG = "en_US"
  are supported and installed on your system.
perl: warning: Falling back to the standard locale ("C").
v-string in use/require non-portable at /Volumes/Software/finkcvs/fink/
bootstrap.pl line 26.
Checking package.. looks good.
Checking system.. powerpc-apple-darwin6.0
This system is supported and tested.
Distribution 10.2
```

```
Fink must be installed and run with superuser (root) privileges. Fink can
automatically try to become root when it's run from a user account. Since
you're currently running this script as a normal user, the method you choose
will also be used immediately for this script. Avaliable methods:

(1) Use sudo
(2) Use su
(3) None, fink must be run as root
Choose a method: [1] 3
ERROR: Can't continue as non-root.
brezup:ray fink $
```

`fink` must be run by the `root` user so that it can modify various things in semiprivileged directories. It's halted here because I don't like giving software the option of "becoming root itself," and I forgot to `su`, or `sudo` at the start of the `bootstrap.sh` process. `fink` is capable of updating many Apple-supplied packages to more current versions, and the maintainers seem committed to keeping their software as Apple-friendly as possible. They appear to be making a conscientious effort to keep their installers from conflicting with Apple installations while providing updated versions of Apple-supplied software. I'm not a big fan of running installations as `root`, but given the level of attention that the `fink` project maintainers are paying to the quality of their code, I feel better about giving this software the go-ahead.

```
brezup:ray fink $ sudo ./bootstrap.sh
Password:
Welcome to Fink.

.
.
.

Fink must be installed and run with superuser (root) privileges. Fink can
automatically try to become root when it's run from a user account. Avaliable
methods:

(1) Use sudo
(2) Use su
(3) None, fink must be run as root
Choose a method: [3] 3
Checking cc.. looks good.
Checking make.. looks good.
```

```
Checking head.. looks good.
Please choose the path where Fink should be installed. [/sw] /sw
OK, installing into '/sw'.

Creating directories...
mkdir -p /sw
mkdir /sw/etc
mkdir /sw/etc/alternatives
.
.
.
mkdir /sw/fink/10.2/local/main/finkinfo
mkdir /sw/fink/10.2/local/main/binary-darwin-powerpc
Copying package descriptions...
.
.
.
USAGE.html ChangeLog VERSION fink.in fink.8.in install.sh setup.sh
postinstall.pl.in perlmod update mirror
Creating initial configuration...

OK, I'll ask you some questions and update the configuration file in
'/sw/etc/fink.conf'.
```

A considerable number of configuration choices follow, enabling you to suggest preferred locations of where you want to download various software bits as the system needs them. If you change your mind later, you can modify these choices with the command `fink configure`. Make choices that are appropriate for your system—I've mostly just chosen the default values here.

```
In what additional directory should Fink look for downloaded tarballs? []
(1) Quiet (don't show download stats)
(2) Low (don't show tarballs being expanded)
(3) Medium (shows almost everything)
(4) High (shows everything)
How verbose should Fink be? [4] 4
Proxy/Firewall settings
Enter the URL of the HTTP proxy to use, or 'none' for no proxy. The URL should
 start with http:// and may contain username, password or
port specifications. [none] none
Enter the URL of the proxy to use for FTP, or 'none' for no proxy. The URL
```

```
should start with http:// and may contain username, password
or port specifications. [none] none
Use passive mode FTP transfers (to get through a firewall)? [Y/n] Y
Mirror selection
Choose a continent:

(1) Africa
(2) Asia
(3) Australia
(4) Europe
(5) North America
(6) South America, Middle America and Caribbean
Your continent? [1] 5
Choose a country:

(1) No selection - display all mirrors on the continent
(2) Canada
(3) Mexico
(4) United States
Your country? [1] 4
Choose a mirror for 'GNU software':

(1) Primary: ftp://ftp.gnu.org/gnu
(2) United States: ftp://gatekeeper.dec.com/pub/GNU/
(3) United States: ftp://ftp.keystealth.org/pub/gnu/
.
.
.
(20) United States: ftp://ftp.nodomainname.net/pub/mirrors/gnu/
(21) United States: ftp://ftp.twtelecom.net/pub/GNU/
Mirror for GNU software? [1] 2
Choose a mirror for 'GNOME':

(1) Primary: ftp://ftp.gnome.org/pub/GNOME/
(2) North America: ftp://ftp.cse.buffalo.edu/pub/Gnome
(3) North America: ftp://ftp.rpmfind.net/linux/gnome.org/
(4) North America: ftp://ftp.yggdrasil.com/mirrors/site/ftp.gnome.org/pub/GNOME/
(5) North America: ftp://gnome.eazel.com/pub/GNOME/
Mirror for GNOME? [1] 1
Choose a mirror for 'The GIMP':
```

```
(1) Primary: ftp://ftp.gimp.org/pub
.
.
.
(6) United States: ftp://ftp.ameth.org/pub/mirrors/ftp.gimp.org/
Mirror for The GIMP? [1] 1
Choose a mirror for 'Comprehensive TeX Archive Network':

(1) Primary: ftp://tug.ctan.org/tex-archive/
.
.
.
(7) United States: ftp://ibiblio.org/pub/packages/TeX/
Mirror for Comprehensive TeX Archive Network? [1] 2
Choose a mirror for 'Comprehensive Perl Archive Network':

(1) Primary: ftp://ftp.funet.fi/pub/languages/perl/CPAN/
(2) United States: http://mirrors.phenominet.com/pub/CPAN/
(3) United States: ftp://mirrors.phenominet.com/pub/CPAN/
.
.
.
(63) United States: http://www.rge.com/pub/languages/perl/
(64) United States: ftp://ftp.rge.com/pub/languages/perl/
(65) United States: ftp://ftp.freesoftware.com/pub/perl/CPAN/
Mirror for Comprehensive Perl Archive Network? [1] 43
Choose a mirror for 'SourceForge':

(1) Primary: http://west.dl.sourceforge.net/sourceforge/
(2) United States: http://umn.dl.sourceforge.net/sourceforge/
(3) United States: http://unc.dl.sourceforge.net/sourceforge/
(4) United States: http://telia.dl.sourceforge.net/sourceforge/
(5) United States: http://twtelecom.dl.sourceforge.net/sourceforge/
(6) North America: http://us.dl.sourceforge.net/sourceforge/
Mirror for SourceForge? [1] 1
BOOTSTRAP PHASE ONE: download tarballs.

pkg gettext version ###
pkg gettext version 0.10.40-3
pkg tar version ###
.
.
.
```

```
gcc -DHAVE_CONFIG_H -I. -I. -I. -I../intl -I/sw/bootstrap/include \
-g -O2 -c `test -f hash.c || echo './'`hash.c
source='human.c' object='human.o' libtool=no \
depfile='.deps/human.Po' tmpdepfile='.deps/human.TPo' \
depmode=gcc /bin/sh ../depcomp \
gcc -DHAVE_CONFIG_H -I. -I. -I. -I../intl -I/sw/bootstrap/include \
-g -O2 -c `test -f human.c || echo './'`human.c
source='modechange.c' object='modechange.o' libtool=no \
depfile='.deps/modechange.Po' tmpdepfile='.deps/modechange.TPo' \
depmode=gcc /bin/sh ../depcomp \
.
.
.
```

(A very long time passes—go have dinner!)

```
.
.
.
BOOTSTRAP DONE. Cleaning up.

rm -rf /sw/bootstrap
dpkg-scanpackages dists/local/main/binary-darwin-powerpc override |
gzip >dists/local/main/binary-darwin-powerpc/Packages.gz
.
.
.
dpkg-scanpackages dists/local/bootstrap/binary-darwin-powerpc override |
gzip >dists/local/bootstrap/binary-darwin-powerpc/Packages.gz
 Wrote 14 entries to output Packages file.

You should now have a working Fink installation in '/sw'. You still need
package descriptions if you want to compile packages yourself. You can get
them from CVS or by installing the packages.tar.gz tarball.

Run 'source /sw/bin/init.csh ; rehash' to set up this Terminal's environment
to use Fink. To make the software installed by Fink available in all of your
shells, add 'source /sw/bin/init.csh' to the init script '.cshrc' in your
home directory. Enjoy.
```

NOTE

In 10.2, `tcsh` was the default shell, now it's `bash`. `bash` doesn't need the `rehash` command, but because `fink` isn't working while we're writing this, we're not sure what it'll say here instead for 10.3.

19

Now you almost have a working copy of the `fink` software installation system. The first thing to do when the prompt returns is to edit the file `/sw/etc/fink.conf` and change the line that reads:

```
Trees: local/main stable/main stable/crypto local/bootstrap
```

to

```
Trees: local/main stable/main stable/crypto local/bootstrap unstable/main
unstable/crypto
```

NOTE

The exact list of trees that you'll want to configure is somewhat variable and depends on the state of the `fink` ports for both your current operating system, and for your version of the developer tools. This list shown is representative of a Mac OS X 10.2 installation using `gcc` 3.1, and allows `fink` to make available a number of applications that haven't been thoroughly tested but that largely work well nonetheless.

If you're interested in only stable release software (by stable, `fink` means "well tested"; much of the unstable software is considerably more stable than many commercial packages you probably use every day, but it hasn't been examined and tested to verify that it qualifies as stable by the rules of the project maintainers), you don't need to add the `unstable/*` entries. There's a fair quantity of interesting software that lives in the unstable branches, though, so it's probably worth leaving in there. You aren't obliged to install any of the software in those branches, but having the entry in the `.conf` file enables you to see the software in them from the installation interface, and you can make an informed choice.

The next thing to do is make that recommended change to your `.bashrc` or `.cshrc` file (add `. /sw/bin/init.sh` or `source /sw/bin/init.csh` to the bottom of the appropriate shell startup file), and at the command line execute the file to load its configuration into your running shell (`. /sw/bin/init.sh` or `source /sw/bin/init.csh ; rehash` as appropriate).

NOTE

This is important! `fink` installs software in a number of noncanonical places and a number of places that won't be in your path as provided by Apple or your previous modifications of your `.bashrc/.cshrc` file. `/sw/bin/init.csh` and `/sw/bin/init.sh` set up a number of directory paths that `fink` uses, and if you don't add lines running these files in your shell startup file, you won't be able to run any of the software the next time you log in.

Now you need to tell fink to update portions of itself using the software it just constructed in the bootstrap phase (Again, tcsh syntax, for the 10.2 version. When fink's working for 10.3, we expect it'll be `. /sw/bin/init.sh`, or something similar.):

```
brezup:ray fink $ source /sw/bin/init.csh ; rehash
brezup:ray fink $ sudo fink selfupdate-cvs
The selfupdate function can track point releases or it can set up your Fink
installation to update package descriptions from CVS. Updating from CVS has
the advantage that it is more up to date than the last point release. On the
other hand, the point release may be more mature or have less bugs.
Nevertheless, CVS is recommended. Do you want to set up direct CVS updating?
[Y/n] Y
Fink has the capability to run the CVS commands as a normal user. That has
some advantages - it uses that user's CVS settings files and allows the
package descriptions to be edited and updated without becoming root
Please specify the user login name that should be used: [root] root
For Fink developers only: Enter your SourceForge login name to set up full CVS
access. Other users, just press return to set up anonymous read-only
access. [anonymous] anonymous
mkdir -p /sw/fink.tmp
Checking to see if we can use hard links to merge the existing tree. Please
ignore errors on the next few lines.
touch /sw/fink/README; ln /sw/fink/README /sw/fink.tmp/README
Now logging into the CVS server. When CVS asks you for a password, just press
return (i.e. the password is empty).
cvs -d:pserver:anonymous@cvs.sourceforge.net:/cvsroot/fink login
(Logging in to anonymous@cvs.sourceforge.net)
CVS password:
Now downloading package descriptions...
cvs -z3 -d:pserver:anonymous@cvs.sourceforge.net:/cvsroot/fink checkout -d fink
dists
cvs server: Updating fink
U fink/.cvsignore
U fink/ChangeLog
.
.
.
pkg apt-shlibs version ###
pkg apt-shlibs version 0.5.4-5
pkg storable-pm version ###
pkg storable-pm version 1.0.14-1
No packages to install.
```

```
The core packages have been updated. You should now update the other packages
using commands like 'fink update-all'.
brezup:ray fink $
```

When this step finishes, you're ready to start using `fink` to install software. `fink` is also done with the `finkcvs` directory (it's the source and build directory for the `fink` command and related software, not for the software `fink` installs), so you can delete it now as well. All other installation, configuration, and updating is carried out in the `/sw` directory (or another location that you specified instead).

You have a choice of using `fink` to carry out software installations directly from the command line or from a menu-driven interface to the `fink` system. These options differ in a fundamental way: The command-line version uses the `fink` system to download and compile source directly on your computer, whereas the menu-driven system downloads precompiled binaries and installs them. There are advantages and disadvantages to each approach. A precompiled binary is usually quicker to download and install, but it might be out of phase with the software on your system, and you could be stuck waiting for someone else to submit a compiled version before you can download something that works on your system.

Using `fink` to compile, on the other hand, is generally slower, and you run a different but similarly annoying risk of the compilation parameters supplied by `fink` not being in sync with the compilers and libraries available on your machine. The maintainers of `fink` packages do a wonderful job of making installation via compilation simple and painless, but regardless of how carefully they try, there are always going to be machines configured by users who "think just a little more differently" than the `fink` maintainers anticipated in their installer scripts.

NOTE

When we were writing for release 10.2 of Mac OS X, (September 17, 2002), the argument for the command-line compilation option won: The binaries available through `fink` hadn't been updated to be 10.2 compatible yet, but the source distribution had been updated to compile on 10.2. As of Sept 14, 2003, the binaries are winning for 10.3, as most of the binaries that work on 10.2 also work on 10.3, whereas the source distribution isn't quite working yet. By the time you're reading this, the binary distribution will probably be behind again (being largely stuck in `gcc` 3.1), and the source distribution will be updated to work with your new OS and corresponding new developer tools.

`fink` and X11

The first bit of software that you'll probably want to install with `fink` is a collection of wrappers that let `fink` see and use Apple's X11 distribution. X11 is required by many traditional Unix applications, and because `fink` knows about the prerequisites for any software it's trying to install, it will want to make sure that you have X11 installed before allowing many other installs to proceed. To satisfy this requirement, you have a choice of telling `fink` to use Apple's X11 version, or of installing the `fink` X11 version instead. If the `fink` version has been updated to a more recent version of X11 than Apple provides, it's a quick and easy way to gain access to the new features. Most users, however, will be satisfied with the version that Apple provides. If you want to install the `fink` distribution, there is quite a bit of documentation on its Web page regarding how to get this up and running.

To install the wrappers to make `fink` work with Apple's vendor-supplied version of XFree86 X11R6 (V4.3.0 at the time of this writing), you need to tell `fink` to install a wrapper for Apple's version:

```
brezup:root fink # fink install system-xfree86-43
```

The `-43` portion of the name changes with different versions of X11 that you might have installed. Note that as specified when building `fink`, you need to be `root`, or `sudo` to use the `fink install` command. `fink` automatically knows about prerequisites for the installation and installs them for you.

To install X11 through `fink`, you need to tell `fink` to acquire the `xfree86-base` and `xfree86-rootless` packages. At the command line, you can do so in this way:

```
brezup:root fink # fink install xfree86-rootless

Information about 1449 packages read in 1 seconds.

pkg xfree86-rootless version ###
pkg xfree86-rootless version 4.3.0
The following package will be installed or updated:
 xfree86-rootless
The following 2 additional packages will be installed:
 dlcompat xfree86-base

Do you want to continue? [Y/n] Y
```


Note that `fink` automatically knows that the `xfree86-base` package is a requirement for `xfree86-rootless`, and downloads and installs it automatically. `fink` understands the interdependencies of its packages, and, for the software it supports, this makes installation much easier than you experienced with the packages we used as examples of manual compilation and configuration in earlier chapters.

A very, very long time passes (maybe go out to a movie?), and you should eventually see this:

```
.
.
.
(Reading database .. 3464 files and directories currently installed.)
Unpacking xfree86-rootless (from .../xfree86-rootless_4.3.0_darwin-powerpc.deb) ...
Selecting previously deselected package xfree86-base.
Unpacking xfree86-base (from .../xfree86-base_4.3.0_darwin-powerpc.deb) ...
Setting up xfree86-base (4.3.0) ...

Setting up xfree86-rootless (4.3.0) ...

brezup:root fink #
```

At this point, you have a working install of an X11 server, as well as several clients on your machine. To start the server, either use the `startx` command, or just double-click the X11 application you'll find in your `Applications/Utilities` folder. (The `fink` version may additionally support `startx -- -quartz -fullscreen` to put the X server in a mode where it runs as a completely isolated window system, rather than intermixed with Aqua, and `startx -- -quartz -rootless` for one that runs with its windows interleaved with Aqua windows.) If you don't have a three button mouse, you'll probably want to add `-fakebuttons` to either command-line incarnation you choose, to allow you to emulate X11's expected three-button mouse with your Command and Option keys. The X11 application allows you to select this functionality as a preference.

NOTE

You now probably want to take a few minutes to browse through the installed X11 software to see what you have. X11R6 binaries traditionally live in `/usr/X11R6/bin/`. In that directory, you'll find more than 130 programs with uses ranging from desktop calculator to window manager, and from OpenGL graphics demos to silly toys that display eyeballs that watch your cursor on the screen. The X11 man pages live in `/usr/X11R6/man` and include good documentation for the installed X11 applications.

Using X11

Whether you've installed X11 from `fink` or `xfree86.org`, or are using Apple's version, starting it is simply a matter of running the `startx` command from the shell or clicking the X11 (XDarwin, if you've installed the `fink`/XFree86 versions) application. When started from the X11 application, you get preference choices between rooted or rootless display and a few other useful features. If you choose to run your X11 server in rooted mode (as a completely separate from Aqua windowing system), you can switch between the X11 desktop and your normal Aqua environment by pressing Command-Option-A.

CAUTION

If it appears that you can't type into any of the windows (you move your cursor over the window and the in-window text cursor highlights, but nothing you type appears), congratulations! You've found a Mac OS X bug. Some versions of the Mac OS X kernel have a bug in which it randomly unloads a table that contains a list of which keys exist on the keyboard. X11 needs this table to map what you type into data to be provided to a program. If you experience this bug, our recommendation is to kill X11, sleep the machine, wake it up, and start X11 again. Apparently, the keymap table is reinjected into the kernel on wake up, and starting X11 immediately afterward seems to be the only consistent fix.

The look and feel of the X Window System are mostly the responsibility of the particular window manager you've chosen to run. (You learn more about window managers in the immediately following section.) But in the general operation of the environment, you'll find that there are a number of constants to the way the X Window System works, regardless of what the interface looks like. Some of these are familiar to anyone who has previously used a computer with a mouse. A few, however, are likely to be new even to users who've been happily using a mouse since the earliest days of the Mac. The significant things to remember are described in the next section.

Common X11 Interface Features

The X Window System is designed for a three-button mouse. Most X software uses the left button for pointing, clicking, and selection. X uses the center button for general functions such as moving or resizing windows, and the right button for application-specific functions such as opening in-application pop-up windows. Of course, any application is capable of modifying these uses, so examination of a program's documentation is always in order.

X also uses its three-button mouse for selection, copying, and pasting in a way that won't be familiar, but that you'll probably come to appreciate quickly. Unlike Mac and Windows, there's no separate command to perform copy functions. Instead, X functions as though whatever has been most recently selected has been placed on the clipboard and can be pasted. The left mouse button allows click-and-drag type selection and picking the start of a selection region. The right mouse button functions like Shift-clicking on the Mac; that is, it extends the selection. And clicking the center mouse button pastes whatever is selected—or has been most recently selected—into whichever window the cursor is in when clicked. This different paradigm for selection, copying, and pasting turns out to be a wonderfully efficient way of enabling you to work with text with the mouse because it requires no coordinated use of a second hand.

The normal Mac mouse, of course, has no middle or right mouse buttons by default. XFree86 deals with this by enabling you to use keyboard modifiers to emulate the middle and right mouse buttons. To enable this mode, add the argument `-fakebuttons` to the `startx` invocation or select it in the X11 application's preferences. This allows clicking while holding down the Command key to emulate the middle mouse button, and the Option key to emulate the right mouse button. So, that benefit of not needing the second hand goes away again, at least for the time being on the Mac. It might be time to put away that cool pro mouse and buy one with multiple buttons or petition Apple to get with the X program!

Of Mice and Buttons

With a single-button mouse, `-fakebuttons` lets you Command-click to send X11 a middle-mouse-button event, and Option-click to send a right-mouse-button event. With a two-button mouse, the right button sends the X11 right-mouse-button event, and you still need the Command-click to send the middle-mouse-button event. Many scroll-wheel mice send a middle-mouse-button event if you push down on (rather than roll) the scroll wheel.

Click Early, Click Often!

X11 likes to make use of the mouse. Under most window managers, there are control and configuration menus that you can access when left-, middle-, and right-clicking on various screen features. Some applications have special menus that appear for certain types of mouse-clicks as well. The menus and options available are context sensitive and change depending on what interface element you're clicking on, and what mouse button (and possibly keyboard key) you're pressing. Application windows, title bars, and the screen background itself all have (or can have, depending on the configuration) their own contextual behaviors for each type of click and keyboard keys in combination with each click. For example Control-clicking in an `xterm` (X11 terminal program) gives you a number of different menus, with options ranging from resetting the font size for that terminal, to turning its scrollbars on and off.

X has the concept of focused input. On Macintosh and Windows platforms, if you type on the keyboard, you generally expect the typing to appear in whatever window or dialog box is in front. On Mac and Windows, the window in front is the active window. In X, the window manager has the option of directing your input where it chooses. The location into which your input is directed is called the input focus. Most window managers can be configured to focus input on the frontmost window, focus input on a selected window (which, on X, doesn't have to be the front window), or focus input on whichever window the cursor is over. These are usually called, respectively, Focus to Front, Click to Focus, and Focus Follows Cursor modes. The last of these, although most unlike the interface you are probably familiar with, is usually considered to be the most powerful.

With the window manager configured in Focus Follows Cursor mode, you can direct typing into a mostly hidden window (for example, to start a noninteractive program) simply by moving the cursor over any visible part of the mostly hidden window and typing. There's no need to waste time bringing a rear window to the front, typing the command, and then shuffling the window back underneath the window that you really wanted to be working in. Figures 19.5 though 19.7 show several examples of working in the different X11 focus modes. Pay careful attention to where the cursor appears (the cursor is an I-beam style text cursor in each), and which window is active. (The active window usually has a solid-block insertion-point cursor, and inactive ones have hollow block insertion-point cursors.) Configuration methods for the different window managers vary, so we cover the options for several in the next section.

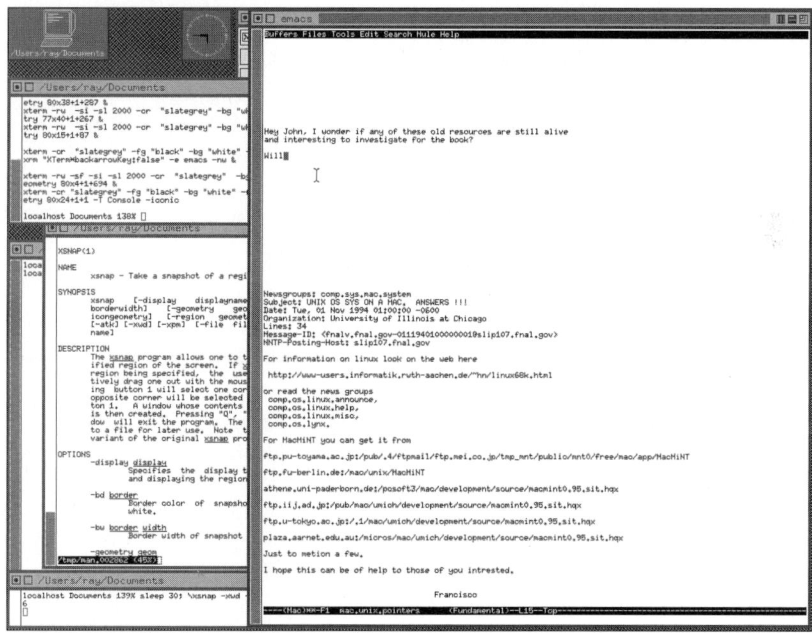

FIGURE 19.5 Focus Follows Cursor mode, with work being done in the frontmost window—this looks like the type of interaction with which you're probably familiar. Note that both the mouse pointer (the I-beam text cursor) and the text insertion point (the dark filled rectangle in the emacs window) are inside the same window.

TIP

If you're typing and you notice that what you're typing isn't appearing where you think it's supposed to, chances are that you've got your input focused in some other window. Make sure that your cursor is where it belongs or, if your system is configured to Click to Focus mode, make sure that you've clicked where you intend to type. It's easy to get confused when moving between platforms using different input focus methods.

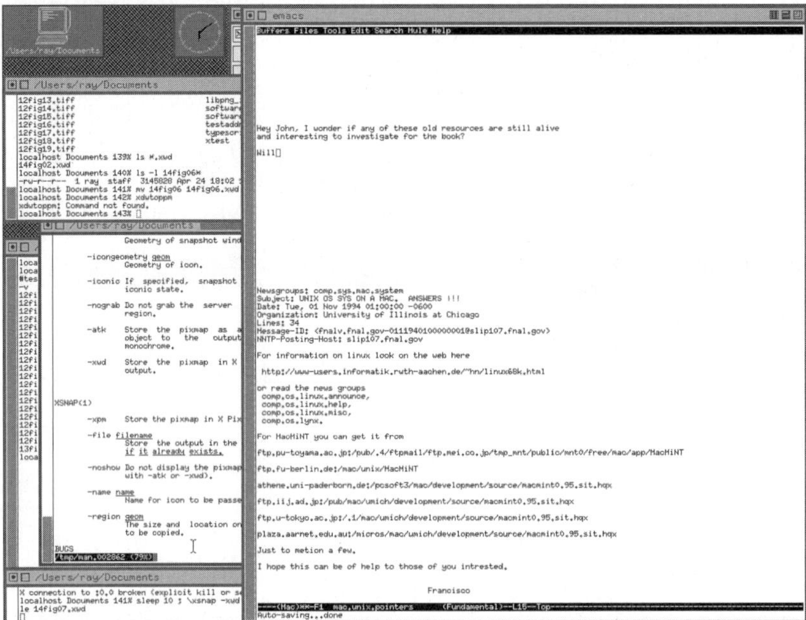

FIGURE 19.6 Focus Follows Cursor mode with work being done in a window that is behind the front window. Notice that the in-window cursor of the emacs window (frontmost) has gone hollow to indicate that it's no longer active. The dark active cursor has followed the mouse pointer to indicate that a different window is active. The window border also changes colors, but that probably doesn't show up well in a black-and-white printed image.

In the X Window System, the window manager or any other program can attach arbitrary commands to arbitrary user actions. For example, a program can attach the action of displaying a menu when a user right-clicks on the title bar. The window manager could pop up a variety of menus when the user left-, right-, or center-clicks in the empty background (root window or desktop) of the windowing system. Or it could happen when the user Shift-left-clicks, Shift-right-clicks, or Shift-center-clicks—the possibilities are endless. One popular terminal program, `xterm`, pops up its configuration menus when the user holds down the Control key and left-, right-, or center-clicks in the window.

Some window managers attach a standard menu with common commands such as Close and Resize to icons in each window's title bar. Others attach these functions to pop-up menus in the title bar. You'll find variations in program behavior even among different installations of X11 on the same version of Unix because local configuration options can exert a significant influence over the interface. Don't be too surprised if your installation of X11 doesn't look or behave quite like what is shown here. With the short generation times for open source software, there's plenty of time for the software to be updated a dozen times between my typing this and your reading it. Also, don't be afraid to read the documentation and the FAQs to find out how things work today, regardless of when *today* happens to be.

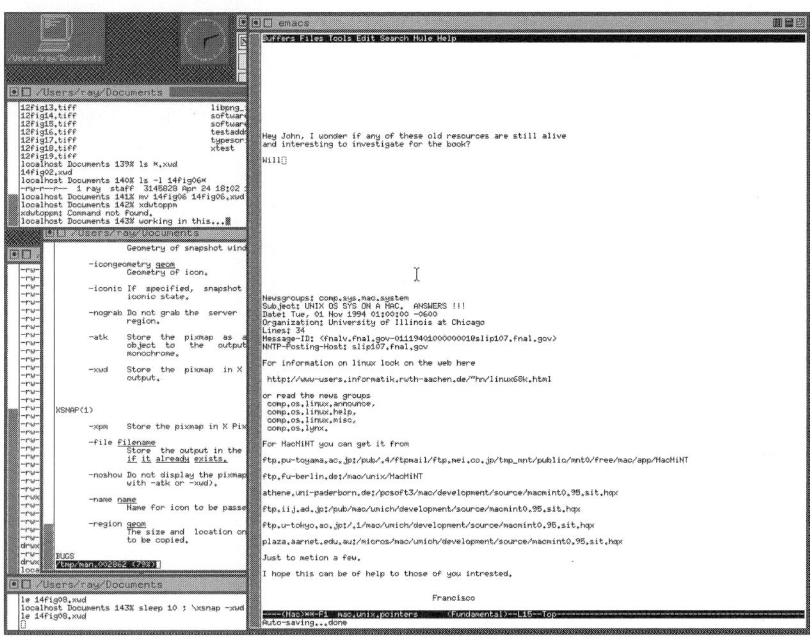

FIGURE 19.7 Click to Focus mode with a window selected other than the one that the cursor is in—this doesn't have to be the front window. Notice that the mouse pointer and active text cursor aren't in the same window. After input is focused into a window in this mode, it doesn't leave until the mouse is clicked elsewhere.

Most window managers can iconize windows. Because the actual display of a client's windows isn't handled by the client, but by the server at the request of the client, the X server and window manager are free to make some useful contributions to the user experience. One of these contributions is that when a client requests a window with particular characteristics, the server isn't obliged to represent the window that way to the user. The server is only obliged to treat it as though it had those characteristics. This enables the server, for example, to scale the window arbitrarily or to shrink it down and display it as an icon.

You're familiar with the concept of files and folders being represented with icons. X11 doesn't know a thing about files or folders. It knows about drawing pictures on the screen (there are file browser applications for X11, much like the Mac OS X Finder, and we talk about them later in this chapter), and it knows that you don't always want all those pictures fighting for display space. So, X11 includes the notion that a window can be turned into an icon displayed in the root window if you don't care to have it taking up space. This is sort of like Mac OS X's capability to minimize a running application into the Dock, but you aren't limited to placing things in one location on the screen. (In fact, the window manager Apple provides with its version of X11 uses the Dock for storing the icons that should be on the root window.) Likewise, some applications can be dynamically resized to provide different functionality than you are familiar with from Mac OS. The xterm terminal window, for example, with most window managers interacts dynamically with the size of the font it's using. Increase the size of the font, and the window increases to show the same data. You can also decrease the font size to a single point—in which case, the terminal shrinks to icon size while remaining a usable terminal and continuing to display output.

Configuring the X Window System

Most configuration of the X Window System is handled by a server resource database. When a client makes a request of the server, the server checks the server resource database to determine user preferences for that client. The server resource database is loaded on a per-user basis via the command `xrdb`, which must be executed automatically after starting X11. `xrdb` loads configuration information from a dotfile, usually named `.X11defaults`. `.X11defaults` usually contains lines similar to the following:

```
1  xbiff*onceOnly:          on
2  xbiff*wm_option.autoRaise:   off
3  xbiff*mailBox          /usr/spool/mail/mymail
```

If you were to include these lines in your `.X11defaults` file, you'd be telling your X server that if `xbiff` (an X11 program that notifies you when you have new mail) starts, it must set certain options.

Line 1 sets an `xbiff`-specific option regarding how frequently to ring the alarm to tell you that you have mail. Here, it's set to ring a single time when mail arrives. Other options are available to set how many times the alarm should ring and at what intervals, if you prefer something other than a single ring.

Line 2 sets an option that belongs to the window manager and tells it how you want `xbiff` treated. Specifically, this tells the window manager not to bring `xbiff` to the front if it's behind other windows when it needs to notify you. Remember, X11 provides the display, and a separate window manager provides such things as window controls.

Line 3 tells `xbiff` where to find the mailbox that it's supposed to look at.

Because each client supports different options and allows the window manager different levels of control, you must consult each client's documentation to learn what you can configure and what you need to do to configure it. As an idea of what you can do, and perhaps as a sample you might like to play with, Listing 19.1 includes a commented listing of my `.X11defaults` file.

LISTING 19.1 A Typical `.X11defaults` File

```
! ~/.X11defaults
!  This file is used by xrdb to initialize the server resource
!  database, which is used by clients when they start up.
!
```

LISTING 19.1 Continued

```
! Default defaults
!
*Font:      *-courier-medium-r-*-*-*-120-*-*-*-*-*-*
*MenuFont:    *-courier-medium-r-*-*-*-140-*-*-*-*-*-*
*BoldFont:    *-courier-bold-r-*-*-*-120-*-*-*-*-*-*
!
! GNU Emacs
!
emacs*BorderWidth:   1
! emacs*Font:      9x15
!
! Clock
!
xclock*borderWidth:       0
xclock*wm_option.title:     off
xclock*wm_option.gadgets:    off
xclock*wm_option.borderContext: off
xclock*wm_option.autoRaise:   off
!
! Load meter
!
xload*font:          *-courier-medium-r-*-*-*-100-*-*-*-*-*-*
xload*wm_option.title:     off
xload*wm_option.gadgets:    off
xload*wm_option.borderContext: off
xload*wm_option.autoRaise:   off
!
! Mail notifier
!
xbiff*wm_option.title:     off
xbiff*wm_option.gadgets:    off
xbiff*wm_option.borderContext: off
xbiff*wm_option.autoRaise:   off
xbiff*wm_option.volume:     20
!
! Terminal Emulator
!
!XTerm*Font:      9x15
XTerm*c132:       true
XTerm*curses:      true
XTerm*jumpScroll:    true
XTerm*SaveLines:    2048
XTerm*scrollBar:    true
```

19

LISTING 19.1 Continued

```
XTerm*scrollInput:   true
XTerm*scrollKey:    true
!
XTerm*fontMenu.Label:       VT Fonts
XTerm*fontMenu*fontdefault*Label: Default
XTerm*fontMenu*font1*Label:    Tiny
XTerm*VT100*font1:          nil2
XTerm*fontMenu*font2*Label:    10 Point
XTerm*VT100*font2:     -*-lucidatypewriter-medium-r-*-*-*-080-*-*-*-*-*-*
XTerm*fontMenu*font3*Label:    14 Point
XTerm*VT100*font3:     -*-lucidatypewriter-medium-r-*-*-*-140-*-*-*-*-*-*
XTerm*fontMenu*font4*Label:    18 Point
XTerm*VT100*font4:     -*-lucidatypewriter-medium-r-*-*-*-180-*-*-*-*-*-*
XTerm*fontMenu*font5*Label:    24 Point
XTerm*VT100*font5:          12x24
XTerm*fontMenu*fontescape*Label:  Escape Sequence
XTerm*fontMenu*fontsel*Label:   Selection
XTerm*VT100.Translations:    #override \n\
  <Key>L1:  set-vt-font(1) set-scrollbar(off) \n\
  <Key>L2:  set-vt-font set-scrollbar(on) \n\
  <Key>R4:  string("0x1b") string("[211z") \n\
  <Key>R5:  string("0x1b") string("[212z") \n\
  <Key>R6:  string("0x1b") string("[213z") \n\
  <Key>R7:  string("0x1b") string("[214z") \n\
  <Key>R9:  string("0x1b") string("[216z") \n\
  <Key>R11:  string("0x1b") string("[218z") \n\
  <Key>R13:  string("0x1b") string("[220z") \n\
  <Key>R15:  string("0x1b") string("[222z")
!
! Netscape
!
netscape*defaultHeight:   850
netscape*anchorColor:    maroon
netscape*visitedAnchorColor:  blue3
!
! screensaver config
!
xscreensaver*programs: \
  xfishtank -c black -r .1 -f 20 -b 20 \n \
  /usr/local/X11R5/bin/flame -root \n \
  /usr/local/X11R5/bin/maze -root
xscreensaver*colorPrograms:
xscreensaver*monoPrograms:
```

In addition to the server resources database, clients frequently have command-line options that can control the client's interaction with X11. For example:

```
brezup:ray test $ xterm -fg "black" -bg "white" -fn 6x10 -geometry 85x30+525+1
```

This starts an xterm terminal session with the following configuration: black as the foreground color, white as the background color (black text on a white window), and a 6×10 point font. It sets the geometry information so that the window is 85 characters wide, 30 characters high, and is placed 525 pixels from the left edge of the screen and 1 pixel down from the top.

Again, different programs have different options available, and your location documentation is your best source for up-to-date information on your exact configuration.

Finally, the applications that start when you start X11 (or most standardized installations of X11, including the default XFree86 installation) are configured by the execution of a file named .xinitrc in your home directory. This is a shell script file containing a collection of commands that you want executed when X11 starts. Therefore, you can put in it lines that start xterm terminals, clocks, editors, and any other X11-based applications that you want to start in your environment. The lines are exactly the commands you'd type at the command line to start these applications, so the earlier comments about the wide variability of the configuration options apply here as well.

NOTE

Under Apple's version of X11, if you don't start a window manager yourself in your own .xinitrc file, an Aqua-like window manager is used, giving your X11 applications standard Mac OS X window appearances and controls.

Listing 19.2 shows the contents of my .xinitrc file, which produces the X11 environment shown previously in Figure 19.1.

LISTING 19.2 A Typical .xinitrc File

```
#!/bin/sh

xrdb -load $HOME/.X11defaults
xset m 2 5 s off
xset fp+ /usr/X11R6/lib/X11/fonts

# xmodmap -e 'keysym BackSpace = Delete'
echo "XTerm*ttyModes:erase ^H" ¦ xrdb -merge

/usr/X11R6/bin/twm &

/usr/X11R6/bin/xclock -bg "slategrey" -fg "lightgrey" -analog ➥-geometry
```

LISTING 19.2 Continued

```
60x60+220+1 -padding 4 &

xterm -rw -si -sl 2000 -cr "slategrey" -bg "white" -fg "black" -fn 6x10 -geometry
80x38+1+287 &
xterm -rw -si -sl 2000 -cr "slategrey" -bg "white" -fg "black" -fn 6x10 -geometry
77x40+1+267 &
xterm -rw -si -sl 2000 -cr "slategrey" -bg "white" -fg "black" -fn 6x10 -geometry
80x15+1+87 &

xterm -cr "slategrey" -fg "black" -bg "white" -fn 6x10 -geometry 82x73+507+1 -xrm
"XTerm*backarrowKey:false" -e emacs -nw &

xterm -rw -sf -si -sl 2000 -cr "slategrey" -bg "white" -fg "black" -fn 6x10 -geome-
try 80x4+1+694 &
xterm -cr "slategrey" -fg "black" -bg "white" -fn 6x10 -title "CONSOLE" -C -geometry
80x24+1+1 -T Console -iconic
```

Window Manager and Application-Specific Configurations

Finally, window managers and applications have their own configuration files that control display options and, possibly, other parameters regarding the user experience. Where and how these are set depends on the window manager and/or application that you are running. Some can be controlled through the server resource database. Others are set in individual control files specific to the window manager, or configured through a control pane-like interface. Yet other options are available through combination mouse-button and keyboard actions. (For example, Control-left-, Control-middle-, and Control-right-clicking provides access to a multitude of options for the `twm` window manager and for `xterm` terminals.)

Window Managers: `twm`, `mwm`, `quartz-wm`

After you've started the X Window System environment, you're presented with a single `xterm` window in the upper left-hand side of your screen, managed with an Aqua-like window manager. This is the current default for a user who has no `.xinitrc` file to control what applications to start and where to put them, and no `.twmrc` file to control what the applications look and feel like. Remember that the X Window System provides only interface, component, and display functionality; additional programs are required to provide a useful user interface. In Figure 19.1, you are actually looking at the result of 10 programs running simultaneously (not counting the X Window System server and associated programs necessary for it to function) just to create the interface. Six display windows, one provides an application dock, one is a clock, one is an editor, and finally, the window manager, `twm`, provides the title bars and border controls associated with the windows.

Startup of the programs occurs in `.xinitrc`, and the configuration of their appearance is controlled by `twm`.

`twm`

One of the most common window managers is `twm` (tabbed window manager, or Tims window manager, depending on who you ask). Shown managing the display in Figure 19.1, `twm` provides very basic window management functions and is the default window manager used by XFree86. Even though it's one of the less fancy window managers, `twm` is convenient and allows an extreme amount of user customization of the environment. If you choose to do so, you can create your own standard buttons that appear in your `twm` title bars and cause them to execute arbitrary commands. You can also build your own pop-up menus, automatically execute commands when the cursor enters windows, customize window manager colors and actions by application name and type, and a host of other customizations. Listing 19.3 is a portion of my `.twmrc` file, which gives you an idea of the range of configuration options. The listing is only a portion of my `.twmrc` file because the entire file contains 284 individual configuration parameters. I'm particular about how my interface functions, and `twm` gives me the flexibility to configure every last one of the 284 tweaks it takes to get it how I like it.

LISTING 19.3 A Representative Sample of a `.twmrc` Configuration File for the `twm` X Window System Window Manager

```
Color
{
  BorderColor "maroon4"

  BorderTileForeground "bisque4"
  BorderTileBackground "darkorchid4"

  TitleForeground "darkslategray"
  TitleBackground "bisque3"

  DefaultBackground "bisque"
  DefaultForeground "slategrey"

  MenuForeground "slategrey"
  MenuBackground "moccasin"

  MenuTitleForeground "slategrey"
  MenuTitleBackground "bisque3"
  MenuShadowColor "bisque4"
  IconForeground "lightgrey"
  IconBackground "slategray"
  IconBorderColor "darkslategray"
```

LISTING 19.3 Continued

```
  IconManagerForeground "darkslategrey"
  IconManagerBackground "bisque"
  IconManagerHighlight "maroon4"
}

BorderWidth   4
FramePadding  2
TitleFont   "8x13"
MenuFont    "8x13"
IconFont    "6x10"
ResizeFont   "fixed"
NoTitleFocus

IconManagerGeometry  "=200x10+290+1"

ShowIconManager

IconManagerFont        "variable"
IconManagerDontShow
{
  "xclock"
  "xbiff"
  "perfmeter"
}

ForceIcons
Icons
{
  "xterm"  "terminal"
}

NoTitle
{
 "TWM"
 "xload"
 "xclock"
 "xckmail"
 "xbiff"
 "xeyes"
 "oclock"
}
```

LISTING 19.3 Continued

```
NoHighlight
{
 "xclock"
 "dclock"
 "xload"
 "xbiff"
}

AutoRaise
{
 "nothing"
}

DefaultFunction f.menu "default-menu"
#WindowFunction f.function "blob"

#Button = KEYS : CONTEXT : FUNCTION
#---------------------------------
Button1 =    : root  : f.menu "button1"
Button2 =    : root  : f.menu "button2"
Button3 =    : root  : f.menu "button3"

Button1 =    : title : f.function "blob"
Button2 =    : title : f.lower

Button1 =    : frame : f.raiselower
Button2 =    : frame : f.move
Button3 =    : frame : f.lower

Button1 =    : icon  : f.function "blob"
Button2 =    : icon  : f.iconify
Button3 =    : icon  : f.menu "default-menu"
Button1 = m  : icon  : f.iconify
Button2 = m  : icon  : f.iconify
Button3 = m  : icon  : f.iconify
Button3 = c  : root  : f.function "beep-beep"

Function "beep-beep"
{
  f.beep
  f.beep
  f.beep
```

LISTING 19.3 Continued

```
  f.beep
  f.beep
}

menu "button1"
{
"Window Ops"    f.title
"(De)Iconify"   f.iconify
"Move"       f.move
"Resize"      f.resize
"Lower"      f.lower
"Raise"      f.raise
"Redraw Window"  f.winrefresh
"Focus Input"   f.focus
"Unfocus Input"  f.unfocus
"Window Info"   f.identify
}

menu "button2"
{
"Window Mgr"    f.title
"Circle Up"    f.circleup
"Circle Down"   f.circledown
 "Refresh All"   f.refresh
"Source .twmrc"  f.twmrc
"Beep"       f.beep
"Show Icon Mgr"  f.showiconmgr
"Hide Icon Mgr"  f.hideiconmgr
"Feel"       f.menu "Feel"
}

menu "button3"
{
"Clients"      f.title
"Xterm"        ! "xterm &"
"Emacs"        ! "emacs -i &"
"Lock Screen"     ! "xnlock &"
"Xman"        ! "xman &"
"X Text Exitor"    ! "xedit &"
"Calculator"     ! "xcalc &"
}
```

LISTING 19.3 Continued

```
menu "default-menu"
{
"Default Menu"    f.title
"Refresh"        f.refresh
"Refresh Window"   f.winrefresh
"twm Version"     f.version
"Focus on Root"    f.unfocus
"Source .twmrc"    f.twmrc
"Cut File"       f.cutfile
"Move Window"     f.move
"ForceMove Window"  f.forcemove
"Resize Window"    f.resize
"Raise Window"    f.raise
"Lower Window"    f.lower
"Focus on Window"   f.focus
"Raise-n-Focus"    f.function "raise-n-focus"
"Zoom Window"     f.zoom
"FullZoom Window"   f.fullzoom
"Kill twm"       f.quit
"Destroy Window"   f.destroy
}

RightTitleButton "down" = f.zoom
RightTitleButton "right" = f.horizoom
LeftTitleButton "icon" = f.destroy
```

mwm

The Motif window manager (mwm) is a popular window manager that evolved from a commercial product, and it's also a popular window manager for others to attempt to emulate. It provides a somewhat different user experience than twm. The difference is partly because twm automatically attaches things such as resize corners to all windows, and partly because of the pretty 3D look it gives to the controls. Figure 19.8 shows mwm managing the same collection of windows managed by twm in Figure 19.1.

19

quartz-wm

quartz-wm makes X11 applications look like native OS X applications. Shown managing some of the windows in Figure 9.9, quartz-wm is an Aqua window manager for X11 applications running in either rooted or rootless mode. It makes X11 applications feel almost exactly like normal Aqua applications and generally makes the whole Aqua versus X11 distinction into a nonissue for the Mac-familiar user.

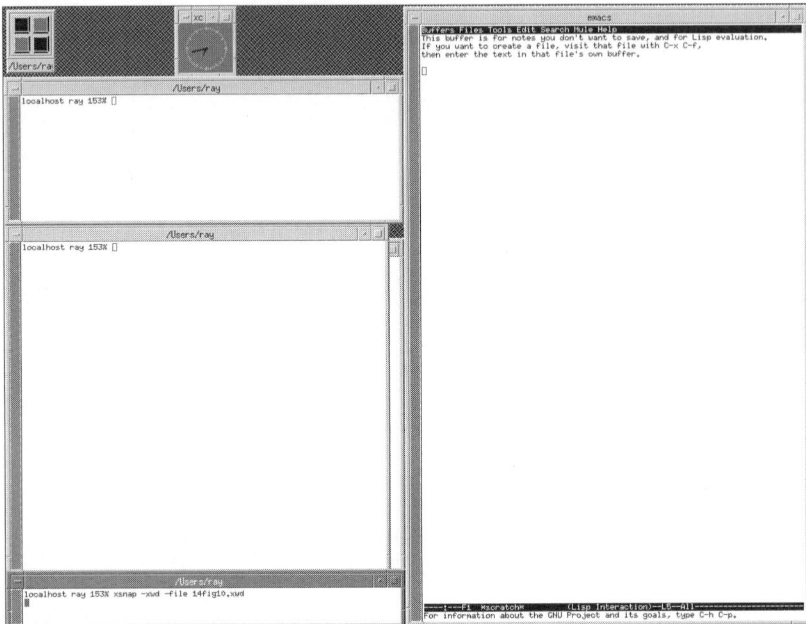

FIGURE 19.8 The `mwm` window manager, managing the same collection of windows shown in Figure 19.1.

> **NOTE**
>
> `quartz-wm` is automatically started by Apple's X11 version if you don't start another window manager of your own in your `.xinitrc` file. If you care to use a different window manager, however, `quartz-wm` still has one useful feature. If it is started with the option `--only-proxy` specified, it relinquishes window management to another window manager but provides an integration layer to assist with mapping copy and paste actions between X11 and native Aqua windows. This feature is tremendously useful if you work back and forth between Aqua and X11 windows frequently because X11's native cut and paste mechanism is not directly compatible with the normal Macintosh methods.

Other Window Managers

New window managers and ports of earlier variants are appearing for Mac OS X at a nice pace. Several nice flavors are already available, and more will probably appear by the time this book is published, so here's a quick list of some of the interesting ones to watch for:

- `tvtwm`—An extension of `twm` that allows you to create an arbitrarily large number of virtual windows and switch between them conveniently.
- `fvwm`—A "3D-ish" version of `twm` with even more flexible configuration options.

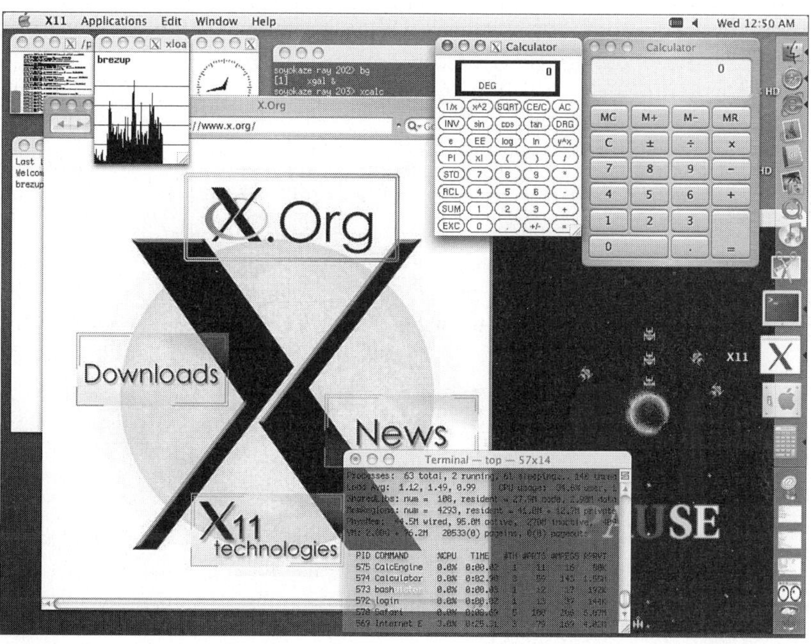

FIGURE 19.9 `quartz-wm` managing some windows. Can you tell which windows are X11 and which are Aqua? What about the minimized applications in the Dock? Visually, and very nearly in any respect, the only clue you get is the odd window names.

- `enlightenment`—A heavyweight (some would say bloated) window manager that belongs to the GNOME desktop environment. GNOME and `enlightenment` are popular on the Linux platform because of the user-friendly environment created under X11. Running `enlightenment` with X11 in rootless mode is interesting. `enlightenment` is another window manager that allows you to have multiple virtual screens that you can toggle among. In `enlightenment`'s case, when you run your cursor off the edge of the screen, the screen slides sideways, and you slide over to a new virtual monitor. When run rootless with Aqua, the Aqua applications of course don't slide, so if you keep one virtual monitor empty of X11 applications, the effect is of being able to slide all the X11 applications off the side of your screen to expose just the Aqua versions, whenever you want. `enlightenment`/GNOME tries to pack every bell and whistle available into an interface that makes Aqua look drab.
- KDE—Another heavyweight window manager and desktop environment. KDE is lighter on the fancy polished graphics than GNOME and `enlightenment`, but it provides powerful interface programming capabilities. Many find its look and feel to be more functional than the `enlightenment`/GNOME combination.

- Window Maker—Another heavyweight window manager, Window Maker is designed to give special support for the GNUstep applications and attempts to provide the elegant look and feel of the OpenStep environment.

When running the X Window System, keep in mind that the window controls, such as title bars and scrollbars, are provided by a separate window manager application. The point of repeating this again is that it's possible for the window manager to exit, leaving you with a collection of unmanaged windows. This is a slightly disconcerting state in which to find the X Window System because the window manager also controls the input focus. Figure 19.10 shows an X Window System session that has lost its window manager.

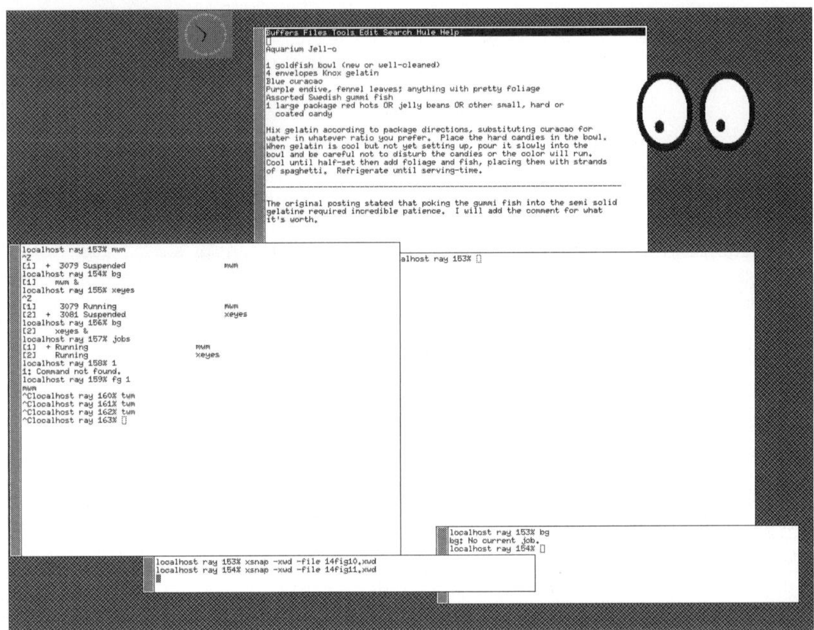

FIGURE 19.10 An X Window System session that has lost its window manager.

> **NOTE**
>
> If your window manager dies while your input is focused somewhere other than a terminal window, you might not be able to refocus. Therefore, you might not be able to type into a window (meaning that you can't type something like `twm` at a prompt, and so you can't restart your window manager). In this case, all is not necessarily lost because the mouse cursor selection and paste method usually still works, even without a window manager. If you can find the letters `t`, `w`, and `m` anywhere on your screen, you can select and paste them at a command prompt, and then select and paste a return/newline, which usually rescues things.

This is a problem with no elegant solution, but if you desperately need to save something you've been working on, it's nice to know there's a fix, even if it's a nuisance. Thankfully, window managers don't frequently die of their own accord. Usually, it takes a user clicking on something like `kill twm` in the menu—in which case, you'll probably be more annoyed at yourself than at having to copy and paste a couple of letters to fix things.

Installing Some Additional Interesting X11 Software

After getting you all excited about how easily the `fink` system installs software, you didn't think we were going to just leave you hanging without showing you around a bit more of the system, did you? Just for kicks, let's use the `fink` system to see what's available (remember, `fink` is always adding new packages) in the way of games. To do this, we use the `fink list` command. `fink list` takes a single argument: a pattern to match in the package name.

fink Isn't Just for X11

The `fink` system isn't just for installing X11 software. That's what we're using it for primarily as an example, but `fink` can install programming languages, networking software, utilities, spreadsheets, you name it. If there's a Unix application that can be ported to Mac OS X, the `fink` project will try to wrap it into its package management system.

To start, let's try looking for packages with `game` in the name:

```
brezup:root Documents # fink list game

Information about 1449 packages read in 1 seconds.

   gnome-games   1.4.0.4-2  GNOME games collection.
   gnome-games-dev 1.4.0.4-2  GNOME games collection.
   gnome-games-shl 1.4.0.4-2  GNOME games collection.
   kdegames3    3.0.7-2   KDE - games
   kdegames3-commo 3.0.7-2   KDE - shared libraries used by KDE games
   kdegames3-dev  3.0.7-2   development headers and libraries for KDE...
```

That's not particularly impressive for a port system boasting more than 1400 packages, is it? Well, let's see what one of them is before we dig further:

```
brezup:root Documents # fink describe gnome-games

Information about 1449 packages read in 1 seconds.

pkg gnome-games version ###
```

```
pkg gnome-games version 1.4.0.4-2

gnome-games-1.4.0.4-2: GNOME games collection.
 The gnome-games package contains a collection of simple games for your
 amusement.
 .
 Web site: http://www.gnome.org/
 .
 Maintainer: Masanori Sekino <msek@users.sourceforge.net>
```

Okay, that could be interesting, let's give it a whirl:

```
brezup:root Documents # fink install gnome-games

Information about 1449 packages read in 1 seconds.

pkg gnome-games version ###
pkg gnome-games version 1.4.0.4-2

fink needs help picking an alternative to satisfy a virtual dependency. The
candidates:

(1) giflib: GIF image format handling library, LZW-enabled version
(2) libungif: GIF image format handling library, LZW-free version

Pick one: [1]
```

`fink` needs help? It's just asking you to make a choice, and it's already suggesting a default, so press Return and let it go:

```
fink needs help picking an alternative to satisfy a virtual dependency. The
candidates:

(1) giflib-bin: GIF image format handling library, LZW-enabled version
(2) libungif-bin: GIF image format handling library, LZW-free version

Pick one: [1]
```

Repeat as necessary!

```
fink needs help picking an alternative to satisfy a virtual dependency. The
candidates:

(1) giflib-shlibs: GIF image format handling library, LZW-enabled version
(2) libungif-shlibs: GIF image format handling library, LZW-free version
```

```
Pick one: [1]

The following package will be installed or updated:
 gnome-games
The following 53 additional packages will be installed:
 audiofile audiofile-bin audiofile-shlibs db3 db3-shlibs docbook-dsssl-nwalsh
 docbook-dtd esound esound-bin esound-common esound-shlibs gdk-pixbuf
 gdk-pixbuf-shlibs giflib giflib-bin giflib-shlibs glib glib-shlibs
 gnome-games-shlibs gnome-libs gnome-libs-dev gnome-libs-shlibs gtk+
 gtk+-data gtk+-shlibs gtk-doc guile guile-dev guile-shlibs imlib
 imlib-shlibs libjpeg libjpeg-bin libjpeg-shlibs libpng libpng-shlibs libtiff
 libtiff-bin libtiff-shlibs libxml libxml-shlibs netpbm netpbm-bin
 netpbm-shlibs openjade orbit orbit-bin orbit-shlibs passwd readline
 readline-shlibs scrollkeeper sgml-entities-iso8879

Do you want to continue? [Y/n] Y
```

Do you want it to install 53 packages for you automatically? Perhaps a better question is, do you want to install 53 packages manually, the way that you did in earlier chapters? Press `Y` and let it roll!

Much time now passes...

```
The following group entries will be added to your NetInfo database:
news:*:250:
mysql:*:251:
pgsql:*:252:
games:*:253:
canna:*:254:
postfix:*:255:
maildrop:*:256:
tomcat:*:257:
jabber:*:258:

Existing entries with these names or numbers will be overwritten or
otherwise affected by this. On the other hand, some Fink packages will
not work unless these entries are in the NetInfo database. You can make
adjustments to the files /sw/etc/passwd-fink and
/sw/etc/group-fink now (from another window), then say yes here. Or
you can say no here and add the users and groups manually (e.g. on your
central NetInfo server). If you don't know what all of this is about,
just say yes.

Do you want to continue? [Y/n] Y
```

Again, accept the default. After this step, and more time, you come back to your command prompt with not much information regarding exactly what software has been installed. Remember that `fink` likes to store its executables in `/sw/bin`. Looking in that directory, you'll find many programs. If you look at the names of the programs, some of them might strike you as familiar. Look back at the list of packages `fink` told you it was going to install—do you recognize `libjpeg`? `libtiff`? How about `netpbm`? All to install a few sample games (`gnometris` is one of them—a simple Tetris-like puzzle-piece game), `fink` has installed some 400 programs and associated libraries, include files, man pages, and so on. The rest of this software is available for you to use as well, so it might be worth a bit of your time to look at some of what's there and check out the man pages. All of this, and you only had to answer a few questions and wait a while.

If you want to try out the software that `fink` installed, start X11 (in case it's an X application) and run some of it. Try out some of the games; `gnometris`, `mahjongg`, `iagno`, `gnibbles`, and `gnobots2` are a few of them. Try out some of the `netpbm` applications—see whether they produce the same output as the ones you built several chapters ago. Figure 19.11 shows a number of the `gnome-game` samples running alongside Aqua windows.

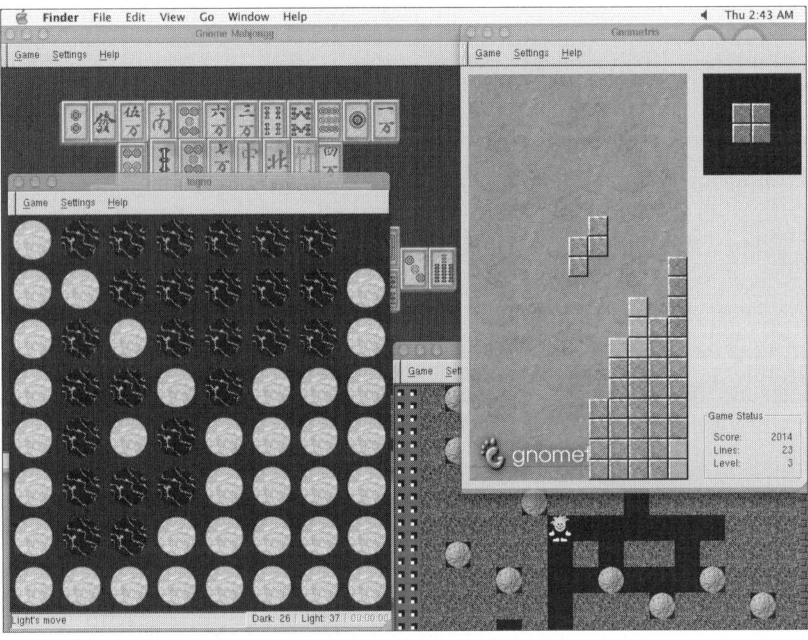

FIGURE 19.11 X11 games running beside Aqua applications.

Let's return to `fink` and see whether there aren't more games. You already know that there's an X11 version of the arcade game Galaga from looking at screenshots earlier in this chapter, so let's see whether it's in `fink`:

```
brezup:root Documents # fink list galaga
Information about 1449 packages read in 2 seconds.

   xgalaga     2.0.34-1   Clone of the classic game of galaga
```

Nifty! Now you know how to install xgalaga if you want it. More importantly, you should observe that although it's a game, xgalaga doesn't have game in its name, only in the comment. This and the grep command should get you started on finding much more software that you might want:

```
brezup:root Documents # fink list ¦ grep "game"
    amaze  0.0-2  3D maze game in curses.
    atlantik    3.0.7-2 KDE - monopoly-like game
    cgoban 1.9.12-1    X11 frontend for the game of Go
    connect4    1.1-2  Text-based Connect Four game.
    crafty-tb-four 18-1  Four piece endgame tablebases for crafty
    crafty-tb-three 18-1  Three piece endgame tablebases for crafty
    crossfire    1.3.0-1 Graphical role-playing adventure game for X11.
    dama  0.5.4-1 Turkish draughts board game. (checkers-like)
    danican 0.5.2-1 International draughts board game. (checkers-like)
    dopewars    1.5.4-1 Drug dealing game set in New York
 i   gnome-games   1.4.0.4-2    GNOME games collection.
    gnome-games-dev 1.4.0.4-2    GNOME games collection.
 i   gnome-games-shlibs   1.4.0.4-2    GNOME games collection.
    gnuboy 1.0.3-2 Opensource gameboy emulator
    gnugo  3.2-12 Plays the game of Go
    grhino 0.6.0-1 Strong othello game for GNOME.
    gtkmonop    0.3.0-5 Client for something resembling the well known
        ➥board game
    katomic 3.0.7-2 KDE - sokoban-like game
    kbackgammon   3.0.7-2 KDE - backgammon board game
    kde-panel-fifteen    3.0.7-2 KDE - moving squares panel game
    kdegames3    3.0.7-2 KDE - games
    kdegames3-common    3.0.7-2 KDE - shared libraries used by KDE games
    kdegames3-dev  3.0.7-2 development headers and libraries for KDE games
    kenolaba    3.0.7-2 KDE - strategy board game
    khangman    3.0.7-2 KDE - hangman word game
    kjumpingcube  3.0.7-2 KDE - tactical game
    klickety    3.0.7-2 KDE - tetris-like game
    klines 3.0.7-2 KDE - Color Lines-like logic game
    kmahjongg    3.0.7-2 KDE - pick-up game based on the ancient
               ➥mandarin Mah Jong
    kmessedwords  3.0.7-2 KDE - mind-training word game
    kmines 3.0.7-2 KDE - minesweeper-like game
```

```
kolf  3.0.7-2 KDE - mini-golf game
konquest    3.0.7-2 KDE - multi-player strategic war game
kpat  3.0.7-2 KDE - collection of solitaire-like card games
kpoker 3.0.7-2 KDE - poker card game
ksame  3.0.7-2 KDE - simple game inspired by SameGame
kshisen 3.0.7-2 KDE - Shisen-So - a Mah Jong-like game
ksokoban    3.0.7-2 KDE - sokoban-like game
kspaceduel   3.0.7-2 KDE - 2-player space arcade game
ktuberling   3.0.7-2 KDE - Mr. Potato Head-like game
lskat  3.0.7-2 KDE - 2-player card game like Offiziersskat
megami 3.0.7-2 KDE - blackjack card game
monopd 0.5.0-3 Monopoly-like game server
nethack 3.4.0-1 Console/X11 based graphical adventure game
nibbles 1.1-2  Text-based color snake game.
robotournament 01.20.02-1   Robot board game inspired by RoboRally
teg   0.10.1-12    Strategy game similar to Risk
xdigger 1.0.10-1    Boulderdash like game for X Windows
xfrisk 1.2-2  Computer version of the Risk boardgame
xgalaga 2.0.34-1    Clone of the classic game of galaga
xlightoff    1.1-1  Light switching game for X11.
xpilot 4.5.4-1 Multi-player 2D space game.
xscorch 0.1.15-2    Scorched Earth - "the mother of all games"
xscrabble    0901-1 Scrabble game for X
```

That's more like it. (Although I'll give you a hint: That isn't all the games. Some of them, such as `kbattleship`, don't have `game` in either the name or the description.) Something to note in the listing is that the lines for `gnome-games` and `gnome-games-shlibs` both now have an `i` before them. This indicates that they're already installed. If there were newer versions available that you might want to install, these would be shown as `(i)`, instead of just `i`.

Should you ever need to update your installed `fink` software to newer versions, you can use `fink update-all`, which automatically downloads everything necessary to update any installed `fink` packages on your system.

Before we leave our quick tour of `fink`, let's look at just a few other types of applications:

Spreadsheets?

```
brezup:root Documents # fink list ¦ grep "pread"
    abs   0.908-1 Opensource spreadsheet
    gnumeric    1.0.9-1 Spreadsheet program for gnome, reads many formats
    kspread 1.2.0-2 KDE - spreadsheet
```

Graphics?

```
brezup:root Documents # fink list ¦ grep "raphics"
    autotrace    0.30-4 Converts bitmap to vector graphics
    gd   1.8.4-11    Graphics generation library
    gd-bin 1.8.4-11    Graphics generation library
    gd-pm  1.33-3 Perl interface to the GD graphics library
    gd-shlibs    1.8.4-11    Graphics generation library
    gd2   2.0.1-4 Graphics generation library
    gd2-bin 2.0.1-4 Graphics generation library
    gd2-shlibs   2.0.1-4 Graphics generation library
    gif2png 2.4.6-1 GIF to PNG graphics file conversion
    gqview 1.0.2-1 Graphics file browser utility
    gri   2.10.1-2    Language for scientific graphics programming.
    kde-kfile-image-plugins 3.0.7-2 KDE - graphics
    kdegraphics3  3.0.7-2 KDE - graphics
    libart2 2.3.9-1 Library for high-performance 2D graphics
    libart2-shlibs 2.3.9-1 Library for high-performance 2D graphics
 i   netpbm 9.25-1 Graphics manipulation programs and libraries
 i   netpbm-bin   9.25-1 Graphics manipulation programs and libraries
 i   netpbm-shlibs  9.25-1 Graphics manipulation programs and libraries
    pgplot 5.2-3  Fortran- or C-callable scientific graphics package.
    pgplot-perl   2.18-2 Perl interfaces for the PGPLOT graphics library
    pymol  0.82-2 Molecular graphics system
    r-base 1.5.1-2 Environment for statistical computing and graphics
    rasmol 2.7.1.1-3    Molecular graphics visualisation tool
    sketch 0.6.13-3    Vector graphics editor
    sodipodi    0.24.1-2    Gnome vector graphics application
    transfig    3.2.3d-7    Converts xfig objects to various graphics formats.
```

Text?

```
brezup:root Documents # fink list ¦ grep "text"
    autogen 5.4.2-1 Tool for automated text generation from templates
    bluefish    0.7-1  Web-oriented text editor
    context 2001.11.13-2  Full-featured macro package written in TeX
    dosunix 1.0.13-1    Converts DOS text files to unix text format
    ee   1.4.2-3 Easy to use text editor.
    emacs-w3    4.0.47-2    Emacs text-based web browser
    emacs21 21.2-9 Flexible real-time text editor, v21.2 with X11 support
    emacs21-nox   21.2-9 Flexible real-time text editor, v21.2 for terminal only
    enscript    1.6.1-1 Converts text files to PostScript
    figlet 22-3  Makes large letters out of ordinary text
    gd-textutil-pm 0.82-1 Perl package for text utilities of GD
 i   gettext 0.10.40-3    Message localization support
```

```
    gnotepad+    1.3.3-1 Simple and feature-rich HTML/text editor
    grep  2.4.2-3 Search text files for patterns
    gtranslator   0.43-1 Gettext po file editor for the GNOME desktop environment
    html-fromtext-pm    1.005-2 Text2html function marks up plain text as HTML
    hyperref    6.72-2 Hypertext marks (clickable links) in LaTeX
    ircii  20020912-1   Popular text based irc client
    jless  358-iso254-1  Featureful text pager with ISO 2022 code extension.
    kbabel 3.0.7-2 KDE - edit and manage gettext PO files
    kedit  3.0.7-2 KDE - simple text editor
    kinput2 3.0-3  Input server for easy input of Japanese text
    kterm  6.2.0-2 X11terminal emulator that can handle multi-lingual text.
    less  376-1  Featureful text pager
    links  0.96-2 Lynx-like text WWW browser with tables
    links-ssl    0.98-1 Lynx-like text WWW browser with tables
    locale-maketext-pm   1.03-1 Perl framework for localization
    mutt-ssl    1.4i-11 Sophisticated text-based mail user agent
    nano  1.0.9-11    Improved clone of the Pico text editor.
    nedit  5.3-5  Multi-purpose text editor X Windows.
    pango1 1.0.3-2 System for Layout and rendering of internationalized text
    pango1-dev    1.0.3-2 System for Layout and rendering of internationalized text
    pango1-shlibs  1.0.3-2 System for Layout and rendering of internationalized text
    text-delimmatch-pm   1.03-1 Perl extension to find regexp delimited strings
    textutils    2.0-4  Text file processing utilities
    vile  9.3-2  Enhanced vi-like text editor.
    w3m-ssl 0.3-13 Pager/text-based WWW browser, with SSL support
    wrap  1-3   Fast text wrapping
    xemacs 21.5.4-3    Highly customizable text editor.
```

Viewers?

```
brezup:root Documents # fink list ¦ grep -i "view"
    aview  1.3.0rc1-4   Ascii art image viewer
    eog   0.6-4  Image viewing and cataloging program
    epstool 2.1-1  Utility to manipulate preview images in EPS files.
    geomview    1.8.1-5 Interactive 3D viewing program
    gkrellkam    0.3.4-1 Gkrellm plugin - Webcam viewer.
    gqview 1.0.2-1 Graphics file browser utility
    kdvi  3.0.7-2 KDE - DVI print file previewer
    kfax  3.0.7-2 KDE - fax file viewer
    kghostview   3.0.7-2 KDE - postscript viewer
    kugar  1.2.0-2 KDE - business report viewer and creator
    kview  3.0.7-2 KDE - image viewer
```

```
lv   4.49.4-2    Powerful Multilingual File Viewer
mgv   3.1.5-3 Motif PostScript viewer loosely based on Ghostview 1.5.
mlview 0.0.1.11-1   Simple XML editor for gnome
orrery 0.9.2-3 Digital model of the solar system, a geomview module
xmakemol    5.05-2 View atomic and molecular systems
xmltv  0.5.0-1 Set of utilities to manage your TV viewing
xpdf  1.01-2 Viewer for Portable Document Format (PDF) files.
xv   3.10a-2 Image viewer
```

Finally, because this one would be difficult to guess what to search for unless you knew what you were looking for, I want to point out the GIMP (GNU Image Manipulation Program):

```
brezup:root Documents # fink describe gimp
Information about 1449 packages read in 1 seconds.

pkg gimp version ###
pkg gimp version 1.2.3-10

gimp-1.2.3-10: The GNU Image Manipulation Program
 .
 Web site: http://www.gimp.org/
 .
 Maintainer: Alexander Strange <astrange@ithinksw.com>
```

The GIMP is an attempt to develop a free-software product to compete with Adobe's Photoshop application. It's definitely not Photoshop 7, but it's an amazingly powerful and configurable application. One of the neatest features is that it's not a closed proprietary application. That means the source is available, the interface to create plug-ins and so on is well documented, and many sample files are floating around the Net containing code that can be used to make custom filters that do exactly what *you* want them to do. You can buy a copy of the GIMP for your Mac if you want to, or you can type **`fink install gimp`** at the command line.

Summary

With the installation of the X Window System on your machine, a whole world of graphical Unix applications has been opened up to you. The particulars of the installation process for the X11 servers might change by the time you read this, but the availability of software that compiles and runs under X11—however you install it—will only continue to increase. For a taste of the range of X11 applications available, peruse the archives of X.org, located at `http://www.x.org/`.

CHAPTER 20

Command-Line Configuration and Administration

IN THIS CHAPTER

- Locating and Editing the OS X Configuration Files
- System Services
- Strong-Arming the System—Brute Force Behavior Modification

You've already been introduced to configuring and controlling the system through GUI utilities such as the control panes. When using older versions of Mac OS, the only access you have to the configuration for the system is through the GUI interface. Now, you have the option of using a GUI or modifying things through the command line. Although you might wonder whether you'd ever want to use the command line for configuration when Apple has provided such nice GUI tools for configuration, we think there are a few arguments to be made for the command line.

- Generally, we agree that Apple's GUI tools are nice. Still, they're GUI tools, and that means you need access to the GUI to use them. If you're trying to manage your machine from a remote location (more on this in Chapter 26, "Remote Access and Control"), access to the GUI might not be possible.
- Even if you're at the console, it generally takes more time for GUI tools to load and display their interface than it takes to tweak configuration files. Sometimes this doesn't make any difference, but sometimes it's simply annoying to wait for a GUI interface to load when only a few keystrokes are necessary to make the same change.
- Configuration files don't need you to change them. A piece of software can make changes to configurations for you. More interestingly, software can change your configurations on a schedule or based on changes that it detects in the operation of the system. This can let you automate things such as location or network settings, as well as a range of other possibilities.

- Finally, just to be pedantic, we'll point out that the GUI interface is software running on top of a non-GUI interface. It's possible for the software that creates the GUI interface to be damaged, and for the rest of the system still to be intact enough to run. If you're limited to knowledge of the GUI tools only, you're limited in your ability to fix the situation. Generally, when dealing with Unix-based things, it's safest to have a handle on the command-line configuration and administration tools. For a pure Unix book, we'd say that it is imperative that you avoid the GUI tools and learn to do everything with the command line. For this book, we'll say that it's a good idea to know the command-line tools—Apple has done a *very* good job.

This chapter introduces you to the tools that you need to modify your machine's configuration from the command line and gives you a few examples of things that you can do. You learn further specifics about the use of these tools in chapters such as Chapter 24, "User Management and Machine Clustering," where we detail specific system configuration topics.

Locating and Editing the OS X Configuration Files

Locating OS X configuration files and figuring out what can be put in them can sometimes be a bit of an adventure. It's difficult to determine the correct information to provide for some items in this chapter. Many configuration options and files that exist in OS X are not actually intended for you to use in the OS X client version. These parts of the configuration system are actually managed by tools provided only (for the moment, at least) by OS X Server. It's possible to diddle around with them, and to do some interesting things, but OS X doesn't provide the tools or the information to do a complete job of documentation or configuration. We'll do our best to provide you with up-to-the-minute information on what's been discovered to be tweakable in the system as of when this book hits the shelves. Do check online information sources such as `http://www.macosxunleashed.com/` and `http://www.macosxhints.com/`, and understand that it seems clear that Apple doesn't intend for the user to ever understand or modify some of these things.

Preference Locations

Unlike previous versions of Mac OS, which kept almost all its preferences in the Preferences folder of the System folder, OS X keeps its preferences in several different locations. Primarily these are the `/etc/` folder, the NetInfo database, and the `~/Library/Preferences/` folders. Many preferences that affect the running of the system, such as what network services are started, the machine name, and global information that does not change from login to login, are kept in the `/etc/` folder or its subfolders. Other preferences of this nature are kept in the NetInfo database. Preferences that affect individual user configuration are primarily kept in files stored in `~/Library/Preferences/`.

Preference Format

Preferences stored in files in the `/etc/` directory generally follow long-standing Unix tradition and are formatted according to their own individual file formats. For example, a number of the network services that your machine will provide to the outside world can be configured in the file `/etc/inetd.conf`, or in the file `/etc/xinetd.conf` and the `/etc/xinetd.d` directory. We choose to look at the `/etc/inetd.conf` file here, rather than `/etc/xinetd.conf` and its associated files, because it is a ubiquitous Unix file, and because its information is easier to read for familiarizing yourself with the basic network services involved. The default `inetd.conf` file as it comes from Apple is shown in Listing 20.1. The # symbol in front of each item indicates that the line is commented out and will not be run. Apple wisely leaves all these network services off by default. Many of them can be security holes, and it's best if you enable them only as you need and understand them.

> **NOTE**
>
> The numbers shown in Listing 20.1 are shown here to make the description of the file easier to follow. The line numbers are not and should not be in the actual file. This is also the case for all the listings in this chapter with line numbers.

LISTING 20.1 A Typical `/etc/inetd.conf` File

```
# WARNING
#
# Mac OS 10.2 and forward uses xinetd instead of the traditional inetd.
# See xinetd.conf(5) if you need to add a service to run out of xinetd.
# Please use /sbin/service to interface over editing the shipped files
# in /etc/xinetd.d directly. For example:
# /sbin/service telnet start
# /sbin/service telnet stop
# /sbin/service --list
#
# Internet server configuration database
#
#    @(#)inetd.conf 5.4 (Berkeley) 6/30/90
#
# Items with double hashes in front (##) are not yet implemented in the OS.
#
#finger stream tcp nowait nobody /usr/libexec/tcpd   fingerd -s
#ftp    stream tcp nowait root   /usr/libexec/tcpd   ftpd -l
#login  stream tcp nowait root   /usr/libexec/tcpd   rlogind
#nntp   stream tcp nowait usenet /usr/libexec/tcpd   nntpd
#ntalk  dgram  udp wait   root   /usr/libexec/tcpd   ntalkd
```

LISTING 20.1 Continued

```
#shell  stream tcp nowait root   /usr/libexec/tcpd   rshd
#telnet stream tcp nowait root   /usr/libexec/tcpd   telnetd
#uucpd  stream tcp nowait root   /usr/libexec/tcpd   uucpd
#comsat dgram  udp wait   root   /usr/libexec/tcpd   comsat
#tftp   dgram  udp wait   nobody /usr/libexec/tcpd   tftpd /private/tftpboot
#bootps dgram  udp wait   root   /usr/libexec/tcpd   bootpd
##pop3  stream tcp nowait root   /usr/libexec/tcpd   /usr/local/libexec/popper
##imap4 stream tcp nowait root   /usr/libexec/tcpd   /usr/local/libexec/imapd
#
# "Small servers" -- used to be standard on, but we're more conservative
# about things due to Internet security concerns. Only turn on what you
# need.
#
#chargen stream tcp    nowait root  internal
#chargen dgram  udp    wait   root  internal
#daytime stream tcp    nowait root  internal
#daytime dgram  udp    wait   root  internal
#discard stream tcp    nowait root  internal
#discard dgram  udp    wait   root  internal
#echo    stream tcp    nowait root  internal
#echo    dgram  udp    wait   root  internal
#time    stream tcp    nowait root  internal
#time    dgram  udp    wait   root  internal
#
# Kerberos (version 5) authenticated services
#
##eklogin   stream tcp  nowait root   /usr/libexec/tcpd  klogind -k -c -e
##klogin    stream tcp  nowait root   /usr/libexec/tcpd  klogind -k -c
##kshd      stream tcp  nowait root   /usr/libexec/tcpd  kshd    -k -c -A
#krb5_prop stream tcp  nowait root   /usr/libexec/tcpd  kpropd
#
# RPC based services (you MUST have portmapper running to use these)
#
##rstatd/1-3   dgram rpc/udp wait root /usr/libexec/tcpd  rpc.rstatd
##rusersd/1-2  dgram rpc/udp wait root /usr/libexec/tcpd  rpc.rusersd
##walld/1      dgram rpc/udp wait root /usr/libexec/tcpd  rpc.rwalld
##pcnfsd/1-2   dgram rpc/udp wait root /usr/libexec/tcpd  rpc.pcnfsd
##rquotad/1    dgram rpc/udp wait root /usr/libexec/tcpd  rpc.rquotad
##sprayd/1     dgram rpc/udp wait root /usr/libexec/tcpd  rpc.sprayd
#
# The following are not known to be useful, and should not be enabled unless
```

LISTING 20.1 Continued

```
63 # you have a specific need for it and are aware of the possible implications.
64 #
65 #exec  stream tcp   nowait root  /usr/libexec/tcpd  rexecd
66 #auth  stream tcp   wait   root  /usr/libexec/identd identd -w -t120
```

This is one of the most important `/etc/` preference files to be familiar with. Its lines tell the system what programs to start in response to certain network events. Briefly, the intent of the services on each line is as follows:

- Lines 1–9—This section provides a comment that Mac OS X now uses `xinetd` by default and lists the syntax for using `/sbin/service` to enable and disable services through `xinetd`.
- Line 17—The `fingerd` daemon allows external users to finger a user ID and find out whether the ID exists; if it does, how recently, and on what terminals the ID has been logged in.
- Line 18—The `ftpd` daemon provides an FTP (file transfer protocol) server.
- Line 19—The `login` service provides service for the `rlogin` remote login terminal program. Don't turn this on.
- Line 20—The `nntp` service is a Usenet newsgroups server. If your machine is configured to receive news from other servers, you can point your newsreader to your local machine to read news.
- Line 21—The `ntalk` (new protocol talk) daemon provides for real-time chat services. If you're familiar with ICQ, iChat, or IRC, this service is somewhat similar.
- Line 22—Provides remote shell service—another way to remotely access machines. This service is required to use certain remote services, such as remote tape archive storage. Because Apple hasn't provided all the software necessary to make full use of these services, we suggest that this be left off as well; it's almost as large a security risk as `rlogin` and `telnet`.
- Line 23—Provides the `telnet` daemon to allow remote `telnet` terminal connections. Don't turn this on.
- Line 24—The `uucpd` service implements the Unix-to-Unix Copy Protocol. This is an antiquated method for networking Unix machines that can't always be connected to the network. Essentially, it allows network traffic between two sites to be queued until both sites are available on the network and then exchanges the data. This service is of limited utility today and presents a significant security risk because it hasn't really been maintained since the days of 1200 baud modems.

- Line 25—The `comsat` daemon provides notification of incoming mail to mail-reader clients.
- Line 26—`tftp` is trivial file transfer protocol and is one of the methods of providing file service to completely diskless network clients. You won't need to enable this service unless you're providing network boot services for diskless Unix clients.
- Line 27—`bootp` is a way of transmitting network configuration information to clients. Chances are you'll use DHCP for this, if you have a need to do so, although it's possible that OS X server could use `bootp` for netboot clients.
- Line 28—`pop3` is a POPmail (Post Office Protocol Mail) server. In the file, Apple indicates that this service is not yet available.
- Lines 35–42—Provide a number of network and network-software diagnostic servers. Unless you are performing network diagnosis and specifically need these, leave them off. They do not cause any known security problems, but if you're not using them, they occupy resources needlessly.
- Lines 43 and 44—Provide the time service (some servers require both stream and datagram connectivity, and these must be defined on separate lines). If you want your machine to be a time server, these can be turned on.
- Lines 48–51—Start a number of Kerberos (security authentication) related servers, but most are unavailable from Apple as of the 10.3 release. The `krb5_prop` service (starting `krpropd`) is the server that propagates a master Kerberos server's database to slave servers.
- Line 55—The `rstatd` daemon allows systems to connect through the network and get machine status information.
- Line 56—The `rusersd` daemon allows systems to connect through the network and to find information about this system's users. This is generally considered to be a bad idea.
- Line 57—The `walld` daemon allows users to write to the screens of all users on the system. This facility is nice if you're root and need to tell your users that the machine is going to go down for maintenance. It's annoying if one of your users starts using it to incessantly ask anyone connected to the machine for help with trivial Unix problems.
- Line 58—The `pcnfsd` daemon provides service for a PC network filesystem product named `pcnfs`. Almost everybody uses `samba` instead nowadays.
- Line 59—The `rquotad` daemon provides disk quota information to remote machines so that they can enforce quotas that your machine specifies on disks that it is serving to them.

- Line 60—sprayd is another network diagnostic server. Simply put, it responds, as rapidly as it can, to packets placed on the network by some other machine's spray process, which places packets on the network as fast as it can. This one would be nice if Apple provided it in a later release because it can be useful for finding problem hardware in your network.
- Line 65—The rexecd daemon allows for the remote execution of parts of programs. Apple claims that it isn't known to be useful, but a programmer can make good use of this service to perform distributed processing tasks by sending parts of programs to many different machines. Of course, it is also a security risk.
- Line 66—Another service that Apple considers to be of no practical use. The identd daemon provides a method for a remote machine to verify the identity of a user causing a connection, inasmuch as any identity can be verified over the network. The service was created because it is easy for a user accessing, for example, a remote FTP site, to pretend to be a different user on your system and potentially cause trouble for the person he is pretending to be.

The service this file controls, inetd (the Internet services daemon), is a bit of a special case because it is a service configured by the inetd.conf file. Its function is to start other services. The configuration of inetd, and how it configures other services, is covered in greater detail later in this chapter.

The inetd service is available on any Unix system. Mac OS X 10.0 and 10.1 include only it. However, some administrators choose to install xinetd, the extended Internet services daemon, as a replacement for inetd. As of Mac OS X 10.2, both services are included. Both inetd and xinetd can start the same types of other services. However, xinetd offers extra features, such as greater access control and better logging. A brief discussion of configuring xinetd is included later in the chapter with the discussion of inetd. However, so that you can start to get a feel for how different the configuration files for inetd and xinetd look, Listing 20.2 shows the default /etc/xinetd.conf file.

LISTING 20.2 The Default /etc/xinetd.conf File

```
# man xinetd.conf for more information

defaults
{
    instances          = 60
    log_type           = SYSLOG daemon
    log_on_success     = HOST PID
    log_on_failure     = HOST
    cps                = 25 30
}

includedir /etc/xinetd.d
```

The `/etc/` preference file with the next most significance to you will be the `/etc/hostconfig` file. This file contains a number of variable assignments that provide information to assorted programs that run on your behalf. The values in the `/etc/hostconfig` come partly from settings in the System Preferences panes and partly from manual modification (even though the file says that it should be touched only by the controls). The `/etc/hostconfig` on your machine should look similar to Listing 20.3.

LISTING 20.3 A Typical `/etc/hostconfig` File

```
 1 ##
 2 # /etc/hostconfig
 3 ##
 4 # This file is maintained by the system control panels
 5 ##
 6
 7 # Network configuration
 8 HOSTNAME=-AUTOMATIC-
 9 ROUTER=-AUTOMATIC-
10
11 # Services
12 AFPSERVER=-NO-
13 AUTHSERVER=-NO-
14 AUTOMOUNT=-YES-
15 CUPS=-YES-
16 IPFORWARDING=-NO-
17 IPV6=-YES-
18 MAILSERVER=-YES-
19 NETINFOSERVER=-AUTOMATIC-
20 NFSLOCKS=-AUTOMATIC-
21 NISDOMAIN=-NO-
22 RPCSERVER=-AUTOMATIC-
23 TIMESYNC=-YES-
24 QTSSERVER=-NO-
25 WEBSERVER=-NO-
26 SMBSERVER=-NO-
27 DNSSERVER=-NO-
28 COREDUMPS=-NO-
29 VPNSERVER=-NO-
30 CRASHREPORTER=-YES-
```

Briefly, the lines of this listing specify the following information:

- Line 8 sets the `HOSTNAME` variable to `AUTOMATIC`. This is used in the system startup scripts to tell the machine what name it has been given in the DNS (Domain Name

Service). With the default value, the system should be able to determine the machine name properly. If you will be using your machine on a network, and it can't determine the name properly, you can't just pick this value arbitrarily. It must be assigned by your network manager. If you're not going to be using your machine on a network, feel free to place any name here that you want to see in your prompt. (You can also change what appears in your prompt by changing your machine's Rendezvous name in the Sharing pane.)

- Line 9 configures a variable that specifies that network routing is handled automatically. That means it is going to use the gateway or DHCP information that you've provided via the GUI Locations manager.
- Line 12 indicates that the machine isn't providing AppleShare Filing Protocol services, which are necessary for serving files via AppleShare.
- Line 13 specifies that the machine isn't providing authentication services.
- Line 14 controls whether the NFS Automounter will run. If you're not using NFS, it seems to make no difference. We aren't fans of NFS automounting for normal Unix installations and aren't sure what to think of it on OS X. You learn more about NFS in Chapter 23, "File and Resource Sharing with NFS and NetInfo."
- Line 15 controls whether the machine has printing services running.
- Line 16 controls IP forwarding. This is a technique by which one machine with a real network connection can make that connection available to other machines connected to it, as though they were also connected to the Internet.
- Line 17 controls whether this machine has the IPv6 protocol enabled.
- Line 18 configures whether the machine functions as its own mail server. Configuration using this option is covered in Chapter 29, "Creating a Mail Server."
- Line 19 configures whether the machine functions as a NetInfo server for other machines.
- Line 20 configures whether NFS locking starts. This is needed for NFS, a Unix file sharing protocol, to properly function.
- Line 21 specifies which, if any, NIS domain the machine belongs to. NIS is the normal Unix way of distributing user ID and password information to multiple machines in a cluster. If you have an existing Unix installation, you can subscribe your OS X machine to the Unix machine's account information.
- Line 22 determines whether the machine functions as an RPC server.
- Line 23 determines whether the machine should use a remote time server to synchronize its clock.

- Line 24 specifies whether the machine functions as a QuickTime streaming server. This technology is detailed in Chapter 27, "Web Serving."
- Line 25 controls whether the machine functions as a Web (HTTPD) server. How to enable and configure your machine as a high-powered Web server is covered in Chapter 27.
- Line 26 configures whether the machine can serve files to Windows machines. How to enable and configure your machine to serve a Windows network is covered in Chapter 30, "Windows Interoperability."
- Line 27 configures whether the machine functions as a DNS server.
- Line 28 sets whether coredumps should be enabled. Coredumps are the contents of memory that an application had at the time that it panicked. The contents are saved to a file on disk and can be used by a programmer for debugging purposes. You may find enabling this option most useful if you are having regular problems with an application or your system. A coredump file might help fix a bug in an application.
- Line 29 sets whether the Virtual Private Network (VPN) server is started. The VPN server allows an external host to connect from an insecure external network to a secure internal network over an encrypted tunnel. It assigns the external host an IP address on the internal network, and it functions as though it were actually on the internal network.
- Line 30 determines whether the machine reports crashes.

NOTE

We've abbreviated the language in the preceding list a bit. The first few entries are worded correctly—the file literally sets the values of variables, and these variables are used elsewhere to configure the properties of the system described. Later items that state that the line *controls* something should be read to mean that it sets a variable that is used by a program elsewhere to control the item.

Other `/etc/` directory preference and configuration files that you should be familiar with are

- `/etc/services`—Configures the service name to port number mapping required for `inetd` and some other network-based services.
- `/etc/hosts`—Configures the set of other machines that this machine knows about, without having to go to the DNS server to get a hostname or IP address.
- `/etc/passwd`—Configures user IDs and associated home directories, passwords, and shells.
- `/etc/group`—Configures groups and group memberships.

These files all use specific internal preferences formats rooted in Unix tradition and documented in the man pages. In OS X, these files are directly used only in single-user mode because Apple has replaced their use with databases from NetInfo. Learning about them isn't completely irrelevant, though. It's often much easier to load the NetInfo database from these files with well-defined formats than it is to enter the data directly into NetInfo. In Chapter 23, we show how to use the traditional `/etc/` configuration file formats to load data into NetInfo.

You might also want to be familiar with the formats for `/etc/fstab` and `/etc/exports`. These files traditionally control the mounting of disks and the serving of disks, respectively. Apple, however, doesn't seem to use them even in single-user mode. But the NetInfo server can load data from these file formats, so it might be useful to learn them if you will be interacting with other types of Unix machines.

Defaults Database

Preferences stored in the `~/Library/Preferences/` files are stored in XML (Extensible Markup Language), an emerging data storage standard. Readers familiar with HTML (Hypertext Markup Language) will find many similarities in the structure of HTML documents and of documents written in XML. The primary differences are that HTML is intended to be (but has wandered away from being) a structurally tagged language in a specified tag set, whereas XML is a language in which structural tagging can be arbitrarily defined.

For those unfamiliar with either language, both are essentially languages in which the content of a document is indicated by surrounding content items with tags. The beginning tag is usually of the form *<TAGNAME>*, where the < and > are required parts of the tag. The ending tag is of the form *</TAGNAME>* where the *TAGNAME* part of the begin/end pair must match. Tags in both languages can be nested, but neither supports tag pairs that overlap. (That is, *<TAG1> some data <TAG2> more data</TAG1> and more data</TAG2>* is not acceptable.) HTML has a defined set of tags that are part of the language, but XML is actually a language in which arbitrary tags can be defined. HTML tags also imply to a browser that the data enclosed by the tags has certain intended display characteristics. XML tags, however, imply only document structure and require an additional style definition to provide display properties. Finally, through design and through degeneration by lack of standards, HTML has come to include a number of tags with purposes and syntaxes outside the logic described earlier. For example, HTML allows "half tags" for certain types of tags, because it uses some tags exclusively for display control, rather than for structural tagging. HTML's `<P>` (paragraph) tag, for instance, can be used alone with no closing `</P>` tag because it specifies only that the browser should move down and start a new line with the next text. It does not delimit the boundaries of a paragraph.

For comparison, Listing 20.4 shows a syntactically correct HTML file, and Listing 20.5 shows similar data encoded in XML.

LISTING 20.4 A File with Typical HTML Tagging

```
<HTML>
<HEAD>
  <META HTTP-EQUIV="Content-type" CONTENT="text/html; charset=iso-8859-1">
  <TITLE>Animate! Ohio State - Not Quite All About Animate!</TITLE>
<LINK REL="stylesheet" HREF="../animate.css" type="text/css">
</HEAD>

<BODY MARGINWIDTH="0" MARGINHEIGHT="0" LEFTMARGIN="0" TOPMARGIN="0"
   BGCOLOR="#FFFFFF" TEXT="#000000" LINK="#C00F00" VLINK="#C00F00"
   ALINK="#808080">
<TABLE BACKGROUND="../scarlet.gif" BORDER=0 CELLSPACING=0 CELLPADDING=0
    WIDTH="100%">
 <TR>
  <TD ALIGN=LEFT VALIGN="TOP"> 
   <IMG SRC="../images/TopMenu/all-animate.gif" WIDTH=146 HEIGHT=30
      BORDER=0 ALT="[ All About Animate! ]" ALIGN="MIDDLE">
  </TD>
  <TD ALIGN=CENTER><IMG SRC="space_scarlet.gif" WIDTH=1 HEIGHT=1></TD>
  <TD ALIGN=RIGHT><A HREF="../animate.html">
   <IMG SRC="../images/TopMenu/association.gif" WIDTH=284 HEIGHT=40
      BORDER=0 ALT="[ The Ohio State University Japanese
      Animation Association ]"></A>
  </TD>
 </TR>
</TABLE>

<TABLE WIDTH="100%" BORDER="0" CELLSPACING="0" CELLPADDING="0"
    BACKGROUND="../grey.gif">
 <TR>
  <TD HEIGHT="25" ALIGN="LEFT" VALIGN="TOP" CLASS="date">
  <IMG SRC="../space_grey.gif" WIDTH=1 HEIGHT=1 BORDER=0>
  <A HREF="find.html" CLASS="date">Find Animate!</A>
  ¦
  <A HREF="joining.html" CLASS="date">Join Animate!</A>
  ¦
  <A HREF="officers.html" CLASS="date">The Officers</A>
  ¦
  <A HREF="helpers.html" CLASS="date">Helpers</A>
  ¦
  <a href="bylaws.html" CLASS="date">The Bylaws</A>
  ¦
  <a href="constitution.html" CLASS="date">The Constitution</A>
```

LISTING 20.4 Continued

```
  </TD>
  <TD ALIGN=CENTER><IMG SRC="space_scarlet.gif" WIDTH=1 HEIGHT=1></TD>
  <TD VALIGN="top" ALIGN="right"><IMG SRC="../space_grey.gif" WIDTH=1
    HEIGHT=1 BORDER=0>
  </TD>
 </TR>
</TABLE>

<TABLE WIDTH="660" BORDER="0" CELLSPACING="0" ALIGN="CENTER">
 <TR>
  <TD ALIGN="left" VALIGN="top" COLSPAN="2"><img src="../space.gif"
    height="20" width="1"></TD>
 </TR>
 <TR>
  <TD WIDTH="360">
  <P CLASS="header">All About Animate!
  <P CLASS="text">As this is a new year, we're busy readying the
  newest club information, so this section is still a little thin.
  Make sure to visit the <A HREF="officers.html">Club Officers</A>
  index and meet the people who keep you in the anime pink, as it
  were, and <A HREF="find.html">how to get to them</A>
  <P CLASS="text">In the meantime, you can go over the
  <A HREF="constitution.html">constitution</A>
  and <A HREF="bylaws.html">club bylaws</A> to learn just how things
  are run at Animate! Ohio State. Also check out the <A HREF="helpers.html">
  helpers</A> page and see just who else lends a hand at Animate!
  <P CLASS="text">This section will be updated as we receive and revise
  </TD>
  <TD WIDTH="340" ALIGN="RIGHT" VALIGN="TOP">
  <P CLASS="caption">
   <IMG SRC="../images/anime/seraphim.jpg" BORDER=1 WIDTH=325 HEIGHT=249
     ALT="[ The 266,613,336 wings of Seraphim. ]">
    The 266,613,336 wings of Seraphim.
  </TD>
 </TR>
  </TD>
 </TR>
 <TR>
  <TD COLSPAN=3>
   <IMG SRC="../space.gif" WIDTH=1 HEIGHT=1 VSPACE=400 BORDER=0>
  </TD>
 </TR>
```

LISTING 20.4 Continued

```
</TABLE>

</BODY>
</HTML>
```

LISTING 20.5 A File with Typical XML Tagging

```
<PAGE>
<SUMMARY>
  <ITEM>charset</ITEM>
   <VALUE>iso-8859-1</VALUE>
  <ITEM>Title</ITEM>
   <VALUE>Animate! Ohio State - Not Quite All About Animate!</VALUE>
</SUMMARY>

<CONTENTS>
<TABLE_FORMAT_1>
 <TABLE_ROW>
  <DATA_1>
   <!ENTITY all-animate SYSTEM "../images/TopMenu/all-animate.gif"
        NDATA GIF87A>
  </DATA_1>
  <DATA_2>
   <!ENTITY spacer SYSTEM "space_scarlet.gif" NDATA GIF87A>
  </DATA_2>
  <DATA_3>
   <LINK XML-LINK="SIMPLE" HREF="animate.html">
    <!ENTITY "The Ohio State University Japanese Animation Association"
         SYSTEM "../images/TopMenu/association.gif" NDATA GIF87A>
   </LINK>
  </DATA_3>
 </TABLE_ROW>
</TABLE_FORMAT_1>

<TABLE_FORMAT_2>
 <TABLE_ROW>
  <DATA_4>
   <!ENTITY spacer2 SYSTEM "../space_grey.gif" NDATA GIF87A>
   <LINK XML-LINK="SIMPLE" HREF="find.html">Find Animate!</LINK>
   :
```

LISTING 20.5 Continued

```
    <LINK XML-LINK="SIMPLE" HREF="joining.html">Join Animate!</LINK>
    ¦
    <LINK XML-LINK="SIMPLE" HREF="officers.html">The Officers</LINK>
    ¦
    <LINK XML-LINK="SIMPLE" HREF="helpers.html">Helpers</LINK>
    ¦
    <LINK XML-LINK="SIMPLE" HREF="bylaws.html">The Bylaws</LINK>
    ¦
    <LINK XML-LINK="SIMPLE" HREF="constitution.html">The Constitution</LINK>
  </DATA_4>
  <DATA_5><!ENTITY spacer SYSTEM "space_scarlet.gif" NDATA GIF87A></DATA_5>
  <DATA_6><!ENTITY spacer2 SYSTEM "../space_grey.gif" NDATA GIF87A></DATA_6>
 </TR>
</TABLE_FORMAT_2>

<TABLE_FORMAT_3>
 <TABLE_ROW>
  <DATA_7>
  <!ENTITY spacer3 SYSTEM "../space.gif" NDATA GIF87A>
  </DATA_7>
 </TABLE_ROW>

 <TABLE_ROW>
  <DATA_8>
  <HEADER_PARAGRAPH>All About Animate!</HEADER_PARAGRAPH>
  <NORMAL_PARAGRAPH>As this is a new year, we're busy readying the newest
  club information, so this section is still a little thin. Make sure
  to visit the <LINK XML-LINK="SIMPLE" HREF="officers.html">Club Officers
  </LINK>index and meet the people who keep you in the anime pink, as it
  were, and <LINK XML-LINK="SIMPLE" HREF="find.html">how to get to them
  </LINK>.</NORMAL_PARAGRAPH>
  <NORMAL_PARAGRAPH>In the meantime, you can go over the
  <LINK XML-LINK="SIMPLE" HREF="constitution.html">constitution</LINK>
  and <LINK XML-LINK="SIMPLE" HREF="bylaws.html">club bylaws</LINK>
  to learn just how things are run at Animate! Ohio State. Also check
  out the <LINK XML-LINK="SIMPLE" HREF="helpers.html">helpers</LINK>
  page and see just who else lends a hand at Animate!</NORMAL_PARAGRAPH>
  <NORMAL_PARAGRAPH>This section will be updated as we receive and revise
  </DATA_8>
  <DATA_9>
  <CAPTION_PARAGRAPH>
```

20

LISTING 20.5 Continued

```
   <!ENTITY "The 266,613,336 wings of Seraphim" SYSTEM
        "../images/anime/seraphim.jpg" NDATA GIF87A>
   The 266,613,336 wings of Seraphim.
  </CAPTION_PARAGRAPH>
  </DATA_9>
 </TABLE_ROW>

 <TABLE_ROW>
  <WIDE_DATA>
   <!ENTITY spacer3 "../space.gif" NDATA GIF87A>
  </WIDE_DATA>
 </TABLE_ROW>
</TABLE_FORMAT_3>

</CONTENTS>
</PAGE>
```

The HTML file renders in a Web browser similar to what is shown in Figure 20.1. The XML file actually has no visual representation because XML is a structural definition and requires an auxiliary style definition to indicate the appropriate visual representation. The auxiliary style definition provides all the style mappings so that tags that have explicit styles in the HTML file (such as `<TD>` elements) with assigned widths, and so on, can be given display style directions. This is why the XML representation has many different `<DATA_*>` tags, instead of a single `<TD>` type tag with parameters. The appropriate display options characteristics for each `<DATA_*>` type are defined in the external style file. We won't provide the style file here because learning its syntax won't help you with Apple's preferences. Still, for this example, you can probably imagine reasonable visual intentions from the tag names and a comparison with the HTML file.

The observant reader will note that the similarities are significant, but that where HTML allows implicitly closed tags for items such as `<P>` (paragraph), XML requires explicitly closed tags. For completely nonenclosing tags, such as HTML's `<HR>` tag (horizontal line), XML substitutes a tag type that is understood to open and close itself in the statement. The XML equivalent would look like `<HR/>`, which is read by the parser as `<HR></HR>`. Apple uses this type of tagging frequently in its XML preferences files. Listing 20.6 shows the `Terminal` preference file (located in `~/Library/Preferences/com.apple.Terminal.plist`) from an installed, but little-used user account.

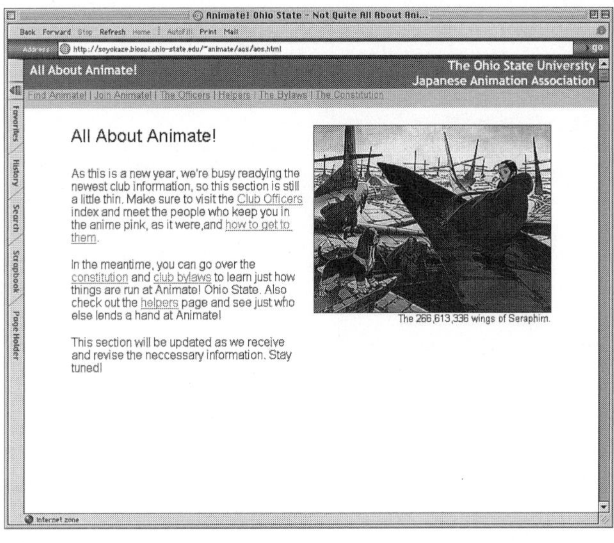

FIGURE 20.1 A Web browser renders the HTML shown in Listing 20.4 like this. The XML shown in Listing 20.5 could render like this as well, but it also could render in any number of other ways as well.

LISTING 20.6 An Almost Bare Preference File for `Terminal`

```
<?xml version="1.0" encoding="UTF-8"?>
<!DOCTYPE plist PUBLIC "-//Apple Computer//DTD PLIST 1.0//EN" "http://www.apple.
com/DTDs/PropertyList-1.0.dtd">
<plist version="1.0">
<dict>
    <key>StartupFile</key>
    <string></string>
</dict>
</plist>
```

The terminal preferences currently contain little of interest other than a reference to a startup file.

Listing 20.7 shows the `Terminal` preferences from a considerably more used account. As you can see, the `plist` files are not required to contain all the preferences for an application and can grow as the user specifies more preferences that aren't just the defaults. One annoyance that this causes is that sometimes hidden preferences aren't accessible through any of the application's Preferences panes. These preferences can find their way into the XML `plist` files only if somebody discovers their existence and adds the preference line to the `plist` file manually.

LISTING 20.7 A Preferences File for `Terminal` That Has Accumulated Some Settings over Time

```
<?xml version="1.0" encoding="UTF-8"?>
<!DOCTYPE plist PUBLIC "-//Apple Computer//DTD PLIST 1.0//EN" "http://www.apple.
com/DTDs/PropertyList-1.0.dtd">
<plist version="1.0">
<dict>
    <key>AutoFocus</key>
    <string>YES</string>
    <key>Autowrap</key>
    <string>YES</string>
    <key>BackgroundImagePath</key>
    <string></string>
    <key>Backwrap</key>
    <string>YES</string>
    <key>Bell</key>
    <string>YES</string>
    <key>BlinkCursor</key>
    <string>YES</string>
    <key>BlinkText</key>
    <string>YES</string>
    <key>CleanCommands</key>
    <string>rlogin;telnet;ssh;slogin</string>
    <key>Columns</key>
    <string>118</string>
    <key>CursorShape</key>
    <string>0</string>
    <key>CustomTitle</key>
    <string>Terminal</string>
    <key>DeleteKeySendsBackspace</key>
    <string>NO</string>
    <key>DisableAnsiColors</key>
    <string>NO</string>
    <key>DoubleBold</key>
    <string>YES</string>
    <key>DoubleColumnsForDoubleWide</key>
    <string>NO</string>
    <key>DoubleWideChars</key>
    <string>YES</string>
    <key>EnableDragCopy</key>
    <string>YES</string>
    <key>ExecutionString</key>
    <string></string>
```

LISTING 20.7 Continued

```
<key>FontAntialiasing</key>
<string>NO</string>
<key>FontHeightSpacing</key>
<string>1</string>
<key>FontWidthSpacing</key>
<string>1</string>
<key>IsMiniaturized</key>
<string>NO</string>
<key>KeyBindings</key>
<dict>
    <key>$F708</key>
    <string>ESC[25~</string>
    <key>$F709</key>
     .
     .
     .
    <key>~F712</key>
    <string>ESC[34~</string>
</dict>
<key>Meta</key>
<string>-1</string>
<key>NSColorPanelMode</key>
<string>6</string>
<key>NSColorPanelVisibleSwatchRows</key>
<integer>1</integer>
<key>NSFixedPitchFont</key>
<string>Monaco</string>
<key>NSFixedPitchFontSize</key>
<real>10</real>
<key>NSFontPanelPreviewHeight</key>
<real>0.0</real>
<key>NSWindow Frame Inspector</key>
<string>102 311 268 435 0 0 1024 746 </string>
<key>NSWindow Frame NSColorPanel</key>
<string>325 263 201 309 0 0 1024 746 </string>
<key>OptionClickToMoveCursor</key>
<string>NO</string>
.
.
.
<key>TermCapString</key>
```

LISTING 20.7 Continued

```
    <string>xterm-color</string>
    <key>TerminalOpaqueness</key>
    <real>1</real>
    <key>TextColors</key>
    <string>1.000 1.000 1.000 0.000 0.000 0.000 1.000 1.000 1.000 1.000 1.00
0 1.000 0.000 0.000 0.000 1.000 1.000 1.000 0.667 0.667 0.667 1.000 1.000 1.000
</string>
    <key>TitleBits</key>
    <string>78</string>
    <key>Translate</key>
    <string>YES</string>
    <key>UseCtrlVEscapes</key>
    <string>YES</string>
    <key>VisualBell</key>
    <string>NO</string>
    <key>WinLocULY</key>
    <string>471</string>
    <key>WinLocX</key>
    <string>67</string>
    <key>WinLocY</key>
    <string>0</string>
    <key>WindowCloseAction</key>
    <string>1</string>
</dict>
</plist>
```

Listing 20.8 shows a preferences file for a shareware product called GraphicConverter. As you can see in Listings 20.7 and 20.8, the items stored in the `~/Library/Preferences/` files are many and varied. You also can see that some preferences are not intuitively parseable.

> **NOTE**
>
> The truly observant might notice that the big block of characters in the middle of Listing 20.8 displays a vague pattern. In fact, it's an icon, encoded and stored in text form. This might give you an idea or two about how you could customize program icons automatically from a script.

LISTING 20.8 The `plist` File for GraphicConverter

```
<?xml version="1.0" encoding="UTF-8"?>
<!DOCTYPE plist PUBLIC "-//Apple Computer//DTD PLIST 1.0//EN"
➥"http://www.apple.com/DTDs/PropertyList-1.0.dtd">
```

LISTING 20.8 Continued

```
<plist version="1.0">
<dict>
    <key>AppleNavServices:ChooseFolder:0:Position</key>
    <data>
    AL4A6A==
    </data>
    <key>AppleNavServices:ChooseFolder:0:Size</key>
    <data>
    AAAAAAFvAjA=
    </data>
    <key>AppleNavServices:GetFile:0:Path</key>
    <string>file://localhost/Volumes/Void/Masa/10030425/</string>
    <key>AppleNavServices:GetFile:0:Position</key>
    <data>
    AJAA6A==
    </data>
    <key>AppleNavServices:GetFile:0:Size</key>
    <data>
    AAAAAAHJAjA=
    </data>
    <key>custom color table</key>
    <data>
    //////////////8zM/////5mZ/////2Zm/////zMz/////wAA///MzP/////MzMzM///M
    zJmZ///MzGZm///MzDMz///MzAAA//+Zmf////+ZmczM//+ZmZmZ//+ZmWZm//+ZmTMz
    //+ZmQAA//9mZv////9mZszM//9mZpmZ//9mZmZm//9mZjMz//9mZgAA//8zM/////8z
    M8zM//8zM5mZ//8zM2Zm//8zMzMz//8zMwAA//8AAP/////8AAMzM//8AAJmZ//8AAGZm
    //8AADMz//8AAAAAzMz/////zMz//8zMzMz//5mZzMz//2ZmzMz//zMzzMz//wAAzMzM
    zP//zMzMzMzMzMzJmZzMzMzGZmzMzMzDMzzMzMzAAAzMyZmf//zMyZmczMzMyZmZmZ
    zMyZmWZmzMyZmTMzzMyZmQAAzMxmZv//zMxmZszMzMxmZpmZzMxmZmZmzMxmZjMzzMxm
    ZgAAzMwzM///zMwzM8zMzMwzM5mZzMwzM2ZmzMwzMzMzzMwzMwAAzMwAAP//zMwAAMzM
    zMwAAJmZzMwAAGZmzMwAADMzzMwAAAAAmZn/////mZn//8zMmZn//5mZmZn//2ZmmZn/
    /zMzmZn//wAAmZnMzP//mZnMzMzMmZnMzJmZmZnMzGZmmZnMzDMzmZnMzAAAmZmZmf//
    mZmZmczMmZmZmZmZmZmZmWZmmZmZmTMzmZmZmQAAmZlmZv//mZlmZszMmZlmZpmZmZlm
    ZmZmmZlmZjMzmZlmZgAAmZkzM///mZkzM8zMmZkzM5mZmZkzM2ZmmZkzMzMzmZkzMwAA
    mZkAAP//mZkAAMzMmZkAAJmZmZkAAGZmmZkAADMzmZkAAAAAZmb/////Zmb//8zMZmb/
    /5mZZmb//2ZmZmb//zMzZmb//wAAZmbMzP//ZmbMzMzMZmbMzJmZZmbMzGZmZmbMzDMz
    ZmbMzAAAZmaZmf//ZmaZmczMZmaZmZmZZmaZmWZmZmaZmTMzZmaZmQAAZmZmZv//ZmZm
    ZszMZmZmZpmZZmZmZmZmZmZmZjMzZmZmZgAAZmYzM///ZmYzM8zMZmYzM5mZZmYzM2Zm
    ZmYzMzMzZmYzMwAAZmYAAP//ZmYAAMzMZmYAAJmZZmYAAGZmZmYAADMzZmYAAAAAMzP/
    ////MzP//8zMMzP//5mZMzP//2ZmMzP//zMzMzP//wAAMzPMzP//MzPMzMzMMzPMzJmZ
    MzPMzGZmMzPMzDMzMzPMzAAAMzOZmf//MzOZmczMMzOZmZmZMzOZmWZmMzOZmTMzMzOZ
```

LISTING 20.8 Continued


```
mQAAMzNmZv//MzNmZszMMzNmZpmZMzNmZmZmMzNmZjMzMzNmZgAAMzMzM///MzMzM8zM
MzMzM5mZMzMzM2ZmMzMzMzMzMzMzMwAAMzMAAP//MzMAAMzMMzMAAJmZMzMAAGZmMzMA
ADMzMzMAAAAAAAD/////AAD//8zMAAD//5mZAAD//2ZmAAD//zMzAAD//wAAAADMzP//
AADMzMzMAADMzJmZAADMzGZmAADMzDMzAADMzAAAAACZmf//AACZmczMAACZmZmZAACZ
mWZmAACZmTMzAACZmQAAAABmZv//AABmZszMAABmZpmZAABmZmZmAABmZjMzAABmZgAA
AAAzM///AAAzM8zMAAAzM5mZAAAzM2ZmAAAzMzMzAAAzMwAAAAAAAAP//AAAAAMzMAAAA
AJmZAAAAAGZmAAAAADMz7u4AAAAA3d0AAAAAu7sAAAAAqqoAAAAAiIgAAAAAd3cAAAAA
VVUAAAAAREQAAAAAIiIAAAAAEREAAAAAAADu7gAAAADd3QAAAAC7uwAAAACqqgAAAACI
iAAAAAB3dwAAAABVVQAAAABERAAAAAAiIgAAAAAREQAAAAAAAO7uAAAAAN3dAAAAALu7
AAAAAKqqAAAAAIiIAAAAAHd3AAAAAFVVAAAAAEREAAAAACIiAAAAABER7u7u7u7u3d3d
3d3du7u7u7u7qqqqqqqqiIiIiIiId3d3d3d3VVVVVVVVREREREREIiIiIiIiERERERER
AAAAAAAA
</data>
<key>dialog last position new</key>
<data>
AAAAAAAAAAAAAAAAAAAAAAAAAAAAAAAAAAAAAAAAAAAAAAAAAAAAAAAAAAAAAAAA
AAAAAAAAAAAAAAAAAAAAAAAAAAAAAAAAAAAAAAAAAAAAAAAAAAAAAAAAAAAAAAAA
AAAAAAAAAAAAAAAAAAAAAAAAAAAAAAAAAAAAAAAAAAAAAAAAAAAAAAAAAAAAAAAA
AAAAAAAAAAAAAAAAAAAAAAAAAAAAAAAAAAAAAAAAAAAAAAAAAAAAAAAAAAAAAAAA
AAAAAAAAAAAAAAAAAAAAAAAAAAAAAAAAAAAAAAAAAAAAAAAAAAAAAAAAAAAAAAAA
AAAAAAAAAAAAAAAAAAAAAAAAAAAAAAAAAAAAAAAAAAAAAAAAAAAAAAAAAAAAAAAA
AAAAAAAAAAAAAAAAAAAAAAAAAAAAAAAAAAAAAAAAAAAAAAAAAAAAAAAAAAAAAAAA
AAAAAAAAAAAAAAAAAAAAAAAAAAAAAAAAAAAAAAAAAAAAAAAAAAAAAAAAAAAAAAAA
AAAAAAAAAAAAAAAAAAAAAAAAAAAAAAAAAAAAAAAAAAAAAAAAAAAAAAAAAAAAAAAA
AAAAAAAAAAAAAAAAAAAAAAAAAAAAAAAAAAAAAAAAAAAAAAAAAAAAAAAAAAAAAAAA
AAAAAAAAAAAAAAEEAIEAAAAAAAAAAAAAAAAAAAAAAAAAAAAAA=
</data>
<key>extension 1</key>
<string>pict</string>
<key>extension 10</key>
<string>tga</string>
<key>extension 11</key>
<string>jpg</string>
<key>extension 12</key>
<string>psd</string>
<key>extension 13</key>
 .
 .
<string>im</string>
<key>extension 71</key>
<string>jp2</string>
```

LISTING 20.8 Continued

```
<key>extension 8</key>
<string>StartupScreen</string>
<key>extension 9</key>
<string>bmp</string>
<key>general</key>
<data>
```

```
AAADcAAVABIBAAAAAAAAAAADAAkAAAAAAAAAAADAAkAAAAAAAAAAAD/pmZmZmZmaP+mZ
mZmZmZo/6ZmZmZmj/pmZmZmaAQAAAAAMAAAAAAAAAAAAAAABAAAAAQEBAAEBAQAAAQBk
AAEAAgACAAEAAQABAAEBAQEAAQAAAwAAAAAEAAAAAwAAAAAAAAAEAAAAAUlNFRAEAAAAA
MgABAAAAAAAABAAEBAAEAAAAAAAAAAAAAAAAAAAAAAAAAAABAAAAAoAAAAHgAAAABAAA
AAgAAABIAAAAAQAABAAAAAAAAAAEAAAABAAAAAAKAAAAB4AAAAAAAAAAAAAAAAAAAAAA
AAAAAAAAAAAAAAAAAAAAAAAAAAAAAAAAAAAAAAAAAAAAAAAAAAAAAAAAAAAAAAAAAAAA
AAAAAAAAAAAAAAAAAAAAAAAAAAAAAAAAAAAAAAAAAAAAAAAAAAAAAAAAAAAAAAAAAAAA
AAAAAAAAAAAAAAAAAAAAAAAAAAAAAAAAAAAAAAAAAAAAAAAAAAAAAAAAAAAAAAAAAAAA
AAAAAAAAAAAAAAAAAAAAAAAAAAAAAAAAAAAAAAAAAAAAAAAAAAAAAAAAAAAAAAAAAAAA
AAAAAAAAAAAAAAAAAAAAAAAAAAAAAAAAAAAAAAAAAAAAAAAAAAAAAAAAAAAAAAAAAAAA
AAAAAAAAAAAAAAAAAAAAAAAAAAAAAAAAAAAAAAAAAAAAAAAAAAAAAAAAAAAAAAAAAAAA
AAAAAAAAAAAAAAAAAAAAAAAAAAAAAAAAAAAAAAAAAAAAAAAAAAAAAAAAAAAAAAAAAAAA
AAAAAAAAAAAAAAAAAAAAAAAAAAAAAAAAAAAAAAAAAAAAAAAAAAAAAAAAAAAAAAAAAAAA
AAAAAAAAAAAAAAAAAAAAAAAAAAAAAAAAAAAAAAAAAAAAAAAAAAAAAAAAAAAAAAAAAAAA
AAAAAAAAAAAAAAAAAAAAAAAAAAAAAAAAAAAAAAAAAAAAAAAAAAAAAABQAFABGAF8AQAA
AAABAQAAAQABAQEAAAABAAAAAAAAAAAAADwEBAAAAAAAAAAAAAAAAAAAAAAAAAAAAQAA
AAAAAAAAAAAAAAAAAAABAAABAQAAAAEAAAA/8AAAAAAAAAAAAAAAP+zMzMzM0/6ZmZmZ
mj/pmZmZmZmaP+mZmZmZmZoBLAAAAIAAAwADAABqcGVnAAAAAAAAAAADAHJwemEAAAAA
AAAAAAMAAAADAAAMAAAAAAAAYAAfQAAAAAAAAAAAMAAAADAAAAAAAABAAAAP9AAAAAAAAAAA
AAAAAAA/1mZmZmZgAAAAAAAD/gAAAAAAAAAAAAAAAAAAAP+ZmZmZmYAAAAAAAA/8AAA
AAAAAAAAAAAAAAD/zMzMzMzAAAAAAAAAAP/MzMzMzMAAAAAAAAAAA/8zMzMzMwAAAAAAAAAAA
AD/QAAAAAAAAAAQFmAAAAAAAAAAAAz/wAAAAAAAAAAAAAAAAAAAAAAAAAAAJagAABvQAQEAAAAA
AAAAAAAAAAAAAAAAAAAAAAAAAAAAAAAAAAAAAAAAAAAAAAAACAAAAyAAAAAAAAAAAAABAAEA
AAADAAAAAAABkAAAAAQAAAAEAAAAAAAAAAAAAAAAAAABAAAAAQAAAAAAAAAAABAAAAAAAAAAA
AUAAAADwAAAABQAAAAAAAAAAAA////////AAAACQAAAAAAAAAAAAAAAAAAAEAAAABAAAA
AQAAAAwAAAAAAAAAAAAAAAAAAAAAAAAAAAAAA//8AAP//AAAAAP//////wAAAAD//wAA
//9ERAAAAAD///////93d3d3d3d3d3//93d///d3d3d////////3d3d3f//3d3////
////AAD///////8AAAABAAAAAQAAAAAAAAAAAAAAAAQAAAAQAAAAAAAAAAAAQAAAAAAAAAAAB
AAAAAAAAAAwAAAAAAAAAAAAAAAAAAAYAAAAAAAAAAABgAAAAAAAAAAAAAAAAAWgAAAAAAAAAAACAAAA
AAAAAAAAAAKAAAAB4AAAAAUAAAABAAAAQAAAADQAAAADAAAACQAAAAAAAAP///////wAA
AAAAAAAAAAAAAAAAAUAAAADIAAAAAQAAAAAAAAAAAAAAAQAAAAEAAAABAAAAAAAAAAAAAUA
AAAAAAAAAAAAAAAAAAAAAAAAAAAAAAAAAAAAAAAAAAAAAAAAQAAAABAAAAAAAAAAAAAAAA
AAAAAAAAAAAAAAAAAAAAAAAAAAAAAAAAAAAAAAAAAAAAAAAAAAAAAAAAAAAAAAAAAAAA
AwAAAAEAAAAAAAAAAAAAAwAAAAIAAAAAAAAAAAAAEAAAAAAAAAAAAQAAAAEAAAAAAAAAAAAAA
AAEAAAAAAAAAAAAQAAAAAAAAAAAAAAAAAQAAAAAAAAAAAAAAAAAAAAIAAAABAAAAAAAAAAAA
```

LISTING 20.8 Continued


```
AAAAAAAAAAAAAAAAAAAAAAAAAAAAAAAAAAAAAAAAAAAAAAAAAAAAAAAAAAAAAAAB
AAAAAAAAAAcAAAABAAAAlgAAAAQAAAABAAAAAAAAoAAAAAAAAAAAAAAAEAAAAAAA
AQAAAAEBcgAAAAAAAFnAAAAAAAAWIAAAAAAAADcGFsAAAAAAAAAAAAAAAAAAAAAD
AAAAAAAAAMAAAAMAAAACQAAAAAAAABAAAAAAAAAAAAAAAAAAAAAAAAAAAAAAAAAA
AAAAAAAAAAAAAAAAAAAAAAAAAAAAAAAAAAAAAAAAAAAAAAAAAAAAAAAAAAEAAAAA
AAAAgAAAAAAAAAAAAAAAQAAAAEAAAAAAAAAQAAAAEAAAABAAAAAAAAAAAAABAAAA
AQAAAAAAAABAAAAAAAAAAAAAABAAAAQAAAAoAAAAKAAAAAAAAAAoAAAAFAAAAQAA
AAAAAAAAAAAAAQAAAAAAAAAAAAAAAAAAAAAAAAAAAAAAAAAAAAAAAAAAAAAAAAAA
AAABAAAABQAFAAAAAQAAAAAAAAAAAZAAAAGQAAAABAAAAAwAAAAEAAAAAAAAAAAA
AAAAAAABAAAABQAAAAMAAAAAAAAAAAzM0AAAABAAAAAQAAAAAAAAAAAAAEdLT04A
AAAAAAAAAAAAAAAAAABAAAAAAAAAAAAAABAAAAAAAAAEAAAABAAAAQAAAAEAAAAA
AAAAAAAAAAAAAAAAAAAAAAAAAAAAAAAAAAAAAAAAAAAAAAEqKioqKioqKgAAAAAA
AAAAAAAAAAABAAAAAFAAAABQAAAAAAAAAAAAAyAAAAMgAAAAAAACCAAAAZAAAAAA
AAAAAAAAAAAAAAAAAAAAAAAAEAAAAAAAAAAFIqY2gAAAAAAACAAAAgAAAAAAAAAA
AAAAAAMAAAABAAAAAAAAAAAAAAAAAAAAAAAEAAAABAAAAAQAAAAEAAAABAAAAQAA
AAEAAAABAAAAQAAAAEAAAABAAAAQAAAAEAAAABAAAAQAAAAEAAAAAAAAAQAAAAEA
AAAAAAAAAAAAAAAAAACAAAAwAAAAAAAAAAAAAAAAAAAEAAAABAAAAAAAAAAAAAAB
AAAAAQAAAAEAAAABAAAAAAAAAAAAAAAAAAAQAAAAIAAAAAAAAAAAAAAEAAAAAAAA
AAAAAAAAAAAAAAAAAAAAEAAAABAAAABAAAAAEAAAAyAAAAMgAAAAAAAAAAAEAAAAA
AAAAAQAAAAEAAAAAAAAFAAAAAAAAAAAAAAAAAAAAAAAABAAAAQAAAABNT1NTAAAA
AgAAAAoAAAABAAAAQAAAAAAAAAAAQYAAQAAABQAAAAUAAAAAAAAAAAAAABAAAAAAA
AAQAAAADAAAAAAAAAEAAAABAAAAAAAAAEAAAAAAAAAAAAAAAAAAAAAAAAQAAAyAA
AAMgAAAAAAAAAAoAAAAAAAAAgAAAAMAAAABAAAAAAAAGQAAAAAAAAAAAAAAEAAAAA
AAAAAAAAAAAAAAAAAAAAAAAAAAAAAAAAAAAAAAAAAAAAAAAAAAAAAAAAAAAAAAAA
AAAAAAAAAAAAAAAAAAAAAAAAAAAAAAAAAAAAAAAAAAAAAAAAAAAAAAAAAAAAAAAA
AAAAAAAAAAAAAAAAAAAAAAAAAAAAAAAAAAAAAAAAAAAAAAAAAAAAAAAAAAAAAAAA
AAAAAAAAAAAAAAAAAAAAAAAAAAAAAAAAAAAAAAAAAAAAAAAAAAAAAAAAAAAAAAAA
AAAAAAAAAAAAAAAAAAAAAAAAAAAAAAAAAAAAAAAAAAAAAAAAAAAAAAAAAAAAAAAA
AAAAAAAAAAAAAAAAAAAAAAAAAAAAAAAAAAAAAAAAAAAAAAAAAAAAAAAAAAAAAAAA
AAAAAAAAAAAAAAAAAAAAAAAAAAAAAAAAAAAAAAAAAAAAAAAAAAAAAAAAAAAAAAAA
AAAAAAAAAAAAAAAAAAAAAAAAAAAAAAAAAAAAAAAAAAAAAAAAAAAAAAAAAAAAAAAA
AAAAAAAAAAAAAAAAAAAAAAAAAAAAAAAAAAAAAAAAAAAAAAAAAAAAAAAAAAAAAAAA
AAAAAAAAAAAAAAAAAAAAAAAAAAAAAAAAAAAAAAAAAAAAAAAAAAAAAAAAAAAAAAAA
AAEAAAABAAAAAAAAAAAAAD6AAAAAAAAAAAAAAAAAAAAABAAAAAAAAAAAAAAAC0AAAA
AAAAAAAAAAAyAAAAUEAAAAAAAAQAAAAAAAAAAAAAABAAAAAAAAAAAAAAAAAAAbgAA
AG4AAAABAAAAAwAAAAQAAAAAAAAAAAAG5irkGAAAAAAAAAAAAAAAAAAAAAQAAAAAA
AAAAAAAAAAAAAAH//////8AAAAAAAAAAAAAgAAAABAAAAgAAAAEAAAABAAAAMv//
/////wAAAAEAAAAAAAAAAAQAAAAEAAAABAAAAQAAAAEAAAABAAAAQAAAAEAAAABAAA
AQAAAAEAAAABAAAAQAAAAEAAAABAAAAQAAAAEAAAABAAAAQAAAAEAAAABAAAAAAA
AAEAAAADAAAAAAAAAAAAAAAAAAAAAAAAAAAAAAAAAAAAAAAAAAAAAAAAlgAAAAEA
AAABAAAAAQAAAAAAAAAAAAAAAAAAAAAAAAAAAAAAAAAAAAAAAAAAAAAAAAAAAAAA
```

LISTING 20.8 Continued

```
    AAAAAAAAAAEAAAAAAAAAAAAAAAAAAAAAAAAACWAAAADIAAAAAAAAAAAAAAAAEAAAe9AAAA
    AAAAAAAAAAAAAAAAAAAAAAAAAAAAAAAAAAgAAAAEAAAABAAAAAAAAAAAAAAAAAAAAAAAAA
    AAEAAAAeAAAAAQAAAAAAAAAAAAAAAAAAAAAAAIAAAAAAAAAAMAAAAAQAAABQAAAAUAAAA
    AAAAAAAAAAAAAAAAAAAAAAAAAAAAAAAAAAAAAAAAAAAAAAAAAAAMgAAAAAAAAAAAAA
    AAAAAAAZAAAAAAAAAAAAAAAAHP9ZmZmZmZmY/8AAAAAAAAD/ZmZmZmZmaP6mZmZmZmZo/
    yZmZmZmZmgAAAAEAAAAAAAAAAAAAAA+gAAAAAAAAACwAAAFAAAAAAAAAAAAAAAAAAAAAB
    AAAAAQAAAAAAAAAA
    </data>
    <key>notification status</key>
    <data>
    AAAAAAAAAAAAAAAAAAAAAAAAAAAAAAAAAAAAAAAAAAAAAAAAAAAAAAAAAAAAAAAAAAAAAA
    AAAAAAAAAAAAAAAAAAAAAAAAAAAAAAAAAAAAAAAAAAAAAAAAAAAAAAAAAAAAAAAAAAAAAA
    AAAAAAAAAAAAAAAAAAAAAAAAAAAAAAAAAAAAAAAAAA
    </data>
    <key>string 0</key>
    <string></string>
    <key>string 1</key>
    <string></string>
    <key>string 10</key>
    .
    .
    .
    <key>string 25</key>
    <string>YYYY-MM-DD HH.NN.SS</string>
    <key>string 26</key>
    <string>TXT HTM HTML EXE DLL P C PAS CC ASM COM SYS LST DOC XLS PST OST
 INI PPT INF SIT ZIP TAR MIM GZIP ARJ</string>
    <key>string 27</key>
    <string>TXT HTM HTML EXE DLL P C PAS CC ASM COM SYS LST DOC XLS PST OST
 INI PPT INF SIT ZIP TAR MIM GZIP ARJ</string>
    <key>string 28</key>
    <string></string>
    <key>string 29</key>
    <string>n-cc-rr.x</string>
    <key>string 3</key>
    <string>en</string>
    <key>string 30</key>
    <string>target="_blank"</string>
    <key>string 31</key>
    <string>ftp://</string>
```

20

LISTING 20.8 Continued

```
    .
    .
    .
</dict>
</plist>
```

As we mentioned, some application preferences are hidden. However, if you are interested, you can spend some time discovering possible preferences. Using the `strings` command can assist in discovering hidden preferences. You see a list of all textual strings in the program. It's reasonable to expect that for the program to read strings out of a `.plist` file, it must contain the string, so the strings found in the program make for potentially interesting things to try as preferences. For example, to try to discover some of the available hidden preferences in the Dock, you might run

```
strings /System/Library/CoreServices/Dock.app/Contents/MacOS/Dock | more
```

Some of the output you get includes the following excerpts:

```
__dyld_mod_term_funcs
__dyld_make_delayed_module_initializer_calls
The kernel support for the dynamic linker is not present to run this program.
showhidden
showshadow
DoesPointToFocusCursorUpdate
ClientMayIgnoreEvents
com.apple.finder
en_US
trashlabel
owensdock
dock
.dock
AppleShowAllExtensions
AppleShowAllFiles
notfound
trashfull
trashempty
finder
openfolder
wvousfloat
wvousfloatselected
wvouscornertl
wvouscornertr
```

```
wvouscornerbl
wvouscornerbr
/System/Library/CoreServices/Finder.app
.app
autohide
magnification
/System/Library/PreferencePanes/Dock.prefPane
poof.png
...
TrashName
TrashRemoveFromDock
Trash
Remove From Dock
default.plist
com.apple.dock
version
persistent-apps
...
orientation
bottom
left
right
pinning
middle
start
mineffect
genie
scale
suck
...
size-immutable
magnify-immutable
autohide-immutable
position-immutable
mineffect-immutable
contents-immutable
...
```


As you can see, the resulting output contains a variety of items, from comments to filenames to possible preference names and possible preference values. From the output, we might guess that `orientation` is a preference and that possible values are `bottom`, `left`, or `right`. We might also guess that `mineffect` is another preference with possible values of `genie`, `scale`, or `suck`. From the Dock control pane, however, we only have the choices of genie or scale, so we've probably already discovered a sort of hidden preference. In that same section of output is pinning, which looks as if it might have possible values of middle or start. In the final section of the shown output, a number of entries that end in immutable, making it seem as if there might be a way to set some preferences so that they don't change. Without experimenting, though, we can't be sure what behavior, if any, to expect. In the middle, there's an entry for poof.png, which is an image file—wonder if that's the Dock "poof" for when you remove things from it by dragging, and whether we could customize that little animation by finding and editing this graphics file?

Instead of requiring you to edit XML files directly, Apple has provided a convenient command-line program for editing the preferences stored in these files. The defaults command allows you to specify a preference to be modified and a value with which to modify it. If the application whose preferences you are trying to modify is currently running, restart the application. As an example of the defaults command in use, the following command pins the Dock at the beginning side of the Dock, as shown in Figure 20.2:

```
defaults write com.apple.dock pinning start
```

Specifically, this command modifies the preference pinning in the file ~/Library/Preferences/com.apple.dock.plist, and sets the value to start. Logging out and logging back in is one way to cause changes to the Dock to take effect. Now this file contains these lines:

```
<key>pinning</key>
<string>start</string>
```

Suppose that you don't want to disable the option to hide the Dock. You might try enabling the autohide-immutable item we saw earlier in the output by using the following command:

```
defaults write com.apple.dock autohide-immutable -bool true
```

The command modifies the preference autohide-immutable to have the Boolean value true. Now the file has these lines:

```
<key>autohide-immutable</key>
<true/>
```

In the Dock control pane, the option to hide the Dock is no longer available, and the option no longer appears under the Apple menu. Figure 20.3 shows the modified Dock control pane.

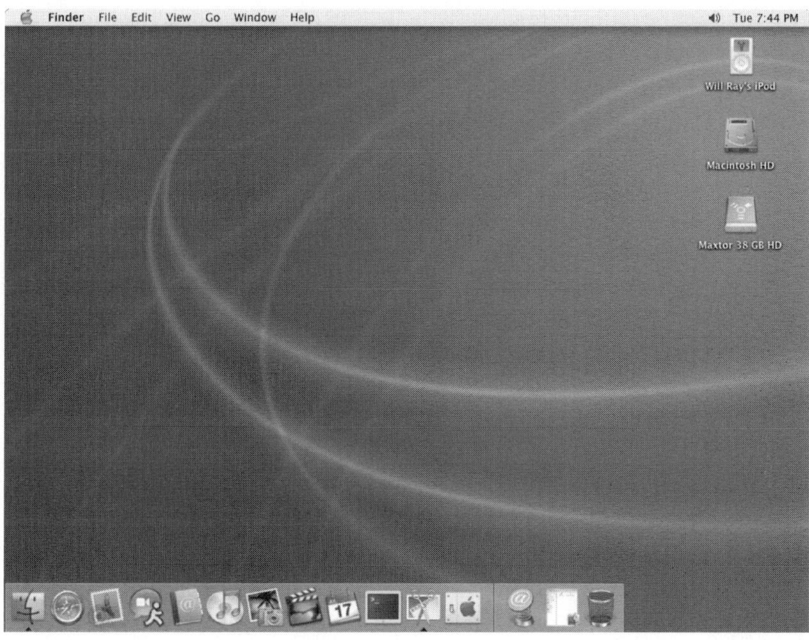

FIGURE 20.2 Here is an example of the Dock with the pinning preference set to start.

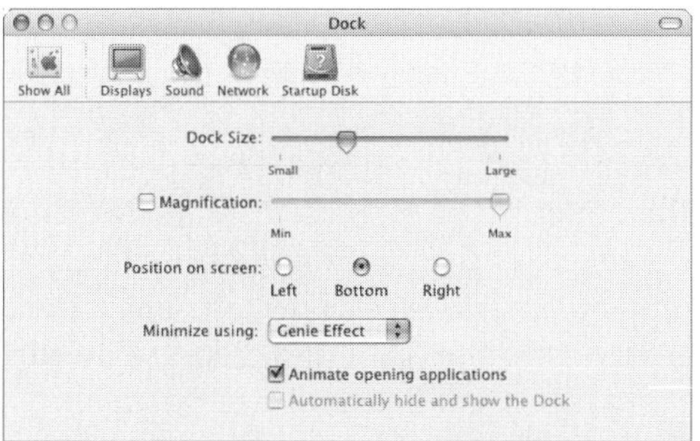

FIGURE 20.3 After setting the autohide-immutable preference to true, the option to hide the Dock is disabled.

As you have seen, preferences files can vary in their complexity. You might sometimes find it easier to edit the actual `plist` file, or use the graphical `/Developer/Applications/Utilities/Property List Editor.app`. For example, from the earlier `strings` output on the Dock preferences, we notice the `persistent-apps` string. This suggests that there might be a way to remove icons that permanently appear in the Dock. However, just from the `persistent-apps` string, it is difficult to guess what you might have to do to remove one of those icons. Because that section in the `~/Library/Preferences/com.apple.dock.plist` file also looks complicated, it might be difficult to guess what the appropriate `defaults` command may be. However, in your favorite text editor, or in the Property List Editor, you can easily locate the section for the application you no longer want to have in your Dock and simply delete it. Figure 20.4 shows removing the `Address Book` section of the `persistent-apps` section of the file using the Property List Editor. You can tell that item 3 of the persistent-apps section, the item to be removed, is the Address Book based on the file-label value.

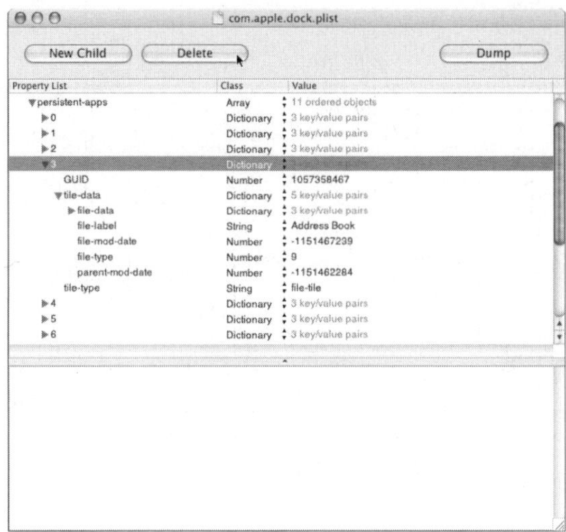

FIGURE 20.4 Using the Property List Editor to remove the Address Book icon from the Dock.

Unfortunately, Apple hasn't provided a definitive list of preferences options for each application. Even a listing of the options that each file contains would not be complete because some applications accept preferences that are not yet stored in the XML files. There are preferences options that some programs take as defaults but that can be overridden by the insertion of specific preferences into the XML files. Because no current preference is stored, we can only make intelligent guesses as to what preference names and values might be accepted. As a matter of fact, making intelligent guesses is exactly what the online community is doing regarding these preferences. With this brief look at discovering and manipulating some preferences in the Dock, you can also start to make some intelligent guesses regarding preferences.

Table 20.1 lists a number of preferences options that have been reported to be interesting, when configured using the `defaults` command. Not all these have known or well-documented functions. We have primarily tested those for the Finder and the Dock. In our testing of the `NSUserKeyEquivalents` preference, we had success in building key equivalents with the `Command` and/or `Shift` characters. However, we list all the reported information on `<keystring>` values, in case it should indeed prove useful. Figure 20.5 shows `Terminal`'s Terminal menu modified so that About Terminal, which normally does not have a keyboard equivalent, now has a keyboard equivalency of Shift-Command-b. You can set this particular equivalency by running this defaults command:

```
defaults write com.apple.Terminal NSUserKeyEquivalents ➥'{"About Terminal"="$@b";}'
```

TABLE 20.1 A Number of the Interesting defaults Preferences Options That Have Been Reported as Having Interesting Effects on the Interface

Issue command as:

defaults write *<domain>* *<key>* *<value>*

<domain>	*<key>*	*<value>*	**Effect**
com.apple.finder	Finder.HasDarkBackground	-bool true -bool false	Some text appears as white with a black outline or as solid black.
	ShowHardDrivesOnDesktop	-bool true -bool false	Does or does not show hard drives on the desktop.
	ShowRemovableMediaOnDesktop	-bool true -bool false	Does or does not show removable media on the desktop.
	ProhibitEmptyTrash	-bool true -bool false	Does or does not remove the option to empty the trash.
	ProhibitFinderPreferences	-bool true -bool false	Does or does not remove the Finder preferences option.
	ProhibitEject	-bool true -bool false	Does or does not remove the option to eject removable media.
	ProhibitBurn	-bool true -bool false	Does or does not remove the option to burn recordable media.
	ProhibitGoToiDisk	-bool true -bool false	Does or does not remove the option to go to the iDisk.
	ProhibitGoToFolder	-bool true -bool false	Does or does not remove the option to go to a folder.
	ProhibitConnectTo	-bool true -bool false	Does or does not remove the option to connect to a server.
	AppleShowAllFiles	-bool true -bool false	Does or does not show all files. Normally false, which hides some files.

TABLE 20.1 Continued

Issue command as:

`defaults write <domain> <key> <value>`

<domain>	<key>	<value>	Effect
	AnimateWindowZoom	-bool true -bool false	"Zoom" windows open from their icon locations, or make them simply appear in place.
com.apple. loginwindow	Finder	<path>	Launches the application specified by <path> at login instead of the Finder.
com.apple.dock	showhidden	-bool true -bool false	Does or does not dim Dock icons for hidden applications.
	showshadow	-bool true -bool false	Does or does not display a slight drop shadow along the edge of the Dock.
	mineffect	genie suck scale	Known values for different Dock minimization effects.
	orientation	left bottom right	Known values for Dock position.
	pinning	start middle end	Known values for anchoring the Dock in its position.
	autohide-immutable	-bool true -bool false	Does or does not make available the option to automatically hide and show the Dock.
<any application domain>	NSUserKeyEquivalents	'{"<menuitem> "=" <keystring>";}'	<menuitem> is any named menu item in a Cocoa application. <keystring> is built from: @ = Command $ = Shift ~ = Option ^ = Control and any other character. Modifies the key equivalent for a menu item.

NOTE

This table includes information from our own investigation as well as excerpts from information collected on the Internet from a variety of places, including

http://www.macosxhints.com/search.php?query=defaults+write&mode=search&datestart=0&dateend=0&topic=0&type=stories&autho=0

http://www.macnn.com/

http://www.pixits.com/defaults.htm

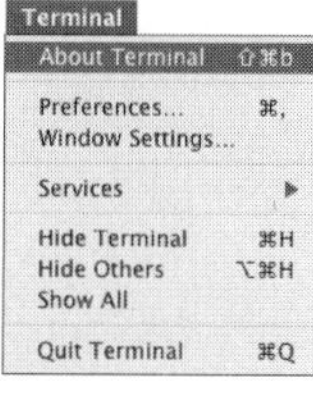

FIGURE 20.5 About Terminal under the Terminal menu of Terminal now has a keyboard equivalency of Shift-Command-b after issuing the appropriate defaults command.

Table 20.2 shows select documentation for the `defaults` command. Note that not only can you use the `defaults` command to write preferences, but you can also use it to read, delete, and search preferences.

TABLE 20.2 Select Documentation Table for the `defaults` Command

defaults	**Accesses the Mac OS X user defaults system.**
defaults [currentHost ¦ -host *<hostname>*] read [*<domain>* [*<key>*]]	
defaults [currentHost ¦ -host *<hostname>*] read-type *<domain>* *<key>*	
defaults [currentHost ¦ -host *<hostname>*] write *<domain>* {'*<plist>*' ¦ *<domain>* *<key>* [']*<value>*[']}	
default [currentHost ¦ -host *<hostname>*] rename *<domain>* *<old-key>* *<new_key>*	
defaults [currentHost ¦ -host *<hostname>*] delete [*<domain>* [*<key>*]]	
defaults [currentHost ¦ -host *<hostname>*] { domains ¦ find *<word>* ¦ help }	
`defaults` allows users to read, write, and delete Mac OS X user defaults from the command line. Applications use the defaults system to record user preferences and other information that must be maintained when applications aren't running, such as the default font for new documents. Because applications do access the defaults system while they are running, you should not modify the defaults of a running application.	

20

TABLE 20.2 Continued

`defaults`	**Accesses the Mac OS X user defaults system.**
User defaults belong to domains, which typically correspond to individual applications. Each domain has a dictionary of keys and values to represent its defaults. Keys are always strings, but values can be complex data structures made up of arrays, dictionaries, strings, and binary data. These data structures are stored as XML Property Lists. Although all applications, system services, and other programs have their own domains, they also share a domain called `NSGlobalDomain`. If a default is not specified in the application's domain, it uses the default listed in the `NSGlobalDomain` instead. *<domain>* is specified as follows: *<domain_name>* ¦ `-app` *<application_name>* ¦ `-globalDomain`	
Subcommands:	
`read`	Prints all the user's defaults for every domain to standard output.
`read` *<domain>*	Prints all the user's defaults for the specified *<domain>* to standard output.
`read` *<domain>* *<key>*	Prints the value for the default of the *<domain>* identified by *<key>*.
`write` *<domain >* *<key>* `'`*<value>*`'`	Writes *<value>* as the value for *<key>* in *<domain>*. *<value>* must be a property list, and must be enclosed in single quotes. For example: `defaults write com.companyname.appname "Default Color" '(255, 0, 0)'` Sets the default color in `com.companyname.appname` to the array containing 255, 0, 0 (red, green, blue components). Note that the key is in quotes because of the space in its name.
`write` *<domain>* `'`*<plist>*`'`	Overwrites the defaults information in *<domain>* with that specified in *<plist>*. *<domain>* must be a property list representation of a dictionary, and must be enclosed in single quotes. For example, `defaults write com.companyname.appname '{ "Default Color" = (255, 0, 0); "Default Font" = Helvetica; }'` Overwrites any previous defaults for `com.companyname.appname` and replaces them with the ones specified.
`delete` *<domain>*	Deletes all default information for *<domain>*.
`delete` *<domain>* *<key>*	Deletes the default named *<key>* in *<domain name>*.
`domains`	Prints the names of all domains in the user's defaults system.

TABLE 20.2 Continued

`defaults`	**Accesses the Mac OS X user defaults system.**
`find <word>`	Searches for *<word>* in the domain names, keys, and values of the user's defaults, and prints out a list of matches.
`help`	Prints a list of possible command formats.
Options:	
`-g`	When specifying a domain, `-g` can be used as a synonym for `NSGlobalDomain`.
Specifying *<value>* **for preference keys:**	
`<value>`	Specifies *<value>* as a string value to use.
`'<value>'`	Specifies *<value>* as a string value to use.
`-string <string_value>`	Specifies *<string_value>* as the string to use.
`-data <hex_digits>`	Specifies *<hex_digits>* as the data to use.
`-int[eger] <integer_value>`	Specifies *<integer_value>* as the integer value to use.
`-bool[ean] true ¦ false ¦ yes ¦ no`	Specifies the Boolean value to use.

System Services

Many programs run on your system to provide an assortment of services to you as a local user and to remote users contacting your system. These services range from obvious things (such as terminal services that allow you to connect to your machine from remote locations and file-sharing services) to less obvious but still useful services (such as the ones that provide wall-clock time information and remote machine status information).

Programs that provide service for all users on a machine are generally started by one of two different mechanisms. Either they are started at machine startup, by a series of shell scripts that execute programs during boot, or they are executed by a daemon that waits for requests for service and starts the appropriate program to handle the request.

Modifying Startup Services

Services that need to be continuously present, such as the software that configures and maintains network connections, are started from startup scripts. These startup scripts are kept in subdirectories of the `/System/Library/StartupItems` directory and are simply shell scripts (such as you learned about in Chapter 18, "Advanced Unix Shell Use: Configuration and Programming [Shell Scripting]") that perform simple logic to make sure that everything is right with the system and start the appropriate software.

NOTE

Remember that in Unix, if you can type it at the command line, you can write it into a shell script. Anything you find that you want to run whenever the system is running can simply be placed in a shell script and that script executed at system startup.

20

As shipped, your OS X machine should have a complement of items in the `StartupItems` folder similar to that shown in Table 20.3. Don't worry if your `/System/Library/StartupItems/` doesn't contain exactly these items. Depending on what installation options you've chosen, and whether any additional software has been installed by the time you're reading this, your system might display some differences.

TABLE 20.3 Typical Items in the `/System/Library/StartupItems/` Directory

StartupItem	Description
`Accounting`	Handles process accounting, if you care to log every action that every user or process takes.
`AMD`	Starts the `amd` automount service.
`Apache`	The Web server.
`AppleShare`	AppleShare file sharing.
`AppServices`	Assorted support services for the overall GUI interface.
`AuthServer`	User authentication services.
`ConfigServer`	Allows the machine to tell itself and, potentially, other machines you want to function similarly, about its configuration.
`CoreGraphics`	Starts the software that makes up the GUI.
`CrashReporter`	Reports system crashes to Apple, if desired.
`Cron`	A service that runs various programs at specified times or specified intervals.
`DirectoryServices`	Manages directory information for exchanging data between the Unix subsystem and the GUI portions of the interface.
`Disks`	Controls disk operations.
`IPServices`	Controls some services related to TCP/IP networking.
`KernelEventAgent`	Starts the kernel event agent. This is an undocumented service. Perhaps it involves communication between parts of the kernel.
`LDAP`	Starts the LDAP (Lightweight Directory Access Protocol) server.
`LoginWindow`	Doesn't actually do anything except denote when the system is ready to bring up the login window.
`NFS`	Controls use of and access to the NFS (Network File System) Unix file sharing protocol.
`NIS`	Starts NIS (Network Information Service).
`NetInfo`	Starts the NetInfo server.
`Network`	Configures and controls the network interface.
`NetworkExtensions`	Loads network kernel modules.
`NetworkTime`	Interacts with the network time server.
`Portmap`	Provides connectivity between remote machines and services on your machine that don't have defined TCP/IP ports that they run on.
`Postfix`	Configures and controls the mail server.
`PrintingServices`	Starts the CUPS (Common Unix Printing System) printing service.
`RemoteDesktopAgent`	Starts the Apple Remote Desktop Client.

TABLE 20.3 Continued

StartupItem	Description
`SNMP`	Starts the SNMP (Simple Network Management Protocol) service. This protocol is used to manage network devices, such as routers.
`SecurityServer`	Part of user authentication software.
`SystemLog`	Configures the system logging daemon.
`SystemTuning`	Apple-specific script that turns on and off assorted services to optimize the system performance.
`UpdateSettings`	This is an undocumented service that, based on the lack of an actual startup script in the English distribution, does not appear to do anything. Perhaps this has certain language functions in other distributions.
`mDNSResponder`	Starts the multicast DNS Responder, the part of the Rendezvous system that listens for and responds to DNS-format query packets.

Each of these directories contains a number of items—typically a file named after the name of the directory, a directory named Resources, and a file named `StartupParameters.plist` (which, oddly, isn't an XML file). The file named after the directory (and service) is the actual shell script that is run at system boot time. The Resources directory typically contains directories of "resource-like" information, such as files that contain language-replacement strings for language localization. The `StartupParameters.plist` contains a collection of variables and associated values that affect the operation of the service started.

Listing 20.9 shows a simple `StartupItems` shell script—this one starts the `Cron` service, which executes scheduled services.

LISTING 20.9 The `Cron` StartupItems Shell Script

```
#!/bin/sh

##
# cron
##

. /etc/rc.common

StartService ()
{
  if ! pid=$(GetPID cron); then
    ConsoleMessage "Starting timed execution services"
    cron
  fi
}

StopService ()
```

LISTING 20.9 Continued

```
18 {
19   if pid=$(GetPID cron); then
20     ConsoleMessage "Stopping timed execution services"
21     kill -TERM "${pid}"
22   else
23     echo "cron is not running."
24   fi
25 }
26
27 RestartService ()
28 {
29   if pid=$(GetPID cron); then
30     ConsoleMessage "Restarting timed execution services"
31     kill -HUP "${pid}"
32   else
33     StartService
34   fi
35 }
36
37 RunService "$1"
```

In this listing, items starting with the # sign are comments. The meaning of the lines in the script can be summarized in a simple manner:

- Line 7 sources the script `/etc/rc.common`, where many systemwide definitions are made.
- Line 9 starts the section for the `StartService` case.
- Line 11 checks whether a process ID for `cron` does not exist using the GetPID portion of `/etc/rc.common`.
- If Line 11 finds that there is not a process ID, line 12 sends a message to the console that says `Starting timed execution services`.
- Line 13 executes the command `cron`.
- Line 14 `fi` is *if* backwards, and it terminates the conditional expression started by the `if` on line 11.
- Line 17 starts the section for the `StopService` case.
- Line 19 checks for the process ID for `cron` using the `GetPID` portion of `/etc/rc.common`.
- If line 19 results in a process ID for `cron`, line 20 displays a message that says `Stopping timed execution services`.

- Line 21 sends a software termination signal that stops the `cron` process.
- Line 22 starts a section on what to do if there is not a `cron` process ID.
- Line 23 sends a message to the console that `cron` is not running.
- Line 24 terminates the conditional expression started by the `if` on line 19.
- Line 27 starts the section for the `RestartService` case.
- Line 29 checks whether a process ID for `cron` exists using the `GetPID` portion of `/etc/rc.common`.
- If line 29 finds a `cron` process ID, line 30 sends a message to the console that says `Restarting timed execution services`.
- Line 31 then sends a hangup signal to the `cron` process ID.
- Line 32 starts a section for what to do if there is no `cron` process ID.
- Line 33 runs the `StartService` section of this script to start the `cron` service.
- Line 34 terminates the conditional expressions of this section.
- Line 37 specifies that `RunService` execute the first command-line argument it receives. For this line to make more sense, it is helpful to look at the `RunService` section of `/etc/rc.common`, where you can see that the expected options are `start`, which executes `StartService`; `stop`, which executes `StopService`; and `restart`, which executes `RestartService`. If none of the expected arguments is given, it returns a response that the argument is an unknown argument. Listing 20.10 shows the `RunService` section of `/etc/rc.common`.

LISTING 20.10 The `RunService` section of `/etc/rc.common`

```
RunService ()
{
  case $1 in
   start ) StartService  ;;
   stop  ) StopService  ;;
   restart) RestartService ;;
   *    ) echo "$0: unknown argument: $1";;
  esac
}
```

The English language locale configuration for the `Cron StartupItems` (`Cron/Resources/English.lproj/Localizable.strings`) is shown in Listing 20.11.

20

LISTING 20.11 The English Language Locale Configuration for the `Cron StartupItems`

```
<?xml version="1.0" encoding="UTF-8"?>
<!DOCTYPE plist SYSTEM "file://localhost/System/Library/DTDs/PropertyList.dtd">
<plist version="0.9">
<dict>
    <key>timed execution services</key>
    <string>timed execution services</string>
    <key>Starting timed execution services</key>
    <string>Starting timed execution services</string>
    <key>Stopping timed execution services</key>
    <string>Stopping timed execution services</string>
    <key>Restarting timed execution services</key>
    <string>Restarting timed execution services</string>
</dict>
</plist>
```

This XML file specifies a key, the expression `timed execution services`, and a local (English) replacement string for that expression `timed execution services`. If everything works as intended, whenever the program attempts to print the key value, the system instead outputs the replacement string value. Because this isn't quite obvious from the English example, Listing 20.12 shows the `Italian.lproj` version of the `Localizable.strings` file.

LISTING 20.12 `Italian.lproj` Version of the `Localizable.strings` File for the `Cron` Service

```
<?xml version="1.0" encoding="UTF-8"?>
<!DOCTYPE plist PUBLIC "-//Apple Computer//DTD PLIST 1.0//EN"
➥"http://www.apple.com/DTDs/PropertyList-1.0.dtd">
<plist version="1.0">
<dict>
    <key>Restarting timed execution services</key>
    <string>Riavvio i servizi di esecuzione con timer</string>
    <key>Starting timed execution services</key>
    <string>Avvio servizi di esecuzione con timer</string>
    <key>Stopping timed execution services</key>
    <string>Interrompo i servizi di esecuzione con timer</string>
    <key>timed execution services</key>
    <string>servizi di esecuzione con timer</string>
</dict>
</plist>
```

Here, it is more obvious that the localization file is requesting a search to find `timed execution services` and replacing it with the Italian equivalent.

If you need to manually start, stop, or restart one of these services, the `SystemStarter` utility may be used. Basic syntax is

```
SystemStarter <action> <path-to-service-directory>
```

For example,

```
SystemStarter restart /System/Library/StartupItems/Cron
```

should restart the `cron` service. However, it does not seem to at this time.

Because Apple recommends using the `SystemStarter` utility, try it first. If it does not work for you, as in this example, try sending the action you want to occur directly to the startup script with this basic syntax:

```
<startup-script> <action>
```

For example, you can restart the `cron` service by running:

```
brezup:sage sage $ sudo /System/Library/StartupItems/Cron/Cron restart
Restarting timed execution services
```

This latter syntax is common in certain flavors of Unix and can therefore be useful to you outside Mac OS X. Depending on the startup script, even the latter syntax may not work properly. In that case, try manually executing the appropriate command from the section of the appropriate portion of the script. For something that requires detailed configuration, you might have to properly configure the service before you get the desired results. Table 20.4 includes select documentation for `SystemStarter`.

TABLE 20.4 Syntax and Selected Options for `SystemStarter`

`SystemStarter`	Starts, stops, and restarts system services.
`SystemStarter [-gvxdDqn] [<action> [<service>]]`	
The `SystemStarter` utility may be used to start, stop, and restart the system services, which are described in the `/Library/StartupItems/` and `/System/Library/StartupItems/` paths.	
The optional `<action>` argument specifies which action `SystemStarter` performs on the startup items.	
The optional `<service>` argument specifies which startup items to perform the action on. If no service is specified, all startup items are acted on; otherwise, only the item providing the service, any items it requires, or any items that depend on it will be acted on.	
Actions	
`Start`	Starts all items, or starts the item that provides the specified `<service>` and all items providing services it requires.

20

TABLE 20.4 Continued

`stop`	Stops all items, or stops the item that provides the specified `<service>` and all items that depend on it.
`Restart`	Restarts all items, or restarts the item providing the specified `<service>`.
Options	
`-g`	Graphical startup.
`-x`	Safe mode startup (only runs Apple-provided items).
`-n`	Doesn't actually perform action on items (no-run mode).

`inetd` Services

As mentioned earlier, the `inetd` service, configured by the `/etc/inetd.conf` file, actually is a service that starts and controls other services. It's not practical to start an unlimited number of some types of network services and leave them running, right from startup. Depending on the use of your machine, some services might be needed in great numbers; for example, the `ftpd` FTP server processes, if you serve particularly interesting data and have many people connecting simultaneously. Others might be used hardly at all, such as the `sprayd` network diagnostic daemon. Or, on your system, the use pattern might be the opposite—but regardless of the use, patterns are likely to vary over time. For many of these types of services, the system relieves you of the task of trying to provide the right number of these servers in some manual configuration process, by using the `inetd` daemon to configure and run them on an as-needed basis.

NOTE

If you want to learn much more about network services in general, you're invited to check out Que Publishing's *Special Edition Using TCP/IP* (ISBN 0-7897-1897-9), another book by John Ray.

The `inetd.conf` file is the file that tells `inetd` which services it should start and how. Listing 20.13 shows a typical `inetd.conf` file and has the form of a set of lines, with each line containing a specification for a service. The service specification lines consist of a set of fields separated by tabs or spaces. The fields that must occur on each line are shown in the following list, with a brief description of the data that belongs in them.

- Service name (used to look up service port in NetInfo services map)
- Socket type (`stream`, `dgram`, `raw`, `rdm`, or `seqpacket`)
- Protocol (`tcp` or `udp`, `rpc/tcp`, or `rpc/udp`)
- Wait/nowait (for `dgrams` only—all others get nowait; should the socket wait for additional connections)
- User (user to run the service as)

- Server program (actual path to binary on disk)
- Server program arguments (how the command line would look, if typed, including server name)

Listing 20.13 shows an `inetd.conf` file from a running machine, with a few useful network services enabled.

LISTING 20.13 An `inetd.conf` File from a Running Machine, with a Few Useful Network Services Enabled

```
#
# Internet server configuration database
#
#  @(#)inetd.conf  5.4 (Berkeley) 6/30/90
#
# Items with double hashes in front (##) are not yet implemented in the OS.
#
#finger stream  tcp  nowait  nobody /usr/libexec/tcpd    fingerd -s
ftp   stream  tcp  nowait  root   /usr/libexec/tcpd    ftpd -l
#login  stream  tcp  nowait  root   /usr/libexec/tcpd    rlogind
#nntp  stream  tcp  nowait  usenet /usr/libexec/tcpd    nntpd
ntalk  dgram  udp  wait   root  /usr/libexec/tcpd   ntalkd
#shell  stream  tcp  nowait  root   /usr/libexec/tcpd    rshd
#telnet stream  tcp  nowait  root   /usr/libexec/tcpd    telnetd
#uucpd  stream  tcp  nowait  root   /usr/libexec/tcpd    uucpd
comsat  dgram  udp  wait   root  /usr/libexec/tcpd    comsat
#tftp  dgram  udp  wait   nobody /usr/libexec/tcpd
  ➥    tftpd /private/tftpboot
#bootp  dgram  udp  wait   root  /usr/libexec/tcpd    bootpd
##pop3  stream  tcp  nowait  root   /usr/libexec/tcpd
  ➥    /usr/local/libexec/popper
##imap4 stream  tcp  nowait  root   /usr/libexec/tcpd
  ➥    /usr/local/libexec/imapd
```

In Listing 20.13, service control lines that have a # symbol in front of them are turned off. Because this machine doesn't provide many network services to the outside world, the majority of the services are turned off. Only the `ftpd` (ftp server), `ntalkd` (talk daemon, provides chatlike services), and `comsat` (provides new mail notification service) are turned on. To turn on additional services, simply uncomment (remove the # sign) the line and restart `inetd` by sending it an HUP signal using either of the following methods:

```
kill -HUP <inetd pid>
killall -HUP inetd
```

20

As you see in the next section, xinetd now comes with an option that allows you to use xinetd to read the /etc/inetd.conf file. If you use /etc/inetd.conf in this way, restart xinetd in the same manner as shown for inetd.

We strongly recommend that you leave your telnet daemon and rlogin daemon disabled because these are both significant security risks. You're already familiar with the ssh (Secure Shell) programs for connecting to remote machines. Chapter 26 covers configuring the sshd daemon on your own machine, and this service provides a secure replacement for the functionality of the telnet and shell daemons.

Notice that according to the file format definition given earlier, the program started by many of the lines is exactly the same: /usr/libexec/tcpd. This is part of a security mechanism, whereby inetd doesn't start the actual service, but instead starts yet another service, which starts the desired final service. The intermediate service, the program /usr/libexec/tcpd, is the TCP Wrappers program. This program can be configured to intercept requests for network services and allow them to continue only if the request comes from an authorized remote host. TCP Wrappers lives as an intermediate service between the inetd service and the end services that it delivers because the inetd-to-end-service method of providing network services was well established before the magnitude of potential Internet security problems was discovered. It turned out to be easier to sneak a wrapper around the end service, and not worry about modifying the model or about having to add security-conscious code to each and every possible service. Chapter 31, "Server Security and Advanced Network Configuration," covers how to configure TCP Wrappers to increase your system security.

xinetd Services

As mentioned earlier, xinetd can also be used to serve some of your basic network services. As a matter of fact, starting with Mac OS X 10.2, xinetd is the default, rather than inetd. It is the default service for serving some network services because of its extra features, such as greater access control and better logging. Table 20.5 shows select runtime options available for xinetd. In OS X it runs by default with the -inetd_compat and -pidfile options: xinetd -inetd_compat -pidfile /var/run/xinetd.pid. The -inetd_compat option is an especially interesting option. With this option enabled, xinetd can also read the /etc/inetd.conf file. It processes /etc/xinetd.conf first and then /etc/inetd.conf. For users who may prefer the /etc/inetd.conf file, this is a way to use a familiar file without any extra work.

TABLE 20.5 Select Runtime Options for xinetd

Option	Description
-d	Enables debug mode.
-syslog *<syslog_facility>*	Enables syslog logging of xinetd-produced messages using the specified syslog facility. The following syslog facilities can be used: daemon, auth, user, local[0-7]. Ineffective in debug mode.

TABLE 20.5 Continued

Option	Description
-filelog <*log_file*>	Specifies where to log xinetd-produced messages. Ineffective in debug mode.
-f <*config_file*>	Specifies which file to use as the config file. Default is /etc/xinetd.conf.
-pidfile <*pid_file*>	Writes the process ID to the file specified. Ineffective in debug mode.
-stayalive	Tells xinetd to stay running even if no services are specified.
-inetd_compat	Causes xinetd to read /etc/inetd.conf in addition to the standard xinetd config files. /etc/inetd.conf is read after the standard xinetd config files.

The default /etc/xinetd.conf file that comes with Mac OS X 10.3 is shown again in Listing 20.14.

LISTING 20.14 The Default /etc/xinetd.conf File

```
 1 # man xinetd.conf for more information
 2
 3 defaults
 4 {
 5     instances           = 60
 6     log_type            = SYSLOG daemon
 7     log_on_success      = HOST PID
 8     log_on_failure      = HOST
 9     cps                 = 25 30
10 }
11
12 includedir /etc/xinetd.d
```

The /etc/xinetd.conf file looks different from the /etc/inetd.conf file. This file has two major sections to it—a defaults section and a services section. The defaults section has controls that are basic defaults for the services. Each service has further controls and can also override or augment controls listed in the defaults section. Briefly, the intent of the lines of this file is as follows:

- Line 3 labels the defaults section of the file.
- Line 4 starts the configuration for the defaults section of the file.
- Line 5 sets the first defaults attribute, instances, which specifies the limit of servers for a given service, to 60.
- Line 6 sets the log_type attribute to the SYSLOG facility at the daemon level.

- Line 7 sets the `log_on_success` attribute to `HOST`, which logs the remote host's IP address, and `PID`, the process ID of the server.
- Line 8 sets the `log_on_failure` attribute to `HOST`, which logs the remote host's IP address.
- Line 9 sets the `cps` attribute, the one that limits the connections per second, to `25` connections per second. When this limit is reached, the service disables itself for the number of seconds specified in the second argument, `30` seconds in this case.
- Line 10 ends the defaults configuration section.
- Line 12 starts the services section by using the `includedir` directive to specify that every file in the `/etc/xinetd.d` directory, excluding files containing `.` or `~`, is parsed as an `xinetd` configuration file. The files are parsed in alphabetical order according to the C locale.

Already you can tell that `xinetd` has more functionality than the traditional `inetd`. For instance, `inetd` cannot limit the number of connections per second. The items listed in this default `/etc/xinetd.conf` file are not the only ones that can be listed in this section, nor are the default values necessarily the only possible values. Table 20.6 shows a listing of select attributes for `xinetd`. Notice that `xinetd` can be set to restrict access based on hosts and even time, redirect services, and display banners.

TABLE 20.6 Select Attributes for `xinetd`

Attribute	Description
`id`	Used to uniquely identify a service. Useful for services that can use different protocols and need to be described with different entries in the configuration file. Default service ID is the same as the service name.
`type`	Any combination of the following can be used: `RPC`: Specifies service as an RPC service. `INTERNAL`: Specifies service as provided by `xinetd`. `TCPMUX/TCPMUXPLUS`: Specifies a service that is started according to the RFC 1078 protocol on the TCPMUX well-known port. `UNLISTED`: Specifies that the service is not listed in a standard system file, such as `/etc/services` or `/etc/rpc`.
`flags`	Any combination of the following can be used: `INTERCEPT`: Intercepts packets or accepted connections to verify that they are coming from acceptable locations. Internal or multithreaded services cannot be intercepted. `NORETRY`: Avoids retry attempts in case of fork failure. `IDONLY`: Accepts connections only when the remote end identifies the remote user. Applies only to connection-based services.

TABLE 20.6 Continued

Attribute	Description
	NAMEINARGS: Causes the first argument to server_args to be the name of the server. Useful for using TCP Wrappers.
	NODELAY: For a TCP service, sets the TCP_NODELAY flag on the socket. Has no effect on other types of services.
	DISABLE: Specifies that this service is to be disabled. Overrides the enabled directive in defaults.
	KEEPALIVE: For a TCP service, sets the SO_KEEPALIVE flag on the socket. Has no effect on other types of services.
	NOLIBWRAP: Disables internal calling of the tcpwrap library to determine access to the service.
	SENSOR: Replaces the service with a sensor that detects accesses to the specified port. Does not detect stealth scans. Should only be used on services you know you don't need. Whenever a connection is made to the service's port, adds the IP address to a global no_access list until the deny_time setting expires.
	IPv4: Sets the service to an IPv4 service.
	IPv6: Sets the service to an IPv6 service.
	REUSE: The REUSE flag is deprecated. All services now implicitly use the REUSE flag.
disable	Has a value of yes or no. Overrides the enabled directive in defaults.
socket_type	Has a value of stream, dgram, raw, or seqpacket.
protocol	Specifies the protocol used by the service. Protocol must exist in /etc/protocols. If it is not defined, the default protocol for the service is used.
wait	Specifies whether the service is single-threaded or multithreaded. If yes, it is single-threaded; xinetd starts the service and stops handling requests for the service until the server dies. If no, it is multithreaded; xinetd keeps handling new service requests.
user	Specifies the UID for the server process. Username must exist in /etc/passwd.
group	Specifies the GID for the server process. Group must exist in /etc/group. If a group is not specified, the group of the user is used.
instances	Determines the number of simultaneous instances of the server. Default is unlimited. The value can be an integer or UNLIMITED.
nice	Specifies server priority.
server	Specifies the program to execute for this service.
server_args	Specifies arguments to be passed to the server. Server name should not be included, unless the NAMEINARGS flag has been specified.
only_from	Specifies to which remote hosts the service is available.
no_access	Specifies the remote hosts to which this service is not available.
access_times	Specifies time intervals when the service is available. An interval has the form: hour:min-hour:min. Hours can range from 0–23; minutes can range from 0–59.

TABLE 20.6 Continued

Attribute	Description
`log_on_success`	Specifies what information is logged when the server is started and exits. Any combination of the following can be specified: `PID`: Logs the server process ID. `HOST`: Logs the remote host's address. `USERID`: Logs remote user Id using RFC 1413 identification protocol. Only available for multithreaded stream services. `EXIT`: Logs the fact that the server exited along with the exit status or termination signal. `DURATION`: Logs the duration of the server session. `TRAFFIC`: Logs the total bytes in and out for a redirected service.
`log_on_failure`	Specifies what is logged when a server cannot start, either from lack of resources or access configuration. Any combination of the following can be specified: `HOST`: Logs the remote host's address `USERID`: Logs remote user ID using RFC 1413 identification protocol. Only available for multithreaded stream services. `RECORD`: Logs as much information about the remote host as possible. `ATTEMPT`: Logs the fact that a failed attempt was made. Implied by use of any of the other options.
`env`	Value of this attribute is a list of strings of the form `<name>=<value>`. These strings are added to the server's environment, giving it `xinetd`'s environment as well as the environment specified by the `env` attribute.
`passenv`	Value of this attribute is a list of environment variables from `xinetd`'s environment to be passed to the server. An empty list implies passing no variables to the server except those explicitly defined by the `env` attribute.
`port`	Specifies the service port. If this attribute is listed for a service in `/etc/services`, it must be the same as the port number listed in that file.
`redirect`	Allows a TCP service to be redirected to another host. Useful for when your internal machines are not visible to the outside world. Syntax is `redirect = <IP address or host name> <port>` The server attribute is not required when this attribute is specified. If the server attribute is specified, this attribute takes priority.
`bind`	Allows a service to be bound to a specific interface on the machine.
`interface`	Synonym for `bind`.
`banner`	Name of the file to be displayed to the remote host when a connection to that service is made. The banner is displayed regardless of access control.
`banner_success`	Name of the file to be displayed to the remote host when a connection to that service is granted. Banner is displayed as soon as access to the service is granted.
`banner_fail`	Name of the file to be displayed to the remote host when a connection to a service is denied. Banner is printed immediately on denial of access.

TABLE 20.6 Continued

Attribute	Description
per_source	Specifies the maximum number of connections permitted per server per source IP address. May be an integer or UNLIMITED.
cps	Limits the rate of incoming connections.
groups	Takes either yes or no. If yes, the server is executed with access to the groups to which the server's effective UID has access. If no, server runs with no supplementary groups. Must be set to yes for many BSD-flavored Unixes.
enabled	Takes a list of service names to enable. Note that the service disable attribute and DISABLE flag can prevent a service from being enabled despite its being listed in this attribute.
include	Takes a filename in the form of include /etc/xinetd/service. File is then parsed as a new configuration file. May not be specified from within a service declaration.
includedir	Takes a directory name in the form of includedir /etc/xinetd.d. Every file in the directory, excluding files containing . or ending with ~, is parsed as an xinetd.conf file.
rlimit_cpu	Sets the maximum number of CPU seconds that the service may use. May either be a positive integer or UNLIMITED.
deny_time	Sets the time span when access to all services to an IP address are denied to someone who sets off the SENSOR. Must be used in conjunction with the SENSOR flag. Options are FOREVER: IP address is not purged until xinetd is restarted. NEVER: Just logs the offending IP address. *<number>*: A numerical value of time in minutes. A typical time would be 60 minutes, to stop most DoS attacks while allowing IP addresses coming from a pool to be recycled for legitimate purposes.

OS X has default xinetd configuration files for the following services:

```
brezup:sage sage $ ls /etc/xinetd.d

auth          echo        nmbd         swat
bootps        echo-udp    ntalk        telnet
chargen       eppc        printer      tftp
chargen-udp   exec        shell        time
comsat        finger      smb-direct   time-udp
daytime       ftp         smbd
daytime-udp   login       ssh
```

As you can see, services that require two lines in /etc/inetd.conf, such as time, require two files in /etc/xinetd.d. Listing 20.15 includes the default listings for the ftp, time, and time-udp files.

LISTING 20.15 Default `xinetd` Configuration Files for the `ftp`, `time`, and `time-udp` Files

```
service ftp
{
    disable        = yes
    socket_type    = stream
    wait           = no
    user           = root
    server         = /usr/libexec/ftpd
    server_args    = -l
    groups         = yes
    flags          = REUSE IPv6
}
service time
{
    disable        = yes
    type           = INTERNAL
    id             = time-stream
    socket_type    = stream
    wait           = no
    user           = root
    groups         = yes
    flags          = REUSE
}
service time-udp
{
    disable        = yes
    type           = INTERNAL
    id             = time-dgram
    socket_type    = dgram
    wait           = yes
    user           = root
    groups         = yes
    flags          = REUSE
}
```

Because FTP is a service that you might possibly enable, let's take a brief look at the attributes of the default `/etc/xinetd.d/ftp` file from Listing 20.15:

- The third line sets the first attribute, `disable`, to `yes`. This means that by default, the FTP service is disabled. `/etc/inetd.conf` simply has a # in front of a service to disable it.

- The fourth line sets the `socket_type` attribute to `stream`. This was the second item in the `ftp` line of `/etc/inetd.conf`.
- The 5th line sets the `wait` attribute to `no`. This was the third item in the `ftp` line of `/etc/inetd.conf`.
- The 6th line sets the `user` attribute to `root`. This was the fourth item in the `ftp` line of `/etc/inetd.conf`.
- The 7th line sets the `server` attribute to `/usr/libexec/ftpd`. This was the fifth item in the `ftp` line of `/etc/inetd.conf`.
- The 8th line sets the `server_args` attribute to `-l`. This was the final item in the `ftp` line of `/etc/inetd.conf`.
- The 9th line sets the `groups` attribute to `yes`. This is required for BSD-flavored Unixes. Because this attribute is required for all your `xinetd` services, you could also move it to the defaults section of `/etc/xinetd.conf` and then remove it from the individual service files.
- Finally, the tenth line sets the `flags` attribute to `REUSE`, which according to the man page is actually deprecated because all services use this flag, and to IPv6.

As was the case with the `/etc/inetd.conf` file, the time service contains the same major descriptors but in a different form. Unlike the `ftp` `xinetd` configuration file, the `time` and `time-udp` also include the `id` attribute to uniquely identify the services.

Perhaps one of the most notable differences between the default `/etc/inetd.conf` file and the `/etc/xinetd.d/ftp` file is that the server is set to `/usr/libexec/tcpd` in the `inetd.conf` file, but in the `ftp` file, it is set to `/usr/libexec/ftpd`. Because `inetd` is not as configurable, it is important to use TCP Wrappers. However, you can configure host access information directly in `xinetd` without having to use TCP Wrappers. We recommend that you use that built-in capability.

If you want to enable any of the default services controlled by `xinetd`, using only the `xinetd` configuration files, simply run `/sbin/service <service> start`.

If you prefer a more manual method, change the `disable` entry to `no` and restart `xinetd` by sending it a HUP signal using either of the following methods:

```
kill -HUP <xinetd_pid>
killall -HUP xinetd
```

If you want to change any of the default configuration files, or add services not included in the initial set of default configuration files, simply restart `xinetd` to have them take effect. Listing 20.16 includes recommended `xinetd` configurations for some services that we've discussed elsewhere in this book that might be of interest to you. If you want to change any of the defaults that appear in `/etc/xinetd.conf` for a given service, be sure to include that updated attribute in the service's file.

LISTING 20.16 Recommended Basic `xinetd` Configurations

```
service ftp
{
    disable        = no
    flags          = REUSE
    socket_type    = stream
    wait           = no
    user           = root
    server         = /usr/libexec/ftpd
    server_args    = -l
    groups         = yes
    only_from      = <host list>
    no_access      = <host list>
    access_times   = <time intervals>
}


service imap
{
     disable       = no
     socket_type   = stream
     wait          = no
     user          = root
     server        = /usr/local/libexec/imapd
     groups        = yes
     flags         = REUSE
}



service pop3
{
     disable       = no
     socket_type   = stream
     wait          = no
     user          = root
     server        = /usr/local/libexec/ipop3d
     groups        = yes
     flags         = REUSE
}
```

NOTE

The Apple-provided `xinetd` `swat` configuration file in Mac OS X 10.3 is sufficient, but the `swat` service also needs a corresponding

```
swat 901/tcp
```

added to the file `/etc/services`.

Strong-Arming the System—Brute Force Behavior Modification

Sometimes, there just isn't a configuration option available to let you make something work the way you want it to. The GUI tools don't have a button for you to click, the configuration files for the software don't list an option for you, and the Defaults database contains no useful parameters. If you're willing to apply what you've learned so far in this book, there still might be ways for you to make your system do what you want. The key is remembering that underneath it all, OS X is running Unix, and the Unix user experience is fundamentally the product of many programs running simultaneously, each providing specific functionality. If you can localize the behavior you want to modify to a single program, you can approach reaching your configuration goal as an exercise in replacing that program's functionality with something that does what you want, instead of what the current version does.

The Sneaky Way—Inserting Imposters

Depending on exactly what you're trying to change, there are two primary ways to go about this. The less obnoxious way is to interpose some software of your own devising between what the system is trying to do and what it's actually doing. Because most everything is a small, special-purpose program, you can often insert an imposter program that looks and talks to the system like the program it thinks it's calling. The imposter can then call the actual program (or not, if you don't need to) with any modifications to inputs that you want, unrestricted by what the system allows you to conveniently configure.

Let's take the Command-Shift-3/Command-Shift-4 screen capture facility that's built into the operating system as an example. Pressing Command-Shift-3 takes a screenshot of what currently appears on the screen. Command-Shift-4 lets you select a region of the screen or a particular window to save an image of instead. Both of these functions unfortunately save their output as Adobe Portable Document Format `.pdf` files. Darned inconvenient, right? If you want to use images captured this way in some truly portable fashion, for example to build a Web page, you have to use Preview to export them as some more universally supported image-file format, such as GIF or JPEG, or find some other way to post-process the `.pdf` files. Wouldn't it be more convenient if the system just saved the screenshots in TIFF format, like it did in OS X 10.1 and earlier?

If you really want that functionality, you're willing to strong-arm the system into giving it to you even though it doesn't appear to be an option, and you accept the consequences of the changes you'll be making, there is a way to accomplish your goal. The solution requires replacing bits of the software underlying the user interface with things that do what you want, instead of what Apple made them do. The consequence is that your system will no longer be quite as Apple delivered it, and there's no telling what an Apple software update will do when it encounters these modified files.

CAUTION

We can't in good conscience suggest that you make this particular modification, or other modifications of this style. We've seen Apple's update installers balk at far less important things, and we wouldn't want to encourage anyone to make a modification that might leave their system in a state that could require a complete reinstallation. Still, we think it's a good example of what can be done with the system if you can keep track of changes you might have to back out to run an update, or if you're willing to live on the wild side and make your system your own. There are many things that we think are pretty cool, that we would be pretty irresponsible if we actually suggested....

The key to solving the problem is to recognize that when you press Command-Shift-3 or Command-Shift-4, the GUI invokes a command-line application, `/usr/sbin/screencapture`. The easiest way to find this out, is by running `top` at the command line and watching the process listing while taking a few screenshots. Armed with this tidbit of information, you should already begin to see the possibilities. At the command line, `screencapture` indicates that its options are as shown in Table 20.7. Unfortunately, none of them appear to be options that allow you to specify a file type for it to save.

TABLE 20.7 Command Documentation for `screencapture`

`screencapture`	Takes pictures of the current state of the screen. `screencapture [-[i¦m]wsWx] <file>` `screencapture [-[i¦m]cwsWx]` `screencapture` takes pictures of the current state of the screen or screens present on the machine, or of windows or selectable regions of the screen. `screencapture` saves its output in `.pdf` format, or places it on the clipboard. `screencapture` lists a `[cursor]` parameter as following the `<file>` parameter when displaying its options, but this parameter is undocumented, and an examination of the `screencapture` executable does not reveal any obvious candidates for parameter values. `screencapture` also accepts an undocumented `-f` option, which is apparently a placeholder option that can be used in `<file>` mode.
`-i`	Captures the screen interactively, by selection or window. Pressing the spacebar toggles between: region selection (crosshair cursor) window selection (camera cursor) Pressing `<esc>` cancels the capture.

TABLE 20.7 Continued

`-c`	Places the screen capture on the clipboard, instead of into a file.
`-m`	Only captures the main monitor. Undefined if `-i` is present.
`-w`	Only allows window selection mode.
`-s`	Only allows mouse selection mode.
`-W`	Starts interaction in window selection mode.
`-x`	Does not play sounds.

Still, the fact that the screen image is captured by a command-line application should immediately bring to mind a possible way that a solution might be approached. You can write small command-line programs, right? You learned how to do this in Chapter 18, when you learned about shell scripts. A shell script looks for all the world just like any other program, but you can fill it with the automated execution of any command-line commands that you want.

So, what would happen when you press Command-Shift-3, if you were to find the `screencapture` program as delivered by Apple, rename it so that the system couldn't find it, and then replace it with a shell script of your own devising? Presuming that you write a syntactically correct shell script, no more, no less than exactly what you put in your shell script. Let's see what happens: You'll find the `screencapture` program in `/usr/sbin/`. As `root`, move it to `/usr/sbin/screencapture-o`.

```
brezup:ray ray $ su
Password:
brezup:root ray # cd /usr/sbin
brezup:root sbin # mv screencapture screencapture-o
```

Now replace it with a small shell script so that you can see what's being passed when Command-Shift-3 and Command-Shift-4 are pressed.

```
brezup:root sbin # cat > screencapture
#!/bin/csh

echo "option 0 $0" > /tmp/screencapopts
echo "option 1 $1" >> /tmp/screencapopts
echo "option 2 $2" >> /tmp/screencapopts
echo "option 3 $3" >> /tmp/screencapopts
```

Press `Control-d` to end the `cat` session; then make the new `screencapture` script executable.

```
brezup:root sbin # chmod 755 screencapture
```

20

Press Command-Shift-3 and see what happens:

```
<Command-Shift-3>
[Racer-X:/usr/sbin] ray# cat /tmp/screencapopts
option 0 /usr/sbin/screencapture
option 1 -f
option 2 /Volumes/Wills_Data/ray/Desktop/Picture 1.pdf
option 3
```

Also check Command-Shift-4 and both variants with Control held down as well (the Control variants are supposed to place the capture on the clipboard):

```
<Command-Shift-4>
[Racer-X:/usr/sbin] ray# cat /tmp/screencapopts
option 0 /usr/sbin/screencapture
option 1 -i
option 2 /Volumes/Wills_Data/ray/Desktop/Picture 2.pdf
option 3

<Command-Control-Shift-3>
[Racer-X:/usr/sbin] ray# cat /tmp/screencapopts
option 0 /usr/sbin/screencapture
option 1 -c
option 2
option 3

<Command-Control-Shift-4>
[Racer-X:/usr/sbin] ray# cat /tmp/screencapopts
option 0 /usr/sbin/screencapture
option 1 -ic
option 2
option 3
```

From these, it's clear that the options are always passed as the first argument to the command (which is apparently what that do-nothing `-f` option is for—filling space as option #1 when no option is required), and the filename, if there is one, is always option 2. This is lucky for us. We don't need to do any fancy option parsing. So long as we can figure out how to convert the output of Apple's `screencapture` (now `screencapture-o`) into a more friendly file format, we can just pass options and parameters straight from our script to it, and all should be well.

The next question is how do we get from a `.pdf` file to a file format such as TIFF? If you remember back to Chapter 10, "Printer, Fax, and Font Management," the Ghostscript application we installed is a PostScript and PDF parser that can render these formats into many different output formats. Those we were interested in, in Chapter 10, were the output formats that were printer languages such as drives the Apple ImageWriter used in the example. Ghostscript, however, isn't limited to printer language outputs. It can also output many image-file formats—TIFF, JPEG, and PNM, to name a few (examine the output of `gs -h` for a listing of supported output formats).

I'm partial to storing my images as TIFFs, so I'm going to use the `tiff24nc` output format, which is uncompressed 24-bit TIFF. Fiddling around at the command line, I find that the syntax shown in the following line, converts a `.pdf` file into a TIFF format file for me.

```
/usr/local/bin/gs -q -dBATCH -dNOPAUSE -sDEVICE=tiff24nc

➥-sOutputFile=<tiffile> <pdffile>
```

For example,

```
brezup:root Desktop # /usr/local/bin/gs -q -dBATCH -dNOPAUSE -sDEVICE=tiff24nc
➥ -sOutputFile="Picture 1.tif" "Picture 1.pdf"
```

creates the file `Picture 1.tif` in my current directory, and it is a properly formatted TIFF file (there's a reason I've used `.tif` instead of `.tiff`, which will be explained shortly).

NOTE

Of course, you aren't restricted to using TIFF files, if you prefer some other format of output on your end. Simply replace the appropriate bits of the filenames, and select the Ghostscript device you require to suit your purposes.

```
brezup:root Desktop # file Picture\ 1.tif
Picture 1.tif: TIFF image data, big-endian
```

Now, all that remains is to put this information together with what you learned in Chapter 18, to make a completely functional shell script wrapper for `screencapture-o`. To summarize:

- Our wrapper needs to be named `screencapture` and be found by the system when we press the Command-Shift-3/4 key combinations.
- It is going to call the original `screencapture` program, now known as `screencap-ture-o`, to do the actual work of capturing the screen images.
- It must accept and store the options and parameters that the system thinks it's handing to the (original) `screencapture` program, so that it can in-turn pass these options and parameters on itself.
- The system is handing `screencapture` parameters for a file with a `.pdf` suffix. This needs to be modified so that the TIFF files are named properly.

All this can be accomplished with the script file shown in Listing 20.17.

LISTING 20.17 Replacement `/usr/sbin/screencapture` Wrapper Script

```
#!/bin/csh

set options="$1";

if ( $%2 > 0 ) then
 set pdffile = "$2"
 set datestr=`date "+%y%m%d-%H:%M:%S"`
 set wrkdir = "$pdffile:h"
 set tmpfile="$wrkdir/.Picture $datestr.tmp"
 set tiffile="$wrkdir/Picture $datestr.tif"

 \rm -f "$pdffile"
 /usr/sbin/screencapture-o $options "$tmpfile"
 \rm -f "$pdffile"
 gs -q -dBATCH -dNOPAUSE -sDEVICE=tiff24nc -sOutputFile="$tiffile" "$tmpfile"
 \rm -f "$tmpfile"
 exit
endif

/usr/sbin/screencapture-o $options
exit
```

This script actually contains a small amount of fiddling that we haven't discussed in the text, but experimentation would quickly lead you to the reasons that it has been included. To most quickly begin to understand what the script does, take the case where the `if` statement fails—the second option, $2, contains no text (there is no filename). In this case, execution falls through to the `endif` statement, and the only thing executed is `/usr/sbin/screencapture-o $options`. It's as if this script weren't even there, which is exactly what we want to happen if there is no filename because that only happens when the user holds down the Control key to save the data to the clipboard.

If there is a filename in $2, we need to process it as follows:

1. First it is stored in the shell variable `$pdffile`.
2. A formatted date is acquired into the shell variable `$datestr`. This date string is necessary because the portion of the `screencapture` process that prevents filename collisions is not part of `screencapture` but instead is part of the GUI server. We'll use this to create a unique filename for the final `.tif` image. (We're trying to create `.tif` files, but the system passes `.pdf` names, so it'll happily keep passing `Picture 1.pdf`

forever, because our `.tif` names will never conflict with it.) The date format specified is `YYMMDD-HH:MM:SS`. You can change this to something more to your liking at your leisure.

3. We get the working directory for saving the file by parsing the path off the `$pdffile` specified by the system.
4. We build a temporary filename and a final name for our TIFF file from these components. The temporary file has a `.` preceding `Picture` so that it won't show up in the Finder (unless we've enabled showing dotfiles in the Finder).
5. We remove the file pointed at by `$pdffile` because the system creates it before starting `screencapture` in an attempt to make it show up on the user's desktop more quickly. Unfortunately, we're not going to be using that file, we're building a TIFF file. I suppose that we could touch the `$tiffile` here to simulate the same behavior.
6. We run `screencapture-o`, with the options passed to our script, and dump its output in the temporary file we've created.
7. We remove the `$pdffile` again, just for good measure.
8. We then run our Ghostscript command, which should read our `$tmpfile` and write our `$tiffile`.
9. Finally, we remove `$tmpfile` and exit.

It's a little difficult to demonstrate in the static text of a printed book, but when installed, this works exactly as described. Using the Command-Shift-3/4 key combinations in the system now results in a file with a name such as `Picture 021009-03/00/58.tif` appearing on the desktop in the Finder.

NOTE

The observant reader who pays attention to man pages will note that the date format we used and what ends up in the filename as shown by the Finder are not identical. We specified colons separating hour, minute, and second, and instead the Finder is showing / characters. If you look at the filename at the command line, it's as expected and contains colons. This is probably a symptom of Apple's attempt to graft the larger Macintosh set of acceptable filename characters onto the Unix filesystem. Those truly bothered by the discrepancy can play with the date format string and pick something they like better than this.

The Brutal Way—Organ Transplants

Sometimes, inserting imposters isn't a clean solution. Other times, it just can't give you all the functionality you really want. In the `screencapture` example given previously, the most annoying issue remaining is that the filename is a bit clunky. Apple's default "Picture

#" names are a bit nicer. There's no elegant way to get that functionality out of a `screencapture` script, though, because it's actually some part of the GUI that's working out what the next available filename is, and it's doing it based on a `.pdf` suffix. We could work out some `csh` syntax to list all `.tif` files and find the highest numbered instance, but that would be some ugly `csh` code, and Apple's already done the work, it's just not *quite* accessible to us. Fixing Apple's software so that it does what we want would be more elegant, but how can we do this without Apple's source code?

CAUTION

This is one of those places where the product carton should say "Kids, don't try this at home—all stunts performed by professional stunt actors." If you try this, or other tweaks of this nature, and you make a mistake, there's a reasonable chance you'll leave your machine unable to boot into anything but single-user mode (see Chapter 23 for more information on what to do if that happens). You really, really, can make a mess of things if you try these techniques and you make a mistake. You also can make some useful customizations if you get it right, but *always* make backups, and never say we didn't warn you!

Remember back in the early chapters covering Unix when we said that Unix doesn't really know or care what's in a file; that if you tried to execute a data file, Unix would let you; and that likewise you could open applications in text editors? Well, `emacs` is your application-modifying friend.

If you dig around the `/System/Library/CoreServices/` directory, you'll eventually find that `SystemUIServer` is the part of the system that's calling `screencapture` when you press the Command-Shift-3/4 key combinations. I found it by using `grep` from `/System/Library/CoreServices/`, as in `grep screencapture /System/Library/CoreServices/*/*/*/* 2>&1 ¦ grep "matches"`. I've piped `grep` back into `grep` (with `STDERR` wrapped into `STDOUT`), so that I don't see all the complaints from the first `grep` about directories.

If you run `strings` on the file that matches, the following interesting tidbits show up:

```
brezup:root sbin # strings /System/Library/CoreServices/SystemUIServer.app/
Contents/MacOS/SystemUIServer
.
.
.
/usr/sbin/screencapture
unknown hot key: %d
screen capture threw exception while handling hot key
OSXDisableScreenGrab
location
com.apple.screencapture
```

```
Picture
InfoPlist
%@ %@.pdf
screen capture failed, could not find screen capture folder
screen capture failed, could not get screen capture name
screen capture failed, could not create picture file %d
screen capture failed, could not create path %d
.
.
.
```

The particularly interesting bit is the line `%@ %@.pdf`. That looks suspiciously like something specifying a filename, where there are two replaceable parameters, separated by a space, and the file suffix is `.pdf`. Sounds a lot like `"Picture 1.pdf"`, doesn't it?

If you're sure that you want to try this, make a backup copy of `/System/Library/CoreServices/SystemUIServer.app/Contents/MacOS/SystemUIServer`; then fire up `emacs` on the file (not the backup) and search for and change the bit of the file containing `%@ %@.pdf` so that it contains `%@ %@.tif` instead. I used `Control-s` to incrementally search for `%@.pdf` and then carefully replaced just the `.pdf` part with `.tif`. Save the file again, and reboot your machine. If you can still log on, things are going well.

CAUTION

If you don't know how to make these edits, don't even try until you're more comfortable with your `emacs` skills. One wrong keystroke and good-bye interface.

CAUTION

Never change the size of a string when you're editing it this way. There's a good chance that the program knows exactly where in itself the various bits of information such as the string specifying the format of the `screencapture` filename are stored. If you changed the `.pdf` to `.tiff`, everything after that string would be off by one position from where the program expects it, and there's no telling exactly what the effect might be.

Presuming that you've successfully made the modification, what you've just done is modify a part of the GUI server so that it no longer passes Picture `#.pdf` to `screencapture`. Instead, it passes `Picture #.tif`. Because the UI handles the collision detection and incrementing the internal number properly, we no longer need to deal with that in our `screencapture` script. Listing 20.18 shows the simplified script that works with this modification of `SystemUIServer`.

20

LISTING 20.18 Replacement `/usr/sbin/screencapture` to Function with Modified `/System/Library/CoreServices/SystemUIServer.app/Contents/MacOS/SystemUIServer`

```
#!/bin/csh

set options="$1";

echo $options >> /tmp/testoutput

if ( $%2 > 0 ) then
 set tiffile="$2"
 set wrkdir = "$tiffile:h"
 set wrkfile = "$tiffile:t"
 set tmpfile = "$wrkdir/.$wrkfile:r.tmp"

 /usr/sbin/screencapture-o $options "$tmpfile"
 /usr/local/bin/gs -dBATCH -dNOPAUSE -sDEVICE=tiff24nc -sOutputFile="$tiffile"
"$tmpfile" >& /tmp/gsout
 \rm -f "$tmpfile"
 exit
endif

/usr/sbin/screencapture-o $options
exit
```

Because the `SystemUIServer` code will be handling collision detection and creating a good filename for us, this code is much simpler than the previous version. The only lines that might be vaguely confusing are where I pull apart the filename passed on `$2`, into a directory and a filename, and then pull the extension off the filename and replace it with `.tmp` for the temporary file (I pulled it apart into directory and filename, so that I could insert that `.` before the filename to keep the `.tmp` file invisible). Study the shell scripting sections of Chapter 18, and this will all make much more sense.

And, as before, it does in fact work as you might hope—TIFF files with convenient "Picture #" names appear on the desktop in response to Command-Shift-3/4.

Both of these examples could, of course, be made much more sophisticated if you were inclined to experiment with the shell scripts. Want Command-Shift-3 to both make a screen capture and print a copy of the file? Easy! Just send the PDF file that `screencapture-o` writes off to `lpr` in your script. Need all of your `screencaptures` to be reduced to grayscale? Pipe them through a some `netpbm` tools before writing them. The possibilities are just about limitless.

CAUTION

Although the benefits available through these sorts of tweaks have been explained, we'll still close with a repeat of our previous warning. There's no telling what an Apple update will do if it sees a modified `screencapture`, or maybe even worse, a modified `SystemUIServer`. It would be a good idea to keep a list of modifications that you make to Apple software, and move original copies back in, before trying to update your system.

Actually, if you've become a sophisticated enough script writer and Unix user to make these sorts of modifications, you should also have become a wise enough Unix user to be maintaining an automated script that lets you back out all your changes to Apple system files with a single command before you execute any system update scripts.

Summary

This chapter provided an overview of the preferences and configuration controls available from and through the command line. Because so much of the system is currently undocumented by Apple, we can't guess whether these items will remain in these places or continue to contain the same options. However, we have a pretty good guess that the general form and style of how the configuration is controlled will remain the same. With the tools provided here, you should be able to cope with any changes that might come your way.

CHAPTER 21

Scripting Languages

IN THIS CHAPTER

- Introduction to AppleScript
- Script Editor
- AppleScript Syntax
- Perl
- Python

Mac OS X's scripting languages open up programming to a wide range of users—from diehard developers to graphic artists. Everyone wants the ability to "tell your computer what to do" and have it respond appropriately—without having to learn complex development environments or wait for hours while your code compiles. Scripting languages provide "instant gratification" programming and can be used to create simple data processing applications to complex client/server systems. This chapter looks at three scripting languages that come with your Mac OS X computer: AppleScript, Perl, and Python.

AppleScript is often referred to as Apple's best-kept secret. It is a command line buried beneath many of the Mac's popular applications, including the Finder. Not surprisingly, Mac OS X integrates AppleScript into the operating system and provides access to the technology from both Carbon and Cocoa applications.

Perl, on the other hand, is a Unix-level scripting language that has proven to be popular on the Web for creating dynamic applications and performs equally well for everything from system automation to SQL database interaction.

Finally, Python is an object-oriented language that offers tremendous benefits in ease of use and readability. It is easy to learn, yet provides more than enough capability and flexibility to satisfy the most hard-core developer.

This chapter uncovers the mystery of using scripting languages and introduces the syntax and tools a user can employ to take control of his or her system at an entirely new level.

Introduction to AppleScript

When creating BSD shell scripts, you are limited to the input and output of the applications being scripted. Complex applications are often impossible to control because of their inability to process standard input. AppleScript works at an entirely different level—within the applications themselves.

To be controlled by AppleScript, an application must implement a scripting dictionary. A scripting dictionary is a collection of commands and functions that can be invoked through AppleScript. Each application determines the features that it makes available for scripting. The result of this approach is that applications can make their most useful functions available through a script, making it possible to create far more complex scripts.

It's also important to note the audience of Mac OS X's AppleScripting capabilities. Python and Perl scripting are the tools of programmers and system administrators. AppleScript was intended to provide a means for normal, everyday Macintosh users to automate tasks on their computers. The syntax is surprisingly simple and can be understood even if you've never seen a programming language before. For example, take the following code:

```
tell application "Finder"
    activate
    close window "Applications"
end tell
```

It doesn't look like a programming language, but it is. This small example instructs Mac OS X to activate the Finder application and then close an open window with the title Applications.

Using a language that can almost be read aloud and understood, normal users can write scripts that combine the capabilities of multiple applications.

Script Editor

The easiest way to get started with AppleScript is with the Script Editor. Besides being a context-sensitive programming editor, it also acts as a script recorder. A user can open the Script Editor, click Record, and generate an AppleScript by using the editor to monitor his actions while interacting with an AppleScriptable application.

NOTE

It's critical to note that AppleScript (and the AppleScript editor) should not be considered a macro system. Macro applications, such as QuicKeys, work by simulating user input to applications. This is similar to shell scripting. From the application's perspective, a user is controlling it.

When AppleScript controls an application, the application understands what is happening. It can return error codes and extended status to the script, enabling it to react and adapt to changing conditions. AppleScript is a powerful tool and offers flexibility beyond simple macros.

Starting with Panther, AppleScript now offers user interface actions that can simulate user input within any application—scriptable or not!

Apple has made remarkable strides in making Mac OS X fully scriptable. Applications such as the Finder and iTunes are fully scriptable. The Script Editor serves as your primary entry and testing point for any AppleScript development—either recorded or entered by hand.

Basic Usage

Launch the Script Editor (`/Applications/AppleScript/Script Editor`) to begin scripting. Figure 21.1 shows the basic editor window.

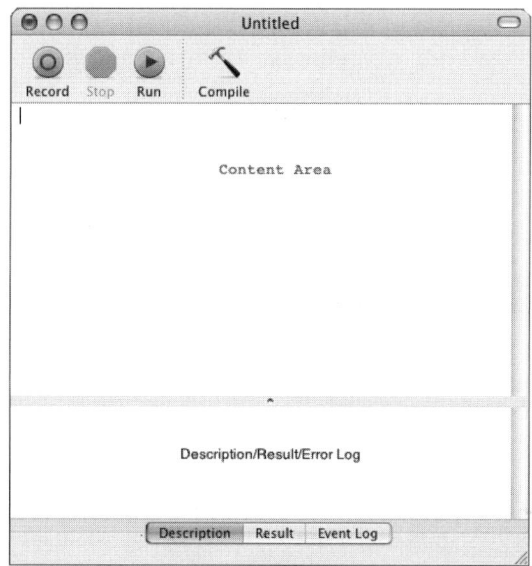

FIGURE 21.1 The Script Editor is used when editing or recording AppleScripts.

The Script Editor is composed of script recording and editing controls, which include

- Recording/Playback—Similar to a tape deck, these buttons are used to control recording and playback of an AppleScript. Click the Record button (Command-D) to start monitoring your system for Apple events within scriptable applications. These events are then stored in a script. The Stop button (Command-.) is used to stop recording, whereas the Run button (Command-R) executes the actions.
- Compile—Reviews the syntax of the current script for errors and automatically reformats the script if needed.
- Content—The content area is used to compose and edit script content. It functions like any Mac OS X text editor, but has the benefit of autoformatting code when syntax is checked or the script is run.
- Description/Result/Error Log—This area is used to display information from or about the script, depending on the active button at the bottom of the window.

To start using the editor, click the Record button, switch to the Finder, and then open and drag a few windows around. As you work in the Finder, an AppleScript will build in the editor window. Click Stop to finish the code block and prepare it for execution. Figure 21.2 displays a script that has just finished generating.

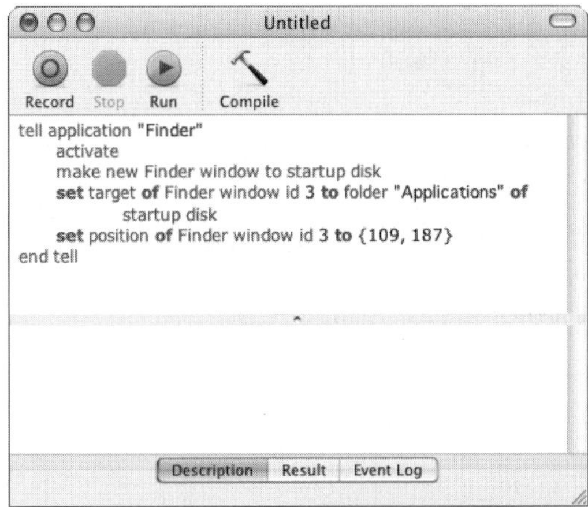
Untitled
Record
Stop
Run
Compile
tell application "Finder"
activate
make new Finder window to startup disk
set target of Finder window id 3 to folder "Applications" of
startup disk
set position of Finder window id 3 to {109, 187}
end tell
Description
Result
Event Log

FIGURE 21.2 Click Record to monitor your actions and build an AppleScript; then click Stop to finish the script.

Scripting Dictionary

Obviously, the biggest draw to AppleScript is the capability to create scripts from scratch. Recording is a good way to get a quick start but can't be used to generate anything truly useful. The basic AppleScript syntax is covered later in the section "AppleScript Syntax". Even this, however, is useless without knowledge of what commands an application can accept. You can view a scripting dictionary that shows the functions and properties offered by a given piece of software.

To access a scripting dictionary for any application, choose File, Open Dictionary from the menu. A list of the available scriptable applications is displayed, as demonstrated by Figure 21.3.

Be aware that some applications might not be shown. The Browse button at the bottom of the window opens a standard File Open dialog for choosing an arbitrary file. After you pick an application from the default or browse view, a dictionary window appears, as shown in Figure 21.4.

Along the left side of the dictionary window is a list of the AppleScript functions provided. These functions are divided into categories, based on their purpose. These categories are called *suites*. To display the syntax for a given item, click its name in the list. Highlighting a suite name displays a description of the commands and classes within that grouping and a complete view of the syntax for each.

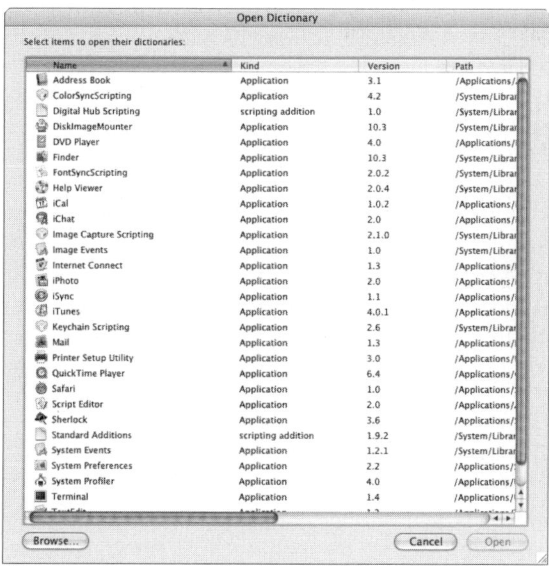

FIGURE 21.3 Choose from the available scriptable applications.

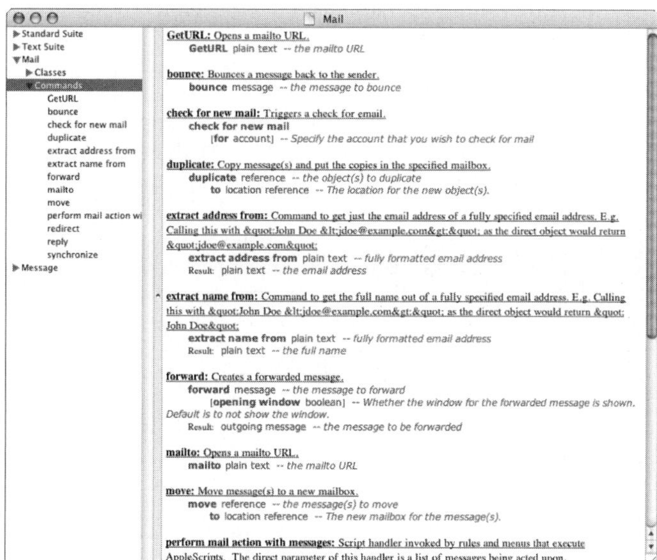

FIGURE 21.4 The dictionary documents the available AppleScript functions.

TIP

Hold down Shift and select all the suite headings to create a master list of the available scripting functions. Choose File, Print (Command-P) from the menu to print a hard-copy reference guide for AppleScripting your favorite applications.

AppleScript abstracts the parts of an application into classes. A class is a "part" of an application you work with, such as a file. When you work with a class, you work with an *instance* of a class, which is called an *object*. Objects have properties that can be `set` or modified to effect changes to the object. The properties can also be retrieved with `get` to return results for evaluation. For example, the Finder has a file object with a file type property. The following script gets and displays the type for an arbitrary file:

```
1: tell application "Finder"
2:   set thisFile to (choose file with prompt "Pick the file to examine:")
3:   set theType to get the file type of thisFile
4:   display dialog theType
5: end tell
```

Line 1 indicates that instructions will be sent to the Finder. Line 2 sets a variable called `thisFile` to point to a file. The `choose` command opens a file selection dialog box for visually selecting a file. Line 3 sets a variable called `theType` to the results of a command that gets the file type of the file reference by `thisFile`. Line 4 displays a dialog box containing the contents of `theType`. Finally, line 5 stops talking to the Finder.

This example introduces the structure you will see in most AppleScript programs. The `tell`, `set`, and `get` statements form the basis of scripts. The objects and the parameters that can be modified, however, will have to be looked up in the application's dictionary.

NOTE

The `display dialog` command used in this script isn't even a function of basic AppleScript. It is provided by the Standard Additions scripting extension, automatically installed on Mac OS X. You can view additional functions offered by the Standard Additions by displaying its dictionary using File, Open Dictionary.

Results

When an AppleScript function returns a result, it is stored in a special temporary variable called `result`. This can be used to access a value without the need for additional variables. For example, lines 3 and 4 of the preceding script could be changed to

```
get the file type of thisFile
display dialog the result
```

To display the contents of the result container within the Script Editor, choose View, Show Result (Command-2) from the menu, or click the Result button at the bottom of the Script Editor window. Mac OS X displays the current value of `result` below the script.

Script Tracing

To trace the execution of a script as it runs, use the Event Log. This log keeps track of the events (commands) sent to an application and displays the results that are returned immediately. Click the Event Log button or press Command-3 to show the Event Log in the lower pane of the Script Editor window. Figure 21.5 shows the Event Log after replaying a simple script to get the location of a Finder window.

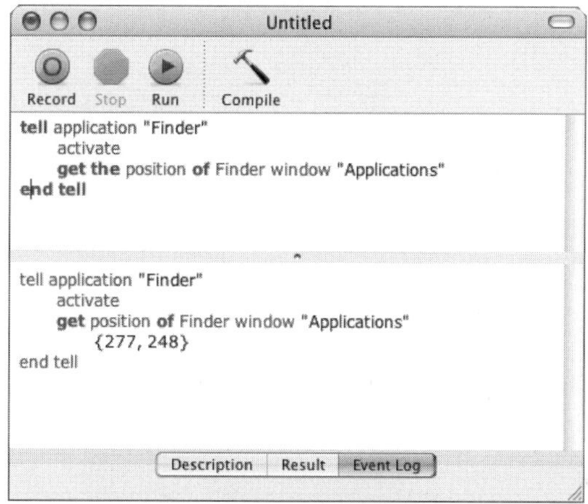

FIGURE 21.5 The Event Log can be used to monitor script execution.

Saving

After creating a script that functions the way you want, you can save it for double-click execution whenever you want. Figure 21.6 displays the Save dialog box.

There are five possible file formats for scripts:

- Compiled Script—Saves the script as a compiled binary file.
- Script Document—A noncompiled binary form of the script.
- Script Text—Saves the contents of the script in a plain-text file.
- `Run-Only`—Protects the script from future edits.
- Application—Saves the script for double-click execution under Mac OS X.

In addition to the file format, you can also choose the line ending format if saving to a text file, and whether the file should be Run Only (not allow editing), display a Startup Screen, Stay Open (after it is finished executing), and Requires Classic (Mac OS 9).

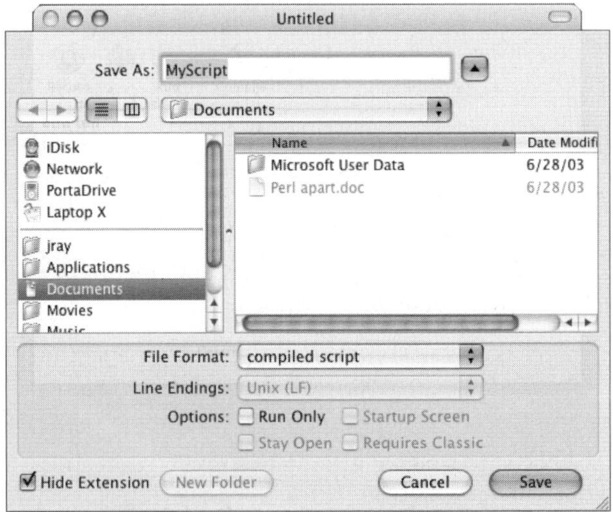

FIGURE 21.6 Save a script for later execution.

Scripting Preferences

The Script Editor automatically highlights and formats AppleScript as you type. To change the default font styles and formatting, choose Preferences from the application menu. Figure 21.7 shows the formatting preferences .

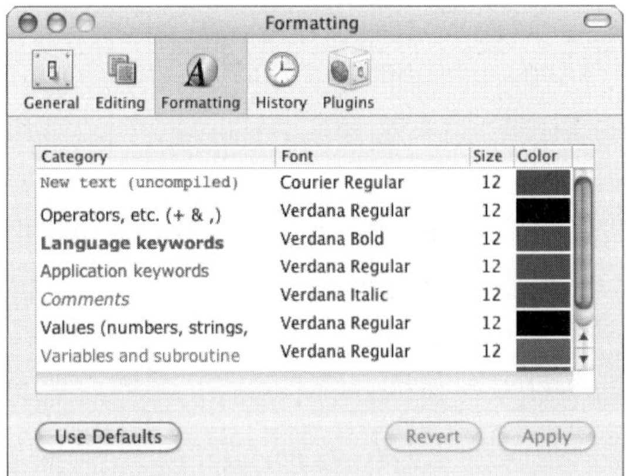

FIGURE 21.7 AppleScript Formatting preferences enable the user to adjust the appearance of the Script Editor.

The five categories of Script Editor preferences are as follows:

- General—The default scripting language to be used. AppleScript is the only language available without installing third-party software.
- Editing—Control Line wrap settings, control tab indentation, and enable/disable the Code Assistant, which attempts to autocomplete functions as you type them in the Script Editor.
- Formatting—Choose font size, color, syntax highlighting, and so on.
- History—Enable or disable a running history of AppleScript-generated results and events.
- Plugins—Display any third-party plug-ins that have been installed.

AppleScript Syntax

Describing the AppleScript syntax to a programmer familiar with a traditional language isn't as straightforward as you might think. AppleScript uses an entirely different programming model based on an English-like structure that, after a few minutes of use, leaves the programmer feeling as though he is having a deep, intellectual conversation with his computer.

`tell`

The basic building block of an AppleScript is the `tell` statement. `tell` is used to address an object and give it instructions to perform. A `tell` line is written in one of two common forms: a block or a single statement. The block format enables the programmer to send multiple commands to an application without stating its name each time.

Single:

```
tell <object> <object name> to <action>
```

Block:

```
tell <object> <object name>
    <action>
    <action>
    <action>
    ...
end tell
```

For example, the following two statements are identical but are structured using the simple and block forms of `tell`:

```
tell application "Finder" to empty trash
```

and

```
tell application "Finder"
    empty trash
end tell
```

Both of these short scripts cause the Finder to empty the Trash. Although the second form might seem more verbose, it is likely to be the most commonly encountered form. Most scripts interact with objects to perform complex compound operations rather than simple commands. In addition, the second version of the AppleScript is easier to read and view the functional components. Maintaining readable code is a good idea no matter what programming platform you're using.

TIP

In addition to breaking up code with `tell` blocks, long lines are typically split using a code-continuation character. To break a single long code line across multiple lines, press Option-Return to insert a code-continuation character.

Variables: `set/get`

In AppleScript, variables are automatically created when they are set. A variable name can be any combination of alphanumerics as long as the first character is a letter. No special prefixes are required to denote a variable within the code.

Although type conversions happen automatically in many cases, a variable type can be explicitly given directly in the `set` statement:

```
set <variable/property> to <value> [as <object type>]
```

For example, both of the following lines set variables (`thevalue` and `thevalue2`) to 5, but the second line forces the variable to be a string:

```
set thevalue to 5
set thevalue2 to 5 as string
```

Variables can take on simple values, such as numbers or strings, or more complex values in the form of lists. Lists are equivalent to arrays in more traditional programming languages. A list is represented by a comma-separated group of values, enclosed in curly brackets {}. For example, the following line sets a variable, `thePosition`, to a list containing two values:

```
set thePosition to {50, 75}
```

Lists are often used to set coordinate pairs for manipulating onscreen objects but can be composed of any object. In fact, lists can even contain lists of lists. For example:

```
set theListOfPositions to {{50, 75}, {65, 45}, {25, 90}}
```

Here, a variable called `theListOfPositions` is set to a list of lists. Item 1 of the list is `{50,75}`, item 2 is `{65,45}`, and so on.

In addition to setting variables, the `set` command can act on the properties of an object to effect changes on the system. Earlier you saw how an AppleScript could get the file type of a given file. Similarly, `set` can alter the file type. For example:

```
1: tell application "Finder"
2:   set thisFile to (choose file with prompt "Pick the file to examine:")
3:   set the file type of thisFile to "JOHN"
4: end tell
```

In line 3 of this code fragment, `set` is used to alter the file type of the chosen file to equal `JOHN`.

NOTE

This is just an example, but chances are you don't want to set your file's type code to `JOHN`. It requires an application that can handle files of type `JOHN` to be able to open it, and I am unaware of what that application would be.

To retrieve values from variables, or properties from objects, you would use the `get` command. `get`, by itself, retrieves the value of an object or variable and stores it in the result variable:

```
get the <property/variable> [of <object>]
```

Traditional programmers might feel uncomfortable with retrieving results into a temporary variable (`result`); in that case, they can combine the `get` and `set` commands to immediately store the results of a `get` in another variable or object property:

```
set <variable/property> [of <object>] to
  get the <property/variable> [of <object>]
```

When dealing with list values, you can reference individual items within a list by referring to them as just that: items. For example, assume that you've run the following command:

```
set thePosition to {50, 75}
```

To retrieve the value of the first item in the list, you can use

```
get item 1 of thePosition
```

When dealing with lists within lists, just embed item statements within one another. Assume that this list has been entered

```
set theListOfPositions to {{50, 75}, {65, 45}, {25, 90}}
```

To retrieve the value of the second item of the second list within a list, you could write

```
get item 2 of item 2 of theListOfPositions
```

Again, the power of these commands is based in the dictionaries of AppleScript applications. FileMaker Pro, for example, can edit, insert, and delete its records via AppleScript.

`If`

A common programming construct is the If-then-else statement. This is used to check the value of an item and then react appropriately. The syntax for a basic `If` statement is

```
If <condition> then
    <action>
end if
```

For example, the following code asks the user to input a value, checks to see whether it equals 5, and outputs an appropriate message if it does.

```
1: display dialog "Enter a number:" default answer ""
2: set theValue to (text returned of the result) as integer
3: if theValue = 5 then
4:   display dialog "Five is my magic number."
5: end if
```

Line 1 displays a dialog prompt for a user to enter a value. Line 2 sets a variable `theValue` to the text returned from the dialog and forces it to be evaluated as an integer. Line 3 checks `theValue`; if it is equal to the number 5, line 4 is executed. Line 4 displays an onscreen message, and line 5 ends the `If` statement.

The `If` statement can be expanded to include an `else` clause that is executed if the original condition is not met.

```
1: display dialog "Enter a number:" default answer ""
2: set theValue to (text returned of the result) as integer
3: if theValue = 5 then
4:   display dialog "Five is my magic number."
5: else
6:   display dialog "That is NOT my magic number."
7: end if
```

In this modified version of the code, line 6 contains an alternative message that will be displayed if the condition in line 3 is not met.

Finally, the `else` itself can be expanded to check alternative conditions using `else if`. This enables multiple possibilities to be evaluated within a single statement:

```
1: display dialog "Enter a number:" default answer ""
2: set theValue to (text returned of the result) as integer
3: if theValue = 5 then
4:   display dialog "Five is my magic number."
5: else if theValue = 3 then
6:   display dialog "Three is a decent number too."
7: else
8:   display dialog "I don't like that number."
9: end if
```

The latest version of the code includes an `else if` in line 5. If the initial comparison in line 3 fails, line 5 is evaluated. Finally, if line 5 fails, the `else` in line 8 is executed.

repeat

Another common programming construct is the loop. AppleScript uses a single-loop type to handle a variety of looping needs. The `repeat` statement has several different forms that cover while, until, and other types of traditional loops.

There are six different forms of the `repeat` statement:

- Repeat indefinitely—Repeat a group of statements indefinitely, or until the `exit` command is called.

  ```
  repeat
    <statements>
  end repeat
  ```

- Repeat #—Using the second loop format, the user can choose the number of times a loop repeats.

  ```
  repeat <integer> times
    <statements>
  end repeat
  ```

- Repeat while—Loop indefinitely while the given condition evaluates to true.

```
repeat while <condition>
  <statements>
end repeat
```

- Repeat until—Loop indefinitely until the given condition evaluates to true. This is the inverse of the `repeat while` loop.

```
repeat until <condition>
  <statements>
end repeat
```

- Repeat with—Called a for/next loop in more traditional languages, this form of the repeat loop counts up or down from a starting number to an ending number. Each iteration updates a variable with the latest loop value.

```
repeat with <variable> from <starting integer> to
<ending integer> [by <increment>]
  <statements>
end repeat
```

- Repeat with list—Like the standard `repeat with` style loop, the `repeat with list` loop runs over a range of values, storing each value in a named variable during the iterations of the loop. The difference is that the value range is specified with a list, rather than an upper and lower integer value. This enables the loop to operate over anything from numbers to strings, to lists of lists.

```
repeat with <variable> in <list>
  <statements>
end repeat
```

Subroutines

The final building block that we will cover in AppleScript is the subroutine. Subroutines help modularize code by breaking it into smaller, more manageable segments that can return specific results to a controlling piece of code. There are two types of subroutines in AppleScript: those with labeled parameters and those that use positional parameters. A *parameter* is a piece of information passed to a subroutine when it is called.

Positional parameters will be the most familiar to anyone who has used another programming language. This type of subroutine, which is the easiest to define and use, depends on being called with a certain number of parameters in a certain order.

Labeled parameters, on the other hand, rely on a set of named parameters and their values, which can be sent to the subroutine in any order. This can be used to create an English-like syntax but adds a level of complexity when reading the code.

Because positional parameters can be used for almost any type of development and fit in with the structure of other languages discussed in this book, they will be the focus here.

The syntax of a positional parameter subroutine is shown here:

```
on <subroutine name> ([<variable 1>,<variable 2>,<variable n>,...])
  <statements>
  [return <result value>]
end <subroutine name>
```

Each positional parameter-based subroutine requires a name, a list of variables that will be supplied when called, and an optional value that will be returned to the main application. For example, the following `beAnnoying` routine takes a string and a number as parameters, and then displays a dialog box with the message. The display will be repeated until it matches the number given.

```
1: on beAnnoying(theMessage, howAnnoying)
2:   repeat howAnnoying times
3:     display dialog theMessage
4:   end repeat
5: end beAnnoying
```

Line 1 declares the subroutine `beAnnoying` and its two parameters: `theMessage` and `howAnnoying`. Line 2 starts a loop that repeats for the number of times set in the `howAnnoying` variable. Line 3 displays a dialog box with the contents `theMessage`. Line 4 ends the loop, and line 5 ends the subroutine.

As expected, running this piece of code does absolutely nothing. It is a subroutine, and, as such, requires that another piece of code call it. To call this particular routine, you could use a line such as

```
beAnnoying("Am I annoying yet?",3)
```

This causes the subroutine to activate and display the message Am I annoying yet? three times.

A more useful subroutine is one that performs a calculation and returns a result. The following example accepts, as input, an integer containing a person's age in years. It returns a result containing the given age in days.

```
on yearsToDays(theYears)
  return theYears * 365
end yearsToDays
```

Because this subroutine returns a value, it can be called from within a set statement to store the result directly into a variable:

```
set dayAge to yearsToDays(90)
```

When working in subroutines, you must explicitly define variables that are only used in the subroutine, as opposed to those that can be accessed from anywhere in the AppleScript application. A variable that is visible to all portions of a script is called a global variable and is defined using the global declaration. Similarly, the local keyword can be used to limit the scope of a variable to only the code contained within a subroutine. For example, try executing the following AppleScript:

```
1: set theValue to 10
2: reset()
3: display dialog theValue
4:
5: on reset()
6:   local theValue
7:   set theValue to 0
8: end reset
```

In line 1, a variable called `theValue` is set to 10. In line 2, the reset subroutine is called, which appears to set the contents of `theValue` to zero. Yet, when the result is displayed in line 3, the original value remains. The reason for this strange behavior is the inclusion of line 6. Line 6 defines `theValue` as a local variable to the reset subroutine. This means that any changes to that variable will not extend outside the subroutine.

To gain the behavior we expect (the contents of `theValue` are set to zero everywhere), swap the local keyword with global:

```
1: set theValue to 10
2: reset()
3: display dialog theValue
4:
5: on reset()
6:   global theValue
7:   set theValue to 0
8: end reset
```

This tiny modification tells the reset subroutine that it should use the global representation of the variable `theValue`. When `theValue` is set to zero in line 7, it replaces the initial value set in line 1.

Accessing the Command Line from AppleScript

AppleScript can easily be integrated with shell scripts using the `do shell` script command, which is part of the AppleScript Standard Additions dictionary. This function returns the results of the command in a variable that you can use in your scripts. For example, to return and display the output of the Unix command `date`:

```
do shell script "date"
set theTime to the result
display dialog theTime
```

If you've worked through the command-line examples, by now you know that sometimes it's useful to execute commands as an administrative user (`root`). There are several additional parameters that you can use with `do shell script` to accomplish this and more. The full syntax follows:

```
do shell script <shell commands>
  [password <admin password> [with administrator privileges]]
```

If the `with administrator privileges` clause is specified, the user is prompted for a password and the script executed with administrative permissions. To eliminate the password prompt, simply use the password keyword followed by your administrator password. For example, to return the contents of `/var/log/secure.log` (which requires administrator access), you could use

```
do shell script "cat /var/log/secure.log" password "mypassword"
  with administrator privileges
```

Combining AppleScript with the power of the command line gives advanced users the ability to control all components of their Mac OS X system.

TIP

Users who just want to activate a shell script can do so by scripting the terminal. This method does not provide a means of returning shell results to the AppleScript.

An example of a Terminal script that uses the `ls` command to display a list of files is shown here:

```
tell application "Terminal"
  do script "ls"
end tell
```

Scripting Additions

Enterprising developers who open the power of their software to the AppleScript model constantly expand AppleScript. The most common type of scripting addition is a new application. Applications that you install under Mac OS X may or may not be scriptable—be sure to check the documentation or try opening the software's dictionary using the Script Editor.

In addition, some developers may deliver extensions to AppleScript in the form of a scripting extension. These extensions are not applications themselves but libraries of additional functions that can be used in any AppleScript.

Downloaded AppleScript extensions should be stored in `~/Library/ScriptingAdditions` or the system-level directory `/Library/ScriptingAdditions` for access by all users.

Script Menu

The Script Menu Installer (path: `Applications/AppleScript/Install Script Menu`) adds a menu extra to your menu bar that can be used to quickly launch AppleScripts from the `/Library/Scripts` folder, or `~/Library/Scripts`.

Figure 21.8 shows the Script menu extra.

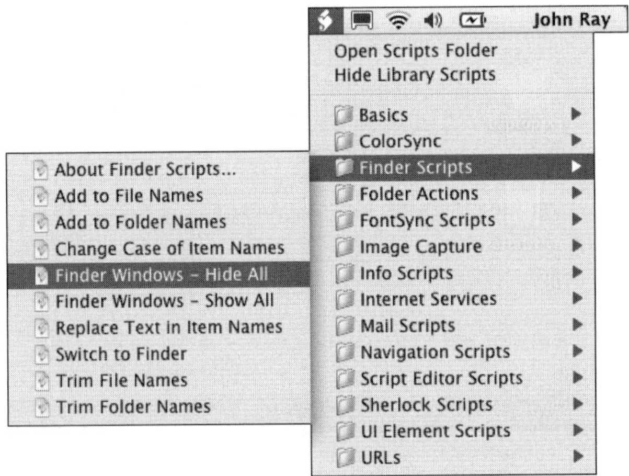

FIGURE 21.8 The Script menu extra adds a menu bar launch point for all your scripts.

Any compiled scripts placed in either of the Scripts locations will become accessible from the menu. To create submenus for categorizing scripts, just create multiple folders within the Scripts folders. As with everything in Mac OS X, items stored in `/Library/Scripts` are accessible by all users, whereas those in your personal `~/Library/Scripts` folders can only be used by you.

TIP

The Script menu can be used to access Perl and Shell scripts in addition to AppleScripts. Any script files placed in Scripts folders will be added to the list.

To remove the Script menu, Command-drag it from the menu bar, or use the Remove Script Menu utility included in the AppleScript folder.

Folder Actions

Folder actions are scripts executed when folders are opened, modified, or moved. Actions can be attached either via the Script menu's Folder Actions submenu or by selecting a Folder in the Finder and choosing Enable Folder Actions from the folder's contextual menu, followed by choosing Add Folder Action or Configure Folder Actions from the same menu. The Add Folder Action prompts you for a folder action script to attach to the highlighted folder, whereas Configure Folder Actions opens the Folder Actions Setup application (path: `/Applications/AppleScript/Folder Actions Setup`), shown in Figure 21.9, that provides access to *all* Folder actions configured for your account.

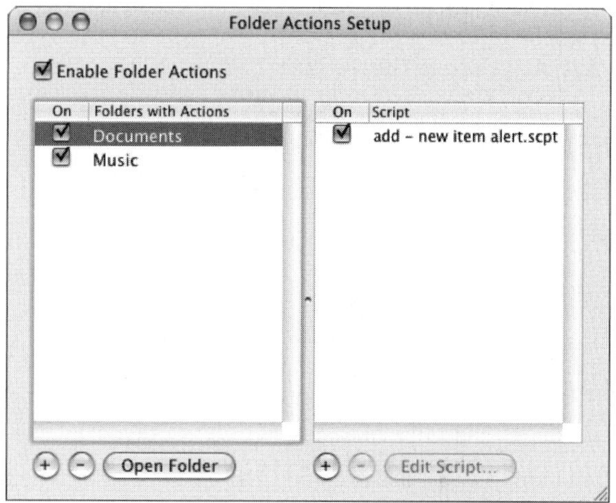

FIGURE 22.9 Configure Folder Actions provides a "control center" for adding and removing folder actions.

Within the Folder Actions Setup window, use the Enable Folder Actions check box to globally enable or disable actions. To add a new action, click the "+" button below the left-hand column and choose a folder you want to attach an action to. When added to the folder list, highlight it and use the "+" button in the right-hand column to choose a folder action script that you want to attach to the folder. The "-" buttons can be used to remove folders and attached scripts, whereas the Open Folder and Edit Script buttons open the highlighted folder and open the selected script in Script Editor.

To get started with folder action scripts, Apple has include three basic scripts in `/Library/Scripts/Folder Action Scripts`:

- `close - close sub-folders.scpt`—Closes any open subfolders when the folder with the attached script is closed.
- `add - new item alert.scpt`—Displays an alert when new items are added to the folder with the attached script.
- `open - show comments in dialog.scpt`—Shows any comments stored when the folder with the attached script is opened.

Properly formed Action scripts should be placed in either `/Library/Scripts/Folder Action Scripts` or `~/Library/Scripts/Folder Action Scripts`. Apple has provided an excellent tutorial on how to set up a folder action script at `http://www.apple.com/applescript/folder_actions/`.

Command-Line AppleScript Tools

AppleScript compilation and execution has been extended to the BSD shell through the use of the `osacompile` and `osascript` commands.

The `osacompile` utility accepts a text file containing AppleScript as input and outputs a compiled script file using the following syntax:

```
osacompile -o <output file> <script file>
```

Although this is probably the form you'll use most, several additional command-line options can fine-tune the compile process. Table 21.1 documents several of these options.

TABLE 21.1 Command Documentation Table for `osacompile`

`-l <language>`	Override the language for any plain text files. Normally, plain text files are compiled as AppleScript.
`-o <name>`	Place the output in the filename. If `-o` is not specified, the resulting script is placed in the file `a.scpt`.
`-t <type>`	Set the output file type to type. Type is a four-character code. If this option is omitted and the output file does not exist, the type is set to `osas`—that is, a compiled script.
`-c <creator>`	Set the output file creator to creator. Creator is a four-character code. If this option is omitted and the output file does not exist, the creator is set to "ToyS"—that is, Script Editor.
`-x`	Save the resulting script as execute only.
`-s`	Run as a stay-open applet (doesn't exit when finished).
`-u`	Display a startup screen when the script runs.

If no options are specified, `osacompile` produces a classic Mac OS format script file—that is, type `osas` (compiled script), creator "ToyS" (Script Editor), with the script data in the `scpt:128` resource and nothing in the data fork. This format is compatible with all Mac OS and Mac OS X systems.

After you've compiled a script, you can run it from the command line using the `osascript` utility by typing:

```
osascript <script filename>
```

If a filename is not specified on the command line, `osascript` attempts to run AppleScript from standard input. This is a great way to test scripts, or run a quick AppleScript command without needing to start the Script Editor. Like the `osacompile` command, `osascript` provides a number of command-line options that advanced users might be interested in. These are displayed in Table 21.2.

TABLE 21.2 Command Documentation Table for `osascript`

Option	Description
`-e` *<command>*	Enter one line of a script. If `-e` is given, `osascript` will not look for a filename in the argument list. Multiple `-e` commands may be given to build up a multiline script. Because most scripts use characters that are special to many shell programs—for example, AppleScript uses single and double quote marks, "(", ")", and "*")—the command has to be correctly quoted and escaped to get it past the shell intact.
`-l` *<language>*	Override the language for any plain text files. Normally, plain text files are compiled as AppleScript.
`-s` *<flags>*	Modify the output style. The *`flags`* argument is a string consisting of any of the modifier characters `e`, `h`, `o`, and `s`. Multiple modifiers can be concatenated in the same string, and multiple `-s` options can be specified. The modifiers come in exclusive pairs; if conflicting modifiers are specified, the last one takes precedence. The meanings of the modifier characters are as follows: `h` Print values in human-readable form (default). `s` Print values in recompilable source form. `osascript` normally prints its results in human-readable form: Strings do not have quotes around them, characters are not escaped, braces for lists and records are omitted, and so on. This is generally more useful but can introduce ambiguities. For example, the lists `'{"foo", "bar"}'` and `'{{"foo", {"bar"}}}'` would both be displayed as `'foo, bar'`. To see the results in an unambiguous form that could be recompiled into the same value, use the `s` modifier. `e` Print script errors to `stderr` (default). `o` Print script errors to `stdout`. `osascript` normally prints script errors to `stderr`, so downstream clients see only valid results. When you're running automated tests, however, using the `o` modifier lets you distinguish script errors, which you care about matching, from other diagnostic output, which you don't.

AppleScript Studio

After you've familiarized yourself with basic AppleScript syntax, you might want to consider moving up to the "next level" of AppleScript development—AppleScript Studio. AppleScript Studio is Apple's integration of the AppleScript programming language with *XCode*.

Using XCode you can quickly create complete GUI applications powered entirely by AppleScript. Although not appropriate for real-time or graphically intense software, AppleScript Studio can quickly create a GUI around Unix-based commands. In fact, a number of utilities (such as Carbon Copy Cloner, discussed in Chapter 32, "System Maintenance") have been written in AppleScript Studio and have received rave reviews.

To get started with AppleScript Studio, install XCode, and browse the examples in `/Developer/Examples/AppleScript Studio`. Apple provides a simple tutorial along with PDF reference guides to get you started. Be warned: AppleScript Studio takes advantage of Apple's development tools. These, although powerful, have been known to take some time to master.

Other Sources of AppleScript Information

AppleScript is a capable language that offers many advanced features impossible to cover in the amount of space this title allows. What is provided here should be an ample start to creating scripts of your own and editing scripts included with Mac OS X. If you're interested in more information on advanced AppleScript syntax, I strongly suggest that you check out the following resources:

- AppleScript Language Guide— `http://developer.apple.com/documentation/AppleScript/Conceptual/AppleScriptLangGuide/index.html`
- AppleScript in Mac OS X—`http://www.apple.com/applescript/macosx/`
- The AppleScript Sourcebook—`http://www.AppleScriptSourcebook.com/`
- *AppleScript in a Nutshell*, Bruce W. Perry, ISBN: 1565928415, O'Reilly, 2001

CAUTION

AppleScript functionality has slowly been evolving with each revision of Mac OS X. If you're lagging a version or two behind, you're likely to notice serious limitations with the version of AppleScript you have installed. Panther's support far exceeds any of the previous releases.

Perl

Although not as user-friendly as AppleScript, Perl (Practical Extraction and Reporting Language) is just as powerful, and, because of its open source and cross-platform nature, significantly more popular.

Originally designed to make working with text data simple, Perl has been expanded by developers to handle tasks such as image manipulation and client/server activities. Because of its ease of use and capability to work with ambiguous user input, Perl is a popular Web development language. For example, assume that you want to extract a phone number from an input string. A user might enter 555-5654, 5552231, 421-5552313, and so on. It is up to the application to find the area code, local exchange, and identifier numbers. In Perl, this is simple:

```
#!/usr/bin/perl
print "Please enter a phone number:";
$phone=<STDIN>;
$phone=~s/[^\d]//g;
$phone=~s/^1//;
if (length($phone)==7) {
  $phone=~/(\d{3,3})(\d{4,4})/;
  $area="???"; $prefix=$1; $number=$2;
} elsif (length($phone)==10) {
  $phone=~/(\d{3,3})(\d{3,3})(\d{4,4})/;
  $area=$1; $prefix=$2; $number=$3;
} else { print "Invalid number!"; exit; }
print "($area) $prefix-$number\n";
```

This program accepts a phone number as input, strips any unusual characters from it, removes a leading 1, if included, and then formats the result in an attractive manner. Applying this capability to mine data from user input to Web development creates opportunities for programmers to write extremely user-friendly software.

Perl programs are similar to shell scripts in that they are interpreted by an additional piece of software. Each script starts with a line that includes the path to the Perl interpreter. In Mac OS X, this is typically `#!/usr/bin/perl`. On entering a script, it must be made executable by typing **`chmod +x`** ***`<script name>`***. Finally, it can be run by entering its complete path at the command line, or by typing **`./`*****`<script name>`*** from the same directory as the script. Alternatively, you can invoke a script by passing it as an argument to Perl—that is, **`perl`** ***`<script name>`***.For more information on this process, refer to Chapter 18, "Advanced Unix Shell Use: Configuration and Programming (Shell Scripting)."

Although this chapter provides enough information to write a program like the one shown here, it is not a complete reference to Perl. Perl is an object-oriented language with thousands of functions. *Sams Teach Yourself Perl in 21 Days* is an excellent read and a great way to beef up on the topic.

TIP

In addition to this introduction, Chapter 22, "MySQL and Database Connectivity," covers Perl's capability to interact with database systems such as MySQL, and Chapter 28, "Web Programming," discusses using Perl as a Web development language.

Variables and Data Types

Perl has a number of different variable types, but the most common are shown in Table 21.3. Perl variable names are composed of alphanumeric characters and are case sensitive, unlike much of Mac OS X. This means that a variable named $mymacosx is entirely different from $myMacOSX. Unlike some languages, such as C, Perl performs automatic type conversion when possible. A programmer can use a variable as a number in one statement and a string in the next.

TABLE 21.3 Common Perl Variable Types

Type	Description
$variable	A simple variable that can hold anything is prefixed with a $. You can use these variables as strings or numbers. These are the most common variables.
FILEHANDLE	Filehandles hold a reference to a file that you are writing or reading. Typically, these are expressed in uppercase and do not have the $ prefix.
@array	The @ references an array of variables. The array does not need to be predimensioned and can grow to whatever size memory allows. You reference individual elements of an array as $array[0], $array[1], $array[2], and so on. The array as a whole is referenced as @array.
%array	This is another type of an array—an associative array. Associative arrays are another of Perl's power features. Rather than using numbers to reference the values stored in this array, you use any string you want. For example, if you have 3 apples, 2 oranges, and 17 grapefruit, you could store these values in the associative array as $array{apple}=3, $array{orange}=2, $array{grapefruit}=17. The only difference between the use of a normal array and an associate array (besides the method of referencing a value) is the type of brackets used. Associative arrays use curly brackets {} to access individual elements, whereas standard arrays use square brackets [].

Input/Output Functions

Because Perl is so useful for manipulating data, one of the first things you'll want to do is get data into a script. There are a number of ways to do this, including reading from a file or the Terminal window. To Perl, however, command-line input and file input are much the same thing. To use either, you must read from an input stream.

Input Streams

To input data into a variable from a file, use $variable=<*FILEHANDLE*>. This inputs data up to a newline character into the named variable. To read from the command line, the filehandle is replaced with a special handle that points to the standard input stream—<STDIN>.

When data is read from an input stream, it contains the end-of-line character (newline) as part of the data. This is usually an unwanted piece of information that can be stripped off using the chomp command. Failure to use chomp often results in debugging headaches as you attempt to figure out why your string comparison routines are failing. For example, the following reads a line from standard (command line) input and removes the trailing newline character:

```
$myname=<STDIN>;
chomp($myname);
```

To read data in from an actual stored file, it must first be opened with open *<FILEHANDLE>*, "*<filename>*". For example, to read the first line of a file named MacOSX.txt:

```
open FILEHANDLE, "MacOSX.txt";
$line1=<FILENAME>;
close FILEHANDLE;
```

When finished reading a file, use close followed by the filehandle to close.

Outputting Data

Outputting data is the job of the print command. print can display text strings or the contents of variables. In addition, you can embed special characters in a print statement that are otherwise unprintable. For example:

```
print "I love Mac OS X!\n---------------\n";
```

In this sample line, the \n is a newline character—this moves the cursor down a line so that subsequent output occurs on a new line, rather than the same line as the current print statement. Table 21.4 contains other common special characters.

TABLE 21.4 Common Special Characters

Escape Sequence	Description
\n	Newline, the Unix equivalent of Return/Enter
\r	A standard return character
\t	Tab
\"	Double quotes
\\	The \ character

Many characters (such as ") have a special meaning in Perl; if you want to refer to them literally, you must prefix them with \—this is called *escaping* the character. In most cases, nonalphanumeric characters should be escaped just to be on the safe side.

File Output

To output data to a file rather than standard output, you must first open a file to receive the information. This is nearly identical to the open used to read data, except for one difference. When writing to a file, you must prefix the name of the file with one of two different character strings:

- >—Output to a file, overwriting the contents.
- >>—Append to an existing file. Creates a new file if none exists.

With a file open, the `print` command is again used for output. This time, however, it includes the filehandle of the output file. For example, this code saves Mac OS X to a file named `MyOS.txt`:

```
open MYFILE, "> MyOS.txt";
print MYFILE "Mac OS X\n";
close MYFILE;
```

Again, the `close` command is used to close the file when all output is complete.

External Results (` `)

One of the more novel (and powerful) ways to get information into Perl is through an external program. For example, to quickly and easily grab a listing of running processes, you could use the output of the Unix `ps axg` command:

```
$processlist=`ps axg`;
```

The backtick (` `) characters should be placed around the command of the output you want to capture. Perl pauses and waits for the external command to finish executing before it continues processing.

This is both a dangerous and powerful tool. You can easily read an entire file into a variable by using the `cat` command with backticks. Unfortunately, if the external program fails to execute correctly, the Perl script might hang indefinitely.

Expressions

Although Perl variables can hold numbers or strings, you still need to perform the appropriate type of comparison based on the values being compared. For example, numbers can be compared for equality using ==, but strings must be compared with `eq`. If you attempt to use == to compare two strings, the expression will evaluate to true because the numeric value of both strings is zero, regardless of the text they contain. Table 21.5 displays common Perl expressions.

TABLE 21.5 Use the Appropriate Comparison Operators for the Type of Data Being Compared

Expression Syntax	Description
`$var1==$var2`	Compares two numbers for equality.
`$var1!=$var2`	Compares two numbers for inequality.
`$var1><$var2`	`Checks $var1 to see whether it is less than $var2.`
`$var1>$var2`	Tests `$var1` to see whether it is a larger number than `$var2`.
`$var1>=$var2`	Tests `$var1` to see whether it is greater than or equal to `$var2`.
`$var1<=$var2`	Compares `$var1` to see whether it is less than or equal to `$var2`.
`$var1 eq $var2`	Checks two strings for equality.
`$var1 ne $var2`	Checks two strings for inequality.
`$var1 lt $var2`	Checks to see whether the string in `$var1` is less than (by ASCII value) `$var2`.
`$var1 gt $var2`	Tests the string in `$var1` to see whether it is greater than `$var2`.
`()`	Parentheses can be used to group the elements of an expression together to force an evaluation order or provide clarity to the code.
`&&/and`	Used to connect two expressions so that both must evaluate to true for the complete expression to be true.
`¦¦/or`	Used to connect two expressions so that if either evaluates to true, the entire expression will evaluate to true.
`!`	Used to negate an expression. If the expression previously evaluated to true, you can place a `!` in front of the expression to force it to evaluate false—or vice versa.

Regular Expressions

Regular expressions (Regex) are a bit more interesting than the expressions in the preceding section. Like one of the previous expressions, a Regex evaluates to a true or false state. In addition, they are used to locate and extract data from strings.

For example, assume that the variable `$mycomputer` contains the information My computer is a Mac.

To create a regular expression that would test the string for the presence of the word "mac," you could write

```
$mycomputer=~/mac/i
```

Although this line might look like an assignment statement, it is in fact looking inside the variable `$mycomputer` for the pattern `mac`. The pattern that a regular expression matches is delimited by the `/` characters (unless changed by the programmer). The `i` after the expression tells Perl that it should perform a case-insensitive search, allowing it to match strings such as `MAC` and `mAC`.

To understand the power of regular expressions, you must first understand the pattern-matching language that comprises them.

Patterns

Regular expressions are made up of groups of pattern-matching symbols. These special characters symbolically represent the contents of a string and can be used to build complex pattern-matching rules with relative ease. Table 21.6 contains the most common components of regular expressions and their purpose.

TABLE 21.6 Use These Pattern-Matching Components to Build a Regular Expression

Pattern	Purpose
`$`	Matches the end of a string
`^`	Matches the beginning of a string
`.`	Matches any character in the string
`[]`	Matches any of the characters within the square brackets
`\s`	Matches any type of white space (space, tab, and so on)
`\n`	Matches the newline character
`\t`	Matches the tab character
`\w`	Matches a word character
`\d`	Matches a digit

The bracket characters enable you to clearly define the characters that you want to match if a predefined sequence doesn't already exist. For example, if you want to match only the uppercase letters A through Z and the numbers 1, 2, and 3, you could write

```
[A-Z123]
```

As seen in this example, you can represent a contiguous sequence of letters or numbers as a range—specifying the start and end characters of the range, separated by a `-`.

Pattern Repetition

With the capability to write patterns, you can match arbitrary strings within a character sequence. What's missing is the capability to match strings of varying lengths. These repetition characters modify the pattern they follow and enable it to be matched once, twice, or as many times as you want:

- `*`—Match any number (including zero) copies of a character.
- `+`—Match at least one copy of a character.
- `{x,y}`—Match at least `x` characters and as many as `y`.

When a repetition sequence is followed by a `?`, the pattern will match as few characters as possible to be considered true. For example, the following expression matches between 5 and 10 occurrences of the numbers 1, 2, or 3:

```
$testnumbers=~/[1-3]{5,10}/;
```

The capability to match an arbitrary number of characters enables programmers to deal with information they might not be expecting.

Extracting Information from a Regular Expression

Although it's useful to be able to find strings that contain a certain pattern, it's even better if the matching data can be extracted and used. To extract pieces of information from a match, enclose the pattern within parentheses (). To see this in action, let's go back to the original telephone number program that introduced Perl in this chapter. One of the regular expressions extracted the parts of a 10-digit phone number from a string of 10 digits:

```
$phone=~/(\d{3,3})(\d{3,3})(\d{4,4})/;
```

There are three parts to the regular expression, each enclosed within parentheses. The first two (`\d{3,3}`) capture strings of three consecutive digits, and the third (`\d{4,4}`) captures the remaining four.

For each set of parentheses used in a pattern, a `$#` variable is created that corresponds to the order in which the parentheses are found. Because the area code is the first set of parentheses in the example, it is `$1`, the local prefix is `$2`, and the final four digits are held in `$3`.

Search and Replace

Because you can easily find a pattern in a string, wouldn't it be nice if you could replace it with something else? Perl enables you to do just that by writing your regular expression line a little bit differently:

```
$a=~s/<search pattern>/<replace pattern>/
```

This simple change (adding the "s" (substitute) flag and a second pattern) enables you to modify data in a variable so that it is exactly what you're expecting—removing extraneous data. For example, to match a phone number in the variable `$phone` and then change it to a standard format could be accomplished in a single step:

```
$phone=~s/(\d{3,3})(\d{3,3})(\d{4,4})/($1) $2-$3/;
```

A new string in the format `(xxx) xxx-xxxx` replaces the phone number found in the original string. This enables a programmer to modify data on-the-fly, transforming user input into a more usable form.

Regular expressions are not easy for many people to learn, and a single misplaced character can trip you up. Don't feel bad if you're confused at first; just keep at it. An understanding of regular expressions is important in many languages, and, if regular expressions are properly used, they can be a powerful development tool.

Flow Control

Flow control statements give Perl the capability to alter its execution and adapt to different conditions on-the-fly. Perl uses standard C-like syntax for its looping and conditional constructs. If you've used C or Java before, these should all look familiar.

`if-then-else`

Perl's `if-then-else` logic is simple to understand. If a condition is met, a block of code is executed. If not, a different piece of programming is run. The syntax for this type of conditional statement is

```
if <expression> {
    <statements...>
} else {
    <statements...>
}
```

For example, to test whether the variable `$mycomputer` contains the string Mac OS X and print Good Choice! if it does, you could write:

```
if ($mycomputer=~/mac os x/i) {
    print "Good Choice!\n";
} else {
    print "Buy a Mac!\n";
}
```

The curly brackets `{}` are used to set off code blocks within Perl. These denote the portion of code that a conditional, looping, or subroutine construct applies to.

`unless-then-else`

The `unless` statement is syntactically identical to the `if-then` statement, except that it operates on the inverse of the expression (and uses the word `unless` rather than `if`). To change the previous example so that it uses `unless`, write

```
unless ($mycomputer=~/mac os x/i) {
    print "Buy a Mac!\n";
} else {
    print "Good Choice!\n";
}
```

The `unless` condition is rarely used in Perl applications and is provided mainly as a way to write code in a more readable manner.

while

The `while` loop enables you to execute while a condition remains true. At the start of each loop, an expression is evaluated; if it returns true, the loop executes. If not, it exits. The syntax for a Perl `while` loop is

```
while <expression> {
    <statements>
}
```

For example, to monitor a process listing every 30 seconds to see whether the application Terminal is running, the following code fragment could be employed:

```
$processlist=`ps axg`;
while (!($processlist=~/terminal/i)) {
    print "Terminal has not been detected.\n";
    sleep 30;
    $processlist=`ps ax`;
}
print "The Terminal process is running.\n";
```

Here the output of the `ps axg` command is stored in `$processlist`. This is then searched using a regular expression in the `while` loop. If the pattern terminal is located, the loop exits, and the message `The Terminal process is running.` is displayed. If not, the script sleeps for 30 seconds and then tries again.

for-next

The `for-next` loop is the bread and butter of all looping constructs. This loop iterates through a series of values until a condition (usually a numeric limit) is met. The syntax for a `for-next` loop is

```
for (<initialization>;<execution condition>;<increment>) {
    <code block>
}
```

The *initialization* sets up the loop and initializes the counter variable to its default state. The *execution condition* is checked with each iteration of the loop; if it evaluates to false, the loop ends. Finally, the *increment* is a piece of code that defines an operation performed on the counter variable each time the loop is run. For example, the following loop counts from 0 to 9:

```
for ($count=0;$count<10;$count++) {
    print "Count = $count";
}
```

The counter, `$count`, is set to 0 when the loop starts. With each repetition, it is incremented by 1 (`$count++`). The loop exits when the counter reaches 10 (`$count<10`).

Subroutines

Subroutines help modularize code by dividing it into smaller functional units. Rather than creating a gigantic block of Perl that does everything under the sun, you can create subroutines that are easier to read and debug.

A subroutine is started with the sub keyword and the name the subroutine should be called. The body of the subroutine is enclosed in curly brackets {}. For example, here is a simple subroutine that prints Mac OS X:

```
sub printos {
    print "Mac OS X\n";
}
```

You can include subroutines anywhere in your source code and call them at any time by prefixing their name with & (&printos). Subroutines can also be set up to receive values from the main program and return results. For example, this routine accepts two strings and concatenates them together (useful, huh?):

```
sub concatenatestring {
    my ($x,$y)=@_;
    return ("$x$y");
}
```

To retrieve the concatenation of the strings Mac and OS X, the subroutine would be addressed as

```
$result=&concatenatestring("Mac","OS X");
```

Data is received by the subroutine through the use of the special variable @_. The two values it contains are then stored in local variables (denoted by the my keyword) named $x and $y. Finally, the return statement returns a concatenated version of the two strings.

CPAN

Perl can be extended to offer additional functionality ranging from Internet access to graphics generation. Just about anything you could ever want to do can be done using Perl—you just need the right module. The best place to find the right Perl module is CPAN—the Comprehensive Perl Archive Network. CPAN contains an ever-increasing list of Perl modules with their descriptions and documentation. To browse CPAN, point your Web browser to http://www.cpan.org.

There are two ways to install modules located in the CPAN archive. The first is using a built-in Perl module that interacts directly with CPAN from your desktop computer. The second is the traditional method of downloading, unarchiving, and installing—just as with any other software. Perl modules are a bit easier to install than most software because the installed code ends up in the Perl directory instead of needing to be placed in a variety of directories across the entire system hierarchy.

Two Perl modules (`DBI::DBD` and `DBD::mysql`) will be used in Chapter 22 to demonstrate Perl/database integration. Conveniently, this corresponds to the two available installation methods. Let's take a look at both methods now and then put them to practice in Chapter 22. Note: These are meant to document the process of installing an arbitrary module. If you try to follow these instructions without MySQL installed, you *will* see errors.

CPAN Installation

Using the interactive method of installing Perl modules is as simple as **`install`** ***<module name>***. To start the interactive module installation shell, type **`sudo perl -MCPAN -e shell`** at a command line. The CPAN installer shell starts:

```
cpan shell -- CPAN exploration and modules installation (v1.70)
''

cpan>
```

> **NOTE**
>
> The first time you start the CPAN shell, it prompts you for manual configuration (for network access and so on). To quickly configure the system, reply with *no*, and the shell automatically configures itself.

> **NOTE**
>
> `sudo` is used to start the CPAN shell because Perl modules must be installed in privileged directories. If you attempt to use the command without running it as `root`, it will work through most of the installation and then fail at the final step.

At the cpan> prompt, type **`install`** ***<modulename>*** to begin the installation process. For example, to add the `DBI::DBD` module:

```
cpan> install DBI::DBD

Issuing "/usr/bin/ftp -n"
Local directory now /private/var/root/.cpan/sources/modules
GOT /var/root/.cpan/sources/modules/03modlist.data.gz
...
CPAN: MD5 security checks disabled because MD5 not installed.
 Please consider installing the MD5 module.
...
Installing /usr/bin/dbiproxy
```

```
Installing /usr/bin/dbish
Writing /Library/Perl/darwin/auto/DBI/.packlist
Appending installation info to /System/Library/Perl/darwin/perllocal.pod
 /usr/bin/make install -- OK
```

Depending on your Perl installation and version, you may notice a number of messages pertaining to different Perl modules during the installation. Each time the CPAN shell is used, it checks for new versions of itself. If a new version is found, it provides instructions on how to install the update (`install Bundle::CPAN`). Don't concern yourself too much about these messages unless the installation fails.

> **TIP**
>
> Many Perl modules ask some basic questions during the install process. Even the highly automated CPAN shell installation method pauses to collect information it needs—so pay attention to your screen during an install.

After CPAN completes the installation process, the module is ready to use—no need to reboot. The next time you invoke Perl, the module will be available.

For more control within the CPAN shell, you can use these additional commands:

- `get` *<module name>*—Download the named module.
- `make` *<module name>*—Download and compile the module, but do not install.
- `test` *<module name>*—Download, compile, and run the named module's tests.
- `install` *<module name>*—Download, compile, test, and install the module.

Modules that have been downloaded are stored in the `.cpan` directory within your home directory. Keep track of the size of this directory because it will continue to grow as long as you install new modules.

Archive-Based Installation

The second form of module installation is archive-based. This is almost identical to installing other types of software, so there shouldn't be many surprises here.

First, download the package to install from CPAN; in this example, I'm using a package called `DBD-mysql`, which you'll use in Chapter 22 to access the MySQL database system:

```
% curl -O ftp://ftp.cpan.org/pub/CPAN/modules/
    ¬by-module/DBD/DBD-mysql-2.0901.tar.gz
```

Next, unarchive the module:

```
% tar zxf DBD-mysql-2.0901.tar.gz
```

Enter the distribution directory and enter this command: **perl Makefile.PL**. This automatically configures the package and generates a makefile that you can use to compile and install the module:

```
% perl Makefile.PL
This is an experimental version of DBD::mysql. For production
environments you should prefer the Msql-Mysql-modules.

I will use the following settings for compiling and testing:

 testpassword (default    ) =
 testhost    (default    ) =
 testuser    (default    ) =
 nocatchstderr (default    ) = 0
 libs      (mysql_config) = -L/usr/local/lib/mysql -lmysqlclient -lz -lm
 testdb     (default    ) = test
 cflags     (Users choice) = -I'/usr/local/mysql/include'

To change these settings, see 'perl Makefile.PL --help' and
'perldoc INSTALL'.

Using DBI 1.18 installed in /Library/Perl/darwin/auto/DBI
Writing Makefile for DBD::mysql
```

NOTE

Some modules may require additional configuration. Be sure to check any README or INSTALL files that come with your CPAN modules.

Now, the installation becomes identical to any other software. The same make commands apply. The best step to take next is to type **make** to compile and then **make test** to test the compiled software:

```
% make
cc -c -I/Library/Perl/darwin/auto/DBI -I'/usr/local/mysql/include'
     -g -pipe -pipe -fno-common -DHAS_TELLDIR_PROTOTYPE
     -fno-strict-aliasing -O3   -DVERSION=\"2.0901\" -DXS_VERSION=
    \"2.0901\" -I/System/Library/Perl/darwin/CORE dbdimp.c
...
t/00base...........ok
t/10dsnlist........ok
t/20createdrop.....ok
t/30insertfetch....ok
```

```
t/40bindparam.......ok
t/40blobs...........ok
t/40listfields......ok
t/40nulls...........ok
t/40numrows.........ok
t/50chopblanks......ok
t/50commit..........ok, 14/30 skipped: No transactions
t/60leaks...........skipped test on this platform
t/ak-dbd............ok
t/akmisc............ok
t/dbdadmin..........ok
t/insertid..........ok
t/mysql2............ok
t/mysql.............ok
All tests successful, 1 test and 14 subtests skipped.
Files=18, Tests=758, 25 wallclock secs ( 3.59 cusr + 0.35 csys = 3.94 CPU)
```

Finally, `sudo make install` to install the Perl module:

```
% sudo make install
Skipping /Library/Perl/darwin/auto/DBD/mysql/mysql.bs (unchanged)
Installing /Library/Perl/darwin/auto/DBD/mysql/mysql.bundle
Files found in blib/arch: installing files in blib/lib into
     ¬architecture dependent tree
...
Installing /usr/share/man/man3/Bundle::DBD::mysql.3
Installing /usr/share/man/man3/DBD::mysql.3
Installing /usr/share/man/man3/DBD::mysql::INSTALL.3
Installing /usr/share/man/man3/Mysql.3
Writing /Library/Perl/darwin/auto/DBD/mysql/.packlist
Appending installation info to /System/Library/Perl/darwin/perllocal.pod
```

The module is installed and ready to use. Chapter 22 demonstrates how to use these Perl modules to communicate with a MySQL database.

Perl Documentation

Retrieving help information on a Perl function or module is as simple as using the `perldoc` command. `perldoc` searches the installed Perl documentation and displays extensive help information on functions, modules, and generalized topics.

There are three common forms for using `perldoc`.

The first, `perldoc -f` *`<function name>`*, returns formatted information about a given built-in Perl function, such as `open`:

```
% perldoc -f open
    open FILEHANDLE,MODE,LIST

    open FILEHANDLE,EXPR

    open FILEHANDLE
        Opens the file whose filename is given by EXPR,
        and associates it with FILEHANDLE. If FILEHANDLE
        is an expression, its value is used as the name of
        the real filehandle wanted. (This is considered a
        symbolic reference, so `use strict 'refs'' should
        not be in effect.)
...
```

Next, `perldoc -q` *`<faq topic>`* retrieves information from the Perl FAQ. For example, to retrieve information on regular expressions:

```
% perldoc -q expressions
Found in /System/Library/Perl/pods/perlfaq6.pod
    How can I hope to use regular expressions without creating
    illegible and unmaintainable code?

    Three techniques can make regular expressions maintainable
    and understandable.

        Comments Outside the Regex
          Describe what you're doing and how you're
          doing it, using normal Perl comments.
```

Finally, use `perldoc` *`<module name>`* to retrieve information about an installed Perl module:

```
% perldoc Shell
Shell(3)    User Contributed Perl Documentation    Shell(3)

NAME
    Shell - run shell commands transparently within perl

SYNOPSIS
    See below.
...
```

Table 21.7 provides many of the flags for the perldoc command.

TABLE 21.7 Command Documentation Table for perldoc

-h	Prints out a brief help message.
-v	Describes search for the item in detail.
-l	Display the filename of the module found.
-f	The -f option followed by the name of a Perl built-in function extracts the documentation of this function from the perlfunc man page.
-q	The -q option takes a regular expression as an argument. It searches the question headings in perl-faq[1-9] and prints the entries matching the regular expression.
-X	The -X option looks for an entry whose basename matches the name given on the command line in the file $Config{archlib}/pod.idx. The pod.idx file should contain fully qualified filenames, one per line.
-U	Because perldoc does not run properly tainted and is known to have security issues, it will not normally execute as the superuser. If you use the -U flag, it will do so, but only after setting the effective and real IDs to nobody's or nouser's account, or -2 if unavailable. If it cannot relinquish its privileges, it will not run.
<PageName¦	The item you want to look up. Nested modules (such as ModuleName¦ProgramName> File::Basename) are specified either as File::Basename or File/Basename. You may also give a descriptive name of a page, such as perlfunc. You may also give a partial or wrong-case name, such as basename for File::Basename, but this will be slower. If there is more than one page with the same partial name, you will only get the first one.

Perl's built-in documentation is an excellent comprehensive reference that provides both usage information as well as complete code examples.

Perl Editors

Although writing Perl in emacs or vi is completely acceptable, it is not necessarily a Mac-like experience. A few commercial and shareware editors that support syntax highlighting and direct Perl execution can make life easier for the serious Perl developer.

- BBEdit—The everything-and-the-kitchen-sink editor. Great for HTML, Perl, PHP, and more—http://www.barebones.com/products/bbedit/.
- AlphaX—Supporting around 50 languages, AlphaX is a serious editor for developers. AlphaX integrates with the command line for accessing tools such as diff, cvs, gcc, and more. http://www.maths.mq.edu.au/~steffen/Alpha/AlphaX/
- SubEthaEdit—A new award-winning piece of software dedicated to collaborative code editing. If you work as a team with other local Mac developers, this is definitely worth a look. http://www.codingmonkeys.de/subethaedit/

Additional Information

The information in this chapter should be enough to get you started authoring and editing Perl scripts. In Chapter 22, you'll learn how to extend Perl to control another free software package—MySQL. In Chapter 28, you'll see how Perl can be used to author online applications.

As with many topics in this book, the space just isn't available for a completely comprehensive text. If you like what you see, you can learn more about Perl through these resources:

- The Perl Homepage—`http://www.perl.org/`—All that is Perl. This page can provide you with links to the latest and most useful Perl information online.
- CPAN—`http://www.cpan.org/`—The Comprehensive Perl Archive Network contains information on all the available Perl modules (extensions). Later in this chapter, you'll learn how to add modules to your Mac OS X Perl distribution.
- *Programming Perl*—O'Reilly Publishing, Larry Wall, ISBN: 0596000278. Written by the developer of Perl, you can't get much closer to the source than this.
- *Sams Teach Yourself Perl in 21 Days*—Laura Lemay, ISBN: 0672313057. An excellent step-by-step guide to learning Perl and putting it to use on your system.

Python

Python, like Perl, is an interpreted scripting language included with Mac OS X. To quote the Python.org Web site, Python is defined as

> **python**, (*Gr. Myth.* An enormous serpent that lurked in the cave of Mount Parnassus and was slain by Apollo) **1.** any of a genus of large, non-poisonous snakes of Asia, Africa and Australia that suffocate their prey to death. **2.** popularly, any large snake that crushes its prey. **3.** totally awesome, bitchin' language that will someday crush the $'s out of certain *other* so-called VHLL's ;-)

Python was built from scratch to be object-oriented and easy to write and read. Although it has the same features as other popular languages, its syntax is cleaner than most—almost to the point of being scary. As such, it can take a bit of time for a long-time C or Perl developer to shake the uncontrollable feeling that somehow what they're writing in Python is wrong.

Languages such as Perl—and even AppleScript—have code structure based on explicitly starting and stopping code blocks with braces `{}` or "`tell application/end tell`" and so on. In Python, the notion of a code block is still present, but rather than being explicitly stated with a keyword or symbol, it is *implied* by indentation.

Consider the following Perl code that prints the numbers between one and ten, and displays a special message with printing the number seven. The code is not indented, because it is not required in Perl, and it is entirely at the whim of the developer to determine *what* proper indentation should be:

```
#!/usr/bin/perl

for ($count=1;$count<11;$count++) {
print "The current value is $count\n";
if ($count==7) {
print "I love the number 7!\n";
}
}
print "This program is finished."
```

Rewritten in Python, this simple loop becomes:

```
for count in range(1,10):
  print "The current value is",count
  if count == 7:
    print "I love the number seven!"
print "This program is finished"
```

Although there are minor differences in the looping and conditional syntax, the obvious difference is in the actual *appearance* of the code. We could have formatted the Perl code nicely to be indented and pretty to look at. Python, on the other hand, *requires* the given formatting. The indentation determines which lines of the program belong to a given code block. If lines are at the same level of indentation, they are part of the same block.

Your initial reaction might be to question why one would want to force themselves into writing pretty code? The answer should be obvious to anyone who has ever tried to debug layers and layers of loops, conditionals, and so on all embedded within one another without proper indentation. Perhaps, you've written a program but missed a closing brace somewhere? In Python this is virtually impossible. You must program so that the visual representation of the program mirrors the intended execution. Python programs tend to be shorter, easier to read, and much easier to debug than languages that follow more traditional structures.

To create an executable Python script, you should include the Python interpreter in the first line (that is, `#!/usr/bin/python`) and make sure that the script has execute permissions by using `chmod +x` *`<script name>`*.

NOTE

Python lines do *not* end in a semicolon like Perl, C, PHP, and so on. You can, however, use a semicolon in Python to include more than a single line of code on a single line in the program file, such as `print "Hello"; print "Goodbye"`.

Variables and Data Types

Python's basic variable types are similar to Perl's, and, like Perl, they are case sensitive and do not require a type definition before their use. Unlike Perl, Python variables gain their meaning based on how they are used. A variable is considered numeric, for example, if you store a number in it, or a string if it contains a string. These are the data types we'll be looking at in this introduction:

- `string`—A variable that contains a text/numeric or mixed value. The line, `myString="Macintosh G5"` is an example of a string assignment in Python. The + symbol is the concatenation operator in Python.
- `numeric`—An assignment such as `processorG=5` creates a numeric variable with an integer value. By default, Python assumes that an operation performed on integers returns an integer, so you must explicitly use floating point numbers where appropriate to avoid rounding errors. Python considers any value a floating point number if it includes decimal places. For example, the assignment `myVal=5/2` results in "2" normally, whereas `myVal=5/2.0` results in "2.5".
- `lists`—A list is the Python equivalent of an array. A list is created by an assignment such as `myList=['This","is","a","test."]`. Individual elements are referenced by indexing into the list starting with 0. For example, `myList[1]` refers to the element "is" in the previously defined list. Unlike most array implementations, lists can be modified using insertion and deletion operators, which we'll get to shortly. Python also supports an immutable list type called a "tuple." Tuples are assigned just like a list, but using parentheses `()` rather than brackets.
- `dictionaries`—A Python dictionary is the equivalent of a Perl associative array. For example, `myDictionary={'Monday': "bad", 'Friday': "good"}`. Here, the strings (keys) `"Monday"` and `"Friday"` are associated with the values `"bad"` and `"good"`, respectively. You can refer to the elements of a dictionary by its keys. The element `myDictionary["Friday"]` returns `"good"`.
- `files`—Like a Perl filehandle, a Python file variable provides a reference to an active file for reading or writing. The statement `$myFile=open("file.txt","r")` opens the file "`file.txt`" for reading and allows file functions to be carried out through the variable `$myFile`.

Python is an *object-oriented* language, and, as such, accessing and manipulating data works a bit differently than in a traditional language. Object-oriented languages apply methods to objects instead of sending data to functions. For example, in Perl I might want to send a string to the `uc()` function to convert it to uppercase:

```
$a="hello";
print uc($a);
```

In Python, however, each of the basic data types is an object, and each has certain methods that that object can perform. String objects, for example, have an `upper()` method that converts them to uppercase. One invokes an object's method by using the syntax *<object>.<method>*. For example:

```
a="hello"
print a.upper()
```

The difference becomes apparent when stringing together multiple methods or functions. To convert to uppercase and then back to lowercase, in Perl you'd embed a function call inside another function call:

```
$a="hello'
print lc(uc($a));
```

In Python, it is simply

```
a="hello"
print a.upper().lower()
```

The `a.upper()` method returns another string object, which also has the `lower()` method and can subsequently be applied. Object-oriented programming has far more nuances than what we can show here. The ultimate goal of object-oriented programming is to create reusable objects that operate independently of the code that ties them together and that abstracts function from implementation.

Our goal is to give you enough information and incentive to get started using Python right away. If you like what you see, we hope that you will pursue learning the language further.

Input/Output Functions

While you take a few minutes to digest the object-oriented nature of Python, let's take a look at how you can get data into (and out of) Python. I've read dozens of language tutorials that spend far too much time discussing language intricacies rather than introducing basic I/O functions. Personally, I find that a language becomes useful as soon as you learn the basics for moving data in and out of a program.

Reading User Input

Basic user input is carried out through the `raw_input(`*<prompt string>*`)` function for strings, or `input(`*<prompt string>*`)` for integer and floating point values. For example:

```
myName=raw_input('What is your name? ')
myAge=input('What is your age? ')
print "Hello",myName+", you are",myAge*365,"days old."
```

This code fragment inputs a name and an age, and then outputs a "hello" message along with the simple calculation of the person's age in days.

Although the raw_input function always returns a string, you can also use it with numeric values by coercing them to the proper type using the int() and float() functions. The second line of this sample, could be written

```
myAge=float(raw_input('What is your age? '))
```

NOTE

In this example, we use the float function wrapped around raw_input instead of using an object method. Certain functions (such as type coercion functions) are global and are not considered an object method. These functions are used just as in Perl.

Because float() and int() can be used to coerce strings to numbers, it stands to reason that numbers can be coerced to strings. This is performed by simply placing the numeric value within backticks (``). For example, to input myAge as a string, you could use the following:

```
myAge=`input('What is your age? ')`
```

Reading from Files

Another common form of input is a text file. To open a file for reading, use the syntax *<filehandle>*=open(*<filename>*,*<file mode>*). In the case of reading, the file mode is simply the string "r". After a file is opened, you can use the object methods readline() or readlines() to return a single line of input, or a list containing all the lines of input from the file. After completing file operations, the file should be closed with the object method close().

For example:

```
myFile=open('MySpecialFile.txt','r')
firstLine=myFile.readline()
otherLines=myFile.readlines()
myFile.close()
```

This example opens the file MySpecialFile.txt for reading and creates the myFile object that can be used to refer to the file. The firstLine variable is used to store the first line of data from the file (retrieved via readline()), whereas otherLines contains a list (think "array") of the remaining lines in the file.

Creating Output

If you've been following along, you probably already know how to output to standard out in Python. The print statement is used to display information for the user. Unlike Perl's print, Python employs a "smart" print function that attempts to format output for you as cleanly as possible. For example, in Perl, you could write:

```
print "Hello, my name is ",$myName," and I am a Mac user.\n";
```

This would print a hello message with the user's name (spaces before and after) and end the message with a newline (`\n`). In Python, the equivalent statement is

```
print "Hello, my name is",myName,"and I am a Mac user."
```

Spaces are automatically inserted between strings in the `print` statement, and a newline is generated automatically at the end. If you want to suppress either of the spaces, you can replace the `,` with +—the Python concatenation character. To suppress the newline, add a lone comma (`,`) to the end of the line.

> **NOTE**
>
> You can use the same escaped characters such as `\n`, `\r`, `\t`, and so on that you use in Perl to refer to newlines, returns, and tabs—among others.

File Output

Outputting data to a file requires, once again, the file-opening function `<filehandle>=open (<filename>,<file mode>)`, this time used with a file mode of `"w"` for writing (and replacing any existing contents) or `"a"` for appending to a new or existing file.

The two object methods used to write information to a file are `write(<string>)` and `writelines(<list>)`. The former writes a single string to the file, whereas the latter writes all the strings contained in the named list.

```
myFile=open('MySpecialFile.txt','w')
myFile.write("Hello World\n")
myFile.close()
```

This creates or replaces the file `MySpecialFile.txt` and writes the contents "Hello World" on a line in the file. Note that the `write` method includes a newline at the end. Unlike the `print` function, `write` requires you to explicitly format the outgoing data.

External Results

One nice feature of Perl is the ease with which you can execute external programs and incorporate their results in your script. You can do the same with Python using the `commands.getoutput(<command to execute>)` method. Before using it, however, you must import the necessary code—simply `import commands`. For example:

```
import commands
myProcesses=commands.getoutput("ps ax")
```

The resulting process list (generated by `ps ax`) is stored as a single string within the `myProcesses` variable.

Expressions

Comparing values in Python is similar but not identical to Perl. Table 21.8 displays common Python expressions.

TABLE 21.8 Common Python Expressions

Expression Syntax	Description
`var1==var2, var1 is var2`	Compares two values for equality.
`var1!=var2, var1 is not var2`	Compares two values for inequality.
`var1><$var2`	Checks `$var1` to see whether it is less than `$var2`.
`$var1>var2`	Tests `var1` to see whether it is a larger number than `var2`, or, when used with strings, whether `var1` is before (based on ASCII value) `var2`.
`var1>=var2`	Tests `var1` to see whether it is greater than or equal to `var2`.
`var1<=var2`	Compares `var1` to see whether it is less than or equal to `var2`.
`()`	Parentheses can be used to group the elements of an expression together to force an evaluation order or provide clarity to the code.
`&,and`	Used to connect two expressions so that both must evaluate to true for the complete expression to be true.
`¦,or`	Used to connect two expressions so that if either evaluates to true, the entire expression evaluates to true.
`not`	Used to logically negate an expression. If the expression previously evaluated to true, you can place a `not` in front of the expression to force it to evaluate false—or vice versa.

Slicing

A unique feature of Python is the capability to "slice" lists for the purpose of retrieving specific information, or inserting/deleting data. For example, assume that you have the following assignment:

```
myList=['one','two','three','four','five']
```

You already know that `myList[0]` returns the first element of the list (that is, "`one`"). It is possible, however, to index into the list using a pair of values, such as `myList[0:2]`. In this case, the first *two* elements of the list (`['one','two']`) are returned. When using this format to dissect a portion of a list, the two numbers specified represent the first element to return and an element to serve as a boundary; the boundary element is *not* returned as part of the results, but the list element preceding it *is*.

As a shortcut for the start and boundary values in a slice, you can leave the first or last number of a slice empty. In the case of an empty initial value, 0 (the first element) is assumed. If the boundary value is left blank, the end of the list (including the final element) is assumed.

For example:

`myList[1:3]` returns `['two','three']`.

`myList[:2]` returns `['one','two']`.

`myList[2:]` returns `['three','four','five']`.

`myList[:]` returns `['one','two','three','four','five']`.

Besides retrieving information, slicing can be used to delete or insert data in lists.

For example, given the previous list, we could change and insert into the second and third elements (`['two','three']`) new values (`['two','two and a half','three','three and a half']`) like this:

```
myList[1:3]=['two','two and a half','three','three and a half']
```

The contents of `myList` are now:

```
['one', 'two', 'two and a half', 'three', 'three and a half', 'four', 'five']
```

Similarly, you can delete elements from the middle of a list by assigning a slice to an empty list. For example, to delete the third, fourth, and fifth elements of the list, use

```
myList[2:5]=[]
```

Common Functions Object Methods

Being able to store and output information is useful, but the ability to manipulate it makes a computer a truly valuable tool. As you've read about Python data types and I/O, you've already seen a few methods used to for manipulating data, such as `readlines` and `writelines` for reading and writing to text files. Table 21.9 contains several more methods and functions, the data types they apply to, and what action they perform.

TABLE 21.9 Common Python Object Methods

Method/Function	Data Type	Description
`abs(<#>)`	number	Returns the absolute value of the given number. Example: `myABSVal=abs(-35)`
`hex(<#>)`	number	Returns a string with the hex equivalent of the given number. Example: `myHexVal=hex(10)`
`round(<#>,<precision>)`	number	Rounds a given number to the specified number of digits (precision) after the decimal place. Example: `MyRoundVal=round(10.05,1)`. Always returns a floating point number.
`append(<element>)`	list	Appends an element to the end of a list. Example: `myList.append('six')`

TABLE 21.9 Continued

Method/Function	Data Type	Description
remove(<*element*>)	list	Removes an element from a list by its value. Example: myList.remove('six')
sort()	list	Sorts a list into alphabetical order. Example: myList.sort()
pop([index])	list	Removes and returns the last element in a list. If an index value is provided, it determines the number of elements returned and removed. Example: myList.pop()
count(<*element*>)	list	Returns a count of the number of occurrences of a value within a list. Example: myG5Count=myList.count('G5')
reverse()	list	Reverses the ordering of a list. Example: myList.reverse()
max(<*list*>)	list	Returns the list element with the highest value. Example: myMaxValue=max(myList)
min(<*list*>)	list	Returns the list element with the lowest value. Example: myMinValue=min(myList)
capitalize()	string	Capitalizes the first letter in a string and lowercases the rest. Example: myString.capitalize()
find(<*search string*> *[,*<*start position*> *[,*<*end position*>*]]*)	string	Searches for a given search string and return the index value (position) where it starts. Returns -1 if no match is found. If a start and end are given, the search only takes place between these index positions. Example: mySearchPos="Find the hidden word.".find('hidden')
isalnum()	string	Returns true if a string is alphanumeric. Example: myAlphaNumeric.isalnum()
isalpha()	string	Returns true if a string is entirely alphabetic. Example: myAlpha.isalpha()
isdigit()	string	Returns true if a string is entirely numeric. Example: myDigit.isdigit()
isupper()	string	Returns true if all characters in a string are uppercase. Example: myUpper.isupper()
islower()	string	Returns true if all characters in a string are lowercase. Example: myLower.islower()
join(<*list*>)	string	Converts the named list to a single string using the object string as the delimiter. Example: myJoinedString=",".join(myList)
upper()	string	Converts a string to uppercase. Example: myString.upper()
lower()	string	Converts a string to lowercase. Example: myString.lower()

TABLE 21.9 Continued

Method/Function	Data Type	Description
rstrip()	string	Removes trailing whitespace from a string. Example: myString.rstrip()
lstrip()	string	Removes leading whitespace from a string. Example: myString.lstrip()
split(<*delimiter*>)	string	Returns a list of strings formed by splitting the object string on the given delimiter. Example: myDateElements="2003-08-25".split('-')
open(<*filename*>, <*file mode*>)	file	Returns a file handle after opening the given filename. The file mode can be 'r','w', or 'a' for read, write, and append. Example: myFile=open('filename.txt','r')
close()	file	Closes the file. Example: myFile.close()
readline([bytes])	file	Reads and returns a string containing a line of input from a file. If the optional byte parameter is specified, input is limited to that number of characters. Example: myInputLine=myFile.readline()
readlines([bytes])	file	Reads and returns a list of input lines from a file. If the optional byte parameter is specified, input is limited to that number of characters. Example: myInputLines=myFile.readlines()
write(<*string*>)	file	Writes the contents of the string to a file. Example: myFile.write('Hello\n')
writelines(<*list*>)	file	Writes the contents of the list to a file. Example: myFile.writelines(myList)
range(<start>,<end>)	list	Returns a list of values between the start and end values. Example: numberList=range(1,10)

Flow Control

Python's flow control is similar to other languages, with just a few syntactical differences. The biggest change from languages such as C, Perl, JavaScript, and so on is, once again, the use of indentation to denote code blocks. We'll use the same examples as in the preceding Perl introduction so that you can compare and contrast the source.

if-then-else

If a condition is met, a block of code is executed. If not, a different piece of programming is run. The syntax for this type of conditional statement is

```
if <expression>:
    <statements...>
else:
    <statements...>
```

For example, to test whether the variable `myComputer` is set to the string "`Mac OS X`" and print Good Choice! if it does, you could write:

```
if myComputer is "Mac OS X":
    print "Good Choice!"
else:
    print "Buy a Mac!"
```

`while`

The `while` loop enables you to execute while a condition remains true. At the start of each loop, an expression is evaluated; if it returns true, the loop executes. If not, it exits. The syntax for a Perl while loop is

```
while <expression>:
    <statements>
}
```

For example, to monitor a process listing every 30 seconds to see whether the application Terminal is running, the following code fragment could be employed:

```
import commands
myProcesses=commands.getoutput("ps axg")
while myProcesses.find('Terminal') is -1:
    print "Terminal has not been detected."
    commands.getoutput("sleep 30")
    myProcesses=commands.getoutput("ps ax")
print "The Terminal process is running."
```

The output of the `ps axg` command is stored in `myProcesses`. This is then searched using `find` in the `while` loop. If the pattern `Terminal` is located, the loop exits, and the message `The Terminal process is running.` is displayed. If not, the script sleeps for 30 seconds and then tries again.

`for-next`

The Python `for-next` loop is slightly different from other implementations. Rather than loop through a series of numbers, it loops through the elements in a list. Frequently, these *are* numbers, but any list values will work. The `range` function is commonly used to provide a list of numbers. Using `range(0,11)`, for example, generates the list `[0, 1, 2, 3, 4, 5, 6, 7, 8, 9, 10]`.

The syntax for a `for-next` loop is

```
for <variable> in <list>:
    <code block>
```

For example, the following loop counts from 0 to 9:

```
for count in range(0,10):
    print "Count =",count
```

Functions

Functions (Python's version of subroutines) help modularize code by dividing it into smaller functional units. A Python function is started with the `def` keyword and the name the function should be called followed by a list of parameters it should receive within parentheses. The body of the function is an indented code block. For example, here is a simple function that prints "Mac OS X":

```
def printos():
    print "Mac OS X"
```

You can include functions anywhere in your source code and call them at any time by their defined name—in this case `printos()`.

Functions can also be set up to receive values from the main program and return results. This example accepts two strings and concatenates them together:

```
def concatenatestring(x,y):
    return x+y
```

To retrieve the concatenation of the strings "Mac" and "OS X," the subroutine would be addressed as

```
myResult=concatenatestring("Mac","OS X")
```

The incoming parameters ("Mac" and "OS X") are stored in the variables `x` and `y` and then returned in concatenated form (courtesy of the `return` keyword and the concatenation operator +).

Jython

As we wrap up the introduction to Python, I'd like to switch gears for a moment to introduce you to *Jython*—a Java implementation of Python. Scripting languages are wonderful, but they don't "package well" for execution on other platforms. Handing out a script to a user is much different from giving him a double-clickable application.

If you want to add GUI support to Python, you need to either use proprietary hooks to aqua—rendering the code inoperable on other platforms—or use a third-party windowing/ GUI module that would need to be installed (if available) on each client computer. Jython eliminates the problem by providing a full implementation of Python within Java. Although there are a few minor incompatibilities, most Python code runs without any changes in Jython. Additionally, Jython provides easy access to Swing within Python ,making it possible to author cross-platform GUI applications with ease. Execution time is slower, but for non-CPU-bound scripts, this is usually not a problem.

Completed Jython applications can be compiled into `.jar` files for easy deployment on any Java-compatible system. For a free downloadable Jython installer, visit `http://www.jython.org/`.

> **NOTE**
>
> If you want to program directly to Cocoa using Python, the PyObjC project is what you're looking for. Using this Open Source project, you can even build interfaces using Interface Builder and then attach your own pure Python code.

Additional Information

Like the introduction to Perl, please realize that this should serve as only a basic primer to the Python language. The language is capable of far more than could be reasonably covered in a few introductory pages.

Thankfully, Python information is in abundance both in printed and electronic formats. If you don't mind reading through Web pages (or printing off a few PDFs), you can find everything from beginner tutorials to complete references available online. Those looking for published products are also in luck; Python books are in ready supply. The following is a list of resources you may want to look into to learn more about the language and its capabilities:

- `http://www.python.org`—The home of Python and a great source of Python documentation links and tutorials. The starting place for both beginners and experienced developers.
- *Instant Hacking: Learn How to Program with Python* (`http://www.hetland.org/python/instant-hacking.php`)—An excellent tutorial for getting up and running quickly with Python.
- *How to Think Like a Computer Scientist: Learning with Python* (`http://www.ibiblio.org/obp/thinkCSpy/`)—An Open Source book that teaches the philosophy of programming through Python.
- *Practical Python*, by Magnus Lie Hetland, ISBN: 1590590066—An excellent book by the author of the *Instant Hacking* tutorial. *Practical Python* is easy to read, understand, and apply.

Summary

AppleScript carries on the tradition of being one of the best secret Apple technologies. It can easily perform advanced functions by using what is built into your existing software. Applications that have never known about each other can be programmed to utilize each other's features. The Script Editor can be used for casual developers to get a feel for the language, whereas AppleScript Studio provides a full IDE for building GUI AppleScript applications.

Perl and Python, on the other hand, are great for writing or controlling command-line processes and provide excellent cross-platform capabilities. With the inclusion of these languages in Mac OS X, potential scripting developers can gain a much wider audience for their software.

Mac OS X has become a wonderful platform for scripting languages, and although only three languages are covered here, enterprising users may want to investigate the powers of Ruby (also included on your system), or install Apple's Aqua Tcl/tk, Expect, or any other of the dozens of Open Source languages available today.

CHAPTER 22

MySQL and Database Connectivity

IN THIS CHAPTER

- Getting Started with MySQL
- Creating a MySQL Database
- Perl/MySQL Integration
- iODBC and ODBC Manager

Thanks to Open Source projects, Macintosh users now enjoy first-class database packages such as MySQL that, only a few years ago we would have never dreamed of running on the Mac OS. Instead of forking over several hundred (or thousand) dollars for a commercial database system, you can take 20 minutes to download and install MySQL and then have a full-featured database at your fingertips.

This chapter covers MySQL, Perl, and iODBC, and discusses how they can be combined to create a powerful database development environment. Without spending a dime, you can host databases capable of handling hundreds of queries a second.

Getting Started with MySQL

The MySQL database system is a free implementation of a database system based on Structured Query Language (SQL). MySQL has been successfully deployed for a number of high-end applications on Web sites such as NASA, Yahoo!, and Slashdot. In addition to the database package itself, MySQL has JDBC and ODBC drivers available, making it accessible from any platform supporting these standards, including Microsoft Windows.

NOTE

The letters SQL are pronounced "S-Q-L," not "sequel" which is typically associated with Microsoft's SQL Server. MySQL, as documented on `www.mysql.com`, is pronounced "My S-Q-L."

Installing MySQL

Starting with Mac OS X Jaguar, MySQL has added the Macintosh platform to its officially supported binary distributions. To install MySQL, all you need to do is download the latest binary distribution from `http://www.mysql.com` Web site and run the installer.

The MySQL software is updated on an ongoing basis, so if you want, you can download the latest source release and compile/install it on your own. We highly recommend, however, that you stick with the official packaged release.

The MySQL disk image can be downloaded from `http://www.mysql.com/downloads/`.

> **NOTE**
>
> Three binary distributions of MySQL are available : Standard, Max, and Debug. The Standard distribution should be fine for most users. Developers may want to use Max because it includes some advanced features that will eventually be incorporated into Standard. The Debug distribution includes debug code and should not be used in a production environment.

Unarchive the distribution, enter the resulting MySQL directory, and use either the `installer` command-line utility or GUI installer to set up the software.

MySQL is installed in a version-tagged directory within `/usr/local`, such as `/usr/local/mysql-max-4.0.13-apple-darwin6.4-powerpc`. This directory, in turn, is symlinked to `/usr/local/mysql`, so it's best to use the link for referencing commands from scripts and so on.

> **TIP**
>
> To compile and install the source distribution of MySQL in the same directory structure as the binary distribution, configure it with

```
./configure --prefix=/usr/local/mysql --localstatedir=/usr/local/mysql/data --
sbindir=/usr/local/mysql/bin
```

> **NOTE**
>
> The Mac OS X installer automatically sets the appropriate directory permissions and runs the command `/usr/local/mysql/bin/mysql_install_db`, which sets up the default MySQL databases.
>
> If you've compiled the software by hand, you *must* first use `chown -R mysql /usr/local/mysql/data` to set the data directory ownership; then run `mysql_install_db` to manually install the initial databases.

Starting the MySQL Daemon

Your MySQL server can be started by changing to the `/usr/local/mysql` directory and then executing the command `./bin/safe_mysqld` as root. Note: You *must* execute `safe_mysqld` from one level above the `/usr/local/mysql/bin` directory, or the daemon will fail to start.

```
brezup:jray jray $ cd /usr/local/mysql ; sudo ./bin/safe_mysqld &
Starting mysqld daemon with databases from /usr/local/mysql/data
```

You should reset the root password immediately after the server is started. Use the command

```
/usr/local/mysql/bin/mysqladmin -u root password '<my new password>'
```

For example, to set my password to "john" (an extremely poor password, by the way), I'd use

```
brezup:jray jray $ /usr/local/mysql/bin/mysqladmin -u root password 'john'
```

NOTE

When creating the new root password, be aware that this password has no effect on the actual Mac OS X root account. For more information on MySQL user management, visit `http://www.mysql.com/documentation/mysql/bychapter/manual_MySQL_Database_Administration.html#User_Account_Management`. I recommend getting a firm grip on MySQL's permissions system before deploying MySQL on a public server.

TIP

The MySQL binaries are installed in `/usr/local/mysql/bin`, which is not part of the default user path. To alter the system to include the directory in your path, see Chapter 20, "Command-Line Configuration and Administration." This eliminates the need to type the full pathname each time you need to access a MySQL utility. Alternatively, you may want to move the `/usr/local/mysql/bin` binaries to `/usr/local/bin` and then create a symbolic link from `/usr/local/mysql/bin` to `/usr/local/bin`.

Creating a Startup Script

Mac OS X uses a special directory structure located in `/Library/StartupItems` or `/System/Library/StartupItems` to automatically start processes when the machine boots. Although some applications install these startup files in the `/System` path, the design of the operating system dictates that add-on software should use the `/Library` directory instead of altering the main system folder.

The three components to a Mac OS X startup script are

- A folder named after the service you are installing (such as MySQL).
- A shell script that bears the same name as the folder. This script should contain the commands needed to start the server process.
- An XML file named `StartupParameters.plist` that contains a description of the process, including its dependencies and the execution order.

Let's take a look at what is exactly needed for Mac OS X and MySQL. At the time of this writing, the official MySQL installer does *not* add this startup script to your system, so you'll need to do it manually, as documented here.

Create the folder MySQL in `/Library/StartupItems` (you may need to create `/Library/StartupItems` if it doesn't exist). Within this folder, add a text file named `MySQL` containing the following shell script:

```
#!/bin/sh

##
# Start MySQL
##

. /etc/rc.common

if [ "${MYSQL:=-NO-}" = "-YES-" ]; then
  ConsoleMessage "Starting MySQL"
  cd /usr/local ; /usr/local/mysql/bin/safe_mysqld &
fi
```

This script checks the `/etc/hostconfig` file for a line that reads `MYSQL=-YES-` and, if it exists, starts the server. Use a text editor to add this to the `hostconfig` file, or just type

```
brezup:jray jray $ sudo echo "MYSQL=-YES-" >> /etc/hostconfig
```

Next, add the `StartupParameters.plist` file to the directory. The contents of this file describe what services the startup item provides, requires, and when it should be started.

```
{
 Description    = "MySQL database server";
 Provides       = ("MySQL");
 Requires       = ("Resolver");
 OrderPreference = "None";
 Messages =
```

```
  {
   start = "Starting MySQL server";
   stop = "Stopping MySQL server";
  };
}
```

As you might guess looking at this example, the `Provides` keyword is used to set a list of the services the startup item provides. The values themselves are arbitrary strings describing the server process and should consist of one or more comma-separated quoted strings contained within parentheses. Similarly, `Requires` values should be set to a list of services required for this service to successfully start, if any. Finally, the `OrderPreference` is used to as a tie breaker for startup items with the same `Requires` values. `OrderPreference` can take on the values of `First`, `Early`, `None`, `Late`, or `Last` (in order of highest to least priority). Despite its existence, Apple does not guarantee that the `OrderPreference` will be followed.

After you add these files, your Mac OS X machine automatically starts MySQL upon booting. It's time to start using your new SQL server.

> **TIP**
>
> For more information on Mac OS X Startup Items, see `http://developer.apple.com/documentation/MacOSX/Conceptual/SystemOverview/BootingLogin/index.html`.

Creating a MySQL Database

The key to using MySQL is an understanding of the SQL syntax itself. If you've used Oracle or another SQL-based system, you'll be right at home interacting with MySQL. For beginners, this introduction should be enough to get started, but we recommend a more complete text such as *MySQL, 2nd Edition* (ISBN: 0-7357-1212-3).

To start MySQL, invoke the client (mysql) using mysql -u<*username*> -p<*password*>. To start, only the root account is available. If you didn't set the password for root, no password is required.

> **TIP**
>
> The MySQL tools (including the client you're using now) can be used to access MySQL servers across a network using the -h <hostname/ip> switch. You could, for example, connect to a server named `my.serverwithmysql.com` running MySQL with the username `kitten` and password `fuzzy4` using `mysql -ukitten -pfuzzy4 -hmy.serverwithmysql.com`.

The first step when working with MySQL is to create the database itself. If you've worked with FileMaker Pro or AppleWorks, this is a very different concept. In MySQL, a database is a container that holds a collection of tables. These tables, in turn, hold actual information.

The FileMaker database model has a single table in a single database. To create relationships between different collections of data requires multiple databases. In MySQL, a single database can contain multiple tables each with unique data.

To create a database, make sure that you've started MySQL and are at a command prompt:

```
brezup:jray jray $ /usr/local/mysql/bin/mysql -uroot -pjohn
Welcome to the MySQL monitor. Commands end with ; or \g.
Your MySQL connection id is 1 to server version: 4.0.13-max

Type 'help;' or '\h' for help. Type '\c' to clear the buffer.

mysql>
```

Next, use create database *<database name>* to set up an empty database. Finally, type use *<database name>* to start working with the new database.

> **NOTE**
>
> The MySQL client requires that all commands end with a semicolon (;). Input can span multiple lines, as long as a semicolon appears at the end.

For example, let's start with an employee database:

```
mysql> create database employee;
Query OK, 1 row affected (0.07 sec)

mysql> use employee;
Database changed
mysql>
```

If you want to delete the database that you've defined, you can use the drop command, which works just like the create command:

```
drop database <database name>
```

> **CAUTION**
>
> A MySQL database can contain multiple tables, each with its own data. Deleting a database removes all information that has been stored in any of the tables.

After a database has been created, you need to set up the internal tables that actually hold the data you want to store.

Tables and Data Types

When making a table, use another create command to tell the system what type of data you want to store—if any.

```
create table <tablename> (<columns...>)
```

For example, let's create some tables for our employee database:

```
create table tblemployee (
  employeeID int not null,
  firstname  varchar(50),
  lastname  varchar(50),
  titleID   int,
  salary   float,
  primary key (employeeID)
);

create table tbljobclassification (
  titleID   int not null,
  title    text,
  minsalary  float,
  maxsalary  float,
  primary key (titleID)
);
```

The first table, `tblemployee`, holds information about each person in the database, such as his name and salary. The second table, `tbljobclassification`, contains job classification data—a general position description, and the minimum and maximum salary ranges for that position.

> **TIP**
>
> The MySQL commands `show databases`, `show tables`, and `describe` *<table name>* can be used to display the available MySQL database, show the tables within the current database, and provide a detailed description of a named table.

When defining a database table, numerous data types are used to build the collection of information that can be stored. Table 22.1 contains a description of the common available data types. This is a summarized version of the documentation supplied at `http://www.mysql.com/`.

TABLE 22.1 Database Tables Are Built with MySQL Data Types

Data Type	Description
TINYINT [UNSIGNED]	A very small integer. The signed range is –128 to 127. The unsigned range is 0 to 255.
SMALLINT [UNSIGNED]	A small integer. The signed range is –32768 to 32767. The unsigned range is 0 to 65535.
MEDIUMINT [UNSIGNED]	A medium-size integer. The signed range is –8388608 to 8388607. The unsigned range is 0 to 16777215.
INT [UNSIGNED]	A normal-size integer. The signed range is –2147483648 to 2147483647. The unsigned range is 0 to 4294967295.
INTEGER [UNSIGNED]	The same as INT.
BIGINT [UNSIGNED]	A large integer. The signed range is –9223372036854775808 to 9223372036854775807. The unsigned range is 0 to 18446744073709551615.
FLOAT	A small (single precision) floating-point number. Cannot be unsigned. Allowable values are –3.402823466E+38 to –1.175494351E–38, 0 and 1.175494351E–38 to 3.402823466E+38.
DOUBLE	A normal-size (double-precision) floating-point number. Cannot be unsigned. Allowable values are –1.7976931348623157E+308 to –2.2250738585072014E–308, 0 and 2.2250738585072014E–308 to 1.7976931348623157E+308.
DECIMAL	An unpacked floating-point number. Cannot be unsigned. Behaves like a CHAR column: unpacked means that the number is stored as a string, using one character for each digit of the value.
DATETIME	A date and time combination. The supported range is 1000-01-01 00:00:00 to 9999-12-31 23:59:59. MySQL displays DATETIME values in YYYY-MM-DD HH:MM:SS format but enables you to assign values to DATETIME columns using either strings or numbers.
TIMESTAMP	A timestamp. The range is 1970-01-01 00:00:00 to some time in the year 2037.
YEAR	A year in two- or four-digit format (the default is four-digit). The allowable values are 1901 to 2155, and 0000 in the four-digit format and 1970–2069 if you use the two-digit format (70–69).
CHAR(<*M*>) [BINARY]	A fixed-length string that is always right-padded with spaces to the specified length when stored. The range of M is 1 to 255 characters. Trailing spaces are removed when the value is retrieved. CHAR values are sorted and compared in case-insensitive fashion according to the default character set unless the BINARY keyword is given.
VARCHAR(<*M*>) [BINARY]	A variable-length string. Note: Trailing spaces are removed when the value is stored. The range of M is 1 to 255 characters. VARCHAR values are sorted and compared in case-insensitive fashion unless the BINARY keyword is given.

TABLE 22.1 Continued

Data Type	Description
`TINYBLOB / TINYTEXT`	A `BLOB` or `TEXT` column with a maximum length of 255 (2^8–1) characters.
`BLOB / TEXT`	A column with a maximum length of 65535 (2^16–1) characters.
`MEDIUMBLOB / MEDIUMTEXT`	A `BLOB` or `TEXT` column with a maximum length of 16777215 (2^24–1) characters.
`LONGBLOB / LONGTEXT`	A `BLOB` or `TEXT` column with a maximum length of 4294967295 (2^32–1) characters.

Fields are defined within a table creation statement by using the syntax `<fieldname> <datatype> <options>`. Two common options are employed to force certain conditions on a table field:

- `not null`—Forces the field to contain a value. If a user attempts to insert data into the database and a not null field is left blank, an error occurs.
- `auto_increment`—When used with an integer field, the value for the field will be determined automatically by MySQL and be incremented with each subsequent record.

The final line of a table creation command should define a primary key (or keys) for the table: `primary key (<fieldname 1,fieldname 2,...>)`. Defining keys is a necessary part of creating a normalized database structure. For more information on normalization, see `http://www.devshed.com/Server_Side/MySQL/Normal/`. We highly recommend reading through this tutorial, at the very least, before designing large-scale database models.

To remove a table that has been defined, type **`drop table <table name>`**.

Inserting Data

There are two ways to insert data into a table; both use the insert command with this structure:

```
insert into <table name> [(<field1,field2,...>)]
        values (<'value1','value2',...>)
```

The difference between the methods comes from the optional field listing. If you want to insert into only a few fields of a table, and want to manually specify the order, you would include the field names, as in this example using the `tblemployee` table created earlier:

```
insert into tblemployee (lastname,firstname,employeeID)
    values ('Ray','John','1');
```

In this example, only the `lastname`, `firstname`, and `employeeID` fields are given in the record, and they don't occur in the same order in which they were defined in the original table.

The second way you can use insert is to provide all the field values at once, in the table definition order. This method doesn't require the field names to be listed:

```
insert into tblemployee values ('1','John','Ray','1','35000.00');
```

It is important to note that you must obey the not null clause for a table definition at all times. In these examples, we had to include a value for the `employeeID` field; otherwise, the insert would have caused an error message to be generated.

To demonstrate the rest of the MySQL syntax, you'll need some data to work with. Go ahead and insert some information into the tables:

```
insert into tbljobclassification values ('1','Programmer/Analyst','20000','80000');
insert into tbljobclassification values ('2','Web Developer','20000','50000');
insert into tbljobclassification values ('3','CEO/President','40000','5000000000');
insert into tblemployee values ('1','John','Ray','1','25300.65');
insert into tblemployee values ('2','Will','Ray','1','32100.25');
insert into tblemployee values ('3','Joan','Ray','1','55300.75');
insert into tblemployee values ('4','Robyn','Ness','2','35000.20');
insert into tblemployee values ('5','Anne','Groves','2','35000.65');
insert into tblemployee values ('6','Julie','Vujevich','2','30300.01');
insert into tblemployee values ('7','Jack','Derifaj','1','12000.00');
insert into tblemployee values ('8','Russ','Schelby','1','24372.12');
insert into tblemployee values ('9','Bill','Gates','3','50000.01');
insert into tblemployee values ('10','Steve','Jobs','3','380000000.00');
```

These statements add three different job classifications (Programmer/Analyst, Web Developer, and CEO/President) to the system, as well as 10 employees who fall under these classifications.

After your database has been populated, you can update or delete individual records using the commands `update`, `delete`, and `replace into`.

TIP

MySQL data can be backed up quickly using `mysqldump -a -A -u<username> -p <password> > <backup filename>`. The resulting file contains all the database, table, and record creation statements.

You can "reload" an empty MySQL database with this data using the mysql client and `mysql -u<username> -p<password> < <backup filename>`.

Modifying Data

Obviously, data in a database must be able to change; otherwise, it would only be useful for a short period of time or for limited applications.

Update

To change existing data, use the `update` command:

```
update <table name> SET <field name 1>=<expression 1>,
    <field name 2>=<expression 2>,<field name n>=<expression n>
    [WHERE <search expression>]
```

To use `update`, you must supply a table name as well as the names of the fields that need to be updated and the new values that they should take on. This leaves one important part of the equation missing: the search expression. If you don't tell update which fields to modify, it modifies all the tables. For example, issuing the command

```
update tblemployee set salary='3000';
```

modifies every listed employee so that the salary field contains '3000'. If this is the desired action, great! If not, you're likely to be smacking your forehead when you discover what you've done.

To be a bit more selective about the update, you must define the `WHERE` search expression. This selects only the records that you want to update. For example, assume that we want to set the salary for `employeeID` 1 to equal 30000.99. The update statement would look like this:

```
update tblemployee set salary='30000.99' where employeeID='1';
```

This update statement searches the database for a field where `employeeID` is equal to 1 and then updates the value in that record's `salary` field.

In addition to =, there are a number of common ways to select a record based on comparing a field to a value; that is, you can select records by creating an expression that evaluates to true or false. Table 22.2 shows some of the most common expression operators and syntax.

TABLE 22.2 Some Common Expression Operators and Syntax

Expression Syntax	Description
`<fieldname> = <value>`	Select records based on a direct comparison to a value.
`<fieldname> > <value>`	Select records where the value of a field is greater than a given value.
`<fieldname> < <value>`	Select records where the value of a field is less than a given value.
`<fieldname> >= <value>`	Select records where the value of a field is greater than or equal to a given value.

TABLE 22.2 Continued

Expression Syntax	Description
`<fieldname> <= <value>`	Select records where the value of a field is less than or equal to a given value.
`<fieldname> LIKE <value>`	Select records based on a simple SQL pattern-matching scheme. The character % matches any number of characters, whereas _ matches a single character.

These basic expressions can be combined to form more complex searches:

NOT *<expression>*—Evaluates to true if the expression evaluates to false.

<expression> OR *<expression>*—Evaluates to true if either of the expressions is true.

<expression> AND *<expression>*—Evaluates to true if both of the expressions are true.

(*<expression>*)—Use parentheses to combine expressions to force an order of evaluation.

Check the MySQL documentation for further information on available mathematical expressions, string comparisons, and other operators that can be used in expression syntax.

Delete

To delete data from a MySQL system, you use a command similar to `update` but without supplying new field values:

```
delete from <table name> [WHERE <search expression>]
```

As with the `update` command, you can leave out the `WHERE` portion of the statement entirely. Unfortunately, the result would be the elimination of all data from the named table. Again, if this is your intention, by all means, use it! For example, to delete employees who make more than $50,000 from the database, you would enter

```
delete from tblemployee where salary>'50000';
```

Replace

There is one final way to conveniently replace existing records with new data. Using the `INSERT` command to try to save a record more than once when one already exists will result in an error. This happens because only one record with a given primary key can exist at a time. For example, assuming that we've filled the database with the following employee record:

```
insert into tblemployee values ('1','John','Ray','1','25300.65');
```

attempting to insert another record using the same employee ID (1) causes an error:

```
mysql> insert into tblemployee values ('1','Maddy','Green','1','41000.00');
ERROR 1062: Duplicate entry '1' for key 1
```

To circumvent this, you could update the existing record; or delete the record and then rerun the insert; or use the `replace into` command.

`replace` replaces an existing record with new data or, if no record exists, simply inserts a record. Think of `replace` as a more powerful version of the basic `insert` command. It can be used to add new records to a table, or replace existing records with new data. The syntax is identical to `insert`. For example, let's retry the insert into the `tblemployee` table—this time using `replace`:

```
mysql> replace into tblemployee values ('1','Maddy','Green','1','41000.00');
Query OK, 2 rows affected (0.00 sec)
```

Success!

CAUTION

`replace` is a useful command unique to the MySQL instruction set. Although convenient, it is best to stick to the basic `insert` statement for most database operations to avoid inadvertently deleting data.

Querying MySQL

After you add data to the tables in a database, you would obviously want to display it. Querying a MySQL database is performed with the `select` statement. The power of relational databases comes from the capability to relate data in one table to that of another, and `select` can do just that:

```
select <field name1>,<field name2>,.. from <table name 1>,<table name 2>,..
    [where <search expression>] [ORDER BY <expression> ASC¦DESC]
```

If this isn't confusing for you, fantastic. If you're like the rest of us, however, some explanation is necessary.

The simplest query that `select` can perform is to pull all the data out of a single table (`select * from <table name>`). For example:

```
mysql> select * from tbljobclassification;
+---------+------------------+----------+----------+
¦ titleID ¦ title            ¦ minsalary ¦ maxsalary ¦
```

```
+---------+------------------+----------+----------+
|    1    | Programmer/Analyst |  20000  |  80000   |
|    2    | Web Developer    |  20000   |  50000   |
|    3    | CEO/President    |  40000   |  5e+09   |
+---------+------------------+----------+----------+
3 rows in set (0.00 sec)
```

Ordering Information

To sort the information based on one of the fields, use `order by` with an expression (often one or more comma-separated field names), and `asc` for ascending order or `desc` for descending order:

```
mysql> select * from tbljobclassification order by maxsalary desc;
+--------      -+------------------+----------+----------+
| titleID      | title            | minsalary | maxsalary |
+-------      --+------------------+----------+----------+
|    3         | CEO/President    |   40000  |   5e+09  |
|    1         | Programmer/Analyst |  20000  |   80000  |
|    2         | Web Developer    |   20000  |   50000  |
+-------      --+------------------+----------+----------+
```

In this example, the `tbljobclassification` table is displayed, and the records are sorted by the maximum salary in descending order (most to least). Obviously, this is great for getting data out of a single table and manipulating its order, but it still doesn't draw on the relational power of MySQL.

Joining Tables

To fully exploit MySQL's capabilities, relationships must be created and used. A relationship links two or more tables based on a common attribute. For example, the `tblemployee` and `tbljobclassification` tables share a `titleID` field. Each employee record has a `titleID` field that can be used to relate to the `tbljobclassification` table. The process of relating tables together is called a *join*.

To see a join in action, let's take a look at how you would display a list of each employee's name, along with his or her job title. The `select` statement looks like this:

```
select firstname,lastname,title from tblemployee,tbljobclassification
    WHERE tblemployee.titleID=tbljobclassification.titleID;
```

Translating this query into English is simple: Select the `firstname`, `lastname`, and `title` fields (`select firstname,lastname,title`) from the `tblemployee` and `tbljobclassification` database tables (`from tblemployee,tbljobclassification`). Relate the two tables by matching the `titleID` field in `tblemployee` to the `titleID` field in `tbljobclassification` (`WHERE tblemployee.titleID=tbljobclassification.titleID`).

The result is a neat display of the employees and their corresponding job titles:

```
mysql> select firstname,lastname,title from tblemployee,tbljobclassification
    WHERE tblemployee.titleID=tbljobclassification.titleID;
+-----------+----------+-------------------+
| firstname | lastname | title             |
+-----------+----------+-------------------+
| Maddy     | Green    | Programmer/Analyst |
| Will      | Ray      | Programmer/Analyst |
| Joan      | Ray      | Programmer/Analyst |
| Jack      | Derifaj  | Programmer/Analyst |
| Russ      | Schelby  | Programmer/Analyst |
| Robyn     | Ness     | Web Developer     |
| Anne      | Groves   | Web Developer     |
| Julie     | Vujevich | Web Developer     |
| Bill      | Gates    | CEO/President     |
| Steve     | Jobs     | CEO/President     |
+-----------+----------+-------------------+
10 rows in set (0.03 sec)
```

TIP

In this example, the two `titleID` fields are referenced by an extended version of their name—`<table name>.<field name>`.

By using this syntax, you remove ambiguity in the SQL statements that would result from multiple tables containing the same names. You can use this when referring to any field, and even use it to refer to a database, table, and fieldname: *`<database name>.<table name>.<field name>`*. In large database projects, with dozens of tables, it helps document the relationships that are being used and is suggested as the standard query format.

A `select` statement can be combined with the `WHERE` search expressions that you've already seen in this chapter. For example, the last query can be modified to show only the employees who are making more than $50,000:

```
select firstname,lastname,title,salary from tblemployee,tbljobclassification
    WHERE tblemployee.titleID=tbljobclassification.titleID
    AND tblemployee.salary>'50000';
```

For example:

```
mysql> select firstname,lastname,title,salary from
    tblemployee,tbljobclassification WHERE
    tblemployee.titleID=tbljobclassification.titleID
    AND tblemployee.salary>'50000';
```

```
+-----------+---------+------------------+---------+
| firstname | lastname | title            | salary  |
+-----------+---------+------------------+---------+
| Joan      | Ray     | Programmer/Analyst | 55300.8 |
| Bill      | Gates   | CEO/President    | 50000   |
| Steve     | Jobs    | CEO/President    | 3.8e+08 |
+-----------+---------+------------------+---------+
3 rows in set (0.00 sec)
```

Of course, expressions can be combined with other expressions to create truly complex queries.

Calculations

Using built-in MySQL functions, you can create virtual fields that contain data calculated as the query is performed. The syntax for an inline calculation is

```
<expression> as '<variable name>'
```

For example, the expression required to calculate the percentage of the maximum salary that each person makes could be represented by

```
tblemployee.salary/tbljobclassification.maxsalary*100 as 'percent'
```

Adding this code into a query of all the employee names and salaries results in

```
mysql> select firstname,lastname,salary,tblemployee.
    salary/tbljobclassification.maxsalary*100 as 'percent'
    from tblemployee,tbljobclassification where
    tblemployee.titleID=tbljobclassification.titleID;
+-----------+----------+---------+------------------+
| firstname | lastname | salary  | percent          |
+-----------+----------+---------+------------------+
| Maddy     | Green    | 41000   | 51.25            |
| Will      | Ray      | 32100.2 | 40.1253125       |
| Joan      | Ray      | 55300.8 | 69.1259375       |
| Jack      | Derifaj  | 12000   | 15               |
| Russ      | Schelby  | 24372.1 | 30.465148925781  |
| Robyn     | Ness     | 35000.2 | 70.0003984375    |
| Anne      | Groves   | 35000.6 | 70.001296875     |
| Julie     | Vujevich | 30300   | 60.60001953125   |
| Bill      | Gates    | 50000   | 0.001000000234375 |
| Steve     | Jobs     | 3.8e+08 | 7.6              |
+-----------+----------+---------+------------------+
10 rows in set (0.01 sec)
```

Suddenly, the database has provided information that didn't even exist previously! Using these methods, you can use the MySQL database engine to perform much of the mathematical work of database applications, leaving the logic to other programming languages.

NOTE

Just because a database system can be used for calculations doesn't mean that it should be. Database systems are optimized for I/O, not necessarily numerics. This is, of course, highly dependent on your project and implementation details.

Summarization and Grouping

Summarizing data is another useful part of any query. Using the summarization functions, you can easily find totals for numeric columns, or count the number of records of a particular type. Here are a few summarization functions that can be used in a query:

- `max()`—The maximum of a given field. Used to match the highest value. For example, if you use `max` on the salary field of the employee table, it should return the highest salary in the group.
- `min()`—The minimum of a given field. Performs the exact opposite of the `max` function.
- `sum()`—The sum of the values in a given field. For example, you could use `sum` to find the total amount paid in salaries.
- `count()`—Provides a count of the number of occurrences of a given field.

For example, you could find the minimum salary of all the employees by typing

```
mysql> select min(salary) from tblemployee;
+-------------+
| min(salary) |
+-------------+
|    12000    |
+-------------+
1 row in set (0.01 sec)
```

Or a count of the occurrences of the `titleID` field:

```
mysql> select count(titleID) from tblemployee;
+----------------+
| count(titleID) |
+----------------+
|       10       |
+----------------+
1 row in set (0.00 sec)
```

This second example obviously isn't very useful—all it did was return the number of times the `titleID` field was used—that is, 10 times, once in each record. Displaying the count of each of the types of `titleIDs` would make more sense. This can be accomplished with one last construct—the `group by` clause.

`group by` organizes the data based on a field name and then makes it available to the summarization function. For example, the previous query could be modified like this:

```
select titleID,count(titleID) from tblemployee group by (titleID);
```

Instead of simply counting the field occurrences and reporting a result, the query groups the records by the `titleID` field and then counts the occurrences within each group. The output looks like this:

```
mysql> select titleID,count(titleID) from tblemployee group by (titleID);
+---------+---------------+
| titleID | count(titleID) |
+---------+---------------+
|    1    |       5       |
|    2    |       3       |
|    3    |       2       |
+---------+---------------+
3 rows in set (0.00 sec)
```

As with all queries, this could be turned into a join to provide information from more than one table. To show the actual job titles rather than just ID numbers, you could modify the query like this:

```
mysql> select title,count(tblemployee.titleID) from
    tblemployee,tbljobclassification where
    tblemployee.titleID=tbljobclassification.titleID
    group by (tblemployee.titleID);

+------------------+--------------------------+
| title            | count(tblemployee.titleID) |
+------------------+--------------------------+
| Programmer/Analyst |            5             |
| Web Developer    |            3             |
| CEO/President    |            2             |
+------------------+--------------------------+
```

This output should be a bit more presentable. Note that in the modified query, the extended name (table name and field name) was used to refer to the `titleID` field. Failure to do this would result in an ambiguity error.

TIP

We highly recommend looking through the official MySQL documentation to get an idea of the full capabilities of the product. This chapter should not be seen as a complete reference to the capabilities of this wonderful application.

Helpers and Alternatives

Several helper applications are available for graphically controlling MySQL and its databases. Personally, I prefer the command-line interface, but your mileage may vary. In addition, Mac OS X boasts several industrial-strength commercial SQL database solutions. If you're interested in pointing and clicking, take a look at these products:

- CocoaMySQL—An excellent free tool for defining, editing, and managing MySQL databases. If you're looking for a GUI to MySQL, try this product first. It's fast, has an attractive interface (see Figure 22.1), and is GPL'd, so even the source code is available. If you find the application useful, consider donating for it future development. `http://cocoamysql.sourceforge.net/`.
- CocoaSQL—Provides a Cocoa interface to MySQL databases, as well as a Service menu item to perform searches from within any other Cocoa application. `http://homepage.mac.com/mxcantor/`.
- MySQL4x Manager—Manage MySQL users and databases from this Cocoa application. An alternative version, SQL4X Manager J, provides a front end to any database with available JDBC drivers, including MS SQL Server. `http://www.macosguru.de/`.
- phpMyAdmin—A Web (PHP) based management tool for MySQL. phpMyAdmin can create, modify, and manage databases from any Web browser. It is easy to install and configure on any PHP-ready system. `http://www.phpmyadmin.net/`.
- FrontBase—A Mac OS X–native SQL database system that features a fully graphical administration and RealBASIC integration. `http://www.frontbase.com/`.
- OpenBase—Another commercial SQL system for Mac OS X. OpenBase features GUI tools for designing database schema, as well as application development using either RealBASIC or RADStudio. `http://www.openbase.com`.
- FileMaker Pro—Apple's "own" database package, FileMaker Pro is available for Mac OS X and Windows and handheld devices. FileMaker Pro is useful for creating desktop database applications and is available in a Server version for developing Web-based applications. `http://www.filemaker.com/`.
- 4D—4DA high-end database development tool for creating desktop and Web applications. 4D provides a far richer development environment than FileMaker Pro but, as a result, has a much higher learning curve. Available on both Windows and Macintosh platforms, 4D is an excellent choice for creating complex data-driven desktop applications. `http://www.4d.com/`.

- PostgreSQL—The PostgreSQL platform is a powerful alternative to MySQL that supports many features that are only "planned" for MySQL, such as subselects. PostgreSQL is available from `http://www.postgresql.org/`.
- SQLite—SQLite is an embeddable SQL database engine. It does not require a server, supports a large subset of SQL (including views and subselects!), writes to a flat file on your system, and is very fast for common operations.

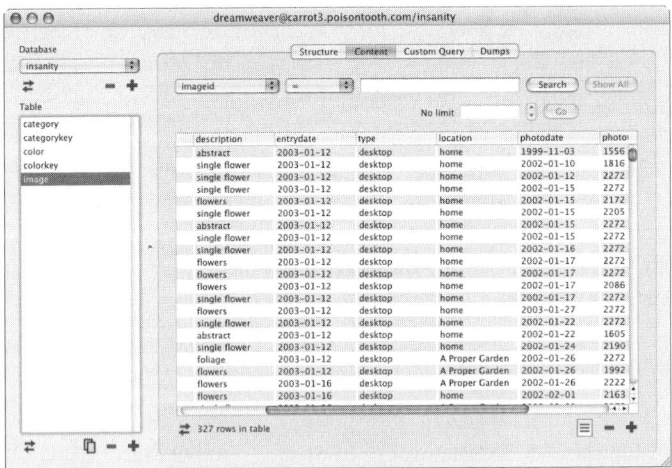

FIGURE 22.1 CocoaMySQL provides an elegant point-n-click interface to the MySQL database.

> **NOTE**
>
> Although not a GUI-based alternative, the PostgreSQL platform is a powerful alternative to MySQL that supports many features that are only "planned" for MySQL, such as subselects. PostgreSQL is available from `http://www.postgresql.org/`.

Perl/MySQL Integration

So, you've got MySQL on your machine. Now what can you do with it? Obviously, you can use one of the previously mentioned utilities to view and manipulate data, but that isn't nearly as useful as being able to apply programmatic logic to the data. Not surprisingly, Perl can be upgraded using DBI (database independent interface) and DBD (database driver) modules to access dozens of database systems, including MySQL.

Perl and MySQL can be combined to create database applications that can be used for anything from storing your personal movie collection to enterprisewide solutions. This portion of the chapter introduces you to the MySQL and Perl connection. You can later apply this knowledge to create Web applications in Chapter 28, "Web Programming."

Installing `DBI::DBD`

As you learned in Chapter 21, "Scripting Languages," installing a Perl module using CPAN requires nothing more than typing `install` *`<module name>`*. To start the interactive module installation shell, type **`sudo perl -MCPAN -e shell`** at a command line.

> **NOTE**
>
> Perl is likely to complain about the version of the CPAN modules you have installed. Although it isn't necessary to upgrade, it won't hurt, and future module installations will be smoother. To upgrade to the latest CPAN modules, type `install Bundle::CPAN` at the `cpan>` prompt.

```
cpan shell -- CPAN exploration and modules installation (v1.70)
ReadLine support enabled

cpan>''
```

At the cpan> prompt, type **`install DBI::DBD`** to begin the installation process:

```
cpan> install DBI::DBD

Local directory now /Users/jray/.cpan/sources/authors/id/T/TI/TIMB
250 OK. Current directory is /
250 OK. Current directory is /pub
250 OK. Current directory is /pub/CPAN
250 OK. Current directory is /pub/CPAN/authors
250 OK. Current directory is /pub/CPAN/authors/id
250 OK. Current directory is /pub/CPAN/authors/id/T
250 OK. Current directory is /pub/CPAN/authors/id/T/TI
250 OK. Current directory is /pub/CPAN/authors/id/T/TI/TIMB
200 TYPE is now 8-bit binary
local: DBI-1.37.tar.gz remote: DBI-1.30.tar.gz
GOT /Users/jray/.cpan/sources/authors/id/T/TI/TIMB/DBI-1.37.tar.gz
...
DBI-1.37
DBI-1.37/DBI.xs
DBI-1.37/t
DBI-1.37/t/80proxy.t
DBI-1.37/t/30subclass.t
DBI-1.37/t/70shell.t
DBI-1.37/t/60preparse.t
```

```
DBI-1.37/t/20meta.t
DBI-1.37/t/40profile.t
...
Installing /usr/share/man/man3/DBI::Shell.3
Installing /usr/share/man/man3/DBI::W32ODBC.3
Installing /usr/share/man/man3/Win32::DBIODBC.3
Installing /usr/bin/dbiproxy
Installing /usr/bin/dbish
Writing /Library/Perl/darwin/auto/DBI/.packlist
Appending installation info to /System/Library/Perl/darwin/perllocal.pod
 /usr/bin/make install -- OK
```

Depending on your Perl installation and version, you might notice several additional messages during the installation. Don't concern yourself too much about these messages unless the installation fails. In the event of a failure, be absolutely sure that you have the latest version of the developer tools installed.

TIP

Many Perl modules ask some basic questions during the install process. Even the highly automated CPAN shell installation method pauses to collect information it needs—so pay attention to your screen during an install.

That's it. The `DBD::DBI` module, which provides the basis for database access from within Perl, is now installed.

Installing `DBD::mysql`

To complete the integration of Perl with MySQL, we need the `DBD::mysql` module. Again, using the CPAN shell, this requires no more effort on our part than `install DBD::mysql`.

Again, invoke CPAN with **`sudo perl -MCPAN -e shell`**:

```
cpan shell -- CPAN exploration and modules installation (v1.70)
ReadLine support enabled
''
cpan>
```

At the cpan> prompt, type **`install DBD::mysql`** to begin the installation process:

```
cpan> install DBD::mysql
GOT /Users/jray/.cpan/sources/authors/id/J/JW/JWIED/DBD-mysql-2.1027.tar.gz
DBD-mysql-2.1027
DBD-mysql-2.1027/t
DBD-mysql-2.1027/t/mysql2.t
```

```
DBD-mysql-2.1027/t/akmisc.t
DBD-mysql-2.1027/t/60leaks.t
DBD-mysql-2.1027/t/10dsnlist.t
DBD-mysql-2.1027/t/ak-dbd.t
DBD-mysql-2.1027/t/50chopblanks.t
...
Installing /usr/share/man/man3/DBD::mysql::INSTALL.3
Installing /usr/share/man/man3/Mysql.3
Writing /Library/Perl/darwin/auto/DBD/mysql/.packlist
Appending installation info to /System/Library/Perl/darwin/perllocal.pod
 /usr/bin/make install -- OK
```

NOTE

If you've already set a root password for MySql, the install will fail when it attempts to connect to mysql as a test. The easiest way around this is to simply force the install by using the command `force install DBD::mysql` within the CPAN shell.

`DBD::mysql` is installed and ready to use. Remember, to view documentation for any of the installed modules, type **perldoc *<module name>***.

Using Perl and MySQL (DBD::mysql)

The `DBD::mysql` module uses an object-oriented model to carry out database translations. Because object-oriented programming is a bit beyond the scope of this book, we'll take a look at two examples: adding information to a database and displaying information contained in a table. You should be able to modify these examples for your own applications, or, if you need more functionality, I recommend adding a Perl book to your library.

Displaying a Table

The easiest way to retrieve information from a MySQL database is to compose a query and retrieve the results, one record at a time. To be able to do this, you must connect to the database, issue the query, determine the number of results, and loop through a display of each one. Listing 22.1 shows the surprisingly short code necessary to do just that.

LISTING 22.1 Display the Result of a MySQL Query

```
#!/usr/bin/perl

use DBI;

$user="";
$pass="";
```

LISTING 22.1 Continued

```
7: $database="employee";
8: $dsn="DBI:mysql:database=$database;host=localhost";
9: $sql="select firstname,lastname,title from tblemployee,tbljobclassification where
tblemployee.titleID=tbljobclassification.titleID";
10:
11: $dbh=DBI->connect($dsn,$user,$pass);
12: $sth=$dbh->prepare($sql);
13: $sth->execute;
14:
15: $numrows=$sth->rows;
16: $numfields=$sth->{'NUM_OF_FIELDS'};
17: nameref=$sth->{'NAME'};
18:
19: for ($x=0;$x<$numrows;$x++) {
20:   $valueref = $sth->fetchrow_arrayref;
21:   print "----------------------------\n";
22:   for ($i=0;$i<$numfields;$i++) {
23:     print "$$nameref[$i] = $$valueref[$i]\n";
24:   }
25: }
```

The following list describes how the Perl code interacts with the MySQL database through the DBI module:

- Line 3—Use the DBI module. This must be included in any Perl application that accesses MySQL.
- Lines 5–9—Set up the username, password, database name, and SQL that will be used to access the database. The `$dsn` variable contains a string that will be used to set up the connection to MySQL. The format of this string cannot change, although the database and hostname can.
- Line 11—Connect to the database using the previously defined connection string and username and password. The variable `$dbh` is a handle that references the database connection.
- Line 12—Prepare the SQL for execution.
- Line 13—Execute the SQL statement and return a reference to the results in the variable `$sth`.
- Line 15—Store the number of returned rows in the `$numrows`.
- Line 16—Store the number of fields (columns) in the result within `$numfields`.

- Line 17—Store a reference to an array containing the field names in the variable `$nameref`.
- Lines 19–25—Loop through each of the rows in the result.
- Line 20—Fetch a row of the result and return the field values in an array referenced by `$valueref`.
- Line 21—Print a divider between each output record.
- Lines 22–24—Loop based on the number of fields in the result. Display each field name followed by the value stored in that field.

Executing the code (assuming that the employee database from earlier in the chapter is in place) produces output like this:

```
% ./display.pl
----------------------------
firstname = Maddy
lastname = Green
title = Programmer/Analyst
----------------------------
firstname = Will
lastname = Ray
title = Programmer/Analyst
----------------------------
firstname = Joan
lastname = Ray
title = Programmer/Analyst
----------------------------
firstname = Jack
lastname = Derifaj
title = Programmer/Analyst
----------------------------
firstname = Russ
lastname = Schelby
title = Programmer/Analyst
----------------------------
firstname = Robyn
lastname = Ness
title = Web Developer
----------------------------
firstname = Anne
lastname = Groves
title = Web Developer
----------------------------
firstname = Julie
```

```
lastname = Vujevich
title = Web Developer
---------------------------
firstname = Bill
lastname = Gates
title = CEO/President
---------------------------
firstname = Steve
lastname = Jobs
title = CEO/President
```

Obviously, the syntax of this code is a bit different from the Perl that you've seen so far, but it should be easy enough to understand that you can modify the code to fit your application.

Storing Data

You probably noticed that the code for displaying the results of a query was very modular. In fact, you can use the same code to insert a record into the database. Listing 22.2 demonstrates the code needed to store data in the `tblemployee` table.

LISTING 22.2 Display the Result of a MySQL Query

```
1: #!/usr/bin/perl
2:
3: use DBI;
4:
5: $user="";
6: $pass="";
7: $database="employee";
8: $id="11"; $firstname="Troy"; $lastname="Burkholder";
9: $titleID="2"; $salary="45000";
10: $dsn="DBI:mysql:database=$database;host=localhost";
11: $sql="insert into tblemployee values
('$id','$firstname','$lastname','$titleID','$salary')";
12:
13: $dbh=DBI->connect($dsn,$user,$pass);
14: $sth=$dbh->prepare($sql);
15: $sth->execute;
```

The only difference between this code and the previous script is the definition of the values for an `insert` (lines 8 and 9) and the definition of the `insert` statement itself (line 11). The SQL statement can be whatever arbitrary SQL code you want. If the statement returns results, they can be read and displayed with the techniques in the previous code.

iODBC and ODBC Manager

Starting in Mac OS X 10.2, the Macintosh once again has ODBC (Open Database Connectivity) support built into the operating system by way of the Open Source iODBC (Independent Open Database Connectivity) software. Before you get excited (or start scratching your head wondering what this is), let's answer a few of the obvious questions.

First, what is ODBC? ODBC is a programming API that allows developers to interact with many different types of databases without having to create custom code for each system. Each database is made accessible by downloading and installing a driver, which plugs into an ODBC manager and hides the details of the server from the programmer and user. There are numerous alternatives to ODBC—such as JDBC (Java), Apple's own Enterprise Objects Framework, and Perl's DBI module, which you just read about. So, with all these different APIs, each doing something similar, why do we need ODBC? ODBC is (one of) Microsoft's standards for database connectivity. It is widely used on the Windows platform and is an accepted developer standard. Is it better than the other options? Nope—but that hasn't stopped other software supported by a monopolistic company from becoming the standard. The Mac OS X iODBC software is a free implementation of the ODBC standard (`http://www.iodbc.org`).

Okay, so what can we do with Mac OS X's ODBC support? To be honest, at the time of this writing, the answer is "not much"—unless you're a programmer. Keep in mind that ODBC is a developer standard for interacting with databases. If developers haven't created applications that use ODBC, users can't do very much with it. ODBC is typically used by software on the Windows platform to allow users to insert live database data into documents. Unfortunately, the support isn't even remotely as pervasive in Mac OS X. Microsoft's current version of Excel, for example, supports Mac OS X's ODBC, but only if the documents that you're using have been created in Mac OS 9 or on Windows. You can't add additional queries or change those that exist.

ODBC Administrator Terminology

The command-line interface to iODBC is not user-friendly. With the benefits of ODBC support coming to GUI applications, it's unreasonable to think that end users will be opening a command prompt to install and manage database connections. Apple has provided (courtesy of OpenLink Software) a simple GUI ODBC manager (path: `/Applications/Utilities/ODBC Administrators`) that allows mere mortals to create and edit connections.

ODBC Administrator works (and looks) like Microsoft's ODBC Data Sources control panel, so if you've used ODBC on Windows, you might experience deja vu. If not, a few terms will be helpful to understand going forward:

- ODBC driver—A driver file that abstracts a database "behind" the ODBC manager. You will need an ODBC driver for any database system you want to access.

- DSN—A *Data Source Name*. For each drive you install, you can create multiple Data Source Names that connect to different databases/database servers. The Data Source Name is a simple word (such as "mydatabase") that identifies a database connection and can contain all the information needed to connect and access a given database.
- User DSN—A DSN accessible only by the user who created it.
- System DSN—A DSN accessible by any user on the Mac OS X system.
- User driver—An ODBC driver accessible only by the user who installed it.
- System driver—An ODBC driver accessible by any user on the Mac OS X system.

To start using the ODBC Administrator, first you need something to manage. Because you've got MySQL on the system, it makes some sense to install a MySQL ODBC driver. You can download a driver packaged to work with Apple's ODBC Administrator from OpenLink: `http://oplweb.openlinksw.com/product/webmatrixst.asp`.

Installing a GUI-Configured ODBC Driver (OpenLink MySQL)

The OpenLink drivers provide a setup GUI for configuring the driver and connection. Unfortunately, they also cost money. For desktop applications, the price tag is reasonable, but costs go up significantly if deploying on a Web server. Thirty-day trials are available for free.

After downloading the MySQL driver, double-click the installation package. You are led through the installation process just as with any other Mac application, as shown in Figure 22.2.

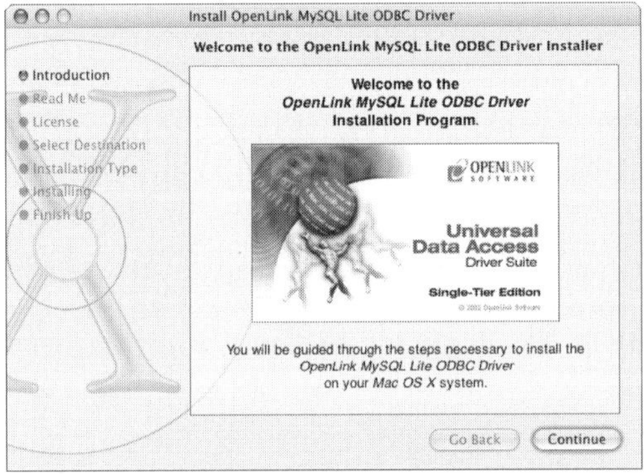

FIGURE 22.2 OpenLink provides easy-to-install ODBC drivers for Mac OS X.

To verify that the driver has installed correctly, open the ODBC Administrator utility and click to the Drivers button. Your display should resemble Figure 22.3.

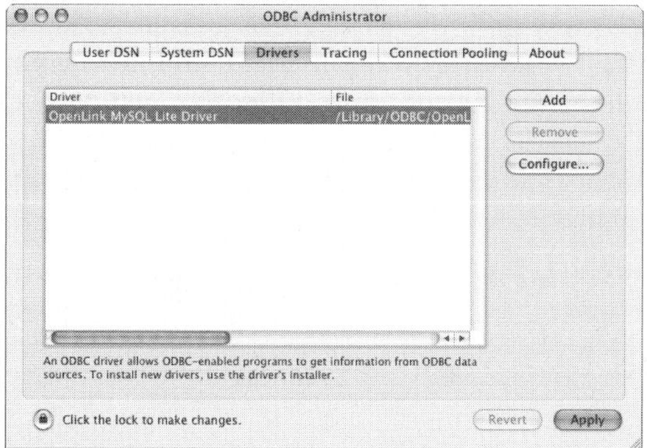

FIGURE 22.3 Use the Drivers pane within the ODBC Administrator to verify that the driver installed correctly.

Not all driver packages will install the same way, but the end result should be the same—a new driver entry in ODBC Administrator. If you don't see this entry, consult the driver documentation.

NOTE

The OpenLink drivers require an additional license file to be emailed to the user and installed. Be sure to follow the licensing instructions before continuing; otherwise, the driver might not work as expected.

Installing a Command-Line Configured ODBC Driver (MyODBC)

Unfortunately, very few "packaged" drivers are available for Mac OS X, and many that are available cost money. For those who have to squeeze every penny out of their IT budgets, there are often free solutions—such as MyODBC for MySQL. MyODBC is an iODBC-compatible ODBC driver that provides much of the same functionality as the OpenLink driver but is available for anyone who wants to compile it, or those with a supported operating system. Although Mac OS X *is* a supported system, the available driver was compiled with paths that do not work with the official version of MySQL, so the driver fails at load time with errors such as the following:

```
dyld errors during link edit for file /Users/mysqldev/venu/local/mysql/lib/
➥mysql/libmysqlclient.10.dylib
dyld: odbctest can't open library: /Users/mysqldev/venu/local/mysql/lib/mysql/
➥libmysqlclient.10.dylib (No such file or directory, errno = 2)
```

So, unless you happen to have the same directory structure shown in the errors, it isn't worth your time to try. Alas, compiling is the only option.

Installing the iODBC Headers

Most drivers require you to manually compile them, and, before you can do that, you'll need to "fix" your iODBC installation. Apple, although including iODBC in the system, neglected to include the header files required to compile iODBC-compatible drivers. So our first step is to retrieve and install the iODBC header files. The good news is that you'll only need to do this once.

First, download the iODBC Manager source code from `http://www.iodbc.org` and unarchive it:

```
brezup:jray jray $ tar zxf libiodbc-3.0.6.tar.gz
```

Next, `cd` into the source distribution and run `./configure` to set up the software. We're not going to compile it, but running `configure` is necessary to create one of the header files:

```
brezup:jray libiodbc-3.0.6 $ ./configure
checking for a BSD-compatible install.. /usr/bin/install -c
checking whether build environment is sane.. yes
checking for gawk.. no
checking for mawk.. no
checking for nawk.. no
checking for awk.. awk
...
```

Finally, we need to create a directory for the header files (`/usr/local/include/iodbc`) and copy the contents of the source distribution's include folder to that location. To do this, issue these commands from inside the iODBC source distribution directory:

```
brezup:jray libiodbc-3.0.6 $ sudo mkdir /usr/local/include/iodbc
brezup:jray libiodbc-3.0.6 $ cd include
brezup:jray include $ sudo cp *.h /usr/local/include/iodbc
```

Now you're ready to compile iODBC drivers. Just make sure that the iODBC headers are in the include path during compilation.

Compiling MyODBC

Download and unarchive the latest MyODBC binary distribution from `http://www.mysql.com/downloads/api-myodbc-3.51.html`.

Now, `cd` into the source distribution and issue the following `configure` command. It is important to type this correctly because it specifies the location of iODBC and MySQL files on your system:

```
brezup:jray myodbc-3.51 $ ./configure --host=powerpc-apple-darwin
 --with-mysql-libs=/usr/local/mysql/lib
 --with-mysql-includes=/usr/local/mysql/include
```

```
--with-iodbc-includes=/usr/local/include/iodbc
--with-iodbc-libs=/usr/lib --with-iodbc-ini=/Library/ODBC/odbc.ini
```

This assumes that you've used the MySQL install discussed in this chapter and have placed the iODBC header files in `/usr/local/include/iodbc`. If any of the information is different on your system, you'll need to adjust it accordingly.

Next, compile the driver by typing **make**:

```
brezup:jray myodbc-3.51 $ make
/bin/sh ./libtool --mode=compile gcc -DHAVE_CONFIG_H -I. -I. -I.
 -I/usr/local/include/mysql -I/usr/local/include/iodbc -g -O2 -c
 catalog.c
gcc -DHAVE_CONFIG_H -I. -I. -I. -I/usr/local/include/mysql
 -I/usr/local/include/iodbc -g -O2 -Wp,-MD,.deps/catalog.pp -c catalog.c
 -o catalog.o
/usr/local/include/iodbc/config.h:80: warning: redefinition of macro PACKAGE
/usr/local/include/mysql/my_config.h:754: warning: this is the location of
 the previous definition
...
```

This took more than 10 minutes on a PowerBook G4 (500), so be patient. When the process has finished, do not use `make install`. The iODBC Manager requires a shared library to be built, which does not happen automatically during the compile. To create the driver in the proper format, type the following:

```
brezup:jray myodbc-3.51 $ cd driver; cc -bundle -undefined error -o .libs/libmyo-
dbc3.so catalog.o connect.o dll.o execute.o handle.o info.o myodbc3.o options.o pre-
pare.o results.o transact.o utility.o cursor.o error.o misc.o -L/usr/local/mysql/lib
-L/usr/local/lib -lz -liodbcinst -lc -lmysqlclient
```

You now have created the file `libmyodbc3.so` in the `.libs` directory of the `driver` source folder. This is the MyODBC driver, ready to be installed. Move the file to an appropriate installation location, such as `/usr/local/lib`, by typing as follows (from inside the `driver` directory):

```
brezup:jray driver $ sudo cp .libs/libmyodbc3.so /usr/local/lib/libmyodbc3.so
```

The driver is installed and ready to use, but if you start ODBC Administrator, you'll notice that it doesn't appear under the Drivers tab. We still need to make a few more changes before it will appear.

Adding the Driver to ODBC Administrator

There are two ways to add drivers to the ODBC Administrator, either through the GUI, or by editing the appropriate configuration file. Because both methods are simple, let's quickly review each.

The iODBC configuration files consist of /Library/ODBC/odbcinst.ini, which contains the installed System Drivers, and /Library/ODBC/odbc.ini, containing the installed System Data Source Names. The "User" level versions of these files are stored in ~/Library/ODBC/odbcinst.ini and ~/Library/ODBC/odbc.ini, respectively.

NOTE

If you've never used the ODBC Administrator before, you will probably need to create the /Library/ODBC directory and odbcinst.ini files by hand.

To add MySQL as system driver, edit the file /Library/ODBC/odbcinst.ini and add the lines

```
[ODBC Drivers]
MyODBC = Installed

[MyODBC]
Driver = /usr/local/lib/libmyodbc3.so
```

The first section [ODBC Drivers] is simply a list of each driver installed on the system. In our case, this is MyODBC. The driver name is arbitrary but should describe what is installed.

For each driver listed under [ODBC Drivers], there should be a corresponding section named identically to the driver name, such as [MyODBC] that contains a Driver = line set to the location of the installed driver file. For our MyODBC driver, this is /usr/local/lib/libmyodbc3.so. There may be additional options that can be set here (see the individual driver instructions for details), but for most cases, this is sufficient.

Now, start ODBC Administrator and click the Drivers button. You see the MyODBC driver listed, as shown in Figure 22.4.

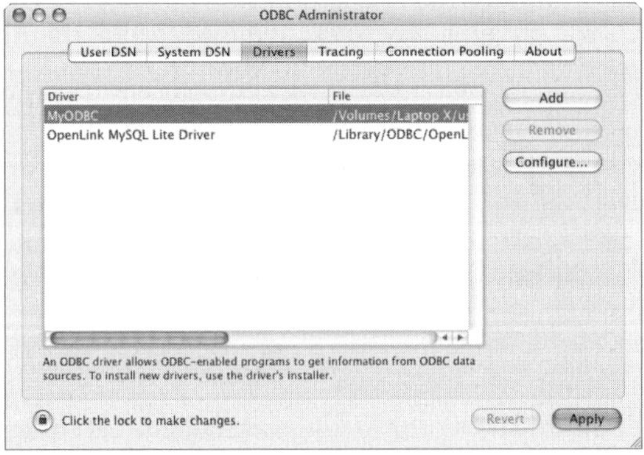

FIGURE 22.4 The Drivers button now lists the MyODBC driver.

If you prefer a more graphical approach to adding the driver, you can avoid editing files altogether by using the Drivers button and the Add button to configure a driver within the Administrator.

Clicking Add displays a dialog box where you can specify a description of the driver, the location of the ODBC driver file, and a setup file (if one is provided with the driver), and choose whether it will be available as a User or System driver. In addition, the Add and Remove buttons within the sheet enable driver-specific variables to be set. Figure 22.5 shows a properly filled-out Add window for adding the MyODBC driver to ODBC Administrator.

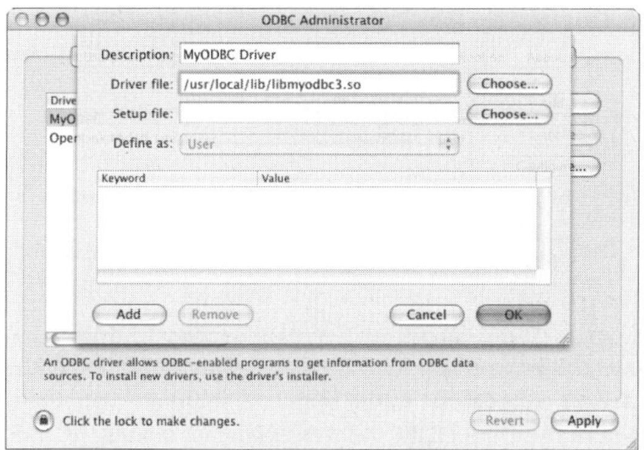

FIGURE 22.5 Use the Add button to add driver files within the ODBC Administrator GUI.

NOTE

System drivers cannot be added unless you first authenticate by clicking the lock button at the bottom of the ODBC Administrator window.

After a driver has been added, you can change its configuration at any time by highlighting the name in the list and clicking the Configure button. Drivers can be removed altogether by clicking Remove.

Defining a Data Source Name

If you chose to install MyODBC, you're probably wondering whether we're finished yet. Those of you with OpenLink drivers are just itching to move on. Regardless of what driver you're using, there's still one more step before we can actively use the ODBC driver—defining a Data Source Name. User Data Sources and System Data Sources function identically—it's just a matter of what users have access to them.

To define a DSN, click the appropriate DSN button at the top of the ODBC Administrator window. For our test purposes, use the User DSN button. Next, click the Add button. You will be presented with a list of the drivers available on your system, as demonstrated in Figure 22.6.

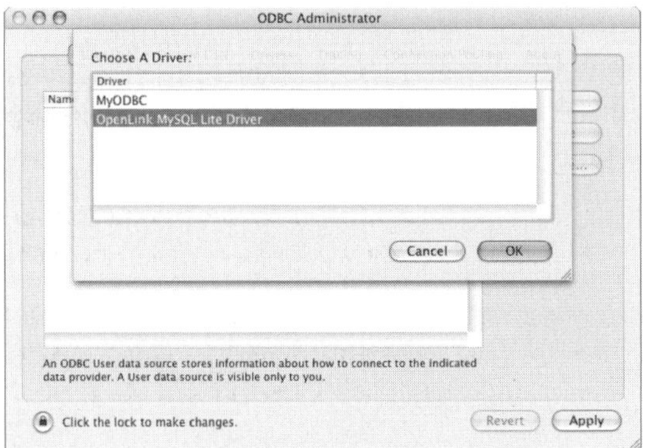

FIGURE 22.6 Choose the ODBC driver you want to use to make a connection.

> **NOTE**
>
> As with the ODBC drivers, you cannot add a System DSN unless you first authenticate by clicking the lock icon at the bottom of the ODBC Administrator window.

After you choose the driver, one of two things happens. If your driver includes an automated setup tool, such as the OpenLink drivers, you are taken to a setup wizard; otherwise, you are presented with a generic setup screen.

Check with your Driver installation instructions to properly complete the setup. In the case of the OpenLink drivers, use the Data Source button to choose a DSN, such as `employeeDB` for the database we created in this chapter. The hostname should be set to the computer running the database server or `localhost` if it is on the same computer as the ODBC driver, and the port number should be left at 3306, the MySQL default. Using the Connection button, you can provide a username and password by which to connect to the database server, and choose the database (such as employee) itself. Again, this is all highly dependent on who packaged the driver, so what works with one ODBC driver might not work with another.

The MyODBC driver, on the other hand, does not include a setup utility, so it must be configured manually. Drivers such as this show a generic setup screen, similar to that in Figure 22.7.

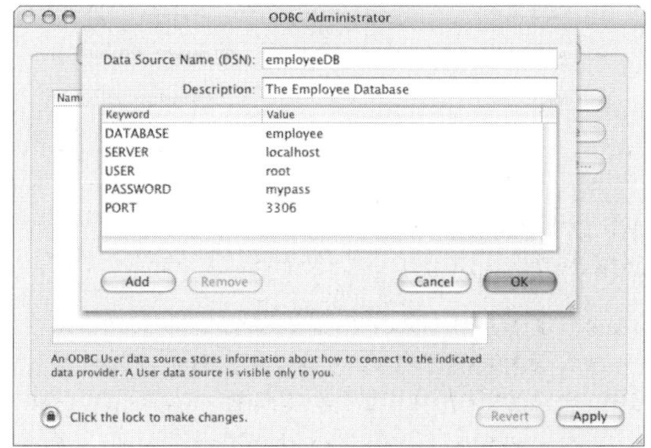

FIGURE 22.7 Drivers without GUI setup wizards must be configured by hand.

Use the DSN field to provide a DSN, such as `employeeDB`, for our example database. In the Description field, provide a brief description of what the DSN will do. Next, use the Add and Remove buttons to add and remove keywords and values that will be used to define the connection. MyODBC is easy to configure by using these keywords:

- `DATABASE`—The name of the database on the MySQL server.
- `SERVER`—The name or IP address of the MySQL server.
- `PORT`—The port that the MySQL server is running on. Always 3306 unless the MySQL Server defaults have been modified.
- `USER`—A MySQL username to connect with.
- `PASSWORD`—The password to use.

Figure 22.7 displays a properly configured connection to the employee database. Click OK to save the DSN definition.

NOTE

As noted earlier, actual DSN setup information is stored in the files `/Library/ODBC/odbc.ini` and `~/Library/ODBC/odbc.ini` for System and User DSNs, respectively. You might find that it is often easier to add these definitions by hand rather than use the ODBC Administrator. For example, the MyODBC employeeDB DSN is defined in my User DSN `odbc.ini` file as follows:

```
[ODBC Data Sources]
employeeDB = MyODBC

[employeeDB]
Driver    = /usr/local/lib/libmyodbc3.so
Description = The Employee Database
DATABASE  = employee
```

```
SERVER    = localhost
USER     = root
PASSWORD  = mypass
PORT     = 3306
```

This is similar to the `odbcinst.ini` file we saw earlier. The `odbc.ini` file simply lists the DSNs and the drivers they use, and then provides a section for each DSN with the necessary keyword/value pairs to connect to the database server.

After a DSN is added (regardless of the means), it can be reconfigured by clicking the Configure button, or removed entirely by clicking Remove.

Testing the DSN

To test a DSN, you can either use an ODBC-enabled application, or the command-line odbctest utility. To use odbctest to connect to a User DSN, simply invoke it at a command prompt:

```
brezup:jray jray $ odbctest
iODBC Demonstration program
This program shows an interactive SQL processor

Enter ODBC connect string (? shows list):
Press ? to display a list of the defined DSNs:
Enter ODBC connect string (? shows list): ?
DSN                | Description
---------------------------------------------------------------
employeeDB             | MyODBC

Enter ODBC connect string (? shows list):
```

Finally, type **DSN=<*DSN*>** to connect to a listed DSN:

```
Enter ODBC connect string (? shows list): DSN=employeeDB
Driver: 03.51.06

SQL>
```

If the driver has been configured successfully, you'll arrive at an `SQL>` prompt where you can issue SQL commands to the database server. This works just like the mysql client application we used earlier:

```
SQL> select * from tblemployee;
```

```
employeeID¦firstname¦lastname¦titleID¦salary
----------+---------+--------+-------+---------
1         ¦John     ¦Ray      ¦1      ¦25300.7
2         ¦Will     ¦Ray      ¦1      ¦32100.2
3         ¦Joan     ¦Ray      ¦1      ¦55300.8
4         ¦Robyn    ¦Ness     ¦2      ¦35000.2
5         ¦Anne     ¦Groves   ¦2      ¦35000.6
6         ¦Julie    ¦Vujevich ¦2      ¦30300
7         ¦Jack     ¦Derifaj  ¦1      ¦12000
8         ¦Russ     ¦Schelby  ¦1      ¦24372.1
9         ¦Bill     ¦Gates    ¦3      ¦50000
10        ¦Steve    ¦Jobs     ¦3      ¦3.8e+08

 result set 1 returned 10 rows.
```

After verifying that the connection works and value results are returned, exit `odbctest` by typing **`exit`**:

```
SQL> exit

Have a nice day.
```

You now have a completely functional ODBC driver and DSN defined. Any software compatible with iODBC should recognize and work with the DSN.

SO NOW WHAT?

You might be asking yourself, "So now what?" The answer, unfortunately, is wait. ODBC-compatible Mac applications will eventually appear. Until then, you'll have to be satisfied with Unix-level utilities.

Perl, for example, provides a DBD ODBC module `DBD::ODBC` that can interact with any database using the same syntax discussed earlier with `DBD::mysql`. This is slower than using a native DBD module (it adds an extra layer of "work" because the DBI module must talk to the DBD driver, which in turn communicates with iODBC and the ODBC driver). However, it is useful for connecting to databases that don't have a native DBD driver.

Additional ODBC Administrator Settings

Two additional buttons in ODBC Administrator can be used to debug or fine-tune your database connections. The first, Tracing, is shown in Figure 22.8.

If you are having problems connecting to your database server, you can enable tracing and choose a log file to hold the trace information. The trace file contains all information sent between the driver and the database server, allowing you to pinpoint where the failure is occurring.

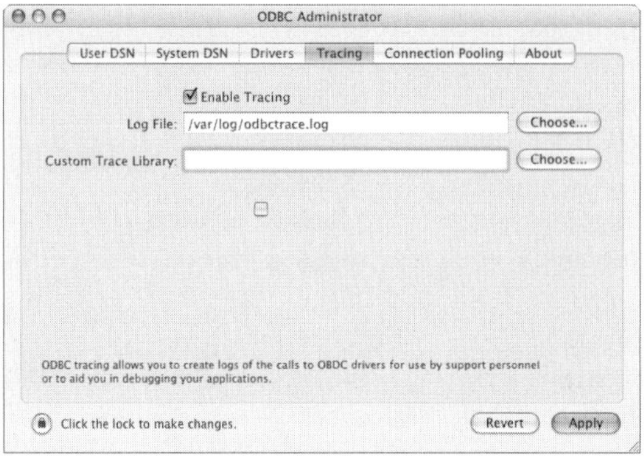

FIGURE 22.8 Enable tracing to debug connection problems.

CAUTION

Trace log files can grow large very quickly and can also slow down the connection to your database server. Enable tracing only when needed.

The second button, Connection Pooling, shown in Figure 22.9, allows you to enable pooling for individual drivers. If a driver is "pooled," it attempts to reuse open connections instead of relocating connection resources each time they are requested.

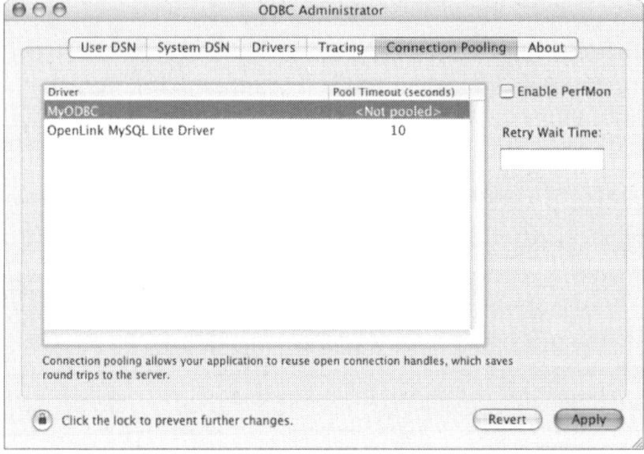

FIGURE 22.9 Connection pooling can reuse server connections.

To enable pooling, authenticate with ODBC Administrator and then enter a timeout value in the Pool Timeout field. This is the length of time a pooled connection exists before it is released.

Summary

This chapter introduced MySQL and ODBC for database development and connection management. MySQL provides a powerful database system that can be used to develop commercial solutions for a fraction of the price. Easily integrated with Perl, MySQL can be used for everything from Web development to your own custom database applications.

ODBC support, at long last, is included in Mac OS X in the form of iODBC and ODBC Administrator. The iODBC software, coupled with Apple's ODBC Administrator, makes it easy to connect to and manage ODBC data sources. Unfortunately, there is very little software that uses ODBC on the Mac platform. Presumably, the integration of this feature with the Mac OS will lead to enhanced database functionality in the near future.

CHAPTER 23

File and Resource Sharing with NFS and NetInfo

IN THIS CHAPTER

In Chapter 11, "Additional System Components," you learned about using the NetInfo database to configure users and information local to your machine. In this chapter, you learn the first half of what you need to do to take full advantage of NetInfo as a resource for grouping multiple OS X (and other flavors of Unix) machines into a cohesive cooperating group of machines.

Single-User Mode

One of the first things you need to become familiar with is single-user mode. Under single-user mode, your machine is most definitely not participating as a working part of a group of machines because it's locked down into a vary minimal state. This is useful exactly because of the capability to so completely intertwine the workings of machines that are operating together—there must be a way to extricate a single machine for maintenance so that its resources aren't being used, and things on it aren't being changed by other machines that it normally interoperates with.

What exactly is single-user mode? It is a "minimally alive" state of the machine. In single-user mode, `root` is the only user who can access the machine. Only a minimum number of processes are running. Only a minimum number of partitions are mounted. Services that are not absolutely necessary for the operation of the system are not started.

To get into single-user mode, press Command-S while the machine is booting or rebooting. When the Macintosh boots into single-user mode, it looks much like a PC. You see a black background and text in various colors scroll by. The final portion of what appears on the screen is this:

```
Singleuser boot - fsck not done
Root device is mounted read-only
If you want to make modifications to files,
run '/sbin/fsck -y' first and then '/sbin/mount -uw /'
localhost:/ root#
```

Not all OS X machines appear to boot into single-user mode with the root device mounted read-only. Be sure to look carefully at the lines of output before the `localhost` prompt. If you need to modify any files, such as making a backup or restoring the NetInfo database, be sure to follow the instructions indicated onscreen. Otherwise, you will not be able to make any changes.

It is helpful to know what behavior to expect from your system in single-user mode before you're required to work in this mode by circumstance. Having your machine land in a state that requires you to go in and fix things under the hood can be a panicky situation, and panicky behavior is exactly what you don't want when you're trying to fix your system. Because `root` is the only user in single-user mode, it is important to be calm and pay close attention to what you're doing.

While you are in single-user mode, you might be interested in running `ps`, just to see what processes run in single-user mode. When you return to multiuser mode, try running `ps` again to see the difference.

To return to multiuser mode, issue the command

```
sync;sync;sync;reboot
```

The first three commands, `sync`, force the system to complete any disk writes before rebooting. It is tradition (stemming from the dark ages of disk cache mechanisms, but good practice nonetheless) to issue the sync command at least two or three times. Then `reboot` is executed.

Alternatively, you can use the `shutdown` command (more details on commands for such maintenance details are available in Chapter 26, "Remote Access and Control").

```
shutdown -r now
```

After seeing your machine once in single-user mode, you are better prepared for any emergencies you might encounter while experimenting with commands in this chapter, and for the future.

We recommend, in general, that you back up and restore shared resources such as your NetInfo domains at the command line, in single-user mode. This helps to prevent any transient changes that might occur due to multiuser operations from corrupting the backup. Even if you don't end up making the backups in single-user mode, there is bound to be a time when you make a change to the NetInfo database that does not work at all and needs to be undone. Or, you might accidentally delete all of it, if you selected the wrong directory. In any case, because normal operation of OS X depends on the NetInfo database, and single-user operation does not, at some point, you may find a need to restore your NetInfo database from single-user mode.

Whether it is for backing up or restoring, it is best to familiarize yourself with single-user mode ahead of time. The appearance of single-user mode on a Macintosh can be disturbing. It is best to have some idea of what to expect before you really need to be in single-user mode.

Creating a Backup of the Local NetInfo Database Using the Command Line

Without a properly functioning NetInfo system, Mac OS X is rendered almost inoperable. Given the importance of the NetInfo database to your machine's functioning, it is best to back up the NetInfo database before making any major changes to it. You've already learned how to back up the database using the NetInfo manager, but to use the NetInfo Manager you must be running in multiuser mode. In the command line, you could use `cp` or `tar` to create your backup. The NetInfo database is in the directory `/var/db/netinfo/local.nidb`. When backing up the NetInfo database from the command line, Apple recommends making the backup in single-user mode.

Because the NetInfo database is stored as a collection of data files in a directory, you can make a backup of the NetInfo database either by copying the directory, or by `tar`ring the directory. Apple seems to prefer the recursive copy of the directory, but I find `tar`ring it into a single file to be more useful.

```
brezup:root ray # cd /var/db/netinfo/
brezup:root netinfo # cp -R local.nidb local.nidb-backup
```

or:

```
brezup:root netinfo # tar -cf local.nidb-backup.tar local.nidb
```

No matter which method you use to make your backup, remember to double-check `/var/db/netinfo` to verify that your backups agree with your actual NetInfo database:

```
brezup:root netinfo # ls -l local.nidb-backup
total 128
-rw------- 1 root wheel    4 4 Sep 21:01 Clean
-rw-r--r-- 1 root wheel    4 4 Sep 21:01 Config
-rw------- 1 root wheel 3072 4 Sep 21:01 Store.1024
-rw------- 1 root wheel 2112 4 Sep 21:01 Store.1056
-rw-r--r-- 1 root wheel 3712 4 Sep 21:01 Store.128
```

```
-rw-r--r-- 1 root wheel 2400 4 Sep 21:01 Store.160
-rw-r--r-- 1 root wheel  576 4 Sep 21:01 Store.192
-rw------- 1 root wheel 2080 4 Sep 21:01 Store.2080
-rw------- 1 root wheel 1568 4 Sep 21:01 Store.224
-rw------- 1 root wheel  256 4 Sep 21:01 Store.256
-rw-r--r-- 1 root wheel 6144 4 Sep 21:01 Store.384
-rw------- 1 root wheel  832 4 Sep 21:01 Store.416
-rw-r--r-- 1 root wheel  512 4 Sep 21:01 Store.512
-rw------- 1 root wheel  672 4 Sep 21:01 Store.672
-rw-r--r-- 1 root wheel 1056 4 Sep 21:01 Store.96
brezup:root netinfo # ls -l local.nidb-backup.tar
-rw-r--r-- 1 root wheel 40960 4 Sep 21:02 local.nidb-backup.tar
```

Some versions of NetInfo Manager provide the capability to create a backup of your NetInfo database directly from the GUI tool. This is mysteriously missing in NetInfo Manager 1.3.1, but given the importance of not breaking the NetInfo database, it's difficult to believe that this omission is intentional. Wherever it gets replaced, we expect it to run much like it previously did, which is to create the same type of backups that the `cp -R` command-line backup does. The default name under which the database was stored by the backup was `local.nibak`.

Using the Command Line to Examine the NetInfo Database

As you have seen throughout this book, command-line tools are frequently available to do what can be done in the graphical tools in OS X. This is also the case with the NetInfo database. You can manage the database graphically in the NetInfo Manager, and you can manage the database through command-line tools. As you become more familiar with the NetInfo database, you will learn that sometimes the graphical tools are more suitable for accomplishing your task, whereas at other times the command-line tools are more suitable.

In this section we take some of the same tour of the NetInfo database as we did using the NetInfo Manager, only this time we use the command line. Having already used the NetInfo Manager makes the introduction to the command line easier.

Before we even begin our tour, we can verify that our machine is indeed a NetInfo server, serving its own local domain by running `ps`:

```
brezup:ray netinfo $ ps -auxw | grep netinfo
root  142 0.0 0.0  27488  344 ?? Ss  8:56PM  0:00.29 netinfod -s local
ray  433 0.0 0.0  18652  92 std R+  9:13PM  0:00.00 grep netinfo
```

As we can see from the `ps` listing, our machine is indeed running a NetInfo server for its `local` domain, and it is the master of its `local` domain.

Now let's look directly at the NetInfo database. We will examine the NetInfo database using the `niutil` command, the NetInfo utility. You can do more than just examine the database with `niutil`, but we will get to that later.

The primary form of `niutil` is

```
niutil <action> [opts] <domain> <path>
```

One of the most confusing parts about using the command-line tools is remembering what term to use to refer to the `local` domain. As you might guess from the NetInfo Manager, / would probably refer to the `local` domain. However, you will also see in man pages and online documentation the use of `.` to refer to the `local` domain. Which is it?


```
brezup:ray netinfo $ niutil -domainname .
/
brezup:ray netinfo $ niutil -domainname /
/
```

GOOD GRIEF, NOT MORE ROOTS AGAIN!

Yes, unfortunately, more roots again. The NetInfo database is described as a directory structure, and so, like other Unix directory structures has a root. The NetInfo database, however, is composed of (potentially many) cooperating directories arranged in their own hierarchical directory structure. Your local domain, therefore, has a `root` directory to its own data structure. This directory may or may not (if your local machine is subscribed to another domain as well) be the `root` of the entire NetInfo domain as your machine sees it. Clear as mud? Don't worry; if you need to make this work, you'll find that it's considerably easier than it sounds. If you don't need to create or work within a multilevel domain, your local domain's `root` is your NetInfo directory's `root`, and you can call it either `.` or /.

As we see from the `niutil` command, we can use either `.` or / to refer to the local domain, as long as the local domain is the only domain we have. If you subscribe to multiple domains, things begin to get more complicated. As you research things on the Internet, you might see both terms being used to refer to the local domain. It isn't necessarily a good idea to follow this imprecise usage because it only works properly if your machine provides its own, only domain. To avoid problems, always (regardless of examples you might find to the contrary) use / to refer to the `root` domain, and `.` to refer to the `local` domain. As we continue with this chapter, we will use this notation, which is as described in the man pages.

Let's look at the `root` directory of our local domain:

```
brezup:ray ray $ niutil -list . /
1     users
2     groups
```

```
3     machines
4     networks
5     protocols
6     rpcs
7     services
8     aliases
9     mounts
10     printers
80     afpuser_aliases
```

This looks familiar! The result we get on the command line looks much like what we see in NetInfo Manager in the center pane, except that the NetInfo Manager listed the directories in alphabetical order rather than by numeric ID.

NOTE

As in Chapter 11, don't be surprised if your listing of NetInfo information isn't identical to what you see here. NetInfo contains much of the information that makes your machine "yours" and my machine "mine." There wouldn't be much point to using a database for all of this, if we didn't Think Different!

We can look at the properties of the `root` directory of the local domain:

```
brezup:ray ray $ niutil -read . /
master: localhost/local
trusted_networks:
```

This looks like the same view we see in the bottom window of the NetInfo Manager when the `root` of the local domain is opened.

Let's do the command-line equivalent of clicking on the `aliases` directory in the NetInfo Manager:

```
brezup:ray ray $ niutil -list . /aliases
58     administrator
59     postmaster
60     MAILER-DAEMON
61     MAILER-AGENT
62     nobody
63     dumper
64     manager
65     operator
```

If we were in the NetInfo Manager, the window to the right would show more data now. If we "click" the `postmaster` directory, we also see in the command line that we have reached the end of the hierarchy:

```
brezup:ray ray $ niutil -list . /aliases/postmaster
brezup:ray ray $
```

Again, we can look at the properties of `postmaster`:

```
brezup:ray ray $ niutil -read . /aliases/postmaster
name: postmaster
members: root
```


As we saw in the NetInfo Manager, `postmaster` appears to be aliased to `root`.

We can also view a specific property using the command line. Here we ask for the value of the `gid` (group ID) property of the `sshd` directory of the `groups` directory in our `local` domain:

```
brezup:ray ray $ niutil -readprop . /groups/sshd gid
75
```

Now we have taken a brief tour of our local NetInfo database using `niutil`. So far, we have seen that using `-list` or some form of `-read` is much like clicking on values in the NetInfo Manager. Specifically, `-list` lists directories in the specified name and path, and `-read` lists associated values of a directory, whereas `-readprop` reads a specific property value. In NetInfo Manager terms, the `-list` action is like navigating the upper windows, but using `-read` is like viewing the contents of a directory being displayed in the upper window in the bottom window.

Table 23.1 shows the command syntax and some of the most useful options for `niutil`. Complete documentation is available in Appendix A. To use the options that write to the NetInfo database, you need to either be `root`, use the `sudo` command, or use the `-p` option, which causes `niutil` and `niload` to prompt you for the `root` password.

TABLE 23.1 The Syntax and Popular Options for `niutil`

niutil	The NetInfo Utility niutil is used to edit the NetInfo database.
niutil -create [*opts*] *<domain>* *<path>*	
niutil -destroy [*opts*] *<domain>* *<path>*	
niutil -createprop [*opts*] *<domain>* *<path>* *<key>* [*<val>*...]	
niutil -appendprop [*opts*] *<domain>* *<path>* *<key>* *<val>*...	
niutil -mergeprop [*opts*] *<domain>* *<path>* *<key>* *<val>*...	
niutil -insertval [*opts*] *<domain>* *<path>* *<key>* *<val>* *<index>*	
niutil -destroyprop [*opts*] *<domain>* *<path>* *<key>*	
niutil -destroyval [*opts*] *<domain>* *<path>* *<key>* *<val>*	

TABLE 23.1 Continued

`niutil -renameprop [opts] <domain> <path> <oldkey> <newkey>`	
`niutil -read [opts] <domain> <path>`	
`niutil -list [opts] <domain> <path>`	
`niutil -readprop <domain> <path> <key>`	
`niutil -readval <domain> <path> <key> <index>`	
`niutil -rparent [opts] <domain>`	
`niutil -resync [opts] <domain>`	
`niutil -statistics [opts] <domain>`	
`niutil -domainname [opts] <domain>`	
`niutil` performs arbitrary reads and writes on the specified NetInfo *<domain>*. To perform writes, `niutil` must be run as `root` on the NetInfo master for the database, unless `-p`, `-P`, or `-u` is specified. The directory specified by *<path>* is separated by / characters. A numeric ID may be used for a path in place of a string. Property names may be given in a path with an =. The default property name is `name`. The following examples refer to a user with user ID 3:	
`/name=users/uid=3`	
`/users/uid=3`	
`-t <host>/<tag>`	Interprets the domain as a tagged domain. For example, `parrish/network` is the domain tagged network on machine `parrish`.
`-p`	Prompts for the `root` password or the password of *<user>* if combined with `-u`.
`-u <user>`	Authenticates as *<user>*. Implies `-p`.
Operations	
`-create <domain> <path>`	Creates a new directory with the specified path.
`-destroy <domain> <path>`	Destroys the directory with the specified path.
`-createprop <domain> <path> <key> [<val>...]`	Creates a new property in the directory *<path>*. *<key>* is the name of the property. Zero or more property values *<key>* `[<val>...]` may be specified. The property is created empty if no `<val>`s are provided. If the named property already exists, it is overwritten.
`-appendprop <domain> <path> <key> <val>...`	Appends new values to an existing property in directory *<path>*. *<key>* is the name of the property. Zero or more property values `<key> <val>..` may be specified. If the named property does not exist, it is created.
`-insertval <domain> <path> <key> <val> <index>`	Inserts a new value into an existing property in the directory *<path>* at position *<index>*. *<key>* is the name of the `<key> <val>` property. If the named property does not exist, it is created.
`-destroyprop <domain> <path> <key>`	Destroys the property with name *<key>* in the specified *<path>*.
`-destroyval <domain> <path> <key> <val>`	Destroys the specified value in the property named *<key>* in the specified *<path>*.

TABLE 23.1 Continued

-read <domain> <path>	Reads the properties associated with the directory <path> in the specified <domain>.
-list <domain> <path>	Lists the directories in the specified <domain> and <path>. Directory IDs are listed along with directory names.
-readprop <domain> <path><path> <key>	Reads the value of the property named <key> in the directory of the specified <domain>.
-readval <domain> <path> <key> <index>	Reads the value at the given <index> of the named <key> property in the specified directory.
-rparent <domain>	Prints the current NetInfo parent of a server. The server should be explicitly given using the -t <host>/<tag> option.
-statistics <domain>	Prints server statistics on the specified <domain>.
-domainname <domain>	Prints the domain name of the given domain.

At the same time you were introduced to the niutil command in Chapter 11 (back when this command-line stuff might have seemed a bit more confusing), you were introduced to the niload command. This command is provided to simplify conversion between traditional Unix flat-file configuration files and NetInfo, as well as to provide a way of getting data into NetInfo on a per-directory basis, instead of the per-value method to which niutil is limited.

Table 23.2 shows the command documentation table for niload, which we will use throughout this chapter.

TABLE 23.2 The Command Documentation Table for niload

niload	niload populates NetInfo directories with multiple properties at once.
niload [-v] [-d] [-m] [-p] [-t] {-r <directory> ¦ <format>} <domain>	
niload loads information from standard output into the specified NetInfo <domain>. If <format> is specified, the input is interpreted according to the flat-file format <format>. Acceptable values for <format> are aliases, bootparams, bootptab, exports, fstab, group, hosts, networks, passwd, printcap, protocols, rpc, and services.	
If -r <directory> is specified instead of a flat-file format, the input is interpreted as raw NetInfo data, as generated by nidump -r, and is loaded into <directory>.	
niload overwrites entries in the existing directory with those contained in the input. Entries that are in the directory, but not in the input, are not deleted unless -d is specified. niload must be run as the superuser on the master NetInfo server for <domain>, unless -p is specified.	
-v	Verbose mode. Prints + for each entry loaded, and - for each entry deleted (flat-file formats only).
-d	Deletes entries that already exist in the directory but that aren't duplicated in the input.
-p	Prompts for the root password of the given domain so that the command can be run from locations other than the master.

TABLE 23.2 Continued

`-m`	Merge into an existing NetInfo structure instead of overwriting in the case of collisions.
`-u` *<user>*	Authenticates as *<user>*. Implies `-p`.
`-P` *<password>*	Provides *<password>* on the command line. Overrides `-p`.
`-t`	Interprets the domain as a tagged domain. For example, `trotter/network` refers to the `domain network` on the machine `trotter`. Machine name can be specified as an actual name or an IP address.
`-r`	Loads entries in raw format, as generated by `nidump -r`. The first argument should be the path of a NetInfo directory into which the information is loaded. The specified directory may be renamed as a result of contents of the input, particularly if the input includes a top-level `name` property. If the specified directory does not exist, it is created.
<domain>	NetInfo *<domain>* that is receiving input. If `.` is the value for *<domain>*, it is referring to the local NetInfo database.

Using the NetInfo Database and NFS to Share Resources

In this section, we demonstrate ways that your OS X machine can share resources with other Unix machines using NFS, the Network File System. We demonstrate two ways to set up your OS X machine as an NFS client and one way to use it as an NFS server.

A Common Way to Set Up an NFS Client in OS X

In this section, we demonstrate a common method for setting up an NFS client on an OS X machine. We show you this method because you will see references to this type of code, for this and other NetInfo-related activities, regularly on the Internet. Sometimes this type of method is the only method you can choose, so you need to be familiar with it. Sometimes, though, an alternative method might work better. For your OS X machine to be a client machine, there has to be another Unix machine that is an NFS server. In other words, there has to be a Unix machine (Mac OS X or another flavor of Unix) on your network that is willing to export one of its filesystems to your OS X machine. So, you cannot just set up your machine as a client and assume that everything will work fine. Discuss your interest in being able to use your OS X machine to access a filesystem on another Unix machine with that machine's system administrator. There is a security risk involved, particularly for the other machine, when it shares its resources with your machine. Therefore, in that machine's interest, the system administrator might not be willing to export its filesystems to your machine.

There might be some additional details to work out with your NFS server system administrator that we will not discuss in depth here, assuming that he feels you will responsibly control your machine and your use of the NFS server's resources. To avoid confusion on the remote host machine, it would be a good idea for users who are accessing the other machine's filesystem from your machine to have the same user and group IDs that they might already have on the remote host machine. Depending on how the remote host is set up, this may be no problem at all, or a considerable annoyance. For example, if the remote host does not have user IDs in the same range as the users on your machine, the unusual user IDs might not be a problem. However, if users on your machine have user IDs in the same range as users on the remote host, files you create on the remote host with your user ID will be viewed by the remote host as being owned by the user native to that system—that is, by whatever user lives on that system and has the same user ID.

At any rate, if the system administrator of the remote machine agrees to export to your machine whichever filesystem you are interested in using, be aware that you still might have to work out some additional details with the system administrator. NFS gives both the client and server considerably more control over exactly how resources are shared (down to details such as how long to wait for a disk to become available again, if the network goes away) than a "point and mount" protocol such as AppleTalk/AppleShare. As your understanding of how to update the NetInfo database continues to improve in this chapter, any changes the system administrator of the remote host might request for your OS X machine should not be difficult to make.

With that said, let's continue to the details of setting up an NFS client on your OS X machine. To be an NFS client, your machine needs to be running the right services. If you did not turn off any of the major default services, you do not need to worry about this. If you turned off NFS in the `/System/Library/StartupItems/` directory, you have to turn it back on to be able to run your NFS client.

NOTE

You're not supposed to need to change these settings, but if your experience is like ours, the "AUTOMATIC" settings for `NFSLOCKS` and `RPCSERVER` specified in `/etc/hostconfig` won't actually work automatically for you. To get things working, we needed to edit `/etc/hostconfig` and set both of these to `YES`.

It would also be a good idea to read the man pages for `mount`, `mount_nfs`, and `fstab`. The information that you will be adding to the NetInfo database is information regarding where your machine should mount a particular filesystem that resides on a remote host. When you are finished updating the NetInfo database, the remote host's filesystem appears to be local to your own machine.

We include the syntax and primary options for the `mount` and `mount_nfs` commands in tables at the end of this section. More complete documentation is in Appendix A, though a complete discussion of how to fully use all the power of NFS is the entire subject of more than one book.

CAUTION

You might need to disable the automounter to get your machine to properly mount NFS directories. This is accomplished by changing the setting in `/etc/hostconfig` to `NO`. This change was not necessary under 10.1.x versions of OS X and, based on some information on the Internet, is not the case for all users of 10.2 and 10.3. However, we have seen several machines where the behavior of NFS is pathologically wrong when the automounter is enabled. The symptoms of the problem are

- The directory to which you attempt to `mount` the remote filesystem is deleted and replaced by a symbolic link to a directory in the `/automount/` directory.
- The directory in the `/automount/` cannot be entered, `ls`ed, or otherwise read, but `mount` claims that the remote directory is mounted.
- The remote directory cannot be `unmount`ed without rebooting the machine; you may also find that any attempt to read the supposedly mounted directory (even just trying to get its name to autoexpand at the command line using `<TAB>`) causes your shell to hang indefinitely.

If you experience these problems and still want to use NFS, disable the automounter by changing its `YES` entry to `NO` in `/etc/hostconfig`, and reboot your machine. With automount off, NFS should work in much more the fashion that the documentation suggests.

AUTOMOUNTER ANTIFANS

We aren't big fans of the automounter (`/usr/sbin/automount`). Even when it's working, it seems like the wrong thing to do. The automounter is supposed to be this magical (or at least poorly documented) utility that remembers filesystems that have been previously mounted and remounts them automatically whenever they're needed. The problem with this idea, other than the fact that in our cumulative 40-odd years of using Unix we've never seen a nontrivial system using `automount` where `automount` actually worked the way anyone wanted it to, is that `automount` removes control from the machine's administrator. You want to mount a directory of data under `/usr/local/data/`? The automounter, in all its wisdom, will insist on mounting it under `/automounter/` and making a symbolic link to its mount point. Have software that won't work through a symbolic link? Tough. What's worse, on some systems, after it's seen a filesystem once, the automounter will keep mounting (or trying to mount) that filesystem forever, even after you've removed the control definition and tried to make it stop. With the exquisite level to which we're used to being able to configure and control our hardware, this behavior is simply unacceptable for a Unix machine.

No, we aren't fans of the automounter at all, and we generally have it turned off on our systems just as a matter of principle. We won't tell you that you have to turn it off, and for lack of documentation, we aren't even sure what unusual twists Apple might have woven into its version. To make NFS work at all on the machines we tested 10.2 with, the automounter needed to be turned off. We haven't had much trouble with 10.3, but it's been enough of a problem that we just don't trust it, so our examples are going to be based on the assumption that it's turned off. Some people make `automount` work on their machines and are happy with how it works, so you very well might be able to make these examples work, or manage a setup in your own preferred configuration without shutting off `automount`. If you can, wonderful—perhaps `automount` just hates us old curmudgeons.

To add a filesystem from a remote host to your OS X machine, do the following:

1. Back up your NetInfo database.
2. Plan where you want your OS X machine to mount the remote host's filesystem. Unlike what you may be familiar with on AppleShare volumes, which mount as "drives" on the desktop, NFS filesystems can be grafted into your directory tree anywhere. Essentially, the directory structure rooted at the directory or filesystem that is exported, can be made to appear exactly as it does on the remote host, as though it were any subdirectory of your choosing on your system.

   The purpose of the remote filesystem might guide you in deciding where to mount it on your machine. For example, it is common, when a filesystem with a users' home directories are involved, that a machine mounting such a filesystem frequently does so in a directory hierarchy of /net/<*remote_host*>/home. If the remote filesystem is simply a filesystem used for storage, any way you want to mount it is probably suitable. Temporary mounts that you don't expect to reuse later are frequently done as subdirectories of /mnt/. Of course, you can change the name of the mount point and remount the filesystem later if you find that you do not like what you picked. Extra thought up front is particularly important, though, when the remote filesystem is used for users' home directories, because more people than just yourself will need to know about and understand any changes that you make later on down the road.

   In our example, we are going to mount a filesystem used for storage. On our machine, we want it to be mounted in a directory called /morespace/mother (mother is the name of the host that will serve the filesystem). We're creating the mount point in a subdirectory of the root directory, rather than directly in the root directory, because we might eventually want to add other storage filesystems from other remote hosts, and we want to be able to keep them straight. Another consideration would be a hierarchy similar to typical user hierarchies, such as /net/<*remote_host*>/morespace. If it's the only filesystem of its type that'll be mounted, there's no real need to have the mount point clearly include the host of origin.

   After you have decided what to call the mount point, make it—mount points are simply directories. They don't even have to be empty if you want the directory to contain one set of files when you have the remote system mounted and another when it's not. (A particularly nifty option available in the OS X NFS client, union filesystems, allows you to see the files in both the local and remote directories simultaneously. See the mount_nfs docs for more information.)

   ```
   brezup:root ray # cd /
   brezup:root / # mkdir morespace
   brezup:root / # mkdir morespace/mother
   brezup:root / # ls morespace/mother
   brezup:root / #
   ```

3. Using your favorite text editor, create a file with the contents of the following form:

```
{
"opts" = ( "w" );
"dir" = ( "/<mountpoint>/" );
"name" = ( "<remote_host>:<remote_filesystem>");
"vfstype" = ( "nfs" );
}
```

Save it with Unix line endings rather than Mac line endings. Check again, to make sure that you really did.

Although many options are available for mounting, the one you will probably find most important initially is the read/write option—after you've got that working, tweaking the nearly endless variety of options to customize the connection can be done at your leisure. On most systems, that option is `rw`. In OS X, that option is `w`, although using the traditional `rw` also appears to work.

Here is a copy of the file we used:

```
{
"opts" = ( "w" );
"dir" = ( "/morespace/mother" );
"name" = ( "192.168.1.4:/innerspace");
"vfstype" = ( "nfs" );
}
```

`/morespace/mother` is where I want the remote filesystem to appear, `192.168.1.4` is the machine (also known as `mother`) serving it to me, and on `mother`, the directory that I'll be mounting is named `/innerspace`. I've named this file `mount-test.txt`, and it's in my current directory.

4. Run `niutil` to create a new directory in the `mounts` directory of the NetInfo database:

```
brezup:root / # niutil -create . /mounts/new1
```

The `new1` directory name is not important, it's going to be overwritten by information we're going to load into the database.

5. Run `niload` to load the file into the NetInfo database:

```
brezup:root / # niload -r /mounts/new1 . < mount-test.txt
```

Notice that because you're providing a `name` and `value` in the data you're loading, the `niload` command renames the `new1` subdirectory you just created. If you type as well as we do, you might have to run that statement a few times before it works. You might get messages indicating that there is an error at some line number in your input file. Just look at your file carefully and fix whatever needs to be fixed (especially, watch for things such as having saved the file with Mac line endings rather than Unix line endings).

6. Look at the updates in the `mounts` section of the NetInfo database either using the command line or the NetInfo Manager. If you are using the command line, you might find it easier to see the values by directory number rather than directory name.

   Here are the command-line results in our example as seen using `niutil`:

```
brezup:root / # niutil -list . /mounts
82      192.168.1.4:/innerspace
brezup:root / # niutil -read . 82
opts: w
dir: /morespace/mother
name: 192.168.1.4:/innerspace
vfstype: nfs
```

7. After you have verified that the updates to your NetInfo database are correct, tell your machine to mount the filesystem, and take a look at what's happened:

```
brezup:root / # ls /morespace/mother/
brezup:root / #
brezup:root / # mount -t nfs -a
brezup:root / # ls /morespace/mother/
apache_1.3.26                tcpwrappers
apache_1.3.26-src.tar            wu-ftpd-2.6.1-linux-anon
danspage                   wu-ftpd-2.6.1-linux-anon.tar.gz
fcsafiles                  wu-ftpd-2.6.1-linux-both
ftpaccess-mother-anon            wu-ftpd-2.6.1-linux-both.tar.gz
.
.
.
```

   Suddenly, there's data in `/morespace/mother/`. However, it's not actually in `/morespace/mother/`; it's actually on the remote machine `192.168.1.4`. This machine is only on the other side of the room, but there's no reason it couldn't be on the other side of the country.

At this point, you're supposed to be able to reboot your machine, and it should automatically mount that filesystem back up, without you needing to use the `mount` command. If your automounter is turned on, it'll definitely try (and it'll probably delete your `/morespace/mother/` mount point for you while it tries). With it turned off, it doesn't appear that Apple takes the customary action of having a `mount -t nfs -a` command in its startup scripts, so you may need to add your own custom startup script to run `mount` for you.

23

When you get this working at startup, or if `automount` is working for you, it might seem as if it takes your machine a little longer to reboot. This is to be expected.

TIP

If you later notice that it's suddenly taking a lot longer to start up, it might be because the NFS server that you've been mounting is not available. Depending on the options you configure, this can cause your machine to hang indefinitely. Such indefinite hangs aren't inevitable, however; check the man pages for the details regarding retries, and under what conditions clients should allow a mount to fail.

In addition to using `mount` to `mount` filesystems, you can run `mount` to see what is `mounted` where:

```
brezup:root / # mount
/dev/disk1s3 on / (local, journaled)
devfs on /dev (local)
fdesc on /dev (union)
<volfs> on /.vol
/dev/disk0s9 on /Volumes/Racer-9 (local)
/dev/disk0s10 on /Volumes/Racer-X (local)
/dev/disk0s11 on /Volumes/Wills_Data (local)
/dev/disk0s12 on /Volumes/Software (local)
/dev/disk0s13 on /Volumes/Temp (local)
192.168.1.4:/innerspace on /morespace/mother
```

The `df` command also tells you a bit about your mounts:

```
brezup:root / # df
Filesystem        512-blocks   Used  Avail Capacity Mounted on
/dev/disk1s3        9715208 9093872 524184  95%   /
devfs             196    196     0   100%  /dev
fdesc              2     2     0   100%  /dev
<volfs>            1024    1024     0   100%  /.vol
/dev/disk0s9        1258104  994768 263336  79%  /Volumes/Racer-9
/dev/disk0s10       10484800 9073632 1411168  87%  /Volumes/Racer-X
/dev/disk0s11       12581856 12147328 434528  97%  /Volumes/Wills_Data
/dev/disk0s12       10484800 8255520 2229280  79%  /Volumes/Software
/dev/disk0s13       4255160 3333520 921640  78%  /Volumes/Temp
192.168.1.4:/innerspace  799494  677500  80716  89%  /morespace/mother
```

Before we go on, let's look a little more closely at the directory that's coming from the `mother` server. Some of the things that you see with `ls` might be slightly unexpected:

```
brezup:root / # ls -l /morespace/mother/
total 150318
drwxr-xr-x 9 ray      ray       1024 27 Jun 2002 apache_1.3.26
-rw-r--r-- 1 ray      ray    9728000 20 Jun 2002 apache_1.3.26-src.tar
drwxr-xr-x 7 software wheel     1024 26 Jul 1999 danspage
drwxr-xr-x 2 ray      wheel     1024 23 Feb 2000 fcsafiles
-rw-r--r-- 1 root     wheel     1918 4 Dec 2001 ftpaccess-mother-anon
-rw-r--r-- 1 root     wheel     2046 4 Dec 2001 ftpaccess-mother-w2ftp
drwxr-xr-x 2 ray      ray       1024 23 Aug 2002 ispell
-rw-r--r-- 1 ray      ray   14239859 28 Apr 2002 j2re-1_3_1_01-linux-i386-rpm
-rw-r--r-- 1 root     wheel 14363657 8 Aug 2001 jre-1.3.1_01.i386.rpm
-rw-r--r-- 1 18940    101   29388800 15 Nov 2002
➥krb5-1.2.7-i686-pc-linux-gnu.tar
-rw-r--r-- 1 18940    101        303 15 Nov 2002
➥krb5-1.2.7-i686-pc-linux-gnu.tar.gz.asc
.
.
.
drwxr-xr-x 8 ray      10        1024 4 Dec 2001 wu-ftpd-2.6.2-linux-anon
-rw-r--r-- 1 root     wheel   956301 4 Dec 2001
➥wu-ftpd-2.6.2-linux-anon.tar.gz
drwxr-xr-x 8 ray      10        1024 4 Dec 2001
➥wu-ftpd-2.6.2-linux-w2ftp
-rw-r--r-- 1 root     wheel   956309 4 Dec 2001
➥wu-ftpd-2.6.2-linux-w2ftp.tar.gz
-rw-r--r-- 1 600      software  351958 4 Dec 2001 wu-ftpd-2.6.2-src.tar.gz
```

Notice how some of the files don't have proper owners and/or groups, and instead show only numeric `UID` and `GID` entries. This is because I don't have the `user` and `groups` list synchronized between these machines. `mother`'s a Linux box that sits in the kitchen and runs my home network, so I have a few users on it that match, but I do most of my work on my OS X laptop. Because of this, I've configured `mother` so that the main user IDs and groups that I use on both machines match up, but there are a number of users on each that are unique to that system. The `UID/GID` matching for mounted directories is done based on the numeric value of the `UID` and `GID`, so the shared users appear to own their own files, but the nonshared users and groups coming from `mother` have no analogous users on my OS X laptop, so they only show up as numbers. As a matter of fact, from NFS's point of view there's really no guarantee that `mother` doesn't think that the numeric `UID` that my laptop knows as `ray`, is really named `fred`. And from my laptop's point of view, it really doesn't care what `mother` thinks the usernames are; it's just showing names based on what its NetInfo users list says goes with the numeric `UID`s and `GID`s that `mother`'s reporting for the files.

In addition to listing and looking at statistics about the remote filesystem, you can of course now access the remote filesystem as if it were local to your machine.

As mentioned earlier, you might have to work out some details with the system administrator of the remote machine. One of the details you might have to work out is making sure that there is a directory on that filesystem that you are allowed to write to. In our example, there is a public directory on the remote filesystem that we are allowed to use. The `mount` options can be configured to allow all users writing access, only some users, only some users to only some directories, and an assortment of other useful combinations.

An Easier Way to Set Up an NFS Client in OS X

As you might recall from the section on adding a printer through the command line, the `niload` command can recognize some regular Unix flat-file formats. The format we saw earlier, `printcap`, is one of them. It turns out that the file that controls mount points, `fstab`, is another of those formats.

We recommend that, where possible, you use `niload` in combination with formats it might already recognize rather than have it load in raw NetInfo format. Because the Unix flat-file formats are easier to type, you will make fewer typos. In addition, if you take the time to familiarize yourself with the regular Unix flat files, you will be even better prepared to understand information that relates to other Unix platforms. Even though your the traditional formats are options for your system, most of the rest of the Unix-using world is comfortable with them and will give advice and suggestions using these formats. When you've loaded data from a file in a traditional control format into NetInfo, always take the time to check the information that's landed in the NetInfo database, not only to confirm that everything was done properly, but also to learn the native OS X formats.

In this section, we show you an easier way to enter the mounts information into the NetInfo database than the one we used for `/morespace/mother/`. Although this is easier, be aware that you still have to coordinate with the system administrator of the remote host.

To set up an NFS client on an OS X machine, you can also do the following:

1. Back up the NetInfo database.
2. Create the local mount point for the remote filesystem.
3. Create a one-line file containing the mount information. The one-line file has these fields, which can be separated by spaces or tabs:

Field	Value
1	Remote filesystem to be mounted, including the machine it's being mounted from. The syntax is as shown earlier: `<machine>:<directory to mount>`.
2	Local `mount` point.
3	Filesystem type (for NFS, it's `nfs`).

4	`mount` options.
5	Interval between dumps.
6	Order in which `fsck` is run at boot time.

Fields `5` and `6` are traditional parts of the format but do not apply to remote filesystems. Those values can either be absent or can be `0`.

Here is the `fstab` used in this examples—note that we can use `rosalyn` as the server name here instead of a fully qualified domain name (complete hostname) because this machine is in the same domain as `rosalyn`, and we have configured this domain as a local search domain via the Network control pane. You may need to use either a FQDN, or an IP address for the server, depending on your configuration:

```
rosalyn:/space /extraspace nfs rw 0 0
```


4. Run `niload` to load the `fstab` format file into the NetInfo database. In our example, we used `fstab-test` as the `fstab` formatted file:

```
brezup:root / # niload fstab . < fstab-test
```

Verify that the data was loaded properly into the NetInfo database using either the command line or the NetInfo Manager.

5. Mount the filesystem with `mount -t nfs -a`, and check your results as previously demonstrated.

Run the same sorts of command-line tools you ran in the previous section, such as `mount` and `ls`. If your automounter is working for you, you might also want to check the list of volumes on your OS X desktop, and/or the `/Computer/Network/Servers` path in the Finder, because you will hopefully find a pleasant surprise there too. Behavior here seems inconsistent, and what mount points will be seen as remote servers and what won't are still a bit of a mystery to us.

NOTE

Any changes you make to the NFS mounts by tweaking the NetInfo database and manually running `mount` are available immediately via the command line. If you want to make the NFS mounts available via the Finder immediately as well, you may need to reboot after making your changes to the mounts in the NetInfo database. There's undoubtedly a process or two that could be restarted to cause the Finder to recognize the existence of the new network disk resources, but we haven't made this work reliably yet. Restarting is slow, but bulletproof.

Table 23.3 shows the syntax and most useful options for `mount`, and Table 23.4 covers `mount_nfs`, the underlying command that `mount` calls. Table 23.5 covers `umount`. The complete documentation is available in Appendix A.

TABLE 23.3 The `mount` Command Syntax and Important Options

`mount`	Mounts filesystems.
`mount`	
`mount [-adfruvw] [-t ufs ¦ lfs ¦ `*<external_type>*`]`	
`mount [-dfruvw]` *<special>* ¦ *<node>*	
`mount [-dfruvw] [-o `*<options>*`] [-t ufs ¦ lfs ¦ `*<external_type>*`]` *<special>* ¦ *<node>*	
`mount` invokes a filesystem-specific program to prepare and graft the *<special>* device or remote node (`rhost:path`) on the filesystem tree at the point *<node>*. If neither *<special>* nor *<node>* is specified, the appropriate information is taken from the `fstab` file.	
The system maintains a list of currently mounted filesystems. If no arguments are given to `mount`, this list is displayed.	
`-a`	All the filesystems described in your NetInfo `mounts` directory or `fstab` (5) control file are mounted. Exceptions are those marked as `noauto` or are excluded by the `-t` flag.
`-r`	Mounts the filesystem read-only (even `root` may not write to it). The same as the `rdonly` subargument to the `-o` option.
`-u`	Indicates that the status of an already mounted filesystem should be changed. Any of the options available in `-o` may be changed. The filesystem may be changed from read-only to read-write, or vice versa. An attempt to change from read-write to read-only fails if any files on the filesystem are currently open for writing unless `-f` is also specified.
`-v`	Enables verbose mode.
`-w`	Sets the filesystem object to read-write.
`-t ufs ¦ lfs ¦`*<external_type>*	Specifies a filesystem type. Default is type `ufs`. The option can also be used to indicate that the actions should be performed only on the specified filesystem type. More than one type may be specified in a comma-separated list. The prefix `no` added to the type list may be used to specify that the actions should not take place on a given type. For example, `mount -a -t nonfs,mfs` indicates that all filesystems should be mounted except those of type NFS and MFS. `mount` attempts to execute a program called `mount_XXX` where `XXX` is the specified typename.
`-o`	Specifies certain options. The options are specified in a comma-separated list.
The following options are available for the `-o` option:	
`noauto`	Skips this filesystem when `mount` is run with the `-a` flag.
`nodev`	Does not interpret character or block special devices on the filesystem. The option is useful for a server that has filesystems containing special devices for architectures other than its own.
`noexec`	Does not allow the execution of any binaries on the mounted filesystem. This option is useful for a server containing binaries for an architecture other than its own.
`nosuid`	Does not allow `set-user-identifier` or `set-group-identifier` bits to take effect.

TABLE 23.3 Continued

`rdonly`	Same as `-r`. Mounts the filesystem read-only. Even `root` may not write to it.
`union`	Causes the namespace (that is, the files that appear there) at the `mount` point to appear as the union of the mounted filesystem `root` and the existing directory. Lookups are done on the mounted filesystem first. If operations fail due to a nonexistent file, the underlying filesystem is accessed instead. All new files and directories are created in the mounted filesystem.
Any additional options specific to a given filesystem type may be passed as a comma-separated list. The options are distinguished by a leading `-`. Options that take a value have the syntax -<*option*>=<*value*>.	

TABLE 23.4 The `mount_nfs` Syntax and Important Options

`mount_nfs`	Mounts NFS filesystems.
mount_nfs [-23KPTUbcdilqs] [-D <*deadthresh*>] [-I <*readdirsize*>] [-L <*leaseterm*>] [-R <*retrycnt*>] [-a <*maxreadahead*>] [-g <*maxgroups*>] [-m <*realm*>] [-o <*options*>] [-r <*read-size*>] [-t <*timeout*>] [-w <*writesize*>] [-x <*retrans*>] <*rhost*>:<*path*> <*node*>	
`-T`	Uses TCP transport instead of UDP. This is recommended for servers not on the same LAN cable as the client. This is not supported by most non-BSD servers.
`-U`	Forces the `mount` protocol to use UDP transport, even for TCP NFS mounts. Necessary for some old BSD servers.
`-b`	Backgrounds the `mount`. If a `mount` fails, forks a child process that keeps trying the `mount` in the background. This option is useful for a filesystem not critical to multiuser operation.
`-c`	Does not do a `connect` (2) for UDP mounts. This must be used for servers that do not reply to requests from the standard NFS port number 2049. It may also be required for servers with more than one IP address, if replies come from an address other than the one specified in the `mount` request.
`-d`	Turns off the dynamic retransmit timeout estimator. This may be useful for UDP mounts that exhibit high retry rates; it is possible for the dynamically estimated timeout to be too short.
`-i`	Makes the `mount` interruptible. The filesystem calls that are delayed due to an unresponsive server fail with `EINTR` when a termination signal is posted for the process.
`-s`	Soft `mount`. Filesystem calls `fail` after <*retrycnt*> round-trip timeout intervals.
-R <*retrycnt*>	Sets the retry count for doing the mount to <*retrycnt*>.
-a <*maxreadahead*>	Sets the read-ahead count to <*maxreadahead*>. This value may be in the 0–4 range, and determines how many blocks are read ahead when a large file is being read sequentially. A value larger than 1 is suggested for `mounts` with a large bandwidth * delay product.
-o <*options*>	Options are specified as a comma-separated list of options. See `mount` (8) for a listing of the available options.

TABLE 23.4 Continued

`-r` *<readsize>*	Sets the `read` data size to *<readsize>*. It should normally be a power of 2 >= 1024. This should be used for UDP mounts when the fragments dropped due to timeout value are getting large while actively using a `mount` point. Use `netstat` (1) `-s` to get the fragments dropped due to timeout value. See the `-w` option.
`-t` *<timeout>*	Sets the initial retransmit timeout to *<timeout>*. May be useful for fine-tuning UDP mounts over networks with high packet loss rates or an overloaded server. Try increasing the interval if `nfsstat` (1) shows high retransmit rates while the filesystem is active, or try reducing the value if there is a low retransmit rate but long response delay observed. Normally the `-d` option is also used when using this option to fine-tune the timeout interval.
`-w` *<writesize>*	Sets the write data size to *<writesize>*. See comments regarding the `-r` option, but using the fragments dropped due to timeout value on the server rather than the client. The `-r` and `-w` options should only be used as a last resort to improve performance when mounting servers that do not support TCP `mounts`.
`-x` *<retrans>*	Sets the retransmit timeout count for soft `mounts` to *<retrans>*.

TABLE 23.5 The Syntax and Primary Options for `umount`

`umount`	Unmounts filesystems.
`umount [-fv]` *<special>* ¦ *<node>*	
`umount -a ¦ -A [-fv] [-h` *<host>*`] [-t` *<type>*`]`	
`-f`	Forcibly unmounts the filesystem. Active special devices continue to work, but all other files return errors if further accesses are attempted. The `root` filesystem cannot be forcibly unmounted.
`-v`	Enables verbose mode.
`-a`	All the filesystems described in `fstab` (5) are unmounted.
`-A`	All the currently mounted filesystems except the `root` are unmounted.
`-h` *<host>*	Unmounts only filesystems mounted from the specified *<host>*. This option implies the `-A` option and, unless otherwise specified with the `-t` option, will only unmount NFS filesystems.
`-t` *<type>*_	Is used to indicate that actions should only be taken on filesystems of the specified *<type>*. More than one type may be specified in a comma-separated list. The list of filesystem types can be prefixed with `no` to specify the filesystem types for which action should not be taken. For example, the `umount` command: `umount -a -t nfs,mfs` unmounts all filesystems of the type NFS and MFS.

Setting Up Your OS X Machine to Be an NFS Server

As the prices of IDE storage continue to drop, the absolute necessity to share disk space is disappearing. Still, it's often convenient if you can share your files and disk space to other machines you use, so that work you do on one is available on all. If you are interested in serving one of your filesystems to another OS X machine, AppleShare might be good enough for some purposes, but NFS works for serving data to any Unix machine. Because we find NFS to be both more powerful and more complicated to get right, and AppleShare to be almost completely automated by the single check box in the Sharing system pane, we'll detail exporting your filesystems as NFS resources.

Just as setting up your machine to be an NFS client requires coordination with the system administrator of the remote Unix machine, so does serving a filesystem to a remote Unix machine. Remember, this reduces security on both systems, especially yours. Do not consider doing this unless you can trust the remote host.

Depending on the system setups, coordination between user IDs might be necessary, especially if you want to make the drive available to users other than yourself. The other system administrator should be able to guide you through any additional details that might need to be coordinated.

The other Unix system administrator will set up the remote host to be able to mount your filesystem. You will have to set up your machine to export a filesystem to a remote host. At this time, you should read the `exports` man page.

If you plan to create your exports through the command line, you might want to take this opportunity to look at the `nidump` command as well. As the name suggests, `nidump` dumps information from the NetInfo database to standard output. It can dump information to a flat file in a number of traditional Unix configuration file formats. It can also dump information in a format that can be read back into and understood by the NetInfo database. This format is both more general and less conveniently human-readable than the typical Unix flat configuration-file format. Because it's a generalized format that works for any NetInfo data, it can be used to import data for directory structures that don't have an analogous Unix flat-file format. To learn more about this format, you might find running `nidump` on one of the NetInfo directories that you know something about to be a useful way of seeing the syntax used to create a new directory and directories under it.

Here is what the `nidump` output from the `mount` examples in the previous section looks like:

```
[localhost:~] software% nidump -r /mounts .

{
 "name" = ( "mounts" );
 CHILDREN = (
  {
   "vfstype" = ( "nfs" );
   "passno" = ( "0" );
   "dir" = ( "/extraspace" );
   "dump_freq" = ( "0" );
   "name" = ( "rosalyn:/space" );
   "opts" = ( "w" );
```

```
  },
  {
   "opts" = ( "w" );
   "dir" = ( "/morespace/mother" );
   "name" = ( "1921.68.1.4:/innerspace" );
   "vfstype" = ( "nfs" );
  }
 )
}
```

Not only does nidump provide an example of the syntax used to create a directory and subdirectories, but the output from an nidump command can also provide the basis for a file that you could edit for setting up your exports. This would already provide much of the complicated part of the syntax and enable you to just edit values suitable for exports instead.

Table 23.6 shows the complete documentation for nidump.

TABLE 23.6 The nidump Utility Can Export NetInfo Data to Plain Text Formats

nidump	Extracts text or flat-file format data from NetInfo.
nidump [-t] { -r *<directory>* ¦ *<format>* } *<domain>*	
nidump reads the specified NetInfo domain and dumps a portion of its contents to standard output. When a flat-file administration format is specified, nidump provides output in the syntax of the corresponding flat file. Allowed values for *<format>* are aliases, bootparams, bootptab, exports, fstab, group, hosts, networks, passwd, printcap, protocols, rpc, and services.	
If -r is used, the first argument is interpreted as a NetInfo directory path, and its contents are dumped in a generic NetInfo format.	
-t	Interprets the domain as a tagged name.
-r	Dumps the specified directory in raw format. Directories are delimited in curly brackets. Properties within a directory are listed in the form property = value;. Parentheses introduce a comma-separated list of items. The special property name CHILDREN is used to hold a directory's children, if any. Spacing and line breaks are significant only within double quotes, which can be used to protect any names with meta characters.

To set up your OS X machine to export a filesystem to a remote Unix host, do the following:

1. Back up the NetInfo database.

2. If you plan to export a filesystem that currently contains a space in the name, change its name to something that does not have a space. Mac OS and now Mac OS X deal with spaces okay, but they confuse many more traditional Unix systems. If

you're only going to be working among Mac OS X systems, spaces might be all right, but you'll probably find that they will eventually be trouble. The same goes for most characters outside basic alphanumerics.

3. Enter `exports` information into the NetInfo database. Unfortunately, despite what the man page says, the `niload` command currently does not understand the typical `exports` format. So, in this case, you cannot make an `exports` format file and load that into NetInfo. You must either make a file that follows the same kind of format we saw in the first `mount` example (the format with braces, parentheses, and quotes), or you must enter the information into the NetInfo database using the NetInfo Manager.

   Because I am so poor at balancing all the appropriate characters, parentheses, and quotes needed to make one of the raw NetInfo files, I prefer to do this through the NetInfo Manager. Our instructions are specifically for the NetInfo Manager. However, you should choose whichever method you are most comfortable with.

   Open the NetInfo Manager, and select the `local` domain. Click in the lock to make changes, and enter the administrator username and password. With the `root` (`/`) directory selected, select Directory, New Subdirectory from the menu. Change the name of `new_directory` to `exports`, and save the change.

4. Click the `exports` directory. Select Directory, New Subdirectory from the menu. Give this subdirectory the name of the filesystem you want to export. Save it. Now select the new directory and add a `clients` property whose value is a list of clients that the filesystem should be exported to—use `insert value` with the `clients` property selected to add multiple client values. Add an `opts` property with any options you want to specify, based on the `exports` man page—`ro` is common if you want the filesystem to be read-only to remote clients that mount it, whereas `rw` allows read-write access. `alldirs` allows clients to mount arbitrary subdirectories from the filesystem instead of the whole filesystem.

   Figure 23.1 shows the settings that we used for exporting our filesystem. Note that you should not use the `maproot` mapping option we used, *`maproot=root`*, unless you can trust the remote system and administrator as highly as you trust your own.

5. Save your changes to the `exports` directory and then restart the NetInfo servers for your local domain. Click the lock to prevent further changes.

6. Reboot the machine and then test the results. Alternatively, you can (as `root`) run `/System/Library/StartupItems/NFS/NFS start` (or, if you've already got NFS exports and are just making changes, `/System/Library/StartupItems/NFS/NFS restart`).

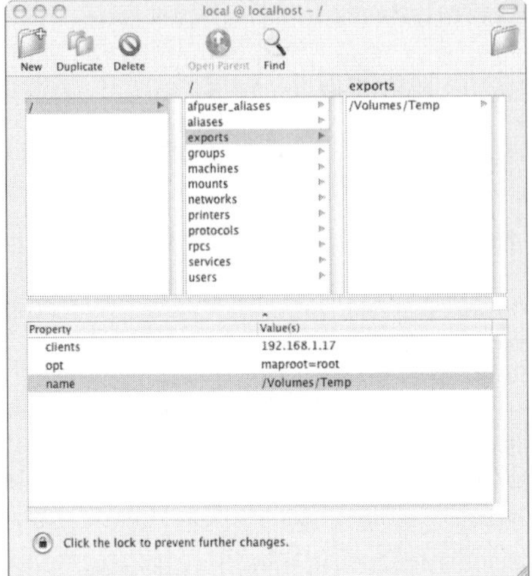

FIGURE 23.1 Here are the settings we used for exporting our `/Volumes/Temp` filesystem.

A quick test you can do on your OS X machine is to run `mount`:

```
brezup:ray ray $ mount
/dev/disk1s3 on / (local, journaled)
devfs on /dev (local)
fdesc on /dev (union)
<volfs> on /.vol
/dev/disk0s9 on /Volumes/Racer-9 (local)
/dev/disk0s10 on /Volumes/Racer-X (local)
/dev/disk0s11 on /Volumes/Wills_Data (local)
/dev/disk0s12 on /Volumes/Software (local)
/dev/disk0s13 on /Volumes/Temp (NFS exported, local)
rosalyn:/space on /extraspace
192.168.1.4:/innerspace on /morespace/mother
```

Note that the OS X machine indicates that `/Volumes/Temp` is being served as an NFS export as well as mounted locally.

Now you need to add your machine to the remote machine's mount list. If the remote machine is an OS X machine, this is just like adding the `morespace` or `extraspace` mount points we used in earlier examples. If the remote machine is a Linux box or other form of Unix boxen, the administrator needs to add an `fstab` line similar to what we used to load the `extraspace` mount into our NetInfo database.

Here, we're mounting brezup's /Volumes/Temp on rosalyn, a Sun Solaris machine at the mount point /net/brezup/huge. After the mount point is defined, run mount -t nfs -a on the remote machine.

Test that the remote host agrees with the OS X machine:

```
Rosalyn joray 87 > ls /net/brezup/huge
AppleShare PDS       TheFindByContentFolder  osx-misc.tar
Desktop DB          TheVolumeSettingsFolder test
Desktop DF          Trash              â¢T+â¢It's HUUUGE
Desktop Folder       lpd-spool-working.tar
```

If we check the filesystem locally, we find the same ls listing:

```
brezup:ray ray $ ls /Volumes/huge
AppleShare PDS        TheFindByContentFolder  osx-misc.tar
Desktop DB           TheVolumeSettingsFolder  test
Desktop DF           Trash              ???T+???It's HUUUGE
Desktop Folder         lpd-spool-working.tar
```

NOTE

Notice the file with the weird characters in the name in each listing. They appear to be different, because the character sets used by the two machines aren't quite the same, and neither one can display that name properly—it has Macintosh special characters in it.

After you are satisfied that the export is working properly, remember that your machine is now serving data to another machine. Consequently, it might seem as if it takes a little longer for it to shut down at shutdown or reboot time. Do not panic. This is expected. If you plan for your exported filesystem to be of regular use, try to keep the number of reboots to a minimum. After your machine starts serving data to another machine, it is not just your machine or a machine for your local users—it is a machine that users on a remote host could come to rely on.

Table 23.7 shows the syntax and primary configuaration options of exports entries. Complete documentation is available in Appendix A.

TABLE 23.7 The Syntax and Primary Configuration Options for exports Settings

exports	Defines remote mount points for NFS requests.

The exports file specifies remote mount points for NFS mount protocol per the NFS server specification. In a mount entry, the first field specifies the directory path within a server filesystem that clients can

TABLE 23.7 Continued

mount. There are two forms of this specification. The first form is to list all `mount` points as absolute directory paths separated by whitespace. The second form is to specify the pathname of the root of the filesystem followed by the `-alldirs` flag. This form allows hosts to mount at any point within the filesystem, including regular files if the `-r` option is used in `mountd`. The pathnames should not have any symbolic links, or . or . components.	
The second component of a line specifies how the filesystem is to be exported to the host set. The options specify whether the filesystem is exported read-only or read-write and how the client UID is mapped to user credentials on the server.	
The third component of a line specifies the client host set. The set may be specified in three ways. The first is to list the host names separated by whitespace. Standard Internet dot addresses may be used instead. The second way is to specify a netgroup, as defined in `netgroup`. The third way is to specify an Internet subnetwork using a network and network mask.	
Export options are as follows:	
`-maproot=user`	Credential of the specified user is used for remote access by `root`. The credential includes all groups to which the user is a member on the local machine. The user may be specified by name or number.
`-mapall=user`	
`-r`	Synonym for `-maproot` for backward compatibility with older export file formats.
When neither `-maproot` nor `-mapall` is specified, remote accesses by `root` result in a credential of `-2:-2`. All other users are mapped to their remote credential. If a `-maproot` option is given, remote access by `root` is mapped according to the specified value instead of `-2:-2`. If `-mapall` is given, the credentials of all users, including `root`, are mapped as specified.	
`-ro`	Specifies that the filesystem should be exported read-only.

If the basic ways available to you in OS X for sharing resources seem a bit overwhelming, you might be interested in a shareware product called NFS Manager, available at `http://www.bresink.de/osx/`. It provides GUI interface controls for both NFS `mounts` and `exports`. Figure 23.2 shows a sample of the interface. At the time of this writing, some portions of it seem to rely on the automounter running, so if you've shut off yours, you may be able to use NFS Manager to create configurations, but you'll need to `mount` them manually at the command line. On the other hand, some people are happy with it running hand-in-hand with the automounter, so this could be a good option for you as well. It's also handy for the exploratory purpose of fiddling with settings and then examining the NetInfo database to see exactly what it's done to configure a mount point or export.

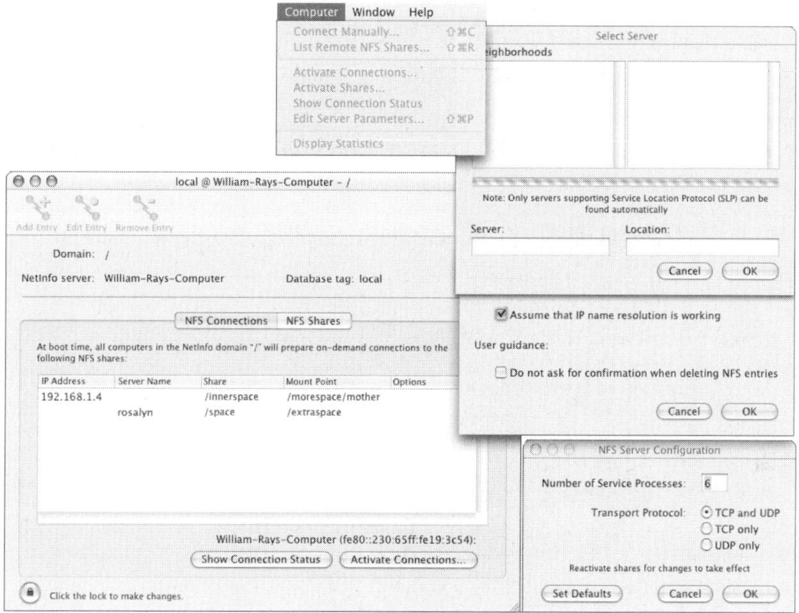

Figure 23.2 Here is a sample of what the interface for the shareware product NFS Manager looks like. It can manage both `mount` and `exports` configuration.

Restoring the Local NetInfo Database

Knowing how to restore your local NetInfo database is just as important as knowing how to back it up.

Exactly how you restore it depends on what method you chose for backing it up or whether you backed up the database as a directory or as a `tar` file. Depending on the situation, you might be running your restore in multiuser mode or in single-user mode. If you are in single-user mode, remember to follow the instructions that appear at the end of the startup so that you are allowed to make modifications.

Be sure not to rush, and pay close attention to what you are doing.

1. If your modification to the NetInfo database was made in conjunction with a change to the `/etc/hostconfig` file, replace the modified `/etc/hostconfig` file with the backup copy.

2. Go to the `/var/db/netinfo`:

```
localhost:/ root# cd /var/db/netinfo
```

List the contents of the directory. You might have multiple backup copies. Make sure that you know which one you want to use for restoring the NetInfo database. The directory called `local.nidb` is the local NetInfo database.

3. Either remove the broken `local.nidb` or rename it to something that lets you know that it is broken. If you rename it, you can remove it later when you have your NetInfo database restored.

   To remove the broken NetInfo database:

```
localhost:/var/db/netinfo root# \rm -rf local.nidb
```

   To rename the broken NetInfo database:

```
localhost:/var/db/netinfo root# mv local.nidb local.nidb-broken
```

4. If you made your backup as a `tar` file, extract the backup copy:

```
localhost:/var/db/netinfo root# tar -xf local.nidb-20010512.tar
```

   Or, if you made your backup as a copy of the directory, rename the backup copy to `local.nidb`:

```
localhost:/var/db/netinfo root# mv local.nidb-backup local.nidb
```

5. Send a `kill -HUP` to the `nibindd` process if it's running—if you are in multiuser mode:

```
brezup:root / # ps -aux ¦ grep nibind

root  6993  0.0 0.0  1288  136 ?? Ss   0:00.04 /usr/sbin/nibindd
root  7777  0.0 0.0  5708    0 std RV  0:00.00 grep nibind

brezup:root / # kill -HUP 6993
```

   If the NetInfo database does not appear to be restored after sending a `kill -HUP` to the `nibindd` process, reboot the machine.

   If you are in single-user mode, reboot the machine:

```
localhost:/var/db/netinfo root# sync;sync;sync;reboot
```

After the restored NetInfo database is up and you have determined that it's fine, if you saved the broken NetInfo database, it is all right to remove it now.

CAUTION

Note that the NetInfo Manager does not appear to provide a way to restore your NetInfo database under OS X 10.3. As of this writing, if something happens to damage your NetInfo database, being comfortable with carrying out these commands at the command line is your only solution.

Summary

The NetInfo database system is used by Mac OS X to store many of its system-critical settings. This database can be used to store and share administrative information across a network. Users can access NetInfo via the NetInfo Manager, or use a handful of command-line utilities such as `niutil`, `nidump`, and `niload`.

NFS disk sharing, enabled through NIS, is one of the most ubiquitous and most configurable disk sharing systems available, and can be used to both mount other systems' disks on your machine and to share your disks with other systems. This sharing can be considerably more complex than what is available with AppleShare, and you can build complex file-sharing setups between groups of machines. To take full advantage of what the system can do, we recommend you find a good book on Unix system administration philosophy; most of it should make sense to you at this point. If you're not quite ready for that, what we cover in Chapter 24, "User Management and Machine Clustering," will get you sharing disk and user information for simple, yet effective clusters.

In this chapter, you learned the basics of working with the NetInfo system from the command line and sharing disk resources with NFS. It is important to remember to back up your NetInfo database before making any changes. Without a properly functioning NetInfo system, Mac OS X will be rendered almost inoperable. Apple, to this point, has released very little information about the data that *is* and can be stored in NetInfo. It is a tool for hard-core administration and should not be considered a beginner's utility.

CHAPTER 24

User Management and Machine Clustering

IN THIS CHAPTER

- Skeleton User Accounts
- Multiple Users and Multiple Machines: Creating Clusters
- Cooperating Without Clusters
- Command-Line Administration Tools

As has been mentioned several times already, Mac OS X, being based on Unix, is designed from the ground up as a multiuser operating system. Where previous versions of Mac OS have supported some types of multiple-user functionality, internally only a single user could be using the machine at once, and the separation of data and resources between user accounts was not particularly strict. With OS X, a nearly unlimited number of users can be simultaneously logged in to a single machine, and from the point of view of each user, the machine is essentially devoted to his use.

One of the consequences of this type of multiple-user operating system, and of the Unix notion of abstraction, is that it is natural to do away with the personal computer notion of a single machine keeping each user's data when several users and several machines are in proximity to each other. Instead, in the Unix world, it is traditional to set up the machines so that all the users can use all the machines, and to distribute the user account information and contents via the network. A collection of machines cooperating in this fashion is called a cluster. In a cluster, any user with an account on the cluster can log in to any machine in the cluster and be presented with his account just as if it were his own personal machine.

In Chapter 23, "File and Resource Sharing with NFS and NetInfo," you learned almost all the techniques necessary to implement a cluster with OS X. This chapter covers some of the management details that you will need to keep in mind to manage a cluster successfully and provides the details needed to actually put a cluster together.

Skeleton User Accounts

If you're going to have any significant number of users on your machine (or machines), you'll soon find that being able to provide a more customized environment than what comes out of the system Accounts control pane by default is a benefit.

Apple has provided a convenient method for you to perform some customization of accounts as created by the Accounts control pane. This is the inclusion of a `User Template` directory, from which the accounts made by the pane are created by duplication. The family of `User Template` directories, individualized by locale, are kept in `/System/Library/User Template`. This system works for simple configuration settings that you might like to configure for each newly created user, but it has some limitations if you want to work with more complex setups. The largest logical limitation is that if you're trying to set up complicated startup scripts and sophisticated environment settings, using a real user account as your default template is nice, because then you can log in for testing and tweaking. The largest practical limitation is that Apple has put the default templates in the `/System/` hierarchy, where they're Apple-sacrosanct, and system updates are likely to tromp on any customizations that you might make.

The easiest way to solve all the problems at once is to create a skeleton user account as a real user account, and to keep it up-to-date with any environmental customizations that you want to provide for new users when you create accounts. If you create the skeleton user as simply another user account, you can log in to it and then conveniently tweak its settings. Using this method, you can create as many skeleton accounts as you need for different collections of settings.

Even if you prefer to use the Accounts control pane, the creation of skeleton users as real users on the system can be useful. You can configure skeleton users who you can actually log in as and test their settings, and then populate the `/System/Library/User Template` directories (if you don't mind incurring the wrath of the Apple installers), as required for customizing the configuration of users under the Users pane in System Preferences. Alternatively, you can create the accounts with Apple's default templates and then overwrite the actual user directories with data from your skeleton account.

As covered in Chapter 12, "Introducing the BSD Subsystem," every user's shell environment is configured by the `.profile` and `.bashrc` files (if the user is using `bash`), or `.login` and `.cshrc` (if the user's using `tcsh` or `csh`) shell scripts in the user's home directory. You might also want to provide a more customized starter Web page or assorted bits of default data or files in the user's home directory. If you're managing student or employee accounts, you might have basic application preferences that you want to come preconfigured. Consider the wealth of personal customizations that you put into your own account. There are certainly many that other users aren't going to be interested in, but there are also undoubtedly many that would be useful starting places for other users on your system. There is also a lot of work involved in putting these preferences together, so despite the extra work involved in making well-customized user templates, you could be saving many hours of work for your users if you can leverage the work you've already put into the system. If you have many users, this can be a real productivity enhancer and timesaver.

After you configure an account in the fashion you want your new users to have, the hard part is done. It would be nice to have a way to use this account directly from the Users pane as the seed for new accounts as they are created, but, unfortunately, we aren't so lucky yet. Instead, you have two options for how to use the starter account information. First, you can create a new user through the Accounts control pane. After the account is created, you can replace the user's home directory (that the Accounts control pane created) with a copy of the skeleton account home directory.

Your other option is to ignore the Accounts control pane and create a new user by duplicating an existing user node from the NetInfo hierarchy, making a copy of the skeleton account home directory for the new user's home directory, and then editing the copy of the NetInfo entry for the new user to reflect the correct information for that user.

The first option is probably easier for novice users, but the second has the benefit of being able to be done from the command line with `nidump` and `niload`, and therefore, of being automatable.

For the rest of the discussion, it is assumed that you've created a skeleton account in which you have made any customizations that you want to install for all new users. The account `UID` is assumed to be `5002`, with a home directory of `/Users/skel` and a `GID` of `101`. It is also assumed that you've added the group `users` to your NetInfo `groups` directory, with a `GID` of `101` (we've previously used `99` for this group, but Apple's put a system group on that ID with 10.3), and that you want to use this `GID` for normal, nonprivileged users. If you prefer to use Apple's new scheme of having every user in a different, unique group, this method is adaptable to that as well.

To implement the first method of providing local customization for a new user, follow these steps:

1. Create the new user with the Accounts control pane. Make any necessary changes to the user's configuration, such as the default `GID`, using NetInfo Manager as shown in earlier chapters.
2. Become `root` (`su`, provide password).
3. Change directories to the skeleton user's directory (`cd ~skel`).
4. Tar the contents of the current directory, using the option to place the output on `STDOUT` (`tar -cf - .`) and then pipe the output of `tar` into a subshell. In the subshell, `cd` to the new user's directory, and untar from `STDIN` (`| ( cd ~<newusername> ; tar -xf - ) )`.

NOTE

If you've created preferences in the skeleton user's account that rely on resource forks, you'll want to use the `ditto` command instead of `tar`, or read ahead to the note regarding `hfstar`.

5. Change directories to one level above the new user's directory (cd ~*<newusername>* ; cd ../).

6. Change the ownership of everything in the new user's directory to belong to the new user and, potentially, to the user's default group if it's not the same as the skel account default group (chown -R *<newusername>*:*<newusergroup>* *<newuserdirectoryname>*). We'll cover the complete documentation for chown at the end of this chapter.

For example, if you've just created a new user named jim, assigned to the group users with the Accounts control pane/NetInfo Manager, and want to put the skel account configuration into jim's home directory, you would enter the following:

```
su (provide password)
cd ~skel
tar -cf - . | ( cd ~jim ; tar -xf - )
cd ~jim
cd ../
chown -R jim:users jim
```

If you'd rather create new users from the command line, either because you can't access the physical console conveniently or because you want to use what you know about shell scripting to automate the process, you can use the second method suggested earlier. You might find this method more convenient for creating users in a NetInfo domain other than localhost/local. The Accounts control pane in the nonserver version of OS X seems incapable of creating users in other NetInfo domains, and this makes using it for managing cluster users difficult.

CAUTION

This process creates a new user by manipulating the NetInfo database directly, so the cautions to back up your database frequently are important to remember here.

To implement the second method, follow these steps:

1. Become root (su, give password).

2. Change directories to the directory in which you want to place the new user's home directory (cd /Users, for example).

3. Make a directory with the short name of the user you're about to create (mkdir *<newusername>* to create a directory for a new user named *<newusername>*).

4. Change directories to the home directory of the skel account (cd ~skel).

5. Tar the contents of the current directory and use the option to place the output on STDOUT (tar -cf - .)

6. Pipe the output of the tar command into a subshell. In the subshell, cd to the new user's directory, and untar from STDIN (¦ (cd <*pathtonewuserdirectory*> ; tar -xf -). Note that you can't use ~<*newusername*> because <*newusername*> doesn't actually exist on the system yet.
7. Dump your skel account (UID 5002 here, remember) NetInfo entry, or some other user's entry, into a file that you can edit (nidump -r /name=users/uid=5002 -t localhost/local > ~/<*sometempfile*>). As an alternative to the uid search, you could specify the skel account with /name=users/name=skel.
8. Edit ~/<*sometempfile*>, changing the entries so that they are appropriate for the new user you want to create. You'll want to change at least _writers_passwd, _writers_tim_password, uid, _writers_hint, _writers_picture, gid, realname, name, passwd, and home. It's probably easiest to leave passwd blank for now.

NOTE

If you want to use the "unique group for every user" management paradigm that Apple has moved to (which frankly we think is a management nightmare), you'll want to change GID here as well.

9. Use niutil to create a new directory for the uid that you've picked for the new user (niutil -p -create -t localhost/local /name=users/uid=<*newuserUID*>; give the root password when asked).
10. Use niload to load the data you modified in ~/<*sometempfile*> back into the NetInfo database (cat ~/<*sometempfile*> ¦ niload -p -r /name=users/uid=<*newuserUID*> -t localhost/local).
11. Set the password for the new user (passwd <*newusername*>;). Provide a beginning password—another BSD utility documented at the end of this chapter.
12. Change back to the directory above the new user's home directory (cd ~<*newusername*>; cd ../).
13. Change the ownership of the new user's directory to the new user's <*username*> and <*defaultgroup*> (chown -R <*username*>:<*usergroup*> <*newuserdirectory*>).

That might look like a lot of typing, but that's what shell scripts are for. If you have two users to create, that's a lot of typing. If you have two hundred, it's much less to type the script once and run it 200 times, than to create each manually with the Accounts preferences pane and NetInfo Manager.

If you've made a mistake somewhere along the way, just restore your NetInfo database from the backup that you made before you started this. You also might need to find the nibindd process, and send it a HUP signal (\ps -auxww ¦ grep "nibindd"; kill -HUP <*whatever PID belongs to nibindd*>, or, killall -HUP nibindd, if you prefer to do things the easy way).

RESOURCE FORKS GET LOST IN THE TAR!

The version of `tar` distributed by Apple doesn't understand file resource forks, and some software vendors haven't caught on to the idea of using `plists` properly yet. The unfortunate consequence is that if you've built a highly customized skeleton user (or are trying to use this as an example to move a real user account), and some of the user's preferences are stored in the resource fork of the preference files, `tar` is going to make a mess of things when you use it to duplicate the user's directory to the new location.

To overcome this problem, you currently have two options:

- metaobject has developed `hfstar`, a GNUtar derivative that supports HFS+, allowing it to properly handle resource forks, type and creator codes, and so on. Because Apple is now distributing GNUtar rather than BSDtar, it's probably safe to do a straight-up replacement of Apple's `tar` with `hfstar` if you want. (BSDtar and GNUtar have sufficient differences that outright replacement was not previously a good option.) Instead of replacement, though, it would be better to keep both `hfstar` and Apple's `tar` around, just in case there turn out to be unexpected differences. Because metaobject has managed to get resource forks working with GNUtar, I'm hopeful that Apple will follow suit with its own updated version of `tar`, obviating the need for replacement. metaobject's `hfstar` can be downloaded from `http://www.metaobject.com/Products.html`.
- Use Apple's already supplied `ditto` command. `ditto` doesn't provide nearly the power of `tar`, but it'll do for copying user directories. More information on `ditto` is provided in Chapter 32, "System Maintenance."

To produce results similar to those from the first method earlier, the following example creates a new user with the username of `james`, `UID 600`, `GID 70` (the web group www), with home directory `/Users/james`. This again assumes the `skel` account with `UID 5002` and characteristics as described earlier.

```
su (provide the password)
cd /Users
mkdir james
cd ~skel
tar -cf - . ¦ ( cd /Users/james ; tar -xf - )
nidump -r /name=users/uid=5002 -t localhost/local > ~/skeltemp
vi ~/skeltemp
```

Change the contents from this

```
{
 "hint" = ( "" );
 "sharedDir" = ( "Public" );
 "_writers_passwd" = ( "skel" );
 "authentication_authority" = ( ";ShadowHash;" );
 "name" = ( "skel" );
 "home" = ( "/Users/skel" );
```

```
 "passwd" = ( "********" );
 "_writers_hint" = ( "skel" );
 "_writers_picture" = ( "skel" );
 "_shadow_passwd" = ( "" );
 "realname" = ( "Skeleton User" );
 "uid" = ( "5002" );
 "shell" = ( "/bin/bash" );
 "generateduid" = ( "66EA85A3-E1A9-11D7-9893-0030654C2E9C" );
 "gid" = ( "101" );
 "_writers_tim_password" = ( "skel" );
 "picture" = ( "/Library/User Pictures/Animals/Jaguar.tif" );
 "_writers_realname" = ( "skel" );
}
```

to this

```
{
 "authentication_authority" = ( ";basic;" );
 "picture" = ( "/Library/User Pictures/Nature/Zen.tif" );
 "_shadow_passwd" = ( "" );
 "hint" = ( "boggle" );
 "uid" = ( "600" );
 "_writers_passwd" = ( "james" );
 "realname" = ( "Sweet Baby James" );
 "_writers_hint" = ( "james" );
 "gid" = ( "70" );
 "shell" = ( "/bin/tcsh" );
 "name" = ( "james" );
 "_writers_tim_password" = ( "james" );
 "passwd" = ( "" );
 "_writers_picture" = ( "james" );
 "home" = ( "/Users/james" );
 "sharedDir" = ( "Public" );
}
```

Then run these commands:

```
niutil -p -create -t localhost/local /name=users/uid=600
(give the root password when asked)
cat ~/skeltemp | niload -p -r /name=users/uid=600 -t localhost/local
(give the root password when asked)
passwd james (fill in a good starting value)
cd ~james
cd ../
chown -R james:www james (GID 70 is group www on this machine)
```

NOTE

Depending on whether your NetInfo daemon is feeling well, you might have to HUP the nibindd process to get it to recognize that you've made the change. Remember that you can always restore your NetInfo database backup to get out of a mess, if you've created one.

TIP

If you need to delete a user account from the command line, you can destroy the NetInfo information for the user by using the command `niutil -p -destroy -t localhost/local /name=users/uid=<userUIDtobedeleted>`. Then `\rm -rf` the user's home directory to delete it and all its contents from the system.

Just to make sure that your user has been created as you think it should have been, you can use `niutil` to list the `/users` NetInfo directory. (Don't be surprised if your listing doesn't look quite like this—this is simply the list of users configured on my machine, so your users are likely to be different.)

```
brezup:root Users # niutil -list -t localhost/local /users
11      nobody
12      root
13      daemon
14      unknown
15      smmsp
16      lp
17      postfix
18      www
19      eppc
20      mysql
21      sshd
22      qtss
23      cyrus
24      mailman
25      appserver
67      ray
69      software
72      sage
74      nermal
76      boris
87      skel
86      james
```

As shown, `james` does now exist in the NetInfo `/users` directory, although this listing shows only the NetInfo node numbers, rather than the users and property values. To see whether `james` has the properties intended, you can use `niutil` to read the info from the node named `james`:

```
brezup:root Users # niutil -read -t localhost/local /users/james
hint: boggle
sharedDir: Public
_writers_passwd: james
authentication_authority: ;ShadowHash;
name: james
home: /Users/james
passwd: ********
_writers_hint: james
_writers_picture: james
_shadow_passwd:
realname: Sweet Baby James
uid: 600
shell: /bin/bash
gid: 70
_writers_tim_password: james
picture: /Library/User Pictures/Animals/Jaguar.tif
_writers_realname: james
```

James can now log in and functions just like a user that you created through the Accounts pane.

NOTE

There are some values in the output from the `nidump` of the user information that we frankly can't figure out what they're for, or whether they affect the system by being present, absent, or changed. Some of these, such as the `generateduid` seem likely to change as Apple matures the password authentication system. This value, for example, is an artifact of the way that Apple's chosen to overcome a security vulnerability in earlier implementations of the NetInfo database. It doesn't seem to actually be used for anything (or rather it seems to be a unique hash value generated to match between the user's information in NetInfo and an encrypted password stored in a file. It seems, however, to be automatically generated and replaced as needed), and nothing seems to break if we remove it. Unfortunately, the root cause is that Apple's new user password storage system makes a portion of the user authentication information local to each machine, instead of allowing it all to be cleanly served from a remote server. This probably means that Apple will supercede this method, and that the requirement for this value will be changed, when Apple implements some secure, yet networkable scheme in the future.

Multiple Users and Multiple Machines: Creating Clusters

Since almost the dawn of computing, the Unix operating system has supported the notion of a cooperating group of machines that share user information between them. The concept of clustering includes the idea that the machines should share not only information but also sufficient resources so that any user with an account on the cluster can use any machine in the cluster, and the experience will be indistinguishable from using any other machine.

The user information traditionally is shared among the machines in the cluster by using a technology known as NIS (the Network Information System, originally known as the Yellow Pages) developed by Sun Microsystems. Filesystems (containing user accounts and software) are shared to members of the cluster using NFS (the Network File System). NFS is still the preferred way of sharing filesystems under OS X, but Apple has provided a slightly more complex, and considerably more powerful, method of sharing user information: the NetInfo system. Not only is the information in NetInfo databases used for configuration of your own machine, but if you choose, this information can be shared to other machines.

As you might guess from what you know of Unix abstraction by now, a machine shouldn't really care whether its NetInfo configuration information comes from its local NetInfo server, or from another NetInfo server that it's talking to over the network. As a matter of fact, a hierarchy of NetInfo servers can be linked together to provide a significant level of sophistication in the distribution of user information.

Creating and managing many-level NetInfo hierarchies is a topic best left for Mac OS X Server, but the creation of a two-level hierarchy is something that can be reasonably done with OS X.

The normal two-level hierarchy includes a local NetInfo domain and a parent NetInfo domain delivered via the network. Each machine that participates in the cluster subscribes to the parent NetInfo domain. (This includes the machine that runs the parent server as well; it subscribes via the network to a domain that it serves via the network. Don't worry; these things will make sense eventually.) Any users defined in the parent domain can use any of the machines that subscribe to the domain. Users defined in the local domain on any machine can use the machine on which they are defined but do not have access to any other machines in the cluster.

Subscribing to a NetInfo Parent Domain

If you want your machine to participate in a cluster, there are two options: Your machine can either subscribe to a parent NetInfo domain or be the provider of the domain. Because subscribing to a domain is necessary in both cases, we'll cover subscription to a domain supplied by another machine first.

For a technique that provides such a powerful method of integrating machines and user accounts, joining a cluster implemented through the NetInfo service is surprisingly easy.

There are essentially only two things that you need to do. First, you need to mount the filesystems from the remote machine so that users' home directories appear on your machine in the same places that they are defined to be in the NetInfo domain to which you will be subscribing.

Second, subscribe to a parent NetInfo domain using the Directory Access utility.

The first of these tasks you've already learned how to do in Chapter 23. For this example, we will assume that users who are intended to be cluster users, with the ability to log in on any of the machines in the cluster, have home directories defined to exist in the directory `/netusers`. Therefore, if we want to be able to log in on our machine as one of the users defined in the parent NetInfo database, we need to mount the remote directory on the server (`192.168.1.16` in this case) named `/netusers` as a local directory `/netusers`. This will allow logins to user accounts listed in the `localhost/local` NetInfo database, as well as to accounts listed in the remote `192.168.1.16/network` database. The following listing shows the `mounts` entry for the machine that is subscribing to the NetInfo cluster:


```
kimagure:root adam # nidump -r /mounts -t localhost/local

{
 "name" = ( "mounts" );
 CHILDREN = (
  {
   "vfstype" = ( "nfs" );
   "dir" = ( "/mnt" );
   "name" = ( "venice.iwaynet.net:/home" );
   "opts" = ( "-i", "net", "-P", "-b", "ro" );
  },
  {
   "vfstype" = ( "nfs" );
   "dir" = ( "/netusers" );
   "name" = ( "192.168.1.16:/netusers" );
   "opts" = ( "-b", "-s", "-P" );
  }
 )
}
```

Note that it is mounting the `/netusers` directory to participate in the cluster, as well as another directory from an entirely different machine. NFS can be used to create arbitrarily complex networks of interconnected filesystems.

Satisfying the second requirement involves only opening the Directory Access utility, enabling subscription to NetInfo services, and entering the machine name or IP address and the NetInfo directory to which to subscribe. For a machine subscribing to the `network` database, served by `192.168.1.16`, this is shown in Figures 24.1 and 24.2.

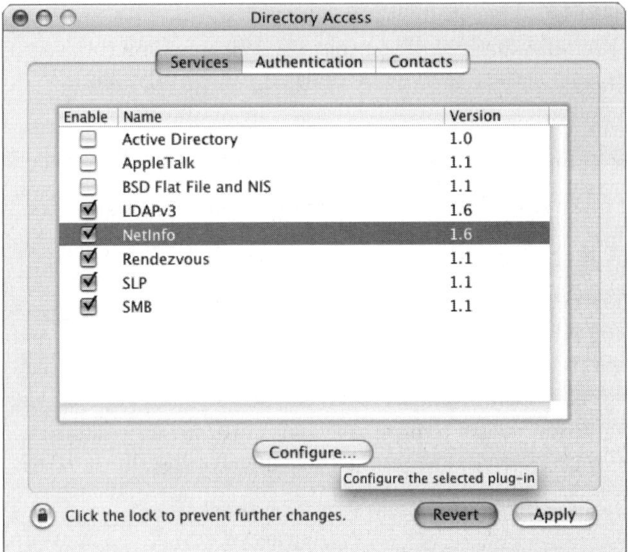

FIGURE 24.1 To subscribe to a parent NetInfo domain, open the Directory Access utility, enable changes, and check the NetInfo box. Then click the Configure button.

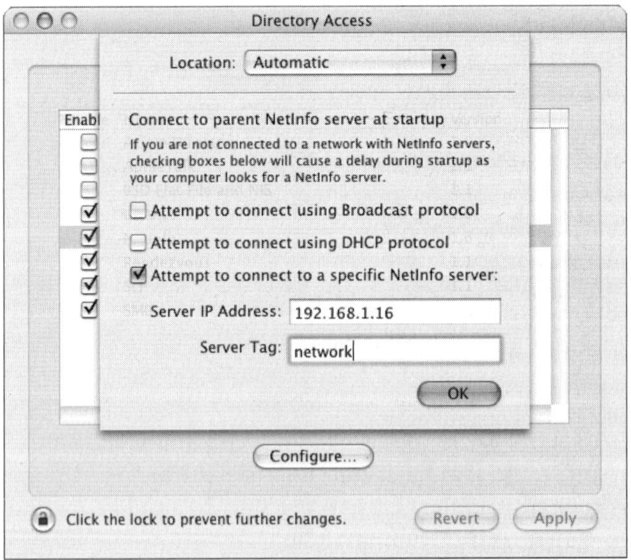

FIGURE 24.2 Subscribing to the parent `network` NetInfo database, served from a machine at IP address `192.168.1.16`. This dialog is reached by clicking Configure as shown in Figure 24.1.

The `network` NetInfo database, to which our machine's NetInfo database is now parented in this example, contains the following users:

```
kimagure:adam / $ niutil -list -t 192.168.1.16/network /users

3	root
4	skel
5	bellchan
```

TIP

Depending on how your name service is configured, you might be able to use an IP address to refer to the remote server's NetInfo domain, or you might have to refer to it by hostname. It's also possible to create a machine entry in your `localhost/local` database that relates the IP address and a machine name, if you prefer to use a nickname for the remote server.

Figures 24.3 and 24.4 show the same user, `bellchan`, logged in to two different machines—`brezup` (`192.168.1.16`) and `kimagure` (`192.168.1.105`). `brezup` is the server of the NetInfo `network` domain, and `kimagure` is subscribed to this as a child of the `network` domain. If you look closely at the figures, you won't see much of a difference—and that is exactly the point. The `bellchan` user has its home directory in the `/netusers` directory on `brezup/192.168.1.16`, and this directory is mounted in the same location on `kimagure/192.168.1.105`. All of `bellchan`'s user information is served via NetInfo and subscribed to by `192.168.1.105`. So, due to Unix abstraction and the power of clustering, there is no difference to the user (other than possible network performance issues) between sitting down in front of either of these machines. Startup applications start the same; preferences are the same. It's as though there's no difference between the machines, unless we look at a view that specifically tells us about the hardware, such as the `df` listing shown in the terminal.

Parenting a NetInfo Domain to Other Machines

If you want to set up your machine to be the server of a NetInfo parent domain to which other machines can subscribe, the process is also straightforward. There are three requirements. First, as you should realize from the previous example, for users who exist in the parent domain to be usable on machines that are clients to the domain, their home directories (or, more usefully, the directory containing all their home directories) must be made available to the client machines.

Next, your machine must be set up to serve a NetInfo directory to the network, and users must exist in it. For example, your machine might serve a NetInfo directory named `network` and make it available to other machines.

FIGURE 24.3 The user `bellchan` logged into `192.168.1.16` (locally named `brezup`) at the console. `bellchan`'s account physically resides on this machine, as does the `network` NetInfo database.

FIGURE 24.4 The user `bellchan` logged in to `192.168.1.105` (locally named `kimagure`) at the console. `bellchan`'s account physically resides on another machine and is coming to this machine via the power of NetInfo, `NFS`, and the notion of Unix clustering.

Finally, your machine must be subscribed to the (network-visible) NetInfo server that it serves, so that your `local` NetInfo database is a child of the network NetInfo database. Following the `bellchan` example you saw earlier, your `local` database would become a child of `network`.

After these requirements are met, others can subscribe as children of your network-served NetInfo database by following the directions given in the section "Subscribing to a NetInfo Parent Domain" earlier in this chapter.

CAUTION

It isn't particularly useful to parent a domain with a machine that switches "locations" frequently. It is difficult to configure the machine to properly parent and not parent the domain when desired. Also, if you're providing domain parenting information to other machines, it's rude to yank their parent domain away when you take the machine down to move it. For this reason, we recommend parenting NetInfo domains only from machines with fixed IP addresses and that are generally intended to be always on.

To configure the server similarly to the one on `192.168.1.16` used in the previous example, the following steps need to be taken:

1. The directory `/netusers` needs to be created, owner set to `root`, and group set to `wheel`, just as the `/Users` directory is set.
2. The directory `/netusers` needs to be exported via NFS. The following listing shows the NetInfo `exports` entry I've used. In this entry, I'm exporting to all machines in my local network (`192.168.1` [the .0 part is a don't-care value for the specific machine]; and mask `255.255.255` [the .0 part indicates part of the IP that's variable; in this case, the mask value is redundant]). Because it's my own local home network, I trust the machines explicitly. `clients` has `<no value>`, not an empty value.

```
[localhost:~/Documents] ray% nidump -r /exports -t localhost/local

{
 "name" = ( "exports" );
 CHILDREN = (
  {
   "clients" = ( );
   "name" = ( "/netusers" );
   "opts" = ( "maproot=root", "network=192.168.1.0",
➥"mask=255.255.255.0" );
  }
 )
}
```

TIP

Remember that the `export` needs to be done in the `local` domain. If you try to use the shareware NFS Manager GUI tool to create this `export`, it creates the `export` in the top-level NetInfo domain. If you've already created a parent master NetInfo server, the `export` information goes into it and not into the `localhost/local` domain where it is needed.

3. A new master NetInfo server needs to be created on your server machine (ours was `192.168.1.16`).

   Under OS X 10.3, you must first edit `/etc/hostconfig` and change the line that says `NETINFOSERVER=-AUTOMATIC-` to `NETINFOSERVER=-YES-` (`AUTOMATIC`, in Apple's world, seems to mean "`NO`"). Restart your machine.

   At the command line run `nidomain -m network`, which should return with no errors or output. Just to make sure that it's been created, run `nidomain -l localhost` and make certain that both `local` and `network` domains are being served by your machine.

   In earlier versions of OS X (and maybe again in the future, given as many revisions as the NetInfo Manager seems to undergo), this could be done through NetInfo Manager, by selecting Manage NetInfo Hierarchy from the Management menu and choosing Create a New Master Server on This Host. A new master server serving a domain named `network` would be created by default.

4. Choose the newly created NetInfo `network` domain as a parent domain for your machine. Yes, you're going to make the machine on which you just created the domain into a client of the domain it now serves. To do this, follow the instructions in the prior example for selecting a parent domain—that is, use Directory Access to enable parenting to a NetInfo domain and provide your IP address (or, the `127.0.0.1` loopback address) and `network` as the domain to use as a parent.

5. Rebooting the machine at this point is probably a wise choice. If the `network` domain was not correctly created, or your NetInfo service doesn't want to connect to it as a parent domain, you'll need to delete the domain and try again.

   Unfortunately, this step seems a little hit or miss on occasion. What appears to be a bug or three in the NetInfo server occasionally results in it dying when trying to connect to the parent domain. The symptom is that the colorful spinning wait cursor appears for the NetInfo Manager and never returns to a pointer cursor. In this case, Force-Quit the NetInfo Manager, restore your NetInfo database from a backup (as discussed in Chapter 23), and reboot your machine).

6. If everything goes well, your machine will reboot cleanly, and you will be able to log in. Verify that your local NetInfo domain is now a child of the `network` domain by opening the `local` domain on `localhost` from the NetInfo Manager and then clicking the Open Parent Domain button (world with up-pointing arrow). The `network` domain you created earlier should open.

7. Create some users in the network domain. This step is currently kind of a catch-22 situation: The Accounts pane won't let you select the domain for new users, but you could create them in the local domain, dump their values out with nidump, and load them back into the network domain. If you created the network domain using the command line nidomain tool, you will need to create at least the users NetInfo directory in network as a place to add the new users. NetInfo Manager won't let you create new directories and properties in the new domain because there are no users in it, so you can't authenticate to it as an administrative user. Once again, the command line comes to the rescue:

```
nidump -r /name=users/uid=0 -t localhost/local > ~/roottemp
niutil -p -create -t localhost/network /name=users/uid=0
cat ~/roottemp ¦ niload -p -r /name=users/uid=0
➥ -t localhost/network
```

You now have a root user in the network domain that NetInfo manager will allow you to authenticate with.

NOTE

There's a bizarre detail that's not obvious from this dump-and-load example. The root user will be created in the network domain, but because of the way that Apple has implemented passwords in OS X 10.3, the password that will be accepted for root will be the one stored on your local machine for the root user. This is because the network version of root will have ShadowHash authentication, and your local root user's generateduid.

You can change this behavior by switching the root user from the network domain to ;basic; authentication instead of ;ShadowHash; authentication, and setting a password with passwd -i netinfo -l <serverip>/network. This change does expose the machine running the network domain to a greater variety of password cracking attempts on this root user's password than are available via ShadowHash password storage. There isn't currently a good way around this problem. If you want to share your user IDs, they will be exposed to more risk than user IDs locked down on your machine alone. Hopefully, Apple will provide a better password system that alleviates this problem in the future, but for now it is a simple fact of life.

Things used to be easier. If you created the parent network domain through the Manage NetInfo Hierarchy capability of NetInfo Manager (if your version sports this capability), you'd find that your root user from the local domain has been duplicated up into the network domain. You could then make more users in the network domain by duplicating the root user and changing the user's information as appropriate.

Either way you go, remember that your new users need to have their home directories located in /netusers. For the example given earlier, we created the skel skeleton account so that we could use it to create other customized users. The skel account was then used as a template as demonstrated earlier, and the bellchan account created from it. If you're going to create the account using the nidump, niutil, and niload command-line tools, remember that you're not inserting users into localhost/local, but instead into localhost/network (or <yourip>/network if localhost isn't recognized).

I created the bellchan user the same way that I created james earlier:

```
nidump -r /name=users/uid=5002 -t localhost/local > ~/skeltemp
vi ~/skeltemp
```

Edit as necessary. Specifically, you need to change UIDs and other parameters to suit the new user you're trying to create, just like you did when following the example for the local user james. Because of a change that Apple made to increase system security, for shared users such as this one, you also need to delete the value of the authentication_authority property (reads ";ShadowHash;" as dumped) and replace it with the value ";basic;". You then need to delete the _shadow_passwd property and change the value of passwd to "".

These changes tell NetInfo to store the encrypted password information in the NetInfo database, instead of in a local disk file. This is somewhat less secure than storing it in the default protected local disk file! Anyone who has permission to view your NetInfo database can see the encrypted value—decrypting it is not trivially possible, but it's also not impossible. Only make this change if you're comfortable that the machines that you're serving user information to are relatively secure, and for users whose passwords you aren't critically concerned about security for. Of course, you should only be serving disks, users, and account information to machines that you trust implicitly, so limiting your exposure to only these machines is only common sense.

```
niutil -p -create -t localhost/network /name=users/uid=10001
```

(I decided to start my network users with uid 10001)

```
cat ~/skeltemp ¦ niload -p -r /name=users/uid=10001
➥ -t localhost/network
cd /Users/skel/
tar -cf - . ¦ (cd /netusers/bellchan/; tar -xf -)
cd /netusers/
chown -R bellchan:users bellchan/
passwd bellchan
```

8. Log out, and try to log in at your console as one of your users from the network domain. If you're successful, you've completed the basic configuration of your machine as a NetInfo and NFS server to provide cluster information to other machines. Other machines can now mount your exported directories and subscribe to your NetInfo network domain, as shown in the earlier example of creating a client.

If you aren't successful, check the user information that you've created in the `network` domain carefully to make sure that you haven't overlapped any `UID`s or usernames with users that exist in your `local` domain. Also make sure that there's now a random-looking string (this is the encrypted password) stored for the value of the user's `passwd` property in your `network` database. If everything else is okay but there are still problems, you can run into trouble because of directories and permissions. Check that things you've specified, such as the home directories, really exist and have the correct ownerships and permissions. If your NetInfo Manager shows that your `local` domain is a child of the `network` domain (by being able to open the network domain as its parent), you're 99% of the way there, and the problem must be in the user account information itself.

NOTE

When you're modifying the `network` domain, the user ID and password required to modify it will belong to one of the users in that domain. Unless you've created a non-`root` administrative user in the `network` domain, you need to use `root` and the `root` password to enable modifications in the `network` domain.

Cooperating Without Clusters

Sometimes it's nice to be able to share information between systems without sharing user accounts. For example, if you manage a number of machines owned by their individual primary users, you may find that they don't particularly want to share access to their hardware with all the other users, and that they would prefer their accounts to be kept entirely contained within their desktop machines. Still, even in a group that prefers for their machines to remain largely autonomous, it's common to find that everyone wants to be able to read and write to some common collection of data, and they don't want to be limited to only having it available when they're online. For these situations, there's little to do other than put a copy of the data on every person's machine and try to keep them in sync. Thankfully, there are two nice Unix utilities already designed for solving exactly this problem: `rsync` and CVS.

Remote Synchronization: `rsync`

The `rsync` program provides the ability to synchronize the contents of directories between machines over the network. The synchronization can be unidirectional or bidirectional and has a host of options regarding how to resolve conflicts. It works particularly well in environments such as that described earlier, where everyone wants his own copy of the data, wants to be able to make modifications to the data, and also wants to be able to push their changes to others and receive other's changes back again. This system is ideal for automating the overnight synchronization of people's computers with a central data repository, or the maintenance of duplicate copies of large data collections on different local networks to reduce network-induced lag in accessing the data.

```
rsync -avz <source path> <destination path>
```

<source path> and *<destination path>* are either full directory or file paths on your local system, or they are specifiers of the form *<user>*@*<host>*:*<path>*. The a option is for archive and forces all files in the destination to be identical to the source (newer files on the destination side are overwritten by the source). If you want to keep newer versions that are on the destination side, add a u option to the -avz. If you want to send the data through Secure Shell for encryption purposes, the syntax is slightly different:

```
rsync -av -e /usr/bin/ssh <source path> <destination path>.
```

The system asks you for a password for remote systems, if they are necessary. For this reason, sending the data through SSH for encryption is probably a good idea. For more information on encrypting your data, and how to make encryption keys that are more secure than normal passwords, see Chapter 26, "Remote Access and Control."

For example, if I were to synchronize the contents of the directory ~/Documents/stylewriter/ between my laptop and a directory owned by the user adam on an iMac living at 192.168.1.17, I could issue an rsync command, using the a flag to get archive mode, the u flag to perform updates rather than overwriting new files, and the v flag twice, to increase verbosity a bit for this example:

```
brezup:ray Documents $ rsync -auvv -e /usr/bin/ssh ~/Documents/stylewriter/
➥ adam@192.168.1.17:Documents/stylewriter/
opening connection using /usr/bin/ssh -l adam 192.168.1.17
➥ rsync --server -vvulogDtpr . Documents/stylewriter/
adam@192.168.1.17's password:
building file list ..
expand file_list to 4000 bytes, did move
done
created directory Documents/stylewriter/
./
.DS_Store
Makefile.atalk
README
README.atalk
README.protocol
README.troubleshooting
adsp.c
adsp.h
lpstyl
lpstyl.c
printcap
printcap.a4
scripts/
scripts/direct_stylpbm
scripts/direct_stylps
scripts/stylascii
```

```
scripts/stylascii-atalk
scripts/stylascii.a4
scripts/stylps
scripts/stylps-atalk
scripts/stylps-color
scripts/stylps-color-atalk
scripts/stylps-color.a4
scripts/stylps-color~
scripts/stylps.a4
styl.ppd
total: matches=0 tag_hits=0 false_alarms=0 data=146820
wrote 148347 bytes read 420 bytes 22887.23 bytes/sec
total size is 146820 speedup is 0.99
```


In this case, I'm copying it to the directory of another user (`adam`) on the remote iMac, so I've must have the password to his account. If I had an account on that machine, I could use my password and have access to write anywhere that my account had permission.

Now if I modify a file on both sides (`README` on the iMac, and `README.atalk` on my laptop) and want to keep the data in sync between them, I need to `rsync` in both directions, from my machine as the source to the iMac as the destination, and from the iMac as the source to my machine as the destination. This is done by simply specifying the `rsync` twice, with the source and destination values switched between them:

```
brezup:ray Documents $ rsync -auvv -e /usr/bin/ssh ~/Documents/stylewriter/
➥ adam@192.168.1.17:Documents/stylewriter/
opening connection using /usr/bin/ssh -l adam 192.168.1.17
➥ rsync --server -vvulogDtpr . Documents/stylewriter/
adam@192.168.1.17's password:
building file list ..
expand file_list to 4000 bytes, did move
done
.DS_Store is uptodate
Makefile.atalk is uptodate
README is newer
README.atalk
README.protocol is uptodate
README.troubleshooting is uptodate
.
.
.
styl.ppd is uptodate
total: matches=5 tag_hits=5 false_alarms=0 data=0
wrote 575 bytes read 66 bytes 116.55 bytes/sec
total size is 146820 speedup is 229.05
```

Notice that the rsync indicates the files that are identical, mentioning that they are uptodate, the file on 192.168.1.17 that's newer (README), and that it's transferred README.atalk. Now to do the same thing in the opposite direction:

```
brezup:ray Documents $ rsync -auvv -e /usr/bin/ssh
➥ adam@192.168.1.17:Documents/stylewriter/ ~/Documents/stylewriter/
opening connection using /usr/bin/ssh -l adam 192.168.1.17 rsync --server --
sender -vvulogDtpr . Documents/stylewriter/
adam@192.168.1.17's password:
receiving file list ..
rsync: expand file_list to 4000 bytes, did move
done
delta transmission enabled
.DS_Store is uptodate
Makefile.atalk is uptodate
README.atalk is uptodate
README.protocol is uptodate
.
.
.
styl.ppd is uptodate
README
total: matches=13 tag_hits=13 false_alarms=0 data=0
wrote 110 bytes read 722 bytes 128.00 bytes/sec
total size is 146820 speedup is 176.47
```

Now everything is uptodate, except for README, which is transferred back to my laptop from 192.168.1.17. Note that I've added the u option to these, so that files will only be updated, instead of allowing the rsync to force the destination to match the source completely. There are, of course, many more options, including such useful features as backing up old files to archival directories instead of overwriting them and synchronization of deletes. Table 24.1 shows the syntax and primary options for rsync. Complete documentation is available in Appendix A.

TABLE 24.1 The Syntax and Primary Options for rsync

Rsync	Synchronizes files and directories; faster, flexible replacement for rcp.
Rsync [OPTION].. SRC [SRC].. [USER@]HOST:DEST	
rsync [OPTION].. [USER@]HOST:SRC DEST	
rsync [OPTION].. SRC [SRC].. DEST	
rsync [OPTION].. [USER@]HOST::SRC [DEST]	
rsync [OPTION].. SRC [SRC].. [USER@]HOST::DEST	
rsync [OPTION].. rsync://[USER@]HOST[:PORT]/SRC [DEST]	
rsync [OPTION].. SRC [SRC].. rsync://[USER@]HOST[:PORT]/DEST	

TABLE 24.1 Continued

Primary uses for `rsync`:

There are eight different ways of using `rsync`. The most useful in day-to day use are:

Copying local files. This is invoked when neither source nor destination path contains a `:` separator.

Copying from the local machine to a remote machine using a remote shell program as the transport (such as `rsh` or `ssh`). This is invoked when the destination path contains a single `:` separator.

Copying from a remote machine to the local machine using a remote shell program. This is invoked when the source contains a `:` separator.

Copying from a remote `rsync` server to the local machine. This is invoked when the source path contains a `::` separator or a `rsync://` URL.

Listing files on a remote machine. This is done the same way as `rsync` transfers except that you leave off the local destination.

Note that in all cases (other than listing) at least one of the source and destination paths must be local.

Setup

`rsync` uses `rsh` for its communications, unless both the source and destination are local.

You can also specify an alternative to `rsh`, either by using the `-e` command-line option, or by setting the `RSYNC_RSH` environment variable.

One common substitute is to use `ssh`, which offers a high degree of security.

Note that `rsync` must be installed on both the source and destination machines.

Usage

You use `rsync` in the same way you use `rcp`. You must specify a source and a destination, one of which may be remote.

Perhaps the best way to explain the syntax is to give some examples:

```
rsync *.c foo:src/
```

This transfers all files matching the pattern `*.c` from the current directory to the directory `src` on the machine `foo`. If any of the files already exist on the remote system, the `rsync` remote-update protocol is used to update the file by sending only the differences.

```
rsync -avz foo:src/bar /data/tmp
```

This recursively transfers all files from the directory `src/bar` on the machine `foo` into the `/data/tmp/bar` directory on the local machine. The files are transferred in archive mode, which ensures that symbolic links, devices, attributes, permissions, ownerships, and so on are preserved in the transfer. Additionally, compression is used to reduce the size of data portions of the transfer.

```
rsync -avz foo:src/bar/ /data/tmp
```

A trailing slash on the source changes this behavior to transfer all files from the directory `src/bar` on the machine `foo` into the `/data/tmp/`. A trailing `/` on a source name means "copy the contents of this directory." Without a trailing slash, it means "copy the directory." This difference becomes particularly important when using the `--delete` option.

You can also use `rsync` in local-only mode, where both the source and destination don't have a `:` in the name. In this case, it behaves like an improved `copy` command.

```
rsync somehost.mydomain.com::
```

This lists all the anonymous `rsync` modules available on the host `somehost.mydomain.com`.

TABLE 24.1 Continued

Connecting to an rsync server It is also possible to use rsync without using rsh or ssh as the transport. In this case, you connect to a remote rsync server running on TCP port 873. You may establish the connection via a Web proxy by setting the environment variable RSYNC_PROXY to a hostname:port pair pointing to your Web proxy. Note that your Web proxy's configuration must allow proxying to port 873. Using rsync in this way is the same as using it with rsh or ssh except that: You use a double colon :: instead of a single colon to separate the hostname from the path. If you specify no pathname on the remote server, the list of accessible paths on the server is shown. If you specify no local destination, a listing of the specified files on the remote server is provided. Some paths on the remote server may require authentication. If so, then you receive a password prompt when you connect. You can avoid the password prompt by setting the environment variable RSYNC_PASSWORD to the password you want to use or using the --password-file option. This may be useful when scripting rsync.	
-h --help	Prints a short help page describing the available options.
-v --verbose	Increases verbosity, can be specified multiple times to increase verbosity more and more.
-q --quiet	Decreases verbosity. Useful when invoking rsync from cron.
-I --ignore-times	Normally rsync skips any files that are already the same length and have the same timestamp. This option turns off this behavior.
--size-only	Normally rsync skips any files that are already the same length and have the same timestamp. With the --size-only option, files are skipped if they have the same size, regardless of timestamp. Useful when starting to use rsync after using another mirroring system that may not preserve time-stamps exactly.
--modify-window	When comparing two timestamps, rsync treats the timestamps as being equal if they are within the value of modify_window.
-c --checksum	Forces the sender to checksum all files using a 128-bit MD4 checksum before transfer. The checksum is then explicitly checked on the receiver, and any files of the same name that already exist and have the same check-sum and size on the receiver are skipped. This option can be quite slow.
-a --archive	Equivalent to -rlptgoD. It is a quick way of saying that you want recursion and want to preserve almost everything. Note, however, that -a does not preserve hardlinks, because finding multi-ply linked files is expensive. You must separately specify -H.

TABLE 24.1 Continued

`-r` `--recursive`	Copies directories recursively. If you don't specify this, `rsync` won't copy directories at all.
`-R` `--relative`	Uses relative paths. This means that the full pathnames specified on the command line are sent to the server rather than just the last parts of the filenames. This is particularly useful when you want to send several different directories at the same time. For example, if you used the command `rsync foo/bar/foo.c remote:/tmp/rsync -R foo/bar/foo.c remote:/tmp/-b` this would create a file called `foo.c` in `/tmp/` on the remote machine. If instead you used a file called `/tmp/foo/bar/foo.c` would be created on the remote machine. The full pathname is preserved.
`--backup`	With this option, preexisting destination files are renamed with a ~ extension as each file is transferred. You can control the backup suffix using the `--suffix` option.
`--backup-dir=<DIR>`	In combination with the `--backup` option, this tells `rsync` to store all backups in the specified directory. This is useful for incremental backups.
`-u` `--update`	Forces `rsync` to skip any files for which the destination file already exists and that have a date later than the source file.
`-l` `--links`	When symlinks are encountered, re-creates the symlink on the destination.
`-L` `--copy-links`	When symlinks are encountered, the file that they point to is copied, rather than the symlink.
`-W` `--whole-file`	With this option, the incremental `rsync` algorithm is not used, and the whole file is sent as-is instead. The transfer may be faster if this option is used when the bandwidth between the source and target machines is higher than the bandwidth to disk (especially when the disk is actually a networked filesystem). This is the default when both the source and target are on the local machine.
`-p` `--perms`	Causes `rsync` to update the remote permissions to be the same as the local permissions.
`-n` `--dry-run`	Tells `rsync` to not do any file transfers; instead it just reports the actions it would have taken.

TABLE 24.1 Continued

`-x` `--one-file-system`	Tells `rsync` not to cross filesystem boundaries when recursing. This is useful for transferring the contents of only one filesystem.
`--existing`	Tells `rsync` not to create any new files—to only update files that already exist on the destination.
`--max-delete=`*<NUM>*	Tells `rsync` not to delete more than *<NUM>* files or directories. This is useful when mirroring large trees to prevent disasters.
`--delete`	Tells `rsync` to delete any files on the receiving side that aren't on the sending side. Files excluded from transfer are excluded from being deleted unless you use `--delete-excluded`. This option has no effect if directory recursion is not selected. This option can be dangerous if used incorrectly! It is a good idea to run first using the dry run option (`-n`) so that you can see what files would be deleted without actually deleting them, and check to make sure that important files aren't listed for deletion. If the sending side detects any I/O errors, the deletion of any files at the destination is automatically disabled. This is to prevent temporary filesystem failures (such as NFS errors) on the sending side causing a massive deletion of files on the destination. You can override this with the `--ignore-errors` option.
`--force`	Tells `rsync` to delete directories even if they are not empty. This applies to both the `--delete` option and to cases where `rsync` tries to copy a normal file but the destination contains a directory of the same name. Because this option was added, deletions were reordered to be done depth-first, so it is hardly ever needed any more except in obscure cases.
`-e` `--rsh=COMMAND`	Allows you to choose an alternative remote shell program to use for communication between the local and remote copies of `rsync`. By default, `rsync` uses `rsh`, but you might want to use `ssh` instead because of its high security. You can also choose the remote shell program using the `RSYNC_RSH` environment variable. See also the `--blocking-io` option, which is affected by this option.
`--rsync-path=`*<PATH>*	Specifies the path to the copy of `rsync` on the remote machine. Useful when it's not in your path. Note that this is the full path to the binary, not just the directory that the binary is in.
`--csum-length=`*<LENGTH>*	By default, the primary checksum used in `rsync` is a strong 16-byte MD4 checksum. In most cases you will find that a truncated version of this checksum is more efficient for making comparisons, and this will decrease the size of the checksum data sent over the link, making things faster. You can choose the number of bytes in the truncated checksum using the `--csum-length` option. Any value less than or equal to 16 is valid.

TABLE 24.1 Continued

`-T` `--temp-dir=<DIR>`	Instructs `rsync` to use *<DIR>* as a scratch directory when creating temporary copies of the files transferred on the receiving side. The default behavior is to create the temporary files in the receiving directory.
`--numeric-ids`	Transfers numeric group and user IDs instead of using user and group names and mapping them at both ends. By default, `rsync` uses the user name and group name to determine what ownership to give files. The special `uid` 0 and the special group 0 are never mapped via user/group names even if the `--numeric-ids` option is not specified. If the source system is a daemon using `chroot`, or if a user or group name does not exist on the destination system, the numeric ID from the source system is used instead.
`--partial`	Delete any partially transferred file if the transfer is interrupted. In some circumstances it is more desirable to keep partially transferred files. Using the `--partial` option tells `rsync` to keep the partial file, which should make a subsequent transfer of the rest of the file much faster.
`--progress`	Tells `rsync` to print information showing the progress of the transfer. This gives a bored user something to watch. This option is normally combined with `-v`. Using this option without the `-v` option produces weird results on your display.
`--bwlimit=<KBPS>`	Allows you to specify a maximum transfer rate in kilobytes per second. This option is most effective when using `rsync` with large files (several megabytes and up). Due to the nature of `rsync` transfers, blocks of data are sent, and then if `rsync` determines that the transfer was too fast, it waits before sending the next data block. The result is an average transfer rate equaling the specified limit. A value of zero specifies no limit.

Cooperatively Working on Projects: CVS

Concurrent Version System (CVS), on the other hand, is a system whereby users “subscribe” to a central repository of information and can check out parts of the information, edit it, and resubmit it to the central repository. One of the useful features of CVS is that through the checkout and checkin methods, a complete history of the whole archive is constructed and maintained. You can revisit any piece of information at any date in the system. This is particularly useful in programming projects where the ability to back out changes or compare current versions to earlier incarnations of code is sometimes a lifesaver. CVS is worth paying attention to even if you don’t have any reason to implement a CVS server on your machine, because it’s one of the prime routes by which open source software is now distributed.

Using Data from CVS

For using CVS, the primary options you'll be interested in are `login`, `checkout`, `add`, `status`, `log`, and `commit`. With these, you can use the most important features of CVS to acquire, edit, and store files. For example, if I were interested in working on a project served by `soyokaze.apple.com`, and the name of the project was `hduc`, contained in the directory `/archive/cvsroot`, I might connect to the system by using the command:

```
brezup:ray cvstest $ ls -l
brezup:ray cvstest $ cvs -d:pserver:ray@soyokaze.apple.com:
➥/archive/cvsroot login
(Logging in to ray@soyokaze.apple.com)
CVS password:
```

NOTE

There is no space between the `:` after `soyokaze.apple.com` and the `/` before `archive/cvsroot` in the preceding command. This command is specifying a server user account and path as `<user>@<machine>:<path>`. No spaces.

At which point I can issue my password for the CVS repository (*not* the same as my password for the system!). At this point, I am authenticated for that directory on the server, but I can't do much of anything until I have made a copy of the data onto my local machine. The data I'm after is a collection of project files called `hduc`, so I'll ask for that archive when I issue the `checkout` command:

```
brezup:ray cvstest $ cvs -d:pserver:ray@soyokaze.apple.com:/archive/cvsroot
checkout hduc
cvs server: Updating hduc
U hduc/Rd.gbk
U hduc/baclocations.gbk
U hduc/hduc-20001122.gbk
U hduc/hduc-20001122.gbk_old
U hduc/hduc-20010920.gbk
U hduc/hduc-20010920_edit.gbk
U hduc/resequence_areas_sorted
```

And now a directory named `hduc` is created and populated:

```
brezup:ray cvstest $ ls -l
drwxr-xr-x 10 ray staff  340 Sep 16 23:35 hduc
brezup:ray cvstest $ ls -l hduc
total 33536
drwxr-xr-x 5 ray staff   170 Sep 16 23:35 CVS
```

```
-rwxr-xr-x 1 ray staff 4175026 Feb 15 2002 Rd.gbk
-rwxr-xr-x 1 ray staff   13898 Jun 14 2001 baclocations.gbk
-rw-r--r-- 1 ray staff 3231636 May 15 2001 hduc-20001122.gbk
-rwxr-xr-x 1 ray staff 3233476 Feb 15 2002 hduc-20001122.gbk_old
-rwxr-xr-x 1 ray staff 3232208 Feb 15 2002 hduc-20010920.gbk
-rwxr-xr-x 1 ray staff 3232832 Feb 15 2002 hduc-20010920_edit.gbk
-rwxr-xr-x 1 ray staff   35968 May 15 2001 resequence_areas_sorted
```

Now I can check on the status of the project, check the logfiles, and so on:

```
brezup:ray cvstest $ cvs -d:pserver:ray@soyokaze.apple.com:➥/archive/cvsroot status
hduc
cvs server: Examining hduc
===================================================================
File: Rd.gbk      Status: Up-to-date
  Working revision:  1.1
  Repository revision: 1.1 /archive/cvsroot/childrens/hduc/Rd.gbk,v
  Sticky Tag:     (none)
  Sticky Date:     (none)
  Sticky Options:   (none)
===================================================================
File: baclocations.gbk Status: Up-to-date
  Working revision:  1.1
  Repository revision: 1.1  /archive/cvsroot/childrens/hduc/baclocations.gbk,v
  Sticky Tag:     (none)
  Sticky Date:     (none)
  Sticky Options:   (none)
===================================================================
File: hduc-20001122.gbk Status: Up-to-date
  Working revision:  1.29
  Repository revision: 1.29 /archive/cvsroot/childrens/hduc/hduc-20001122.gbk,v
  Sticky Tag:     (none)
  Sticky Date:     (none)
  Sticky Options:   (none)
===================================================================
File: hduc-20001122.gbk_old   Status: Up-to-date
  Working revision:  1.1
  Repository revision: 1.1  /archive/cvsroot/childrens/hduc/hduc-20001122.gbk_old,v
  Sticky Tag:     (none)
  Sticky Date:     (none)
  Sticky Options:   (none)
===================================================================
```

24

```
File: hduc-20010920.gbk Status: Up-to-date
  Working revision:  1.1
  Repository revision: 1.1  /archive/cvsroot/childrens/hduc/hduc-20010920.gbk,v
  Sticky Tag:     (none)
  Sticky Date:     (none)
  Sticky Options:   (none)
===================================================================
File: hduc-20010920_edit.gbk  Status: Up-to-date
  Working revision:  1.1
  Repository revision: 1.1  /archive/cvsroot/childrens/hduc/hduc-20010920_edit.gbk,v
  Sticky Tag:     (none)
  Sticky Date:     (none)
  Sticky Options:   (none)
===================================================================
File: resequence_areas_sorted  Status: Up-to-date
  Working revision:  1.2
  Repository revision: 1.2
➥/archive/cvsroot/childrens/hduc/resequence_areas_sorted,v
  Sticky Tag:     (none)
  Sticky Date:     (none)
  Sticky Options:   -kb
```

If I want to see the comments that have been made for various revisions of a file, I can check its log:

```
brezup:ray cvstest $ cvs -d:pserver:ray@soyokaze.apple.com:➥/archive/cvsroot log
hduc/hduc-20001122.gbk
RCS file: /archive/cvsroot/childrens/hduc/hduc-20001122.gbk,v
Working file: hduc/hduc-20001122.gbk
head: 1.29
branch:
locks: strict
access list:
symbolic names:
keyword substitution: kv
total revisions: 29;  selected revisions: 29
description:
----------------------------
revision 1.29
date: 2001/05/15 18:13:43; author: ray; state: Exp; lines: +20537 -20570
Many gene identification updates - post multocita availability
```

```
----------------------------
revision 1.28
date: 2001/01/08 22:47:37; author: ray; state: Exp; lines: +7 -6
Fixed a few note errors
----------------------------
revision 1.27
date: 2001/01/02 05:40:26; author: ray; state: Exp; lines: +101 -74
Finished annotation uniforming, WCR pass 1
----------------------------
.
.
.
----------------------------
revision 1.12
date: 2000/12/10 08:21:44; author: ray; state: Exp; lines: +132 -88
location., but that have no good starts near the expected
----------------------------
revision 1.11
date: 2000/12/08 20:58:44; author: ray; state: Exp; lines: +30 -0
remaining tRNAs added
----------------------------
revision 1.10
date: 2000/12/08 20:41:23; author: ray; state: Exp; lines: +57 -1
tRNAs Arg, Asn, Asp, cys, Gln, gly, His, Ile, Leu, Lys, Met added
----------------------------
.
.
.
revision 1.2
date: 2000/11/22 18:05:52; author: ray; state: Exp; lines: +1 -1
test commit
----------------------------
revision 1.1
date: 2000/11/22 16:51:30; author: ray; state: Exp;
Early revision H. ducreyi GenBank file
=============================================================================
```

As you can see from the output, a plethora of information is maintained on each of the files. The status information tells you about the current state of each file, and the log information tells you about each of the past versions of the file queried.

If I now wanted to edit one of these files and make the changes available in the archive, I could modify the file in whatever editor I choose, and then simply use the `commit` option to upload it to the archive as a new revision. When `commit` is run, the first thing that happens is that an editor window appears allowing the entry of information regarding the changes that have been made. This is actually a CVS repository that I use for real work, so here I'm providing a comment for myself so that I know I didn't really change anything in this file. To start the process, I execute the cvs `commit` command:

```
brezup:ray cvstest $ cvs -d:pserver:ray@soyokaze.apple.com:/archive/cvsroot commit
hduc/baclocations.gbk
```

An editor opens. This is what I see and have entered in the editor window:

```
Just a quick change to tickle the revision number.
No modifications of any significance, just ignore this one.
CVS: ----------------------------------------------------------------------
CVS: Enter Log. Lines beginning with `CVS:' are removed automatically
CVS:
CVS: Committing in .
CVS:
CVS: Modified Files:
CVS:  hduc/baclocations.gbk
CVS: ----------------------------------------------------------------------
```

After that, the update runs, and the file is added to the archive:

```
Checking in hduc/baclocations.gbk;
/archive/cvsroot/childrens/hduc/baclocations.gbk,v <-- baclocations.gbk
new revision: 1.2; previous revision: 1.1
done
```

If I now listed the log for `baclocations.gbk`, the new revision of the file, tagged with the comment I just entered, would show up at the top of the list, with revision 1.2.

If I found a problem with something in a current version of a file and I wanted to check an older version, I could check out files with a `-D date_spec` option:

```
brezup:ray cvstest $ cvs -d:pserver:ray@soyokaze.apple.com:/archive/cvsroot
checkout -D 7/21/2001 hduc/hduc-20001122.gbk
```

This checks out the file `hduc/hduc-20001122.gbk` in whatever state it existed in the repository on 7/21/2001 (July 21, 2001).

If I decide I'm not interested in changes that I've made to the files and don't want to check back in the edits I've made on them, I can `release` my version back to the CVS server. This discards any changes I might have made to any files in the checked-out directory, though the directory and files it contains remain on your system.

```
brezup:ray cvstest $ cvs -d:pserver:ray@soyokaze.apple.com:/archive/cvsroot
release hduc
U hduc-20010920.gbk
You have [0] altered files in this repository.
Are you sure you want to release directory 'hduc': y
```

There are, of course, numerous other options to the CVS system. Enough in fact, that the official man page has entered the popular open source developer lingo as "The Cederqvist," after one of the prime authors. The Cederqvist is available in a number of forms from `http://www.cvshome.org/docs/manual`. Apple also provides documentation in the Developers tools located at `file://localhost/Developer/Documentation/DeveloperTools/cvs/cvsclient_toc.html` and `file://localhost/Developer/Documentation/DeveloperTools/cvs/cvs_toc.html`.

Command-Line Administration Tools

A number of command-line tools are of assistance in the configuration and maintenance of user accounts. Some of these have functionality duplicated in graphical tools, and some do not. For truly sophisticated user management, we again suggest looking to Mac OS X Server because it provides tools that are considerably more powerful.

NetInfo Utilities

The `nidump`, `niutil`, and `niload` commands are particularly useful for user account creation and deletion. It's also a good idea to be familiar with the `tar` command for backing up NetInfo databases. The command documentation tables for each of the NetInfo-specific commands are provided in Chapter 23. `tar` is documented in Chapter 12. We wouldn't be surprised if someone creates a graphical tool that scripts the sort of account maintenance that has been shown in this chapter and makes it available on the Net. If we managed to pique your interest in shell programming in the earlier chapters, this would be an ideal problem to attack as a learning experience. Because NetInfo is so vital to the operation of the machine, we recommend that you verify, by using `print` statements, that the scripts you create output exactly what you want—before you turn them loose on the NetInfo database.

Common BSD Tools

In addition to the NetInfo commands for creating and modifying user accounts themselves, you have access to a number of standard BSD utilities. Primarily, these allow you to operate on the files in user accounts; but one, the `passwd` command, inserts `crypted` passwords into the NetInfo user record. (This is a little odd because Apple has circumvented most BSD tools of this nature and incorporated their functionality into the NetInfo commands. It wouldn't be too surprising if Apple replaces or supercedes this command with another in the future.)

Changing File Ownership: `chown`

The `chown` command is used to change the ownership of files. Only the `root` user can execute the `chown` command. The simplest form, and the one you'll end up using the most frequently, is `chown` *<username>* *<filename>*, which changes the ownership property of *<filename>* to belong to the user *<username>*. The command can optionally be given as `chown` *<username>*:*<groupname>* *<filename>* to change the user and group at the same time. Additionally, `-R` can be specified after the command to cause a recursive change in an entire directory, instead of to a single file. Table 24.2 shows the command documentation table for `chown`.

TABLE 24.2 The Command Documentation Table for `chown`

chown	Changes file owner and group.
chown [-R [-H ¦ -L ¦ -P]] [-fhv] *<owner>* *<file1>* *<file2>* ...	
chown [-R [-H ¦ -L ¦ -P]] [-fhv] :*<group>* *<file1>* *<file2>* ...	
chown [-R [-H ¦ -L ¦ -P]] [-fhv] *<owner>*:*<group>* *<file1>* *<file2>* ...	
-R	Recursively descends through directory arguments to change the user ID and/or group ID.
-H	If -R is specified, symbolic links on the command line are followed. Symbolic links encountered in tree traversal are not followed.
-L	If -R is specified, all symbolic links are followed.
-P	If -R is specified, no symbolic links are followed.
-f	Forces an attempt to change user ID and/or group ID without reporting any errors.
-h	If the file is a symbolic link, the user ID and/or group ID of the link is changed.
-v	Be verbose about changes.

The `-H`, `-L`, and `-P` options are ignored unless `-R` is specified. Because they also override each other, the last option specified determines the action that is taken.

The `-L` option cannot be used with the `-h` option.

It is not necessary to provide both *<owner>* and *<group>*; however, one must be specified. If group is specified, it must be preceded with a colon (`:`).

The owner may be either a numeric user ID or a username. If a username exists for a numeric user ID, the associated username is used for the owner. Similarly, the group may be either a numeric group ID or a group name. If a group name exists for a group ID, the associated group name is used for the group.

Unless invoked by the superuser, `chown` clears `set-user-id` and `set-group-id` bits.

Changing File Group Ownership: chgrp

The chgrp command functions like the chown command, except that it changes only the group ownership of a file. This can be particularly useful when you want to give a user, or group of users, access to files owned by a number of different users. Instead of changing the ownership of each, or issuing a separate chown *<userid>*:*<groupid>* for each file, you can instead change the file's groups *en masse* to one that the intended user or group can read, while not affecting the actual ownership of the files.

Table 24.3 shows the command documentation table for chgrp.

TABLE 24.3 The Command Documentation Table for chgrp

chgrp	Changes group.
chgrp [-R [-H ¦ -L ¦ -P]] [-fhv] *<group>* *<file1>* *<file2>* ...	
-R	Recursively descends through directory arguments to change the group ID.
-H	If -R is specified, symbolic links on the command line are followed. Symbolic links encountered in tree traversal are not followed.
-L	If -R is specified, all symbolic links are followed.
-P	If -R is specified, no symbolic links are followed.
-f	Forces an attempt to change group ID without reporting any errors.
-h	If the file is a symbolic link, the group ID of the link is changed.
-v	Be verbose about changes.
Unless -h, -H, or -L is specified, chgrp on symbolic links always succeeds and has no effect.	
The -H, -L, and -P options are ignored unless -R is specified. Because they also override each other, the last option specified determines the action that is taken.	
The group may be either a numeric group ID or a group name. If a group name exists for a group ID, the associated group name is used for the group.	
The user invoking chgrp must belong to the specified group and be the owner of the file, or be the superuser.	
Unless invoked by the superuser, chgrp clears set-user-id and set-group-id bits.	

Setting a User's Password: passwd

The passwd command, somewhat unexpectedly, changes a user's password. passwd as a command is a holdover from the days of entirely files-based (no databases) BSD administration. A number of related password and account management commands come from BSD Unix, but with the exception of the passwd command, all the others appear to operate on the local files only. passwd alone has been updated to work cleanly with the NetInfo database. Because the local authentication files (such as /etc/passwd and /etc/group) are usually used only in single-user mode, none of the other commands currently have any significant use in OS X. (We'd like to think that Apple is working on making more of them operate with the NetInfo database, but with OS X 10.3, more BSD things seem to be newly broken than newly fixed, so we aren't too hopeful on this.)

Simply issued as passwd, with no other options, the passwd command enables a user to change her password. The root user has the ability to issue passwd *<username>* to force the password for the user *<username>* to change. Table 24.4 shows the command documentation table for passwd.

TABLE 24.4 The Command Documentation Table for passwd

passwd	Modifies a user's password.
passwd [-i infosystem -l location] [*<user>*]	
passwd changes the user's password in any of a number of authentication systems. The user is first prompted for her old password. The user is next prompted for a new password and then prompted again to retype the new password for verification.	
The new password should be at least six characters in length. It should use a variety of lowercase letters, uppercase letters, numbers, and metacharacters.	
-i *<infosystem>*	Specifies an information system/directory service in which to update the information. Supported options are netinfo (the default), file (for BSD flat files such as /etc/master.passwd), nis (for using Sun's ubiquitous Network Information Systems directory service), and opendirectory (for using LDAP directory services).
-l *<location>*	Specifies a location for the change. Locations are infosystem specific. netinfo accepts domains, or server/tag locations. file accepts filenames. nis accepts NIS domainnames (not the same as Internet domain names). opendirectory accepts LDAP node names.
If no flags are specified, the following occurs:	
If no infosystem and/or location are specified, the change is made in the first infosystem/location in which the user appears. The parent NetInfo domain is searched first and then NetInfo subdomains. Files are used last. Traditional methods of specifying the search order for directory services don't work under OS X, so we aren't sure whether NIS or LDAP have precedence.	

Summary

This chapter covered the techniques used to make your machine into a member of a cooperating cluster of computers, or to make it into a server for such a cluster. It also covered techniques that can be used to automate the creation and customization of user accounts on your machine or in your cluster.

The most important thing to remember is the Unix abstract notion that it doesn't matter where things like user account information are coming from or where drives are coming from. The OS is designed so that it can acquire such information and resources from any compatible system, and so can be combined with any compatible systems to provide a seamless user experience across any number of machines.

Although Mac OS X uses slightly different protocols by default than most Unix systems, the principles are identical to those used by other Unix flavors. If you want to construct a system that is more complex than what we've covered here, don't hesitate to consult references for other Unixes—you'll have to use the information here and in other resources to do a bit of translation, but you should be able to interpret such references with only a little effort.

If you're planning on using your machine only as a personal machine, you'll have only minor need for the material covered here. Do keep in mind that you can use these techniques to network multiple computers in your home or office, so that you have less maintenance and less software configuration to do. If you've no interest in doing even this, don't let the seemingly complex processes outlined here intimidate you. You've got no real need to understand them unless you plan on clustering your machines.

CHAPTER 25
FTP Serving

IN THIS CHAPTER

- Activating the FTP Server
- FTP Server Options
- Setting Up Anonymous FTP
- Using `wu-ftpd` as a Replacement for the Default `ftpd`
- Alternatives to FTP

Sometimes it's helpful to be able to transfer files between machines. If you're collaborating on a project, you and your collaborators might need to exchange files. Because mail spools frequently have file size limits, an FTP server can provide an alternative means to exchange files. If you've built a Web site on one machine but want to transfer it to your Mac OS X machine because you have a Web server running on it, an FTP server can provide a way to do so. With little effort, your Mac OS X machine can run an FTP server to facilitate this activity. In this chapter, we look at the FTP server included in the Mac OS X distribution. Then we look at an alternative, highly configurable FTP server that you could install in place of the default FTP server. Finally, we take a brief look at alternatives that can be used in place of, or in conjunction with, an FTP server.

Activating the FTP Server

The Mac OS X distribution includes an FTP server called `lukemftpd`, which is a port of the NetBSD FTP server. Because Apple is concerned about the security of your machine, this service is not turned on by default. Currently, you can FTP only from your Mac OS X machine to other FTP servers. After you've turned on the FTP service, you can FTP directly to your Mac OS X machine. Unfortunately, this service also makes your machine more vulnerable to outside attacks. Throughout the chapter, we provide suggestions for some simple precautions that you can take to protect your machine. Of course, the best protection is to not turn on the FTP server.

To activate the FTP server, check the FTP Access box under the Services tab of the Sharing pane, as shown in Figure 25.1.

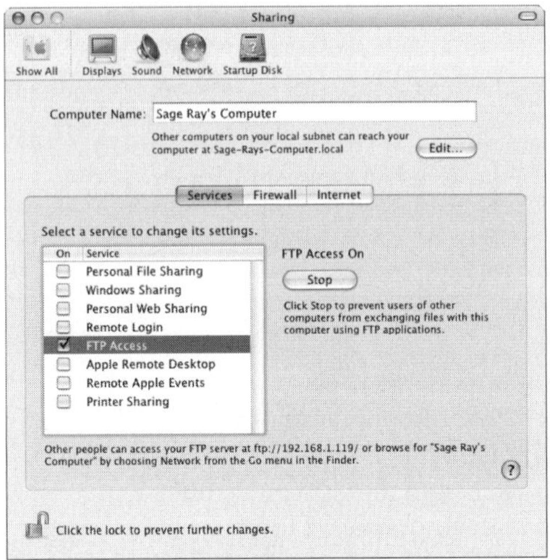

FIGURE 25.1 The FTP server is activated in the Sharing pane.

Behind the scenes, this changes the disable line in `/etc/xinetd.d/ftp` to `disable=no` and forces `xinetd` to reread its configuration file. See Chapter 20, "Command-Line Configuration and Administration," for basic comments about the `/etc/xinetd.d/ftp` file. If, for whatever reason, you're using `inetd` rather than the default `xinetd`, uncomment the `ftp` line and then run `killall -HUP inetd` to have `inetd` reread its configuration file.

When you activate the FTP service, you're opening a service that accepts user IDs and passwords in clear text over your network connection, making that information visible to anyone watching your network. Even though activating the FTP server isn't difficult, we recommend that you look at the "Alternatives to FTP" section later in this chapter first, before you actually activate the FTP server, in case an alternative is more suitable for your needs.

FTP Server Options

You've just turned on your FTP server. If you looked at the `/etc/xinetd.d/ftp` file, you noticed that the server runs by default with the `-l` option (`server_args = -l`), which is the option that forces the logging of successful and unsuccessful FTP sessions.

Many other options are available in the FTP server, and selected ones are detailed in Table 25.1. The complete documentation table is in Appendix A. To implement any of the options, edit the `server_args` entry in `/etc/xinetd.d/ftp` to reflect the options you want to use. Then run `killall -HUP xinetd` to have `xinetd` reread its configuration. Alternatively, if you are using `inetd` instead, edit the ftp entry in `/etc/inetd.conf` to include the desired server arguments and have `inetd` reread its configuration file.

Note that whenever you turn the FTP service on or off via the System Preferences pane, any other configuration changes you have made to the service are retained instead of being reset. Nonetheless, it is a good idea to keep a copy of the file with your configuration changes, in case this default behavior ever changes.

TABLE 25.1 Command Documentation Table for `ftpd`

ftpd	**Internet File Transfer Protocol Server**
`ftpd [-dHlqQrsuUwWX] [-a` *<anondir>*`] [-c` *<confdir>*`] [-C` *<user>*`] [-e` *<emailaddr>*`] [-h` *<hostname>*`] [-P` *<dataport>*`] [-V` *<version>*`]`	
`ftpd` is the Internet File Transfer Protocol process. It uses the TCP protocol and runs on the port specified as `ftp` in the services directory of the NetInfo database.	
`-a` *<anondir>*	Defines *<anondir>* as the directory to `chroot(2)` into for anonymous logins. Default is the home directory for the `ftp` user. This can also be specified with the `ftpd.conf(5) chroot` directive.
`-c` *<confdir>*	Changes the root directory of the configuration files from `/etc` to *<confdir>*. This changes the directory for the following files: `/etc/ftpchroot`, `/etc/ftpusers`, `/etc/ftpwelcome`, `/etc/motd`, and the file specified by the `ftpd.conf(5)` limit directive.
`-h` *<hostname>*	Explicitly sets the hostname to advertise as *<hostname>*. Default is the hostname associated with the IP address that `ftpd` is listening on. This capability (with or without `-h`), in conjunction with `-c` *<confdir>*, is useful when configuring virtual FTP servers, each listening on separate addresses as separate names.
`-H`	Equivalent to `-h` *<hostname>*.
`-l`	Logs each successful and failed FTP session using syslog with a facility of `LOG_FTP`.
`-P` *<dataport>*	Uses *<dataport>* as the data port, overriding the default of using the port one less than the port `ftpd` is listening on.
`-q`	Enables the use of PID files for keeping track of the number of logged-in users per class. This is the default.
`-U`	Doesn't log each concurrent FTP session to `/var/run/utmp`. This is the default.
`-V` *<version>*	Uses *<version>* as the version to advertise in the login banner and in the output of `STAT` and `SYST` instead of the default version information. If version is `-` or empty, it doesn't display any version information.

Restricting Access

The FTP server uses three main configuration files for restricting access: `/etc/ftpusers`, `/etc/ftpchroot`, and `/etc/ftpd.conf`. By using these files, you can place restrictions on who can use FTP to access your machine—blocking certain users and allowing others. You can also configure limitations to the type and frequency of access granted by limiting the number of connections, and setting timeouts and other server-related limits on FTP server availability and capability.

An /etc/ftpusers file comes by default. This file contains the list of users who aren't allowed FTP access to the machine. Here's the default file:

```
brezup:sage Documents $ more /etc/ftpusers
# list of users disallowed any ftp access.
# read by ftpd(8).
Administrator
administrator
root
uucp
daemon
unknown
www
```

If you have additional users who shouldn't be granted FTP access, include them in this file. Also include any system logins that might not be listed by default in this file. Because the syntax for this file can be more complex, its documentation is included in Table 25.2.

The FTP server also allows for chrooted FTP access, which is a compromise between full access and anonymous-only access. With this compromise access, a user is granted FTP access to only his home directory. List any users who should have this type of access in the /etc/ftpchroot file.

The last major configuration file for the default ftpd is /etc/ftpd.conf. In this file, you can define classes and various types of restrictions for a given class. This FTP server is supposed to understand three classes of user: REAL, CHROOT, and GUEST. A REAL user has full access to your machine. A CHROOT user is restricted to his home directory or a directory otherwise specified in /etc/ftpd.conf. A GUEST user can connect to the machine for anonymous FTP only.

The basic form of a line in ftpd.conf is

```
<directive> <class> <argument>
```

Although there's no default /etc/ftpd.conf file, these are the defaults that the FTP server uses:

```
checkportcmd all
classtype    chroot CHROOT
classtype    guest  GUEST
classtype    real   REAL
display      none
limit        all    -1    # unlimited connections
maxtimeout   all    7200  # 2 hours
modify       all
motd         all    motd
notify       none
passive      all
```

```
timeout     all   900  # 15 minutes
umask       all   027
upload      all
modify      guest off
umask       guest 0707
```

Directives that appear later in the file override directives that appear earlier. This gives you the opportunity to define defaults as wildcards. In addition to the defaults you see listed in the preceding file, other available controls include ones for limiting the upload and download storage rates, maximum uploadable file size, and port ranges. The last control can be useful for setting up your FTP server to work while a firewall is also running on your machine. Table 25.3 details select directives for the `/etc/ftpd.conf` file. The complete documentation is available in Appendix A.

TABLE 25.2 Documentation for `/etc/ftpusers`

`ftpusers`	`ftpd` **access control files.**
`ftpchroot`	
`/etc/ftpusers`	The `/etc/ftpusers` file provides user access control for `ftpd(8)` by defining which users may log in. If the `/etc/ftpusers` file does not exist, all users are denied access. The syntax of each line is `<userglob>[:<groupglob>][@<host>] [<directive> [<class>]]`
These elements are	
<userglob>	is matched against the username, using `fnmatch(3)` glob matching (for example, `f*`).
<groupglob>	is matched against all the groups that the user is a member of, using `fnmatch(3)` glob matching (for example, `*src`).
<host>	is either a `CIDR` address (refer to `inet_net_pton(3)`) to match against the remote address (for example, `1.2.3.4/24`), or an `fnmatch(3)` glob to match against the remote hostname (for example, `*.netbsd.org`).
<directive>	allows access to the user if set to `allow` or `yes`. Denies access to the user if set to `deny` or `no`, or if the directive is not present.
<class>	defines the class to use in `ftpd.conf(5)`.
If *<class>*	isn't given, it defaults to one of the following:
`chroot`	if there's a match in `/etc/ftpchroot` for the user.
`guest`	if the username is `anonymous` or `ftp`.
`real`	if neither of the preceding conditions is true.
No further comparisons are attempted after the first successful match. If no match is found, the user is granted access. This syntax is backward compatible with the old syntax.	
If a user requests a guest login, the `ftpd(8)` server checks to see that both `anonymous` and `ftp` have access. So, if you deny all users by default, you must add both `anonymous allow` and `ftp allow` to `/etc/ftpusers` to allow guest logins.	
`/etc/ftpchroot`	
The file `/etc/ftpchroot` is used to determine which users will have their session's root directory changed (using `chroot(2)`), either to the directory specified in the `ftpd.conf(5) chroot` directive (if set), or to the home directory of the user. If the file doesn't exist, the root directory change is not performed.	

TABLE 25.3 Documentation for `/etc/ftpd.conf`

ftpd.conf	`ftpd(8)` **configuration file.**

The `ftpd.conf` file specifies various configuration options for `ftpd(8)` that apply after a user has authenticated his connection.

`ftpd.conf` consists of a series of lines, each of which may contain a configuration directive, a comment, or a blank line. Directives that appear later in the file override settings by previous directives. This allows wildcard entries to define defaults and then have class-specific overrides.

A directive line has the format:

`<command> <class> [<arguments>]`

Each authenticated user is a member of a class, which is determined by `ftpusers(5)`. Class is used to determine which `ftpd.conf` entries apply to the user. The following special classes exist when parsing in entries:

`all` matches any class.

`none` matches no class.

Each class has a type, which may be one of the following:

`GUEST` Guests (as per the `anonymous` and `ftp` logins). A `chroot(2)` is performed after login.

`CHROOT` `chroot(2)`ed users (as per `ftpchroot(5)`). A `chroot(2)` is performed after login.

`REAL` Normal users.

The `ftpd(8)` `STAT` command returns the class settings for the current user, unless the private directive is set for the class.

`advertise <class> host`	Sets the address to advertise in the response to the `PASV` and `LPSV` commands to the address for host (which may be either a hostname or IP address).
`chroot <class> [<pathformat>]`	If `<pathformat>` is not given or `<class>` is none, uses the default behavior. Otherwise, `<pathformat>` is parsed to create a directory to create as the root directory with `chroot(2)` into on login.

The default root directory is

`CHROOT` The user's home directory.

`GUEST` If `-a` *<anondir>* is given, uses *<anondir>*; otherwise, uses the home directory of the FTP user.

`REAL` By default, no `chroot(2)` is performed.

`classtype <class> <type>`	Sets the class type of `<class>` to `<type>`.
`conversion <class> <suffix> [<type> <disable> <command>]`	Defines an automatic inline file conversion.
`homedir <class> [<pathformat>]`	If `<pathformat>` isn't given or `<class>` is none, uses the default behavior. Otherwise, `<pathformat>` is parsed to create a directory to change to on login, and to use as the home directory of the user for tilde expansion in pathnames, and so on.
`limit <class> <count> [<file>]`	Limits the maximum number of concurrent connections for `<class>` to `<count>`, with 0 meaning unlimited connections.

TABLE 25.3 Continued

ftpd.conf	`ftpd(8)` configuration file.
`maxfilesize <class> <size>`	Sets the maximum size of an uploaded file to size.
`maxtimeout <class> <time>`	Sets the maximum timeout period that a client may request, defaulting to two hours. This cannot be less than 30 seconds or the value for `timeout`. If `<class>` is none or time is not specified, sets to default of two hours.
`passive <class> [off]`	If `<class>` is none or off is given, prevents passive (`PASV`, `LPSV`, and `EPSV`) connections. Otherwise, enables them.
`portrange <class> <min> <max>`	Sets the range of port numbers for the passive data port.
`rateget <class> <rate>`	Sets the maximum get (`RETR`) transfer rate throttle for `<class>` to rate bytes per second.
`rateput <class> <rate>`	Sets the maximum put (`STOR`) transfer rate throttle for `<class>` to `<rate>` bytes per second, which is parsed as per `rateget` rate.
`timeout <class> <time>`	Sets the inactivity timeout period.
`upload <class> [off]`	If `<class>` is none or off is given, disables the following commands: `APPE`, `STOR`, and `STOU`, as well as the modify commands: `CHMOD`, `DELE`, `MKD`, `RMD`, `RNFR`, and `UMASK`. Otherwise, enables them.

25

Logging

The FTP server logs connections to `/var/log/ftp.log`. Typical entries in the log look like this:

```
Sep 14 00:41:26 localhost ftpd[532]: connection from ? to
brezup
Sep 14 04:41:35 localhost ftpd[532]: ANONYMOUS FTP LOGIN FROM
192.168.1.200, joray@ (class: guest, type: GUEST)
Sep 14 04:43:16 localhost ftpd[532]: Data traffic: 1087050 bytes in 1
file
Sep 14 04:43:16 localhost ftpd[532]: Total traffic: 1088966 bytes in
3 transfers
Sep 14 00:44:13 localhost ftpd[542]: connection from ? to
brezup
Sep 14 04:44:17 localhost ftpd[542]: FTP LOGIN FROM ? as
miwa (class: chroot, type: CHROOT)
Sep 14 04:44:37 localhost ftpd[542]: Data traffic: 2485381 bytes in 2
files
Sep 14 04:44:37 localhost ftpd[542]: Total traffic: 2488561 bytes in 3
transfers
```

```
Sep 14 00:45:28 localhost ftpd[546]: connection from ? to brezup
Sep 14 00:45:33 localhost ftpd[546]: FTP LOGIN FROM ? as
sage (class: real, type: REAL)
Sep 14 00:45:46 localhost ftpd[546]: Data traffic: 1562810 bytes in 1
file
Sep 14 00:45:46 localhost ftpd[546]: Total traffic: 1563473 bytes in 1
transfer
```

The `ftp.log` file shows who logged in, where the user logged in from, and what FTP class the user belongs to. In the case of an anonymous connection, the password used can identify the user. The file logs data size, the number of files transferred, the total amount of data, and the total number of files for a given session. Note that some versions of this FTP server show the IP address for where the user logged in from, but this version shows `?`.

Setting Up Anonymous FTP

As you've seen, setting up the FTP server to allow real users to have FTP access is not difficult. Unfortunately, it suffers from the basic design vulnerability of transmitting the user's information in clear text. In some instances, you can reduce this risk by setting up an anonymous FTP server instead. Anonymous FTP servers allow users to connect, upload, and (potentially) download files without the use of a real-user user ID and password. Of course, this brings the risk that you will not know who is logging in to your system via the anonymous FTP service, and preventing unauthorized users from accessing the system is difficult if everyone is known only as "anonymous." But if anonymous users can't do anything damaging, or see any data that's private while so connected, this might be a good trade-off for the security of not allowing real user connections and the problems this brings. Anonymous FTP servers also are useful for enabling users with no account on your machine to acquire or provide information, such as to download product literature, or upload suggestions or possible modifications to a project on which you're working. In other words, anonymous FTP servers provide an easy cross-platform way to conveniently distribute or receive files.

CAUTION

Remember, even if you set up an anonymous-only FTP server, there's nothing to prevent your real users from trying to enter their user IDs and passwords at the prompts.

Setting up the FTP server to allow anonymous FTP takes some work, however. Be warned that setting up anonymous FTP makes your machine vulnerable to more attacks. We recommend that you do not enable anonymous FTP unless you need it. However, we more strongly recommend against enabling unprotected FTP for real users

Setting up anonymous FTP involves making an `ftp` user, whose home directory is where anonymous FTP users connect. Additionally, you copy the necessary system components to ftp's account so that users can run ls properly. When a user requests a list of files via the FTP ls command, the command that is actually executed is a server-side binary program kept in a special directory for the FTP server's use, the home directory of the ftp user. When the FTP server is chrooted, it can't access /bin/ls; therefore, placing a copy of ls and any other system components that the FTP server needs in its special directory is normally an important step. However, starting with the Mac OS X 10.2 release, the system components don't seem to help for running ls. This isn't a problem with the default ftpd in the 10.3 release or with the wu-ftpd that we discuss later because both FTP servers can provide an internal ls. Because it's difficult to predict how a new release of either system software or FTP server software will change things, we include the steps for the system components to install in case Apple modifies OS X so that you don't have to rely on the FTP server having its own ls again. Steps 4–10 listed in the following pages include the instructions for copying the appropriate system components.

To set up an anonymous FTP site, do the following:

1. Create an ftp user in the NetInfo database. Follow the pattern of one of the generic users, such as user unknown. You might start by duplicating the unknown user and editing the duplicate user. Create your ftp user with the basic parameters shown in Table 25.4.

TABLE 25.4 Basic Parameters for an ftp User

Property	Value
name	ftp
realname	*<some generic reference to ftp>*
uid	*<some unused uid number>*
passwd	*
home	*<some suitable location>*
shell	/dev/null
gid	*<some unused gid number>*
change	0

Figure 25.2 shows the values we used for our ftp user.

2. Create an ftp group in the NetInfo database. Make sure that you assign the same gid to the ftp group that you indicated for the ftp user.

3. Create a home directory for user ftp. Make sure that you create the directory that you specified in the NetInfo database (/Users/ftp in this example). The directory should be owned by root and have permissions 555.

4. Create a ~ftp/bin/ directory, owned by root with permissions 555.

5. Copy the system's /bin/ls to ~ftp/bin/.

6. Create ~ftp/usr/lib/. Each of those directories should be owned by root with permissions 555.

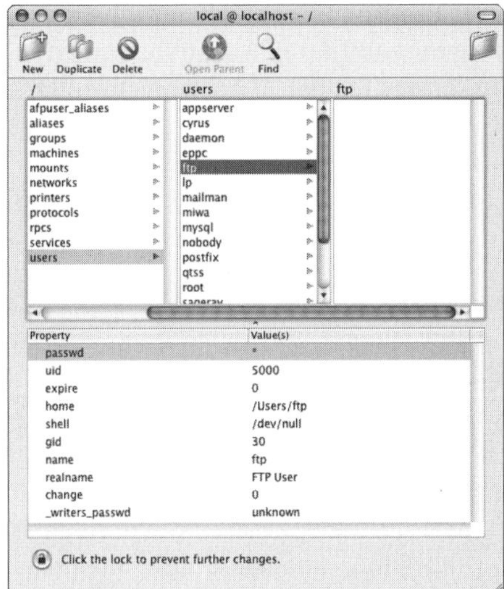

FIGURE 25.2 Here's how we chose to create our `ftp` user as shown in NetInfo Manager.

7. Copy the system's `/usr/lib/dyld` to `~ftp/usr/lib/`. This is one of the files that helps `ls` function properly in this `chroot`ed environment.

8. Copy the system's `/usr/lib/libSystem.B.dylib` to `~ftp/usr/lib/`. This is another file that helps `ls` function properly in the `chroot`ed environment.

9. Create `~ftp/System/Library/Frameworks/System.framework/Versions/B/`. Each of the directories in this path should be owned by `root` with permissions `555`.

10. Copy the system's `/System/Library/Frameworks/System.framework/ Versions/B/ System` to `~ftp/System/Library/Frameworks/System.framework/Versions/B/`. This is another file that helps `ls` function properly in the `chroot`ed environment.

11. Create a `~ftp/pub/` directory in which files can be stored for download. Recommended ownership of this directory includes some user and group `ftp` or user `root`. Typical permissions for this directory are `755`.

12. If you also want to make a drop location where files could be uploaded, create `~ftp/incoming/`, owned by `root`. Recommended permissions include `753`, `733`, `1733`, `3773`, or `777`. You could also create `~ftp/incoming/` with permissions `751` and subdirectories that are used as the drop locations with any of the recommended drop-off permissions.

If you decide to allow anonymous FTP, make sure that you regularly check the anonymous FTP area and your logs for any unusual activity. In addition, regularly check Apple's Web site for any updates for Mac OS X that include `ftp` updates. Security holes are regularly found in `ftpd` and regularly fixed.

For your convenience, here's a listing of our `ftp` user's home directory:

```
brezup:sage Users $ ls -lRaF ftp
total 0
dr-xr-xr-x 7 root wheel 238 Sep 13 00:04 ./
drwxrwxr-t 8 root wheel 272 Sep 12 23:56 ../
dr-xr-xr-x 3 root wheel 102 Sep 13 00:00 System/
dr-xr-xr-x 3 root wheel 102 Sep 12 23:57 bin/
drwxr-x-wx 2 root wheel  68 Sep 13 00:04 incoming/
drwxr-xr-x 2 root wheel  68 Sep 13 00:04 pub/
dr-xr-xr-x 3 root wheel 102 Sep 12 23:57 usr/

ftp/System:
total 0
dr-xr-xr-x 3 root wheel 102 Sep 13 00:00 ./
dr-xr-xr-x 7 root wheel 238 Sep 13 00:04 ../
dr-xr-xr-x 3 root wheel 102 Sep 13 00:01 Library/

ftp/System/Library:
total 0
dr-xr-xr-x 3 root wheel 102 Sep 13 00:01 ./
dr-xr-xr-x 3 root wheel 102 Sep 13 00:00 ../
dr-xr-xr-x 3 root wheel 102 Sep 13 00:02 Frameworks/

ftp/System/Library/Frameworks:
total 0
dr-xr-xr-x 3 root wheel 102 Sep 13 00:02 ./
dr-xr-xr-x 3 root wheel 102 Sep 13 00:01 ../
dr-xr-xr-x 3 root wheel 102 Sep 13 00:02 System.framework/

ftp/System/Library/Frameworks/System.framework:
total 0
dr-xr-xr-x 3 root wheel 102 Sep 13 00:02 ./
dr-xr-xr-x 3 root wheel 102 Sep 13 00:02 ../
dr-xr-xr-x 3 root wheel 102 Sep 13 00:02 Versions/

ftp/System/Library/Frameworks/System.framework/Versions:
total 0
dr-xr-xr-x 3 root wheel 102 Sep 13 00:02 ./
dr-xr-xr-x 3 root wheel 102 Sep 13 00:02 ../
dr-xr-xr-x 3 root wheel 102 Sep 13 00:03 B/
```

```
ftp/System/Library/Frameworks/System.framework/Versions/B:
total 2440
dr-xr-xr-x 3 root wheel    102   Sep 13 00:03 ./
dr-xr-xr-x 3 root wheel    102   Sep 13 00:02 ../
-r-xr-xr-x 1 root wheel 1546264 Sep 13 00:03 System*

ftp/bin:
total 56
dr-xr-xr-x 3 root wheel  102    Sep 12 23:57 ./
dr-xr-xr-x 7 root wheel  238    Sep 13 00:04 ../
-r-xr-xr-x 1 root wheel 32464   Sep 12 23:57 ls*

ftp/incoming:
total 0
drwxr-x-wx 2 root wheel  68     Sep 13 00:04 ./
dr-xr-xr-x 7 root wheel 238     Sep 13 00:04 ../

ftp/pub:
total 0
drwxr-xr-x 2 root wheel  68     Sep 13 00:04 ./
dr-xr-xr-x 7 root wheel 238     Sep 13 00:04 ../

ftp/usr:
total 0
dr-xr-xr-x 3 root wheel 102     Sep 12 23:57 ./
dr-xr-xr-x 7 root wheel 238     Sep 13 00:04 ../
dr-xr-xr-x 4 root wheel 136     Sep 12 23:59 lib/

ftp/usr/lib:
total 3128
dr-xr-xr-x 4 root wheel    136   Sep 12 23:59 ./
dr-xr-xr-x 3 root wheel    102   Sep 12 23:57 ../
-r-xr-xr-x 1 root wheel  385956 Sep 12 23:58 dyld*
-r-xr-xr-x 1 root wheel 1546264 Sep 12 23:59 libSystem.B.dylib*
```

For additional thoughts on anonymous FTP configuration, you might want to check these Web sites:

- CERT Coordination Center's Anonymous FTP Configuration Guidelines—`http://www.cert.org/tech_tips/anonymous_ftp_config.html`
- WU-FTPD Resource Center's Documents link—`http://www.landfield.com/wu-ftpd/`
- AppleCare Service & Support—`http://www.info.apple.com/`

Using wu-ftpd as a Replacement for the Default ftpd

If you decide to activate anonymous FTP, especially anonymous FTP with an upload directory, consider replacing the default ftpd with a more modifiable ftpd. A popular, highly configurable replacement ftpd is wu-ftpd, available at http://www.wu-ftpd.org/. In addition to being highly configurable, it easily compiles under Mac OS X 10.2 and earlier, and with some modifications in 10.3.

Although popular and highly configurable, wu-ftpd is not exempt from security problems. It's still important to regularly monitor the anonymous FTP area, if you have one, as well as make sure that you have the latest version of wu-ftpd, which is version 2.6.2 as of this writing.

NOTE

As of this writing, if you decide to replace the default ftpd with wu-ftpd, or even with the latest version of the default ftpd, now tnftpd, available from ftp://ftp.netbsd.org/pub/NetBSD/misc/tnftp/, anonymous ftp works fine. However, real and, in the case of wu-ftpd, guest users cannot use the FTP server. Default user accounts in 10.3 use ;ShadowHash; authentication, which apparently has not yet been well integrated into the system. We expect that this problem will be corrected in the future. However, if you change the default FTP server to another one, whether or not it is one mentioned here, and your real users can not use the FTP server, change their authentication method in NetInfo to ;basic; authentication. Details on this are covered in Chapter 24, "User Management and Machine Clustering."

How to Replace ftpd with wu-ftpd

To replace the default ftpd with wu-ftpd, first download, compile, and install wu-ftpd. wu-ftpd is one of the packages that follows this basic format for compilation and installation:

```
./configure
make
make install
```

When you download the wu-ftpd source files, also download any patches available for the source. After a patch file is copied to the root directory of the source, run patch as follows:

```
brezup:software wu-ftpd-2.6.2 350 $ patch -p0 < realpath.patch
```

The default config.guess and config.sub files that come with the wu-ftpd source don't work with Mac OS X. Use the files that come with Mac OS X:

```
brezup:software wu-ftpd-2.6.2 351 $ cp /usr/share/automake-1.6/config.guess ./
brezup:software wu-ftpd-2.6.2 352 $ cp /usr/share/automake-1.6/config.sub ./
```

If you are using Mac OS X 10.3, at the top of the wu-ftpd source directory, do the following:

1. In src/proto.h change

   ```
   char *strcasestr(register char *s, register char *find);
   ```

   to

   ```
   /* char *strcasestr(register char *s, register char *find); */
   ```

2. Run grep "nameser" */* and then change all occurrences of

   ```
   #include <arpa/nameser.h>
   ```

   to

   ```
   #include <arpa/nameser_compat.h>
   ```

3. In src/Makefile, change

   ```
   LIBS= -lsupport
   ```

   to

   ```
   LIBS= -lsupport -lresolv
   ```

If you haven't already done so, create a bin user. The bin user is needed for wu-ftpd to install properly. The bin user should have a relatively low uid. Mac OS X already comes with a bin group with gid 7. In many other Unix variants, the bin user has the same uid and gid. As with the ftp user, follow the basic parameters of a generic user, such as the unknown user. You might consider duplicating the unknown user and editing values. Table 25.5 shows suggested values for the bin user.

TABLE 25.5 Suggested Parameters for a bin User

Property	Value
name	bin
realname	System Tools Owner
uid	7
passwd	*
home	/bin
shell	/bin/sync
gid	7
change	0

Next, you're ready to run ./configure. Being the highly configurable package that it is, you can pass many parameters to configure, common and/or interesting ones of which are detailed in Table 25.6. Make sure that you read the installation documentation for more details.

TIP

To have an ls that works properly under Mac OS X 10.2 or 10.3 for anonymous FTP or guest FTP, you may need to use the --enable-ls option.

TABLE 25.6 Select Options to Configure for wu-ftpd

Option	Description
--with-etc-dir=<PATH>	Path for configuration files; usually /etc.
--with-pid-dir=<*PATH*>	Path for run/pid files; usually /var.
--with-log-dir=<*PATH*>	Path for log files (xferlog); usually /var/log.
--prefix=<*PATH*>	Path for the files not specified by --with-etc-dir, --with-pid-dir, and --with-log-dir.
--disable-upload	Disables support for the upload keyword in the ftpaccess file.
--disable-overwrite	Disables support for the overwrite keyword in the ftpaccess file.
--enable-anononly	Allows only anonymous FTP connections.
--enable-paranoid	Disables some features that might possibly affect security.
--disable-map-chdir	Doesn't keep track of user's path changes. This leads to worse symlink handling.
--enable-crackers	Doesn't wait for password entry if someone tries to log in with a wrong username. Although convenient, it's a security risk in that crackers can find out names of valid users.
--disable-virtual	Disables support of virtual servers.
--disable-closedvirt	Allows guests to log in to virtual servers.
--disable-dns	Skips all DNS lookups.
--disable-port	Disallows port mode connections.
--disable-pasv	Disallows passive mode connections.
--disable-pasvip	Doesn't require the same IP for control and data connection in passive mode. This is more secure but can cause trouble with some firewalls.
--disable-anonymous	Allows only real users to connect.
--enable-ls	Uses the internal ls command instead of /bin/ls in the chroot directory. This is experimental and has known problems.

To distinctly separate the wu-ftpd installation from the default ftpd, consider specifying paths in the various path parameters. In addition, you might consider running ./configure with --prefix=<*some-directory-for-wu-ftpd*> so that the wu-ftpd binaries and man pages are all in one place. You might also find it interesting that you can create either an anonymous-only or a real users-only FTP server. Next, run `make` and `make install`.

After you have a `wu-ftpd` binary, update the `/etc/xinetd.d/ftp` file to reflect the location of the new `ftpd` as well as any runtime options that should be used. After you've adjusted `/etc/xinetd.d/ftp`, have `xinetd` reread its configuration file. Table 25.7 details some runtime options available in `wu-ftpd`. Complete documentation is located in Appendix A.

TABLE 25.7 Select Runtime Options Available in `wu-ftpd`

`ftpd`	**Internet File Transfer Protocol server.**
`ftpd`	`[-d] [-v] [-l] [-t` *<timeout>*`] [-T` *<maxtimeout>*`] [-a] [-A] [-L] [-i] [-I] [-o] [-p` *<ctrlport>*`] [-P` *<dataport>*`] [-q] [-Q] [-r` *<rootdir>*`] [-s] [-S] [-u` *<mask>*`] [-V] [-w] [-X]`. `ftpd` is the Internet File Transfer Protocol process. It uses the TCP protocol and runs on the port specified as `ftp` in the services directory of the NetInfo database.
`-d`	Logs debugging information to the syslog.
`-l`	Logs each FTP session to the syslog.
`-t` *<timeout>*	Sets the inactivity timeout period to *<timeout>* seconds. Default is 15 minutes.
`-T` *<maxtimeout>*	A client may also request a different timeout period. The maximum period may be set to *<maxtimeout>* seconds. Default is two hours.
`-a`	Enables the use of the `ftpaccess (5)` configuration file.
`-A`	Disables the use of the `ftpaccess (5)` configuration file. This is the default.
`-L`	Logs commands sent to the `ftpd` server to the syslog. Overriden by the use of the `ftpaccess` file.
`-o`	Logs files transmitted by the `ftpd` server to the `xferlog (5)`. Overridden by the use of the `ftpaccess (5)` file.
`-P` *<dataport>*	Override port numbers used by the daemon.
`-p` *<ctrlport>*	
`-q -Q`	Determine whether the daemon uses the PID files required by the limit directive to determine the number of current users in each access class. Disabling the use of PID files disables user limits. Default, `-q`, is to use PID files.
`-r` *<rootdir>*	Instructs the daemon to `chroot (2)` to *<rootdir>* immediately on loading. This can improve system security by limiting the files that can be damaged in a break-in. Setup is much like anonymous FTP, with additional files required.
`-u` *<umask>*	Sets the default `umask` to *<umask>*.
`-V`	Displays the copyright and version information and then terminates.
`-w`	Records every login and logout. This is the default.

Limiting Access

Access to wu-ftpd can be limited through the use of the ftpusers, ftphosts, and ftpaccess files.

ftpusers

Like the default ftpd, wu-ftpd also uses an ftpusers file as a way of restricting access on a per-user basis. Copy the default /etc/ftpusers file to the etc directory of your wu-ftpd installation and add any users who should not be granted FTP access.

ftphosts

The ftphosts file is used to allow or deny access on a user/host basis. The basic syntax of a rule is as follows:

```
allow <username> <addrglob> [<addrglob> …]
deny <username> <addrglob> [<addrglob> …]
```

The *<addrglob>* may be a specific hostname, IP address, or pattern of each. Additionally, *<addrglob>* may also be specified as address/cidr or address:netmask.

As you may expect, the order of the allow and deny rules can be important; the rules are processed sequentially on a first-match-wins basis. When you create these rules, be sure to think about rule order, particularly with any allow and deny pairs.

For example, to grant user marvin access from only marvin.biosci.ohio-state.edu, but not any other machines on the biosci.ohio-state.edu network, use this set of rules:

```
allow marvin marvin.biosci.ohio-state.edu
deny marvin *.biosci.ohio-state.edu
```

If the rules were reversed, then wu-ftpd would encounter the deny rule first, which would deny access to user marvin from all biosci.ohio-state.edu machines, including marvin.biosci.ohio-state.edu.

ftpaccess

Although wu-ftpd provides a lot of configuration options with its compile-time and runtime options, more controls can be set in the ftpaccess file. To enable the use of the ftpaccess file, be sure to run wu-ftpd with the -a option.

Table 25.8 documents selected useful controls in ftpaccess. Be sure to read the ftpaccess man page thoroughly for information about these and other available controls.

TABLE 25.8 Selected Controls Available for `ftpaccess`

Control	Function
`loginfails <number>`	Logs a "repeated login failures" message after `<number>` login failures. Default is 5.
`class <class> <typelist> <address> [<address>...]`	Sets up classes of users and valid access addresses. `<typelist>` is a comma-separated list of any of these keywords: `real`, `anonymous`, or `guest`. If `real` is included, the class can include users FTPing to real accounts. If anonymous is included, the class can include anonymous FTP users. If `guest` is included, the class can include members of guest access accounts.
`guestgroup <groupname> [<groupname>...]`	For `guestgroup`, if a real user is a member of any specified `<groupname>`, the session is set up exactly as with anonymous FTP. In other words, a `chroot` is done and the user is no longer permitted to issue the `USER` and `PASS` commands. `<groupname>` is a valid group from NetInfo. In other words, a real user whose group is `<groupname>` is treated as a guest FTP user. A guest user's home directory must be properly set up, exactly as anonymous FTP would be. The group name may be specified by either name or numeric ID. To use a numeric group ID, place a `%` before the number. Ranges may be given. Use an asterisk to mean all groups.
`guestuser <username> [<username> ...]`	`guestuser` works like `guestgroup`, except it uses the username (or numeric ID).
`realgroup <groupname> [<groupname> ...]`	
`realuser <username> [<username> ...]`	`realuser` and `realgroup` have the same syntax, but reverse the effect of `guestuser` and `guestgroup`. They allow real user access when the remote user would otherwise be determined a guest.
`limit <class> <number> <times> <message_file>`	Limits the number of users belonging to `<class>` to access the server during the `<times>` indicated and posts `<message_file>` as the reason for access denial.
`file-limit [<raw>] <in ¦ out ¦ total> <count> [<class>]`	Limits the number of files a user in `<class>` may transfer. Limit may be placed on files in, out, or total. If no class is specified, the limit is the default for classes that do not have a limit specified. `<raw>` applies the limit to the total traffic rather than just data files.

TABLE 25.8 Continued

Control	Function
data-limit [<raw>] <in ¦ out ¦ total> *<count>* [*<class>*]	Limits the number of data bytes a user in *<class>* total> *<count>* [*<class>*]may transfer. Limit may be placed on bytes in, out, or total. If no class is specified, the limit is the default for classes that do not have a limit specified. <raw> applies the limit to the total traffic rather than just data files.
limit-time {* ¦ anonymous ¦ guest} *<minutes>*	Limits the total time a session can take. By default, there is no limit. Real users are never limited.
log commands *<typelist>*	Logs individual commands issued by users in *<typelist>*, where *<typelist>* is a comma-separated list of any of the keywords real, anonymous, or guest.
log transfers *<typelist>* *<directions>*	Logs the transfers of users belonging to <typelist> in the specified *<directions>*. *<typelist>* is a comma-separated list of any of the keywords real, anonymous, or guest. *<directions>* is a comma-separated list of the keywords inbound or outbound, where inbound refers to transfers to the server, and outbound refers to transfers from the server.
log syslog	Redirects logging messages for incoming and outgoing transfers to the system log. Default is xferlog.
log syslog+xferlog	Logs transfer messages to both the system log and xferlog.
defaultserver deny *<username>* [*<username>*...]	
defaultserver allow *<username>* [*<username>*...]	By default all users are allowed access to the default, nonvirutal FTP server. defaultserver <deny> denies access to specific users. You could use defaultserver <deny> * to deny access to all users, and then use defaultserver <allow> to allow specific users.
guestserver [*<hostname>*]	Controls which hosts may be used for anonymous or guest access. If used without *<hostname>*, denies all guest or anonymous access to this site. More than one *<hostname>* may be specified. Guest and anonymous access are allowed only on the named machines. If access is denied, the user is asked to use the first *<hostname>* listed.

TABLE 25.8 Continued

Control	Function
`passwd-check` *<level> <enforcement>*	Defines the level and enforcement of password checking done by the server for anonymous FTP. *<level>* can be `none`, `trivial` (must contain an `@`), or `rfc822` (must be an RFC822-compliant address). *<enforcement>* can be `warn` (warns the user but allows him to log in) or *`enforce`* (warns the user and logs him out).
`chmod <yes ¦ no>` *<typelist>* `delete <yes ¦ no> <typelist>` `overwrite <yes ¦ no>` *<typelist>* `rename <yes ¦ no>` *<typelist>* `umask <yes ¦ no>` *<typelist>*	Sets permissions for `chmod`, `delete`, `overwrite`, `rename`, and `umask` as `yes` or `no` for users in *<typelist>*, where *<typelist>* is a comma-separated list of any of the keywords `real`, `anonymous`, or `guest`.
`upload [absolute ¦ relative] [class=<classname>]... [-]` *<root-dir> <dirglob>* `<yes ¦ no>` *<owner> <group> <mode>* `[dirs ¦ nodirs] [`*<d_mode>*`]`	Specifies upload directory information. *<root-dir>* `[class=<classname>]... [-]` *<root-dir> <dirglob>* `<yes ¦ no>` *<owner> <group> <mode>* `[dirs ¦ nodirs] [`*<d_mode>*`]`specifies the FTP root directory. *<dirglob>* specifies a directory under the *<root-dir>*. `<yes ¦ no>` indicates whether files can be uploaded to the specified directory. If `yes`, files will be uploaded as belonging to *<owner>* and *<group>* in *<mode>*. `[dirs ¦ nodirs]` specifies whether new subdirectories can be created in the upload directory. If `dirs`, they are created with mode *<d_mode>*, if it is specified. Otherwise, they are created as defined by *<mode>*. If `<mode>` is not specified, they are created with mode `777`. Upload restrictions can be specified by class with *`class=<classname>`*.
`path-filter` *<typelist> <mesg> <allowed_charset>* `[`*<disallowed regexp>*`...]`	Defines regular expressions that control what a filename can or cannot be for users in *<typelist>*, where *<typelist>* is a comma-separated list of any of the keywords `real`, `anonymous`, or `guest`.

TABLE 25.8 Continued

Control	Function
noretrieve [absolute¦relative] [class=<*classname*>] .. [-] <*filename*> <*filename*> ...	Always denies the ability to retrieve these files. If the files are a path specification (begin with a / character), only those files are marked irretrievable. Otherwise, all files matching the filename are refused transfer. For example:
noretrieve /etc/passwd core	specifies no one can get the file /etc/passwd, but users will be allowed to transfer a file called passwd if it is not in /etc. On the other hand, no one can get files named core, wherever they are. Directory specifications mark all files and subdirectories in the named directory irretrievable. The <*filename*> may be specified as a file glob. For example: noretrieve /etc /home/*/.htaccess specifies no files in /etc or any of its subdirectories may be retrieved. Also, no files named .htaccess anywhere under the /home directory may be retrieved. The optional first parameter selects whether names are interpreted as absolute or relative to the current chrooted environment. The default is to interpret names beginning with a slash as absolute. The noretrieve restrictions may be placed on members of particular classes. If any class= is specified, the named files are not retrievable only if the current user is a member of any of the given classes.
throughput <*root-dir*> <*subdir-glob*> <*file-glob-list*> <*bytes-per-second*> <*bytes-per-second-multiply*> <*remote-glob-list*>	Restricts throughput to <*bytes-per-second*> on download of files in the comma-separated <*file-glob-list*> in the subdirectory matched by <*subdir-glob*> under <*root-dir*> when the remote host or IP address matches the comma-separated <*remote-glob-list*>.
anonymous-root <*root-dir*> [<class>]	Specifies <*root-dir*> as the chroot path for anonymous users. If no anonymous-root is matched, the old method of parsing the home directory for the FTP user is used.
guest-root <*root-dir*> [<*uid-range*>]	Specifies <*root-dir*> as the chroot path for guest users. If no guest-root is matched, the old method of parsing the user's home directory is used.

TABLE 25.8 Continued

Control	Function

`deny-uid` *<uid-range>* `[...]`
`deny-gid` *<gid-range>* `[...]`
`allow-uid` *<uid-range>* `[...]`
`allow-gid` *<gid-range>* `[...]`
	The `deny` clauses specify UID and GID ranges that are denied access to the FTP server. The `allow` clauses are then used to allow access to those who would otherwise be denied access. `deny` is checked before `allow`. Default is to allow access. Use of these controls can remove the need for the `/etc/ftpusers` file. Wherever `uid` or `gid` can be specified in the `ftpaccess` file, either names or numbers may be used. Put `%` before numeric `uid` or `gid`.

`restricted-uid` *<uid-range>* `[...]`
`restricted-gid` *<gid-range>* `[...]`
`unrestricted-uid` *<uid-range>* `[...]`
`unrestricted-gid` *<gid-range>* `[...]`
	Controls whether real or guest users are allowed access to areas on the FTP server outside their home directories. Not intended to replace the use of `guest-group` and `guestuser`. The unrestricted clauses may be used to allow users outside their directories when they would have been otherwise restricted.

`passive ports` *<cidr>* *<min>* *<max>*	Allows control of the TCP port numbers that may be used for a passive data connection. If the control connection matches *<cidr>*, a port in the *<min>* to *<max>* range is randomly selected for the daemon to listen on. This control allows firewalls to limit the ports that remote clients use for connecting to the protected network. *<cidr>* is shorthand for an IP address in dotted-quad notation, followed by a slash and the number of left-most bits that represent the network address. For example, for the reserved class-A network `10`, instead of using a netmask of `255.0.0.0`, use a `CIDR` of `8`, and `10.0.0.0/8` represents the network. Likewise, for a private class-C home network, you could use `192.168.1.0/24` to represent your network.

TABLE 25.8 Continued

Control	Function
deny *<addrglob>* *<message_file>*	Always denies access to host(s) matching *<addrglob>* and displays *<message_file>* to the host(s). *<addrglob>* may be !nameserved to deny access to sites without a working nameserver. It may also be the name of a file, starting with a slash (/), which contains additional address globs, as well as in the form *<address>*:*<netmask>* or *<address>*/*<cidr>*.
dns refuse_mismatch *<filename>* [override]	Refuses FTP sessions when the forward and reverse lookups for the remote site do not match. Displays *<filename>* to warn the user. If override is specified, allows the connection after complaining.
dns refuse_no_reverse *<filename>* [override]	Refuses FTP sessions when there is no reverse DNS entry for the remote site. Displays *<message>* to warn the user. If override is specified, allows the connection after complaining.

Understanding Basic ftpaccess Controls As you saw in Table 25.8, even a selective list of ftpaccess controls is large. Because many controls are available, let's take a look at some of the basic configuration controls in the ftpaccess file.

class Look at this statement:

```
class  staff  real  *.biosci.ohio-state.edu
```

In this example, a class called staff is defined as being a real user coming from anywhere in the biosci.ohio-state.edu domain.

In the following statement, a class called local is defined as being a guest user coming from anywhere in the ohio-state.edu domain:

```
class  local  guest  *.ohio-state.edu
```

In the following statement, a class called remote is defined as being an anonymous user whose connection comes from anywhere:

```
class  remote anonymous    *
```

You can create as many classes as suit your needs.

`limit` In the following statement, there's a limit of five users belonging to class `remote` who can access the FTP server on Saturdays and Sundays and on any day between 6:00 p.m. and 6:00 a.m.:

```
limit  remote 5    SaSu|Any1800-0600    /usr/local/etc/msgs/msg.toomany
```

When the limit is reached, any additional user sees a posting of the message file, `msg.toomany`, in `/usr/local/etc/msgs`.

In the following statement, no users belonging to the class `staff` can access the FTP server at any time:

```
limit  staff 0    Any         /usr/local/etc/msgs/msg.notallowed
```

Whenever any user in class `staff` attempts to log in, she sees a message indicating that she is not allowed to access the FTP server.

`upload` In the following statements, the guest user, `bioftp`, can upload files to the `~ftp/public/` directory. The files are uploaded with permissions **`600`** (that is, read and write permissions) for guest user `bioftp`:

```
upload /home/ftp  /public     yes   bioftp  ftponly   0600
upload /home/ftp  /public/*   yes   bioftp  ftponly   0600
```

However, in the following statement, no user can upload to the `~ftp/bin/` directory:

```
upload /home/ftp  /bin     no
```

Note that the upload control also has a `nodirs` option that does not allow directories to be uploaded. If you decide to run an anonymous FTP server, make sure that you include the `nodirs` option to the upload control.

`restricted-uid` and `restricted-gid` Although `restricted-uid` and `restricted-gid` are straightforward controls, it's useful to note that these controls function like the `/etc/ftpchroot` file for the default `ftpd`.

A restricted control entry such as this:

```
restricted-uid marvin
```

restricts user `marvin` to his home directory for FTP access. The numeric `uid` for `marvin`, preceded by `%`, could be used instead, as well as a range of `uids`.

Controlling Bandwidth and Other Advanced Features The controls available in ftpaccess range from basic to advanced. With the advanced features, you can control many aspects of an FTP session. Some interesting controls include limiting the throughput, limiting the number of bytes that can be transferred, limiting the number of files that can be transferred, refusing sessions from hosts whose forward and reverse name lookups don't match or if a DNS lookup can't be done, and specifying a passive port range for a passive data connection.

`throughput` The `throughput` directive is one that you can use to help make your anonymous FTP site less attractive. Here is a sample `throughput` directive:

```
throughput /Users/ftp /pub* *zip  22000 0.5 *
```

The sample statement limits the throughput of a Zip file downloaded from the `pub` directory to approximately 22000 bytes/second from any remote host. Furthermore, because a multiply factor of 0.5 is also specified, the second Zip file is downloaded at a rate of approximately 11000 bytes/second; the third, 5500 bytes/second, and so on.

`file-limit` The number of files uploaded, downloaded, or transferred in total by a user in a given class can be restricted with the `file-limit` directive. For example, this directive

```
file-limit in 1 remote
```

limits the number of files uploaded to your site by a user belonging to class `remote` to just one file.

`data-limit` Use the `data-limit` directive to limit the number of data bytes that can be uploaded, downloaded, or transferred in total by a user in a given class. In this statement

```
data-limit total 5000000 remote
```

the total number of data bytes that may be transferred by a user in class `remote` is restricted to approximately 5000000 bytes.

`dns refuse_mismatch` To deny access to a host whose forward and reverse DNS lookups don't match, use the `dns refuse_mismatch` directive. In this example

```
dns refuse_mismatch mismatch-warning override
```

the file, `mismatch-warning`, is displayed for the offending host, but with the override option in place, the host is granted access anyway.

`dns refuse_no_reverse` To deny access to a host for which a reverse DNS lookup can't be done, use the `dns refuse_no_reverse` directive. In this statement

```
dns refuse_no_reverse noreverse-warning
```

the file named `noreverse-warning` is displayed, and the connection from the offending host is refused.

`passive ports` At this time, the `passive ports` directive might not seem important. However, if you decide to use the built-in firewall package, `ipfw`, you might find the `passive ports` directive useful for allowing passive connections through your firewall. In this example

```
passive ports 140.254.12.0/24 15001 19999
```

ports in the range of 15001 to 19999 for passive data connections from 140.254.12.* have been specified. This directive could be used in conjunction with an `ipfw` rule to permit a passive data connection through the firewall.

Understanding the `xferlog`

By default, `wu-ftpd` logs transfers to a file called `xferlog`. Each entry in the log consists of an entry in this format:

```
<current-time> <transfer-time> <remote-host> <file-size> <filename>
<transfer-type> <special-action-flag> <direction> <access-mode> <username>
<service-name> <authentication-method> <authenticated-user-id>
<completion-status>
```

At a casual glance, that format might seem a bit overwhelming. Let's look at some sample entries to better understand that format.

Here's an entry resulting from someone contacting the anonymous FTP server:

```
Fri May 11 13:32:19 2001 1 calvin.biosci.ohio-state.edu 46
➥ /Users/ftp/incoming/file4 b _ i a joray@ ftp 0 * c
```

Immediately apparent are the date and time when the transfer occurred. The next entry, the `1`, indicates that the transfer time was only one second. The remote host was `calvin.biosci.ohio-state.edu`. The file size was 46 bytes. The file transferred was `file4` in the incoming area of the anonymous FTP server. The transfer was a binary transfer. No special action, such as compressing or tarring, was done. From the `i`, you can see that this was an incoming transfer; that is, an upload. From the `a`, you can see that this was an anonymous user. The string identifying the username in this case is `joray@`. That is the password that the user entered. The `ftp` indicates that the FTP service was used. The `0` indicates that no authentication method was used. The `*` indicates that an authenticated user ID is not available. The `c` indicates that the transfer completed.

Here's an entry resulting from a guest user contacting the FTP server:

```
Fri May 11 16:32:24 2001 5 calvin.biosci.ohio-state.edu 5470431
➥ /Users/guests/betty/dotpaper.pdf b _ i g betty ftp 0 * c
```

It looks much like the anonymous entry. In this entry, we see that the transfer time was 5 seconds. The file transfer was larger than in the previous example, 5470431 bytes. The i indicates that this transfer was also an incoming transfer, an upload. The g indicates that the user involved was a guest user. The guest user was user betty.

Here's an entry resulting from a real user contacting the FTP server:

```
Fri May 11 15:34:14 2001 1 ryoohki.biosci.ohio-state.edu 277838
➥ /Users/marvin/introduction.ps b _ o r marvin ftp 0 * c
```

Again, this entry is much like the other two entries we've seen. In this example, we learn from the o that the transfer was an outgoing transfer; that is, a download. The r indicates that a real user made the transfer. In this case, the real user was marvin.

You'll probably find that wu-ftpd logs to /var/log/ftpd.log as well. However, the log entries are more detailed than what you saw for the default FTP server. Take a look at them, too. They contain a lot of the same information as the xferlog, but they also include information on passive mode, ports that were used, and so on.

Guest User Accounts

As you've seen, wu-ftpd understands three types of users: real, anonymous, and guest. Real users are users who have full login access to your machine. You can restrict your real users' FTP access to their home directories, if you so choose. Whether you choose to do so is up to you. If you trust your users enough to give them full login access to your machine in the first place, you might also trust them with full FTP access. Anonymous users are users who have access to only the anonymous area of your machine, if you chose to create an anonymous FTP area. Guest users are users who have accounts on your machine but aren't granted full access to your machine. Guest user accounts might be suitable for users who have Web sites on your machine and need FTP access only to occasionally update their Web sites.

A guest user account is a cross between a real user account and an anonymous FTP account. A guest user has a username and password but doesn't have shell access to his account. This allows him to use FTP to access files on the server via a user ID and password but prevents him from being able to log in to the machine either through the network or at the console. Guest user accounts are useful if, for example, you need to set up a place where a group of collaborators can share sensitive information and data, but where you don't really want members of the group to be full users of your machine. If you set up a single guest user account for this group of users, they can all access it with a user ID and password, and people without the user ID and password can't, so their information remains private. Because they don't have real shells, however, they can't log in to your machine and use any resources other than those available through the FTP server.

Guest user accounts are set up similarly to the anonymous FTP account. The users are restricted to their home directories only, as is the anonymous FTP account, and their accounts contain the commands that they might need to run while accessing their accounts via FTP.

If you decide that you need guest user accounts, do the following to implement a guest user:

1. Decide where the guest user's home directory should be. You could put your guest users in the same location as your regular users. You also could create a directory somewhere for guest users and place guest user directories in that location.

2. After you've decided where the guest account should reside, make a guest account. You could create your user in the Accounts pane in System Preferences. Your guest user, however, might not really have a need for all the directories that are made in a user account created in this way. You can decide what directories might be necessary. If you anticipate having many guest users, you could create a guest skeleton user as your basis for guest accounts.

3. The guest user should belong to some sort of guest group. Create a guest group with an unused GID number. Edit the guest user's account to belong to the guest group. The guest user's shell should be modified to some nonexistent shell. Make sure that the guest user's home directory and everything in it are owned by the guest user with the guest group.

4. There are two possible ways to list the guest user's home directory. The traditional way is to include a `.` where the FTP server should `chroot` to as the root FTP directory. For example, we could create a guest user called `betty`, with a home directory located in `/Users/guests/betty/`. To indicate that the root directory that we want `betty` to see when she accesses the FTP server to be `/Users/guests/betty`, we would edit the home directory to be `/Users/guests/betty/./`. If we wanted betty to be able to see a listing of other guest users' directories before changing to her directory, we could list her home directory as `/Users/guests/./betty/`. By listing her home directory this way, her guest root directory does not need to be specifically listed in the `ftpaccess` file. Figure 25.3 shows how the guest user's home directory appears in NetInfo Manager when indicated by this method.

   The other way to list a guest user's home directory is to list the home directory as usual in NetInfo Manager. In the `ftpaccess` file, list the guest user with the `guestuser` control. With this method, the user's directory in the NetInfo database looks like the notation for any real user's home directory, as we see for guest user `ralph` in Figure 25.4.

   The entry for the guest user in `ftpaccess` looks like this:

   ```
   guestuser ralph
   ```

5. Include the shell that you use for the guest in `/etc/shells`. You might want the contents of your fake guest user shell to be something like this:

   ```
   #! /bin/sh
   exit 1
   ```

6. Update the ownership information of the guest user's account to include the guest group GID indicated in the NetInfo database.

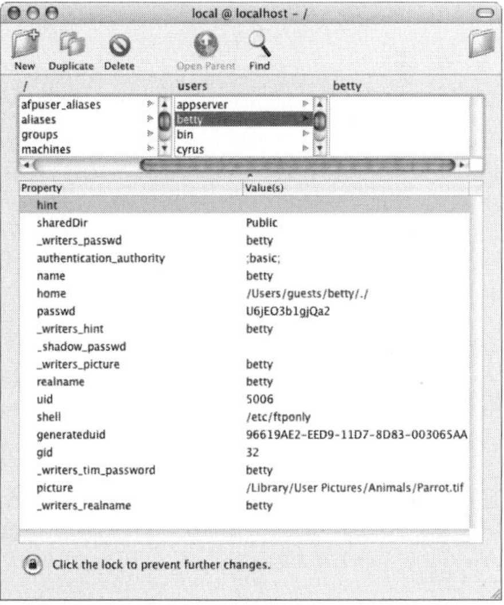

FIGURE 25.3 Here are the parameters we used for our guest user `betty`. Her home directory is listed in the traditional notation for a guest user, which includes a `.` to indicate the root directory that the user sees when she FTPs.

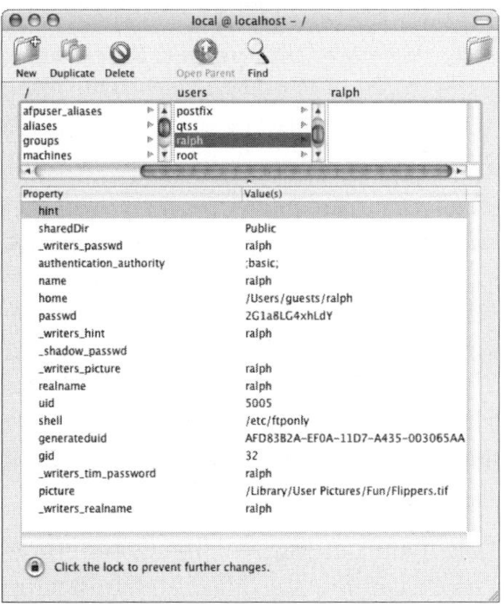

FIGURE 25.4 The home directory for this guest user is indicated in the regular fashion. The root directory for FTP for this guest user is indicated instead using the `guestuser` control in the `ftpaccess` file.

7. Copy the same system files used for the anonymous FTP user to the guest user's account. Specifically, make sure that the system files

```
/bin/ls
/usr/lib/dylib
/usr/lib/libSystem.B.dylib
/System/Library/Frameworks/System.framework/Versions/B/System
```

are included in the guest user's home directory. In this example, for user `ralph`, the files would be placed in

```
/Users/guests/ralph/bin/
/Users/guests/ralph/usr/lib/
/Users/guests/ralph/System/Library/Frameworks/System.framework/Versions/B/
```

with the same permissions and ownerships that are used for an anonymous FTP account.

If you create a skeleton guest user account, these are files that would be useful to include in the skeleton guest user account. Note that this step isn't necessary if you used the `--enable-ls` option.

Alternatives to FTP

As we've mentioned, turning on the FTP server makes your machine more vulnerable to attacks from the outside. There are other, more secure options you could consider using as alternatives to FTP.

`scp` and `sftp`

If you turn on the SSH server (detailed in Chapter 26, "Remote Access and Control"), two alternatives become available. You can transfer files either with secure copy (`scp`) or secure FTP (`sftp`). Transfers made using `scp` or `sftp` are encrypted, thereby providing an extra level of security. Specifically, the client creates a tunnel through SSH, using the standard port 22, and executes an `sftp-server` process on the server end, which sends data back through the encrypted channel. The `sftp` and `sftp-server` executables are part of the SSH package. Unlike SSH, the FTP protocol and servers we've covered earlier in this chapter transmit passwords in clear text, adding yet another vulnerability to FTP itself. This makes `scp` or `sftp` a strongly preferred option for users who can use them (appropriate clients are necessary on the client end).

With the SSH server turned on,)you can transfer files to other machines running SSH servers. Likewise, those machines can transfer files to your machine by using `scp` or `sftp`. In addition, there exists a freely available (Classic) Mac OS client that has built-in `scp` capabilities. For PCs, there's a client that has a built-in `sftp` client. Running SSH removes most needs for an FTP server for real users of your machine. It does not provide a useful substitute for providing data or data-exchange capabilities to anonymous users, or ftp-guest type users. For these purposes, FTP still rules the roost. We discuss SSH in detail in Chapter 26.

FTP and SSH

As you might recall, the `wu-ftpd` can be built as an anonymous-only FTP server. If your real users are transferring files via `scp` or `sftp`, but you still need to distribute files to anonymous users, you might then consider compiling an anonymous-only FTP server and running that alongside your SSH server.

Regularly checking the anonymous FTP area for any irregularities and keeping your `wu-ftpd` current are still important activities to do.

Tunneling FTP over SSH

If, for whatever reason, running the SSH server is not sufficient to meet your users' needs, you can tunnel FTP connections through `ssh` logins. This enables you to protect the command channel but can't easily protect the FTP data channel. If you're administering an FTP server, you can moderately increase your system security by using an FTP configuration that encourages users to tunnel their FTP connections into your machine.

As mentioned earlier, if you provide an open FTP port for your users to connect to, they'll be likely to try it, and likely to enter their user ID and password on the clear-text data channel to attempt login. You can bias your users against this behavior by exploiting `wu-ftpd`'s capability for configuration and creating specialized FTP servers to handle real and anonymous users. By creating a real-users-only FTP server, using the `--disable-anonymous` compile-time option for `wu-ftpd`, you can create a server that allows only real users to log in. To protect this server, you can restrict access to it to only connections originating from the server machine itself. This way, the data from the connections never visibly passes over the network, and any connections that come in over the network are rejected, preventing users from unintentionally disclosing their information. SSH can then be used to create tunnels between the users' client machines and the server, so that their command channels are carried encrypted over the network to the server and unpacked on the server. Because the connection to the command channel looks (to the FTP server) as if it's coming from the server machine itself (where it's being unpacked), it is allowed, and because it came to the server over the encrypted SSH tunnel, it is protected against prying eyes. Here you'll learn how to configure a `wu-ftpd` server for this use. In Chapter 26, we discuss in detail how to set up a client to tunnel an FTP connection.

To make tunneling work on the server side, you have to wrap the FTP server to accept connections only from itself. The easiest way to set up the restriction is to use the `only_from` directive in `xinetd`. For machine `192.168.1.19`, such an entry looks like:

```
only_from     = 127.0.0.1 192.168.1.19 localhost
```

Another easy way to set up the restriction is to use the TCP Wrappers program that comes with the Mac OS X distribution.

In an enhanced `/etc/hosts.allow` file, you would do this with the following syntax:

```
in.ftpd: <machine-IP> 127.0.0.1 localhost: allow
in.ftpd: deny
```

If you use TCP Wrappers, you must also indicate this in `/etc/xinetd.d/ftp`, if you're using the default `xinetd`, or in `/etc/inetd.conf`, if you're using `inetd` instead. For `xinetd`, you need to add `NAMEINARGS` to the `flags`, which tells `xinetd` that the server itself and its runtime options are listed in the `server_args` directive. The server directive then lists `tcpd`. Here is a sample `/etc/xinetd.d/ftp` file using TCP Wrappers:

```
service ftp
{
    disable         = no
    socket_type     = stream
    wait            = no
    user            = root
    server          = /usr/libexec/tcpd
    server_args     = /usr/local/WUftpd/sbin/in.ftpd -l -d -a
    groups          = yes
    flags           = REUSE NAMEINARGS
}
```

Finally, have `xinetd` re-read its configuration file by running `killall -HUP xinetd`.

If you're using `inetd`, the default `/etc/inetd.conf` is already set up to use TCP Wrappers. Uncomment the `ftp` line, change the `ftpd -l` portion that lists the `ftp` server to whatever is appropriate for yours, add any runtime options, and have `inetd` re-read its configuration file.

If you must also have an anonymous FTP server running, or even if you don't, it's a good idea to run the FTP server you're trying to make secure on non-canonical ports for FTP (such as `31` for `ftp`, `30` for `ftp-data`). If you're running an anonymous-only server, leave it running on the standard FTP ports (`21` for `ftp`, `20` for `ftp-data`).

As you've seen, you don't need to edit anything to run an FTP server on the standard ports. All that's left, then, is to configure your real-user FTP server and install it on an alternative set of ports. Follow these steps:

1. For ease of administration, it's a good idea to have each FTP server installed in a distinctly separate location. For example, you could install your anonymous FTP server in `/usr/local/ftp` and your real users' FTP server in `/usr/local/wuftp`.

2. Pick a set of unused port numbers. We like ports close to the standard FTP ports for convenience—`31` and `30` are our favorites.

3. Edit the `/etc/services` file to include the alternative services. You could call them something like `wuftp` and `wuftp-data`. Whichever port number you assign to the `wuftp` service is the one to which the clients wanting to connect need to tunnel.
4. Again for convenience, name the alternative FTP server itself something similar to the service name, such as `wuftpd`. It is automatically installed as `in.ftpd` in whatever location you specified during the build, but you can rename that file.
5. Finally, wrap the alternative FTP server to allow only connections from itself, but allow the anonymous FTP server access from all machines.

If you also decide to run Mac OS X's built-in firewall, `ipfw`, you must add statements to allow `ipfw` to grant access to the alternative FTP server. In addition, set the passive ports control to the `ftpaccess` file to a range of ports, such as 15001-19999. Then add a statement to the rules for `ipfw` to allow access to whatever range of ports you specified with passive ports. You might find that you have to keep tweaking your `ipfw` and anonymous and real FTP configurations until everything works in harmony. Be sure to check your logs as you're doing this. They're more informative than you might realize now.

Don't worry if the wrapping concept or `ipfw` seems confusing right now. Use of TCP Wrappers and `ipfw` is discussed in Chapter 31, "Server Security and Advanced Network Configuration." These details are mentioned here so that you can quickly find a summary of the important information about running two FTP servers in one place. Shortly, `scp` and `sftp` should suit most of your needs. We recommend that, where possible, you use `scp` and `sftp` instead of running an FTP server.

NOTE

If you decide to run the types of FTP servers suggested in this section, you might find that guest accounts do not work. This appears to be a version-specific bug, or an unexpected consequence of some recent change, because we've used all these capabilities simultaneously before. Also, note that only the channel that carries the username, password, and command information can be tunneled. The channel that travels between machines when you actually transfer a file using FTP can't be protected in this fashion. For many users, though, this protection is sufficient.

Summary

This chapter looked at how to make the optional FTP process more secure. Although OS X comes with an FTP server provided by Apple, we suggest that if you do want to provide FTP services, you run the more configurable `wu-ftpd`. No matter which server you decide to run, restrict access to the server as much as possible, regularly check your logs, and keep the FTP server up-to-date. For the default FTP server, you can do this with the OS X software updates, or by compiling and installing the more recent versions by hand. For `wu-ftpd`, you have to update manually.

You also saw alternative suggestions to simply using FTP. Most preferable is using `scp` or `sftp`. If you need an anonymous FTP server, have the regular users use `scp` and `sftp` while you provide an anonymous FTP server. However, you may also discover a need for having an FTP server available for your real users. In that case, consider compiling a real users only FTP server, wrapping it with TCP Wrapper, and teaching your users to tunnel connections to it over SSH.

You might have found some parts of the chapter confusing. However, as your needs evolve, so does your understanding. You can always return to this chapter to get a start on customizing your FTP needs.

CHAPTER **26**

Remote Access and Control

IN THIS CHAPTER

- Security-Minded Thinking
- What Is Secure Shell?
- Activating the SSH Server
- Basic Configuration
- Basic Use
- Advanced Use
- Clients
- Control Commands

Apple advertises that with OS X, you now have the power of Unix. With the power of Unix also come some unfamiliar security issues. Many Unix machines run various types of services, such as Telnet, that increase your machine's vulnerability to attacks from crackers. In general, crackers are interested in either wiping your machine or installing a packet sniffer that saves passwords transmitted on your network for future devious uses. To keep your machine most secure, you should not hook it up to the Internet. That solution is rather impractical in an age in which Internet communication is one of the many reasons why people buy computers. Therefore, it becomes your responsibility to pay attention to security issues, if not for yourself, for the other machines on your network.

Fortunately, Apple realizes that Macintosh users are not used to worrying about security issues. In fact, Macintosh users have always had the luxury of knowing that their Macintosh is practically impenetrable. So, unlike some Unix operating systems, OS X ships with all the services turned off. You have to decide, as you start using your machine more, which services, if any, you should try to turn on. Remember that the more services you turn on, the more vulnerable your machine becomes.

Security-Minded Thinking

Although Chapter 31, "Server Security and Advanced Network Configuration," goes into security details in considerably more depth, it's a good idea to start thinking about security issues now. In this chapter, you're going to configure your machine so that you can connect to it from other machines.

If you can connect to it, so can anyone else, and it's time to start thinking about security. Here are some common sense guidelines that you can use when thinking about your machine's security:

- Regularly apply updates to the operating system. It is common for the Unix vendors to fix security problems and make the fixes available as downloadable updates, usually called *patches*.
- Do not turn on any unnecessary services. If you don't know what the service is, you probably don't need it.
- Do not turn on the `telnet` service. `telnet` transmits passwords in clear text. That is exactly what some of the crackers are looking for.
- Restrict as many of the TCP-based services as possible with `xinetd`'s access attributes or with TCP Wrappers.
- Use secure shell (SSH) for remote logins to your machine.

It is the last item, secure shell, that we will discuss in depth in this chapter. You were first introduced to the secure shell software via `slogin`, in Chapter 15, "Command-Line Applications and Application Suites." In that chapter, you learned how to use `slogin` on your Mac OS X box to connect to outside machines as well as how to use `scp` and `sftp`. In this chapter, we will look at secure shell configuration, basic and advanced use, and available clients.

What Is Secure Shell?

SSH, also known as secure shell, is a protocol for secure remote login, file transfer, and tunneling. It can be used as a secure replacement for the more familiar `telnet` and `rlogin` protocols without any noticeable difference to the user. For file transfers, SSH can be used as a secure replacement for `rcp` and `ftp`. Finally, SSH can be used to tunnel traffic over an encrypted channel. In other words, SSH can be used to transport otherwise insecure traffic more securely. For example, it can be used to encrypt the username and password data transmitted by `ftp`.

SSH is a more secure protocol than the traditional protocols because it encrypts traffic. The other protocols transmit data in clear text, which can then be captured by packet sniffers.

There are two versions of the SSH protocol: SSH1 and SSH2. As you might have guessed, SSH1 is the original version, and SSH2 is a later development. The SSH2 protocol is the version currently being developed, although fixes are occasionally released for SSH1 because it is still in use.

The SSH protocol was first developed by Tatu Ylonen in 1995. In that same year he also founded SSH Communications Security and currently serves as its President and CEO. SSH Communications Security offers commercial and free versions of its SSH server and client products. The company originally sold products through another company called Data

Fellows, which is now F-Secure. F-Secure has marketing rights for SSH and also sells SSH servers and clients. Both companies work on further developing SSH2.

There is also an SSH open source project called OpenSSH. This is the SSH distribution that Apple includes with Mac OS X. It is also based on Tatu Ylonen's early SSH code. OpenSSH provides support for both SSH1 and SSH2 protocols. There is little noticeable difference in using the SSH servers from one of the companies and from the OpenSSH package.

Because the OpenSSH package is included with Mac OS X, it is the package on which we will concentrate our discussion.

Activating the SSH Server

If you are just interested in connecting from your OS X machine to another machine running an SSH server, you do not need to activate the SSH server on your machine. However, if you want to be able to access your Macintosh remotely, consider turning on the SSH server. To activate the SSH server, check the Remote Login box in the Services section of the Sharing pane, as shown in Figure 26.1.

Behind the scenes, this changes the `disable` line in `/etc/xinetd.d/ssh` to `disable=no` and forces `xinetd` to reread its configuration file. The SSH server listed in `/etc/xinetd.d/ssh` is a script called `/usr/libexec/sshd-keygen-wrapper` that ultimately runs `/usr/sbin/sshd`. Whenever someone connects to the machine via SSH, an SSH server for that session is started. When the user logs out, the session is terminated. In previous releases of Mac OS X, an SSH server ran all the time and started `sshd` processes for each login. 10.3 uses `xinetd` to start each `sshd` process. This gives you the ability to use `xinetd`'s control features for SSH.

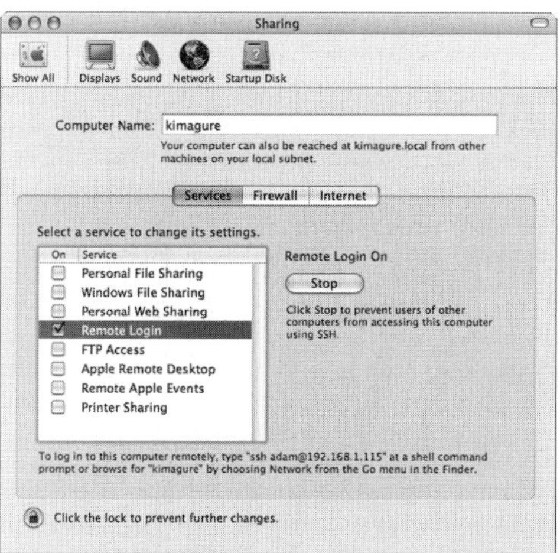

FIGURE 26.1 To start the SSH server on your machine, check the Remote Login box under Services in the Sharing pane.

Basic Configuration

There are two basic configuration files for SSH: /etc/sshd_config and /etc/ssh_config. The first file is the configuration file for the SSH server itself, sshd. The second file is the configuration file for the client, ssh. You can also use command-line options at startup for configuring sshd. Command-line options override settings in /etc/sshd_config.

/etc/sshd_config

The default configuration file for sshd, /etc/sshd_config, is shown in the following code fragment. Because sshd processes run for each incoming connection, it is easiest to make changes to your sshd from the console. A brief explanation for the sections is included.

```
#     $OpenBSD: sshd_config,v 1.59 2002/09/25 11:17:16 markus Exp $

# This is the sshd server system-wide configuration file. See
# sshd_config(5) for more information.

# This sshd was compiled with PATH=/usr/bin:/bin:/usr/sbin:/sbin

# The strategy used for options in the default sshd_config shipped with
# OpenSSH is to specify options with their default value where
# possible, but leave them commented. Uncommented options change a
# default value.

#Port 22
#Protocol 2,1
#ListenAddress 0.0.0.0
#ListenAddress ::

# HostKey for protocol version 1
#HostKey /etc/ssh_host_key
# HostKeys for protocol version 2
#HostKey /etc/ssh_host_rsa_key
#HostKey /etc/ssh_host_dsa_key

# Lifetime and size of ephemeral version 1 server key
#KeyRegenerationInterval 3600
#ServerKeyBits 768
```

This section of the configuration file sets some general configuration settings. By default, sshd runs on port 22. The protocol option allows you to specify which SSH protocols sshd should support. The default is 2,1. By default, sshd listens on all local addresses. However, there can be multiple ListenAddress statements, where you can specify settings for each interface.

```
# Logging
#obsoletes QuietMode and FascistLogging
#SyslogFacility AUTH
#LogLevel INFO
```

This section controls the facility code and level of logging that `sshd` does.

```
# Authentication:

#LoginGraceTime 120
#PermitRootLogin yes
#StrictModes yes

#RSAAuthentication yes
#PubkeyAuthentication yes
#AuthorizedKeysFile   .ssh/authorized_keys

# rhosts authentication should not be used
#RhostsAuthentication no
# Don't read the user's ~/.rhosts and ~/.shosts files
#IgnoreRhosts yes
# For this to work you will also need host keys in /etc/ssh_known_hosts
#RhostsRSAAuthentication no
# similar for protocol version 2
#HostbasedAuthentication no
# Change to yes if you don't trust ~/.ssh/known_hosts for
# RhostsRSAAuthentication and HostbasedAuthentication
#IgnoreUserKnownHosts no

# To disable tunneled clear text passwords, change to no here!
#PasswordAuthentication yes
#PermitEmptyPasswords no

# Change to no to disable s/key passwords
#ChallengeResponseAuthentication yes

# Kerberos options
#KerberosAuthentication no
#KerberosOrLocalPasswd yes
#KerberosTicketCleanup yes

#AFSTokenPassing no
```

```
# Kerberos TGT Passing only works with the AFS kaserver
#KerberosTgtPassing no

# Set this to 'yes' to enable PAM keyboard-interactive authentication
# Warning: enabling this may bypass the setting of 'PasswordAuthentication'
#PAMAuthenticationViaKbdInt no
```

This section addresses various authentication issues. By default, `PermitRootLogin` is set to `yes`. Possible values for this directive are `yes`, `without-password`, `forced-commands-only`, or `no`. `without-password` disables password authentication for `root`. The `forced-commands-only` option permits `root` to log in using public key authentication, but only if the command has been specified on a key in the `authorized_keys` file using the `command=..` option. This option can be useful for doing remote backups on a system where `root` is not normally permitted to log in.

This section also provides some settings for a user's session. By default, `~/.rhosts` and `~/.shosts` are ignored for `RhostsAuthentication`, `RhostsRSAAuthentication`, or `HostbasedAuthentication`. The `/etc/hosts.equiv` files and `/etc/shosts.equiv` are still used. The `~/.rhosts` and `~/.shosts` files allow users to specify trusted hosts. Typically, the `/etc/hosts.equiv` and `/etc/shosts.equiv` files specify systemwide trusted hosts.

This section also specifies what authentication methods are allowed. The `RhostsRSAAuthentication` and `RSAAuthentication` are protocol 1 directives. Public key authentication is allowed by default for protocol 2.

```
#X11Forwarding no
#X11DisplayOffset 10
#X11UseLocalhost yes
#PrintMotd yes
#PrintLastLog yes
#KeepAlive yes
#UseLogin no
#UsePrivilegeSeparation yes
#PermitUserEnvironment no
#Compression yes
```

In this section, you can also set whether to allow X11 forwarding, the printing of the message of the day, when the user last logged in, and whether the server sends TCP keepalive messages. Having the server send TCP keepalive messages prevents a connection from hanging if the network goes down or the client crashes.

```
#MaxStartups 10
# no default banner path
#Banner /some/path
#VerifyReverseMapping no
```

This section includes options for more general settings for sshd. The MaxStartups option allows you to specify the maximum number of concurrent unauthenticated connections to sshd. When specified as a set of three colon-separated numbers, this option specifies a random early drop as start:rate:full. The point at which random early dropoff starts is when the number of unauthenticated connections reaches start. When the number of unauthenticated connections reaches full, all the connections are refused. The sshd refuses connections with a probability of rate/100 if the number of connections is start. The probability increases linearly to 100% as the number of unauthenticated connections reaches full. The VerifyReverseMapping directive specifies whether sshd should verify the remote hostname for an IP address by checking that the resolved hostname maps back to the same IP address.

```
Subsystem     sftp  /usr/libexec/sftp-server
```

The default configuration file ends with the preceding line. This option activates the sftp server. It is on by default. In earlier versions of Mac OS X, this option was commented out, and therefore off by default. If you don't think you will have a need for the sftp functionality, you can turn it off here.

Some additional interesting directives are noted in Table 26.1.

TABLE 26.1 Select Additional Options for /etc/sshd_config

Option	Function
AllowGroups	Takes a list of group name patterns, separated by spaces. If this option is specified, login is allowed only for users whose primary group or supplementary group list matches one of the patterns. * and ? can be used as wildcards in the patterns. Only group names are valid; a numerical group ID is not recognized. By default, login is allowed for all groups.
AllowUsers	Takes a list of username patterns, separated by spaces. If this option is specified, login is allowed only for usernames that match one of the patterns. * and ? can be used as wildcards in the patterns. Only usernames are valid; a numerical user ID is not recognized. By default, login is allowed for all users. If the pattern is of the form USER@HOST, USER and HOST are separately checked, restricting logins to particular users from particular hosts.
Ciphers	Specifies the ciphers allowed for protocol version 2. Multiple ciphers must be comma-separated. The default is aes128-cbc,3des-cbc,blowfish-cbc,cast128-cbc,arcfour, aes192-cbc,aes256-cbc
ClientAliveInterval	Sets a timeout interval in seconds after which if no data has been received from the client, sshd sends a message through the encrypted channel to request a response from the client. The default is 0, indicating that these messages will not be sent to the client. Protocol version 2 option only.

TABLE 26.1 Continued

Option	Function
ClientAliveCountMax	Sets the number of client alive that may be sent without sshd receiving any messages back from the client. If this threshold is reached while client alive messages are being sent, sshd disconnects the client, terminating the session. The default value is 3. If ClientAliveInterval is set to 15, and ClientAliveCountMax is left at the default, unresponsive ssh clients will be disconnected after approximately 45 seconds.
DenyGroups	Takes a list of group name patterns, separated by spaces. Login is disallowed for users whose primary group or supplementary group list matches one of the patterns. * and ? can be used as wildcards in the patterns. Only group names are valid; a numerical group ID is not recognized. By default, login is allowed for all groups.
DenyUsers	Takes a list of username patterns, separated by spaces. Login is disallowed for usernames that match one of the patterns. * and ? can be used as wildcards in the patterns. Only usernames are valid; a numerical user ID is not recognized. By default, login is allowed for all users. If the pattern takes the form USER@HOST, then USER and HOST are separately checked, restricting logins to particular users from particular hosts.
MACs	Specifies the available MAC (message authentication code) algorithms. The MAC algorithm is used in protocol version 2 for data integrity protection. Multiple algorithms must be comma-separated. The default is hmac-md5,hmac-sha1,hmac-ripemd160,hmac-sha1-96,hmac-md5-96
PidFile	Specifies the file that contains the process identifier of sshd.
PubkeyAuthentication	Specifies whether public key authentication is allowed. Argument must be yes or no. Default is yes. Protocol version 2 option only.
UsePrivilegeSeparation	Specifies whether sshd separated privileges by creating an unprivileged child process to deal with incoming network traffic. After successful authentication, another process will be created that has the privilege of the authenticated user. The goal of privilege separation is to prevent privilege escalation by containing any corruption within the unprivileged processes. The default is yes.
VerifyReverseMapping	Specifies whether sshd should try to verify the remote hostname by checking that the resolved hostname for the remote IP address maps back to the same IP address. The default is no.
X11DisplayOffset	Specifies the first display number available for sshd's X11 forwarding. This prevents sshd from interfering with real X11 servers. The default is 10.
X11Forwarding	Specifies whether X11 forwarding is permitted. The default is no. Note that disabling X11 forwarding does not improve security in any way because users can always install their own forwarders. X11 forwarding is automatically disabled if UseLogin is enabled.

TABLE 26.1 Continued

Option	Function
`X11UseLocalhost`	Specifies whether `sshd` should bind the X11 forwarding server to the loopback address or to the wildcard address. By default, `sshd` binds the forwarding server to the loopback address and sets the `hostname` part of the `DISPLAY` environment variable to `localhost`. This prevents remote hosts from connecting to the proxy display. However, some older X11 clients may not function with this configuration. `X11UseLocalhost` may be set to `no` to specify that the forwarding server should be bound to the wildcard address. The argument must be `yes` or `no`. The default is `yes`.
`XAuthLocation`	Specifies the full pathname of the `xauth` program. The default is `/usr/X11R6/bin/xauth`.

`sshd` Command-Line Options

By default, `sshd` does not start with any command-line options, but you can use command-line options at startup for configuring `sshd`. Command-line options override settings in `/etc/sshd_config`. If you choose to have `sshd` start with certain command-line options, edit the `/usr/sbin/sshd` line of the `/usr/libexec/sshd-keygen-wrapper` script that `xinetd` runs. Table 26.2 provides a listing of select runtime options. Complete documentation is available in Appendix A.

TABLE 26.2 Command-Line Options to `sshd`

`sshd`	OpenSSH daemon
`sshd [-deiqtD46] [-b <bits>] [-f <config_file>] [-g <login_grace_time>] [-h <host_key_file>] [-k <key_gen_time>] [-o <option>] [-p <port>] [-u <len>]`	
`-d`	Debug mode.
`-f <configuration_file>`	Specifies the name of the configuration file. Default is `/etc/sshd_config`. `sshd` refuses to start if there is no configuration file.
`-g <login_grace_time>`	Gives the grace time for clients to authenticate themselves. If the client fails to authenticate the user within this many seconds, the server disconnects and exits. A value of zero indicates no limit. Default is 600 seconds.
`-h <host_key_file>`	Specifies a file from which a host key is read. This option must be given if `sshd` is not run as `root` (because the normal host key files are normally not readable by anyone but `root`). Defaults are `/etc/ssh_host_key` for protocol version 1, and `/etc/ssh_host_rsa_key` and `/etc/ssh_host_dsa_key` for protocol version 2. It is possible to have multiple host key files for the different protocol versions and host key algorithms.

TABLE 26.2 Continued

-i	Runs sshd from inetd. sshd is normally not run from inetd because it needs to generate the server key before it can respond to the client, and this may take tens of seconds. Clients would have to wait too long if the key was regenerated every time. However, with small key sizes (for example, 512) using sshd from inetd may be feasible.
-o *<option>*	Can be used to give options in the format used in the configuration file. Useful for specifying options for which there is no separate command-line flag.
-p *<port>*	Specifies the port on which the server listens for connections. Default is 22.
-t	Test mode. Only checks the validity of the configuration file and sanity of the keys. Useful for updating sshd reliably as configuration options may change.
-u *<len>*	Specifies the size of the field in the utmp structure that holds the remote hostname. If the resolved hostname is longer than *<len>*, the dotted decimal value will be used instead.
-D	sshd does not detach and does not become a daemon. Allows for easy monitoring of sshd.
-4	Forces sshd to use IPv4 addresses only.
-6	Forces sshd to use IPv6 addresses only.

/etc/ssh_config

/etc/ssh_config, the default systemwide configuration file for the client, ssh, is shown following. The configuration file is divided into host sections. Because parameters are determined on a first-match-wins basis, more host-specific values should be given at the beginning of the file, with general values at the end of the file. Users can also configure the ssh client to suit their needs by creating a ~/.ssh/config file. Specifying Host as * sets parameters for all hosts.

```
#	$OpenBSD: ssh_config,v 1.16 2002/07/03 14:21:05 markus Exp $

# This is the ssh client system-wide configuration file. See
# ssh_config(5) for more information. This file provides defaults for
# users, and the values can be changed in per-user configuration files
# or on the command line.

# Configuration data is parsed as follows:
# 1. command line options
# 2. user-specific file
# 3. system-wide file
# Any configuration value is only changed the first time it is set.
# Thus, host-specific definitions should be at the beginning of the
```

```
# configuration file, and defaults at the end.

# Site-wide defaults for various options

# Host *
#   ForwardAgent no
#   ForwardX11 no
#   RhostsAuthentication no
#   RhostsRSAAuthentication no
#   RSAAuthentication yes
#   PasswordAuthentication yes
#   BatchMode no
#   CheckHostIP yes
#   StrictHostKeyChecking ask
#   IdentityFile ~/.ssh/identity
#   IdentityFile ~/.ssh/id_rsa
#   IdentityFile ~/.ssh/id_dsa
#   Port 22
#   Protocol 2,1
#   Cipher 3des
#   Ciphers aes128-cbc,3des-cbc,blowfish-cbc,cast128-cbc,arcfour,aes192-cbc,aes
256-cbc
#   EscapeChar ~
```


The default /etc/ssh_config file lists some options that you may want to set. Table 26.3 includes a description of some of the options shown in this file, along with other selected options. For more details, be sure to read the man page for ssh.

CAUTION

Options that you can set in a systemwide /etc/ssh_config include LocalForward and RemoteForward. We discourage setting up any tunnels in a systemwide configuration. If an intruder does gain access to your machine, your systemwide forwarding settings make it that much easier for an intruder to access other machines.

TABLE 26.3 Select Options for /etc/ssh_config or ~/.ssh/config

Option	Function
Host	Restricts the following declarations (up to the next Host keyword) to be only for those hosts that match one of the patterns given after the keyword. * and ? can be used as wildcards in the patterns. A single * as a pattern can be used to provide global defaults for all hosts. The host is the hostname argument given on the command line (that is, the name is not converted to a canonicalized hostname before matching).

TABLE 26.3 Continued

Option	Function
`BatchMode`	If set to `yes`, disables passphrase/password querying. Useful in scripts and other batch jobs where no user is present to supply the password. The argument must be `yes` or `no`. Default is `no`.
`BindAddress`	Specifies the interface to transmit from on machines with multiple interfaces or aliased addresses. Option does not work if `UsePrivilegedPort` is set to `yes`.
`CheckHostIP`	If set to `yes`, `ssh` also checks the host IP address in the `known_hosts` file. This allows `ssh` to detect whether a host key changed due to DNS spoofing. If set to `no`, the check is not executed. Default is `yes`.
`Cipher`	Specifies the cipher to use for encrypting the session in protocol version 1. `blowfish`, `3des`, and `des` are supported, although `des` is only supported in the `ssh` client for interoperability with legacy protocol 1 implementations that do not support the `3des` cipher. Its use is strongly discouraged due to cryptographic weaknesses. Default is `3des`.
`Ciphers`	Specifies the ciphers allowed for protocol version 2 in order of preference. Multiple ciphers must be comma-separated. The default is `aes128-cbc,3des-cbc,blowfish-cbc,cast128-cbc,arcfour,aes192-cbc,aes256-cbc`
`ClearAllForwardings`	Specifies that all local, remote and dynamic port forwardings specified in the configuration files or on the command line be cleared. Primarily useful when used from the `ssh` command line to clear port forwardings set in configuration files, and is automatically set by `scp` and `sftp`. Argument must be `yes` or `no`. Default is `no`.
`ForwardX11`	Specifies whether X11 connections will be automatically redirected over the secure channel and `DISPLAY` set. Argument must be `yes` or `no`. Default is `no`.
`GlobalKnownHostsFile`	Specifies a file to use for the global host key database instead of `/etc/ssh_known_hosts`.
`HostKeyAlgorithms`	Specifies in order of preference the protocol version 2 host key algorithms that the client should use. Default is `ssh-rsa,ssh-dss`
`HostKeyAlias`	Specifies an alias that should be used instead of the real hostname when looking up or saving the host key in the host key database files. Useful for tunneling `ssh` connections or for multiple servers running on a single host.
`HostName`	Specifies the real hostname to log in to. This can be used to specify nicknames or abbreviations for hosts. Default is the name given on the command line. Numeric IP addresses are also permitted, both on the command line and in `HostName` specifications.
`IdentityFile`	Specifies a file from which the user's RSA or DSA authentication identity is read. Defaults are `$HOME/.ssh/identity` for protocol version 1, and `$HOME/.ssh/id_rsa` and `$HOME/.ssh/id_dsa` for protocol version 2.

TABLE 26.3 Continued

Option	Function
	Additionally, any identities represented by the authentication agent will be used for authentication. The filename may use the tilde syntax to refer to a user's home directory. It is possible to have multiple identity files specified in configuration files; all these identities will be tried in sequence.
`LocalForward`	Specifies that a TCP/IP port on the local machine be forwarded over the secure channel to the specified host and port from the remote machine. The first argument must be a port number, and the second must be `host:port`. IPv6 addresses can be specified with an alternative syntax: `host/port`. Multiple forwardings may be specified, and additional forwardings can be given on the command line. Only the superuser can forward privileged ports.
`MACs`	Specifies the MAC (message authentication code) algorithms in order of preference. The MAC algorithm is used in protocol version 2 for data integrity protection. Multiple algorithms must be comma-separated. Default is `hmac-md5,hmac-sha1,hmac-ripemd160,hmac-sha1-96,hmac-md5-96`
`NumberOfPasswordPrompts`	Specifies the number of password prompts before giving up. Argument must be an integer. Default is 3.
`Port`	Specifies the port number to connect to on the remote host. Default is 22.
`PreferredAuthentications`	Specifies the order in which the client should try protocol 2 authentication methods. Default is `hostbased,publickey,keyboard-interactive,password`
`Protocol`	Specifies the protocol versions `ssh` should support in order of preference. The possible values are 1 and 2. The default is `2,1`. In other words, `ssh` tries version 2 and falls back to version 1 if version 2 is not available.
`PubkeyAuthentication`	Specifies whether to try public key authentication. Argument must be `yes` or `no`. Default is `yes`. Protocol version 2 option only.
`RemoteForward`	Specifies that a TCP/IP port on the remote machine be forwarded over the secure channel to the specified host and port from the local machine. The first argument must be a port number, and the second must be `host:port`. IPv6 addresses can be specified with an alternative syntax: `host/port`. Multiple forwardings may be specified, and additional forwardings can be given on the command line. Only the superuser can forward privileged ports.
`StrictHostKeyChecking`	Argument must be `yes`, `no`, or `ask`. Default is `ask`. If set to `yes`, `ssh` never automatically adds host keys to the `$HOME/.ssh/known_hosts` file and refuses to connect to hosts whose host key has changed. This provides maximum protection against Trojan

26

TABLE 26.3 Continued

Option	Function
	horse attacks but can be annoying when the /etc/ssh_known_hosts file is poorly maintained, or connections to new hosts are frequently made. Forces the user to manually add all new hosts.
	If set to no, ssh automatically adds new host keys to the user known hosts files.
	If set to ask, new host keys are added to the user known host files only after the user has confirmed that is what he really wants to do, and ssh refuses to connect to hosts whose host key has changed.
	The host keys of known hosts are verified automatically in all cases.
UsePrivilegedPort	Specifies whether to use a privileged port for outgoing connections. Argument must be yes or no. Default is no.
User	Specifies the user's login. This can be useful when a different username is used on different machines. This saves the trouble of having to remember to give the username on the command line.
UserKnownHostsFile	Specifies a file to use for the user host key database instead of $HOME/.ssh/known_hosts.

Basic Use

SSH provides for secure encrypted traffic transmission across a network. Most SSH software, including that provided by Apple, includes both the encrypted transmission facility and rudimentary tools for making use of that functionality. These tools include the ability to use the encryption to provide secure terminal services and file transfer support. Other functionality can be added as needed by the user, by using just the secure transport portion of the software to encrypt the traffic between otherwise insecure external software packages.

A common use for the SSH package is for making remote terminal connections. Although you can set a number of options to ssh in a user configuration file, you will probably find yourself using ssh with command-line options initially. This is actually the easiest way to start using ssh. After you have been using ssh with command-line options for a while, you will get a feel for what options, if any, you may want to specify in either ~/.ssh/config or /etc/ssh_config.

To use the ssh client, you can either run ssh or slogin. If you are used to using rlogin on a system, slogin will be the natural choice for you. Otherwise, you probably won't have any preferences.

The most commonly used syntax for ssh is

```
ssh -l <username> <remote_host>
ssh <username>@<remote_host>
```

To quickly test that sshd works on your machine, it is easiest to log in to your own machine, as shown here:

```
brezup:nermal nermal $ ssh 192.168.1.17
The authenticity of host '192.168.1.17 (192.168.1.17)' can't be established.
RSA key fingerprint is 51:bd:78:92:34:8e:b8:a7:aa:e5:bc:92:05:83:fb:06.
Are you sure you want to continue connecting (yes/no)? yes
Warning: Permanently added '192.168.1.17' (RSA) to the list of known hosts.
nermal@192.168.1.17's password:
Welcome to Darwin!
brezup:nermal nermal $
```

Note that the first time you try an ssh action to a remote host, you are told that the remote machine's identity can't be verified, and you are asked whether it should be trusted.

After you have verified that your SSH server is running, you should be able to connect to your OS X machine from another machine by using an SSH client.

Chapter 15 shows the command documentation for ssh and slogin in Table 15.4.

Advanced Use

In addition to its terminal capabilities, the SSH suite provides utilities for securely transferring files, tunneling connections, and public key authentication. Some of these topics you have already seen in other chapters in the book. However, we briefly include those here for your convenience. Table 26.4 includes a listing of the primary utilities available in OpenSSH.

TABLE 26.4 Primary Utilities in OpenSSH

Utility	Description
sshd	SSH server.
ssh	SSH client.
sftp	An interactive secure file transfer program.
scp	A copy program for copying files between hosts.
sftp-server	SFTP server subsystem started automatically by sshd.
ssh-keygen	A utility that generates keys for public key authentication.
ssh-agent	Authentication agent that manages keys for public key authentication users so that they don't have to enter a passphrase when logging in to another machine. It starts at the beginning of an X11 session or login session, and windows and programs start as its children.
ssh-add	Utility that adds keys to the ssh-agent.

Transferring Files

The SSH suite includes the scp (secure copy) and sftp (secure FTP) utilities for securely transferring files.

The basic syntax for scp is

```
scp <from> <to>
```

The *<from>* or *<to>* can be specified as a remote host and file, expanding the basic syntax to

```
scp [[<username>@]<remote_host>:]<pathtofile>
➥[[<username>@]<remote_host>:]<pathtofile>
```

The *<remote_host>* can be a name or IP address. Here is sample output from copying a file on the remote host, ~sage/terminal/term-display-1.tiff, to the current directory on the local machine:

```
brezup:nermal nermal $ scp sage@192.168.1.17:terminal/term-display-1.tiff ./
sage@192.168.1.17's password:
term-display-1.tiff 100% |*********************************|  900 KB  00:01
```

While the transfer occurs, the percentage and amount transferred increase over time. You cannot use scp to copy files from your OS X machine unless you have activated the SSH server.

Chapter 15 shows the command documentation for scp in Table 15.5.

The sftp command can also be used to securely transfer files. Its basic syntax, shown following, initiates an interactive session that works much like regular ftp:

```
sftp [<usesrname>@]<remote_host>
```

Here is sample output from an interactive sftp session:

```
brezup:nermal nermal $ sftp sage@192.168.1.17
Connecting to 192.168.1.17...
sage@192.168.1.17's password:
sftp> get terminal/term-display-2.tiff
Fetching /Users/sage/terminal/term-display-2.tiff to term-display-2.tiff
sftp> quit
```

In this example, sftp is used to transfer a file on the remote host, ~sage/terminal/term-display-2.tiff, to the current directory on the local machine. As with scp, you cannot use sftp to transfer files from your OS X machine unless you have activated the SSH server.

Chapter 15 shows the command documentation for sftp in Table 15.6. Only SSH2 servers include sftp.

Tunneling Connections

As you may recall from Chapter 15, secure shell can be used to set up an encrypted tunnel between two machines to transfer data. Services that you might be most interested in tunneling include FTP, POP, IMAP, and X11. Recall that X11 forwarding is off by default in the /etc/sshd_config file.

When tunneling a connection, you can optionally choose to restrict access to a particular service by restricting it to accept connections only from the server machine. Depending on the service, this can be done as an entry to the appropriate /etc/xinetd.d/ file or as an entry in the /etc/hosts.allow file for the server machine, 127.0.0.1. This type of setup increases the security of your machine.

To set up the tunnel, use an SSH client, such as ssh or slogin. Later in this chapter, we will look at setting up an SSH client to do this in Mac OS 8/9 or Classic mode.

At the command line on a machine running an OpenSSH version of SSH, such as another Mac OS X machine, you could run the following to set up a tunnel without having a terminal connection:

```
[creampuf:~] joray% slogin 192.168.1.119 -l sageray -N -L 2121:192.168.1.119:21
sageray@192.168.1.119's password:
```


In the preceding statement, a tunnel is set up between the local machine and the remote host 192.168.1.119 for user sage. The remote host can be specified as a hostname or an IP address. The tunnel is created between the local host at port 2121 and the remote host at port 21, where ftpd on the remote host is listening. The -N option allows us to set up a tunnel without initiating a terminal session. Please note that only root can forward ports under 1024. So if you wanted to use a port number under 1024 on the local machine, you would have to have root privileges.

After the port forwarding is set up in the SSH client, use the regular client for the service, providing it with the appropriate local port to use and localhost or 127.0.0.1 as the host. Although localhost is easier to remember, you may find that only 127.0.0.1 works.

An FTP session over this encrypted channel would look like the following output. Please note that for ftp, it is necessary for the session to be in passive mode. To accomplish this, sometimes you have to issue the passive command at the ftp>. Sometimes passive mode is the default for the ftp client. In this particular case, to get this to work properly from one Mac OS X machine to another, the extended passive mode for IPv4 had to be turned off. However, so far for us, connections from Mac OS X machines to other Unix platforms have not required turning off the extended passive mode.

```
[creampuf:~] joray% ftp 127.0.0.1
Connected to localhost.
220 brezup FTP server (lukemftpd 1.1) ready.
Name (127.0.0.1:joray): sageray
331 Password required for sageray.
Password:
230-
  Welcome to Darwin!
230 User sageray logged in.
Remote system type is UNIX.
Using binary mode to transfer files.
ftp> epsv4 off
EPSV/EPRT on IPv4 off.
ftp> binary
200 Type set to I.
ftp> get snap.jpg
local: snap.jpg remote: snap.jpg
227 Entering Passive Mode (192,168,1,119,195,57)
150 Opening BINARY mode data connection for 'snap.jpg' (561347 bytes).
100% |*************************************|  548 KB 934.85 KB/s  00:00 ETA
226 Transfer complete.
561347 bytes received in 00:00 (927.11 KB/s)
ftp> quit
221-
  Data traffic for this session was 561347 bytes in 1 file.
  Total traffic for this session was 562228 bytes in 1 transfer.
221 Thank you for using the FTP service on brezup.
```

Although tunneling FTP is pertinent to some of you, tunneling SMTP and a protocol such as POP may be more useful. To tunnel SMTP and POP connections over SSH, use a command such as this one:

```
brezup:nermal nermal $ slogin rosalyn.biosci.ohio-state.edu -l ralph
➥-N -L 2110:rosalyn.biosci.ohio-state.edu:110
➥-L 2125:rosalyn.biosci.ohio-state.edu:25
ralph@rosalyn.biosci.ohio-state.edu's password:
```

For the sample statement, in the POP mail client, the POP server is `127.0.0.1`, and its port is `2110`. For some POP mail clients, this is entered as `127.0.0.1:2110`. The SMTP server is 127.0.0.1, and its port is `2125`. Again, for some POP mail clients, this is entered as `127.0.0.1:2125`. The 110 and 25 in the preceding statements are the ports where `popper` and `smtp` are listening on the remote host. Those are standard ports for those services. The administrator of the remote host can tell you which ports the remote host is using. The

2110 and 2125 are port numbers we picked over 1024 so that `root` privileges would not be required for the tunnel. If you are using a POP mail client that does not allow you to specify an alternate port, you may have to use 110 and 25. Figure 26.2 shows the incoming mailbox of a POP account checked using our tunnel and Mailsmith.

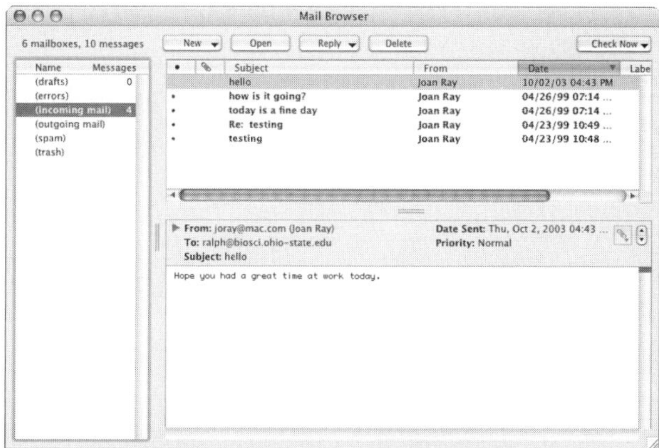

FIGURE 26.2 The incoming mailbox of a POP account checked via SSH tunnels and Mailsmith.

In short, the basic procedure to follow for tunneling a given protocol is as follows:

1. Optionally restrict access by setting up the server to accept connections only from the server machine. Depending on your circumstances, you may have to have this restriction anyway.
2. Set up an `ssh` client with port and server information.
3. Set up the client for the service being tunneled with the local port number to use and `localhost` or `127.0.0.1` as the host.
4. Use the client for the tunneled service as you ordinarily would.

A notable exception to this basic procedure is the procedure for tunneling X11 connections. The SSH server on the remote machine whose display you want to have displayed to your local machine should have X11 forwarding enabled. From your local machine, simply connect with the `ssh` or `slogin` command with the `-X` option, which tunnels an X11 connection. Because SSH takes care of handling everything else to make it work, you don't have to worry about details such as setting the `DISPLAY` environment variable. However, if this doesn't work for you, it may also be necessary for the remote host to add a line to `/etc/hosts.allow` to allow your IP address to have access to `the sshdfwd-X11` service. The `/etc/hosts.allow` file is discussed in Chapter 31.

Figure 26.3 shows remotely running X11 applications being displayed to an OS X machine via SSH tunneling. This is the same XGalaga application you saw in Chapter 19, "X Window System Applications," but because it is running more securely, nobody will know my score!

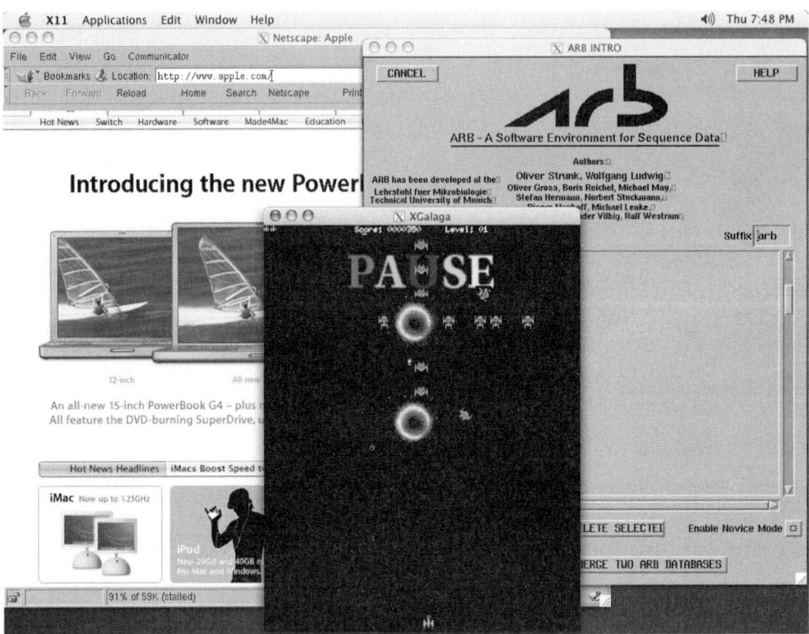

FIGURE 26.3 Remotely running X11 applications are being displayed on an OS X machine via SSH tunneling.

Public Key Authentication

In addition to the standard method of user authentication—a username and password—SSH provides another method: public key authentication. With the traditional authentication method, the remote host stores a username and password pair for a user. With public key authentication, the user creates a key-pair on a given host. The key-pair consists of a private key and a public key protected with a passphrase. Then the user transfers the public key to the remote host to which she wants to connect. So, the remote host stores a set of public keys for machines on which you have generated a key-pair and transferred a copy of your public key. Furthermore, you protect your keys with a passphrase, rather than a password.

Why might you want to use public key authentication? Passwords do not provide much randomness, even if a user tries to create a password that he thinks can't be easily guessed. With today's technology, a machine can guess the password space in a matter of months. Passphrases, on the other hand, provide more randomness and are more difficult to guess.

The procedure for enabling public key authentication is similar for both SSH1 and SSH2. Table 26.5 provides select documentation on `ssh-keygen`, the utility that generates key-pairs. Complete documentation is available in Appendix A. To enable public key authentication, do the following:

1. Generate a key-pair on the host from which you want to access another host. (We will call the host from which you want to connect the local host, and the host to which you want to connect the remote host.) Use a good passphrase to protect your key. It is recommended that a good passphrase be 10–30 characters long and not simple sentences or otherwise easily guessable. Include a mix of uppercase, lowercase, numeric, and nonalphanumeric characters.
2. Transfer the public key of the key-pair generated on the local host to the remote host. The public key is public, so you can use any method necessary to transfer it to the remote host. Depending on the SSH servers involved, you might have to convert your key to a different format first.
3. Add the public key you just transferred to the file on the remote host that stores public keys. Depending on the version of SSH that the remote host is running, this could entail actually adding the key to a file, or just adding a reference to the key in the appropriate file.
4. Test logging in to the remote host. You should now be prompted for the passphrase that you used to generate your key-pair because the private key of the local host is paired with its public key that was transferred to the remote host.

TABLE 26.5 Select Documentation for `ssh-keygen`

`ssh-keygen` Tool for authentication key generation, management and conversion

```
ssh-keygen [-q] [-b <bits>] -t <type> [-N <new_passphrase>] [-C <comment>] [-f
<output_keyfile>]
ssh-keygen -p [-P <old_passphrase>] [-N <new_passphrase>] [-f <keyfile>]
ssh-keygen -i [-f <input_keyfile>]
ssh-keygen -e [-f <input_keyfile>]
ssh-keygen -y [-f <input_keyfile>]
ssh-keygen -c [-P <passphrase>] [-C <comment>] [-f <keyfile>]
ssh-keygen -l [-f <input_keyfile>]
ssh-keygen -B [-f <input_keyfile>]
```

`ssh-keygen` generates, manages, and converts authentication keys for `ssh`. `ssh-keygen` can create RSA keys for use by 1, and RSA or DSA keys for use by SSH2. The type of key to be generated is specified with the `-t` option.

Normally each user who wants to use SSH with RSA or DSA authentication runs this once to create the authentication key in `$HOME/.ssh/identity`, `$HOME/.ssh/id_dsa`, or `$HOME/.ssh/id_rsa`. Additionally, the system administrator may use this to generate host keys.

`-b <bits>`	Specifies the number of bits in the key to create. Minimum is 512 bits. Generally 1024 bits is considered sufficient, and key sizes above that no longer improve security but make things slower. Default is 1024 bits.

TABLE 26.5 Continued

`-e`	Reads a private or public OpenSSH key file and prints the key in a SECSH Public Key File Format to `stdout`. This option allows exporting keys for use by several commercial SSH implementations.
`-f` *<filename>*	Specifies the filename of the key file.
`-i`	Reads an unencrypted private (or public) key file in SSH2-compatible format and prints an OpenSSH-compatible private (or public) key to `stdout`. `ssh-keygen` also reads the SECSH Public Key File Format. This option allows importing keys from several commercial SSH implementations.
`-p`	Requests the changing of the passphrase of a private key file instead of creating a new private key.
`-t` *<type>*	Specifies the type of the key to create. The possible values are `rsa1` for protocol version 1 and `rsa` or `dsa` for protocol version 2.
`-C` *<comment>*	Provides the new comment.
`-N` *<new_passphrase>*	Provides the new passphrase, *<new_passphrase>*.
`-P` *<passphrase>*	Provides the (old) passphrase, *<passphrase>*.

Not only are there differences in public key authentication between SSH1 and SSH2, but there are differences between SSH packages as well. The keys for SSH1 and SSH2 generated by OpenSSH differ from the ones made by SSH Communications Security's SSH servers, the other ones you are most likely to encounter. Be sure to thoroughly read the `ssh-keygen`, `ssh`, and `sshd` man pages for the SSH servers you have to connect to because the information you need to know for connecting via public key authentication will most likely be spread among those man pages. The keys look a bit different for the different protocols and can look quite different between the SSH packages. Fortunately, OpenSSH's `ssh-keygen` can import and export keys.

To give you an idea of how the various public keys look, some sample public keys are shown following. Default file locations were accepted when creating the keys. This first key is a sample SSH2 public key generated in OpenSSH with the DSA algorithm option (`ssh-keygen -t dsa`), stored as `~/.ssh/id_dsa.pub`:

```
ssh-dss AAAAB3NzaC1kc3MAAACBALzT9RbceziStHPmMiHmg78hXUgcMP14sJZ/7MH/p2NX
/fB0cmbULPNgEN8jrs8w9N73J7yUFHSPR/LVfBj+UwkIzwjyXUW/z/VmCs25IDF/UBn1OQK5
PCi16rF0F+Cx0hMN4R3AaFAetXBdLqoom5x4Yo9gdspPqhhB44QnT43JAAAAFQDWTkKDJ2m4
SApHZ/qRnRpMN5whTQAAAIAVADOsHpnUdUOFKjIgxZ0Hwh7IaMQ2ofGt/6PmbmNG/8zXRdxm
u/JrBzieWHq6sSRSkWDSDIjuEuTkZyJ4wx3KsLmhIrtlBw3NCcsJT2GfGQ9gEBm8fkUpeQyK
AQcirbx4Hw93iMFC3g9A8cwqmA4DalKSX3un7cweNU32Irhq+gAAAIAz+lDSjqjFzuTV4vJ/
P83nH2uwb62/iCSIB9cL32hrOm234imaAceu8pN9qqEAPr9AilCWa+lqGvgcdyDK0vZTvKQn
k6KOU3TJfDyMR7i/gzW4P4TA/== miwa@brezup
```

This is a sample SSH2 public key generated in OpenSSH with the RSA algorithm option (`ssh-keygen -t rsa`), stored as `~/.ssh/id_rsa.pub`:

```
ssh-rsa AAAAB3NzaC1yc2EAAAABIwAAAIEAnMV/YAmJdEoRFC3Fa91YVloqivKeAwD62bd4
+zSsd1lMr6JV4oE9EIfVPM3BL98UgmDzfhlh5b2PAP1YFwalXNksPeCQ0TNoBYIO1qloPwGr
00l4sllJDCgMGKphT3saumDCVryGof4g9tm3itMri/c8sA04MqOb0NS2tfBCQRc= miwa@br
ezup
```

This is a sample SSH1 public key generated in OpenSSH with the RSA algorithm, the only choice for SSH1 (`ssh-keygen -t rsa1`), stored as `~/.ssh/identity.pub`:

```
1024 35 155721298510659584179944539389589685520184296531692648011618717 8
47931275273178693642653436228988381482922069944869579300829219135525658 1
25248351354000991356228685632047778649000628072666080837001969287828694 1
83286791348827043363003985437592043458504034267132999021632074427678357 6
664388358911747235081029563 87 miwa@brezup
```

This key is a sample SSH2 public key generated in SSH Communications Security's SSH server with the DSA algorithm (`ssh-keygen2 -t dsa`), stored in `~/.ssh2/id_dsa_1024_a.pub`:

```
---- BEGIN SSH2 PUBLIC KEY ----
Subject: miwa
Comment: "1024-bit dsa, miwa@Rosalyn, Thu May 16 2002 23:33:30 -0500"
AAAAB3NzaC1kc3MAAACBAIxEJgV24AtDzKyFzMAD5agu/YHOZnhUma12zVX31Ov5Xj9hU/
0VB/FdxtctLKbUMRra5b9azzHFsdJl/f1VqoQ8feEfFZ/4nTcSVbL5f5KydmSe0Mmyq4vq
IqSC4jyDjIHMUcDfj2Z/kRhF9o6VxCdCUd5OvkpZmEfWqLNR9oPlAAAAFQD02rAsEPS2uU
VTAa/pHqKhcrC6mwAAAIB3UDIDjP9TOJNaap34/9o0qW1o7agFMXcJftlUgZEtUfc5v/jX
MplQiL77CggJU+rdv9WQbyefaFjWLQAibV5M71kt2mdkYVtuQzbmBTDW9v8YP1/QMnnjOK
v8xRmrsplC/lv9/rmzS0gI1Hfbbuq60zW/ULdg6c61y7HyZ/Qf5AAAAIArWb/PIWRhMxLR
aY9VZvFZOYjOxcIR66aoybkneODPaAwZsW5yq1q2XEpxxza4q2yTyZ7drTYLCUBbXwG4Cu
RVv3CMTiXQ47AXlKYPECVT0I4bTZyY60GuLI4TUsyHLk5HFF0Ctt/6OB8WEHOn6LGDNNoN
DF4M7MlGbyOVNZnGCw==
---- END SSH2 PUBLIC KEY ----
```

This is a sample SSH2 public key generated in SSH Communications Security's SSH server with the RSA algorithm (`ssh-keygen2 -t rsa`), stored in `~/.ssh2/id_rsa_1024_a.pub`:

```
---- BEGIN SSH2 PUBLIC KEY ----
Subject: miwa
Comment: "1024-bit rsa, miwa@Rosalyn, Sun Sep 08 2002 23:00:14 -0500"
AAAAB3NzaC1yc2EAAAADAQABAAAAgQDenNONzW2v+TB/ZeRHZvKRWJk24Lk7LsA4+uWsYL
5L+bNoPYV0oKD3UMYddEacM47gcSd2e1E511Wlx/+X0MjrvPqEIlqw9owkjwOukm38iISz
qypT4uvawOW9GcKE7c5KH8BD9tfhvCkwZE+oAsJk3jfTBRSdOdxhvhF87RgbcQ==
---- END SSH2 PUBLIC KEY ----
```

This is a sample SSH1 public key generated in SSH Communications Security's SSH server with the RSA algorithm (`ssh-keygen1`), stored in `~/.ssh/identity.pub`:

```
1024 35 150523262886747450533481402006467053649597280355648477085483985
712083176768664660899834191983286561976032166628443720186802736469866695
561784637378345179225111133633075841684444147236898954804613540972039555
146309834605363142493240937409415470774407489421467610336509326725169131
15515061714916853690571025084316 3 miwa@Rosalyn
```

After you have transferred your public key to the remote host, you have to let the remote host know that you want to allow public key authentication from your local host. How this is done depends on the SSH server. For OpenSSH, authorized public keys for SSH1 and SSH2 keys are stored in `~/.ssh/authorized_keys`. Each line of a basic `authorized_keys` file contains a public key. Blank lines and lines starting with # are ignored. However, limitations can be further placed on an authorized public key using options listed in Table 26.6. A sample `~/.ssh/authorized_keys` file follows:

```
1024 35 155721298510659584179944539389589685520184296531692648011618717 8
479312752731786936426534362289883814829220699448695793008292191355256581
252483513540009913562286856320477786490006280726660808370019692878286941
832867913488270433630039854375920434585040342671329990216320744276783576
6643883589117472350810295638 7 miwa@brezup

ssh-dss AAAAB3NzaC1kc3MAAACBALPMiCqdPDGxcyB1IwPrPXk3oEqvpxR62EsspxGKGGbO
M6mf60i1hwTvjZzDhUSR7ViGeCopKtjJIqn2ljgeLbhFsQUX2UyJ6A1cFVuef0x6GVAsybqb
tJc8JBh41U+iSXJKppEY5BI+REMydpBXJf2qT/8yZeq3NPjiOiMb6TyjAAAAFQDYvvV4WQK1
Zu23q/7iLKg5j/zi5wAAAIBR7vgrQpjKW2cprIUJsnenTm4hnBrEO7NMUomjgezrY23iZdIS
QlU1ESMgx9W9nnZstd2vjeqHDSmmcD2p/aGqhl3N1WlYk8zgFYYJilPwRxVm77Np/vXz/MQp
ygJE7ToXGvfHqVmdBpUyakyfx6DveWhFPis1Ab8N1RCPWm6PMwAAAIAytHjAAMYscqX2tl4i
cw3oOku3HIvoHBCx9D6Q9LjCqt7DqqgMN2e5vuvNz0hzqBaBDJsjNA/A4bI88ZrgLhfJM/Nh
s2xkcb7AYeHEtuGKVbsbB0EjsECtLRHydfmk3wDQjUVT92HsodFvsIl4Je7seWUuiAEe0V1x
fF7XrXuwNQ== miwa@hobbes
```

For an SSH1 server by SSH Communications Security, the authorized public keys are also stored in `~/.ssh/authorized_keys`. An SSH2 server by SSH Communications Security, however, stores references to files that contain authorized public keys in `~/.ssh2/authorization`. Here is a sample `~/.ssh2/authorization` file:

```
Key hobbes.pub
Key ryoohki.pub
```

As an example, suppose that you want to allow public key authentication from a machine running an SSH Communications Security SSH2 server. First, generate a key-pair on the remote SSH2 machine using `ssh-keygen2`.

Then transfer the public key of the key-pair to your Mac OS X machine by whatever method you choose.

In this case, because you want to allow public key authentication from a machine running a non-OpenSSH SSH server, you have to convert the public key file that was transferred to something compatible with your OpenSSH server. The `ssh-keygen` utility can convert between SSH formats. Run a command of the following form:

```
ssh-keygen -i -f <transferred_public_key> > <converted_transferred_public_key>
```

The preceding statement imports the transferred public key file and directs the converted output to a file specified by *<converted_transferred_public_key>*. We recommend including the name of the remote host in your filename to make things easier for you. OpenSSH's `ssh-keygen` can also export its keys to the IETF SECSH format.

Then add that file to the `~/.ssh/authorized_keys` file, the file that contains your public keys from machines authorized to connect via public key authentication. This can be done in whatever way you feel most comfortable. Issuing the following statement does this quite neatly:

```
cat <converted_transferred_public_key> >> .ssh/authorized_keys
```

Now that the public key from the non-OpenSSH machine has been transferred and converted to a format used by OpenSSH, you can log in to your Mac OS X machine from the remote host via pubic key authentication.

Logging in to a machine running a non-OpenSSH SSH server from your OS X machine is similar. First generate the key-pair on your OS X machine using `ssh-keygen`. Then convert the public key file to the IETF SECSH format by running a command of the form:


```
ssh-keygen -e -f <public_key> > <converted_public_key>
```

Transfer the converted public key file to the remote host by whatever method you choose. Then add a reference to the `~/.ssh2/authorization` file of the form:

```
Key <public_key_filename>
```

Now that the public key generated on your OS X machine has been transferred to the remote host running a non-OpenSSH SSH server, and a reference to it has been added to the `~/.ssh2/authorization` file, you are logged in to the remote host via public key authentication.

The details provided here address logging in via public key authentication between the major different SSH servers using the SSH2 protocol. Because the SSH1 protocol is not under active development, we are not discussing the details involved there. However, if you need to connect to an SSH1 server via public key authentication, it is easier than what needs to be done for the SSH2 protocol. You do not have to convert the key formats. On the non-OpenSSH machine, the file that contains the public keys is `~/.ssh/authorized_keys`, and you add public keys themselves to the file rather than references to the public key files.

If you don't like the command line, you might try Gideon Softworks' `SSH Helper`, available at `http://www.gideonsoftworks.com/sshhelper.html`. It is a freely available package.

TABLE 26.6 Options for `~/.ssh/authorized_keys`

Option	Function
`From="pattern-list"`	Specifies that in addition to RSA authentication, the canonical name of the remote host must be present in the comma-separated list of patterns. `*` and `?` serve as wildcards. The list may also contain patterns negated by prefixing them with !. If the canonical hostname matches a negated pattern, the key is not accepted.
`Command="command"`	Specifies that the command is executed whenever this key is used for authentication. The command supplied by the user (if any) is ignored. The command is run on a `pty` if the client requests a `pty`; otherwise, it is run without a `tty`. If an 8-bit clean channel is required, one must not request a `pty` or should specify `no-pty`. A quote may be included in the command by quoting it with a backslash. This option might be useful to restrict certain RSA keys to perform just a specific operation. An example might be a key that permits remote backups but nothing else. Note that the client may specify TCP/IP and/or X11 forwarding unless they are explicitly prohibited. Note that this option applies to shell, command, or subsystem execution.
`environment="NAME=value"`	Specifies that the string is to be added to the environment when logging in using this key. Environment variables set this way override other default environment values. Multiple options of this type are permitted. This option is automatically disabled if `UseLogin` is enabled.
`no-port-forwarding`	Forbids TCP/IP forwarding when this key is used for authentication. Any port forward requests by the client will return an error. This might be used, for example, in connection with the command option.
`no-X11-forwarding`	Forbids X11 forwarding when this key is used for authentication. Any X11 forward requests by the client will return an error.
`no-agent-forwarding`	Forbids authentication agent forwarding when this key is used for authentication.
`no-pty`	Prevents `tty` allocation (a request to allocate a `pty` will fail).
`permitopen="host:port"`	Limits local `ssh -L` port forwarding such that it may only connect to the specified host and port. IPv6 addresses can be specified with an alternative syntax: `host/port`. Multiple permit open options may be applied separated by commas. No pattern matching is performed on the specified hostnames; they must be literal domains or addresses.

A Butler to Hold Your Wallet: `ssh-agent`

The SSH suite of applications is wonderful for protecting your communications, but although entering a passphrase instead of a password for logins through `ssh` is only a minor inconvenience, repeating it over and over to copy files using scp can be a real annoyance. Thankfully, the designers thought of this and have created an auxiliary application that allows you to authenticate yourself once to it, and it can then use the stored private keys and the passphrases associated with your SSH identities (SSH keypairs generated by ssh-keygen and authorized on another host), to authenticate to remote hosts for you automatically. Essentially, this software acts as your agent and responds for you, whenever a remote host asks for your passphrase. This eliminates any need for you to respond to passphrase queries from remote hosts for which the agent knows a proper response, and can drastically decrease the effort involved in using the SSH applications.

If you're dealing with SSH on a daily basis, using ssh-agent is almost certainly the way you'll want to use the SSH software because it will make your life much easier. The process for using the agent is simple as well and can be summarized as follows:

1. Start the ssh-agent.
2. Set up your environment so that SSH applications can find the agent.
3. Add identities to the agent.
4. Use SSH applications (slogin, scp, and so on), and never get asked for your passphrase.

However, although the difference in practice is significant, the difference in print is subtle. Previously in this chapter you learned how to perform all the steps necessary to work through SSH, but for the sake of clarity with respect to what ssh-agent can actually do for you, we'll recap from the position of a user who's never used SSH to authenticate to remote hosts. In the following examples, we've left the prompt intact so that you can tell which machine and directory we're working in. The input/output fragments that follow were collected as a single stream of actions by our test user miwa, and we've split them up to intersperse some comments on what he's doing. If you follow along, by the end of this section you'll have set up a user with two independent SSH identities that can be used to authenticate against both ssh.com and openssh.org type sshd servers.

1. Let's see what files miwa has in his ~/.ssh directory.

```
brezup:miwa miwa $ ls -l .ssh
ls: .ssh: No such file or directory
```

2. We're starting with a clean slate. We've deleted miwa's ~/.ssh directory so that it's as if he's never used the SSH software before.

```
brezup:miwa miwa $ ssh-keygen -t rsa -b 1024
Generating public/private rsa key pair.
Enter file in which to save the key (/Users/miwa/.ssh/id_rsa):
Created directory '/Users/miwa/.ssh'.
Enter passphrase (empty for no passphrase):
```

```
Enter same passphrase again:
Your identification has been saved in /Users/miwa/.ssh/id_rsa.
Your public key has been saved in /Users/miwa/.ssh/id_rsa.pub.
The key fingerprint is:
b3:c9:1f:91:25:ea:31:4d:28:b0:78:34:8a:16:f1:9e miwa@brezup
```

3. To use SSH applications, miwa needs keys. Create his default key as an RSA key of 1024 bits. We enter a passphrase for miwa, but it's not echoed to the screen.

```
brezup:miwa miwa $ ls -l .ssh
total 16
-rw------- 1 miwa miwa 951 2 Oct 18:50 id_rsa
-rw-r--r-- 1 miwa miwa 221 2 Oct 18:50 id_rsa.pub
```

4. And in his ~/.ssh directory, there are now two files, containing the private and public keypair for his default identity.

```
brezup:miwa miwa $ slogin ryoko.biosci.ohio-state.edu
The authenticity of host 'ryoko.biosci.ohio-state.edu
➥(140.254.104.240)' can't be established.
DSA key fingerprint is 17:07:3d:f6:44:55:7d:8a:a2:00:89:b7:76:43:ad:f4.
Are you sure you want to continue connecting (yes/no)? yes
Warning: Permanently added 'ryoko.biosci.ohio-state.edu,
➥140.254.104.240' (DSA) to the list of known hosts.
 miwa@ryoko.biosci.ohio-state.edu's password:
Last login: Mon Feb 17 2003 19:15:54 -0500 from cvl232015.columb
You have new mail.
ryoko miwa 1 > ls -l .ssh2
.ssh2: No such file or directory
ryoko miwa 2 >mkdir .ssh2
ryoko miwa 3 >exit
Connection to ryoko.biosci.ohio-state.edu closed.
```

5. miwa logs in to ryoko.biosci.ohio-state.edu using his password for the system. ryoko is a Sun Enterprise Server running ssh.com's version of the SSH software. It doesn't keep its key files in the same place as does our Macintosh's openssh.org version. miwa creates the required ~/.ssh2 directory in his home directory on ryoko and then logs off the machine. For the best security, we recommend disabling passworded logins from the network entirely and only accepting passphrases, but this requires physical access to both machines for at least a little while, or some other way of transferring a public key without being able to log in to the remote machine via the network.

```
brezup:miwa miwa $ cd .ssh
brezup:miwa .ssh $ ls -l
```

```
total 24
-rw------- 1 miwa miwa 951 2 Oct 18:50 id_rsa
-rw-r--r-- 1 miwa miwa 221 2 Oct 18:50 id_rsa.pub
-rw-r--r-- 1 miwa miwa 633 2 Oct 18:56 known_hosts
brezup:miwa .ssh $ ssh-keygen -e -f id_rsa
---- BEGIN SSH2 PUBLIC KEY ----
Comment: "1024-bit RSA, converted from OpenSSH by miwa@brezup"
AAAAB3NzaC1yc2EAAAABIwAAAIEAv09dKFr46dK+U43m8h9hV0JtooRdyf8hbPJcf1y+kX
cpcOpHWz7NBqGI3FsZZUrJDrgP3Q/1VHa8SiDsCkYFuG55HobfNfrsGVvW7LqHn9ApzYhi
fPUGpLSQnML4/qzTLNn2JmUiEvlcdYrnZoi+b23Om4mLu1zez7nT91EGTnk=
---- END SSH2 PUBLIC KEY ----
```

6. miwa needs to get the public key for the identity he wants to use on ryoko into a form that ryoko's sshd can understand. Pleasantly, ssh-keygen can not only generate keys, it can also translate them into the standard format that ssh.com's server version wants. A known_hosts file has appeared in miwa's .ssh directory along with his id_rsa identity files. In this file is recorded the public host-key for ryoko.

```
brezup:miwa .ssh $ ssh-keygen -e -f id_rsa > home_rsa.ietf
brezup:miwa .ssh $ ls -l
total 32
-rw-r--r-- 1 miwa miwa 328 2 Oct 19:05 home_rsa.ietf
-rw------- 1 miwa miwa 951 2 Oct 18:50 id_rsa
-rw-r--r-- 1 miwa miwa 221 2 Oct 18:50 id_rsa.pub
-rw-r--r-- 1 miwa miwa 633 2 Oct 18:56 known_hosts
```

7. Using ssh-keygen, miwa writes out an IETF formatted version of the public key for his id.rsa key and puts it in his .ssh directory. Because the SSH implementation on Mac OS X won't use this key for anything, he could actually store it just about anywhere, but this seems like as good and safe a place as any.

```
brezup:miwa .ssh $ scp ./home_rsa.ietf
➥miwa@ryoko.biosci.ohio-state.edu:.ssh2/home_rsa.ietf
miwa@ryoko.biosci.ohio-state.edu's password:
scp: warning: Executing scp1 compatibility.
home_rsa.ietf    100% |*****************************| 347    00:00
```

8. miwa copies the key to ryoko using scp. Because it's a public key, it wouldn't be a problem even if he had to copy it over a protocol where data is visible. If passworded logins are blocked, this key transfer needs to be done in some other fashion, such as transporting it on removable media.

```
brezup:miwa .ssh $ slogin ryoko.biosci.ohio-state.edu
miwa@ryoko.biosci.ohio-state.edu's password:
```

```
Last login: Thu Oct 02 2003 17:56:28 -0500 from dhcp065-024-074-
You have new mail.
ryoko miwa 1 >ls -l .ssh2
total 2
-rw-r--r--  1 miwa   class    328 Oct 2 19:07 home_rsa.ietf
ryoko miwa 2 >cd .ssh2
ryoko .ssh2 3 >cat >> authorization
Key home_rsa.ietf
^D
```

9. An `authorization` file must be created on `ryoko`, listing the key `miwa` just transferred as valid for logins. `miwa` just `cat`s the line in append mode onto his `authorization` file. The file doesn't exist, so it'll get created, but if it did exist, this Key line would simply be added as new data at the end of the file. The `cat` command is terminated with a `Control-D` on a line by itself.

```
ryoko .ssh2 4 >ls -l
total 4
-rw-r--r--  1 miwa   class     18 Oct 2 19:10 authorization
-rw-r--r--  1 miwa   class    328 Oct 2 19:07 home_rsa.ietf
ryoko .ssh2 5 >chmod 600 authorization home_rsa.ietf
ryoko .ssh2 6 >ls -l
total 4
-rw-------  1 miwa   class     18 Oct 2 19:10 authorization
-rw-------  1 miwa   class    328 Oct 2 19:07 home_rsa.ietf
ryoko .ssh2 7 >cat authorization
Key home_rsa.ietf
ryoko .ssh2 8 >exit
Connection to ryoko.biosci.ohio-state.edu closed.
```

10. The authorization file now exists and contains the data expected. Even though it's a public key and theoretically can't be usefully abused, `miwa` `chmod`s both files in his `.sshd` directory so that only he can read them, just to be sure.

```
brezup:miwa .ssh $ slogin ryoko.biosci.ohio-state.edu
Enter passphrase for key '/Users/miwa/.ssh/id_rsa':
Last login: Thu Oct 02 2003 18:08:34 -0500 from dhcp065-024-074-
You have new mail.
ryoko miwa 1 >exit
Connection to ryoko.biosci.ohio-state.edu closed.
```

11. Back on brezup, `miwa` can now `slogin` to `ryoko` and be asked for a passphrase instead his considerably weaker password.

```
brezup:miwa .ssh $ ssh-keygen -t rsa -b 1024
Generating public/private rsa key pair.
Enter file in which to save the key (/Users/miwa/.ssh/id_rsa):
➥/Users/miwa/.ssh/internal_rsa
Enter passphrase (empty for no passphrase):
Enter same passphrase again:
Your identification has been saved in /Users/miwa/.ssh/internal_rsa.
Your public key has been saved in /Users/miwa/.ssh/internal_rsa.pub.
The key fingerprint is:
d4:b9:f7:7a:1f:49:96:b4:9d:ac:1a:3a:5d:0a:57:3b miwa@brezup
```

12. For some reason, `miwa` wants another, separate identity for use on his internal (private) network. Perhaps it's because he's going to allow (against our good advice) other users to log in to his account and use it for connecting to other machines on the internal network. By using a separate identity, and only giving out the passphrase to his internal identity, he can mitigate the danger in this scheme and protect his external identity. Here, `miwa`'s chosen to create it into the nondefault file `internal_rsa`, again as a 1024-bit RSA key.

```
brezup:miwa .ssh $ ls -l
total 48
-rw-r--r-- 1 miwa miwa 328 2 Oct 19:05 home_rsa.ietf
-rw------- 1 miwa miwa 951 2 Oct 18:50 id_rsa
-rw-r--r-- 1 miwa miwa 221 2 Oct 18:50 id_rsa.pub
-rw------- 1 miwa miwa 951 2 Oct 19:27 internal_rsa
-rw-r--r-- 1 miwa miwa 221 2 Oct 19:27 internal_rsa.pub
-rw-r--r-- 1 miwa miwa 633 2 Oct 18:56 known_hosts
```

13. Now there are files in `~miwa/.ssh/` for both his default `id_rsa` identity and his `internal_rsa` identity. `miwa` needs to transfer the public key from in the `internal_rsa` keypair to any of our private, internal-network hosts he wants to be able to access via passphrase. In this case, `192.168.1.200`, otherwise known as `creampuf`, is used as an example.

```
brezup:miwa .ssh $ slogin 192.168.1.200
The authenticity of host '192.168.1.200 (192.168.1.200)'
➥can't be established.
RSA key fingerprint is f3:62:16:8e:25:7f:75:ab:4c:cd:99:5d:39:bc:3c:b7.
Are you sure you want to continue connecting (yes/no)? yes
Warning: Permanently added '192.168.1.200' (RSA) to the list of known hosts.
miwa@192.168.1.200's password:
Welcome to Darwin!
[creampuf:~] miwa% ls -l .ssh
ls: .ssh: No such file or directory
```

```
[creampuf:~] miwa% mkdir .ssh
[creampuf:~] miwa% touch .ssh/authorized_keys
[creampuf:~] miwa% chmod 600 .ssh/authorized_keys
[creampuf:~] miwa% exit
Connection to 192.168.1.200 closed.
```

14. Again, `miwa` hasn't logged in to this host before, so creating the directory to contain SSH keys is necessary. This time it's a Mac OS X machine, so it uses the `openssh.org` way of specifying authorized remote users, that being a single `authorized_keys` file of (concatenated) authorized keys. `miwa` creates the file and sets its permissions to owner-read/write only.

```
brezup:miwa .ssh $ ls -l
total 48
-rw-r--r-- 1 miwa miwa 328 2 Oct 19:05 home_rsa.ietf
-rw------- 1 miwa miwa 951 2 Oct 18:50 id_rsa
-rw-r--r-- 1 miwa miwa 221 2 Oct 18:50 id_rsa.pub
-rw------- 1 miwa miwa 951 2 Oct 19:27 internal_rsa
-rw-r--r-- 1 miwa miwa 221 2 Oct 19:27 internal_rsa.pub
-rw-r--r-- 1 miwa miwa 856 2 Oct 19:31 known_hosts
```

15. Back on brezup, the `known_hosts` file has grown because it's accumulated the host key from `192.168.1.200` now as well.

```
brezup:miwa .ssh $ scp internal_rsa.pub
➥miwa@192.168.1.200:.ssh/miwa_brezup_rsa.pub
miwa@192.168.1.200's password:
internal_rsa.pub   100% |*****************************|  240    00:00
brezup:miwa .ssh $ slogin 192.168.1.200
miwa@192.168.1.200's password:
Welcome to Darwin!
[creampuf:~] miwa% cd .ssh
[creampuf:~/.ssh] miwa% ls -l
total 8
-rw------- 1 miwa staff   0 Oct 2 19:33 authorized_keys
-rw-r--r-- 1 miwa staff 221 Oct 2 19:51 miwa_brezup_rsa.pub
[creampuf:~/.ssh] miwa% cat miwa_brezup_rsa.pub >> authorized_keys
[creampuf:~/.ssh] miwa% cat authorized_keys
ssh-rsa AAAAB3NzaC1yc2EAAAABIwAAAIEAzc9VaVwZEG8lWJ5SO/t1LfCpZK7dHGbz
uTnLXdN2sTLd09Ei0567vLHSxRmDddGej79ShvqKh+4EXXZsCjwvuIyJsQvW61FC/IQJ
HkCJjCxxmrEaxphPEG5Iu5M2k5JsshmoLL89aKYWYadv1vsBLZ5PxgDTtGE2h+pd8PBa
q/0= miwa@brezup
[creampuf:~/.ssh] miwa% chmod 600 miwa_brezup_rsa.pub
[creampuf:~/.ssh] miwa% exit
Connection to 192.168.1.200 closed.
```

16. miwa transfers his public key from his internal_rsa key-pair to 192.168.1.200 and saves it as miwa_sage_rsa.pub in his .ssh directory on 192.168.1.200. It's good to come up with a standardized naming scheme for keys that gives you some idea of what user the key was for and what host it allows access from. In this case, because miwa might be allowing other users to log in to his account, he might eventually have many other users' public keys stored in his authorized_keys files in his various accounts around our internal network. Keeping a copy of each of them named in terms of who it allows access, and from which machine, gives him the ability to sort through his authorized_keys file and delete entries if it becomes necessary to limit access in the future.

    After he's transferred his internal_rsa public key to creampuf, he logs in to creampuf (again using his password) and cats the key (in append mode) onto the end of his ~/.ssh/authorized_keys file. He also chmods it to owner read/write only, again, just to be safe.

```
brezup:miwa .ssh $ cd ~
brezup:miwa .ssh $ slogin 192.168.1.200
miwa@192.168.1.200's password:
^C
```

17. Back on brezup, miwa tests his setup and lands at a password prompt. That wasn't the expected behavior. Everything was copied over properly, so maybe it's something about slogin that miwa doesn't yet understand—maybe it's not smart enough to pick the correct identity credentials from the ones he's created, and it's trying to authenticate to the internal server with his default ID? Reading the man page, he discovers that you can specify an ID explicitly, and he tries that option.

```
brezup:miwa .ssh $ slogin 192.168.1.200 -i internal_rsa
Warning: Identity file internal_rsa does not exist.
miwa@192.168.1.200's password:
^C
```

    Again, not the desired response, but this time it's a complaint that the identity doesn't exist. Perhaps slogin's not smart enough to look in the default location for anything other than the default identity as well?

```
brezup:miwa miwa $ slogin 192.168.1.200 -i .ssh/internal_rsa
miwa@192.168.1.200's password:
Welcome to Darwin!
[creampuf:~] miwa% tail -3 /var/log/system.log
Oct 2 21:40:08 creampuf sshd[618]: Could not reverse map address
192.168.1.119.
Oct 2 21:40:08 creampuf sshd[618]: Authentication refused: bad ownership or
modes for directory /Users/miwa
```

```
Oct 2 21:40:08 creampuf sshd[618]: Accepted password for miwa from
192.168.1.119 port 49656 ssh2
```

Although it doesn't show up in print, there was actually a fairly long pause after `miwa` issued this `slogin` command before it brought up the `password` prompt. Clearly it knows about the ID because it didn't complain about the specification this time, so maybe something's wrong with the server on the remote host. A quick look at the diagnostics from `sshd` in `system.log` reveals the problem. There's something about the permissions of `miwa`'s home directory that `sshd` doesn't like, and it's therefore refusing to allow passphrased access.

```
[creampuf:~] miwa% ls -ld /Users/miwa/
drwxrwxr-x 29 miwa staff 986 Oct 2 19:33 /Users/miwa/
```

The problem is that `miwa` has been being sloppy with security and has left his home directory with write-access for the staff group. This would enable a malicious user who was a member of group staff to potentially edit or overwrite files in `miwa`'s directory. Because this could allow them to modify `miwa`'s `~/.ssh/authorized_keys` file without permission, `sshd` recognizes this as a security hole and disables use of that file for authorization.

```
[creampuf:~] miwa% chmod 755 .
[creampuf:~] miwa% ls -ld /Users/miwa/
drwxr-xr-x 29 miwa staff 986 Oct 2 19:33 /Users/miwa/
[creampuf:~] miwa% exit
Connection to 192.168.1.200 closed.
```

18. `miwa` changes the permissions on his home directory to disallow write access for anyone except himself, and logs out to try again.

```
brezup:miwa miwa $ slogin 192.168.1.200 -i .ssh/internal_rsa
Enter passphrase for key '.ssh/internal_rsa':
Welcome to Darwin!
```

19. Success! `miwa` can now log in to either `ryoko.biosci.ohio-state.edu` or to `192.168.1.200`, and each uses an independent ID with independent passphrases. This brings us to the conclusion of the recap, and to where `miwa` uses `ssh-agent` to make his life easier, by removing the need for him to constantly type passphrases to use SSH tools.

```
brezup:miwa miwa $ ssh-agent
SSH_AUTH_SOCK=/tmp/ssh-kyJ6HQ6T/agent.6989; export SSH_AUTH_SOCK;
SSH_AGENT_PID=6990; export SSH_AGENT_PID;
echo Agent pid 6990;
```

20. When run, ssh-agent prints out some information regarding how it can be contacted, and forks itself into the background. At that point, it's your agent, ready and willing to answer passphrase requests for you, but it doesn't yet have copies of any of your credentials, and none of the software that needs access to your credentials knows how to find it. The information that it prints out (by default) is commands in the syntax of your shell that will set up a shell so that SSH tools run in that shell can find the agent.

    In tcsh, the preceding output would be

```
setenv SSH_AUTH_SOCK /tmp/ssh-kyJ6HQ6T/agent.6989;
setenv SSH_AGENT_PID6990;
echo Agent pid 6990;
```

    To use the information, simply copy the lines that ssh-agent prints and execute them as commands at the command-line prompt.

```
brezup:miwa miwa $ SSH_AUTH_SOCK=/tmp/ssh-kyJ6HQ6T/agent.6989;
➥export SSH_AUTH_SOCK;
brezup:miwa miwa $ SSH_AGENT_PID=6990; export SSH_AGENT_PID;
```

TIP

Instead of copying and pasting the default ssh-agent output, you could just execute ssh-agent at the command-line as `` `ssh-agent` `` to have that output executed for you.

21. miwa runs the two commands to set the environment variables and ignores the echo. The output of ssh-agent is designed so that you can wrap it into a script that calls it and executes its suggested shell commands automatically. The echo is only there so that you get diagnostic output to your terminal if you use it in this fashion.

    Next, miwa must supply the credentials that he wants the agent to provide in response to queries from SSH programs. This is accomplished with the ssh-add command.

```
brezup:miwa miwa $ ssh-add
Enter passphrase for /Users/miwa/.ssh/id_rsa:
Identity added: /Users/miwa/.ssh/id_rsa (/Users/miwa/.ssh/id_rsa)
brezup:miwa miwa $ ssh-add .ssh/internal_rsa
Enter passphrase for .ssh/internal_rsa:
Identity added: .ssh/internal_rsa (.ssh/internal_rsa)
```

22. miwa uses ssh-add to add his default identity and then to add his internal_rsa identity. Both identities require that he supply the passphrase, just as if he were logging in to the remote systems that accept these identities by using slogin.

```
brezup:miwa miwa $ ssh-add -L
ssh-rsa AAAAB3NzaC1yc2EAAAABIwAAAIEAv09dKFr46dK+U43m8h9hV0JtooRdyf8
hbPJcf1y+kXcpcOpHWz7NBqGI3FsZZUrJDrgP3Q/1VHa8SiDsCkYFuG55HobfNfrsGV
vW7LqHn9ApzYhifPUGpLSQnML4/qzTLNn2JmUiEvlcdYrnZoi+b23Om4mLu1zez7nT9
1EGTnk= /Users/miwa/.ssh/id_rsa
ssh-rsa AAAAB3NzaC1yc2EAAAABIwAAAIEAzc9VaVwZEG8lWJ5SO/t1LfCpZK7dHGb
z uTnLXdN2sTLd09EiO567vLHSxRmDddGej79ShvqKh+4EXXZsCjwvuIyJsQvW61FC/
IQJ HkCJjCxxmrEaxphPEG5Iu5M2k5JsshmoLL89aKYWYadv1vsBLZ5PxgDTtGE2h+p
d8PBaq/0= .ssh/internal_rsa
```

23. Just for good measure, miwa checks the credentials that ssh-agent is holding for him and then goes on to test whether slogin now works without requiring him to supply his passphrase:

```
brezup:miwa miwa $ slogin ryoko.biosci.ohio-state.edu
Last login: Thu Oct 02 2003 18:24:46 -0500 from dhcp065-024-074-
You have new mail.
ryoko miwa 1 >exit
Connection to ryoko.biosci.ohio-state.edu closed.
brezup:miwa miwa $ slogin 192.168.1.200
Welcome to Darwin!
[creampuf:~] miwa% exit
Connection to 192.168.1.200 closed.
```

The end demonstration is almost anticlimactic, but it's what miwa doesn't do here that's significant. It looks like there's no authentication—as though ryoko and creampuf simply allowed him to slogin in, without bothering to check his credentials. This isn't the case. His ID was validated, but it was ssh-agent acting as his assistant that answered the query and responded with the appropriate credentials. ssh-agent will continue to do so for any SSH commands run in this terminal, or for any other terminal that has had the environment variables set so that SSH commands run in it, can find the ssh-agent to talk to it.

Table 26.7 provides documentation for ssh-agent. Table 26.8 provides documentation for ssh-add.

CAUTION

It should be noted that using ssh-agent in this fashion is, as they say, putting all your eggs in one basket. If a malicious user could find a way to co-opt the use of your ssh-agent, it would allow him to spoof connections as you, and your ssh-agent would happily provide your credentials to verify his false claim. Properly configured file permissions for keys in your .ssh directory go a long way toward minimizing this problem. However, if a cracker has actually managed to break into your account, he can access your key files with your permissions, and a running ssh-agent that you've started will have no way to tell you apart. Should this happen, using ssh-agent does materially weaken your security.

If you only use SSH in a mode where the remote systems require you to enter your passphrase directly out of your brain, a cracker who has broken one of your accounts is no closer to cracking your others. If you use `ssh-agent` to hold all your credentials, and the cracker happens along while you have a running copy of `ssh-agent` that's serving credentials for you, the cracker will have full access to your accounts on machines for which `ssh-agent` holds credentials.

TABLE 26.7 Documentation for `ssh-agent`

`ssh-agent` Authentication agent

`ssh-agent [-a <bind_address>] [-c ¦ -s] [-t <life>] [-d] [<command> [<args> ...]]`

`ssh-agent [-c ¦ -s] -k`

`ssh-agent` is a program to hold private keys used for public key authentication (RSA, DSA). `ssh-agent` is started in the beginning of an X-session or a login session, and all other windows or programs are started as clients to the `ssh-agent` program. Through use of environment variables the agent can be located and automatically used for authentication when logging in to other machines using `ssh`(1).

`-a <bind_address>`	Binds the agent to the `unix-domain socket <bind_address>`. The default is `/tmp/ssh-XXXXXXXX/agent.<ppid>`.
`-c`	Generates C-shell commands on `stdout`. This is the default if `SHELL` looks like it's a `csh` style of shell.
`-s`	Generates Bourne shell commands on `stdout`. This is the default if `SHELL` does not look like it's a `csh` style of shell.
`-k`	Kills the current agent (given by the `SSH_AGENT_PID` environment variable).
`-d`	Debug mode. When this option is specified, `ssh-agent` does not fork.

26

TABLE 26.8 Documentation for `ssh-add`

`ssh-add` Adds RSA or DSA identities to the authentication agent

`ssh-add [-lLdDxXc] [-t <life>] [<file> ...]`

`ssh-add` adds RSA or DSA identities to the authentication agent, `ssh-agent(1)`. When run without arguments, it adds the files `$HOME/.ssh/id_rsa`, `$HOME/.ssh/id_dsa`, and `$HOME/.ssh/identity`. Alternative filenames can be given on the command line. If any file requires a passphrase, `ssh-add` asks for the passphrase from the user. The passphrase is read from the user's `tty`. `ssh-add` retries the last passphrase if multiple identity files are given.

The authentication agent must be running and must be an ancestor of the current process for `ssh-add` to work.

`-l`	Lists fingerprints of all identities currently represented by the agent.
`-L`	Lists public key parameters of all identities currently represented by the agent.
`-d`	Deletes the identity from the agent.
`-D`	Deletes all identities from the agent.
`-x`	Locks the agent with a password.
`-X`	Unlocks the agent.
`-c`	Indicates that added identities should be subject to confirmation before being used for authentication.
`-t <life>`	Sets a maximum life time when adding identities to an agent. The life time may be specified in seconds or in a time format specified in `sshd(8)`.

A Better-Looking, More Helpful Butler: SSH Agent (the GUI Version)

If you're comfortable with the risks that using ssh-agent brings, there's a useful GUI tool that you might want to consider using, because it, the Mac OS X Keychain, and some Terminal.app features all working together can make for wonderfully convenient secure remote connections. Xander Schrijen is actively developing a useful front end to the ssh-agent command-line utility and endowing it with some nice auxiliary functions. SSH Agent acts sort of like a meta-agent for ssh-agent. It provides a GUI front end for the features of ssh-agent and further can be configured to use your login credentials to store your passphrases in the OS X Keychain, thereby allowing for ssh-agent functionality without you needing to do anything but successfully log in. To try out SSH Agent, download it from http://www.phil.uu.nl/~xges/ssh/ and follow the Quick-Start installation instructions. At this time, this means performing the following steps:

1. Download the software from http://www.phil.uu.nl/~xges/ssh/.
2. Mount the disk image and copy the SSH Agent application to some convenient place on your drive. If you want it to be available to all your users, putting it in /Applications/ would be appropriate. Eject the disk image when you're finished.
3. Run the SSH Agent application and open the Preferences pane.
4. In the Startup tab, shown in Figure 26.4, check the Make Agent Global setting.

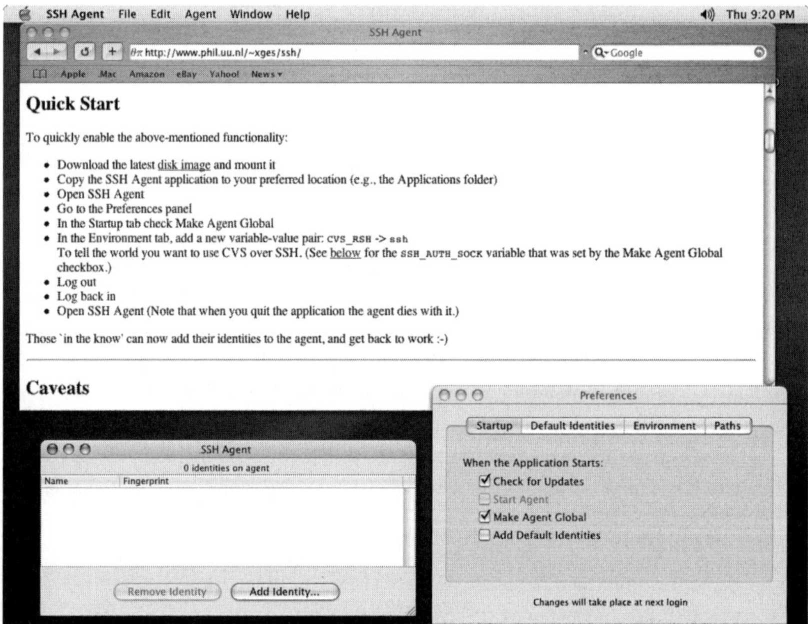

FIGURE 26.4 Setting the SSH Agent application to serve credentials globally.

5. In the Environment tab, use the Add Variable button to add a variable named CVS_RSH and set its value to ssh (see Figure 26.5).

FIGURE 26.5 Setting Environment variables through SSH Agent.

6. Log out, log back in, and restart SSH Agent. Open the Preferences pane again, and go to the Default Identities pane. Initially, it appears as shown in Figure 26.6. Click on the Add Identity button, and the dialog shown in Figure 26.7 appears. The IDs shown in this dialog should be familiar from our recap of miwa's SSH key generation earlier in this section. Select the private key from the keypair for any identity you want to use by default. In this example, we're adding both IDs that miwa created earlier.

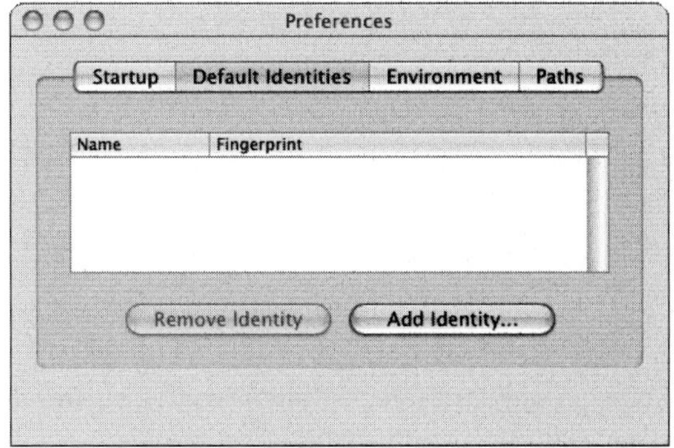

FIGURE 26.6 Like ssh-agent, out of the box, SSH Agent knows no identities.

After you've selected the identities to add, the IDs appear in the Default Identities tab, as shown in Figure 26.8.

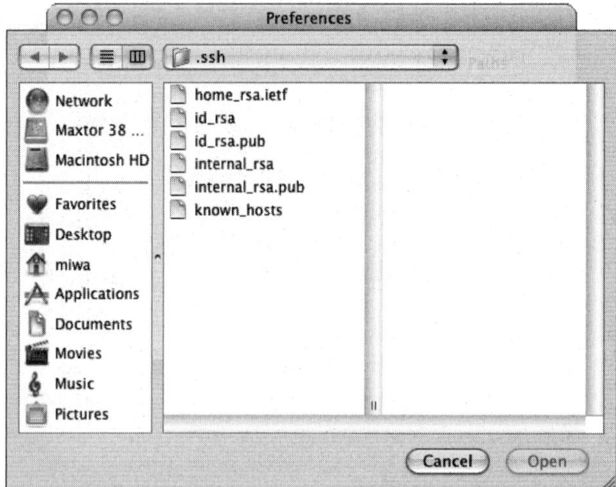

FIGURE 26.7 Clicking the Add Identity button allows you to select among any SSH identities that you've previously created. There's also a New Identity function under the File menu where you can create key pairs in `SSH Agent` denovo. Here, you need to select the private keys of each keypair you want to use.

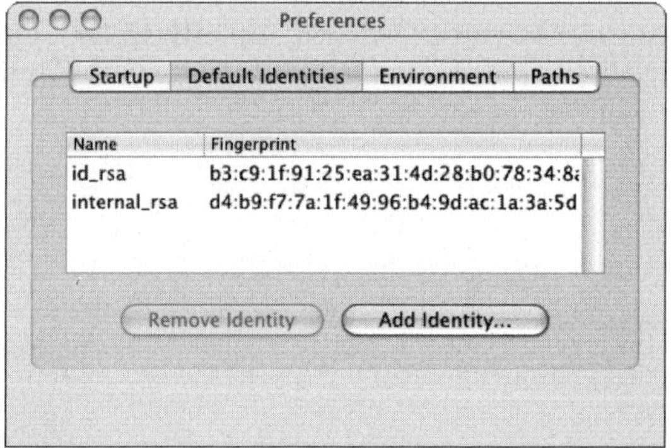

FIGURE 26.8 The Default Identity pane after adding some IDs.

7. Go back to the Startup pane and select Add Default Identities as shown in Figure 26.9 and then quit `SSH Agent` again.

When you start `SSH Agent` again, you'll see a dialog as shown in Figure 26.10, where `SSH Agent` is asking you for the passphrase for an ID. Pay attention to the path shown for the identity because `SSH Agent` asks you for the passphrase for each identity you've configured it to load by default. Figure 26.11 shows what `SSH Agent` looks like after you've successfully supplied the requested passphrases.

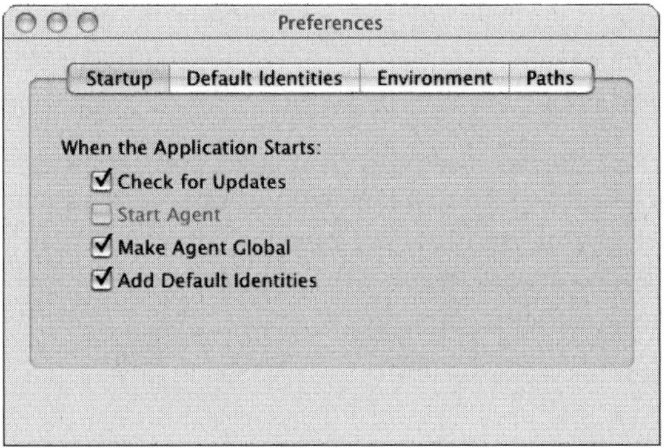

FIGURE 26.9 Setting the final preference that you need to configure before you can start using `SSH Agent`.

FIGURE 26.10 `SSH Agent` prompts for the passphrases for each identity you've asked it to hold for you.

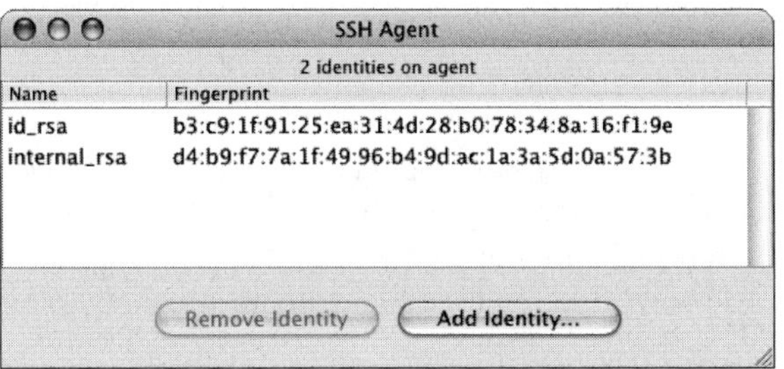

FIGURE 26.11 After you've supplied the requested passphrases, `SSH Agent` shows the loaded identities. From this window (which you can bring up from the Agent menu if the window is closed), you can also load additional nondefault identities selectively and as needed.

Now, if you start a terminal you can use the credentials held by `SSH Agent`, and you don't even need to execute the `setenv` commands as you needed to for the command-line `ssh-agent`. Figure 14.10 shows our `miwa` user using these IDs in a terminal.

If you want to avoid even the work of having to enter the passphrases once at the startup of `SSH Agent`, you can select the Add to Keychain option seen in Figure 26.12, and the passphrases you enter for your identities are saved in your Keychain. If you do this, your default identities are loaded automatically when you start `SSH Agent`, and you don't need to enter the passphrases for them again.

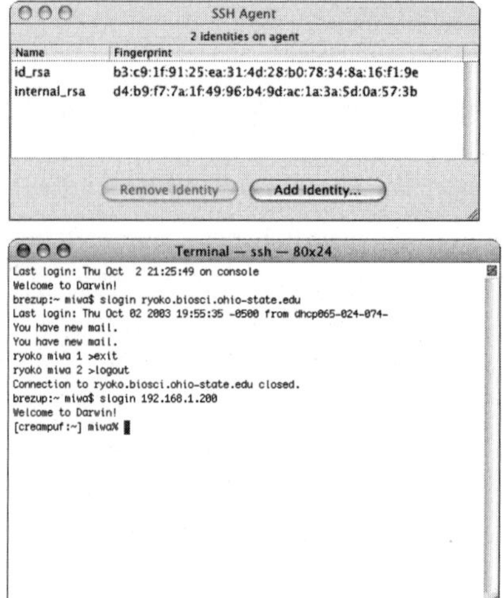

FIGURE 26.12 Now `SSH Agent` can provide the conveniences of `ssh-agent`, without you needing to set environment variables. This is nice, but the good part is still to come.

Combining this capability with some of the capabilities of `Terminal.app` is where the big payoff in ease-of-use comes in. `Terminal.app` has an infrequently used function under the File menu listed as New Command. This function gives you the ability to execute a command and open a terminal window containing the executing results of that command. Figure 26.13 shows it being used to set up an `slogin` session to `192.168.1.200`.

Not surprisingly, the result of running the command in a shell, is a connection to `creampuf` (`192.168.1.200`). The neat thing is that we can now use another little-used feature of `Terminal.app` to save this terminal. Select the File, Save As from Terminal.app's menu. This brings up a dialog like the one shown in Figure 26.14. In this dialog, provide a useful name that helps you remember where these terminal settings will take you. Also, remember to set the save location to some place that you'll actually find useful.

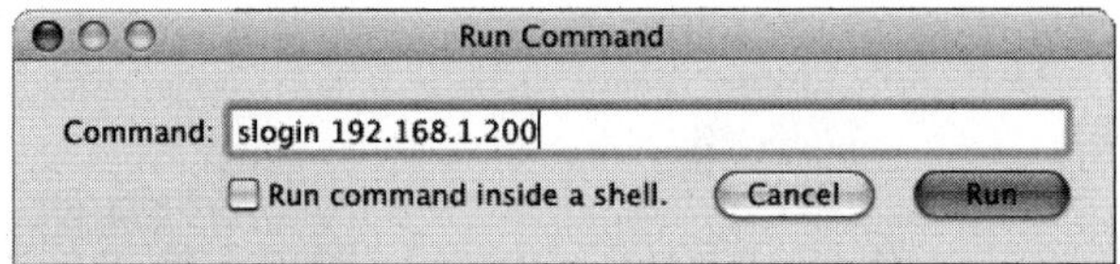

FIGURE 26.13 Setting up a terminal session to run a command. Usually, you would just run the command in a terminal session yourself, but this use is special.

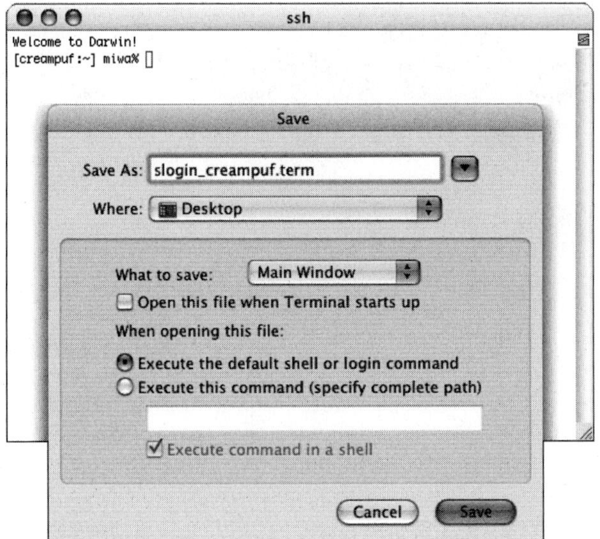

FIGURE 26.14 Saving a `Terminal.app` terminal session. This isn't saving the contents; it's saving what the terminal is doing.

And finally the nifty part. Figure 26.15 shows what `miwa`'s done with his `SSH Agent` supplied identities, and with saved `Terminal.app` terminal sessions. Two icons are shown in the Dock. The one labeled `slogin_ryoko.term` is a saved terminal file for one of `miwa`'s IDs. The icon next to it is another saved `.term` file that `miwa` created for his `creampuf` ID. He's applied interesting icons to each, to make them a bit more distinctive than the default little white rectangle icons they come with. Clicking on either launches a terminal session, using the command `miwa` set for it from the New Command menu item. That command queries the running `SSH Agent` and gets the appropriate passphrase for `miwa` as necessary, and the connection to the remote server is made with no further interaction needed on `miwa`'s part.

Single-click secure, encrypted connections to remote servers. What could be slicker than that?

FIGURE 26.15 Saved `.term` files allow you to rerun their saved commands, in this case, saved `slogin` commands, which `SSH Agent` allows to create secure connections with no further authentication required.

Clients

From other Unix machines with an SSH server installed, you should be able to use `ssh` or `slogin` to connect to your Mac OS X machine from remote. But you don't need a Unix machine to connect to your Mac OS X machine. Windows and traditional Mac OS clients are also available. This section includes a listing of popular client software, including a brief description of each client's features.

Windows

A number of Windows SSH clients are available. Among the available clients are

- Tera Term Pro with TTSSH—A free terminal emulation program available at `http://hp.vector.co.jp/authors/VA002416/teraterm.html`. A free extension DLL called TTSSH is available for Tera Term at `http://www.zip.com.au/~roca/ttssh.html`. With the extension, Tera Term can be used as an SSH client. It supports only the SSH1 protocol. Additionally, it can handle public key authentication, tunneling, and X11 forwarding.

- PuTTY—A free Telnet and SSH client available at `http://www.chiark.greenend.org.uk/~sgtatham/putty/`. PuTTY supports both the SSH1 and SSH2 protocols, with SSH1 being the default protocol. It also supports public key authentication, tunneling, and X11 forwarding. Additionally, it includes `scp` (PSCP) and `sftp` (PSFTP) clients.
- F-Secure SSH—A commercial SSH client. It is available for Windows 95/98/ME/NT 4.0/2000/XP. It supports both the SSH1 and SSH2 protocols. It also supports public key authentication, tunneling, and X11 forwarding. Additionally, it includes a built-in `sftp` client and command-line `ssh` tools. For more product information, see `http://www.f-secure.com/`.
- SSH Secure Shell—SSH Communications Security has both a commercial and free SSH client for Windows 95/98/ME/NT 4.0/2000/XP. It supports both the SSH1 and SSH2 protocols. It also supports public key authentication, tunneling, and X11 forwarding. Additionally, it includes a built-in `sftp` client. For more product information, see `http://www.ssh.com/`. To download the freely available client, go to `ftp://ftp.ssh.com/pub/ssh/` and select the latest Windows client.
- SecureCRT—A commercial SSH client available from `http://www.vandyke.com/products/securecrt/`. It supports both the SSH1 and SSH2 protocols. It also supports public key authentication, tunneling, X11 forwarding, and `sftp`.

Macintosh 8/9

A few `ssh` clients are available for the traditional Mac OS. The clients that work in the traditional Mac OS probably also work in Mac OS X's classic mode. As a matter of fact, to tunnel connections in classic mode, you will need one of these clients with tunneling capabilities. Available clients include

- NiftyTelnet 1.1 SSH r3—A free Telnet and SSH client available at `http://www.lysator.liu.se/~jonasw/freeware/niftyssh/`. It supports only the SSH1 protocol. It also supports public key authentication and has a built-in `scp` function.
- MacSSH—A free client for SSH, Telnet, and various other protocols available at `http://www.macssh.com/`. For SSH, it supports only the SSH2 protocol. Additionally, it supports public key authentication, tunneling, and X11 forwarding.
- MacSFTP—A shareware `sftp` client available at `http://www.macssh.com/`. It supports both SSH1 and SSH2. You can download a 15-day trial. If you decide to keep it, the shareware cost is $25. It has an interface similar to Fetch's.
- F-Secure SSH—A commercial SSH client. It supports both the SSH1 and SSH2 protocols. Additionally, it supports public key authentication, tunneling, and X11 forwarding. For more product information, see `http://www.f-secure.com/`.

Mac OS X

Mac OS X, of course, has the command-line `ssh` tools available. However, if you are new to the command line, you may also be wondering whether any SSH GUI tools are available. As you might recall from Chapter 12, "Introducing the BSD Subsystem," even `Terminal.app` provides some basic SSH GUI tools. For `sftp` and `scp` alternatives, you should also check whether your favorite FTP client includes or will include such support. Available clients include

- JellyfiSSH—A freeware product available from `http://www.arenasoftware.com/grepsoft/`. It provides a GUI login interface and bookmarking capabilities. After you enter your login information, it brings up a terminal window to the remote host, showing the command that was issued. If you are comfortable with using `slogin` or `ssh` to log in to a remote host, this application might not be useful to you. If you like the basic GUI login interface of the clients for traditional Mac OS, this application might be useful to you. If you want to learn how to use the `ssh` command-line client, this application might be useful to you because you can see how the command was issued.
- `Terminal.app`—As of Mac OS X 10.3, `Terminal.app`'s Connect to Server option under the File menu offers a graphical interface to the `ssh` and `sftp` commands. Enter the information in the graphical interface, and a terminal opens up running the command. If you are comfortable with the basic command-line `ssh` and `sftp`, this interface might not interest you. Otherwise, you might find it useful for learning how to issue the commands.
- Fugu—A freeware product available from `http://rsug.itd.umich.edu/software/fugu/`. It is an `scp/sftp/ssh` tunneling client.
- SSH Tunnel Manager—A freeware product available from `http://projects.tynsoe.org/en/stm/`. As the name suggests, this is a graphical application that helps you set up and manage your SSH tunnels.
- MacSFTP—Also works in OS X. This shareware `sftp` client is available at `http://www.macssh.com/`. It supports both the SSH1 and SSH2 protocols. You can download a 15-day trial. If you decide you like it, the shareware cost is $25. It has an interface similar to Fetch's.
- Gideon—A shareware `sftp/ftp` client available at `http://www.gideonsoftworks.com/gideon.html`. The shareware cost is $25, payable if you like it.
- RBrowser—An application available from `http://www.rbrowser.com/`. It provides a finder interface to `ssh`, `scp`, and `sftp`, and also supports tunneling. If you do not like the command line at all, this might be the application for you. The `sftp` feature works by dragging files from one "finder" to the other. This is a shareware product with two levels of licensing: a basic level that covers `ftp` and `sftp` features and a

professional level that includes `ftp`, `sftp`, Unix, `ssh`, and `ssh` tunneling. Demo licenses are also available.

- F-Secure SSH—As of this writing, F-Secure is working on a client for OS X. However, it is not yet available. Because it is supposed to be similar to the F-Secure SSH 2.4 client, it is expected to be able to do tunneling. Check `http://www.f-secure.com/` for more information.

Using an SSH Client in Traditional Mac OS

As mentioned earlier, if you activate the SSH server on your OS X machine, you can log in to it not only from a remote Unix machine but also from Windows or Mac OS machines. In this section, we take a brief look at using an SSH client in traditional Mac OS. This basic information can also be useful for OS X users who might need to tunnel a connection to a machine while in Classic mode.

In particular, we will look at F-Secure SSH 2.4. Although the client can support both the SSH1 and SSH2 protocols, we will only use it for SSH2 protocol connections. A 30-day trial version is available from `http://www.f-secure.com/`.

Setting Up a Terminal

To set up a terminal, do the following:

1. Start F-Secure SSH 2.4. The Connection Manager will probably appear.
2. Click on the terminal window icon in the Connection Manager (the second icon) or choose File, New Terminal from the menu. A Properties dialog box appears with Connect highlighted. Note that in the top left of the window the term "Terminal" appears.
3. Enter the remote machine as the SSH server.

   The default server port is 22. There is no need to change this unless you have been informed that the SSH2 server is running on a different port.
4. Enter your username and password, as shown in Figure 26.16; then click Connect.
5. The first time you connect to an unknown host, you are asked whether you should accept the host key for the unknown host. If you plan to connect regularly to the remote host, click Accept & Store in the message box shown in Figure 26.17.

Assuming that you have entered your username and password correctly, you should be logged in to the remote host.

Note that the status connection of the terminal appears in the bottom left of the terminal window. In Figure 26.18, the status is SSH Shell Connected. When you have logged out, the status changes to Disconnected.

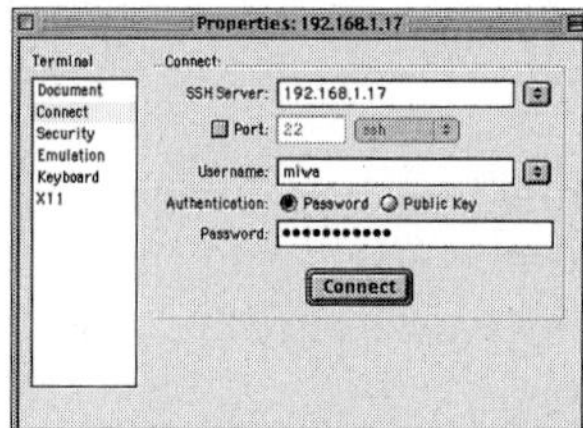

FIGURE 26.16 Fill in the connection parameters in the Connect section of the Properties dialog box.

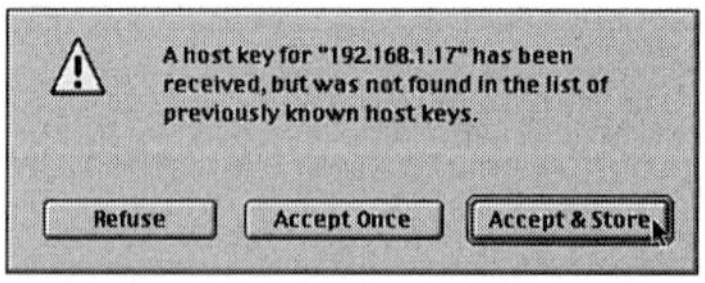

FIGURE 26.17 Click Accept & Store to store the remote host's host key.

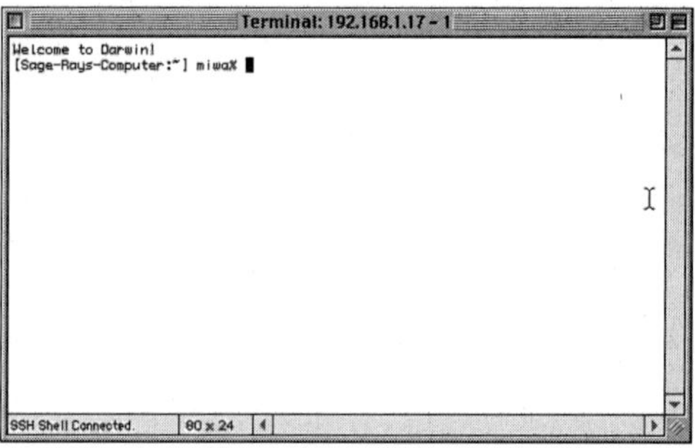

FIGURE 26.18 Connected terminal window.

If you plan to connect to the remote host regularly, you might want to choose File, Save from the menu and then save the connection as an alias to your desktop.

There are various ways to end your terminal connection. You can type `exit` at the command line. You can also select the terminal connection in the Connection Manager and then click on the Disconnect button. You will probably find that the connection to the remote host times out after some period. Of course, you can quit the F-Secure program. If you have a connection in progress, it asks whether you really want to close the connection.

Setting Up an FTP Tunnel

To set up an FTP tunnel, perform the following steps:

1. Click on the FTP icon in the Connection Manager, or select FTP Tunnel in the Tunnel list under the File menu.

   A Properties box appears, with Connect highlighted. Note that in the top left of the window, the description FTP Tunnel appears.

2. Name your tunnel by first clicking Document in the FTP Tunnel menu and then add a tunnel name in the Name box. Next, check the Auto-Connect on Open box. Note that there is an Auto-launch on Connect feature, as shown in Figure 26.19. With this feature enabled, you can set F-Secure to automatically open another application upon connection.

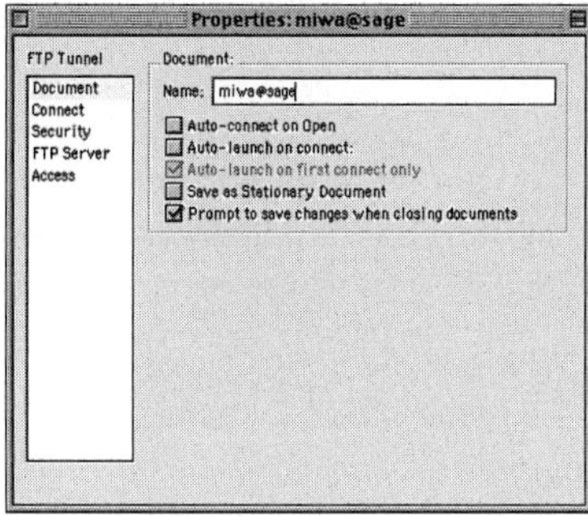

FIGURE 26.19 You can set a name for your FTP tunnel in the Document section of the Properties box. You can also do this for a terminal connection.

3. Next, select FTP Server in the FTP Tunnel menu, as shown in Figure 26.20. It is all right to click in the FTP Server Port boxes, even if you are using the default 21 port. SSH Server comes selected as the default item. If you do not do anything with this section, the client assumes port 21 for the local and remote ports and that the SSH server is the remote server.

   If you will be accessing a machine that might be running an FTP server on an alternative port, be sure to change the port number appropriately. If you should ever have to do that, you will lose the `ftp` descriptor, but the tunnel will still work.

4. Select Connect in the FTP Tunnel menu, and enter the remote machine as the SSH server.

5. Next, enter your username and password; then click Connect. Note that the Properties window now says Connected at the bottom left, and the Connection Manager shows an FTP connection.

6. Choose File, Save. For your convenience, also save this alias directly to your desktop.

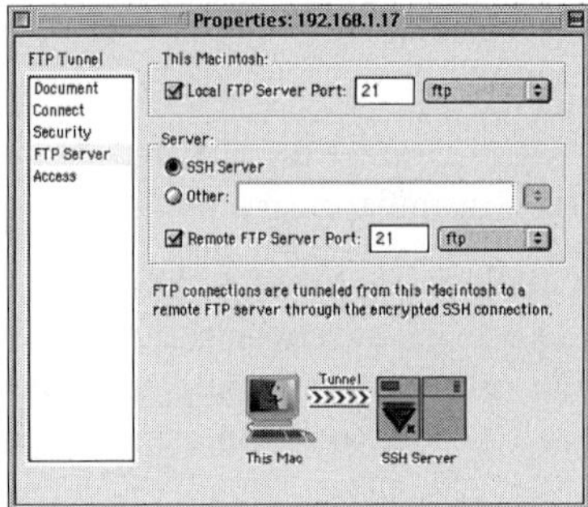

FIGURE 26.20 FTP server settings are set in the FTP Server section of the Properties box.

Setting Up the FTP Client

After your FTP tunnel is set up, you are ready to set up the FTP client. Although we only demonstrate with Fetch in this section, the basic concepts shown here and in earlier command-line sections should prepare you to use other FTP clients, too.

1. Set Fetch to FTP using PASV mode. Select Customize, Preferences in the menu. At the Firewall tab, check the Use Passive Mode Transfers (PASV) box and then click OK. This setting is shown in Figure 26.21.

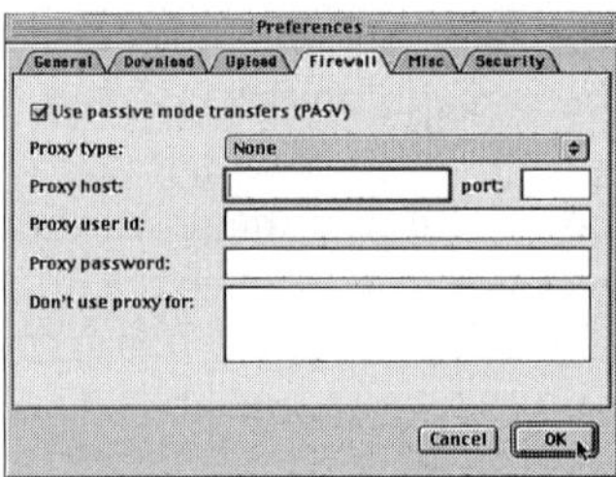

FIGURE 26.21 Set PASV mode in Fetch at the Firewall tab in Preferences under the Customize menu.

2. Make a connection by choosing File, New Connection from the menu. Enter **`localhost`** or **`127.0.0.1`** as the host. Enter your username and password. Enter an initial directory, if applicable. If your FTP tunnel uses the default port of 21, you do not need to enter a port number. If your tunnel uses another local port, enter that number in the Non-Standard Port Number box. Click OK. Figure 26.22 shows the New Connection dialog box.

3. Choose File, Save Bookmark under the menu to save an alias to your desktop for your convenience if you will want to FTP regularly.

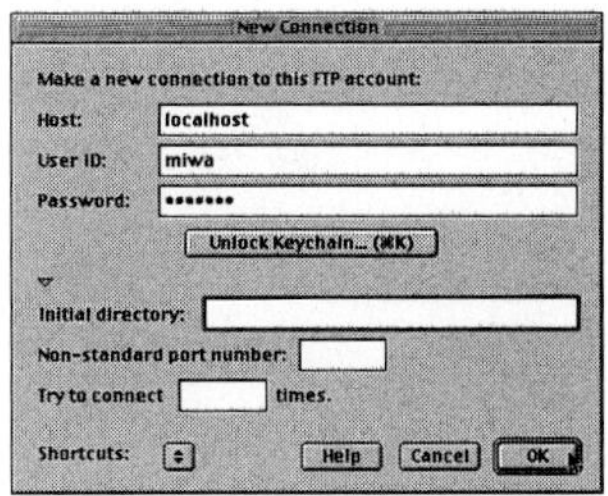

FIGURE 26.22 Initiating a connection in Fetch to a remote host via an FTP tunnel in the SSH client.

To briefly summarize the FTP process, whenever you want to FTP, first open an FTP tunnel connection to the FTP server in the F-Secure SSH client. Then make a connection to `localhost` or `127.0.0.1` in the FTP client. The connection will be tunneled from one server, the Mac OS machine, to the other server, the remote FTP server, as you have specified in the F-Secure client. Figure 26.23 shows a connection in Fetch to an OS X machine via a tunnel.

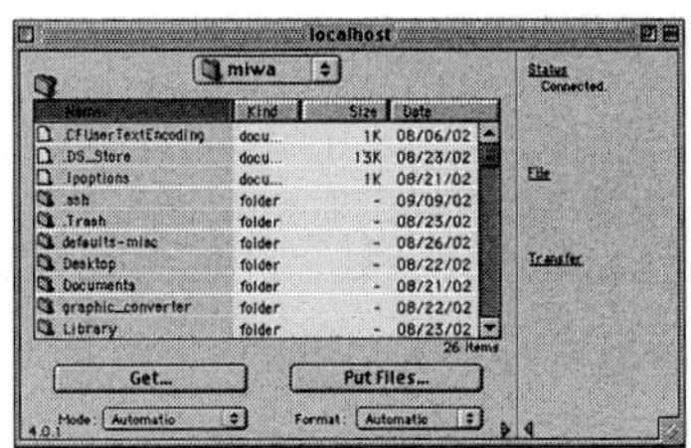

FIGURE 26.23 A connection to a remote host using Fetch via an FTP tunnel in the SSH client.

Setting Up an Email Tunnel and Client

Another type of tunnel that you might want to make is a tunnel for your POP/IMAP account. Making a mail tunnel is much like making an FTP tunnel.

In the F-Secure Connection Manager, click the email icon (fourth icon) or select E-Mail Tunnel from the Tunnel list under the File menu. In the Properties box that appears, provide all the usual information.

The Services section of the Properties box is where you specify what email services are to be tunneled. If you will be accessing a POP account, deselect the IMAP tunnel service. If you will be accessing an IMAP account, deselect the POP tunnel service. This section also includes a section to enter server names. These need to be filled out only if the email services are on a host other than the server to which you are connecting. Figure 26.24 shows a basic Services configuration for a POP account.

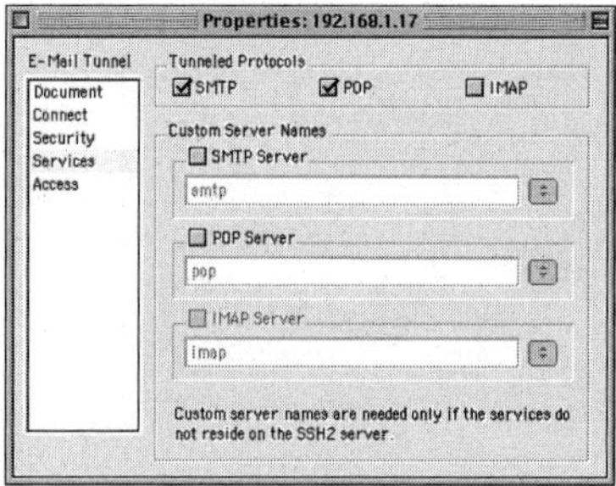

FIGURE 26.24 The Services section of the Properties box is where you specify what email services are to be tunneled.

After the tunnel is set up, you can use an email client to read the account's mail. Setting up the email client varies with the client and your machine's settings. You might need to specify `localhost`, `127.0.0.1`, or your Mac OS machine's fully qualified domain name (FQDN). We have tested tunneling a POP mail connection using Claris Emailer, which is no longer supported, and Mailsmith.

Setting Up Other Tunnels

F-Secure SSH 2.4 also allows you to forward arbitrary TCP services, for which prelabeled services might not already be listed in the TCP Tunnel Properties box. If you need to tunnel other TCP services, tunnel them using the TCP Tunnel type, which is the third icon in the Connection Manager, or the TCP Tunnel in the Tunnels section under the File menu.

For example, if you typically accessed a program on a remote host by a special telnet client (one that did something more special than show you a command-line prompt; otherwise, the SSH terminal is a perfectly sufficient alternative), you could forward the telnet connection through an arbitrary TCP tunnel in the SSH client. As with FTP clients, the remote host you would list in the telnet client would be `localhost`.

In addition to arbitrary TCP tunnels, you can also tunnel X11 connections. Starting with Mac OS X 10.3 Apple's X11 application is available as an optional install. If you installed it, you might start to find certain X11 applications to be useful, and if you have an older Mac, you might also want to use them from it from time to time. The ability to tunnel X11 connections can also be of particular use with applications on other Unix machines.

If you discover a need for X11 tunneling, simply check the Tunnel X11 Connections box in the X11 section of the Properties box for a terminal connection, as shown in Figure 26.25. The option to specify eXodus (a commercial X Window System server for Mac OS and Windows) as the local X server is even available. Remember to have X11 forwarding enabled on your OS X machine.

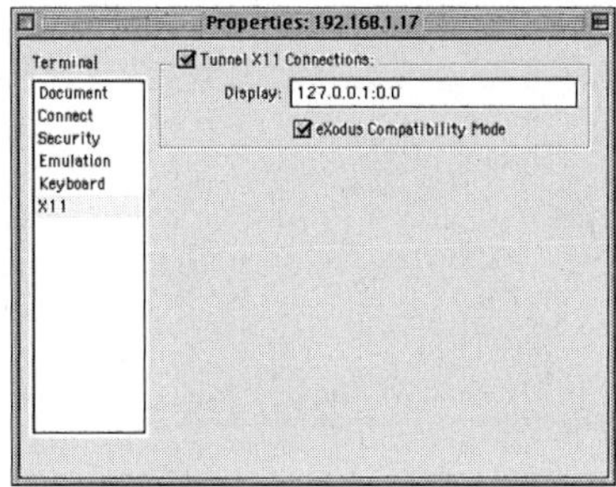

FIGURE 26.25 Enable X11 tunneling in the X11 section of the Properties box for terminal connection in the SSH client.

Managing Your Connections

So far in this section, we have been creating independent tunnels in F-Secure 2.4. Because our tunnels are independent, we can choose, for example, to use only the FTP tunnel without having to log in to the remote host. We have been saving our independent tunnels as separate aliases on the desktop. If you made at least a terminal alias and an FTP alias, you now have two aliases on your desktop. This might be precisely what you need, especially if you regularly plan to access the remote host with only one type of connection. However, if you expect to regularly use both types of connections to the host, you might be interested in grouping your independent tunnels together.

When you group a set of independent tunnels that you have already made, the group alias you save on the desktop replaces the aliases for the independent tunnels. When you use the group alias, you automatically make all the desired connections at once. If you decide to terminate all the connections at once, you can select the appropriate folder in the Connection Manager and then select Disconnect. You still have the freedom to terminate any given connection without terminating the other connections in your group by selecting the appropriate connection in the Connection Manager and then selecting Disconnect.

Although we tend to group our connections by host, you can also group connections to different hosts, if that is more suitable to your needs. For example, you might regularly use a terminal connection to one host, but the FTP server might be on another host. You can set up your individual connection types, group them together, and save that group as an alias on the desktop. When you connect using that alias, you are asked for both passwords right away. Figure 26.26 shows a sample of the Connection Manager with a group of connections and two other connections.

Public Key Authentication

Setting up public Key authentication with the F-Secure SSH client involves converting key files. However, from what you have already seen, that can be done on the OS X machine itself.

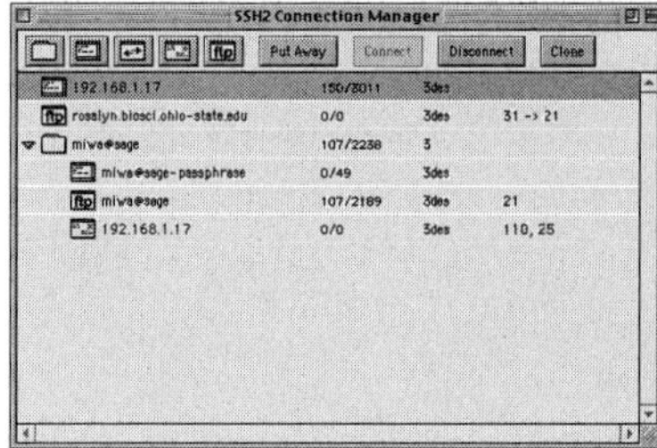

FIGURE 26.26 The sample of the Connection Manager shows a grouped set of connections as well as two other connections.

To set up public key authentication in the F-Secure SSH client, do the following:

1. Select File, Create Public Key from the menu. The Public Key Authentication Key Generator dialog box appears, as shown in Figure 26.27.

FIGURE 26.27 Indicate parameters for public key generation in the Public Key Authentication Key Generator dialog box.

2. Enter a comment. A comment of the form `<user>@<macos-host>` can be useful.

3. Select an encryption algorithm. For an SSH2 server, either DSA or RSA is acceptable. For an SSH1 server, RSA is the only choice.

4. Enter a length of no less than 1024 bits and no longer than 2048 bits. 1024 is the default.

5. Enter a passphrase to encrypt the private key. Again, it is recommended that the passphrase be at least 10 characters long and include as many character types as possible: uppercase letters, lowercase letters, numbers, and special characters. Spaces may be included as part of the passphrase.

6. Select a Clipboard option. The Copy Install Script option copies a script to the Clipboard for transferring the public key to the server. Although it is probably all right to use this option, we avoid this as a precaution. The Copy Public Key option copies only the contents of the public key to the Clipboard. We recommend this option as an easy option. The Leave Alone option does nothing, but you can still transfer the file separately by whatever method you choose.

7. Click on Create New Key Pair.

8. Save the public key and private key. Do not add an extension to the private key, and do not change the .pub extension of the public key. The filenames default to key and key.pub. If multiple users use the Mac OS machine, it is recommended that, for easy sorting, each user store his keys in his own folder in the F-Secure SSH folder.

9. Log in to the OS X machine and copy the key from the Clipboard into a file, using the editor of your choice, and save the file.

10. Convert the transferred public key to an OpenSSH format key using ssh-keygen. Again something like ssh-keygen -i -f *<transferred_public_key>* > *<converted_transferred_public_key>* should work.

11. Add that key to your ~/.ssh/authorized_keys file using whatever method you prefer.

12. Now you are ready to try to connect from the Mac OS machine using public key authentication. When you are setting up your connection, select Public Key instead of Password. The first time you try public key authentication, you have to select your private key. Then enter your passphrase and connect.

13. Save the public key authentication connection setting to your desktop for your convenience.

Tunneling Connections in Mac OS X

Although a number of graphical SSH clients are available for Mac OS X, so far only a few include tunneling capability. and SSH Tunnel Manager are two such clients.

To tunnel a connection in Fugu, supply the following information: Remote Host, Remote Port, Local Port, Tunnel Host, Username, and Port. If you take another look at the example used in the "Advanced Use" section earlier in this chapter, slogin 192.168.1.119 -l sage -N -L 2121:192.168.1.119:21, the values to use in Fugu would be

Remote Host:	192.168.1.119
Remote Port:	21

Local Port:	`2121`
Tunnel Host:	`192.168.1.119`
Username:	`sageray`
Port:	(Can be left blank if the remote host's SSH server is running on the standard SSH port, 22.)

After you establish an SSH tunnel, either via the command line or via a graphical SSH client, you can then start the application that needs to use the tunnel, as we saw earlier with Mailsmith. Figure 26.28 shows in FTP over an SSH tunnel in Fetch 4.0.2. The ability to use an FTP tunnel in a graphical application is especially useful in Web editing suites that include built-in FTP clients. As Web editing suites start to support SFTP, the need to use an FTP tunnel may decline.

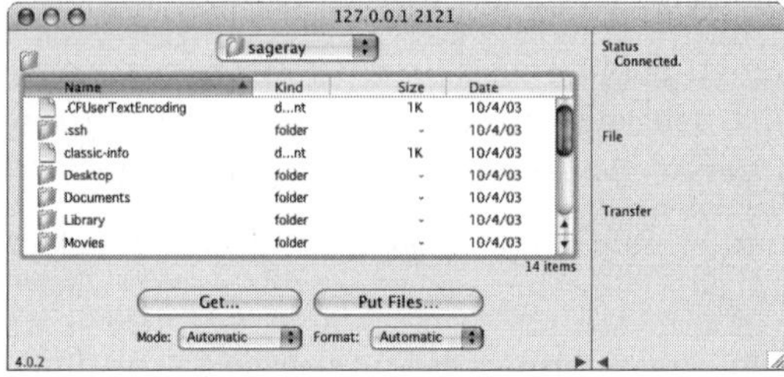

FIGURE 26.28 A Fetch 4.0.2 connection tunneled via the `slogin` command in the terminal.

Unfortunately, you cannot at this time create a tunnel in the terminal and have Classic mode obey the tunnel. You can, however, tunnel connections in Classic mode almost as you would on a traditional Mac OS machine. This can be especially helpful if you are using a Web editing suite with a built-in FTP client in Classic mode.

If you are using Mac OS X 10.1 or 10.3, the behavior in Classic mode is identical to using a Mac OS machine. However, if you are using Mac OS X 10.2, the machine appears to behave differently. For example, for FTP, the service we would expect you to most likely need to tunnel in Classic mode, it automatically uses port 65488 as the local port, if you use the default local port in the F-Secure SSH client. It is unclear whether it actually obeys any alternative port entries you might try for the local port. For 10.2 and 10.3 make sure that you use `127.0.0.1` for the host rather than `localhost`. Figure 26.29 shows a tunneled FTP connection in Classic mode using F-Secure SSH 2.4 and Interarchy 4.

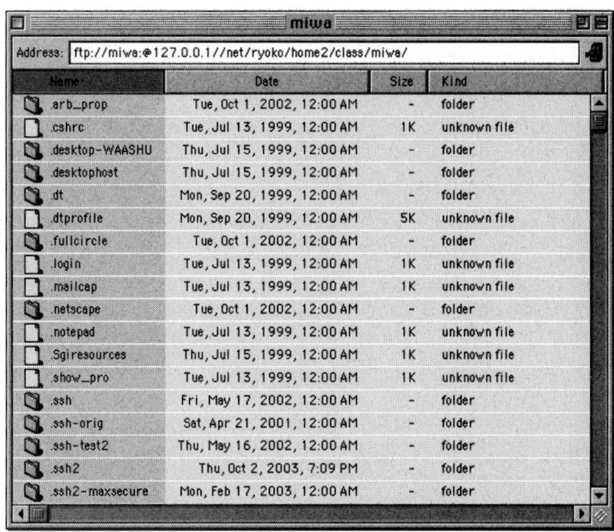

FIGURE 26.29 A tunneled FTP connection in Classic mode using F-Secure SSH 2.4 and Interarchy 4.

Control Commands

A reason why you might want to activate the SSH server on your machine is to be able to control your machine from remote. In addition to knowing how to use the SSH suite to access your OS X machine remotely, being familiar with some commands that you might have to use in controlling your machine could be helpful. This section includes a summary of some of the important commands you might need to use from remote.

`disktool`

`disktool` is a command-line utility that assists with disk activities such as mounting and unmounting disks, listing the disks currently on the system and ejecting disks. Table 26.9 shows command documentation for `disktool`.

TABLE 26.9 Command Documentation for `disktool`

`disktool`	Disk Arbitration Command Tool
`disktool -[r][a][u][e][m][p][n][d][s][g][A][S][D][l]` *`<deviceName>`* `[`*`<options>`*`]`	
Renames, ejects, mounts, or unmounts disks and volumes	
Information about disks:	
`-l`	Lists the disks currently known and available on the system.

TABLE 26.9 Continued

Controlling arbitration:	
`-r`	Refreshes Disk Arbitration. Causes arbitration to refresh its internal tables and look for new mounts/unmounts.
Managing disks:	
`-u`	Unmounts a disk (for example, `disktool -u disk2`).
`-p`	Unmounts a partition (for example, `disktool -p disk1s2`).
`-e`	Ejects a disk (for example, `disktool -e disk2`).
`-m`	Mounts a disk (for example, `disktool -m disk2`). Useful when a disk has been unmounted by hand (using `-p` or `-u` parameters).
`-a`	Notifies of mount.
`-d`	Notifies of dismount.Controlling disk parameters:
`-n`	Renames volume. Renames the volume specified as the first argument (for example, `disktool -n disk1s2 <newName>`).
`-g`	Gets the HFS encoding on a volume (for example, `disktool -g disk1s2`).
`-s`	Sets the HFS encoding on a volume (for example, `disktool -s disk1s2 4`).
`-A`	Adopts the given device into the volinfo database.
`-D`	Disowns the given device from the volinfo database.
`-S`	Displays the status of the device in the volinfo database.

shutdown

`shutdown` is a convenient command to use to shut down the machine or to reboot it, especially when users are on the system. The `shutdown` command notifies users that the system is about to go down and gives them the opportunity to save what they are doing. Additionally, it does not allow logins five minutes before shutdown, or immediately, if the impending shutdown is in less than five minutes. The two most common uses of shutdown are

```
shutdown -h <time>
shutdown -r <time>
```

The `-h` option halts the machine, and the `-r` option reboots the machine. The specified *<time>* can be `now` or in minutes or a specific date. Table 26.10 shows the command documentation for `shutdown`.

TABLE 26.10 Command Documentation for `shutdown`

`shutdown`	Closes down the system at a given time.
`shutdown [-] [-fhkrn] <time> [<warning_message>]`	
`shutdown` provides an automatic way for the superuser to nicely notify users of an impending shutdown.	
`-f`	`shutdown` arranges for filesystems to not be checked on reboot.
`-h`	Halts the system at the specified *<time>* when shutdown executes `halt(8)`.

TABLE 26.10 Continued

`-k`	Kicks everybody off. The `-k` option does not actually halt the system but does leave the system multiuser with logins disabled for all users except the superuser.
`-r`	Shuts down the system and executes `reboot(8)` at the specified `<time>`.
`-n`	Prevents normal `sync(2)` before stopping.
`<time>`	The time when the system is to be brought down. `<time>` can be the word now for immediate shutdown, or a future time in one of two formats: `<+number>` or `<yymmddhhmm>`, where the year, month, and day may be defaulted to the current system values. The first form brings the system down in `<number>` minutes and the second at the absolute time specified.
`<warning_message>`	Any other arguments comprise the warning message that is broadcast to users currently logged on the system.
`-`	Reads the warning message from standard input.

`halt` and `reboot`

In addition to `shutdown`, `halt` and `reboot` can also be used to halt or reboot the system, as appropriate. The `shutdown` command is more polite for the users and is therefore the recommended command to use. However, if you do end up using `halt` or `reboot`, they are traditionally invoked in combination with `sync`, as follows:

```
sync;sync;sync;reboot
sync;sync;sync;halt
```

The `sync` command forces the completion of disk writes. `halt`, `reboot`, and `shutdown` also do this before closing down the machine. However, the wisdom of defying tradition is left to you. Table 26.11 shows command documentation for `halt` and `reboot`.

TABLE 26.11 Command Documentation for `halt` and `reboot`

`halt`	Stops the system.
`reboot`	Restarts the system.
`halt [-lnq]`	
`reboot [-lnq]`	
The `halt` and `reboot` utilities flush the system cache to disk, send all running processes a `SIGTERM` and subsequently a `SIGKILL`, and, respectively, halts or restarts the system. The action is logged, including adding a shutdown record into the login accounting file.	
`-l`	Does not log the `halt` or `reboot` to the system log. Intended for applications such as `shutdown(8)`, that call `reboot` or `halt` and log this themselves.
`-n`	Does not flush the filesystem cache. This option probably should not be used.
`-q`	Quickly and ungracefully halts/restarts the system, and only flushes the filesystem cache. This option probably should not be used.
Normally, `shutdown(8)` is used when the system needs to be halted or restarted to warn users of their impending doom.	

Summary

This chapter provided an overview of SSH, from the server to basic and advanced SSH usage for SSH2. Although we only looked at SSH2, the basics are the same for SSH1, if you should need to interact with an SSH1 server. Topics included an examination of the configuration files for SSH as well as securely transferring files, tunneling connections, and enabling public key authentication.

The chapter finished with a brief overview of some important commands you may have to use remotely to control your machine.

CHAPTER 27

Web Serving

IN THIS CHAPTER

- Apache
- Apache Configuration
- Rebuilding and Securing Apache
- WebDAV—`mod_dav`
- Streaming MP3s—`mod_mp3`
- Show Me Something to Impress My Friends!

The early Macintosh was never been a major contender in the Web-serving arena. As a platform, it was unstable and suffered from a slow network stack. Users had only a few choices—either expensive proprietary software, or Apple's built-in Web Sharing application. As an enterprise-level Web server, the Macintosh had almost nothing to offer. Being involved in Web development, I became accustomed to sitting in front of my Mac and remotely accessing Linux servers for development and production.

The introduction of Mac OS X signaled the end of the agony. Mac OS X ships bundled with Apache as a replacement to the Mac OS 8/9 Web Sharing server. Apache, an open source project similar to Mac OS X itself, is a high-speed extensible server supported by thousands of developers around the world. Never before has a personal Web server been so powerful. This chapter introduces Apache, its capabilities, extensions, and basic administration.

Apache

Apache is an open source project developed by a worldwide group of volunteers known as the Apache group (`http://www.apache.org`). It is available on dozens of operating systems including Microsoft Windows. Apache's appeal comes from its flexibility and extensibility. The base server package excels at serving HTML, but to truly exploit the power of Apache, you can install a number of extension modules, including MP3 streaming servers, SSL security, Java Server Pages, and much more. With a total expenditure of $0, you can set up a secure e-commerce server that processes credit cards in real-time and delivers SQL database access.

Apache Versus Personal Web Sharing

If you're looking for the features of the Mac OS 8/9 personal Web server, look elsewhere. The Apache server under Mac OS X does not offer the Finder mode, nor does it offer the SimpleText-to-HTML conversion of the previous operating system. To place information online, you'll need to create HTML documents. This isn't difficult, but there is no direct upgrade path if you have a collection of SimpleText documents you've been serving to the Internet.

Although Mac OS 8/9 allowed you to use the primary address of your computer as the address for your Web site, the Mac OS X Web sharing system forces a URL based on your username. For example, if your computer's address is `http://192.168.0.1` and your username is joeuser, your Web site address would be `http://192.168.0.1/~joeuser`. This change is because of the multiuser capabilities of Mac OS X. Regardless of how many users are on the system, each can have his personal Web site online, simultaneously. To use this feature, users must place their Web pages within the Sites folder of their home directory. If you want a single server without usernames, a master Web site can be created by placing documents in the /Library/WebServer/Documents folder.

> **TIP**
>
> If you are not connected directly to the Internet and want to view an Apache-served Web site on your local computer, you can refer to your local machine as either localhost or 127.0.0.1. The previous example for joeuser could be written as `http://127.0.0.1/~joeuser`.

Regardless of whether Apache is being used for an entire Web site or a few personal pages, users can take advantage of the server's advanced features. A personal page can execute CGI applications, use embedded programming languages, and so on.

Capabilities

This chapter addresses the base features of Apache, but it also includes some interesting add-ons that will make your system into a Web-serving powerhouse. Literally hundreds of Apache modules are available for download (`http://modules.apache.org/`), so we'll try to focus on a select few:

`mod_ssl`—The standard for Web server security is SSL, the Secure Socket Layer. Through the use of OpenSSL and the `mod_ssl` module, Apache can be configured for completely secure transactions.

`mod_dav`—Mac OS X supports built-in WebDAV (Distributed Authoring and Versioning) file system access. This open standard defines a file-sharing protocol based on standard HTTP. The cross-platform nature of WebDAV means that both Macintosh and Windows users can access the same files from the same server.

`mod_mp3`—Have an MP3 library? Want to stream it to the world? Upset that Apple removed this feature in iTunes 4.0.1? This module creates an MP3 stream accessible by any MP3 player supporting the Shoutcast protocol.

If you're not interested in these features, take a look at the other Apache modules available. It's best to install only the modules you really use. Additional modules can add overhead and potentially weaken the overall security of the server.

NOTE

I don't mean to imply that the modules included in this chapter are inherently dangerous. "Less is better" is always a good rule of thumb, whether talking about Apache modules or full-blown server applications.

Activating Web Sharing

To activate Web sharing (and the Apache Web server), open the System Preferences application (path: `/Applications/System Preferences`) and click the Sharing icon. You've seen this screen, shown in Figure 27.1, before.

With the Services button selected, highlight the Personal Web Sharing line. Assuming that the screen reads Web Sharing Off, click the Start button to start Apache. After a few seconds, the server status should change to Web Sharing On. Your Web pages are now online.

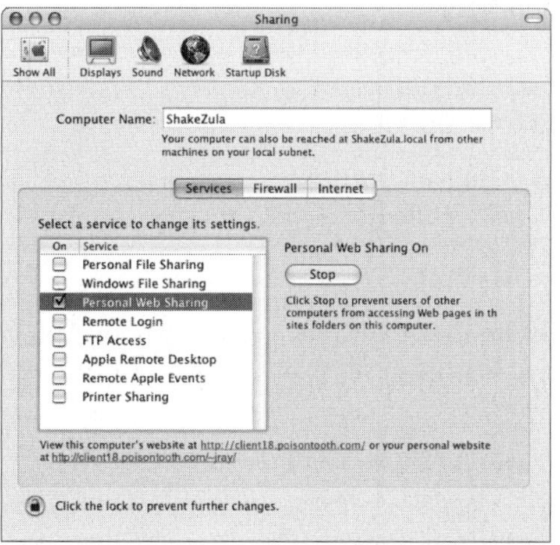

FIGURE 27.1 Use the Sharing Preference panel to activate Apache.

The Sharing button does two things. First, it configures the Mac OS X Server to start Apache when it boots. The `/etc/hostconfig` file is modified to read WEBSERVER=-YES-:

```
##
# /etc/hostconfig
##
```

```
# This file is maintained by the system control panels
##

# Network configuration
HOSTNAME=-AUTOMATIC-
ROUTER=-AUTOMATIC-

# Services
AFPSERVER=-NO-
APPLETALK=en1
AUTHSERVER=-NO-
AUTOMOUNT=-YES-
CONFIGSERVER=-NO-
CUPS=-YES-
IPFORWARDING=-NO-
IPV6=-YES-
MAILSERVER=-NO-
NETBOOTSERVER=-NO-
NETINFOSERVER=-AUTOMATIC-
NISDOMAIN=-NO-
RPCSERVER=-AUTOMATIC-
TIMESYNC=-YES-
QTSSERVER=-NO-
SSHSERVER=-NO-
WEBSERVER=-YES-
SMBSERVER=-NO-
DNSSERVER=-NO-
CRASHREPORTER=-YES-
```

Second, it activates the Apache server with no need to reboot. You can start, stop, and restart Apache at any time using the `/usr/sbin/apachectl` utility. For example, to restart the server, type

```
brezup:jray jray $ sudo /usr/sbin/apachectl restart
```

TIP

The Start/Stop buttons and check box within the Sharing Preference panel can also be used to start and stop the Apache process.

Table 27.1 documents all of the available `apachectl` options.

TABLE 27.1 The `apachectl` Administration Application Accepts These Commands

Options	Functions
`start`	Starts the Apache server.
`stop`	Stops the Apache server.
`restart`	Restarts Apache. This is equivalent to stopping and then starting the server. Current connections are closed.
`fullstatus`	Displays a full status of the server. This requires lynx to be installed.
`status`	Displays a summary of the server status. The lynx text browser is required.
`graceful`	Restarts the server gracefully. Current connections are not dropped.
`configtest`	Checks the configuration files for errors. Can be used regardless of the current server state.

There is an interface problem that occurs with Apple's use of the Personal Web Sharing metaphor when it is applied to Apache. Each user has his own directory. When Web sharing is turned on for one user, it is activated for everyone.

If the computer is a all of the available `apachectl` optionsmultiuser system, you cannot be certain that Web sharing is on or off. The only way to guarantee that your files aren't being displayed on the Web is to manually disable viewing files using Apache configuration directives, or to remove the files from your `~/Sites` directory.

NOTE

This isn't Apple's fault, but just part of the growing pains associated with moving to a multiuser environment. The `/etc/hostconfig` file is the definitive checkpoint for figuring out what your server will be doing when it starts up.

Apache Configuration

Apache is an extremely large piece of software that has hundreds of configuration options and possible setups. A number of books have been written about Apache. This section looks at the most common attributes that can be configured and how they affect your system. It is not meant to be a complete reference to Apache. Version 2.0 of Apache is available from `http://www.apache.org`, but it is not yet distributed with Mac OS X and still lacks support for many popular modules including PHP (which you'll learn about in the next chapter). The current shipping version, 1.3.27, is discussed here.

File Locations

Apple has done an excellent job of making the Apache Web server configuration manageable for machines with large numbers of personal Web sites. Instead of a single monolithic configuration, like the standard Linux or Windows installation, the server can be configured on two different levels:

System-wide configuration—(path: `/etc/httpd/httpd.conf`) This is the master configuration file. It contains information about the system as a whole—what directories are accessible, what plug-ins are in use, and so on. Changes to the Web server as a whole are included here.

User-directory configuration—(path: `/etc/httpd/users/<username>.conf`) When the Mac OS X Users System Preference panel creates a new account, it automatically adds a basic configuration file for that user within the `/etc/httpd/users` directory. This mini-configuration file determines the security for the Web pages within a user's Sites folder.

By splitting up the configuration, the administrator can quickly adjust Web permissions on a given account. To edit the user or system configuration, you must either log in (or su) as `root`, or use `sudo`.

> **NOTE**
>
> Although the user configuration files are stored based on the user's name, they have no real connection to the actual user other than containing the path to a personal Sites folder. These files can contain any Apache configuration option, including those that affect other users. The division by username is for ease of editing only.

Apache approaches configuration in a very object-oriented manner. The configuration files are XML like, but not compliant, so don't attempt to edit them using the plist editor. Apache calls each configuration option a directive. The two types of configuration directives are

Global—Global directives affect the entire server, everything from setting a name for the Web server to loading and activating modules.

Container-based—An Apache container is one of a number of objects that can hold Web pages. For example, a directory is a container, a virtual host is a container, and an aliased location is also a container. If you don't know what these are, don't worry; we'll get there. For now, just realize that each container can be configured to limit who has access to what it contains, and what pages within it can do.

Global Options

The global options can fall anywhere within the server configuration file. If you're running a heavy-traffic Web site, you'll definitely want to change the defaults. By default, Apache starts only one server and keeps a maximum of five running at any given time. These numbers do not enable the server to quickly adapt to increased server load.

Table 27.2 documents the some of the most important configuration directives contained in the `/etc/httpd/httpd.conf` file. They are listed in the order in which you're likely to encounter them in the `httpd.conf` file.

> **NOTE**
>
> Several of the Apache directives refer to the number of server processes that should be started. These processes are subprocesses of the parent Apache process. When you use `apachectl` to control the server, you are controlling all the Apache processes.

TABLE 27.2 Global Apache Directives

Directive	Description
`ServerType` `<standalone¦inetd>`	The Server type determines how Apache starts. Standalone servers are the default. Inetd-based servers use the `inetd` process to activate a server only when it is accessed. This is inefficient and not recommended for all but the lowest-traffic systems.
`ServerRoot` `<path>`	The base path of the Apache binary files.
`PidFile` `<path/filename>`	The path (and filename) of the file that should store Apache's process ID.
`Timeout` `<seconds>`	The number of seconds that Apache will wait for a response from a remote client. After the time period expires, the connection will be closed.
`KeepAlive` `<On¦Off>`	Allows more than one request per connection. This is the default behavior of HTTP/1.1 browsers. Shutting this off might result in a higher server load and longer page load times for clients.
`MaxKeepAliveRequests` `<#>`	The maximum number of requests that can be made on a single connection.
`KeepAliveTimeout` `<seconds>`	The number of seconds to wait between requests on a single connection.
`MinSpareServers` `<#>`	Apache automatically regulates the number of running servers to keep up with incoming requests. This is the minimum number of servers kept running at any given time.
`MaxSpareServers` `<#>`	The maximum number of servers that will be kept running when there is no load. This is not a limit on the total number of server processes to start; it limits the number of unused processes that will be kept running to adapt to changes in load.
`StartServers` `<#>`	The number of servers to start when Apache is first launched.
`MaxClients` `<#>`	The `MaxClients` directive sets an upper limit on the number of servers that can be started at a given time. Keeping this number low can help prevent denial of service attacks from eating up all system resources. A heavy-volume server should rarely need more than 100.
`MaxRequestsPerChild` `<#>`	Some systems have memory leaks. A memory leak is a portion of the system software in which memory usage slowly grows in size. Apache recognizes that memory leaks might exist and automatically kills a server after it has processed a given number of requests, freeing up any memory it was using. The server process is then restarted, fresh and ready to go.

TABLE 27.2 Continued

Directive	Description
LoadModule *<modulename>*	Loads an Apache module. Many modules will be *<modulepath>* installed automatically, so you rarely need to adjust anything.
AddModule *<modulename.c>*	Activates a loaded module.
Port *<#>*	The port number that the Apache server will use. The standard HTTP port is 80.
User *<username>*	The user ID under which Apache will run. Apache has the full access permissions of this user, so never, ever, EVER, set this to the root account. Mac OS X has the user www configured for the purpose of running Apache.
Group *<groupname>*	The group ID under which Apache will run. Like the User directive, this should never be set to a privileged value. If it is, any broken Web applications could compromise your entire computer. You should use the www group for this purpose on Mac OS X.
ServerAdmin *<Email Address>*	The email address of the Web server operator.
ServerName *<Server Name>*	If your server has several different hostnames assigned, use the ServerName directive to set the one that will be returned to the client browser. This cannot be an arbitrary name; it *must* exist!
DocumentRoot *<path to html files>*	This defines the path to the main server HTML files. The Mac OS X default is /Library/WebServer/Documents.
UserDir *<name of user's website directory>* Apache installs is	The personal Web site directory within each user's home directory. As you already know, OS X uses Sites; the default used in most public_html. Removing this directive will make individual users to unable to create Web sites.
DirectoryIndex *<Default HTML file>*	When a URL is specified by only a directory name, the Web server attempts to display a default HTML file with this name.
AccessFileName *<Access Filename>*	The name of a file that, if encountered in a directory, will be read for additional configuration directives for that directory. Typically used to password-protect a directory. The default name is htaccess.
DefaultType	The default MIME type for outgoing documents. The text/html type should be used to serve HTML files.
HostnameLookups *<On¦Off>*	If activated, Apache stores the full hostname of each computer accessing the server rather than its IP address. This is *not* recommended for servers with more than a trivial load. Hostname lookups can greatly slow down response time and overall server performance.
TypesConfig *<mime-type configuration file>*	The path to a file that contains a list of MIME types and file extensions that should be served with that MIME type. For example, the type text/html is applied to files with the .html extension. The default MIME types are located at /private/etc/httpd/mime.types.

TABLE 27.2 Continued

Directive	Description
LogLevel <*level*>	One of eight different error log levels: debug, info, notice, warn, error, crit, alert, or emerg.
LogFormat <*Log Format*> <*short name*>	Defines a custom log format and assigns it to a name. Discussed shortly.
CustomLog <*Log filename*><*short name*>	Sets a log filename and assigns it to one of the LogFormat types.
Alias <*URL path*> <*server pathname*>	Creates a URL path that aliases to a different directory on the server.
ScriptAlias <*URL path*> *pathname*>	Creates a URL path that aliases to a directory containing CGI <*server* applications on the server.
Redirect <*old URL*> <*new URL*>	Redirects (transfers) a client from one URL to another. Can be used to transfer between URLs on the same server or to transfer a client accessing a local Web page to a remote site.
AddType <*MIME-type*> <*extension(s)*>	Adds a MIME-type without editing the mime.types file.
AddHandler server-parsed <*file extension*>	Activates server-side includes for files with the specified extension. The default SSI extension is .shtml.
AddHandler send-as-is <*file extension*>	When activated, files with the defined extension are sent directly to the remote client as is.
AddHandler imap-file <*file extension*>	Sets the extension for server-side imagemap features. All modern Web browsers use client-side image maps, but if you need compatibility with Netscape 1.0 browsers, you need to use server-side maps.
ErrorHandler <*error number*> <*Error Handler*>	Sets an error handler from any one of the standard HTML error messages. This will be discussed in greater detail shortly.
Include <*directory*>	Reads multiple configuration files from a directory. This is set to /etc/httpd/users.

This is only a partial list of commonly used directives—for a complete list, visit Apache's Web site. To get a handle on configuration, let's take a look at a few different directives in use. Each of these commands, because of its global nature, can be used anywhere within the /etc/httpd/httpd.conf configuration file.

Aliases

As you build a complex Web server, you'll probably want to spread files out and organize them using different directories. This can lead to extremely long URLs, such as /mydocuments/work/project1/summary/data/. This URL is a bit bulky to be considered convenient if it were commonly accessed or publicly advertised.

Thankfully, you can shorten long URLs by creating an alias. Aliases work in a similar manner as the Mac OS X Finder aliases. A short name is given that, when accessed, will automatically retrieve files from another location. To alias the long data URL to something shorter, such as /data/, you would use the following command:

```
Alias /data/ /mydocuments/work/project1/summary/data
```

Aliases can be used to access files anywhere on the server, not just within the server document root. Obviously, the files in the alias directory need to be readable by the Apache process owner.

Redirection

Web sites change. URLs change. For established Web sites, changing the location of a single page can be a nightmare for users—bookmarks break and advertised URLs fail. Although this might seem trivial to experienced Web surfers, some users might not be persistent enough to figure out where the page has gone.

Many Web sites put a redirection page up in place of the missing page. This type of redirection relies on a browser tag to take the user to another URL after a set timeout period. This is effective for most modern browsers, but it takes several seconds between loading the original page and the redirection. In addition, a page needs to be created for each location that might be accessed by the client. This could be hundreds of pages!

A simpler, faster, neater way is to use the Redirect directive. Redirect forces the client browser to transfer to a different URL before the original page even opens. Entire URL structures can be redirected using a single command. The destination URL can even be on a remote server!

For example, if you've decided to move all the files under a URL called /ourcatalog/toys to a new server with the URL www.mynewstoreonline.com/toys, you could use

```
Redirect /ourcatalog/toys http://www.mynewstoreonline.com/toys
```

If a user attempted to access the URL /ourcatalog/toys/cooltoy1.html, he would immediately be transferred to http://www.mynewstoreonline.com/toys/cooltoy1.html.

Using redirects is more reliable and transparent for the end user. Avoid using HTML-based redirects, and rely on the Apache Redirect directive to hide changes in the structure of your Web site.

Logs

Apache on Mac OS X stores its log files in the directory /var/log/httpd. By default, there are two logs—access_log and error_log.

The access_log file contains a record of what remote computers have accessed Apache, what they asked for, and when they did it. For example,

```
140.254.85.2 - - [02/September/2003:16:49:47 -0400] "GET /extimage/images/
        26_thumb.jpg HTTP/1.1" 200 27012
140.254.85.2 - - [02/September/2003:16:49:47 -0400] "GET /extimage/images/
        27_thumb.jpg HTTP/1.1" 200 35793
140.254.85.2 - - [02/September/2003:16:49:47 -0400] "GET /extimage/images/
        28_thumb.jpg HTTP/1.1" 200 26141
140.254.85.2 - - [02/September/2003:16:49:47 -0400] "GET /extimage/images/
        30_thumb.jpg HTTP/1.1" 200 29316
140.254.85.2 - - [02/September/2003:16:49:47 -0400] "GET /extimage/images/
        29_thumb.jpg HTTP/1.1" 200 33626
```

This log excerpt shows five requests for `.jpg` images from the Apache server. Five fields are stored with each log entry:

- **Remote Client**—The machine accessing the Apache Web server. In these examples, that client is 140.254.85.2.
- **Date and Time**—A time and date stamp for when the request was made. These five requests were made on September 2, 2003, at 4:49 p.m.
- **Request String**—The actual request that the remote machine made. Most requests begin with GET and are followed by the resource to retrieve, and then the version of the HTTP protocol to retrieve it with. The five requests in the example are for files within the `/extimage/images/` directory of the server's documents folder.
- **Response Code**—Identifies how the remote server responded to the request. The code 200 shows that the request was successfully served. A 404, on the other hand, indicates that the request couldn't be satisfied because the resource wasn't found. The response codes for HTTP 1.1 are available from `http://www.w3.org/Protocols/rfc2616/rfc2616-sec6.html`.
- **Response Size**—The number of bytes sent to the remote client to satisfy the request.

NOTE

There are actually seven fields in this log format. The second and third fields contain a `-` that indicates a value could not be determined. It is unlikely that you'll see values here.

Apache knows this style of access log as the common log format. Log formats are completely customizable using the LogFormat directive. The common format is defined as

```
LogFormat "%h %l %u %t \"%r\" %>s %b" common
```

Each of the %h elements denotes an element to be stored in the log file. The \" is an escaped quote, meaning that a quote will also be stored in that location. You can build a log format using:

%h—Hostname of the requesting computer.

%a—IP address of the remote computer.

%r—Request string.

%t—Time of request.

%T—Amount of time taken to serve the request.

%b—Bytes sent.

%U—URL path requested.

%P—Process ID of the child that served the request.

%>s—The last status reported by the server.

%{Referer}i—The referring URL (the URL that contained the link to current page).

%{User-Agent}i—The string identifies the remote browser.

TIP

This is only a partial listing. You can find a complete list of the Apache log elements at http://httpd.apache.org/docs/mod/mod_log_config.html#logformat.

You define a log format by using the LogFormat line, a string containing the format elements, and a name for the file. For example, to define a log called mylog that stores only the hostname of the remote client for each request, you would use

```
LogFormat "%h" mylog
```

Except for custom solutions, you'll be best served by one of Apache's default log formats. Although the common log is common, it probably isn't the best thing for doing extensive reporting. A better choice is Apache's combined log format. The combined log format includes referer and user-agent strings with each request. Most Web analysis packages use the combined log style.

To activate a log format, use the CustomLog directive, followed by the pathname for the log and the log name. To activate the combined log format, use within the /etc/httpd/httpd.conf file:

```
CustomLog "/private/var/log/httpd/access_log" combined
```

Log files are an important part of any Web server. They can provide important data on the popular pages of the server, errors that have occurred, and how much traffic your system is getting.

NOTE

The `error_log` is not shown here because it should only contain startup and shutdown messages. If a security violation or configuration error occurs, it is recorded to this file. In addition, programmers can find detailed information about program errors written to this location.

Log Analysis Software An abundance of log analysis software is available for Unix operating systems (and thus Mac OS X). Log analysis is more of an art than a science. As you've seen by looking at the logfile formats, you can determine the remote host, requested resource, and time of request from the logfile. Unfortunately, many analysis packages try to go even further by providing information on how long visitors were at your page, or where (geographically) they are located. Neither of these pieces of information is tracked in the Apache logs.

To determine how long someone has been at your site, the analysis software must look at all accesses and determine which are related, and the amount of time between them. This is entirely guesswork on the part of the server. Assume that a user opens her browser, views a page, walks away for 15 minutes, and then accidentally clicks on another page before closing her browser. If the software is set with a session timeout period greater than 15 minutes, it sees two separate hits on the page. The software assumes that the user spent at least 15 minutes reading both pages and registers that the browser spent 30 minutes on the site. In reality, only a minute or two was spent looking at the site content.

When determining geographic information, analysis software performs an even more amazing task—locating what city a user is coming from. To do this, the analysis utility looks up the domain of the client accessing the system. It retrieves the city and state that the domain was registered in. Unfortunately, this is almost completely worthless data. I recently ran a WebTrends report on a local (Columbus, Ohio) e-commerce site to see how it would perform.

The results showed that more than 95% of the remote requests are coming from Herndon, VA. In fact, an analysis of other (non-related) sites shows a similar amount of traffic from Virginia. The reason is simple—the RoadRunner cable model network. The rr.com domain is registered in Herndon, VA. There are thousands of users with RoadRunner-based access—no matter where they are actually coming from, the report displays Herndon, VA. That isn't very useful, is it?

The final Web statistic fallacy is the number of hits a page receives. Many people are delighted when they find that they're getting a few thousand hits a day, but they don't realize what constitutes a hit. The Apache Web server counts any information requested as a hit. If a Web page has 10 tiny icons on it, it takes at least 11 hits to load the page (1 for the page, 10 for the icons). As pages become more graphically rich, it takes even more requests to load them. A 10,000-hit-per-day site might only be serving a few hundred pages per day!

As long as you realize that log analysis data can be deceiving, it can still provide useful information. Here are a few popular Web statistics packages available for Mac OS X:

Analog—The world's most popular statistics software, Analog provides all the basics in a very simple layout. Analog doesn't create DTP-quality graphs or have the snazziest interface you've ever seen, but it's fast, does a good job, and it's free. `http://www.summary.net/soft/analog.html`

Sawmill—The Sawmill software provides complete statistics including search engine identification and a unique Calendar view for located information by month and date. Sawmill is a commercial package costing $99 and up. `http://www.flowerfire.com/sawmill/samples.html`

Summary—Summary is a great entry-level piece of software with advanced reporting features. Data can be exported directly to spreadsheet format for external graphing. Single-user licenses for Summary start at $59. `http://summary.net/download.html`

AWStats—Advanced Web Statistics is a relative newcomer to the Web stats arena, but brings with it extensive reporting and built-in graphing. A bit flashier than analog and free for anyone's use, it is a good choice for budget-conscious Web manager who wants to provide as complete and easy-to-read statistics as possible. `http://awstats.sourceforge.net`.

Urchin—Urchin has, without a doubt, the most user-friendly and attractive interface, as shown in Figure 27.2. Behind the interface is one of the most comprehensive Web statistics applications available—exceeding such industry standbys as WebTrends. Urchin is the ultimate stats solution for serious Web sites. Urchin starts at $199 for an individual server license, but can operate in Lite mode free. `http://www.urchin.com/download/`

NOTE

I do not endorse any stats package over another. The primary difference in Web statistics packages is the interface and data presentation. Remember, there is a very finite amount of data stored in the log file. The best log analysis software is one that creates the reports with the information you need in the format you need it.

Container Options

The second type of Apache directives are "container based." These directives control how Apache serves a certain group of files. Files are chosen based on pattern, location (URL), or directory and are denoted by a start and end tag in the Apache configuration file. For example, the `/etc/httpd/users/` configuration files define a container consisting of each user's `Sites` directory. This is the configuration file created for my `jray` user account (in my case, that file would be `/etc/httpd/users/jray.conf`):

```
<Directory "/Users/jray/Sites/">
  Options Indexes MultiViews
  AllowOverride None
  Order allow,deny
  Allow from all
</Directory>
```

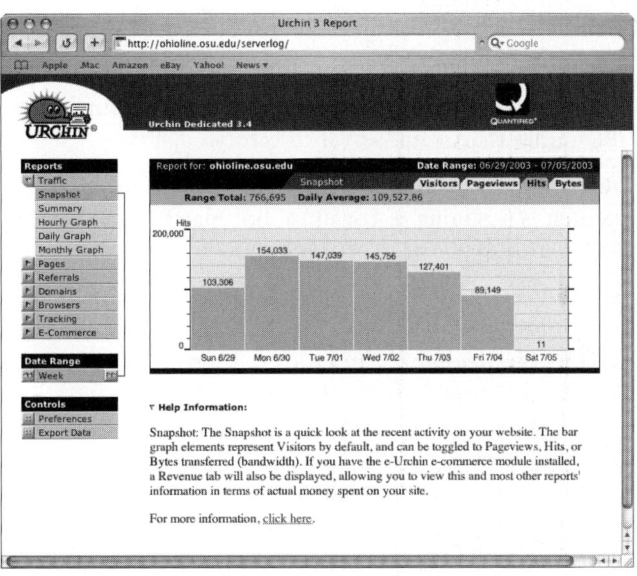

FIGURE 27.2 Web statistics can provide valuable information about your site's operation. The Urchin log analysis software is shown here.

In this example, the directory `/Users/jray/Sites` is the container. Web pages within this container can use the `Indexes` and `Multiviews` options. The `AllowOverride`, `Order`, and `Allow` directives control who has access to the files within this container. This will be explained in more detail shortly.

Besides a directory container, there are other constructs that can also be added to the configuration file(s):

- **Directory**. Creates a directory-based container. All files within the named directory are part of the container.
- **DirectoryMatch**. Like Directory, but uses a regular expression to match directory names. Check out "So What's A $#!%% Regular Expression, Anyway?!" for a nice introduction to writing and understanding regular expressions, `http://www.devshed.com/Server_Side/Administration/RegExp/page1.html`, or Chapter 21, "Scripting Languages."
- **Files**. Groups files based on their names. All files matching the specified name are included in the container. The filename should be given exactly, or you should use the `?` and `*` wildcards to match a single unknown character or any number of unknown characters.

- **FilesMatch**. Similar to Files, but matches filenames based on a regular expression rather than an exact name.
- **Location**. The Location container is similar to Directory, but matches Web content based on a URL, rather than a full-server directory.
- **LocationMatch**. If you've been following along, you'll probably guess correctly that LocationMatch is the same as Location, but matches the URL based on a regular expression.
- **VirtualHost**. The VirtualHost container defines a virtual server within the main server. For external clients, the virtual host appears identical to any other Web server. To you, the system administrator, it is a directory on your server that gets its very own domain name. You'll see how this can be set up shortly.

Within the container objects, the administrator can add a number of directives to control access to the contents or what special features are available in that location. Table 27.3 includes the container directives you'll encounter most often. We're going to explicitly set up password protection and virtual hosting shortly because this can be a bit tricky just going on the directive definitions alone.

TABLE 27.3 Apache Container Directives

Options <*Option List*>	Sets the special capabilities of the server container. There are eight possible options; each can be preceded by an optional + or - to add or remove it.
AllowOverride <*All*>¦<*None*>¦<*Directive Type*>	Chooses the server-defined directives that a local .htaccess file can override. The .htaccess file is used to apply directives outside of the main Apache server configuration and can be edited by any user with access to the directory. For that reason, it is important to allow only trusted users to override options. None disables all overrides; All allows all server directives to be overridden or specifies a combination of AuthConfig, FileInfo, Indexes, Limit, or Options to allow these directive types to be overridden.
Order <*Deny*¦*Allow*>, <*Deny*¦*Allow*>¦mutual-failure (Allow) or denied hosts (Deny) is	Controls the order in which security controls are evaluated—whether or not the list of allowed hosts checked first.
Allow from <*allowed networks*¦all>	A list of IP addresses, networks and subnets, or domain names that can be *allowed* access to the resource.
Deny from <*allowed networks*¦all>	A list of IP addresses, networks and subnets, or domain names that should be *denied* access to the resource.
AuthType <Basic¦Digest>	Attaches HTTP authorization password protection to a directory.

TABLE 27.3 Continued

`AuthName` *`<text string>`*	Identifies the password-protected resource to the end user.
`AuthUserFile` *`<userfile path>`*	Sets a path to the userfile being used for basic authentication.
`AuthDigestFile` *`<digest userfile path>`*	Sets a path to the MD5 Digest password file used with Digest authentication.
`AuthGroupFile` *`<groupfile path>`*	Sets the path to a file containing group definitions for use with authentication.
`Require user¦group¦ valid-user` *`<user/group list>`*	Allows only listed users, groups, or any valid user to access a directory. The users and groups are *not* Mac OS X users unless you're using `mod_auth_apple`, discussed shortly. They are created with the `htpasswd` command.
`ErrorDocument` *`<Error ID><Document Path>`*	Used to substitute a custom-error page in place of the default Apache pages. Use the standard HTTPD error codes (such as 404) and a path to the HTML page to display when the error occurs within the given resource.
`ServerAdmin`	The email address of the administrator of a virtual host.
`DocumentRoot`	The root-level directory for a virtual host.
`ServerName`	The fully qualified domain name for a virtual host, such as `www.poisontooth.com`.

Now let's see how these directives can be used to refine and secure your Apache Web server.

27

Password Protection: `htpasswd`

Password-protecting a directory is extremely simple. For example, suppose a user wants to password-protect his entire public Web site for development purposes. The first step is to set up a username and password file that will contain the login information for those who are allowed to access the resource. This is accomplished using `htpasswd`. There are two steps to the process—first, create a new password file with a single user; second, add additional usernames/passwords to it.

To create a new file, use the syntax `htpasswd -c` *`<pathname> <initial username>`*. For example,

```
brezup:jray jray $ htpasswd -c /Users/jray/webpasswords jray
New password:
Re-type new password:
Adding password for user jray
```

A new password file (/Users/jray/webpasswords) is created, and the initial user jray is added.

Subsequent users can be added by calling `htpasswd -b` *<pathname><username> <password>*:

```
brezup:jray jray $ htpasswd -b /Users/jray/webpasswords testuser testpass
Adding password for user testuser
```

The password file now has two entries: the initial jray user, and testuser.

Next, create a directory container that encompasses the files that need to be protected. Because this example is protecting a personal Web site, the container already exists as a <username>.conf file in /etc/httpd/users:

```
<Directory "/Users/jray/Sites/">
  Options Indexes MultiViews ExecCGI
  AllowOverride None
  Order allow,deny
  Allow from all
</Directory>
```

NOTE

This file from this example has been modified slightly since the initial Mac OS X installation. The `options` directive includes `ExecCGI` to enable CGI development to take place.

To this directory container, add `AuthType`, `AuthName`, `AuthUserFile`, and Require directives. You must be root or using `sudo` to edit the file:

```
<Directory "/Users/jray/Sites/">
  AuthType Basic
  AuthName "John's Development Site"
  AuthUserFile /Users/jray/webpasswords
  Require valid-user
  Options Indexes MultiViews ExecCGI
  AllowOverride None
  Order allow,deny
  Allow from all
</Directory>
```

The `AuthUserFile` is set to the name of the password file created with `htpasswd`, whereas the `Require valid-user` directive allows any user in the password file to gain access to the protected resource. To activate the authentication, use **`sudo /usr/sbin/apachectl restart`**:

```
brezup:jray jray $ sudo /usr/sbin/apachectl restart
/usr/sbin/apachectl restart: httpd restarted
```

Attempting to access the /Users/jray/Sites directory (~jray) now opens an HTTP authentication dialog, as seen in Figure 27.3.

FIGURE 27.3 The directory is now password-protected.

Access to a directory can be restricted even further using the Allow, Deny, and Order directives.

Authenticating Against User Accounts with mod_auth_apple

Using the basic is fine in many cases, but you might find yourself wanting to protect resources based on actual user accounts on your computer. Although it's simple enough to create a password file for each user, these passwords will not be updated as users update their Mac OS X passwords. The *real* solution is to provide an authentication mechanism by which resources could be protected by actual system accounts and system passwords. This is entirely possible courtesy of Apple's mod_auth_apple Apache module.

Included with Mac OS X Server by default, Mac OS X client users can download and install mod_auth_apple with very little trouble. There are two components to the install: First, a missing header file Security/checkpw.h must be copied from the Darwin CVS repository or mirror, and then the source code for mod_auth_apple can be downloaded and installed.

The header file can be downloaded directly from Apple at http://developer.apple.com/darwin/projects/darwin/darwinserver/, but you'll need to register before downloading. Alternatively, download the header from http://www.opendarwin.org/cgi-bin/cvsweb.cgi/src/Security/checkpw/. After downloading, make a new directory /usr/include/Security, and copy the header file to the new location:

```
brezup:jray jray $ curl -O "http://www.opendarwin.org/cgi-bin/cvsweb.cgi/~check-
out~/src/Security/
 checkpw/checkpw.h"
brezup:jray jray $ sudo mkdir /usr/include/Security
brezup:jray jray $ sudo mv checkpw.h /usr/include/Security/
```

Next, download the latest `mod_auth_apple` package from `http://developer.apple.com/darwin/projects/darwin/darwinserver/`, unarchive it, and then enter the source distribution directory:

```
brezup:jray jray $ tar zxf mod_auth_apple-XS-10.3.tgz
brezup:jray jray $ cd mod_auth_apple
```

Be sure to check the Apple README file for installation instructions; they might change between versions. The instructions shown here are "modified" from Apple's directions so that the software configures automatically. Use `make` followed by `apxs -i -a mod_auth_apple.so` (as root) to compile and install the module:

```
brezup:jray mod_auth_apple $ make
/usr/sbin/apxs -c -Wc,"-traditional-cpp -Wno-four-char-constants
 -F/System/Library/PrivateFrameworks -DUSE_CHKUSRNAMPASSWD"
 -Wl,"-bundle_loader /usr/sbin/httpd -framework Security"
 -o mod_auth_apple.so mod_auth_apple.c
gcc -DDARWIN -DUSE_HSREGEX -DUSE_EXPAT -I../lib/expat-lite
 -g -Os -pipe -DHARD_SERVER_LIMIT=2048 -DEAPI -DSHARED_MODULE
 -I/usr/include/httpd -traditional-cpp -Wno-four-char-constants
 -F/System/Library/PrivateFrameworks -DUSE_CHKUSRNAMPASSWD -c mod_auth_apple.c
...
brezup:jray mod_auth_apple $ sudo apxs -i -a mod_auth_apple.so
[activating module 'apple_auth' in /private/etc/httpd/httpd.conf]
cp mod_auth_apple.so /usr/libexec/httpd/mod_auth_apple.so
chmod 755 /usr/libexec/httpd/mod_auth_apple.so
cp /private/etc/httpd/httpd.conf /private/etc/httpd/httpd.conf.bak
cp /private/etc/httpd/httpd.conf.new /private/etc/httpd/httpd.conf
rm /private/etc/httpd/httpd.conf.new
```

The `mod_auth_apple` module is now compiled and installed. Using it is identical to the examples we've already seen for Basic authentication, except no password file is needed. For example, to protect my `Sites` directory so that only my account (jray) can access it, I would use the following in my `/etc/httpd/users/jray.conf` file:

```
<Directory "/Users/jray/Sites/">
  AuthType Basic
  AuthName "John's Development Site"
  Require user jray
```

```
  Options Indexes MultiViews ExecCGI
  AllowOverride None
  Order allow,deny
  Allow from all
</Directory>
```

To verify against any account on the machine, one would replace `Require user jray` with `Require valid-user`. Alternatively, to validate against a group, `Require group <groupname>` could be employed.

CAUTION

The authentication methods shown here use Basic authentication, which passes clear-text information (usernames/passwords) over the network. A more secure form called Digest authentication is also available, which encrypts passwords before sending them. In addition, Apple offers a digest form of their authentication module that you can use to gain a bit of security. (See `http://httpd.apache.org/docs/howto/auth.html#digest` for more information on Digest authentication.)

Unfortunately, Digest authentication should not be considered truly secure because the encrypted password itself is sent as plaintext and could simply be provided to the remote server to authenticate. To *truly* be secure, you'll need SSL support, which we'll cover very shortly.

Restricting Access by Network

To create more stringent control over the users who can access a given resource, use Allow and Deny to set up networks that should or shouldn't have access to portions of your Web site. This is extremely useful for setting up intranet sites that should only be accessible by a given subnet. For example, assume that you want to restrict access to a resource from everyone except the subnet 192.168.0.x. The following rules define the access permissions:


```
Allow from 192.168.0.0/255.255.255.0
Deny from all
```

Because there isn't an ordering specified, what really happens with these rules is ambiguous. Is the connection allowed because of the allow statement? Or denied because all the connections are denied?

To solve the problem, insert the `Order` directive:

```
Order Deny,Allow
Allow from 192.168.0.0/255.255.255.0
Deny from all
```

With this ordering, an incoming connection is first compared to the deny list. Because all access is denied by default, any address matches this rule. However, the `Allow` directive is used for the final evaluation of the connection and will allow any connection from the network 192.168.0.0 with the subnet 255.255.255.0.

Using different orderings and different Allow/Deny lists, you can lock down a Web site to only those people who should have access, or disable troublesome hosts that misuse the site.

TIP

As with any change to the Apache configuration file, you must use `/usr/sbin/apachectl` to restart the server.

An alternative to restarting is to add a `.htaccess` file to the directory you want to protect. This file can contain any of the standard directory container directives and will be automatically read when Apache attempts to read any file from the directory.

Virtual Hosts

A virtual host is a unique container object, in that it can define an entirely separate Web space unrelated to the main Apache Web site or user sites. For example, the three domains poisontooth.com, vujevich.com, and shadesofinsanity.com are all being served from a single computer. To the end user, these appear to be different and unique hosts. To Apache, however, they're just different directories on the same hard drive.

There are two types of virtual hosts, name-based and IP-based:

Name-based—These hosts rely on the HTTP/1.1 protocol to work. A single IP address is used on the server, but there are multiple DNS name entries for that single address. When connecting to the server, the client browser sends a request for a Web page, along with the name of the server it should come from. Apache uses that information to serve the correct page. This works for all but the oldest 2.0 revision browsers.

IP-based—These hosts rely on Apache's capability to listen to multiple IP addresses simultaneously. Each domain name is assigned to a different IP address. Apache can differentiate between the different incoming addresses and serve the appropriate documents for each. This works on any browser, but is costly in terms of the IP addresses that it consumes.

To set up a virtual host, you must first have an IP address and a domain name assigned for the host. If you're using name-based hosts, you will have a single IP address but multiple hostnames. Your ISP or network administrator should be able to help set up this information.

TIP

Mac OS X users who are attempting to configure IP-based virtual hosts will find that no GUI currently exists for adding multiple addresses to a single machine. Luckily, they can be added from the command line using `ifconfig` *<interface>* `alias` *<additional IP address>* `255.255.255.255`. For most single network card systems, the interface will be `en0`. AirPort cards are usually identified with `en1`. For example,

```
sudo ifconfig en0 alias 192.168.0.200 255.255.255.255
```

This adds the IP address 192.168.0.200 as an additional address to the Mac OS X system. You will need to add any aliases to either a new StartupItem or one of the /etc/rc files.

There are only two differences in the Apache configuration of name-based and IP-based virtual hosts. Name-based hosts must include the NameVirtualHost directive, whereas IP-based hosts will need to use Listen to inform Apache of all the available addresses.

Let's take a look at two different ways to configure the virtual hosts www.mycompany.com and www.yourcompany.com. First, we'll use named-based hosting.

Assume that both mycompany and yourcompany domain names point to the IP address 192.168.0.100. To configure name-based virtual hosts, you could add the following directives to the end of the /etc/httpd/httpd.conf file:

```
NameVirtualHost 192.168.0.100

<VirtualHost 192.168.0.100>
    ServerName www.mycompany.com
    DocumentRoot /Users/jray/mycompany
    ServerAdmin president@mycompany.com
</VirtualHost>

<VirtualHost 192.168.0.100>
    ServerName www.yourcompany.com
    DocumentRoot /Users/jray/yourcompany
    ServerAdmin president@yourcompany.com
</VirtualHost>
```


The NameVirtualHost sets up the IP address that Apache will expect multiple domain name requests to come in on. The two VirtualHost directives define the basic properties of the two sites: what their real domain names are, where the HTML documents are loaded, and the email address for the person who runs the site.

Creating this same setup using IP-based hosts doesn't require much additional effort. For this sample configuration, assume that www.mycompany.com has the address 192.168.0.100 and that www.yourcompany.com uses 192.168.0.101. The configuration becomes

```
Listen 192.168.0.100
Listen 192.168.0.101

<VirtualHost 192.168.0.100>
    ServerName www.mycompany.com
    DocumentRoot /Users/jray/mycompany
    ServerAdmin president@mycompany.com
</VirtualHost>
```

```
<VirtualHost 192.168.0.101>
    ServerName www.yourcompany.com
    DocumentRoot /Users/jray/yourcompany
    ServerAdmin president@yourcompany.com
</VirtualHost>
```

This time, the `Listen` directive is used to tell Apache to watch for incoming Web connections on both of the available IP addresses. The `VirtualHost` containers remain the same, except they now use different IP addresses for the two different sites.

Virtual hosting provides an important capability to the Mac OS X Web server. Although available with a GUI configuration tool in the Mac OS X Server, the Apache distribution included in Mac OS X is every bit as powerful. It just takes a bit of manual editing to get things done!

Rebuilding and Securing Apache

Many of today's hot Web sites include e-commerce or other private areas that require secure communications. Unfortunately, although Mac OS X does ship with SSL support built into Apache, it is neither enabled nor easily configured. In addition, the version of Apache shipped with Mac OS X lags behind the current release by several version numbers. Don't worry; this isn't cause for great alarm, but it does make things tricky for system administrators who want to stay current with the supplied BSD software.

There are two goals to rebuilding and securing Apache. The first is, obviously, to rebuild Apache with the latest source code from `http://www.apache.org`. The second, and intimately related, goal is to configure Apache for SSL communications during the rebuild process. If you have no need for secure Web services, just skip this section.

What Is SSL?

SSL stands for Secure Sockets Layer. It is a protocol developed by Netscape for transmitting sensitive data over the HTTP protocol. All data that passes over SSL is encrypted using a variable-length key. The key size determines the level of encryption. SSL-enabled Web sites are typically used in banking and e-commerce applications to provide security during credit card and other money transactions. In addition, SSL provides support for digitally signed certificates that are used to verify that a server or client is who it claims to be. We highly recommend that anyone who hasn't set up an SSL server before read this introduction before continuing: `http://www.modssl.org/docs/2.8/ssl_intro.html`.

NOTE

The `mod_ssl` that comes with Mac OS X 10.2 can be enabled easily if you simply want to test SSL security on your system. We recommend rebuilding Apache with the latest release of both Apache and `mod_ssl`, but, for the impatient, enabling SSL is a good way to get your feet wet.

Apple has posted full documentation on using the existing mod_ssl/Apache installation at http://developer.apple.com/internet/macosx/modssl.html.

One advantage of building a mod_ssl Apache yourself (besides having the latest version of everything) is that you also get the mkcert.sh script, which greatly eases the process of making and installing your certificate files.

Building Apache

To build Apache with SSL support, you need a few components before you can get started. Unlike most Apache modules, the mod_ssl software must be compiled at the same time as the Apache source code. In addition, you need to download the OpenSSL software that mod_ssl uses for security. Enabling the module, although faster than recompiling, is not as clean as using the certificate management tools in the full Apache distribution, and isn't likely to be as up-to-date. If you're interested in using the existing module, visit http://developer.apple.com/internet/macosx/modssl.html for instructions. Otherwise, follow along to recompile from scratch.

First, download the latest Apache source from http://httpd.apache.org/, the most current version of mod_ssl from http://www.modssl.org, and the Darwin-patched OpenSSL distribution from http://www.openssl.org. Note that the version numbers shown in the text are not likely to be the most recent versions available when you read this. Place the downloads in a common build directory:

```
brezup:jray jray $ mkdir apachebuild
brezup:jray jray $ cd apachebuild/
brezup:jray apachebuild $ curl -O
ftp://www.modssl.org/source/mod_ssl-2.8.10-1.3.27.tar.gz
brezup:jray apachebuild $ curl -O
http://www.apache.org/dist/httpd/apache_1.3.27.tar.gz
brezup:jray apachebuild $ curl -O
ftp://ftp.openssl.org/source/openssl-0.9.6g.tar.gz
```

Now, decompress and untar (tar zxf *<filename>*) each of the archives:

```
brezup:jray apachebuild $ tar zxf apache_1.3.27.tar.gz
brezup:jray apachebuild $ tar zxf mod_ssl-2.8.10-1.3.27.tar.gz
brezup:jray apachebuild $ tar zxf openssl-0.9.6g.tar.gz
```

All done! Let's move on.

Preparing mod_ssl

The next step is to prepare mod_ssl—this can be skipped if you are simply upgrading Apache and have no desire to add SSL support. Use the command ./configure --with-apache=*<path to apache source distribution>* from within the mod_ssl distribution directory, substituting in the appropriate name of your Apache distribution:

27

```
brezup:jray mod_ssl-2.8.10 $ ./configure --with-apache=../apache_1.3.27
Configuring mod_ssl/2.8.10 for Apache/1.3.27
 + Apache location: ../apache_1.3.27 (Version 1.3.27)
 + Auxiliary patch tool: ./etc/patch/patch (local)
 + Applying packages to Apache source tree:
  o Extended API (EAPI)
  o Distribution Documents
  o SSL Module Source
  o SSL Support
  o SSL Configuration Additions
  o SSL Module Documentation
  o Addons
Done: source extension and patches successfully applied.
```

The `mod_ssl` configuration will include several additional instructions on how to finish the Apache installation. *Do not* follow them or your compiled Apache server will be missing some important functions.

Preparing OpenSSL

Now it's time to set up the OpenSSL system—again, skip this step if you have no intention of running an SSL-enabled server.

> **NOTE**
>
> If you already have a fresh install of OpenSSL on your system, there's no need to recompile. Just be sure to set the `SSL_BASE` to the appropriate location in the next step (in the section "Building Apache").

Compiling might take quite a while, depending on your system speed. You might want to start this process, and then walk away for a few minutes. If you're lucky enough to have a new G5, ignore that comment. To configure OpenSSL for compilation, enter the distribution directory and type **`./config`**:

```
brezup:jray openssl-0.9.6g $ ./config
Operating system: ppc-apple-darwin
Configuring for darwin-ppc-cc
Configuring for darwin-ppc-cc
IsWindows=0
...
```

After the software has been configured, use `make` to compile OpenSSL:

```
brezup:jray openssl-0.9.6g $ make
+ rm -f libcrypto.0.dylib
+ rm -f libcrypto.dylib
```

```
+ rm -f libcrypto.0.9.6.dylib
+ rm -f libssl.0.dylib
+ rm -f libssl.dylib
+ rm -f libssl.0.9.6.dylib
making all in crypto...
```

Finally, it's time to compile and install Apache.

Building Apache

Building Apache is straightforward. Apple has worked with the Apache group to incorporate information about the Mac OS X (Darwin) operating system into the source code distribution. What this means to *you* is that Apache, when compiled and installed, will correctly integrate itself with the Mac OS X operating system.

To configure Apache for installation, first move into the source distribution directory. If you are compiling with SSL support, you must set the `SSL_BASE` environment variable to point to the directory containing the OpenSSL source distribution:

```
brezup:jray apache_1.3.27 $ SSL_BASE=../openssl-0.9.6g
```

Next, use `./configure --enable-module=all --enable-shared=max` to set up the distribution for the Mac OS X environment:

```
brezup:jray apache_1.3.27 $ ./configure --enable-module=all --enable-shared=max
Configuring for Apache, Version 1.3.27
 + using installation path layout: Darwin (config.layout)
Creating Makefile
Creating Configuration.apaci in src
Creating Makefile in src
 + configured for Darwin platform
 + setting C compiler to gcc
 + setting C pre-processor to gcc -E -traditional-cpp
 + checking for system header files
 + adding selected modules
  o rewrite_module uses ConfigStart/End
   enabling DBM support for mod_rewrite
  o dbm_auth_module uses ConfigStart/End
  o db_auth_module uses ConfigStart/End
   using Berkeley-DB/1.x for mod_auth_db (-lc)
  o ssl_module uses ConfigStart/End
   + SSL interface: mod_ssl/2.8.10
   + SSL interface build type: DSO
   + SSL interface compatibility: enabled
   + SSL interface experimental code: disabled
   + SSL interface conservative code: disabled
```

```
+ SSL interface vendor extensions: disabled
+ SSL interface plugin: Configured DBM (-ldbm)
+ SSL library path: /Users/jray/apachebuild/openssl-0.9.6g
+ SSL library version: OpenSSL 0.9.6b 9 Jul 2001
+ SSL library type: source tree only (stand-alone)
```

If an error occurs, make sure that you have correctly set the `SSL_BASE` and typed the command-line options exactly as they appear here.

Now, one tiny correction needs to be made to the SSL module `Makefile`. From within the main Apache source distribution, go into `src/modules/ssl/`. Open the file `Makefile` in your favorite text editor and look for the line that reads

```
SSL_LIBS= -ldbm -lssl -lcrypto -L/usr/lib -lgcc
```

Change it to

```
SSL_LIBS= -lssl -lcrypto -L/usr/lib -lgcc
```

If you fail to follow these steps, the compilation process will complain of a missing library.

Finally, compile your new version of Apache by typing **make** from within the root level of the Apache source directory:

```
brezup:jray apache_1.3.27 $ make
===> src
===> src/regex
sh ./mkh -p regcomp.c >regcomp.ih
...
```

The compile should finish in roughly three minutes on a base 1GHz G4. When the compile finishes, Apache displays a success message with the following instructions:

```
+---------------------------------------------------------------------+
| Before you install the package you now should prepare the SSL      |
| certificate system by running the 'make certificate' command.      |
| For different situations the following variants are provided:      |
|                                                |
| % make certificate TYPE=dummy  (dummy self-signed Snake Oil cert) |
| % make certificate TYPE=test   (test cert signed by Snake Oil CA) |
| % make certificate TYPE=custom  (custom cert signed by own CA)     |
| % make certificate TYPE=existing (existing cert)                |
|    CRT=/path/to/your.crt [KEY=/path/to/your.key]            |
|                                                |
| Use TYPE=dummy  when you're a vendor package maintainer,       |
```

```
| the TYPE=test   when you're an admin but want to do tests only,  |
| the TYPE=custom  when you're an admin willing to run a real server |
| and TYPE=existing when you're an admin who upgrades a server.    |
| (The default is TYPE=test)                            |
|                                                       |
| Additionally add ALGO=RSA (default) or ALGO=DSA to select       |
| the signature algorithm used for the generated certificate.      |
|                                                       |
| Use 'make certificate VIEW=1' to display the generated data.     |
|                                                       |
| Thanks for using Apache & mod_ssl.    Ralf S. Engelschall     |
|                   rse@engelschall.com     |
|                   www.engelschall.com     |
+----------------------------------------------------------------------+
```

You now have the most recent version of Apache, and it is ready to start handling secure Web traffic! All that remains is a few more minutes of setting up a basic certificate. If you are not using SSL, you can type **`sudo make install`** to start using the new version of Apache immediately.

Creating a Certificate and Installing

Secure Web servers rely on a CA (Certificate Authority) signed certificate to prove their identity and open a secure connection with a client. Unfortunately, obtaining a certificate isn't as simple as going to a Web site and buying one. An official certificate can be issued only by a CA, and only after you generate and send a CSR (Certificate Signing Request) to it. Luckily, for the purposes of testing SSL-enabled Apache, you can sign your own certificate. This will create a secure server, but most Web browsers will display a dialog box when accessing a server that isn't signed by a known CA. For the purposes of this chapter, we'll assume that you want to get up and running quickly, and that you'll want to use a VeriSign or other CA signed certificate later on.

27

Assuming that you're in top level of the Apache distribution directory, type **`make certificate TYPE=test`**. This will take you through the steps of setting up a certificate, allowing you to automatically sign it with a fictional CA so that it can be used immediately, and then creating a CSR file so that you can send in a request for a real certificate in the future. During the certification creation, you are asked a series of questions related to your business or organization. Of all the questions, it is most important to correctly answer the Common Name prompt. This is your Web server's hostname (for example, `www.poisontooth.com`). Any questions you are unsure of can be left with their default values:

```
% make certificate TYPE=test
SSL Certificate Generation Utility (mkcert.sh)
```

```
Copyright (c) 1998-2000 Ralf S. Engelschall, All Rights Reserved.

Generating test certificate signed by Snake Oil CA [TEST]
WARNING: Do not use this for real-life/production systems
______________________________________________________________________

STEP 0: Decide the signature algorithm used for certificate
The generated X.509 CA certificate can contain either
RSA or DSA based ingredients. Select the one you want to use.
Signature Algorithm ((R)SA or (D)SA) [R]:
______________________________________________________________________

STEP 1: Generating RSA private key (1024 bit) [server.key]
2529186 semi-random bytes loaded
Generating RSA private key, 1024 bit long modulus
..........................++++++
......++++++
e is 65537 (0x10001)
______________________________________________________________________

STEP 2: Generating X.509 certificate signing request [server.csr]
Using configuration from .mkcert.cfg
You are about to be asked to enter information that will be incorporated
into your certificate request.
What you are about to enter is what is called a Distinguished Name or a DN.
There are quite a few fields but you can leave some blank
For some fields there will be a default value,
If you enter '.', the field will be left blank.
-----
1. Country Name       (2 letter code) [XY]:US
2. State or Province Name  (full name)   [Snake Desert]:Ohio
3. Locality Name      (eg, city)   [Snake Town]:Dublin
4. Organization Name    (eg, company)  [Snake Oil, Ltd]:PoisonTooth, Ent.
5. Organizational Unit Name (eg, section)  [Webserver Team]:
6. Common Name      (eg, FQDN)   [www.snakeoil.dom]:www.poisontooth.com
7. Email Address    (eg, name@FQDN) [www@snakeoil.dom]:jray@poisontooth.com
8. Certificate Validity   (days)     [365]:
______________________________________________________________________

STEP 3: Generating X.509 certificate signed by Snake Oil CA [server.crt]
Certificate Version (1 or 3) [3]:
Signature ok
subject=/C=US/ST=Ohio/L=Dublin/O=PoisonTooth, Ent./OU=Webserver Team/CN=www.poison-
tooth.com/Email=jray@poisontooth.com
```

```
Getting CA Private Key
Verify: matching certificate & key modulus
read RSA key
Verify: matching certificate signature
../conf/ssl.crt/server.crt: OK
______________________________________________________________________

STEP 4: Enrypting RSA private key with a pass phrase for security [server.key]
The contents of the server.key file (the generated private key) has to be
kept secret. So we strongly recommend you encrypt the server.key file
with a Triple-DES cipher and a Pass Phrase.
Encrypt the private key now? [Y/n]: n
Warning, you're using an unencrypted RSA private key.
Please notice this fact and proceed at your own risk.
______________________________________________________________________

RESULT: Server Certification Files

o conf/ssl.key/server.key
  The PEM-encoded RSA private key file which you configure
  with the 'SSLCertificateKeyFile' directive (automatically done
  when you install via APACI). KEEP THIS FILE PRIVATE!

o conf/ssl.crt/server.crt
  The PEM-encoded X.509 certificate file which you configure
  with the 'SSLCertificateFile' directive (automatically done
  when you install via APACI).

o conf/ssl.csr/server.csr
  The PEM-encoded X.509 certificate signing request file which
  you can send to an official Certificate Authority (CA)
  to request a real server certificate (signed by this CA instead
  of our demonstration-only Snake Oil CA), which later can replace
  the conf/ssl.crt/server.crt file.

WARNING: Do not use this for real-life/production systems
```

In this example, there is only one nonintuitive response: the use of encryption for the server key (`Encrypt the private key now? [Y/n]: n`). If the server key *is* encrypted, you have to manually enter a password to unlock the key each time the server is started or write a script to supply the password to the server. When the key is left unencrypted, the assumption is made that your server protection is sufficient to keep the file safe from prying eyes. The Apache server and certificate are ready to install. Type **`sudo make install`** to prepare the software:

```
brezup:jray apache_1.3.27 $ sudo make install
===> [mktree: Creating Apache installation tree]
./src/helpers/mkdir.sh /usr/bin
./src/helpers/mkdir.sh /usr/sbin
...
+--------------------------------------------------------+
| You now have successfully built and installed the     |
| Apache 1.3 HTTP server. To verify that Apache actually |
| works correctly you now should first check the        |
| (initially created or preserved) configuration files   |
|                                                        |
|  /etc/httpd/httpd.conf
|                                                        |
| and then you should be able to immediately fire up    |
| Apache the first time by running:                     |
|                                                        |
|  /usr/sbin/apachectl start
|                                                        |
| Or when you want to run it with SSL enabled use:       |
|                                                        |
|  /usr/sbin/apachectl startssl
|                                                        |
| Thanks for using Apache.     The Apache Group          |
|                   http://www.apache.org/ |
+--------------------------------------------------------+
```

Unfortunately, the installation of the newly compiled Apache needs a modified version of the configuration file, so you still need to make two final changes before you're done. Open the file `/etc/httpd/httpd.conf.default` and add the following line to the bottom of the file:

```
Include /private/etc/httpd/users
```

Next, search for the directive

```
UserDir public_html
```

and change it to

```
UserDir Sites
```

Save the configuration file and copy it to take the place of `/etc/httpd/httpd.conf`. *Now* you're ready to go. Stop the existing Apache server (**`apachectl stop`**) and start the new SSL-enabled server with **`apachectl startssl`**.

```
% sudo /usr/sbin/apachectl stop
/usr/sbin/apachectl stop: httpd stopped
# /usr/sbin/apachectl startssl
Processing config directory: /private/etc/httpd/users
 Processing config file: /private/etc/httpd/users/jray.conf
 Processing config file: /private/etc/httpd/users/robyn.conf
 Processing config file: /private/etc/httpd/users/test.conf
 Processing config file: /private/etc/httpd/users/test2.conf
/usr/sbin/apachectl startssl: httpd started
```

To configure Mac OS X to automatically start Apache in SSL mode each time it boots, edit the file `/System/Library/StartupItems/Apache/Apache` and change the line

```
apachectl start
```

to read

```
apachectl startssl
```

That wasn't so bad, was it? Your Mac OS X machine is now a full-fledged secure Web server. To test it, open a Web browser and point to a URL on the machine, prefacing the URL with `https://` rather than the usual `http://`. Your browser might display a message about the certificate and signing authority not being recognized. You can expect to see these messages until you send in a certificate-signing request to a recognized CA.

Certifying Authorities

When you created your server certificate, you also created a CSR that can be sent to a CA to generate a real certificate. The certificate signing request file is stored in `/etc/httpd/ssl.csr/server.csr`. This file can be sent to a CA, such as

VeriSign—`http://digitalid.verisign.com/server/apacheNotice.htm`

Thawte—`http://www.thawte.com/html/RETAIL/ssl/index.html`

After processing your request, the CA will return a new digitally signed certificate file. Replace the existing `/etc/httpd/ssl.crt/server.crt` certificate with the CA signed certificate, and your server will be official.

NOTE

A large number of SSL configuration directives can be included to fine-tune Apache's secure services. The default configuration file is sufficient for most, but if you'd like to alter the setup, read the `http://www.modssl.org/` documentation. SSL is not a simple topic and will require resources beyond the scope of this book.

Reinstalling mod_hfs_apple Support

Any time you recompile Apache manually, you should add mod_hfs_apple support back into the system; otherwise you put yourself at risk for a serious case-sensitivity security exploit.

Apache assumes that HFS+ is case sensitive, but it *isn't*. As a result, one could create a directory named privatedocs that was blocked to everyone but a select few. As long as the resource was accessed exactly as it was defined, the block would work. Unfortunately, however, if you attempt to access the resource using a different case variation, such as PRIVATEdocs, the block would not be applied, and the information would be served. To get around this, Apple created the mod_hfs_apple Apache module, which correctly deals with case-sensitivity between requests. When recompiling Apache, you lose support for the module, and the security hole reappears.

To reinstall mod_hfs_apple, download the source distribution from Apple's Darwin repository at http://www.opensource.apple.com/projects/darwin/6.0/projects.html or from http://www.opendarwin.org/cgi-bin/cvsweb.cgi/src/apache_mod_hfs_apple/.

The distribution consists of a Makefile and a source file—which you install much the same was as you did the mod_auth_apple. Unarchive and enter the module distribution. As always, the installation needs to take place as root, or use sudo for the final step:

```
brezup:jray jray $ tar zxf apache_mod_hfs_apple-3.tar.gz
brezup:jray jray $ cd apache_mod_hfs_apple-3
```

Next, edit the Makefile line. Look for the section reading

```
all build $(MODULE): $(MODULE_SRC) $(OTHER_SRC)
    ln -sf $(SRCROOT)$(SRCPATH)/Makefile $(OBJROOT)/Makefile
    ln -sf $(SRCROOT)$(SRCPATH)/mod_hfs_apple.c $(OBJROOT)/mod_hfs_apple.c
```

Comment out the two ln link lines:

```
all build $(MODULE): $(MODULE_SRC) $(OTHER_SRC)
    #ln -sf $(SRCROOT)$(SRCPATH)/Makefile $(OBJROOT)/Makefile
    #ln -sf $(SRCROOT)$(SRCPATH)/mod_hfs_apple.c $(OBJROOT)/mod_hfs_apple.c
```

While you're still in the file, look for the commented out line that looks like

```
# /usr/sbin/apxs -i -a -n hfs_apple $(MODULE)
```

Uncomment it so that it reads

```
/usr/sbin/apxs -i -a -n hfs_apple $(MODULE)
```

You're now ready to compile and install using make DSTROOT=. OBJROOT=. and make install DSTROOT=. OBJROOT=., respectively:

```
brezup:jray apache_mod_hfs_apple-3 $ make DSTROOT=. OBJROOT=.
#ln -sf /Makefile ./Makefile
#ln -sf /mod_hfs_apple.c ./mod_hfs_apple.c
cd . ; /usr/sbin/apxs -c -S LDFLAGS_SHLIB="-bundle -bundle_loader
...
brezup:jray apache_mod_hfs_apple-3 $ sudo make install DSTROOT=. OBJROOT=.
Installing product...
/bin/mkdir -p ./usr/libexec/httpd
/bin/cp ./mod_hfs_apple.so ./usr/libexec/httpd
/bin/chmod 755 ./usr/libexec/httpd/mod_hfs_apple.so
/usr/bin/strip -x ./usr/libexec/httpd/mod_hfs_apple.so
/usr/sbin/apxs -i -a -n hfs_apple mod_hfs_apple.so
[activating module `hfs_apple' in /private/etc/httpd/httpd.conf]
cp mod_hfs_apple.so /usr/libexec/httpd/mod_hfs_apple.so
chmod 755 /usr/libexec/httpd/mod_hfs_apple.so
cp /private/etc/httpd/httpd.conf /private/etc/httpd/httpd.conf.bak
cp /private/etc/httpd/httpd.conf.new /private/etc/httpd/httpd.conf
rm /private/etc/httpd/httpd.conf.new
```

The `mod_hfs_apple` module is now compiled and installed, and your server is again protected from case-sensitivity issues.

WebDAV—mod_dav

Something that Apple hasn't advertised with Mac OS X is the integration of WebDAV as a native file-sharing format. If you're the proud owner of a .Mac account, you already use WebDAV to access your iDisk. WebDAV (Distributed Authoring and Versioning) is a relatively new protocol that operates on top of HTTP. What makes this attractive is the fact that it doesn't require additional inetd or system daemons to be present, and works great through HTTP proxies.

27

WebDAV is entirely cross-platform, is integrated into the Windows operating system, and is supported natively in software such as Macromedia Dreamweaver MX. Using WebDAV, you can distribute authoring and editing Web sites across a number of different computers and operating systems—or just use it to share files. Best of all, WebDAV is easy to use and, because it operates through Apache, the same configuration directives you've already seen can apply directly to its setup.

Installing and Configuring WebDAV

You can download the WebDAV Apache module (`mod_dav`) from `http://www.webdav.org/mod_dav/`. Installing WebDAV is an excellent example of a typical Apache module compilation.

NOTE

Apple also includes a precompiled version of WebDAV on your Mac OS X CD. To enable it, open your `/etc/httpd/httpd.conf` file and look for the two (nonconsecutive) lines:

```
#LoadModule dav_module     libexec/httpd/libdav.so
#AddModule mod_dav.c
```

Uncomment both lines so that they read:

```
LoadModule dav_module     libexec/httpd/libdav.so
AddModule mod_dav.c
```

You can now restart Apache (`/usr/sbin/apachectl restart`) and skip ahead to the setup.

Be aware that it is recommended practice to recompile modules when you recompile Apache. If you followed the previous steps in the chapter to secure Apache, you should download and recompile `mod_dav` from the source.

First, unarchive and uncompress the software:

```
brezup:jray jray $ tar zxf mod_dav-1.0.3-1.3.6.tar.gz
```

Next, enter the source directory and configure the application. You should use the `--with-apxs` flag to enable automatic configuration and installation of the Apache module:

```
brezup:jray mod_dav-1.0.3 $ ./configure --with-apxs
creating cache ./config.cache
checking for gcc.. no
checking for cc.. cc
checking whether the C compiler (cc ) works.. yes
checking whether the C compiler (cc ) is a cross-compiler.. no
checking whether we are using GNU C.. yes
checking whether cc accepts -g.. yes
checking for ranlib.. ranlib
```

Finally, make and install the module:

```
brezup:jray mod_dav-1.0.3 $ sudo make install
cc -c  -I/usr/include/httpd -I/usr/include/httpd/xml -g -O2 -DDARWIN -DUSE
     _HSREGEX -DUSE_EXPAT -I../lib/expat-lite -g -O3 -pipe
     -DHARD_SERVER_LIMIT=1024 -DEAPI -DSHARED_MODULE
     dav_props.c -o dav_props.o
...
cp libdav.so /usr/libexec/httpd/libdav.so
chmod 755 /usr/libexec/httpd/libdav.so
[activating module `dav' in /private/etc/httpd/httpd.conf]
```

NOTE

Modules that are installed using the apxs utility are automatically placed in the appropriate location and have the appropriate LoadModule and AddModule directives added to the http.conf file.

To finish the configuration and activation of WebDAV service on your Apache server, you need to create a directory that will hold WebDAV lock files and then turn on the service for a particular directory or location.

Use the DAVLockDB directive to set the directory and base filename for WebDAV's lockfiles. This should fall anywhere after the LoadModule/AddModule lines in the /etc/httpd/httpd.conf file:

```
DAVLockDB /var/tmp/davlock
```

This example specifies that the directory /var/tmp will be used to hold lock files and that davlock will be the base filename for the lock files. Be sure to include the base filename, not just a directory name. If the lockfile is not properly set, mod_dav will start, but won't operate correctly.

Now, choose one of the directory or container objects that will support WebDAV service and add the DAV On directive:

```
<Directory "/Library/WebServer/Documents">
   DAV On
   Options Indexes FollowSymLinks MultiViews
   AllowOverride None
   Order allow,deny
   Allow from all
</Directory>
```


You should limit access to the DAV services using the same require directive in the standard Apache configuration. WebDAV relies on the HTTP protocol to authenticate users for editing. This means that you will need to create a password file using htpasswd just as we did earlier or use Apple's authentication module to limit access to user accounts on the computer. Unlike the previous example, however, a valid user will be required only when performing a modification to the file system. To create this sort of selective authentication, we'll use the Limit directive. For example, the following configuration file fragment defines an authentication scheme and limits it to the operations that WebDAV uses to add and update files.

```
AuthType Basic
AuthName "The Poisontooth Webserver"
AuthUserFile /Users/jray/webpasswords
```

```
<Limit PUT DELETE PROPPATCH MKCOL COPY MOVE LOCK UNLOCK>
     Require valid-user
</Limit>
```

To finish things up, just combine the authentication block with the resource that WebDAV support has been enabled (DAV On):

```
1: <Directory "/Library/WebServer/Documents">
2:   DAV On
3:   Options Indexes FollowSymLinks MultiViews
4:   AllowOverride None
5:   Order allow,deny
6:   Allow from all
7:   AuthType Basic
8:   AuthName "The Poisontooth Webserver"
9:   AuthUserFile /Users/jray/webpasswords
10:   <Limit PUT DELETE PROPPATCH MKCOL COPY MOVE LOCK UNLOCK>
11:     Require valid-user
12:   </Limit>
13: </Directory>
```

Line 1 sets up the directory to WebDAV enable. This can be a directory that is already defined in the main Apache http.conf or one of the user configuration files.

Line 2 turns on DAV support, and lines 3–6 are standard directory security directives—not WebDAV related.

Lines 7–9 set up basic HTTP authentication. This will be used to authenticate potential WebDAV clients. Lines 10–12 limit the HTTP authentication to only those actions that would be triggered by a WedDAV client.

One small thing still needs to be adjusted before WebDAV can be used—the permissions on the directory that has WebDAV support enabled. Because WebDAV is nothing more than an extension to Apache, it has no more user rights than the Apache server process. This means that if Apache can't write to a resource (that is, it isn't owned by www or isn't set to world-writable), WebDAV won't be able to modify the resource either. To make a directory editable using DAV, you must use chown to modify the file and directory ownership. Type **chown -R www:admin <*directory to DAV-enable*>** and you're done!

Restart Apache (**/usr/sbin/apachectl restart**) to begin using WebDAV.

Mounting WebDAV Shares

First, from within a Finder window, use the Go menu to choose Connect to Server (Command+K). The dialog box shown in Figure 27.4 will appear.

FIGURE 27.4 Use the Connect to Server menu item to connect to WebDAV-enabled servers.

Fill in the URL of the directory with DAV access in the Address field. This should be the Web path to the resource, not the actual file path on the server. In the screenshot shown, the main root directory of the Web server `http://www.shadesofinsanity.com/` has been enabled, so the URL given is just set to the main Web site URL. When satisfied that your settings are correct, click Connect. You will be prompted for a username and password for the resource. Use the username/password pair defined by your HTTP authentication configuration.

After a few seconds, the remote site should be mounted as if it were a local drive on your computer.

TIP

Although not entirely practical for high-volume sharing, WebDAV volumes work just like AppleShare or NFS volumes under Mac OS X. Unlike the implementation on certain other platforms, Mac OS X users can store and execute applications directly on WebDAV shares. In Mac OS X 10.2 and up, your iDisk is accessed entirely via the WebDAV protocol. This enables it to appear to be connected all the time. The end result is more convenient access for you and less of a load on Apple's servers.

Using WebDAV on Windows

Like Mac OS X, WebDAV is integrated into recent releases of the Windows operating system. To access a WebDAV share from your Mac OS X Web server, you must create a new Network Place.

Double-click My Network Places to open the Network Places window. Next, double-click Add Network Place to start the Network Place Wizard. If prompted, tell the Network Place Wizard to Choose Another Network Location, and then click Next. Windows will ask for the address of the network place, as seen in Figure 27.5.

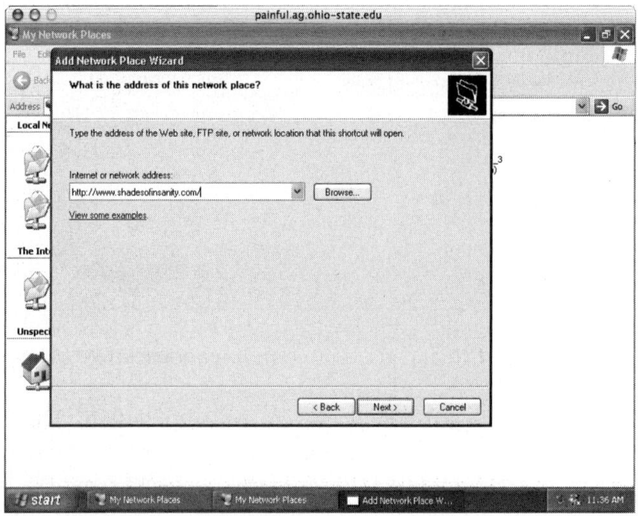

FIGURE 27.5 The Network Place Wizard will help set up a WebDAV resource in Windows.

Fill in the URL of the WebDAV resource, and then click Next. As with Mac OS X, you will be prompted for the username and password that were set using `htpasswd` or accessed by `mod_auth_apple`. Click Next to finish and mount the resource.

WebDAV support is an integral part of Mac OS X and Windows and can be used to unite a multiplatform environment for collaboration on Web sites and other projects. In a pinch, WebDAV can even serve as a file server for things other than Web-related files.

Using `mod_rendezvous`

Another module that Apple has included in Mac OS X (and neglected to tell anyone about) is their self-authored `mod_rendezvous` module. `mod_rendezvous` registers sites with Rendezvous-enabled browsers (like Safari) on your local network. Rather than bookmarking your local servers, the servers advertise their own bookmarks!

Unfortunately, Apple failed to provide a mechanism for disabling this—so if you happen to be running a private test server, there's a good chance your machine is advertising it via Rendezvous to every other computer on your network. Let's take a look at how you can manually control `mod_rendezvous` and what it does.

To disable the module completely, just comment out the appropriate `LoadModule` and `AddModule` lines from `/etc/httpd/httpd.conf`:

```
#LoadModule rendezvous_apple_module libexec/httpd/mod_rendezvous_apple.so
#AddModule mod_rendezvous_apple.c
```

If, instead, you prefer to control which services are advertised, find the mod_rendezvous directive block at the end of httpd.conf. The default block should look like this:

```
<IfModule mod_rendezvous_apple.c>
RegisterUserSite all-users
RegisterDefaultSite
</IfModule>
```

There are two directives included within the block—the first, RegisterUserSite all-users, registers *all* personal sites (~*<username>*) for users with configuration files within /etc/httpd/users. To only register specific user sites, use RegisterUserSite *<username>* [*<username>* ...]. The second directive, RegisterDefaultSite, registers the default /Library/Webserver/Documents Web site via Rendezvous. A final directive, RegisterResource *<resource name>* *<resource URI>*, allows you to register any URL on your server with an arbitrary resource name.

For example, to register my personal Web site (username jray) along with a URL /bulletinboard/bbs.cgi, I'd change the Rendezvous directives in /etc/httpd/httpd.conf to read:

```
<IfModule mod_rendezvous_apple.c>
RegisterUserSite jray
RegisterResource "My Local BBS" "/bulletinboard/bbs.cgi"
</IfModule>
```

After making the changes, restarting Apache puts them into effect immediately, removing the default site advertisement and adding my two custom rendezvous-enabled sites.

That's enough work for now. On to something a bit more entertaining—streaming audio from Apache!

27

Streaming MP3s—mod_mp3

If you've been using iTunes, you've probably got quite a collection of MP3 files that have been building up on your drive. Rather than taking the MP3s with you wherever you go, you can create your own Internet radio station and broadcast music to your computer at work, home, or wherever your MP3s aren't. Apple briefly introduced this feature with iTunes 4.0, and then removed it because of pressure from the recording industry.

Using the Apache mod_mp3 module, you bring this feature back in the form of a Shoutcast-compatible streaming MP3 server. Of course, it goes without saying that anyone who listens to your streams has a legitimate copy of the music. Absolutely no sarcasm intended. None.

Installing mod_mp3 only takes a few minutes of time. Download the latest release from http://media.tangent.org/ and then decompress the archive:

```
brezup:jray jray $ tar zxf mod_mp3-0.40.tar.gz
```

First, cd into the distribution directory, and use **configure --with-apxs** to prepare the module:

```
brezup:jray jray $ cd mod_mp3-0.40
brezup:jray mod_mp3-0.40 $ ./configure --with-apxs
ARGS --with-apxs
checking for ghttp for yp.. could not find ghttp for yp support
checking for perl.. found
checking for apxs.. found
adding support for internal dispatch
Writing proto.h
Writing Makefile
...
```

Next, type **make** to compile:

```
brezup:jray mod_mp3-0.40 $ make
`/usr/sbin/apxs -q CC` -I`/usr/sbin/apxs -q INCLUDEDIR` `/usr/sbin/apxs -q
 CFLAGS` -DCONTENT_DISPOSITION -DSELECT_ENABLED  -c src/mod_mp3.c
 -DCONTENT_DISPOSITION -DSELECT_ENABLED  -o src/mod_mp3.o
`/usr/sbin/apxs -q CC` -I`/usr/sbin/apxs -q INCLUDEDIR` `/usr/sbin/apxs -q
 CFLAGS` -DCONTENT_DISPOSITION -DSELECT_ENABLED  -c src/directives.c
 -DCONTENT_DISPOSITION -DSELECT_ENABLED  -o src/directives.o
`/usr/sbin/apxs -q CC` -I`/usr/sbin/apxs -q INCLUDEDIR` `/usr/sbin/apxs -q
 CFLAGS` -DCONTENT_DISPOSITION -DSELECT_ENABLED  -c src/ice.c
 -DCONTENT_DISPOSITION -DSELECT_ENABLED  -o src/ice.o
`/usr/sbin/apxs -q CC` -I`/usr/sbin/apxs -q INCLUDEDIR` `/usr/sbin/apxs -q
 CFLAGS` -DCONTENT_DISPOSITION -DSELECT_ENABLED  -c src/load.c
 -DCONTENT_DISPOSITION -DSELECT_ENABLED  -o src/load.o
 ...
```

Finally, use **sudo make install** to add the module to /etc/httpd/httpd.conf:

```
brezup:jray mod_mp3-0.40 $ sudo make install
/usr/sbin/apxs -c -I`/usr/sbin/apxs -q INCLUDEDIR` src/mod_mp3.o
 src/directives.o src/ice.o src/load.o src/shout.o src/utility.o
 src/ogg.o src/common.o src/id3.o src/log.o src/internal_dispatch.o
 src/encode.o
cc -bundle -undefined suppress -flat_namespace -Wl,-bind_at_load -o
 src/mod_mp3.so src/mod_mp3.o src/directives.o src/ice.o src/load.o
 src/shout.o src/utility.o src/ogg.o src/common.o src/id3.o
 src/log.o src/internal_dispatch.o src/encode.o
/usr/sbin/apxs -i -a -n 'mp3' src/mod_mp3.so
...
```

```
+--------------------------------------------------+
¦ All done.                                        ¦
¦ If you want to use the default mod_mp3 configure file ¦
¦ go add:                                          ¦
¦                                                  ¦
¦ Include /private/etc/httpd/mp3.conf              ¦
¦                                                  ¦
¦ to your httpd.conf for apache.                   ¦
¦ If not, cat its content into your httpd.conf file. ¦
¦                                                  ¦
¦ Thanks for installing mod_mp3.                   ¦
+--------------------------------------------------+
```

The MP3-streaming module is now installed and ready for use.

Configuring mod_mp3

The mod_mp3 module is activated by setting up an Apache virtual host that will serve as the contact point for iTunes or any other streaming MP3 client. There are two ways to approach this—either by using a name-based or IP-based host, as you've already seen, or using a virtual host running on a port address rather than the standard Web server port 80. We shall use the latter.

A handful of directives are used to control the mod_mp3 streaming features. Several of these are documented in Table 27.4.

TABLE 27.4 These Directives Control mod_mp3's Capability to Stream Music

Directive	Purpose
MP3 <file or pathname>	Adds an MP3 file or directory containing MP3 files to the list of files to be served.
MP3Engine <on¦off>	Turns on the streaming engine.
MP3CastName <stream	Sets a name for the streaming music *collection.name*>
MP3Genre <stream genre>	Sets a music genre for the stream.
MP3Random <on¦off>	Randomizes the order that MP3 files will be served.
MP3Loop <on¦off>	Loops through the music files indefinitely.
MP3LimitPlayConnections <connection limit>	The number of simultaneous streaming connections that will be supported.
MP3ReloadRequest <on¦off>	If turned on, mod_mp3 will reload all files with each request. This is useful if you're adding to the available files during the broadcast.
MP3Playlist <playlist file>	Accepts the name of a file that contains a list of MP3 filenames.
MP3Cache <on¦off>	When on, the module will attempt to cache all MP3 files in memory. This can speed up the server, but will probably take up way too much memory if you have more than a handful of files.

Use these directives, coupled with a virtual host, to set up and start streaming. The following is a typical sample virtual host entry for the `/etc/httpd/httpd.conf` file:

```
1: Listen 8000
2: <VirtualHost music.poisontooth.com:8000>
3:    ServerName music.poisontooth.com
4:    MP3Engine On
5:    MP3CastName "Johns Tunes"
6:    MP3Genre "Hard Rock and 80s"
7:    MP3 /Users/jray/Music
8:    MP3Random On
9:    Timeout 1200
10: </VirtualHost>
```

Line 1 sets the port number for listening to incoming streaming requests. The default Web port is 80, so if you're using the hostname for a Web site as well as streaming music, be sure to pick a different port.

Line 2 sets up the virtual host and port number for connections.

Line 4 turns on MP3 support.

Lines 5 and 6 set some identifying information for the streaming server.

Line 7 adds a directory containing MP3 files to the stream (you can add as many MP3 directives as you'd like).

Line 8 randomizes the playback order.

Line 9 sets a high timeout so that connections are properly serviced.

TIP

A sample `mod_mp3` configuration is installed under the filename `/etc/httpd/mp3.conf`. Feel free to use it rather than typing out all the directives by hand.

Restart Apache to turn on your new `mod_mp3`-streaming server: **`/usr/sbin/apachectl restart`**.

NOTE

Starting the Apache Web server with `mod_mp3` and a reasonably sized MP3 collection can take several seconds. Don't worry if the system appears to stall momentarily.

To access your new MP3 server using iTunes, select Open Stream from the Advanced menu (Command+U) and enter the URL of your MP3 virtual host. The sample `mod_mp3` configuration used in this chapter would be referenced with the URL `http://music.poisontooth.com:8000`, as seen in Figure 27.6.

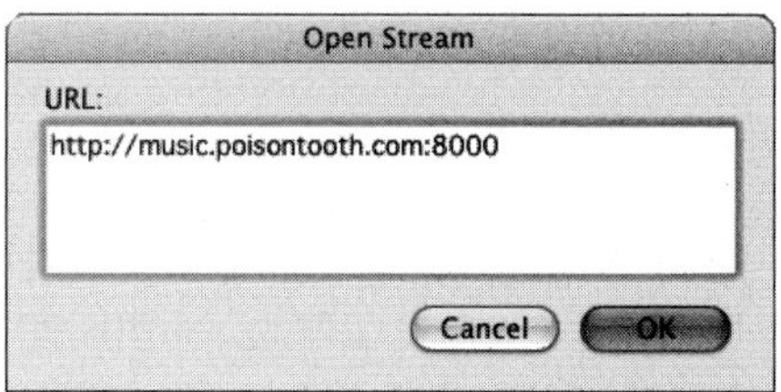

FIGURE 27.6 Open the Apache-served MP3 stream from within iTunes.

Alternatives

If you'd like to try another method of streaming MP3s, there are quite a few available (including Apple's own QuickTime Streaming Server available at `http://www.apple.com`). Here are a few you might be interested in checking out:

SHOUTcast—An official SHOUTcast server from nullsoft. Uses a command-line interface, but is fast and effective. `http://www.shoutcast.com/download/files.phtml`.

NetJuke—NetJuke provides a Web interface (PHP-based) to your music collection. This very popular Open Source project is extremely flexible and, once installed, offers a wonderful Web-based interface that you can access anywhere. `http://netjuke.sourceforge.net`.

LeanStream—A drag-and-drop approach to MP3 streaming, LeanStream is very easy to set up and use. Although not as configurable as other streaming servers, it can get your collection online in a flash. `http://www.melonsoft.com/products/leanstream`.

MP3 Sushi—An excellent Rendezvous-enabled streaming server for Mac OS X. If you're not interested in tons of bells and whistles, but want a great interface to streaming music, this is it. `http://www.maliasoft.com/mp3sushi/index.html`.

Show Me Something to Impress My Friends!

Apache and its associated modules can be configured to do some reasonably "amazing" things. As one more useful example, I offer up these two configuration lines that you can add to your `/etc/httpd/httpd.conf` file (after the `<Directory />` container is a good place):

```
RewriteEngine On
RewriteRule (.+\.pdf)\.html
http://access.adobe.com/perl/convertPDF.pl?url=http://%{HTTP_HOST}$1 [P]
```

I originally wrote these lines to avoid installing a PDF indexer for my Web site's search engine. So, what does this code do?

First, it activates the Apache `mod_rewrite` module, and then adds a rule to which Apache will compare every incoming request.

Assume that you have a PDF file on your site named `"mydocument.pdf"`. You want to serve the document online as HTML. You could convert it with a third-party piece of software or use Adobe's online PDF conversion service. This rule automates the process by looking for requests for `"mydocument.pdf.html"` (which doesn't exist). If it sees a matching request, it immediately sends the corresponding PDF file to Adobe's online conversion service, and then returns the results back to your browser—entirely transparently.

From the user's perspective, the file `mydocument.pdf.html` exists and is served from your Web server.

Try that with IIS.

Summary

Apache is an extremely configurable and a very powerful Web server platform. The basic Apache software can be configured with network and user-level security and used to set up multiple virtual hosts on a single computer. If the basic software isn't enough, Apache can be expanded to include SSL support, MP3 streaming, and integrated file-sharing capabilities. The Apache module library continues to grow and add new features daily. As you might have guessed, Apache is a very large and capable server application. If you'd like to learn more, I suggest looking at an Apache-dedicated title, such as *Sams Apache Server Unleashed,* ISBN 0672318083. Apple's Personal Web server is capable of publishing a few pages or your entire corporate Web site.

CHAPTER 28
Web Programming

IN THIS CHAPTER

- Introduction to Web Programming
- Programming CGIs in Perl
- PHP
- Alternative Development Environments

A Web server is only as good as its content. Creating a Web site that changes over time is an important step in keeping users interested. The Mac OS X BSD base provides access to dozens of different programming and scripting languages, each of which can be used for creating dynamic Web applications that run from within Apache.

This chapter serves as a beginner's guide to CGI (Common Gateway Interface) programming and introduces topics ranging from CGI security to Perl and PHP programming. As in many of the Unix chapters in *Mac OS X Panther Unleashed,* it is important to remember that the information provided is appropriate for learning about the technology available in the operating system. If you're starting from scratch, you might want to look into additional references on Web development.

Introduction to Web Programming

Writing an application for the Web is not as simple as writing an application or script that executes on a local machine. Web applications must obey the HTTP protocol, which, by design, is stateless and connectionless. This poses a problem for anything beyond simple programs that submit a form.

To understand the problem, consider the steps in running a normal piece of software from the Mac OS X desktop (this is a generic fictitious application):

1. Double-click the application to display the Welcome screen.
2. Provide basic input into the application screen by typing or clicking.
3. The application provides feedback based on your input.
4. Repeat steps 2 and 3 as necessary.

5. Choose Quit from the application menu.
6. The application saves your changes and preferences, and then exits.

To translate these operations into a Web application, however, requires working around the limitations of the HTTP protocol.

HTTP

When HTTP (Hypertext Transfer Protocol) was developed, the Web was never expected to become the consumer-driven mish-mash that it is today. HTTP was created to be simple and fast. When retrieving a Web page, the client performs four actions. It first opens a connection to the remote server. The client then requests a resource from the server and sends form data, if necessary. Next, the client receives the results, and finally, it closes the connection.

This happens repeatedly for different page elements (or, depending on the browser and server, multiple requests can be made in one connection). When the browser has finished downloading data, that data is displayed on the user's screen. At this point in time, there is no connection between the client computer and the server. They have effectively forgotten each other's existence.

If the user clicks a link to visit another page on the server, the same process is repeated. The server has no advance knowledge of who the client is, even though they've just been talking. If you've seen the movie *Memento*, you'll understand this concept. The HTTP protocol suffers from a severe lack of short-term memory (statelessness).

Applying this new knowledge to the steps of using an application, the problems becomes obvious:

1. Double-click the application. This is the equivalent of clicking a link on a Web page or entering a URL into a browser. Launching a Web application is nothing more than browsing its URL. No problems so far.
2. It starts, displaying a welcome screen. An HTML welcome page is easily built with a link into the main application. Still no problems.
3. You provide basic input into the application screen by typing or clicking. The trouble begins. Data entered on an HTML form is sent all at once. Providing live feedback to data isn't possible, except for rudimentary JavaScript functionality. Clicking links transports the browser to other pages, effectively losing any information you've already entered.
4. The application provides feedback based on your input. The Web application has access only to information provided as input in the form immediately preceding it. For example, assume that there are two forms in which a user inputs data, one right after the other. The first form submits to the second form. The second form, in turn, submits its data to a page that calculates results based on the entries in both form

pages. Only the data in the second form will be taken into account. The first form's information no longer exists after submitting the second.

5. Repeat steps 3 and 4 as necessary. During each repetition, the server is entirely unaware of what has come before. The application cannot build on previous input.
6. Choose Quit from the application menu. This is a tough one. Remember that the connection to the Web server lasts only long enough to retrieve a single page and send form data. This means that the Web application effectively quits after any step of execution. Web software must be developed with the knowledge that the user can quit his browser at any given point in time. Doing so must not pose either a functional or security risk to the original software.
7. The application saves your changes and preferences, and then exits. If a user quits in the middle of running an online application, there is no way for the software to know that this has occurred. It is up to the programmer to make sure that the Web site keeps track of a user's actions each time it is accessed.

So, how do you work around a protocol that was never designed to keep information between accesses? By employing session management techniques.

Session Management

A *session*, in Web-speak, is the equivalent to the process of running an application from start to finish. The goal of session management is to help the Web server remember information about a user and what that user has done in previous requests for the server. Using session management techniques, you can quickly create Web applications that function like conventional desktop applications. Unfortunately, there is no perfect session management technique. There are several ways to approach the problem, but none offers a completely satisfying solution.

URL Variable Passing

URL variable passing is the simplest form of session management. To make a value available on any number of Web pages, you can use the URL to pass information from page to page. For example, suppose that I had a variable, name, with the value of `johnray` that I wanted to be available even after clicking a link to another portion of the program. I could create links that looked like this:

```
http://www.acmewebsitecomp.com/webapp.cgi?name=johnray
http://www.acmewebsitecomp.com/reportapp.cgi?name=johnray
http://www.acmewebsitecomp.com/accountapp.cgi?name=johnray
```

Each of the three Web applications would receive the variable name with the value `johnray` upon clicking the links. These applications could then pass the values along even further by appending the same information (`?name=johnray`) to links within themselves. Obviously, this would require the Web applications to generate links dynamically, but it's a small price to pay for being able to reliably pass information from page to page.

This technique relies on the HTTP GET method. When a browser sends a GET request for a Web resource, it can append additional data onto the request by adding it in the format:

```
?<variable>=<value>[&<variable>=<value>...]
```

The trouble with this approach is that to send large amounts of data between pages, you must construct extremely large URLs. Visually, this creates an ugly URL reference in the browser's URL field and could lead users to bookmark a URL that contains information about the current execution of the Web application that might not be valid in subsequent executions—such as the date, or other time-sensitive information.

In addition, users can easily modify the URL line of the browser to send back any information to the server that they want. If you've just created a shopping cart application that passes a user's total to a final billing page where it is charged against that user's credit card, it is unlikely that you want him to be able to adjust the price of the merchandise he's purchasing.

Form Variable Passing

Similar to passing variables within a URL (the GET method) is using the POST method of transferring data. Instead of passing data directly in the request for a page, data is sent *after* the initial page request and cannot be directly modified by the user.

With POST, developers can use hidden form fields to hold values before they are needed. Assume that you have two forms: the first collects a first and last name, and the second collects an email address and phone number. Submitting the first form opens the second form, which, when submitted, saves the data to a file.

Each form could save its data to a file independently, but this is problematic when considering applications in which all data must be present before it can be saved. Session management can be used to ensure that all data is present when the final form is submitted.

For example, assume that the first form looks something like this:

```
<form action="form2.cgi" method="post">
First Name: <input type="text" name="first"><br>
Last Name: <input type="text" name="last"><br>
<input type="submit">
</form>
```

This form submits two fields (`first` and `last`) to the `form2.cgi`. If the second form must collect an email address and phone number and submit them simultaneously with the first and last values, the `form2.cgi` could dynamically create a form that stored the original two fields in two hidden input fields:

```
<form action="savedata.cgi" method="post">
Email Address: <input type="text" name="email"><br>
```

```
Phone Number: <input type="text" name="phone"><br>
<input type="hidden" name="first" value="first-value">
<input type="hidden" name="last" value="last-value">
<input type="submit">
</form>
```

Submitting this form would make all the field data available to the subsequent page (`savedata.cgi`).

NOTE

These examples show how you might use different techniques to pass data between Web pages. For them to be effective, you must be able to dynamically generate the URLs and forms that contain your data. We're getting to that—don't panic!

Unfortunately, the trouble with this approach is that only pages with forms can transfer data between one another. Form variable passing is usually used in conjunction with URL passing to cover all bases.

Data integrity is also an issue with this method because a savvy user could easily save an HTML form locally, edit the hidden field values, and then submit the data from the edited form.

NOTE

The URL and form variable passing methods are much more closely related than they appear. The technique of specifying variables and values within a URL is actually also a way of submitting a form called the GET method. When using the GET method, the values sent from a form are appended to the URL requested from the server. By doing this manually, we are simulating a form submission using GET.

The POST method, shown in these examples, sends the variable/value data to the server after requesting a resource. It does not append information to the URL and can only be used to send data via an actual form submission. In some cases, these two methods are used together, but this is not a common coding practice.

In general, POST is a cleaner code choice because it doesn't clutter your URL line. GET, however, creates bookmark-able URLs.

Cookies

Another way to pass information is to use a cookie. *Cookies* are variable/value pairs that are stored on a user's computer and can be retrieved by the remote Web server. Many people are cautious about cookies because of the fear of information being stolen from the cookie without their knowledge. Cookies, however, can be a valuable tool for Web developers and users alike.

From the developer's perspective, assigning a cookie is much like setting a variable. You can name the cookie and give it a value and an expiration day/time. That value then becomes globally available regardless of whether the user jumps to another page, retypes the URL, or starts over. Only if the cookie is reassigned or reaches its expiration does the value cease to exist. There is even a special type of cookie expiration that can limit a cookie's lifetime to the current browser session. In this case, the values are never stored on the client computer and are forgotten when the user exits the program. Using this special type of expiration, a programmer can create a Web application that, after the user exits, leaves no remnants of the login information. This is as close to traditional programming-language variables as a Web developer can hope to get.

From the user's perspective, cookies offer both security and ease-of-use advantages. If a Web application stores a user's identifier in a cookie, that user can immediately be recognized when visiting a Web site. This is commonly used on sites such as Apple's Livepage (`http://livepage.apple.com/`) and Amazon.com to provide a personalized appearance. Because cookies can span multiple pages and applications, a single login can apply to many different portions of a Web site. Using URL or form variable passing, each link and form on a site must be constructed on-the-fly. No changes need to be made to the links when cookies are used. In the case of the former, the chance of programming error is much greater.

Cookies are saved to the local computer's drive and can be viewed in many popular browsers. Safari, for example, enables the user to examine stored cookies within the Security Preferences pane, shown in Figure 28.1.

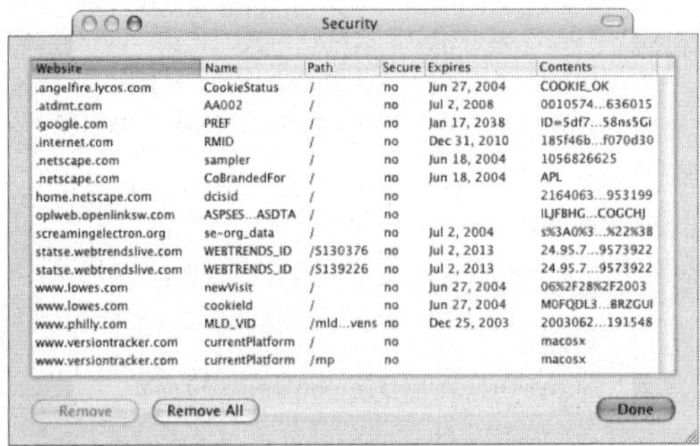

FIGURE 28.1 Popular browsers, such as Internet Explorer, enable the user to browse stored cookies.

Cookies—Are They Evil?

Many people still view cookies as evil. I've heard everything from concerns about a cookie stealing credit card numbers to cookies being used to upload viruses to client computers.

Contrary to popular belief, cookies are not retrieved by a remote server; they are made available by the client browser. When a cookie is first set, it is given a path (URL) for which it is valid.

If your browser comes across a request for a resource (HTML page, image, and so forth) that includes the path, the cookie is automatically sent to that server along with the request. Your browser will send cookies only to the paths where they belong, not to all Web sites you view.

The contents of a cookie are, indeed, determined by the remote server and can be set to any arbitrary string. They do not provide the capacity to upload binary files or executable applications. It's certainly possible that a cookie could hold a credit card number, but you would have had to enter that number into a Web page before it could be stored in a cookie. I have never seen an e-commerce or banking site that worked in this manner, but it is possible that one might exist. If this were the case, other users on your system might be able to find the cookie and extract the sensitive information.

If you're concerned about using cookies on your system, the best advice is to inform your users about how cookies are being employed and make sure that they are comfortable with the information being stored. The dangers of cookies have been greatly exaggerated. Use of common sense and caution while programming with cookies will lead to applications that users will trust and enjoy.

Although it is possible to use other techniques for passing information, cookies are the fastest and easiest. Regardless of the technique used to maintain information two final elements are missing from the big picture—the session database and session ID. Together they form the Holy Grail of session management, session variables.

Session Variables

A *session variable* is a variable that can be set to any value, will be accessible by any portion of a Web application, and will last only while the Web application is being used. In principle, any of the techniques we've looked at so far can do this. Unfortunately, they all fall short when applied to a large system.

For example, imagine that you're passing variables using the URL method:

```
http://www.mywebsite.com/mywebapp.cgi?variable1=value&variable2=value
```

This works great for one or two variables, but extend it to a few thousand! Suddenly a two or three line URL seems short. There is a limit to the amount of data that can be contained within a URL, making this impossible for large amounts of information.

When using cookies or forms to pass data, you aren't necessarily limited by the size of the request string but by the overhead and complexity of the coding. For each variable that must be stored, a hidden field must be added to a form, or a cookie sent back to the server. This process must be repeated on every page. This adds up, in terms of transmission time and processing.

Luckily, there is a solution that can be used with any of the approaches to variable passing—the use of a session database and a session ID.

The concept is simple—when a user comes to a Web site, his session starts. He is assigned a unique ID, called the *session ID*, by the remote Web application. As the user interacts with the Web site, the Web application passes the session ID from page to page. This process can be done using the URL, forms, or cookies. When the Web application software wants to store a value, it stores it on the server, in a local database that is keyed to that particular session ID.

For programmers, this is a dream come true. They can store any information they want (including sensitive data), and it is never transmitted over the network. The only piece of data that is visible on the network wire is the session ID.

Because a single piece of information can keep track of an unlimited number of variables, the session management system can be written to pass the session ID using URL/form methods, or a cookie. Either way is entirely feasible. To make things even easier, developers have included these capabilities in programming languages such as JSP and PHP. For example, in PHP, you can activate session management and store a variable for use on another Web page using syntax like this:

```
<?php
session_start();
$x=$x+1;
session_register('x');
print $x;
?>
```

This example uses `session_start()` to create a new session ID, which is automatically stored in a cookie. Next, the variable `x` is incremented and then registered (stored) with the session. Finally, the value of `x` is displayed. The result is a Web page that displays an increasing count each time a user loads it.

NOTE

It is important to make the distinction that this is not the same as a Web counter. A session ID is specific to a single user, as are all the variables registered with that session. If 50 users were accessing this script simultaneously, each would see a result independent of all the others.

More traditional languages (such as Perl or C) weren't created with Web programming in mind. To implement session variables within Perl, you must create, manipulate, and manage session IDs and session databases. This has already been done so many times that a number of prebuilt solutions are available to work with, but none is as elegant as a language designed for the purposes of creating Web applications.

That said, let's look at using Perl for creating simple CGI applications. What? Didn't I just say that Perl is not nearly as elegant as languages such as PHP? Although this is true, Perl is an excellent starting point for anyone learning Web application development and can extend to developing applications beyond just the Web. Perl is robust, easy to use, and forces the user to understand the basics of Web programming.

What Is a CGI?

CGI stands for Common Gateway Interface. A CGI application is written to conform to a Web server/application communication standard (the CGI). CGI applications pass and read their information to and from an underlying Web server. The generic definition of CGI is just a standalone Web application.

This chapter looks at two types of CGI applications: those programmed within a traditional language, such as Perl, and others based on embedded programming languages, such as PHP. The latter is not truly considered a CGI language because it uses a different mechanism for exchanging information with the Web server, but the end result of each is a Web application.

Programming CGIs in Perl

This chapter assumes that you either know a reasonable amount of Perl basics, or have diligently read the introduction to Perl scripts in Chapter 22, "MySQL and Database Connectivity." In addition, you must have set ExecCGI permissions for the directory you are programming in and have uncommented the CGI AddHandler directive, as described in Chapter 27, "Web Serving."

NOTE

For many Web applications, you can create your CGIs in the Mac OS X folder /Library/WebServer/CGI-Executables. This location is already configured for CGI execution and can be accessed through the URL http://localhost/cgi-bin/*<your cgi name>*.

Unfortunately, CGI-Executables is a special directory that can only contain CGI files. The examples in this chapter use a CGI to display images in the same directory with the CGI and will fail when run from this location. In addition, CGI-Executables is a serverwide repository for CGI scripts. Because this is a learning exercise, use your own personal site ~/Sites for development.

Remember, files within your personal Web space can be accessed with the URL http://localhost/~*<your username>*/*<file or CGI name>*.

Let's start with the most basic CGI example possible—Hello World. Your initial reaction is probably (hopefully!) to create a Perl script (helloworld.cgi) in your Sites directory along the lines of

```
#!/usr/bin/perl
print "Hello World! I have a Mac, shouldn't you?";
exit;
```

After enabling execution (chmod +x helloworld.cgi), try running the application from the command line (./helloworld.cgi) and then by accessing its URL through a Web browser (http://localhost/~*<your username>*/helloworld.cgi). Although the command-line version runs fine, the browser reports an execution error message, as shown in Figure 28.2.

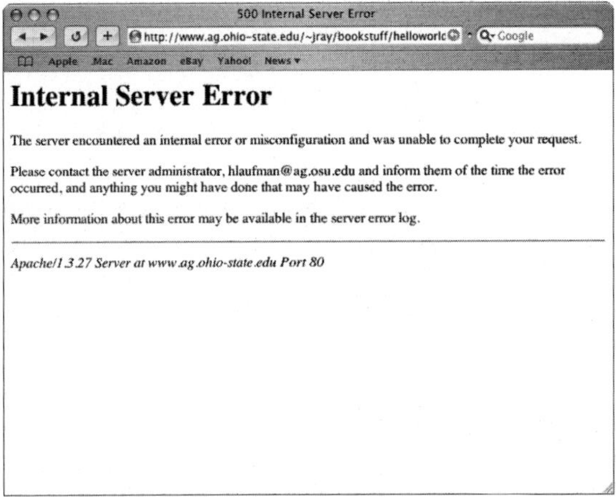

FIGURE 28.2 A simple Hello World isn't quite so simple.

So, what went wrong? Why is this program, which runs perfectly from a command prompt, broken when it tries to send its results over the Web?

The answer lies in the way the Web servers communicate their results back to a client browser.

HTTP Headers

For the simple Hello World application to work, it must produce the sort of output that a Web browser expects. To the browser, it should send the same response as when a standard `.html` static Web page is loaded. The easiest way to see that response is to generate one manually by using telnet to connect to a Web server and request a page. For example, to retrieve the primary page from the local Mac OS X box, you would telnet to `localhost` (or `127.0.0.1`) on port 80, and then use `GET / HTTP/1.0` (followed by two carriage returns to terminate the request) to retrieve the root level of the Web site:

```
% telnet localhost 80
Trying 127.0.0.1...
Connected to localhost.
Escape character is '^]'.
GET / HTTP/1.0

HTTP/1.1 200 OK
Date: Sun, 28 Jul 2002 03:39:06 GMT
Server: Apache/1.3.26 (Darwin)
Content-Location: index.html.en
Vary: negotiate,accept-language,accept-charset
```

```
TCN: choice
Last-Modified: Wed, 18 Jul 2001 23:44:21 GMT
ETag: "81b5e-5b0-3b561f55;3d3ba024"
Accept-Ranges: bytes
Content-Length: 1456
Connection: close
Content-Type: text/html
Content-Language: en
Expires: Sun, 28 Jul 2002 03:39:06 GMT
```

NOTE

This example does not include the text of the Web page, just the headers that are sent from the server. If you attempt this on your own machine, you'll get similar results, along with the contents of the `index.html` file within your `/Library/WebServer/Documents` folder.

There are quite a few interesting lines in the group of headers that are returned, such as the language content and an expiration date (used to keep a page from being cached beyond a certain day and time). Only one of these headers, however, is required.

The `Content-Type` header tells the remote Web browser what MIME type of file it is about to receive. When a user requests a JPEG image file, the server sends a header that reads

```
Content-Type: image/jpeg
```

Each type of file has a different MIME type (determined by the file `/private/etc/httpd/mime.types`). The server can decide what type of file it is about to serve based on the filename. Unfortunately, when working with CGIs, the Web server cannot be certain what type of information is going to be sent back. In fact, a single CGI could easily send an image with one request and an HTML page with another.

To create a fully working CGI, the first thing that the Web application must send is an appropriate MIME type. The initial version of `helloworld.cgi` did nothing but print out the Hello World message. The browser, however, was expecting a `Content-Type` header; when the header didn't appear, an error was generated. To correct the problem, the `Content-Type` must be printed before any other output occurs:

```
#!/usr/bin/perl
print "Content-Type: text/html\n\n";
print "Hello World! I have a Mac, shouldn't you?";
exit;
```

After making the small change to the script, this smallest of Web applications will happily run, as demonstrated in Figure 28.3.

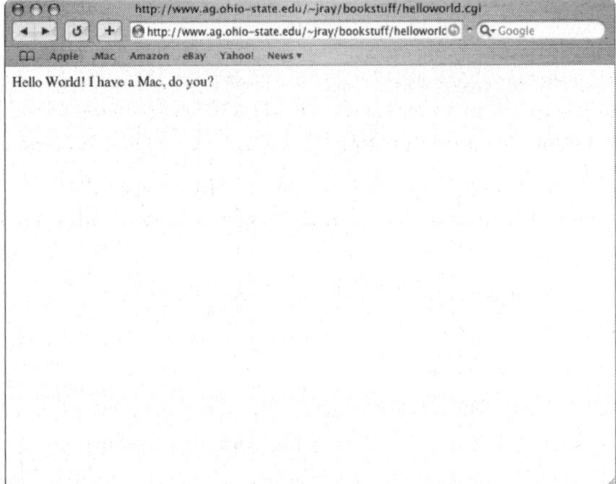

FIGURE 28.3 When the appropriate header is added to the CGI script, everything works as planned.

NOTE

You can add any valid headers to the output that you want. The `Content-Type` header is the only one required. Each header needs to be printed with a single newline character at the end of each line. The final header must have two newline characters at the end.

These headers must come before any other output but not necessarily at the start of the program. As long as no parts of the page body are produced before a `Content-Type` header is sent, the headers can occur anywhere within the script.

HTML Output

Creating the output of a CGI is the second step of developing a Web application. Unlike normal Perl scripts that produce plain text output, Web applications produce HTML. This can take a while to get used to, but keep in mind that the goal is to produce a dynamic Web page, not a plain text file.

When creating output from a CGI script, you can use any tags that you normally would in an HTML document. The trouble with doing this in Perl is that you have to escape all quotes when printing the HTML.

For example:

```
<table border="0" cellpadding="0" cellspacing="0">
```

When printed in Perl, this becomes

```
print "<table border=\"0\" cellpadding=\"0\" cellspacing=\"0\">";
```

When creating complicated output, this can get a bit tedious. It can also lead to programmers taking shortcuts and leaving out quotes around HTML tag attributes. The easiest way to display large amounts of complex HTML is to use Perl's alternative print method:

```
print <<ENDOFHTML;
  <table border="0" cellpadding="0" bgcolor="#FFDDDD" cellspacing="0">
  <tr><td align="right">This is more HTML</td></tr>
  </table>
ENDOFHTML
```

So, let's take a look at an example of CGI output in action. This is CGI output, so don't think that you won't be able to get information into your Web application. We're going to get there; just be patient!

Let's start with something simple, such as creating a script that displays all the images and the associated filenames in a given folder.

To start the CGI, build a simple Perl script that lists all the JPEG (`.jpg`) files in a folder. Listing 28.1 shows such a script.

LISTING 28.1 When Building a CGI, It's Often Easiest to Start with Something That Runs from the Command Line

```
1: #!/usr/bin/perl
2:
3: $imagedir="imagefolder";
4: @imagelist=glob("$imagedir/*jpg");
5:
6: for ($x=0;$x<@imagelist;$x++) {
7:     $imagename=$imagelist[$x];
8:     print "Image $x = $imagename\n";
9: }
```


Line 3 sets the variable `$imagedir` to the directory that contains the images. In this case, I'm using `imagefolder` inside my `Sites` directory, which is also where this script is located. I have not specified the entire path because I'm only interested in the location of the images relative to the script.

NOTE

CGIs only have access to the files within "Web space." You must use an image folder located in the same directory as your CGI, or you must dynamically build the URL for the images so that it matches a valid Web URL.

Line 4 loads all the filenames within `$imagedir` that end in `.jpg` into the array `@imagelist`. The Perl `glob()` function takes a path and filename pattern as input and then returns any results that match.

Lines 6–9 loop through each element in the `@imagelist` array, temporarily storing them in the `$imagename` variable. Print a line that displays the image and its name.

When run, the CGI-in-the-making, which I've named `showimages.cgi`, produces the list we were hoping for:

```
% ./showimages.cgi
Image 0 = imagefolder/897.jpg
Image 1 = imagefolder/920.jpg
Image 2 = imagefolder/921.jpg
Image 3 = imagefolder/922.jpg
Image 4 = imagefolder/923.jpg
Image 5 = imagefolder/924.jpg
Image 6 = imagefolder/925.jpg
Image 7 = imagefolder/927.jpg
Image 8 = imagefolder/928.jpg
Image 9 = imagefolder/929.jpg
Image 10 = imagefolder/94.jpg
Image 11 = imagefolder/940.jpg
Image 12 = imagefolder/942.jpg
Image 13 = imagefolder/944.jpg
Image 14 = imagefolder/945.jpg
Image 15 = imagefolder/947.jpg
Image 16 = imagefolder/948.jpg
Image 17 = imagefolder/949.jpg
Image 18 = imagefolder/96.jpg
```

So, how can this be translated into a CGI that displays the actual images in a Web browser? The first step, as mentioned earlier, is to produce a `Content-Type` header. Without this information, the browser has no idea what type of data it is receiving. At the same time, it's a good idea to translate any `\n` (newline) characters in the program into their XHTML equivalent: `<br/>`. Listing 28.2 shows the new CGI, which is capable of running in a browser.

LISTING 28.2 Adding a Content-Type and Fixing Line Breaks Is All You Need to Turn a Simple Command-Line Script into a CGI

```
1: #!/usr/bin/perl
2: print "Content-Type: text/html\n\n";
3: $imagedir="imagefolder";
4: @imagelist=glob("$imagedir/*jpg");
5:
6: for ($x=0;$x<@imagelist;$x++) {
7:     $imagename=$imagelist[$x];
8:     print "Image $x = $imagename<br/>";
9: }
```

NOTE

The `\n` (newline) characters that come after the `Content-Type` header should not be translated to HTML breaks. The browser interprets data after the header lines and always expects the final (and in this case, only) header to be followed by two newlines.

Figure 28.4 shows the result of running the new CGI in a Web browser.

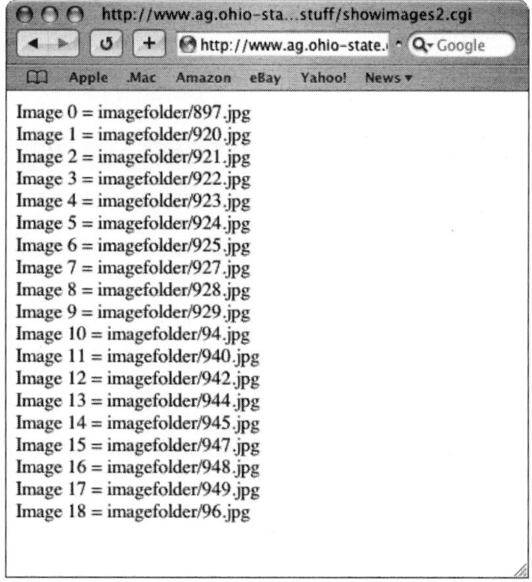

FIGURE 28.4 The command-line application now runs within a Web browser.

Unfortunately, things still aren't quite where we want them. What good is a CGI that lists pictures but doesn't display them? To be able to show the pictures, the CGI must be modified so that the name is used within an `<img>` (image) tag rather than just displayed on the screen. Try adding a new line that uses an image, rather than the image name, as shown in Listing 28.3.

LISTING 28.3 The Revised Code Displays an Image as Well as Its Name

```
#!/usr/bin/perl
print "Content-Type: text/html\n\n";
$imagedir="imagefolder";
@imagelist=glob("$imagedir/*jpg");

for ($x=0;$x<@imagelist;$x++) {
    $imagename=$imagelist[$x];
```

LISTING 28.3 Continued

```
8:     print "<img src=\"$imagename\" width=\"120\" height=\"90\"><br/>";
9:     print "Image $x = $imagename<br/>";
10: }
```

Line 8 performs the magic in the application. Using the same `$imagename` variable used to print an image's name (now in line 9), the variable is instead used to set an image source within an `<img>` tag. I've also added a width and height to the image tag to maintain some consistency in the display.

When viewed in a Web browser, the result resembles Figure 28.5.

> **NOTE**
>
> When setting an image size within the image tag, be aware that it doesn't change the physical size of the images being sent to the browser. The amount of data transmitted is identical to what would be sent if the width and height tags were not included. To resize the image in real-time requires the use of additional software, such as the GD Perl module, downloadable from CPAN.org.

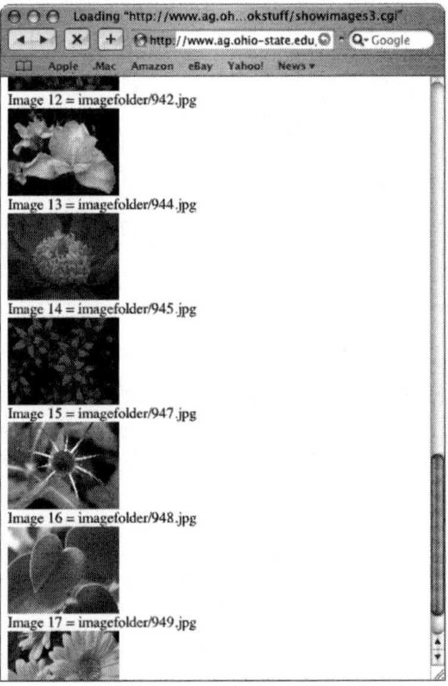

FIGURE 28.5 With the addition of the `<img>` tag, the images themselves can now be seen in the listing.

Hopefully, by now, you're starting to see the method to the madness. CGIs are just applications that write HTML as their output. The example we've been looking at is barely modified from the original command-line version, yet it includes full images for each file it finds. To fully realize the potential of a CGI, you must use HTML to its fullest. So far, the Perl script we've been developing is nothing but a simple port of the initial command-line utility. With only a small amount of work, we can turn it into something far more useful. Listing 28.4 shows a more developed version of the application. Unlike the previous version of the CGI, this revision uses an HTML table to structure the layout of the images.

LISTING 28.4 With a Little Work, the CGI Can Take Advantage of All of HTML's Layout Capabilities

```
1: #!/usr/bin/perl
2: print "Content-Type: text/html\n\n";
3:
4: $imagedir="imagefolder";
5: $columns=3;
6:
7: @imagelist=glob("$imagedir/*jpg");
8:
9: print "<table bgcolor=\"#FFFFFF\" border=\"1\" bordercolor=\"#000000\">";
10: while ($x<@imagelist) {
11:   print "<tr>";
12:   for ($y=0;$y<$columns;$y++) {
13:    $imagename=$imagelist[$x];
14:    if ($x<@imagelist) {
15:     $x++;
16:     print "<td align=\"center\">";
17:     print "<img src=\"$imagename\" width=\"120\" height=\"90\"><br/>";
18:     $imagename=~s/$imagedir\///;
19:     print "<font type=\"Arial\">$imagename</font>";
20:     print "</td>";
21:    }
22:   }
23:   print "</tr>";
24: }
25: print "</table>";
```


Line 5 sets a limit for the number of columns in the table (how many images will be displayed in a single line), whereas line 9 sets up the table structure using a table with a white (`#FFFFFF`) background and a black (`#000000`) border. In line 10, instead of using a `for` loop to go through each image, the counter `$x` is incremented when an image tag is output. The `while` loop continues as long as the counter is less than the total number of images.

Line 11 starts a new table row (<tr>). Lines 12–22 loop through the number of columns set for the table. For each column, increment the variable `$x`. If `$x` has not exceeded the total number of images available, output a table data cell (<td>) that contains the image and its name. Line 18 removes the path from the image filename. This is done using a simple Perl regular expression search and replace. After displaying all the data cells for a row, line 23 ends the table row (</tr>). Line 24 repeats lines 11–23 until all images have been displayed, and line 25 ends the table (</table>).

Figure 28.6 shows the output from the finalized CGI.

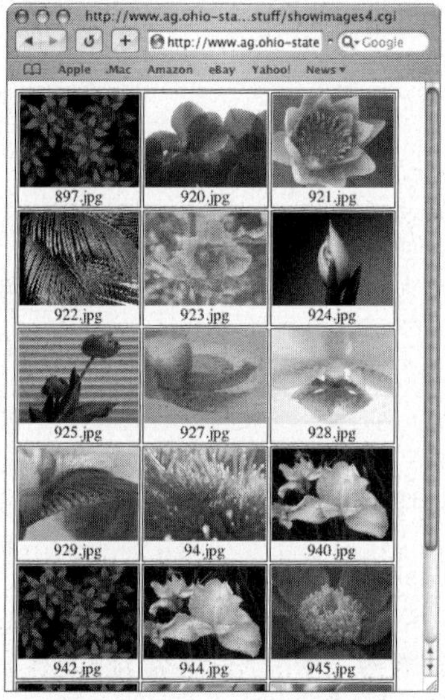

FIGURE 28.6 The final version of the CGI outputs the image directory in a nicely formatted table.

NOTE

The most common type of CGI/Web-application output is `text/html`. This doesn't mean that a Web application can't output other types of data. If your script opens, reads, and outputs a JPEG file, it would use `Content-type: image/jpeg`. Any type of media that can be sent by a Web server can also be sent from a CGI.

CGI Input: `CGI.pm`

This quick-and-dirty image viewer provides a reasonable start to CGI programming, but it is lacking in the one area that can be used to create truly dynamic and user-driven sites—user input. Getting input into a CGI can be a bit of a challenge if you're starting from scratch.

Thankfully, others have been here before, and Perl includes a module (CGI.pm) that handles most of the dirty work for you. Because we're only going to be using a few of the functions to handle incoming data, you might want to read http://stein.cshl.org/WWW/software/CGI/ for full documentation. We will be using the software in *function* mode rather than *object-oriented* mode to avoid delving into the complexities of Perl's object-oriented model.

We'll introduce three functions:

- use CGI qw(:standard)—Makes the CGI.pm functions available to your Perl code.
- header(<*MIME-type*>)—Sends an appropriate Content-type header to the client browser. If no header is specified (that is, header()), the type text/html is assumed.
- param(<variable name>)—Returns the value of a submitted form variable.

Let's take a look at practical CGI input by altering the Hello World application we used previously so that it personalizes the message. If your name happens to be World, you might skip this exercise. Listing 28.5 shows the helloworld.cgi modified to display a person's name. I'll refer to this new version as helloworld2.cgi.

LISTING 28.5 Using the CGI.pm Module, Any Script Can Receive Input

```
1: #!/usr/bin/perl
2: use CGI qw(:standard);
3:
4: $myname=""param('name');
5:
6: ""header;
7: print "Hello $myname! I have a Mac, shouldn't you?";
```

Although mostly apparent, the breakdown of the code is as follows:

Line 2 loads CGI.pm—the Perl CGI module. Line 4 sets the variable $myname to the submitted variable name. Line 6 sends the required content-type, and line 7 prints a greeting containing the name submitted to the CGI in the name variable.

As you can see, the number of changes to the original application is small. This CGI should now correctly allow a name to be sent to it for use in a customized greeting. The problem remains, however, how do you go about actually sending the variable and value to the application?

Because the parse() function handles either POST or GET method transmission, there are two ways that this new CGI can be called. Using the URL to pass a variable is the easiest, so let's start there. Start a Web browser and enter the URL for the new CGI, adding **?name=John** (or whatever is appropriate for you) to the end:

http://localhost/~<*your username*>/helloworld2.cgi?name=**<*your name*>**

My test system, for example, looks like this:

```
http://localhost/~john/helloworld2.cgi?name=John
```

Figure 28.7 shows the new personalized message.

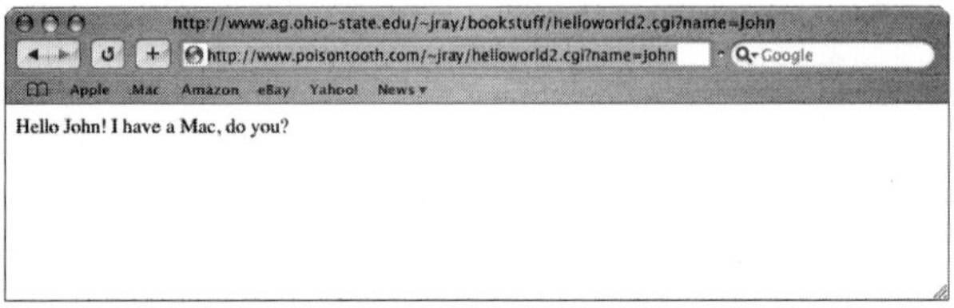

FIGURE 28.7 Providing an input method for CGIs enables you to customize their output.

To use the POST method to send information to the CGI, create an HTML form that submits its data to the Web application. For `helloworld2.cgi`, the form needs nothing more than a name field and a submit button:

```
<form action="helloworld2.cgi" method="post">
Enter your name: <input type="text" name="name">
<input type="submit" name="submit">
</form>
```

Save the form code in a new HTML file (`hello.html`) in the same directory as the `helloworld2.cgi`. Open the new Web page in your browser, type a name, and click Submit. You should see results identical to the earlier URL-based input shown in Figure 28.7.

NOTE

If you don't include the `method="post"` attribute for the form, or use `method="get"`, submitting the form actually passes the name data through the URL.

As it stands, if you're using a separate HTML page to submit information to the CGI, two files compose the entire project: `helloworld2.cgi` and `hello.html`. This isn't excessive, but it can be consolidated. Rather than `hello.html` containing the form, it can be added directly to `helloworld2.cgi`. Listing 28.6 consolidates the form and application into a single CGI file.

LISTING 28.6 A CGI Can Encapsulate HTML and Application Logic

```
#!/usr/bin/perl
use CGI qw(:standard);

```

LISTING 28.6 Continued

```
4: $myname=param('name');""
5: ""header;
6:
7: if ($myname eq "") {
8:   print <<ENDOFHTML;
9:     <form action="helloworld2.cgi" method="post">
10:     Enter your name: <input type="text" name="name">
11:     <input type="submit" name="submit">
12:     </form>
13: ENDOFHTML
14:   exit;
15: }
16:
17: print "Hello $myname! I have a Mac, shouldn't you?";
```

Consolidating the code into the single CGI brings into play some of the session management techniques discussed earlier in the chapter. This revision of `helloworld2.cgi` has two states—prior to entering the name and after entering the name. To determine what the program should be doing, it checks the value of `$myname`—if a name hasn't been set, the HTML form should be displayed. If a name is defined, the Hello message is shown. A more detailed analysis of the changes follows:

Line 7 checks to see whether the `$myname` variable is empty. If it is, this is the first time the CGI has been executed—the user hasn't entered his name yet.

Lines 8–13 display the HTML form, and line 14 exits the CGI. This line is more important than it might appear. If it is not included, the CGI will continue to execute after displaying the HTML form; this will generate an empty hello message immediately following the form. Finally, line 17 displays the hello message with the user's name.

This demonstrates the fundamental workings of CGI applications. Although the example is only a two-step process, it could easily be extended to multiple steps by passing data from screen to screen. For an encore, let's add another form to the hello page that collects the user's age. After submitting this second form, a third page is shown with the user's name, age, and a few comments. Listing 28.7 shows the final version of this overly long Hello World application.

LISTING 28.7 The Extended Version of Hello World Now Includes Three Steps and Demonstrates CGI Input and Variable Passing

```
#!/usr/bin/perl
use CGI qw(:standard);""

```

LISTING 28.7 Continued

```
4: $myname"=param('name')";
6: $myage=param('age')"";
7:
8: ""header;
9:
10: if ($myname eq "") {
11:   print <<ENDOFHTML;
12:     <form action="helloworld2.cgi" method="post">
13:     Enter your name: <input type="text" name="name">
14:     <input type="submit" name="submit">
15:     </form>
16: ENDOFHTML
17:   exit;
18: }
19:
20: if ($myage eq "") {
21:   print "Hello $myname!";
22:   print "</br>";
23:   print <<ENDOFHTML2;
24:     <form action="helloworld2.cgi" method="post">
25:     Enter your age: <input type="text" name="age"><br/>
26:     <input type="hidden" name="name" value="$myname">
27:     <input type="submit" name="submit">
28:     </form>
29: ENDOFHTML2
30:   exit;
31: }
32:
33: $dayage=$myage*365;
34: $hourage=$dayage*24;
35: $minage=$hourage*60;
36: print "Hello again $myname!<br\/>";
37: print "You have lived for $dayage days...<br\/>";
38: print ".. or $hourage hours...<br\/>";
39: print ".. or $minage minutes!<br\/>";
```

This final revision adds an additional form and output screen. Lines 20–31 display the standard hello message but also show a form where the user is prompted for his age. What makes this form unique is that it includes a hidden name field set to the original `$myname` value. This shows how information can be carried from page to page.

The final page, generated in lines 33–39, calculates a user's name in days, hours, and minutes. This demonstrates that the name has indeed been carried through each of the CGI screens.

As an exercise, you might want to try adding a search screen to the image catalog creator that was built earlier in the chapter. Suppose, for instance, that there are multiple image folders to view, a need for the number of columns to be adjusted, or even searching based on the image filename—these features can all be added easily to the application. Listing 28.8 is a two-step version of the image catalog application.

LISTING 28.8 This New Version of the Image Catalog CGI Now Offers Searching and Display Settings

```
#!/usr/bin/perl

use CGI qw(:standard);""

$imagedir=param('"imagedir')";
$imagename=param('"imagename');"
$columns=param('"columns');"
$match=param('"match')"
if ($imagedir=~/\//) { $imagedir="imagefolder"; }
if ($imagename=~/\//) { $imagename=""; }

""header;
if ($imagedir eq "") {
  print <<ENDOFHTML;
    <form action="showimages5.cgi" method="post">
Image dir: <input type="text" name="imagedir" value="imagefolder"><br/>
    Select the number of columns in the display: <select name="columns">
      <option>1</option>
      <option>2</option>
      <option>3</option>
      <option>4</option>
    </select><br/>
    Show images that match: <input type="text" name="match">
    <input type="submit" name="submit">
    </form>
ENDOFHTML
}

@imagelist=glob("$imagedir/*$match*jpg");

print "<table bgcolor=\"#FFFFFF\" border=\"1\" bordercolor=\"#000000\">";
```

28

LISTING 28.8 Continued

```
32: while ($x<@imagelist) {
33:   print "<tr>";
34:   for ($y=0;$y<$columns;$y++) {
35:    $imagename=$imagelist[$x];
36:    if ($x<@imagelist) {
37     $x++;
38:     print "<td align=\"center\">";
39:     print "<img src=\"$imagename\" width=\"120\" height=\"90\"><br/>";
40:     $imagename=~s/$imagedir\///;
41:     print "<font type=\"Arial\">$imagename</font>";
42:     print "</td>";
43:    }
44:   }
45:   print "</tr>";
46: }
47: print "</table>";
```

The only modifications to the original image catalog are the addition of lines 3–27. The rest remains the same.

Line 3 loads the `CGI.pm` module.

Lines 5–8 store values for the columns to display, image directory to use, and a string to search for in the image names.

Lines 9–10 are very important. When processing user input, an application can never trust the incoming data. If the image catalog blindly accepted an arbitrary path, it could pose a serious security risk and give the user access to other parts of the filesystem. For that reason, any input that includes a / is disregarded. This eliminates the potential for the user to input any path information.

If an image directory has not been set (such as the application has not received the search criteria yet), lines 13–27 display a search form. This is a simple HTML form that includes elements for setting the image directory, number of columns, and a search string for the image name.

A modification to the original `glob`, this line 29 variation adds the `$match` string to the pattern, displaying only images that match the specified string.

By now, you should have a grasp of the basics of CGI programming, and how Perl can be used to create quick-and-dirty Web applications.

Enabling `mod_perl`

If you've decided on Perl for your Apache development environment, you might want to look into the `mod_perl` module. This add-on attaches a Perl interpreter to the Apache process, greatly speeding up CGI execution. If your site makes extensive use of large Perl applications, give it a try.

mod_perl can be enabled by following these steps:

1. Create a directory /Library/Webserver/perl-bin/ to hold your mod_perl-based CGIs.
2. Uncomment the following lines in /etc/httpd/httpd.conf by removing the pound (#) signs:

   ```
   #LoadModule perl_module libexec/httpd/libperl.so
   ```

   and

   ```
   #AddModule mod_perl.c
   ```

3. Add the following lines to the end of your /etc/httpd/httpd.conf file:

   ```
   <IfModule mod_perl.c>
     Alias /perl-bin/ /Library/WebServer/perl-bin/
     <Location /perl-bin/>
       SetHandler perl-script
       PerlHandler Apache::Registry
       Options +ExecCGI
       PerlSendHeader On
     </Location>
   </IfModule>
   ```

4. Restart Apache using the Sharing System Preferences pane or /usr/sbin/apachectl restart.
5. Perl CGIs run from the new /Library/WebServer/perl-bin directory (via the URL http://<*hostname or localhost*>/perl-bin/<*cgi name*>) will be accelerated.

28

Although Perl is certainly capable of generating large-scale applications, many developers have had their heads turned by the popular PHP language. If you've grasped the basics of Perl, moving on to PHP will be no problem.

NOTE

Depending on what you're doing, and the state of Apple's Apache implementation when you read this, you may need to compile Apache with mod_perl statically, rather than a dynamically loaded Apache module (DSO). There are known stability problems with the included dynamically loaded module. Linking issues also plague the module and result in partial or unpredictable execution of popular Perl applications.

You compile mod_perl easily by following the instructions at http://david.wheeler.net/osx.html.

PHP

PHP (PHP Hypertext Preprocessor; it's recursive) is a relatively new language that integrates with the Apache Web server. Whereas Perl is a general-purpose programming language, PHP provides Web-specific functions that can speed up development time significantly.

One of the primary differences between Perl and PHP is how it is programmed. With Perl, the focus is on the application logic; integrating an interface is secondary. When using PHP, the logic is embedded into the HTML. Yes, there are means of writing embedded Perl, but the PHP language itself was designed to be used in this fashion from the start.

A PHP developer can use traditional Web development tools, such as Macromedia Dreamweaver MX or Adobe GoLive, to create an interface and then attach logic. For example, in Perl, we used code like this to print a variable within some HTML:

```
print <<HTML;
    print "<tr>";
    print "<td align=\"center\">$myname</td>";
    print "</tr>";
HTML
```

The equivalent code in PHP looks like this:

```
<tr>
<td align="center"><?php print $myname; ?></td>
</tr>
```

As you can see, the application code is entirely isolated from the HTML. PHP code is contained with its own tags: `<?php` to start and `?>` to end. As Apache reads a PHP file, it executes the code in the PHP tags and then sends the final result to the waiting browser. The remote user cannot see these special tags in the HTML source—your application logic is safe from prying eyes. In addition to a clean programming model, PHP offers features such as built-in database access, advanced security, and real-time graphic generation.

Activating PHP

Your Mac OS X 10.3 system comes with a fully functioning version of PHP installed. Activating it is simply a matter of uncommenting a few lines in the `/etc/httpd/httpd.conf` file. You'll need to be logged in as root, or use `sudo` from the command line to edit the file. Open it, and look for the following lines:

```
#LoadModule php4_module    libexec/httpd/libphp4.so
#AddModule mod_php4.c
```

NOTE

These lines are noncontiguous in the configuration file—they're shown together here to save space. Activate PHP by removing the comment (#) symbol from the front of each line.

Next, at the bottom of the http.conf file, add the following two lines:

```
AddType application/x-httpd-php .php
AddType application/x-httpd-php-source .phps
```

The AddType Apache directives tell your Web server that files ending in .php should be processed as PHP applications, whereas .phps files will be displayed as syntax-highlighted source code.

TIP

PHP's source-code syntax highlighting is a helpful feature of the programming language. If you have a PHP source file with the extension .phps on your Web site, you can retrieve it and see an automatically highlighted and formatted version of the code.

Unfortunately, this implies that you need to have two copies of a PHP file to both run it and view the source code. You can avoid this limitation by creating a symbolic link from the .php file to the .phps file:

```
ln -s <your file>.php <your file>.phps
```

When the link is in place, you can both run your Web application and view the source code at the same time.

To fine-tune the PHP configuration, you'll need to install a PHP .ini file in /etc/php.ini. Apple has included the file /etc/php.ini.default on your system. Copy this file to /etc/php.ini, then open it in your text editor of choice.

First, make sure that any system-specific settings are set. Usually, the default settings work perfectly fine. You might want to look at the resource settings, however, because they can be used to make sure that renegade scripts don't eat up the memory and CPU time on your system. Look in the php.ini for these lines:

```
;;;;;;;;;;;;;;;;;;;
; Resource Limits ;
;;;;;;;;;;;;;;;;;;;

max_execution_time = 30  ; Maximum execution time of each script, in seconds
memory_limit = 8M       ; Maximum amount of memory a script may consume (8MB)
```

By default, scripts can use up to 8MB of memory and take 30 seconds to execute. For many CGIs, these are rather liberal values. You can reduce them as you want; I've cut them in half on my system and haven't had any problems thus far.

Additionally, you should enable safe mode (safe_mode = On) on a public-use production server. This virtually eliminates the need to worry about environment variables being modified and misused:

```
; Safe Mode
safe_mode         =    On
safe_mode_allowed_env_vars = PHP_ ; Setting certain environment variables
                 ; may be a potential security breach.
                 ; This directive contains a comma-delimited
                 ; list of prefixes. In Safe Mode, the
                 ; user may only alter environment
                 ; variables whose names begin with the
                 ; prefixes supplied here.
                 ; By default, users will only be able
                 ; to set environment variables that begin
                 ; with PHP_ (e.g. PHP_FOO=BAR).
                 ; Note: If this directive is empty, PHP
                 ; will let the user modify ANY environment
                 ; variable!
safe_mode_protected_env_vars = LD_LIBRARY_PATH; This directive is a comma-
                 ; delimited list of environment variables,
                 ; that the end user won't be able to
                 ; change using putenv().
                 ; These variables will be protected
                 ; even if safe_mode_allowed_env_vars is
                 ; set to allow to change them.
disable_functions    =     ; This directive allows you to disable certain
                 ; functions for security reasons. It receives
                 ; a comma separated list of function names.
                 ; This directive is *NOT* affected by whether
                 ; Safe Mode is turned on or off.
```

This combination of settings enables you, the administrator, to prohibit environment variables from being modified unless they begin with one of the listed prefixes (`safe_mode_protected_env_vars`). You can also specify environment variables that, under no circumstances, should ever be allowed to change, regardless of the prefix settings. Finally, if there are certain functions you'd rather not be available to users, you can list these here as well (`disable_functions`).

Finally, to activate the changes, restart the Apache Web server using the Sharing Preferences pane, or by typing **`sudo /usr/sbin/apachectl restart`** from the command line.

To verify that PHP is working, create a file (`test.php`) within one of your Web directories (such as `Sites` within your home directory):

```
<?php
  phpinfo();
?>
```

Load this test page using a Web browser. If the installation was successful, you should see a screen similar to Figure 28.8.

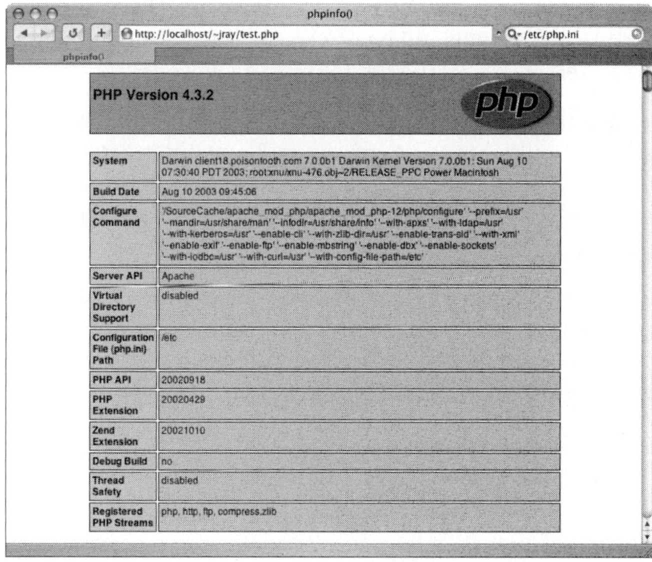

FIGURE 28.8 The `phpinfo()` function generates a screen of PHP installation information.

> **NOTE**
>
> In the first edition of *Mac OS X Unleashed*, we provided instructions on compiling PHP directly. Unfortunately, within weeks of writing the chapter, PHP compilation "broke" on Mac OS X. Subsequent distributions of PHP have had similar but slightly different problems. For that reason, we're foregoing the direct compilation because it would be outdated by the time you read the text.
>
> Luckily, Apple has started to take PHP seriously and has been actively updating the Apple-provided version of PHP as new distributions become available. If, however, you want to compile the latest version on your own, visit `http://www.entropy.ch/software/macosx/php/`. The Entropy site has consistently provided up-to-date information on compiling the latest PHP software for Mac OS X.

PHP Syntax

The best introduction to programming PHP is a background in C or Perl. Check out Chapter 22 as a starter guide for that language. PHP borrows heavily from Perl's free-form open scripting model and auto data conversion. What truly makes PHP shine is the built-in Web functions. Let's take a brief look at what you need to get started and then examine some of the unique features.

Syntax

PHP programs are created as standard text files within any of your Web-enabled directories. To execute the script, you must have the extension `.php`. This does not have a bearing on the HTML contents of the file. In fact, you can have an HTML file that contains no PHP code but ends in `.php`—it will still be served correctly, although with a slight performance penalty as the server checks the file for executable code.

PHP code itself is typically embedded within the `<?php` and `?>` brackets. Failing to place these tags around code results in the programming being interpreted as text within an HTML document. Even if you are working with a file that contains no HTML at all, it must still place all the PHP script within the brackets. There can be multiple PHP start and end tags in a single document.

If you've written JavaScript, this is similar to the behavior of the `<script>` and `</script>` tags that embed JavaScript code into a document. Regardless of how many PHP code segments are in your program, the code can be considered all part of one big global block. The variables defined in one section are available in another. For example:

```
<?php $myname="John"; ?>
This is some standard HTML in the middle...<BR><BR>
<?php print $myname; ?>
```

This code fragment assigns the value John to `$myname`, includes a bit of HTML, and finally prints the value of `$myname` (John). Even though `$myname` occurs within two separate PHP blocks, the value is still maintained.

NOTE

Perhaps not surprisingly, PHP can be embedded with the `<script>` and `</script>` tags. To use this format, just include PHP as the scripting language within the first `tag: <script language="php">`.

Each line of PHP code must end in a semicolon (;) to be correctly executed. Because of this requirement, extremely long lines of code can be broken across multiple lines to improve legibility.

Data Types

Like Perl, PHP's data types are typecast from one to another internally. Although there is one primary data type, PHP is an object-oriented language and is used to create arbitrary object types with their own properties. Object-oriented programming is beyond the scope of this text, so only the basics are covered here. Don't worry; there's more than enough to start building complex Web applications.

- `$<variable name>`—PHP defines a variable as an alphanumeric string prefaced by a `$`. Variable names cannot begin with a number. The variable can contain text, binary data, numbers, and so on. Type conversion happens automatically during program execution.

- $<*variable name*>[<*index*>]—Arrays offer more flexibility than Perl. An array can be defined during the course of program execution by adding an [index] to the end of a variable name. Unlike Perl, which differentiates between a standard array and associative arrays, an array index in PHP can be either a number or a string.

PHP variables are unique creatures and can be used in interesting ways. For example, the contents of a variable can be interpreted as variables themselves. Assume that you have a variable named $peach. Obviously, you can reference this variable by name ($peach). Now assume that a second variable, $fruit, contains the string peach "peach". Using this second variable, you can reference the contents of the first variable through $$fruit. This works because $$fruit is functionally identical to typing $"peach", which in turn is equivalent to $peach. This same technique can be applied to function calls to create a logic flow that changes itself based on variables in the program.

NOTE

Although not commonly used in simple applications, PHP does support passing variables by reference. As in C, you can pass a reference to a variable by placing an ampersand (&) in front: &<$*variable name*>.

Basic Operators

The comparison and assignment operations work much like a simplified version of their Perl counterparts. The primary difference is that string comparisons are identical to numeric comparisons in syntax within PHP. Table 28.1 contains the common PHP operators.

TABLE 28.1 Common PHP Operators

Operator	Action	Description
==	Equals	Tests for equality
!=	Not equal	Tests for inequality
=	Assignment	Assigns the value on the right to the variable on the left
*	Multiplication	Multiplies two values together
/	Division	Divides two values
+	Addition	Adds two numbers together
-	Subtraction	Subtracts one number from another
.	Concatenation	Concatenates two strings together
&&	AND	Performs a logical AND on two values
||	OR	Performs a logical OR on two values

As previously mentioned, PHP automatically handles type conversions for you, making it possible to write code that looks like this:

```
<?php
$a="1";
$b="3";
$c=$a.$b;
$c=$c*2;
?>
```

Here, two strings, 1 and 3, are concatenated together and stored in `$c`. This new value is then multiplied by 2. Printing the result would display 26—even though the only true number used in the calculation was 2 (during the multiplication).

There are a few shortcuts to the assignment as well. For example, incrementing or decrementing a number is common. Written in long form, adding 1 to the existing value of a variable `$a` looks like this:

```
$a=$a+1;
```

This can be shortened to

```
$a++;
```

The same applies to subtraction, using the minus (`-`) symbol.

Another shortcut applies to concatenating, adding, or subtracting to an existing value. For example, this line of code concatenates `$b` onto the end of `$a`:

```
$a=$a.$b;
```

The same thing can be written as

```
$a.=$b;
```

For addition and subtraction, just substitute the appropriate operator in place of the period (`.`). The basic syntax remains the same.

Control Structures

Two types of control structures will be discussed here: linear flow operators and looping constructs. Linear flow operators can change the course of a program based on variables and other conditions. Looping constructs, on the other hand, can repeat sections of code based on similar criteria. Together they enable software to adapt to a particular task, instead of being hard-coded to work with one set of input.

`if-then-else`

The most common linear flow control structure is the `if-then-else` statement. This can evaluate one or more conditions and act on them accordingly. The basic PHP `if-then` statement is structured like this:

```
if <condition> {
    <do something>;
}
```

This statement can be expanded to include an alternative course of action if the original condition is not met. This is considered an `if-then-else` statement:

```
if <condition> {
    <do something>;
} else {
    <do something else>;
}
```

One final variation of the statement exists that can evaluate multiple conditions within the single statement. This last variation is the `if-then-elsif` statement.

```
if <condition> {
    <do something>;
} elsif <another condition> {
    <do something else>;
} else {
    <do yet another thing>;
}
```

This example includes a single `elsif` line, but, depending on the needs of the programmer, this can be repeated as many times as necessary. A less verbose way to accomplish the same goal is to use the `switch` statement.

switch

The `switch` statement takes a value as input and defines a set of possible outcomes that can occur, depending on that value. The best way to understand how this works is to look at an example:

```
switch ($x) {
    case 0:
        print "x=0";
        break;
    case 1:
        print "x=1";
        break;
    case 2:
```

```
        print "x=2";
        break;
    default:
        print "none of the above";
        break;
}
```

This piece of code examines the value of $x. If it is 0, PHP prints x=0. If $x equals 1, the code prints x=1..., and so on. If $x doesn't match any of the listed values (0, 1, 2), it uses the default value and prints none of the above.

The switch statement can be extended to include as many cases as needed. In addition, the cases do not have to be numeric. You can just as easily include strings:

```
switch ($name) {
    case 'John':
        print "John has a dog named Maddy";
        break;
    case 'Robyn':
        print "Robyn has a dog named Coco";
        break;
    case 'Jack':
        print "Jack has a bag of M&Ms";
        break;
    case default:
        print "I don't know you!";
        break;
}
```

The two portions of the switch statement that might require a bit more explanation are the break statement and the default case.

The break causes the switch statement to exit. If break is not executed, all code after the matching case is executed. If John is matched, all the print statements are executed until a break is encountered.

The default case is optional. It is executed only if none of the other cases is matched. It's usually a good idea to have a default case to keep untrapped errors from occurring.

for

The for loop is the most commonly encountered loop in programming, regardless of the language. This loop executes a block of code until a condition is met. Each iteration of a for-next loop increments (or decrements) a counter variable. The loop is constructed using this syntax:

```
for (<initialization>;<execution condition>;<increment>) {
    <code block>
}
```

The *initialization* sets up the loop and initializes the counter variable to its default state. The *execution condition* is checked in each iteration of the loop; if it evaluates to false, the loop ends. Finally, the increment is a piece of code that defines an operation performed on the counter variable each time the loop is run. For example, the following loop counts from 0 to 9:

```
for ($count=0;$count<10;$count++) {
    print "Count = $count";
}
```

The counter, `$count`, is set to 0 when the loop starts. With each repetition, it is incremented by 1 (`$count++`). The loop exits when the counter reaches 10 (`$count<10`).

The format for the PHP for loop is identical to the Perl syntax.

`while`

The `while` loop executes while a condition evaluates to true. Unlike a `for` loop, which usually ends based on a change in the counter, the `while` loop requires that something change within the code block that causes the condition to evaluate as false.

```
while (<execution condition>) {
    <code block>
}
```

The previous `for` example counted from 0 to 9. This same loop translated into a `while` loop looks like this:

```
$count=0;
while ($count<10) {
    print "Count = $count";
    $count++;
}
```

When you're using `while`/`do-while` loops, be sure that the execution condition eventually evaluates to false. It's easy to write infinite loops using this structure.

`do-while`

Similar to the basic `while` loop, a `do-while` loop runs until a preset condition evaluates to false. The difference between the two loop styles is where the execution condition is checked. In a `while` loop, the condition is evaluated at the start of the loop. `do-while` loops, on the other hand, evaluate the condition at the end:

```
do {
    <code block>
} while (<execution condition>);
```

Again, let's translate the count from 0 to 9 into a `do-while` loop. As you can see, the difference is slight.

```
$count=0;
do {
    print "Count = $count";
    $count++;
} while ($count<10);
```

> **NOTE**
>
> Many languages have a similar loop structure known as a `do-until` loop. The only difference is that the `do-until` loop exits after a condition is met, not after it has become false.

Functions

Like any good programming language, PHP supports the notion of *functions*—independent pieces of code that can act on input and return a result. As you develop Web applications, you'll find that a reasonable amount of code is reused each time. If applications are programmed as modularly as possible, you can create a library of commonly used functions to share among multiple applications and developers.

A function is set up using the function keyword; values are returned to the main program using `return`. For example:

```
function addnumbers($arg1,$arg2) {
    $result=$arg1+$arg2;
    return($result);
}
```

This function accepts two arguments (`$arg1` and `$arg2`), adds them together, and then returns the result to the main program. The `addnumbers` function could be called like this:

```
$theresult=&addnumbers(1,5);
```

In this example, the function is called with a preceding ampersand (`&`). This is optional but is required in code where the function's definition occurs after the function call is used in the code.

By default, all variables used in a function are automatically considered local to that function and cannot be accessed outside the function code. To make a variable's scope global, use the `global` keyword within a function:

```
global <variable name>;
```

A variable that is declared global can be accessed from the main program block as well as the declaring function.

Common Functions

It's pointless to try to document all PHP's capabilities in this chapter. More than 1,500 functions are available in the PHP 4.3.x release. Table 28.2 provides a quick reference to some of the more interesting and useful functions. For those who are interested, when compiling this list I surveyed more than a dozen PHP scripts and noted the most frequently used operations as well as those needed for the examples in the chapter.

TABLE 28.2 With More Than 1,500 Available Functions, PHP Is Anything But Limited

Function	Purpose
addslashes(<*string*>)	Escapes special characters within strings (such as '"') and returns the resulting string.
chop(<*string*>)	Removes trailing whitespace from a string and returns the result.
file(<*url*>)	Reads a file from a URL (local, FTP, Web) and returns an array of each line in the file.
header(<*string*>)	Outputs a header before processing any HTML output.
join(<*glue string*>,<*array*>)	Returns a single string containing all the elements of a given array joined together with the "glue" string. Same as implode.
mysql_connect(<*host*>,<*user*>, <*pass*>)	Returns a link to a MySQL server on a given host.
mysql_close(<*link*>)	Given a database link, closes the connection.
mysql_db_query(<*database*>, <*sql statement*>)	Sends an SQL statement to the MySQL server. Returns a pointer to the resulting data.
mysql_fetch_array(<*result*>)	Returns an array with the next available row of MySQL data from the resultset. The array is indexed by field name.
mysql_num_rows(<*result*>)	Returns the number of rows in a query result, or an error if the original query was invalid.
preg_replace(<*regex*>, <*replace string*>,<*string*>)	Searches a string for a Perl-style regular expression, replaces it with another, and returns the new string.
print "<*output*>"	Displays an output string. This is identical to the echo keyword.
opendir(<*directory name*>)	Opens a directory for reading and returns a file handle.
readdir(<*file handle*>)	Returns the next filename within a directory opened with opendir. Returns false if no more files are available.
require(<*filename*>)	Includes the contents of another file within the PHP code.
session_start()	Initializes a new session.
session_register(<*variable*>)	Registers a variable with a session—making it available in subsequent Web page accesses. Do not include the $ with the name of the variable.
session_unregister(<*variable*>)	Unregisters a session variable.

TABLE 28.2 Continued

Function	Purpose
`session_destroy()`	Removes the active session.
`sort(<array>)`	Sorts an array.
`soundex(<string>)`	Returns a soundex value for a given string. This value is based on the sound of a string and can be used to compare two strings that sound similar but are spelled differently.
`split(<pattern>,<string>)`	Splits a string based on the characters in `<pattern>` and returns each of the results as the element in an array.
`stripslashes(<string>)`	Removes slashes from a string—the opposite of `addslashes`—and returns the result.
`strlen(<string>)`	Returns the length of a given string.

Visit `http://www.php.net/quickref.php` for a full list of the PHP functions.

PHP in Practice

In the Perl portion of this chapter, we created a simple image catalog. Let's see how that catalog can be rewritten in PHP. Listing 28.9 shows a PHP version of the Perl-image catalog.

LISTING 28.9 The Image Catalog, Rewritten in PHP

```
<?php if (!$imagedir) { ?>
    <form action="showimages1.php" method="post">
Choose image dir: <input type="text" name="imagedir" value="imagefolder"><br>
    Select the number of columns in the display: <select name="columns">
      <option>1</option>
      <option>2</option>
      <option>3</option>
      <option>4</option>
    </select><br>
    Show images that match: <input type="text" name="match">
    <input type="submit" name="submit">
    </form>
<?php exit; } ?>

<table bgcolor="#FFFFFF" border="1" bordercolor="#000000">
<?php
$handle=opendir("$imagedir");
while ($imagename = readdir($handle)) {
  if ($count==0 && $loop==0) { print "<tr>"; $loop=1; }
  if (preg_match("/.*$match.*\.jpg$/i",$imagename)) { ?>
    <td align=center>
```

LISTING 28.9 Continued

```
22:<img src="<?php print"$imagedir/$imagename"; ?>" width="120" height="90"><br>
23:     <font type="Arial"><?php print $imagename; ?></font>
24:     </td><?php
25:     $count++;
26:     if ($count==$columns) { print "</tr>"; $count=0; $loop=0; }
27:   }
28: }
29: if ($count!=0) { print "</tr>"; }
30: ?>
31: </table>
```

The first two things you should notice looking at this code are that it is shorter than the Perl code and that the PHP is embedded in the HTML, rather than the HTML being embedded in the programming.

As the PHP application begins sending output, it automatically adds a `text/html` `Content-Type` header. In addition, no additional library or module, such as `CGI.pm`, is required. When a form posts information to a PHP program, the form variables are automatically translated into PHP variables. For example, an input field with the name address becomes the variable `$address` when submitted to a PHP script. These shortcuts enable you to focus on the code rather than the specifics of HTTP.

A breakdown of the changes in the code follows:

Lines 1–13 check whether the variable `$imagedir` is defined. If it isn't, the user hasn't submitted a search request yet, and the search form should be displayed. Unlike Perl, which used `print` to show the form, PHP `if-then` tags can encompass HTML blocks. In this case, if the variable isn't defined, the HTML in the `if-then` is sent to the browser; otherwise, it is skipped.

Line 15 starts the HTML output table. Line 17 opens the image directory for reading. PHP, sadly, doesn't support a `glob` function, like Perl. Although there are files in the opened directory, lines 18–28 read them into `$filename`.

If at the start of a row, send a `<tr>` tag. Line 19 must also set a flag (`$loop`) to indicate that the loop has started; this prevents multiple `<tr>` from being sent if the first few files read in the directory are not image files. Line 20 uses a Perl regular expression to match the filename to a file that ends in `.jpg` and includes the search string (`$match`).

Lines 21–24 display the table data cell for the image. Note that the image name is added to the HTML by embedded PHP `print` statements. Lines 25–26 increment the number of images displayed. If it is equal to the selected number of image columns, output a `</tr>`.

If the last file displayed occurred in the middle of a row, the program must add a final `</tr>` to close the row. This is done with line 29. Line 31 closes the output table.

For the most part, the programming syntax should closely resemble what you've seen in Perl. The lack of a `glob` function adds a few extra lines but doesn't prevent the PHP version from coming in 20% shorter.

You might have noticed that this version of the script does not attempt to check the input variables for `/`. This is because PHP automatically escapes troublesome characters in user input. For example, `/example` becomes `\/example`. This gives developers some peace of mind during programming.

PHP and Sessions

I've made such a big deal about sessions and how they make life easier; it's probably time to see one in use. Unfortunately, it's difficult to fabricate the use for a session in a reasonable amount of space. So, let's take a look at a simple case of sessions at work.

Imagine having a Web page that remembers how many times you've visited it during your current browser session (since you last quit out of your Web browser). This can't be done using a form because an action would be needed to submit the form each time you load the page. URL parameters can't be used because, likewise, the page would have to alter all the links it contains to include the number of visits using URL variable passing. With sessions, this is beyond simple. In fact, the following example keeps track of the cumulative number of visits to two distinct pages.

Create two Web pages (`one.php` and `two.php`) that link to one another. In `one.php`, type the following:

```
<?php
session_start();
$x++;
session_register(x);
print "You've been to page one and two $x times";
?>
</br>
<A HREF="two.php">Go to page two</a>
```

And in `two.php`, type this:

```
<?php
session_start();
$x++;
session_register(x);
print "You've been to page one and two $x times";
?>
</br>
<a href="one.php">Go to page one</a>
```

Loading one of the pages (either one) creates a page similar to that shown in Figure 28.9.

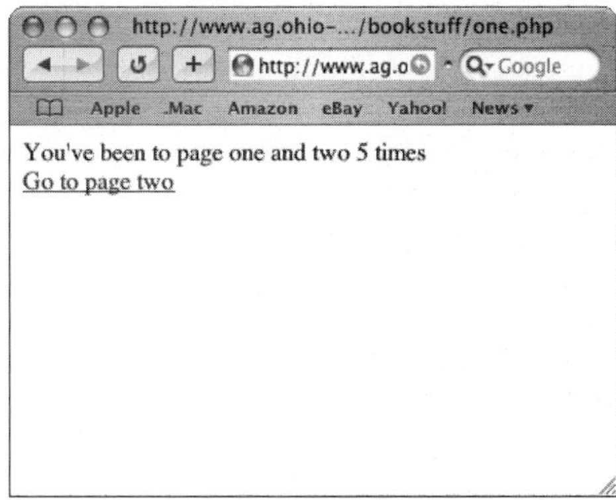

FIGURE 28.9 The two Web pages (`one.php` and `two.php`) share a single variable `$x`.

Clicking the link to toggle between the two pages increments the counter, and the displayed number starts counting up. Although this is not a groundbreaking Web site, it demonstrates the capabilities of built-in session management. The two pages share a single counter variable `$x`. The `session_start()` command starts a new PHP session, if one doesn't already exist. The `session_register(x)` registers the variable `$x` with the current session—effectively saving its value until another page is accessed. It is important to provide variables to `session_register` without the preceding dollar sign ($).

The incrementing of `$x` doesn't depend in any way on the links between `one.php` and `two.php`. You can reload one of the pages 30 times, and the counter will increment 30 times. You can even visit another Web site and then come back to either of the Web pages, and the count is still present. The only way to lose the value of `$x` is to drop the session—that is, close your Web browser.

28

PHP and MySQL

Finally, as an example of PHP's capability to work with databases, let's take a look at how easily code can be written to interact with MySQL (covered in detail in Chapter 22). Because most database-driven Web sites require a bit of setup, this example assumes that your Mac OS X computer is running a MySQL database server with a username `databaseuser` and password `databasepass`.

The database itself is named `employee` and contains a table `tblemployee` with at least the two fields, `firstname` and `lastname`. You should easily be able to adapt this short script to work with any MySQL database you can design, or just use the sample database in Chapter 22. Listing 28.10 demonstrates PHP that retrieves and prints each person's name from `employee`.

LISTING 28.10 PHP/MySQL Example

```
1: <?php
2: $link=mysql_connect("localhost","databaseuser","databasepass");
3: $result=mysql_db_query("employee","select * from tblemployee");
4: $count=mysql_num_rows($result);
5: for ($x=0;$x<$count;$x++) {
6:    $record=mysql_fetch_array($result);
7:     $firstname=$record[FirstName];
8:    $lastname=$record[LastName];
9:    print "$lastname, $firstname<br/><$count;$x++) {
6:    $record=mysql_fetch_array($result);
7:    $firstname=$record[firstname];
8:    $lastname=$record[lastname];
9:    print "$lastname, $firstname<br/>";"
10: }
11: mysql_close($link);
12: ?>
```

Line 2 makes the initial connection to the MySQL database located on the same computer as the Web server (`localhost`) and accessed via the username/password pair `databaseuser/databasepass`. The variable `$link` can be used to refer to the connection.

Line 3 queries the MySQL database `employee` by sending it the SQL query `select * from tblemployee`. A pointer to the resultset is returned to the variable `$result`.

Line 4 stores the total number of records in the result in the variable `$count`.

Lines 5–10 loop through the number of available records. Line 6 stores each row (one per loop) in the array `$record`. Lines 7 and 8 retrieve the `firstname` and `lastname` fields from the record, storing them in the `$firstname` and `$lastname` variables, respectively. Line 9, finally, outputs the name.

Line 11 closes the connection created in Line 2.

TIP

This example demonstrates how to pull information from MySQL, but the process for storing data is identical. The `mysql_db_query` function can be used to send any SQL statement to the database server and retrieve the results. You could just as easily use an insert or update SQL command in place of the select shown here.

The virtues of PHP could be touted for pages, but, unfortunately, the room is not available. If you want more information on PHP development, look at any of these fine sites:

- PHP Home—`http://www.php.net/`
- PHP Builder—`http://www.phpbuilder.net/`
- comp.lang.php—PHP's official Usenet newsgroup

Additionally, Zend Technologies (`http://www.zend.org`) has released its Zend IDE for Mac OS X, which makes creating and debugging PHP applications much like working with traditional desktop applications.

Alternative Development Environments

Many alternative Web development environments can run under Mac OS X, including Apple's own WebObjects. Personally, I have a thing for open source products, but depending on your needs, PHP or Perl might not be appropriate.

TIP

If you love Python (covered in Chapter 21, "Scripting Languages"), check out `http://www.modpython.org/` for information on an Apache module for creating an embedded Python server.

WebObjects, for example, is a Java-based development environment that includes RAD tools, distributed application logic and load handling, and a steep learning curve. WebObjects is used to deploy large-scale applications and requires a decent knowledge of the Mac OS X object model to begin programming. WebObjects comes with a reasonably high price tag outside the range of smaller groups. On the plus side, it is widely recognized as a superior Web application server and has won numerous awards in the enterprise marketplace (`http://www.apple.com/webobjects/`).

Active Server Pages (ASP/ASP.NET) is usually associated with the Windows platform. Stryon Software's iASP product brings Active Server Pages to the Mac OS X platform. This offers a great opportunity to ISPs and those entrenched in an NT environment to migrate to a better solution. iASP pricing ranges from $500 to $1,500 depending on your deployment requirements. PHP offers a great solution to the cross-platform scripting problem, but doesn't necessarily fit the corporate model just yet (that is, it's free). iASP is a great way to incorporate a Mac into a Windows-centric development environment (`http://www.halcyonsoft.com/`). In addition, Stryon also offers iNet—a complete Java implementation of Microsoft's .NET framework, enabling enterprise users seamless integration with Microsoft's Internet services.

Java Server Pages (JSP) is a fast-growing application development solution that leverages the cross-platform nature of Java. Like WebObjects, JSP requires knowledge of the Java programming language and has a similarly steep learning curve. A big advantage to JSP is that it is a supported server platform in software packages such as Macromedia's

Dreamweaver MX—enabling graphical development of Web applications. In addition, the JBoss (`http://www.jboss.org/`) application server is available as a custom install with the Mac OS X developer tools, allowing you to get started with JSP right away. See `http://developer.apple.com/internet/java/enterprisejava.html` for information on getting started with JBoss on Mac OS X.

Summary

Professional Web application development finally comes to the Macintosh platform. Perl offers a great starting language for programmers. A more Web-centric development environment is PHP, which works by embedding development code into HTML, rather than embedding HTML into the code.

Even if the Perl/PHP development solutions don't meet your needs, a number of other options are available for Mac OS X that can create enterprise-level Web sites and online applications.

CHAPTER 29

Creating a Mail Server

IN THIS CHAPTER

- Running a Mail Server
- Activating Postfix
- Postfix Configuration
- University of Washington `imapd`
- Web-Based Email

The Unix operating system started the email phenomenon by running the servers that first brought mail to the electronic age. Mac OS X continues the tradition by bundling the full-featured server Postfix with every copy of Panther. It can provide email services for a small workgroup or an entire corporation.

This chapter explores the steps needed to activate the dormant Mac OS X Postfix installation and implement basic security features. In addition, you'll learn how to install POP3 and IMAP servers to deliver email to client computers across a network.

Running a Mail Server

The first step in running a successful email server is determining that you actually *need* an email server. Unlike more basic services, such as Apache, email is a more intrusive process that enables complete strangers to store information on your computer. In addition, administration of an email server is an ongoing process. Monitoring and detecting problems is a must. Email has been around for more than 20 years, but it's still growing and evolving. Because it is one of the most highly utilized pieces of software on the Internet, it is also one of the most prone to attacks.

Mail server security is unlike basic server security because it occurs on two levels. First, you must protect the physical server software from being exploited. Remote users have found numerous holes in Sendmail (previously included in Mac OS X) that enabled them to gain unauthorized access. Monitoring server logs for unexplained connections and abnormal mail transmissions is standard practice. This aspect of mail server security should seem familiar because it should be a common practice for other basic system services, such as FTP or HTTP.

The second security problem is mail server abuse. This doesn't necessarily equate to compromising the email server, but the results can be even more far-reaching. Email spam, for example, is the result of poorly implemented email security. In the case of spam, there are two possible problems. The first is that an authorized user is inappropriately using your email resources; the second is that an unauthorized user is taking advantage of an open relay on your mail server to do the work of distributing his or her spam.

In either case, the result is the same. The second scenario is the most serious when considering the security of your network. It is much akin to hacking but without necessarily needing to exploit any program flaws on your system.

WHAT IS AN OPEN RELAY?

An **open relay** is an SMTP server that accepts and delivers mail for any user from any user. Mail servers should be configured to allow only certain clients to send email; otherwise, they can be used by anyone in the world to send spam or other harmful data.

For these reasons, you should seriously consider alternatives to running your own mail server. Users in need of controlling their own email accounts and the privacy of storing their own messages, or requiring complex mail relaying or automated processing are the best candidates for running their own server.

A properly configured server requires little maintenance and will perform well on Mac OS X. An improperly configured server, however, could be a disaster.

Activating Postfix

Sendmail is a monster of a mail server, and, although included in Mac OS X 10.0–10.2.x, it's not surprising that Apple made the switch to a smaller product—Postfix. To quote the author of Postfix:

Postfix attempts to be fast, easy to administer, and secure, while at the same time being sendmail compatible enough to not upset existing users. Thus, the outside has a sendmail-ish flavor, but the inside is completely different.

Many people are hesitant to move away from mainstream software such as sendmail, but Postfix has gained a following as one of the easiest and most stable Unix SMTP servers available. Better yet, it installs as a drop-in sendmail replacement, meaning that any other software or scripts that rely on sendmail (such as CGI scripts) can use it to function without additional modifications.

Postfix supports Mac OS X, integrates with NetInfo, and is much easier to configure than Sendmail.

Assuming that you've decided to go ahead and create a mail server, the first step is to turn on the server application itself. Mac OS X includes the Postfix software, but it is not activated when the system first boots.

TIP

The assumption is made that the Mac OS X machine you're going to use as a mail server already has a registered hostname. If this is not the case, be sure to register with a domain name system (DNS) before continuing. In addition to the standard A record (address record), a mail server typically also registers an MX record for the base-level domain. For example, although the server `postoffice.ag.ohio-state.edu` receives mail for accounts addressed directly to itself, there also is an MX record setup for `ag.osu.edu` that points to `postoffice.ag.ohio-state.edu`. This enables mail sent to an account at `ag.osu.edu` to be sent to the `postoffice.ag.ohio-state.edu` hostname transparently.

To automate Postfix startup, open the file `/etc/hostconfig` in your favorite text editor. Edit the line that reads `MAILSERVER=-NO-` to `MAILSERVER=-YES-`:

```
##
# /etc/hostconfig
##
# This file is maintained by the system control panels
##

# Network configuration
HOSTNAME=-AUTOMATIC-
ROUTER=-AUTOMATIC-

# Services
AFPSERVER=-NO-
APPLETALK=-NO-
AUTHSERVER=-NO-
AUTOMOUNT=-YES-
CONFIGSERVER=-NO-
CUPS=-YES-
IPFORWARDING=-NO-
IPV6=-YES-
MAILSERVER=-YES-
NETBOOTSERVER=-NO-
NETINFOSERVER=-AUTOMATIC-
NISDOMAIN=-NO-
RPCSERVER=-AUTOMATIC-
TIMESYNC=-YES-
...
```

Basic Host Settings

When you reboot your Mac OS X computer, Postfix starts and runs under the user ID `postfix`. (You can also start it at any time by typing **`sudo /usr/sbin/postfix start`**.) Unfortunately, you need to make a few more settings before the software will run successfully.

Edit the `/etc/postfix/main.cf` file now. To get up and running quickly, you need to tell Postfix what your server's hostname and domain are by using the `mydomain` and `myhostname` directives.

Look for the `myhostname` and `mydomain` lines, both of which are initially commented out with the # character. Uncomment both of the lines and change them to accurately reflect the state of your server and network. For example, my server is `mail.poisontooth.com` on the domain `poisontooth.com`. Thus, my `mail.cf` file contains the following lines:

```
myhostname = mail.poisontooth.com
mydomain = poisontooth.com
```

> **NOTE**
>
> After assignment, these setting variables (`myhostname`,`mydomain`,`etc`) can be referenced with a dollar sign ($) in other configuration directives as discussed in the section "Postfix Configuration" later in this chapter.

Verifying the Setup

Your Postfix server should now be ready to run. To verify the configuration, run `sudo /usr/sbin/postfix check`. This checks for errors in your setup. Start the server itself by rebooting or typing `sudo /usr/sbin/postfix start`.

```
brezup:jray jray $ sudo /usr/sbin/postfix start
postfix/postfix-script: starting the Postfix mail system
```

Verify that Postfix is running by Telneting to port 25 on your server computer. Use the `QUIT` SMTP command to exit:

```
brezup:jray jray $ telnet localhost 25
Trying 127.0.0.1...
Connected to localhost.poisontooth.com.
Escape character is '^]'.
220 client1.poisontooth.com ESMTP Postfix
QUIT
```

Assuming that your system responds similarly, everything has gone according to plan, and you're ready to fine-tune the Postfix system. For simple setups, this may be as far as you need to go. Postfix automatically configures itself to relay only for those machines on the same class subnet to which you're connected. All others are denied.

Congratulations. Your Mac OS X computer is now running an enterprise-class SMTP server.

Postfix Configuration

All the Postfix configuration we'll look at is done in the `/etc/postfix/main.cf`, and options within `main.cf` consist of lines in the form

```
<setting>=<value>[,<value>]
```

where *<setting>* is one of the Postfix directives, and *<value>* is a simple setting (such as a hostname, timeout value, and so on), a path to a hash file, such as `hash:/etc/aliases`, or, in the case of Mac OS X, a NetInfo path, such as `netinfo:/aliases`. In some cases, lists of values can be used, separated by commas.

A hash file is a binary lookup table that holds key and value pairs. There are two specific types of hash files you'll be interested in with Postfix—map files and alias files, generated with the `postmap` or `postalias` commands, respectively.

Alias files contain *<key>* and *<value>* fields, separated by a colon (`:`) and whitespace, such as this example `/etc/postfix/aliases` file:

```
postmaster: root
operator: jray
admin: jray
```

All other hash files simply contain *<key>* and *<value>* fields separated by whitespace. The `postalias` command works exclusively on alias files, whereas `postmap` is used to generate all other hash files.

To use the Postfix utilities to generate hash files from the corresponding text file, type either **`postmap <text file>`** or **`postalias <alias text file>`**. Within a few seconds, a binary hash is created in the same location as the original file, with the extension `.db`.

29

Local Domain Names

If your mail server has several different domain names that all are capable of receiving mail, you must explicitly list them using the `mydestination` Postfix directive; otherwise, mail to any name other than your server's primary domain name will be rejected.

Add a line to the `main.cf` file with all the names for which your mail server should accept email. For example, I want to be able to accept email for `poisontooth.com`, `mail.poisontooth.com`, and `mail.shadesofinsanity.com`. Each of these hostnames' DNS entries points directly to the server. By default, the names $myhostname and localhost.$mydomain are used—so when adding new names, be sure to add the defaults back in as well.

To make sure that Postfix accepts email for all the names, my mydestination directive would look like this:

```
mydestination = $myhostname, localhost.$mydomain,
➥ poisontooth.com, mail.poisontooth.com, mail.shadesofinsanity.com
```

Aliases

Aliases provide simple mailing list functionality, enable users to receive email under multiple names, or forward messages to another email account. Aliases are added to the file /etc/postfix/aliases. The alias file contains lines with the username that will receive email, followed by a colon, and then the email address (local or remote) that should get the message:

```
<email username>: <recipient email address>
```

For example:

```
webmaster: jray
jraywork: ray.30@osu.edu
root: jray, hlaufman
```

After editing, the aliases hash file must be rebuilt by running newaliases at the command line or postalias /etc/postfix/aliases. If the database is not rebuilt, Postfix will not "notice" the changes you've made.

In this simple alias file, email addressed to Webmaster would be sent to the local user jray, whereas email addressed to jraywork would be forwarded to the account ray.30@osu.edu. Finally, any messages sent to root are automatically sent to both jray and hlaufman—two local-user accounts.

To simplify and modularize aliases that direct email to multiple users, you can include files that list several email addresses. Take a line such as

```
job-info: :include:/etc/mail/job.list
```

When this entry is added in the aliases file, it includes the list of email addresses in the file /etc/postfix/job.list. This is a convenient way to create a mailing list with little work.

Mac OS X's Postfix implementation offers an alternative way to add mail aliases: via the NetInfo database system. This results in a setup that isn't directly transferable to other Unix systems but allows you to use the NetInfo Manager or nicl command-line utility to quickly add aliases.

To add aliases directly to the /aliases directory within the NetInfo database, you must first create a NetInfo directory with the name of the alias and then add a member's key with the appropriate alias information. Think of this as splitting the lines in the alias file on the first : character. The information to the left of the : is the NetInfo alias name, and the information to the right is the member name. For example, consider this line, as it appears in /etc/mail/aliases:

```
jraywork: ray.30@osu.edu
```

This information could be added directly to NetInfo using

```
brezup:jray jray $ sudo nicl / -create /aliases/jraywork
brezup:jray jray $ sudo nicl / -append /aliases/jraywork members ray.30@osu.edu
```

The NetInfo GUI tools can be used to perform this action as well. Chapter 23, "File and Resource Sharing with NFS and NetInfo," discusses the use of the NetInfo Manager utility.

NOTE

Although the /etc/postfix/aliases file or NetInfo /aliases database can set up systemwide forward information for email addresses, individual users can do the same for their accounts by creating a .forward file in their home directory (path: ~/.forward).

Within the .forward file, add a single line containing the email address where email should be forwarded.

Relaying

By default, Postfix only serves as a relay for (only transmits messages for) your local subnet. This means that you can start the server without worrying about whether it will be used to send spam. As the administrator, you will, however, need to make choices on what relaying capabilities the server should have.

In a situation where you need to relay for multiple domains or subnets, use the relay_domains directive to list the subnets that are allowed to transmit mail through your server. For example, assume that I want people in the subnet 192.168.10.0/24 along with those in the domain mysaferelayusers.com to be able to send messages via my Postfix installation. To enable this, I could add

```
relay_domains = 192.168.10.0/24, mysaferelayusers.com
```

to the main.cf file. If you want to break this out into a separate file, you can do so using a hash table, or a simple text file with one network/domain listed per line:

```
relay_domains = $config_directory/my-safe-relay-domains
```

Here, the file /etc/postfix/my-safe-relay-domains would be filled with any networks, clients, or domain names that should be allowed to use the server for relaying.

Protecting Postfix

When you changed the myhostname and mydomain directives to enable Postfix, you edited two out of hundreds of configuration options available for use in the /etc/postfix/main.cf file. Table 29.1 contains a number of settings you may find useful.

TABLE 29.1 Common Postfix main.cf Settings

Setting	Description
myhostname = <*Postfix server name*>	Sets *unqualified* hostname for the machine running the mail server.
mydomain = <*Postfix server domain*>	The domain of the Postfix server.
inet_interfaces = <*all¦hostname¦ip,...*>	A list of the network interfaces on which Postfix is active. By default, it works on all active interfaces.
mydestination = <*domain name, ...*>	A list of domain names and hostnames for which Postfix accepts email. By default, Postfix accepts email for $myhostname and $myhostname.localhost. If your server accepts email for the entire domain, you should add $mydomain and $myhostname.$mydomain.
mynetworks_style = <*class¦subnet¦host*>	Sets how Postfix determines what portion of the local network it should trust for relaying. By default, the local subnet is trusted. To trust clients in the same class, use the class setting. Finally, to trust only the local computer, use host.
mynetworks = <*network/netmask,...*>	Used in lieu of mynetwork_style, mynetworks sets a list of network addresses that should be considered local clients. Specified in the format network/netmask, such as 10.0.1.1/24. This can also be set to a hash file, or any of the supported Postfix table lookup methods, including a NetInfo path.
relay_domains = <*host¦domain¦file*>	A list of domains for which Postfix relays mail. The list can consist of host or domain names, files containing hostnames, or lookup tables (such as hash tables or NetInfo paths). These are in addition to the mydestination and mynetworks settings.
local_recipient_maps = <*user lookup tables*>	A list of lookup tables for usernames accepted as local for the mail server. By default, this is set to the local user accounts and any alias lookup tables that exist.

TABLE 29.1 Continued

Setting	Description
alias_maps = <*alias lookup tables*>	One or more lookup tables that contain the alias lists for the database. The defaults are hash:/postfix/aliases and netinfo:/aliases. Remember, postalias is used to regenerate the alias hash file.
home_mailbox = <*mail box path*>	The path to the local mailbox files. Mac OS X users should use the default /var/mail.
smtpd_banner = $myhostname <*banner text*>	Sets banner text to be displayed when a host connects. RFC requirements state that the hostname must come at the start of the banner ($myhostname).
local_destination_concurrency_limit = <*limit integer*>	A limit on the number of local simultaneous deliveries that can be made to a single user. The default is 2.
default_destination_concurrency_limit = <*limit integer*>	The number of simultaneous connections that Postfix makes to deliver mail. The default is 10. Keeping this number low can help protect against inappropriate use of your server if it is compromised. It is unlikely that your server will ever need to make 10 simultaneous connections to a single domain at a time.
disable_vrfy_command = <yes¦no>	Disables the VRFY SMTP command, which can be used by spammers to verify that an account exists on the server.
smtpd_recipient_limit = <*limit integer*>	The maximum number of recipients accepted per message. Keeping this limit low makes your server unusable for mass spam.
smtpd_timeout = <*timeout* s¦m¦h¦d¦w>	The timeout period to wait for a response from an SMTP client (in seconds, minutes, hours, days, or weeks).
strict_rfc821_envelopes = <yes¦no>	Sets a requirement for RFC821-compliant messages. If set to "yes," MAIL FROM and RCPT TO addresses must be specified within <>.
smtpd_helo_required = <yes¦no>	Determines whether postfix requires the HELO or EHLO SMTP greeting at the start of a connection.
smtpd_client_restrictions = < *restrictions*>	Used to fine-tune the restrictions on the Postfix clients and can handle everything from real-time blacklisting to access control lists.
smtpd_helo_restrictions = <*restrictions*>	Used to fine-tune the restrictions on what machines are permitted within a HELO or EHLO greeting.

TABLE 29.1 Continued

`smtpd_sender_restrictions = <restrictions>`	Used to fine-tune the restrictions on what machines are permitted within a MAIL FROM address.
`smtpd_recipient_restrictions = <restrictions>`	Used to fine-tune the restrictions on what machines are permitted within a RCPT TO address.

If you plan to operate a successful and secure mail server, you should learn how to control external access to Postfix. The smtpd *XXXXX*_restrictions directives provide a wide range of restrictions. These directives control access to the server and can be applied against client addresses, HELO/EHLO headers, and MAIL FROM/RCPT TO addresses.

Four different types of restrictions are considered here: client (smtpd_client_restrictions), helo (smtpd_helo_restrictions), sender (smtpd_sender_restrictions), and recipient (smtpd_recipient_restrictions). In addition to a standard access hash table (see /etc/postfix/access as an example), they each share some common additional restriction options, so rather than list them separately, Table 29.2 combines them.

TABLE 29.2 Common Options for Setting the smtpd Restrictions

Restriction	Description	Use In
reject_unknown_client	Reject the client if the hostname is unknown.	client, helo, sender, recipient
reject_invalid_hostname	Reject the connection if the HELO/ELHO hostname is invalid.	helo, sender, recipient
reject_unknown_hostname	Reject the connection if the HELO/ELHO hostname does not have a matching DNS A or MX record.	helo, sender, recipient
reject_unknown_sender_domain	Reject if the HELO/ELHO sender does not have a matching DNS A or MX record.	sender
reject_non_fqdn_sender	Reject sender addresses that are not fully qualified.	recipient, sender
reject_non_fqdn_recipient	Reject recipient addresses that are not fully qualified.	recipient
reject_rbl_client *<RBL name>*	Rejects the connection, message, or so on, based on blacklisting DNS.	client, helo, sender, recipient

Let's take a look at a few examples of restrictions that can be made in your main.cf file.

Access Controls

Access controls determine who can connect to your Postfix SMTP server. Using the restriction directives, you can limit access based on the client address connection, HELO headers, and so on.

For example, assume that you have three possibilities for clients:

```
goodclient.mydomain.com
gooddomain.com
badbadbad.com
```

The first (goodclient.mydomain.com) is an individual host that should always be allowed; the second is a domain (gooddomain.com) that, likewise, should always be considered a valid client. Finally, the last domain (badbadbad.com) should explicitly be denied. Because these connections should be allowed or denied based on the client IP or hostname, the directive to use is smtpd_client_restrictions.

To add these controls to your server, create a new access map file, such as /etc/postfix/clientaccess, and then add these lines:

```
goodclient.mydomain.com  OK
gooddomain.com           OK
.gooddomain.com          OK
.badbadbad.com           REJECT Client not allowed
badbadbad.com            REJECT Client not allowed
```

The lines of the file are made up of a pattern (in this case, domain or client names) and an action. Domain names that begin with a "." match any subdomain within that domain. For restrictions that match against MAIL FROM addresses (such as smtpd_sender_restrictions), you can also provide full or partial email addresses to match and allow/reject individual senders.

In this example, two actions are used: REJECT [rejection message] and OK. As their names imply, the first rejects connections from the client and provides an optional error message, whereas the second allows the connection to be made.

Documentation for other actions can be found in the file /etc/postfix/access.

After creating the appropriate /etc/postfix/clientaccess file, "compile it" using postmap /etc/postfix/clientaccess.

Finally, add the configuration line to main.cf that will impose the restriction:

```
smtpd_client_restrictions = hash:/etc/postfix/clientaccess
```

If you also wanted to block clients without a proper hostname, you could add the directive reject_unknown_client to the list of restrictions (refer to Table 29.2). The line for main.cf would become:

```
smtpd_client_restrictions = hash:/etc/postfix/clientaccess,
➥ reject_unknown_client
```

Real-time Blacklisting

One of the first protection features to enable on any spam-sensitive Internet-connected Postfix server should be real-time blacklisting (RBL). RBL services maintain a list of known open relay mail servers and spammers. If you enable RBL service on the Mac OS X mail server, it automatically checks each incoming message to determine whether it is from a known open relay or spammer. If it is, the message is returned as undeliverable.

To test for blacklisted addresses, a standard DNS lookup is performed on a specially constructed version of a hostname. For example, if you want to check the IP address 140.254.85.225 to see whether it is blacklisted, you would look up the special address 225.85.254.140.spam.dnsrbl.net. As you can probably tell, this is nothing but the IP address reversed with .spam.dnsrbl.netadded to the end. If a lookup on the address *fails*, it is not blacklisted:

```
brezup:jray jray $ host 225.85.254.140.spam.dnsrbl.net
Host 225.85.254.140.spam.dnsrbl.net not found: 3(NXDOMAIN)
```

To see an example of a "successful" (or blacklisted) lookup, use the IP address 127.0.0.2—or 2.0.0.127. .spam.dnsrbl.net. This address, reserved for testing, should return a valid DNS lookup:

```
brezup:jray jray $ host 2.0.0.127.spam.dnsrbl.net
2.0.0.127.spam.dnsrbl.net is an alias for test.dnsrbl.net.spam.spam.dnsrbl.net.
test.dnsrbl.net.spam.spam.dnsrbl.net has address 127.0.0.4
```

Searching for RBL or RBL DNS is the easiest way to find the "latest and greatest" blacklisting servers that are currently active. Here are a few to try:

- spam.dnsrbl.net
- spamguard.leadmon.net
- korea.services.net
- sbl.spamhaus.org

To enable RBL screening for client connections, simply use the `reject_rbl_client <RBL name>` restriction from Table 29.2. For example, to add an RBL filter using `spam.dnsrbl.net` to the client restrictions in the previous section, just change the line to read:

```
smtpd_client_restrictions = hash:/etc/postfix/clientaccess,
➥ reject_unknown_client, reject_rbl_client spam.dnsrbl.net
```

Additional Information

For more information about Postfix and its operation and configuration, look into these resources:

- *Postfix*, by Richard Blum, Sams Publishing—The only printed reference specifically for Postfix, this book covers the use and configuration of the Postfix MTA in an easy-to-follow format.
- `http://www.postfix.net`—The Postfix home page provides links to the latest software release, FAQs, and supporting documentation.
- `http://groups.google.com/groups?oi=djq&as_ugroup=mailing.postfix.users`—An archive of the Postfix mailing list. (For information on subscribing to the list itself, see the Postfix home page.)

University of Washington imapd

Postfix makes up only part of the mail-server picture. Although Postfix handles sending and receiving email on the server side, it does not have any provisions for the client software, such as Eudora or Outlook Express. To provide email for remote clients, Mac OS X needs an IMAP server, a POP3 server, or both. Thankfully, the University of Washington has created an easy-to-install software package that kills two birds with one stone.

The UW `imapd` server is capable of handling both IMAP and POP3 traffic, and it is already Mac OS X–aware, so it takes very little work to install. Even better, there is absolutely no configuration file for the software, so after it's installed, it's ready to use.

NOTE

If you're scratching your head wondering what POP3 and IMAP are, refer to Chapter 4, "Internet Applications." These two mail delivery protocols are explained during the introduction to the Mail application.

A straightforward comparison between POP3 and IMAP can be found at the IMAP Connection: `http://www.imap.org/imap.vs.pop.brief.html`.

Installing UW imapd

Installing imapd is straightforward but requires a few additional modifications to be able to perform smoothly on your OS X computer. To start, fetch the current sources from ftp://ftp.cac.washington.edu/imap/. Unarchive the source and cd into the distribution directory:

```
brezup:jray jray $ curl -O ftp://ftp.cac.washington.edu/imap/
➥imap-2003.DEV.SNAP-0305291356.tar.gz
brezup:jray jray $ tar zxf imap-2003.DEV.SNAP-0305291356.tar.gz
brezup:jray jray $ cd imap-2003.DEV.SNAP-0305291356
```

Before compiling there, an important change should be made to the file src/osdep/unix/env_unix.c. By default, the IMAP server attempts to create all mailboxes directly in the user's home directory. In fact, it assumes that any directory in the home directory is an IMAP folder. This results in potentially hundreds (or thousands) of folders being downloaded and displayed. To get around this, the env_unix.c file must be adjusted so that a directory other than the main home directory is used. This can be any directory, as long as it exists in every user's account. A good choice is ~/Library/Mail/Mailboxes because it contains the mailboxes created by the Mail application. This enables remote access to mail downloaded onto the Mac OS X computer. Just remember to create the directory name you choose in each account that accesses the IMAP server.

Edit the src/osdep/unix/env_unix.c file to add the mailbox directory name you've chosen. Look for a line reading

```
static char *mailsubdir = NIL; /* mail subdirectory name */
```

Change the text to include the directory you've chosen. For example:

```
static char *mailsubdir = "Library/Mail/Mailboxes"; /* mail subdirectory name */
```

The source code is now ready to compile by typing **make osx SSLTYPE=unix**. This builds a *partially* noncompliant IESG (Internet Engineering Steering Group) version of the software. This simply means that the software does *not* force the use of SSL encryption for transferring mail/passwords.

```
brezup:jray imap-2003.DEV.SNAP-0305291356 $ make osx SSLTYPE=unix
make sslunix
+++++++++++++++++++++++++++++++++++++++++++++++++++++++++++++++++
+ Building in PARTIAL compliance with IESG security requirements:
+ Compliant:
++ TLS/SSL encryption is supported
+ Non-compliant:
++ Unencrypted plaintext passwords are permitted
```

```
Applying an process to sources...
tools/an "ln -s" src/c-client c-client
tools/an "ln -s" src/ansilib c-client
tools/an "ln -s" src/charset c-client
tools/an "ln -s" src/osdep/unix c-client
tools/an "ln -s" src/mtest mtest
...
```

The compile process takes only a minute or two because the server application is really quite small. Unfortunately, installation of the compiled software is not automated, so you will need to copy the binary files to an appropriate location.

The Mac OS X /etc/inetd.conf file already has entries for the IMAP and POP servers, so we'll just use the standard setting (/usr/local/libexec/). You'll have to create the libexec directory within /usr/local, and then copy the files imapd and ipop3d (created within the imapd and ipopd directories of the source distribution) to the new directory:

```
brezup:jray imap-2003.DEV.SNAP-0305291356 $ sudo mkdir /usr/local/libexec
% sudo cp imapd/imapd /usr/local/libexec/
% sudo cp ipopd/ipop3d /usr/local/libexec/
```

NOTE

Depending on what additional BSD software you've installed, you might already have the /usr/local/libexec directory on your system.

Next, you'll need to configure xinetd to automatically start the POP and IMAP servers when there is an incoming request. To do this add two files (pop and imap) to your /etc/xinetd.d directory:

The file /etc/xinetd.d/pop should read like this:

```
service pop3
{
    disable         = no
    socket_type     = stream
    wait            = no
    user            = root
    server          = /usr/local/libexec/ipop3d
    groups          = yes
    flags           = REUSE
}
```

The file `/etc/xinetd.d/imap` should read like this:

```
service imap
{
    disable         = no
    socket_type     = stream
    wait            = no
    user            = root
    server          = /usr/local/libexec/imapd
    groups          = yes
    flags           = REUSE
}
```

Finally, reboot the Mac OS X computer, or force the `xinetd` process to reload its configuration using `kill -HUP` and the `xinetd` process ID.

Test to make sure that the services you want to run are running by Telneting into port 110 (POP3) and port 143 (IMAP):

```
# telnet localhost 110
Trying 127.0.0.1...
Connected to localhost.
+OK POP3 client1.poisontooth.com v2003.529 server ready
Escape character is '^]'.
Connection closed by foreign host.
```

and

```
# telnet localhost 143
Trying 127.0.0.1...
Connected to localhost.
Escape character is '^]'.
* OK [CAPABILITY IMAP4REV1 LOGIN-REFERRALS AUTH=LOGIN]
   client1.poisontooth.com IMAP4rev1
   2003.529 at Sun, 10 Aug 2002 14:42:25 -0400 (EDT)
```

Both services are running, as we intended. As a rule, remember that less is more when it comes to servers. If you aren't going to use the IMAP or POP3 servers, don't activate them in your configuration.

The UW `imapd` server is now ready for use. You can connect to the Mac OS X machine to pick up email that has been received by the Postfix SMTP daemon.

TIP

The IMAP and POP3 servers are both installed and configured to use TCP Wrappers. TCP Wrappers, as you'll learn in Chapter 31, "Server Security and Advanced Network Configuration," can be used to limit access to any `inetd`-controlled services. It is recommended that you use TCP Wrappers to block mail services except for those domains that must have access—these servers offer hackers an excellent entry point for their activities.

POP Before SMTP

A common problem with mail servers is that many require you to enumerate the networks that can send email (which is difficult for mobile users) and don't include built-in support for SMTP authentication methods. As a result, SMTP servers are stuck with either having to act as an open relay in cases where they shouldn't or force restrictions on mobile users.

A clever way around this is to allow your IMAP/POP server software to "okay" connections to your SMTP server. Because both IMAP and POP require a username and password, these servers can authenticate a user and then pass on the authenticated IP address to the SMTP server, which can temporarily allow messages to be sent from that IP address. One easy solution that works with the Postfix and UW `imapd` software you've installed is `Pop-before-smtp` (`http://popbsmtp.sourceforge.net/`).

Written entirely in Perl, this utility watches your POP/IMAP server logs for a valid login and then authorizes that IP to send email through Postfix for 30 minutes. Because this software requires no changes to the Postfix or `imapd` applications, you can install and use it with a minimum amount of configuration. If you're comfortable with installing Perl modules, you can jump right in at `http://popbsmtp.sourceforge.net/quickstart.shtml`. Otherwise, you might want to review Chapter 21, "Scripting Languages," first.

Web-Based Email

There are a number of packages that you can install to create Web-based email, such as ZOE (`http://guests.evectors.it/zoe/`) and IMP (`http://www.horde.org/imp/download`). In addition, the PHP Web development language has the capability to talk directly to the IMAP servers, but you'll need to recompile it with IMAP support, or download a version with compiled-in support from `http://www.entropy.ch`.

If you're interested in a solution that is easy to set up, you might want to check out the Majora software, which can be downloaded from `http://www.macosxunleashed.com/downloads/majora.tar.gz`.

Written in Perl, Majora is easy to understand and simple to set up. Assuming that you've enabled CGI support in Apache, you can add a Web front end to your mail server in a minute or two. The software *isn't* overly robust, nor does it support SSL, but, in a pinch, it can provide quick and dirty email access.

To install Majora, first download and unarchive the Majora distribution, placing it in a Web-accessible directory. In this example, the files are placed in my local `Sites` directory:

```
% curl -O http://www.macosxunleashed.com/downloads/majora.tar.gz
% tar zxf majora.tar.gz
```

Next, `cd` into the Majora directory and open the file `majora.cgi`. A few lines at the start of the file can be configured to better suit your site.

The following lines affect the coloring of the message output table. Alter the colors to adjust the HTML display in the client browser:

```
#### Color information for the display
$NormalColor="BGCOLOR=\"#FFFFE9\"";
$SelectedColor="BGCOLOR=\"#A0A0DD\"";
$HeadingColor="BGCOLOR=\"#D3D3FA\"";
$NumberColor="BGCOLOR=\"#CDCDDD\"";
$SubjectColor="BGCOLOR=\"#FFEDED\"";
$DateColor="BGCOLOR=\"#EDFFED\"";
```

When viewing messages in a Web browser, you don't want to worry about downloading several megabytes of attachments to the remote Web browser. To get around this potential problem, set the `$bigmessage` variable to the largest message size (in bytes) to transfer.

```
#### Largest message (in bytes) to allow the user to view online
$bigmessage=10000;
```

The variable `$popmailcgi` should only be changed if, for some reason, you've modified the name of the Majora CGI.

```
#### URL to this CGI
$popmailcgi="majora.cgi";
```

Finally, the `$smtpserver` and `$thishost` variables should be set to the SMTP server that will be used for sending email, and the hostname of the local computer, respectively.

```
#### SMTP server used to send mail..
$smtpserver="poisontooth.com"
#### This server's hostname (in case `hostname` doesn't work)
$thishost="poisontooth.com";
```

Save these changes to the Majora CGI file, and the system will be ready to go. To test it, start your Web browser and open the URL where Majora has been installed. Figure 29.1 shows the Majora login screen.

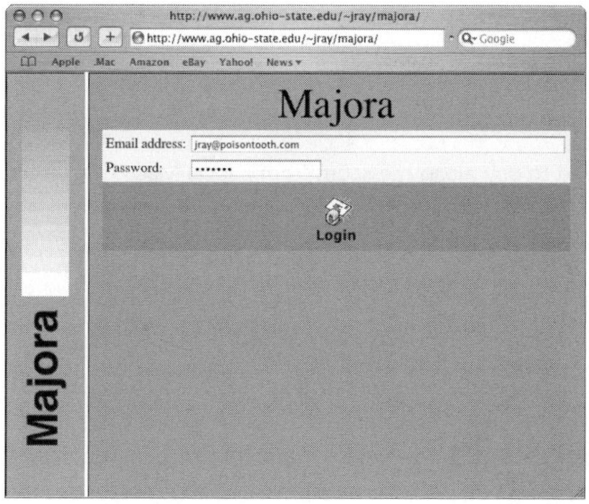

FIGURE 29.1 Log in to your email account.

After logging in to the system, the available options Compose, Get Mail, and Logout are displayed along the left side of the browser window. Those should be reasonably self-explanatory.

Waiting for the Get Mail function might take quite a while, depending on the size of your inbox. After information has been collected about each message, a listing is displayed for each one, as shown in Figure 29.2. Click the number at the start of each line to read the corresponding message.

http://www.ag.ohio-state.edu/~jray/majora/

Compose
Get Mail
Logout

POP Server is responding. Username accepted. Password accepted. 1857 messages are waiting

#	From	Date	Subject
1	applereg@apple.com	Sat, 15 Sep 2001 05:09:22	Thank you for registering your new Apple Computer
2	Thomas Michael Archer	Tue, 18 Sep 2001 16:19:58	Welcome!!!
3	Harrington B. Laufman	Mon, 1 Oct 2001 12:01:25	Re: web advice handout
4	customerservice@macromedia.com	Mon, 1 Oct 2001 13:34:32	Your Macromedia Membership Account
5	Martha Filipic	Thu, 4 Oct 2001 08:52:20	Unknown
6	Jessica Chapel	Tue, 09 Oct 2001 11:16:28	Re: Zeitgeist
7	Robyn Ness	Fri, 12 Oct 2001 21:31:07	desktop metaphor link
8	Joe Bonnell	Thu, 25 Oct 2001 18:20:52	Praise for R. Ness
9	John Ray	Fri, 2 Nov 2001 16:10:54	Ticker
10	John Ray	Wed, 5 Sep 2001 09:48:29	Re: We're done!!!!
11	John Ray	Mon, 13 Aug 2001 14:58:42	Ag Eng contact
12	Robyn Ness	Fri, 16 Nov 2001 16:16:01	Re: bulletin boards/postings
13	Joan Thomson	Mon, 19 Nov 2001 13:31:08	Current JOE useage
14	John Ray	Mon, 19 Nov 2001 14:52:52	Thumbnail viewer
15	John Ray	Mon, 19 Nov 2001 15:19:56	Re: Thumbnail viewer
16	Joe Bonnell	Fri, 16 Nov 2001 15:34:22	Sites to look at
17	Joan Thomson	Mon, 19 Nov 2001 16:52:18	response: Current JOE useage
18	John Ray	Sun, 25 Nov 2001 22:53:53	Urchin/joe.org
19	John Ray	Sun, 25 Nov 2001 22:56:07	Joe logs
20	Joe Bonnell	Mon, 26 Nov 2001 13:50:56	Fwd:
21	Unknown	Unknown	Unknown
22	John Ray	Tue, 27 Nov 2001 12:08:13	www.ag search engine updated
23	Joe Bonnell	Fri, 30 Nov 2001 08:22:42	Watershed site
24	Satish Verma	Tue, 04 Dec 2001 00:26:14	Electronic version

FIGURE 29.2 The messages in the inbox are listed.

The Majora code is open and can be modified as you see fit. Feel free to edit the Perl code to your heart's content.

> **TIP**
>
> Majora isn't required to download messages from a local Mac OS X server. The software attempts to access whatever email server is specified in the email login line.

Summary

Mail servers require disk space and a commitment from the administrator to monitor traffic and usage. An improperly configured mail server can be used to spread spam and viruses to remote clients around the world. Before setting up a server, you should first evaluate whether a local server is truly needed, and what alternative solutions are available.

Assuming that you *do* decide to enable Postfix, most installations will want to install a server such as UW `imapd` to deliver messages to client applications such as Eudora, Outlook Express, and Mail. In addition, Web clients can be added to create a mail solution that enables users to access email from anywhere there is Web access.

CHAPTER 30

Windows Interoperability

IN THIS CHAPTER

- Introduction to SMB and CIFS
- Accessing and Sharing Windows Resources
- Samba

There's no denying it. There's no ignoring it. We live in a world dominated by Windows-based computers. Granted, this dominance will last only a few more years until the current generation of Unix-heads (Mac OS X users included!) takes over. In the meantime, despite the example set by the opposition, it's still a good idea to play nice with Windows computers.

This chapter introduces the Mac OS X software that will help your computer exchange files over a Windows network and take the place of a Windows server for file and print sharing. Best of all, you can do everything from within the familiar Mac OS X interface.

Introduction to SMB and CIFS

The Simple Message Block (SMB) protocol provides the basis for Windows file and print sharing. SMB provides support for file browsing, and two levels of security:

- User—A user must authenticate with the SMB server during the initial connection. The supplied username and password determine what resources the user can access.
- Share—Share-level security operates on an individual shared resource. The resource has a single password. Anyone with access to the password can access the resource.

SMB is implemented on top of a transport protocol. Think of this as similar to the way that AppleTalk exists on top of LocalTalk (serial networking) and EtherTalk (ethernet-based networks).

The SMB protocol has gone through several phases in its existence. Early in life, it used NetBEUI as its transport protocol. NetBEUI is independent of TCP/IP and, as such, was only suited for local-area networks. Today, most SMB services run on top of NetBIOS (NetBT/NBT). NetBIOS is the equivalent of NetBEUI, but running on top of TCP/IP. This creates a routable file/print serving system that can be used across the Internet as well as in LAN situations.

Unfortunately, things aren't that clean and simple. The NetBEUI protocol used a simple broadcast protocol to enable browsing of local resources. When SMB moved to NetBIOS (and thus TCP/IP), finding remote resources became a bigger problem. Machines needed a new way to locate each other, besides sending broadcast packets. This was the only way to successfully handle spanning across multiple subnets.

The Windows Internet Naming Service (WINS) protocol was created to provide a central registration point for Windows computers. When coming online, a computer can register itself with a WINS server, as well as look up other machines for creating a connection.

NOTE

Yes, WINS is a proprietary name resolution system that bears a resemblance to DNS (domain name service). Versions of Windows later than 98 and NT 4.0 support DNS resolution of remote computer names. Microsoft's latest attempt at a proprietary directory service is the Active Directory Service. ADS offers greater support for open standards, but continues to be based on a proprietary system.

The latest version of SMB is known as Common Internet File System (CIFS) and is backed by Microsoft as well as several third-party companies. CIFS is an open version of SMB with Internet-specific modifications. For the sake of remaining reasonably sane, you can assume that CIFS and SMB are synonymous.

TIP

The history of SMB, NetBEUI, NetBIOS, and how everything fits together is documented on the What Is SMB? page: `http://samba.anu.edu.au/cifs/docs/what-is-smb.html`.

Accessing and Sharing Windows Resources

Panther provides integrated browsing of Windows shares directly in the Finder and the capability to connect to Microsoft Exchange servers for email and address book synchronization. In addition, the system enables you to serve your files and printers to Windows clients—all within the Mac OS X GUI. These features are supported by the Samba software package, which we'll look at later in the chapter.

Browsing and Mounting Windows Shares

To browse available Windows shares, open the Network level in the Finder (Go, Network, or Shift-Command-K), as shown in Figure 30.1. Windows workgroups, domains, and computers will be mixed in with Apple SLP domains and AppleTalk zones. Figure 30.1 shows two workgroups: `WORKGROUP` and `POISONTOOTH`.

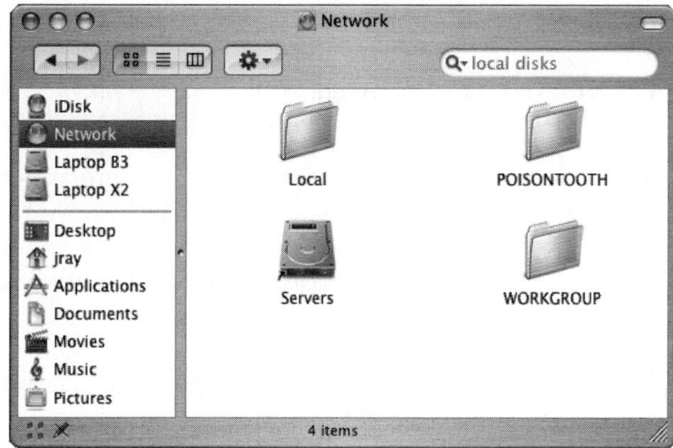

FIGURE 30.1 The Panther Finder can browse Windows workgroups on your local network.

To connect to a server, double-click it within the Finder. You are prompted for login information, just like a Mac OS X shared volume, as demonstrated in Figure 30.2. If you plan to connect to the volume in the future, you can choose to store the login information in your keychain. Mounted volumes behave just like any other network share.

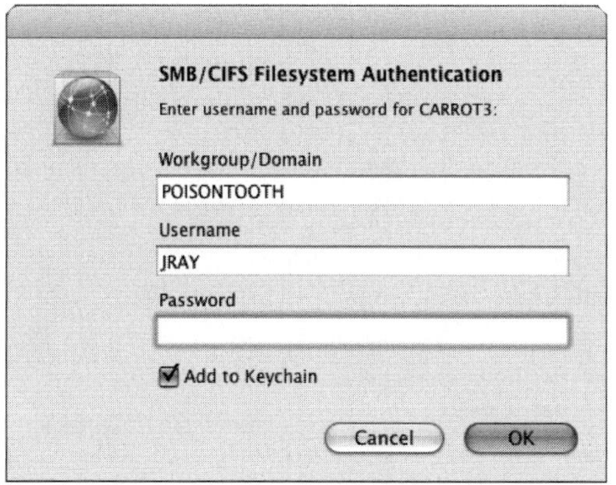

FIGURE 30.2 Log on to the Windows share.

30

Mounting by Name

Often it is easier to mount a share by its IP address or hostname than by browsing—especially if the server is located on another subnet. Panther supports connecting to Windows shares using the following naming conventions:

```
smb://<server name or ip>/[<volume>]

cifs://<server name or ip>/[<volume>]
```

You may also have luck with the standard Windows format: `\\<server name or ip>\[<volume>]` which worked on and off throughout the Panther beta cycle.

To mount a volume by name, choose Go, Connect to Server (Command-K). Enter the connection string within the Server Address field and then click Connect. If a volume name is not supplied, you are presented with a list of available shares to choose from. The connection proceeds exactly as it would if you had browsed to the server directly.

Using smbtree

To browse the Windows network from the command line, use the `smbtree` command, which prints a hierarchical view of the available network resources. For example, to browse the publicly visible volumes on your network, use `smbtree -N`:

```
$ smbtree -N
WORKGROUP
        \\CLIENT19              Samba 2.2.3a (build 26)
        \\CLIENT19\ADMIN$              IPC Service (Samba 2.2.3a (build 26))
        \\CLIENT19\IPC$                IPC Service (Samba 2.2.3a (build 26))
        \\CLIENT18              Mac OS X
        \\CLIENT18\Test_on_10.0.       PT Laser
        \\CLIENT18\Darkness@clie       Darkness
        \\CLIENT18\ADMIN$              IPC Service (Mac OS X)
        \\CLIENT18\IPC$                IPC Service (Mac OS X)
POISONTOOTH
        \\PAINFUL               Painful
        \\PAINFUL\C$                  Default share
        \\PAINFUL\ADMIN$              Remote Admin
        \\PAINFUL\SharedDocs
        \\PAINFUL\IPC$                Remote IPC
        \\PAINFUL\Secret Stuff
    \\CARROT3               Mac OS X Server
        \\CARROT3\ADMIN$              IPC Service (Mac OS X Server)
        \\CARROT3\IPC$                IPC Service (Mac OS X Server)
        \\CARROT3\Groups              macosx
        \\CARROT3\www.cutelittl       macosx
        \\CARROT3\Websites            macosx
        \\CARROT3\Users               macosx
        \\CARROT3\Public              macosx
```

Here, the two workgroups, WORKGROUP and POISONTOOTH, are shown with two clients in each. Many of the shares shown here are default administrative shares that are normally invisible in Windows (those that end in $), so the list isn't exactly what you would see within the Mac browser.

You can modify the operation of smbtree to query using a username/password, or only display machines visible by responding to broadcast requests. Table 30.1 contains the most useful of the smbtree options.

TABLE 30.1 smbtree Command-Line Options

Option	Description
-b	Use broadcasts requests to query available network resources. Typically a "master browser" is queried. The master browser contains a browse list that servers register with. Using a broadcast query displays all machines that are online and responding directly.
-D	Only display workgroup/domain names on the network.
-S	Only display workgroup/domain and servers—not individual shares.
-N	Suppress the smbtree password prompt.
-U=*<username>*%*<password>*	Set a username and password.
-k	Attempt to authenticate with Kerberos for Active Directory lookups.

Mounting with mount_smbfs

To mount a network volume from the command line, use mount_smbfs. In its simplest form, the mount_smbfs syntax is mount_smbfs "//*<server name>*/*<share>*" *<mount point>*. Note that the slashes have changed direction from the output of smbtree and the direction typically used in Windows.

For example, to mount the volume \\PAINFUL\Secret Stuff in the directory /tmp/mysmbmount, use

```
brezup:jray jray $ mount_smbfs "//PAINFUL/Secret Stuff" /tmp/mysmbmount
Password: *******
```

A quick look at the output of the mount command displays that the mount succeed (of course, looking in the /tmp/mysmbmount directory would do the same).

```
brezup:jray jray $ mount
/dev/disk0s11 on / (local, journaled)
devfs on /dev (local)
fdesc on /dev (union)
<volfs> on /.vol
/dev/disk0s9 on /Volumes/Laptop X2 (local, journaled)
automount -nsl [315] on /Network (automounted)
automount -fstab [320] on /automount/Servers (automounted)
automount -static [320] on /automount/static (automounted)
//JRAY@PAINFUL/SECRET STUFF on /tmp/thing (nodev, nosuid, by jray)
```

NOTE

When making the connection, mount_smbfs prompts for a password but not a username. By default it uses your login username for authentication. You can change this behavior using a command-line switch.

A common problem with using mount_smbfs in this fashion is failure of server name resolution. If you experience any trouble finding the server, try specifying the fully qualified domain name or IP address in the connection string. Alternatively, you can provide a connection hostname using the -I command-line switch—that is, -I carrot3.poisontooth.com. Table 30.2 contains a list of useful switches.

TABLE 30.2 Useful mount_smbfs Switches

Option	Description
-I *<hostname>*	Manually specify the name of the host that you are connecting to.
-U *<username>*	Set the username to be used when making the connection. Rather than use this option, you may want to modify the connection string to include the username and password, like this: //*<username>*:*<password>*@*<server name>*/*<share>*
-W *<workgroup>*	Set the workgroup name you are connecting to.
-N	Do not prompt for a password.
-u *<uid>*	Set the user ID assigned to files on the mounted volume.
-g *<gid>*	Set the group ID assigned to files on the mounted volume.
-h	Print mount_smbfs help.

Interactive File Transfers with smbclient

If you prefer to interact with your SMB servers much as you would an FTP server, the smbclient utility (part of Samba), provides an interactive client that can query and transfer files to and from a server. Unlike mount_smbfs, smbclient doesn't mount the filesystem and can be run by any user.

To connect, use the syntax smbclient -U *<username>* "//*<servername>*/*<share name>*" *<password>*. For example, to connect to my local share \\carrot3\Websites with the username admin and password mypass, I'd use

```
brezup:jray jray $ smbclient -U admin "//carrot3/Websites" mypass
Domain=[POISONTOOTH] OS=[Unix] Server=[Samba 2.2.3a (build 26)]
smb: \>
```

When connected, smbclient presents the smb: \> prompt, indicating that you are located at the root level of the server (\) and it is ready to receive commands. If you've ever used command-line FTP, you'll feel at home here. For example, to list files, use ls:

```
smb: \> ls
  .                        D       0 Sat Jul 26 03:00:29 2003
  .                        D       0 Tue Jul  1 23:09:45 2003
```

```
 .DS_Store                   AH    15364 Sat Jul 26 03:00:29 2003
 .VolumeIcon.icns            H     46531 Sat Nov 10 00:46:21 2001
 calendar.poisontooth.com    D     0 Wed Nov  7 00:23:14 2001
 coco.shadesofinsanity.com   D     0 Wed Nov  7 22:38:52 2001
 html                        D     0 Wed Nov  7 21:39:54 2001
 icbins.poisontooth.com      D     0 Sun Nov 18 01:39:09 2001
 julie.vujevich.com          D     0 Tue Jul 29 14:37:48 2003
 Network Trash Folder        D     0 Mon Aug 26 14:23:01 2002
...
```

To enter a directory, use cd:

```
smb: \> cd www.macosxunleashed.com
smb: \www.macosxunleashed.com\>
```

To get/put files, use, surprise, get and put:

```
smb: \www.macosxunleashed.com\> put INSTALL.TXT
putting file INSTALL.TXT as \www.macosxunleashed.com\INSTALL.TXT (4.1 kb/s)
(average 4.1 kb/s)
```

The easiest way to learn the complete smbclient syntax is to use the help function to get a list of available interactive commands and then help *<command>* to get detailed help for a specific command. Table 30.3 contains the most important functions you'll need to manage your files.

TABLE 30.3 Interactive Commands for Use with smbclient

Command	Description
ls	List the files in the current directory of the server.
cd *<directory>*	Change to a different server directory.
get *<filename>*	Retrieve a file from the server.
put *<local filename>*	Send a local file to the server.
mget *<filename(s)>*	Transfer multiple files from the server.
mput *<filename(s)>*	Transfer multiple files to the server.
prompt	Toggle prompting on and off for unattended file transfer operation.
del *<filename>*	Delete the given filename from the server.
mkdir *<directory>*	Create a new directory on the server.
rmdir *<directory>*	Remove a directory from the server.
exit	Quit smbclient.

Using smbutil

Another command-line utility that you might want to keep your eye on is smbutil. Provided by Apple, this utility promises to provide several functions, such as login, logout, and printing on SMB servers. Unfortunately, at the time of this writing, smbutil doesn't actually seem to work as described by the Apple documentation. Three functions that are working, however, are `view`, `lookup`, and `status`. The first lists resources shared from a named host; the second translates NetBIOS names to IP addresses, and the third translates IPs to names. The basic syntax of `smbutil` is `smbutil <function> <name or ip>`.

For example, to display the shared resources on `painful`, use

```
brezup:jray jray $ smbutil view //painful
Password: ******
Share         Type    Comment
-------------------------------
Secret Stuff disk
IPC$          pipe    Remote IPC
SharedDocs    disk
ADMIN$        disk    Remote Admin
C$            disk    Default share

5 shares listed from 5 available
```

TIP

Although this example just uses `//painful`, you can use the same connection string and *upper-case* options that were used in `mount_smbfs` to customize the connection.

To look up the IP address associated with `painful`, use the `lookup` function:

```
brezup:jray jray $ smbutil lookup painful
Got response from 10.0.1.107
IP address of painful: 10.0.1.107
```

Finally, to reverse the lookup, use the `view` function to find a NetBIOS name given the IP address:

```
brezup:jray jray $ smbutil status 10.0.1.107
Workgroup: POISONTOOTH
Server: PAINFUL
```

Presumably, the rest of `smbutil` will work as described in the man page at *some* point, but for now the command is only partially functional.

Sharing to Windows

To share files and printers with a Windows system, open the Mac OS X System preferences and click the Sharing pane. A single option—Windows Sharing—activates printer and folder sharing, as shown in Figure 30.3.

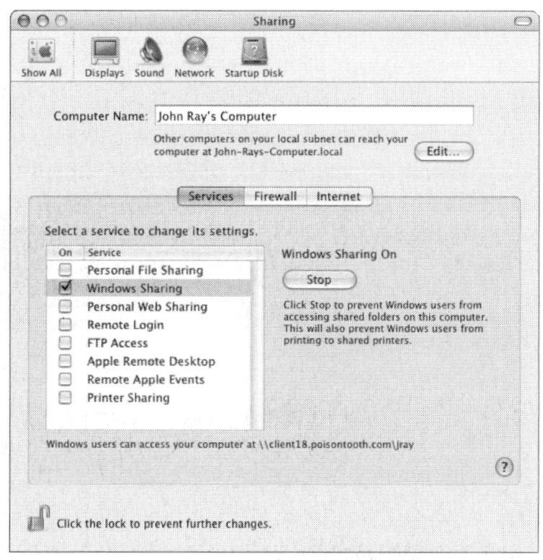

FIGURE 30.3 Activate file and printer sharing with a single click.

NOTE

Jaguar required that user accounts be "enabled" for login from windows. This is no longer the case in Panther.

After sharing is started, the window refreshes with the connection string that Windows users can use to connect to your computer. For example, in Figure 30.3, the connection string is `\\client18.poisontooth.com\jray`. Windows machines should also be able to browse to your computer and connect to shares and printers.

You can verify that the shares are active using the `smbutil` command discussed previously:

```
brezup:jray jray $ smbutil view //client18.poisontooth.com
Password: *****
Share           Type      Comment
-------------------------------
IPC$            pipe      IPC Service (Mac OS X)
ADMIN$          pipe      IPC Service (Mac OS X)
Darkness@clie printer  Darkness
Test_on_10.0. printer  PT Laser
jray            disk      User Home Directories

5 shares listed from 5 available
```

In this example, the default `IPC$` and `ADMIN$` shares are visible, along with two printers and my home directory—`jray`.

Setting Your Workgroup and WINS Server

By default, Mac OS X registers your computer in the workgroup `WORKGROUP`. Although this might be amusing for you, it can be annoying for Windows users who expect to find a little order on their network. To fix the problem, you can use SWAT to edit the Samba configuration (which we'll see shortly), or use the Directory Access utility (`/Applications/Utilities/Directory Access`) to edit it through a GUI.

To change your workgroup, start the utility and authenticate, if necessary, by clicking the lock button. Next, highlight the SMB line and click the Configure button. A dialog appears, as shown in Figure 30.4.

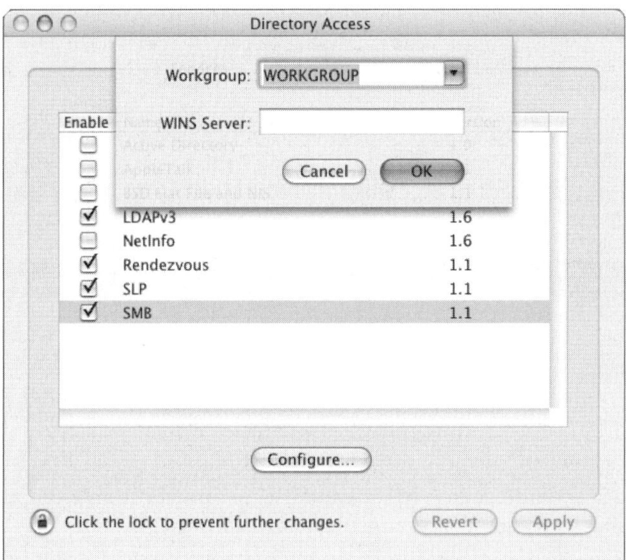

FIGURE 30.4 Set your workgroup and WINS server.

Enter the name of the workgroup that you want to join and specify a WINS server that Samba should register with, if desired. Click OK to save your changes.

> **NOTE**
>
> If you uncheck SMB within the Directory Access utility, it disables browsing and SMB connections within Mac OS X.

Exchange Integration

Mac OS X Panther offers rudimentary Exchange support in the form of Address Book synchronization and the capability to connect to an Exchange server via IMAP and

Outlook Web Access. No, this does not mean that you'll be synchronizing calendars and scheduling with your Windows brethren. It does mean, however, that the Mac OS X Mail application can read email from an Exchange server, and Address Book (by way of iSync) can synchronize with your Exchange contacts.

Mail and Exchange

To use Mail with Exchange, the Exchange server must be configured for IMAP support. If the server also supports Outlook Web Access, the OWA server can be specified so that non-email related information is filtered from the email. If OWA is *not* available, Mail still can access the account but may display extraneous information that, although useful in Outlook, has no purpose in Mac OS X. To add an Exchange IMAP account to Mail, follow the instructions in Chapter 4, "Internet Applications," but, when choosing an account type, pick Exchange, as shown in Figure 30.5.

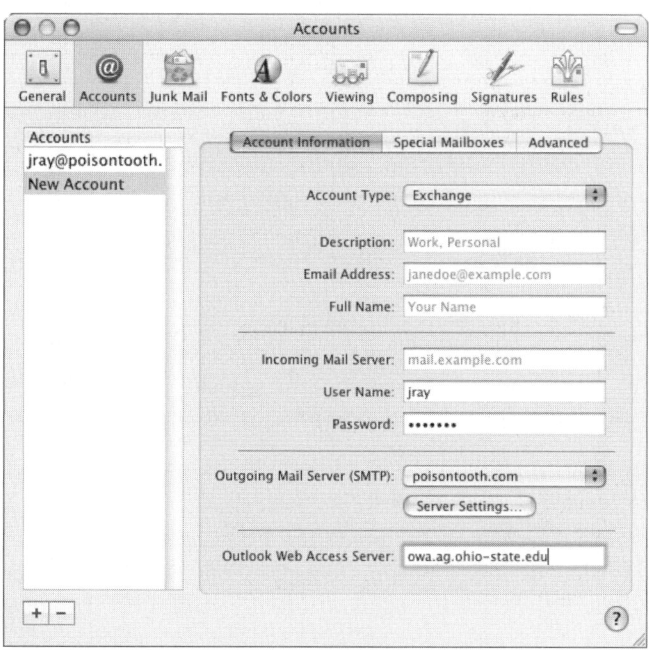

FIGURE 30.5 Configure your Mail application to access Exchange.

The settings are identical to IMAP, with the exception of the Outlook Web Access Server. Again, this is an optional field; talk to your network administrator to determine whether OWA is even available for your server.

After the account is configured, Mail operates identically to a standard IMAP account. Refer to Chapter 4 for more information.

Address Book, iSync, and Exchange

Address Book also supports synchronization with Exchange's contact information by way of Outlook Web Access and iSync. To configure synchronization, open Address Book and then choose the General pane from the application preferences pane. Make sure that the Synchronize with Exchange check box is checked; then click the Configure button. A dialog appears as shown in Figure 30.6.

FIGURE 30.6 Configure Address Book synchronization with Exchange.

Enter your Exchange username and password along with the address or hostname of your Outlook Web Access Server. If OWA is *not* available, synchronization will fail.

Click the Synchronize Every Hour check box to automatically synchronize hourly via iSync. If this is not checked, you can force a sync at any time using the iSync menu extra or by clicking Sync Now in iSync.

After synchronization is activated, a new device appears in iSync, the Exchange device, as shown in Figure 30.7.

As with other devices, you can choose what happens the first time a synchronization takes place. Subsequent synchronization work as described in the iSync section of Chapter 3, "Applications and Utilities."

To disable synchronization, you must return to the General pane of the Address Book preferences. It cannot be removed from within iSync.

Active Directory Integration

If your company is primarily Windows-based, it probably has or is moving to Microsoft's Active Directory. Active Directory (AD) is Microsoft's enterprise directory service. It provides centralized resource and user management for tens, hundreds, or thousands of users.

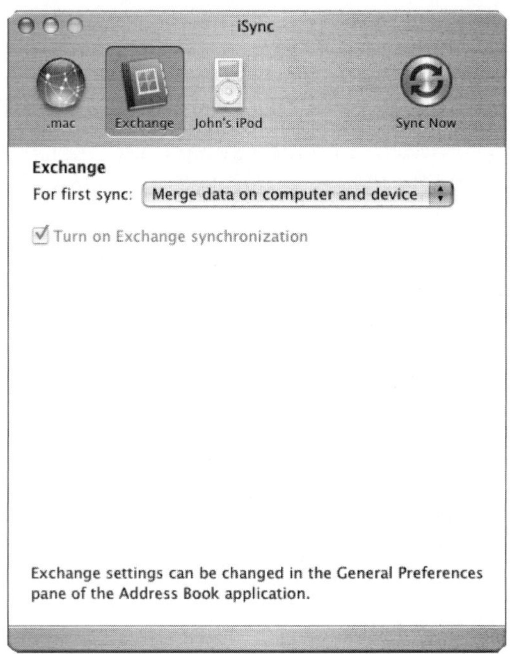

FIGURE 30.7 A new device is automatically added to iSync.

Apple's Mac OS X also supports directory services, such as NetInfo and LDAP, and can even integrate into an AD-based network without resorting to installing special software, or compromising the way you use your computer. Panther introduces direct AD integration as a part of the Apple Open Directory architecture. Open Directory allows Mac OS X computers to interact with directory servers, local files, and network resources to create distributed administration systems that can be used in a wide variety of settings.

A properly configured Mac OS X AD client is subject to the same login/password policies as a Windows client. Mac users will also automatically have their Windows home directory mounted as a share on their Panther desktop. Authenticated AD administrators will even have administrative access on Mac OS X.

To start setting up the connection, open up the Directory Access utility (path: `/Applications/Utilities/Directory Access`).

To use an AD server, you need the following information:

- The name of AD forest host
- The domain that you are joining.
- The Computer ID that has been assigned to your system in the AD and the search path for the OU (organizational unit) that contains it.

Collect this information from your Windows administrator before continuing.

Authenticate by clicking the lock button in the lower-left corner of the window. Highlight the Active Directory item (make sure that it's checked) and then click Configure.

A dialog appears, and Directory Access prompts you for information about your AD server. Click the Show Advanced Options disclosure pushbutton to show all the setting options, shown in Figure 30.8.

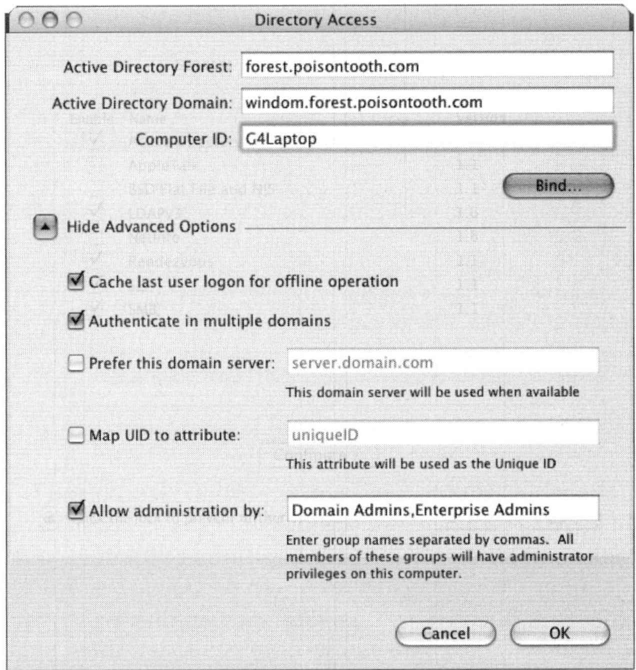

FIGURE 30.8 Enter the information necessary to connect to the Active Directory.

The first three pieces of information, which identify the AD forest, your domain, and computer ID are required. The rest are optional but can affect how your machine operates within the Active Directory. Use these five advanced settings as directed by your administrator:

- Cache Last User Logon for Offline Operation—When checked (the default), an AD user who authenticates with a Mac OS X computer will have a local home directory created and their login credentials stored. If the AD server goes offline, they can still log in to Mac OS X using the cached credentials. If you disable this feature, the AD server must be online for the user to log in.

- Authenticate in Multiple Domains—If selected, users throughout the AD forest can log in. If unchecked, you must choose the specific domains that can authenticate with Mac OS X when adding Active Directory to the Directory Access Authentication settings (discussed shortly).
- Prefer This Domain Server—If a preferred domain server is listed, Mac OS X attempts to use it by default. Otherwise, the AD is consulted and a nearby domain controller located.
- Map UID to Attribute—Specify a user account attribute in the AD that can be mapped to a user ID. This assumes that the AD schema has been extended beyond the default. If unchecked, Mac OS X generates a UID based on the GUID of the AD object. Changing this value at a later time can cause problems when accessing the user account.
- Allow Administration By—Choose the groups in the AD that are considered administrators by Mac OS X; `Domain Admins` and `Enterprise Admins` are the defaults.

After choosing your options, click the Bind button. Panther prompts for a username, password, and search path to identify your computer OU in the Active Directory, as shown in Figure 30.9. This is an AD username and password, not your local Mac OS X admin account. Click OK to continue.

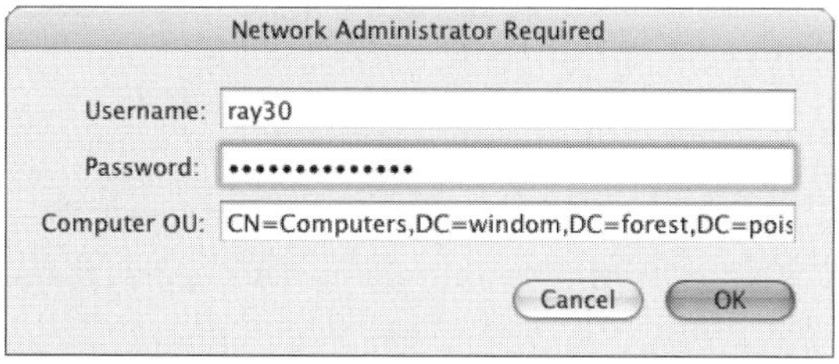

Network Administrator Required

Username: ray30

Password: ••••••••••••••

Computer OU: CN=Computers,DC=windom,DC=forest,DC=pois

Cancel OK

FIGURE 30.9 Authenticate with the Active Directory.

Panther takes a few moments to complete five steps in connecting to the Active Directory. If any errors occur along the way, you are given specific information to help correct the problem.

Finally, you need to add a search policy to Mac OS X so that it can query information from the server when appropriate. Click OK to return to the Directory Services application's main display.

Adding Search Policies

From within the Directory Access utility, click either the Authentication or Contacts button bar depending on whether you are using the directory server to provide administration information (logins, passwords, and so on) or simply contact data (names, email addresses, and so on). You can, of course, use both, but because they're configured identically, we'll only look at one.

After clicking the option (Authentication or Contacts) you want to connect to the directory server, use the Search pop-up menu to choose Custom Path. The default Automatic search policy searches local directory information as well as any DHCP-provided LDAP servers, but you must manually enter a search policy for Active Directory servers you've entered by hand.

After choosing Custom Path, click the Add button that appears at the bottom of the window. Mac OS X shows a list containing the Active Directory server you've added. Make sure that it is highlighted and then click Add to add it to your directory search list. By default, Mac OS X always searches the `/NetInfo/root` directory. You can reorder the search order of any directory by dragging it within the list, but the local NetInfo directory must always remain first.

As soon as it is added, Mac OS X should be able to query the directory server. If you're retrieving authentication data from the directory server, you should be able to log out and then log back in using the authentication information stored on the Windows server.

With Panther, connecting to an Active Directory server is almost as easy as connecting from a Windows client. Although many of AD's benefits are lost on the Mac (such as group policies), it goes a long way toward getting the Mac accepted as a viable corporate desktop client.

Samba

Over the past few years, Windows-only shops have been slowly adding Linux systems to their server arsenal. The reason for this seemingly unnatural acceptance of an alternative operating system is a piece of software called Samba. Samba provides the Windows sharing services that you've already seen in Mac OS X but is capable of much more than simply sharing your home directory. It is capable of replacing Windows NT and 200x servers on your network.

Samba offers comparable performance, features, and a price that can't be beat (free, of course). To quote *eWEEK*:

> Samba is capable, flexible, mature, and fairly well-documented; runs on several Unix operating systems; offers Web-based configuration and administration; and is free.
>
> Samba is now a viable option as a file and print server for many more Windows shops than before and earns an *eWEEK* Labs Analyst's Choice award for this remarkable technical accomplishment.
>
> To add this functionality, Samba Team developers (including those who are part of the Samba: The Next Generation project) had to reverse-engineer the proprietary protocols Microsoft Corp. uses to authenticate users and systems over the network, using, in many cases, nothing but a packet sniffer.

Samba offers Web-based configuration and administration. Even if you've never used a Windows computer and don't know the first thing about Windows file sharing, you'll be able to get a basic server up and running in only a few minutes.

Samba supports several advanced features, including file and printer sharing, user and share security, WINS, and emulation of a Windows NT domain. Best of all, it runs natively on Mac OS X. Now Windows users can come to the Mac, rather than vice versa.

What Is an NT Domain?

A *domain* is a collection of computers, much like a basic Windows workgroup or a zone in the traditional Mac AppleShare model. Besides organizing multiple computers into a unit, a domain provides centralized authentication and administration. When starting a computer, a user logs in to a domain. Doing so grants him or her access to resources within the domain.

In addition, a domain controller can manage roaming profiles for users; wherever they log in to the network, they see their personal desktop.

Interestingly enough, these features are available natively on Mac OS X using the NetInfo network directory system. NetInfo has existed since the late 1980s and predates the NT domain model by several years. A Mac OS X Server machine can be used to manage NetInfo Domains and perform Windows domainlike system administration.

Samba is a large piece of software—approaching Apache in terms of complexity and number of configuration options. In this chapter, the focus is on setting up solid, general-purpose servers. High-end needs are best served by other sources, such as *Sams Teach Yourself Samba in 24 Hours* (ISBN: 0672316099). The Samba Web site is also a great source for information (`http://www.samba.org`).

NOTE

Apple has been reasonably good about including a new version of Samba with Mac OS X and keeping up with security patches. If you prefer to install from scratch and have about 30 minutes, you can easily compile and install Samba on your own. Download the latest Samba source from `http://www.samba.org/`.

Let's get down to business.

Activating SWAT

Although Samba can be activated and used with Apple's default configuration (stored in `/etc/smb.conf`), you'll be missing 99% of the functionality. Samba offers many advanced features that can only be accessed when you manually edit the setup. In its early days, Samba was configured entirely by hand by editing the `smb.conf` file. It worked but wasn't really useful to anyone but the most die-hard Unix users. Today, however, configuration is handled entirely through a Web-based GUI called SWAT.

CAUTION

Although Samba can still be configured by hand (which you're welcome to do!), it is recommended that SWAT be used at all times. Some small changes are easy enough to accomplish with a text editor, but the Samba configuration file is extremely sensitive to invalid settings.

If, at any point in time, you want to return to the original Mac OS X Samba configuration, just copy the file `/etc/smb.conf.template` over `/etc/smb.conf`, and all the changes you've made will be replaced.

SWAT is included with your system but not ready for use. SWAT requires additional setup that enables it to activate when a Web browser accesses port 901 on your computer.

Open your `/etc/services` file and add the following line:

```
swat     901/tcp # SWAT
```

Next, you need to configure `xinet` to start SWAT (see Chapter 20, "Command-Line Configuration and Administration," for the details of `xinet`).

Edit the file `/etc/xinetd.d/swat`, changing the line that reads `disable = yes` to `disable = no`:

```
swat
service swat
{
    port  = 901
    socket_type   = stream
    wait  = no
    only_from = localhost
    user  = root
    server = /usr/sbin/swat
    log_on_failure += USERID
    groups = yes
    disable = no
}
```

SWAT is ready to run. Either reboot Mac OS X to enable SWAT access on port 901, or kill -HUP the `xinetd` process (`sudo killall -1 xinetd` will suffice).

NOTE

SWAT is not related, in any way, to the Apache process. Even if Apache is not activated, you'll still be able to use a Web browser to configure the Samba server. The Internet Daemon (`inetd` or `xinetd`) process listens on port 901 for incoming TCP connections, and then launches `/usr/sbin/swat` to service the request.

Configuring Samba

To configure Samba, start a Web browser and point it at port 901 of the Samba server (`http://localhost:901`). SWAT prompts for an administrative username and password. All screenshots shown in this section assume that the controlling user is `root`. Figure 30.10 shows the SWAT home screen.

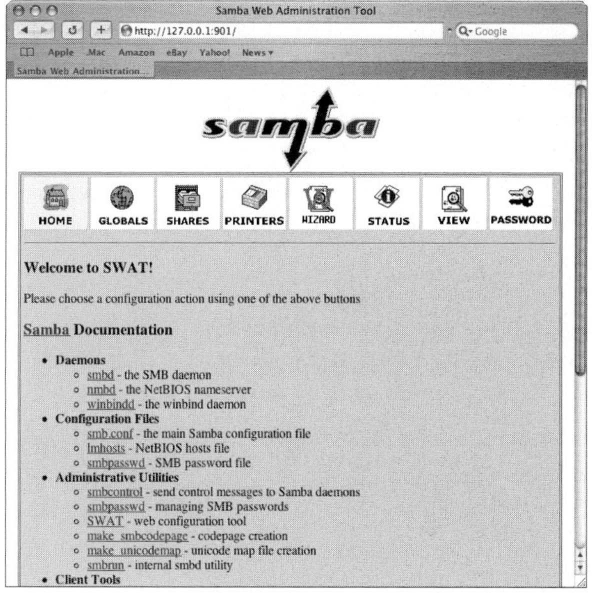

FIGURE 30.10 SWAT opens with a page providing easy access to Samba documentation.

The top of the SWAT display includes eight buttons to control the operation of the server:

- Home—Provides links to Samba documentation and supplemental material.
- Globals—Settings that affect the entire server, such as its name and security model.
- Shares—Shared file resources. If you used the sample configuration file that comes with the Apache distribution, a single home directory share already should be configured.
- Printers—Shared printers. To share a printer, it must first be set up so that it can be accessed from Mac OS X. By default, all configured printers are shared.
- Wizard—A quick-start for configuring Samba to be a standalone server, domain controller, or domain member. Because Mac OS X already includes a standalone configuration with setup specific to Mac OS X, starting over isn't recommended.

- Status—Monitor and view the status of the server. If logged in as `root`, you can restart or stop the server process.
- View—View a copy of the text configuration file.
- Password—Set and edit Samba user passwords. Samba authenticates against Mac OS X passwords by default, so it is unlikely you'll need these settings.

Let's step through these configuration screens to see the options used in a typical sharing environment.

Globals

The Global Variables page, shown in Figure 30.11, is the starting point for setting up your Samba server. Many people jump the gun and immediately start setting up file shares. Failure to properly configure the global options might make it impossible to mount or browse shared resources.

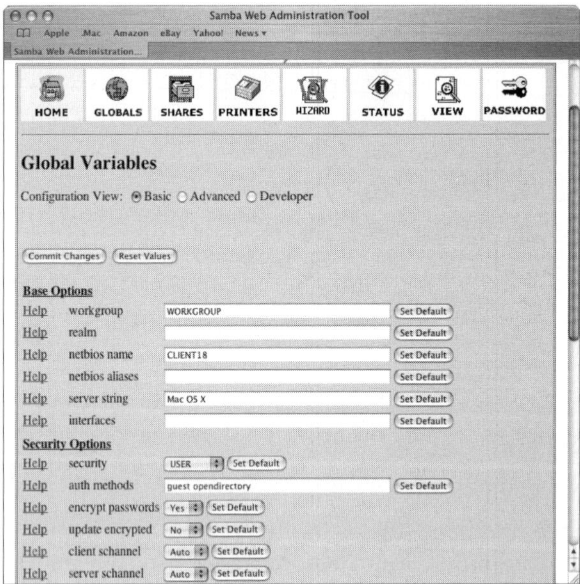

FIGURE 30.11 Global options set the operating parameters for the Samba server.

Two buttons can save (Commit Changes) server settings and reset changes (Reset Values). Choosing the Basic, Advanced, or Developer View radio buttons shows additional options—a number of which are listed in Table 30.4. If you don't see the setting you're looking for, move to the Advanced mode.

TABLE 30.4 Common Global Options and Their Purpose

Option	Purpose
`workgroup`	Sets the workgroup or domain that the server belongs to. Set this to the same value as the workgroup/domain of local Windows clients; otherwise, they cannot browse the server. This is the same value that can be set in the Directory Access application.
`netbios name`	The Windows (NetBIOS) name of the server.
`netbios aliases`	A list of additional NetBIOS names to which the Samba server responds.
`server string`	A string used to describe the server. This is entirely arbitrary.
`interfaces`	The network interfaces that Samba broadcasts over. For example, Mac OS X's primary interface is `en0`. By default, all active interfaces are used. To limit the interfaces, enter the interface names to use, or the network address followed by a subnet mask (that is, 192.168.0.0/255.255.255.0).
`password level`	The number of case-changes checked between the client login and the server password. Because client operating systems might transmit passwords in uppercase, they have to be altered to authenticate with the server. (Advanced)
`username level`	The same as the password level but alters the username in a similar manner. For example, if I have a Mac OS X username of `jray` and a Windows login of `JRAY`, I must set this value to 4 for it to be successfully permuted into the lowercase version. (Advanced)
`security`	The type of security model to use. User security bases access on a user login. Share password-protects individual shared resources. Domain and server security passes authentication duties to other NT or Samba servers, respectively. You'll probably want user or share-level security.
`encrypt passwords`	Sets encrypted password negotiation with the client. Encrypted passwords are required to access Samba from Windows 98 and later.
`guest account`	The local user that should be used for guest access and resource browsing. Mac OS X should use `unknown`.
`hosts allow`	A list of hostnames, IP addresses, IP addresses with subnet masks (`192.168.0.0/255.255.255.0`), or partial addresses (`192.168.0.`) that can access the server. The `except` keyword can create an exception to a rule. For example, `192.168.0.0/255.255.255.0 except 192.168.0.5` would allow any host in the `192.168.0.0` subnet, except `192.168.0.5`, to access the server. If left blank, all remote hosts can access the server.
`hosts deny`	Like hosts allow but used to list servers that should not have access to the server. Configure using the same method as `hosts allow`.
`log file`	The log file to store server accesses in. The `%m` in the default path appends the name of the remote machine to the log file name.
`max log size`	The maximum size in kilobytes that a log file should be allowed to reach before rolling over.

TABLE 30.4 Continued

Option	Purpose
`domain logon`	Accept domain logins. This allows Windows clients to recognize the Samba server as a PDC (primary domain controller). (Advanced)
`preferred master`	If set to yes, the Samba server attempts to force an election for master browser. Do not use on networks with multiple servers that want to be masters.
`local master`	Enables Samba to try to become the master browser for the local area network. If set to no, it does not attempt to assume this role.
`domain master`	Enables Samba's `nmbd` component to become a domain master browser that collects browse lists from remote subnets.
`os level`	A number used to determine the ranking of Samba when a master browser is being elected on a Windows network. If Samba is the only server on the network, use the default 20. If NT/2000/XP machines are on the network, and you want Samba to be the master browser, set this to a value greater than 32.
`dns proxy`	Attempts to resolve WINS queries through DNS if they cannot be resolved from locally registered machines.
`wins server`	A remote WINS server that Samba should register with.
`wins support`	Enables Samba's WINS service. Only a single machine should act as a WINS server on a given subnet.

The default settings should be sufficient for most small networks, with the exception of the base and security options (such as `hosts allow` and `hosts deny`). The best rule for Samba is that if you aren't sure what something does, or whether you even need it, don't touch it.

Shares

The Share Parameters page sets up file shares that can be mounted on networked Windows-based computers. To create a new share, type a share name in the Create Share field and then click the Create Share button. To edit an existing share, choose its name from the pop-up list and then click Choose Share—or click Delete Share to remove it completely.

With the default Panther Samba configuration file, a single `homes` share should already be available. `homes` is unique because it is equivalent to each user sharing his home directory. Figure 30.12 shows this share loaded.

The basic share parameters are listed in Table 30.5. Again, a few advanced options are also included.

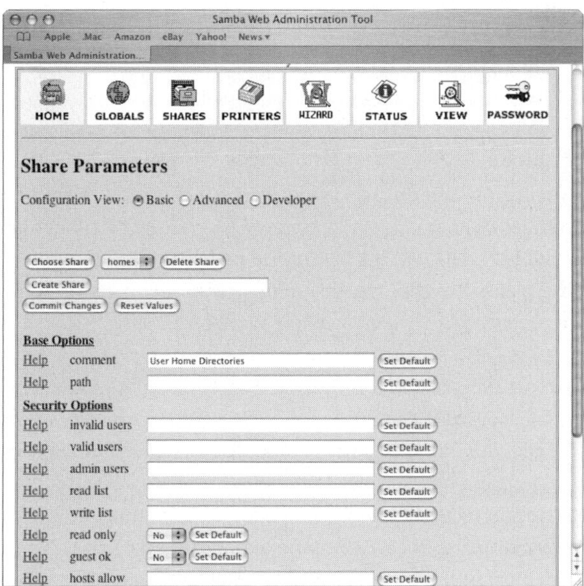

FIGURE 30.12 Use the Share Parameters page to set up your Windows SMB file shares.

TABLE 30.5 File-Sharing Options and Values

Option	Purpose
`comment`	A comment to help identify the shared resource.
`path`	The pathname of the directory to share. Be aware that in user-level security, you must make sure that the corresponding Mac OS X user accounts have access to this directory. When using share-level security, a single-user account is used—usually the guest account. In that case, the next setting becomes very important.
`guest account`	The account used to access the share if the remote client is logged in as a guest. The default is unknown, but, if set to another username, the guest user will have the read/write permissions of that local user account. If you want to use share-level access control, you can set this value to the account whose permissions should be used when accessing the share.
`force user`	If entered, the `force user` username is used for all accesses (read/write) to the file share, regardless of the username used to log in. (Advanced)
`force group`	Similar to force user but forces a group rather than a user. (Advanced)
`read only`	When set to Yes, users cannot write to the share, regardless of the Mac OS X file permissions.
`read list`	A list of users that should only have read-access to the volume, regardless of any other settings.

30

TABLE 30.5 Continued

Option	Purpose
`write list`	A list of users that should have read/write access regardless of any other settings.
`create mask`	A set of permissions that newly created files will have. By default, the mask is set to 0744. (Advanced)
`guest ok`	If set to Yes, guests can log in to the server without a password.
`hosts allow`	A list of hostnames, IP addresses, IP addresses with subnet masks (`192.168.0.0/255.255.255.0`), or partial addresses (`192.168.0.`) that can access the share. The `except` keyword can create an exception to a rule. For example, `192.168.0.0/255.255.255.0 except 192.168.0.5` would allow any host in the `192.168.0.0` subnet, except `192.168.0.5`, to access the server. If left blank, all remote hosts can access the server.
`hosts deny`	Like `hosts allow` but used to list servers that should not have access to the server. Configure using the same method as allow.
`max connections`	Restricts the number of simultaneous users who can access the share. (Advanced)
`browseable`	When set to Yes, the share shows up in the Windows network browser. If no, the share still exists, but remote users cannot see its name.
`available`	If set to Yes, the share is made available over the network. Setting to No disables access to the share.

The trickiest part of setting up a share is figuring out user access rights. Regardless of whether Samba is using user-level or share-level access, a Unix user must be mapped to the incoming connection.

The easiest security model is user-level (the default), which requires Windows users to log in to their computers using the same username and password set up on the Mac OS X machine. When using user-level access, Windows users are mapped directly to Samba users. The Mac OS X file permissions apply directly to the permissions of the connected user.

Assume, for example, that the Mac OS X user `jray` has read/write permissions to the folder `/Stuff`, which is also set to be a Samba share. If `jray` logs in to a Windows computer using the same username as on Mac OS X, he can access the `Stuff` share and have read/write access. The SWAT Password page can be used to map Unix users to the passwords that they will use on the remote Windows client if the Windows password doesn't match their default OS X password.

Things are a bit different with share-level access. In these cases, a single password is needed to access the share for all users, and no matter who is logged in, a single account is used by Samba when interacting with the Mac OS X filesystem. To simplify share-level security, create a new Mac OS X user to use for logging in to your shares; then set the guest account for the share equal to the Mac OS X username. You should disable other login access (set the shell to `/dev/null`) if you *do* distribute a password among multiple people for the purpose of file sharing.

Wizard

The Samba Wizard options configure a Samba server to act as either a standalone server, domain member, or domain controller. Use the radio buttons to choose your basic server settings, how WINS will be used (as either a client, server, or not at all), and finally, whether home directories should be enabled. Click Commit to save the changes.

> **NOTE**
>
> Samba maintains the basic share settings and parameters configured before the wizard is used. The wizard feature tweaks only a handful of global options—nothing that can't be handled just as easily on the Globals page.

Printers

Samba can act as a full print server for a Windows network. By default, all configured printers are shared through a share called `printers` that operates much like the `homes` share does for home directories. Check out Chapter 10, "Printer, Fax, and Font Management," for setting up Mac OS X printers.

There are a few options for setting up printer sharing. You can go with the default of sharing every printer available through the `printers` share. You can also modify the settings of the `printers` share or any specific shared printer to control its use. A final option is to delete the `printers` share and configure each device manually. Because Mac OS X normally does most of the work for you automatically, this last option really just makes life more difficult.

Shared printers can be configured using the options in Table 30.6.

TABLE 30.6 Printer Sharing Options

Option	Purpose
`comment`	A comment used to identify the printer share.
`path`	A directory where print spool files are saved before printing. The directory must be configured to be world-writable and have the sticky bit set.
`guest account`	The guest account used to access the printer resource, if guest access is enabled.
`guest ok`	If set to Yes, guests may access the printer. This is not a wise idea on a publicly networked device.
`hosts allow`	A list of hostnames, IP addresses, IP addresses with subnet masks (`192.168.0.0/255.255.255.0`), or partial addresses (`192.168.0.`) that can access the share. The `except` keyword can create an exception to a rule. For example, `192.168.0.0/255.255.255.0 except 192.168.0.5` would allow any host in the `192.168.0.0` subnet, except `192.168.0.5`, to access the server. If left blank, all remote hosts can access the server.
`hosts deny`	Like `hosts allow` but used to list servers that should not have access to the server. Configure using the same method as `allow`.
`printable`	Allows authenticated clients to write to the print spool directory.

TABLE 30.6 Continued

Option	Purpose
`printer name`	The CUPS name for the printer; used if configuring the printer manually. You must switch to Advanced View to see this option. To view a list of the CUPS-recognized printers on your system, type **`lpstat -p`**. Any available printer can be shared.
`max print jobs`	The maximum number of print jobs that can be submitted to the print queue at one time.
`browseable`	When set to Yes, the printer shows up in the Windows network browser. If no, the printer share still exists, but remote users cannot see its name.
`available`	If set to Yes, the printer is made available over the network. Setting to No disables access to the printer.

Enter the options needed to create the printer share and then click Commit Changes. Windows clients should be able to browse and print the device immediately.

Status

Figure 30.13 shows the SWAT Server Status page. This page gives a quick overview of the server's current conditions, including active connections, shares, and files. The administrator can use this screen to restart the server or disable any active connections.

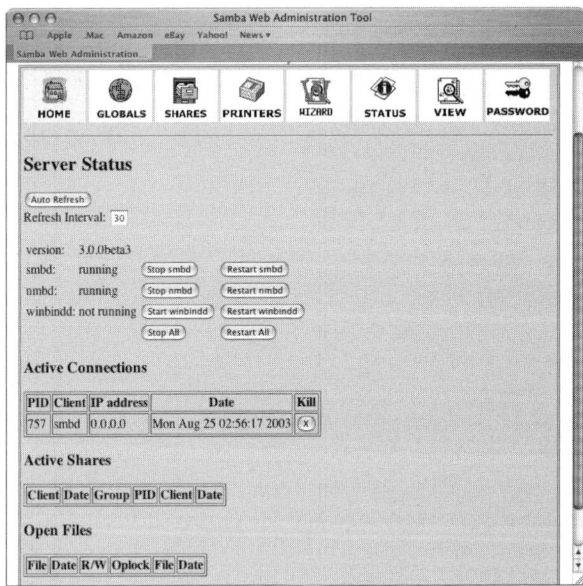

FIGURE 30.13 Use the Status page to monitor active connections.

Each of the visible buttons effects a change on the server:

- Auto Refresh—Sets the SWAT status page to autorefresh based on the Refresh Interval field. This is useful for monitoring server activity.
- Stop/Start/Restart `smbd`—Stops, starts, or restarts `smbd`—the Samba SMB file/print server. All active connections are terminated.
- Stop/Start/Restart `nmbd`—Stops, starts, or restarts `nmbd`—the Samba NetBIOS name server. Does not affect active connections.
- Stop/Start/Restart `winbindd`—Stops, starts, or restarts `winbindd`—A process that binds to a Windows domain to retrieve account information. Does not affect active connections.
- Kill—The Kill button (an "X") appears to the right of every listed connection. Clicking the button immediately terminates the link.

NOTE

Terminating an active connection might result in data loss for the remote user. Although certainly a tempting prank, it isn't a nice thing to do.

View

View offers a glimpse at the configuration file behind SWAT's GUI. Sometimes it's easier to scan through a text file to locate a problem than to work with the Web interface. The View page has two modes. The Normal view (default) shows the minimum configuration file needed to implement your settings.

Switching to the Full view displays all the settings, including default options, for the Samba configuration. Each option is explicitly listed, regardless of its necessity.

Password

The Password page is used to set up Samba passwords for existing Mac OS X users, or change remote user passwords if using domain-level security and a remote host for user authentication.

If you've enabled a Mac OS X user so that she can log in to her account from Windows, you've effectively already used this feature. Because Apple has tied Samba to the Mac OS X authentication system, there is little need to use these settings; use the Mac OS X Accounts preferences pane instead.

If Samba uses domain-level security, another server (such as a Windows primary domain controller) is the source for all authentication information. To change a user's password on the remote server, use the Client/Server Password Management features of the password screen:

- User Name—The remote user to change.
- Old Password—The user's existing password.
- New Password—The new password to set on the remote server.
- Re-type New Password—The same as the New Password option; used to verify typing.
- Remote Machine—The remote server that contains the username/password mappings.

Click the Change Password button to send the password changes to the remote server.

Creating a Sample Share

Now let's go through the process of accessing a shared volume from a Windows computer. This example uses Windows XP. By the time you read this, five or six new versions of Windows will probably be available, so I apologize if the instructions don't match up entirely.

First, set up the server defaults. For my machine, POINTY, I've created a bare global configuration. Rather than including a screenshot for the share, I'm including the configuration from the `/etc/smb.conf` file. Each resource has its own block in the `config` file. Within that block, the options we've covered are listed, along with their associated value. This is the global configuration block for my simple Samba server:

```
[global]
    auth methods = guest, opendirectory
    passdb backend = opendirectorysam, guest
    guest account = unknown
    workgroup = POISONTOOTH
    netbios name = POINTY
    server string = Poisontooth SAMBA Server
    encrypt passwords = Yes
    preferred master = Yes
    dns proxy = No
    wins support = Yes
```

The workgroup, NetBIOS name, and server string are personalized for my server and local area network. I've also chosen to have the server act as a WINS server and register as the preferred master browser on the network. It's important to note that encrypted passwords are enabled; otherwise, newer Windows clients (such as Windows 2000/XP) wouldn't be able to connect.

Next, the file share. I've created a folder `/filestorage/mp3s` on my Mac OS X computer to hold my library of iTunes MP3 files. My user account (`jray`) owns the folder and has read/write permission to it. This simple share, named MyMP3s, is defined as

```
[MyMP3s]
      path = /filestorage/mp3
      read only = No
```

Now, with only a few clicks of the mouse (barring Windows lockups), I'll be happily listening to my iTunes music on a Windows computer.

Mapping the Share in Windows

There are a number of different ways to mount a network drive under Windows. If your Windows XP computer is set up with the same workgroup name as the Samba server, you can simply double-click My Network Places and then View Workgroup Computers. The Samba server should appear using the NetBIOS name you specified in the Global configuration.

Right-clicking My Network Places (or My Computer) and choosing Map Network Drive from the pop-up menu is the fastest mounting method. The screen shown in Figure 30.14 is displayed.

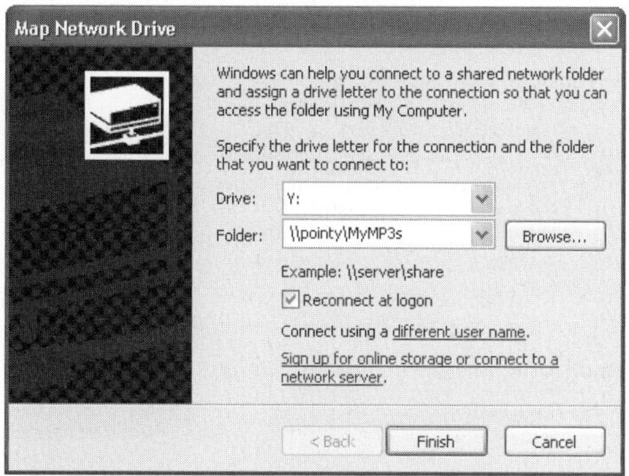

FIGURE 30.14 Map the shared folder in one simple step.

Choose a drive letter to use for the mounted volume and then enter the share path in the Folder field. The share path is entered as `\\`***`<NetBIOS name>`***`\`***`<share name>`***. For the sample share I've set up, the path is `\\pointy\MyMP3s\`. Click the Reconnect at Logon button to automatically mount the shared resource when you log in to the Windows computer.

The Mac OS X Folder, shared through Samba, becomes usable like any other network drive on Windows.

It's too bad that Windows doesn't play as nicely, isn't it?

Viewing Connections with smbstatus

Although the SWAT interface is fully capable of telling you who is accessing your server, sometimes a Web browser isn't convenient. In these cases, the smbstatus utility provides information about the active connections and users. For example:

```
brezup:root root # smbstatus
NOTE: Service printers is flagged unavailable.

Samba version 3.0.0beta3
PID   Username   Group    Machine
-------------------------------------------------------------------
 951  jray      jray     client19   (10.0.1.119)
 965  jray      jray     painful    (10.0.1.107)

Service   pid  machine    Connected at
-------------------------------------------------------
IPC$      965  painful    Sat Aug 23 00:38:22 2003
jray      951  client19   Sat Aug 23 00:11:29 2003
jray      965  painful    Sat Aug 23 00:38:35 2003
No locked files
```

In this example, two client computers (client19 and painful) are connected using the process IDs 951 and 965, respectively. The painful client is using the default IPC$ and jray shares, whereas client19 is just using jray. You can force a connection to close by killing the associated process ID.

Table 30.7 shows the most useful smbstatus options.

TABLE 30.7 smbstatus Options

Option	Purpose
-b	Summary of connected users.
-d	Detailed connection listing. This is the default mode.
-L	Lists locked files only.
-p	Lists the smbd process IDs and exit.
-S	Lists connected shares only.
-s *<config file>*	Chooses the smb.conf file to use.
-u *<username>*	Displays only information relevant to a given username.
-v	Verbose output.

Summary

This chapter introduced the reader to the Windows SMB/CIFS file-sharing protocols and how they can be used on the Mac OS X platform. Mac OS X already offers integration features with Windows, such as file and printer sharing and basic Exchange server synchronization. For users wanting to share more than just their home directories, Panther includes Samba 3.

Samba is a full-featured server product that is easy to install and set up, and can replace a Windows XP/2000 server for file and print sharing. Samba has so many configuration options that additional resources, such as *Sams Teach Yourself Samba in 24 Hours*, are required for complex configuration. To access Samba or Windows shares from a Mac OS X desktop, you can use the built-in SMB/CIFS client, or mount and access the data using command-line utilities. For users in a corporate environment, Apple's support of Windows technologies makes it possible to integrate and interoperate with Microsoft-centric networks.

PART VII

System and Server Health

IN THIS PART

CHAPTER 31

Server Security and Advanced Network Configuration

IN THIS CHAPTER

- Why Bother with Network Security
- Disabling Access
- Intrusion Detection
- Where to Go from Here

In earlier chapters, we touched on the idea of making your machine as secure as possible. In this chapter, we cover the topic in greater depth. We discuss why security is important, types of attacks you might encounter, some suggestions for securing your machine, and some security tools that can help you.

Why Bother with Network Security

Before we can reasonably discuss ways to make your Mac OS X machine more secure, it's important to understand why you should care and what you're facing.

You might be wondering, "Why bother with security?" You've never cared about securing your Mac before. In fact, prior to Mac OS X, security has rarely been an issue for a Mac owner. However, as a Unix-based operating system, Mac OS X brings with it not only the advantages of a Unix operating system—it also brings the disadvantages. Unfortunately, one of those disadvantages is security, which has always been a problem for networked, multitasking operating systems. This is unsettling at the beginning, but the simple fact is that nothing can be done to make any network-connected Unix machine (Mac OS X or otherwise) completely secure. To paraphrase one system administrator's feeling about securing a Unix machine, "I'd pull the plug and the network, put the machine in a safe, fill the safe with concrete, lock it, and drop it in the middle of Hudson Bay—and even then I wouldn't be sure."

That take might be a little extreme, but you get the point. If your machine is on a network, and/or the hardware is physically accessible, it's vulnerable to something somehow. Your best efforts at security are only capable of increasing the effort, time, and creativity required for a cracker to access your hardware—you simply can't make it impossible.

Crackers target anything they can find on your computer or network. Your Mac OS X computer runs a variety of server processes that enable it to communicate with the outside world. A single programming flaw in one of these daemons could open administrative access to anyone. If a cracker can't find a way in directly, he can direct attacks on your network hardware or your ISP's hardware. Switches, routers, and other devices are also susceptible to attack. If your computer has blocked access to outside networks, the intruder might resort to IP spoofing to fake his real location.

The threat of computer break-ins is very real and a very real concern—even if you're doing everything right. For example, earlier versions of Sendmail (the mail server that used to be included with the Mac OS X installation) suffered from a bug that allowed remote crackers to send a specially formatted email to the server and force it to execute pieces of code with full administrator privileges. Imagine it: A person, anywhere in the world, could potentially take over control of your computer by sending it an email message. Even experienced administrators were at risk from this bug. Although Sendmail has since been patched, this is an excellent example of the type of attack that's possible. For more information about this particular exploit, check out `http://ciac.llnl.gov/ciac/bulletins/h-23.shtml`.

NOTE

Crackers, not hackers: There seems to be a popular misconception that the term *hacker* means someone who breaks into computers. This hasn't always been the case, and annoys the hackers out there who do not break into computers. To many hackers, the term *hacker* means a person who hacks on code to make it do new and different things—frequently with little regard to corporate-standard good programming, but also frequently with a Rube Goldberg–like, elegant-but-twisted logic.

Hackers, to those who don't break into computers, are some of the true programming wizards—the guys who can make a computer do almost anything. These are people you want on your side, and dirtying their good name by associating them with the average scum that try to break into your machine isn't a good way to accomplish this.

So, to keep the real hackers happy, we refer to the people who compromise your machine's security as *crackers* in this book. We hope you follow our lead in your interactions with the programmers around you.

You might still be wondering, "Why bother?" If the machine can't be made completely secure, why try? When your machine is brand new and not very customized, perhaps you can afford to have that attitude. Reinstalling the operating system is not all that traumatic at that stage. However, because you've made it to this chapter, you've seen Mac OS X from many angles and perhaps even implemented some customizations to your system. Hence, you might not feel like doing it all over again.

So, if you can't be *completely* secure, what can you do? You can be *reasonably* secure. Exactly how secure is reasonable differs from case to case, and depends on a wide range of factors. Later in this chapter, we discuss some of these factors and how to assess your needs. For now, understand that when designing security measures, there's a threshold beyond which expending extra effort does not produce a sufficient increase in security to make that effort worthwhile. You can liken this to the somewhat facetious advice given for how to protect yourself when hiking in bear country—"always hike with someone who runs slower than you do." Your goal in securing your system is to make your machine and your network less attractive than the next guy's system to the cracker. In this chapter, we look at some ways to accomplish that goal.

Security Assessment

There are a number of factors that you need to keep in mind when assessing what reasonable security means to you. How you weigh each of these factors and the decisions you make regarding implementation details are up to you. There are, however, some good rules of thumb that you can live by. You might not fully understand some of these items, but we recommend that you follow them anyway. Some might sound like overt paranoia until you've been in the trenches for a while. After you've been there and done that a few times, you'll probably come to realize that when it comes to security, paranoia is usually your friend.

The four questions that you should ask yourself before deciding on a strategy are "Why do I want security?" "Who is going to try to compromise my security?" "How worried about it am I?" and "How much effort do I want to invest in stopping them?"

"Because" is a perfectly reasonable answer to the first question, but if you have a better answer, such as "because my system contains sensitive financial transaction data," your mission in securing your machine will be much more focused.

The answer to the second question is instrumental in deciding what security precautions are appropriate for your site. If you're trying to secure a system that contains important industrial secrets, you have much more at stake. Therefore, you'll also meet a very different kind of cracker than on something like a student-organization Web server at a college.

The answer to the third question should be "very." First, if you aren't very worried, you're putting forth a lot of effort to protect something that you're not very worried about. Second, paranoia is an admirable quality in a system administrator. You might not feel like a system administrator, but with your Mac OS X machine, not only have you become a Unix user, but you're also a system administrator. A good system administrator always prepares for the worst possible scenario that she can imagine. The worst (or something closely approximating it) happens to everyone eventually, and it's the paranoid system administrator who planned for the worst three years ago who keeps the system up and running like nothing ever happened. When the system administrator's job is done right, nobody ever notices that she's done it and nobody ever says thank you. You might not have many users on your Mac OS X machine, so you might not be in quite the same shoes as your system administrator. Nevertheless, you should take the time to brighten your system administrator's day and say thank you. If you want to make her even happier, let her know that you're taking steps to make your machine reasonably secure.

On the final question, if your answer isn't "a lot," you should realize up front that your system won't be very secure for very long. All flavors of Unix are such complex systems that it's impossible to completely debug them, and new holes and exploits are being found on a weekly basis. Although there are more interesting things to do on your Mac OS X machine, as a responsible Unix machine owner, you should try to keep up with the latest patches to software and watch the latest developments in the cracker world.

Private Data Versus Secret Data

Understanding the reasons that the data or contents of your system need to be protected is important. If you're proposing to create a secure system for something like a K–12 student-teaching lab network, your main reason for wanting to protect your system is probably simply the principle of the matter. On the other hand, if you're protecting a system that contains important industrial secrets, preventing intrusion is probably a necessity. Essentially, this assessment comes down to a question of whether your data is simply private or actually secret. Allowing the disclosure of private data is never a good thing, but you won't find many people with the motivation to try to compromise your system if the data in it is simply private. On the other hand, if your data contains secrets, such as industrial trade secrets, financial records, or some types of highly sensitive personal information, you'll find attackers who are much more motivated to crack your system.

The point of this examination goes back to that issue of making your system less attractive than the next guy's. If your system contains only private data, you won't have much trouble making it more secure than the vast majority of other systems out there. If your only concern is the random curious cracker rather than the dedicated and motivated one, you can make your system unattractive to him with little work.

If, on the other hand, you're in the unfortunate position of needing to defend truly secret data, you might find crackers motivated enough that they won't leave you alone no matter what you do. Against these individuals, you've little choice but to simply do your best to stay one step ahead of them.

Types of Attackers

We divide the types of attackers you're likely to meet into three subsets. Although it might not seem obvious at first consideration, the variety that you're the most likely to meet—regardless of the type of data you're protecting—is frequently both the most and least dangerous.

The Motivated Cracker

The type of cracker you're probably least likely to meet is the dedicated and motivated professional or amateur cracker with a mission. This person might be an industrial spy trying to discover your company's trade secrets, a student trying to change his grade, or a hobbyist who simply finds your security measures a challenge.

> **CAUTION**
>
> Obscurity isn't to be relied on, but it sure doesn't hurt!
>
> Many system administrators, and even OS vendors, have historically had a bad habit of attempting to implement security measures based only on the fact that people didn't know about the holes in them. This is a concept known as *security through obscurity*, and is generally considered a bad thing to rely on. On the other hand, obscurity in addition to other security measures certainly doesn't hurt. Keeping your system and security measures low profile is always a good idea. If you have a system with extra-tight security measures, telling people just how tight they are is the surest way to attract the person who delights in cracking systems "just because."
>
> Rely neither on security through obscurity nor on the invincibility of your security measures. The best way to motivate a person to try to crack your system just because it's there is to let on that you think it can't be done.

The motivated cracker isn't likely to leave a large amount of evidence of his comings and goings. These types vary between unlikely to do any significant damage (other than observing your data), to making insidious and difficult-to-detect modifications to the contents of your system.

To defeat this type of cracker, you must understand his motivation and either remove it or resign yourself to a constant battle to stay ahead. The only way to actually stop these people permanently is to track them down and pursue legal remedies against them.

The Casual Experimenter

The next type of attacker you're likely to meet is the casual experimenter. These individuals don't usually intend any significant harm and aren't usually very motivated to invade your system. They're frequently just a bit overcurious, and are trying out something that they stumbled across somewhere on the Internet. This doesn't mean that they're not dangerous—their lack of intent can't prevent simple typing mistakes that can be disastrous to a person with root access. Thankfully, these individuals aren't usually too difficult to defend against because they're usually not particularly sophisticated. They also don't tend to be worth investing much effort in tracking down legally.

The Script Kiddie

The most common type of cracker doesn't even deserve to be called a cracker. Historically, crackers have been frequently thought of as Robin Hood characters, with a sort of romantic fascination with their exploits. Not to minimize the impropriety of the legendary crackers' actions, but you can appreciate the creativity and tenacity of these individuals without approving of their actions. By the standards set by the crackers of old, the vast majority of today's crackers barely qualify as cracker-wannabe wannabes.

Today's prototypical cracker is a young adult with too much free time who found a cracking script on a Web site somewhere and is trying to use it to show his friends he's an "lEEt HaCkEr dOOd." In fact, these new crackers are called script kiddies.

These individuals are both a trivial and significant concern. If you keep your system up-to-date and pay attention to the latest cracking scripts and to the patches against them, you're almost invulnerable to actual intrusion at the hands of these people. They don't generally try anything more complicated than running a script they've borrowed from someone else, so if you keep your system secure against these scripts, you're usually secure against cracker wannabes. That doesn't mean they're completely innocuous because they can still consume your network resources while trying to break into your system.

However, they can be very dangerous if you don't keep your system completely up-to-date because there are so darned many of them, and because they're basically glory hounds interested in nothing more than self-aggrandizement. To give you a perspective on the magnitude of their numbers, here at The Ohio State University, we see unsophisticated cracking attempts of this sort multiple times every week, directed at the thousands of machines on campus. A Linux machine, installed out of the box and not immediately secured against intrusion, stands a better than 50% chance of being cracked within 24 hours if it's attached to the network here. Fortunately, a Mac OS X machine installed out of the box is a bit more secure, but that doesn't mean it's invincible.

Also, because their basic goal is self-aggrandizement, and also because they don't get that much glory for using someone else's script, these people are rarely content to break into a system, tread lightly, and leave without a trace. Instead, they're more likely to erase the contents of your hard drive, or replace your corporate Web page with pornography, so they have some evidence to show their "lEEt HaCkEr dOOd" friends.

Securing your system against these attacks is simply a matter of watching every security discussion list and cracker site for signs of trouble and postings of new cracking scripts, and then applying every security patch as quickly as it becomes available. Simple, no? As satisfying as tracking them down and squashing them like the insects they are might be, it's usually impractical. Ninety percent of these attacks come from users with transient accounts, and the best you'll usually do is chase them to a different account. If you do happen to catch one, please do let the Internet system administration community know—the newsgroup `alt.sysadmin.recovery` is a good venue—public lynchings are always well attended.

Types of Attacks

Next, let's look at what methods attackers might use to access your machine. This is especially important if your machine is connected to an unprotected network or if it serves as a firewall.

Software and OS Flaws

The most common type of attack you'll encounter is one that attempts to exploit flaws in application or operating system software. There's probably not much you can do about most software flaws other than hoping that the providers find and fix the problems promptly. Although this is a problem from a security standpoint, the positive side is that if you're spending the time to watch the cracking Web pages and the security mailing lists, you'll know about the problems as soon as the crackers do. With the information you get from these sources and your understanding of the special risks your site incurs, you can assess whether leaving that software on your machine is an acceptable risk until the vendor fixes it.

You need to be aware that some of these flaws require prior access to your system to exploit, whereas others can be exploited from a remote site over the network. Don't make the mistake of assuming that because no one has actually logged in to your machine, you can't or haven't been attacked.

Brute Force Attacks

Although not a particularly elegant form of attack, the brute force attack is one that you can only partially prevent. In its simplest form, this attack is a cracker attempting to log in to a system by sitting at a machine and iteratively typing attempts at passwords into the prompt. There's not much you can do to keep people from trying this sort of thing.

Keep an eye on the system logs, and you'll see the trivial attempts as they occur. However, there's typically much more danger from this sort of attack when a cracker manages to get your password file and can attempt to crack the passwords on his own machine at his leisure. To prevent this, some systems use a shadow password facility to keep the password file from being readable by a normal user. However, Mac OS X does not have a shadow password facility. Instead, you might want to consider restricting the executable permission on your NetInfo utilities, such as `nidump` and `niutil`, to root only.

Denial of Service

Denial of service (DoS) attacks are generally destructive attempts rather than attempts to access your system. When the attacks come from a network of multiple machines, they're known as distributed denial of service attacks. Both types of attacks are targeted at preventing you and your users from using your machines instead of allowing an intruder access. Because this can be effectively accomplished without the aid of your system, there's little that you can do about many of these attacks. Because a denial of service attack rarely results in an actual security violation or illegitimate access of your system, your best defense is detection and elimination.

Although the specific methods employed in different varieties of denial of service attacks vary, they share a common feature: the exhausting of some service or resource that your machines require or provide. Why do people do this? Good question. You might expect this sort of behavior from a disgruntled ex-employee attacking a former employer or from a student who thinks it's a funny practical joke. Less expected are denial of service attacks that seem to happen as random vandalism just because the attacker can do it.

Certain denial of service attacks can be mitigated or prevented with software or hardware updates. In general, these updates tend to be installation of OS patches to disallow certain types of connections or installation of filtering hardware to block certain types of network traffic. Denial of service attacks range from flooding users' email, to absorbing all your HTTP server connections, to running your printer out of paper, to flooding your network with ICMP ping packets. Unfortunately, there's little you can count on to be reliably effective other than constant vigilance and swift retribution.

NOTE

Not all denial of service attacks are devoid of security risks. Some attacks are targeted at services that are known to break inelegantly and that sometimes allow privileged access when broken. Just because a denial of service attack looks relatively harmless, don't allow yourself to be complacent. It could be less harmless than it looks, or it could be a prelude to more unpleasant attacks.

Most attacks can generally be thwarted by taking the following precautions:

- Vigilance is your best defense against denial of service attacks. Watching your machine's load and network performance are the best ways to discover an attack in progress.
- Consider building a monitoring Web page that collects this information from all your machines and provides you with a continuously updated representation of the state of the world.
- A gateway between your cluster and the outside world can be used to deny traffic from a problematic outside host. Unfortunately, this can't prevent an outside host from effectively denying your network services just by banging away at your gateway until your network bandwidth is consumed.
- Enlist the help of system administrators upstream from your site in tracking and blocking denial of service attacks as they occur. Because you can't effectively prevent users on the other side of the world from running flood-ping against your machines, you'll need to find someone between you and them who can help.

Physical Attacks

Many administrators in charge of system security overlook this area of obvious weakness in their security strategy. Computers don't need to be logged in for a person to access their data. A person unscrupulous enough to crack your machines is just as happy to simply yank a hard drive out of your machine to steal the data on it. These sorts of attacks are usually easy to detect, but can cause significant downtime while critical hardware is replaced.

Although distributed computing and distributed storage are popular in certain environments, if security is a goal, especially data security, you should severely restrict access to all hardware with mission-critical data.

By far the easiest physical attack on your hardware is the power switch or reset button combined with the capability to boot the machine into single-user mode without a password or to boot off of a device specified at startup, also without a password. When in single-user mode, an attacker can get a dump of your passwords, change your root password, and so on.

Disabling Access

An important part of securing your machine is limiting access to it. In this section, we look at choosing services that run on your machine, using TCP Wrappers to restrict access, and some commonsense preventive measures you can take.

Selecting Services in the Graphical User Interface

As you might recall, Apple ships Mac OS X with many services disabled. In many of the Unix operating systems, you have to be careful to disable some common services that are turned on by default, but that you might not actually need. With Mac OS X, however, many of these common services are disabled. Instead, if you want to run a common service, such as a remote login service, you have to turn it on specifically in Mac OS X.

In the Sharing pane of System Preferences, controls to enable or disable a variety of services, such as the SSH, FTP, Web, and AppleShare services, are available. Choose only those services that you really need. Remember: The more services you turn on, the more vulnerable to attack your machine becomes.

Selecting Services Manually

As you saw earlier in the book, the actual controls that can be accessed via a graphical user interface are stored in a variety of places on the system.

`/etc/xinetd.d`

If you're using the default setup, `xinetd` is starting some of your common services, such as FTP. The controls for each of the services it handles are located in the `/etc/xinetd.d` directory. All of those services are initially off by default. In other words, each file in that directory contains a `disable=yes` line. Some services are disabled by not even having a configuration file in `/etc/xinetd.d`.

If you decide to turn on a service, make a backup copy of the appropriate service file, change the `disable` entry to `no`, add any server arguments to the `server_args` entry, and add any `xinetd` directives that you want to enable for the given service. Have `xinetd` reread its configuration file after you've made your changes. Consider using directives such as

- `only_from`—Restricts connections to a service only to the listed hosts
- `no_access`—Doesn't allow connections to a service from the listed hosts
- `access_times`—Restricts a service to being available only during the listed access times
- `per_source`—Specifies the maximum instances of a service per source IP address
- `cps`—Limits the rate of incoming connections

Please note that you can also start a service using `/sbin/service <service> start`, but if you need to make any adjustments to the server_args or directives, you have to edit the appropriate `xinetd` configuration file. Likewise, to turn off a service, you can also use `/sbin/service <service> stop`.

`/etc/inetd.conf`

Alternatively, you may also decide to have `inetd` control some of the common services on your system. Those services are configured in `/etc/inetd.conf`. As with `xinetd`, all the services controlled in `/etc/inetd.conf` are turned off by default in Mac OS X. For `/etc/inetd.conf`, that means there's a comment at the beginning of each service line.

If you decide to turn on a service, as a precaution, make a backup copy of the `/etc/inetd.conf` file. Next, uncomment the line containing the service you want to enable and save the file. Finally, restart the `inetd` process. If you decide to disable a service that starts out of `inetd`, simply comment the line that contains the service, save the file, and restart the `inetd` process.

One of the services that comes disabled in `/etc/inetd.conf` (and does not have a configuration file in `/etc/xinetd.d`) is the `identd` service. Although this is not a problem, you might experience some delays with your mail server.

You might have noticed that some of the services listed in `/etc/inetd.conf` have `##` at the beginning of the line, rather than `#`. These services are not yet implemented in the operating system.

StartupItems

As you also saw earlier in the book, some of the services that run in Mac OS X are started in `/System/Library/StartupItems`. Some of the services started in `/System/Library/StartupItems` also have controls in `/etc/hostconfig` that the startup scripts in `/System/Library/StartupItems` check. The Web server, the mail server, and AppleShare are controlled in such a fashion.

If you enabled those services, but later decide to disable them, set the appropriate `/etc/hostconfig` variable to `-NO-` and kill their current processes. The next time you reboot, the services won't start. To manually start one of those services, set the appropriate variable in `/etc/hostconfig` to `-YES-` and manually execute the startup script. How this is done depends on the startup script. For some, using `SystemStarter` (`SystemStarter start <path-to-service-directory>`) might be appropriate. For others, passing the start action to the script (`<startup script> start`) might work instead. For others, simply executing the startup script without passing the start action is sufficient. For others, you might have to execute the appropriate command within the script. For example, for AppleShare, you would make the `AFPSERVER` line in `/etc/hostconfig` read `AFPSERVER =-YES-`. Then you would execute `/System/Library/StartupItems/AppleShare/AppleShare start`. To disable a service that doesn't have a control in `/etc/hostconfig`, simply rename the startup script and kill its process.

TIP

Some third-party applications install their startup scripts in the /Library/StartupItems folder. Be sure to check this location as well as the main system-level folder.

Using TCP Wrappers

A common way to restrict access to some TCP services is to use the TCP Wrappers program. TCP Wrappers is a package that monitors and filters requests for TCP (Transmission Control Protocol) services. We don't look at the protocol in any detail here—that's a book subject in itself. Suffice it to say the protocol has enough control information in it that we can use a package like TCP Wrappers to filter some of that traffic. TCP Wrappers can be used to restrict certain network services to individual computers or networks.

To make use of this program on some flavors of Unix, TCP Wrappers must be installed by the system administrator. This isn't a necessary step in Mac OS X because the TCP Wrappers program comes preinstalled on the system. The `/etc/inetd.conf` file in Mac OS X already assumes that you use TCP Wrappers, as evidenced by a line such as the following:

```
#ftp  stream tcp   nowait root  /usr/libexec/tcpd        ftpd -l
```

The `/usr/libexec/tcpd` portion of the previous line indicates that TCP Wrappers is used to call `ftpd`.

Although using TCP Wrappers with `inetd` is the default in Mac OS X, it isn't the default for using `xinetd`. That's because of the controls already available in `xinetd`. Recall that `xinetd` has the `only_from` and `no_access` directives, which can help you to restrict access to services. If you decide that you want to use TCP Wrappers for host access restrictions on a service controlled by `xinetd`, you need to add a flag, `NAMEINARGS`, to the service and further expand the `server_args` line to include the full path to the service. Replace the original path to the server with the path to `tcpd`. Here's an example for using TCP Wrappers for restricting access to the FTP service in `xinetd`:

```
service ftp
{
    flags       = REUSE NAMEINARGS
    socket_type = stream
    protocol    = tcp
    wait        = no
    user        = root
    server      = /usr/libexec/tcpd
    server_args = /usr/libexec/ftpd -l
}
```

NOTE

To make use of TCP Wrappers with `xinetd`, `libwrap` support has to be compiled in. The `xinetd` that comes with Mac OS X has `libwrap` support. If you check your logs, you will see a line indicating this:

```
Sep 9 00:01:41 localhost xinetd[370]: xinetd Version 2.3.11 started
➥with libwrap options compiled in.
```

If you decide to update your `xinetd`, and you're using TCP Wrappers or think that you might want to use it, be sure to compile in the `libwrap` option.

Configuring TCP Wrappers

The particularly difficult part about using TCP Wrappers is configuring it. In this section, we look at two ways you can configure TCP Wrappers in Mac OS X: the traditional method of using two control files and a newer method that uses only one control file.

Traditionally, TCP Wrappers has two control files: `/etc/hosts.allow` and `/etc/hosts.deny`. We look at the traditional method in more detail because it's the default setup for a machine when extended processing options aren't enabled. An understanding of the traditional method should carry over to the new method. Be sure to read the `hosts_access` and `hosts_options` man pages for detailed information.

Here's the format of the access control files:

```
daemon_list : client_list : option : option ...
```

Through `/etc/hosts.allow`, you can allow specific services for specific hosts.

Through `/etc/hosts.deny`, you can deny services to hosts and provide global exceptions.

The easiest way to think of and use these configuration files is to think of TCP Wrappers as putting up a big fence around all the services on your machine.

The specifications in /etc/hosts.deny tell the fence what services are on the outside of the fence and, therefore, aren't denied. The fence can appear to be around different sets of services for different clients. For example, an /etc/hosts.deny file might look like this:

```
ALL EXCEPT ftpd : 192.168.1. : banners /usr/libexec/banners
ALL : 140.254.12.100 140.254.12.135 : banners /usr/libexec/banners
ALL EXCEPT ftpd sshd : ALL : banners /usr/libexec/banners
```

This file says

- For the subdomain 192.168.1., deny all connections except connections to the FTP daemon, ftpd.
- For the specific machines 140.254.12.100 and 140.254.12.135 (maybe they're troublemakers), deny absolutely all connections.
- For all other IP addresses, deny everything except connections to ftpd and to the secure-shell daemon sshd.

The banners /usr/libexec/banners entry is an option that tells tcpd that if it denies a connection to a service based on this entry, try to find an explanation file in this location. Use this option if you need to provide an explanation as to why the service isn't available.

The specifications in /etc/hosts.allow make little gates through the fences erected by /etc/hosts.deny for specific host and service combinations. For example, an /etc/hosts.allow file might look like this:

```
ALL: 140.254.12.137 192.168.2. 192.168.3.
popper: 140.254.12.124 140.254.12.151 192.168.1.36
```

This file says

- Allow connections to any TCP service from the host 140.254.12.137 and all hosts in the 192.168.2. and 192.168.3. subdomains. (Perhaps the 192.168.2. and 192.168.3. subdomains are known highly secure networks, and we really trust 140.254.12.137 because it's so well run.)
- Allow connections to the popd service for three specific machines: 140.254.12.124, 140.254.12.151, and 192.168.1.36.

If used in combination with the previous /etc/hosts.deny file, these allowances still stand. They override the denials in /etc/hosts.deny; even though the 192.168.1. subdomain is denied all access except to ftpd by /etc/hosts.deny, the specific machine 192.168.1.36 has its own private gate that allows it access to the popd service as well.

NOTE

Services with a smile or without? There can be a bit of confusion as to the name of the service to put in an `/etc/hosts.allow` or `/etc/hosts.deny` file. If it's a service out of inetd.conf, the name to use generally is the service name from the leftmost column of the inetd.conf file, or of the `/etc/services` file (or corresponding NetInfo directory). If this doesn't work, try adding a d to the end of the service name (`ftp` -> `ftpd`).

Other services use names that don't seem to be recorded officially anywhere. Other services that you encounter and decide to wrap with TCP Wrappers might require a bit of experimenting on your part. So far, my experience has been that their names are relatively easy to guess.

Now that you've seen how the traditional method of controlling TCP Wrappers works, let's take a brief look at a newer method that uses only the `/etc/hosts.allow` file. The newer method can be used on systems where extended option processing has been enabled. This is indeed the case with Mac OS X. Nevertheless, both methods work in Mac OS X.

In the single file, `/etc/hosts.allow`, you specify allow and deny rules all in the same file. With the `/etc/hosts.allow` only method, `tcpd` reads the file on a first-match-wins basis. Consequently, it's important that your allow rules appear before your deny rules.

For example, to restrict access to `ftpd` only to our host, `140.254.12.124`, we would use these rules:

```
ftpd: 140.254.12.124 127.0.0.1 localhost: ALLOW
ftpd: ALL: DENY
```

In the first line, we allow our host, `140.254.12.124`, access to `ftpd` using various addresses that it knows for itself. On the second line, we deny access to all other hosts. If we reversed these lines, even the host that we want to allow `ftpd` access to would be denied access.

After you've sufficiently tested that you have properly set up your allow and deny rules, there's nothing else you need to do to keep TCP Wrappers running. As you're testing your rules, check your logs carefully to see where, if at all, the behaviors are logged. You'll rarely see entries for `tcpd` itself in your logs, but you might see additional logging for a wrapped service under that service.

Wrapping Services to Allow Tunneling over SSH

As you saw earlier in the book, it's possible to tunnel connections over SSH. If you do decide to run the FTP service on your machine, you might be interested in restricting access to the service so that anyone who uses the service has to tunnel it through SSH. You saw in detail how to configure a Mac client running traditional Mac OS to do this, and you saw how to set up a tunnel in the command line in Mac OS X. We've not yet officially seen how to configure the Mac OS X machine to permit this.

The key to setting this up is restricting access to the desired service to your host by its IP address and as `localhost` addresses. Sometimes it can be helpful to include your machine by its name, too, but we haven't encountered this problem on a Mac OS X machine.

To restrict access to `ftpd` so that a user would have to tunnel her FTP connection, you could have an `/etc/hosts.deny` file like this:

```
ALL EXCEPT sshd: ALL
```

In this example, all services are denied except `sshd`.

In the `/etc/hosts.allow` file, add a line for your host that includes your host's IP address, `127.0.0.1` and `localhost`.

```
ftpd: 140.254.12.124 127.0.0.1 localhost
```

In this example, our host, `140.254.12.124`, is the only host allowed access to `ftpd`.

In the `/etc/hosts.allow` only method

```
sshd: ALL: ALLOW
ftpd: 140.254.12.124 127.0.0.1 localhost: ALLOW
ftpd: ALL: DENY
```

Commonsense Preventive Measures

We've reached a good time to point out some commonsense preventive measures to provide basic security for your machine. They don't guarantee the safety of your machine, of course, but they provide good basic guidelines for you. These commonsense activities apply not only to Mac OS X, but also to any other operating system.

The commonsense preventive security measures that you should always keep in mind are

- Keep your operating system current. You can easily do this by setting Software Update to a regular update schedule. If you prefer not to have Software Update check for updates automatically, make sure that you check Apple's Web site regularly for any updates and subsequently run Software Update. This is perhaps the most important commonsense activity you can do.
- For Mac OS X, don't turn on any network services that you don't need. For other operating systems, this often means turning off services you don't need because many operating services tend to come with many network services turned on by default.
- Restrict access to the services you have to run. Using TCP Wrappers is one method for restricting access to some services.

- Replace insecure services with secure services. For many systems, this advice especially targets using `sshd` instead of telnetd because `sshd` typically has to be installed separately. For Mac OS X, enabling remote login in the Sharing pane automatically starts `sshd`, which is included in the Mac OS X distribution, rather than telnetd.
- Run services with the least privilege necessary for the job. Check the documentation for the service to see advice about this.

Using BrickHouse as an Interface to the Built-in Firewall Package

As you've already seen, Mac OS X has basic tools available to help you secure your machine. In addition to the basic tools, Mac OS X comes with a firewall package called `ipfw`. A nice graphical interface to configuring and using `ipfw` is a shareware product called BrickHouse, available at `http://personalpages.tds.net/~brian_hill/`.

There's also a graphical firewall package, called Firewalk X, which we don't discuss. It's available from `http://www.pliris-soft.com/`. You can download a demo that is good for up to two hours after a reboot. The package installs as a System Preferences pane under the Internet & Network section. We aren't discussing the Firewalk X package because BrickHouse provides a better demonstration for learning how to use the `ipfw` package.

Preparation

Because you'll probably want to see some of the before-and-after effects of BrickHouse, we suggest that you take a quick look at a couple commands before you get started with the application.

Run this command:

```
brezup:root root # ipfw show
65535 49873 13969242 allow ip from any to any
```

What you just did was ask `ipfw` to show you the current firewall settings. As you probably guessed, `ipfw` on Mac OS X ships in an open state.

To correctly configure a firewall, you need to know the network interfaces being used on your system. The `ifconfig` command displays and sets interface information on your system. Try this command, especially if you are also hoping to use BrickHouse to help you set up your Mac OS X machine as a gateway for your home network. This process requires you to correctly identify the interface of your internal (private) network and main Internet connection.

```
brezup:sage sage $ ifconfig -a
lo0: flags=8049<UP,LOOPBACK,RUNNING,MULTICAST> mtu 16384
    inet6 ::1 prefixlen 128
    inet 127.0.0.1 netmask 0xff000000
gif0: flags=8010<POINTOPOINT,MULTICAST> mtu 1280
```

```
stf0: flags=0<> mtu 1280
en0: flags=8863<UP,BROADCAST,SMART,RUNNING,SIMPLEX,MULTICAST> mtu 1500
    inet6 fe80::230:65ff:feaa:37ae prefixlen 64 scopeid 0x4
    inet 192.168.1.16 netmask 0xffffff00 broadcast 192.168.1.255
    ether 00:30:65:aa:37:ae
    media: autoselect (10baseT/UTP <half-duplex>) status: active
    supported media: none autoselect 10baseT/UTP <half-duplex>
➥10baseT/UTP <full-duplex> 10baseT/UTP <full-duplex,hw-loopback>
➥100baseTX <half-duplex> 100baseTX <full-duplex> 100baseTX
➥<full-duplex,hw-loopback>
fw1: flags=8822<BROADCAST,SMART,SIMPLEX,MULTICAST> mtu 2030
    tunnel inet -->
    lladdr 00:30:65:ff:fe:aa:37:ae
    media: autoselect <full-duplex> status: inactive
    supported media: autoselect <full-duplex>
```

The utility `ifconfig` enables you to configure interface parameters. As shown previously, `ifconfig -a` produces a full listing of available interfaces.

Because the firewall package can be tricky to work with, what you try to do in BrickHouse might make your machine completely unusable. This is no fault of BrickHouse, but you should be prepared to remove components that you might have BrickHouse install. Depending on your situation, this might be possible only in single-user mode. If you haven't yet put your machine in single-user mode, we suggest that you do so before you do anything in BrickHouse. If you tried single-user mode a while ago but have forgotten what you did, take this moment to try again. Press Command+S while rebooting to get into single-user mode. The last few lines that appear are as follows (the actual prompt may vary):

```
Singleuser boot - fsck not done
Root device is mounted read-only
If you want to make modifications to files,
run '/sbin/fsck -y' first and then '/sbin/mount -uw /'
localhost#
```

Using BrickHouse

After you've downloaded and uncompressed the BrickHouse disk image, you're ready to start using it.

1. The Setup Assistant appears. Please note that you can also use the Setup Assistant at any time later by clicking on the Assistant button in the main BrickHouse window. The first part of the Setup Assistant is the External Network sheet, shown in Figure 31.1. Select your connection type and IP address assignment method (dynamic or static). Connection-type choices are DSL or Cable Ethernet (Regular Ethernet), Dialup Modem (PPP), DSL or Cable PPPoE, AirPort (+ External AirPort Base Station).

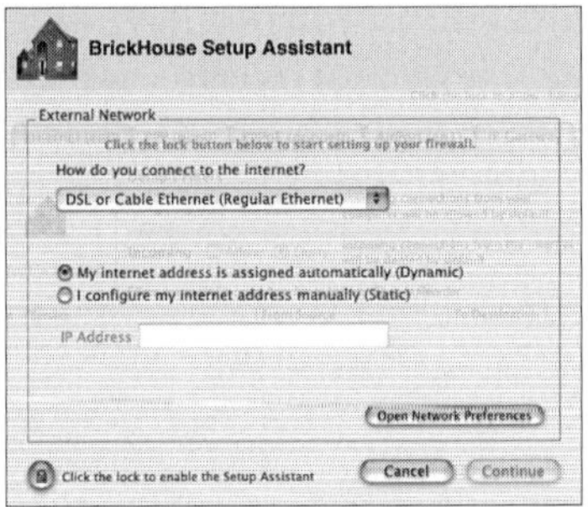

FIGURE 31.1 The BrickHouse Setup Assistant begins with your External Network settings.

2. The Public Services sheet, shown in Figure 31.2, is next. Check the boxes by the services that you want your machine to run. If you're not sure what a service is, select it, and a description appears at the bottom of the window. If you typically share your machine over an AppleTalk network, don't forget to check the appropriate AppleTalk services.

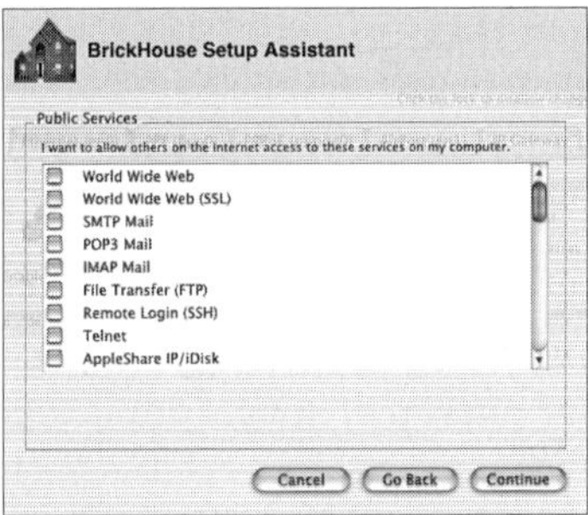

FIGURE 31.2 In the Public Services sheet, select the services you want your machine to run.

3. The Blocked Services sheet, shown in Figure 31.3, is where you select specific ports to be blocked. The list primarily includes ports aimed at various known attacks. The sheet notes that incoming traffic is blocked by default.

4. The next sheet to appear is the Firewall Setup Complete sheet, shown in Figure 31.4. To enable the configuration, click Apply Configuration. To install a startup script, click Install Startup Script. If you're interested in using your Mac OS X machine as a gateway for an internal network, click the Setup IP Sharing button. If you decide that you want to make changes to your configuration, you can make changes in the main window and apply a new configuration. Additionally, you can install or remove a startup script under the application's Options menu.

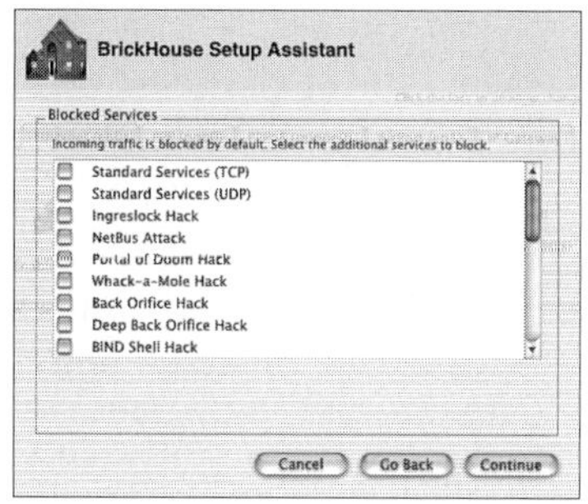

FIGURE 31.3 In the Blocked Services sheet, select additional ports to have blocked.

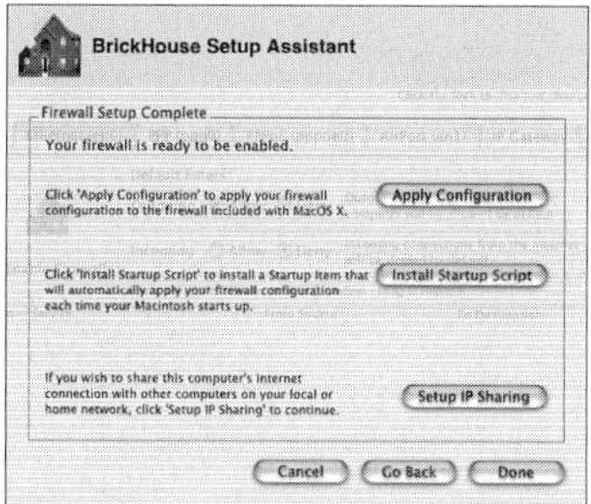

FIGURE 31.4 In the Firewall Setup Complete sheet, you can preliminarily finalize your setup or you can continue your setup by clicking on the Setup IP Sharing button to configure your machine to serve as a gateway for an internal network.

5. If you plan to set up your Mac OS X machine as a gateway for your internal network, the next sheet that appears is the IP Sharing sheet, shown in Figure 31.5. Here you select how your machine connects to the internal network and what internal IP address should be used for the machine. Connection choices are Ethernet Card (en0), AirPort or Second Ethernet Card (en1).

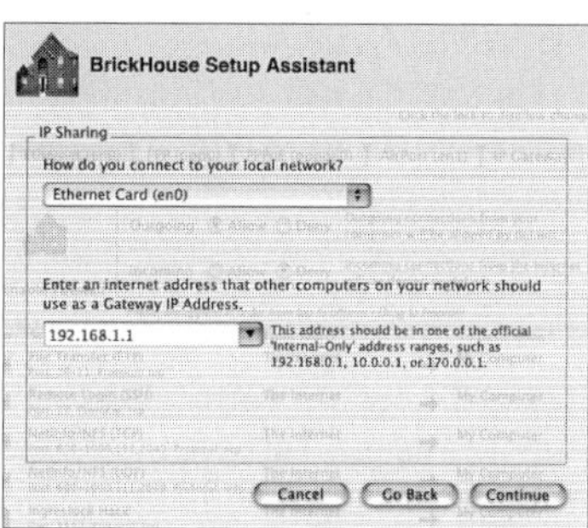

FIGURE 31.5 Make specifications about your local network in the IP Sharing sheet.

After you're done with this sheet, this version of BrickHouse then displays another sheet giving you instructions on starting IP sharing in BrickHouse. At this time, BrickHouse doesn't configure IP sharing to start at boot time.

You've just completed the initial BrickHouse setup. Now let's take the time to examine the rest of the BrickHouse interface. The default interface is the Quick Configuration, shown in Figure 31.6. The filters you selected during the setup process are shown under the tab for your interface. The IP Gateway tab shows information that pertains to any IP sharing that you've set up.

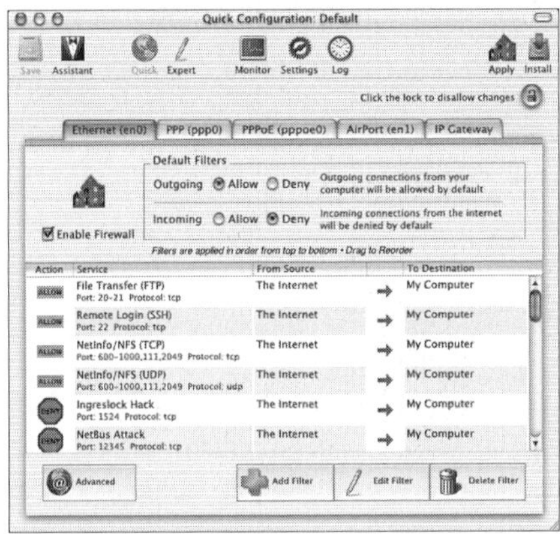

FIGURE 31.6 The default BrickHouse interface is the Quick Configuration interface.

The Advanced button, shown in Figure 31.7, enables you to edit some additional settings involving rules for some select protocols, DHCP, and your domain name service. The bottom-right buttons enable you to add, edit, and delete filters. When you add a filter, you can choose among the same options you saw in the Setup Assistant, as well as Custom Service, which enables you to specify a port or port range. The interface for adding a filter is shown in Figure 31.8. You can rearrange the order of filter rules by dragging them around in the main window.

From the toolbar, you can access the Setup Assistant at any time by clicking the Assistant button. The Setup Assistant always starts from scratch. The Monitor button enables you to monitor the firewall. An example of what it looks like is shown in Figure 31.9.

Settings enable you to manipulate settings files. You can duplicate, rename, delete, import, or export. By clicking the Log button, you can access the Daily Firewall Log window, shown in Figure 31.10, from which you can enable logging. If you want logging to be enabled at startup, be sure to reinstall the startup script, which you can do by either clicking the Install button or under the Options menu. Even if you don't think you want to have logging all the time, you might find that having logging on at this stage helps you troubleshoot problems with the firewall configuration.

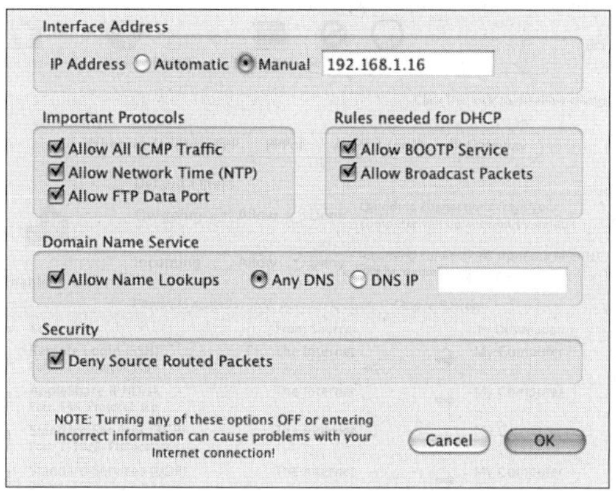

FIGURE 31.7 The Advanced button enables you to edit rules involving some select protocols, DHCP, and your domain name service.

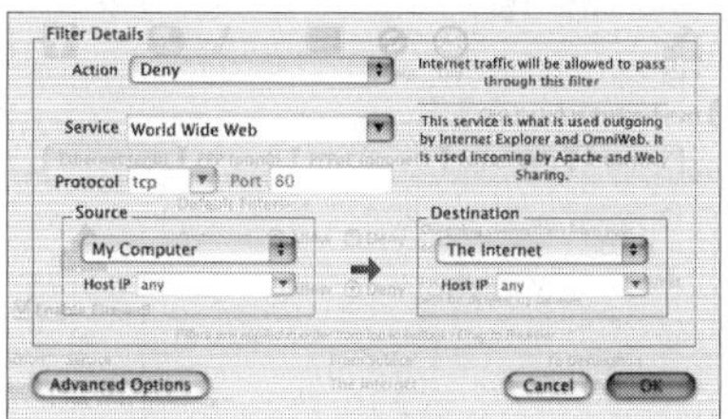

FIGURE 31.8 The Add Filter button opens this sheet, from which you can add another filter. Specify the action, service, protocol, port, source host, and destination host.

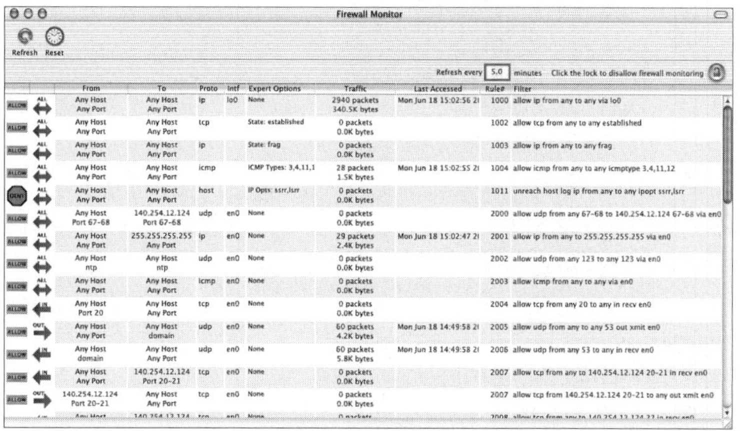

FIGURE 31.9 The Firewall Monitor window is where you can monitor the firewall's activity.

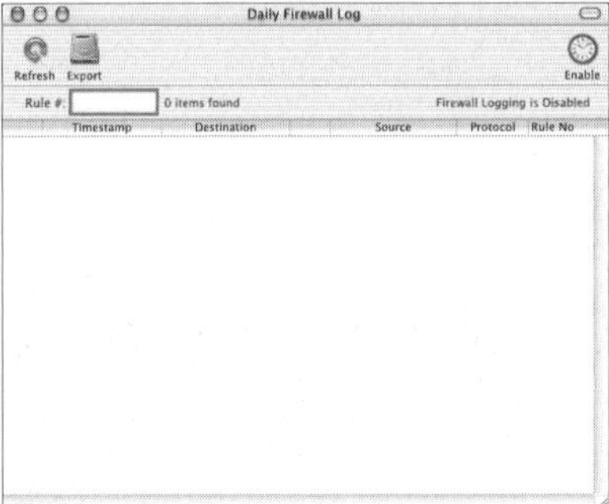

FIGURE 31.10 Click the Enable button at the top right in the Daily Firewall Log window to enable firewall logging. If you want to enable logging at startup, reinstall the startup script.

In addition to the default Quick Configuration mode is the Expert Configuration mode, accessible by clicking the Expert button. The Expert Configuration window, shown in Figure 31.11, is a split window that displays the rules that are being passed to `ipfw` as well as a configuration file for `natd`, which redirects packets to another machine if you configured your machine as a gateway.

FIGURE 31.11 In the Expert Configuration window, you can edit the firewall rules more precisely.

It's worthwhile to experiment with some filters that you might be most concerned about while you're still in the BrickHouse interface. With each set you want to try, just click the Apply button to apply those settings. The Quick Configuration mode is useful for adding basic filters, whereas the Expert Configuration mode enables you to tweak the configuration. After you have a set that you are happy with, don't forget to save the settings. If you're working in the Expert Configuration mode, you might also want to save the settings in a text file in a Terminal window just to be sure that you can easily find the file without the graphical interface. After you're relatively satisfied with the results, install the startup script if you want the firewall to start at startup.

If your Mac OS X machine is an NFS client, don't test to see whether the mounts still work in the graphical interface. If your mounts aren't working properly, you might hang your console when you check. If you check in the Terminal, you can continue testing until you're finally satisfied. For a Mac OS X machine that's an NFS client, you might ultimately find it necessary to add a line in the Expert mode that allows all traffic from your NFS server.

Finally, you should be aware of the options available under the Options menu: Allow Changes, Quick Configuration, Expert Configuration, Apply Settings, Install Startup Script, Clear All Rules, and Remove Startup Script. Only some of those options are available in the toolbar.

When you're satisfied with your firewall configuration, reboot your machine—especially if you had BrickHouse install a startup script for you. This tells you exactly what behavior to expect from the firewall starting from scratch. If something undesirable occurs, the potential cause for the behavior is fresh in your mind and more easily fixed.

Behind the Scenes: `ifconfig`, `ipfw`, `natd`

So, what are some of the things that BrickHouse did for you?

First, if you had BrickHouse install a startup script for you, you should've noticed a comment about the firewall starting.

Run the first command that you ran before you started:

```
brezup:root root # ipfw show
01000 6810 451096 allow ip from any to any via lo0
01002  98  10104 allow tcp from any to any established
01003   0      0 allow ip from any to any frag
01004   0      0 allow icmp from any to any icmptype 3,4,11,12
02000   0      0 allow udp from any 67-68 to 192.168.1.16 67-68 via en0
02001   0      0 allow ip from any to 255.255.255.255 via en0
02002   0      0 unreach host log logamount 500 ip from any to any via
➥en0 ipopt ssrr,lsrr
02003   0      0 allow udp from any 123 to any 1024-65535 via en0
02004   0      0 allow icmp from any to any via en0
02005   0      0 allow tcp from any 20-21 to any 1024-65535 in recv en0
02006   7    504 allow udp from any 1024-65535 to any 53 out xmit en0
02007   6    894 allow udp from any 53 to any 1024-65535 in recv en0
02008   2     96 allow tcp from any to 192.168.1.16 22 in recv en0
02008   0      0 allow tcp from 192.168.1.16 22 to any out xmit en0
02009   0      0 allow tcp from any to 192.168.1.16 548 in recv en0
```

```
02009   0     0 allow tcp from 192.168.1.16 548 to any out xmit en0
02010   0     0 deny log logamount 500 tcp from any to 192.168.1.16
➥1-1023 in recv en0
02011   0     0 deny log logamount 500 udp from any to 192.168.1.16
➥1-1023 in recv en0
02012   0     0 deny log logamount 500 tcp from any to 192.168.1.16
➥1524 in recv en0
02013   0     0 deny log logamount 500 tcp from any to 192.168.1.16
➥12345 in recv en0
02014   0     0 deny log logamount 500 udp from any to 192.168.1.16
➥10067 in recv en0
02015   0     0 deny log logamount 500 tcp from any to 192.168.1.16
➥12361 in recv en0
02016   0     0 deny log logamount 500 udp from any to 192.168.1.16
➥31337 in recv en0
02017   0     0 deny log logamount 500 udp from any to 192.168.1.16
➥31338 in recv en0
02018   0     0 deny log logamount 500 tcp from any to 192.168.1.16
➥31337 in recv en0
02019   0     0 deny log logamount 500 udp from any to 192.168.1.16
➥2140 in recv en0
02020   0     0 deny log logamount 500 udp from any to 192.168.1.16
➥31785 in recv en0
02021   0     0 deny log logamount 500 tcp from any to 192.168.1.16
➥31789,31791 in recv en0
02022   0     0 deny log logamount 500 tcp from any to 192.168.1.16
➥21554 in recv en0
02023   0     0 deny log logamount 500 tcp from any to 192.168.1.16
➥6969 in recv en0
02024   0     0 deny log logamount 500 tcp from any to 192.168.1.16
➥23456 in recv en0
02025   0     0 deny log logamount 500 tcp from any to 192.168.1.16
➥1243,6776 in recv en0
02026   0     0 deny log logamount 500 tcp from any to 192.168.1.16
➥15104,12754 in recv en0
02027   0     0 deny log logamount 500 udp from any to 192.168.1.16
➥10498,6838 in recv en0
02028   0     0 deny log logamount 500 udp from any to 192.168.1.16
➥31335 in recv en0
02029   0     0 deny log logamount 500 tcp from any to 192.168.1.16
➥27665,27444 in recv en0
02030   0     0 deny log logamount 500 tcp from any to 192.168.1.16
➥20432 in recv en0
```

```
02031    0     0 deny log logamount 500 udp from any to 192.168.1.16
➥18753,20433 in recv en0
52032    2   154 allow ip from 192.168.1.16 to any out xmit en0
52033    0     0 deny log logamount 500 ip from any to 192.168.1.16 in recv en0
65535 39626 6340835 allow ip from any to any
```

You should now have a bit more output than you did previously. The open rule, which was the only rule before you started, is now the last rule. The Firewall Monitor in BrickHouse appears to be a graphical view of `ipfw show`.

Next run `ifconfig -a`. If you configured your machine to be a gateway, you should now see information about your machine's interface to the internal and external networks. If you didn't configure your machine to be a gateway, you shouldn't see any changes. Select command documentation for `ifconfig` is included in Table 31.1.

TABLE 31.1 Command Documentation Table for `ifconfig`

`ifconfig`	Configures network interface parameters
`ifconfig [-L] [-m] `*<interface>*` [create] `*<address_family>*` [`*<address[/prefixlength]>* `[`*<dest address>*`]] [`*<parameters>*`]`	
`ifconfig `*<interface>*` destroy`	
`ifconfig -a [-L] [-d] [-m] [-u] [<address_family>]`	
`ifconfig -l [-d] [-u] [<address_family>]`	
`ifconfig [-L] [-d] [-m] [-u]`	
`ifconfig` assigns an address to a network interface and/or configures network interface parameters. It must be used at boot time to define the network address of each network interface. It may also be used at a later time to redefine an interface's network address or other operating parameters. Only the super user can modify the configuration of a network interface.	
`-m`	If passed before an interface name, `ifconfig` displays all the supported media for the specified interface.
`-a`	Produces a full listing of all available interfaces.
`-l`	Produces a name-only listing of all available interfaces.
`-d`	Limits a listing to those interfaces that are down.
`-u`	Limits a listing to those interfaces that are up.
Available options for `ifconfig` are	
<address>	For the DARPA-Internet family, the address is either a hostname in the hostname database or a DARPA-Internet address expressed in the Internet standard dot notation.
<address family>	Specifies the *<address family>*, which affects the interpretation of the remaining parameters. The address or protocol families currently supported are inet, iso, and ns.
<dest address>	Specifies the address of the correspondent on the other end of a point to point link.

TABLE 31.1 Continued

<interface>	The *<interface>* parameter is a string of the form *<name of physical unit>*, such as `en0`.
The following parameters may be set with `ifconfig`:	
`add`	Another name for the alias parameter. Introduced for compatibility with BSD/OS.
`alias`	Establishes an additional network address for this interface.
`-alias`	Removes the network address specified.
`broadcast`	(inet only) Specifies the address to use to represent broadcasts to the network. The default broadcast address is the address with a host part of all 1s.
`delete`	Removes the network address specified. This is used if you incorrectly specified an alias or if it's no longer needed.
`down`	Marks an interface as down. When an interface is marked down, the system does not attempt to transmit messages through that interface. If possible, the interface is reset to disable reception as well. This doesn't automatically disable routes using the interface.
`tunnel <src-addr> <dest-addr>`	(IP tunnel devices only.) Configures the physical source and destination address for IP tunnel interfaces (gif(4)). The arguments `<src_addr>` and `<dest_addr>` are interpreted as the outer source/destination for the encapsulating IPv4/IPv6 header.
`deletetunnel`	Unconfigures the physical source and destination address for IP tunnel interfaces previously configured with `tunnel`.
`create`	Creates the specified network pseudo-device.
`destroy`	Destroys the specified network pseudo-device.
`mtu <n>`	Sets the maximum transmission unit of the interface to n; default is interface specific. The MTU is used to limit the size of packets that are transmitted on an interface. Not all interfaces support setting the MTU, and some interfaces have range restrictions.
`netmask` *<mask>*	(inet and ISO) Specifies how much of the address to reserve for subdividing networks into subnetworks. The mask includes the network part of the local address and the subnet part, which is taken from the host field of the address.
`up`	Marks an interface as up. Can be used to enable an interface after `ifconfig down` has been run. It happens automatically when setting the first address on an interface. If the interface was reset when previously marked down, the hardware is reinitialized.

If you had BrickHouse install a startup script, you now have a `/Library/StartupItems/Firewall` directory:

```
brezup:sage sage $ ls -l /Library/StartupItems/Firewall/
total 24
-rwxrwxr-x 1 root admin  535 10 Sep 23:00 Firewall
-rw-rw-r-- 1 root admin  552 10 Sep 23:00 StartupParameters.plist
-rwxrwxr-x 1 root admin 2393 10 Sep 23:00 openniports.pl
```

Just as you saw earlier in the book with fonts and sounds, you can also place local startup items in the `/Library` directory, following the basic structure seen in `/System`; in this case, `/Library/StartupItems`. Here's a sample startup script installed by BrickHouse to start the firewall and its logging facilities:

```
brezup:sage sage $ more /Library/StartupItems/Firewall/Firewall
#!/bin/sh
# Firewall Boot Script
# Generated by BrickHouse


#============================================================
# Enable IP Firewall Logging
#============================================================
/usr/sbin/sysctl -w net.inet.ip.fw.verbose=1

# Put a limit on each rule's logging
/usr/sbin/sysctl -w net.inet.ip.fw.verbose_limit=500


#============================================================
# Process Firewall Rules File
#============================================================
/sbin/ipfw -q /etc/firewall.conf
```

As you can see from the startup script, BrickHouse installed a configuration file that it called `firewall.conf` in `/etc`. Look at the configuration file, especially if you didn't switch to the Expert Configuration mode in BrickHouse. The file is nicely commented. If you need to make additional changes to the ruleset, you can do so either in the BrickHouse interface or you can directly edit the `/etc/firewall.conf` file. Be sure to check the `ifpw` man page for specific details. This configuration file works in a similar manner to the newer TCP Wrappers configuration method. The `ipfw` program reads the configuration file on a first-match-wins basis.

The general format of the lines BrickHouse created in the `/etc/firewall.conf` file is

```
add <rule_number> <action> <protocol> from <source> to
  <destination> [<options>] [via <interface>]
```

If you selected AppleShare as one of your services, you have entries that look approximately like this:

```
#################################################
## AppleShare IP/iDisk
#################################################
```

```
add 2009 allow tcp from any to 192.168.1.16 548 in via en0
add 2009 allow tcp from 192.168.1.16 548 to any out via en0
```

The first line is a rule that enables incoming TCP packets from any host to the host machine on port 548 via the interface `en0`. The second AppleShare rule enables outgoing TCP packets from the host machine on port 548 to any host via the `en0` interface.

As mentioned in the previous section, if your Mac OS X machine is an NFS client, you might have to allow all incoming packets to the NFS server. You could do that with a rule like this:

```
add <rule_number> allow ip from <NFS_Server-IP> to <host_IP> via en0
```

The `ip` packet description means all packets. You can also use `all`. Select command documentation for `ipfw` is included in Table 31.2.

TABLE 31.2 Command Documentation Table for `ipfw`

`ipfw` Controlling utility for IP firewall

```
ipfw [-q] [-p <preproc> [-D macro[=value]] [-U macro]] pathname
   ipfw [-f ¦ -q] flush
   ipfw [-q] {zero ¦ resetlog ¦ delete} [number ...]
   ipfw [-s [field]] [-aftN] {list ¦ show} [number ...]
   ipfw [-q] add [number] rule-body
```

`ipfw` is the user interface for controlling the `ipfirewall`(4) and the `dummynet`(4) traffic shaper in FreeBSD.

Each incoming or outgoing packet is passed through the `ipfw` rules. If host is acting as a gateway, packets forwarded by the gateway are processed by `ipfw` twice. In case a host is acting as a bridge, packets forwarded by the bridge are processed by `ipfw` once.

A firewall configuration is made of a list of numbered rules, which is scanned for each packet until a match is found and the relevant action is performed. Depending on the action and certain system settings, packets can be reinjected into the firewall at the rule after the matching one for further processing. All rules apply to all interfaces, so it is the responsibility of the system administrator to write the ruleset in such a way as to minimize the number of checks.

A configuration always includes a DEFAULT rule (numbered 65535) which cannot be modified by the programmer and always matches packets. The action associated with the default rule can be either deny or allow depending on how the kernel is configured.

If the ruleset includes one or more rules with the keep-state option, `ipfw` assumes a stateful behavior; that is, upon a match will create dynamic rules matching the exact parameters (addresses and ports) of the matching packet.

These dynamic rules, which have a limited lifetime, are checked at the first occurrence of a check-state or keep-state rule, and are typically used to open the firewall on demand to legitimate traffic only.

All rules (including dynamic ones) have a few associated counters: a packet count, a byte count, a log count, and a timestamp indicating the time of the last match. Counters can be displayed or reset with `ipfw` commands.

TABLE 31.2 Continued

Rules can be added with the `add` command; deleted individually with the `delete` command, and globally with the `flush` command; displayed, optionally with the content of the counters, using the `show` and `list` commands.

Available commands:

`add`	Adds a rule.
`delete`	Deletes the first rule with number *<number>*, if any.
`list`	Prints out the current rule set.
`show`	Equivalent to `ipfw -a list`.
`flush`	Removes all rules.

The following options are available:

`-a`	Shows counter values while listing. Also see `show`.
`-t`	Shows last match timestamp while listing.
`-N`	Tries to resolve addresses and service names in output.

To ease configuration, rules can be put into a file that is processed using `ipfw` as shown in the first synopsis line. An absolute pathname must be used. The file will be read line by line and applied as arguments to the `ipfw` utility.

Rule Format

The `ipfw` rule format is the following:

```
[prob <match_probability>] <action> [log [logamount <number>]] <proto> from <src> to
<dst> [<interface-spec>] [<options>]
```

Each incoming and outgoing packet is sent through the `ipfw` rules. In the case of a host acting as a gateway, packets forwarded by the host are processed twice: once when entering and once when leaving. Each packet can be filtered based on the following associated information:

Transmit and receive interface (by name or address)

Direction (incoming or outgoing)

Source and destination IP address (possibly masked)

Protocol (TCP, UDP, ICMP, and so on)

Source and destination port (lists, ranges, or masks)

TCP flags

IP fragment flag

IP options

ICMP types

User/group ID of the socket associated with the packet

Note that it might be dangerous to filter on source IP address or source TCP/UDP port because either or both could be spoofed.

The `ipfw` utility works by going through the rule list for each packet until a match is found. All rules have two associated counters: a packet count and a byte count. These are updated when a packet matches the rule.

Rules are ordered by line number from `1` to `65534`. Rules are tried in increasing order, with the first matching rule being the one that applies. Multiple rules may have the same number and are applied in the order they were added.

TABLE 31.2 Continued

If a rule is added without a number, it's numbered `100` higher than the highest defined rule number unless the highest rule number is `65435` or greater—in which case, the new rules are given that same number.

One rule is always present: `65535 deny all from any to any.`

This rule, not to allow anything, is the default policy.

If the kernel option `IPFIREWALL_DEFAULT_TO_ACCEPT` has been enabled, the default rule is `65535 allow all from any to any.`

The previous rule is the default rule in Mac OS X.

`log [logamount number]`	If the kernel was compiled with `IPFIREWALL_VERBOSE`, when a packet matches a rule with the log keyword, a message will be logged to `syslogd`(8) with a `LOG_SECURITY` facility
`proto`	An IP protocol specified by number or name. (For a complete list, see `/etc/protocols`.) The `ip` or `all` keywords mean any protocol will match. `tcp`, `udp`, `icmp` are commonly used ones.

Available options for <*action*>:

`allow`	Allows packets that match rule. The search terminates. Aliases are pass, permit, and accept.
`deny`	Discards packets that match rule. The search terminates. Alias is drop.
`check-state`	Checks the packet against the dynamic ruleset. If a match is found, the search terminates; otherwise we move to the next rule. If no `check-state` rule is found, the dynamic ruleset is checked at the first `keep-state` rule.
`fwd <ipaddr>` dotted	Changes to the next hop on matching packets to <*ipaddr*>, which can be a
`[,<port>]`	quad address or hostname. If <*ipaddr*> is not directly reachable, the route as found in the local routing table for that IP address is used instead.
`pipe <pip-nr>`	Pass packet to a `dummynet`(4) pipe (for bandwidth limitation, delay, and so on. The search terminates; however, on exit from the pipe and if the `sysctl`(8) variable `net.inet.ip.fw.one_pass` is not set, the packet is passed again to the firewall code starting from the next rule.
`queue <queue-nr>`	Pass packet to a `dummynet`(4) queue (for bandwidth limitation using `WF2Q`).

`src` and `dst`:

`any ¦ me ¦ [not] <address/mask> [<ports>]`

Specifying `any` makes the rule match any IP number.

Specifying `me` makes the rule match any IP number configured on an interface in the system. This is a computationally semi-expensive check that should be used with care.

The sense of the match can be inverted by preceding an address with the `not` modifier, causing all other addresses to be matched instead. This does not affect the selection of port numbers.

With the TCP and UDP protocols, optional ports may be specified as

`{port¦port-port¦port:mask}[,port[,...]]`

TABLE 31.2 Continued

Some combinations of the following specifiers are allowed for <interface-spec>	
in	Only matches incoming packets.
out	Only matches outgoing packets.
via ifX	Packet must be going through interface ifX.
via any	Packet must be going through some interface.
via ipno	Packet must be going through the interface having IP address ipno.
The via keyword causes the interface to always be checked. If recv or xmit is used instead of via, the only receive or transmit interface (respectively) is checked. By specifying both, it is possible to match packets based on both receive and transmit interface, for example:	
ipfw add 100 deny ip from any to any out recv en0 xmit en1	
The recv interface can be tested on either incoming or outgoing packets, whereas the xmit interface can only be tested on outgoing packets.	
Options available for *<options>*:	
keep-state[<method>]	Upon a match, the firewall will create a dynamic rule, whose default behavior is to matching bidirectional traffic between source and destination IP/port using the same protocol. The rule has a limited lifetime (controlled by a set of sysctl(8) variables), and the lifetime is refreshed every time a matching packet is found.
ipoptions *<spec>*	Matches if the IP header contains the comma-separated list of options specified in *<spec>*. The supported IP options are ssrr (strict source route), lsrr (loose source route), rr (record packet route), and ts (timestamp). The absence of a particular option can be denoted with a !.
tcpoptions <spec>	Matches if the TCP header contains the comma-separated list of options specified in spec. The supported TCP options are mss (maximum segment size), window (tcp window advertisement), sack (selective ack), ts (rfc1323 timestamp) and cc (rfc1644 t/tcp connection count). The absence of a particular option can be denoted with a !.
established	TCP packets only. Matches packets that have the RST or ACK bits set.
setup	TCP packets only. Matches packets that have the SYN bit set but no ACK bit.
tcpflags *<spec>*	Matches if the TCP header contains the comma-separated list of flags specified in *<spec>*. The supported TCP flags are fin, syn, rst, psh, ack, and urg. The absence of a particular flag can be denoted by an !. A rule that contains a tcpflags specification can never match a fragmented packet that has a nonzero offset.
Important points to consider when designing your rules:	
Remember that you filter packets both going in and out. Most connections need packets going in both directions.	
Remember to test very carefully. It's a good idea to be at the console at the time.	
Don't forget the loopback interface.	

BrickHouse might also have installed a configuration file, /etc/natd.conf, for natd. Here's a sample /etc/natd.conf created by BrickHouse:

```
interface en0
use_sockets yes
same_ports yes
```

This configuration file specifies the interface to be used. In addition, the use_sockets option is included as well as the same_ports option. The use_sockets option allocates a socket for the connection, and is useful for guaranteeing connections when ports conflict. The same_ports option specifies that natd should try to keep the same port number when altering outgoing packets. This also aids in guaranteeing the success of the connection. Command documentation for natd is included in Table 31.3.

TABLE 31.3 Command Documentation Table for natd

natd	Network Address Translation Daemon

natd [-unregistered_only ¦ -u] [-log ¦ -l] [-proxy_only] [-reverse] [-deny_incoming ¦ -d] [-use_sockets ¦ -s] [-same_ports ¦ -m] [-verbose ¦ -v] [-dynamic] [-in_port ¦ -i <port>] [-out_port ¦ -o <port>] [-port ¦ -p <port>] [-alias_address ¦ -a <address>] [-target_address ¦ -t <address>] [-interface ¦ -n <interface>] [-proxy_rule <proxyspec>] [-redirect_port <linkspec>] [-redirect_proto <linkspec>] [-redirect_address <linkspec>] [-config ¦ -f <configfile>] [-log_denied] [-log_facility <facility_name>] [-punch_fw <firewall_range>] [-clamp_mss]

This program provides a Network Address Translation facility for use with divert(4) sockets under FreeBSD. It is intended for use with NICs—if you want to do NAT on a PPP link, use the -nat switch to ppp(8).

The natd normally runs in the background as a daemon. It is passed raw IP packets as they travel into and out of the machine, and will possibly change these before reinjecting them back into the IP packet stream.

It changes all packets destined for another host so that their source IP number is that of the current machine. For each packet changed in this manner, an internal table entry is created to record this fact. The source port number is also changed to indicate the table entry applying to the packet. Packets that are received with a target IP of the current host are checked against this internal table. If an entry is found, it is used to determine the correct target IP number and port to place in the packet.

-d -deny_incoming	Rejects packets destined for the current IP number that have no entry in the internal translation table.
-m -same_ports	Tries to keep the same port number when allocating outgoing packets
-u	Only alters outgoing packets

TABLE 31.3 Continued

`-unregistered_only`	with an unregistered source address. According to RFC 1918, unregistered source addresses are `10.0.0.0/8`, `176.16.0.0/12` and `192.168.0.0/16`.
`-log_denied`	Logs denied incoming packets via syslog (*see also* `log_facility`).
`-log_facility` *<facility_name>*	Uses specified log facility when logging information via syslog. Facility names as in `syslog.conf`(5).
`-dynamic`	If the `-n` or `-interface` option is used, `natd` monitors the routing socket for alterations to the *<interface>* passed. If the interface IP number is changed, `natd` dynamically alters its concept of the alias address.
`-i` *<inport>* `-in_port` *<inport>*	Reads from and writes to *<inport>*, treating all packets as packets coming into the machine.
`-o` *<output>* `-out_port` *<outport>*	Reads from and writes to *<outport>*, treating all packets as packets going out of the machine.
`-p` *<port>* `-port` *<port>*	Reads from and writes to *<port>*, distinguishing packets as incoming or outgoing using the rules specified in `divert`
`-a` *<address>* `-alias_address` *<address>*	Uses *<address>* as the alias address. If this option is not specified, the `-n` or `-interface` option must be used. The specified address should be the address assigned to the public-network interface.
`-t` *<address>* `-target_address` *<address>*	Sets the target address. When an incoming packet not associated with any pre existing link arrives at the host machine, it will be sent to the specified address.

TABLE 31.3 Continued

-n *<interface>* -interface *<interface>*	Uses *<interface>* to determine the alias address.
-f *<configfile>* -config *<configfile>*	Reads the configuration from
-redirect_port <proto> <targetIP>:<targetPORT> [<aliasIP>:]<aliasPORT> [<remoteIP>[:<remotePORT>]	Redirects incoming connections arriving to given port to another host and port.
redirect_address network.	Redirects traffic for public IP address to a machine on the local
<localIP> <publicIP>	This function, known as static NAT, is normally useful if your ISP has allocated a small block of IP addresses to you, but it can be used in the case of a single address.
-punch_fw <basenumber>: <count>	This option directs natd to punch holes in an ipfirewall(4) based firewall for FTP/IRC DCC connections.

Recovery

While you're experimenting with BrickHouse, you might leave your machine in an unusable state. It's a bit inconvenient, but it's supposed to protect your machine from attacks. If you're simulating attacks to test it, you can't really fault it for trying to lock you out. If you need to uninstall BrickHouse while you work out a solution, the documentation suggests that you select Remove Startup Script under the Options menu and reboot, or throw out the /Library/StartupItems/Firewall folder and reboot. The documentation also points out that Clear All Rules under the Options menu temporarily uninstalls the firewall.

If your machine is so unusable that you can't do any of the previous suggestions, reboot into single-user mode and remove the /Library/StartupItems/Firewall directory. You can also remove the /etc/firewall.conf and /etc/natd.conf files. On reboot, your machine is restored to the condition it was in before you used BrickHouse. The next time you're ready to use BrickHouse, start with the Setup Assistant and work from there.

Virtual Private Networks

Sometimes the simplest solution for protecting your machine against unwanted outside access is to strictly control what external machines can reach it. In some situations, this is relatively easily done by use of a Virtual Private Network (VPN). A VPN is a collection of cooperating software that simulates a situation in which your machine is directly wired into some remote network, via an unbroken cable. Additionally, the traffic on this virtual wire is encrypted, protecting it against prying eyes. If you set up this type of connection, you can then restrict your various servers to only talk to this virtual connection; only machines that are also members of this virtual (and private) network can talk to your services.

The capabilities of SecureShell can be used to implement this type of connection on a point-to-point basis without any special server software, but it's not a convenient solution for protecting all the communications between a cluster of machines. The VPN software built into Mac OS X can make securing these types of connections easier. Currently, this software supports PPTP (Point-to-Point Tunneling Protocol)–type VPNs, which include VPNs served by Mac OS X Server, MS Windows XP/2000, and L2TP over IPSec (Layer 2 Tunneling Protocol), which is supported by Linux, Microsoft operating systems, and hardware VPNs by companies such as Cisco. Setting up your Mac OS X machine as a member of a VPN network is almost anticlimactically simple. Almost all the configuration is handled on the server side, so as a client, you've little to do other than fill in a few pieces of information in a dialog and a VPN connection is installed automatically. You can also set up and save multiple VPN configurations. Figure 31.12 shows the connection dialog for setting up a VPN connection—this dialog is accessed from the New VPN Connection Window selection under the File menu of the Internet Connect application.

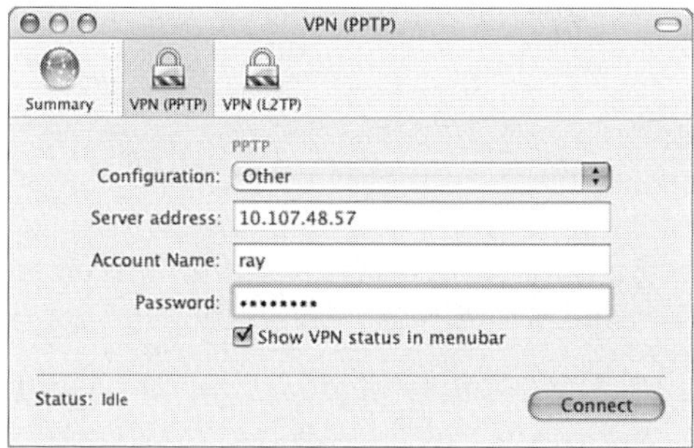

FIGURE 31.12 Setting up a VPN in the Internet Connect application.

After it's configured from the dialog box in Figure 31.12, your machine should believe it has a new network interface. Traffic to the private subnet can be routed over this interface, and, if you choose, you can route traffic to other network sites through it as well by setting up routes through its gateway to the outside network at large. While the VPN network interface is up, `ifconfig` should show output such as this:

```
lo0: flags=8049<UP,LOOPBACK,RUNNING,MULTICAST> mtu 16384
    inet6 ::1 prefixlen 128
    inet 127.0.0.1 netmask 0xff000000
gif0: flags=8010<POINTOPOINT,MULTICAST> mtu 1280
stf0: flags=0<> mtu 1280
en0: flags=8863<UP,BROADCAST,SMART,RUNNING,SIMPLEX,MULTICAST> mtu 1500
    inet6 fe80::230:65ff:feaa:37ae prefixlen 64 scopeid 0x4
    inet 192.168.1.16 netmask 0xffffff00 broadcast 192.168.1.255
    ether 00:30:65:aa:37:ae
    media: autoselect (10baseT/UTP <half-duplex>) status: active
    supported media: none autoselect 10baseT/UTP <half-duplex> 10baseT/UTP <
```

```
full-duplex> 10baseT/UTP <full-duplex,hw-loopback> 100baseTX <half-duplex> 100ba
seTX <full-duplex> 100baseTX <full-duplex,hw-loopback>
fw1: flags=8822<BROADCAST,SMART,SIMPLEX,MULTICAST> mtu 2030
    tunnel inet -->
    lladdr 00:30:65:ff:fe:aa:37:ae
    media: autoselect <full-duplex> status: inactive
    supported media: autoselect <full-duplex>
ppp0: flags=8051<UP,POINTOPOINT,RUNNING,MULTICAST> mtu 1448
     inet 10.107.48.132 --> 10.107.48.190 netmask 0xffff0000
```

Here, you can see the normal network interfaces that you'd see using `ifconfig`, as well as the `ppp0` network interface that PPTP has configured. In this case, the machine now has two IP addresses—`192.168.1.16`, which is the configured IP address on its `en0` ethernet interface, and `10.107.48.132`, which is the IP address on which it will answer connections to the virtual ppp0 interface created by the VPN. Based on the netmask, any traffic destined for the `10.107` network will be carried, encrypted, over the `ppp0` virtual interface. It will be conveyed in encrypted form to the remote VPN server, where it will be unpacked and distributed to the `10.107` network.

After you have a VPN set up, you can configure many of your services, either directly, or through `inetd`/`xinetd`, to respond to only queries coming from your private network. The result is that all traffic into or out of these services will be encrypted. Better yet, only a very limited and tightly controlled collection of machines can connect to the services.

The log window, reached from the Window menu of Internet Connect, lets you monitor the progress and status of your VPN connection as it occurs. Figure 31.13 shows typical log output from a successful VPN connection.

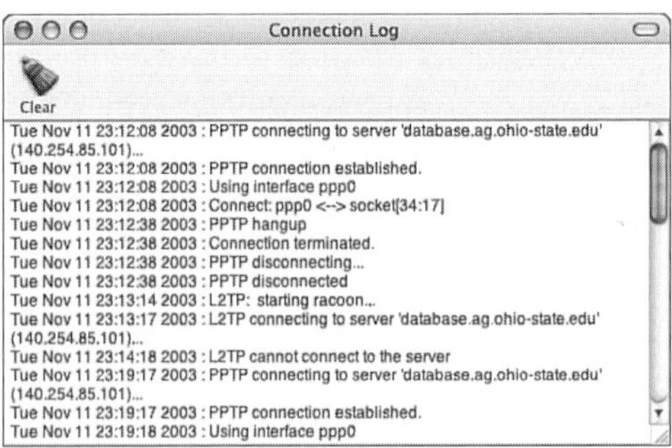

FIGURE 31.13 A VPN log from Internet Connect.

Limited-Access Administrative Accounts: `sudo` and `/etc/sudoers`

Finally, one of the most important things that you can do to limit access to your machine is to limit access to the abilities of the `root` account. The configuration with which Apple ships Mac OS X includes an `admin` group, any members of which can execute any command they want with `root` privileges. If you have multiple people with user accounts that you want to be able to perform various administrative functions, giving them all complete access to run any command as `root` is a serious security threat.

Your best option is to use the capabilities of the `sudo` command in the fashion it was originally intended: to provide limited access to specific privileged functions to specific users. Covering the complete syntax and configuration options for `sudo` is a topic best suited for an entire chapter, but we'll cover enough to get you started here.

`sudo`, and which users it will allow to execute which commands, is controlled by the file `/etc/sudoers`. This file is composed of a number of lines in Extended Backus-Naur Form (EBNF), which is a formalized way of writing definitions when the definitions are of the form "An A is a B or a C; Cs can be Ds or Es and Fs; and Es are types of fruit." That is, descriptions where left-side terms are equated to right-side definitions, and definitions may be other terms, ordered lists of terms, or terminal nodes. Terminal nodes are final, non-subdividable entries. BNF and EBNF (the differences are beyond the scope of this book) are used, either directly or indirectly, in a number of computer configuration methods. BNF form definitions lend themselves to being used either as the direct content of a configuration file where the configuration must be a set of hierarchical definitions (such as who's allowed to run what commands), or the syntax of the configuration may be explained in terms of its BNF definition. (And, in fact, many computer languages, programs that can be thought of as very large configuration specifications, can be usefully defined in BNF.)

As an example of how BNF works, a simple first attempt at creating a BNF description for the English language might look something like this:

```
sentence  : ([subject] [verb] [object]), ([subject] [verb])
subject   : [phrase]
object    : (a [phrase])
phrase    : [noun], ([adjective] [noun])
verb      : hit, threw, chased
noun      : tommy, ball
adjective : red, big
```

If we consider things in parentheses to be ordered lists of terms, things separated by commas to indicate choices between multiple things, things in square braces to be terms, and things without square braces to be terminal nodes, we have a BNF definition that can be used to build potential English-language sentences. Using this BNF to construct valid sentences, we can come up with things such as

"tommy hit a ball"

"tommy hit a big ball"

"big tommy hit a red ball"

or

"tommy hit"

Although English makes a good example for explaining simple BNF grammars, it's much too complex a language to completely codify in BNF form. Because of this, the BNF grammar I've constructed also would allow sentences such as "ball threw" and "red ball chased a big tommy." Fortunately, the language required for most things such as constructing configuration files is not nearly as complex as English. For `/etc/sudoers`, the language required is simply a way of specifying users, the commands they are allowed to run, and the user IDs under which the commands are run when these users invoke `sudo`. In the case of `sudo`, the configuration file consists of individual configuration lines specifying aspects of the configuration. There can be as many configuration lines as you need to completely specify the users and permissions desired. `/etc/sudoers` contains two types of configuration lines: alias lines and user-specification lines.

The alias lines are used to build a hierarchical specification of users, user IDs, or commands. The user-spec lines are then used to combine these into useful definitions as to who is allowed to do what and how. The alias lines conform to `LINE`s created by the following EBNF—here I'm using commas to separate choices and square braces to indicate non-terminal terms. Parentheses again indicate an ordered grouping of terms, and angle braces denote textual explanations of a valid value. Single quotes surround characters that appear verbatim in a value, where those verbatim characters might be misunderstood as part of the EBNF itself. Exclamation point characters are used to negate a value.

```
LINE        : [User_Line],  [Runas_Line], [Cmnd_Line]
User_Line   : (User_Alias   [NAME] = [User_List])
Runas_Line  : (Runas_Alias  [NAME] = [Runas_List])
Host_Line   : (Host_Alias   [NAME] = [Host_List])
Cmnd_Line   : (Cmnd_Alias   [NAME] = [Cmnd_List])
NAME        : <A NAME is a string containing upper-case letters, numbers,
              and the underscore characters '_'. A NAME must start with
              an uppercase letter.>

User_List   : [User], ([User]',' [User_List])
User        : [UserType], ![UserType]
UserType    : <username>, %<groupname>, <NAME where NAME is a
              defined User_Alias>
```

A `User_List` is made up of one or more usernames, system groups (prefixed with `%`), and other `User_Alias` aliases. Each item can be prefixed with an `!` to negate the sense of the definition.

```
Runas_List   : [RunasUser], ([RunasUser]',' [Runas_List])
RunasUser    : [RunasType], ![RunasType]
RunasType    : <username>, #<userid>, %<group>, <NAME where NAME is a
               defined Runas_Alias>
```

A Runas_List is similar to a User_List except that it can also contain numeric user IDs (prefixed with #) and instead of User_Aliases, it can contain Runas_Aliases.

```
Host_List   : [Host], ([Host]',' [Host_List])
Host        : [HostType], ![HostType]
HostType    : <hostname>, <ipaddress>, <network range>, <NAME where NAME is
              a Host_Alias>
```

A Host_List is made up of one or more hostnames, IP addresses, network numbers, and other Host_Alias aliases. The Host_Alias directive is of only minor use if you're not building a cooperating group of machines. By allowing host specifications, the same /etc/sudoers file can be used on all machines of a cluster, yet have customized and specific actions on each. This allows much more convenient maintenance than if you needed to create and configure the file on each machine individually.

```
Cmnd_List   : [Cmnd], ([Cmnd]',' [Cmnd_List])
Cmnd        : [CmndType], ![CmndType]
CmndType    : [CommandName], <directory path>, <NAME where NAME is a
              defined Cmnd_Alias>
CommandName : <command path>, (<commandpath> <args>), (<commandpath> '""')
```

A Cmnd_List is a list of one or more CommandNames, directories, and other Cmnd_Alias aliases. A CommandName is a fully qualified file path that might include shell-style wildcards. A simple filename enables the user to run the command with any arguments she wants. However, you can also specify command-line arguments (including wildcards). Alternately, you can specify "" to indicate that the command can be run only without command-line arguments. A directory path is a fully qualified path to a directory ending in a /. When you specify a directory in a Cmnd_List, the user can run any file within that directory (but not in any subdirectories therein). If a Cmnd has associated command-line arguments, the arguments given by the user on the command line must exactly match those in the Cmnd (or match the wildcards, if there are any). Note that the following characters must be escaped with a \ if they're used in command arguments: “,”, “:”, “=”, and “\.”

TIP

In the actual file, a \ alone at the end of a line indicates that the line continues on to the next line unbroken.

After you've defined the various elements you need using the alias line syntax, you use these to define who may do what, using ULINEs in the following user-specification syntax:

```
ULINE          : ([User_list] [WhereWhat])
WhereWhat      : ([Host_List] = [Cmnd_Spec_List]),
                 ([Host_List] = [Cmnd_Spec_List] : [WhereWhat])
Cmnd_Spec_List : [Cmnd_Spec], ([Cmnd_Spec]',' [Cmnd_Spec_List])
Cmnd_Spec      : [Runas_Spec] [Passwd_Spec] [Cmnd]
Runas_Spec     : '(' [Runas_List] ')', ''
Passwd_Spec    : 'PASSWD:', 'NOPASSWD:', ''
```

A user-specification line consists of a User_List (constructed by the EBNF rules shown previously), for which this particular rule is true. This is followed by a Host_List defining the set of hosts on which the commands specified may be run. To this Host_List is assigned a Cmnd_Spec_List defining the commands that this user is allowed to run on the hosts that match the Host_List. There may be additional [Host_List] = [Cmnd_Spec_List] entries on the same line, separated from each other by colons. Each Cmnd_Spec_List is composed of previously defined Cmnd definitions (which, by convoluted logic, you'll note may be Cmnd_Aliases, to lists of Cmnds). For each of these, the Cmnd may optionally be preceded by a Runas_List enclosed in parentheses, or by the flags PASSWD: or NOPASSWD:. Inclusion of a Runas_List overrides the default root user ID as the commands run through sudo are executed. Inclusion of NOPASSWD: or PASSWD: allows overriding (or making explicit) the requirement for the user to enter a password to run commands in the Cmnd_Spec as the alternative user ID. Password checking can be turned on for some commands and off for others in the same ULINE by prefixing the respective group's Cmnd_Specs with PASSWD: and NOPASSWD: as appropriate.

All this might seem a bit complex, especially when you start looking at a definition like that for a Cmnd, where a Cmnd may be the name of a defined Cmnd_Alias, which may be a Cmnd_List, which may be a Cmnd. But it's actually rather simple when you start following concrete examples through the EBNF grammar.

First, let's look at the /etc/sudoers file that comes with Mac OS X by default:

```
# sudoers file.
#
# This file MUST be edited with the 'visudo' command as root.
#
# See the sudoers man page for the details on how to write a sudoers file.
#
# Host alias specification
# User alias specification
# Cmnd alias specification
# Defaults specification
# User privilege specification
```

```
root   ALL=(ALL) ALL
%admin ALL=(ALL) ALL
```

Not much to it, so it couldn't be too difficult to interpret, could it? Two lines of user specification. They both make rather copious use of the built-in ALL alias, which functions as "All valid values in this position." Parsing these lines is particularly easy. For the first ULINE, the User_List portion is simply root, so it's a line that specifies some things that root's allowed to do through sudo. The Host_List portion is ALL, so root's allowed to do the things listed anywhere. The optional Runas_Spec is ALL as well, so root's allowed to do (some as yet unspecified) things, as anyone through sudo. Finally, the Cmnd_Spec_List portion is again ALL, indicating that root is allowed to do anything, as anyone, anywhere, using the sudo command. This isn't particularly surprising. If root wanted to do something under an alternative user ID, even if it couldn't be done by specifying an alternative user ID to sudo, root can always su to anyone.

The second ULINE, which is quite similar to the first, is the one that's a bit disturbing for your day-to-day system security. Its User_List portion is specified by group name, instead of by user ID, and it enables anyone in the group admin to have exactly the same complete access to the system as root. If you're the only user on your machine, this isn't a concern. But if your machine is a multiuser machine, having everyone who needs *any* administrative access getting *all* administrative access is a bad idea and a recipe for an eventual security disaster.

NOTE

The command visudo is used to edit the /etc/sudoers file. This command is functionally the vi editor, but it locks the /etc/sudoers file so that only one person can edit it at a time, and provides basic syntax checking to help eliminate parsing errors in the /etc/sudoers file.

Instead of this rather poor configuration, consider something that limits sub-administrator access to specific commands. Even with limited access, there might be ways for a person with malicious intent to find a way to do harm, but there's no sense in giving everyone the combination to the bank vault if what they need to do their job is only a key to the utility closet. Your needs will be as individual as your system, but you should be able to build a much more competent administrative hierarchy for sudo by studying the following example and adapting it to your needs.

Let's consider an /etc/sudoers file that contains the following definitions (lines that start with # are comments):

```
# User alias specification
User_Alias   FULLTIMERS  = john, will, joan
User_Alias   PARTTIMERS  = adam, robyn, jack
User_Alias   WEBMASTERS  = sandy, rich
User_Alias   PROGRAMMERS = dave, bob
User_Alias   SECRETARIES = karen, nancy, dan
```

Here, the file defines five named groups of users: FULLTIMERS, PARTTIMERS, WEBMASTERS, PROGRAMMERS, and SECRETARIES. You might imagine that these separate full-time administrative staff from part-time staff, and Webmaster type administrators (who probably aren't experienced Unix administrators, but who need some root-like functions to do things such as stop and start the Web server) from programmers and secretaries. Programmers might have some reason to have limited special privileges, such as installing software, and our secretaries can do some general maintenance without needing an administrator around.

```
# Runas alias specification
Runas_Alias  OP = root
Runas_Alias  DB = mysql
Runas_Alias  SW = software
```

Three aliases are constructed to specific users to allow the commands to be run with their user IDs:

```
# Host alias specification
Host_Alias   SPARC   = soyokaze, rosalyn, ryoko, rodan :\
             SGI     = waashu, oni, halo :\
             ALPHA   = godzilla :\
             LINUX   = mother, venice, hedora
Host_Alias   CUNETS  = 140.254.12.0
Host_Alias   SERVERS = ftp, mail, www
Host_Alias   CDROM   = waashu, ryoko, soyokaze
```

The first Host_Alias line uses the : separator to define several aliases simultaneously for a number of different machines by name. The next line (remember that \ in the file itself causes the next physical line to be read as a continuation of this one) specifies a network range. They are all machines in the 140.254.12. C-class network; there's an additional netmask parameter available if you're building truly complex configurations—see the sudoers man page for more information. Next, an alias for some server machines is constructed, and finally an alias for some machines that have CD-ROMs. Note that membership in one Host_Alias doesn't preclude membership in others. All the machines that have CD-ROMs are also members of their respective hardware-type alias groups.

```
# Cmnd alias specification
Cmnd_Alias   DUMPS    = /usr/bin/mt, /usr/sbin/dump, /usr/sbin/rdump,\
             /usr/sbin/restore, /usr/sbin/rrestore
Cmnd_Alias   KILL     = /usr/bin/kill
Cmnd_Alias   INSTALL  = /usr/bin/make install
Cmnd_Alias   PRINTING = /usr/sbin/lpc, /usr/bin/lprm
Cmnd_Alias   SHUTDOWN = /usr/sbin/shutdown
Cmnd_Alias   HALT     = /usr/sbin/halt, /usr/sbin/fasthalt
```

```
Cmnd_Alias   REBOOT  = /usr/sbin/reboot, /usr/sbin/fastboot
Cmnd_Alias   SHELLS  = /usr/bin/sh, /usr/bin/csh, /usr/bin/ksh, \
             /usr/local/bin/tcsh, /usr/bin/rsh, \
             /usr/local/bin/zsh
Cmnd_Alias   SU      = /usr/bin/su
```

Now we have some `Cmnd_Alias` lines configured with a few useful groups of commands. The `DUMPS` `Cmnd_Alias` includes commands you'd need to run to do `dump/restore` type backups. `PRINTING` includes control programs for `lpr/lpd` access to CUPS. `SHELLS` includes those applications that can also function as user login shells. The others are fairly self-explanatory.

Making use of all these definitions is now rather easy: Simply construct `ULINE` entries that tie them together to explain who can do what and where it can be done. Perhaps we want to allow our full-time staff complete access to any machine as `root`, while our part-time staff should be able to run various commands as `root`, but we don't want them to be able to start up a `root` shell:

```
FULLTIMERS   ALL = (OP) ALL
PARTTIMERS   ALL = (OP) ALL, !SU, !SHELLS
```

CAUTION

The negated `SU` and `SHELL` entries here should be considered to be mostly informative, rather than a strict preventative measure. If the `PARTTIMERS` really wanted shell access, they could easily get it by invoking a command shell out of some application that they're allowed to run.

We have an additional administrative user (`scott`) who's only responsible for backup and restore functions on the server machines:

```
scott      SERVERS = (OP) DUMPS
```

We want the secretaries to be able to kill off printer jobs that are causing problems. We'd also like them to be able to use the CD-ROM burner to write a user's files to CD-R without needing them to be able to `su` to that user ID to access the files, so the secretaries need `hdiutil` and `ditto`:

```
SECRETARIES  ALL = (OP) PRINTING, /usr/bin/hdiutil, \
                   /usr/bin/ditto
```

We also have a few of people who fiddle with and compile software, who we trust enough to install it as under the auspices of our `software` user, but to whom we don't want to give full access to the software user's account:

```
PROGRAMMERS  ALL = (SW) INSTALL
```

On the Linux boxes, we'd like scott to be able to do shutdown and reboot type administrative tasks:

```
scott      LINUX = (OP) SHUTDOWN, HALT, REBOOT
```

User dave needs to have access to kill hung processes on his desktop machine:

```
dave       192.168.1.18 = (OP) KILL
```

The Webmasters need to have permission to run any command on the Web server (a machine named www), with a generic webmaster user ID (which won't necessarily be able to do much). They also need to be able to restart the Web server as root because it's run by the system startup scripts and the parent server is owned by root:

```
WEBMASTERS    www = (webmaster) ALL, \
          (OP) /System/Library/StartupItems/Apache/Apache start,\
          (OP) /System/Library/StartupItems/Apache/Apache stop, \
          (OP) /System/Library/StartupItems/Apache/Apache restart
```

Because we've been having a bit of trouble with the power in the room where the SGI workstations live, we're going to let any user run sync on them as root. This way, if any user happens to be around when the power goes out, she might be able to sync the drives before the uninterruptible power supplies die. We're not even going to require a password for this because it would be hard to hurt the machines by syncing the drives:

```
ALL       SGI = (OP) NOPASSWD: /bin/sync
```

This is nowhere near a complete iteration of what can be configured using sudo and /etc/sudoers, or even a complete itemization of what can be built using the simple alias lines constructed in the first part of the example. It should, however, be enough to demonstrate how you can compartmentalize your administrative needs into separate tasks and users who can perform them. This compartmentalization, combined with a judicious use of reassigning directory and application ownerships, will enable you to vastly increase your machine's day-to-day security because it removes much of the need and/or temptation to run as the root user. If you believe your cluster configuration would benefit from greater richness in what can be permitted and limited via sudo, please see the sudoers man page—the discussion here only brushes the surface.

CAUTION

The examples given here are somewhat contrived to show the possible uses, and aren't specifically an indication of good thinking when it comes to security practices. A user who wants to abuse the system could probably find ways to circumvent the limitations placed on their access, and gain complete root access to the machine though a number of these rules. If you're going to allow users sudo access to run some commands with root privileges, you must be either very certain your users are trustable or very careful when you pick which commands they're allowed to run.

For example, imagine that the WEBMASTER users own the executable file that's the Apache Web server, and they want to usurp root powers. All they would need to do is replace apache with a shell script of their own devising and issue a root-privileged apache restart to have whatever commands they choose run as root.

When you design your /etc/sudoers rules, you need to consider this type of subterfuge and plan your permissions accordingly.

Intrusion Detection

In the previous section, you saw some basic methods you can use for securing your machine, including the use of TCP Wrappers. Additionally, you saw that Mac OS X comes with a firewall package, `ipfw`, which can be used for further securing your machine. In this section, we look at a couple intrusion detection tools that you can install to further secure your machine and discuss detecting and reacting to a break-in.

Tripwire

Tripwire is a utility that monitors the integrity of important files or directories. It stores information in a database about files and directories that you've specified. You can then use Tripwire to check whether there have been any changes to your files. It checks the current state of the files against the information in its database. The academic source release of Tripwire 1.3.1 is available from `http://www.tripwire.com/ products/tripwire_asr/`. Tripwire Security Systems also has a commercial version of Tripwire, but it might not be available for Mac OS X. An open source version for linux is available from `http://sourceforge.net/projects/tripwire`.

Remember that Tripwire can't detect any unauthorized changes that have already been made on your system. If you have any doubts about the system's current integrity, you can reinstall the operating system and then install Tripwire.

To start using Tripwire, edit your `tw.config` file. The sample configuration file provides details on the syntax of the file. You can specify directories or files for Tripwire to check and what kind of checking it should do in the `tw.config` file. The basic form of a line in the file is `<file> <flags>`. The sample `tw.config` file provides a rather detailed description about the available flags and modifiers to `<file>`, and the man page provides even more details. Basically, there are flags for a number of things to have Tripwire check, such as permissions, user ID, access time, modification time, and so on. Additionally, there are template definitions for certain combinations of the flags. You can use the template definitions for assigning how you want a file or directory to be checked, you can just assign flags, or you can assign a combination of the template with instructions to ignore something in the template or not to ignore something that's being ignored in the template.

After you feel you have a good basic `tw.config` file, you must initialize the Tripwire database by running `tripwire -initialize`. If you put your `tw.config` file in the wrong place,

Tripwire tells you so at this step. When you initialize Tripwire, it creates a `databases` directory with a database called `tw.db_`*<hostname>*. Pay attention to the output because it tells you where Tripwire expects to find the `tw.db_`*<hostname>* database that was just created. Put the database in that location.

The documentation suggests that you store your database in a read-only location and that you immediately make a hard copy of the database contents as added protection. A hard copy of the database contents enables you to make a manual comparison if you become suspicious of the database's integrity. Last, the documentation suggests that you might want to generate a set of signatures for the database, the configuration file, and the Tripwire executable by using the `siggen` utility that's included with the Tripwire package. Make a hardcopy of these as well.

Tripwire has four basic modes: database generation, integrity checking, database update, and interactive. You've already experienced the database generation mode. The integrity-checking mode is the mode you're probably most interested in at this point. To run Tripwire in integrity-checking mode, simply execute `tripwire`. In integrity-checking mode, Tripwire checks the integrity of whatever you specified in `tw.config` and provides a report of what's changed.

Here's an example of what the output looks like when Tripwire finds no changes:

```
brezup:root root # tripwire
Tripwire(tm) ASR (Academic Source Release) 1.3.1
File Integrity Assessment Software
(c) 1992, Purdue Research Foundation, (c) 1997, 1999 Tripwire
Security Systems, Inc. All Rights Reserved. Use Restricted to
Authorized Licensees.
### Phase 1:  Reading configuration file
### Phase 2:  Generating file list
### Phase 3:  Creating file information database
### Phase 4:  Searching for inconsistencies
###
###           All files match Tripwire database. Looks okay!
###
```

Here's an example of what the output looks like when Tripwire finds changes:

```
brezup:root root # tripwire
Tripwire(tm) ASR (Academic Source Release) 1.3.1
File Integrity Assessment Software
(c) 1992, Purdue Research Foundation, (c) 1997, 1999 Tripwire
Security Systems, Inc. All Rights Reserved. Use Restricted to
Authorized Licensees.
### Phase 1:  Reading configuration file
### Phase 2:  Generating file list
```

```
### Phase 3:  Creating file information database
### Phase 4:  Searching for inconsistencies
###
###           Total files scanned:      4398
###              Files added:       0
###              Files deleted:      0
###              Files changed:      1
###
###           Total file violations:     1
###
changed: -rwxr-xr-x root      0 8cô,=? /bin/ls
### Phase 5:  Generating observed/expected pairs for changed files
###
### Attr    Observed (what it is)     Expected (what it should be)
### =========== ============================= =============================
/bin/ls
    st_mode: 100755              100555
    st_ino: 231005              7009
    st_size: 32420               32464
   st_mtime: Wed Sep 10 22:09:22 2003   Sun Aug 17 12:52:47 2003
   st_ctime: Wed Sep 10 22:09:22 2003   Mon Aug 25 21:17:34 2003
  md5 (sig1): 0hpZEjBPxNLjZY84dSZwXl     28:qV1vILkgEYwn2Up5KYN
```

If you weren't expecting any changes, you should be suspicious. If you were expecting changes, there are two ways you can update your database to eliminate the false alarm. You can run `tripwire -interactive`. This puts Tripwire in interactive mode. Whenever it comes across a discrepancy, it prompts the user whether the database should be updated. You can also update your database by running `tripwire -update` *`<filename>`*, where *`<filename>`* can be a file or directory. This tells Tripwire to update the specified entry.

To make Tripwire useful, you should run it regularly. The easiest way to do so is to run Tripwire in a daily `cron` job and have the results mailed to you.

Be sure to read the man pages for `tripwire`, `tw.config`, and `siggen` for more detailed information.

Snort and HenWen

Snort, available from `http://www.snort.org/`, is a freely available package that has a packet sniffer mode and a network intrusion detection system mode. HenWen, available from `http://seiryu.home.comast.net/henwen.html`, is a graphical interface to `snort`. HenWen also includes a slightly modified version of `snort` in its distribution. It's free for personal, education, and government users, but commercial users are asked to pay a shareware fee. Just as BrickHouse does for `ipfw`, HenWen provides an opportunity for you to learn how the `snort` configuration file works. The current version of HenWen, HenWen

1.2.1, runs on Mac OS X 10.2 or later. The site does make an older version available for Mac OS X 10.1 and 10.0.

If you want to download and compile Snort yourself, it compiles and installs easily on Mac OS X. It follows the basic approach:

```
./configure
make
make install
```

By default, Snort installs in `/usr/local`. There are a number of compile-time options, including support for `openssl` and `mysql`. The `mysql` option can be useful for a number of reporting packages for Snort.

After you have Snort compiled, you might want to run it in packet-sniffing mode for a few seconds just to see how that looks and to verify that it runs. If you're interested in doing so, run `snort -v`. If you get no activity upon issuing this command, you may need to specify an interface. The `snort -v` output indicates which interface it is checking. Use `snort -v -i <interface>` to specify the interface. This prints TCP/IP packet headers to the screen. Here's an example of the very end of some output:

```
09/10-00:12:14.508492 192.168.1.112:49160 -> 192.168.1.16:22
TCP TTL:255 TOS:0x0 ID:46032 IpLen:20 DgmLen:84 DF
***AP*** Seq: 0xBD89D1D4 Ack: 0x2020CE5D Win: 0x8000 TcpLen: 20
=+=+=+=+=+=+=+=+=+=+=+=+=+=+=+=+=+=+=+=+=+=+=+=+=+=+=+=+=+=+=+=+=+=+=+=+=+=+

09/10-00:12:14.508554 192.168.1.16:22 -> 192.168.1.112:49160
TCP TTL:64 TOS:0x0 ID:35079 IpLen:20 DgmLen:40 DF
***A**** Seq: 0x2020CE5D Ack: 0xBD89D200 Win: 0xFFFF TcpLen: 20
=+=+=+=+=+=+=+=+=+=+=+=+=+=+=+=+=+=+=+=+=+=+=+=+=+=+=+=+=+=+=+=+=+=+=+=+=+=+

09/10-00:12:14.509890 192.168.1.16:22 -> 192.168.1.112:49160
TCP TTL:64 TOS:0x0 ID:35079 IpLen:20 DgmLen:40 DF
***A**** Seq: 0x2020CE5D Ack: 0xBD89D200 Win: 0xFFFF TcpLen: 20
=+=+=+=+=+=+=+=+=+=+=+=+=+=+=+=+=+=+=+=+=+=+=+=+=+=+=+=+=+=+=+=+=+=+=+=+=+=+

^C

===============================================================================
Snort analyzed 267 out of 267 packets, dropping 0(0.000%) packets

Breakdown by protocol:        Action Stats:
  TCP:  243    (91.011%)      ALERTS: 0
  UDP:  0      (0.000%)       LOGGED: 0
  ICMP: 0      (0.000%)       PASSED: 0
```

```
  ARP:   1     (0.375%)
 EAPOL:  0     (0.000%)
  IPv6:  0     (0.000%)
  IPX:   0     (0.000%)
 OTHER:  0     (0.000%)
DISCARD: 0     (0.000%)
===============================================================================
Wireless Stats:
Breakdown by type:
  Management Packets: 0     (0.000%)
  Control Packets:    0     (0.000%)
  Data Packets:       0     (0.000%)
===============================================================================
Fragmentation Stats:
Fragmented IP Packets: 0     (0.000%)
  Fragment Trackers:   0
  Rebuilt IP Packets:  0
  Frag elements used:  0
Discarded(incomplete): 0
  Discarded(timeout):  0
 Frag2 memory faults:  0
===============================================================================
TCP Stream Reassembly Stats:
    TCP Packets Used:    0     (0.000%)
      Stream Trackers:   0
      Stream flushes:    0
       Segments used:    0
  Stream4 Memory Faults: 0
===============================================================================
Snort exiting
```

To run Snort in intrusion detection mode, however, you must edit the configuration file and run it as a daemon. The distribution comes with a default `snort.conf` file that you can edit. You should periodically get updates to the rules from `http://www.snort.org/dl/rules/`.

To be able to run Snort in intrusion detection mode, manually complete your installation as follows:

```
brezup:root snort-2.0.1 # mkdir -p /usr/local/etc/snort/rules
brezup:root snort-2.0.1 # cp rules/* /usr/local/etc/snort/rules/
brezup:root snort-2.0.1 # cp etc/* /usr/local/etc/snort
brezup:root snort-2.0.1 # chmod -R 600 /usr/local/etc/snort
brezup:root snort-2.0.1 # mkdir /var/log/snort
```

In the configuration file, `snort.conf`, you configure network variables, preprocessor statements, output options, and Snort rules. The preprocessor statements determine how packets are handled before actually matching them against any rules. The output options determine how the Snort output is handled. Options include logging to a syslog or a database, such as MySQL. The rules are set up as separate files in a rules directory, like the services files for `xinetd`. It's easier to update the rules by storing them in a separate directory and having `include` statements in the configuration file for the rules rather than including them directly in the configuration file.

If you manually complete the installation as described earlier, the rules are copied to a separate rules directory located in `/usr/local/etc/snort/rules`, and snort.conf, like the rules directory, is also located in `/usr/local/etc/snort`. At the very least, the snort.conf file has to be edited to reflect this. Change the

```
var RULE_PATH ../rules
```

line to

```
var RULE_PATH rules
```

To run Snort in daemon mode, try a statement like this:

```
sort -D -c <path-to-snort.conf> -i <interface>
```

In this example, to run Snort on an airport interface, that would be

```
snort -D -c /usr/local/etc/snort/snort.conf -i en1
```

If you're satisfied with what Snort does, you might want to consider adding it to the startup scripts.

You might find HenWen useful for familiarizing yourself with the configuration file. It provides a graphical interface for setting up a basic `snort.conf` file and also comes with a detailed manual on setting up the configuration file. You can either use HenWen as its own package or for creating a base `snort.conf` file. By default, it creates a `snort.conf` file within its own hierarchy, but you can also choose to save a copy elsewhere. Additionally, you can have it start at boot.

Figure 31.14 shows the Network section of HenWen setup. This is HenWen's interface for setting up the network variables in the `snort.conf` file. The Preprocessors tab configures the preprocessors portion of the `snort.conf` file. The Output section configures the output options section of `snort.conf`. The Alerts section configures the rules portion; the Snort section, snort decoder and detection engine; the Spoof Detector section, the arpspoof section of the preprocessors portion of `snort.conf`.

HenWen's `snort.conf` file and `rules` directory are located in `HenWen.app/Contents/Resources`. If you install HenWen, you can still periodically update the rules statements as you can with the regular Snort distribution.

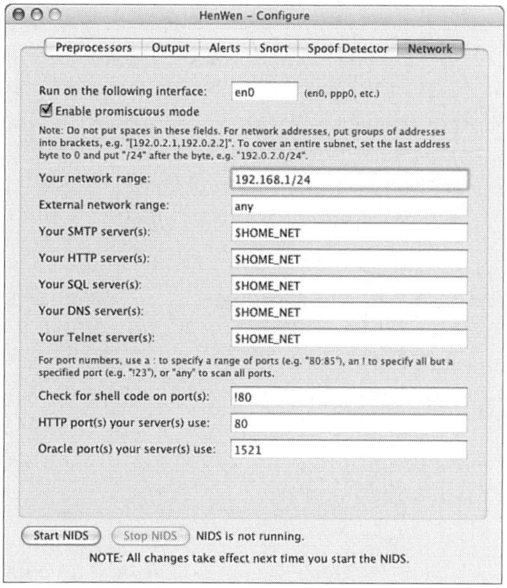

FIGURE 31.14 You can configure the network variables for `snort.conf` under the Network section in HenWen's interface.

Here's an example of what you might see in the Snort alert log:

```
[**] [1:618:4] SCAN Squid Proxy attempt [**]
[Classification: Attempted Information Leak] [Priority: 2]
09/10-22:27:31.943601 192.168.1.200:54268 -> 192.168.1.16:3128
TCP TTL:44 TOS:0x0 ID:1439 IpLen:20 DgmLen:40
******S* Seq: 0x13C3248A Ack: 0x0 Win: 0x400 TcpLen: 20

[**] [1:615:4] SCAN SOCKS Proxy attempt [**]
[Classification: Attempted Information Leak] [Priority: 2]
09/10-22:27:31.986179 192.168.1.200:54268 -> 192.168.1.16:1080
TCP TTL:44 TOS:0x0 ID:11200 IpLen:20 DgmLen:40
******S* Seq: 0x13C3248A Ack: 0x0 Win: 0x400 TcpLen: 20
[Xref => http://help.undernet.org/proxyscan/]

[**] [1:1420:2] SNMP trap tcp [**]
[Classification: Attempted Information Leak] [Priority: 2]
09/10-22:27:31.986428 192.168.1.200:54268 -> 192.168.1.16:162
TCP TTL:44 TOS:0x0 ID:4532 IpLen:20 DgmLen:40
******S* Seq: 0x13C3248A Ack: 0x0 Win: 0x400 TcpLen: 20
[Xref => http://cve.mitre.org/cgi-bin/cvename.cgi?name=CAN-2002-0013][Xref => ht
tp://cve.mitre.org/cgi-bin/cvename.cgi?name=CAN-2002-0012]
```

PortSentry

PortSentry 1.2 is a utility available from `http://sourceforge.net/projects/sentrytools/`. It's part of the Sentry Tools suite, a suite of free host-based security and intrusion tools. Sentry Tools also include LogSentry, which helps you monitor your system logs and HostSentry, which detects anomalous login behavior. The project recently moved to SourceForge, and is in the process of updating its licenses. As a result, HostSentry and PortSentry 2.x are not yet available.

PortSentry monitors connections to ports specified in the `portsentry.conf` file. If PortSentry detects a connection on one of those ports, you can choose to have it simply log the connection. You can also configure PortSentry to immediately block the connection. PortSentry adds a deny line for the host to your `/etc/hosts.deny` or `/etc/hosts.allow`, depending on which way you're using TCP Wrappers. It then blocks the connection via `route` or `ipfw`. You can also provide PortSentry with a list of hosts whose connections it should ignore. You must do some testing until you're completely satisfied with your PortSentry configuration.

PortSentry cleanly compiles on Mac OS X, so be sure to read the documentation carefully before you begin. The author clearly outlines the installation procedure in a step-by-step manner. Compiling with `make generic` works fine. By default, the package installs in `/usr/local/psionic/portsentry`.

The most important file you'll work with is `portsentry.conf`. The first part of the configuration file is the Port Configurations section. Here you specify which TCP and UDP ports are monitored. The author has provided three basic selections: `anal`, `aware`, and `bare-bones`. Of course, you can add any additional ports to whichever set you select.

Next is the Advanced Stealth Scan Detection Options section. Because these options apply only to Linux, you can ignore this section. PortSentry 2.0 is supposed to be able to detect stealth scans. That version is not available on SourceForge yet, but if you would like to try it, the source code for it is still available at `http://www.macosxunleashed.com/downloads/portsentry-2.0b1.tar.gz`. If you choose to `make bsd`, in portsentry.h, in the section that starts with `#ifdef BSD`, comment out the line that reads `#include <netinet/ip_ether.h>` by placing `//` at the beginning of that line.

The section that follows is the Configuration Files section, where you specify the location of `portsentry.ignore`, `portsentry.history`, and `portsentry.blocked`. The `portsentry.ignore` file is where you specify which hosts' connections the program should ignore. The `portsentry.history` file is where PortSentry logs a history of the actions it has taken. The `portsentry.blocked` file is where PortSentry logs a history of its actions for the current session.

The next section is the Misc. Configurations Options section, which only has one configuration option. Here you set whether DNS lookups are done on attacking hosts. The default is off.

The next section is the Response Options section. In this section, you specify what the automatic response should be for TCP and UDP connections. In the Ignore Options subsection, you specify what level of `ignore` PortSentry should follow for TCP and UDP connections. You can have PortSentry block scans, not block them, or execute some external command. The Dropping Routes subsection is where you select what the blocking response should be. The program can be configured to block via `route` or via `ipfw`. I recommend using `ipfw` if you have it running. If you select `ipfw`, PortSentry, by default, adds a deny rule to `ipfw`. Of course, you can modify that rule. In the TCP Wrappers subsection, select the correct TCP Wrappers syntax for the way you are using it. An external command can be specified in the External Commands subsection. In the Scan Trigger Value subsection, you configure the number of port connects that are allowed before an alarm is given. In the Port Banner section, you can specify what text, if any, should be displayed when PortSentry is tripped.

After you have a basic `portsentry.conf` file, and you've installed the package, run the following to start PortSentry:

```
/usr/local/psionic/portsentry/portsentry -tcp
/usr/local/psionic/portsentry/portsentry -udp
```

Check `/var/log/system.log` for the PortSentry startup response. For each PortSentry, you'll see some initial startup lines, a line for each port it's monitoring, and a final line indicating that PortSentry is active and listening.

If PortSentry is set to immediately block a connection, here's the type of response you will see in the log:

```
Sep 11 01:11:51 localhost portsentry[1164]: attackalert: Host 192.168.1.200
➥has been blocked via wrappers with string: "ALL: 192.168.1.200"
Sep 11 01:11:51 localhost portsentry[1164]: attackalert: Host 192.168.1.200
➥has been blocked via dropped route using command: "/sbin/ipfw add
➥1 deny all from 192.168.1.200:255.255.255.255 to any"
Sep 11 01:11:51 localhost portsentry[1164]: attackalert: Connect from host:
➥192.168.1.200/192.168.1.200 to TCP port: 1
Sep 11 01:11:51 localhost portsentry[1164]: attackalert: Host: 192.168.1.200
➥is already blocked. Ignoring
```

Check your `/etc/hosts.deny` and run `ipfw show`. You'll see that it does add the offending host to the `/etc/hosts.deny` file and add an `ipfw` rule.

If PortSentry isn't set to block connections, here is a sample response in the log file:

```
Sep 11 01:03:52 localhost portsentry[1125]: attackalert: Connect
➥from host: 192.168.1.200/192.168.1.200 to TCP port: 21
Sep 11 01:03:52 localhost portsentry[1125]: attackalert: Ignoring
➥TCP response per configuration file setting.
```

Detecting a Break-in

In spite of the tools we've looked at so far, it isn't necessarily easy to detect a break-in, even with Tripwire. If your machine has been compromised, the intruder might update your Tripwire database for you. The tools certainly help, but they provide no guarantee of protection.

A Linux cluster that we put up a few years ago for a class experienced a break-in within days of being up. That Linux cluster was an out-of-the-box Linux installation, and we didn't follow the commonsense, preventive security measures outlined earlier in this chapter. Unlike Mac OS X, many Linux distributions come with services turned on by default. How did we detect the break-in? Actually, we didn't. The university's security group, which monitors the university's network traffic—among their various duties—told our administration staff that we had a break-in. Not only did they tell us we had a break-in, but they also told us where on our machines to find the culprit software and evidence. Obviously, the security group keeps up-to-date on the latest vulnerabilities and popular cracking software. The break-in was well hidden from us. Common commands such as `ls` had been replaced, and the software was put in a directory called `..` that not only usually requires using `ls -a` rather than `ls` to see, but the replacement version of `ls` wouldn't show at all. The crackers also replaced the `ps` command with one that wouldn't show their sniffing processes even as the processes were still running, and they tried to delete all other traces of their presence from the machines. A couple of people from the security group came with a floppy that had noncompromised versions of useful commands, and we were indeed able to see the `..` directory and the unusual processes that were running.

There are some things that you and your facility, if your machine is part of a facility, can do to detect a break-in. Who knows? You might detect one in progress. Your network administrator, who is probably monitoring network traffic, might be able to tell you whether the network is being or was recently probed. This might give you the opportunity to check your logs for any unusual activity. If your machines seem sluggish, someone else could be tying up your resources. Check your logs; check to see who is logged on and check what processes are running. It's possible that you'll discover that a normally inactive account has had a recent flourish of activity. Depending on how far along the cracker is, your useful commands for detecting unusual activity might have been replaced. Try using `ls-F` in `tcsh`, instead of your normal `ls`, to see whether you can detect the presence of any unusual software or directories. Even if your network administrator hasn't alerted you to any unusual network activity, or even if your machine isn't sluggish, check your logs regularly. You never know what you might find. You might want to consider downloading the LogSentry utility to assist you with monitoring your logs.

NOTE

The `tcsh` shell has a built-in `ls` command named `ls-F`. Because most cracker wannabes don't know what they're doing, they won't add a fake `ls-F` or replace `tcsh` with a broken version, as well as replacing the normal `ls` command in `/usr/bin`. Of course, you shouldn't rely on this as a 100% certain way to detect problem directories or compromised commands. As soon as you trust something, a cracker wannabe with above-average smarts adds it to one of the automated scripts. It's another tool in your arsenal, however, and you need all the tools you can get.

Regularly checking your machine's logs, processes, and so on really is useful. Recently, a machine on our building's network was compromised. How long it was compromised is unknown. The system administrator noticed an odd FTP process that root was running, but the process had no reason to be running. When he killed the process, the machine became unusable. When the machine was finally restored, which involved reinstalling the operating system, it was compromised again within two weeks. This time, the system administrator noticed that he had four new users who he didn't create.

In addition, be especially paranoid around holidays. Crackers know that users won't be around on holidays and that many system administrators won't be around either. This makes holidays, weekends, and early mornings prime time for crackers because they know they'll have at least a few hours to play before any human is likely to notice them.

Responding to a Break-in

How you respond to a break-in depends on the circumstances surrounding it.

If your security group personnel discovers the break-in, follow their instructions to the letter. What they tell you depends somewhat on the circumstances of the break-in. In the case of a sniffer, the security group personnel will advise you to secure your machines and have everyone change their passwords. By *changing passwords*, they mean passwords for any accounts the users on your network might have accessed during the time in question. Yes, that's all passwords on any accounts they might have accessed from your network—including ones on other networks that they've accessed from your machines. However, even in the case of a sniffer, sometimes your security group will advise you to reinstall the operating system. If you have a sniffer, all the traffic that's been across your network has been compromised, including outgoing traffic to other sites, so this might impact machines far beyond yours.

What Is a Sniffer?

A sniffer is an application that watches network traffic as it moves past the sniffer machine. Most modern sniffers can extract usernames, passwords, and other sensitive information from the traffic flow. Recall that Snort can be used as a sniffer. For another example of a network sniffer for Mac OS X, check out the Ettercap project at `http://ettercap.sourceforge.net/`. Note: You should never use a sniffer on a network that you do not administer, nor should you activate it without the knowledge of the other users on the network.

If your security group learns that your machine was used for attacking another site, the response they'll suggest might surprise you. This time, they might not ask you to secure your machine right away. The site that was attacked might request the cooperation of your site in capturing the culprit.

If, however, you detect a break-in before your security group does, you need to decide what your response will be. Do you close down the machine? Do you keep it open to try to catch the culprit? Do you ask your security group what to do? Certainly, there's nothing wrong with asking your security group, but depending on the time of day and number of security problems, you might not be able to find them. Think about how you might respond to a break-in before it actually occurs.

If the break-in caused no obvious damage to anyone else's site, swiftly closing down services on your machine and fixing what was done might be the right solution. If damage is done to someone else's site, you might want to keep your machine open for a while in a cooperative effort to catch the culprit. On the other hand, if your site is being used to break into someone else's site and the other site doesn't know about it yet, you have a responsibility to stop the attack before the crackers can do any more damage. Cooperation is the name of the game here, and you should behave as reasonably and as professionally as possible. If a remote site requests your help, do everything you can to help—you'd want the same courtesy. If a remote site is being attacked through your site, bend over backward to limit the damage. You wouldn't want someone to tell you, "Oh, we could have stopped that, but we were in the middle of a game of Quake and didn't want to shut down." Some of this might seem like advice to a system administrator, but remember, you are a system administrator for your Mac OS X machine as well as one of its users.

No matter what you decide to do, if you have a security group in your company, tell them about the incident and what you did. The security group personnel need to know everything to best assess your company's security needs.

If your machine might have been compromised but you can't find any obvious evidence in your logs or some helpful logs aren't available, you might have no recourse but to wipe out your machine and start over. Your users might not like it, but it's better for you to have a machine that you know you can trust, even if that means starting over from scratch. Your users probably prefer the downtime to the potential loss of their data. Again, tell your security group folks what you've done. In all likelihood, they'll support your decision to wipe out your machine and start over from scratch. They'd rather have you do that if you have any doubt about your machine than have you let even one suspect machine stay on the network. Roughly one-third of our campus network and a related government site were taken down for several days a while ago when someone persisted in allowing one compromised machine to stay on the university's network. Fortunately, our machines weren't involved in that one.

Given that one day you might have to wipe your machine in response to an attack, there are some commonsense measures you can take to make restoring your data easier:

- Keep a copy of your Mac OS X CDs in a location where you can find them.
- Keep your software CDs and registration numbers in a location where you can find them.
- Archive to CD-R any additional third-party software you downloaded and installed, especially if it was difficult to compile or is important to you.
- Archive to CD-R any data you don't want to lose.

Yes, that's it. Don't lose your Mac OS X CDs and software CDs. Back up any additional software you compiled and your data. That seems too obvious, doesn't it? It should be, but even the best of us need that reminder. Remember the machine on our network that was compromised twice in one month? When the initial break-in was discovered, the system administrator killed off just one suspicious process, but the machine was rendered completely non-functional as a result. In the end, it had to be wiped clean with a freshly formatted hard drive, and everything reinstalled from scratch. Because they didn't perform regular backups, they lost a large amount of user-account data in the process. They also lost a software package that was the key to one faculty member's research, but which wasn't stored anywhere else except in the (by then long-departed) student's directory where it had been written. Those folks spent at least $5,000 for their machine, and didn't bother to spend the additional $200 on a tape drive or CD recorder for backup. After investing in the latest hardware, you can't afford not to spend a few dollars more and a little bit of time to preserve your data. With the current cost of CD-Rs, you should even be able to afford good CD-Rs for your data. In other words, if your machine has been compromised, it's best to be prepared to have the smoothest recovery possible. Backups and your original software CDs should help with this.

Where to Go from Here

The Ohio State University's security group says it hasn't experienced any security incidents involving Mac OS X on campus, yet. The security group personnel do point out, however, that as Mac OS X becomes more widespread, crackers will start to target Mac OS X machines. Of course, they recommend that you take a proactive security stance with your machine.

In this chapter, we attempted to help you do just that. You've seen some basic security measures that you can follow in securing your machine. In addition, you learned about `ipfw`, the built-in firewall package that comes with Mac OS X. You also learned about some intrusion detection tools. After reading this chapter, you should follow those basic security measures at the very least. Hopefully, you'll also decide to use some combination of the firewall package and intrusion detection tools, and if you're wise, you'll start making regular backups.

Backup, Backup, Backup: Disk Images with `hdiutil`

You can never have too many backups. If you think you do, it's only because you haven't needed one that you decided not to make. In Chapter 32, "System Maintenance," you'll learn about the `dump` and `restore` commands that are the traditional Unix way of doing backups (and still quite useful for many things). But for many users, tape isn't a particularly convenient way of archiving things, and if it's not convenient, it often gets overlooked. To make life a little easier for those of you who have writable CD-R, CD-RW, and DVD-R drives, Apple has provided the `hdiutil` command. `hdiutil` is a command-line interface to disk image files. It allows their creation and configuration, and burning them to a writable CD/DVD. Combined with the ditto command (a resource-fork–enabled file copying program that's covered in Chapter 32), or GNU-tar (the resource-fork savvy version of tar), hdiutil makes for a handy backup utility.

Many users will probably be primarily interested in the fact that hdiutil enables you to burn already existing disk image files to recordable media, creating a copy of the original:

```
hdiutil burn myImage.dmg
```

Of interest to other users will be the -fs option that enables a blank disk image to be created and then populated with the contents of a segment of your filesystem.

```
brezup:ray ray $ du -s unleashed
290160 unleashed
brezup:ray ray $ hdiutil create -sectors 291160 -fs HFS+
➥-volname MyUnleashed_Files Unleashed_Image
Initializing...
Creating...
.................................................................
.................................................................
....
Formatting...
Finishing...
created: /Users/ray/Unleashed_image.dmg
brezup:ray ray $ hdiutil attach Unleashed_Image.dmg
Initializing...
Attaching...
Finishing...
Finishing...
/dev/disk2          Apple_partition_scheme
/dev/disk2s1        Apple_partition_map
/dev/disk2s2        Apple_HFS           /Volumes/MyUnleashed_Files
brezup:ray ray $ ditto -rsrcFork unleashed/ /Volumes/MyUnleashed_Files/
brezup:ray ray $ hdiutil detach /dev/disk2
"disk2" unmounted.
"disk2" ejected.
```

NOTE

Observant readers will note that I've added a bit to the sector size value compared to the size result that du told me. This is to provide room for the overhead involved in being a completely separate volume structure, as opposed to a branch of a directory tree, and possible differences in the way du counts space occupied by resource forks as compared with the Finder and ditto. Apple's recommendation is to add 100 sectors, but I've found this to sometimes be too small.

See Chapter 32 for further information on the use of ditto.

At this point, I have a file named Unleashed_Image.dmg in my home directory. If I double-click it to mount it, it mounts as a desktop disk image named MyUnleashed_Files, and it contains the contents of the unleashed directory that lives in my home directory. If I'd like it a bit smaller, I can additionally use hdiutil to convert the file into an alternative, compressed storage format.

NOTE

Remember to unmount images, either at the command line or in the Finder, before manipulating their format!

```
brezup:ray ray $ hdiutil convert -format UDZO -o
➥Unleashed_Image.Z.dmg Unleashed_Image.dmg
Preparing imaging engine...
Reading DDM...
  (CRC32 $D1902EA3: DDM)
Reading Apple_partition_map (0)...
  (CRC32 $CE981B6A: Apple_partition_map (0))
Reading Apple_HFS (1)...
.................................................................
.................................................................
....
  (CRC32 $C12AA10D: Apple_HFS (1))
Reading Apple_Free (2)...
.................................................................
.................................................................
....
  (CRC32 $00000000: Apple_Free (2))
Terminating imaging engine...
Adding resources...
.................................................................
.................................................................
....
Elapsed Time: 1m 16.019s
 (1 task, weight 100)
File size: 45959867 bytes, Checksum: CRC32 $4FE0F26F
Sectors processed: 295160, 295137 compressed
Speed: 1.9Mbytes/sec
Savings: 69.6%
created: Unleashed_Image.Z.dmg
```

Now I have a considerably smaller version of the file, as well as the large version that I haven't disposed of yet. This version takes longer to mount, but is just barely more than 30% the size of the original file.

Of course, hdiutil is capable of a considerable number of other manipulations of disk image files as well, including a multitude of burn options for how images are written to recordable media, and a number of conversions between different standard disk image formats. Table 31.4 includes an abbreviated version of the command documentation table showing the options most relevant for system backup and recovers. The full version is available in Appendix A, "Command-Line Reference."

TABLE 31.4 The Command Documentation Table for hdiutil

hdiutil	Manipulates disk images
hdiutil *<verb>* [*<options>*]	
hdiutil uses the DiskImages framework to manipulate disk image files. Common verbs include attach, detach, verify, create, convert, and burn.	
The rest of the verbs are help, info, load, checksum, eject (historical synonym for detach), flatten, unflatten, imageinfo, mount (historical synonym for attach), mountvol, unmount, plugins, resize, segment, and pmap.	
Options	
All hdiutil verbs accept these options:	
-verbose	Verbose; default is less output. This option is useful if it's unclear why a particular operation failed. At a minimum, the probing for each image type of any given files will be shown.
-quiet	Minimizes output in most cases.
-debug	Very verbose. This option is useful if a large amount of information about what hdiutil and the DiskImages framework are doing is needed.
Many hdiutil verbs understand the following options:	
-encryption [*<crypto_method>*]	Specifies a particular type of encryption or, if not specified, the default CEncrypedEncoding.
-passphrase *<passphrase>*	Provides a passphrase for an encrypted image. -passphrase is very insecure because the passphrase is visible to who can run ps(1).
-shadow [*<shadowfile>*]	Uses a shadow file in conjunction with the data in the image. This option prevents modification of the original image and enables read-only images to be used as read/write images. When blocks are being read from the image, blocks present in the shadow file override blocks in the base image. When blocks are being written, the writes will be redirected to the shadow file. If not specified, -shadow defaults to *<imagename>*.shadow. If the shadow file doesn't exist, it's created.
For the verbs that create images, it should be noted that the correct extension is added to the filenames if the extension is not present. The creation engine also examines the filename extension of the provided filename and changes its behavior accordingly. For example, a sparse image can be created without specifying -type SPARSE simply by appending the .sparseimage extension to the provided filename.	

TABLE 31.4 Continued

Verbs

Each verb is listed with its description and individual arguments. Arguments to the verbs can be passed in almost any order. A sector is 512 bytes.

`help`	Displays the usage information for each verb.
`attach <imagename> [<options>]`	Mounts an image file. `attach` calls `hdid` with its arguments.
`detach <dev_name> [-force]`	Detaches a disk image and terminates any associated `hdid` process. `-force`. Similar to `umount -f`. `unmounts` any filesystems and `detaches` the image file, regardless of any open files on the image.
`verify <imagename> [<options>]`	Computes the checksum of a read-only (or compressed) image file, and verifies it against the value stored in the image. `verify` accepts the common options `-encryption`, `-srcimagekey`, `-tgtimagekey`, `-passphrase`, and `-shadow`.
`create <imagename> <size_spec> [<options>]`	Creates a new blank image. If *`imagename`* already exists, `-ov` must be specified or `create` will fail. Common options: `-plist`, `-encryption`, and `-passphrase`.
`convert <imagefile> -format <format> -o <outfile> [<options>]`	Converts `<imagefile>` to type `<format>` and writes the result to `<outfile>`. The correct filename extension is added only if it isn't part of the provided name. `<format>` is one of `UDRW` `UDIF` read/write image `UFBI` `UDIF` entire image with MD5 checksum `UDRO` `UDIF` read/only image `UDCO` `UDIF` ADC-compressed image `UDTO` DVD/CD-R export image `UDxx` `UDIF` stub image `DC42` Disk Copy 4.2 image In addition to the compression offered by some formats, the `UDIF` and `NDIF` non-read/write image formats completely remove unused space in HFS and UFS filesystems. For `UDZO`, `-imagekey-zlib-level=<value>` enables you to set the `zlib` compression level as with `gzip(1)`. The default compression level is `1` (fastest). `<options>` are any of Common options: `-shadow`, `-encryption`, and `-passphrase` Other options: `-align <sector_alignment>` Default is `4` (2KB)

TABLE 31.4 Continued

	`-pmap` Add a partition map. When converting a `NDIF` to a any variety of `UDIF`, or when converting a partition-less `UDIF` to `UDIF`, the default is `true`.

`burn` *`<imagename>`* `[`*`<options>`*`]`	Burns *`<imagename>`* to optical media in an attached drive. In all cases, a prompt for media is printed when an appropriate drive has been found.
	`<options>` are any of
	
	Common options: `-shadow`, `-srcimagekey`, `-encryption`, and `-passphrase`
	
	Other options:
	`-testburn`
	Doesn't turn on laser (laser defaults to on).
	`-noeject`
	Doesn't eject disc after burning.
	`-eject`
	Ejects disc after burning (default).
	`-verifyburn`
	Verifies disc contents after burn (default).
	`-noverifyburn`
	Doesn't verify disc contents after burn.
	`-addpmap`
	Adds partition map if necessary. Some filesystem types aren't recognized when stored on optical media unless they're enclosed in a partition map. This option adds a partition map to any bare filesystem that needs a partition map to be recognized when burned to optical media. This is the default behavior.
	`-noaddpmap`
	Doesn't add partition map.
	`-skipfinalfree`
	Skips final free partition. If there's a partition map on the image specifying an `Apple_Free` partition as the last partition, that `Apple_Free` partition is not burned. The burned partition map still references the empty space. This is the default behavior.
	`-noskipfinalfree`
	Doesn't skip any trailing `Apple_Free` partition.
	`-optimizeimage`
	Optimizes filesystem for burning. Optimization can reduce the size of an `HFS` or `HFS+` volume to the size of the data contained

TABLE 31.4 Continued

	on the volume. This option changes what is burned such that the disc has a different checksum than the image it came from. -nooptimizeimage Doesn't optimize. Burns all blocks of the image (minus any blocks in trailing Apple_Free partitions unless -noskipfinalfree is specified). This is the default behavior. -forceclose Forces the disc to be closed after burning. Further burns to the disc are impossible. -noforceclose Doesn't force disc to be closed (default) -speed *<x_factor>* *<x_factor>* may be 1, 2, 4, 6, .. max Specifies the desired ×-factor. For example, 8 means that the drive will burn at 8× speed. max causes the burn to proceed at the maximum speed of the drive. max is the default speed. -sizequery Only calculates the size of disc required. (The size returned is in sectors.) -erase Prompts for optical media (DVD-RW/CD-RW) and then, if the hardware supports it, quickly erases the media. -fullerase Erases all sectors of the disc. (This usually takes quite a bit longer than -erase.)
unmount *<volume>*	Unmounts a mounted volume. *<volume>* can be a full path to a /dev entry or the name of a mountpoint.
imageinfo *<imagename>* [*<options>*]	Prints out information about a disk image. Common options are -plist, -encryption, and -passphrase.
resize *<size_spec>* *<imagename>* [*<options>*]	For a read/write-partitioned UDIF device image, if the last partition is Apple_HFS (either HFS or HFS+), it attempts to resize the partition to the end of the device file, or to the last used block in the embedded HFS/HFS+ filesystem. Common options are -encryption and -passphrase.
pmap *<image_source>* [*<options>*]	Displays partition map from image or device. *<image_source>* is either a plain file or special file (that is, a /dev/disk entry).

Other Tools and Resources

Is there anything else you can do to protect your machine? If your company has a security group, contact the group to find out whether it holds any security meetings or has a mailing list that issues any security advisories that could be important for you. If you live near a university, find out whether the university has a security group. The university's security group probably holds meetings that are also open to the public. Attending meetings where you can meet some of the experts in security gives you the opportunity to ask any security question you might have face-to-face.

Earlier in this chapter, we mentioned that you should update Mac OS X regularly. You can extend that to third-party services software that you have installed, such as `wu-ftpd` and `sendmail`. In addition, we mentioned replacing basic services with secure services where possible.

You might also be interested in installing additional tools to enhance your security. Many of the sites listed in the following paragraphs contain links to the various types of available tools.

Finally, it's important to keep informed on security issues. The following list describes some resources that can be of assistance:

CERT Coordination Center—`http://www.cert.org/`

The CERT Coordination Center grew out of the Computer Emergency Response Team, which was formed in 1988 by the Defense Advanced Research Project Agency (DARPA), in response to the Internet worm of the day. The CERT Coordination Center issues security advisories that you can receive as they come out if you're on the mailing list. The site provides advice on many security matters, including those for the home user.

SecurityFocus.com—`http://www.securityfocus.com/`

This site provides a wealth of information on tools, vulnerabilities, and so on. In addition, this site hosts the BugTraq mailing list, a mailing list that discusses vulnerabilities, how to exploit them, and how to fix them. You can sign up to be on the mailing list or view the archives.

Apple Computer Product Security Incident Response—`http://www.info.apple.com/usen/security/security.html`

This page is Apple's general security page from which Apple provides some formal information on Apple security as well as a link to a page on which you can sign up to be on Apple's security announcement mailing list.

MacSecurity.org—`http://www.macsecurity.org/`

This is a nice site dedicated to Macintosh security issues.

SecureMac—`http://www.securemac.com/`

This site is dedicated to Macintosh security issues. At this time, it doesn't appear to be as current on security issues for Mac OS X as MacSecurity.org.

National Infrastructure Protection Center—`http://www.nipc.gov/cybernotes/cybernotes.htm`

The center provides some interesting security reports, called Cybernotes, that break down into three sections: Bugs, Holes & Patches; Recent Exploit Scripts; and Viruses.

SANS Institute—`http://www.sans.org/`

The SANS (SysAdmin, Audit, Network, Security) Institute is a cooperative research and education organization. It sponsors a variety of conferences and training sessions

CERIAS—`http://www.cerias.purdue.edu/`

Purdue University's Center for Education and Research in Information Assurance and Security is an education and research area for security issues. Probably the item of most interest here is the link to the FTP archive from which you can download a number of security tools. The archive includes many security tools, even ones that CERIAS didn't necessarily develop. Although you might prefer to download a specific tool from the home developing site, browsing this FTP archive is a convenient way to read the basic READMEs for many tools.

Summary

Network security has never been as important on the Macintosh as it is with Mac OS X. The new Mac operating system, based on a BSD core, provides a wider variety of network services than any previous release. Luckily, Mac OS X includes a variety of tools that can fend off attacks before they occur—without the need for additional software.

Many users find that their needs are met simply by applying TCP Wrappers to their critical services and shutting down those protocols that aren't being used. Advanced users can employ `ipfw` or BrickHouse to provide low-level control over the flow of network traffic to and from the Mac OS X computer. In addition, administrators might want to take proactive measures by employing an intrusion detection tool such as Tripwire or Snort. These applications can detect an attack and react to it—potentially saving your system, data, and peace of mind.

CHAPTER 32

System Maintenance

IN THIS CHAPTER

With every book, there are topics that don't quite fit into any of the other chapters. In Mac OS X Panther Unleashed, these topics, related to system maintenance and troubleshooting, have been included in this, the last chapter. Here you'll find information on how to maintain your system and what products are available to aid your efforts.

Software Updates

An important part of maintaining a functioning and secure Mac OS X system is staying on top of the operating system updates. With a BSD core, Mac OS needs more frequent attention than the Classic Mac operating system. Critical security utilities such as SSH are revised regularly and, unless updated, might open your system to outside attack. An update in mid-2003 fixed a screensaver hole that could potentially allow a local user to bypass password protection. Although it may be tempting to let your system "coast" for a few months and then perform all the updates at once, this is not wise. A machine with a full-time Internet connection is vulnerable from the moment that a new software exploit is found and very likely will be compromised.

For example, consider my home computer, which logs each connection attempt made (via PortSentry):

```
07/13/2003 03:38:28 Host: www.allstat.com/216.168.220.18 Port: 137 UDP Blocked
07/13/2003 03:51:47 Host: 211.109.221.80/211.109.221.80 Port: 27374 TCP Blocked
07/13/2003 04:22:09 Host: 71dial170.xnet/213.233.71.170 Port: 27374 TCP Blocked
07/13/2003 07:46:43 Host: 92dial132.xnet/213.233.92.132 Port: 27374 TCP Blocked
07/13/2003 08:03:51 Host: 65.103.240.60/65.103.240.60 Port: 1433 TCP Blocked
07/13/2003 08:10:57 Host: pc172.jeleniag.sdi.tpnet/217.96.243.172 Port: 22 TCP Blocked
07/13/2003 09:49:30 Host: rrcs-central-24-12/24.123.46.10 Port: 515 TCP Blocked
07/13/2003 10:35:34 Host: 64dial26.xnet.ro/213.233.64.26 Port: 27374 TCP Blocked
07/13/2003 12:53:05 Host: 211.137.136.118/211.137.136.118 Port: 111 TCP Blocked
07/13/2003 14:15:47 Host: 6535208hfc65.tampa/65.35.208.65 Port: 137 UDP Blocked
07/13/2003 15:00:20 Host: Sherbrooke-HSE/65.93.184.161 Port: 27374 TCP Blocked
07/13/2003 19:01:57 Host: 210.0.179.119/210.0.179.119 Port: 21 TCP Blocked
07/13/2003 19:51:48 Host: 67-92-203-151/67.92.203.151 Port: 1433 TCP Blocked
07/13/2003 20:26:33 Host: AC83C299.ipt.aol/172.131.194.153 Port: 23 TCP Blocked
07/13/2003 21:05:20 Host: 66.84.150.13/66.84.150.13 Port: 1433 TCP Blocked
07/13/2003 23:19:13 Host: 195.113.153.9/195.113.153.9 Port: 21 TCP Blocked
07/13/2003 23:32:48 Host: 61-220-153-179.HINET-IP./61.220.153.179 Port: 1433 TCP Blocked
```

In the course of one day, there are more than 15 connection attempts. Some are innocuous—simple probes for Internet sharing services such as Kazaa—whereas others are attempts to connect to well-known services, such as telnet, SSH, and FTP, presumably for the purpose of exploitation. On a production computer with a real Internet connection running real services, you might experience hundreds of inappropriate connection attempts a day, and unless you want to spend your time reinstalling Mac OS X, you should keep your system updated and prepared to handle the threat.

Checking for Updates

Mac OS X automates the process of upgrading software through the use of the Software Update System Preferences pane (path: `/Applications/System Preferences`), shown in Figure 32.1.

Use the check box to choose whether to run the software update application automatically, or invoke it manually. If you've chosen an automatic install, use the pop-up menu to select a schedule (Daily, Weekly, Monthly) for the update library to be queried. If you want the system to automatically download updates in the background and then notify you when they're ready to be installed, click Download Important Updates in the Background.

NOTE

Unlike Mac OS 9.2, when the update runs automatically, it does not install the software it finds. It first prompts the user to select the module's installation.

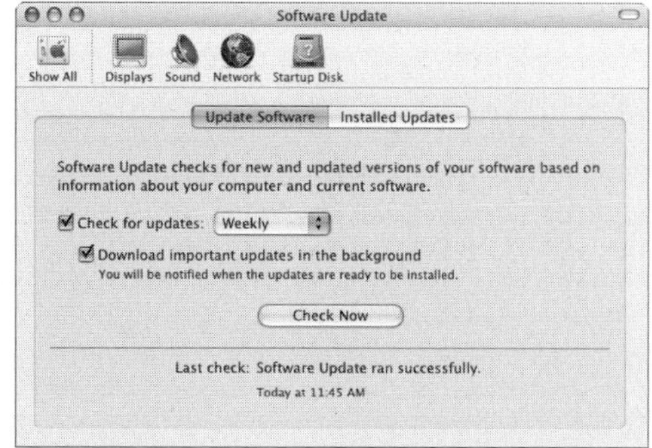

FIGURE 32.1 The Software Update pane controls automatic system updates.

To force the system to look for updates immediately, click the Check Now button. Your Mac OS X computer contacts Apple and detects available software packages.

If updates are found, a system update application is launched, as shown in Figure 32.2.

FIGURE 32.2 Check the items that you want to install.

Downloading Updates

Click the check box in front of each package that you want to download and then click Install to start the process. You are prompted for an administrator password before continuing.

During the download, the system displays an installation status bar for each update. Some downloads could take a long time, depending on your connection and how much bandwidth the latest Windows IIS virus is consuming, so you might want to take a break while your system is updated.

Depending on the software package, you might see a license agreement at some point in time during the installation. In addition, the install process is likely to pause for a long period of time while it optimizes your installed packages. This is completely normal, albeit slightly annoying. I've seen the optimization process take longer than 30 minutes for a small update.

When finished, the software might prompt you to restart. All updates to the base operating system require a reboot before becoming active.

> **NOTE**
>
> For those who want to put the update on a CD or file server, Apple offers normal file downloads for all the available system updates. To download an update file to your desktop through the Software Update application, select the item in the update list; then choose Update, Download Checked Items to Desktop from the menu.

Disabling Unnecessary Updates

If there are updates that don't apply to your system, select them and choose Update, Make Inactive (Command--) from the menu. This prevents Software Update from attempting to install them in the future.

To *show* updates that you've previously made inactive, choose Update, Show Inactive Updates (Command-Shift--).

Installed Files

Many users, for good reason, want to keep track of what software has been installed on their system. Opening the Software Update preferences pane and clicking the Installed Updates tab displays a log of installed updates. Figure 32.3 shows this listing.

In the event of an installation failure, Apple suggests manually forcing an update, and then reselecting and reinstalling the failed upgrade. I've found that downloading the update package to the desktop and installing manually often works.

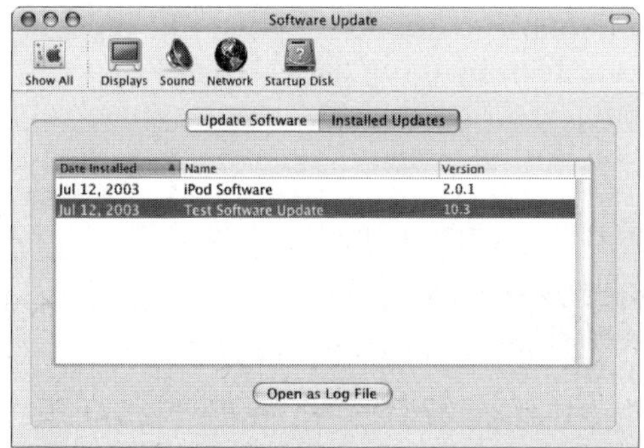

FIGURE 32.3 The Software Update pane displays a list of installed update packages.

In some cases, packages that are "partially" installed might not show up as an available upgrade. This means that Mac OS X thinks the software was installed even if it wasn't. To make OS X forget about an update so that it can be reinstalled, open the directory `/Library/Receipts`. This folder contains receipt files for all software installed using Apple's built-in Installer program. The receipts are named based on the updated package; for example, Security Update July 2003 has the receipt file `SecurityUpd2003-07-14.pkg`.

Throwing out a receipt file will usually effectively convince Mac OS X that the update was never installed.

BOM and `lsbom`

The receipt files, in addition to keeping track of which packages have been installed, also contain a bill of materials (BOM). The BOM tracks every single file that was updated or installed. Users can access the BOM using the command-line `lsbom` command. You'll need to dig deep into the receipt files, accessing a directory with this pattern: `<receipt package>.pkg/Contents/Resources/<receipt package>.bom`. For example, to view the BOM for the Security Update July 2002 receipt file:

```
brezup:jray jray $ sudo lsbom /Library/Receipts/SecurityUpd2003-07-14.pkg
➥/Contents/Resources/SecurityUpd2003-07-14.bom

.	41775	0/80
./System	40755	0/0
./System/Library	40755	0/0
./System/Library/Frameworks	40755	0/0
./System/Library/Frameworks/Security.framework 40755	0/0
./System/Library/Frameworks/Security.framework/Versions 40755	0/0
./System/Library/Frameworks/Security.framework/Versions/A	40755	0/0
...
```

The `lsbom` command can limit its output to only specific types of files contained in the BOM, such as directories or files, by using flags such as `-d` and `-f`, respectively. The Apple `lsbom` documentation, contained in Table 32.1, displays many of the available options and filters for viewing BOMs as documented in the man page.

TABLE 32.1 Command Documentation Table for `lsbom`

Option	Description
`lsbom`	View Bill of Material files
`-b`	List block devices
`-c`	List character devices
`-d`	List directories
`-f`	List files
`-l`	List symbolic links
`-m`	Print modified times (for plain files only)
`-s`	Print only the path of each file
`-x`	Suppress modes for directories and symlinks
`-arch`	`archVal` when displaying plain files that represent fat `mach-o` binaries, print the size and checksum of the file contents for the specified `archVal` (either "ppc" or "i386")
`-p` *<param>*	Print only some of the results (Each option can only be used once):
`c`	32-bit checksum
`f`	Filename
`F`	Filename with quotes (that is, `"/usr/bin/lsbom"`)
`g`	Group ID
`G`	Group name
`m`	File mode (permissions)
`M`	Symbolic file mode (that is, "dr-xr-xr-x")
`s`	File size
`S`	Formatted size
`t`	Mod time
`T`	Formatted mod time
`u`	User ID
`U`	Username
`/`	User ID/group ID
`?`	Username/group name

BOM files can be useful) in determining what has changed on your system. If you've modified the location of system software or configuration files, a system update might modify or move these files. Viewing the BOM can tell you exactly what happened during a system update.

32

Command-Line Updates

Starting in Mac OS X 10.1.5, the Software Update component can be accessed through the command-line utility `softwareupdate`. Invoking `softwareupdate` as `root` produces a list of the available updates:

```
brezup:root jray # softwareupdate

Software Update Tool
Copyright 2002 Apple Computer, Inc.

Software Update found the following new or updated software:

  - SecurityUpd2003-07-14-1.0
    Security Update 2003-07-14 (1.0), 1740K - restart required

To install an update, run this tool with the item name as an argument.
    e.g. 'softwareupdate <item> ...'''
```

Included with each package description is a short single "word" by which you can refer to the update. To install an update, simply invoke `softwareupdate` followed by the short name for each update. You can specify as many updates on a single line as you want, and each will be downloaded and installed in turn:

```
softwareupdate <update name> <update name> ...
```

For example:

```
brezup:root jray # softwareupdate SecurityUpd2003-07-14-1.0

Software Update Tool
Copyright 2002 Apple Computer, Inc.

Downloading "Security Update 2003-07-14".. 10% 20% 30% 40% 50%
➥2003-07-17 22:07:05.574 softwareupdate[742] File verification succeeded

Unarchiving "Security Update 2003-07-14".. 50%
Installing "Security Update 2003-07-14".. 50%
Installing "Security Update 2003-07-14".. 50%
...
```

If an update requires a system restart to become active, it prompts you to reboot after the installation has completed. You can reboot from the command line by typing **`sudo /sbin/reboot`**.

> **NOTE**
>
> Failing to reboot after installing an update that requires a restart may result in unusual and unpredictable system behavior.

Backups

Keeping an archive of your important applications and data is a crucial part of maintaining a Mac OS X computer, as it is with any operating system. Backups generally fall into two categories: *full* and *incremental*. A full backup is an exact duplicate of everything within your filesystem (or a branch thereof, such as `/Users` or `/usr/local`). From a full backup you can quickly restore the state of all the backed up files as they existed at the time the backup was made. Full backups are time consuming (all files must be copied each time the backup is run) and cannot efficiently be used to store multiple versions of files over an extended period of time. If, for example, you want to have a copy of each day's updates to your file server for the period of a year, you would need to make 365 full copies of each of the files—this can quickly add up in terms of storage media. Full backups are usually reserved for mostly static information that can be copied and stored.

An incremental backup, on the other hand, is used to archive filesystems that aren't static. You start with a single full backup and then periodically back up the files that have changed since the full backup took place. Incremental backups can take place at multiple "levels," with each level backing up only the files that have changed since the preceding level was backed up.

The biggest problem with backups and Mac OS X is that few backup solutions cover both Unix and Macintosh sides of the operating system. The Unix users out there are probably scratching their heads asking, "What about `tar`, `dump`, and `restore`?" Although those are all perfectly good solutions for Mac OS X installations based on the Unix filesystem (UFS), or Unix and Cocoa apps based on HFS+, they are not suitable for Classic or Carbon applications. The dependency of these types of software on the HFS+ resource fork greatly limits what software can be used to back them up.

Traditional Unix utilities "see" the data fork only when looking at a dual-forked file. Attempting to back up a file with a resource fork will probably lead to an entirely unusable archive. Apple has included a command-line copy utility called `ditto` that is capable of copying HFS+ files intact, but it lacks incremental backup capabilities.

This section of the chapter looks at what is currently available for backing up Mac OS X files and volumes. Because of a lack of GUI backup options, the focus will be on what can be done from the Unix command line.

Mac OS X Native GUI Backup Utilities

For most people, backing up the contents of their `/Users/<username>` home directories will suffice for protecting personal information. This, of course, doesn't help much with applications and Unix system services that have been installed, nor does it cover additional accounts for other family members or friends.

Let's go ahead and take a look at what is available, and what they're appropriate for. Finally, we'll review several command-line tools that can be employed to back up both Carbon/Classic applications and generic data files.

Retrospect

Retrospect is, by far, the most well-known and accepted backup solution for Mac OS X, featuring the capability to back up and restore Windows, Red Hat, and Macintosh systems; store backups on Internet FTP servers; and more. Figure 32.4 displays Retrospect Backup for Mac OS X.

The Retrospect client is available for Mac OS X, Mac OS 9, and MS Windows. After Retrospect is installed, the Retrospect Backup administrator can locate the client computers, select the files to back up, and store them on a variety of media including CDRW, DVD, DAT, and Internet storage sites. Backups can be scripted for automatic execution, or run at any time with the click of a mouse. Restoring files from a backup is a simple point-and-click operation that automatically copies files from the source media back to the client.

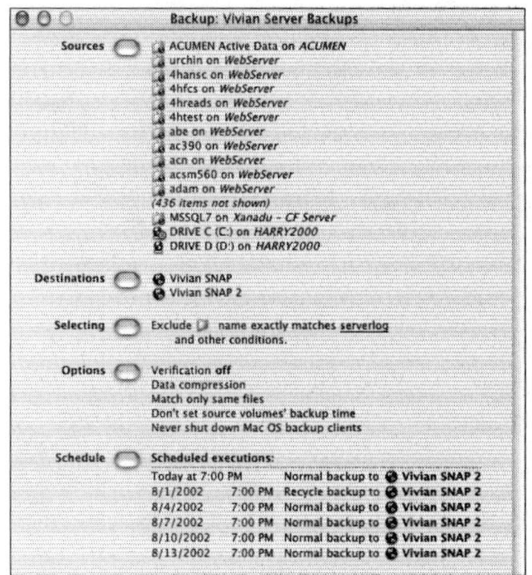

FIGURE 32.4 Retrospect 5.1 is a complete backup solution for Mac OS X.

Mixed-platform networks will be happy to find that Retrospect clients are available for older Mac systems as well as Windows. Unfortunately, Retrospect still has a few annoying "gotchas" that may affect users with advanced setups. I strongly urge that you read the Dantz forums to figure out whether there is any known issue with your setup.

Retrospect 5.1 comes in several different versions, ranging from a single desktop backup solution to workgroup and server editions. Find out more about Retrospect from `http://www.dantz.com/`.

Backup

For the home user who just wants to make sure that his critical data is backed up to CD, DVD, or iDisk, Apple's aptly named Backup may be the right answer. Backup is Apple's long-overdue consumer backup utility for Mac OS X.

Shown in Figure 32.5, Backup is a simple piece of software that is capable of selecting common file types (such as Word documents), system information (such as Safari preferences), or arbitrary files and folders and backing them up to your Mac's optical drive or .Mac iDisk. It does not currently offer a command-line interface, incremental backups, nor a way of performing unattended backups.

Unfortunately, besides the entry-level capabilities, there's another catch to the software. Backup is a .Mac membership exclusive application. This means that to download and use the tool, you'll need to pay the $100 entrance fee (`http://www.mac.com/`).

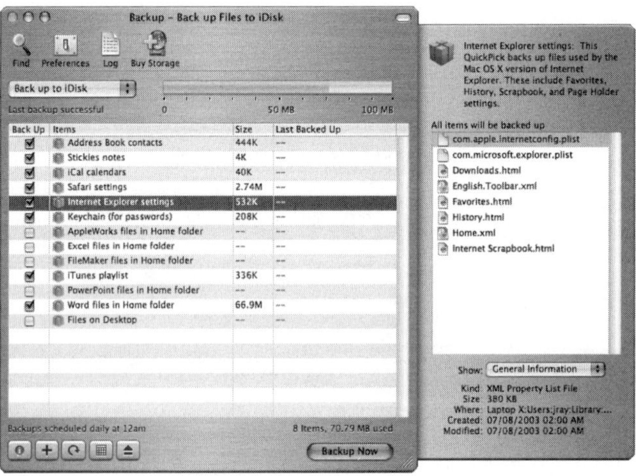

FIGURE 32.5 Apple's Backup is a simple tool for backing up data files.

NOTE

On a positive note, .Mac membership also buys you a copy of Virex virus scanning software, along with the mac.com email, iDisk, and iSync capabilities. For Mac users who aren't running servers or using Unix tools, this might be a wise investment. For others, however, the money might be better spent on a third-party backup solution.

Data Backup X

Data Backup from ProSoft Engineering (`http://www.prosoftengineering.com/products/data_backup.php`) is a complete personal backup system that picks up where Apple's tool left off. It offers advanced features such as scheduling, compression, mirroring, synchronization, incremental backups, and an "evolutive" mode that preserves different versions of files as they change across backups. For personal workstations, Data Backup X is hard to beat. If you can afford the $50 expense, Data Backup X is one of the most feature-filled personal backup software currently available.

Synk

The Synk application is an Open Source Cocoa-based utility that provides synchronization and backup services between folders and volumes. Synk allows the creation of AppleScript "Run" documents that can be used to launch a specific backup configuration with a simple double-click from the desktop. When used to synchronize storage locations, Synk even offers the capability to archive files that would normally be replaced or deleted during a synchronization process. Download Synk from `http://www.decimus.net/synk/`.

Carbon Copy Cloner

An entirely different backup approach is to mirror your system and data disks exactly. With Mac OS X, this is a simple process of using the `ditto` command, which we'll look at in the section "Command-Line Backups." Although this feature is built into the operating system, a number of graphic utilities have sprung up around it to provide a more Mac-like experience.

The most popular of these utilities is Carbon Copy Cloner (`http://www.bombich.com/software/ccc.html`). Written in AppleScript Studio, Carbon Copy Cloner adds a user-friendly interface, shown in Figure 32.6, to the `ditto` command and enables quick, easy, and even scheduled drive mirroring. Copied volumes are bootable and are created with all file permissions intact.

Although not an efficient solution for those who just want to back up changed data files, Carbon Copy Cloner, along with an external FireWire drive, makes a fantastic "complete system" backup for servers and other machines with complex configurations.

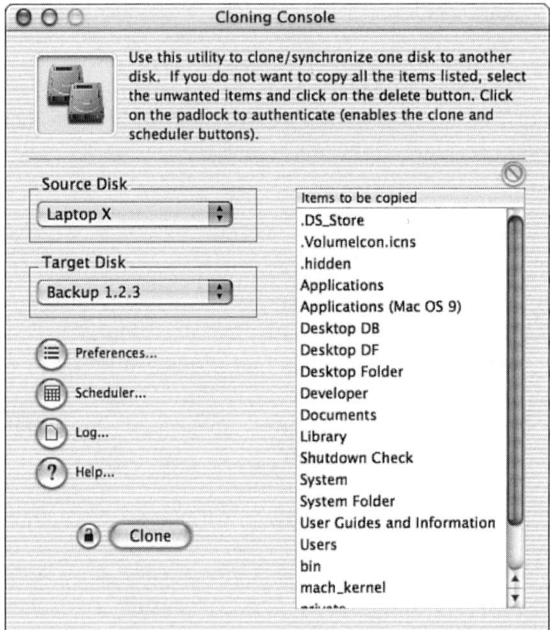

FIGURE 32.6 Carbon Copy Cloner uses `ditto` to create duplicates of your system volumes.

> **TIP**
>
> Carbon Copy Cloner (or `ditto`) can be used to replicate an existing partition onto a different partition or volume. Because Mac OS X does not currently have any tools for resizing partitions (except for HD Toolkit, currently only available for Classic —`http://www.fwb.com/html/hard_disk_toolkit.html`), the only option is to copy data to another drive, repartition, and then copy the data back. `ditto`'s capability to keep file permissions intact and create bootable volumes makes the process at least bearable.

Command-Line Backups

Traditional Mac users are obviously the target audience of most of the GUI backup software. Unfortunately, this has led to a plethora of tools that can only be controlled or configured if you are sitting in front of your computer. Remote command-line administration of Retrospect, for example, is virtually impossible.

The Unix side of Mac OS X provides some command-line backup tools, but the HFS+ filesystem complicates their use. You have several basic options—some with HFS+ support, some without—choose your poison.

Mirroring with ditto

The ditto function (for those who don't remember the addictively good-smelling purple copies from grade school that share the name) creates a duplicate of a file or folder structure on your system. Unlike the Unix cp command, ditto is capable of dealing with the HFS+ filesystem and can quickly and easily replicate entire bootable system volumes. The basic syntax of ditto is


```
ditto [-<options>] <source file/folder> <destination file/folder>
```

ditto can be used to copy multiple files or folders to a folder, or a single file to another file. In the case of the former, the destination directory is created if it doesn't already exist.

Many users will also want to take advantage of two of the ditto options: -V and -rsrcFork. The -V flag creates verbose output, listing each file and link being duplicated, whereas -rsrcFork preserves HFS+ data, making completely "Mac file friendly" copies.

For example, to copy the entire /Applications folder (and subfolders) to another location, /Volume/NewDisk, I'd use

```
brezup:jray jray $ ditto -V-rsrcFork /Applications /Volumes/NewDisk

>>> Copying /Applications
copying file Applications/.DS_Store .. 15364 bytes
copying file Applications/.localized .. 0 bytes
copying file Applications/Acrobat Reader 5.0/Info-macos.plist .. 3043 bytes
copying file Applications/Acrobat Reader 5.0//ACELiteCarbonLib .. 417634 bytes
copying file Applications/Acrobat Reader 5.0/Acrobat Reader
 5.0 .. 4285090 bytes
...
```

and so on.

> **NOTE**
>
> ditto is compatible with non-HFS+ volumes, such as network NFS shares, and automatically creates the appropriate AppleDouble (HFS+ resource forks on a flat filesystem) files transparently.

Another use for ditto is to copy only files that are contained within a given BOM (bill of materials). Using the -bom option followed by a valid BOM file limits the files copied to those contained within a given BOM file. For more information on BOM files, read about the lsbom command, earlier in this chapter.

Table 32.2 provides Apple's options for ditto.

TABLE 32.2 Command Documentation Table for `ditto`

Option	Description
`-v`	Print a line of output for each source directory copied.
`-V`	Print a line of output for every file, symbolic link, and device copied.
`-c`	Create an archive at the destination path.
`-z`	Use PKZip archives instead of CPIO.
`-x`	The first source is an archive to decompress.
`-arch` *<arch>*	Thin multi-architecture binaries ("fat binaries") to the specified architecture. If multiple `-arch` options are specified, the resulting destination file will be multi-architectural containing each of the specified architectures (if they are present in the source file). `arch` should be specified as "ppc", "i386", and so on.
`-bom` *<bom>*	If this option is given, only files, links, devices, and directories that are present in the specified BOM file are copied.
`-rsrcFork`	Preserve resource forks and HFS metadata. `ditto` stores this data in AppleDouble files on filesystems that do not support resource forks.

Synchronizing Files: `rsync`

Having a backup of critical files is the best way to avert disaster, but restoring a backup can be time consuming and creating an exact mirror is often impractical on a day-to-day basis. In many cases, the best solution is to synchronize files between two or more machines as changes are made. Starting in Mac OS X 10.2, Apple has included `rsync`, an Open Source utility designed to make folder synchronization fast, scriptable, and painless.

NOTE

The version of `rsync` included in Mac OS X 10.2 does not include support for HFS+ resource forks but a work-alike HFS+ compatible version is available for download through the Open Darwin Web site CVS—`http://www.opendarwin.org/cgi-bin/cvsweb.cgi/proj/rsync_hfs/`.

`rsync` can operate locally to synchronize files between directories on a single machine, or can work over a network. An especially nice feature of the software is its capability to use several different transport mechanisms for network transfers. The `rsync` utility, for example, can operate as a server and be used to host `rsync`-accessible directories on remote machines. But if setting up an additional dedicated server process isn't desirable, you don't have to. An alternative (and often overlooked) method of providing `rsync` access is through a remote shell such as SSH. If your Mac OS X machines are running SSH, they are ready to use `rsync` immediately, without any additional software or configuration.

Using rsync

The rsync syntax is simple: rsync [options] *<source>* *<destination>*. For example, to synchronize the contents of the folder /Users/jray/source with /Users/jray/destination, I would use the following:

```
brezup:jray jray $ rsync -va source/ destination
rsync: building file list...
rsync: 6 files to consider.
./
Icon
apache_pb.gif
index.html
macosxlogo.gif
web_share.gif
wrote 25079 bytes read 100 bytes 50358.00 bytes/sec
total size is 24711 speedup is 0.98
```

In this example, the -v (verbose) and -a (archive) options are included so that rsync displays files being copied and includes all attributes (permissions, owner, and so on) of the original files. Running the command again produces slightly different output because rsync doesn't need to re-copy the files:

```
brezup:jray jray $ rsync -va source/ destination
rsync: building file list...
rsync: 6 files to consider.
wrote 172 bytes read 20 bytes 128.00 bytes/sec
total size is 24711 speedup is 128.70
```

Here, no files were copied because the directories are already in sync.

> **NOTE**
>
> Trailing slashes mean something to rsync. If a path is given with a trailing slash, it refers to the contents of the named directory. If the slash is excluded, it means the directory itself.

Although synchronizing local directories may be useful, the true power of rsync is revealed when it is used over a remote network connection. To do this, all that is needed is a running SSH daemon on the remote side, and an account with access to the directory you want to sync. If you've ever used scp, you'll recognize the syntax for an SSH-tunneled rsync immediately; for example, assume that I want to synchronize the directory /Users/jray/Tools located on a remote server www.poisontooth.com with a local directory Tools—and, at the same time, compress the data as it is sent:

```
brezup:jray jray $ rsync -vaze ssh jray@www.poisontooth.com:/Users/jray/Tools/ Tools
jray@www.poisontooth.com's password: ******
```

```
receiving file list .. done
./
htdigsearch/
adduser
authuser.pl
backupdisdain.pl
cgiinput.pl
deluser
footer.html
...
runindex.pl
setupconfig.pl
ticker.tar
wrote 448 bytes read 216031 bytes 18824.26 bytes/sec
total size is 1262138 speedup is 5.83
```

This example introduces the use of `-e ssh` to specify that `ssh` should be used as the remote shell that `rsync` connects through and `-z`, which compresses data in real-time to increase the transfer rate. A number of additional switches can be used with `rsync` to change its behavior. Table 32.3 documents many of the useful options.

TABLE 32.3 Useful `rsync` Options

Option	Description
`-v`	Use verbose output.
`-a`	Recursively copy files, preserving as much information as possible.
`-c`	Calculate a checksum before sending and after receiving to verify file integrity.
`-b`	Create a backup of existing files. Any file that would be replaced is renamed with a ~ (tilde) extension.
`--suffix=<string>`	Set the string used as a suffix when using the -b option. By default, the suffix is "~".
`-u`	Skip any files that are already newer (have a more recent date stamp) at the destination.
`-n`	Perform a "dry-run" of the operation, displaying what would be copied but without making any changes.
`--existing`	Do not copy any files that don't already exist on the destination.
`--delete`	Delete files on the destination that are not in the source.
`--max-delete=<#>`	Sets the maximum number of files that can be deleted (to avoid disaster).
`--delete-after`	Delete files only after they have been successfully transferred.
`--exclude=<pattern>`	Exclude files from the operation based on a pattern, such as `*.dmg`.
`--include=<pattern>`	Do not exclude files that match the given pattern (used in conjunction with `--exclude`).

TABLE 32.3 Continued

Option	Description
-z	Compress transferred data.
-p	Transfer file permissions. Implied by -a.
-o	Transfer file ownership (must be root). Implied by -a.
-g	Transfer file group membership. Implied by -a.
-t	Transfer file modification times. Implied by -a.

Make sure to read through the rsync man page for additional information on command usage. The include and exclude options can be used to generate complex file selection rulesets beyond simple wildcards. Also, if you want to run a dedicated rsync server rather than use an SSH, you can view a tutorial on the setup of an rsync daemon at http://www.macosxhints.com/article.php?story=20021023063424701.

More Synchronization with psync

A fast and easy-to-install alternative to rsync is psync, a Perl script based on the MacOSX::File module, which handles reading and writing data to and from the HFS+ filesystem. psync does not require any special server daemons to be running; it simply works across whatever local or remote volumes you have mounted on your system. The psync home page is located at http://www.dan.co.jp/cases/macosx/psync.html.

To install psync, all that is required is installation of the MacOSX::File module—psync is included. To install the module, use the same CPAN steps covered in Chapter 21, "Scripting Languages.":

First, as root, invoke the interaction Perl CPAN shell:

```
brezup:root jray # perl -MCPAN -e shell

cpan shell -- CPAN exploration and modules installation (v1.70)
ReadLine support enabled
```

Next, use **install MacOSX::File** to download, compile, and install the required Perl module. (Note: You must have the current developer tools installed for this to be successful.)

```
cpan> install MacOSX::File

CPAN: Net::FTP loaded ok
Fetching with Net::FTP:
Scanning cache /Users/jray/.cpan/build for sizes
MacOSX-File-0.66
MacOSX-File-0.66/bin
```

```
MacOSX-File-0.66/bin/pcpmac
MacOSX-File-0.66/bin/pgetfinfo
...
MacOSX-File-0.66/t/spec.t

 CPAN.pm: Going to build D/DA/DANKOGAI/MacOSX-File-0.66.tar.gz

Checking if your kit is complete...
Looks good
Writing Makefile for MacOSX::File::Catalog
Writing Makefile for MacOSX::File::Copy
Writing Makefile for MacOSX::File::Info
Writing Makefile for MacOSX::File::Spec
Writing Makefile for MacOSX::File
...
Installing /usr/local/bin/pgetfinfo
Installing /usr/local/bin/pmvmac
Installing /usr/local/bin/psetfinfo
Installing /usr/local/bin/psync
Writing /Library/Perl/darwin/auto/MacOSX/File/.packlist
Appending installation info to /System/Library/Perl/darwin/perllocal.pod
  /usr/bin/make install -- OK
```

NOTE

A binary distribution of psync is available at http://www.dan.co.jp/cases/macosx/MacOSX-File-0.66.dmg.

Using psync

The basic psync syntax is psync [options] *<source>* *<destination>*. For example, to copy my Sites directory (/Users/jray/Sites) to /Volume/backup, I'd use psync /Users/jray/Sites /Volumes/backup. All file attributes are retained during the copy, including permissions and HFS+ resource forks.

```
brezup:root jray # psync /Users/jray/Sites /Volumes/backup
Scanning Destination Directory /Volumes/backup ...
     0:.
65 items found.
Scanning Source Item /Users/jray/Sites ...
     0:..
```

```
178 items found.
    0 items to delete,
   68 items unchanged,
   117 items to copy.
copying items ...
+f /Users/jray/Sites/imagefolder/Classic Aqua Blue.jpg
+f /Users/jray/Sites/imagefolder/Classic Aqua Graphite.jpg
...
f /Users/jray/Sites/joestuff/feed.sql
+d /Users/jray/Sites/joestuff/files
+f /Users/jray/Sites/joestuff/files/1/left.htm
+f /Users/jray/Sites/webdav.key
fixing directory attributes ...
00777,jray,staff /Volumes/backup/joestuff/images
00777,jray,staff /Volumes/backup/joestuff/files/6
00777,jray,staff /Volumes/backup/joestuff/files/5
...
```


Subsequent executions of psync to synchronize the same directory do not result in any files being copied:

```
brezup:root jray # psync /Users/jray/Sites /Volumes/backup
Scanning Destination Directory /Volumes/backup ...
     0:..
178 items found.
Scanning Source Item /Users/jray/Sites ...
     0:..
178 items found.
    0 items to delete,
   185 items unchanged,
    0 items to copy.
copying items ...
fixing directory attributes ...
```

psync can create incremental backups across Samba, NFS, and AppleTalk volumes in addition to other HFS volumes. If you're backing up to a remote filesystem, use the -r option to store permission information in the file .psync.db on the remote system. If psync finds a .psync.db file in the source volume, it uses the file to restore the permissions to the destination. Although -r is usually the only psync option you'll need, there are several more, documented in Table 32.4, that you might find somewhat useful.

TABLE 32.4 psync Options

Option	Description
`-r`	Remote backup/restore mode. Uses the `.psync.db` file for storing ownership and permission information for copied files.
`-d`	Deletes files from the destination that no longer exist on the source.
`-f`	Force all files to be copied—even those that haven't changed.
`-n`	Run as a simulation, showing what would be copied or deleted, but do not carry out any of the actions.
`-v<1-3>`	Set the verbosity of the output (from 1 (the least) to 3 (the most)).
`-q`	Quiet—silence all output.

`psync` can be combined with a `cronjob` (discussed later in this chapter) to create an effective (and free) incremental backup solution. If you want to add a GUI front end, `psyncX` can be downloaded from `http://sourceforge.net/projects/psyncx/`.

NOTE

If you still aren't satisfied with command-line options available, you may want to download Hfstar (an HFS+ aware version of `tar`) from `http://www.metaobject.com/Products.html` or hfspax from `http://homepage.mac.com/howardoakley/`.

For a full-featured (and full priced) command-line backup system, check out BRU (`http://www.tolisgroup.com/products/CLI/`). Although definitely not for home use, BRU can be a godsend for those managing headless Xserves.

Incremental Backups with `dump/restore`

If you have created a Unix filesystem (UFS) partition for your OS X machine, you can use the `dump` utility to back up the data on that partition. The `dump` utility that currently comes with the OS X distribution cannot be used to back up HFS+ partitions. Because OS X does not provide an `mt` utility that can be used to communicate directly with a local tape drive, you might need to have access to a remote tape drive. If you do have access to a tape drive, we recommend that you store your important data on the UFS partition, because you can back it up regularly.

The version of `dump` that OS X provides supports incremental backups. As the phrase incremental backups suggests, you do not back up everything on your UFS partition every time. Instead, you decide on a backup schedule that consists of doing whatever is necessary to maintain reliability for your site. At the very least, you will run full backups every few months. At the very best, you will run full backups every few months, a monthly backup once a month, a weekly backup once a week, and a daily backup once a day. In practice, though, your schedule may fall somewhere in between.

The key to understanding incremental dumps is realizing that you will not back up everything on your UFS partitions every time you run the `dump` command. You can issue different levels, or degrees, of the `dump` command. You can issue the `dump` command from levels 0 through 9. Except for level 0, which is the level used for a complete backup that backs up everything on the partition, you have the freedom to assign what a number means. Each dump level with a level number higher than 0 backs up only files that have changed since the most recent dump that has a lower-level number. Note that I didn't say since the most recent dump, but rather since the most recent with a lower-level number. This facility allows you to conserve tapes and save on equipment wear by doing most of your backups of only files that change and infrequently backing up files that stay the same for long periods of time.

In the example we will look at, the level numbers have the following meaning:

0	Full
2	Monthly
4	Weekly
6	Daily

You don't have to choose even numbers. Odd numbers are just fine, too. I've chosen to space mine out so that I can add an unexpected backup for whatever reason. It doesn't matter what arbitrary values you assign as long as the numeric values increase with the frequency of the scheduled dump, but, to make your life easier, be consistent from use to use.

It's fairly easy to be confused by the idea of incremental backups, but an example should help to clear things up.

Let's say that last month I ran a full dump (level 0) on a filesystem. Every day initially following the full dump, I ran dailies (level 6). A week after the full dump was made, I decided to run a weekly dump (level 4). In the days following the weekly dump, I ran dailies (level 6). The second week after the full dump, I ran another weekly (level 4). And I continued the pattern until today, a month after the full dump. Today I decide to run a monthly (level 2). Table 32.5 shows a sort of calendar the sample backup schedule follows. For purposes of the example, today is the last identified day in the schedule, Monday of week 5.

TABLE 32.5 Sample Backup Schedule

Week	Mon	Tues	Wed	Thurs	Fri	Sat	Sun
1	0	6	6	6	6	6	6
2	4	6	6	6	6	6	6
3	4	6	6	6	6	6	6
4	4	6	6	6	6	6	6
5	2						

To reiterate, remember that dumps are incremental. Keeping that in mind, what do the numbers in Table 32.5 mean? Here is what lands on each of the tapes:

On Monday of week 1, a full dump, level 0, was done. Everything on the filesystem was backed up to the dump level 0 tape.

On Tuesday of week 1, a daily, level 6 dump was done. That is, everything that had changed since the most recent dump with a lower level was backed up. In this case, Monday's dump level 0 has a lower level and is the most recent dump with a lower level. So, anything that changed between Monday's level 0 dump and Tuesday's level 6 was backed up to the dump level 6 tape.

What about Wednesday of the first week? Again, with the Wednesday dump, level 6, only files that have changed since the most recent dump with a lower level have been backed up. What's the most recent dump with a lower-level number? Yes, it's the level 0 dump from Monday. Again, only files that changed between Monday, level 0, and Wednesday, level 6, were backed up. Wednesday's dump is not a reflection of the changes in files between Tuesday and Wednesday because both of those dumps were level 6.

Thursday, Friday, Saturday, and Sunday's dumps for the first week mimic the behavior of Tuesday's and Wednesday's. For each of these dumps, the most recent dump with a lower number will be Monday's level 0 dump, and each of these will contain a backup of all files that changed between Monday and the day of the dump.

On Monday of the second week, a dump level 4 was done. What does this mean? Again, the files that changed between the most recent dump with a lower dump level number and the current date were backed up. Again, the dump level 0 dump from the previous Monday was the most recent dump with a lower number. The dump from Monday of the second week reflects changes that were made between the previous Monday and that Monday. The significance of using level 4 for this dump will appear with the dump for the next day.

What about Tuesday of the second week? On this Tuesday we ran a dump level 6, but this time the most recent dump with a lower dump level than 6 is not the first Monday's level 0 dump, but the second Monday's level 4 dump instead. Tuesday's dump, then, consists of the files that changed between Monday of week 2 and Tuesday of week 2.

Likewise, the dump from Wednesday of week 2 reflects the changes between Monday of week 2 and Wednesday of week 2.

What files did the dump level 2 on Monday of week 5 capture? If we look at the chart, we see that the most recent dump with a dump level lower than our dump level of 2 is the dump level 0 of Monday on week 1. So, the dump level 2 on Monday of week 5 is a dump of the files that changed between Monday of week 1 and Monday of week 5.

TOMORROW, TOMORROW, AND ALL TOMORROW'S TOMORROWS

Notice that if we do a dump level 6 tomorrow, today's dump level 2 will be the most recent lower number. The most recent lower number isn't looking for any sort of order in the numbers; it just goes back looking for the most recent lower number dump performed in the past, and backs up everything since then.

When you are restoring files, the same incremental approach applies. Dumps are incremental, so the restores must be incremental as well. If a user deletes a directory, to rebuild that directory to its most recent state will take one restore at each of the dump levels that you use.

For example, if I accidentally deleted a directory midday on Tuesday of week 5, sometime after the daily dump (level 6) was done, I would have to restore my directory from the dump level 0 of Monday of week 1, the dump level 2 of Monday of week 5, and Tuesday morning's daily dump, level 6.

Why do I have to restore my directory from multiple different archives? Because other than the level 0 dump that provides a complete snapshot of my directory, the others only provide differences over time. I need to restore the dump level 0 to get back files that have been around in my directory for ages, the dump level 2 for changes in the last week, and the dump level 6 for changes since yesterday. What comes from each tape is as follows:

- The dump level 0 tape would provide the base level restore of my directory as it existed on Monday of week 1 because it's a full dump and captures everything as of when it is made.
- To this, the dump level 2 tape adds any changes that occurred between the dump level 0 dump of week 1 and the date of the level 2 dump, the day before I made the mistake. Any new files that I added during that time, or older files that I changed, would be backed up on this tape, but files that I had not changed would not be included.
- Tuesday's dump level 6 fills in any changes that occurred between the dump level 2 of the day before and Tuesday.

As you can see, the directory has to be restored incrementally. If Tuesday's daily dump ran at 4:00 a.m., and I made some spectacular changes at noon, just before I accidentally deleted everything after lunch, I can't get the spectacular changes back. I can only restore to the state of the directory as it was at 4:00 a.m.

Using `dump`

The `dump` utility has a variety of options. Options to make sure you include are the dump level, the blocking factor, any special tape size information you have to provide, and the name of the tape device. The blocking factor is information used by `dump` to determine how to group the data and control information on the tape. The man page mentions a maximum blocking size, which should probably be fine. The man page also mentions an option that could be used for automatic size detection. Unfortunately, this option is not currently available in the OS X distribution of dump. So, you probably will have to work out some density and feet numbers. For a remote tape device, definitely ask the system administrator of the machine with the tape drive for advice. If you are lucky, that system administrator has had to use a similar dump.

Always record on the tape packaging the date, dump level, blocking factor, and the filesystems that were dumped in the order in which they were dumped. Record the blocking factor, even if you are just using the default. It might save someone else time restoring from your tape if she knows the blocking factor right away, instead of having to guess.

The clever system administrator will work out a schedule whereby tapes that are used for weekly or daily dumps will be rotated into duty as full-dump tapes and (semi-) permanently archived after some period of time. Magnetic media has a finite lifetime when running over record and playback heads, so moving a frequently used tape to a "use once and forget" status near the end (or middle, more practically) of its useful life is a way to economize on tape costs.

Here's the basic form of a dump command:

```
dump options <filesystem_to_dump>
```

Here is a sample of dump output:

```
brezup:root jray # dump 0bdsfu 64 83333 6000 rosalyn:/dev/rmt/0n /dev/rdisk2s9

 DUMP: Date of this level 0 dump: Fri Jun 29 12:31:03 2001
 DUMP: Date of last level 0 dump: the epoch
 DUMP: Dumping /dev/rdisk2s9 to /dev/rmt/0n on host rosalyn
 DUMP: mapping (Pass I) [regular files]
 DUMP: mapping (Pass II) [directories]
 DUMP: estimated 613411 tape blocks on 0.29 tape(s).
 DUMP: dumping (Pass III) [directories]
 DUMP: dumping (Pass IV) [regular files]
 DUMP: 23.54% done, finished in 0:16
 DUMP: 50.81% done, finished in 0:09
 DUMP: 75.19% done, finished in 0:04
 DUMP: 96.47% done, finished in 0:00
 DUMP: DUMP: 613410 tape blocks on 1 volumes(s)
 DUMP: level 0 dump on Fri Jun 29 12:31:03 2001
 DUMP: Closing /dev/rmt/0n
 DUMP: DUMP IS DONE
```

In this particular instance of dump, the level is 0. After the 0, you see the string bdsfu. This string specifies that it is followed by a collection of data values:

b is the blocking factor.

d is the density in bytes per inch (bpi).

s is the size of the tape in feet.

f is the tape device or file.

u is an indication to update /etc/dumpdates on successful completion of dump.

Following the bdsfu string are the numeric values corresponding to each item specified, in the order specified. The filesystem to be dumped is specified as the last thing on the line; here it's the raw device, /dev/rdisk2s9. With some versions of dump, you can specify the mount point of the filesystem, but that does not work with the dump that comes with OS X. As you can see by the naming convention, rosalyn:/dev/rmt/0n, the tape drive is not local to the machine. The magical numbers used for density and size have been determined from various man pages and trial and error as something that works on a 120m DAT tape for this particular tape drive on a different operating system.

The dump output includes this line:

```
DUMP: estimated 613411 tape blocks on 0.29 tape(s).
```

Some versions of dump also include output information in total MB, KB, or bytes dumped. Although the OS X dump does not provide that precise translation, from df -k we see a convenient correlation—the tape blocks must be approximately 1KB blocks:

```
brezup:jray jray $ df -k /dev/disk2s9

Filesystem  1K-blocks   Used  Avail Capacity Mounted on
/dev/disk2s9  692795  612336  45820  93%  /new1
```

Table 32.6 includes the command documentation for dump. The dump syntax used in the earlier sample follows traditional dump syntax. However, from the man page, we would expect the following statement to work also:

```
dump -0u -b 64 -d 83333 -s 6000 -f rosalyn:/dev/rmt/0n /dev/rdisk2s9
```

In the resulting /etc/dumpdates file, we see

```
brezup:jray jray $ more /etc/dumpdates

/dev/rdisk2s9  0 Fri Jun 29 12:31:03 2001
```

From the file, we see that so far there has only been one dump of /dev/rdisk2s9 and that it was a level 0. When another dump level is performed on /dev/rdisk2s9, a new line will be added with the date and time for that dump level.

NOTE

Most classical versions of dump have arguments more appropriate for 9-track streaming tape drives of the type you see in 1960s and 1970s sci-fi films. The parameters were not really designed to accommodate today's high-capacity cartridge drives, so you must fudge the length and density values until you achieve a working selection that makes reasonable use of the tape's capacity. Usually it is sufficient to provide size and density values that are bigger than the actual tape capacity because most modern tape drives will detect when EOM (end of media) is reached. However, if the values are significantly larger, dump's estimate of the number of tapes required will be useless, so you probably will want to attempt to make a reasonably accurate guess. Usually the man pages make helpful suggestions on making these guesses, but given the rapid advances in tape capacity in recent years, even the man pages seem to be out-of-date as far as accurate predictions go.

TABLE 32.6 Command Documentation Table for dump

Option	Description
-0-9	Dump levels. A level 0, full backup, guarantees that the entire filesystem is copied. A level number above 0, an incremental backup, tells dump to copy all files new or modified since the last dump of the same or lower level. The default level is 9.
-c	Changes the defaults for use with a cartridge tape drive, with a density of 8000 bpi and a length of 1700 feet.
-n	Notifies all operators in the group operator whenever dump requires operator attention.
-u	Updates the file /etc/dumpdates after a successful dump. The format of /etc/dumpdates is readable by people, consisting of one free format record per line: filesystem name, increment level, and ctime (3). There may be only one entry per filesystem at each level.
-B *<records>*	The number of kilobytes per volume, rounded down to a multiple of the blocksize. This option overrides the calculation of the tape size.
-b *<blocksize>*	The number of kilobytes per dump record. Because the IO system slices all requests into chunks of MAXBSIZE (typically 64KB), it is not possible to use a larger block size without having problems later with restore. Therefore, dump constrains writes to MAXBSIZE.
-d *<density>*	Sets the tape density to *<density>*. The default is 1600 bpi.
-f *<file>*	Writes the backup to *<file>*. *<file>* may be a special device file, such as a tape drive or disk drive, an ordinary file, or - (standard output). Multiple filenames may be given as a single argument separated by commas. Each file will be used for one dump volume in the order listed. If the dump requires more volumes than the number of names listed, the last filename is used for all remaining volumes after prompting for media changes. If the name of the file is of the form *<host>*:*<file>* or *<user>*@*<host>*:file, dump writes to the named file on the remote host using rmt.

TABLE 32.6 Continued

Option	Description
-h <*level*>	Honors the user nodump flag only for dumps at or above the given <*level*>. The default honor level is 1 so that incremental backups omit such files but full backups retain them.
-s <*feet*>	Attempts to calculate the amount of tape needed at a particular density. If this amount is exceeded, dump prompts for a new tape. It is recommended to be a bit conservative on this option. The default tape length is 2300 feet.
-T <*date*>	Uses the specified date as the starting time for the dump instead of the time determined from looking in /etc/dumpdates. The format of the date is the same as that of ctime (3). This option is useful for automated dump scripts that want to dump over a specified period of time. The -T flag is mutually exclusive with the -u flag.
-W	Tells the operator what filesystems need to be dumped. The information is gleaned from /etc/dumpdates and /etc/fstab. The -W flag causes dump to print out, for each filesystem in /etc/dumpdates, the most recent dump date and level and highlights of those filesystems that should be dumped. If the -W flag is set, all other options are ignored, and dump exits immediately.
-w	Similar to W, but prints only those filesystems that need to be dumped.

Troubleshooting dump

If dump works fine on the machine with the tape drive, but not on your remote OS X client, you might need to double-check your coordination with the system administrator of the machine with the tape device.

Make sure that you are using the right device name for the remote tape drive. Ask the system administrator whether she has placed an entry for your OS X machine in root's .rhosts file. An entry in the .rhosts file has a form like this:

```
mother.politically.correct.com root
```

Also, if the system administrator has closed services on the machine with the tape drive, ask whether rsh has been enabled and whether she has placed an entry in her /etc/hosts.allow for rsh for your OS X machine. Only machines that are allowed to have access to the tape drive should be given access to the rsh service. Make sure that any other possible firewall issues have been addressed.

Restoring Your Data from Tape: Using restore

It's one thing to get dump to work and another to successfully restore from tape. Make sure that you test restoring data from tape before you actually have to do it. Take notes as you do it. Do your testing in noncritical locations on your system. Get an approximate idea of what you have to do. You might not end up restoring to the exact location you hope for, but you can always move the data around.

Preparing to Restore The information that you will most likely need for `restore` is the blocking factor and the name of the tape drive. If you choose an interactive restore session, you don't need to worry about too many other options.

Which tapes you need for your restore vary with what you have to restore. If you only have to restore a file that you last updated yesterday before today's dump, today's tape is sufficient. Recall, however, that you might need to restore from the appropriate combination of the most recent full, monthly, weekly, and daily tapes.

When you restore from tape, you have to navigate the tape to the location that has the filesystem with the data you need to restore. This shouldn't be too problematic, assuming that you have written, somewhere on the tape package, the dump date, dump level, blocking factor, and what was dumped in the order it was dumped. If you do not write this information down, your tapes are all but useless. With sufficient experimentation, you might be able to determine the contents of a tape that you haven't recorded this information for, but realistically you should consider the contents of a tape with no written information to be lost.

Doing a Restore

What I am going to restore first is actually data created by another operating system's dump of a UFS filesystem.

The data I am most interested in is a collection of patches for SunOS 4.1.4 and scripts to install the patches. Because my UFS partition is large enough to hold all the available data, I will restore all of it, and sort through it to see what I don't really need.

To complete this task, I need the tapes from the most recent appropriate levels. In my case, I need the most recent level 0, level 2, and level 4 tapes.

I first restore the base contents from the level 0 tape. My label indicates that a blocking factor of 126 was used, and that the directory I'm looking for is on the 17th filesystem on the tape.

On the remote host, I have to position the tape, using the `mt` command. First, I rewind the tape to make sure that I am at the beginning of the tape. Then I fast-forward the tape to the end of the 16th filesystem. As you saw in the `dump` example, the tape device on this host machine is `/dev/rmt/0n`.

```
brezup:root jray # mt -f /dev/rmt/0n rewind
brezup:root jray # mt -f /dev/rmt/0n fsf 16
```

The `fsf 16` instructs `mt` to fast-forward to the end of the 16th file. Some versions of `restore`, including the one for OS X, have a `-s` option that allows you to skip to the **n**th file on the tape. This `restore` option could alleviate some need for an `mt` utility.

With the tape properly positioned, I can now restore from it:

```
brezup:root jray # restore ibf 126 rosalyn:/dev/rmt/0n
Connection to rosalyn.biosci.ohio-state.edu established.
restore > ls
.:
ftp/        installed-950421/ stacker.mods
installed/    lost+found/
```

Because I have chosen an interactive restore mode, I am given a prompt from which I can run `ls`, which as you might expect, lists the contents of the tape. A / at the end of a name indicates that the entry is a directory. Items that you want to restore can be selected with the `add` command. Because I want everything on this filesystem, I can just enter **`add *`**. If I wanted only certain files, I could navigate and select certain files and directories with the `add` command. Here is my `add` command:

```
restore > add *
```

After everything is selected, I tell `restore` to extract the data with the `extract` command:

```
restore > extract
```

The `restore` command responds with a request for which volume to read. I've always backed up one tape at a time, so I enter **`1`**. If you do multitape dumps for one filesystem, you will want to answer this question with the highest tape number for a given filesystem. The restore process instructs you as to how to proceed from there. It's much more convenient to work with single-volume dumps and restores, however, and with today's high-capacity tape drives and a bit of planning, you should be able to avoid the necessity for multitape dumps entirely.

```
You have not read any tapes yet.
Unless you know which volume your file(s) are on you should start
with the last volume and work towards the first.
Specify next volume #: 1
```

Then I wait a while, or so it seems. Finally, `restore` asks whether I want to set modes:

```
set owner/mode for '.'? [yn] y
restore > quit
```

You might want to experiment with the set owner/modes question. The results of choosing yes and no are similar, but not exactly identical. When you choose y, the hierarchy of the filesystem on the tape is restored to the restore directory, with permissions and ownership of the restore directory itself ('.') set to those of the filesystem on the tape. If root owns the filesystem that you're restoring from on the tape, and you used your home directory as the temporary restore location, your home directory is now owned by root.

If you choose n, the permissions and ownerships of the filesystem on the tape are not given to the directory that you're restoring in ('.'). But the hierarchy as it appears on the tape is still restored into the restore directory with the permissions and ownerships that belong to the hierarchy.

In this example, because I am restoring an entire filesystem, choosing yes is the best answer.

Because I am now done with the level 0 tape, I can continue with the level 2 tape. To eject the level 0 tape, or start the ejection process, depending on the tape drive, I can issue this command:

```
> mt -f /dev/rmt/0n offline
```

Here is how the restore goes on the level 2 tape:

```
brezup:root jray # restore ibf 126 rosalyn:/dev/rmt/0n

Connection to rosalyn.biosci.ohio-state.edu established.
restore > ls
.:
ftp/

restore > add ftp
warning: ./ftp: File exists
warning: ./ftp/incoming: File exists
warning: ./ftp/incoming/ISSR: File exists
warning: ./ftp/incoming/rtr: File exists
warning: ./ftp/incoming/galloway: File exists
warning: ./ftp/incoming/reeve: File exists
warning: ./ftp/incoming/reeve/990726: File exists
warning: ./ftp/incoming/reeve/05-1098: File exists
warning: ./ftp/incoming/reeve/05-1098-2: File exists
warning: ./ftp/incoming/njohnson: File exists
restore > extract
You have not read any tapes yet.
Unless you know which volume your file(s) are on you should start
with the last volume and work towards the first.
Specify next volume #: 1
set owner/mode for '.'? [yn] y
restore > quit
```

From the warnings that `restore` issues, I learn that there are probably new files in directories that now already exist on my machine.

Because the restore from the level 4 tape looks almost the same as the one from the level 2 tape, except for warnings about different directories, its output is not shown.

ALWAYS SOMETHING THERE TO REWIND ME

If you can't seem to get off file number 1 on the tape drive, it's because you're using the rewind version of your tape device. Read the man pages on the tape host machine to find out how to use the nonrewinding interface to your tape. Currently, your tape is being helpful by automatically rewinding itself after every command. So, if you're using the rewind device and ask the drive to skip forward 16 files, it will dutifully do so. Then it will be most helpful and automatically rewind itself again before you can issue another command.

So far, you have seen that the OS X `restore` can restore UFS data dumped from another operating system. It can also restore UFS data dumped from the OS X dump. Here is a demonstration of restoring a file from the OS X dump that you saw earlier:

```
brezup:root jray # restore ibf 64 rosalyn:/dev/rmt/0n

Connection to rosalyn.biosci.ohio-state.edu established.
restore > ls
.:
ftp/       installed-950421/ stacker.mods
installed/    lost+found/

restore > cd ftp
restore > ls
./ftp:
 /              home.html
BuiltByNOF.gif        incoming/
Home_HProfessional_down.gif  index.html
Home_NProfessionalBanner.gif l3seqmotifs.pdf
INSTALL-BINARY        l4datsearch.pdf
If-250.jpg          l5apat.pdf
L1a-Intro.pdf         l5bprotfam.pdf
L1b-Molbio.pdf        public/
L2-database.pdf        talks.htm
L2b-genomeDBs.pdf       usr/
L3a-homology.pdf       whatsnew.txt
L3b-globalaln.pdf       ws_ftp.exe
L6-phylogenetics.pdf     ws_ftp.ext
bin/             ws_ftp.hlp
clearpixel.gif        ws_ftp.ini
dev/             ws_ftp.log
error.wav           ws_ftp.txt
etc/             ws_read.me
guest/
```

```
restore > cd public
restore > ls
./ftp/public:
.ADeskTop        dilbert.tar       patches-sunos-0010/
.IDeskTop        grasp.tar        patches-y2k/
.afpvols        jk1           pfu_clean_leaders.tfa
.finderinfo/      lib-libMagick.tar    pfu_clean_leaders.tfa~
.resource/       mix           ph_clean_leaders.tfa
BACK          pab_clean_leaders    ph_clean_leaders.tfa~
ISSR.programs/     pab_clean_leaders.tfa  sendmail.8.11.1.tar.gz
Network Trash Folder/  pab_clean_leaders.tfa~ ssh-2.0.13-src.tar
assets/         patches-aug98/     tbtupmc1.zip
bigfile.af-mt      patches-more/      yst.tar
delphin.tar       patches-security/

restore > cd patches-sunos-0010
restore > ls
./ftp/public/patches-sunos-0010:
100523-26/        100626-10.tar     Solaris1.1.2.PatchReport
100523-26.tar       106859-01/       install-patches-0010
100626-10/        106859-01.tar

restore > add Solaris1.1.2.PatchReport
restore > extract
You have not read any tapes yet.
Unless you know which volume your file(s) are on you should start
with the last volume and work towards the first.
Specify next volume #: 1
set owner/mode for '.'? [yn] n
restore > quit
```

If we do a quick check for the data, we see that the temporary restore directory, ~joray/temp-restore2, has the desired file and that it was restored in the hierarchy seen while running restore.

```
brezup:jray jray $ ls -RaF temp-restore2

./  ../ ftp/

temp-restore2/ftp:
./   ../   public/
```

```
temp-restore2/ftp/public:
./          ../         patches-sunos-0010/

temp-restore2/ftp/public/patches-sunos-0010:
./             ../            Solaris1.1.2.PatchReport
```

Table 32.7 shows partial command documentation for the interactive mode of restore.

After dumping to a tape, it is a good idea to randomly check the tape to make sure that your data is readable, especially on a level 0 dump tape. It should be sufficient to use `restore` and run `ls` rather than actually restore something. If the tape is not readable, the tape drive informs you right away. Sometimes there is a bad tape in the package, and you find that out only when you try to restore from it.

TABLE 32.7 Command Documentation Table for Interactive Mode of `restore`

Option	Description
`-i`	Interactive. After reading in the directory information from the media, `restore` invokes an interactive interface that allows you to browse through the dump files' directory hierarchy and select individual files to be extracted. See the listing of interactive commands later in this table.
`-b <blocksize>`	Specifies the block size, the number of kilobytes per dump record. If the option is not specified, it tries to determine the media block size dynamically.
`-f <file>`	Reads the backup from `<file>`. `<file>` may be a special device, such as a tape drive or disk drive, an ordinary file, or `-` (standard input). If `<file>` is of the form `<host>:<file>` or `<user>@<host>:<file>`, `restore` reads from the named file on the remote host using `rmt (8)`.
`-s <filenumber>`	Skips to `<filenumber>` when there are multiple files on the same tape. File numbering starts at 1.
`-h`	Extract the actual directory rather than the files it references.
`-v`	Work verbosely
`-y`	Do not prompt in the event of an error.
`add <file>`	Adds the specified file or directory to the list of files to be extracted. If the argument is a directory, it and all its descendants are added to the list. Files that are on the extraction list are prepended with a "*" when they are listed by `ls`.
`delete <file>`	Deletes the current file or directory and its descendants from the list of files to be extracted.
`extract`	Extracts all files on the extraction list from the dump.
`cd <directory>`	Changes to the specified directory.
`ls <directory>`	Lists the current or specified directory.
`pwd`	Prints the full pathname of the current working directory.
`help`	Lists the available commands.
`quit`	Ends the session, even if there are files listed for extraction.

The utilities dump and restore are excellent examples of how the availability of Unix-based solutions often exceeds that of what is available natively on Mac OS X. Users who have abandoned non-native Classic and Carbon applications can easily use these utilities to back up their entire system. For everyone else, all we can do is wait.

Diagnostics and Repairs

With a complex operating system like Mac OS X, things can sometimes go wrong, and the user is left with little recourse for solving the problem. Thankfully, operations such as repairing damaged Mac OS X installations, resetting the root password, and fixing damaged disks can all be performed even if your machine is not booting into the operating system properly.

Verbose Boot

Mac OS 8 and 9, although they hid much of the system operation from the user, gave a clearer picture of what was going on during a system boot. When Mac OS X starts, dozens of support processes and drivers are loaded at the same time. If something fails, it is left to the imagination of the user to guess exactly what has gone wrong. In many cases, users might not even be aware that there are problems with their system configuration because the boot process hides behind a simple GUI startup screen.

To view exactly what is happening as the Mac OS X system boots, you can hold down Command-V at power-on to force a verbose startup. The verbose boot displays all status and error messages while the computer starts. This can be a bit startling to many Mac users because instead of the usual blue or gray background present during startup, the screen is black and filled with text. Windows and Linux users will feel right at home.

The verbose startup messages are similar to those contained in /var/log/system.log. For example:

```
Jun 29 17:30:30 localhost mach_kernel: .Display_RADEON: i2cPower 1
Jun 29 17:30:30 localhost mach_kernel: .Display_RADEON:
➥user ranges num:1 start:9c008000 size:640080
Jun 29 17:30:30 localhost mach_kernel: .Display_RADEON:
➥using (1600x1024@0Hz,32 bpp)
Jun 29 17:30:30 localhost mach_kernel: AirPortDriver:
➥Ethernet address 00:30:65:11:37:15
Jun 29 17:30:30 localhost mach_kernel: ether_ifattach called for en
Jun 29 17:30:30 localhost mach_kernel: kmod_create:
➥com.apple.nke.ppp (id 58), 6 pages loaded at 0xc20, header size 0x1000
Jun 29 17:30:30 localhost mach_kernel: kmod_create:
➥ com.apple.nke.SharedIP (id 59), 5 pages loaded at 0x0, header size 0x0
Jun 29 17:30:30 localhost mach_kernel: kmod_create:
➥IPFirewall (id 60), 5 pages loaded at 0xc292000, header size 0x1000
```

```
Jun 29 17:30:30 localhost mach_kernel: ipfw_load
Jun 29 17:30:30 localhost mach_kernel:
➥IP packet filtering initialized, divert enabled, rule-based forwarding
➥enabled, default to accept, logging disabled
Jun 29 17:30:31 localhost sharity[161]: [0] Sharity daemon version 2.4 started
Jun 29 17:30:39 localhost ntpdate[204]:
➥ntpdate 4.0.95 Sat Feb 17 02:38:39 PST 2001 (1)
Jun 29 17:30:43 localhost ntpdate[204]:
➥no server suitable for synchronization found
Jun 29 17:30:43 localhost ntpd[206]:
➥ntpd 4.0.95 Thu Apr 26 13:40:11 PDT 2001 (1)
Jun 29 17:30:43 localhost ntpd[206]: precision = 7 usec
Jun 29 17:30:43 localhost ntpd[206]:
➥frequency initialized 0.000 from /var/run/ntp.drift
Jun 29 17:30:43 localhost ntpd[206]: server 128.146.1.7 minpoll 12 maxpoll 17
```

This small sample of the verbose output shows the Apple Radeon driver loading, followed by the AirPort software, Classic SharedIP driver, firewall, Sharity, and `ntp` (network time protocol) software.

Interestingly enough, in capturing this example, I ascertained what I had suspected for several weeks: The `ntpdate` utility, which is responsible for automatically contacting a remote time server for synchronization, has been failing:

```
Jun 29 17:30:39 localhost ntpdate[204]:
➥ntpdate 4.0.95 Sat Feb 17 02:38:39 PST 2001 (1)
Jun 29 17:30:43 localhost ntpdate[204]:
➥no server suitable for synchronization found
```

Similar feedback is provided for almost all the services on the computer, from low-level device drivers to Apache and Postfix. If your computer hangs during boot, you can use the verbose startup mode to determine exactly where the sequence has gone amiss.

TIP

If you want to permanently boot into verbose mode, you can (as root) use the command `nvram boot-args="-v"` to set the Mac OS X boot arguments to always include the verbose boot flag. You can disable this by unsetting the flag with `nvram boot-args=""`.

TIP

You can use the `dmesg` command on a booted system to show the current contents of the system message buffer at any time, including error messages.

Getting Access to Your Drive

The original Mac OS (7/8/9) allowed you to disable extensions by holding down the Shift key while booting your computer. This simplified the process of debugging by providing a way "in" to your computer so that you could figure out what software had been installed that was messing things up and then remove it.

Safe Boot

In Mac OS X, the Extensions Off mode has been replaced with Safe Boot. In Safe Boot mode, only the components necessary to get your Mac booted and running are loaded. Additional software, even networking, is disabled.

When you're running in Safe Boot mode, you can manually remove any software you've added and perform most basic repair tasks from within the Mac OS X GUI. To start your computer in Safe Boot mode, hold down the Shift key while starting up, until the Mac OS X startup screen appears with the words "Safe Boot." You can then release the Shift key and allow your Mac to finish booting.

NOTE

You may notice that startup takes longer than usual when in Safe Boot mode. This is because Safe Boot forces your Mac to run the disk check and repair process on the system volume during startup.

Single-User Mode

Another modification to the startup process is booting into single-user mode. Holding down Command-S starts Mac OS X in single-user mode, allowing an administrator to directly access the system through a command-line interface. This is a last-resort method of booting your computer that should be used only if absolutely necessary.

Single-user mode boots in a text-only fashion, just like the verbose startup mode. The process finishes by dropping the user to a shell:

```
Singleuser boot -- fsck not done
Root device is mounted read-only
If you want to make modifications to files,
run '/sbin/fsck -y' first and them '/sbin/mount -uw /'
localhost#
```

CAUTION

Be aware that the single-user mode command prompt carries with it full root access. This is not a place for playing games or learning Unix.

fsck

Using the `fsck` command, you can repair local filesystems from the command line. To fix a damaged filesystem, type **`fsck -y`** at the single-user prompt. This is equivalent to running the First Aid Disk Utility:

```
brezup:root jray # fsck -y
** /dev/rdisk0s9
** Root file system
** Checking HFS Plus volume
** Checking Extents Overflow file.
** Checking Catalog file.
** Checking multi-linked files.
** Checking Catalog heirarchy.
** Checking volume bitmap.
** Checking volume information.
** The volume Rmac OS XS appears to be OK.
```

If an error occurs during this process, you might have to tell the system that it is okay to perform repairs. Table 32.8 lists additional command-line arguments for `fsck`.

TABLE 32.8 `fsck` Command-Line Options

Option	Purpose
`-d`	Debugging mode. Displays the commands that `fsck` will execute without actually carrying them out.
`-f`	Forces a check of the filesystems, even if they are considered clean.
`-l` *<max parallel processes>*	Sets the number of scans that `fsck` will run in parallel. Usually defaults to one scan per disk.
`-n`	Assumes that the answer to all interactive questions is no.
`-p`	Preen (clean) the filesystems marked as dirty.
`-y`	Answers yes to all interactive questions.

TIP

If you just want to run a disk repair, the easiest way to do it is to perform a Safe Boot, which forces a repair automatically.

Alternatively, boot from the Mac OS X installation disk and then choose Open Disk Utility from the application menu. Chapter 3, "Applications and Utilities," discusses the use of Disk Utility for repairing volumes.

When booted into single-user mode, the Mac OS X filesystem is mounted read-only as a precaution. If you've installed a new daemon or script that is stalling the system at startup, it would be useful to be able to edit files from within single-user mode. To mount the filesystem with write permissions, use `/sbin/mount -uw /`.

Again, be aware that changes made while in single-user mode are made as the root user.

Logging into the Console

If your problem lies not with the bootup process, but with logging in, you might want to try a standard boot followed by a non-GUI login. To do this, you must have username and password fields enabled in the login window. If you do, allow the system to boot to a standard login window; then type **`>console`** as your username and click the Login button.

Your screen goes black, and you see a prompt similar to

```
Darwin/BSD (brezup.poisontooth.com) (console)

login:
```

Type your username and password to log in and use the system via the console. Logging out of the console restarts the window manager and takes you back to a GUI login screen.

Finding the Problem

When dealing with stalled startups, take the same approach as with extensions and control panels under Mac OS 8 and 9: Remove the last item to load before the system failure and then reboot.

Assuming that you haven't found what is crashing the machine in your `system.log` or by running a Verbose boot, disable any new software that runs with root privileges or drivers for add-on devices. After you've gained access to your system (either through a Safe Boot, Single User Mode, or Console login), search the list of "usual suspects" to find newly installed files:

As you already know, both the `/Library/Startupitems` and `/System/Library/Startupitems` directories contain the services that are started at boot time. If software in your auto-launch Login Items list is causing the problem, they're stored in `~/Library/Preferences/loginwindow.plist`.

`/Library/Components` and `/System/Library/Extensions` provide two more common hiding places for installed drivers and kernel extensions.

In addition, the `/etc/hostconfig` and `/private/var/db/SystemConfiguration/preferences.xml` files hold information on your machine's network configuration and boot parameters. Although editing these files isn't a guaranteed cure for any problem, they're a good place to start.

Testing Kernel Extensions

If you suspect an extension is causing a problem but aren't sure, you can use the capability of Mac OS X to dynamically load and unload kernel extensions to test your hypothesis.

Viewing Active Extensions: `kextstat` To list the currently loaded extensions, use the utility **`kextstat`** with the argument **`-k`** to hide kernel components (which you wouldn't want to touch):

```
brezup:jray jray $ kextstat -k
Index Refs Address Size  Wired   Name (Version) <Linked Against>
 11  9  0x14ec8 0x9000 0x8000 com.apple.iokit.IOPCIFamily (1.2)
 12  0  0x14f52 0x18000 0x17000 com.apple.driver.AppleMacRISC2PE (1.3) <11>
 13  0  0x14f80 0x6000 0x5000 com.apple.BootCache (12.3)
 14  3  0x1504a 0x2d000 0x2c000 com.apple.iokit.IOHIDFamily (1.2.5)
 15  3  0x150a6 0x2000 0x1000 com.apple.iokit.IOHIDSystem (1.2) <14>
 16  5  0x1514e 0x1c000 0x1b000 com.apple.iokit.IOGraphicsFamily (1.2) <11>
 17  0  0x1518b 0x4000 0x3000 com.apple.driver.AppleGossamerPE (2.0) <11>
...
 72  0  0x15015 0x7000 0x6000   com.apple.nke.asp_atp (2.1)
 73  0  0x193f7 0x48000  0x47000 com.apple.filesystems.afpfs (3.8.2)
 74  0  0x1512c 0x6000 0x5000 com.apple.nke.IPFirewall (1.2.1)
 75  1  0x19e08 0xe3000 0xe2000 com.apple.NVDAResman (2.2) <22 16 11>
 76  0  0x15198 0x28000 0x27000 com.apple.GeForce (2.2) <75 22 16 11>
```

A "normal" system should have roughly 60–75 extensions loaded.

Each line contains the name of the extension and information about where it is loaded in memory. The fields you'll be most interested in are the Name field (such as **`com.apple.GeForce`**) and the Ref field. The Name is the name by which the system refers to the loaded extension and is what you will need to use to unload it. The Ref field contains the number of active references to that extension. If other components are using an extension, it cannot be unloaded. For example, the `com.apple.NVDAResman` extension has a reference count of "1", (which I happen to know is because it is being used by the `com.apple.GeForce` extension), so it cannot be unloaded without first unloading `com.apple.GeForce`.

Unloading an Extension: `kextunload`

To unload a kernel extension, you must be root (or use **`sudo`**) and issue the command **`kextunload -b`** **<*extension name*>**. For example, in the **`kextstat`** listing we looked at previously, to unload the **`com.apple.NVDAResman`** extension, you would type:

```
brezup:root jray # kextunload -b com.apple.NVDAResman
unload id com.apple.NVDAResman failed (result code 0xe00002c2)
```

This is syntactically correct, but the unload failed because of the Reference count. To unload the extension, you must first unload **com.apple.GeForce** and then com.apple.NVDAResman:

```
brezup:root jray # kextunload -b com.apple.GeForce
unload id com.apple.GeForce succeeded (any personalities also unloaded)
brezup:root jray # kextunload -b com.apple.NVDAResman
unload id com.apple.NVDAResman succeeded (any personalities also unloaded)
```

TIP

You can also unload a kernel extension based on its filesystem name by simply typing **kextunload** ***<full path to extension>*****.**

Loading an Extension: kextload

Loading an extension is virtually identical to unloading but uses the command kextload instead—kextload *<path to extension>*. For example, to reload the GeForce extension, you would type

```
brezup:root jray # kextload /System/Library/Extensions/GeForce.kext
kextload: /System/Library/Extensions/GeForce.kext loaded successfully
```

Reinstall

Most Windows users are familiar with the word "reinstall." I've listened in on many support calls, only to hear the technician give up and tell the end user to reinstall. Unfortunately, Mac OS X users might find themselves doing the same thing. The difference, however, is that reinstalling Mac OS X does not replace your system accounts, information, or configuration.

I have found on numerous occasions that rerunning the Mac OS X installer is the fastest and easiest way to return to a viable system. There are, however, a few drawbacks—most notably, the system updates are replaced by the original version of the operating system. After running the Mac OS X Installer to recover a damaged system, be sure to open the /Library/Receipts folder, throw away any receipt files stored by system updates, and then manually force a software update to reinstall the latest versions of the Mac OS X support software.

Another anomaly is that if you've moved or removed any of the system-installed applications, they will be restored during the install process.

Restoring the Administrator Password

If the Mac OS X administrator password is forgotten or misplaced, Apple has provided a facility for restoring a password. Boot your computer from the Mac OS X install CD (hold down the C key while turning on your computer with the CD in the CD-ROM drive).

When the Installer application starts, choose Reset Password from the Installer application menu. Figure 32.7 shows the interface to the Password Reset facility.

Detected Mac OS X volumes are listed along the top of the Window. Click the main boot drive to load the password database for that volume.

Next, use the pop-up menu to choose the user account that you want to reset. Fill in the new password in both of the password fields provided.

Finally, click Save to store the new password.

FIGURE 32.7 Use the boot CD and Password Reset application to ease your forgetful head.

This really isn't useful for much beyond resetting the administrator password. As long as there is access to the administrator account from the command line, you can easily use passwd <*username*> to reset the named user's password:

```
brezup:jray jray % sudo passwd jackd
Changing password for jackd.
New password:
Retype new password:
```

TIP

It is not possible to recover a password that has been forgotten—it is only possible to reset it. Mac OS X passwords are encrypted and can only be decrypted using the user's own password. If you're setting up a large-scale network with dozens of accounts, it's a good idea to develop a default password policy. Several organizations that I've worked for base the user's passwords on a combination of their initials and the last four digits of the user's Social Security number. This enables the administrators to reset passwords to a safe default value that the user can remember.

Commercial Repair, Prevention, and Recovery Tools

Although Mac OS X provides a number of tools for recovering from system trouble, there are certain issues that the supplied tools cannot deal with. If you've been using a Mac for a few years and have ever run the Apple Disk Repair tools, you've almost certainly run across an instance of the repair process stating "Disk Repair cannot fix this problem." The usual reaction (immediately following the "Oh Poop!") is, "well, what can solve the problem?"

Several commercial utilities can aid you in keeping your system running smoothly and error free. Even if you never have a problem, it's a good idea to keep one or two of these packages around:

- Drive 10 by Micromat Inc. (`http://www.micromat.com/`)—Offers extensive disk diagnostic utilities ranging from power supply tests and buffer validation to disk optimization. Unfortunately, it is lacking several of the more generalized system diagnostics of its big brother, TechTool Pro.
- TechTool Pro by Micromat Inc. (`http://www.micromat.com/`)—The undisputed king of diagnostics. It can locate problems with almost any hardware component, from memory to CPU failures. It also includes extensive drive repair and optimization facilities. A version of TechTool Pro is included as part of Apple's AppleCare package.
- DiskWarrior by Alsoft (`http://www.alsoft.com/DiskWarrior/index.html`)—An award-winning piece of software that takes a different approach to repairing disk problems. Rather than fix damaged drive information, it rebuilds the data from scratch, often offering superior results to traditional utilities such as Norton's.
- Virtual Lab by Binary Biz (`http://www.binarybiz.com/vlab/mac.php`)—The software you need if you've lost files from disk problems or carelessness. It is fast, thorough, and intuitive. You can even download a free trial capable of retrieving 1MB of data directly from its Web site. Its purpose is to *retrieve* data, not fix your drive, so make sure that this is what you need before you buy.
- Data Rescue X by Prosoft Engineering (`http://www.prosoftengineering.com/products/data_rescue.php`)—Another tool, like Virtual Lab, that provides data recovery features for damaged drives. Unlike Virtual Lab, Data Rescue's focus is on recovering from failing disks, not undeleting files. For that, they have a separate product.
- Data Recycler by Prosoft Engineering (`http://www.prosoftengineering.com/products/data_recycler.php`)—Although not the only product capable of undeleting files on Mac OS X, it is currently the only one capable of doing it *well*. Data Recycler maintains separate storage for holding deleted files and offering safe recovery if you find yourself in an "oops" situation. Undeletes are virtually instantaneous and do not require scanning your drive.
- Norton Utilities by Symantec, Inc., (`http://www.symantec.com/product/home-mac.html`)—The oldest and best-known Macintosh repair software available. NU focuses entirely on drive repair, optimization, and data loss prevention.

- Virex by McAfee by way of Apple (`http://www.mac.com/`)—As part of the .Mac membership, Apple offers an enhanced version of McAfee/NAI's Virex utility. Virex 7.2 provides virus protection for your Macintosh as well as any Windows files stored on it. Because Mac OS X 10.3 offers superb integration with Windows networks, any user who shares files in a cross-platform environment will find this a valuable preventative tool. Provides command-line virus scanning capabilities in `/usr/local/vscanx`.
- Norton AntiVirus by Symantec, Inc., (`http://www.symantec.com/nav/nav_mac/index.html`)—Norton AntiVirus is an easy-to-use alternative to Virex that offers the same basic features in a cost-effective and user-friendly package. If you're accustomed to the Norton Utilities package, this may be the right virus solution for your system.

NOTE

It is recommended that any system requiring fault-tolerance utilize the RAID and (at least) journaling features built into Mac OS X. These functions are built into Disk Utility, discussed in Chapter 3.

Housekeeping

The Mac OS X Unix subsystem can schedule tasks for automatic execution whenever you want. As with the automatic software updates, you can write your own maintenance scripts that execute at given intervals. This chapter covered several tools that could be used to create your own free incremental backup system. Combine those utilities with the ability to schedule their execution at regular intervals, and you've got a headache-free disaster recovery system. In fact, you might be surprised to find there are already several scripts that help keep your system running clean.

`cron`

The `cron` process is used to schedule repeating tasks for execution by adding entries to either a user or system `crontab` file. The system-level file is located in `/etc/crontab`. The default `crontab` file looks like this:

```
brezup:root jray # /etc/crontab
SHELL=/bin/sh
PATH=/etc:/bin:/sbin:/usr/bin:/usr/sbin
HOME=/var/log
#
#minute hour  mday  month  wday  who   command
#
```

```
#*/5  *    *    *    *    root  /usr/libexec/atrun
#
# Run daily/weekly/monthly jobs.
15   3    *    *    *    root  periodic daily
30   4    *    *    6    root  periodic weekly
30   5    1    *    *    root  periodic monthly
```

At the start of the file, a handful of environment variables are set (SHELL, PATH, HOME), which are made available to the commands executing from the file. Additional environment variables can be added using the same syntax: *<variable name>*=*<value>*.

One special crontab variable is the MAILTO variable, which can be set to a user account name. Output from the crontab commands (errors, and so on) is sent via email to that user's account.

The body of the crontab file is laid out in seven columns, separated by spaces or tabs. These seven fields control different aspects of when a command is run:

- Minute—The minutes after an hour that a command should be executed (0–59).
- Hour—The hour a command should run (0–23).
- Day of the month—The day of the month to run the command (0–31).
- Month—The month, specified numerically (1–12), or by name that the command should execute.
- Weekday—The day of the week the command should execute, set numerically (0–7, 0 or 7 specifies Sunday) or by name.
- User—The user ID to use while executing the command.
- Command—The command string to execute. This field can point to a shell script or other file to run a sequence of commands.

Fields that contain an asterisk (*) indicate that the command will run whenever the other columns' values are matched. For example, assume that there is an asterisk in every column (except for the User and Command fields, obviously):

```
* * * * * <my user> <my command>
```

The command will be started every minute, of every hour, of every day, of every day of the week, and so on. In addition, you can set a command to run at multiple different intervals within a time period without having to use additional lines. Just use integers separated by commas to set off multiple times within one of the columns.

For example, to run a command every 10 minutes, you could use

```
0,10,20,30,40,50 * * * * <my user> <my command>
```

Even this, however, can be shortened to be a bit more manageable. Regular intervals can be shortened using the syntax */<*interval length*>. The previous example, could be rewritten like this:

```
*/10 * * * * <my user> <my command>
```

Additions made to the /etc/crontab file are read every minute without additional user interaction.

Three jobs are run by default from the Mac OS X /etc/crontab file: periodic daily, periodic weekly, and periodic monthly. As the names suggest, these are run at repeating intervals each day, week, and month, respectively. The periodic program is used to execute periodic cron tasks—in this case, daily, weekly, and monthly scripts located in the /etc/daily, /etc/weekly, and /etc/monthly files, respectively. They handle cleaning up temporary system files, log rotation, and other menial maintenance tasks. You can take advantage of these files or add additional script files to perform other common tasks.

CAUTION

It might be tempting to set up scripts that run in tight intervals (for monitoring system activity and so forth). If you set up commands to execute at frequent intervals make absolutely sure that they can finish executing within that interval. If a command tends to run long, you might find that your system slowly grinds to a halt as more copies are started and system resources are exhausted.

cron for Normal Users

The systemwide /etc/crontab file should be used only for system tasks. Users, however, might want to add their own commands and scripts that are executed within their accounts. To do this, a user can create a crontab-style file within his directory. This file should contain all the fields as the previously documented /etc/crontab file, with one notable exception: there is no User field. Any commands executed from a personal crontab file are executed with the permissions of that user.

For example:

```
*/15 * * * * /Users/jray/myscript.pl
```

Putting this line in a file gives me a personal crontab that executes a Perl script in my home directory every 15 minutes.

Unlike the system-level crontab file, personal crontab files are loaded into a privileged system area rather than run directly from the file you've created. To load a personal crontab file into the system, use the crontab utility followed by the name of your personal file: crontab <*my crontab file*>.

Assuming that I've stored my crontab entries in mycrontab, I can load them into the system with

```
brezup:jray jray $ crontab mycrontab
```

After the file is loaded into the system, you can safely delete the local copy of your crontab file—it is no longer needed. A user can display the loaded crontab information (and thereby regenerate the original file) by typing **crontab -l**:

```
brezup:jray jray $ crontab -l
# DO NOT EDIT THIS FILE - edit the master and reinstall.
# (mycrontab installed on Sun Jul 1 10:01:20 2001)
# (Cron version -- $FreeBSD: src/usr.sbin/cron/crontab/crontab.c,v 1.12
# 1999/08/28 01:15:52 peter Exp $)
*/15 * * * * /Users/jray/myscript.pl
```

Users can also use the -e option to edit the currently stored crontab information, or use -r to remove it entirely.

NOTE

The root user (or a user executing sudo) can work with the contents of any user's personal crontab file by adding -u<*username*> to the crontab -l command-line utility.

The crontab information is stored in /etc/cron/tabs/<*username*> if you want direct access to the data.

TIP

Users wanting to access cron services from a GUI interface might want to check out CronniX. CronniX can create and edit crontab files for any system user from within a point-and-click environment. Download it from http://www.koch-schmidt.de/cronnix/.

Limiting Access to cron Services

On a system with many users, it isn't necessarily a good idea to give all of them access to cron services. You might find that your poor system performance is due to a few hundred copies of SETI@home that start automatically every night. To limit access to the crontab command for adding personal crontab entries, use either /var/cron/allow or /var/cron/deny.

As you might infer, the allow file controls who is allowed to access crontab. Adding entries to this file denies access for anyone who isn't listed.

Likewise, the deny file, if it exists, provides access to crontab for anyone who isn't listed.

This isn't intentionally tricky, but it is important to note that the act of creating one of these files implicitly denies or allows access to all the accounts on the system. Obviously, you should not be running a system where both files exist simultaneously because it leads to an ambiguity of what happens to "everyone else" who isn't listed in one of the files.

Over time, you'll discover that there are small tasks you carry out on a day-to-day basis. Using the power of the `cron` daemon along with shell scripts, Perl, or AppleScript can automate many of these processes.

Summary

Mac OS X, although not nearly as easy to debug as Mac OS 9, is still reasonably straightforward to diagnose. Third-party support has done a great job of filling in the holes left by Apple. This chapter demonstrated the use of single-user and verbose boot modes, introduced tools for backing up your system, and discussed automating system processes.

Eventually, Mac OS X will probably mature into a system that can be documented entirely without ever seeing a command line (unless you want to!). For now, we hope that this book provides a balanced view of what you can do through the GUI and via the command line. Best of luck!

Sincerely,

John Ray (`jray@macosxunleashed.com`)

Will Ray (`wray@macosxunleashed.com`)

PART VIII

Appendix

IN THIS PART

To access Appendix A, "Command-Line Reference," visit our Web site at `www.samspublishing.com`. Type the ISBN (excluding hyphens) or the title of the book in the Search box to find the book you're looking for.

Index

Symbols & Numbers

A

B

C

D

F

G

H

I

J

K

L

M

N

O

P

Q

R

S

T

U

V

X

Y - Z